David Hansford / Alamy

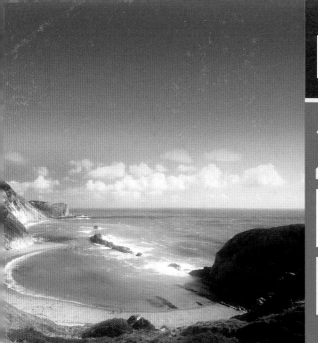

PHILIP'S RO

2015 ESSENTIAL BRITAIN & IRELAND

II	**Key to map symbols**
III	**The Death of the Full English?**
VI	**Restricted motorway junctions**
VIII	**Route planning maps**
XVIII	**Road map of Ireland**
XX	**Distances and journey times**
1	**Key to road map pages**
2	**Road maps of Britain**
161	**Urban approach maps**
161	Glasgow *approaches*
162	Birmingham *approaches*
164	London *approaches*
168	Manchester *approaches*
169	**Town plans**
169	Aberdeen, Birmingham
170	Bath, Bradford, Bristol
171	Cambridge, Cardiff, Coventry, Derby
172	Edinburgh, Glasgow
173	Gloucester, Hull, Leeds
174	London
176	Liverpool, Manchester
177	Leicester, Middlesbrough, Newcastle upon Tyne, Norwich
178	Nottingham, Oxford, Plymouth, Portsmouth
179	Reading, Sheffield, Southampton
180	Stoke-on-Trent (Hanley), Swansea, Worcester, York
181	**Index to road maps of Britain**

www.philips-maps.co.uk

Published by Philip's
a division of Octopus Publishing Group Ltd
www.octopusbooks.co.uk
Endeavour House, 189 Shaftesbury Avenue
London WC2H 8JY
An Hachette UK Company
www.hachette.co.uk

First edition 2014
First impression 2014

ISBN 978-1-84907-320-2

Cartography by Philip's

While every reasonable effort has been made to ensure that the information compiled in this atlas is accurate, complete and up-to-date at the time of publication, some of this information is subject to change and the Publisher cannot guarantee its correctness or completeness.

The information in this atlas is provided without any representation or warranty, express or implied and the Publisher cannot be held liable for any loss or damage due to any use or reliance on the information in this atlas, nor for any errors, omissions or subsequent changes in such information.

The representation in this atlas of any road, drive or track is no evidence of the existence of a right of way.

Data for the speed cameras provided by **PocketGPSWorld.com Ltd**.

Information for National Parks, Areas of Outstanding Natural Beauty, National Trails and Country Parks in Wales supplied by the Countryside Council for Wales.

Information for National Parks, Areas of Outstanding Natural Beauty, National Trails and Country Parks in England supplied by Natural England. Data for Regional Parks, Long Distance Footpaths and Country Parks in Scotland provided by Scottish Natural Heritage.

Gaelic name forms used in the Western Isles provided by Comhairle nan Eilean.

Data for the National Nature Reserves in England provided by Natural England. Data for the National Nature Reserves in Wales provided by Countryside Council for Wales. Darparwyd data'n ymwneud â Gwarchodfeydd Natur Cenedlaethol Cymru gan Gyngor Cefn Gwlad Cymru.

Information on the location of National Nature Reserves in Scotland was provided by Scottish Natural Heritage.

Data for National Scenic Areas in Scotland provided by the Scottish Executive Office. Crown copyright material is reproduced with the permission of the Controller of HMSO and the Queen's Printer for Scotland. Licence number C02W0003960.

Printed in China.

*Independent research survey, from research carried out by Outlook Research Limited, 2005/06.

**Nielsen BookScan Travel Publishing Year Book 2013 data

Road map symbols

M6	Motorway, toll motorway
4 — 5	Motorway junction – full, restricted access
S — S	Motorway service area – full, restricted access
	Motorway under construction
A453	Primary route – dual, single carriageway
S — S	Service area, roundabout, multi-level junction
4 — 5	Numbered junction – full, restricted access
	Primary route under construction
	Narrow primary route
Derby	Primary destination
A34	A road – dual, single carriageway
	A road under construction, narrow A road
B2135	B road – dual, single carriageway
	B road under construction, narrow B road
	Minor road – over 4 metres, under 4 metres wide
	Minor road with restricted access
2	Distance in miles
	Scenic route
40 — 40	Speed camera – single, multiple
TOLL	Toll, steep gradient – arrow points downhill
	Tunnel
	National trail – England and Wales
	Long distance footpath – Scotland
	Railway with station
	Level crossing, tunnel
	Preserved railway with station
	National boundary
	County / unitary authority boundary
	Car ferry, catamaran
	Passenger ferry, catamaran
	Hovercraft
CALAIS Ferry	Ferry destination
	Car ferry – river crossing
	Principal airport, other airport

National park

Area of Outstanding Natural Beauty – England and Wales National Scenic Area – Scotland
forest park / regional park / national forest

Woodland

Beach

Linear antiquity

Roman road

Hillfort, battlefield – with date

Viewpoint, nature reserve, spot height – in metres

Golf course, youth hostel, sporting venue

Camp site, caravan site, camping and caravan site

Shopping village, park and ride

29 Adjoining page number – road maps

Approach map symbols

M6	Motorway
	Toll motorway
6 — 5	Motorway junction – full, restricted access
S	Service area
	Under construction
A6	Primary route – dual, single carriageway
S	Service area
	Multi-level junction
	roundabout
	Under construction
A195	A road – dual, single carriageway
B1288	B road – dual, single carriageway
	Minor road – dual, single carriageway
	Ring road
3	Distance in miles
	Congestion charge area
COSELEY	Railway with station
LOXDALE	Tramway with station
M ⊖ — •	Underground or metro station

Town plan symbols

	Motorway
	Primary route – dual, single carriageway
	A road – dual, single carriageway
	B road – dual, single carriageway
	Minor through road
→	One-way street
	Pedestrian roads
	Shopping streets
	Railway with station
City Hall	Tramway with station
	Bus or railway station building
	Shopping precinct or retail park
	Park
	Building of public interest
	Theatre, cinema
P	Parking, shopmobility
Bank ⊖	Underground station
West St •	Metro station
H	Hospital, Police station
PO	Post office

Tourist information

† Abbey, cathedral or priory	Farm park	Roman antiquity
Ancient monument	Garden	Safari park
Aquarium	Historic ship	Theme park
Art gallery	House	Tourist information centre
Bird collection or aviary	House and garden	i open all year
Castle	Motor racing circuit	i open seasonally
Church	Museum	Zoo
Country park England and Wales Scotland	Picnic area	Other place of interest
	Preserved railway	
	Race course	

Speed Cameras

Fixed camera locations are shown using the 40 symbol.

In congested areas the 40 symbol is used to show that there are two or more cameras on the road indicated.

Due to the restrictions of scale the camera locations are only approximate and cannot indicate the operating direction of the camera. Mobile camera sites, and cameras located on roads not included on the mapping are not shown. Where two or more cameras are shown on the same road, drivers are warned that this may indicate that a SPEC system is in operation. These cameras use the time taken to drive between the two camera positions to calculate the speed of the vehicle.

Relief

Feet	metres
3000	914
2600	792
2200	671
1800	549
1400	427
1000	305
0	0

Road map scales

3·15 miles to 1 inch • 1:200 000

0 1 2 3 4 5 6 miles
0 1 2 3 4 5 6 7 8 9 10 km

Parts of Scotland

4.18 miles to 1 inch • 1:265 000

0 1 2 3 4 5 6 miles
0 2 4 6 8 12 km

Scottish Highlands and Islands

5.24 miles to 1 inch • 1:332 000

0 1 2 3 4 5 6 7 8 miles
0 2 4 6 8 10 12 km

Orkney and Shetland Islands 1:400 000, 6.31 miles to 1 inch

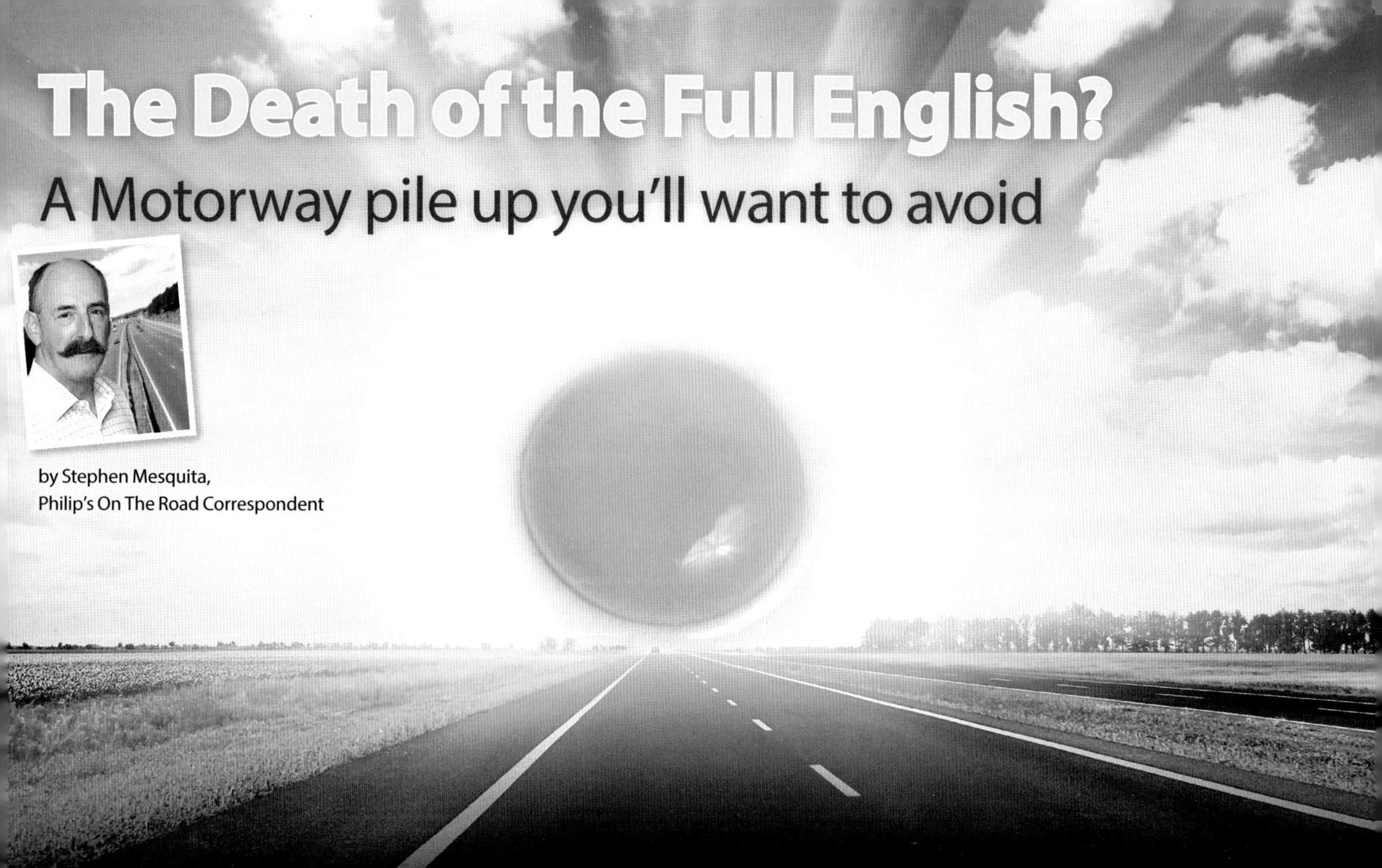

The Death of the Full English?

A Motorway pile up you'll want to avoid

by Stephen Mesquita,
Philip's On The Road Correspondent

Now come on. Be honest. When you're away from home and on the road early, haven't you been tempted by a Full English? Live it up. Put the new diet on hold. Build up your strength for the day ahead. Won't have to eat again till dinner. (A full list of excuses may be available on our web site).

shutterstock

One Full English can be a struggle. But, on a hot and sunny day last August, your intrepid Philip's On The Road Correspondent, ably assisted by his right-hand man Stuart the Sales Supremo, consumed eight of them. Our location: a typical stretch of Middle England – otherwise known as Milton Keynes. Our guide: The Philip's atlas, dotted with Post-it notes for each location (we won't mention the sat-nav). Our mission: to see if the hungry early-morning motorist is adequately catered for. I'm sad to report that, in my view, The Full English for the motorist in a hurry has become an endangered species. Here are a few of the threats to one of our great traditions:

- **Low-quality ingredients** – most of the sausages and bacon served up seem to be from the 'we've got something cheaper out the back' counter.
- **Sausages have more than one side** – the striped sausage reigns supreme, burnt on two sides.
- **Baked Beans** – OK for the Full American but they alter the taste of the Full English. They should be offered as an option only.
- **Triangles of frozen Hash Browns** – these have no place in the Full English and should not be allowed through Passport Control.
- **Bring back the Fried Bread, please** – it may be horribly unhealthy but it's the forbidden pleasure of the Full English, the apple in the Garden of Eden. Where is it now?
- **Tinned tomatoes** – some people may prefer them but we don't. We like a lightly cooked ripe tomato, not one that's been refrigerated for six months and then burnt.
- **Cold, lukewarm or barely warm?** These seem to be the thermal options. None of the breakfasts were piping hot and many were stone cold.
- **Value for money** – not a concept understood by Motorway Service Areas.

So here is what we thought of what we tasted – a bite-by-bite account of the whole gory episode:

1 Moto Toddington Services Eat and Drink Company

🕐 6.20am **Price**: £8.49

The Highlights

- **Eggs cooked to order and cover provided** (but still not hot)
- **Fried bread** (hurrah – the only one)
- **A decent amount for your money** (but needs to be for £8.49)
- **Sausages like rubber**
- **Bacon unappetising**
- **Hash browns superfluous and tasted of frozen goo**
- **Black pudding** – a terrible mistake

Verdict: 5 out of 10

Comment: a reasonable attempt let down by less than adequate ingredients.

▼ 6.20am Moto Toddington, Stuart decides

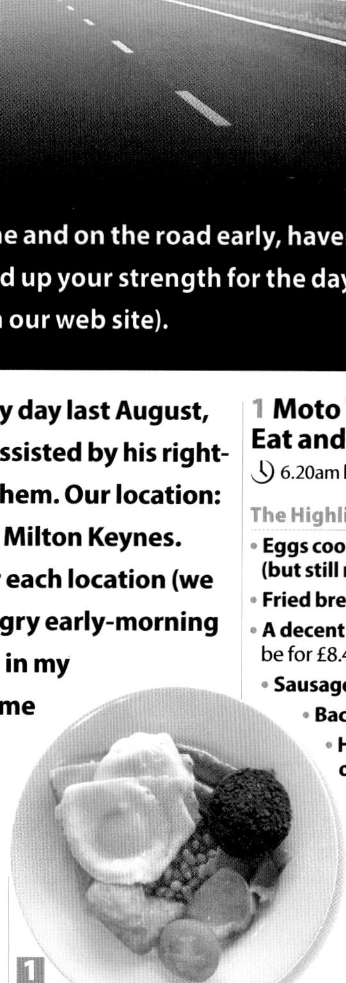

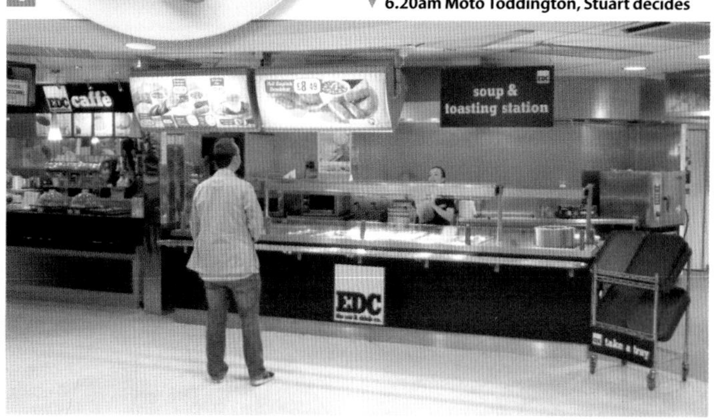

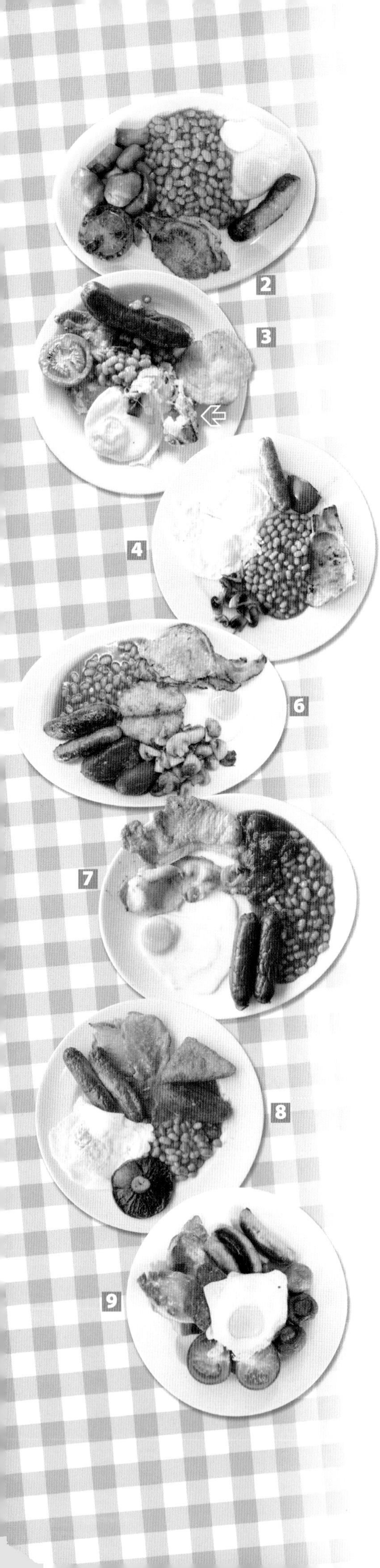

2 Premier Inn ⏱ 7.30am Price: £8.25

The Highlights

- **Egg** – rubbery and covered in grease (with an extra greasy bit thrown in)
- **Tomato** – unripe
- **Sausage** –not a disaster but rather sweet
- **Bacon** – mainly salt
- **Mushrooms** – a bit chewy
- **Swamped** by baked beans
- **Intrusive drivel** from local radio station

Comment: Lovely location, pity about the breakfast. We liked the windmill.

Verdict: 4 out of 10

3 Toby Carvery, Travel Lodge

⏱ 8.05am **Price**: £3.99

The Highlights

- **Egg** –beyond repair
- **Sausage** – seemed to be a veteran of many campaigns
- **Bacon** – tasted like 99% salt
- **Hash brown** – completely tasteless pancake
- **Tomato** – unripe
- **2 orange juices** cost nearly as much as the breakfast

Comment: The unseemly mess highlighted by the arrow is a triumph of innovation over taste. Overall, this breakfast was not what you want to be faced with first thing in the morning.

Verdict: 2 out of 10

4 Comfort Inn Milton Keynes Hotel

⏱ 8.45am **Price**: £7.50 but didn't accept credit cards or have change so accepted £6.70 (all the change we had)

The Highlights

- **An unspeakable experience**
- **Mushrooms** – like cardboard filings, late 20th Century
- **Eggs** – greasy and unappetising
- **Sausage** – tasted as if it had made only passing contact with meat.
- **Tomato** – a quarter, slightly burnt

Comment: The website says this hotel is an unrivalled experience. That's true.

Verdict: 1 out of 10

5 McDonald's

Price: Big Breakfast £3.39 including OJ/ Sausage and Egg McMuffin £3.29 including OJ

The Highlights:

- **The Full American** – not really an English breakfast as we know it
- **You can't fault the price**
- **Couldn't look more unappetising**
- **Hash brown slab mainly fat**
- **A confession:** the sausage burger's quite nice
- **Stick to the scrambled egg in the Big Breakfast** – the flying saucer in the Egg McMuffin is dire
- **Here's what the others don't tell you:** the Big Breakfast is 550 calories

Verdict: 4 out of 10

Comment: It doesn't pretend to be an English breakfast but you know what you're getting.

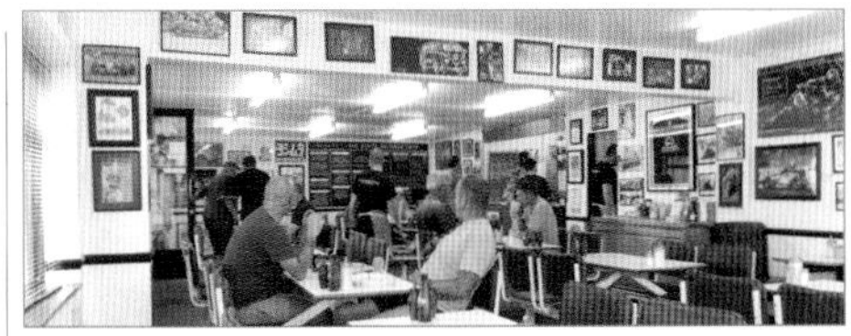

6 Super Sausage A5 Towcester

⏱ 9.50am, **Price**: £6.20

The Highlights

- **Tasty sausages** (bravo!)
- **Good value for money**
- **Egg** – nicely cooked and not too greasy
- **Bacon** –tasted of bacon
- **A bit let down by some of the extras** (hash browns were tasteless, except slightly burnt)
- **Excellent service**

Comment: not a classic Full English but by some way the best we tasted. Great for families as well as motorists.

Verdict: 7 out of 10

7 Jack's Hill Café A5/A43

⏱ 10.20am **Price**: £4.50

The Highlights

- **Excellent value for money**
- **Reasonably tasty**
- **Ingredients** – you get what you pay for

Comment: you expect truck stops to be cheap and filling and this fits the bill. You won't (and we didn't) get a gourmet experience.

Verdict: 6 out of 10

8 Road Chef Watford Gap Services Fresh Food Cafe ⏱ 11.00am

The Highlights

- **Arrived in 1 minute**
- **All lukewarm**
- **Egg** – cooked both sides (not asked for)
- **Bacon** – like salty mdf
- **Hash Brown** – a fried mush
- **A real mushroom (hurrah)** but rubbery and watery
- **Comment:** As Julius Caesar said, 'We Came, We Saw, We Left'.

Verdict: 3 out of 10

9 Welcome Break Newport Pagnell Services

⏱ 11.55 **Price**: £7.99

The Highlights

- **Mushrooms** –a bit wizened
- **Bacon** – tough, cold and horrible, with watery white residue
- **3 sausages** with the designer 'zebra' look
- **Hash brown** – like a fishcake without the fish
- **Tomatoes** – lukewarm
- **Egg specially cooked (hurrah!)** – two cooked, only one put on plate. Where did it go?

Comment: sausages would win a 'Find the Meat' competition

Verdict: 3 out of 10

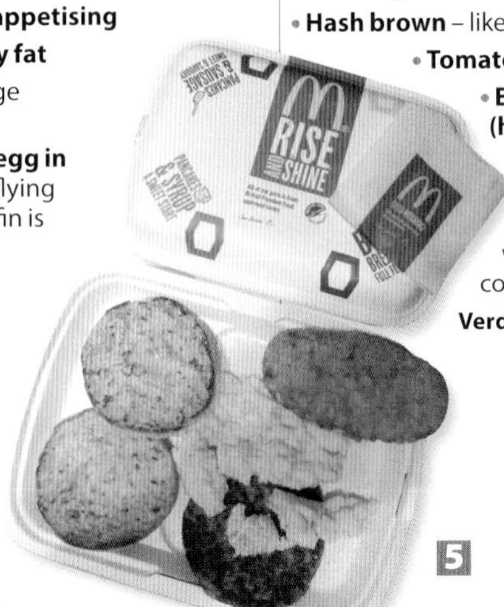

10 Home – the £2 Challenge

The Price: £1.98

I've been impolite about almost all the breakfasts we tasted – so it seems only fair that I have a go myself.

And to make things harder, I set myself a stiff challenge. To create a Full English with the best ingredients I could find for no more than £2.

Why £2? Because then I could sell it for a four times mark up for £7.99. That's a reasonable price for good breakfast. And – I'm sure you'll agree, beleaguered consumers and travellers, a more than generous profit margin for me as the supplier. I'm sure that most of the breakfasts we ate on the road were making substantially more profit – great for them but not so good for us.

Part 1: The shopping

Off to the market in my local town of Halesworth in Suffolk and the tension is mounting. Armed with a calculator, I was asking the big question: could I buy the ingredients for my Under £2 Full English and bring it in under budget?

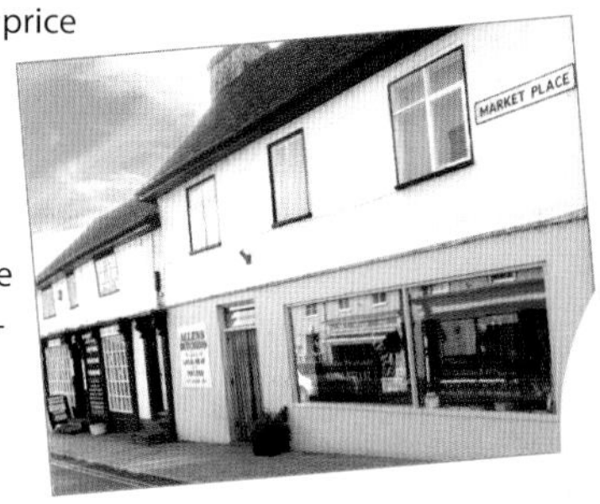

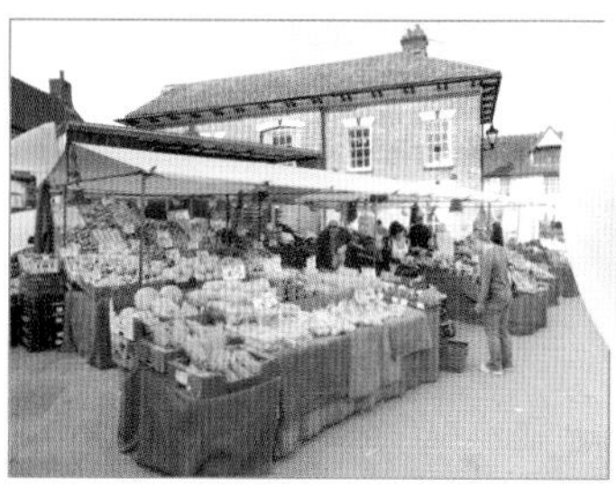

First stop – the local farm for absolutely fresh, speckled eggs, laid in the last 24 hours. Then to the Wednesday market stall for the tomatoes and mushrooms. Next the Farmhouse Bakery for a small granary loaf and – last stop – Allen's The Butcher for the meat (best Suffolk pork, of course).

That was the easy bit. Now the fun really started, as I retired to Frapa's for a cup of their excellent coffee and agonised over the costings with a calculator. The ingredients were great: fresh, wholesome and local. But could I bring it in on budget?

The shopping list – in the best traditions of male shopping, created on a spreadsheet – reveals all.

▲ Allen's Butchers Halesworth

▼ Halesworth Market

Ingredients	Price per portion	Notes
Eggs (2)	£0.33	Six farm-laid eggs £1.00
Bacon (1)	£0.30	Best Suffolk Pork Smoked Bacon £10.99 per kilo £1.21 for 4 rashers
Sausages (2)	£0.84	Best Suffolk Pork Sausages £6.99 per kilo £1.68 for 4
Tomato (1)	£0.145	Ripe English vine tomatoes £0.60 per lb
Mushrooms (4)	£0.28	Fresh mushrooms £1.20 per lb
Bread (1)	£0.085	Granary loaf £0.95 for 11 slices

The spreadsheet

The total cost: £1.98. Just 2p to spare! I'd done it! Now I had to cook it.

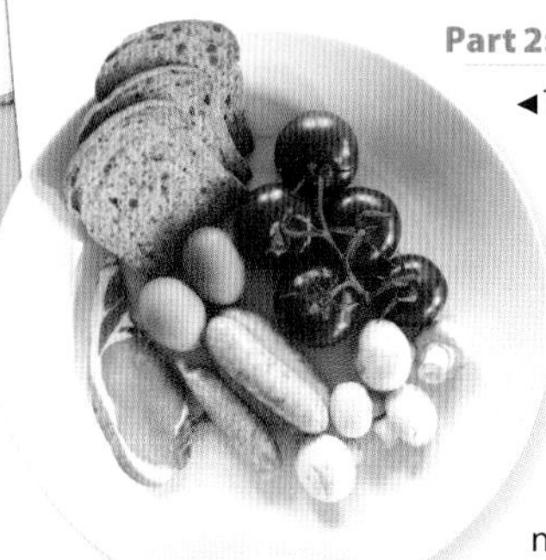

Part 2: The Preparation

◀ The picture says it all

Part 3: The Cooking

I took the view that a Full English shouldn't pretend to be 100% healthy – but my personal preference was for something not too cholesterol-soaked. So the sausages, bacon and tomatoes were cooked in the oven, the bread was toasted not fried and the eggs fried in almost no olive oil. Here are the results:

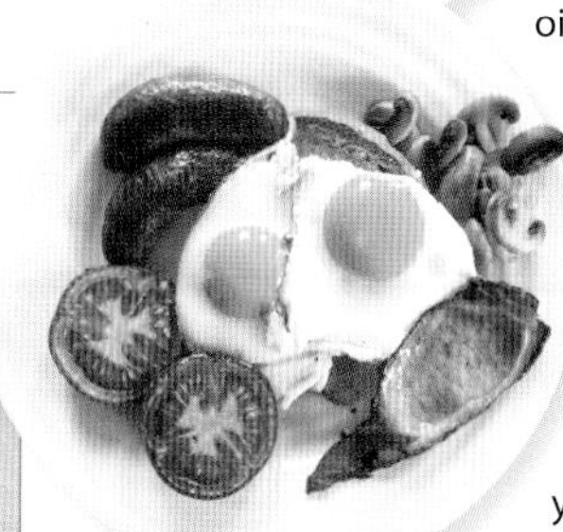

Part 4: The Eating

It may sound immodest to say this – but this was the most pleasurable 10 minutes of the whole exercise. Actually, it isn't immodest because the pleasure had almost nothing to do with my cooking and almost everything to do with the ingredients. They were yummy. Where do I start?

- **The eggs were as good as they looked**
- **The sausages tasted of meat and were not too salty.**
- **The bacon was lean and beautifully flavoured**
- **The tomatoes were ripe and succulent**
- **The mushrooms were juicy and nicely flavoured**
- **Even the toast had a pleasant aroma**

This Full English actually tasted quite healthy (all right – the bacon and sausage were a bit of an indulgence) and didn't require 3 litres of water to recover from it. All for £1.98.

Enter the 'Death of the Full English Breakfast' competition

and you could win a copy of the Royal Geographical Society Atlas of the World (worth £100).
Create the Full English Breakfast from Hell using the numbered pictures in this article.

THE ROYAL GEOGRAPHICAL SOCIETY
ATLAS OF THE WORLD

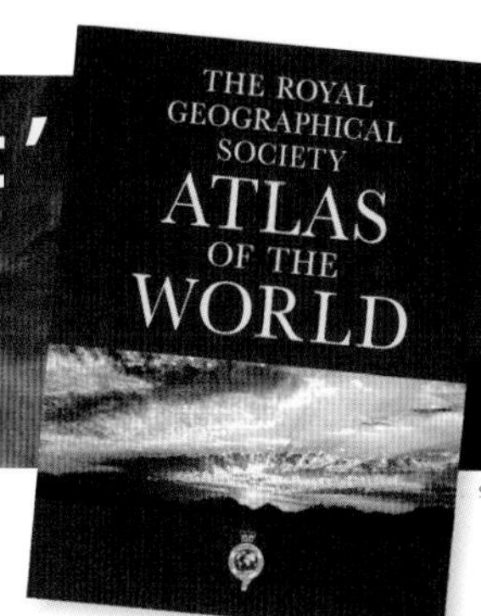

shutterstock

Here's how you enter:

Look at the pictures and read the text of this article. Choose the picture which you think has the worst ingredient from the list on the right. So, for example, if you think that Picture 1 has the worst eggs (check the text and look at the pictures), choose that one.

E-mail your list to **deadenglishbreakfast@octopusbooks.co.uk** or tweet it to **@deadenglishbrek**

The competition closes 15th March 2015. The first 25 winners drawn out of a hat will receive a copy of the Royal Geographical Society Atlas of the World, the magnificent flagship atlas of the Philip's range, with a retail price of £100.

Here's the list:

Eggs	Picture ☐
Bacon	Picture ☐
Sausage	Picture ☐
Mushrooms	Picture ☐
Tomatoes	Picture ☐
Black Pudding	Picture ☐

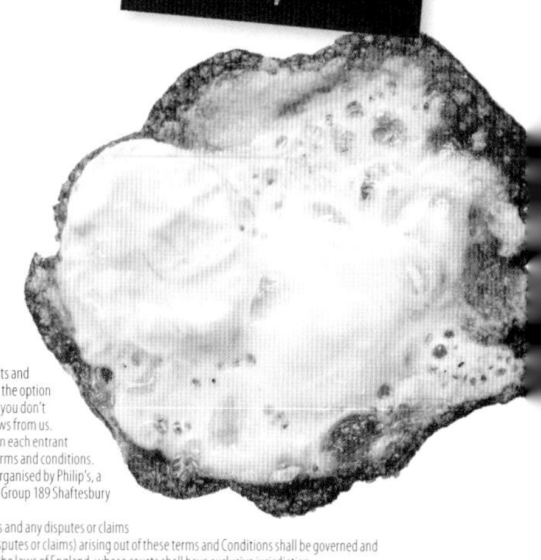

Restricted motorway junctions

M1 Junction 34

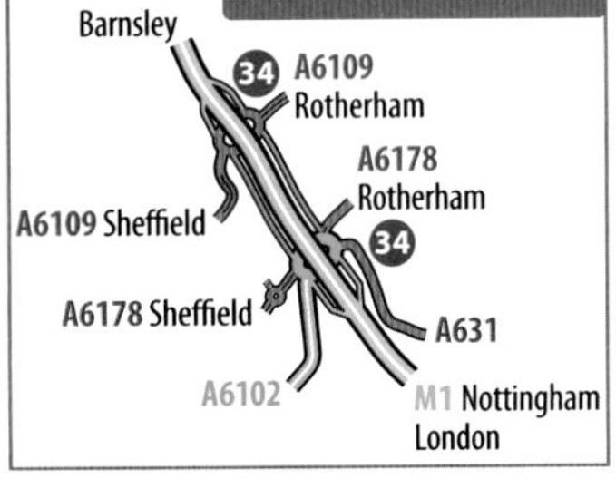

M1 Junctions 6, 6A
M25 Junctions 21, 21A

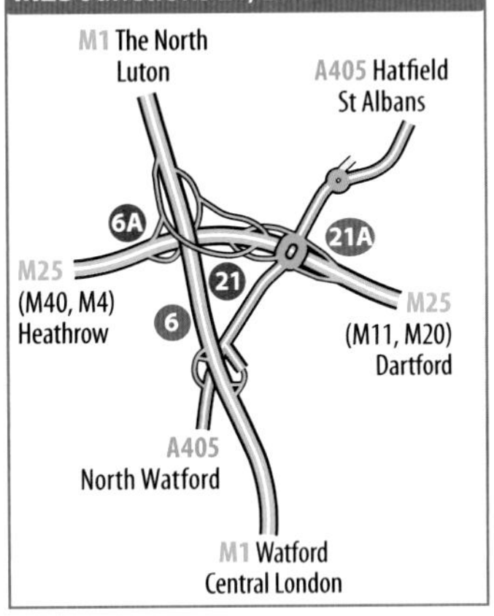

M4 Junctions 25, 25A, 26

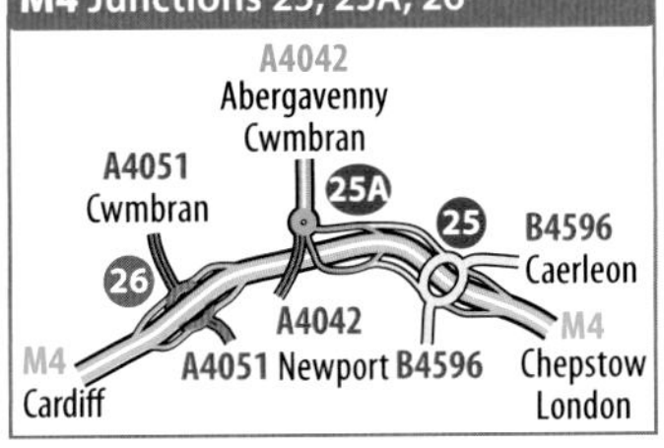

M5 Junction 11A

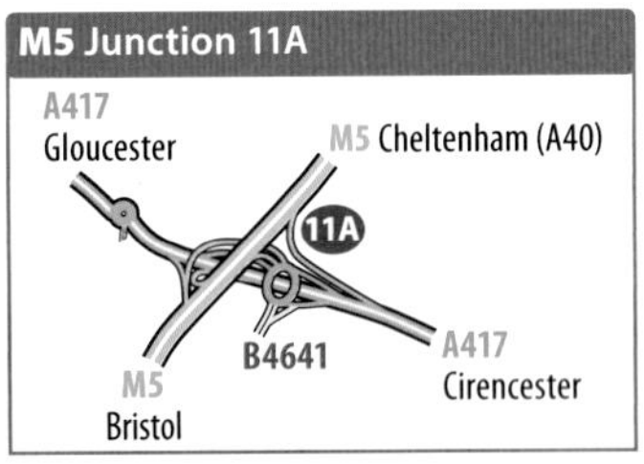

M8 Junctions 8, 9 · M73 Junctions 1, 2
M74 Junctions 2A, 3, 3A, 4

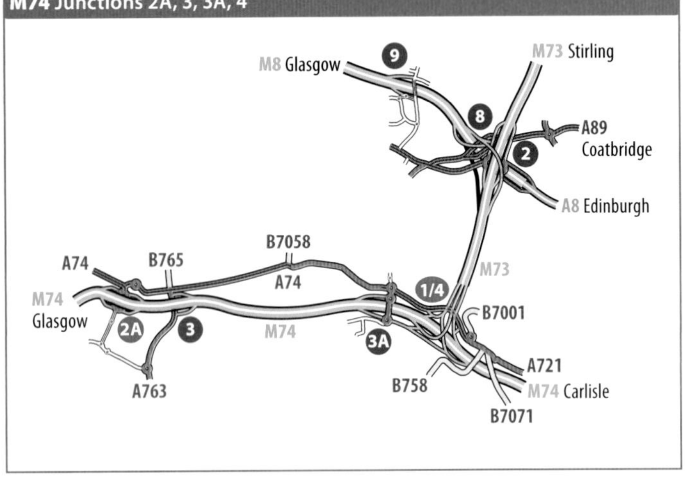

M1	Northbound	Southbound
2	No exit	No access
4	No exit	No access
6A	No exit. Access from M25 only	No access. Exit to M25 only
7	No exit. Access from A414 only	No access. Exit to A414 only
17	No access. Exit to M45 only	No exit. Access from M45 only
19	No exit to A14	No access from A14
21A	No access	No exit
23A		Exit to A42 only
24A	No exit	No access
35A	No access	No exit
43	No access. Exit to M621 only	No exit. Access from M621 only
48	No exit to A1(M) southbound	

M3	Eastbound	Westbound
8	No exit	No access
10	No access	No exit
13	No access to M27 eastbound	
14	No exit	No access

M4	Eastbound	Westbound
1	Exit to A4 eastbound only	Access from A4 westbound only
2	Access from A4 eastbound only	Access to A4 westbound only
21	No exit	No access
23	No access	No exit
25	No exit	No access
25A	No exit	No access
29	No exit	No access
38		No access
39	No exit or access	No exit
41	No access	No exit
41A	No exit	No access
42	Access from A483 only	Exit to A483 only

M5	Northbound	Southbound
10	No exit	No access
11A	No access from A417 eastbound	No exit to A417 westbound

M6	Northbound	Southbound
3A	No access. Exit to M42 northbound only	No exit. Access from M6 eastbound only
4A	No exit. Access from M42 southbound only	No access. Exit to M42 only
5	No access	No exit
10A	No access. Exit to M54 only	No exit. Access from M54 only
11A	No exit. Access from M6 Toll only	No access. Exit to M6 Toll only
20	No exit to M56 eastbound	No access from M56 westbound
24	No exit	No access
25	No access	No exit
30	No exit. Access from M61 northbound only	No access. Exit to M61 southbound only
31A	No access	No exit
45	No access	No exit

M6 Toll	Northbound	Southbound
T1		No exit
T2	No exit, no access	No access
T5	No exit	No access
T7	No access	No exit
T8	No access	No exit

M8	Eastbound	Westbound
8	No exit to M73 northbound	No access from M73 southbound
9	No access	No exit
13	No exit southbound	Access from M73 southbound only
14	No access	No exit
16	No exit	No access
17	No exit	No access
18		No exit
19	No exit to A814 eastbound	No access from A814 westbound
20	No exit	No access
21	No access from M74	No exit
22	No exit. Access from M77 only	No access. Exit to M77 only
23	No exit	No access
25	Exit to A739 northbound only. Access from A739 southbound only	Access from A739 southbound only
25A	No exit	No access
28	No exit	No access
28A	No exit	No access

M9	Eastbound	Westbound
1A	No exit	No access
2	No access	No exit
3	No exit	No access
6	No access	No exit
8	No exit	No access

M11	Northbound	Southbound
4	No exit. Access from A406 only	No access. Exit to A406 only
5	No access	No exit
9	No access	No exit
13	No access	No exit
14	No exit to A428 westbound	No exit. Access from A14 westbound only

M20	Eastbound	Westbound
2	No access	No exit
3	No exit Access from M26 eastbound only	No access Exit to M26 westbound only
11A	No access	No exit

M23	Northbound	Southbound
7	No exit to A23 southbound	No access from A23 northbound
10A	No exit	No access

M25	Clockwise	Anticlockwise
5	No exit to M26 eastbound	No access from M26 westbound
19	No access	No exit
21	No exit to M1 southbound. Access from M1 southbound only	No exit to M1 southbound. Access from M1. southbound only
31	No exit	No access

M27	Eastbound	Westbound
10	No exit	No access
12	No access	No exit

M40	Eastbound	Westbound
3	No exit	No access
7	No exit	No access
8	No exit	No access
13	No exit	No access
14	No access	No exit
16	No access	No exit

M42	Northbound	Southbound
1	No exit	No access
7	No access Exit to M6 northbound only	No exit Access from M6 northbound only
7A	No access. Exit to M6 southbound only	No exit
8	No exit. Access from M6 southbound only	Exit to M6 northbound only. Access from M6 southbound only

M45	Eastbound	Westbound
M1 J17	Access to M1 southbound only	No access from M1 southbound
With A45	No access	No exit

M48	Eastbound	Westbound
M4 J21	No exit to M4 westbound	No access from M4 eastbound
M4 J23	No access from M4 westbound	No exit to M4 eastbound

M49	Southbound	Northbound
18A	No exit to M5 northbound	No access from M5 southbound

M53	Northbound	Southbound
11	Exit to M56 eastbound only. Access from M56 westbound only	Exit to M56 eastbnd only. Access from M56 westbound only

M56	Eastbound	Westbound
2	No exit	No access
3	No access	No exit
4	No exit	No access
7		No access
8	No exit or access	No exit
9	No access from M6 northbound	No access to M6 southbound
15	No exit to M53	No access from M53 northbound

M57	Northbound	Southbound
3	No exit	No access
5	No exit	No access

M58	Eastbound	Westbound
1	No exit	No access

M60	Clockwise	Anticlockwise
2	No exit	No access
3	No exit to A34 northbound	No exit to A34 northbound
4	No access from M56	No exit to M56
5	No exit to A5103 southbound	No exit to A5103 northbound
14	No exit	No access
16	No exit	No access
20	No access	No exit
22		No access
25	No access	
26		No exit or access
27	No exit	No access

M61	Northbound	Southbound
2	No access from A580 eastbound	No exit to A580 westbound
3	No access from A580 eastbound. No access from A666 southbound	No exit to A580 westbound
M6 J30	No exit to M6 southbound	No access from M6 northbound

M62	Eastbound	Westbound
23	No access	No exit

M65	Eastbound	Westbound
9	No access	No exit
11	No access	No exit

M66	Northbound	Southbound
1	No access	No exit

M67	Eastbound	Westbound
1A	No access	No exit
2	No exit	No access

M69	Northbound	Southbound
2	No exit	No access

M73	Northbound	Southbound
2	No access from M8 or A89 eastbound. No exit to A89	No exit to M8 or A89 westbound. No access from A89

M74	Northbound	Southbound
3	No access	No exit
3A	No exit	No access
7	No exit	No access
9	No exit or access	No access
10		No exit
11	No exit	No access
12	No exit	No exit

M77	Northbound	Southbound
4	No exit	No access
6	No exit	No access
7	No exit or access	
8	No access	No access

M80	Northbound	Southbound
4A	No access	No exit
6A	No exit	
8	Exit to M876 northbound only. No access	Access from M876 southbound only. No exit

M90	Northbound	Southbound
2A	No access	No exit
7	No exit	No access
8	No access	No exit
10	No access from A912	No exit to A912

M180	Eastbound	Westbound
1	No access	No exit

M621	Eastbound	Westbound
2A	No exit	No access
4	No exit	
5	No exit	No access
6	No access	No exit

M876	Northbound	Southbound
2	No access	No exit

A1(M)	Northbound	Southbound
2	No access	No exit
3		No access
5	No exit	No access
14	No exit	No access
40	No access	No access
43	No exit. Access from M1 only	No access. Exit to M1 only
57	No access	No exit
65	No access	No exit

A3(M)	Northbound	Southbound
1	No exit	No access
4	No access	No exit

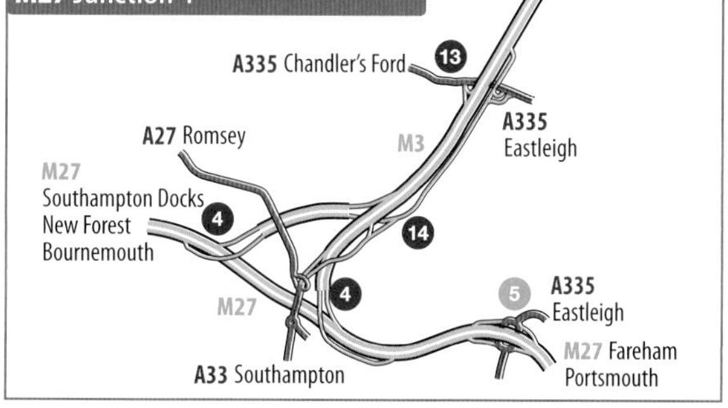

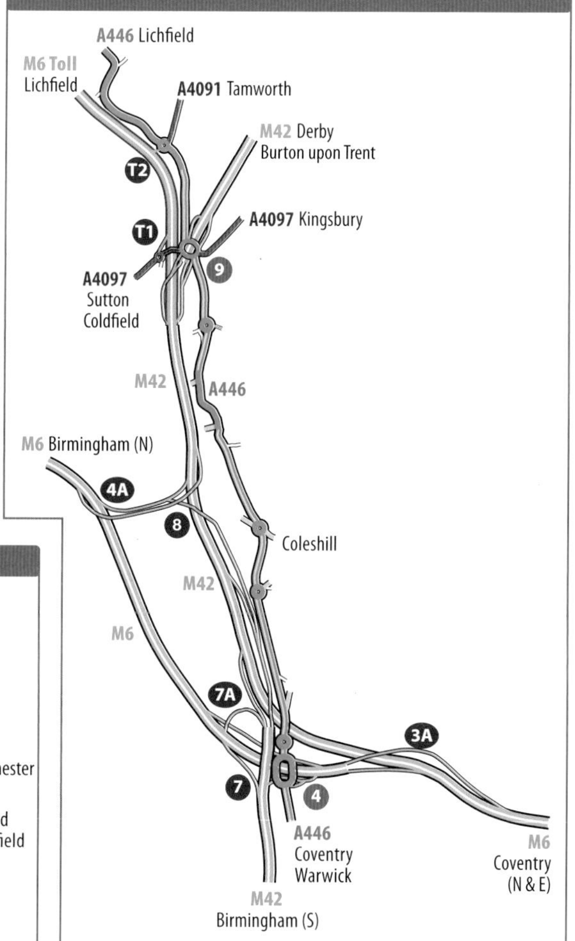

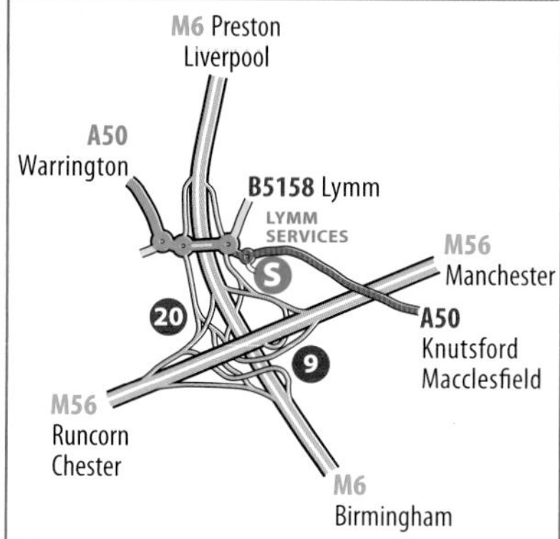

A38(M)	Northbound	Southbound
With Victoria Rd, (Park Circus) Birmingham	No exit	No access

A48(M)	Northbound	Southbound
M4 Junc 29	Exit to M4 eastbound only	Access from M4 westbound only
29A	Access from A48 eastbound only	Exit to A48 westbound only

A57(M)	Eastbound	Westbound
With A5103	No access	No exit
With A34	No access	No exit

A58(M)		Southbound
With Park Lane and Westgate, Leeds		No access

A64(M)	Eastbound	Westbound
With A58 Clay Pit Lane, Leeds	No access	No exit
With Regent Street, Leeds	No access	No access

A74(M)	Northbound	Southbound
18	No access	No exit
22		No exit

A194(M)	Northbound	Southbound
A1(M) J65 Gateshead Western Bypass	Access from A1(M) northbound only	Exit to A1(M) southbound only

M3 Junctions 13, 14 · **M27** Junction 4

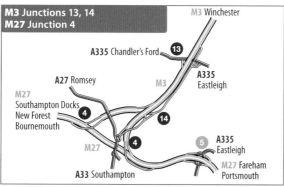

M6 Junctions 3A, 4A · **M42** Junctions 7, 7A, 8, 9
M6 Toll Junctions T1, T2

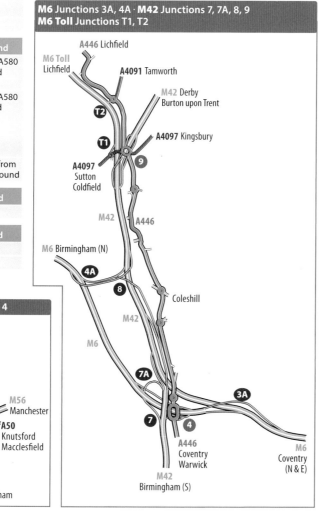

M6 Junction 20 · **M56** Junction 4

M62 Junctions 32A, 33 · **A1(M)** Junctions 40, 41

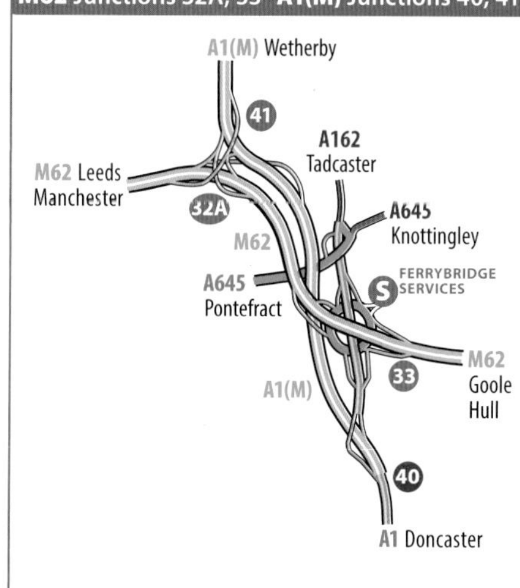

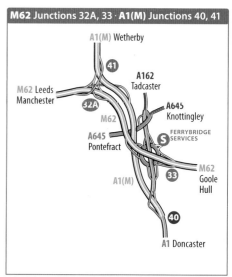

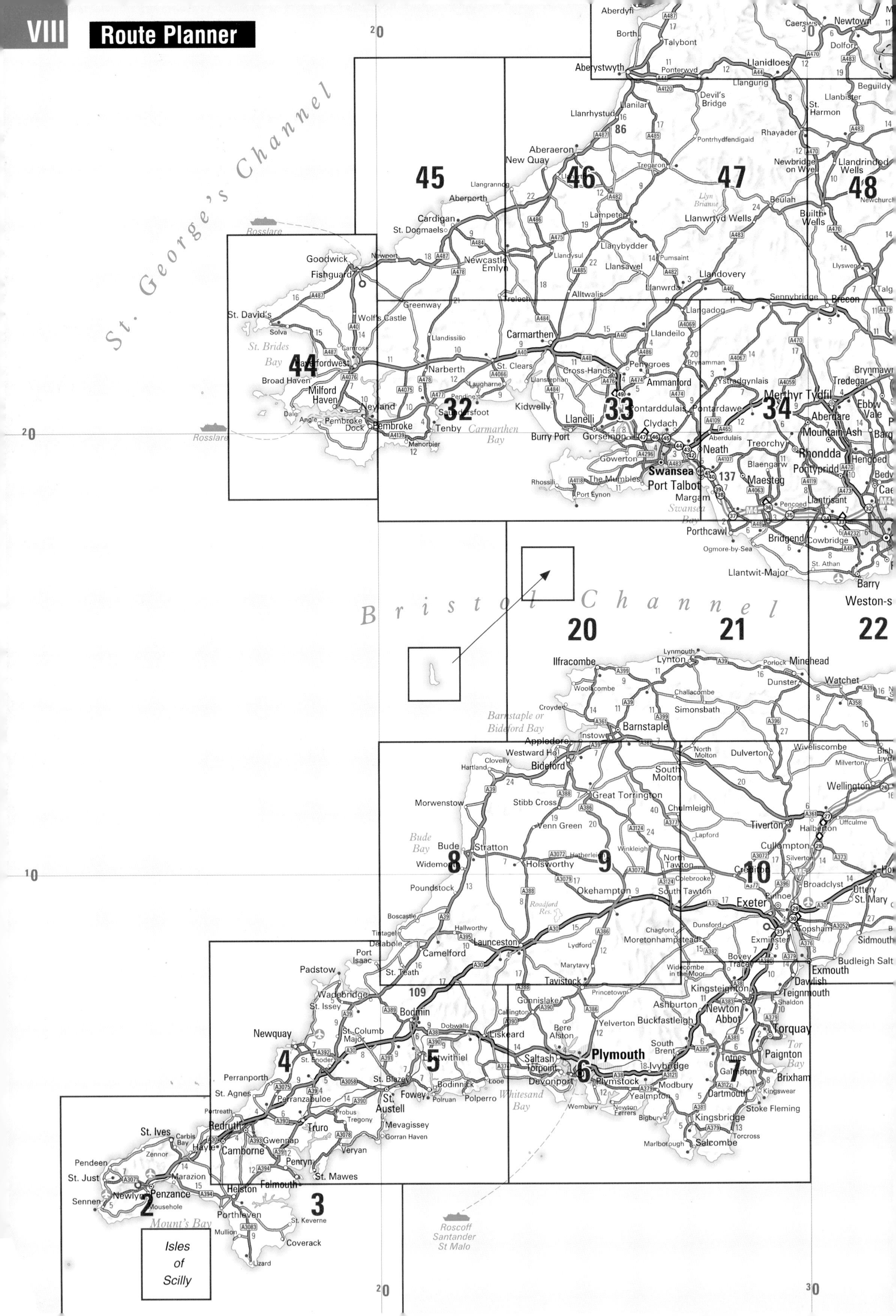

St. George's Channel

Bristol Channel

| 45 | 46 | 47 | 48 |

Aberdyfi
Aberystwyth
New Quay
Aberaeron
Cardigan
Aberporth
St. Dogmaels
Goodwick
Fishguard
St. David's
Solva
44
Broad Haven
Milford Haven
Neyland
Pembroke Dock
Pembroke
Dale
Angle
Manorbier

| 32 | 33 | 34 |

Newcastle Emlyn
Carmarthen
Narberth
Saundersfoot
Tenby
Carmarthen Bay
Kidwelly
Burry Port
Llanelli
Gorseinon
Gowerton
Swansea
The Mumbles
Port Eynon
Rhossili
Swansea Bay
Port Talbot
Margam
Porthcawl
Ogmore-by-Sea
Llantwit-Major

Llandovery
Llandeilo
Ammanford
Pontarddulais
Pontardawe
Clydach
Neath
Treorchy
Aberdare
Mountain Ash
Rhondda
Merthyr Tydfil
Ebbw Vale
Tredegar
Brynmawr
Maesteg
Pontypridd
Bridgend
Cowbridge
St. Athan
Barry
Weston-s

| 20 | 21 | 22 |

Ilfracombe
Lynmouth
Lynton
Minehead
Porlock
Dunster
Watchet
Woolacombe
Croyde
Simonsbath
Challacombe
Barnstaple
Barnstaple or Bideford Bay
Appledore
Instow
Westward Ho!
Bideford
Clovelly
Hartland
North Molton
South Molton
Dulverton
Wiveliscombe
Milverton
Wellington
Morwenstow
Great Torrington
Stibb Cross
Chulmleigh
Tiverton
Halberton
Uffculme
Bude Bay
Bude
Stratton
Venn Green
Winkleigh
North Tawton
Lapford
Cullompton
Silverton
Widemouth
8
Holsworthy
9
Hatherleigh
10
Crediton
Poundstock
Okehampton
Colebrooke
Broadclyst
Roadford Res.
South Tawton
Pinhoe
St. Mary
Boscastle
Hallworthy
Chagford
Dunsford
Exeter
Tintagel
Launceston
Lydford
Moretonhampstead
Exminster
Topsham
Sidmouth
Delabole
Marytavy
Bovey Tracey
Port Isaac
Camelford
Tavistock
Widecombe in the Moor
Kingsteignton
Budleigh Salt
Padstow
St. Teath
Princetown
Ashburton
Newton Abbot
Exmouth
Wadebridge
Gunnislake
Yelverton
Buckfastleigh
Teignmouth
Dawlish
St. Issey
109
Bodmin
Callington
Bere Alston
South Brent
Shaldon
Torquay
Newquay
St. Columb Major
Dobwalls
Liskeard
Plymouth
Ivybridge
Totnes
Paignton
Tor Bay
Perranporth
4
St. Enoder
St. Austell
5
Lostwithiel
Saltash
Torpoint
Devonport
6
Plymstock
Modbury
Galmpton
Brixham
St. Agnes
Bodinnick
Fowey
Polruan
Looe
Polperro
Whitesand Bay
Yealmpton
Dartmouth
Kingswear
Redruth
St. Blazey
Probus
Tregony
Mevagissey
Wembury
Newton Ferrers
Bigbury
7
Stoke Fleming
Pendeen
Zennor
St. Ives
Carbis Bay
Hayle
Camborne
Gwennap
Truro
Veryan
Gorran Haven
Marlborough
Kingsbridge
Salcombe
Torcross
St. Just
Newlyn
Marazion
Penryn
Falmouth
St. Mawes
3
2
Penzance
Mousehole
Helston
Porthleven
St. Keverne
Mount's Bay
Mullion
Coverack
Isles of Scilly
Lizard

Rosslare

Roscoff Santander St Malo

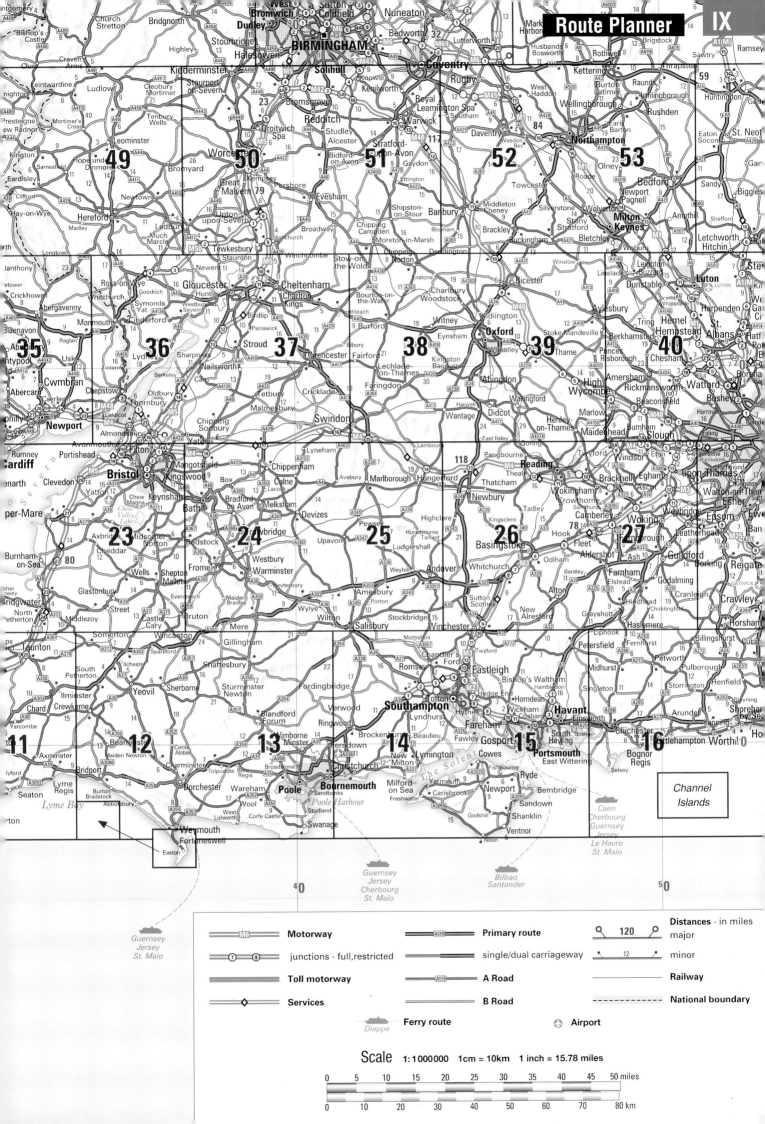

Motorway	**Primary route**	**Distances** - in miles major
junctions - full, restricted	single/dual carriageway	minor
Toll motorway	**A Road**	**Railway**
Services	**B Road**	**National boundary**
Ferry route	**Airport**	

Scale **1:1 000 000 1cm = 10km 1 inch = 15.78 miles**

0 5 10 15 20 25 30 35 40 45 50 miles

0 10 20 30 40 50 60 70 80 km

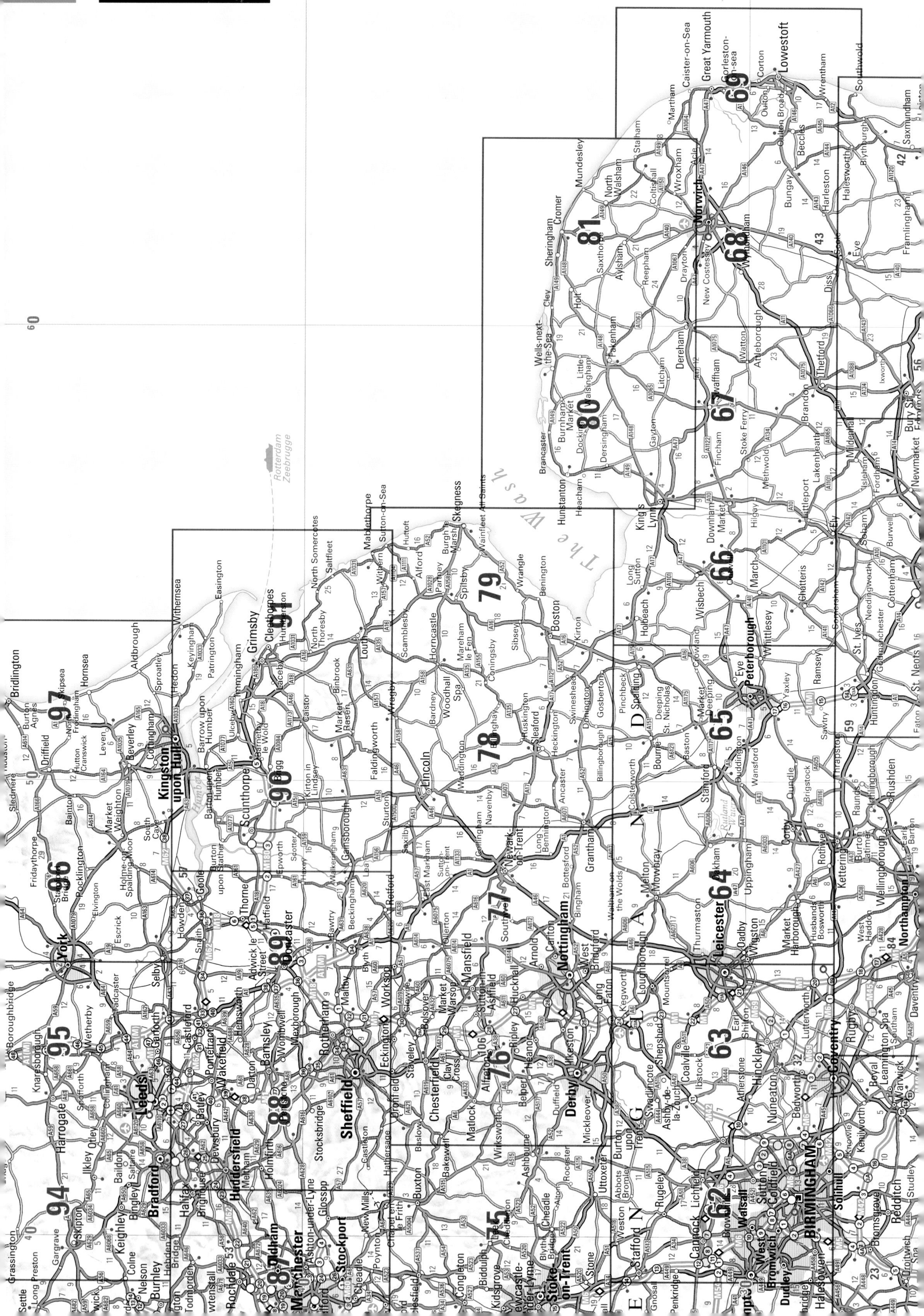
York
Leeds
Bradford
Harrogate
Huddersfield
Halifax
Wakefield
Sheffield
Doncaster
Rotherham
Barnsley
Manchester
Oldham
Stockport
Kingston upon Hull
Grimsby
Cleethorpes
Scunthorpe
Lincoln
Skegness
Boston
Nottingham
Derby
Leicester
Peterborough
Northampton
Coventry
BIRMINGHAM
Walsall
Norwich
Great Yarmouth
Lowestoft
Cromer
King's Lynn
Wisbech
Spalding
Grantham
Newark-on-Trent
Mansfield
Chesterfield
Stoke-on-Trent
The Wash
Rotterdam
Zeebrugge
Humber
Rutland Water
75
76
77
78
79
80
81
87
88
89
90
91
94
95
96
97
62
63
64
65
66
67
68
69

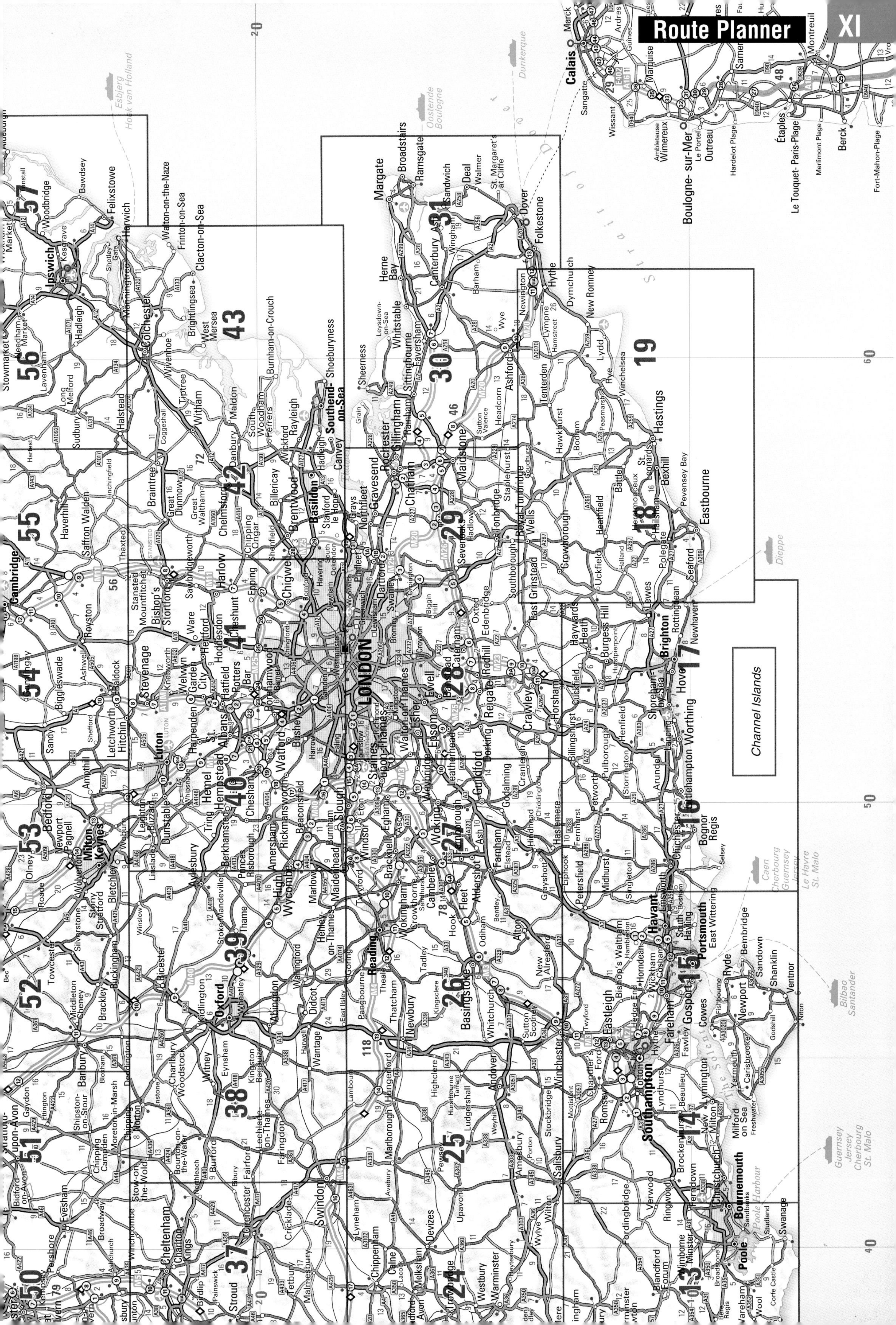

LONDON
Channel Islands
Calais
Boulogne-sur-Mer
Le Touquet-Paris-Plage
Étaples
Berck
Dunkerque
Oostende
Dieppe
Margate
Ramsgate
Canterbury
Dover
Folkestone
Ashford
Maidstone
Chatham
Gillingham
Rochester
Gravesend
Sevenoaks
Tonbridge
Royal Tunbridge Wells
Hastings
Eastbourne
Brighton
Hove
Worthing
Crawley
Horsham
Reigate
Guildford
Woking
Basingstoke
Reading
Slough
Windsor
Maidenhead
High Wycombe
Oxford
Swindon
Cheltenham
Cirencester
Salisbury
Winchester
Southampton
Portsmouth
Havant
Chichester
Bognor Regis
Bournemouth
Poole
Newport
Chelmsford
Basildon
Southend-on-Sea
Colchester
Ipswich
Felixstowe
Harwich
Cambridge
Stevenage
Luton
Bedford
Milton Keynes
Watford
Harlow
Clacton-on-Sea
13
14
15
16
17
18
19
24
25
26
27
28
29
30
31
37
38
39
40
41
42
43
50
51
52
53
54
55
56
57

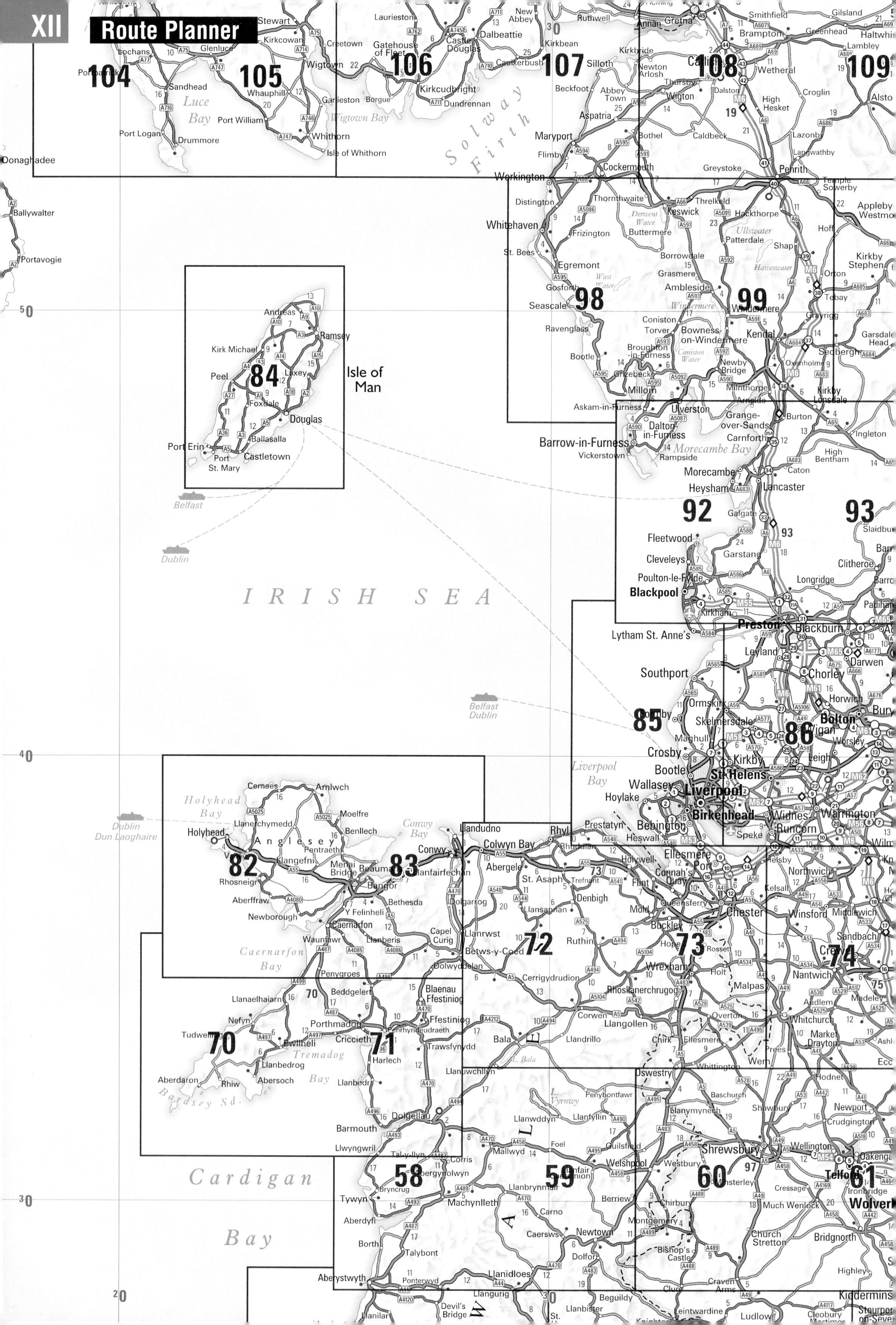
104
105
106
107
108
109
Stewart
Kirkcowan
Creetown
Laurieston
Gatehouse of Fleet
Castle Douglas
Dalbeattie
New Abbey
Ruthwell
Annan
Gretna
Smithfield
Gilsland
Brampton
Greenhead
Haltwhistle
Lambley
Lochans
Glenluce
Portpatrick
Sandhead
Luce Bay
Port William
Port Logan
Drummore
Whauphill
Wigtown
Garlieston
Borgue
Wigtown Bay
Whithorn
Isle of Whithorn
Kirkcudbright
Dundrennan
Kirkbean
Caulkerbush
Silloth
Kirkbride
Newton Arlosh
Carlisle
Wetheral
Dalston
High Hesket
Croglin
Alston
Beckfoot
Abbey Town
Thursby
Wigton
Aspatria
Solway Firth
Maryport
Bothel
Caldbeck
Lazonby
Langwathby
Flimby
Donaghadee
Workington
Cockermouth
Greystoke
Penrith
Temple Sowerby
Ballywalter
Portavogie
Distington
Thornthwaite
Keswick
Threlkeld
Hackthorpe
Appleby-in-Westmorland
Whitehaven
Frizington
Derwent Water
Buttermere
Ullswater
Patterdale
Hoff
Shap
St. Bees
Borrowdale
Egremont
Grasmere
Haweswater
Orton
Kirkby Stephen
Gosforth
Wast Water
Ambleside
Tebay
Seascale
98
99
Windermere
Grayrigg
Garsdale Head
Coniston
Torver
Bowness-on-Windermere
Kendal
Sedbergh
Ravenglass
Broughton-in-Furness
Coniston Water
Oxenholme
Bootle
Newby Bridge
Grizebeck
Millom
Milnthorpe
Kirkby Lonsdale
Arnside
Burton
Ingleton
Askam-in-Furness
Ulverston
Grange-over-Sands
Dalton-in-Furness
Carnforth
Barrow-in-Furness
Vickerstown
Rampside
Morecambe Bay
High Bentham
Caton
Morecambe
Heysham
Lancaster
92
93
Galgate
Slaidburn
Fleetwood
Garstang
Cleveleys
Clitheroe
Poulton-le-Fylde
Longridge
Blackpool
Kirkham
Preston
Blackburn
Lytham St. Anne's
Leyland
Darwen
Chorley
Southport
Horwich
Ormskirk
Bury
Formby
85
86
Skelmersdale
Bolton
Wigan
Maghull
Worsley
Crosby
Kirkby
Leigh
Bootle
St Helens
Liverpool Bay
Wallasey
Liverpool
Hoylake
Birkenhead
Widnes
Warrington
Bebington
Runcorn
Prestatyn
Heswall
Speke
Rhyl
Rhuddlan
Ellesmere Port
Helsby
Holywell
Connah's Quay
Northwich
Flint
Kelsall
Mold
Queensferry
Winsford
Middlewich
Buckley
Chester
Sandbach
Hope
Rossett
Crewe
Wrexham
Holt
Nantwich
Malpas
Madeley
Rhosllanerchrugog
Audlem
Overton
Whitchurch
Market Drayton
Chirk
Ellesmere
Prees
Wem
Whittington
Oswestry
Hodnet
Baschurch
Newport
Shawbury
Crudgington
Llanymynech
Shrewsbury
Wellington
Oakengates
Telford
Ironbridge
Westbury
Minsterley
Cressage
Much Wenlock
Wolverhampton
Chirbury
Church Stretton
Bridgnorth
Montgomery
Bishop's Castle
Highley
Craven Arms
Clun
Kidderminster
Leintwardine
Ludlow
Cleobury Mortimer
Stourport-on-Severn
Knighton
Beguildy
Llanbister
Isle of Man
84
Andreas
Ramsey
Kirk Michael
Peel
Laxey
Foxdale
Douglas
Ballasalla
Port Erin
Port St. Mary
Castletown
Belfast
Dublin
IRISH SEA
Belfast
Dublin
82
83
Cemaes
Amlwch
Holyhead Bay
Moelfre
Llanerchymedd
Benllech
Conwy Bay
Holyhead
Anglesey
Pentraeth
Llandudno
Llangefni
Menai Bridge
Beaumaris
Conwy
Colwyn Bay
Abergele
Llanfairfechan
Bangor
Rhosneigr
Aberffraw
Bethesda
Newborough
Y Felinheli
Caernarfon
Llanberis
Capel Curig
Waunfawr
Caernarfon Bay
Dolgarrog
Llanrwst
Betws-y-Coed
St. Asaph
Trefnant
Denbigh
Llansannan
Ruthin
72
73
Penygroes
Dolwyddelan
Cerrigydrudion
Dublin
Dun Laoghaire
70
71
Llanaelhaiarn
Beddgelert
Blaenau Ffestiniog
Ffestiniog
Nefyn
Porthmadog
Penrhyndeudraeth
Tudweiliog
Pwllheli
Criccieth
Trawsfynydd
Tremadog Bay
Harlech
Llanbedrog
Aberdaron
Rhiw
Abersoch
Bay
Llanbedr
Bardsey Sd.
Bala
L. Bala
Corwen
Llangollen
Llandrillo
Llanuwchllyn
L. Vyrnwy
Penybontfawr
Llanwddyn
Llanfyllin
Dolgellau
Barmouth
Llwyngwril
Mallwyd
Foel
Guilsfield
Welshpool
Tal-y-llyn
Corris
Cardigan Bay
58
59
60
61
Aberdyfi
Bryncrug
Tywyn
Machynlleth
Llanbrynmair
Llanfair Caereinion
Berriew
Carno
Caersws
Newtown
Dolfor
Borth
Talybont
Aberystwyth
Llanidloes
Ponterwyd
Llangurig
Devil's Bridge
Llanilar
WALES

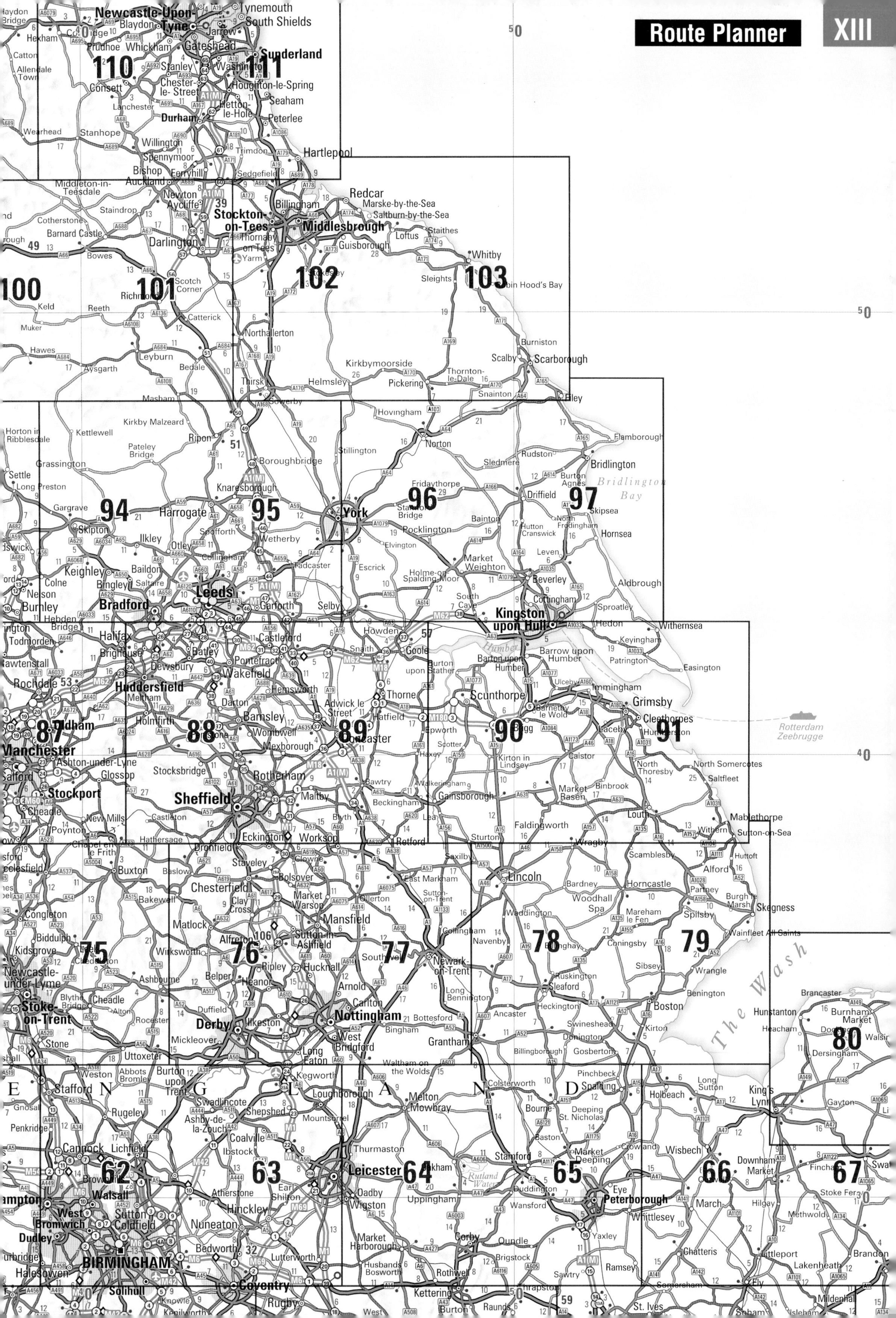

Newcastle-Upon-Tyne
Tynemouth
South Shields
Blaydon
Jarrow
Gateshead
Hexham
Prudhoe
Whickham
Sunderland
Washington
Stanley
Consett
Chester-le-Street
Houghton-le-Spring
Seaham
Lanchester
Durham
Hetton-le-Hole
Peterlee
Wearhead
Stanhope
Willington
Spennymoor
Trimdon
Hartlepool
Bishop Auckland
Ferryhill
Sedgefield
Middleton-in-Teesdale
Newton Aycliffe
Billingham
Redcar
Marske-by-the-Sea
Saltburn-by-the-Sea
Staindrop
Stockton-on-Tees
Middlesbrough
Cotherstone
Barnard Castle
Thornaby-on-Tees
Loftus
Staithes
Darlington
Guisborough
Yarm
Whitby
Bowes
Sleights
Robin Hood's Bay
Scotch Corner
Richmond
Keld
Reeth
Muker
Catterick
Northallerton
Hawes
Leyburn
Aysgarth
Bedale
Burniston
Scalby
Scarborough
Kirkbymoorside
Helmsley
Pickering
Thornton-le-Dale
Snainton
Thirsk
Sowerby
Filey
Masham
Kirkby Malzeard
Hovingham
Horton in Ribblesdale
Kettlewell
Ripon
Norton
Flamborough
Pateley Bridge
Stillington
Rudston
Boroughbridge
Sledmere
Bridlington
Grassington
Settle
Long Preston
Knaresborough
Burton Agnes
Bridlington Bay
Fridaythorpe
Driffield
Gargrave
Harrogate
York
Stamford Bridge
Skipsea
Skipton
Spofforth
Wetherby
Bainton
Hutton Cranswick
North Frodingham
Hornsea
Ilkley
Otley
Pocklington
Elvington
Collingham
Leven
Keighley
Baildon
Tadcaster
Escrick
Market Weighton
Beverley
Colne
Bingley
Saltaire
Holme-on-Spalding-Moor
Aldbrough
Nelson
Burnley
Bradford
Leeds
Garforth
Selby
South Cave
Cottingham
Kingston upon Hull
Sproatley
Hebden Bridge
Todmorden
Halifax
Castleford
Howden
Hedon
Withernsea
Brighouse
Batley
Pontefract
Snaith
Goole
Humber
Barrow upon Humber
Keyingham
Patrington
Rawtenstall
Dewsbury
Wakefield
Barton-upon-Humber
Burton upon Stather
Easington
Rochdale
Huddersfield
Hemsworth
Thorne
Ulceby
Immingham
Meltham
Darton
Adwick le Street
Scunthorpe
Grimsby
Oldham
Holmfirth
Barnsley
Hatfield
Barnetby le Wold
Cleethorpes
Wombwell
Doncaster
Epworth
Brigg
Laceby
Humberston
Rotterdam Zeebrugge
Manchester
Mexborough
Scotter
Ashton-under-Lyne
Stocksbridge
Haxey
Kirton in Lindsey
Caistor
North Somercotes
Glossop
Rotherham
North Thoresby
Saltfleet
Salford
Stockport
Maltby
Bawtry
Walkeringham
Market Rasen
Binbrook
Beckingham
Gainsborough
Cheadle
Sheffield
Castleton
Blyth
Lea
Louth
Mablethorpe
New Mills
Poynton
Eckington
Worksop
Retford
Faldingworth
Withern
Sutton-on-Sea
Hathersage
Sturton
Wragby
Chapel en le Frith
Dronfield
Saxilby
Scamblesby
Huttoft
Macclesfield
Buxton
Baslow
Staveley
Clowne
Lincoln
Alford
Bolsover
East Markham
Bardney
Horncastle
Partney
Chesterfield
Market Warsop
Sutton-on-Trent
Woodhall Spa
Burgh le Marsh
Skegness
Bakewell
Clay Cross
Ollerton
Mareham le Fen
Spilsby
Congleton
Mansfield
Waddington
Matlock
Sutton-in-Ashfield
Collingham
Navenby
Coningsby
Wainfleet All Saints
Biddulph
Alfreton
Southwell
Newark-on-Trent
Branston
Sibsey
Kidsgrove
Cheddleton
Wirksworth
Ripley
Hucknall
Ruskington
Wrangle
Newcastle-under-Lyme
Ashbourne
Belper
Heanor
Arnold
Long Bennington
Sleaford
Benington
The Wash
Brancaster
Stoke-on-Trent
Blythe Bridge
Cheadle
Alton
Duffield
Carlton
Heckington
Boston
Hunstanton
Burnham Market
Rocester
Derby
Ilkeston
Nottingham
Bottesford
Ancaster
Swineshead
Kirton
Heacham
Docking
Walsingham
Stone
Mickleover
West Bridgford
Bingham
Grantham
Donington
Dersingham
Uttoxeter
Long Eaton
Billingborough
Gosberton
Weston
Abbots Bromley
Burton upon Trent
Kegworth
Waltham on the Wolds
Colsterworth
Pinchbeck
Long Sutton
Stafford
ENGLAND
Loughborough
Melton Mowbray
Spalding
Holbeach
King's Lynn
Gnosall
Rugeley
Swadlincote
Shepshed
Bourne
Deeping St. Nicholas
Gayton
Penkridge
Ashby-de-la-Zouch
Mountsorrel
Coalville
Baston
Cannock
Lichfield
Ibstock
Thurmaston
Stamford
Market Deeping
Crowland
Wisbech
Downham Market
Fincham
Brownhills
Leicester
Oakham
Rutland Water
Eye
Outwell
Walsall
Atherstone
Earl Shilton
Oadby
Uppingham
Duddington
Peterborough
March
Hilgay
Stoke Ferry
West Bromwich
Sutton Coldfield
Hinckley
Wigston
Wansford
Whittlesey
Methwold
Dudley
Nuneaton
Market Harborough
Corby
Oundle
Yaxley
Bedworth
Lutterworth
Chatteris
Littleport
Brandon
Halesowen
BIRMINGHAM
Husbands Bosworth
Brigstock
Ramsey
Lakenheath
Coventry
Rothwell
Sawtry
Somersham
Ely
Solihull
Knowle
Kenilworth
Rugby
Kettering
Burton
Raunds
Thrapston
St. Ives
Mildenhall
Soham

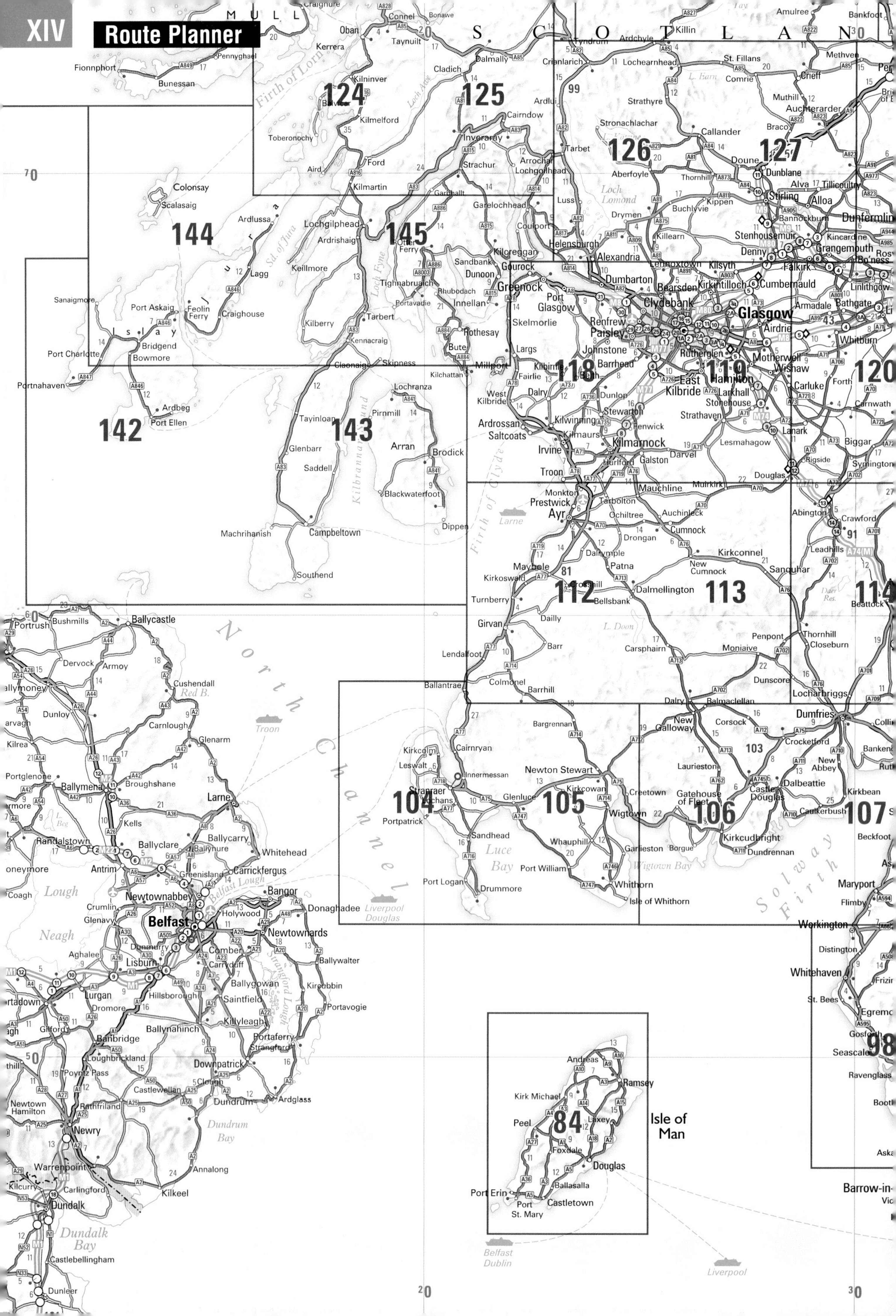
SCOTLAND
North Channel
Firth of Clyde
Solway Firth
Firth of Lorn
Mull
Jura
Islay
Arran
Isle of Man
124
125
126
127
144
145
142
143
118
119
120
112
113
114
104
105
106
107
103
84
91
81
99
98
Oban
Kerrera
Taynuilt
Connel
Bonawe
Dalmally
Tyndrum
Crianlarich
Killin
Lochearnhead
St. Fillans
Comrie
Crieff
Methven
Amulree
Muthill
Auchterarder
Braco
Callander
Doune
Dunblane
Stirling
Alloa
Alva
Tillicoultry
Dunfermline
Bannockburn
Stenhousemuir
Kincardine
Grangemouth
Bo'ness
Falkirk
Denny
Kilsyth
Cumbernauld
Linlithgow
Bathgate
Armadale
Whitburn
Airdrie
Glasgow
Clydebank
Bearsden
Kirkintilloch
Lennoxtown
Renfrew
Paisley
Johnstone
Barrhead
Rutherglen
Motherwell
Wishaw
Hamilton
East Kilbride
Larkhall
Stonehouse
Carluke
Lanark
Carnwath
Biggar
Strathaven
Lesmahagow
Douglas
Abington
Crawford
Leadhills
Sanquhar
Thornhill
Closeburn
Dumfries
Lochmaben
Locharbriggs
Dalbeattie
Castle Douglas
Kirkcudbright
Dundrennan
Gatehouse of Fleet
Creetown
Newton Stewart
Wigtown
Whithorn
Isle of Whithorn
Garlieston
Port William
Glenluce
Stranraer
Cairnryan
Portpatrick
Drummore
Port Logan
Sandhead
Ballantrae
Girvan
Maybole
Turnberry
Ayr
Prestwick
Troon
Irvine
Kilmarnock
Kilwinning
Ardrossan
Saltcoats
West Kilbride
Largs
Greenock
Gourock
Port Glasgow
Dumbarton
Helensburgh
Alexandria
Balloch
Dunoon
Rothesay
Inveraray
Strachur
Arrochar
Tarbet
Lochgilphead
Ardrishaig
Tarbert
Kilmartin
Kilmelford
Kilninver
Campbeltown
Machrihanish
Southend
Brodick
Lochranza
Colonsay
Port Askaig
Bowmore
Port Ellen
Port Charlotte
Portnahaven
Craighouse
Fionnphort
Bunessan
Cumnock
Dalmellington
Mauchline
Galston
Darvel
Kirkconnel
New Cumnock
Dalry
New Galloway
Moniaive
Penpont
Maryport
Workington
Whitehaven
Egremont
Seascale
Barrow-in-Furness
Ramsey
Peel
Douglas
Laxey
Castletown
Port Erin
Port St. Mary
Kirk Michael
Andreas
Foxdale
Ballasalla
Ballycastle
Bushmills
Portrush
Ballymoney
Ballymena
Larne
Antrim
Randalstown
Carrickfergus
Whitehead
Newtownabbey
Belfast
Bangor
Donaghadee
Holywood
Newtownards
Comber
Lisburn
Dunmurry
Ballyclare
Lurgan
Portadown
Banbridge
Ballynahinch
Downpatrick
Newcastle
Dundrum
Newry
Warrenpoint
Kilkeel
Carlingford
Dundalk
Dundalk Bay
Castlebellingham
Dunleer
Lough Neagh
Strangford Lough
Portaferry
Ardglass
Cushendall
Glenarm
Carnlough
Portavogie
Killyleagh
Saintfield
Hillsborough
Dromore
Gilford
Rathfriland
Belfast Dublin
Liverpool
Troon
Larne
Liverpool Douglas

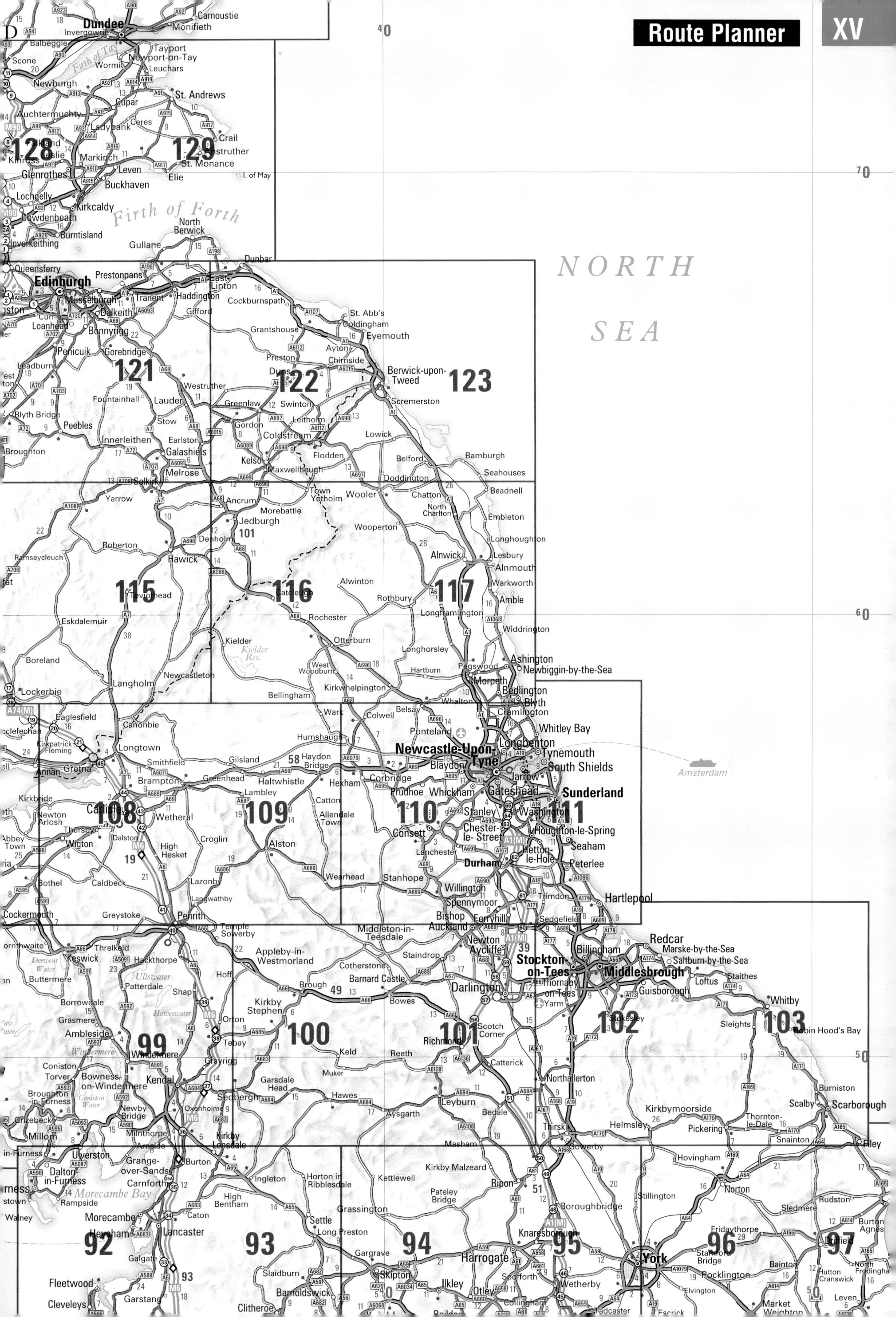

NORTH

SEA

Firth of Tay

Firth of Forth

128

129

121

122

123

115

116

117

101

108

109

110

111

99

100

101

102

103

92

93

94

95

96

97

Amsterdam

Dundee

Edinburgh

Newcastle-Upon-Tyne

Sunderland

Durham

Middlesbrough

Stockton-on-Tees

York

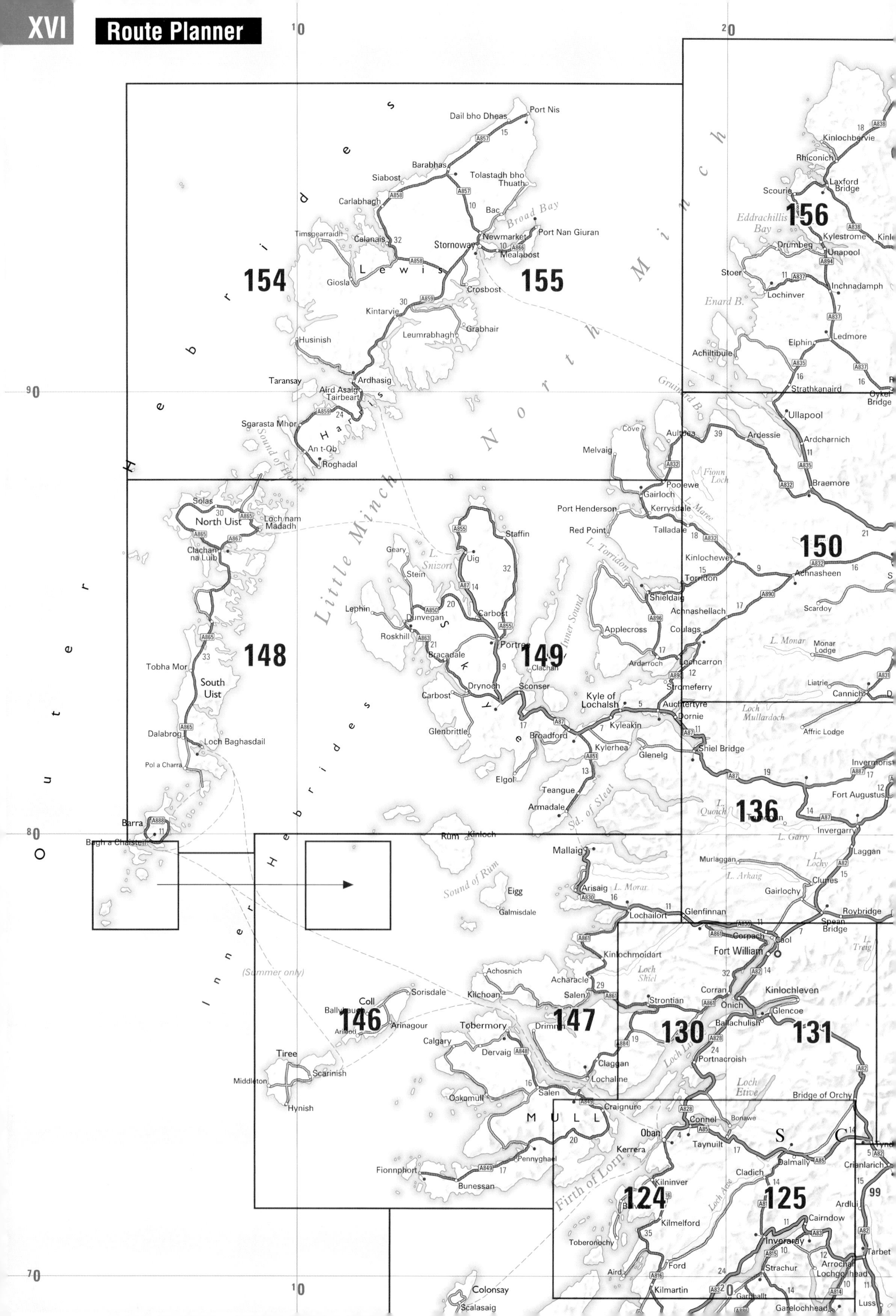
Outer Hebrides
Inner Hebrides
North Minch
Little Minch
154
155
156
148
149
150
136
146
147
130
131
124
125
99
Stornoway
Lewis
Harris
North Uist
South Uist
Barra
Skye
Portree
Kyle of Lochalsh
Ullapool
Mallaig
Fort William
Oban
Tobermory
MULL
Coll
Tiree
Eigg
Rum
Colonsay
Inveraray
(Summer only)

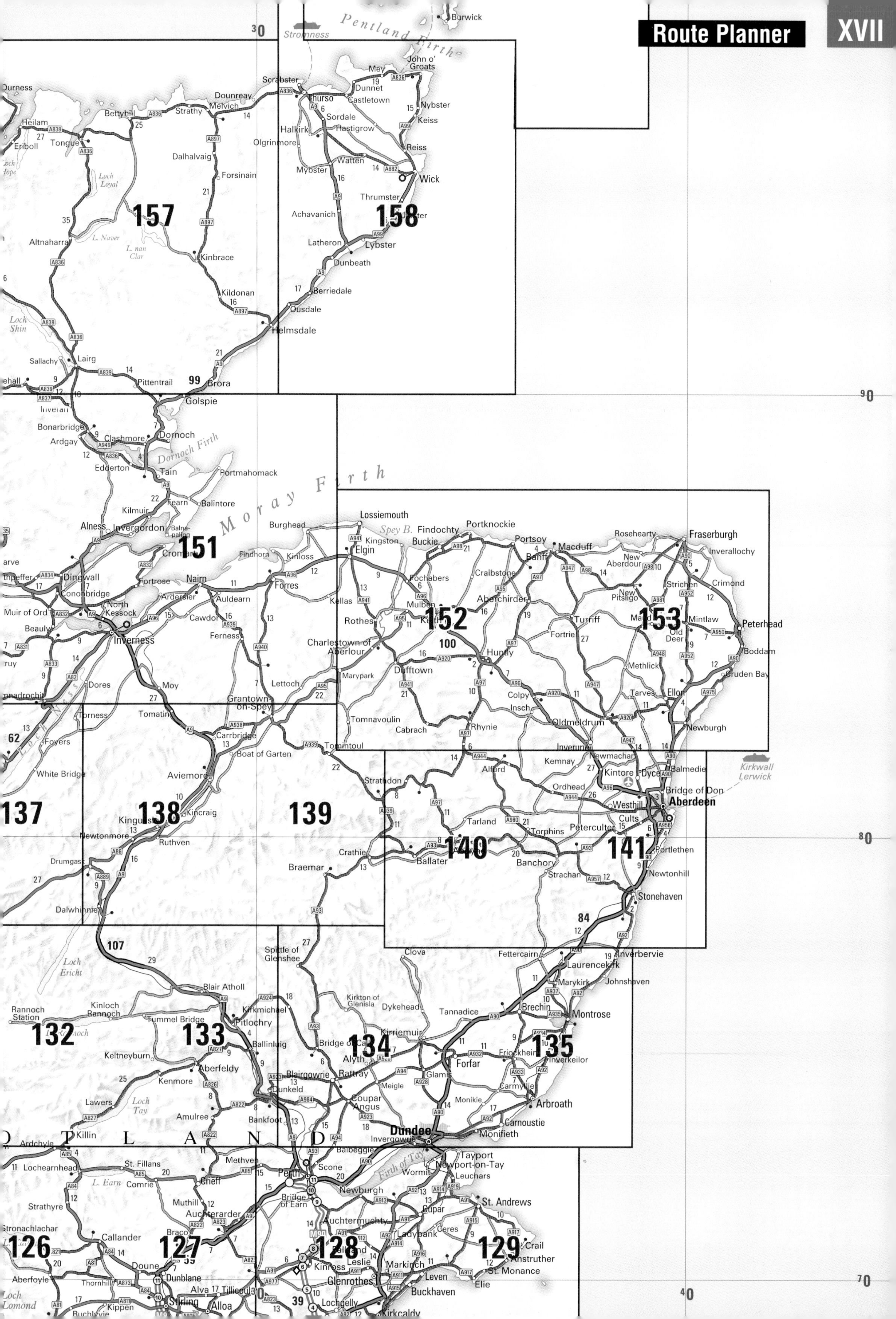
Pentland Firth
Stromness
Burwick
John o' Groats
Mey
Dunnet
Castletown
Nybster
Keiss
Scrabster
Thurso
Durness
Dounreay
Melvich
Bettyhill
Strathy
Heilam
Tongue
Eriboll
Sordale
Halkirk
Hastigrow
Olgrinmore
Reiss
Watten
Mybster
Wick
Dalhalvaig
Forsinain
Loch Loyal
157
158
Thrumster
Achavanich
Altnaharra
L. Naver
L. nan Clar
Latheron
Lybster
Kinbrace
Dunbeath
Berriedale
Kildonan
Ousdale
Loch Shin
Helmsdale
Sallachy
Lairg
Pittentrail
Brora
99
Golspie
Inveran
Bonarbridge
Ardgay
Clashmore
Dornoch
Dornoch Firth
Edderton
Tain
Portmahomack
Moray Firth
Fearn
Balintore
Kilmuir
Alness
Invergordon
Balnapaling
Cromarty
151
Burghead
Findhorn
Kinloss
Lossiemouth
Spey B.
Findochty
Portknockie
Kingston
Buckie
Elgin
Portsoy
Banff
Macduff
Rosehearty
Fraserburgh
Inverallochy
New Aberdour
Craibstone
Strichen
Crimond
New Pitsligo
Dingwall
Conon Bridge
Fortrose
Nairn
Auldearn
Forres
Ardersier
North Kessock
Muir of Ord
Beauly
Cawdor
Inverness
Ferness
Kellas
Rothes
Fochabers
Mulben
Keith
152
Aberchirder
Turriff
Maud
153
Mintlaw
Peterhead
Old Deer
Fortrie
Charlestown of Aberlour
100
Huntly
Boddam
Methlick
Cruden Bay
Marypark
Dufftown
Lettoch
Dores
Moy
Grantown-on-Spey
Colpy
Insch
Tarves
Ellon
Oldmeldrum
Newburgh
Tomnavoulin
Cabrach
Rhynie
Torness
Tomatin
Foyers
Carrbridge
Boat of Garten
Tomintoul
Inverurie
Kemnay
Newmachar
Kintore
Dyce
Balmedie
Kirkwall Lerwick
White Bridge
Aviemore
Alford
Strathdon
Ordhead
Westhill
Bridge of Don
Aberdeen
137
138
139
Kingussie
Kincraig
Newtonmore
Ruthven
Tarland
Torphins
Cults
Peterculter
140
141
Crathie
Ballater
Banchory
Portlethen
Drumgask
Braemar
Strachan
Newtonhill
Stonehaven
84
Dalwhinnie
107
Loch Ericht
Spittle of Glenshee
Clova
Fettercairn
Inverbervie
Laurencekirk
Marykirk
Johnshaven
Blair Atholl
Kirkton of Glenisla
Dykehead
Tannadice
Brechin
Montrose
Rannoch Station
Kinloch Rannoch
Kirkmichael
Tummel Bridge
Pitlochry
132
133
Ballinluig
Bridge of Cally
134
Kirriemuir
Alyth
Friockheim
135
Inverkeilor
Forfar
Keltneyburn
Aberfeldy
Kenmore
Blairgowrie
Rattray
Glamis
Meigle
Carmyllie
Dunkeld
Coupar Angus
Arbroath
Monikie
Lawers
Loch Tay
Amulree
Bankfoot
Carnoustie
Killin
Dundee
Monifieth
Invergowrie
SCOTLAND
Ardchyle
Balbeggie
Tayport
Newport-on-Tay
Firth of Tay
Wormit
Leuchars
Lochearnhead
St. Fillans
Methven
Perth
Scone
L. Earn
Comrie
Crieff
Newburgh
Bridge of Earn
St. Andrews
Strathyre
Muthill
Auchterarder
Cupar
Auchtermuchty
Ceres
Stronachlachar
Callander
Braco
Ladybank
Crail
126
127
128
129
Falkland
Leslie
Markinch
Anstruther
St. Monance
Doune
Kinross
Leven
Elie
Aberfoyle
Thornhill
Dunblane
Glenrothes
Loch Lomond
Kippen
Stirling
Alva
Tillicoultry
Alloa
Lochgelly
Buckhaven
Kirkcaldy
Buchlyvie
30
40
90
80
70

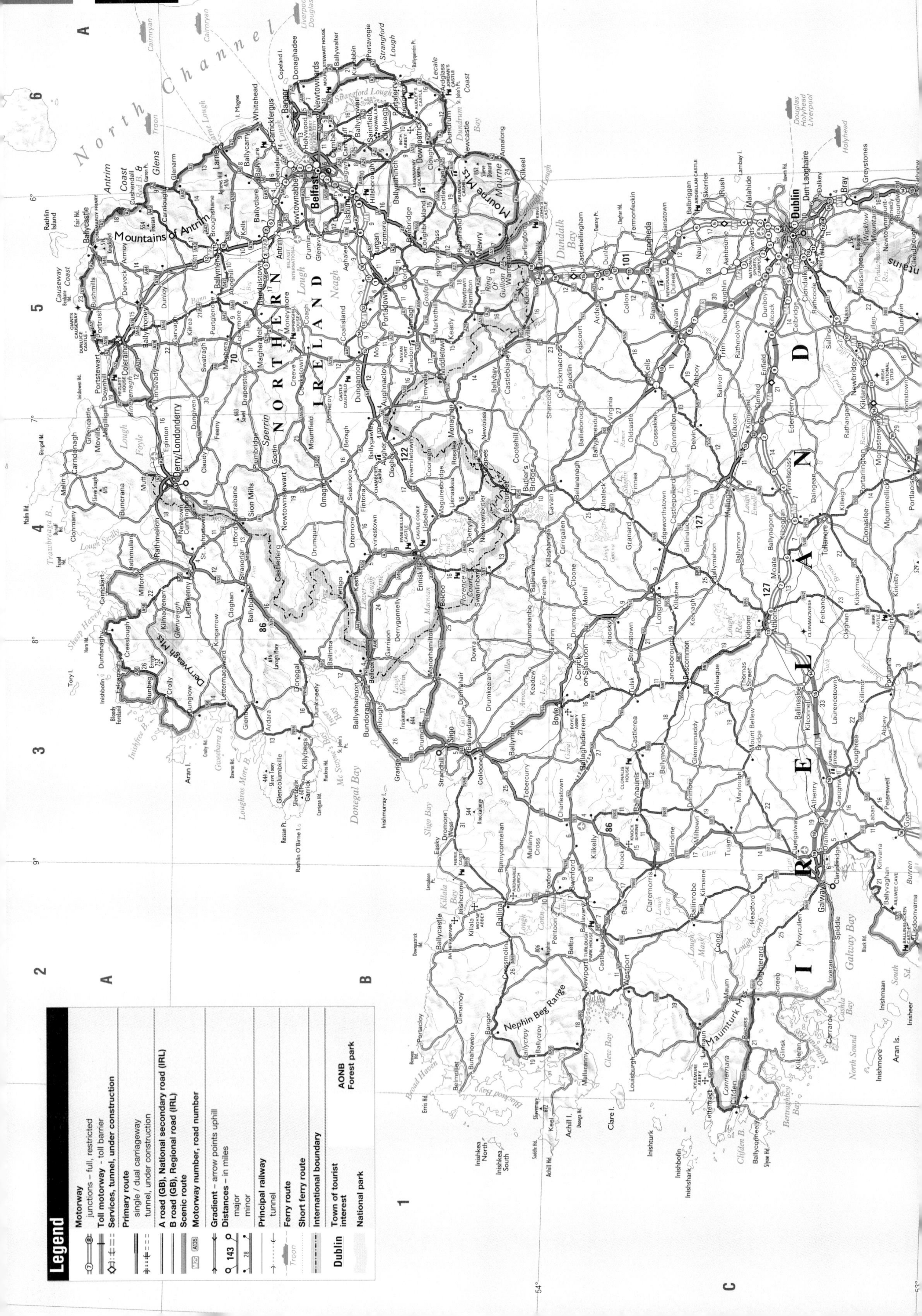
Legend
Motorway
junctions – full, restricted
Toll motorway - toll barrier
Services, tunnel, under construction
Primary route
single / dual carriageway
tunnel, under construction
A road (GB), National secondary road (IRL)
B road (GB), Regional road (IRL)
Scenic route
Motorway number, road number
Gradient – arrow points uphill
Distances – in miles
major
minor
Principal railway
tunnel
Ferry route
Short ferry route
International boundary
Dublin
Town of tourist interest
National park
AONB
Forest park
NORTHERN IRELAND
IRELAND
North Channel
Mountains of Antrim
Mourne Mts.
Derryveagh Mts.
Nephin Beg Range
Maumturk Mts.
Donegal Bay
Galway Bay
Dublin
Belfast
Derry/Londonderry
Galway
Sligo

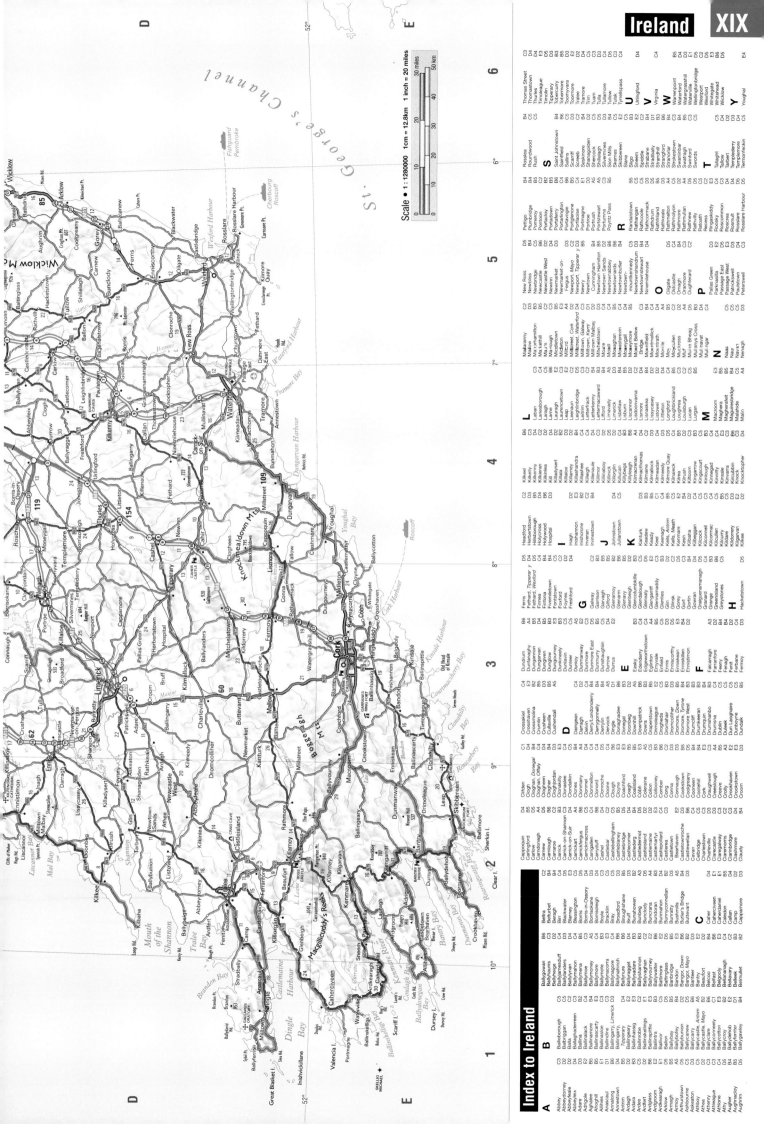

Scale 1 : 1280000   1cm = 12.8km   1 inch = 20 miles

St. George's Channel

Index to Ireland

Distance table

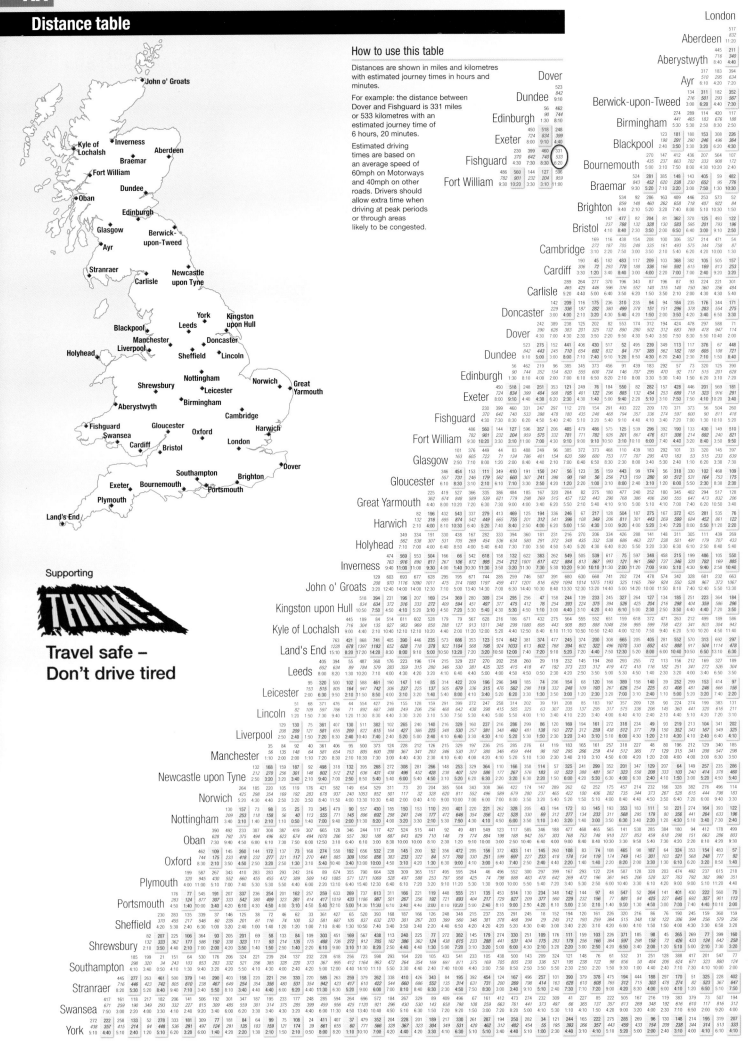

How to use this table

Distances are shown in miles and kilometres with estimated journey times in hours and minutes.

For example: the distance between Dover and Fishguard is 331 miles or 533 kilometres with an estimated journey time of 6 hours, 20 minutes.

Estimated driving times are based on an average speed of 60mph on Motorways and 40mph on other roads. Drivers should allow extra time when driving at peak periods or through areas likely to be congested.

Dover					
Dundee					523 / 842 / 9:10
Edinburgh				56 / 90 / 1:30	462 / 744 / 8:10
Exeter			450 / 724 / 8:00	518 / 834 / 9:10	248 / 399 / 4:40
Fishguard		230 / 370 / 4:30	399 / 642 / 7:30	460 / 740 / 8:30	331 / 533 / 6:20
Fort William	486 / 782 / 9:30	560 / 901 / 10:20	144 / 232 / 3:30	127 / 204 / 3:10	596 / 959 / 11:00

London																																																	
Aberdeen																																																	517 / 832 / 11:20
Aberystwyth																																																445 / 716 / 8:40	211 / 340 / 4:40
Ayr																																															317 / 510 / 6:10	183 / 295 / 4:20	394 / 634 / 7:20
Berwick-upon-Tweed																																														134 / 216 / 3:00	311 / 501 / 6:20	182 / 293 / 4:40	352 / 567 / 7:30
Birmingham																																													274 / 441 / 5:30	289 / 465 / 5:30	114 / 183 / 2:50	420 / 676 / 8:30	117 / 188 / 2:50
Blackpool																																												123 / 198 / 2:40	181 / 291 / 3:50	180 / 290 / 3:30	153 / 246 / 3:20	308 / 496 / 6:20	226 / 364 / 4:30
Bournemouth																																											270 / 435 / 5:00	147 / 237 / 3:10	412 / 663 / 7:50	436 / 702 / 8:00	207 / 333 / 4:30	564 / 908 / 10:20	107 / 172 / 2:40
Braemar																																										524 / 843 / 9:30	281 / 452 / 5:20	385 / 620 / 7:10	148 / 238 / 3:20	143 / 230 / 3:00	405 / 652 / 7:50	59 / 95 / 1:30	482 / 776 / 10:30
Brighton																																									534 / 859 / 9:40	92 / 148 / 2:10	286 / 460 / 5:20	163 / 262 / 3:20	409 / 658 / 7:40	446 / 718 / 8:00	253 / 407 / 5:10	573 / 922 / 10:30	52 / 84 / 1:50
Bristol																																								147 / 237 / 4:10	477 / 768 / 8:40	82 / 132 / 2:30	204 / 328 / 3:50	81 / 130 / 2:00	362 / 583 / 6:50	370 / 595 / 6:40	125 / 201 / 3:00	493 / 793 / 9:10	122 / 196 / 2:50
Cambridge																																							169 / 272 / 3:10	116 / 187 / 2:20	438 / 705 / 7:50	154 / 248 / 3:00	208 / 335 / 3:50	100 / 161 / 2:10	306 / 493 / 5:40	357 / 575 / 6:20	214 / 344 / 4:20	471 / 758 / 10:00	54 / 87 / 1:30
Cardiff																																						190 / 306 / 3:30	45 / 72 / 1:20	182 / 293 / 3:40	483 / 778 / 8:40	117 / 188 / 3:00	209 / 336 / 4:00	103 / 166 / 2:20	368 / 592 / 7:00	382 / 615 / 7:00	105 / 169 / 2:40	505 / 813 / 9:20	157 / 253 / 3:20
Carlisle																																					289 / 465 / 5:20	264 / 425 / 4:40	277 / 446 / 5:00	370 / 596 / 6:40	196 / 316 / 3:50	343 / 552 / 6:20	87 / 140 / 1:50	196 / 315 / 3:50	87 / 140 / 2:10	93 / 150 / 2:00	224 / 360 / 4:30	221 / 356 / 4:30	301 / 484 / 5:40
Doncaster																																				142 / 229 / 3:00	209 / 336 / 4:00	116 / 187 / 2:10	175 / 282 / 3:20	236 / 380 / 4:30	310 / 499 / 5:40	235 / 378 / 4:20	94 / 151 / 1:50	94 / 151 / 2:00	184 / 296 / 3:50	235 / 378 / 4:20	176 / 283 / 3:40	344 / 554 / 6:50	171 / 275 / 3:30
Dover																																			242 / 390 / 4:30	389 / 626 / 7:00	238 / 383 / 4:30	125 / 201 / 2:30	202 / 325 / 3:50	82 / 132 / 2:20	553 / 890 / 9:50	174 / 280 / 4:30	312 / 502 / 5:40	194 / 312 / 3:50	424 / 683 / 7:50	478 / 769 / 8:30	297 / 478 / 5:50	588 / 947 / 10:40	71 / 114 / 2:00
Dundee																																		523 / 842 / 9:10	275 / 443 / 5:00	152 / 245 / 3:00	441 / 710 / 8:00	406 / 654 / 7:10	430 / 692 / 7:40	517 / 832 / 9:10	52 / 84 / 1:20	495 / 797 / 8:50	239 / 385 / 4:30	349 / 562 / 6:20	113 / 182 / 2:40	117 / 188 / 2:30	376 / 605 / 7:10	67 / 108 / 1:50	448 / 721 / 8:40
Edinburgh																																	56 / 90 / 1:30	462 / 744 / 8:10	219 / 352 / 4:00	96 / 154 / 2:00	385 / 620 / 7:00	345 / 555 / 6:10	373 / 600 / 6:50	456 / 734 / 8:20	91 / 146 / 2:10	439 / 707 / 8:00	183 / 295 / 3:30	292 / 470 / 5:30	57 / 92 / 1:40	73 / 117 / 1:50	320 / 515 / 6:20	125 / 201 / 3:10	390 / 628 / 7:20
Exeter																																450 / 724 / 8:00	518 / 834 / 9:10	248 / 399 / 4:40	251 / 404 / 4:30	353 / 568 / 6:20	121 / 195 / 2:30	249 / 401 / 4:30	76 / 122 / 1:40	184 / 296 / 5:00	550 / 885 / 9:40	82 / 132 / 2:20	282 / 454 / 5:10	157 / 253 / 3:10	428 / 689 / 7:50	446 / 718 / 7:50	201 / 323 / 4:10	569 / 916 / 10:20	181 / 291 / 3:40
Fishguard																															230 / 370 / 4:30	399 / 642 / 7:30	460 / 740 / 8:30	331 / 533 / 6:20	247 / 398 / 4:50	297 / 478 / 5:40	112 / 180 / 2:40	270 / 435 / 5:10	154 / 248 / 3:20	291 / 468 / 5:40	493 / 794 / 9:10	222 / 357 / 4:40	209 / 336 / 4:10	170 / 274 / 3:40	371 / 597 / 7:20	373 / 600 / 7:00	56 / 90 / 1:30	504 / 811 / 10:10	260 / 418 / 5:20
Fort William																														486 / 782 / 9:30	560 / 901 / 10:20	144 / 232 / 3:30	127 / 204 / 3:10	596 / 959 / 11:00	357 / 575 / 7:00	206 / 332 / 4:30	485 / 781 / 9:10	479 / 771 / 9:00	486 / 782 / 9:10	575 / 926 / 10:50	125 / 201 / 3:10	539 / 867 / 10:10	296 / 476 / 6:00	392 / 631 / 7:40	190 / 306 / 4:40	133 / 214 / 3:20	430 / 692 / 8:40	149 / 240 / 3:50	510 / 821 / 9:50
Glasgow																													101 / 163 / 2:50	376 / 605 / 7:10	449 / 723 / 8:00	44 / 71 / 1:20	83 / 134 / 2:00	488 / 786 / 8:40	249 / 401 / 4:40	96 / 154 / 2:10	385 / 620 / 7:00	372 / 599 / 6:40	373 / 600 / 6:50	468 / 753 / 8:30	110 / 177 / 2:30	439 / 707 / 8:00	183 / 295 / 3:40	292 / 470 / 5:30	101 / 163 / 2:40	33 / 53 / 1:10	320 / 515 / 6:20	145 / 233 / 3:30	397 / 639 / 7:30
Gloucester																												346 / 557 / 6:10	454 / 731 / 8:30	153 / 246 / 3:10	111 / 179 / 2:10	349 / 562 / 6:10	410 / 660 / 7:10	191 / 307 / 3:30	150 / 241 / 2:50	247 / 398 / 4:20	56 / 90 / 1:20	123 / 198 / 2:20	35 / 56 / 1:00	159 / 256 / 3:10	443 / 713 / 8:00	99 / 159 / 2:40	174 / 280 / 3:10	56 / 90 / 1:20	318 / 512 / 6:00	330 / 531 / 5:50	102 / 164 / 2:30	468 / 753 / 8:30	109 / 175 / 2:30
Great Yarmouth																											225 / 362 / 4:40	419 / 674 / 8:00	527 / 848 / 10:20	366 / 589 / 7:20	335 / 539 / 6:30	386 / 621 / 7:30	484 / 779 / 9:00	185 / 298 / 4:00	167 / 269 / 3:40	320 / 515 / 6:20	284 / 457 / 5:50	82 / 132 / 2:10	275 / 443 / 5:40	180 / 290 / 4:10	477 / 768 / 9:10	240 / 386 / 5:00	252 / 406 / 5:10	180 / 290 / 4:10	345 / 555 / 7:00	402 / 647 / 7:40	294 / 473 / 6:20	517 / 832 / 10:50	128 / 206 / 3:40
Harwich																										82 / 132 / 2:10	196 / 316 / 4:00	432 / 695 / 8:10	543 / 874 / 10:30	337 / 542 / 6:40	279 / 449 / 5:20	413 / 665 / 7:40	469 / 755 / 8:40	125 / 201 / 2:50	194 / 312 / 4:00	336 / 541 / 6:20	246 / 396 / 5:00	67 / 108 / 1:50	217 / 349 / 4:30	128 / 206 / 3:00	504 / 811 / 9:20	187 / 301 / 4:00	275 / 443 / 5:20	167 / 269 / 3:40	372 / 599 / 7:20	425 / 684 / 8:00	281 / 452 / 5:50	535 / 861 / 11:20	76 / 122 / 2:20
Holyhead																									349 / 562 / 7:10	334 / 538 / 7:00	191 / 307 / 4:00	330 / 531 / 6:40	438 / 705 / 8:50	167 / 269 / 4:00	282 / 454 / 5:40	333 / 536 / 6:40	394 / 634 / 7:30	360 / 580 / 7:00	181 / 291 / 3:50	231 / 372 / 4:50	216 / 348 / 5:40	270 / 435 / 5:20	206 / 332 / 4:30	334 / 538 / 6:40	426 / 686 / 8:20	288 / 463 / 5:50	141 / 227 / 3:20	148 / 238 / 3:30	311 / 501 / 6:30	305 / 491 / 6:10	111 / 179 / 2:50	439 / 707 / 8:40	269 / 433 / 5:40
Inverness																								474 / 763 / 9:40	569 / 916 / 11:00	553 / 890 / 11:00	504 / 811 / 9:30	166 / 267 / 4:00	66 / 106 / 1:40	542 / 872 / 10:30	618 / 995 / 11:30	158 / 254 / 3:50	132 / 212 / 3:20	622 / 1001 / 11:30	383 / 617 / 7:30	262 / 422 / 5:30	549 / 884 / 10:20	505 / 813 / 9:30	539 / 867 / 10:10	617 / 993 / 11:30	75 / 121 / 2:00	597 / 961 / 11:20	348 / 560 / 7:00	458 / 737 / 9:00	215 / 346 / 5:10	199 / 320 / 4:30	486 / 782 / 9:40	105 / 169 / 2:50	550 / 885 / 10:40
John o' Groats																							129 / 208 / 3:20	603 / 970 / 12:40	693 / 1116 / 14:00	677 / 1090 / 14:00	628 / 1011 / 12:30	295 / 475 / 7:10	195 / 314 / 5:00	671 / 1080 / 13:40	744 / 1197 / 14:30	285 / 459 / 7:00	259 / 417 / 6:30	746 / 1201 / 14:40	507 / 816 / 10:30	391 / 629 / 8:40	680 / 1094 / 13:30	630 / 1014 / 12:30	668 / 1075 / 13:20	741 / 1193 / 14:40	202 / 325 / 5:00	724 / 1165 / 14:20	478 / 769 / 10:00	574 / 924 / 11:50	342 / 550 / 8:10	328 / 528 / 7:40	601 / 967 / 12:40	232 / 373 / 5:50	663 / 1067 / 13:30
Kingston upon Hull																						518 / 834 / 10:50	394 / 634 / 7:50	231 / 372 / 4:50	196 / 316 / 4:10	207 / 333 / 5:20	169 / 272 / 3:10	254 / 409 / 4:50	369 / 594 / 7:20	280 / 451 / 5:30	309 / 497 / 5:40	234 / 377 / 4:30	295 / 475 / 5:30	256 / 412 / 4:50	47 / 76 / 1:10	158 / 254 / 3:00	244 / 393 / 4:40	139 / 224 / 3:10	233 / 375 / 4:20	245 / 394 / 4:40	327 / 526 / 6:10	264 / 425 / 5:00	127 / 204 / 2:30	134 / 216 / 2:50	185 / 298 / 3:50	251 / 404 / 4:40	223 / 359 / 4:40	364 / 586 / 7:20	184 / 296 / 3:50
Kyle of Lochalsh																					445 / 716 / 9:00	189 / 304 / 4:40	84 / 135 / 2:10	514 / 827 / 10:40	611 / 983 / 12:10	602 / 969 / 12:10	528 / 850 / 10:20	179 / 288 / 4:40	79 / 127 / 2:00	567 / 913 / 11:20	628 / 1011 / 12:00	216 / 348 / 5:20	186 / 299 / 4:40	671 / 1080 / 12:50	432 / 695 / 8:40	275 / 443 / 6:10	564 / 908 / 11:10	555 / 893 / 10:50	552 / 888 / 10:50	651 / 1048 / 12:40	159 / 256 / 4:00	618 / 995 / 12:10	372 / 599 / 7:50	471 / 758 / 9:40	263 / 423 / 6:20	212 / 341 / 5:10	499 / 803 / 10:20	189 / 304 / 4:50	586 / 943 / 11:40
Land's End																				763 / 1228 / 15:10	421 / 678 / 8:20	868 / 1397 / 17:20	741 / 1193 / 14:20	405 / 652 / 8:30	390 / 628 / 8:00	446 / 718 / 9:10	235 / 378 / 5:00	573 / 922 / 10:50	686 / 1104 / 13:20	353 / 568 / 7:20	123 / 198 / 3:20	574 / 924 / 10:50	642 / 1033 / 12:00	381 / 613 / 7:40	374 / 602 / 7:20	477 / 768 / 9:10	245 / 394 / 5:20	374 / 602 / 7:20	200 / 322 / 4:40	308 / 496 / 7:50	665 / 1070 / 12:30	205 / 330 / 5:20	405 / 652 / 8:00	281 / 452 / 6:00	552 / 888 / 10:40	570 / 917 / 10:50	313 / 504 / 6:50	692 / 1114 / 13:10	297 / 478 / 6:30
Leeds																			405 / 652 / 8:00	394 / 634 / 8:20	55 / 89 / 1:30	487 / 784 / 10:20	360 / 579 / 7:10	176 / 283 / 4:00	223 / 359 / 4:30	196 / 315 / 4:20	174 / 280 / 3:20	215 / 346 / 4:10	329 / 530 / 6:40	237 / 381 / 4:40	270 / 435 / 5:00	202 / 325 / 4:00	258 / 415 / 4:50	260 / 418 / 4:50	29 / 47 / 0:50	119 / 192 / 2:30	232 / 373 / 4:20	145 / 233 / 2:50	194 / 312 / 3:50	260 / 419 / 5:00	293 / 472 / 5:30	255 / 410 / 4:50	72 / 116 / 1:40	113 / 182 / 2:30	156 / 251 / 3:20	212 / 341 / 4:00	169 / 272 / 3:40	327 / 526 / 6:50	189 / 304 / 3:50
Leicester																		95 / 153 / 2:00	320 / 515 / 6:30	500 / 805 / 9:50	102 / 164 / 2:10	588 / 947 / 11:50	461 / 742 / 8:50	190 / 306 / 4:00	147 / 237 / 3:10	140 / 225 / 3:20	85 / 137 / 1:40	314 / 505 / 5:40	422 / 679 / 8:00	209 / 336 / 4:10	196 / 315 / 3:40	296 / 476 / 5:20	349 / 562 / 6:20	185 / 298 / 3:30	74 / 119 / 1:30	206 / 332 / 3:50	154 / 248 / 3:00	68 / 109 / 1:20	120 / 193 / 2:30	166 / 267 / 3:20	389 / 626 / 7:00	158 / 254 / 3:10	140 / 225 / 2:40	39 / 63 / 1:10	252 / 406 / 5:00	299 / 481 / 5:20	153 / 246 / 3:20	414 / 666 / 7:40	97 / 156 / 2:20
Lincoln																	51 / 82 / 1:20	68 / 109 / 1:50	371 / 597 / 7:30	476 / 766 / 9:40	44 / 71 / 1:20	554 / 892 / 11:30	427 / 687 / 8:30	216 / 348 / 4:40	155 / 249 / 3:30	128 / 206 / 3:20	159 / 256 / 3:10	291 / 468 / 5:30	399 / 642 / 7:50	272 / 438 / 5:30	247 / 398 / 4:40	258 / 415 / 5:00	314 / 505 / 5:50	202 / 325 / 4:00	39 / 63 / 1:10	191 / 307 / 3:40	208 / 335 / 4:10	85 / 137 / 2:20	183 / 295 / 3:40	197 / 317 / 4:00	357 / 575 / 6:40	209 / 336 / 4:10	128 / 206 / 2:40	90 / 145 / 2:10	224 / 360 / 4:40	274 / 441 / 5:10	199 / 320 / 4:20	383 / 616 / 7:20	131 / 211 / 3:10
Liverpool																129 / 208 / 2:50	130 / 209 / 2:40	75 / 121 / 1:50	361 / 581 / 7:20	407 / 655 / 8:30	130 / 209 / 2:40	511 / 822 / 10:40	382 / 615 / 7:40	102 / 164 / 2:40	265 / 427 / 5:20	240 / 386 / 5:00	140 / 225 / 2:40	216 / 348 / 4:10	329 / 530 / 6:40	160 / 257 / 3:30	237 / 381 / 4:30	216 / 348 / 4:10	286 / 460 / 5:20	299 / 481 / 5:30	86 / 138 / 1:50	120 / 193 / 2:30	169 / 272 / 3:20	194 / 312 / 3:40	161 / 259 / 3:10	272 / 438 / 5:10	318 / 512 / 6:00	234 / 377 / 4:30	49 / 79 / 1:20	93 / 150 / 2:10	219 / 352 / 4:30	213 / 343 / 4:10	104 / 167 / 2:40	341 / 549 / 6:40	202 / 325 / 4:10
Manchester															35 / 56 / 1:10	84 / 135 / 2:00	92 / 148 / 2:00	40 / 64 / 1:10	361 / 581 / 7:20	406 / 654 / 8:30	95 / 153 / 2:10	500 / 805 / 10:30	373 / 600 / 7:30	124 / 200 / 3:00	228 / 367 / 4:40	212 / 341 / 4:30	126 / 203 / 2:30	215 / 346 / 4:10	329 / 530 / 6:40	197 / 317 / 4:00	236 / 380 / 4:20	215 / 346 / 4:10	285 / 459 / 5:20	276 / 444 / 5:10	61 / 98 / 1:30	119 / 192 / 2:30	183 / 295 / 3:40	165 / 266 / 3:10	161 / 259 / 3:10	257 / 414 / 4:50	318 / 512 / 6:00	227 / 365 / 4:20	48 / 77 / 1:20	80 / 129 / 2:00	196 / 315 / 4:00	212 / 341 / 4:00	129 / 208 / 3:00	340 / 547 / 6:30	185 / 298 / 3:50
Newcastle upon Tyne														132 / 212 / 2:50	168 / 270 / 3:20	159 / 256 / 3:20	187 / 301 / 3:40	92 / 148 / 2:10	498 / 802 / 9:40	318 / 512 / 7:00	132 / 212 / 2:50	395 / 636 / 8:50	268 / 431 / 5:40	272 / 438 / 5:40	308 / 496 / 6:00	281 / 452 / 5:40	266 / 428 / 4:50	148 / 238 / 3:10	253 / 407 / 5:20	329 / 529 / 6:20	364 / 586 / 6:30	110 / 177 / 2:20	166 / 267 / 3:20	358 / 576 / 6:30	114 / 183 / 2:20	57 / 92 / 1:50	325 / 523 / 6:00	241 / 388 / 4:20	299 / 481 / 5:30	352 / 567 / 6:30	201 / 323 / 4:00	347 / 558 / 6:30	129 / 208 / 2:40	207 / 333 / 4:10	64 / 103 / 1:50	149 / 240 / 3:00	257 / 414 / 5:20	235 / 378 / 4:50	286 / 460 / 5:40
Norwich													264 / 425 / 5:20	185 / 298 / 4:30	220 / 354 / 4:40	105 / 169 / 2:50	119 / 192 / 3:20	176 / 283 / 3:50	421 / 678 / 8:40	582 / 937 / 11:50	149 / 240 / 4:00	654 / 1053 / 13:30	529 / 852 / 10:30	311 / 501 / 6:40	73 / 117 / 2:00	20 / 32 / 0:40	204 / 328 / 4:10	385 / 620 / 9:00	504 / 811 / 10:00	343 / 552 / 7:00	308 / 496 / 6:00	366 / 589 / 7:00	422 / 679 / 8:00	174 / 280 / 3:50	147 / 237 / 3:20	289 / 465 / 5:40	262 / 422 / 5:20	62 / 100 / 1:50	252 / 406 / 5:10	175 / 282 / 4:00	457 / 735 / 8:40	214 / 344 / 4:40	232 / 373 / 4:50	166 / 267 / 3:50	328 / 528 / 6:40	382 / 615 / 7:20	276 / 444 / 6:00	496 / 798 / 9:40	114 / 183 / 3:30
Nottingham												130 / 209 / 3:40	157 / 253 / 3:10	73 / 118 / 1:40	98 / 158 / 2:10	35 / 56 / 1:10	25 / 40 / 0:50	70 / 113 / 1:40	345 / 555 / 7:00	479 / 771 / 9:40	90 / 145 / 2:00	557 / 896 / 11:30	430 / 692 / 8:20	185 / 298 / 4:00	150 / 241 / 3:20	153 / 246 / 3:30	110 / 177 / 2:10	293 / 472 / 5:30	401 / 646 / 7:50	220 / 354 / 4:30	221 / 356 / 4:10	262 / 422 / 4:50	328 / 528 / 6:00	205 / 330 / 3:50	43 / 69 / 1:10	194 / 312 / 3:40	172 / 277 / 3:20	83 / 134 / 1:40	145 / 233 / 3:00	193 / 311 / 3:50	353 / 568 / 6:30	183 / 295 / 3:40	111 / 179 / 2:20	50 / 80 / 1:20	221 / 356 / 4:30	274 / 441 / 5:10	164 / 264 / 3:40	393 / 633 / 7:30	122 / 196 / 2:40
Oban											390 / 628 / 7:30	492 / 792 / 9:40	233 / 375 / 4:50	307 / 494 / 6:00	308 / 496 / 6:10	387 / 623 / 7:30	419 / 674 / 7:50	307 / 494 / 6:00	665 / 1070 / 12:50	128 / 206 / 3:10	346 / 557 / 6:40	244 / 393 / 6:10	117 / 188 / 3:00	427 / 687 / 8:30	524 / 843 / 10:00	515 / 829 / 10:00	441 / 710 / 8:10	92 / 148 / 2:30	49 / 79 / 1:20	481 / 774 / 9:10	549 / 884 / 10:00	123 / 198 / 3:00	117 / 188 / 2:50	585 / 942 / 10:40	346 / 557 / 6:40	188 / 303 / 4:00	477 / 768 / 9:00	468 / 753 / 8:40	465 / 748 / 8:40	565 / 910 / 10:30	141 / 227 / 3:30	530 / 853 / 9:50	285 / 459 / 5:40	384 / 618 / 7:30	180 / 290 / 4:20	94 / 151 / 2:20	412 / 663 / 8:10	178 / 286 / 4:20	499 / 803 / 9:30
Oxford										462 / 744 / 8:30	109 / 175 / 2:10	145 / 233 / 3:50	260 / 418 / 4:50	144 / 232 / 2:50	172 / 277 / 3:20	137 / 221 / 2:50	73 / 117 / 1:30	168 / 270 / 3:10	274 / 441 / 5:40	550 / 885 / 10:40	192 / 309 / 3:40	656 / 1056 / 13:00	532 / 856 / 10:00	238 / 383 / 4:50	145 / 233 / 3:10	200 / 322 / 4:20	52 / 84 / 1:30	356 / 573 / 6:30	472 / 760 / 9:00	205 / 330 / 4:10	156 / 251 / 3:00	372 / 599 / 6:40	433 / 697 / 7:40	141 / 227 / 2:50	145 / 233 / 2:40	260 / 418 / 4:40	108 / 174 / 2:20	83 / 134 / 1:40	74 / 119 / 1:40	108 / 174 / 2:20	465 / 749 / 8:20	90 / 145 / 2:00	187 / 301 / 3:30	64 / 103 / 1:30	324 / 521 / 6:10	353 / 568 / 6:20	154 / 248 / 3:20	483 / 777 / 8:50	57 / 92 / 1:40
Plymouth									199 / 320 / 4:00	587 / 945 / 11:00	267 / 430 / 5:10	343 / 552 / 7:00	410 / 660 / 7:40	283 / 455 / 5:30	283 / 455 / 5:30	293 / 472 / 5:50	242 / 389 / 4:40	316 / 509 / 6:00	89 / 143 / 2:20	674 / 1085 / 13:10	355 / 571 / 6:40	790 / 1271 / 15:40	664 / 1069 / 12:30	328 / 528 / 6:40	309 / 497 / 6:10	365 / 588 / 7:20	157 / 253 / 3:20	495 / 797 / 9:10	595 / 958 / 11:20	264 / 425 / 5:30	46 / 74 / 1:30	496 / 798 / 9:00	552 / 888 / 10:00	300 / 483 / 5:50	297 / 478 / 5:40	399 / 642 / 7:20	167 / 269 / 3:40	293 / 472 / 5:30	122 / 196 / 2:50	224 / 361 / 6:00	587 / 945 / 10:40	128 / 206 / 3:30	328 / 528 / 6:10	203 / 327 / 4:20	474 / 763 / 9:00	492 / 792 / 9:00	237 / 382 / 5:10	615 / 990 / 11:20	218 / 351 / 4:40
Portsmouth								176 / 283 / 4:50	77 / 124 / 1:40	545 / 877 / 10:00	191 / 307 / 3:40	207 / 333 / 4:20	337 / 542 / 6:10	236 / 380 / 4:30	254 / 409 / 4:50	201 / 323 / 4:00	162 / 261 / 3:10	257 / 414 / 4:50	259 / 417 / 5:40	633 / 1019 / 12:10	269 / 433 / 5:00	737 / 1186 / 14:30	613 / 987 / 11:30	311 / 501 / 6:10	166 / 267 / 3:40	221 / 356 / 4:40	119 / 192 / 3:00	448 / 721 / 8:10	555 / 893 / 10:20	251 / 404 / 5:00	135 / 217 / 2:40	453 / 729 / 8:10	514 / 827 / 9:00	130 / 209 / 2:50	234 / 377 / 4:20	348 / 560 / 6:10	142 / 229 / 3:00	144 / 232 / 2:50	97 / 156 / 2:10	48 / 77 / 1:40	547 / 881 / 9:50	52 / 84 / 1:30	264 / 425 / 4:50	141 / 227 / 3:00	401 / 645 / 7:30	430 / 692 / 7:40	222 / 357 / 4:40	560 / 901 / 10:10	70 / 113 / 2:00
Sheffield							230 / 370 / 4:20	283 / 455 / 5:30	135 / 217 / 2:40	339 / 546 / 6:30	37 / 60 / 1:00	146 / 235 / 3:20	125 / 201 / 2:40	38 / 61 / 1:00	72 / 116 / 1:40	46 / 74 / 1:20	62 / 100 / 1:20	33 / 53 / 1:00	361 / 581 / 7:10	427 / 687 / 8:40	65 / 105 / 1:30	520 / 837 / 10:50	393 / 632 / 7:40	168 / 270 / 3:40	187 / 301 / 3:50	166 / 267 / 3:40	126 / 203 / 2:20	248 / 399 / 4:40	348 / 560 / 6:50	215 / 346 / 4:20	237 / 381 / 4:20	235 / 378 / 4:20	291 / 468 / 5:20	245 / 394 / 4:30	18 / 29 / 0:40	152 / 245 / 3:00	194 / 312 / 3:40	120 / 193 / 2:20	161 / 259 / 3:10	226 / 364 / 4:20	320 / 515 / 6:00	216 / 348 / 4:10	86 / 138 / 1:50	76 / 122 / 1:50	190 / 306 / 4:00	245 / 394 / 4:30	159 / 256 / 3:30	360 / 579 / 6:50	159 / 256 / 3:20
Shrewsbury						82 / 132 / 2:10	207 / 333 / 3:50	225 / 362 / 4:40	106 / 171 / 2:10	364 / 586 / 7:00	93 / 150 / 2:00	205 / 330 / 4:20	201 / 323 / 3:50	69 / 111 / 1:40	58 / 93 / 1:50	133 / 214 / 2:50	84 / 135 / 1:40	109 / 175 / 2:20	303 / 488 / 6:10	451 / 726 / 9:00	169 / 272 / 3:10	567 / 912 / 11:30	438 / 705 / 8:20	113 / 182 / 2:50	240 / 386 / 4:40	225 / 362 / 4:40	77 / 124 / 1:30	272 / 438 / 5:00	382 / 615 / 7:20	145 / 233 / 3:10	179 / 288 / 3:20	274 / 441 / 5:00	330 / 531 / 6:00	251 / 404 / 4:30	109 / 175 / 2:10	176 / 283 / 3:20	111 / 179 / 2:20	159 / 256 / 3:00	103 / 166 / 2:50	226 / 364 / 4:20	371 / 597 / 6:50	185 / 298 / 3:40	98 / 158 / 2:00	45 / 72 / 1:20	265 / 426 / 5:10	269 / 433 / 5:00	77 / 124 / 2:10	399 / 642 / 7:30	160 / 258 / 3:20
Southampton					185 / 298 / 4:10	199 / 320 / 3:40	21 / 34 / 0:50	151 / 243 / 4:10	64 / 103 / 1:30	530 / 853 / 9:40	176 / 283 / 3:20	206 / 332 / 4:20	324 / 521 / 5:50	221 / 356 / 4:10	239 / 385 / 4:30	204 / 328 / 4:00	137 / 220 / 2:40	232 / 373 / 4:20	228 / 367 / 5:00	618 / 995 / 12:00	256 / 412 / 4:40	723 / 1164 / 14:10	598 / 963 / 11:10	293 / 472 / 5:50	164 / 264 / 3:30	220 / 354 / 4:40	105 / 169 / 2:40	433 / 697 / 7:40	541 / 871 / 10:00	233 / 375 / 4:40	105 / 169 / 3:00	438 / 705 / 7:50	500 / 805 / 8:50	143 / 230 / 2:50	209 / 336 / 3:50	324 / 521 / 5:50	121 / 195 / 2:30	148 / 238 / 2:50	76 / 122 / 2:20	61 / 98 / 1:50	532 / 856 / 9:30	31 / 50 / 1:00	251 / 404 / 4:40	128 / 206 / 2:40	388 / 624 / 7:10	417 / 671 / 7:30	201 / 323 / 4:10	547 / 880 / 10:00	77 / 124 / 2:00
Stranraer				445 / 716 / 8:20	277 / 446 / 5:30	263 / 423 / 5:20	461 / 742 / 8:40	500 / 805 / 9:40	379 / 610 / 7:10	148 / 238 / 3:40	290 / 467 / 5:50	403 / 649 / 8:10	158 / 254 / 3:40	220 / 354 / 4:40	221 / 356 / 4:40	298 / 480 / 6:00	330 / 531 / 6:20	220 / 354 / 4:40	585 / 942 / 11:30	263 / 423 / 6:30	259 / 417 / 5:20	379 / 610 / 9:00	262 / 422 / 6:00	338 / 544 / 7:00	410 / 660 / 8:10	426 / 686 / 8:40	343 / 552 / 6:30	84 / 135 / 2:30	195 / 314 / 4:50	392 / 631 / 7:50	454 / 731 / 8:30	124 / 200 / 3:00	167 / 269 / 3:40	496 / 798 / 9:10	257 / 414 / 5:10	101 / 163 / 2:40	390 / 628 / 7:30	379 / 610 / 7:10	378 / 608 / 7:20	475 / 765 / 9:00	194 / 312 / 4:20	444 / 715 / 8:30	188 / 303 / 4:00	297 / 478 / 6:00	170 / 274 / 4:10	51 / 82 / 1:20	325 / 523 / 6:50	228 / 367 / 5:10	402 / 647 / 7:50
Swansea			417 / 671 / 7:50	161 / 259 / 3:00	118 / 190 / 2:20	217 / 349 / 4:00	182 / 293 / 3:30	206 / 332 / 4:10	141 / 227 / 2:40	506 / 815 / 9:20	192 / 309 / 3:40	301 / 485 / 6:00	347 / 559 / 6:20	187 / 301 / 3:30	195 / 314 / 3:40	233 / 375 / 4:30	177 / 285 / 3:20	248 / 399 / 4:40	285 / 459 / 6:00	594 / 956 / 11:30	264 / 425 / 4:50	696 / 1120 / 13:40	572 / 921 / 10:40	184 / 296 / 4:50	267 / 430 / 5:10	329 / 530 / 6:30	89 / 143 / 1:50	409 / 658 / 7:20	496 / 798 / 9:20	67 / 108 / 1:50	161 / 259 / 3:00	412 / 663 / 7:20	473 / 761 / 8:20	274 / 441 / 5:00	232 / 373 / 4:10	309 / 497 / 5:30	41 / 66 / 1:10	227 / 365 / 4:10	85 / 137 / 1:50	222 / 357 / 4:20	505 / 813 / 9:00	167 / 269 / 3:20	216 / 348 / 4:00	119 / 192 / 2:30	383 / 616 / 7:10	379 / 610 / 6:50	73 / 117 / 2:00	507 / 816 / 9:20	194 / 312 / 4:00
York		272 / 438 / 5:10	222 / 357 / 4:40	258 / 415 / 5:10	133 / 214 / 2:40	52 / 84 / 1:20	278 / 448 / 5:10	333 / 536 / 6:20	181 / 291 / 3:20	309 / 497 / 6:00	77 / 124 / 1:40	181 / 291 / 4:20	84 / 135 / 2:20	64 / 103 / 1:30	99 / 159 / 2:10	75 / 121 / 1:50	108 / 174 / 2:10	24 / 39 / 0:50	411 / 661 / 8:00	407 / 655 / 8:20	37 / 60 / 1:10	479 / 771 / 10:10	352 / 566 / 7:00	204 / 328 / 4:20	228 / 367 / 4:40	201 / 323 / 4:20	189 / 304 / 3:30	217 / 349 / 4:10	330 / 531 / 6:30	261 / 420 / 5:10	287 / 462 / 5:10	194 / 312 / 3:40	250 / 402 / 4:40	282 / 454 / 5:10	34 / 55 / 1:00	121 / 195 / 2:30	244 / 393 / 4:40	165 / 266 / 3:10	222 / 357 / 4:10	275 / 443 / 5:10	285 / 459 / 5:20	269 / 433 / 5:00	96 / 154 / 2:00	130 / 209 / 2:40	148 / 238 / 3:10	214 / 344 / 4:00	195 / 314 / 4:10	319 / 513 / 6:10	207 / 333 / 4:10

Supporting

THINK!

Travel safe – Don't drive tired

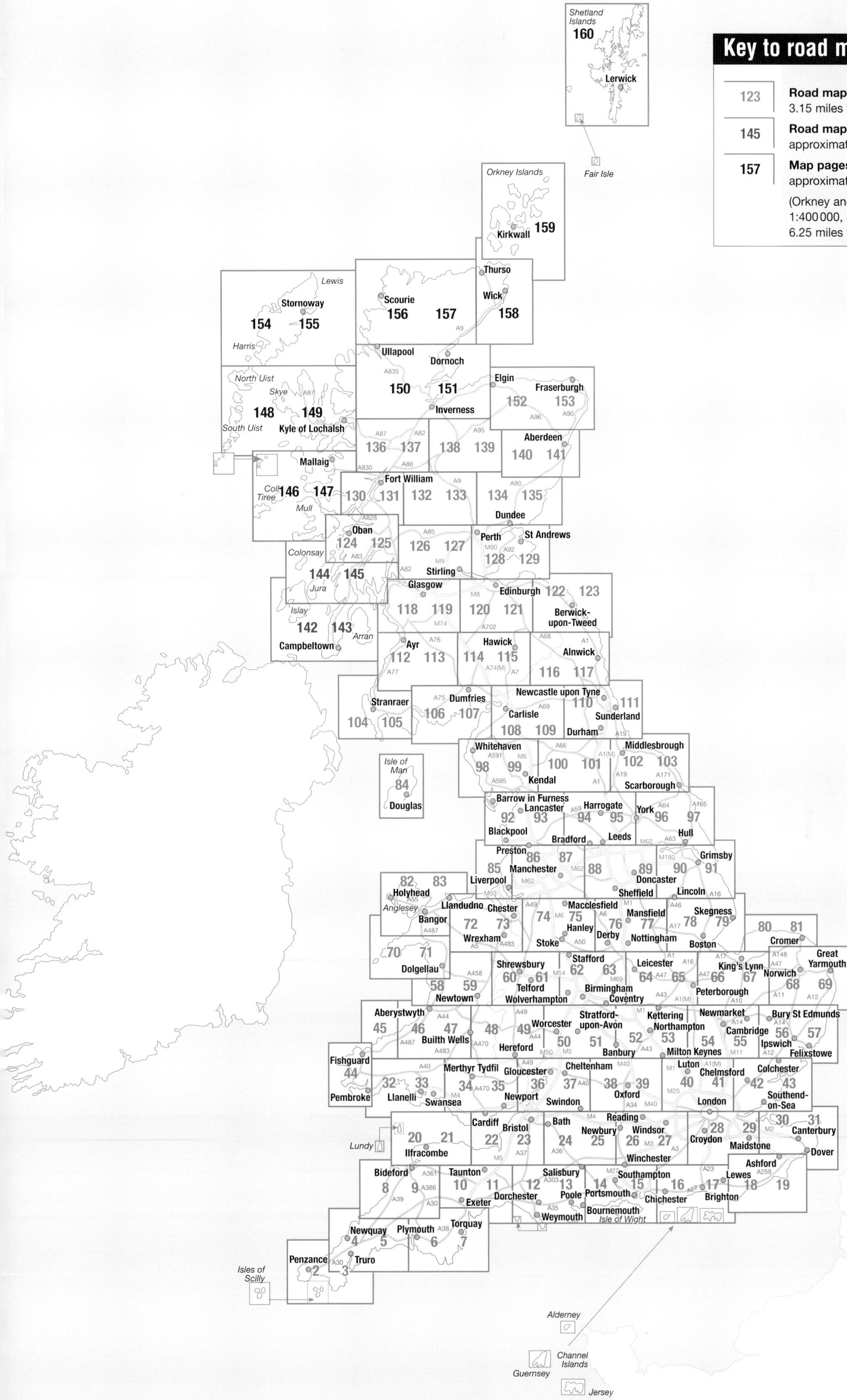

Key to road map pages

123	**Road map pages at 1:200 000** 3.15 miles to 1 inch
145	**Road map pages at 1:265 000** approximately 4 miles to 1 inch
157	**Map pages at 1:332 000** approximately 5 miles to 1 inch (Orkney and Shetland Islands at 1:400 000, approximately 6.25 miles to 1 inch)

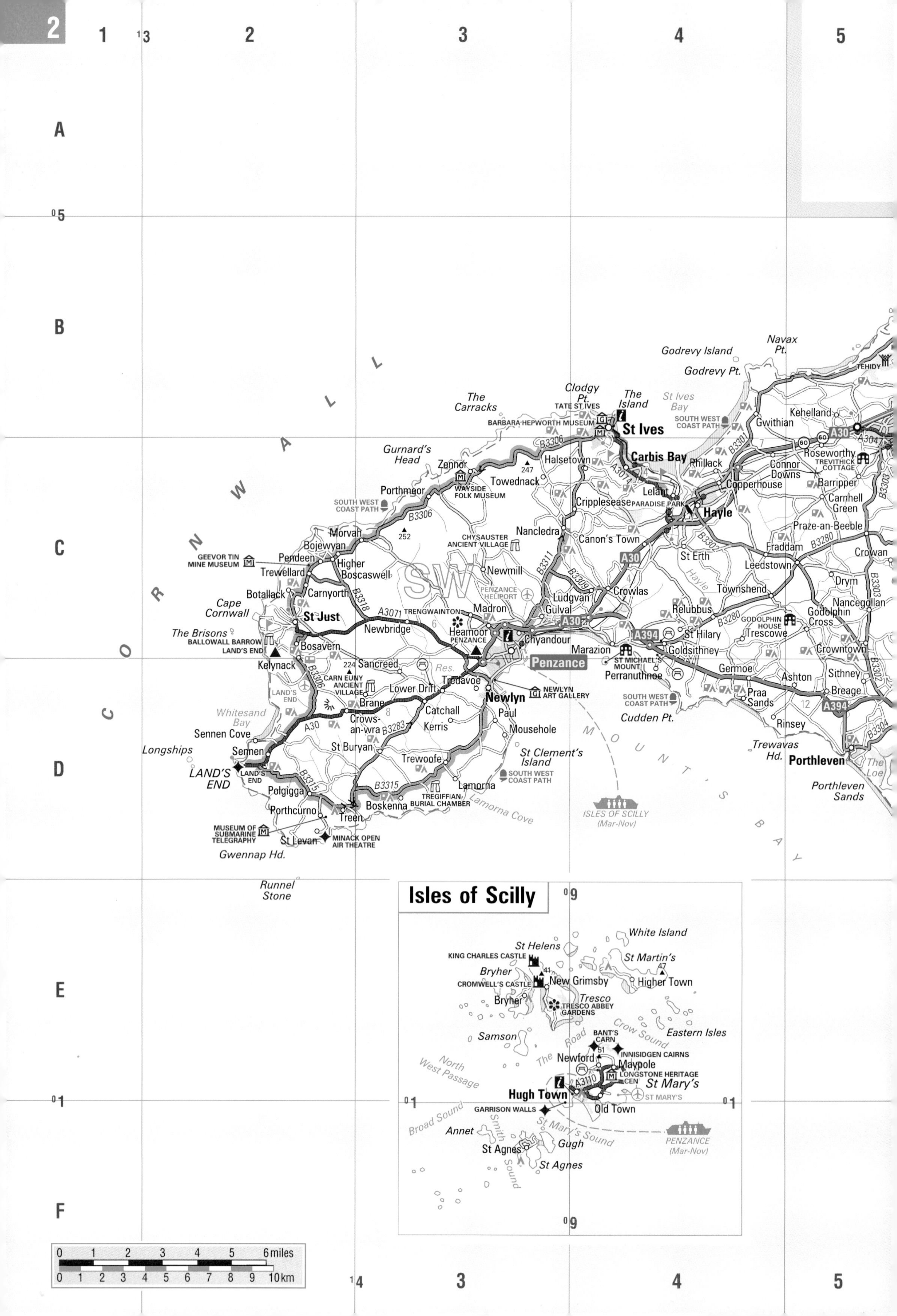
CORNWALL
SW
St Ives
Carbis Bay
Hayle
Penzance
Newlyn
St Just
Porthleven
Marazion
Godrevy Island
Godrevy Pt.
Navax Pt.
TEHIDY
The Carracks
Clodgy Pt.
The Island
TATE ST IVES
BARBARA HEPWORTH MUSEUM
St Ives Bay
SOUTH WEST COAST PATH
Gwithian
Kehelland
Halsetown
Phillack
Connor Downs
Roseworthy
TREVITHICK COTTAGE
Gurnard's Head
Zennor
WAYSIDE FOLK MUSEUM
Towednack
Lelant
Copperhouse
Barripper
Porthmeor
Cripplesease
PARADISE PARK
Carnhell Green
Morvah
CHYSAUSTER ANCIENT VILLAGE
Nancledra
Praze-an-Beeble
Bojewyan
Canon's Town
St Erth
Fraddam
Crowan
GEEVOR TIN MINE MUSEUM
Pendeen
Higher Boscaswell
Newmill
Leedstown
Trewellard
Drym
Botallack
Carnyorth
PENZANCE HELIPORT
Ludgvan
Crowlas
Townshend
Nancegollan
Cape Cornwall
Gulval
Relubbus
Godolphin Cross
TRENGWAINTON
Madron
GODOLPHIN HOUSE
Newbridge
Heamoor
Trescowe
The Brisons
BALLOWALL BARROW
LAND'S END
Bosavern
Chyandour
St Hilary
Crowntown
Kelynack
Sancreed
ST MICHAEL'S MOUNT
Goldsithney
Perranuthnoe
Germoe
Ashton
Sithney
CARN EUNY ANCIENT VILLAGE
Tredavoe
Lower Drift
NEWLYN ART GALLERY
Breage
Whitesand Bay
Brane
Catchall
Praa Sands
Crows-an-wra
Kerris
Paul
Cudden Pt.
Sennen Cove
Mousehole
Rinsey
Longships
Sennen
St Buryan
Trewoofe
St Clement's Island
Trewavas Hd.
LAND'S END
Polgigga
Lamorna
TREGIFFIAN BURIAL CHAMBER
Porthleven Sands
The Loe
Porthcurno
Boskenna
Treen
Lamorna Cove
ISLES OF SCILLY (Mar-Nov)
MUSEUM OF SUBMARINE TELEGRAPHY
St Levan
MINACK OPEN AIR THEATRE
Gwennap Hd.
Runnel Stone
MOUNT'S BAY
Isles of Scilly
White Island
St Helens
St Martin's
KING CHARLES CASTLE
Bryher
New Grimsby
Higher Town
CROMWELL'S CASTLE
Tresco
TRESCO ABBEY GARDENS
Samson
Eastern Isles
Crow Sound
BANT'S CARN
INNISIDGEN CAIRNS
The Road
Newford
Maypole
North West Passage
LONGSTONE HERITAGE CEN
St Mary's
Hugh Town
ST MARY'S
GARRISON WALLS
Old Town
Broad Sound
Smith Sound
St Mary's Sound
PENZANCE (Mar-Nov)
Annet
St Agnes
Gugh
A30
A394
A3071
A3074
A3047
A3110
B3306
B3311
B3309
B3318
B3315
B3283
B3280
B3301
B3302
B3303
B3304
0 1 2 3 4 5 6 miles
0 1 2 3 4 5 6 7 8 9 10 km

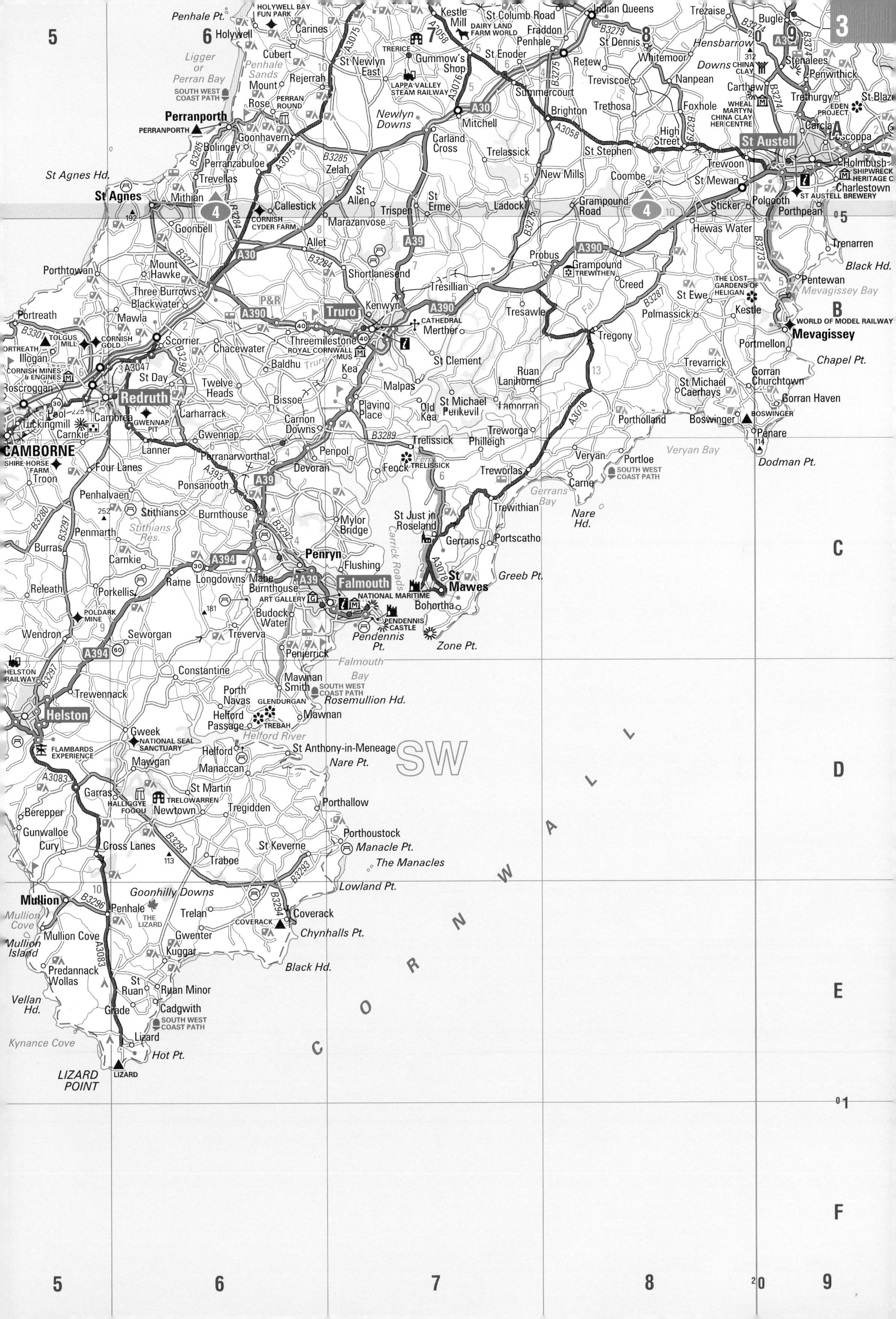

5
6
7
8
9
A
B
C
D
E
F
SW
CORNWALL
Penhale Pt.
Holywell
HOLYWELL BAY FUN PARK
Carines
Cubert
Ligger or Perran Bay
Penhale Sands
Mount
Rejerrah
Rose
PERRAN ROUND
SOUTH WEST COAST PATH
Perranporth
PERRANPORTH
Goonhavern
Bolingey
Perranzabuloe
Trevellas
St Agnes Hd.
St Agnes
Mithian
Callestick
CORNISH CYDER FARM
Goonbell
Porthtowan
Mount Hawke
Three Burrows
Blackwater
Portreath
Mawla
TOLGUS MILL
CORNISH GOLD
Illogan
CORNISH MINES & ENGINES
Roscroggan
Scorrier
Chacewater
St Day
Redruth
Pool
Tuckingmill
Carnkie
Cambrea
GWENNAP PIT
CAMBORNE
SHIRE HORSE FARM
Troon
Four Lanes
Lanner
Gwennap
Carharrack
Twelve Heads
Penhalvaen
Stithians
Stithians Res.
Penmarth
Burras
Carnkie
Releath
Porkellis
POLDARK MINE
Wendron
Seworgan
HELSTON RAILWAY
Trewennack
Helston
FLAMBARDS EXPERIENCE
Gweek
NATIONAL SEAL SANCTUARY
Mawgan
Garras
HALLIGGYE FOGOU
TRELOWARREN
Newtown
Berepper
Gunwalloe
Cury
Cross Lanes
Mullion
Mullion Cove
Mullion Island
Predannack Wollas
Vellan Hd.
Kynance Cove
LIZARD POINT
LIZARD
Lizard
Hot Pt.
Grade
St Ruan
Ruan Minor
Cadgwith
SOUTH WEST COAST PATH
Kuggar
Gwenter
Trelan
Penhale
THE LIZARD
Goonhilly Downs
Coverack
COVERACK
Chynhalls Pt.
Black Hd.
Lowland Pt.
St Keverne
Traboe
Tregidden
St Martin
Manaccan
Helford
Helford River
Helford Passage
TREBAH
GLENDURGAN
Porth Navas
Constantine
Mawnan Smith
Mawnan
Rosemullion Hd.
St Anthony-in-Meneage
Nare Pt.
Porthallow
Porthoustock
Manacle Pt.
The Manacles
Treverva
Rame
Longdowns
Mabe Burnthouse
Budock Water
Penjerrick
Falmouth
Falmouth Bay
ART GALLERY
NATIONAL MARITIME
PENDENNIS CASTLE
Pendennis Pt.
Penryn
Flushing
Mylor Bridge
Carrick Roads
Burnthouse
Ponsanooth
Perranarworthal
Devoran
Penpol
Carnon Downs
Bissoe
Playing Place
Kea
Feock
TRELISSICK
Baldhu
Threemilestone
ROYAL CORNWALL MUS
Truro
Kenwyn
CATHEDRAL
Merther
St Clement
Malpas
Old Kea
St Michael Penkevil
Lamorran
Ruan Lanihorne
Tresawle
Tresillian
Shortlanesend
Allet
Marazanvose
Trispen
St Erme
St Allen
Zelah
Carland Cross
Newlyn Downs
Mitchell
St Newlyn East
TRERICE
Gummow's Shop
LAPPA VALLEY STEAM RAILWAY
Kestle Mill
DAIRY LAND FARM WORLD
St Columb Road
Fraddon
Penhale
St Enoder
Indian Queens
St Dennis
Retew
Summercourt
Treviscoe
Whitemoor
Nanpean
Trezaise
Bugle
Hensbarrow Downs
CHINA CLAY
Stenalees
Penwithick
Carthew
WHEAL MARTYN CHINA CLAY HER CENTRE
Trethurgy
EDEN PROJECT
St Blazey
Carclaze
Boscoppa
Holmbush
SHIPWRECK HERITAGE C
Charlestown
ST AUSTELL BREWERY
St Austell
Foxhole
High Street
Trethosa
Brighton
Trelassick
New Mills
Ladock
St Stephen
Coombe
Grampound Road
Trewoon
St Mewan
Sticker
Polgooth
Porthpean
Hewas Water
Trenarren
Black Hd.
Pentewan
Mevagissey Bay
THE LOST GARDENS OF HELIGAN
Kestle
St Ewe
Polmassick
WORLD OF MODEL RAILWAY
Mevagissey
Portmellon
Chapel Pt.
Gorran Churchtown
Gorran Haven
Trevarrick
St Michael Caerhays
Boswinger
BOSWINGER
Penare
Dodman Pt.
Porthholland
Veryan Bay
Portloe
Veryan
SOUTH WEST COAST PATH
Carne
Nare Hd.
Gerrans Bay
Treworlas
Trewithian
Treworga
Philleigh
Tregony
Creed
Probus
Grampound
TREWITHEN
Trelissick
St Just in Roseland
Gerrans
Portscatho
St Mawes
Bohortha
Greeb Pt.
Zone Pt.
A30
A39
A390
A393
A394
A3075
A3076
A3078
A3083
A3058
A3047
A3274
B3285
B3284
B3277
B3298
B3300
B3280
B3297
B3291
B3289
B3293
B3294
B3296
B3287
B3273
B3275
B3279
B3374
P&R

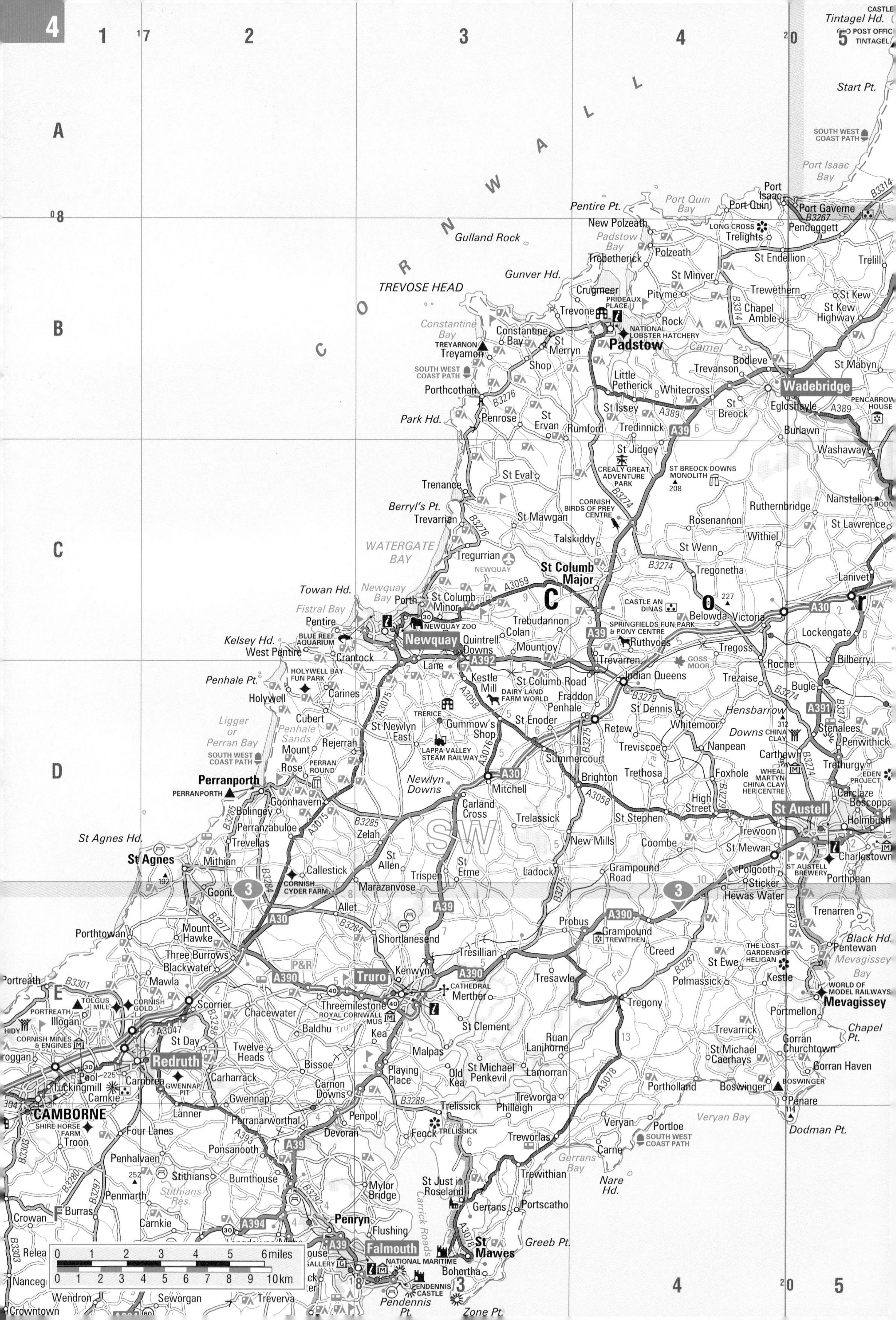
1
2
3
4
5
A
B
C
D
E
F
C O R N W A L L
Tintagel Hd.
Start Pt.
Port Isaac Bay
Port Isaac
Port Quin
Port Gaverne
Pentire Pt.
New Polzeath
Padstow Bay
Gulland Rock
Polzeath
Trebetherick
Gunver Hd.
TREVOSE HEAD
St Minver
Pityme
Rock
Trevone
Padstow
Constantine Bay
Treyarnon
St Merryn
Camel
Porthcothan
Park Hd.
Penrose
St Ervan
Rumford
St Issey
Little Petherick
Whitecross
Wadebridge
Trenance
Berryl's Pt.
Trevarrian
St Eval
St Mawgan
Talskiddy
St Jidgey
WATERGATE BAY
Tregurrian
St Columb Major
Towan Hd.
Newquay Bay
Porth
St Columb Minor
Fistral Bay
Pentire
Kelsey Hd.
West Pentire
Crantock
Newquay
Quintrell Downs
Colan
Mountjoy
Trebudannon
Indian Queens
St Columb Road
Penhale Pt.
Holywell
Carines
Cubert
St Newlyn East
Gummow's Shop
Kestle Mill
Fraddon
Penhale
St Enoder
Ligger or Perran Bay
Penhale Sands
Rejerrah
Mount
Rose
Perranporth
Goonhavern
Bolingey
Perranzabuloe
Newlyn Downs
Mitchell
Summercourt
Carland Cross
Zelah
St Agnes Hd.
St Agnes
Mithian
Trevellas
Callestick
St Allen
Trispen
St Erme
Ladock
Marazanvose
Allet
Goonbell
Porthtowan
Mount Hawke
Three Burrows
Blackwater
Mawla
Portreath
Illogan
Scorrier
Chacewater
Truro
Kenwyn
Threemilestone
Shortlanesend
Tresillian
Merther
St Clement
Baldhu
Kea
Malpas
Redruth
St Day
Twelve Heads
Bissoe
Carharrack
Pool
Carn Brea
Tuckingmill
Carnkie
CAMBORNE
Troon
Four Lanes
Lanner
Gwennap
Carnon Downs
Playing Place
Old Kea
St Michael Penkevil
Lamorran
Ruan Lanihorne
Tregony
Tresawle
Probus
Grampound
Creed
Perranarworthal
Devoran
Penpol
Feock
Trelissick
Philleigh
Treworga
Ponsanooth
Penhalvaen
Stithians
Burnthouse
Stithians Res.
Mylor Bridge
Penmarth
Carnkie
Burras
Crowan
Penryn
Flushing
Falmouth
Carrick Roads
St Just in Roseland
Gerrans
Portscatho
St Mawes
Bohortha
Pendennis Pt.
Zone Pt.
Greeb Pt.
Gerrans Bay
Nare Hd.
Trewithian
Treworlas
Carne
Veryan
Portloe
Veryan Bay
Portholland
Boswinger
Penare
Dodman Pt.
Gorran Haven
Gorran Churchtown
St Michael Caerhays
Trevarrick
Portmellon
Mevagissey
Chapel Pt.
Mevagissey Bay
Pentewan
Black Hd.
Kestle
St Ewe
Polmassick
Trenarren
Porthpean
Charlestown
St Austell
Polgooth
Sticker
Hewas Water
St Mewan
Trewoon
Coombe
Grampound Road
New Mills
Trelassick
St Stephen
High Street
Foxhole
Nanpean
Trethosa
Treviscoe
Brighton
Retew
St Dennis
Whitemoor
Hensbarrow Downs
Carthew
Trethurgy
Stenalees
Penwithick
Bugle
Roche
Trezaise
Tregoss
Ruthvoes
Trevarren
Belowda
Victoria
Tregonetha
St Wenn
Rosenannon
Withiel
Ruthernbridge
Lanivet
Lockengate
Bilberry
Nanstallon
St Lawrence
Washaway
Burlawn
Egloshayle
St Breock
Trevanson
Bodieve
St Mabyn
Chapel Amble
St Kew
St Kew Highway
Trewethern
St Endellion
Trelights
Pendoggett
Trelill
Tredinnick
Wendron
Seworgan
Treverva
Crowntown
Relea
Nancegollan
0 1 2 3 4 5 6 miles
0 1 2 3 4 5 6 7 8 9 10 km

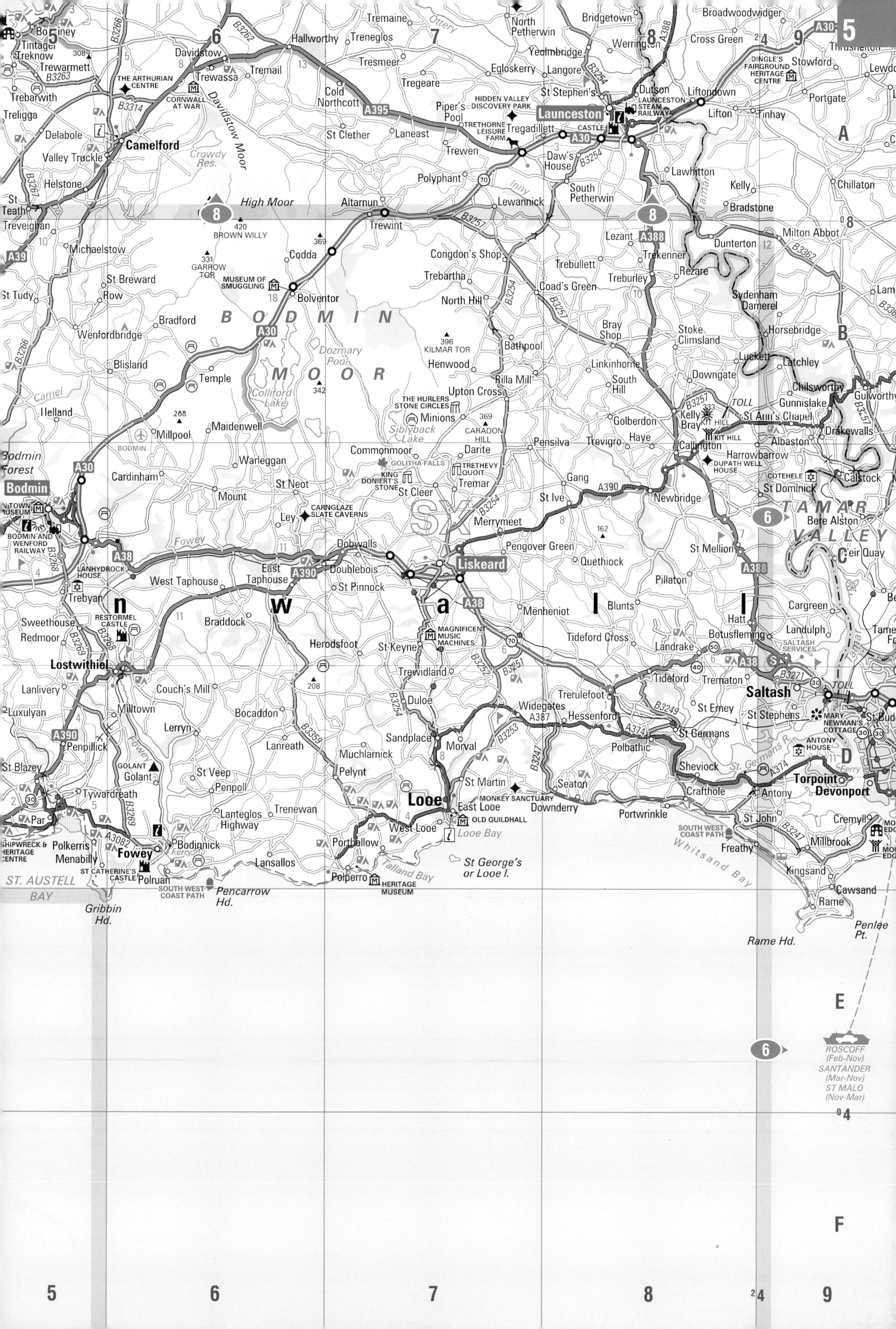

Bossiney
Tintagel
Treknow
Trewarmett
B3263
Trebarwith
Treligga
Delabole
Valley Truckle
Camelford
Helstone
St Teath
Treveighan
Michaelstow
St Breward
Row
St Tudy
Wenfordbridge
Bradford
Blisland
Helland
Camel
Bodmin Forest
Bodmin
Cardinham
Millpool
Maidenwell
Temple
Warleggan
Mount
St Neot
Ley
CARNGLAZE SLATE CAVERNS
Davidstow
Trewassa
Tremail
THE ARTHURIAN CENTRE
CORNWALL AT WAR
Davidstow Moor
Crowdy Res.
High Moor
420 BROWN WILLY
331 GARROW TOR
MUSEUM OF SMUGGLING
Codda
Bolventor
B O D M I N
M O O R
Dozmary Pool
Colliford Lake
Hallworthy
Treneglos
Tremaine
Tresmeer
Tregeare
Cold Northcott
A395
St Clether
Laneast
Altarnun
Trewint
Trewen
Polyphant
Piper's Pool
TRETHORNE LEISURE FARM
HIDDEN VALLEY DISCOVERY PARK
Tregadillett
Egloskerry
North Petherwin
Bridgetown
Werrington
Yeolmbridge
Langore
St Stephen's
Launceston
LAUNCESTON STEAM RAILWAY
CASTLE
Dutson
Daw's House
South Petherwin
Lewannick
Inny
Congdon's Shop
Trebartha
North Hill
396 KILMAR TOR
Henwood
Bathpool
Rilla Mill
Upton Cross
THE HURLERS STONE CIRCLES
Minions
Siblyback Lake
369 CARADON HILL
Darite
Commonmoor
GOLITHA FALLS
KING DONIERT'S STONE
TRETHEVY QUOIT
St Cleer
Tremar
Trebullett
Treburley
Coad's Green
Lezant
Trekenner
Bray Shop
Linkinhorne
South Hill
Golberdon
Pensilva
Trevigro
Haye
Callington
Kelly Bray
KIT HILL
Stoke Climsland
Downgate
Luckett
Latchley
Chilsworthy
Gunnislake
St Ann's Chapel
Drakewalls
Albaston
Harrowbarrow
DUPATH WELL HOUSE
COTEHELE
Calstock
St Dominick
TAMAR VALLEY
Bere Alston
Ceir Quay
Gulworthy
Broadwoodwidger
Cross Green
Stowford
DINGLE'S FAIRGROUND HERITAGE CENTRE
Liftondown
Lifton
Tinhay
Portgate
Lawhitton
Kelly
Bradstone
Chillaton
Milton Abbot
Dunterton
Rezare
Sydenham Damerel
Horsebridge
Lewdown
Lamerton
Thrushelton
A30
A39
A38
A390
A388
A387
A374
A3082
B3266
B3262
B3314
B3267
B3257
B3254
B3362
B3268
B3269
B3359
B3252
B3251
B3253
B3247
B3249
B3271
Gang
St Ive
Newbridge
Merrymeet
Pengover Green
Quethiock
St Mellion
Pillaton
Liskeard
Dobwalls
Doublebois
East Taphouse
West Taphouse
St Pinnock
LANHYDROCK HOUSE
BODMIN AND WENFORD RAILWAY
Trebyan
Sweethouse
Redmoor
RESTORMEL CASTLE
Braddock
Lostwithiel
Lanlivery
Luxulyan
Milltown
Couch's Mill
Herodsfoot
St Keyne
MAGNIFICENT MUSIC MACHINES
Menheniot
Blunts
Tideford Cross
Trewidland
Duloe
Bocaddon
Lerryn
Lanreath
Muchlarnick
Sandplace
Morval
Widegates
Hessenford
Trerulefoot
Tideford
Landrake
Botusfleming
Hatt
Cargreen
Landulph
SALTASH SERVICES
Trematon
Saltash
St Erney
St Stephens
St Germans
Polbathic
MARY NEWMAN'S COTTAGE
ANTONY HOUSE
Sheviock
Crafthole
Antony
Torpoint
Devonport
Portwrinkle
St John
Millbrook
Cremyll
Kingsand
Cawsand
Rame
Rame Hd.
Penlee Pt.
Whitsand Bay
SOUTH WEST COAST PATH
Freathy
Seaton
Downderry
MONKEY SANCTUARY
St Martin
Looe
East Looe
West Looe
OLD GUILDHALL
Looe Bay
St George's or Looe I.
Pelynt
Trenewan
Lanteglos Highway
Portlooe
Polperro
HERITAGE MUSEUM
Talland Bay
Lansallos
Polruan
Bodinnick
Fowey
Golant
Penpillick
Tywardreath
Par
St Blazey
Polkerris
Menabilly
SHIPWRECK & HERITAGE CENTRE
ST CATHERINE'S CASTLE
ST. AUSTELL BAY
Gribbin Hd.
Pencarrow Hd.
SOUTH WEST COAST PATH
St Veep
Penpoll
ROSCOFF (Feb-Nov)
SANTANDER (Mar-Nov)
ST MALO (Nov-Mar)
TOLL
A
B
C
D
E
F
5
6
7
8
9

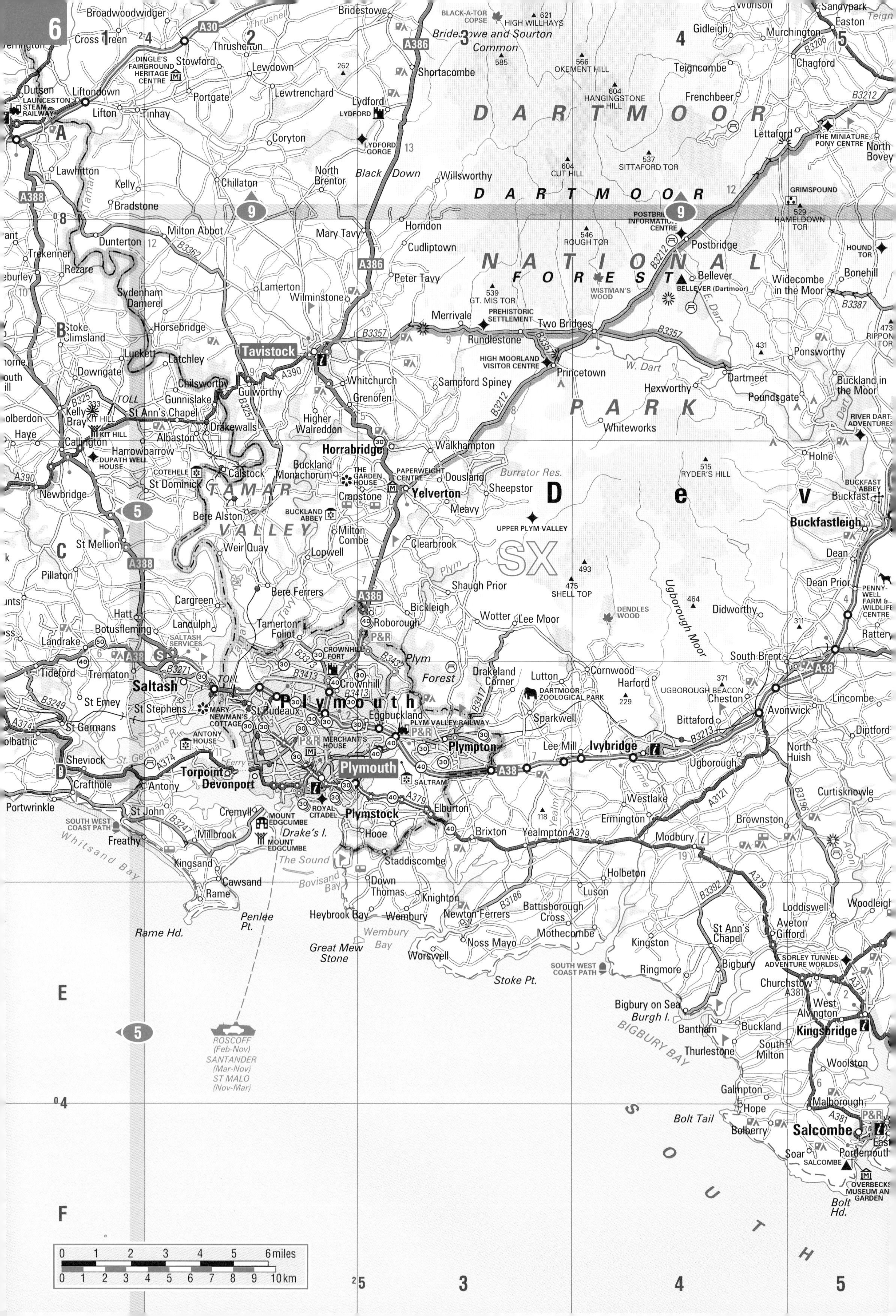
Broadwoodwidger
Bridestowe
BLACK-A-TOR COPSE
621 HIGH WILLHAYS
Cross Green
Thrushelton
A30
Bridestowe and Sourton Common
585
Gidleigh
Murchington
Sandypark
Easton
Teign
DINGLE'S FAIRGROUND HERITAGE CENTRE
Stowford
Lewdown
A386
Shortacombe
566 OKEMENT HILL
Teigncombe
Chagford
B3206
Dutson
LAUNCESTON STEAM RAILWAY
Liftondown
Lifton
Tinhay
Portgate
Lewtrenchard
Lydford
LYDFORD
604 HANGINGSTONE HILL
Frenchbeer
B3212
DARTMOOR
Coryton
LYDFORD GORGE
Lettaford
THE MINIATURE PONY CENTRE
North Bovey
Lawhitton
Kelly
Chillaton
North Brentor
Black Down
Willsworthy
604 CUT HILL
537 SITTAFORD TOR
GRIMSPOUND
A388
Bradstone
DARTMOOR
529 HAMELDOWN TOR
POSTBRIDGE INFORMATION CENTRE
Milton Abbot
Mary Tavy
Horndon
546 ROUGH TOR
Postbridge
Dunterton
Trekenner
B3362
Cudliptown
HOUND TOR
Rezare
NATIONAL
FOREST
A386
Peter Tavy
Bellever
Bonehill
Widecombe in the Moor
Sydenham Damerel
Lamerton
Wilminstone
539 GT. MIS TOR
WISTMAN'S WOOD
BELLEVER (Dartmoor)
E. Dart
B3387
PREHISTORIC SETTLEMENT
Merrivale
Two Bridges
Stoke Climsland
Horsebridge
B3357
Rundlestone
B3357
431
473 RIPPON TOR
Tavistock
Luckett
Latchley
HIGH MOORLAND VISITOR CENTRE
Princetown
W. Dart
Ponsworthy
Downgate
Chilsworthy
A390
Whitchurch
Sampford Spiney
Dartmeet
Hexworthy
Buckland in the Moor
B3257
TOLL
Gulworthy
Grenofen
B3212
Poundsgate
Kelly Bray
333 KIT HILL
Gunnislake
St Ann's Chapel
B3257
PARK
Dart
Higher Walreddon
Whiteworks
Drakewalls
RIVER DART ADVENTURES
Callington
Albaston
Horrabridge
Walkhampton
Harrowbarrow
DUPATH WELL HOUSE
Holne
COTEHELE
Calstock
Buckland Monachorum
THE GARDEN HOUSE
PAPERWEIGHT CENTRE
Dousland
Burrator Res.
515 RYDER'S HILL
A390
St Dominick
TAMAR
Sheepstor
BUCKFAST ABBEY
Newbridge
Crapstone
Yelverton
D
e
V
Buckfast
Meavy
BUCKLAND ABBEY
Bere Alston
UPPER PLYM VALLEY
Buckfastleigh
VALLEY
Milton Combe
St Mellion
Weir Quay
Clearbrook
Dean
Lopwell
SX
A388
Plym
493
Dean Prior
Pillaton
Shaugh Prior
475 SHELL TOP
Ugborough Moor
PENNYWELL FARM & WILDLIFE CENTRE
Bere Ferrers
A386
464
Cargreen
Bickleigh
Didworthy
Hatt
DENDLES WOOD
Landulph
Tamerton Foliot
Roborough
Wotter
Lee Moor
311
Botusfleming
Ratter
Landrake
SALTASH SERVICES
P&R
CROWNHILL FORT
Plym
Forest
South Brent
A38
Tideford
Trematon
B3373
B3432
Drakeland Corner
Cornwood
A38
Saltash
B3271
TOLL
B3413
Crownhill
Lutton
371
Harford
UGBOROUGH BEACON
B3249
St Erney
B3413
DARTMOOR ZOOLOGICAL PARK
Lincombe
St Stephens
MARY NEWMAN'S COTTAGE
St Budeaux
Plymouth
Eggbuckland
B3417
229
Cheston
A374
St Germans
PLYM VALLEY RAILWAY
Sparkwell
Avonwick
Bittaford
Diptford
ANTONY HOUSE
P&R
MERCHANT'S HOUSE
P&R
B3213
St Germans R.
Plympton
Lee Mill
Ivybridge
North Huish
Sheviock
A374
Ferry
Plymouth
Ugborough
Torpoint
SALTRAM
A38
Crafthole
Antony
Devonport
Erme
B3196
Curtisknowle
Portwrinkle
A379
Elburton
Westlake
A3121
St John
Cremyll
ROYAL CITADEL
Plymstock
118
Yealm
Ermington
Brownston
SOUTH WEST COAST PATH
MOUNT EDGCUMBE
Drake's I.
Brixton
Yealmpton
A379
Modbury
B3247
Millbrook
Hooe
Freathy
MOUNT EDGCUMBE
Avon
Whitsand Bay
The Sound
Staddiscombe
Kingsand
Holbeton
A379
Cawsand
Bovisand Bay
B3392
Rame
Down Thomas
Luson
Knighton
B3186
Loddiswell
Woodleigh
Penlee Pt.
Heybrook Bay
Wembury
Newton Ferrers
Battisborough Cross
Aveton Gifford
Rame Hd.
Mothecombe
St Ann's Chapel
Wembury Bay
Great Mew Stone
Noss Mayo
Kingston
SORLEY TUNNEL ADVENTURE WORLDS
Worswell
SOUTH WEST COAST PATH
Bigbury
Ringmore
Stoke Pt.
Churchstow
A381
A379
E
Bigbury on Sea
West Alvington
Burgh I.
BIGBURY BAY
Bantham
Buckland
Kingsbridge
5
ROSCOFF (Feb-Nov)
SANTANDER (Mar-Nov)
ST MALO (Nov-Mar)
Thurlestone
South Milton
Woolston
Galmpton
04
Hope
Malborough
Bolt Tail
A381
P&R
Bolberry
Salcombe
SOUTH
Soar
Portlemouth
SALCOMBE
OVERBECKS MUSEUM AND GARDEN
F
Bolt Hd.
0 1 2 3 4 5 6 miles
0 1 2 3 4 5 6 7 8 9 10 km
25
3
4
5
A
B
C
D
1
2
3
4
5
9
9
5
08

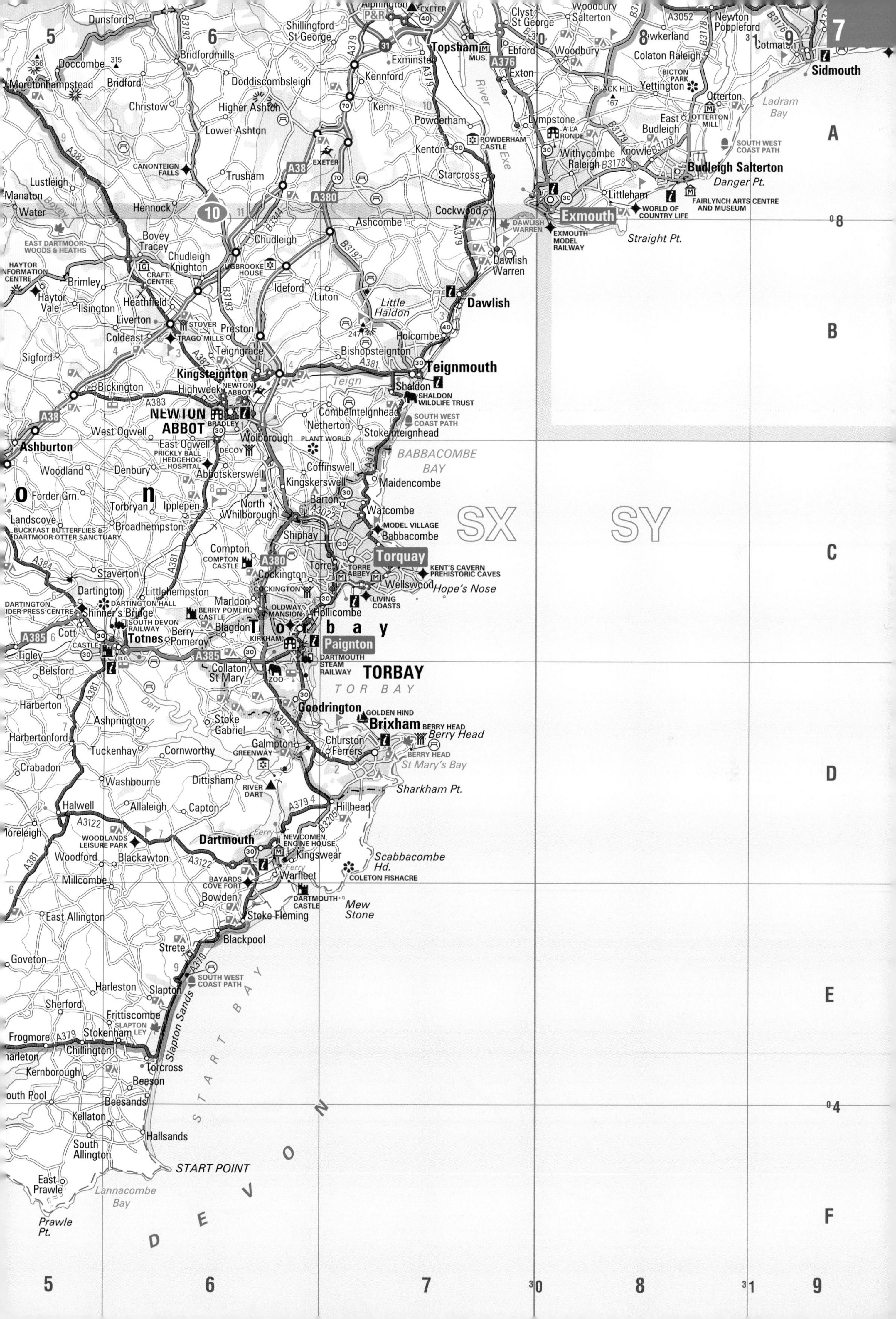

7
Dunsford
Doccombe
Moretonhampstead
Bridford
Bridfordmills
Christow
Doddiscombsleigh
Higher Ashton
Lower Ashton
Shillingford St George
Alphington
EXETER
Topsham
Exminster
Kennford
Kenn
Powderham
POWDERHAM CASTLE
Kenton
Starcross
Cockwood
Clyst St George
Woodbury Salterton
Ebford
Woodbury
Exton
Lympstone
A LA RONDE
Withycombe Raleigh
Exmouth
EXMOUTH MODEL RAILWAY
Littleham
WORLD OF COUNTRY LIFE
Straight Pt.
Budleigh Salterton
Danger Pt.
FAIRLYNCH ARTS CENTRE AND MUSEUM
East Budleigh
Knowle
Otterton
OTTERTON MILL
Yettington
BICTON PARK
BLACK HILL
Colaton Raleigh
Newton Poppleford
Sidmouth
Cotmaton
Ladram Bay
SOUTH WEST COAST PATH
DAWLISH WARREN
Dawlish Warren
Dawlish
Holcombe
Teignmouth
Shaldon
SHALDON WILDLIFE TRUST
Little Haldon
Bishopsteignton
Luton
Ideford
Ashcombe
Chudleigh
UGBROOKE HOUSE
Trusham
CANONTEIGN FALLS
Hennock
Lustleigh
Manaton
Water
EAST DARTMOOR WOODS & HEATHS
HAYTOR INFORMATION CENTRE
Haytor Vale
Bovey Tracey
Chudleigh Knighton
CRAFT CENTRE
Brimley
Heathfield
Ilsington
Liverton
STOVER
TRAGO MILLS
Coldeast
Preston
Teigngrace
Sigford
Kingsteignton
Bickington
Highweek
NEWTON ABBOT
NEWTON ABBOT
BRADLEY
Wolborough
Combeinteignhead
Netherton
Stokeinteignhead
PLANT WORLD
BABBACOMBE BAY
Ashburton
West Ogwell
East Ogwell
DECOY
PRICKLY BALL HEDGEHOG HOSPITAL
Abbotskerswell
Woodland
Denbury
Coffinswell
Kingskerswell
Maidencombe
Forder Grn.
Torbryan
Ipplepen
North Whilborough
Barton
Watcombe
MODEL VILLAGE
Babbacombe
Landscove
BUCKFAST BUTTERFLIES & DARTMOOR OTTER SANCTUARY
Broadhempston
Shiphay
SX
SY
Compton
COMPTON CASTLE
Torquay
KENT'S CAVERN PREHISTORIC CAVES
Staverton
Torre
TORRE ABBEY
Wellswood
Hope's Nose
Cockington
COCKINGTON
Dartington
DARTINGTON HALL
Littlehempston
Marldon
DARTINGTON CIDER PRESS CENTRE
Shinner's Bridge
BERRY POMEROY CASTLE
OLDWAY MANSION
Hollicombe
LIVING COASTS
SOUTH DEVON RAILWAY
Cott
Berry Pomeroy
Blagdon
Torbay
CASTLE
Totnes
KIRKHAM
Paignton
Tigley
Collaton St Mary
ZOO
DARTMOUTH STEAM RAILWAY
TORBAY
TOR BAY
Belsford
Harberton
Ashprington
Dart
Stoke Gabriel
Goodrington
GOLDEN HIND
Brixham
BERRY HEAD
Berry Head
Harbertonford
Tuckenhay
Cornworthy
Galmpton
GREENWAY
Churston Ferrers
St Mary's Bay
Crabadon
Washbourne
Dittisham
RIVER DART
Sharkham Pt.
Halwell
Allaleigh
Capton
Hillhead
Moreleigh
WOODLANDS LEISURE PARK
Dartmouth
NEWCOMEN ENGINE HOUSE
Kingswear
Scabbacombe Hd.
Woodford
Blackawton
COLETON FISHACRE
Millcombe
BAYARDS COVE FORT
Warfleet
Bowden
DARTMOUTH CASTLE
Mew Stone
East Allington
Stoke Fleming
Blackpool
Strete
Goveton
SOUTH WEST COAST PATH
Harleston
Slapton
Sherford
Frittiscombe
SLAPTON LEY
Slapton Sands
START BAY
Frogmore
Stokenham
Charleton
Chillington
Torcross
Kernborough
Beeson
South Pool
Beesands
Kellaton
South Allington
Hallsands
START POINT
East Prawle
Lannacombe Bay
Prawle Pt.
DEVON
A
B
C
D
E
F
5
6
7
8
9

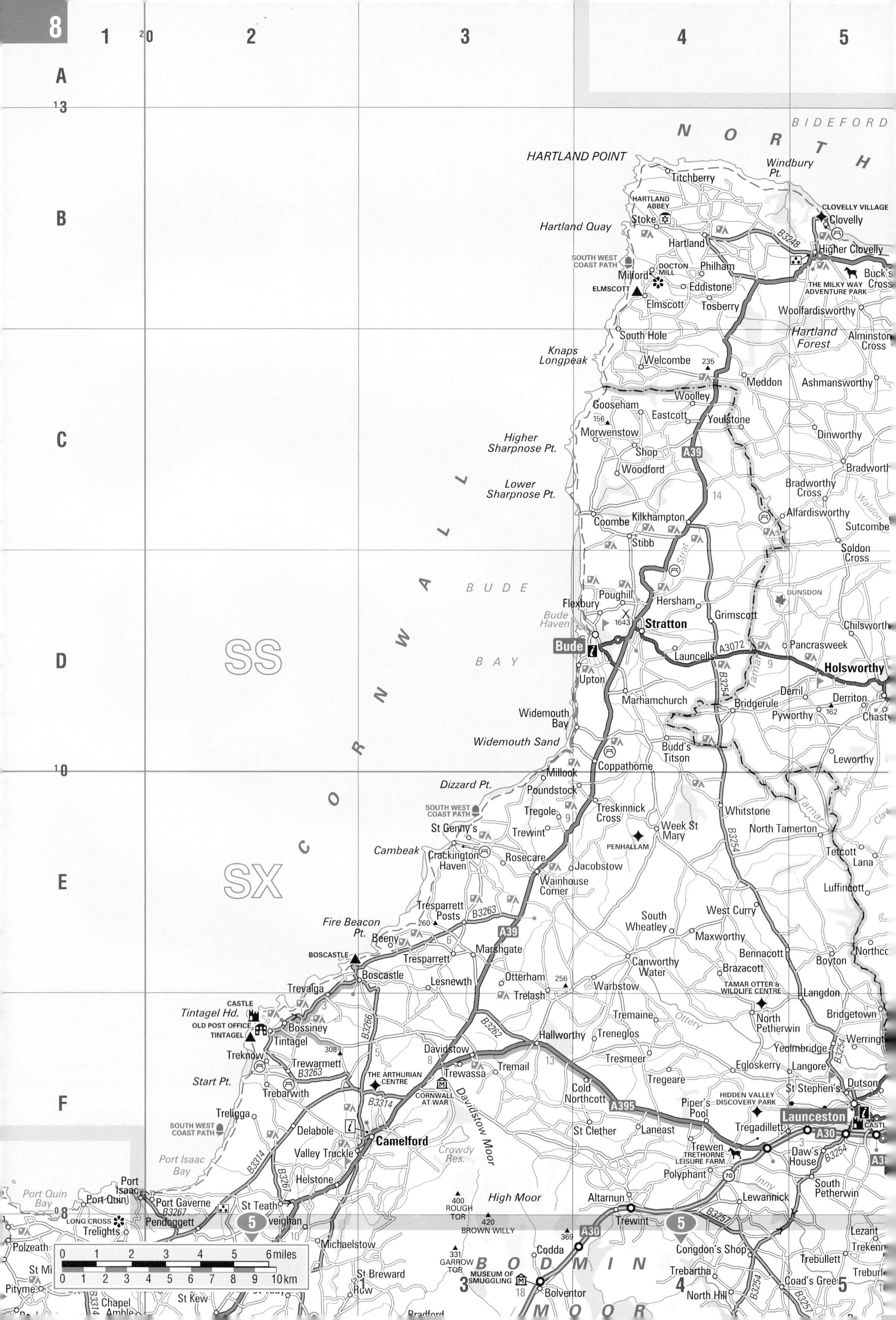
1
2
3
4
5
A
B
C
D
E
F
N O R T H
BIDEFORD
HARTLAND POINT
Windbury Pt.
Titchberry
HARTLAND ABBEY
Stoke
CLOVELLY VILLAGE
Clovelly
Hartland Quay
Hartland
B3248
Higher Clovelly
SOUTH WEST COAST PATH
DOCTON MILL
Philham
Milford
Buck's Cross
ELMSCOTT
Eddistone
THE MILKY WAY ADVENTURE PARK
Elmscott
Tosberry
Woolfardisworthy
South Hole
Hartland Forest
Alminston Cross
Knaps Longpeak
Welcombe
235
Meddon
Ashmansworthy
Woolley
Gooseham
Eastcott
Youlstone
156
Morwenstow
Dinworthy
Higher Sharpnose Pt.
Shop
A39
Woodford
Bradworthy
Lower Sharpnose Pt.
Bradworthy Cross
14
Waldon
Coombe
Kilkhampton
Alfardisworthy
Sutcombe
Stibb
Soldon Cross
Strat
C O R N W A L L
BUDE
DUNSDON
Poughill
Flexbury
Hersham
Grimscott
Bude Haven
1643
Stratton
Chilsworthy
SS
Bude
A3072
Pancrasweek
Launcells
Tamar
9
Holsworthy
BAY
B3254
Upton
Derril
Derriton
Marhamchurch
Bridgerule
162
Pyworthy
Chasty
Widemouth Bay
Widemouth Sand
Budd's Titson
Lewworthy
Coppathorne
Millook
Dizzard Pt.
Poundstock
Deer
SOUTH WEST COAST PATH
Treskinnick Cross
Whitstone
Tregole
9
St Genny's
Week St Mary
North Tamerton
Trewint
PENHALLAM
B3254
Cambeak
Crackington Haven
Rosecare
Tetcott
Jacobstow
Lana
SX
Wainhouse Corner
Luffincott
Tresparrett Posts
B3263
South Wheatley
West Curry
Fire Beacon Pt.
260
A39
Maxworthy
Beeny
6
Marshgate
Bennacott
BOSCASTLE
Tresparrett
Canworthy Water
Northcott
Brazacott
Boyton
Boscastle
Otterham
256
Lesnewth
TAMAR OTTER & WILDLIFE CENTRE
Trevalga
Warbstow
Langdon
Trelash
CASTLE
Tintagel Hd.
3
North Petherwin
Bridgetown
OLD POST OFFICE
Tremaine
Bossiney
TINTAGEL
B3262
Ottery
Treneglos
Werrington
Tintagel
Hallworthy
B3266
308
Yeolmbridge
B3254
Trewarmett
Davidstow
Treknow
5
Tresmeer
8
13
Egloskerry
Langore
B3263
Tremail
Tregeare
Start Pt.
THE ARTHURIAN CENTRE
Trewassa
Dutson
Trebarwith
St Stephen's
CORNWALL AT WAR
Cold Northcott
Davidstow Moor
HIDDEN VALLEY DISCOVERY PARK
B3314
A395
Piper's Pool
F
Treligga
Launceston
SOUTH WEST COAST PATH
St Clether
Laneast
Tregadillett
A30
Delabole
3
Camelford
Crowdy Res.
Trewen
Daw's House
B3254
TRETHORNE LEISURE FARM
Valley Truckle
Port Isaac Bay
B3314
Polyphant
B3267
70
Helstone
Inny
South Petherwin
Port Isaac
Port Quin Bay
400 ROUGH TOR
High Moor
Altarnun
Lewannick
Port Quin
Port Gaverne
B3267
St Teath
LONG CROSS
Pendoggett
Trelights
420 BROWN WILLY
Trewint
B3257
5
Lezant
10
369
A30
Polzeath
Michaelstow
Trekenn
Codda
Congdon's Shop
331 GARROW TOR
B O D M I N
Trebullett
St Breward
Trebartha
Treburl
MUSEUM OF SMUGGLING
Pityme
Bolventor
18
Coad's Green
Chapel Amble
St Kew
M O O R
North Hill
B3254
B3257
0
1
2
3
4
5
6 miles
0
1
2
3
4
5
6
7
8
9
10 km

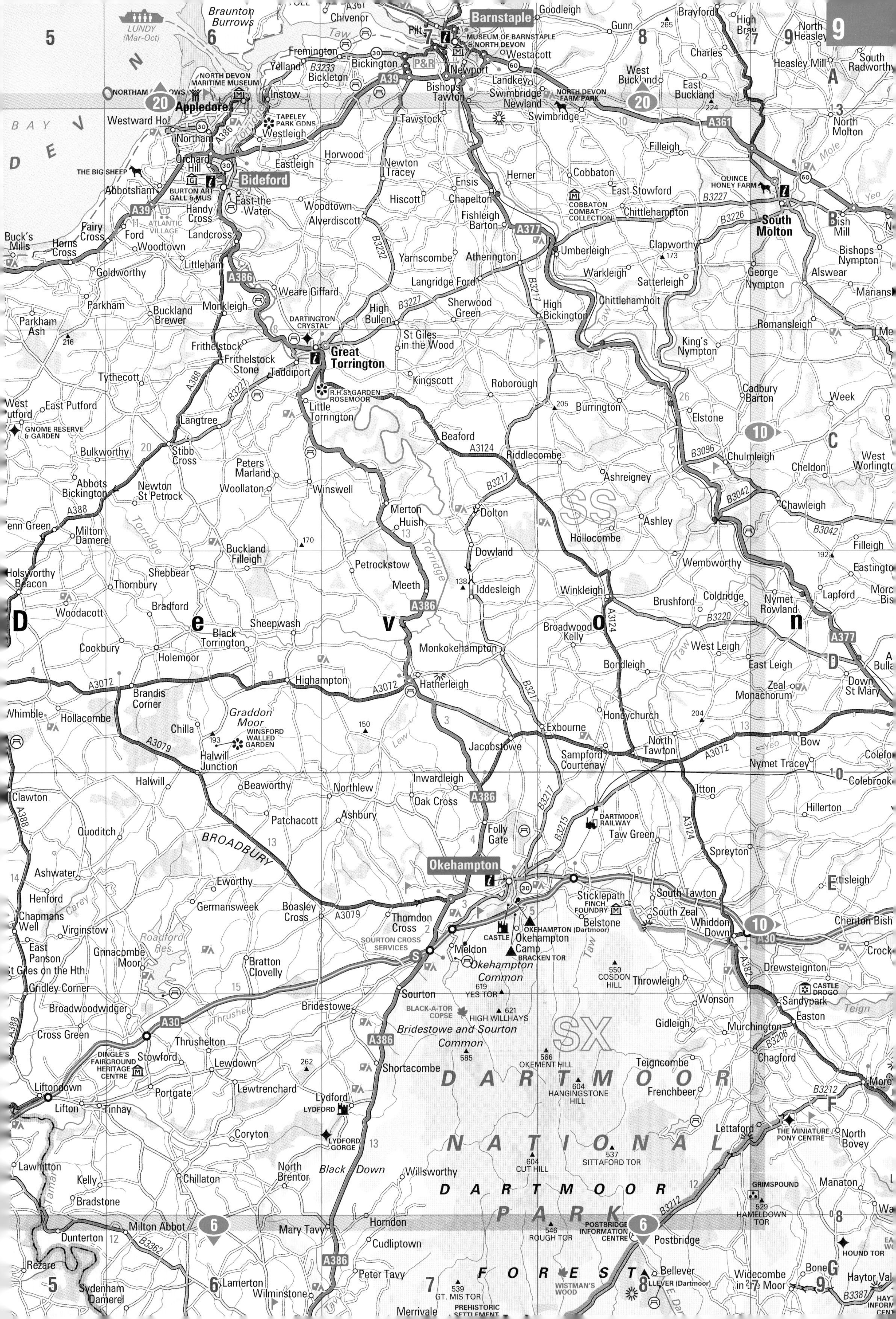
LUNDY (Mar-Oct)
Braunton Burrows
Chivenor
Barnstaple
Goodleigh
Brayford
High Bray
North Heasley
MUSEUM OF BARNSTAPLE & NORTH DEVON
Westacott
Gunn
Heasley Mill
South Radworthy
Charles
Fremington
Yelland
Bickington
Bickleton
Newport
Landkey
West Buckland
East Buckland
NORTH DEVON MARITIME MUSEUM
NORTHAM BURROWS
Appledore
Instow
Bishops Tawton
Swimbridge Newland
NORTH DEVON FARM PARK
Swimbridge
North Molton
BAY
DEVON
Westward Ho!
Northam
TAPELEY PARK GDNS
Westleigh
Tawstock
Filleigh
Orchard Hill
THE BIG SHEEP
Abbotsham
Bideford
Eastleigh
Horwood
Newton Tracey
Herner
Cobbaton
East Stowford
QUINCE HONEY FARM
BURTON ART GALL & MUS
East-the-Water
Handy Cross
Woodtown
Hiscott
Ensis
Chapelton
COBBATON COMBAT COLLECTION
Chittlehampton
South Molton
Bish Mill
Fairy Cross
ATLANTIC VILLAGE
Buck's Mills
Horns Cross
Ford
Landcross
Alverdiscott
Fishleigh Barton
Woodtown
Umberleigh
Clapworthy
Bishops Nympton
Littleham
Goldworthy
Yarnscombe
Atherington
Warkleigh
Satterleigh
George Nympton
Alswear
Langridge Ford
Weare Giffard
Marians
Parkham
Buckland Brewer
Monkleigh
High Bullen
Sherwood Green
High Bickington
Chittlehamholt
Parkham Ash
DARTINGTON CRYSTAL
Great Torrington
St Giles in the Wood
Romansleigh
Frithelstock
Frithelstock Stone
Taddiport
King's Nympton
Tythecott
Kingscott
Roborough
R.H.S. GARDEN ROSEMOOR
Little Torrington
Burrington
Cadbury Barton
Week
West Putford
East Putford
GNOME RESERVE & GARDEN
Langtree
Elstone
Beaford
Riddlecombe
Chulmleigh
West Worlington
Bulkworthy
Stibb Cross
Cheldon
Peters Marland
Ashreigney
Abbots Bickington
Newton St Petrock
Woollaton
Winswell
Chawleigh
Merton
Huish
Dolton
Ashley
Milton Damerel
Hollocombe
Torridge
Dowland
Filleigh
Buckland Filleigh
Wembworthy
Eastington
Holsworthy Beacon
Shebbear
Petrockstow
Meeth
Iddesleigh
Winkleigh
Thornbury
Coldridge
Brushford
Nymet Rowland
Lapford
Bradford
Woodacott
Broadwood Kelly
Devon
Sheepwash
Black Torrington
Monkokehampton
West Leigh
Cookbury
Holemoor
Bondleigh
East Leigh
Highampton
Hatherleigh
Zeal Monachorum
Down St Mary
Brandis Corner
Whimble
Hollacombe
Graddon Moor
Honeychurch
Chilla
WINSFORD WALLED GARDEN
Exbourne
Halwill Junction
Jacobstowe
Sampford Courtenay
North Tawton
Bow
Nymet Tracey
Colebrook
Halwill
Clawton
Beaworthy
Northlew
Inwardleigh
Oak Cross
Itton
DARTMOOR RAILWAY
Hillerton
Quoditch
Patchacott
Ashbury
Folly Gate
Taw Green
BROADBURY
Spreyton
Ashwater
Okehampton
Eworthy
Germansweek
Boasley Cross
Thorndon Cross
Sticklepath
FINCH FOUNDRY
South Tawton
South Zeal
Belstone
Whiddon Down
Henford
Chapmans Well
Virginstow
SOURTON CROSS SERVICES
CASTLE
OKEHAMPTON (Dartmoor)
Okehampton Camp
BRACKEN TOR
Cheriton Bishop
East Panson
Grinacombe Moor
Roadford Res.
Meldon
Okehampton Common
550 COSDON HILL
Throwleigh
Drewsteignton
Crockernwell
St Giles on the Hth.
Bratton Clovelly
CASTLE DROGO
Gridley Corner
Sourton
619 YES TOR
Wonson
Sandypark
Broadwoodwidger
Bridestowe
BLACK-A-TOR COPSE
621 HIGH WILLHAYS
Teign
Easton
Thrushel
Bridestowe and Sourton Common
SX
Gidleigh
Murchington
Cross Green
Thrushelton
Chagford
DINGLE'S FAIRGROUND HERITAGE CENTRE
Stowford
Lewdown
585
566 OKEMENT HILL
Teigncombe
Shortacombe
DARTMOOR
604 HANGINGSTONE HILL
Frenchbeer
Moreton
Liftondown
Portgate
Lewtrenchard
Lydford
LYDFORD CASTLE
Lifton
Tinhay
Lettaford
THE MINIATURE PONY CENTRE
North Bovey
Coryton
LYDFORD GORGE
NATIONAL
604 CUT HILL
537 SITTAFORD TOR
Lawhitton
North Brentor
Black Down
Willsworthy
Kelly
Chillaton
DARTMOOR
GRIMSPOUND
Manaton
Bradstone
PARK
529 HAMELDOWN TOR
Milton Abbot
Horndon
POSTBRIDGE INFORMATION CENTRE
Postbridge
Dunterton
Mary Tavy
546 ROUGH TOR
Cudliptown
HOUND TOR
Rezare
Peter Tavy
Bellever
Widecombe in the Moor
Bonehill
Haytor Vale
Sydenham Damerel
Lamerton
Wilminstone
539 GT. MIS TOR
FOREST
WISTMAN'S WOOD
LLEVER (Dartmoor)
Merrivale
PREHISTORIC SETTLEMENT
A39
A361
A377
A386
A388
A3124
A3072
A3079
A30
A382
B3227
B3232
B3217
B3226
B3096
B3042
B3220
B3215
B3212
B3206
B3362
B3387
B3233
Taw
Torridge
Yeo
Mole
Lew
Carey
Tamar
Tavy
Teign
20
10
6
A
B
C
D
E
F
G
5
6
7
8
9

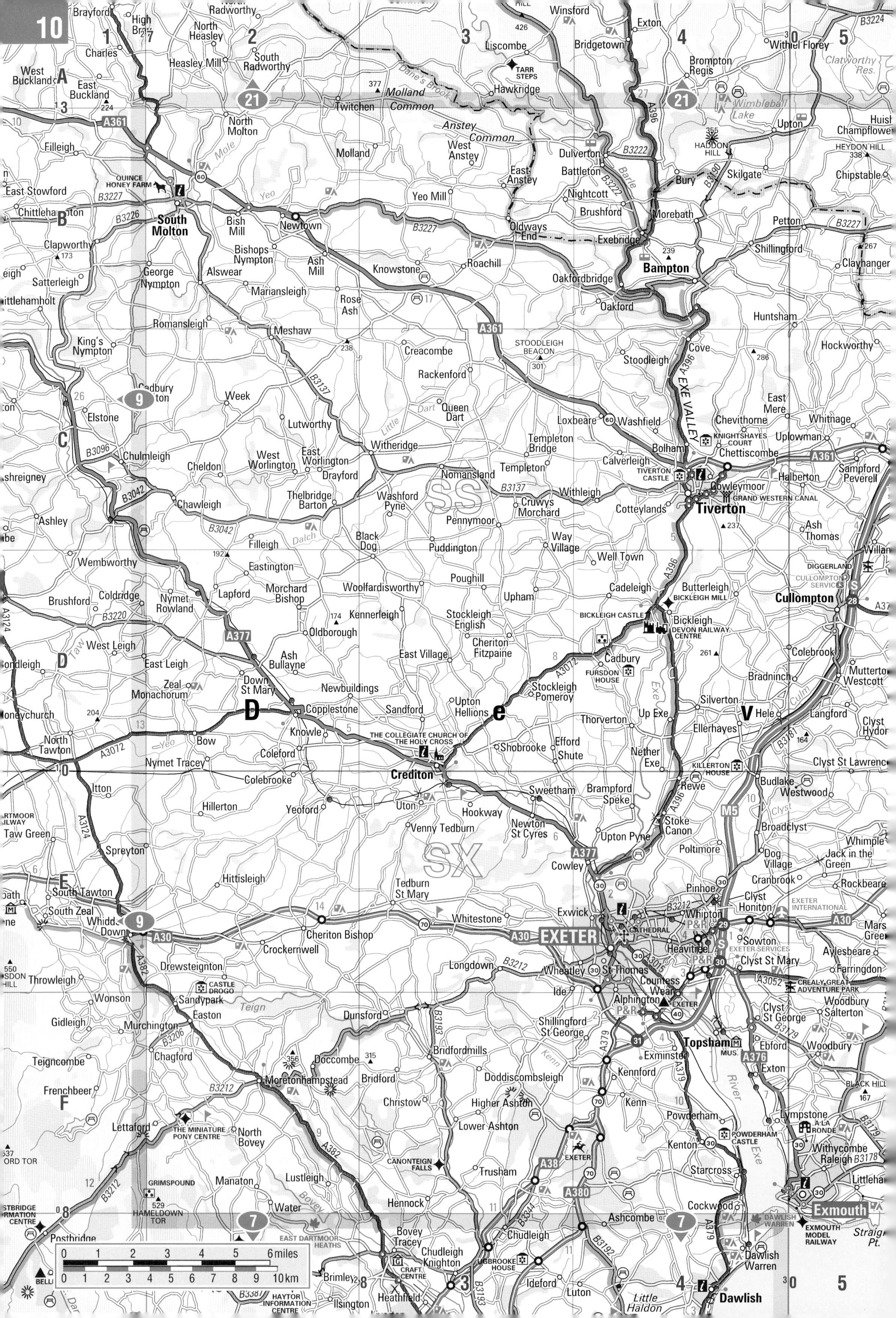

Brayford
High Bray
Radworthy
North Heasley
Heasley Mill
South Radworthy
Charles
West Buckland
East Buckland
Twitchen
Molland Common
Dane's Brook
Liscombe
TARR STEPS
Hawkridge
Winsford
Exton
Bridgetown
Brompton Regis
Withiel Florey
Clatworthy Res.
Wimbleball Lake
Upton
Huish Champflower
HADDON HILL
HEYDON HILL
Skilgate
Chipstable
Filleigh
North Molton
Molland
Anstey Common
West Anstey
East Anstey
Dulverton
Battleton
Barle
Nightcott
Brushford
Bury
Morebath
QUINCE HONEY FARM
East Stowford
Chittlehampton
South Molton
Bish Mill
Newtown
Yeo Mill
Oldways End
Exebridge
Bampton
Petton
Shillingford
Clayhanger
Clapworthy
George Nympton
Satterleigh
Alswear
Bishops Nympton
Ash Mill
Knowstone
Roachill
Oakfordbridge
Oakford
Mariansleigh
Rose Ash
Romansleigh
Meshaw
Huntsham
King's Nympton
Creacombe
STOODLEIGH BEACON
Stoodleigh
Cove
Hockworthy
Rackenford
Cadbury
Week
Elstone
Queen Dart
Little Dart
Lutworthy
Loxbeare
Washfield
East Mere
Chevithorne
Whitnage
EXE VALLEY
KNIGHTSHAYES COURT
Uplowman
Chulmleigh
Cheldon
West Worlington
East Worlington
Witheridge
Templeton Bridge
Templeton
Calverleigh
Bolham
Chettiscombe
Sampford Peverell
Halberton
TIVERTON CASTLE
Cowleymoor
GRAND WESTERN CANAL
Tiverton
Drayford
Nomansland
Thelbridge Barton
Washford Pyne
Pennymoor
Cruwys Morchard
Withleigh
Cotteylands
Chawleigh
Ashley
Ash Thomas
Way Village
Well Town
Filleigh
Dalch
Black Dog
Puddington
Wembworthy
Eastington
DIGGERLAND
CULLOMPTON SERVICES
Cullompton
Brushford
Coldridge
Nymet Rowland
Lapford
Morchard Bishop
Woolfardisworthy
Poughill
Upham
Cadeleigh
Butterleigh
BICKLEIGH MILL
BICKLEIGH CASTLE
Bickleigh
DEVON RAILWAY CENTRE
Kennerleigh
Stockleigh English
Oldborough
Cheriton Fitzpaine
Colebrook
West Leigh
East Leigh
Ash Bullayne
East Village
Cadbury
FURSDON HOUSE
Bradninch
Mutterton
Westcott
Zeal Monachorum
Down St Mary
Newbuildings
Stockleigh Pomeroy
Silverton
Hele
Langford
Clyst Hydon
Honeychurch
Copplestone
Sandford
Upton Hellions
Thorverton
Up Exe
Ellerhayes
North Tawton
Knowle
Bow
THE COLLEGIATE CHURCH OF THE HOLY CROSS
Shobrooke
Efford
Shute
Nether Exe
Nymet Tracey
Coleford
Crediton
KILLERTON HOUSE
Clyst St Lawrence
Itton
Colebrooke
Sweetham
Brampford Speke
Rewe
Budlake
Westwood
Hillerton
Yeoford
Uton
Hookway
Newton St Cyres
Stoke Canon
Broadclyst
Taw Green
Venny Tedburn
Upton Pyne
Poltimore
Whimple
Spreyton
Cowley
Dog Village
Jack in the Green
Hittisleigh
Tedburn St Mary
Pinhoe
Cranbrook
Rockbeare
South Tawton
South Zeal
Whiddon Down
Whitestone
Exwick
Whipton
Clyst Honiton
EXETER INTERNATIONAL
Cheriton Bishop
EXETER
CATHEDRAL
Heavitree
Sowton
EXETER SERVICES
Crockernwell
Aylesbeare
Marsh Green
Drewsteignton
Longdown
Wheatley
St Thomas
Clyst St Mary
Farringdon
Throwleigh
CASTLE DROGO
Countess Wear
Ide
Alphington
CREALY GREAT ADVENTURE PARK
Wonson
Sandypark
Easton
Teign
Dunsford
Shillingford St George
Clyst St George
Woodbury Salterton
Gidleigh
Murchington
Topsham
Ebford
Woodbury
Exminster
Chagford
Doccombe
Bridfordmills
Teigncombe
Moretonhampstead
Bridford
Doddiscombsleigh
Kennford
Exton
Frenchbeer
Christow
Higher Ashton
Kenn
Powderham
BLACK HILL
Lower Ashton
POWDERHAM CASTLE
Lympstone
A LA RONDE
Lettaford
THE MINIATURE PONY CENTRE
North Bovey
Kenton
Withycombe Raleigh
CANONTEIGN FALLS
Trusham
Starcross
Littleham
GRIMSPOUND
Manaton
Lustleigh
HAMELDON TOR
Water
Bovey
Hennock
Cockwood
Exmouth
STBRIDGE INFORMATION CENTRE
Postbridge
EAST DARTMOOR HEATHS
Bovey Tracey
Chudleigh
Ashcombe
DAWLISH WARREN
EXMOUTH MODEL RAILWAY
Straight Pt.
Chudleigh Knighton
CRAFT CENTRE
UGBROOKE HOUSE
Dawlish Warren
Brimley
Ideford
Luton
Heathfield
Ilsington
HAYTOR INFORMATION CENTRE
Little Haldon
Dawlish
A361
A396
A3072
A377
A3124
A30
A382
A38
A380
A379
A376
M5
B3227
B3226
B3222
B3190
B3224
B3137
B3096
B3042
B3220
B3212
B3206
B3193
B3344
B3192
B3181
B3179
B3178
B3052
B3015
SS
SX
0 1 2 3 4 5 6 miles
0 1 2 3 4 5 6 7 8 9 10 km

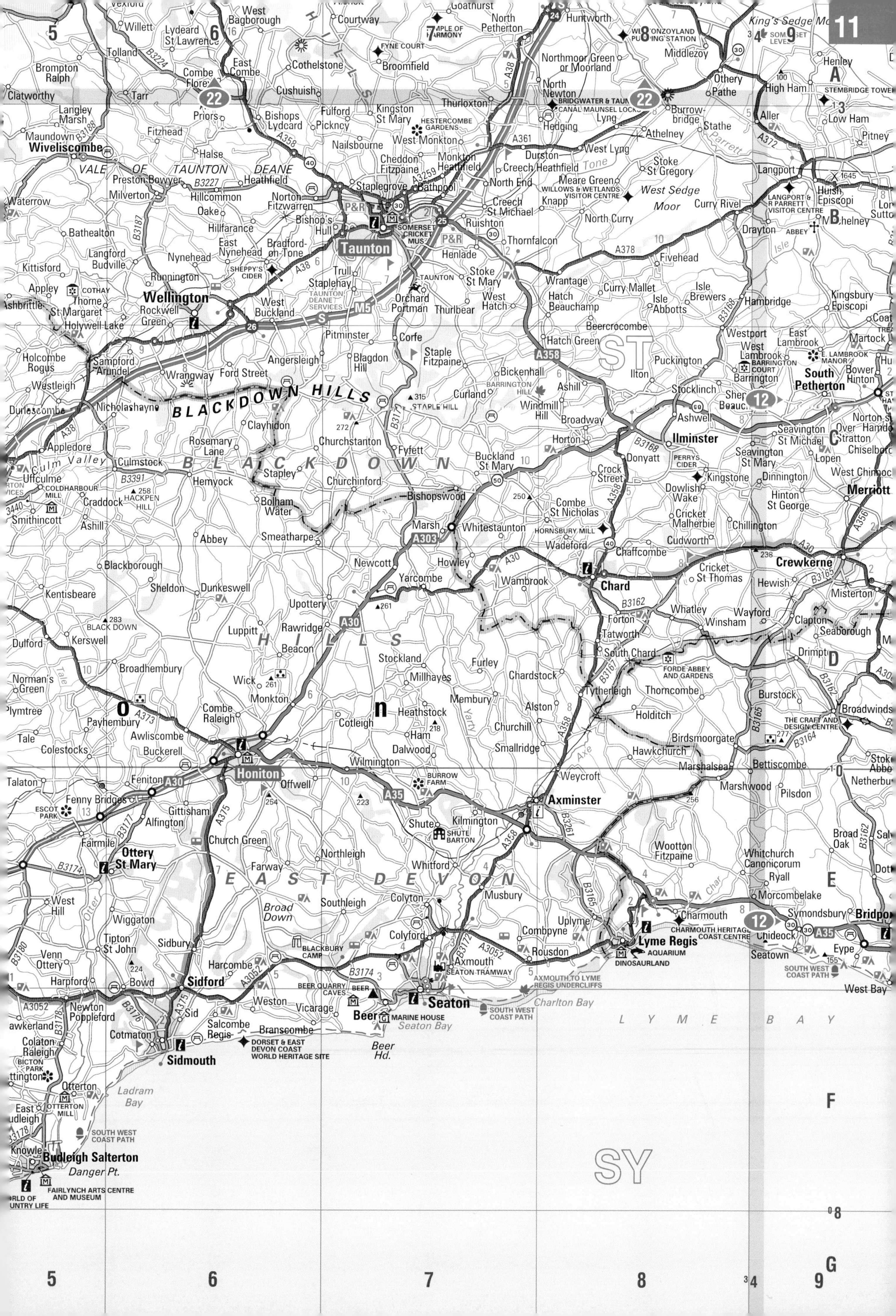

West Bagborough
Willett
Lydeard St Lawrence
Courtway
Goathurst
North Petherton
Huntworth
Westonzoyland Pumping Station
Middlezoy
King's Sedge Moor
Somerset Levels
Temple of Harmony
Fyne Court
Tolland
East Combe
Cothelstone
Broomfield
Brompton Ralph
Combe Florey
Northmoor Green or Moorland
Othery
Henley
Pathe
High Ham
Stembridge Tower
Clatworthy
Tarr
Cushuish
North Newton
Bridgwater & Taunton Canal: Maunsel Locks
Burrow-bridge
Low Ham
Langley Marsh
Priors
Bishops Lydeard
Fulford
Kingston St Mary
Thurloxton
Hedging
Lyng
Stathe
Aller
Maundown
Fitzhead
Picknoy
Hestercombe Gardens
Athelney
Pitney
Wiveliscombe
Halse
Nailsbourne
West Monkton
Durston
West Lyng
Parrett
Vale of Taunton Deane
Cheddon Fitzpaine
Monkton Heathfield
Creech Heathfield
Tone
Stoke St Gregory
Langport
Preston Bowyer
Heathfield
Staplegrove
Bathpool
North End
Meare Green
Willows & Wetlands Visitor Centre
West Sedge Moor
Huish Episcopi
Waterrow
Milverton
Hillcommon
Norton Fitzwarren
Creech St Michael
Knapp
Curry Rivel
Langport & R Parrett Visitor Centre
Muchelney
Oake
Bishop's Hull
North Curry
Ruishton
Drayton
Abbey
Bathealton
Hillfarance
Somerset Cricket Mus
Thornfalcon
East Nynehead
Bradford-on-Tone
Taunton
Henlade
Isle
Langford Budville
Nynehead
Sheppy's Cider
Trull
Stoke St Mary
A378
Fivehead
Kittisford
Runnington
Staplehay
Wrantage
Curry Mallet
Isle Brewers
Appley
Cothay
Thorne St Margaret
Wellington
Taunton Deane Services
Orchard Portman
Thurlbear
West Hatch
Hatch Beauchamp
Isle Abbotts
Hambridge
Kingsbury Episcopi
Ashbrittle
Rockwell Green
West Buckland
Holywell Lake
Beercrocombe
Westport
East Lambrook
Martock
Pitminster
Corfe
Hatch Green
ST
Puckington
West Lambrook
Barrington Court
E. Lambrook Manor
Holcombe Rogus
Sampford Arundel
Angersleigh
Blagdon Hill
Staple Fitzpaine
Barrington
South Petherton
Wrangway
Ford Street
Bickenhall
Barrington Hill
Ilton
Bower Hinton
Westleigh
Ashill
Stocklinch
Shepton Beauchamp
Blackdown Hills
Curland
Staple Hill
Windmill Hill
Ashwell
Norton sub Hamdon
Durlescombe
Nicholashayne
Clayhidon
Broadway
Seavington St Michael
Over Stratton
Appledore
Rosemary Lane
Churchstanton
Fyfett
Horton
Ilminster
Culm Valley
Culmstock
Donyatt
Seavington St Mary
Lopen
Chiselborough
Uffculme
Blackdown
Buckland St Mary
Crock Street
Perrys Cider
West Chinnock
Coldharbour Mill
Hemyock
Stapley
Churchinford
Kingstone
Dinnington
Hackpen Hill
Bishopswood
Dowlish Wake
Hinton St George
Merriott
Craddock
Bolham Water
Combe St Nicholas
Cricket Malherbie
Smithincott
Ashill
Marsh
Whitestaunton
Hornsbury Mill
Chillington
Abbey
Smeatharpe
Wadeford
Cudworth
Chaffcombe
Blackborough
Newcott
Howley
Cricket St Thomas
Crewkerne
Yarcombe
Wambrook
Sheldon
Dunkeswell
Chard
Hewish
Misterton
Kentisbeare
Upottery
Black Down
Forton
Whatley
Wayford
Clapton
Winsham
Seaborough
Luppitt
Rawridge
Tatworth
Dulford
Kerswell
Hills
Beacon
South Chard
Drimpton
Stockland
Furley
Forde Abbey and Gardens
Broadhembury
Chardstock
Norman's Green
Millhayes
Tytherleigh
Thorncombe
Burstock
Wick
Membury
Broadwindsor
Plymtree
Monkton
Alston
Holdich
Payhembury
Combe Raleigh
Cotleigh
Heathstock
Churchill
The Craft and Design Centre
Tale
Awliscombe
Ham
Birdsmoorgate
Colestocks
Buckerell
Dalwood
Smallridge
Hawkchurch
Wilmington
Marshalsea
Bettiscombe
Stoke Abbott
Talaton
Honiton
Feniton
Offwell
Burrow Farm
Weycroft
Marshwood
Netherbury
Fenny Bridges
Pilsdon
Escot Park
Gittisham
Axminster
Alfington
Shute
Kilmington
Shute Barton
Fairmile
Church Green
Wootton Fitzpaine
Broad Oak
Ottery St Mary
Northleigh
Whitford
Whitchurch Canonicorum
Farway
East Devon
Ryall
West Hill
Musbury
Morcombelake
Broad Down
Southleigh
Colyton
Charmouth
Symondsbury
Bridport
Wiggaton
Uplyme
Chideock
Charmouth Heritage Coast Centre
Tipton St John
Sidbury
Colyford
Combpyne
Lyme Regis
Eype
Blackbury Camp
Rousdon
Aquarium
Venn Ottery
Axmouth
Dinosaurland
Seatown
South West Coast Path
Harcombe
Seaton Tramway
Axmouth to Lyme Regis Undercliffs
Harpford
Bowd
Sidford
Beer Quarry Caves
Beer
West Bay
Newton Poppleford
Weston
Vicarage
Seaton
Charlton Bay
Sid
Marine House
Seaton Bay
Lyme Bay
Hawkerland
Salcombe Regis
Branscombe
Colaton Raleigh
Cotmaton
Dorset & East Devon Coast World Heritage Site
Beer Hd.
Bicton Park
Sidmouth
Otterton
Ladram Bay
Otterton Mill
East Budleigh
South West Coast Path
Knowle
Budleigh Salterton
Danger Pt.
Fairlynch Arts Centre and Museum
World of Country Life
SY
A
B
C
D
E
F
G
5
6
7
8
9

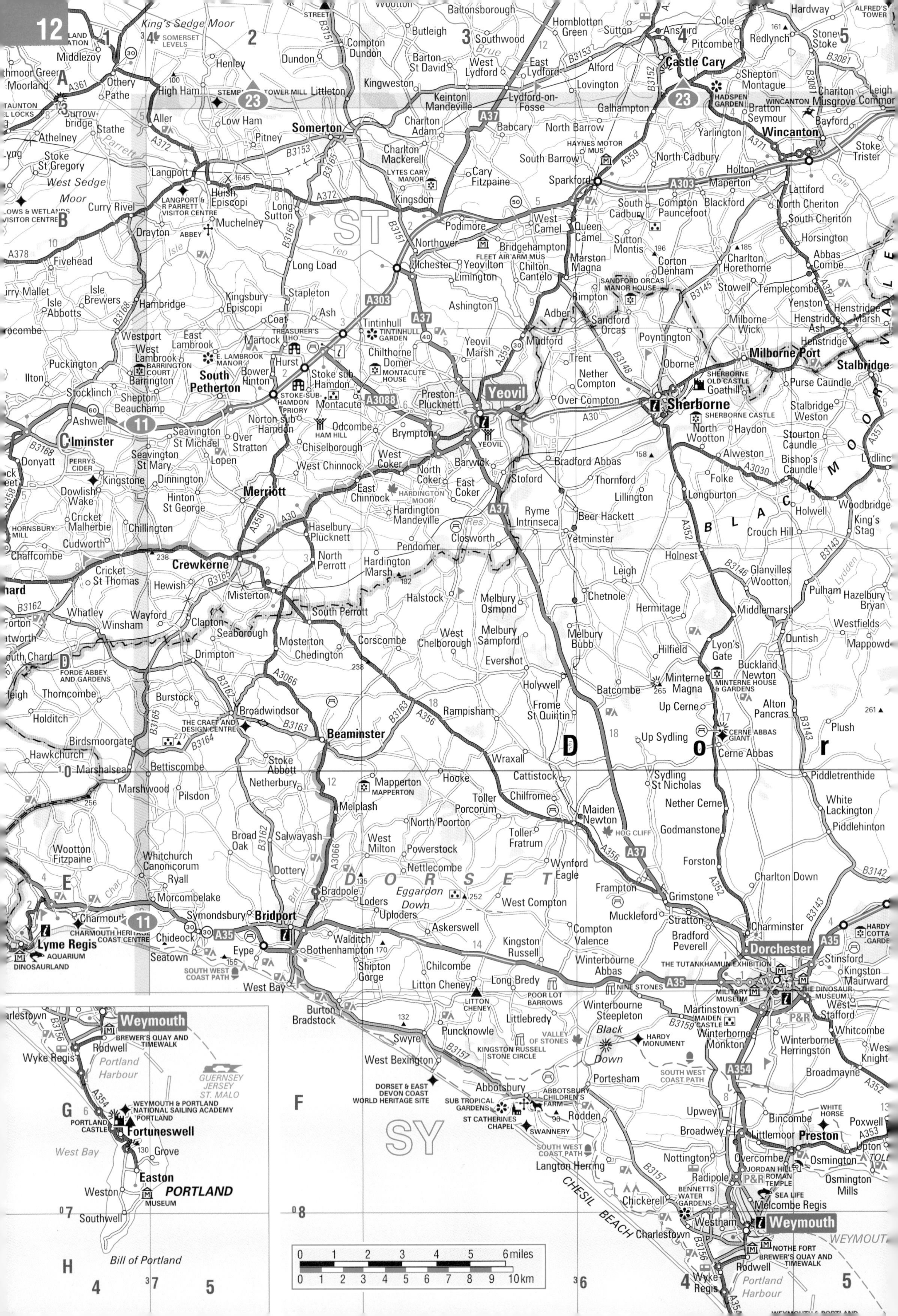
King's Sedge Moor
SOMERSET LEVELS
Middlezoy
Othery
Pathe
Moorland
Burrow-bridge
Stathe
Athelney
Stoke St Gregory
West Sedge Moor
Henley
High Ham
Low Ham
Aller
Pitney
Dundon
Compton Dundon
Littleton
Somerton
TOWER MILL
Langport
Huish Episcopi
LANGPORT & R PARRETT VISITOR CENTRE
Muchelney
ABBEY
Curry Rivel
Drayton
Fivehead
Isle Brewers
Isle Abbotts
Hambridge
Kingsbury Episcopi
Long Sutton
Long Load
Stapleton
Ash
Coat
Martock
Westport
East Lambrook
West Lambrook
E. LAMBROOK MANOR
BARRINGTON COURT
Barrington
Puckington
Ilton
South Petherton
Bower Hinton
Hurst
Stocklinch
Shepton Beauchamp
Ashwell
Ilminster
Seavington St Michael
Seavington St Mary
Over Stratton
Lopen
Donyatt
PERRYS CIDER
Kingstone
Dowlish Wake
Dinnington
Hinton St George
Merriott
Cricket Malherbie
Chillington
Cudworth
HORNSBURY MILL
Chaffcombe
Crewkerne
Cricket St Thomas
Hewish
Misterton
Whatley
Winsham
Wayford
Clapton
Seaborough
Drimpton
FORDE ABBEY AND GARDENS
Thorncombe
Holditch
Burstock
Broadwindsor
THE CRAFT AND DESIGN CENTRE
Birdsmoorgate
Hawkchurch
Marshalsea
Bettiscombe
Marshwood
Pilsdon
Stoke Abbott
Netherbury
Wootton Fitzpaine
Whitchurch Canonicorum
Ryall
Morcombelake
Charmouth
CHARMOUTH HERITAGE COAST CENTRE
Lyme Regis
AQUARIUM
DINOSAURLAND
Chideock
Seatown
Symondsbury
Bridport
Eype
SOUTH WEST COAST PATH
West Bay
Bothenhampton
Walditch
Shipton Gorge
Broad Oak
Salwayash
Dottery
Bradpole
Loders
Uploders
Melplash
Beaminster
Mapperton
MAPPERTON
West Milton
Powerstock
Nettlecombe
North Poorton
Hooke
DORSET
Eggardon Down
Askerswell
Chilcombe
Litton Cheney
Puncknowle
Swyre
West Bexington
Burton Bradstock
DORSET & EAST DEVON COAST WORLD HERITAGE SITE
Abbotsbury
SUB TROPICAL GARDENS
ABBOTSBURY CHILDREN'S FARM
ST CATHERINES CHAPEL
SWANNERY
Rodden
Langton Herring
CHESIL BEACH
Charlestown
Chickerell
Long Bredy
Littlebredy
KINGSTON RUSSELL STONE CIRCLE
VALLEY OF STONES
Kingston Russell
POOR LOT BARROWS
Winterbourne Steepleton
Black Down
HARDY MONUMENT
Portesham
Winterbourne Abbas
NINE STONES
West Compton
Compton Valence
Wynford Eagle
Toller Porcorum
Toller Fratrum
Chilfrome
Maiden Newton
HOG CLIFF
Frampton
Muckleford
Cattistock
Wraxall
Rampisham
Frome St Quintin
Holywell
Evershot
Melbury Sampford
Melbury Osmond
Melbury Bubb
West Chelborough
Corscombe
Halstock
Chedington
Mosterton
South Perrott
North Perrott
Haselbury Plucknett
Hardington Marsh
Pendomer
Closworth
Hardington Mandeville
HARDINGTON MOOR
East Chinnock
West Chinnock
Chiselborough
West Coker
North Coker
East Coker
Barwick
Stoford
Odcombe
HAM HILL
Montacute
MONTACUTE HOUSE
Norton sub Hamdon
STOKE-SUB-HAMDON PRIORY
Stoke sub Hamdon
TREASURER'S HO
Tintinhull
TINTINHULL GARDEN
Chilthorne Domer
Preston Plucknett
Brympton
Yeovil
Yeovil Marsh
Mudford
Ashington
Ilchester
Yeovilton
FLEET AIR ARM MUS
Limington
Northover
Podimore
Kingsdon
LYTES CARY MANOR
Charlton Mackerell
Charlton Adam
Keinton Mandeville
Kingweston
Barton St David
Butleigh
Baltonsborough
West Lydford
East Lydford
Lydford-on-Fosse
Southwood
Brue
Alford
Lovington
Hornblotton Green
Sutton
Ansford
Castle Cary
Pitcombe
Cole
Hardway
Redlynch
Stoney Stoke
ALFRED'S TOWER
Shepton Montague
HADSPEN GARDEN
Bratton Seymour
Charlton Musgrove
WINCANTON
Wincanton
Leigh Common
Bayford
Stoke Trister
Yarlington
North Cadbury
Galhampton
North Barrow
South Barrow
Babcary
HAYNES MOTOR MUS
Cary Fitzpaine
Sparkford
Holton
Maperton
Lattiford
North Cheriton
South Cheriton
Horsington
Abbas Combe
Templecombe
Yenston
Henstridge
Henstridge Marsh
Henstridge Ash
Stalbridge
Milborne Port
Milborne Wick
Stowell
Charlton Horethorne
Corton Denham
Compton Pauncefoot
Blackford
South Cadbury
Queen Camel
West Camel
Sutton Montis
Marston Magna
Bridgehampton
Chilton Cantelo
Rimpton
SANDFORD ORCAS MANOR HOUSE
Sandford Orcas
Adber
Trent
Nether Compton
Over Compton
Poyntington
Oborne
SHERBORNE OLD CASTLE
Goathill
Sherborne
SHERBORNE CASTLE
Purse Caundle
Stalbridge Weston
North Wootton
Haydon
Stourton Caundle
Bishop's Caundle
Alweston
Folke
Longburton
Bradford Abbas
Thornford
Lillington
Beer Hackett
Yetminster
Ryme Intrinseca
Leigh
Chetnole
Holnest
Glanvilles Wootton
BLACKMOOR VALE
Holwell
Crouch Hill
King's Stag
Woodbridge
Lydlinch
Pulham
Hazelbury Bryan
Middlemarsh
Westfields
Mappowder
Dunstish
Hermitage
Hilfield
Lyon's Gate
Buckland Newton
MINTERNE HOUSE & GARDENS
Minterne Magna
Batcombe
Up Cerne
Alton Pancras
Plush
CERNE ABBAS GIANT
Cerne Abbas
Up Sydling
Sydling St Nicholas
Piddletrenthide
White Lackington
Piddlehinton
Nether Cerne
Godmanstone
Forston
Charlton Down
Grimstone
Stratton
Bradford Peverell
Charminster
Dorchester
THE TUTANKHAMUN EXHIBITION
HARDY COTTAGE
Stinsford
Kingston Maurward
THE DINOSAUR MUSEUM
MILITARY MUSEUM
MAIDEN CASTLE
Martinstown
Winterborne Monkton
Winterborne Herringston
West Stafford
Whitcombe
West Knight
Broadmayne
Upwey
Bincombe
WHITE HORSE
Poxwell
Broadwey
Littlemoor
Preston
Osmington
Osmington Mills
Upton
Nottington
Radipole
Overcombe
JORDAN HILL ROMAN TEMPLE
SEA LIFE
BENNETTS WATER GARDENS
Melcombe Regis
Westham
Weymouth
NOTHE FORT
BREWER'S QUAY AND TIMEWALK
Rodwell
Portland Harbour
Wyke Regis
Charlestown
Weymouth
BREWER'S QUAY AND TIMEWALK
Rodwell
Wyke Regis
Portland Harbour
GUERNSEY JERSEY ST. MALO
WEYMOUTH & PORTLAND NATIONAL SAILING ACADEMY
PORTLAND CASTLE
Fortuneswell
Grove
West Bay
Easton
PORTLAND
Weston
MUSEUM
Southwell
Bill of Portland
ST
SY
0 1 2 3 4 5 6 miles
0 1 2 3 4 5 6 7 8 9 10 km

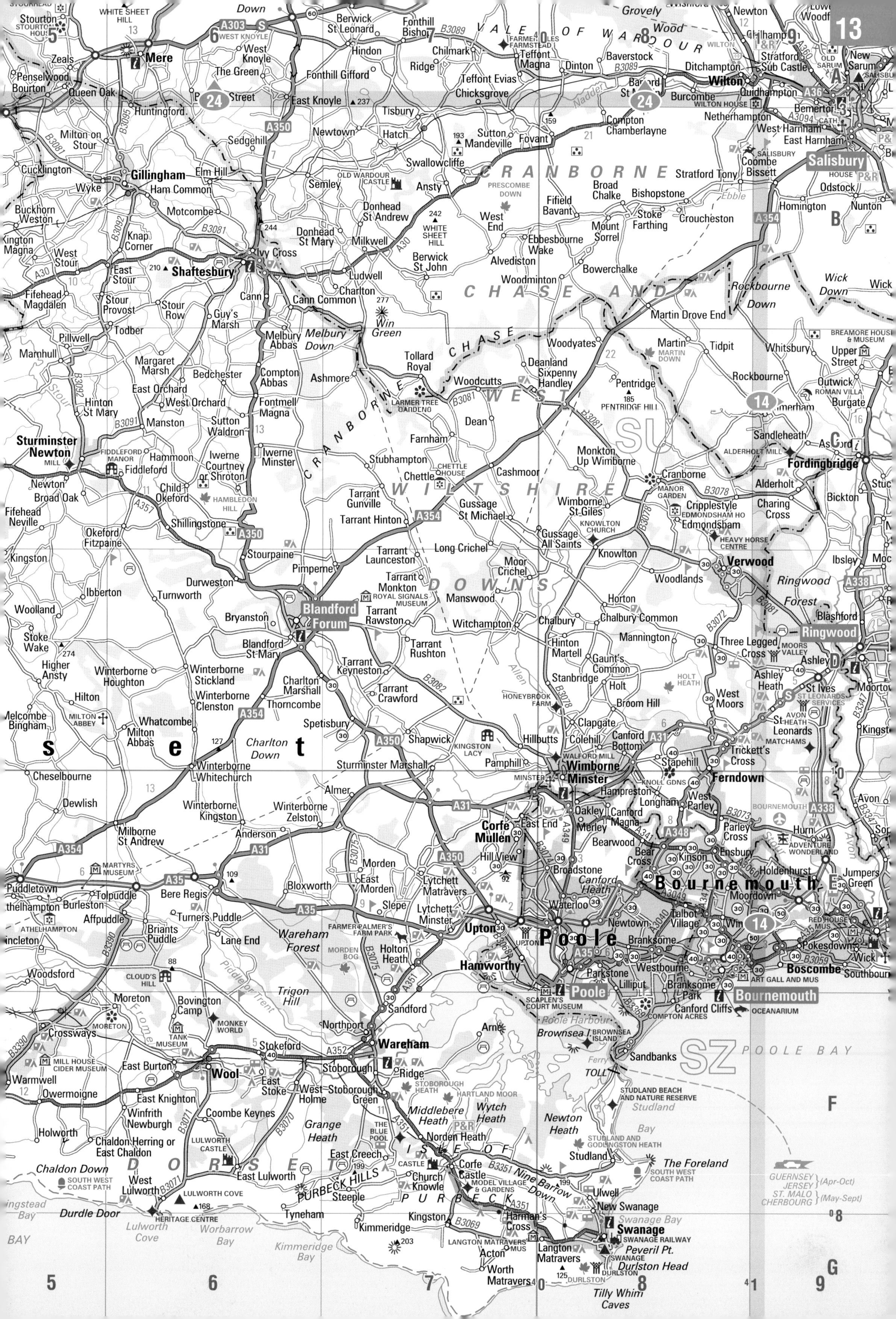

White Sheet Hill
Down
Berwick St Leonard
Fonthill Bishop
Vale of Wardour
Grovely Wood
Newton
Stourton
Mere
West Knoyle
Hindon
Chilmark
Teffont Magna
Dinton
Baverstock
Ditchampton
Stratford sub Castle
Old Sarum
Zeals
Penselwood
Bourton
Queen Oak
The Green
Fonthill Gifford
Ridge
Teffont Evias
Chicksgrove
Barford St Martin
Wilton
Burcombe
Quidhampton
Bemerton
Wilton House
Netherhampton
Salisbury
Huntingford
East Knoyle
Tisbury
Compton Chamberlayne
West Harnham
East Harnham
Milton on Stour
Sedgehill
Newtown
Hatch
Sutton Mandeville
Fovant
Cucklington
Gillingham
Elm Hill
Semley
Old Wardour Castle
Swallowcliffe
Ansty
Cranborne
Stratford Tony
Coombe Bissett
Wyke
Ham Common
Prescombe Down
Broad Chalke
Bishopstone
Odstock
Buckhorn Weston
Motcombe
Donhead St Andrew
Fifield Bavant
Ebble
Croucheston
Homington
Nunton
Kington Magna
Knap Corner
Donhead St Mary
White Sheet Hill
West End
Stoke Farthing
Mount Sorrel
Ebbesbourne Wake
West Stour
Ivy Cross
Shaftesbury
Milkwell
Berwick St John
Alvediston
Bowerchalke
East Stour
Ludwell
Woodminton
Wick Down
Fifehead Magdalen
Cann
Charlton
Chase and
Rockbourne Down
Stour Provost
Stour Row
Cann Common
Win Green
Martin Drove End
Guy's Marsh
Todber
Melbury Abbas
Melbury Down
Woodyates
Martin
Martin Down
Tidpit
Whitsbury
Breamore House & Museum
Upper Street
Marnhull
Pillwell
Margaret Marsh
Tollard Royal
Chase
Deanland
Sixpenny Handley
Bedchester
Compton Abbas
Ashmore
Woodcutts
Pentridge
Pentridge Hill
Rockbourne
Outwick
Roman Villa
Burgate
East Orchard
West Orchard
Fontmell Magna
Larmer Tree Gardens
West
Hinton St Mary
Manston
Sutton Waldron
Dean
Sandleheath
Ashford
Farnham
Monkton Up Wimborne
Sturminster Newton
Mill
Fiddleford Manor
Fiddleford
Hammoon
Iwerne Courtney or Shroton
Iwerne Minster
Stubhampton
Chettle House
Chettle
Cashmoor
Cranborne
Alderholt Mill
Fordingbridge
Newton
Broad Oak
Child Okeford
Hambledon Hill
Tarrant Gunville
Wiltshire
Manor Garden
Cripplestyle
Alderholt
Charing Cross
Bickton
Fifehead Neville
Shillingstone
Tarrant Hinton
Gussage St Michael
Wimborne St Giles
Edmondsham House
Edmondsham
Okeford Fitzpaine
Knowlton Church
Gussage All Saints
Heavy Horse Centre
Kingston
Stourpaine
Long Crichel
Knowlton
Verwood
Ibsley
Tarrant Launceston
Pimperne
Moor Crichel
Ringwood Forest
Durweston
Tarrant Monkton
Downs
Woodlands
Ibberton
Turnworth
Royal Signals Museum
Manswood
Horton
Woolland
Bryanston
Blandford Forum
Tarrant Rawston
Witchampton
Chalbury
Chalbury Common
Blashford
Ringwood
Stoke Wake
Blandford St Mary
Tarrant Rushton
Hinton Martell
Mannington
Three Legged Cross
Moors Valley
Higher Ansty
Winterborne Houghton
Winterborne Stickland
Tarrant Keyneston
Gaunt's Common
Ashley
Charlton Marshall
Stanbridge
Ashley Heath
St Ives
Holt
Holt Heath
Hilton
Winterborne Clenston
Tarrant Crawford
Honeybrook Farm
West Moors
Melcombe Bingham
Milton Abbey
Whatcombe
Thorncombe
Broom Hill
Milton Abbas
Spetisbury
Clapgate
St Leonards
Colehill
Canford Bottom
Matchams
Charlton Down
Shapwick
Kingston Lacy
Hillbutts
Trickett's Cross
Winterborne Whitechurch
Sturminster Marshall
Pamphill
Walford Mill
Wimborne Minster
Stapehill
Ferndown
Cheselbourne
Almer
Knoll Gdns
Hampreston
Dewlish
Winterborne Kingston
Winterborne Zelston
Longham
West Parley
Corfe Mullen
East End
Oakley
Merley
Canford Magna
Bournemouth
Parley Cross
Hurn
Milborne St Andrew
Anderson
Bearwood
Adventure Wonderland
Martyrs Museum
Morden
Hill View
Bear Cross
Kinson
Ensbury
Holdenhurst
Jumpers Green
Puddletown
Tolpuddle
Bere Regis
Bloxworth
East Morden
Lytchett Matravers
Broadstone
Canford Heath
Moordown
Athelhampton
Burleston
Affpuddle
Turners Puddle
Slepe
Lytchett Minster
Waterloo
Newtown
Talbot Village
Briants Puddle
Wareham Forest
Farmer Palmer's Farm Park
Upton
Poole
Branksome
Red House Mus
Pokesdown
Lane End
Morden Bog
Holton Heath
Hamworthy
Westbourne
Boscombe
Southbourne
Woodsford
Cloud's Hill
Parkstone
Lilliput
Branksome Park
Art Gall and Mus
Bovington Camp
Trigon Hill
Sandford
Scaplen's Court Museum
Compton Acres
Canford Cliffs
Oceanarium
Moreton
Monkey World
Tank Museum
Northport
Poole Harbour
Brownsea Island
Arne
Crossways
Wareham
Stokeford
Sandbanks
Poole Bay
Mill House Cider Museum
East Burton
Wool
Stoborough
Ridge
Ferry
Toll
Warmwell
East Stoke
West Holme
Stoborough Green
Stoborough Heath
Hartland Moor
Studland Beach and Nature Reserve
Owermoigne
East Knighton
Middlebere Heath
Wytch Heath
Studland
Winfrith Newburgh
Coombe Keynes
Grange Heath
Newton Heath
Bay
Holworth
Chaldon Herring or East Chaldon
Lulworth Castle
The Blue Pool
Norden Heath
Studland and Godlingston Heath
East Creech
Isle of
Corfe Castle
Studland
The Foreland
Chaldon Down
Dorset
East Lulworth
Church Knowle
Nine Barrow Down
South West Coast Path
West Lulworth
Lulworth Cove
Purbeck Hills
Steeple
Model Village & Gardens
Purbeck
Ulwell
Guernsey Jersey (Apr-Oct)
St. Malo Cherbourg (May-Sept)
Durdle Door
Heritage Centre
Tyneham
Kingston
Harman's Cross
New Swanage
Swanage Bay
Swanage
Swanage Railway
Worbarrow Bay
Kimmeridge
Langton Matravers Mus
Langton Matravers
Peveril Pt.
Durlston Head
Kimmeridge Bay
Acton
Worth Matravers
Durlston
Tilly Whim Caves
Bay

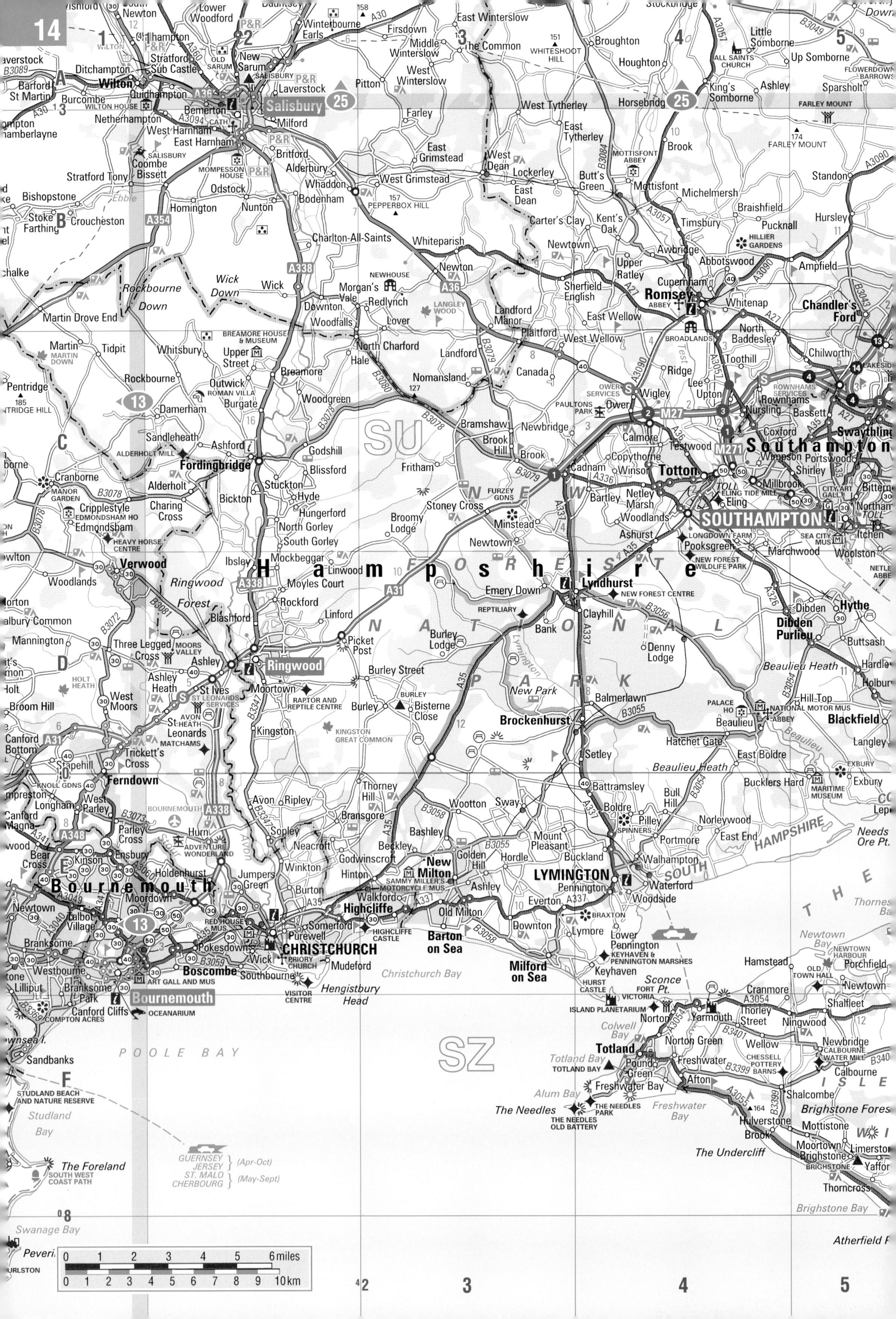

Newton
Lower Woodford
Winterbourne Earls
East Winterslow
Firsdown
Middle Winterslow
The Common
WHITESHOOT HILL
Broughton
Houghton
Little Somborne
Up Somborne
ALL SAINTS CHURCH
Wilton
Ditchampton
Stratford sub Castle
OLD SARUM
New Sarum
Salisbury
Laverstock
Pitton
West Winterslow
Barford St Martin
Burcombe
WILTON HOUSE
Quidhampton
Bemerton
Netherhampton
West Harnham
East Harnham
Milford
Farley
West Tytherley
East Tytherley
Horsebridge
King's Somborne
Ashley
Sparsholt
FARLEY MOUNT
Brook
Britford
Coombe Bissett
Stratford Tony
MOMPESSON HOUSE
Alderbury
East Grimstead
West Dean
Lockerley
MOTTISFONT ABBEY
Mottisfont
Butt's Green
Michelmersh
Standon
Bishopstone
Odstock
Whaddon
West Grimstead
Bodenham
East Dean
PEPPERBOX HILL
Homington
Nunton
Stoke Farthing
Croucheston
Ebble
Carter's Clay
Kent's Oak
Braishfield
Timsbury
Pucknall
Hursley
Charlton-All-Saints
Whiteparish
Newtown
Awbridge
HILLIER GARDENS
Abbotswood
Ampfield
Newton
NEWHOUSE
Morgan's Vale
Redlynch
Upper Ratley
Sherfield English
Romsey
ABBEY
Cupernham
Whitenap
Chandler's Ford
Wick Down
Wick
Rockbourne Down
Martin Drove End
Downton
Woodfalls
Lover
LANGLEY WOOD
Landford Manor
East Wellow
Plaitford
West Wellow
BROADLANDS
North Baddesley
Chilworth
Martin
MARTIN DOWN
Tidpit
Whitsbury
BREAMORE HOUSE & MUSEUM
Upper Street
North Charford
Hale
Landford
Canada
Toothill
Ridge
Pentridge
PENTRIDGE HILL
Rockbourne
Outwick
ROMAN VILLA
Breamore
Nomansland
OWER SERVICES
Wigley
Lee
Upton
ROWNHAMS SERVICES
Rownhams
Nursling
Bassett
Damerham
Burgate
Woodgreen
PAULTONS PARK
Ower
M27
Swaythling
Sandleheath
Ashford
ALDERHOLT MILL
Fordingbridge
Godshill
SU
Bramshaw
Brook Hill
Newbridge
Calmore
Testwood
Southampton
Wimpson
Portswood
Shirley
Cranborne
MANOR GARDEN
Alderholt
Bickton
Blissford
Stuckton
Fritham
Brook
Cadnam
Copythorne
Winsor
Totton
Millbrook
Bitterne
Cripplestyle
EDMONDSHAM HO
Edmondsham
Charing Cross
Hyde
Hungerford
FURZEY GDNS
Stoney Cross
Bartley
Netley Marsh
ELING TIDE MILL
Eling
SOUTHAMPTON
CITY ART GALL
Northam
HEAVY HORSE CENTRE
North Gorley
South Gorley
Broomy Lodge
Minstead
Woodlands
Ashurst
LONGDOWN FARM
Pooksgreen
SEA CITY MUS
Itchen
Verwood
Ibsley
Mockbeggar
Linwood
Newtown
NEW FOREST WILDLIFE PARK
Marchwood
Woolston
Woodlands
Ringwood Forest
Moyles Court
Hampshire
Lyndhurst
Emery Down
NEW FOREST CENTRE
Hythe
Dibden
Dibden Purlieu
Rockford
REPTILIARY
Clayhill
Blashford
Linford
Bank
Denny Lodge
Buttsash
Mannington
Three Legged Cross
MOORS VALLEY
Picket Post
Burley Lodge
NEW FOREST NATIONAL PARK
Beaulieu Heath
Hardley
Holbury
Ashley
Ringwood
Burley Street
Holt Heath
Ashley Heath
St Ives
ST LEONARDS SERVICES
Moortown
RAPTOR AND REPTILE CENTRE
BURLEY
Burley
Bisterne Close
New Park
Balmerlawn
Hill Top
West Moors
AVON HEATH
St Leonards
Kingston
KINGSTON GREAT COMMON
Brockenhurst
PALACE HO
NATIONAL MOTOR MUS
ABBEY
Beaulieu
Blackfield
Broom Hill
Canford Bottom
MATCHAMS
Hatchet Gate
Langley
Trickett's Cross
Setley
East Boldre
Stapehill
Ferndown
Beaulieu Heath
EXBURY
Exbury
KNOLL GDNS
Longham
West Parley
Thorney Hill
Avon
Ripley
Wootton
Sway
Battramsley
Bull Hill
Bucklers Hard
MARITIME MUSEUM
BOURNEMOUTH
Canford Magna
Bransgore
Boldre
Pilley
SPINNERS
Norleywood
Parley Cross
Sopley
Bashley
Mount Pleasant
Portmore
East End
HAMPSHIRE
Needs Ore Pt.
Hurn
ADVENTURE WONDERLAND
Neacroft
Beckley
Golden Hill
Hordle
Buckland
Walhampton
Bear Cross
Kinson
Ensbury
Holdenhurst
Jumpers Green
Winkton
Godwinscroft
Hinton
SAMMY MILLER'S MOTORCYCLE MUS
New Milton
Ashley
LYMINGTON
Pennington
Waterford
Woodside
Bournemouth
Moordown
Burton
Walkford
Everton
SOUTH
Newtown
Talbot Village
RED HOUSE MUS
Somerford
Highcliffe
Old Milton
Downton
BRAXTON
Thorness Bay
Purewell
HIGHCLIFFE CASTLE
Barton on Sea
Lymore
Lower Pennington
Newtown Bay
NEWTOWN HARBOUR
Branksome
Pokesdown
CHRISTCHURCH
PRIORY CHURCH
Wick
Mudeford
KEYHAVEN & PENNINGTON MARSHES
Keyhaven
Hamstead
Porchfield
OLD TOWN HALL
Westbourne
Boscombe
Southbourne
Christchurch Bay
Milford on Sea
Sconce Pt.
HURST CASTLE
FORT VICTORIA
Cranmore
Newtown
Lilliput
Branksome Park
ART GALL AND MUS
VISITOR CENTRE
Hengistbury Head
ISLAND PLANETARIUM
Yarmouth
Thorley Street
Shalfleet
Ningwood
Canford Cliffs
COMPTON ACRES
OCEANARIUM
Norton
Colwell Bay
Norton Green
Wellow
Newbridge
CALBOURNE WATER MILL
Calbourne
POOLE BAY
SZ
Totland
Totland Bay
TOTLAND BAY
Pound Green
Freshwater
CHESSELL POTTERY BARNS
Sandbanks
Alum Bay
Freshwater Bay
Afton
Shalcombe
ISLE OF WIGHT
STUDLAND BEACH AND NATURE RESERVE
Studland Bay
The Needles
THE NEEDLES PARK
THE NEEDLES OLD BATTERY
Freshwater Bay
Brighstone Forest
Hulverstone
Brook
Mottistone
The Foreland
SOUTH WEST COAST PATH
GUERNSEY JERSEY (Apr-Oct)
ST. MALO CHERBOURG (May-Sept)
The Undercliff
Moortown
Brighstone
BRIGHSTONE
Limerstone
Yafford
Thorncross
Swanage Bay
Brighstone Bay
Atherfield Point
Peveril
0 1 2 3 4 5 6 miles
0 1 2 3 4 5 6 7 8 9 10 km

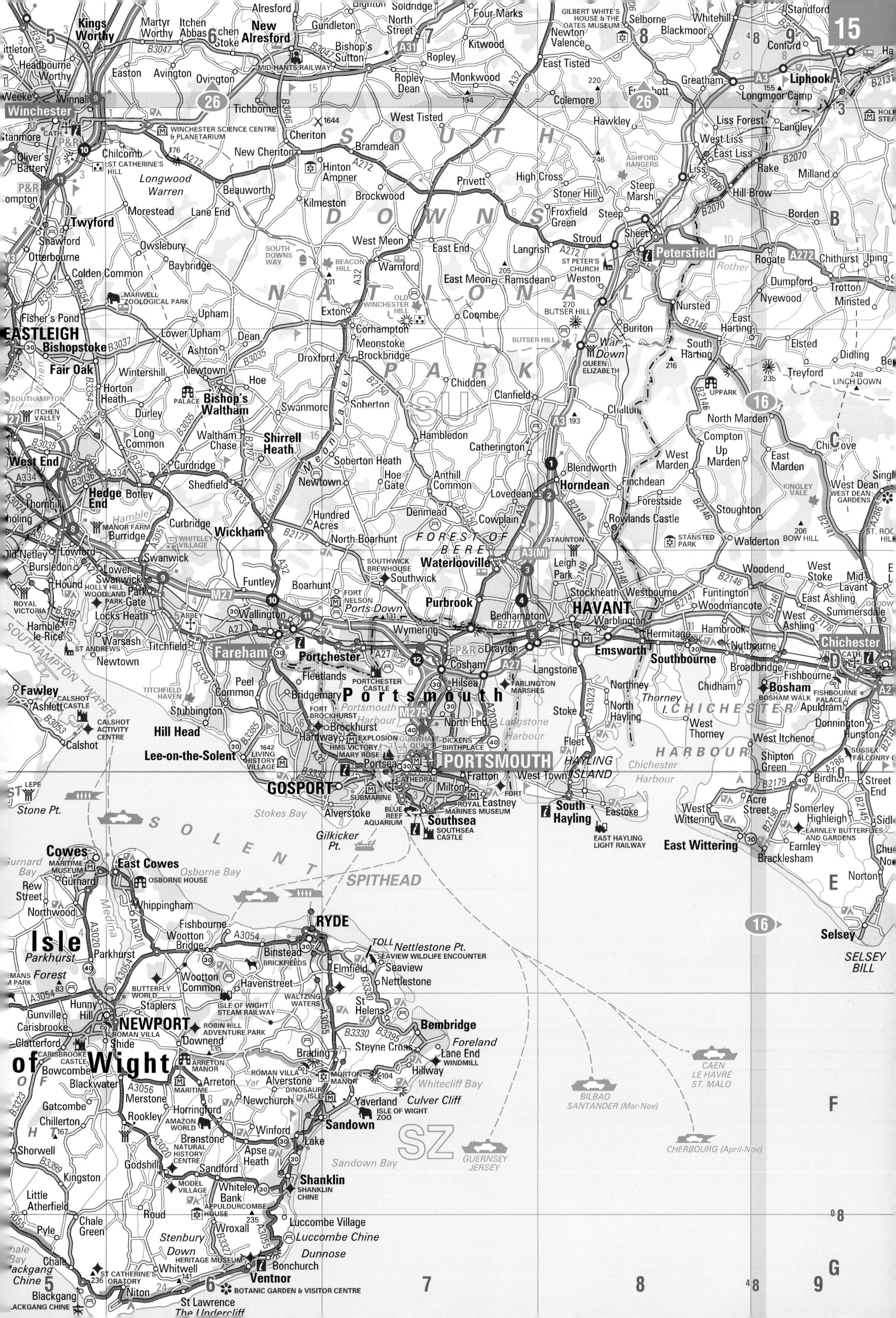
Winchester
Kings Worthy
Headbourne Worthy
Martyr Worthy
Itchen Abbas
Itchen Stoke
New Alresford
Alresford
Gundleton
Bishop's Sutton
MID-HANTS RAILWAY
North Street
Ropley
Ropley Dean
Four Marks
Kitwood
Monkwood
Easton
Avington
Ovington
Tichborne
Winnall
Weeke
WINCHESTER SCIENCE CENTRE & PLANETARIUM
Cheriton
West Tisted
East Tisted
Colemore
Newton Valence
Selborne
GILBERT WHITE'S HOUSE & THE OATES MUSEUM
Blackmoor
Whitehill
Standford
Conford
Liphook
Greatham
Longmoor Camp
Liss Forest
Langley
West Liss
East Liss
Liss
Rake
Milland
Hill Brow
Borden
Chilcomb
ST CATHERINE'S HILL
Oliver's Battery
Longwood Warren
New Cheriton
Bramdean
Hinton Ampner
Beauworth
Kilmeston
Brockwood
Privett
High Cross
Hawkley
ASHFORD HANGERS
Steep Marsh
Stoner Hill
Froxfield Green
Steep
Sheet
Petersfield
Twyford
Morestead
Lane End
West Meon
East End
Langrish
Stroud
Shawford
Otterbourne
Owslebury
Baybridge
SOUTH DOWNS WAY
BEACON HILL
Warnford
East Meon
Ramsdean
ST PETER'S CHURCH
Weston
Rogate
Chithurst
Dumpford
Trotton
Nyewood
Minsted
Rother
Colden Common
MARWELL ZOOLOGICAL PARK
Fisher's Pond
EASTLEIGH
Bishopstoke
Fair Oak
Upham
Lower Upham
Ashton
Dean
Exton
OLD WINCHESTER HILL
Corhampton
Meonstoke
Brockbridge
Coombe
BUTSER HILL
Buriton
Nursted
East Harting
South Harting
Elsted
Didling
Treyford
LINCH DOWN
War Down
QUEEN ELIZABETH
UPPARK
SOUTH DOWNS NATIONAL PARK
Droxford
Wintershill
Newtown
Hoe
Bishop's Waltham
Horton Heath
Durley
Swanmore
Soberton
Chidden
Clanfield
Chalton
North Marden
Compton
Up Marden
West Marden
East Marden
Chilgrove
West Dean
KINGLEY VALE
SOUTHAMPTON
ITCHEN VALLEY
West End
Hedge End
Botley
Long Common
Waltham Chase
Shirrell Heath
Meon Valley
Hambledon
Catherington
Soberton Heath
Hoe Gate
Anthill Common
Blendworth
Horndean
Finchdean
Forestside
Rowlands Castle
Stoughton
Walderton
BOW HILL
STANSTED PARK
Curdridge
Shedfield
Newtown
Lovedean
Denmead
Cowplain
Curbridge
Burridge
MANOR FARM
WHITELEY VILLAGE
Wickham
Hundred Acres
North Boarhunt
FOREST OF BERE
STAUNTON
Thornhill
Lowford
Old Netley
Bursledon
Swanwick
Lower Swanwick
Park Gate
Hound
ROYAL VICTORIA
Locks Heath
Funtley
Boarhunt
SOUTHWICK BREWHOUSE
Southwick
Waterlooville
Leigh Park
Woodend
West Stoke
Mid Lavant
East Ashling
West Ashling
Funtington
Woodmancote
Hambrook
Nutbourne
Summersdale
Hamble-le-Rice
ST ANDREWS
Warsash
Newtown
ABBEY
Titchfield
Wallington
FORT NELSON
Ports Down
Purbrook
Bedhampton
Stockheath
Westbourne
HAVANT
Warblington
Hermitage
Emsworth
Southbourne
Chichester
Fareham
Portchester
PORTCHESTER CASTLE
Fleetlands
Wymering
Drayton
Cosham
Langstone
Broadbridge
Fishbourne
Bosham
Chidham
Fawley
CALSHOT CASTLE
Ashlett
CALSHOT ACTIVITY CENTRE
Calshot
SOUTHAMPTON WATER
TITCHFIELD HAVEN
Peel Common
Stubbington
Bridgemary
Portsmouth
Portsmouth Harbour
FORT BROCKHURST
Brockhurst
Hilsea
FARLINGTON MARSHES
Northney
North Hayling
Thorney
West Thorney
Stoke
I. CHICHESTER HARBOUR
Apuldram
Donnington
Hunston
Hill Head
Lee-on-the-Solent
LIVING HISTORY VILLAGE
Hardway
EXPLOSION
HMS VICTORY, MARY ROSE
GUNWHARF QUAYS
DICKENS BIRTHPLACE
North End
Langstone Harbour
Fleet
HAYLING ISLAND
West Itchenor
Shipton Green
Chichester Harbour
SUSSEX FALCONRY
PORTSMOUTH
Fratton
West Town
Birdham
Street End
LEPE
Stone Pt.
GOSPORT
Portsea
CATHEDRAL
SUBMARINE
Milton
ROYAL MARINES MUSEUM
FORT
Eastney
South Hayling
Eastoke
EAST HAYLING LIGHT RAILWAY
Acre Street
West Wittering
East Wittering
Somerley
Highleigh
EARNLEY BUTTERFLIES AND GARDENS
Earnley
Bracklesham
Sidlesham
SOLENT
Stokes Bay
Alverstoke
BLUE REEF AQUARIUM
Southsea
SOUTHSEA CASTLE
Gilkicker Pt.
Cowes
Gurnard Bay
MARITIME MUSEUM
Gurnard
East Cowes
OSBORNE HOUSE
Osborne Bay
SPITHEAD
Rew Street
Whippingham
Northwood
Medina
Fishbourne
Wootton Bridge
RYDE
Isle
Parkhurst
Parkhurst Forest
Binstead
BRICKFIELDS
Elmfield
TOLL
Nettlestone Pt.
SEAVIEW WILDLIFE ENCOUNTER
Seaview
Nettlestone
Wootton Common
Havenstreet
BUTTERFLY WORLD
ISLE OF WIGHT STEAM RAILWAY
WALTZING WATERS
St Helens
Hunny Hill
Gunville
Carisbrooke
NEWPORT
Staplers
ROBIN HILL ADVENTURE PARK
ROMAN VILLA
Downend
Bembridge
Foreland
Clatterford
Shide
Brading
Steyne Cross
Lane End
WINDMILL
CARISBROOKE CASTLE
of Wight
Bowcombe
ARRETON MANOR
Arreton
ROMAN VILLA
Alverstone
MORTON MANOR
Hillway
Whitecliff Bay
Blackwater
MARITIME
DINOSAUR ISLE
Culver Cliff
Merstone
Yaverland
ISLE OF WIGHT ZOO
Newchurch
Gatcombe
Horringford
Sandown
Chillerton
Rookley
AMAZON WORLD
Winford
Branstone
Lake
Shorwell
NATURAL HISTORY CENTRE
Apse Heath
Sandown Bay
Godshill
Sandford
Kingston
MODEL VILLAGE
Whiteley Bank
Shanklin
SHANKLIN CHINE
Little Atherfield
APPULDURCOMBE HOUSE
Roud
Chale Green
Luccombe Village
Luccombe Chine
Pyle
Wroxall
Stenbury Down
Dunnose
Chale
HERITAGE MUSEUM
Bonchurch
Whitwell
ST CATHERINE'S ORATORY
Ventnor
Blackgang
BLACKGANG CHINE
Niton
BOTANIC GARDEN & VISITOR CENTRE
St Lawrence
The Undercliff
CAEN LE HAVRE ST. MALO
BILBAO SANTANDER (Mar-Nov)
GUERNSEY JERSEY
CHERBOURG (April-Nov)
Selsey
SELSEY BILL
Norton
SU
SZ
M27
M275
A3(M)
A3
A27
A32
A31
A272
B3047
B2177
B2150
B2146
B2149
B2148
B2147
B2070
B3006
B2179
B2145
B2198
A286
A3054
A3020
A3021
A3055
A3056
B3330
B3395
B3399
B3327
B3323
B3385
B3333
B3334
B3035
B3037
B3354
B3335
B3046
A334
A335
A3024
A3025
A3051
B3397
B3053
A2030
A3023
B2141
B2178
B2201
26
16

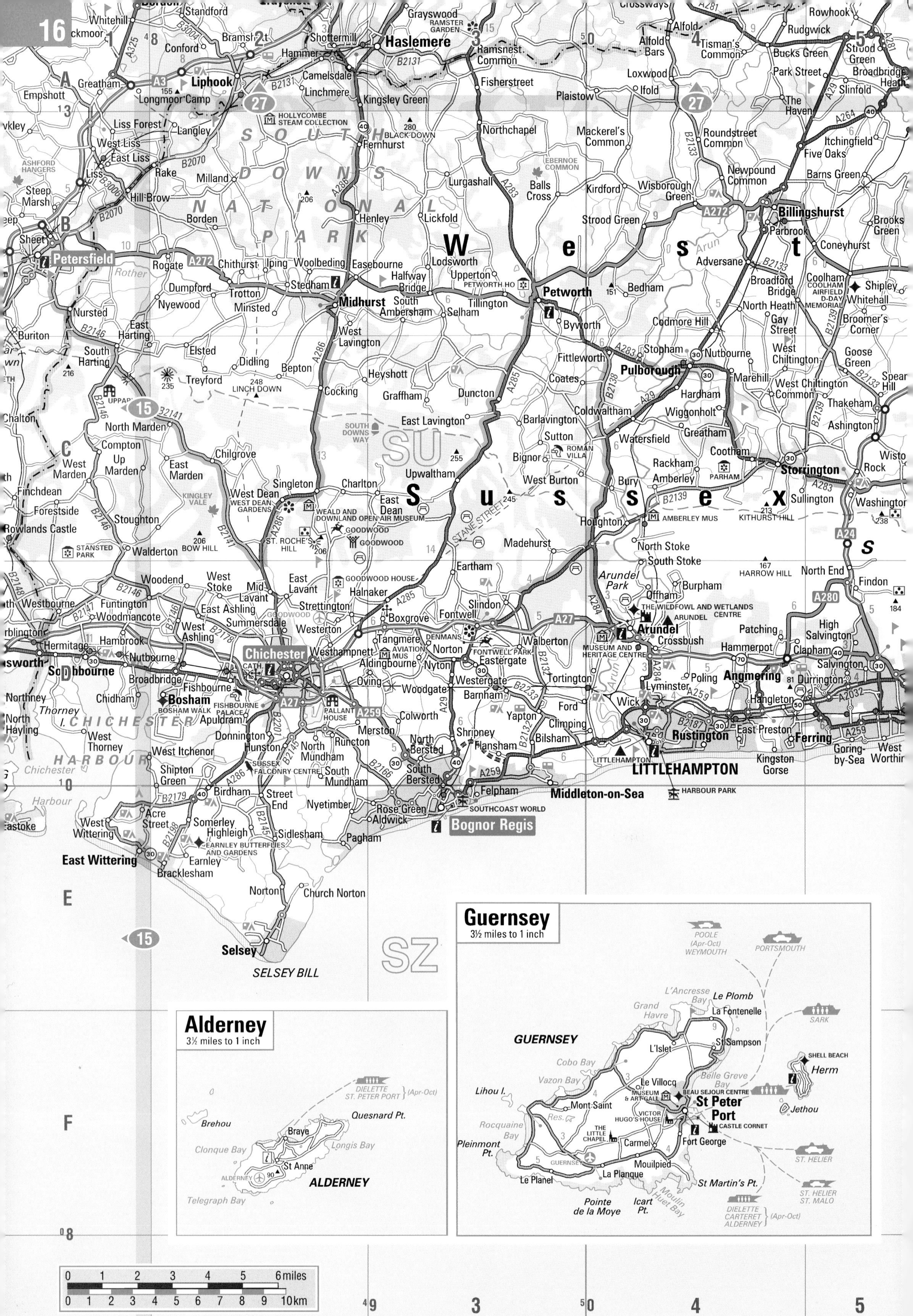

Standford
Whitehill
Grayswood
Ramster Garden
Rowhook
Rudgwick
Alfold
Alfold Bars
Tismans Common
Bucks Green
Strood Green
Broadbridge Heath
Slinfold
Conford
Bramshott
Shottermill
Haslemere
Ramsnest Common
Hammer
Camelsdale
Liphook
Greatham
Empshott
Longmoor Camp
Linchmere
Kingsley Green
Fisherstreet
Plaistow
Loxwood
Ifold
Park Street
The Haven
Hollycombe Steam Collection
Black Down
Fernhurst
Northchapel
Mackerel's Common
Roundstreet Common
Itchingfield
Five Oaks
Liss Forest
Langley
West Liss
East Liss
Ashford Hangers
Liss
Rake
Milland
Steep
Marsh
Hill Brow
Lurgashall
Ebernoe Common
Balls Cross
Kirdford
Wisborough Green
Newpound Common
Barns Green
South Downs National Park
Borden
Henley
Lickfold
Strood Green
Billingshurst
Parbrook
Brooks Green
Sheet
Petersfield
Rogate
Chithurst
Iping
Woolbeding
Easebourne
Lodsworth
Halfway Bridge
Upperton
Petworth Ho
West Sussex
Adversane
Coneyhurst
Rother
Dumpford
Trotton
Stedham
Nyewood
Minsted
Midhurst
South Ambersham
Selham
Tillington
Petworth
Byworth
Bedham
Broadford Bridge
Coolham
Coolham Airfield D-Day Memorial
Shipley
Whitehall
North Heath
Codmore Hill
Gay Street
Broomer's Corner
Nursted
East Harting
West Lavington
Buriton
South Harting
Elsted
Didling
Bepton
Stopham
Nutbourne
Fittleworth
Pulborough
West Chiltington
Goose Green
Treyford
Linch Down
Heyshott
Cocking
Graffham
Duncton
Coates
Marehill
West Chiltington Common
Spear Hill
Thakeham
Hardham
Chalton
Uppark
North Marden
Compton
Up Marden
West Marden
East Marden
Chilgrove
South Downs Way
East Lavington
Barlavington
Coldwaltham
Wiggonholt
Sutton
Watersfield
Greatham
Ashington
Bignor
Roman Villa
Cootham
Storrington
Wiston
Rock
Upwaltham
Rackham
Amberley
Parham
Finchdean
Forestside
Rowlands Castle
Stoughton
Kingley Vale
Singleton
West Dean
West Dean Gardens
Charlton
East Dean
Weald and Downland Open Air Museum
Goodwood
St. Roche's Hill
Stane Street
West Burton
Bury
Houghton
Amberley Mus
Kithurst Hill
Sullington
Washington
Stansted Park
Walderton
Bow Hill
Madehurst
North Stoke
South Stoke
Harrow Hill
Eartham
Westbourne
Woodend
West Stoke
Mid Lavant
East Lavant
Goodwood House
Halnaker
Arundel Park
Offham
Burpham
North End
Findon
Funtington
Woodmancote
East Ashling
Strettington
Slindon
The Wildfowl and Wetlands Centre
Arundel
West Ashling
Summersdale
Westerton
Boxgrove
Fontwell
Patching
High Salvington
Emsworth
Hermitage
Hambrook
Nutbourne
Chichester
Westhampnett
Tangmere
Aviation Mus
Denmans
Fontwell Park
Walberton
Norton
Eastergate
Museum and Heritage Centre
Crossbush
Hammerpot
Clapham
Salvington
Southbourne
Broadbridge
Fishbourne
Cath.
Aldingbourne
Nyton
Westergate
Tortington
Poling
Angmering
Durrington
Oving
Woodgate
Lyminster
Northney
Thorney I.
Chidham
Bosham
Bosham Walk
Fishbourne Palace
Pallant House
Barnham
Ford
Wick
Hangleton
North Hayling
Chichester Harbour
Apuldram
Colworth
Yapton
Climping
Rustington
East Preston
Ferring
West Thorney
Donnington
Merston
North Bersted
Shripney
Bilsham
Runcton
Flansham
Littlehampton
Goring-by-Sea
West Worthing
West Itchenor
Hunston
North Mundham
Sussex Falconry Centre
South Mundham
South Bersted
Kingston Gorse
Shipton Green
Birdham
Street End
Felpham
Middleton-on-Sea
Harbour Park
Nyetimber
Rose Green
Aldwick
Southcoast World
Bognor Regis
West Wittering
East Wittering
Acre Street
Somerley
Highleigh
Earnley Butterflies and Gardens
Earnley
Bracklesham
Sidlesham
Pagham
Norton
Church Norton
Selsey
Selsey Bill
SU
SZ
Alderney
3½ miles to 1 inch
Dielette
St. Peter Port
(Apr-Oct)
Quesnard Pt.
Brehou
Braye
Clonque Bay
Longis Bay
St Anne
Alderney
Telegraph Bay
Guernsey
3½ miles to 1 inch
Poole
(Apr-Oct)
Weymouth
Portsmouth
L'Ancresse Bay
Le Plomb
Grand Havre
La Fontenelle
Sark
St Sampson
L'Islet
Shell Beach
Herm
Cobo Bay
Belle Greve Bay
Vazon Bay
Le Villocq
Lihou I.
Museum & Art Gall
Beau Sejour Centre
Mont Saint
St Peter Port
Jethou
Victor Hugo's House
Castle Cornet
Rocquaine Bay
The Little Chapel
Carmel
Fort George
Pleinmont Pt.
Mouilpied
St. Helier
Le Planel
La Planque
Moulin Huet Bay
St Martin's Pt.
St. Helier
St. Malo
Pointe de la Moye
Icart Pt.
Dielette
Carteret
Alderney
0 1 2 3 4 5 6 miles
0 1 2 3 4 5 6 7 8 9 10 km

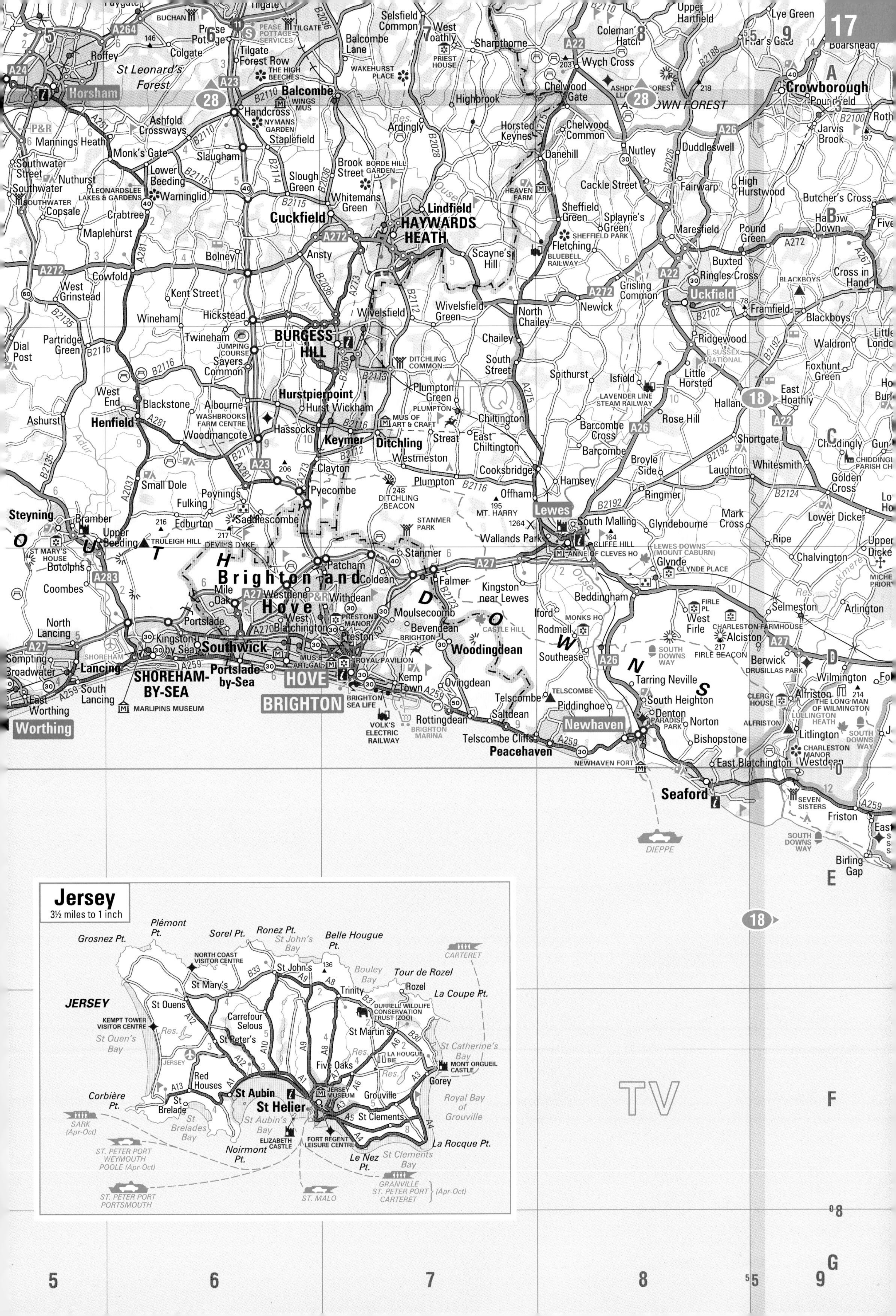
Horsham
Roffey
Colgate
St Leonard's Forest
Pease Pottage Services
Tilgate
Tilgate Forest Row
Buchan
The High Beeches
Balcombe
Balcombe Lane
Selsfield Common
West Hoathly
Priest House
Wakehurst Place
Sharpthorne
Coleman's Hatch
Wych Cross
Upper Hartfield
Lye Green
Friar's Gate
Boarshead
Crowborough
Poundfield
Jarvis Brook
Rotherfield
Chelwood Gate
Ashdown Forest
Highbrook
Ardingly
Wings Mus
Handcross
Nymans Garden
Staplefield
Ashfold Crossways
Mannings Heath
Monk's Gate
Slaugham
Southwater Street
Southwater
Nuthurst
Lower Beeding
Leonardslee Lakes & Gardens
Warninglid
Copsale
Crabtree
Maplehurst
Slough Green
Brook Street
Borde Hill Garden
Whitemans Green
Cuckfield
Lindfield
Haywards Heath
Horsted Keynes
Chelwood Common
Danehill
Nutley
Duddleswell
Fairwarp
High Hurstwood
Cackle Street
Heaven Farm
Sheffield Green
Sheffield Park
Splayne's Green
Fletching
Bluebell Railway
Maresfield
Pound Green
Butcher's Cross
Hadlow Down
Five Ashes
Buxted
Ringles Cross
Cross in Hand
Blackboys
Uckfield
Framfield
Grisling Common
Newick
Bolney
Ansty
Scayne's Hill
Cowfold
West Grinstead
Kent Street
Wineham
Hickstead
Twineham
Jumping Course
Burgess Hill
Wivelsfield
Wivelsfield Green
North Chailey
Chailey
South Street
Sayers Common
Ditchling Common
Partridge Green
Dial Post
West End
Henfield
Ashurst
Blackstone
Albourne
Washbrooks Farm Centre
Hurstpierpoint
Hurst Wickham
Hassocks
Keymer
Ditchling
Mus of Art & Craft
Plumpton Green
Plumpton
Streat
East Chiltington
Chiltington
Westmeston
Spithurst
Isfield
Lavender Line Steam Railway
Little Horsted
Ridgewood
E. Sussex National
Blackboys
Waldron
Little London
Foxhunt Green
East Hoathly
Halland
Rose Hill
Barcombe Cross
Barcombe
Broyle Side
Laughton
Shortgate
Whitesmith
Chiddingly
Chiddingly Parish Church
Golden Cross
Woodmancote
Small Dole
Poynings
Fulking
Edburton
Saddlescombe
Truleigh Hill
Devil's Dyke
Clayton
Pyecombe
Ditchling Beacon
Cooksbridge
Hamsey
Offham
Mt. Harry
Lewes
Ringmer
South Malling
Glyndebourne
Mark Cross
Lower Dicker
Upper Dicker
Steyning
Bramber
Upper Beeding
St Mary's House
Botolphs
Coombes
Stanmer Park
Stanmer
Wallands Park
Cliffe Hill
Anne of Cleves Ho
Lewes Downs (Mount Caburn)
Glynde
Glynde Place
Ripe
Chalvington
Patcham
Coldean
Falmer
Kingston near Lewes
Beddingham
Selmeston
Arlington
Michelham Priory
Brighton and Hove
Mile Oak
Westdene
Withdean
Portslade
West Blatchington
Preston Manor
Moulsecoomb
Bevendean
Castle Hill
Iford
Monks Ho
Rodmell
Firle Pl
West Firle
Charleston Farmhouse
Alciston
Berwick
Drusillas Park
Wilmington
Folkington
North Lancing
Kingston by Sea
Southwick
Preston
Woodingdean
Southease
South Downs Way
Firle Beacon
Sompting
Broadwater
Lancing
Shoreham
Shoreham-by-Sea
Portslade-by-Sea
Mus & Art Gal
Royal Pavilion
Hove
Brighton
Kemp Town
Ovingdean
Telscombe
Piddinghoe
Tarring Neville
South Heighton
Clergy House
Alfriston
The Long Man of Wilmington
Lullington Heath
East Worthing
South Lancing
Marlipins Museum
Worthing
Brighton Sea Life
Volk's Electric Railway
Brighton Marina
Rottingdean
Saltdean
Telscombe Cliffs
Peacehaven
Newhaven
Denton
Paradise Park
Norton
Bishopstone
Litlington
Charleston Manor
Westdean
Newhaven Fort
East Blatchington
Seaford
Seven Sisters
Friston
Eastdean
Birling Gap
Dieppe
South Downs Way
South Downs
TQ
TV
Jersey
3½ miles to 1 inch
Grosnez Pt.
Plémont Pt.
Sorel Pt.
Ronez Pt.
St John's Bay
Belle Hougue Pt.
Carteret
North Coast Visitor Centre
St John's
Bouley Bay
Tour de Rozel
Rozel
La Coupe Pt.
Trinity
St Mary's
JERSEY
St Ouens
Kempt Tower Visitor Centre
St Ouen's Bay
Carrefour Selous
Durrell Wildlife Conservation Trust (Zoo)
St Martin's
St Peter's
St Catherine's Bay
La Hougue Bie
Mont Orgueil Castle
Gorey
Five Oaks
Red Houses
St Aubin
Jersey Museum
St Helier
Grouville
Royal Bay of Grouville
Corbière Pt.
St Brelade
St Brelades Bay
St Aubin's Bay
St Clements
Sark (Apr-Oct)
St. Peter Port Weymouth Poole (Apr-Oct)
Noirmont Pt.
Elizabeth Castle
Fort Regent Leisure Centre
Le Nez Pt.
St Clements Bay
La Rocque Pt.
Granville St. Peter Port Carteret (Apr-Oct)
St. Peter Port Portsmouth
St. Malo

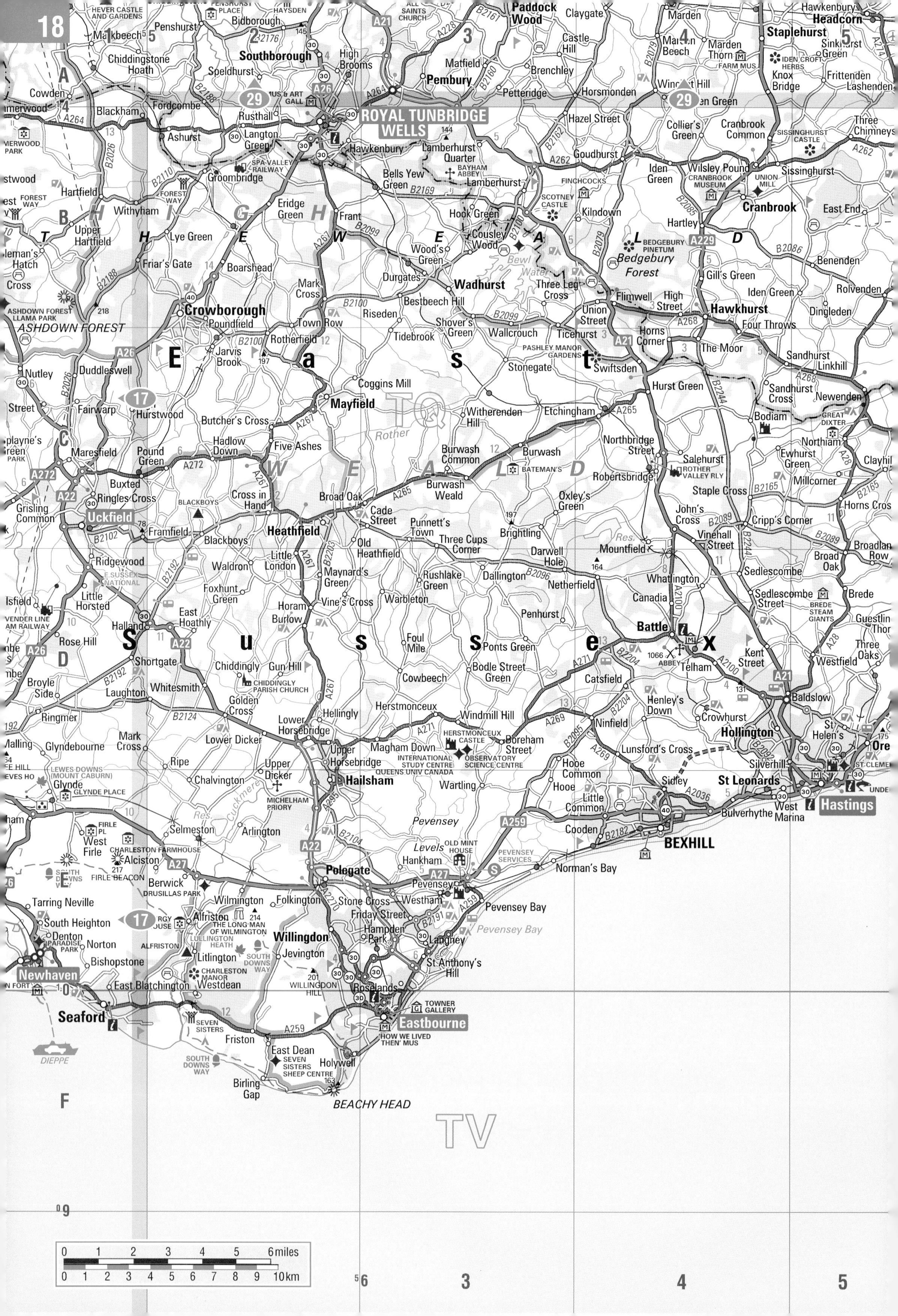
HEVER CASTLE AND GARDENS
Penshurst
PENSHURST PLACE
Haysden
Bidborough
ALL SAINTS CHURCH
Paddock Wood
Claygate
Marden
Hawkenbury
Headcorn
Markbeech
Southborough
High Brooms
Pembury
Matfield
Castle Hill
Marden Beech
Marden Thorn
Staplehurst
Sinkhurst Green
IDEN CROFT HERBS
FARM MUS
Knox Bridge
Frittenden
Lashenden
Chiddingstone Hoath
Speldhurst
Brenchley
Cowden
Petteridge
Horsmonden
Winchet Hill
Green
Blackham
Fordcombe
Rusthall
ROYAL TUNBRIDGE WELLS
Hazel Street
Collier's Green
Cranbrook Common
SISSINGHURST CASTLE
Three Chimneys
Ashurst
Langton Green
Hawkenbury
Lamberhurst Quarter
Goudhurst
Iden Green
Wilsley Pound
Sissinghurst
SPA VALLEY RAILWAY
Groombridge
Bells Yew Green
BAYHAM ABBEY
Lamberhurst
FINCHCOCKS
CRANBROOK MUSEUM
UNION MILL
Cranbrook
East End
Hartfield
FOREST WAY
Withyham
Eridge Green
Frant
Hook Green
SCOTNEY CASTLE
Kilndown
Hartley
Upper Hartfield
Lye Green
Cousley Wood
Wood's Green
BEDGEBURY PINETUM
Bedgebury Forest
Benenden
Friar's Gate
Boarshead
Durgates
Bewl Water
Wadhurst
Three Leg Cross
Gill's Green
Mark Cross
Flimwell
High Street
Iden Green
Rolvenden
Cross
ASHDOWN FOREST LLAMA PARK
ASHDOWN FOREST
Crowborough
Poundfield
Riseden
Bestbeech Hill
Union Street
Hawkhurst
Dingleden
Town Row
Rotherfield
Tidebrook
Shover's Green
Wallcrouch
Ticehurst
Horns Corner
Four Throws
Jarvis Brook
PASHLEY MANOR GARDENS
Swiftsden
The Moor
Sandhurst
Linkhill
Nutley
Duddleswell
Stonegate
Coggins Mill
Hurst Green
Sandhurst Cross
Newenden
Fairwarp
Hurstwood
Mayfield
Butcher's Cross
Witherenden Hill
Etchingham
Bodiam
GREAT DIXTER
Rother
Northbridge Street
Northiam
Maresfield
Pound Green
Hadlow Down
Five Ashes
Burwash Common
Burwash
Salehurst
ROTHER VALLEY RLY
Ewhurst Green
Clayhill
BATEMAN'S
Robertsbridge
Millcorner
Buxted
Ringles Cross
Burwash Weald
Oxley's Green
Staple Cross
BLACKBOYS
Cross in Hand
Broad Oak
Cade Street
Horns Cross
Grisling Common
Uckfield
Framfield
Heathfield
Punnett's Town
Brightling
John's Cross
Cripp's Corner
Blackboys
Old Heathfield
Three Cups Corner
Mountfield
Vinehall Street
Broadland Row
Ridgewood
E. SUSSEX NATIONAL
Waldron
Little London
Darwell Hole
Broad Oak
Foxhunt Green
Maynard's Green
Rushlake Green
Dallington
Netherfield
Whatlington
Sedlescombe
Little Horsted
Vine's Cross
Warbleton
Canadia
Sedlescombe Street
Brede
BREDE STEAM GIANTS
Isfield
LAVENDER LINE STEAM RAILWAY
East Hoathly
Horam
Burlow
Penhurst
Battle
Guestling Thorn
Halland
Foul Mile
Ponts Green
Rose Hill
Shortgate
Chiddingly
Gun Hill
Bodle Street Green
ABBEY
Telham
Kent Street
Westfield
Three Oaks
CHIDDINGLY PARISH CHURCH
Cowbeech
Catsfield
Broyle Side
Laughton
Whitesmith
Golden Cross
Baldslow
Henley's Down
Ringmer
Hellingly
Herstmonceux
Windmill Hill
Crowhurst
Ninfield
Lower Horsebridge
Hollington
St Helen's
Ore
Malling
Glyndebourne
Mark Cross
Lower Dicker
HERSTMONCEUX CASTLE
Boreham Street
Magham Down
Lunsford's Cross
Silverhill
Upper Horsebridge
Ripe
Upper Dicker
INTERNATIONAL STUDY CENTRE
QUEENS UNIV CANADA
OBSERVATORY SCIENCE CENTRE
Hooe Common
LEWES DOWNS (MOUNT CABURN)
Chalvington
Hailsham
Wartling
Hooe
Sidley
St Leonards
Glynde
GLYNDE PLACE
MICHELHAM PRIORY
Little Common
West Marina
Hastings
Bulverhythe
Pevensey
FIRLE PL
Selmeston
Arlington
Cooden
BEXHILL
West Firle
CHARLESTON FARMHOUSE
Levels
OLD MINT HOUSE
PEVENSEY SERVICES
Alciston
Hankham
Norman's Bay
SOUTH DOWNS WAY
FIRLE BEACON
Berwick
Polegate
Pevensey
DRUSILLAS PARK
Westham
Tarring Neville
Wilmington
Folkington
Stone Cross
Pevensey Bay
South Heighton
Alfriston
THE LONG MAN OF WILMINGTON
Friday Street
Pevensey Bay
Denton
PARADISE PARK
Norton
LULLINGTON HEATH
Hampden Park
ALFRISTON
Willingdon
Langney
Bishopstone
Litlington
Jevington
St Anthony's Hill
Newhaven
CHARLESTON MANOR
WILLINGDON HILL
East Blatchington
Westdean
Roselands
Seaford
SEVEN SISTERS
TOWNER GALLERY
Eastbourne
Friston
HOW WE LIVED THEN' MUS
DIEPPE
East Dean
SEVEN SISTERS SHEEP CENTRE
Holywell
Birling Gap
BEACHY HEAD
TQ
TV
E a s t
S u s s e x
W E A L D
H I G H W E A L D
0 1 2 3 4 5 6 miles
0 1 2 3 4 5 6 7 8 9 10 km

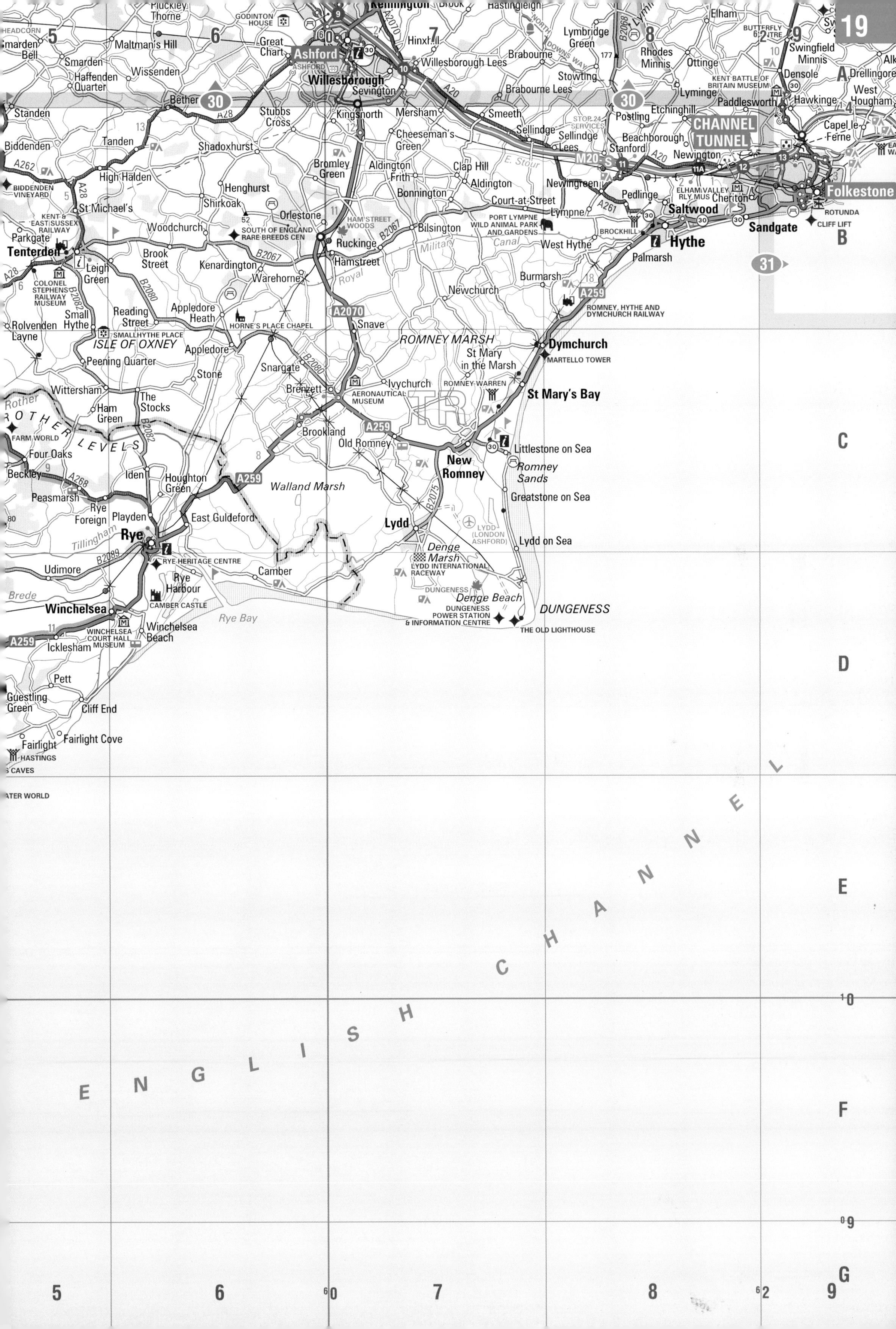

HEADCORN **5** **6** 7 **8** 9

Maltman's Hill
Smarden Bell
Smarden
Wissenden
Haffenden Quarter
Standen

Great Chart
Ashford
Willesborough Lees
Hinxhill
Brabourne

Pluckley Thorne
GODINTON HOUSE
Kennington
Brook
Hastingleigh

Elham
Lymbridge Green
Rhodes Minnis
Ottinge
BUTTERFLY CENTRE
Swingfield Minnis
Densole
Drellingore
West Hougham
Capel le Ferne

A

Bether
30
Stubbs Cross
Kingsnorth
Sevington
Mersham
Smeeth
Sellindge
Sellindge Lees
Stowting
Brabourne Lees
Postling
Etchinghill
Lyminge
Paddlesworth
KENT BATTLE OF BRITAIN MUSEUM
Hawkinge
30

Biddenden
BIDDENDEN VINEYARD
Tanden
Shadoxhurst
Bromley Green
Aldington Frith
Bonnington
Aldington
Clap Hill
Court-at-Street
STOP 24 SERVICES
Stanford
Beachborough
Newington
Newingreen
Pedling
ELHAM VALLEY RLY MUS
Cheriton
CHANNEL TUNNEL
ROTUNDA

High Halden
St Michael's
Henghurst
Shirkoak
Orlestone
HAM STREET WOODS
Bilsington
PORT LYMPNE WILD ANIMAL PARK AND GARDENS
Lympne
Saltwood
Sandgate
Folkestone
CLIFF LIFT

B

KENT & EAST SUSSEX RAILWAY
Parkgate
Tenterden
Leigh Green
Woodchurch
Brook Street
Kenardington
Ruckinge
Hamstreet
Warehorne
Newchurch
West Hythe
Burmarsh
Palmarsh
Hythe
ROMNEY, HYTHE AND DYMCHURCH RAILWAY

COLONEL STEPHENS RAILWAY MUSEUM
Small Hythe
Reading Street
Appledore Heath
SOUTH OF ENGLAND RARE BREEDS CEN
HORNE'S PLACE CHAPEL
Snave
31

Rolvenden Layne
SMALLHYTHE PLACE
Appledore
Stone
Snargate
Brenzett
AERONAUTICAL MUSEUM
Ivychurch
ROMNEY WARREN
St Mary in the Marsh
Dymchurch
MARTELLO TOWER

ISLE OF OXNEY
Peening Quarter
Wittersham
Ham Green
The Stocks
Brookland
Old Romney
St Mary's Bay

C

Rother
ROTHER LEVELS
FARM WORLD
Four Oaks
Beckley
Peasmarsh
Iden
Houghton Green
A259
Walland Marsh
New Romney
Littlestone on Sea
Romney Sands
Greatstone on Sea

Rye Foreign
Playden
East Guldeford
Lydd
LYDD (LONDON ASHFORD)
Lydd on Sea

Tillingham
Rye
RYE HERITAGE CENTRE
Camber
Denge Marsh
LYDD INTERNATIONAL RACEWAY
Denge Beach
DUNGENESS

Udimore
Rye Harbour
CAMBER CASTLE
Rye Bay
DUNGENESS POWER STATION & INFORMATION CENTRE
THE OLD LIGHTHOUSE

Brede
Winchelsea
WINCHELSEA COURT HALL MUSEUM
Winchelsea Beach

D

A259
Icklesham
Pett
Guestling Green
Cliff End
Fairlight
Fairlight Cove
HASTINGS CAVES

WATER WORLD

E

E N G L I S H   C H A N N E L

F

5 **6** **7** **8** **9**

G

1 2³ 2 3 4 5

A

¹8

B

15
²2

North West Point   North East Point

LUNDY MARINE NATURE RESERVE   LUNDY

C   142▲   ILFRACOMBE BIDEFORD (Mar-Oct)

South West Point   Surf Point

²1
¹4

SS

NORTH DEVON

LUNDY (Mar-Oct)   Rillage Pt.   OLD CORN MILL   Combe Martin Bay   Trentishoe

Bull Pt.   Ilfracombe   ILFRACOMBE MUSEUM   Hele   WATERMOUTH CASTLE   Girt Down   Heale

Rockham Bay   Lee   Whitestone   Slade   206   Berrynarbor   Combe Martin   10   349

D

Morte Point   Mortehoe   B3230   Sterridge   WILDLIFE & DINOSAUR PARK

E   Woolacombe   Trimstone   269   A3123   Berry Down Cross   Kentisbury

MORTE BAY   B3343   Cheglinch   Berry Down   Patchole   Kentisbury Ford

Woolacombe Sand   210   Dean   West Down   Bittadon   East Down

SOUTH WEST COAST PATH   North Buckland   A361   Churchill   Arlington   ARLINGTON COURT

Pickwell   Nethercott   Halsinger   Milltown   Muddiford   Loxhore   11

Baggy Pt.   Putsborough   Darracott   Muddiford

Croyde Bay   Georgeham   Knowle   Marwood   Guineaford   Shirwell   Bratton Fleming

B3231   158   Croyde   Lobb   Pippacott   MARWOOD HILL GARDENS   Kingsheanton   Prixford   198   Shirwell Cross   Stoke Rivers

Saunton   14   Braunton   Heanton   BROOMHILL

F   ELLIOT GALLERY   Punchardon   Ashford   Burridge   Barnstaple   Goodleigh   Gunn

Saunton Sands   Wrafton   TOLL   Chivenor   A361   Pilton   MUSEUM OF BARNSTAPLE & NORTH DEVON   Westacott

Braunton Burrows   Taw   Fremington   Newport   Landkey   NORTH DEVON FARM PARK

LUNDY (Mar-Oct)   B3233   Bickington   P&R   Bishops Tawton   Swimbridge

NORTH DEVON MARITIME MUSEUM   Yelland   Instow   Newland   Swimbridge

BIDEFORD BAY   NORTHAM BURROWS   TAPELEY PARK GDNS   Newton Tracey   A377   Herner   Cobbaton   East Stowford

¹3   Appledore   Westward Ho!   Westleigh   COBBATON COMBAT COLLECTION

9   Northam   Horwood   Ensis   Chapelton

THE BIG SHEEP   Orchard Hill   Eastleigh

Titch   0 1 2 3 4 5 6miles   Bideford   Woodtown   Hiscott

0 1 2 3 4 5 6 7 8 9 10km   BURTON ART GALL & MUS   ²4   4   A377

LAND BBEY   ²4   Abbotsham   East the   5

CLOVELLY VILLAGE   Handy

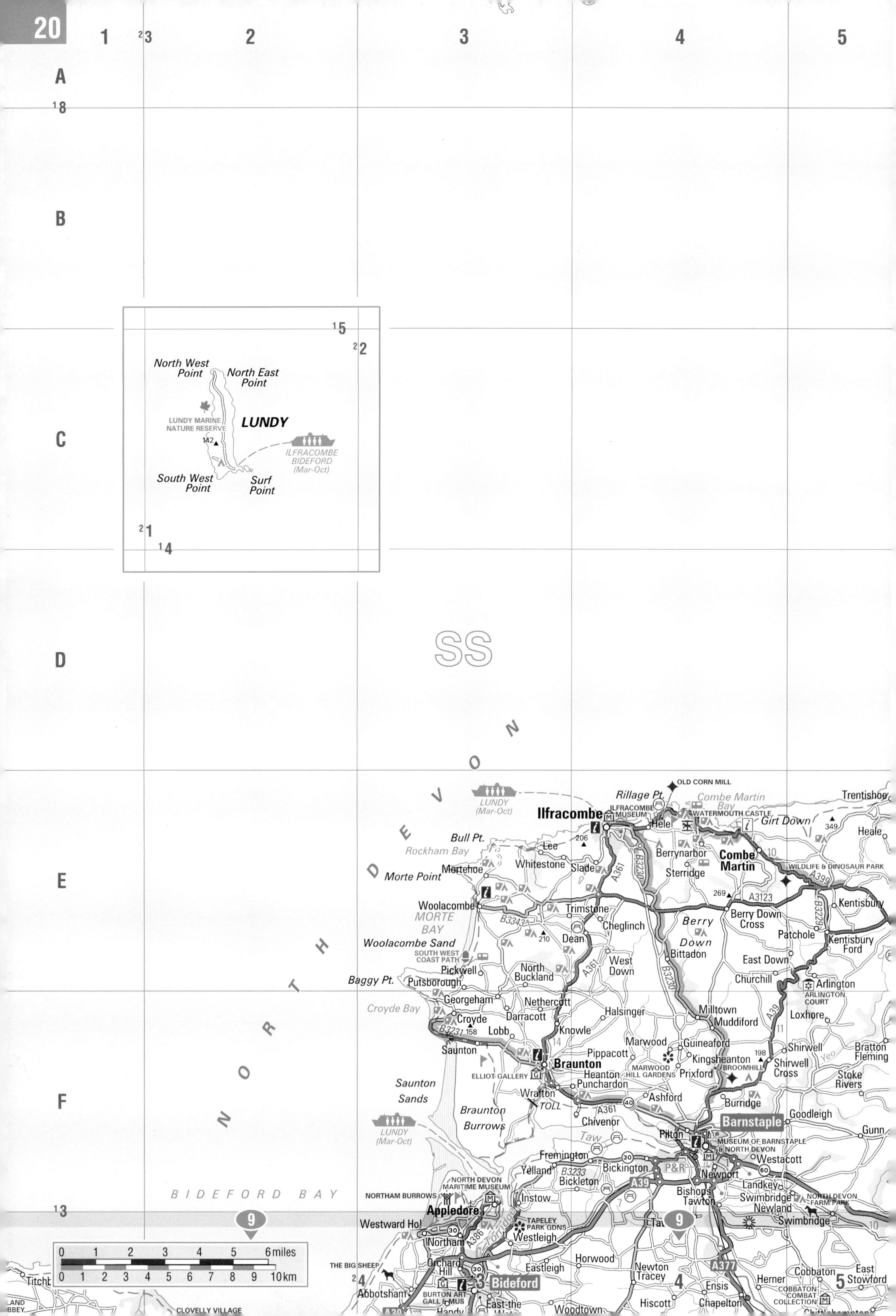

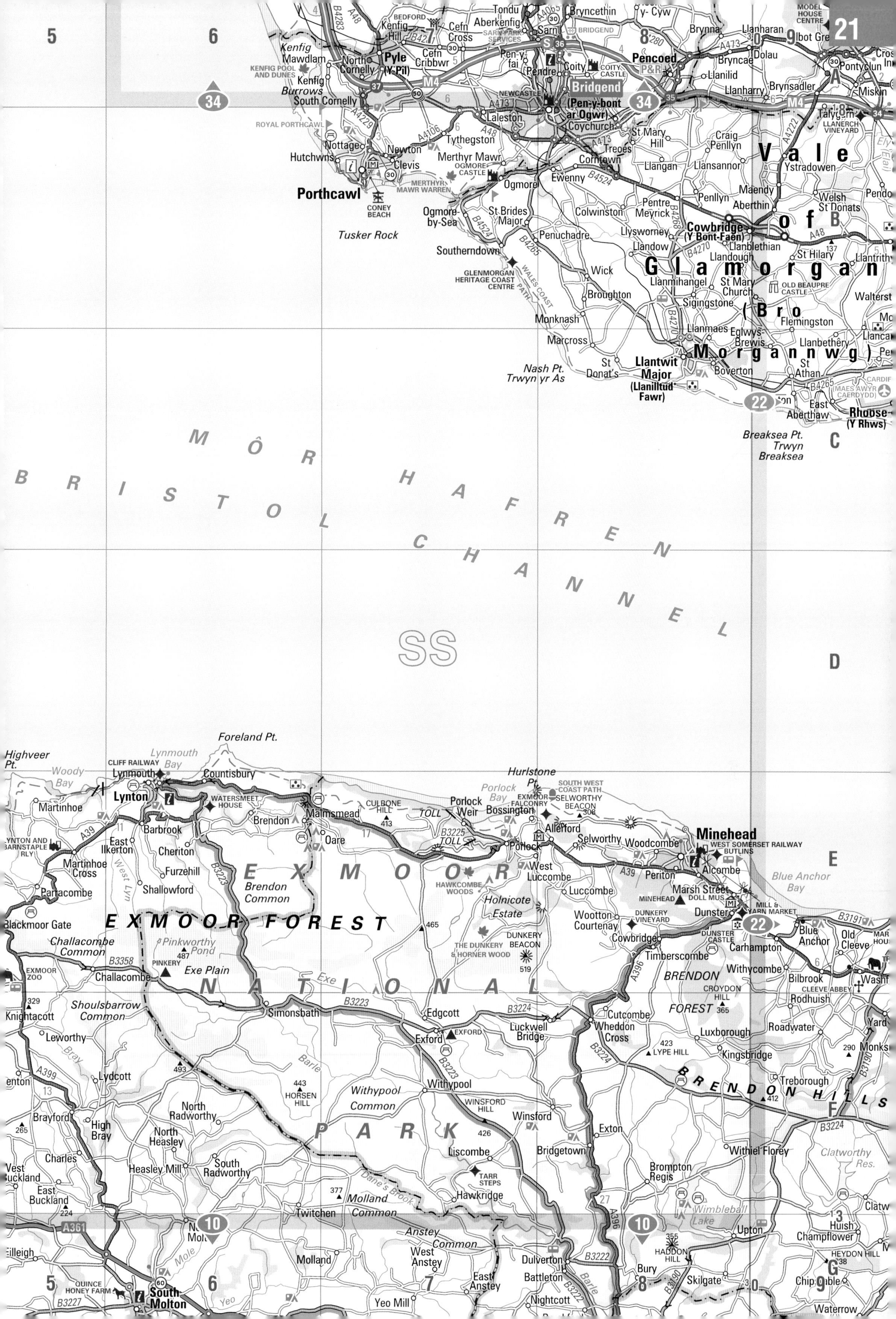

5
6
8
9
Tondu
Aberkenfig
Bryncethin
y- Cyw
Bedford
Kenfig Hill
Cefn Cross
Sarn Park Services
Sarn
Bridgend
Brynna
Llanharan
Talbot Green
Model House Centre
Kenfig
Mawdlam
Kenfig Pool and Dunes
Kenfig Burrows
North Cornelly
Pyle (Y Pîl)
Cefn Cribbwr
Pen-y-fai
Pendre
Coity
Coity Castle
Pencoed
Bryncae
Dolau
Llanilid
Pontyclun
Cross Inn
Miskin
34
South Cornelly
Newcastle
Bridgend (Pen-y-bont ar Ogwr)
Laleston
Coychurch
Llanharry
Brynsadler
Talygarn
Llanerch Vineyard
Royal Porthcawl
Nottage
Newton
Tythegston
St Mary Hill
Craig Penllyn
Hutchwns
Clevis
Merthyr Mawr
Treoes
Corntown
Llangan
Llansannor
Vale of Glamorgan (Bro Morgannwg)
Ystradowen
Ogmore Castle
Merthyr Mawr Warren
Ogmore
Ewenny
Porthcawl
Coney Beach
Penllyn
Maendy
Aberthin
Welsh St Donats
Pendoylan
Ogmore-by-Sea
St Brides Major
Colwinston
Pentre Meyrick
Cowbridge (Y Bont-Faen)
Tusker Rock
Southerndown
Penuchadre
Llysworney
Llandow
Llanblethian
Llandough
St Hilary
Llantrithyd
Glenmorgan Heritage Coast Centre
Wales Coast Path
Wick
Llanmihangel
St Mary Church
Old Beaupre Castle
Walterston
Broughton
Sigingstone
Flemingston
Monknash
Llanmaes
Eglwys-Brewis
Llanbethery
Llancarfan
Marcross
Nash Pt. Trwyn yr As
St Donat's
Llantwit Major (Llanilltud Fawr)
Boverton
St Athan
Cardiff (Maes Awyr Caerdydd)
22
East Aberthaw
Rhoose (Y Rhws)
Breaksea Pt. Trwyn Breaksea
C
MÔR HAFREN
BRISTOL CHANNEL
SS
D
Foreland Pt.
Highveer Pt.
Lynmouth Bay
Woody Bay
Cliff Railway
Lynmouth
Countisbury
Lynton
Watersmeet House
Martinhoe
Brendon
Malmsmead
Culbone Hill
Toll
Porlock Weir
Porlock Bay
Hurlstone Pt.
South West Coast Path
Exmoor Falconry
Selworthy Beacon
Bossington
Allerford
Oare
Porlock
Selworthy
Woodcombe
Minehead
West Somerset Railway
Butlins
Lynton and Barnstaple Rly
Barbrook
East Ilkerton
Cheriton
Martinhoe Cross
Furzehill
West Lyn
Parracombe
Shallowford
EXMOOR
Brendon Common
Hawkcombe Woods
West Luccombe
Luccombe
Holnicote Estate
Periton
Alcombe
Marsh Street
Minehead Doll Mus
Dunster
Mill & Yarn Market
Blue Anchor Bay
Blue Anchor
Old Cleeve
E
Blackmoor Gate
EXMOOR FOREST
465
Wootton Courtenay
Dunkery Vineyard
Dunster Castle
Carhampton
Challacombe Common
Pinkworthy Pond
487
Pinkery
Exe Plain
The Dunkery & Horner Wood
Dunkery Beacon
519
Cowbridge
Timberscombe
Withycombe
Exmoor Zoo
Challacombe
Exe
NATIONAL
Brendon
Croydon Hill
365
Bilbrook
Cleeve Abbey
Washford
329
Knightacott
Shoulsbarrow Common
Simonsbath
Edgcott
Luckwell Bridge
Cutcombe
Wheddon Cross
Forest
Rodhuish
Roadwater
Leworthy
Exford
Luxborough
Kingsbridge
Yard
Monksilver
Lydcott
493
Barle
443 Horsen Hill
Withypool Common
Withypool
423 Lype Hill
290
Brendon Hills
Treborough
412
F
Brayford
North Radworthy
Winsford Hill
Winsford
Exton
High Bray
North Heasley
PARK
426
Bridgetown
Withiel Florey
Clatworthy Res.
Charles
Heasley Mill
South Radworthy
Liscombe
Brompton Regis
West Buckland
East Buckland
Tarr Steps
Hawkridge
Wimbleball Lake
Clatworthy
224
377
Molland Common
Dane's Brook
Twitchen
Huish Champflower
North Molton
10
Anstey Common
Upton
355 Haddon Hill
Heydon Hill
Filleigh
Mole
West Anstey
Molland
Dulverton
Bury
Skilgate
338
G
East Anstey
Battleton
Chipstable
Quince Honey Farm
South Molton
Yeo
Yeo Mill
Nightcott
Waterrow
7

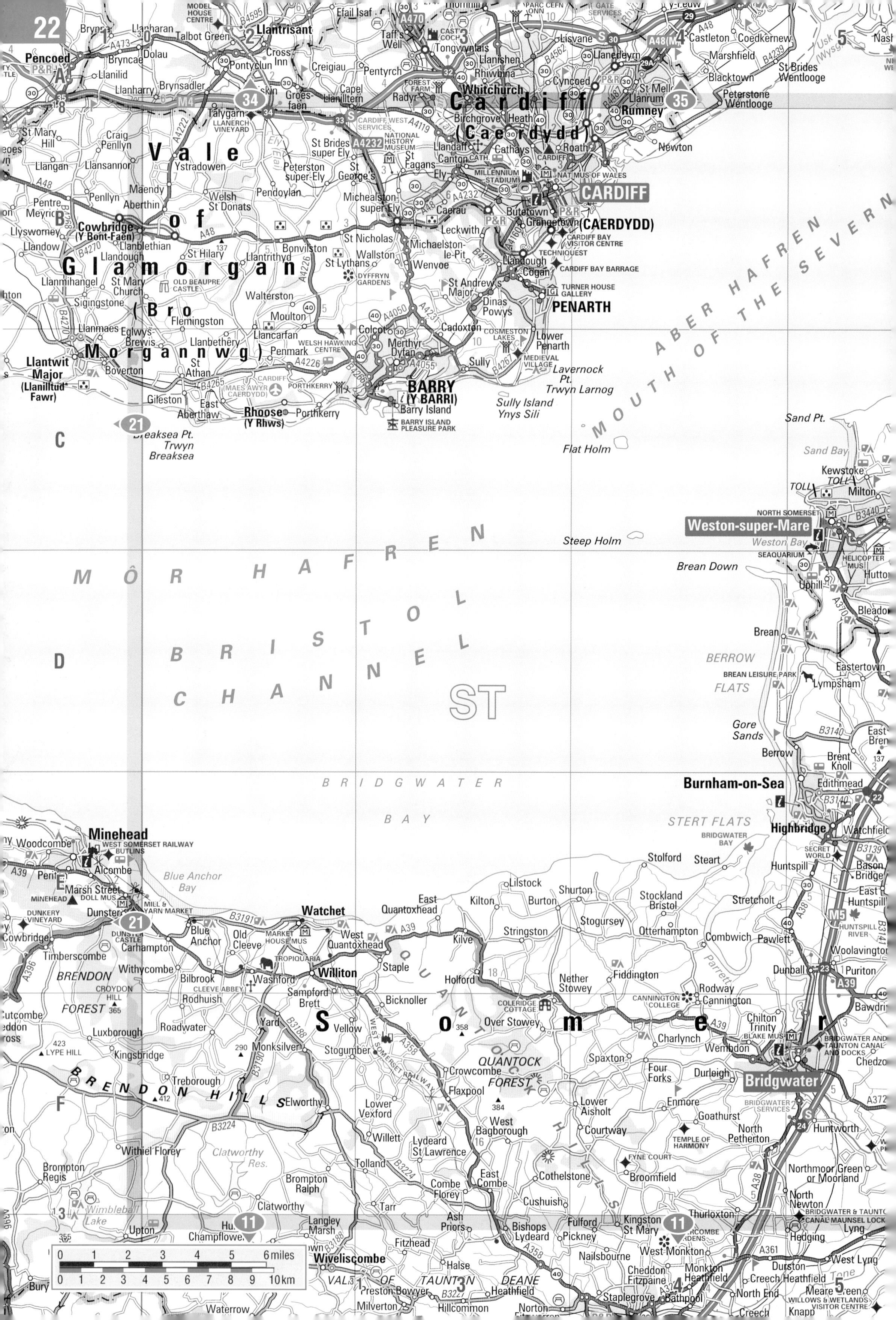
Pencoed
Llantrisant
Talbot Green
Pontyclun
Cross Inn
Creigiau
Pentyrch
Efail Isaf
Taff's Well
Tongwynlais
Llanishen
Lisvane
Rhiwbina
Whitchurch
Cyncoed
Llanedeyrn
Castleton
Coedkernew
Marshfield
Blacktown
St Brides Wentlooge
Peterstone Wentlooge
St Mellons
Llanrumney
Rumney
Cardiff
(Caerdydd)
Radyr
Birchgrove
Heath
Cathays
Roath
Llandaff
Canton
Ely
St Fagans
Newton
MILLENNIUM STADIUM
NAT MUS OF WALES
CARDIFF
(CAERDYDD)
Butetown
Grangetown
CARDIFF BAY VISITOR CENTRE
TECHNIQUEST
CARDIFF BAY BARRAGE
Llandough
Cogan
TURNER HOUSE GALLERY
PENARTH
Vale of Glamorgan
(Bro Morgannwg)
Brynsadler
Llanharry
Talygarn
Groes-faen
Capel Llanilltern
St Brides super Ely
Peterston super-Ely
St George's
Michaelston-super-Ely
Caerau
Leckwith
Pendoylan
Welsh St Donats
Ystradowen
Craig Penllyn
Llansannor
Llangan
St Mary Hill
Maendy
Aberthin
Penllyn
Pentre Meyrick
Cowbridge
(Y Bont-Faen)
Llysworney
Llandow
Llanblethian
St Hilary
Llandough
Llantrithyd
Bonvilston
St Nicholas
Wallston
St Lythans
DYFFRYN GARDENS
Wenvoe
Michaelston-le-Pit
St Andrews Major
Dinas Powys
Llanmihangel
St Mary Church
OLD BEAUPRE CASTLE
Sigingstone
Walterston
Flemingston
Moulton
Llanmaes
Eglwys-Brewis
Llanbethery
Llancarfan
WELSH HAWKING CENTRE
Penmark
Colcot
Merthyr-Dyfan
Cadoxton
COSMESTON LAKES
MEDIEVAL VILLAGE
Lower Penarth
Sully
Lavernock Pt.
Trwyn Larnog
Sully Island
Ynys Sili
Llantwit Major
(Llanilltud Fawr)
Boverton
St Athan
CARDIFF (MAES AWYR CAERDYDD)
PORTHKERRY
Gileston
East Aberthaw
Rhoose
(Y Rhws)
Porthkerry
BARRY
(Y BARRI)
Barry Island
BARRY ISLAND PLEASURE PARK
Breaksea Pt.
Trwyn Breaksea
Flat Holm
ABER HAFREN
MOUTH OF THE SEVERN
Sand Pt.
Sand Bay
Kewstoke
Milton
NORTH SOMERSET
Weston-super-Mare
Weston Bay
SEAQUARIUM
HELICOPTER MUS
Steep Holm
Brean Down
Uphill
Hutton
Bleadon
Brean
BERROW FLATS
BREAN LEISURE PARK
Eastertown
Lympsham
Gore Sands
Berrow
Brent Knoll
East Brent
Burnham-on-Sea
Edithmead
Highbridge
Watchfield
MÔR HAFREN
BRISTOL CHANNEL
ST
BRIDGWATER BAY
STERT FLATS
BRIDGWATER BAY
SECRET WORLD
Huntspill
Bason Bridge
East Huntspill
HUNTSPILL RIVER
Minehead
WEST SOMERSET RAILWAY
BUTLINS
Woodcombe
Alcombe
Periton
Marsh Street
MINEHEAD
DOLL MUS
DUNKERY VINEYARD
Dunster
MILL & YARN MARKET
DUNSTER CASTLE
Blue Anchor Bay
Blue Anchor
Old Cleeve
Carhampton
MARKET HOUSE MUS
Watchet
West Quantoxhead
East Quantoxhead
Kilton
Lilstock
Burton
Shurton
Stolford
Steart
Stockland Bristol
Stogursey
Stringston
Otterhampton
Combwich
Pawlett
Stretcholt
Kilve
Cowbridge
Timberscombe
Withycombe
TROPIQUARIA
Williton
Staple
Holford
Nether Stowey
Fiddington
Rodway
Cannington
CANNINGTON COLLEGE
Dunball
Puriton
Woolavington
BRENDON
CROYDON HILL
FOREST
Bilbrook
Washford
CLEEVE ABBEY
Rodhuish
Sampford Brett
Bicknoller
QUANTOCK
COLERIDGE COTTAGE
Over Stowey
Somerset
Charlynch
Chilton Trinity
BLAKE MUS
Wembdon
BRIDGWATER AND TAUNTON CANAL AND DOCKS
Chedzoy
Bawdrip
Cutcombe
Luxborough
Roadwater
Yard
Vellow
Monksilver
Stogumber
LYPE HILL
Kingsbridge
WEST SOMERSET RAILWAY
Crowcombe
QUANTOCK FOREST
Spaxton
Four Forks
Durleigh
Bridgwater
BRENDON HILLS
Treborough
Elworthy
Flaxpool
Lower Vexford
West Bagborough
Lower Aisholt
Enmore
Goathurst
BRIDGWATER SERVICES
Huntworth
North Petherton
Courtway
TEMPLE OF HARMONY
Withiel Florey
Clatworthy Res.
Willett
Lydeard St Lawrence
Brompton Regis
Tolland
FYNE COURT
Broomfield
Brompton Ralph
Combe Florey
East Combe
Cothelstone
Northmoor Green
or Moorland
North Newton
Wimbleball Lake
Clatworthy
Tarr
Cushuish
Thurloxton
BRIDGWATER & TAUNTON CANAL MAUNSEL LOCK
Lyng
Upton
Huish Champflower
Langley Marsh
Ash Priors
Bishops Lydeard
Fulford
Pickney
Kingston St Mary
Hestercombe Gardens
Hedging
Fitzhead
Wiveliscombe
Halse
Nailsbourne
West Monkton
Monkton Heathfield
Durston
West Lyng
Cheddon Fitzpaine
Creech Heathfield
VALE OF TAUNTON DEANE
Heathfield
Preston Bowyer
Milverton
Hillcommon
Norton Fitzwarren
Staplegrove
Bathpool
North End
Meare Green
WILLOWS & WETLANDS VISITOR CENTRE
Creech
Knapp
Bury
Waterrow
0 1 2 3 4 5 6 miles
0 1 2 3 4 5 6 7 8 9 10 km

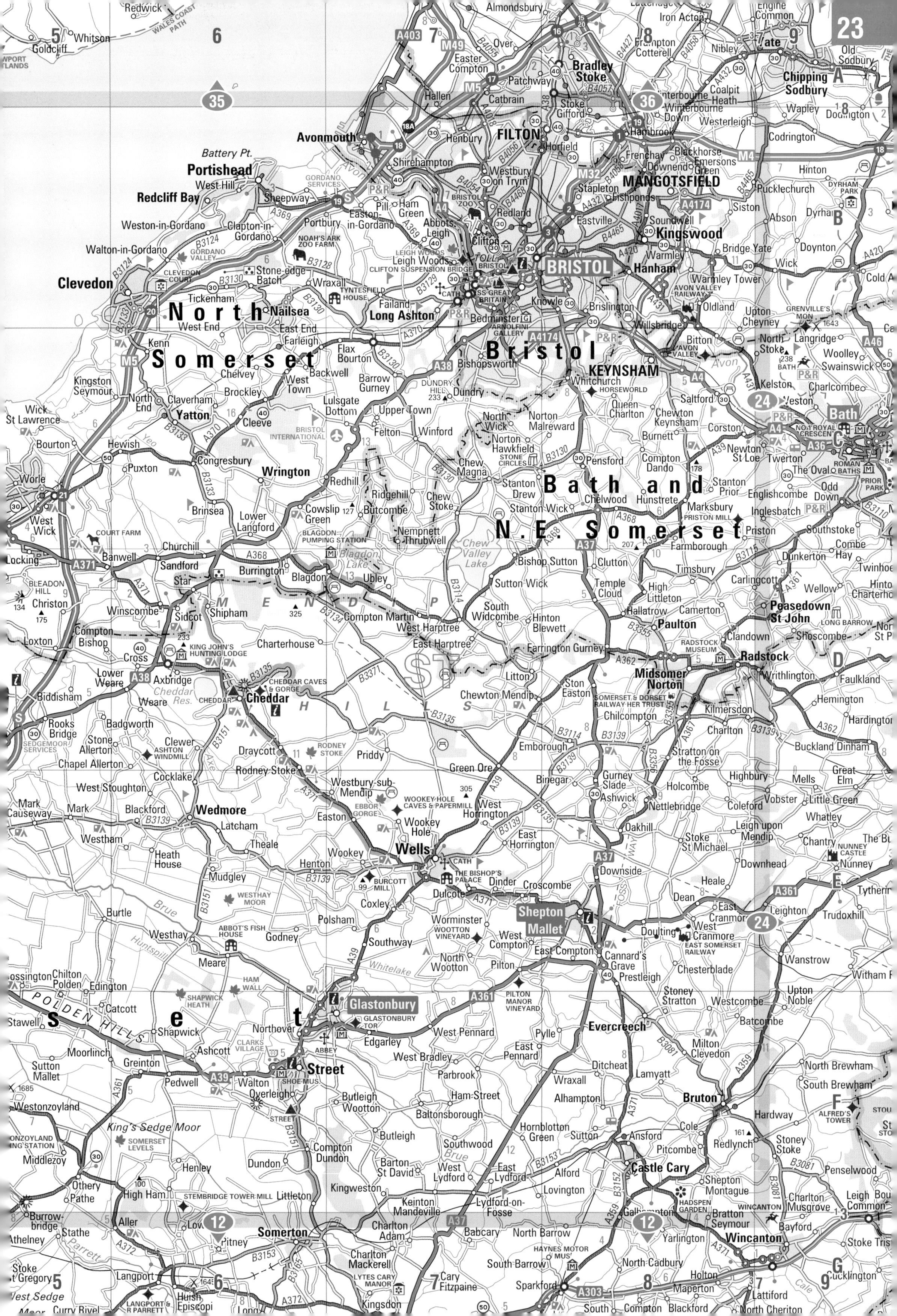
North Somerset
Bristol
Bath and N.E. Somerset
Mendip Hills
Polden Hills
Almondsbury
Iron Acton
Frampton Cotterell
Yate
Old Sodbury
Chipping Sodbury
Redwick
Goldcliff
Whitson
Easter Compton
Over
Bradley Stoke
Patchway
Hallen
Catbrain
Stoke Gifford
Winterbourne
Coalpit Heath
Winterbourne Down
Westerleigh
Wapley
Dodington
Avonmouth
Henbury
Filton
Horfield
Hambrook
Codrington
Battery Pt.
Portishead
West Hill
Redcliff Bay
Sheepway
Shirehampton
Westbury on Trym
Frenchay
Blackhorse
Emersons Green
Downend
Mangotsfield
Hinton
Pucklechurch
Dyrham Park
Stapleton
Fishponds
Pill
Ham Green
Easton-in-Gordano
Abbots Leigh
Redland
Portbury
Eastville
Soundwell
Kingswood
Siston
Abson
Dyrham
Weston-in-Gordano
Clapton-in-Gordano
Walton-in-Gordano
Gordano Valley
Noah's Ark Zoo Farm
Leigh Woods
Clifton Suspension Bridge
Clifton
Bristol Zoo
Warmley
Bridge Yate
Doynton
Hanham
Wick
Clevedon
Clevedon Court
Stone-edge Batch
Wraxall
Tyntesfield House
SS Great Britain
Warmley Tower
Avon Valley Railway
Cold Ash
Tickenham
Nailsea
Failand
Long Ashton
Bedminster
Arnolfini Gallery
Knowle
Brislington
Oldland
Upton Cheyney
Grenville's Mon
West End
East End
Farleigh
Willsbridge
Bitton
Langridge
Kenn
Flax Bourton
Bishopsworth
Avon Valley
North Stoke
Woolley
Swainswick
Chelvey
Backwell
West Town
Keynsham
Whitchurch
Horseworld
Kingston Seymour
Brockley
Barrow Gurney
Dundry Hill
Dundry
Saltford
Kelston
Charlcombe
Weston
Bath
North End
Claverham
Yatton
Lulsgate Bottom
Upper Town
Queen Charlton
Chewton Keynsham
Wick St Lawrence
Cleeve
Bristol International
Felton
Winford
North Wick
Norton Malreward
Corston
Burnett
No. 1 Royal Crescent
Newton St Loe
Twerton
Bourton
Hewish
Norton Hawkfield
Stone Circles
Pensford
Compton Dando
Roman Baths
The Oval
Congresbury
Puxton
Wrington
Chew Magna
Prior Park
Worle
Redhill
Stanton Drew
Stanton Prior
Odd Down
Englishcombe
Ridgehill
Chew Stoke
Chelwood
Hunstrete
Marksbury
Inglesbatch
West Wick
Brinsea
Cowslip Green
Butcombe
Stanton Wick
Priston Mill
Priston
Lower Langford
Court Farm
Blagdon Pumping Station
Nempnett Thrubwell
Chew Valley Lake
Farmborough
Southstoke
Combe Hay
Churchill
Locking
Banwell
Sandford
Burrington
Blagdon Lake
Blagdon
Ubley
Bishop Sutton
Clutton
Timsbury
Dunkerton
Twinhoe
Star
Sutton Wick
Temple Cloud
High Littleton
Carlingcott
Wellow
Bleadon Hill
Christon
Winscombe
Sidcot
Shipham
Compton Martin
West Harptree
South Widcombe
Hinton Blewett
Hallatrow
Camerton
Paulton
Peasedown St John
Long Barrow
Compton Bishop
Loxton
Charterhouse
East Harptree
Farrington Gurney
Radstock Museum
Clandown
Shoscombe
Radstock
Cross
King John's Hunting Lodge
Lower Weare
Axbridge
Cheddar Res.
Cheddar Caves & Gorge
Cheddar
Litton
Midsomer Norton
Writhlington
Faulkland
Biddisham
Weare
Chewton Mendip
Ston Easton
Somerset & Dorset Railway Her Trust
Kilmersdon
Hemington
Hardington
Rooks Bridge
Badgworth
Sedgemoor Services
Chilcompton
Charlton
Stone Allerton
Clewer
Ashton Windmill
Draycott
Rodney Stoke
Priddy
Emborough
Stratton on the Fosse
Buckland Dinham
Chapel Allerton
Green Ore
Gurney Slade
Highbury
Great Elm
Mells
Cocklake
Binegar
Holcombe
Vobster
Little Green
West Stoughton
Westbury-sub-Mendip
Ashwick
Mark Causeway
Mark
Blackford
Wedmore
Wookey Hole Caves & Papermill
Ebbor Gorge
West Horrington
Nettlebridge
Coleford
Whatley
Easton
Wookey Hole
Latcham
Oakhill
Leigh upon Mendip
Westham
Theale
East Horrington
Stoke St Michael
Chantry
Nunney Castle
Nunney
Heath House
Wookey
Wells
Cath
The Bishop's Palace
Downside
Downhead
Henton
Mudgley
Burcott Mill
Dinder
Croscombe
Heale
Westhay Moor
Dulcote
Coxley
Dean
Shepton Mallet
East Cranmore
West Cranmore
Leighton
Trudoxhill
Burtle
Polsham
Worminster
Wootton Vineyard
Doulting
East Somerset Railway
Westhay
Abbot's Fish House
Godney
Southway
West Compton
East Compton
Cannard's Grave
Prestleigh
Wanstrow
Witham Friary
Meare
North Wootton
Pilton
Chesterblade
Chilton Polden
Edington
Ham Wall
Whitelake
Upton Noble
Shapwick Heath
Glastonbury
Pilton Manor Vineyard
Stoney Stratton
Westcombe
Catcott
Stawell
Shapwick
Northover
Glastonbury Tor
Evercreech
Batcombe
Moorlinch
Ashcott
Clarks Village
Abbey
Edgarley
West Pennard
Pylle
East Pennard
Milton Clevedon
Sutton Mallet
Greinton
West Bradley
Ditcheat
Lamyatt
North Brewham
South Brewham
Pedwell
Walton
Street
Shoe Mus
Overleigh
Parbrook
Wraxall
Westonzoyland
Butleigh Wootton
Ham Street
Alhampton
Bruton
Hardway
Alfred's Tower
King's Sedge Moor
Somerset Levels
Baltonsborough
Hornblotton Green
Sutton
Ansford
Cole
Redlynch
Stoney Stoke
Butleigh
Southwood
Pitcombe
Middlezoy
Compton Dundon
Henley
Dundon
Barton St David
West Lydford
East Lydford
Alford
Castle Cary
Penselwood
Othery
Pathe
High Ham
Stembridge Tower Mill
Littleton
Kingweston
Keinton Mandeville
Lovington
Shepton Montague
Hadspen Garden
Charlton Musgrove
Leigh Common
Burrowbridge
Athelney
Stathe
Aller
Low Ham
Pitney
Somerton
Charlton Adam
Babcary
Lydford-on-Fosse
North Barrow
Galhampton
Yarlington
Bratton Seymour
Wincanton
Bayford
Stoke Trister
Haynes Motor Mus
South Barrow
North Cadbury
Charlton Mackerell
Lytes Cary Manor
Cary Fitzpaine
Sparkford
Holton
Maperton
Cucklington
Stoke St Gregory
West Sedge Moor
Langport
Langport & R Parrett
Huish Episcopi
Curry Rivel
Kingsdon
South Compton
Blackford
North Cheriton
Lattiford
River Avon
River Yeo
River Axe
River Brue
River Parrett
River Cale
Huntspill
M4
M5
M32
M49
A4
A36
A37
A38
A39
A303
A361
A362
A367
A368
A369
A370
A371
A372
A403
A420
A431
A432
A4174
B3124
B3128
B3130
B3133
B3134
B3135
B3139
B3151
B3153
B3114
B3355
B3081
P&R
35
36
24
12

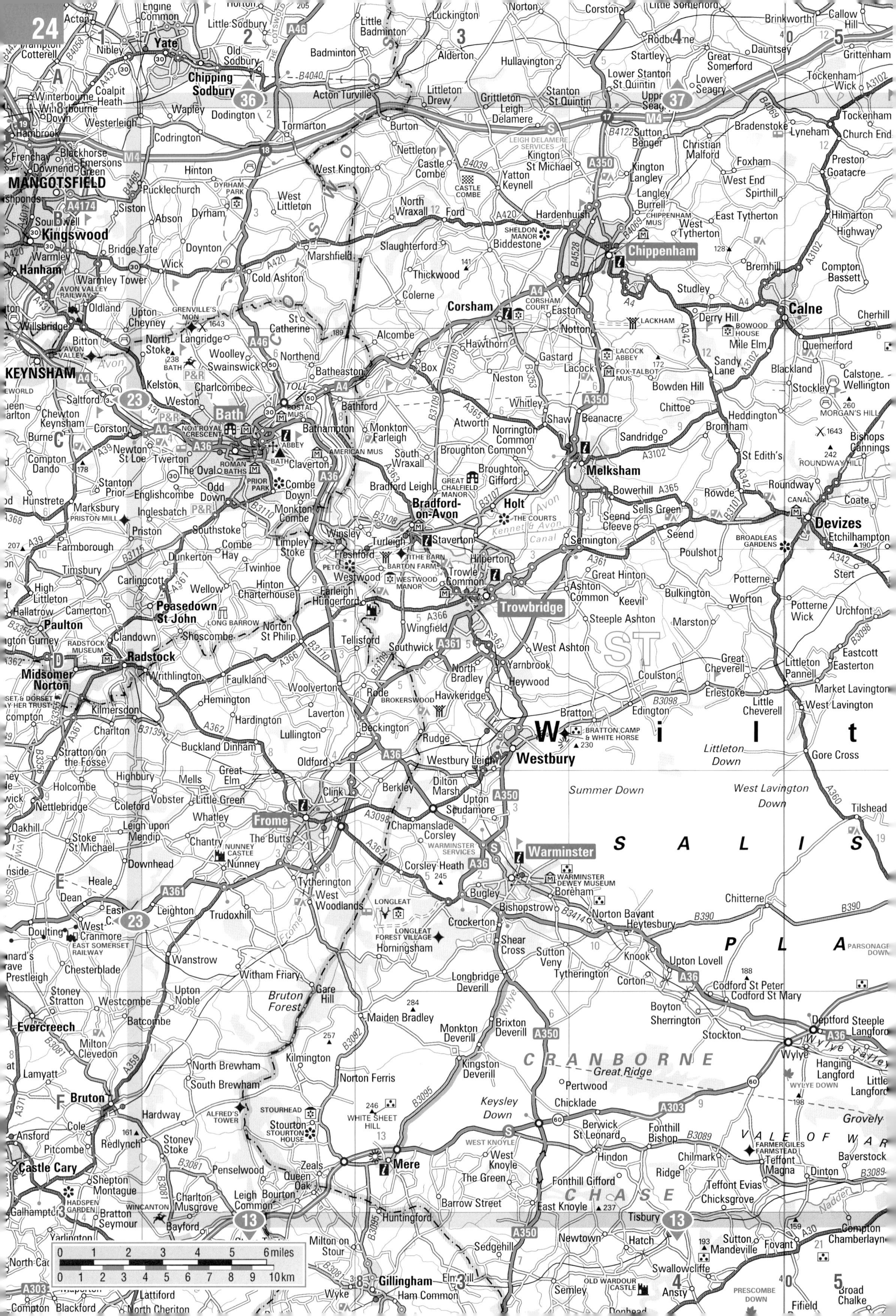

Acton
Engine Common
Yate
Nibley
Little Sodbury
Old Sodbury
Chipping Sodbury
Little Badminton
Badminton
Luckington
Alderton
Norton
Hullavington
Corston
Little Somerford
Rodbourne
Startley
Great Somerford
Lower Stanton St Quintin
Lower Seagry
Upper Seagry
Brinkworth
Dauntsey
Callow Hill
Grittenham
Tockenham Wick
Tockenham
Lyneham
Church End
Coalpit Heath
Winterbourne
Winterbourne Down
Westerleigh
Wapley
Dodington
Acton Turville
Tormarton
Burton
Littleton Drew
Grittleton
Leigh Delamere
Stanton St Quintin
Leigh Delamere Services
Kington St Michael
Sutton Benger
Christian Malford
Bradenstoke
Foxham
Preston
Goatacre
West End
Spirthill
Hambrook
Frenchay
Blackhorse
Emersons Green
Downend
Codrington
Hinton
Nettleton
West Kington
Castle Combe
Yatton Keynell
Kington Langley
Langley Burrell
Mangotsfield
Pucklechurch
Dyrham Park
Dyrham
Siston
Abson
West Littleton
North Wraxall
Ford
Hardenhuish
Chippenham Mus
East Tytherton
West Tytherton
Hilmarton
Highway
Soundwell
Kingswood
Hanham
Warmley
Bridge Yate
Doynton
Wick
Marshfield
Slaughterford
Sheldon Manor
Biddestone
Chippenham
Bremhill
Compton Bassett
Warmley Tower
Avon Valley Railway
Cold Ashton
Thickwood
Colerne
Corsham
Corsham Court
Easton
Studley
Derry Hill
Calne
Cherhill
Oldland
Upton Cheyney
Grenville's Mon
Willsbridge
Bitton
North Stoke
Langridge
Woolley
St Catherine
Alcombe
Hawthorn
Notton
Lackham
Bowood House
Mile Elm
Quemerford
Keynsham
Bath
Swainswick
Northend
Batheaston
Box
Gastard
Lacock Abbey
Lacock
Fox-Talbot Mus
Sandy Lane
Blackland
Calstone Wellington
Kelston
Charlcombe
Neston
Bowden Hill
Stockley
Saltford
Weston
Bathford
Whitley
Chittoe
Morgan's Hill
Chewton Keynsham
No 1 Royal Crescent
Postal Mus
Atworth
Shaw
Beanacre
Heddington
Bishops Cannings
Burnett
Corston
Newton St Loe
Twerton
Abbey
Bathampton
Monkton Farleigh
Norrington Common
Sandridge
Bromham
Compton Dando
The Oval
Roman Baths
Claverton
American Mus
South Wraxall
Broughton Common
Melksham
St Edith's
Roundway Hill
Stanton Prior
Odd Down
Prior Park
Combe Down
Bradford Leigh
Great Chalfield Manor
Broughton Gifford
Bowerhill
Roundway
Rowde
Canal
Coate
Hunstrete
Marksbury
Priston Mill
Englishcombe
Inglesbatch
Monkton Combe
Bradford-on-Avon
Holt
The Courts
Seend Cleeve
Sells Green
Devizes
Priston
Southstoke
Winsley
Turleigh
Staverton
Kennet & Avon Canal
Seend
Semington
Broadleas Gardens
Etchilhampton
Farmborough
Combe Hay
Dunkerton
Limpley Stoke
Freshford
Tithe Barn
Barton Farm
Hilperton
Poulshot
Timsbury
Twinhoe
Peto
Westwood
Westwood Manor
Trowle Common
Ashton Common
Great Hinton
Potterne
Stert
High Littleton
Carlingcott
Wellow
Hinton Charterhouse
Farleigh Hungerford
Keevil
Bulkington
Worton
Potterne Wick
Urchfont
Hallatrow
Camerton
Peasedown St John
Trowbridge
Steeple Ashton
Marston
Paulton
Long Barrow
Norton St Philip
Wingfield
Tellisford
Southwick
West Ashton
Eastcott
Radstock Museum
Radstock
Shoscombe
Midsomer Norton
Writhlington
Faulkland
North Bradley
Yarnbrook
Heywood
Coulston
Great Cheverell
Littleton Pannell
Easterton
Woolverton
Rode
Brokerswood
Hawkeridge
Erlestoke
Market Lavington
Kilmersdon
Hemington
Hardington
Laverton
Bratton
Edington
Little Cheverell
West Lavington
Charlton
Lullington
Beckington
Rudge
Bratton Camp & White Horse
Westbury
Gore Cross
Littleton Down
Stratton on the Fosse
Buckland Dinham
Oldford
Westbury Leigh
Wilt
Highbury
Great Elm
Mells
Dilton Marsh
Summer Down
West Lavington Down
Holcombe
Vobster
Little Green
Clink
Berkley
Upton Scudamore
Tilshead
Nettlebridge
Coleford
Whatley
Frome
Chapmanslade
Oakhill
Leigh upon Mendip
Chantry
The Butts
Corsley
Warminster Services
Stoke St Michael
Nunney Castle
Nunney
Warminster
Salis
Downhead
Corsley Heath
Warminster Dewey Museum
Heale
Tytherington
West Woodlands
Longleat
Bugley
Boreham
Dean
Leighton
Trudoxhill
Bishopstrow
Norton Bavant
Chitterne
Doulting
Cranmore
East Somerset Railway
Crockerton
Heytesbury
Longleat Forest Village
Horningsham
Shear Cross
Sutton Veny
Pla
Parsonage Down
Chesterblade
Wanstrow
Knook
Upton Lovell
Prestleigh
Witham Friary
Longbridge Deverill
Tytherington
Corton
Codford St Peter
Codford St Mary
Stoney Stratton
Westcombe
Upton Noble
Bruton Forest
Gare Hill
Boyton
Sherrington
Evercreech
Batcombe
Maiden Bradley
Brixton Deverill
Monkton Deverill
Stockton
Deptford
Steeple Langford
Milton Clevedon
Kilmington
Cranborne
Wylye
Wylye Valley
Hanging Langford
Lamyatt
North Brewham
Kingston Deverill
Great Ridge
Little Langford
South Brewham
Norton Ferris
Pertwood
Wylye Down
Bruton
Stourhead
White Sheet Hill
Keysley Down
Chicklade
Grovely
Hardway
Alfred's Tower
Stourton
Stourton House
Berwick St Leonard
Fonthill Bishop
Cole
Ansford
Redlynch
Stoney Stoke
West Knoyle
Vale of Wardour
Pitcombe
Zeals
Mere
Hindon
Chilmark
Farmer Giles Farmstead
Baverstock
Teffont Magna
Dinton
Castle Cary
Penselwood
Queen Oak
The Green
Fonthill Gifford
Ridge
Teffont Evias
Shepton Montague
Charlton Musgrove
Leigh Common
Bourton
Chase
Chicksgrove
Hadspen Garden
Bratton Seymour
Wincanton
Barrow Street
East Knoyle
Tisbury
Nadder
Galhampton
Yarlington
Bayford
Huntingford
Newtown
Hatch
Sutton Mandeville
Fovant
Compton Chamberlayne
Milton on Stour
Sedgehill
Swallowcliffe
North Cadbury
Gillingham
Ham Common
Semley
Old Wardour Castle
Ansty
Prescombe Down
Fifield
Broad Chalke
Lattiford
Compton
Blackford
North Cheriton
Wyke
Donhead
M4
A46
A4
A36
A350
A361
A303
A420
A4174
A39
A367
A366
A363
A362
A342
A3102
A360
A30
A359
A371
A365
A3098
B4040
B4039
B4069
B4122
B4528
B3109
B3108
B3107
B3110
B3115
B3139
B3098
B390
B3414
B3089
B3092
B3095
B3081
B3087
B3355
B3356
0 1 2 3 4 5 6 miles
0 1 2 3 4 5 6 7 8 9 10 km

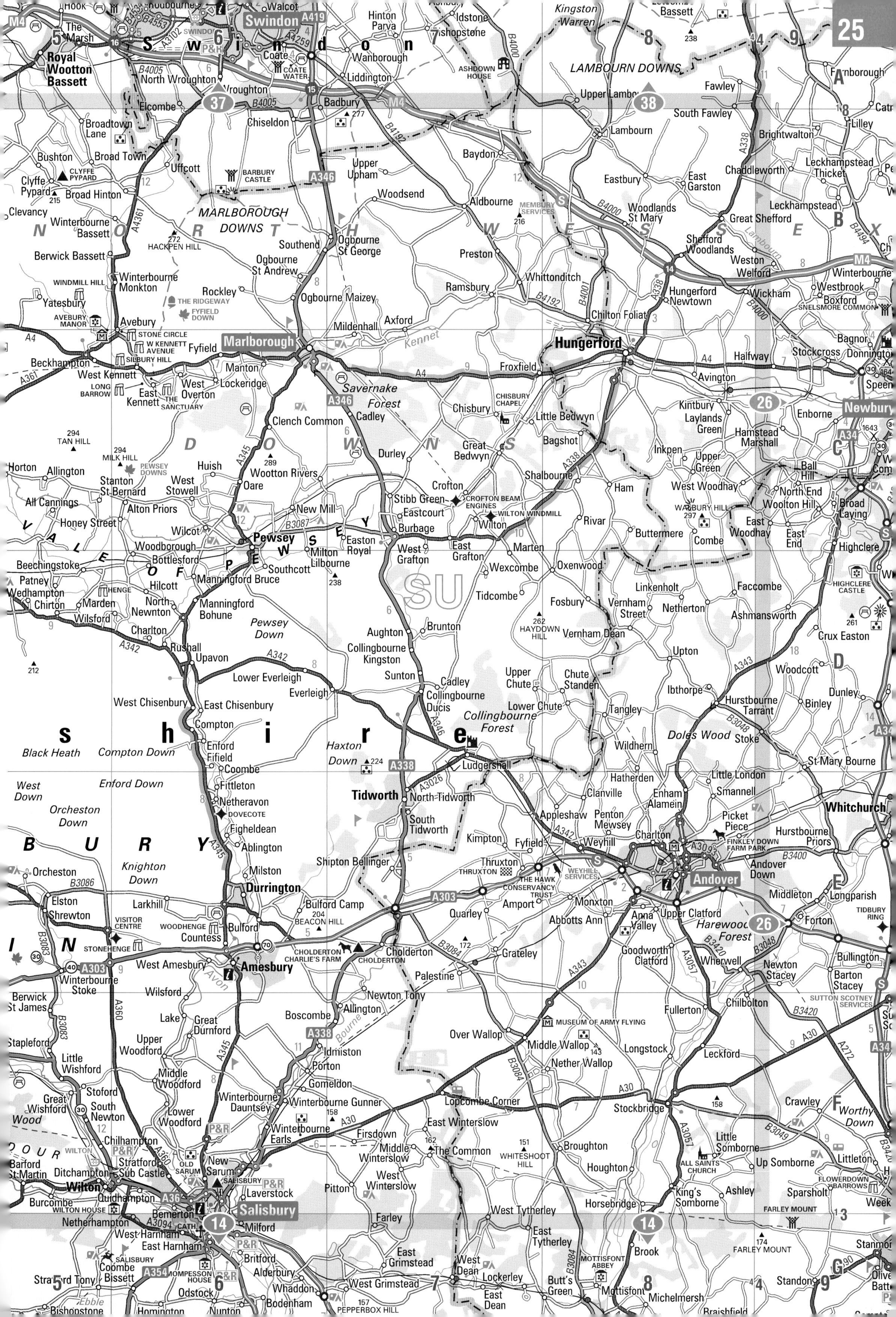
Swindon
Royal Wootton Bassett
The Marsh
Hook
Walcot
Coate
Coate Water
North Wroughton
Wroughton
Elcombe
Chiseldon
Badbury
Hinton Parva
Wanborough
Liddington
Bishopstone
Idstone
Ashdown House
Kingston Warren
Bassett
Lambourn Downs
Upper Lambourn
Lambourn
Fawley
South Fawley
Farnborough
Catmore
Lilley
Brightwalton
Leckhampstead Thicket
Chaddleworth
Leckhampstead
Great Shefford
Shefford Woodlands
Weston
Welford
Winterbourne
Westbrook
Boxford
Snelsmore Common
Wickham
East Garston
Eastbury
Woodlands St Mary
Baydon
Aldbourne
Membury Services
Preston
Whittonditch
Ramsbury
Chilton Foliat
Hungerford
Hungerford Newtown
Bagnor
Donnington
Stockcross
Halfway
Avington
Speen
Newbury
Broadtown Lane
Bushton
Broad Town
Clyffe Pypard
Uffcott
Barbury Castle
Upper Upham
Woodsend
Broad Hinton
Clevancy
Winterbourne Bassett
Marlborough Downs
Hackpen Hill
Berwick Bassett
Windmill Hill
Winterbourne Monkton
Yatesbury
The Ridgeway
Fyfield Down
Avebury
Avebury Manor
Stone Circle
W Kennett Avenue
Silbury Hill
Fyfield
Marlborough
Beckhampton
West Kennett
Long Barrow
East Kennett
The Sanctuary
West Overton
Lockeridge
Manton
Southend
Ogbourne St George
Ogbourne St Andrew
Rockley
Ogbourne Maizey
Mildenhall
Axford
Kennet
Savernake Forest
Cadley
Froxfield
Chisbury
Chisbury Chapel
Little Bedwyn
Great Bedwyn
Bagshot
Shalbourne
Kintbury
Laylands Green
Hamstead Marshall
Enborne
Inkpen
Upper Green
Ball Hill
North End
West Woodhay
Woolton Hill
Broad Laying
Walbury Hill
Combe
East Woodhay
East End
Highclere
Highclere Castle
Buttermere
Ham
Rivar
Crofton
Crofton Beam Engines
Wilton Windmill
Wilton
Stibb Green
Eastcourt
Burbage
Durley
Marten
Oxenwood
Wexcombe
East Grafton
West Grafton
Clench Common
Wootton Rivers
Tan Hill
Milk Hill
Pewsey Downs
Horton
Allington
Stanton St Bernard
West Stowell
Huish
Oare
All Cannings
Alton Priors
Honey Street
Wilcot
New Mill
Pewsey
Vale of Pewsey
Woodborough
Beechingstoke
Bottlesford
Easton Royal
Milton Lilbourne
Southcott
Manningford Bruce
Patney
Wedhampton
Chirton
Marden
Henge
Hilcott
North Newnton
Manningford Bohune
Wilsford
Charlton
Rushall
Upavon
Pewsey Down
Tidcombe
Fosbury
Linkenholt
Vernham Street
Netherton
Faccombe
Ashmansworth
Crux Easton
Haydown Hill
Vernham Dean
Upton
Brunton
Aughton
Collingbourne Kingston
Sunton
Cadley
Collingbourne Ducis
Upper Chute
Chute Standen
Lower Chute
Collingbourne Forest
Tangley
Ibthorpe
Hurstbourne Tarrant
Woodcott
Dunley
Binley
Doles Wood
Stoke
Wildhern
St Mary Bourne
Lower Everleigh
Everleigh
West Chisenbury
East Chisenbury
Compton
Enford
Fifield
Coombe
Black Heath
Compton Down
Haxton Down
Wiltshire
Ludgershall
Tidworth
North Tidworth
South Tidworth
Hatherden
Little London
Smannell
Clanville
Enham Alamein
Appleshaw
Penton Mewsey
Picket Piece
Whitchurch
Charlton
Hurstbourne Priors
Finkley Down Farm Park
Weyhill
Weyhill Services
Kimpton
Fyfield
Thruxton
Andover
Andover Down
Middleton
Longparish
West Down
Enford Down
Orcheston Down
Fittleton
Netheravon
Dovecote
Figheldean
Ablington
Salisbury
Orcheston
Knighton Down
Milston
Durrington
Shipton Bellinger
The Hawk Conservancy Trust
Amport
Monxton
Abbotts Ann
Anna Valley
Upper Clapford
Harewood Forest
Forton
Tidbury Ring
Elston
Shrewton
Larkhill
Bulford Camp
Beacon Hill
Quarley
Visitor Centre
Woodhenge
Bulford
Countess
Stonehenge
Cholderton
Cholderton Charlie's Farm
Grateley
Goodworth Clatford
Wherwell
Bullington
Newton Stacey
Barton Stacey
Sutton Scotney Services
Winterbourne Stoke
West Amesbury
Amesbury
Avon
Palestine
Newton Tony
Allington
Boscombe
Chilbolton
Fullerton
Berwick St James
Wilsford
Lake
Great Durnford
Upper Woodford
Over Wallop
Museum of Army Flying
Middle Wallop
Nether Wallop
Longstock
Leckford
Stapleford
Little Wishford
Middle Woodford
Idmiston
Porton
Gomeldon
Bourne
Stoford
Great Wishford
South Newton
Wishford Wood
Lower Woodford
Winterbourne Dauntsey
Winterbourne Gunner
Winterbourne Earls
Lopcombe Corner
East Winterslow
Stockbridge
Crawley
Worthy Down
Chilhampton
Firsdown
Middle Winterslow
The Common
Whiteshoot Hill
Broughton
Little Somborne
Up Somborne
Littleton
Barford St Martin
Wilton
Stratford sub Castle
Old Sarum
New Sarum
Houghton
All Saints Church
Ditchampton
Burcombe
Quidhampton
Wilton House
Salisbury
Laverstock
Pitton
West Winterslow
Horsebridge
King's Somborne
Ashley
Sparsholt
Flowerdown Barrows
Weeke
Farley Mount
Netherhampton
Bemerton
West Harnham
East Harnham
Milford
Farley
West Tytherley
East Tytherley
Brook
Stanmore
Salisbury Racecourse
Coombe Bissett
Britford
East Grimstead
West Dean
Lockerley
Mottisfont Abbey
Mottisfont
Butt's Green
Standon
Olivers Battery
Stratford Tony
Ebble
Bishopstone
Homington
Longford Castle
Odstock
Nunton
Alderbury
Whaddon
Bodenham
West Grimstead
Pepperbox Hill
East Dean
Michelmersh
Braishfield

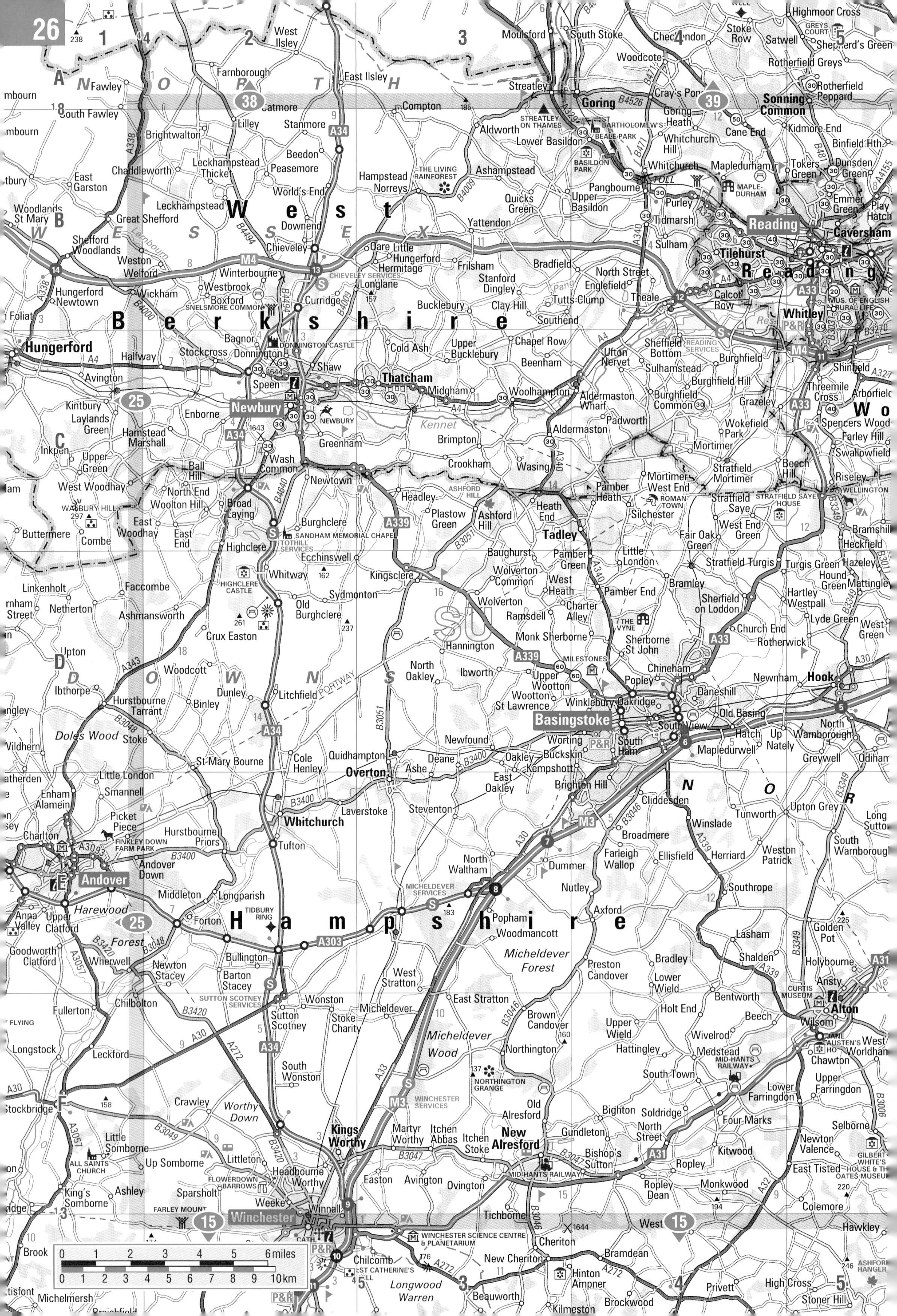
West Berkshire
Berkshire
Hampshire
Reading
Newbury
Hungerford
Thatcham
Basingstoke
Andover
Winchester
Whitchurch
Overton
Tadley
Kings Worthy
New Alresford
Alton
Hook
Goring
Caversham
Tilehurst
Whitley
Sonning Common
West Ilsley
East Ilsley
Farnborough
Fawley
South Fawley
Catmore
Compton
Lilley
Brightwalton
Stanmore
Beedon
Peasemore
Chaddleworth
Leckhampstead Thicket
Leckhampstead
East Garston
Woodlands St Mary
Great Shefford
Shefford Woodlands
Weston
Welford
Wickham
Hungerford Newtown
World's End
Downend
Chieveley
Hampstead Norreys
THE LIVING RAINFOREST
Ashampstead
Yattendon
Quicks Green
Upper Basildon
Pangbourne
Aldworth
Lower Basildon
BASILDON PARK
Streatley
STREATLEY ON THAMES
BEALE PARK
Moulsford
South Stoke
Checkendon
Stoke Row
Highmoor Cross
Satwell
Shepherd's Green
Rotherfield Greys
Rotherfield Peppard
Woodcote
Cray's Pond
Goring Heath
Whitchurch Hill
Cane End
Kidmore End
Binfield Hth.
Mapledurham
MAPLEDURHAM
Tokers Green
Dunsden Green
Emmer Green
Play Hatch
Purley
Tidmarsh
Sulham
Calcot Row
Theale
Englefield
Tutts Clump
North Street
Bradfield
Southend
Frilsham
Stanford Dingley
Bucklebury
Clay Hill
Upper Bucklebury
Cold Ash
Chapel Row
Beenham
Oare
Little Hungerford
Hermitage
Longlane
Curridge
CHIEVELEY SERVICES
Winterbourne
Westbrook
Boxford
SNELSMORE COMMON
Bagnor
DONNINGTON CASTLE
Donnington
Stockcross
Shaw
Speen
Halfway
Avington
Kintbury
Laylands Green
Inkpen
Upper Green
Hamstead Marshall
Enborne
West Woodhay
Ball Hill
North End
Woolton Hill
Wash Common
Greenham
NEWBURY
Kennet
Brimpton
Crookham
Wasing
Midgham
Woolhampton
Aldermaston Wharf
Aldermaston
Padworth
Ufton Nervet
Sheffield Bottom
READING SERVICES
Sulhamstead
Burghfield
Burghfield Hill
Burghfield Common
Grazeley
Shinfield
Threemile Cross
Arborfield
Spencers Wood
Farley Hill
Swallowfield
Riseley
WELLINGTON
Wokefield Park
Mortimer
Stratfield Mortimer
Mortimer West End
Beech Hill
Pamber Heath
ROMAN TOWN
Silchester
Stratfield Saye
STRATFIELD SAYE HOUSE
West End Green
Fair Oak Green
Stratfield Turgis
Turgis Green
Hazeley
Bramshill
Heckfield
Hound Green
Mattingley
Hartley Wespall
Lyde Green
West Green
Rotherwick
Church End
Sherfield on Loddon
Bramley
Little London
Pamber End
Pamber Green
Baughurst
Heath End
Wolverton Common
West Heath
Charter Alley
Wolverton
Ramsdell
THE VYNE
Sherborne St John
Monk Sherborne
Hannington
Kingsclere
Ecchinswell
Sydmonton
Old Burghclere
Burghclere
SANDHAM MEMORIAL CHAPEL
TOTHILL SERVICES
Highclere
HIGHCLERE CASTLE
Whitway
Newtown
Headley
Plastow Green
ASHFORD HILL
Ashford Hill
Broad Laying
East End
East Woodhay
Buttermere
Combe
WALBURY HILL
Linkenholt
Faccombe
Netherton
Ashmansworth
Crux Easton
Upton
Ibthorpe
Hurstbourne Tarrant
Woodcott
Dunley
Binley
Litchfield
PORTWAY
North Oakley
Ibworth
Upper Wootton
Wootton St Lawrence
MILESTONES
Winklebury
Oakridge
Popley
Chineham
Daneshill
Old Basing
Newnham
South View
South Ham
Worting
Buckskin
Kempshott
Brighton Hill
Hatch
Up Nately
Mapledurwell
Greywell
Warnborough
Odiham
Cliddesden
Winslade
Tunworth
Upton Grey
Long Sutton
South Warnborough
Weston Patrick
Herriard
Ellisfield
Farleigh Wallop
Dummer
Nutley
Axford
Southrope
Lasham
Golden Pot
Shalden
Holybourne
Bradley
Lower Wield
Bentworth
CURTIS MUSEUM
Wilsom
Holt End
Beech
Wivelrod
Medstead
MID-HANTS RAILWAY
JANE AUSTEN'S HO
Chawton
West Worldham
Upper Farringdon
Lower Farringdon
Four Marks
Selborne
Newton Valence
GILBERT WHITE'S HOUSE & THE OATES MUSEUM
East Tisted
Colemore
Hawkley
Ropley
Ropley Dean
Monkwood
Kitwood
Bishop's Sutton
Gundleton
North Street
Soldridge
Bighton
South Town
Hattingley
Upper Wield
Preston Candover
Brown Candover
Northington
NORTHINGTON GRANGE
Old Alresford
Micheldever Forest
Micheldever Wood
Popham
Woodmancott
North Waltham
Steventon
Deane
East Oakley
Oakley
Newfound
Quidhampton
Ashe
Laverstoke
Cole Henley
Freefolk
Tufton
Hurstbourne Priors
Longparish
Middleton
Forton
TIDBURY RING
Bullington
Barton Stacey
Newton Stacey
SUTTON SCOTNEY SERVICES
Sutton Scotney
Wonston
South Wonston
Stoke Charity
Micheldever
MICHELDEVER SERVICES
West Stratton
East Stratton
WINCHESTER SERVICES
Martyr Worthy
Itchen Abbas
Itchen Stoke
Avington
Ovington
Easton
Headbourne Worthy
Weeke
Winnall
Tichborne
Cheriton
New Cheriton
Hinton Ampner
Bramdean
Beauworth
Kilmeston
Brockwood
Privett
High Cross
Stoner Hill
ASHFORD HANGER
West
Chilcomb
ST CATHERINE'S HILL
Longwood Warren
WINCHESTER SCIENCE CENTRE & PLANETARIUM
FARLEY MOUNT
Sparsholt
Littleton
FLOWERDOWN BARROWS
Crawley
Worthy Down
Little Somborne
Up Somborne
Ashley
King's Somborne
ALL SAINTS CHURCH
Stockbridge
Brook
Michelmersh
Leckford
Longstock
Fullerton
Chilbolton
Wherwell
Goodworth Clatford
Upper Clatford
Anna Valley
Harewood Forest
Andover Down
FINKLEY DOWN FARM PARK
Picket Piece
Charlton
Enham Alamein
Smannell
Little London
St Mary Bourne
Stoke
Doles Wood
Vernham Street
M4
M3
A34
A4
A339
A303
A30
A33
A340
A343
A31
A32
A272
A3057
A338
A3093
A329
B4009
B4494
B4000
B4526
B4640
B3051
B3400
B3048
B3420
B3046
B3047
B3049
B3349
0 1 2 3 4 5 6 miles
0 1 2 3 4 5 6 7 8 9 10 km

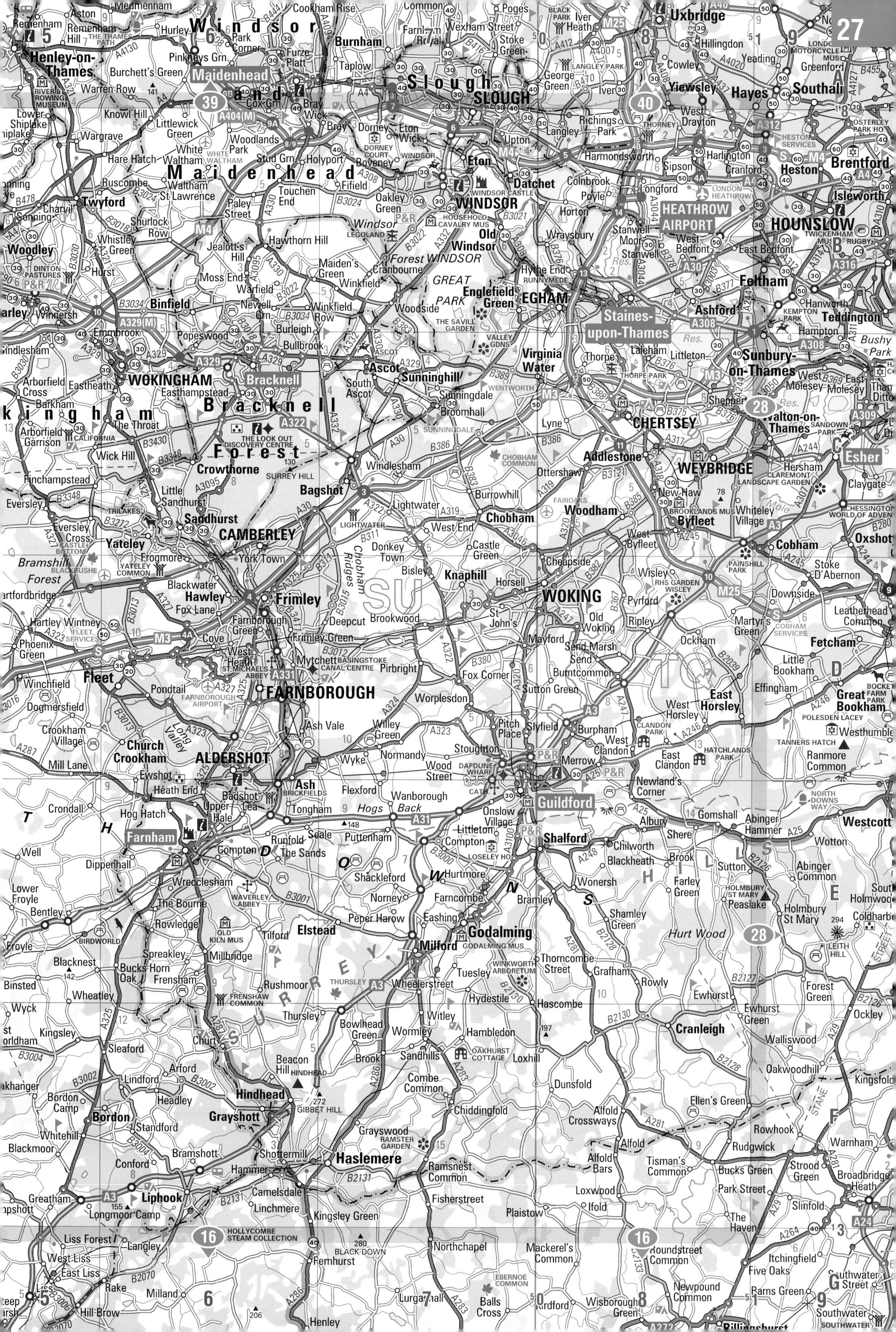
Windsor and Maidenhead
Henley-on-Thames
Remenham
Remenham Hill
Aston
Medmenham
Hurley
Cookham Rise
Burnham
Farnham Royal
Wexham Street
Stoke Poges
Stoke Green
Iver Heath
Uxbridge
Hillingdon
Cowley
Yeading
Greenford
Southall
Hayes
Yiewsley
West Drayton
Maidenhead
Slough
SLOUGH
Pinkneys Grn.
Burchett's Green
Warren Row
Knowl Hill
Littlewick Green
Woodlands Park
White Waltham
Hare Hatch
Wargrave
Shiplake
Cox Grn.
Bray Wick
Bray
Dorney
Eton Wick
Eton
Upton
Langley
Richings Park
Harmondsworth
Sipson
Harlington
Cranford
Heston
Brentford
Isleworth
HOUNSLOW
Twyford
Ruscombe
Waltham St Lawrence
Paley Street
Touchen End
Holyport
Stud Grn.
Fifield
Oakley Green
WINDSOR
Datchet
Colnbrook
Poyle
Longford
HEATHROW AIRPORT
Horton
Wraysbury
Old Windsor
Stanwell
Stanwell Moor
West Bedfont
East Bedfont
Feltham
Hanworth
Teddington
Woodley
Sonning
Charvil
Shurlock Row
Whistley Green
Hurst
Jealott's Hill
Hawthorn Hill
Maiden's Green
Cranbourne
Winkfield
Forest WINDSOR
GREAT PARK
Englefield Green
EGHAM
Staines-upon-Thames
Ashford
Sunbury-on-Thames
Hampton
Winnersh
Binfield
Moss End
Warfield
Newell Grn.
Winkfield Row
Woodside
Burleigh
Emmbrook
Popeswood
Bullbrook
Ascot
Sunninghill
South Ascot
Sunningdale
Virginia Water
Thorpe
Laleham
Littleton
Shepperton
West Molesey
East Molesey
Sindlesham
Arborfield Cross
Eastheath
WOKINGHAM
Bracknell
Easthampstead
Barkham
Wokingham
The Throat
Arborfield Garrison
Broomhall
Lyne
CHERTSEY
Walton-on-Thames
Esher
Wick Hill
Finchampstead
Forest
Crowthorne
Windlesham
Addlestone
Ottershaw
WEYBRIDGE
Hersham
Claygate
Eversley
Little Sandhurst
Sandhurst
Bagshot
Lightwater
Burrowhill
Chobham
Woodham
New Haw
Byfleet
Whiteley Village
Eversley Cross
Yateley
CAMBERLEY
York Town
Frogmore
West End
Donkey Town
Castle Green
West Byfleet
Cobham
Oxshott
Bramshill Forest
Chobham Ridges
Bisley
Knaphill
Horsell
Cheapside
Wisley
Stoke D'Abernon
Hartfordbridge
Blackwater
Hawley
Frimley
Fox Lane
WOKING
Pyrford
Downside
Hartley Wintney
Farnborough Green
Deepcut
Brookwood
St John's
Old Woking
Ripley
Martyr's Green
Leatherhead Common
Phoenix Green
Cove
Frimley Green
Mayford
Send Marsh
Send
Ockham
Fetcham
Fleet
West Heath
Mytchett
Pirbright
Burntcommon
Little Bookham
Winchfield
Pondtail
FARNBOROUGH
Fox Corner
Sutton Green
Effingham
East Horsley
West Horsley
Great Bookham
Dogmersfield
Worplesdon
Crookham Village
Church Crookham
Long Valley
Ash Vale
Willey Green
Pitch Place
Slyfield
Burpham
West Clandon
East Clandon
Westhumble
Mill Lane
ALDERSHOT
Wyke
Normandy
Wood Street
Stoughton
Merrow
Ranmore Common
Ewshot
Heath End
Badshot Lea
Ash
Flexford
Wanborough
Guildford
Newland's Corner
Crondall
Hog Hatch
Upper Hale
Tongham
Hogs Back
Onslow Village
Gomshall
Abinger Hammer
Westcott
Farnham
Runfold
Seale
Puttenham
Littleton
Compton
Shalford
Chilworth
Albury
Shere
Wotton
Well
Dippenhall
The Sands
Blackheath
Brook
Abinger Common
Wrecclesham
Shackleford
Hurtmore
Wonersh
Farley Green
Sutton
Lower Froyle
The Bourne
Norney
Farncombe
Bramley
Shamley Green
Peaslake
Holmbury St Mary
Bentley
Rowledge
Peper Harow
Eashing
Godalming
Hurt Wood
Tilford
Elstead
Milford
Thorncombe Street
Grafham
Froyle
Blacknest
Spreakley
Millbridge
Bucks Horn Oak
Frensham
Rushmoor
Wheelerstreet
Tuesley
Rowly
Ewhurst
Forest Green
Binsted
Wheatley
Hydestile
Hascombe
Ewhurst Green
Ockley
Wyck
Kingsley
Thursley
Bowlhead Green
Witley
Wormley
Hambledon
Cranleigh
Walliswood
Sleaford
Churt
Beacon Hill
Brook
Sandhills
Loxhill
Oakwoodhill
Arford
Lindford
Headley
Bordon Camp
Bordon
Hindhead
Combe Common
Dunsfold
Grayshott
Chiddingfold
Ellen's Green
Kingsfold
Whitehill
Standford
Alfold Crossways
Rowhook
Warnham
Blackmoor
Bramshott
Grayswood
Shottermill
Haslemere
Alfold
Rudgwick
Conford
Hammer
Ramsnest Common
Alfold Bars
Tisman's Common
Bucks Green
Strood Green
Broadbridge Heath
Greatham
Liphook
Longmoor Camp
Camelsdale
Linchmere
Kingsley Green
Fisherstreet
Plaistow
Loxwood
Ifold
Park Street
The Haven
Slinfold
Liss Forest
Langley
West Liss
East Liss
Fernhurst
Northchapel
Mackerel's Common
Roundstreet Common
Itchingfield
Five Oaks
Rake
Milland
Lurgashall
Balls Cross
Kirdford
Wisborough Green
Newpound Common
Barns Green
Southwater
Southwater Street
Hill Brow
Henley
Billingshurst
Liss

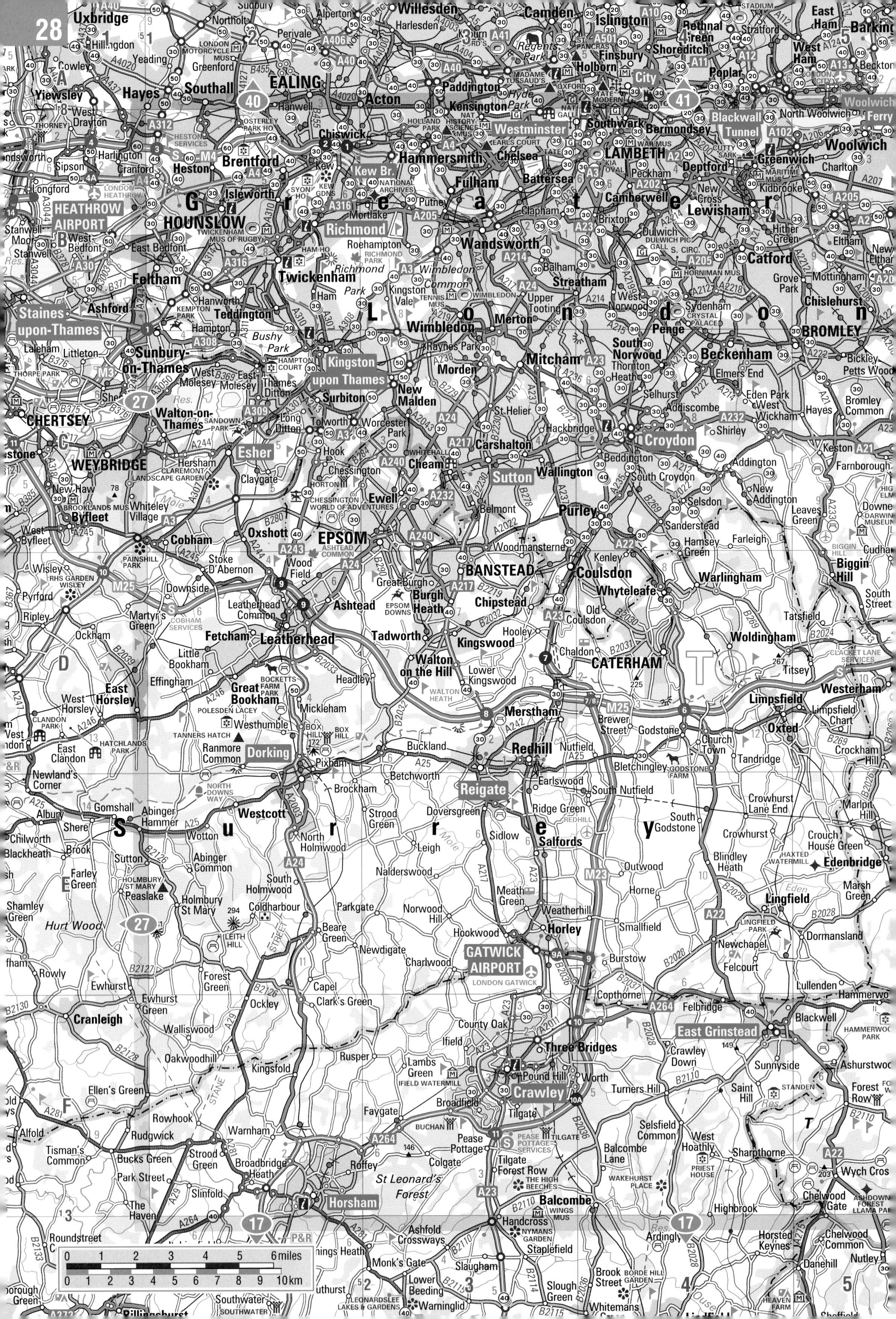
Uxbridge
Hillingdon
Cowley
Yiewsley
West Drayton
Hayes
Southall
EALING
Acton
Willesden
Harlesden
Perivale
Northolt
Greenford
Camden
Islington
Bethnal Green
Stratford
East Ham
Barking
Shoreditch
Finsbury
Holborn
City
Poplar
West Ham
Beckton
Paddington
Kensington
Hyde Park
Westminster
Southwark
Bermondsey
Blackwall Tunnel
Woolwich
North Woolwich
Chiswick
Hammersmith
Chelsea
LAMBETH
Greenwich
Deptford
Harlington
Sipson
Cranford
Heston
Brentford
Kew Br.
Fulham
Battersea
Peckham
Charlton
Longford
HEATHROW AIRPORT
Isleworth
HOUNSLOW
Richmond
Putney
Mortlake
Wandsworth
Clapham
Brixton
Camberwell
New Cross
Lewisham
Kidbrooke
Stanwell
West Bedfont
East Bedfont
Roehampton
Wimbledon Common
Balham
Dulwich
Catford
Eltham
Feltham
Twickenham
Kingston Vale
Streatham
Grove Park
Mottingham
Staines upon-Thames
Ashford
Hanworth
Teddington
Ham
Upper Tooting
Sydenham
Chislehurst
Laleham
Littleton
Sunbury-on-Thames
Hampton
Bushy Park
Wimbledon
Merton
Penge
BROMLEY
Kingston upon Thames
Raynes Park
Mitcham
South Norwood
Beckenham
Bickley
Petts Wood
West Molesey
East Molesey
Thames Ditton
Surbiton
New Malden
Morden
Thornton Heath
Elmers End
Selhurst
Eden Park
West Wickham
Hayes
Bromley Common
CHERTSEY
Walton-on-Thames
Long Ditton
Tolworth
Worcester Park
St Helier
Hackbridge
Addiscombe
Shirley
Croydon
Carshalton
Beddington
WEYBRIDGE
Esher
Hersham
Hook
Chessington
Cheam
Sutton
Wallington
South Croydon
Addington
Keston
Farnborough
Claygate
Ewell
Belmont
Purley
Selsdon
New Addington
New Haw
Whiteley Village
Byfleet
West Byfleet
Cobham
Oxshott
EPSOM
Woodmansterne
Sanderstead
Hamsey Green
Farleigh
Leaves Green
Downe
Wisley
Stoke D'Abernon
Wood Field
Great Burgh
BANSTEAD
Coulsdon
Kenley
Whyteleafe
Warlingham
Biggin Hill
Pyrford
Downside
Leatherhead Common
Ashtead
Burgh Heath
Chipstead
Old Coulsdon
Ripley
Martyr's Green
Fetcham
Leatherhead
Tadworth
Kingswood
Hooley
Tatsfield
Woldingham
Ockham
Little Bookham
Walton on the Hill
Lower Kingswood
Chaldon
CATERHAM
Titsey
Effingham
Headley
Great Bookham
West Horsley
East Horsley
Mickleham
Merstham
Brewer Street
Godstone
Limpsfield
Westerham
Oxted
Limpsfield Chart
Westhumble
Ranmore Common
Dorking
Buckland
Redhill
Nutfield
Church Town
Crockham Hill
East Clandon
Newland's Corner
Pixham
Betchworth
Bletchingley
Tandridge
Brockham
Earlswood
South Nutfield
Reigate
Gomshall
Abinger Hammer
Albury
Westcott
Strood Green
Doversgreen
Ridge Green
Crowhurst Lane End
Marlpit Hill
Shere
Chilworth
Wotton
North Holmwood
Sidlow
Salfords
South Godstone
Crowhurst
Crouch House Green
Blackheath
Brook
Sutton
Abinger Common
Leigh
Blindley Heath
Edenbridge
Farley Green
Peaslake
Holmbury St Mary
South Holmwood
Nalderswood
Outwood
Horne
Marsh Green
Lingfield
Shamley Green
Coldharbour
Parkgate
Norwood Hill
Meath Green
Weatherhill
Smallfield
Dormansland
Hurt Wood
Beare Green
Hookwood
Horley
Newchapel
Newdigate
Charlwood
GATWICK AIRPORT
Burstow
Felcourt
Rowly
Ewhurst
Forest Green
Lullenden
Ewhurst Green
Ockley
Capel
Clark's Green
Copthorne
Felbridge
Blackwell
Cranleigh
Walliswood
County Oak
Ifield
Three Bridges
Crawley Down
East Grinstead
Oakwoodhill
Kingsfold
Rusper
Lambs Green
Pound Hill
Worth
Sunnyside
Ashurstwood
Ellen's Green
Turners Hill
Saint Hill
Forest Row
Broadfield
Crawley
Tilgate
Faygate
Rowhook
Warnham
Pease Pottage
Selsfield Common
West Hoathly
Sharpthorne
Alfold
Rudgwick
Balcombe Lane
Wych Cross
Tisman's Common
Bucks Green
Strood Green
Colgate
Broadbridge Heath
Roffey
Tilgate Forest Row
Park Street
Slinfold
St Leonard's Forest
Highbrook
Chelwood Gate
The Haven
Horsham
Balcombe
Handcross
Roundstreet
Ashfold Crossways
Staplefield
Ardingly
Horsted Keynes
Chelwood Common
Monk's Gate
Slaugham
Danehill
Nutley
Lower Beeding
Brook Street
Slough Green
Southwater
Warninglid
Whitemans
0 1 2 3 4 5 6 miles
0 1 2 3 4 5 6 7 8 9 10 km

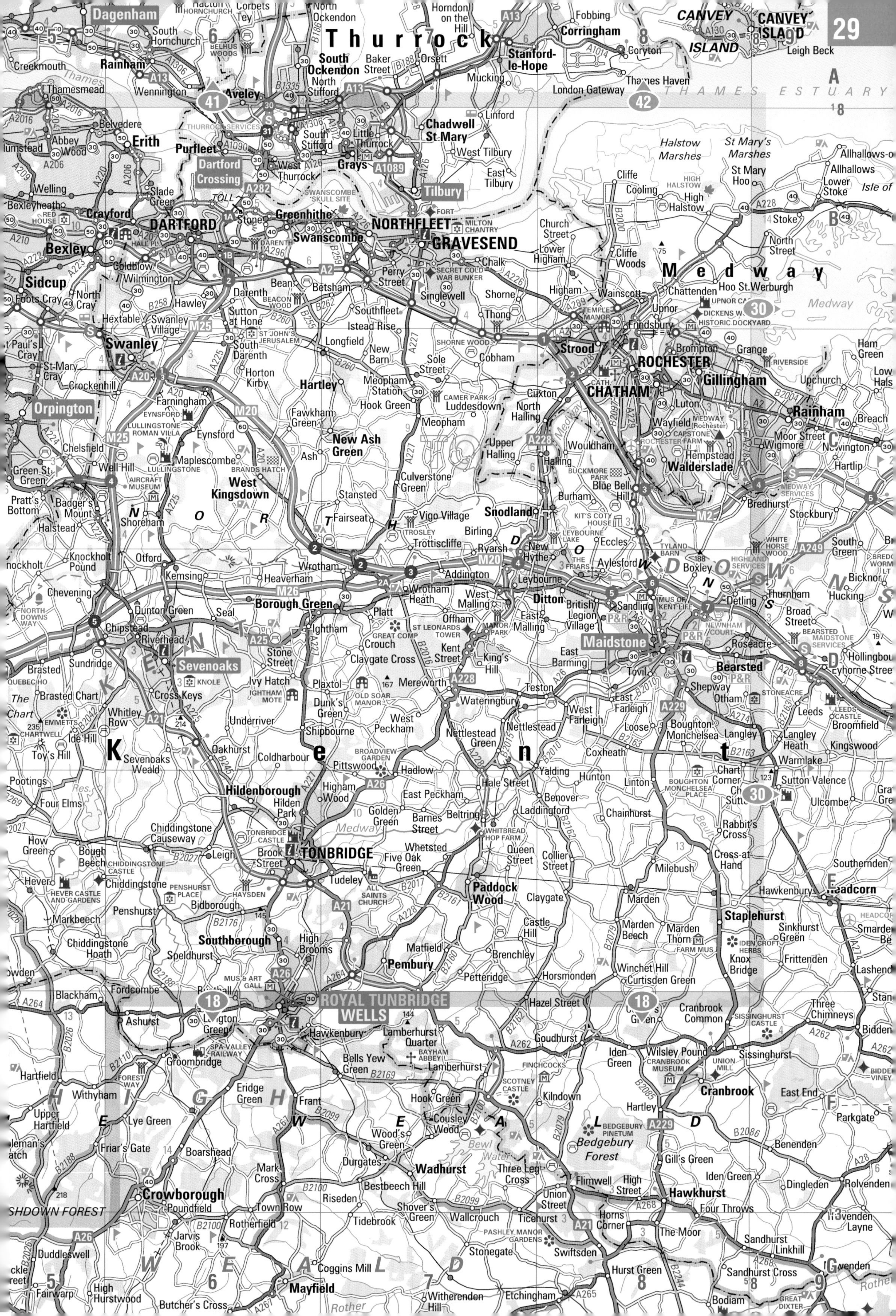
Dagenham
Hornchurch
Corbets Tey
North Ockendon
Horndon on the Hill
Fobbing
Corringham
Canvey Island
Thurrock
South Hornchurch
Rainham
Creekmouth
Wennington
Aveley
South Ockendon
Baker Street
Orsett
Stanford-le-Hope
Coryton
Mucking
Leigh Beck
Thamesmead
North Stifford
London Gateway
Thames Haven
Thames Estuary
Belvedere
Erith
Purfleet
Thurrock Services
Chadwell St Mary
Linford
Abbey Wood
Dartford Crossing
South Stifford
Little Thurrock
Grays
West Thurrock
West Tilbury
East Tilbury
Tilbury
Halstow Marshes
St Mary's Marshes
Allhallows-on-Sea
Allhallows
Welling
Bexleyheath
Slade Green
Swanscombe Skull Site
Cliffe
Cooling
High Halstow
St Mary Hoo
Lower Stoke
Isle of Grain
Crayford
Dartford
Stone
Greenhithe
Northfleet
Milton Chantry
Gravesend
Stoke
North Street
Bexley
Swanscombe
Chalk
Church Street
Lower Higham
Cliffe Woods
Sidcup
Coldblow
Wilmington
Bean
Betsham
Perry Street
Secret Cold War Bunker
Singlewell
Shorne
Higham
Wainscott
Chattenden
Hoo St.Werburgh
Medway
Foots Cray
North Cray
Hawley
Darenth
Beacon Wood
Southfleet
Thong
Temple Manor
Upnor
Upnor Castle
Dickens World
Historic Dockyard
Hextable
Swanley Village
Sutton at Hone
St John's Jerusalem
Istead Rise
Frindsbury
Swanley
South Darenth
Longfield
New Barn
Shorne Wood
Cobham
Strood
Rochester
Brompton
Grange
Ham Green
St Paul's Cray
St Mary Cray
Horton Kirby
Sole Street
Riverside
Crockenhill
Hartley
Meopham Station
Camer Park
Luddesdown
Cuxton
Chatham
Gillingham
Upchurch
Lower Halstow
Orpington
Farningham
Eynsford
Fawkham Green
Hook Green
North Halling
Luton
Rainham
Lullingstone Roman Villa
Meopham
Wayfield
Medway (Rochester)
Capstone Farm
Breach
Chelsfield
Maplescombe
New Ash Green
Upper Halling
Wouldham
Rochester Farm
Moor Street
Newington
Well Hill
Lullingstone
Brands Hatch
Ash
Halling
Hempstead
Wigmore
Green Street Green
Aircraft Museum
West Kingsdown
Culverstone Green
Buckmore Park
Walderslade
Hartlip
Pratt's Bottom
Badger's Mount
Shoreham
Stansted
Snodland
Burham
Blue Bell Hill
Medway Services
Bredhurst
Halstead
North
Fairseat
Vigo Village
Trosley
Birling
Kit's Coty House
Stockbury
Trottiscliffe
Ryarsh
Leybourne Lake
New Hythe
Eccles
Tyland Barn
White Horse Wood
South Green
Knockholt Pound
Knockholt
Otford
Kemsing
Heaverham
Wrotham
Addington
The Friars
Aylesford
Boxley
Highland Services
Bicknor
Chevening
Borough Green
Wrotham Heath
West Malling
Leybourne
Ditton
British Legion Village
Sandling
Mus of Kent Life
Detling
Thurnham
Hucking
North Downs Way
Dunton Green
Seal
Platt
Offham
Manor Park
East Malling
Broad Street
Chipstead
Riverhead
Ightham
Great Comp
St Leonards Tower
Kent Street
Newnham Court
Roseacre
Bearsted
Maidstone Services
Hollingbourne
Brasted
Sundridge
Sevenoaks
Stone Street
Crouch
Claygate Cross
King's Hill
East Barming
Maidstone
Tovil
Bearsted
Eyhorne Street
Quebec House
Brasted Chart
The Chart
Knole
Ivy Hatch
Ightham Mote
Plaxtol
Old Soar Manor
Mereworth
Teston
East Farleigh
Shepway
Otham
Stoneacre
Leeds
Leeds Castle
Emmetts
Whitley Row
Cross Keys
Dunk's Green
Wateringbury
West Farleigh
Loose
Boughton Monchelsea
Langley
Broomfield
Chartwell
Ide Hill
Underriver
West Peckham
Shipbourne
Nettlestead Green
Nettlestead
Langley Heath
Kingswood
Toy's Hill
Kent
Sevenoaks Weald
Oakhurst
Coldharbour
Broadview Garden
Pittswood
Hadlow
Coxheath
Yalding
Hunton
Linton
Chart Corner
Chart Sutton
Warmlake
Sutton Valence
Pootings
Hildenborough
Higham Wood
Hale Street
Benover
Boughton Monchelsea Place
Ulcombe
Four Elms
Hilden Park
East Peckham
Golden Green
Barnes Street
Beltring
Laddingford
Chainhurst
Rabbit's Cross
Chiddingstone Causeway
Medway
Whitbread Hop Farm
How Green
Bough Beech
Tonbridge Castle
Leigh
Brook Street
Tonbridge
Whetsted
Five Oak Green
Queen Street
Collier Street
Cross-at-Hand
Chiddingstone Castle
Hever
Chiddingstone
Penshurst Place
Haysden
Tudeley
All Saints Church
Paddock Wood
Claygate
Milebush
Southernden
Hever Castle and Gardens
Penshurst
Bidborough
Marden
Hawkenbury
Headcorn
Markbeech
Staplehurst
Castle Hill
Marden Beech
Marden Thorn
Farm Mus
Sinkhurst Green
Iden Croft Herbs
Smarden
Chiddingstone Hoath
Southborough
High Brooms
Matfield
Brenchley
Knox Bridge
Frittenden
Speldhurst
Pembury
Winchet Hill
Curtisden Green
Lashenden
Petteridge
Horsmonden
Mus & Art Gall
Fordcombe
Blackham
Royal Tunbridge Wells
Hazel Street
Cranbrook Common
Three Chimneys
Ashurst
Langton Green
Hawkenbury
Lamberhurst Quarter
Goudhurst
Sissinghurst Castle
Biddenden
Spa Valley Railway
Groombridge
Bayham Abbey
Bells Yew Green
Lamberhurst
Iden Green
Wilsley Pound
Cranbrook Museum
Union Mill
Sissinghurst
Hartfield
Forest Way
Finchcocks
Scotney Castle
Kilndown
Biddenden Vineyard
Withyham
Eridge Green
Frant
Hook Green
Cranbrook
East End
Upper Hartfield
Lye Green
Cousley Wood
Bedgebury Pinetum
Bedgebury Forest
Hartley
Parkgate
Wood's Green
Bewl Water
Benenden
Friar's Gate
Boarshead
Mark Cross
Durgates
Wadhurst
Three Leg Cross
Gill's Green
Iden Green
Flimwell
High Street
Dingleden
Rolvenden
Crowborough
Bestbeech Hill
Union Street
Hawkhurst
Ashdown Forest
Poundfield
Town Row
Riseden
Shover's Green
Wallcrouch
Ticehurst
Four Throws
Rolvenden Layne
Jarvis Brook
Rotherfield
Tidebrook
Pashley Manor Gardens
Horns Corner
The Moor
Swiftsden
Sandhurst
Linkhill
Duddleswell
Stonegate
Coggins Mill
Hurst Green
Sandhurst Cross
Newenden
Fairwarp
High Hurstwood
Mayfield
Witherenden Hill
Etchingham
Bodiam
Great Dixter
Butcher's Cross
Rother

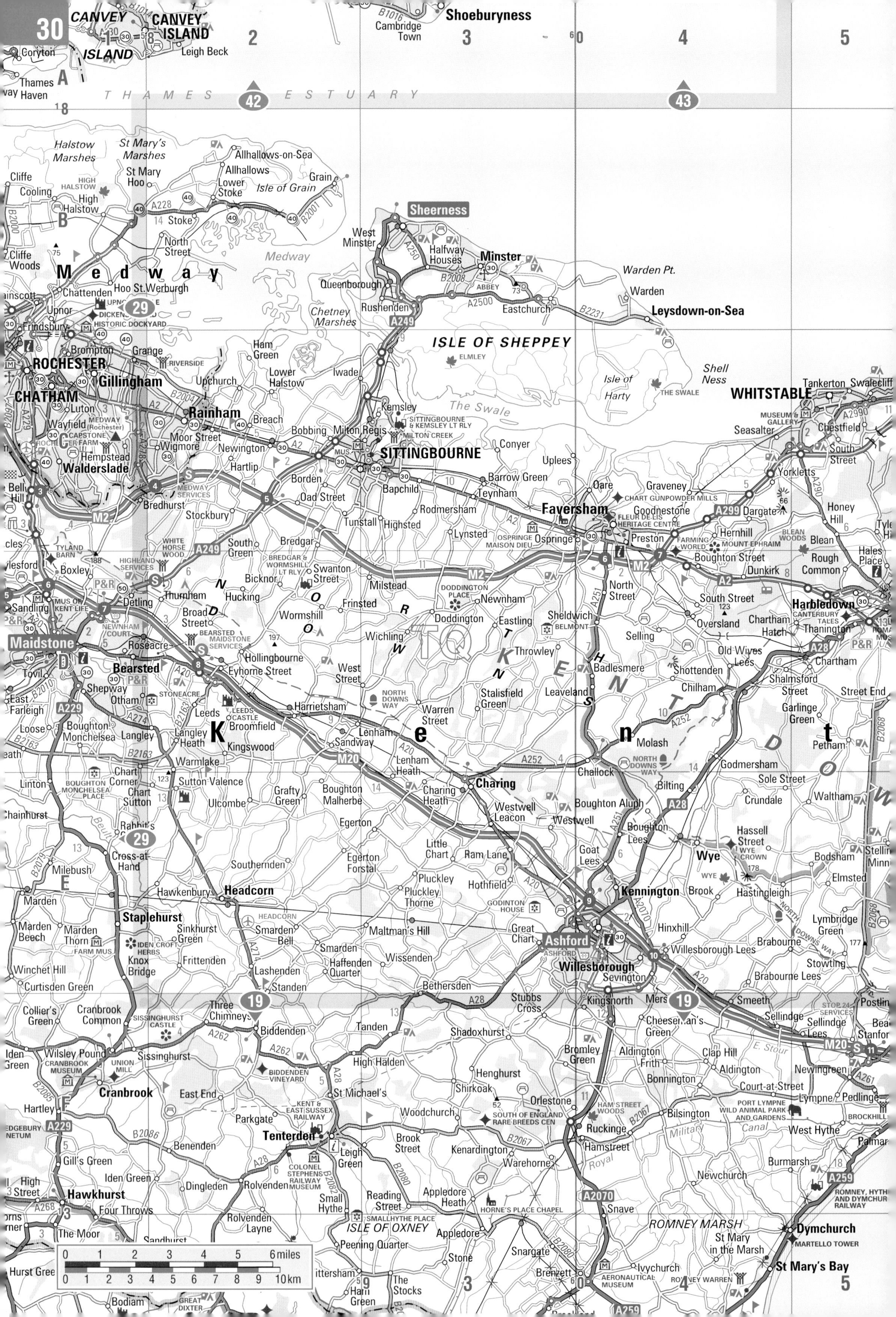
CANVEY ISLAND
Coryton
Thames Haven
Leigh Beck
Cambridge Town
Shoeburyness
THAMES ESTUARY
42
43
Halstow Marshes
St Mary's Marshes
Allhallows-on-Sea
Allhallows
Grain
Isle of Grain
Lower Stoke
St Mary Hoo
Cliffe
Cooling
HIGH HALSTOW
High Halstow
Stoke
North Street
Cliffe Woods
Medway
Sheerness
West Minster
Halfway Houses
Minster
ABBEY
Warden Pt.
Warden
Leysdown-on-Sea
Queenborough
Rushenden
Eastchurch
Chetney Marshes
ISLE OF SHEPPEY
ELMLEY
Isle of Harty
THE SWALE
Shell Ness
Chattenden
Hoo St.Werburgh
Upnor
HISTORIC DOCKYARD
Frindsbury
Brompton
Grange
RIVERSIDE
Ham Green
Upchurch
Lower Halstow
Iwade
ROCHESTER
Gillingham
CHATHAM
Rainham
Luton
Wayfield
Breach
Kemsley
SITTINGBOURNE & KEMSLEY LT RLY
MILTON CREEK
The Swale
Tankerton
Swalecliffe
WHITSTABLE
Seasalter
Chestfield
South Street
Moor Street
Wigmore
Newington
Bobbing
Milton Regis
SITTINGBOURNE
Conyer
Hempstead
Walderslade
Hartlip
Borden
Uplees
Barrow Green
Bapchild
Teynham
Oare
Graveney
Yorkletts
Bell Hill
Bredhurst
MEDWAY SERVICES
Oad Street
Rodmersham
Faversham
CHART GUNPOWDER MILLS
Goodnestone
Dargate
Honey Hill
Stockbury
Tunstall
Highsted
FLEUR DE LIS HERITAGE CENTRE
Hernhill
Lynsted
OSPRINGE MAISON DIEU
Ospringe
Preston
Blean
FARMING WORLD
MOUNT EPHRAIM
BLEAN WOODS
WHITE HORSE WOOD
South Green
Bredgar
Boughton Street
Rough Common
Hales Place
TYLAND BARN
BREDGAR & WORMSHILL LT RLY
Swanton Street
Dunkirk
Aylesford
Boxley
HIGHLAND SERVICES
Bicknor
Milstead
North Street
South Street
Harbledown
Thurnham
Hucking
DODDINGTON PLACE
Newnham
Sandling
MUS OF KENT LIFE
Detling
Broad Street
Frinsted
Doddington
Eastling
Sheldwich
BELMONT
Oversland
Chartham Hatch
CANTERBURY TALES
Thanington
Wormshill
NEWNHAM COURT
BEARSTED MAIDSTONE SERVICES
Maidstone
Roseacre
Wichling
Throwley
Selling
Old Wives Lees
Chartham
Bearsted
Hollingbourne
West Street
Badlesmere
Shottenden
Shalmsford Street
Tovil
Eyhorne Street
NORTH DOWNS WAY
Stalisfield Green
Leaveland
Chilham
Street End
East Farleigh
Shepway
Otham
STONEACRE
LEEDS CASTLE
Harrietsham
Warren Street
Garlinge Green
Loose
Boughton Monchelsea
Langley
Leeds
Broomfield
Lenham
Sandway
Molash
Petham
Langley Heath
Kingswood
Kent
Warmlake
Lenham Heath
A252
Challock
NORTH DOWNS WAY
Godmersham
Linton
Chart Corner
BOUGHTON MONCHELSEA PLACE
Chart Sutton
Sutton Valence
Grafty Green
Boughton Malherbe
Charing Heath
Charing
Bilting
Sole Street
Crundale
Waltham
Ulcombe
Westwell Leacon
Boughton Aluph
Westwell
Chainhurst
Rabbit's Cross
Cross-at-Hand
Egerton
Boughton Lees
Hassell Street
WYE CROWN
Little Chart
Ram Lane
Goat Lees
Wye
Bodsham
Milebush
Southernden
Egerton Forstal
Pluckley
Hothfield
Brook
Elmsted
Marden
Hawkenbury
Headcorn
Pluckley Thorne
Kennington
Hastingleigh
Staplehurst
HEADCORN
GODINTON HOUSE
Great Chart
Hinxhill
Lymbridge Green
Marden Beech
Marden Thorn
FARM MUS
IDEN CROFT HERBS
Sinkhurst Green
Smarden Bell
Maltman's Hill
Ashford
Willesborough Lees
Brabourne
Knox Bridge
Frittenden
Smarden
Haffenden Quarter
Wissenden
Willesborough
Sevington
Stowting
Winchet Hill
Curtisden Green
Lashenden
Standen
Bethersden
Brabourne Lees
Collier's Green
Cranbrook Common
SISSINGHURST CASTLE
Three Chimneys
Stubbs Cross
Kingsnorth
Mersham
Smeeth
Postling
Sellindge
Biddenden
Tanden
Shadoxhurst
Cheeseman's Green
STOP 24 SERVICES
Sellindge Lees
Stanford
Iden Green
Wilsley Pound
CRANBROOK MUSEUM
UNION MILL
Sissinghurst
BIDDENDEN VINEYARD
High Halden
Bromley Green
Aldington Frith
Clap Hill
Aldington
Newingreen
Cranbrook
Henhurst
Shirkoak
Bonnington
Court-at-Street
Hartley
East End
St Michael's
Orlestone
HAM STREET WOODS
PORT LYMPNE WILD ANIMAL PARK AND GARDENS
Lympne
Pedlinge
BEDGEBURY PINETUM
KENT & EAST SUSSEX RAILWAY
Parkgate
Woodchurch
SOUTH OF ENGLAND RARE BREEDS CEN
Ruckinge
Bilsington
BROCKHILL
West Hythe
Tenterden
Leigh Green
Brook Street
Kenardington
Hamstreet
Royal Military Canal
Gill's Green
Benenden
COLONEL STEPHENS RAILWAY MUSEUM
Warehorne
Burmarsh
Iden Green
Dingleden
Rolvenden
Small Hythe
Reading Street
Appledore Heath
Newchurch
ROMNEY, HYTHE AND DYMCHURCH RAILWAY
High Street
Hawkhurst
Four Throws
SMALLHYTHE PLACE
HORNE'S PLACE CHAPEL
Snave
The Moor
Rolvenden Layne
ISLE OF OXNEY
Appledore
ROMNEY MARSH
Dymchurch
MARTELLO TOWER
Sandhurst
Peening Quarter
Snargate
St Mary in the Marsh
Stone
Ivychurch
Hurst Green
Wittersham
The Stocks
Brenzett
AERONAUTICAL MUSEUM
ROMNEY WARREN
St Mary's Bay
Bodiam
GREAT DIXTER
Ham Green
0 1 2 3 4 5 6 miles
0 1 2 3 4 5 6 7 8 9 10 km

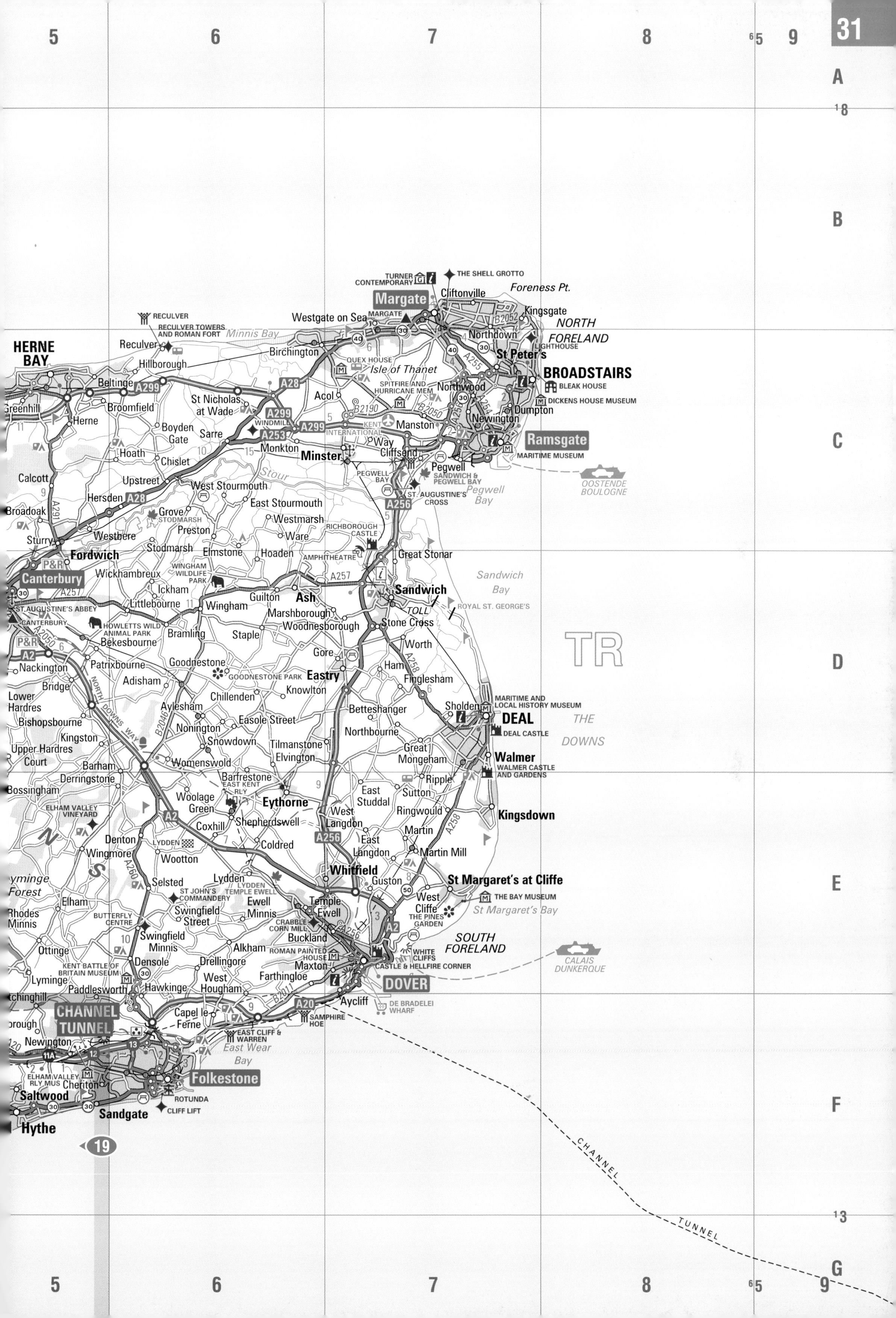

5 6 7 8 6 5 9

A

8

B

5 6 7 8 6 5 9

G

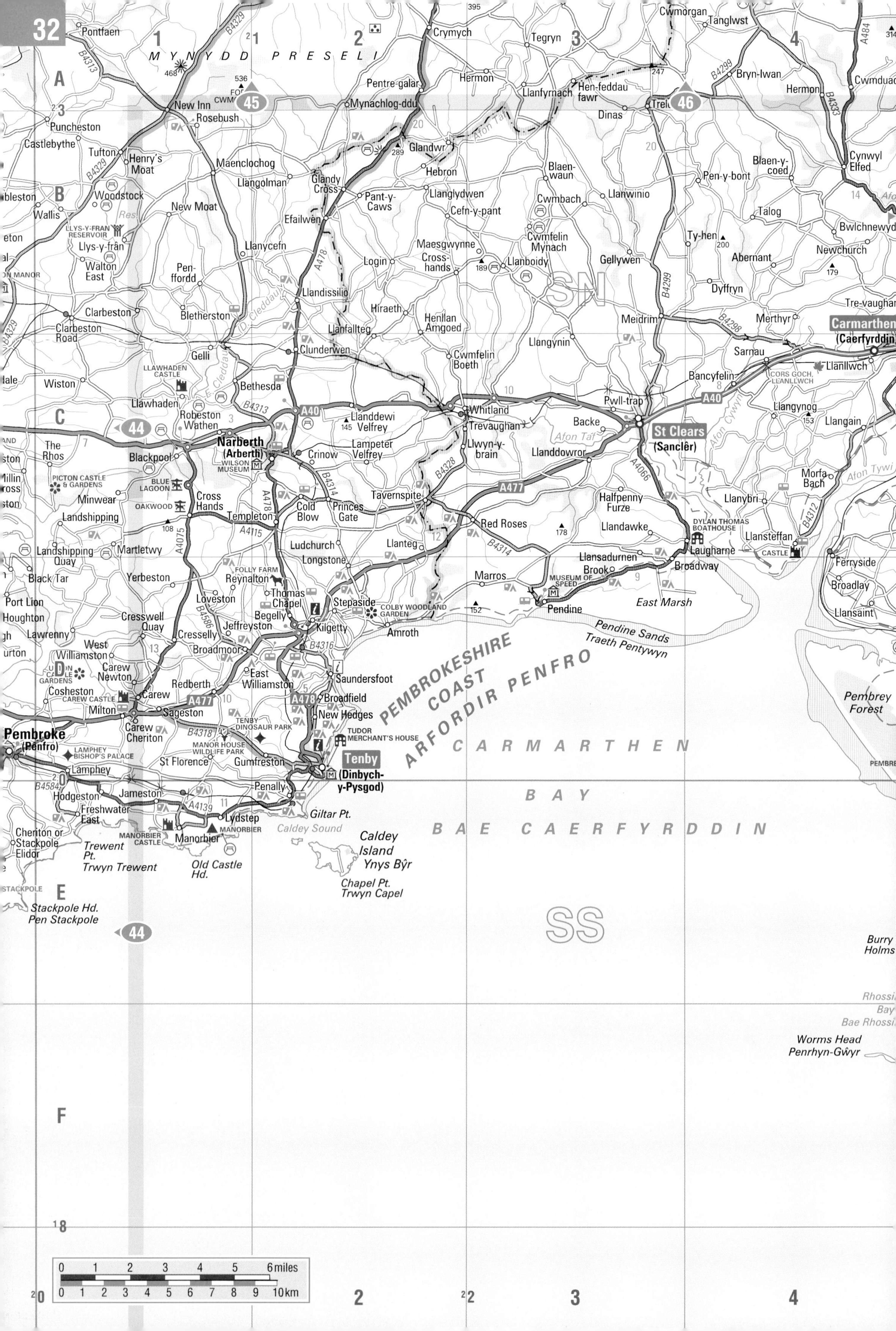
MYNYDD PRESELI
PEMBROKESHIRE COAST
ARFORDIR PENFRO
CARMARTHEN BAY
BAE CAERFYRDDIN
SN
SS
Pembroke (Penfro)
Narberth (Arberth)
Tenby (Dinbych-y-Pysgod)
St Clears (Sanclêr)
Carmarthen (Caerfyrddin)
Whitland
Laugharne
Pendine
Saundersfoot
Kilgetty
Amroth
Manorbier
Lamphey
Carew
Crymych
Llanboidy
Meidrim
Clunderwen
Efailwen
Maenclochog
Puncheston
Letterston
Rosebush
New Inn
Pontfaen
Llangolman
Llys-y-frân
Walton East
Clarbeston Road
Wiston
Llawhaden
Robeston Wathen
Templeton
Begelly
Jeffreyston
Cresselly
East Williamston
Redberth
Sageston
St Florence
Gumfreston
Penally
Lydstep
Jameston
Hodgeston
Freshwater East
Stackpole
Stackpole Hd.
Pen Stackpole
Old Castle Hd.
Caldey Island
Ynys Bŷr
Chapel Pt.
Trwyn Capel
Giltar Pt.
Caldey Sound
Trewent Pt.
Trwyn Trewent
Pendine Sands
Traeth Pentywyn
East Marsh
Marros
Llansadurnen
Llandawke
Red Roses
Tavernspite
Llanteg
Ludchurch
Longstone
Stepaside
Princes Gate
Cold Blow
Lampeter Velfrey
Llanddewi Velfrey
Crinow
Llandissilio
Llanfallteg
Henllan Amgoed
Cwmfelin Boeth
Llangynin
Llanddowror
Backe
Pwll-trap
Bancyfelin
Sarnau
Llanllwch
Llangynog
Llangain
Llanybri
Llansteffan
Ferryside
Broadlay
Llansaint
Pembrey Forest
Burry Holms
Worms Head
Penrhyn-Gŵyr
Rhossili Bay
Bae Rhossili
Tegryn
Hermon
Llanfyrnach
Glandwr
Hebron
Blaenwaun
Cwmbach
Llanwinio
Cwmfelin Mynach
Gellywen
Dinas
Trelech
Cynwyl Elfed
Bryn-Iwan
Cwmduad
Talog
Bwlchnewydd
Newchurch
Abernant
Dyffryn
Tre-vaughan
Merthyr
Pen-y-bont
Blaen-y-coed
Ty-hen
Cwmorgan
Tanglwst
Mynachlog-ddu
Pentre-galar
Glandy Cross
Pant-y-Caws
Llanglydwen
Cefn-y-pant
Maesgwynne
Cross-hands
Login
Hiraeth
Llanycefn
New Moat
Pen-ffordd
Bletherston
Gelli
Bethesda
Clarbeston
Castlebythe
Tufton
Henry's Moat
Woodstock
Wallis
Blackpool
Minwear
Landshipping
Landshipping Quay
Martletwy
Black Tar
Yerbeston
Reynalton
Loveston
Thomas Chapel
Cresswell Quay
Lawrenny
West Williamston
Carew Newton
Cosheston
Milton
Carew Cheriton
Broadmoor
New Hedges
Broadfield
Cross Hands
Halfpenny Furze
Brook
Broadway
Morfa Bach
Llwyn-y-brain
Trevaughan
Port Lion
Houghton
The Rhos
Cheriton or Stackpole Elidor
LLYS-Y-FRAN RESERVOIR
LLAWHADEN CASTLE
PICTON CASTLE & GARDENS
BLUE LAGOON
OAKWOOD
WILSON MUSEUM
FOLLY FARM
COLBY WOODLAND GARDEN
MUSEUM OF SPEED
DYLAN THOMAS BOATHOUSE
CASTLE
CORS GOCH, LLANLLWCH
CAREW CASTLE
TENBY DINOSAUR PARK
MANOR HOUSE WILDLIFE PARK
LAMPHEY BISHOP'S PALACE
TUDOR MERCHANT'S HOUSE
MANORBIER CASTLE
A40
A477
A478
A4075
A4115
A4066
A4139
B4313
B4314
B4316
B4318
B4328
B4329
B4298
B4299
B4312
B4333
B4584
B4586
44
45
46
0 1 2 3 4 5 6 miles
0 1 2 3 4 5 6 7 8 9 10 km

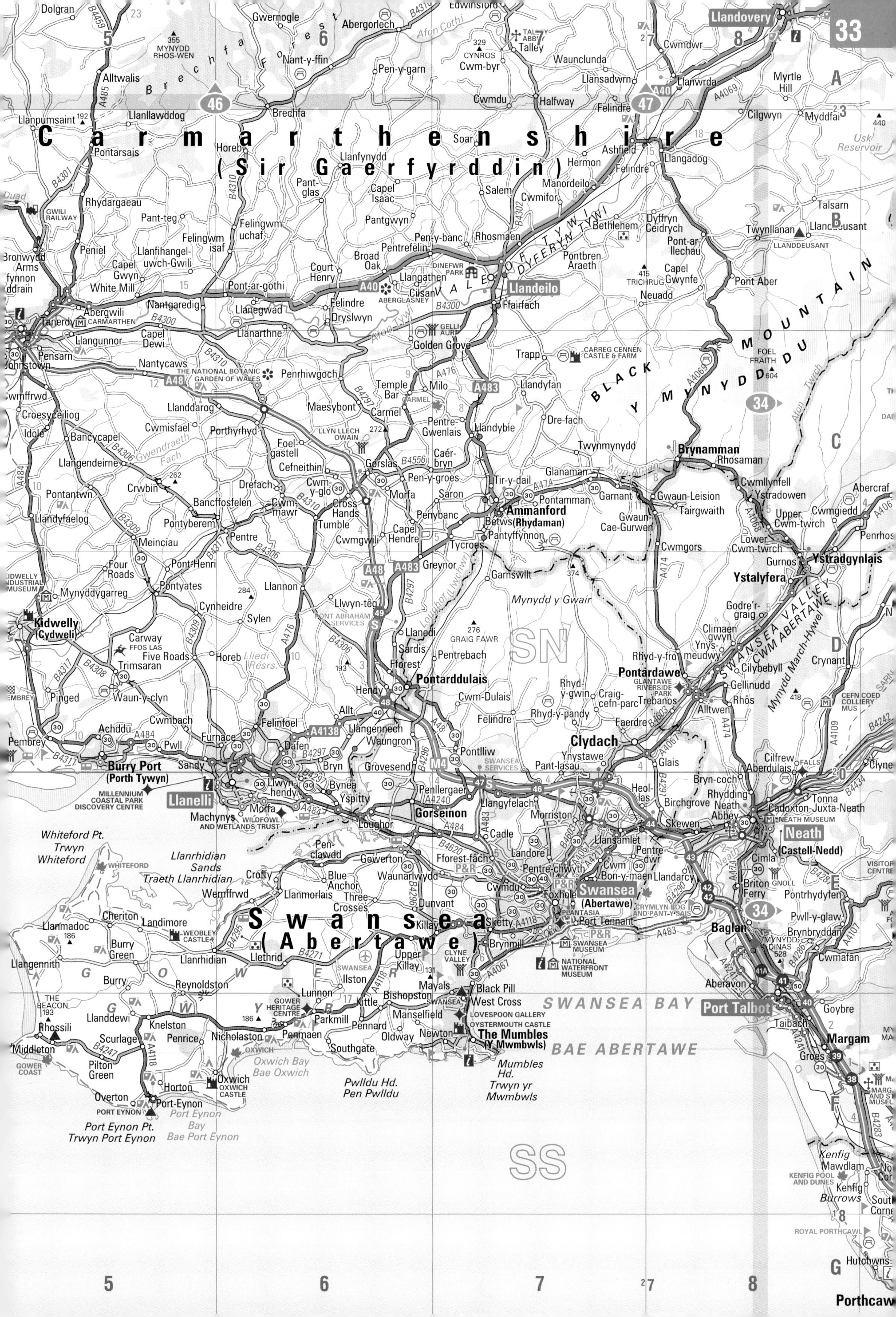
Carmarthenshire
(Sir Gaerfyrddin)
Swansea
(Abertawe)
Brechfa Forest
Dolgran
Gwernogle
Abergorlech
Afon Cothi
Edwinsford
Talley
Llandovery
Cwmdwr
355 MYNYDD RHOS-WEN
Nant-y-ffin
Pen-y-garn
329 CYNROS
Cwm-byr
Waunclunda
Llansadwrn
Llanwrda
Myrtle Hill
Alltwalis
46
Brechfa
Cwmdu
Halfway
Felindre
47
Cilgwyn
Myddfai
Llanpumsaint
Llanllawddog
Soar
Ashfield
Llangadog
Usk Reservoir
Pontarsais
Horeb
Llanfynydd
Hermon
Felindre
Pant-glas
Capel Isaac
Salem
Manordeilo
Cwmifor
Rhydargaeau
GWILI RAILWAY
Pant-teg
Felingwm uchaf
Pantgwyn
Bethlehem
Dyffryn Ceidrych
Talsarn
Felingwm isaf
Pen-y-banc
Rhosmaen
Twynllanan
Llanddeusant
Bronwydd Arms
Peniel
Llanfihangel-uwch-Gwili
Pentrefelin
Broad Oak
DINEFWR PARK
Vale of Tywi
Dyffryn Tywi
Pont-ar-llechau
Pontbren Araeth
Capel Gwyn
Court Henry
415 TRICHRUG
Capel Gwynfe
Pont Aber
White Mill
Pont-ar-gothi
Llangathen
Cilsan
Llandeilo
Neuadd
ABERGLASNEY
Abergwili
Nantgaredig
Felindre
Dryslwyn
B4300
Ffairfach
Tanerdy
CARMARTHEN
Llanegwad
Afon Tywi
Llanarthne
GELLI AUR
Golden Grove
Llangunnor
Capel Dewi
CARREG CENNEN CASTLE & FARM
Trapp
Black Mountain
Y Mynydd Du
FOEL FRAITH 604
Pensarn
Johnstown
Nantycaws
THE NATIONAL BOTANIC GARDEN OF WALES
Penrhiwgoch
Temple Bar
Milo
A483
Llandyfan
A48
Llanddarog
Maesybont
Carmel
34
Croesyceiliog
Cwmisfael
Porthyrhyd
Pentre-Gwenlais
Llandybie
Dre-fach
Idole
Bancycapel
Gwendraeth Fach
LLYN LLECH OWAIN
Foel-gastell
Twynmynydd
Brynamman
Rhosaman
Llangendeirne
Cefneithin
Gorslas
Caer-bryn
Glanaman
Afon Aman
262
Cwm-y-glo
Pen-y-groes
Tir-y-dail
Cwmllynfell
Abercraf
Pontantwn
Crwbin
Drefach
Morfa
Saron
Pontamman
Garnant
Gwaun-Leision
Ystradowen
Cwmgiedd
Bancffosfelen
Cwm-mawr
Cross Hands
Ammanford
Tairgwaith
Upper Cwm-twrch
Llandyfaelog
Pontyberem
Tumble
Penybanc
Betws (Rhydaman)
Gwaun-Cae-Gurwen
Penrhos
Pentre
Capel Hendre
Pantyffynnon
Lower Cwm-twrch
Meinciau
Cwmgwili
Tycroes
Cwmgors
Ystradgynlais
Four Roads
Pont-Henri
Greynor
Gurnos
Ystalyfera
KIDWELLY INDUSTRIAL MUSEUM
Pontyates
Garnswllt
374
Mynyddygarreg
284
Llannon
Mynydd y Gwair
Godre'r-graig
Kidwelly (Cydweli)
Cynheidre
Llwyn-têg
PONT ABRAHAM SERVICES
Swansea Valley
Cwm Abertawe
Sylen
Llanedi
276 GRAIG FAWR
Climaen gwyn
Ynys-meudwy
Carway
FFOS LAS
Sardis
Pentrebach
Rhyd-y-fro
Cilybebyll
Crynant
Five Roads
Horeb
Lliedi Resrs.
Fforest
Pontardawe
GLANTAWE RIVERSIDE PARK
Trimsaran
193
Pontarddulais
Rhyd-y-gwin
Gellinudd
Mynydd March-Hywel
Pinged
Waun-y-clyn
Hendy
Cwm-Dulais
Craig-cefn-parc
Trebanos
Rhôs
418
CEFN COED COLLIERY MUS
Cwmbach
Allt
Alltwen
Achddu
Felinfoel
Llangennech
Felindre
Rhyd-y-pandy
Faerdre
Pembrey
Pwll
Furnace
A4138
Waungron
Clydach
Cilfrew
Burry Port (Porth Tywyn)
Sandy
Dafen
Bryn
Grovesend
Pontlliw
M4
SWANSEA SERVICES
Ynystawe
Pant-lasau
Glais
Aberdulais
Clyne
MILLENNIUM COASTAL PARK DISCOVERY CENTRE
Llanelli
Llwyn-hendy
Bynea
Yspitty
Penllergaer
Llangyfelach
Heol-las
Bryn-coch
Rhydding
Neath Abbey
Cadoxton-Juxta-Neath
Machynys
Morfa
WILDFOWL AND WETLANDS TRUST
Loughor
Gorseinon
Morriston
Birchgrove
Skewen
NEATH MUSEUM
Neath (Castell-Nedd)
Whiteford Pt.
Trwyn Whiteford
WHITEFORD
Llanrhidian Sands
Traeth Llanrhidian
Pen-clawdd
Gowerton
Cadle
Fforest-fach
Landore
Llansamlet
Pentre-dwr
Cimla
Crofty
Blue Anchor
Waunarlwydd
Pentre-chwyth
Cwm
Bon-y-maen
Llandarcy
Briton Ferry
GNOLL
Pontrhydyfen
Wernffrwd
Llanmorlais
Three Crosses
Dunvant
Cwmdu
Foxhole
Swansea (Abertawe)
CRYMLYN BOG AND PANT-Y-SAIS
Cheriton
Landimore
Killay
Sketty
PLANTASIA
Port Tennant
Baglan
Pwll-y-glaw
Llanmadoc
WEOBLEY CASTLE
Burry Green
Llethrid
Brynmill
SWANSEA MUSEUM
Brynbryddan
MYNYDD DINAS 528
Llangennith
Llanrhidian
Gower
Upper Killay
CLYNE VALLEY
NATIONAL WATERFRONT MUSEUM
Cwmafan
Burry
Reynoldston
Ilston
SWANSEA
Black Pill
Aberavon
THE BEACON 193
Lunnon
GOWER HERITAGE CENTRE
Mayals
Bishopston
West Cross
Swansea Bay
Port Talbot
Goybre
Llanddewi
186
Parkmill
Kittle
Manselfield
LOVESPOON GALLERY
OYSTERMOUTH CASTLE
Taibach
Rhossili
Knelston
Penrice
Nicholaston
Penmaen
Pennard
Oldway
Newton
The Mumbles (Y Mwmbwls)
Bae Abertawe
Margam
Middleton
Scurlage
OXWICH
Southgate
Groes
GOWER COAST
Pilton Green
Oxwich Bay
Bae Oxwich
Mumbles Hd.
Trwyn yr Mwmbwls
Oxwich
OXWICH CASTLE
Pwlldu Hd.
Pen Pwlldu
Horton
Overton
PORT EYNON
Port-Eynon
Port Eynon Bay
Bae Port Eynon
Port Eynon Pt.
Trwyn Port Eynon
SN
SS
Kenfig
Mawdlam
KENFIG POOL AND DUNES
Kenfig Burrows
ROYAL PORTHCAWL
Hutchwns
Porthcawl
A
B
C
D
E
F
G
5
6
7
8

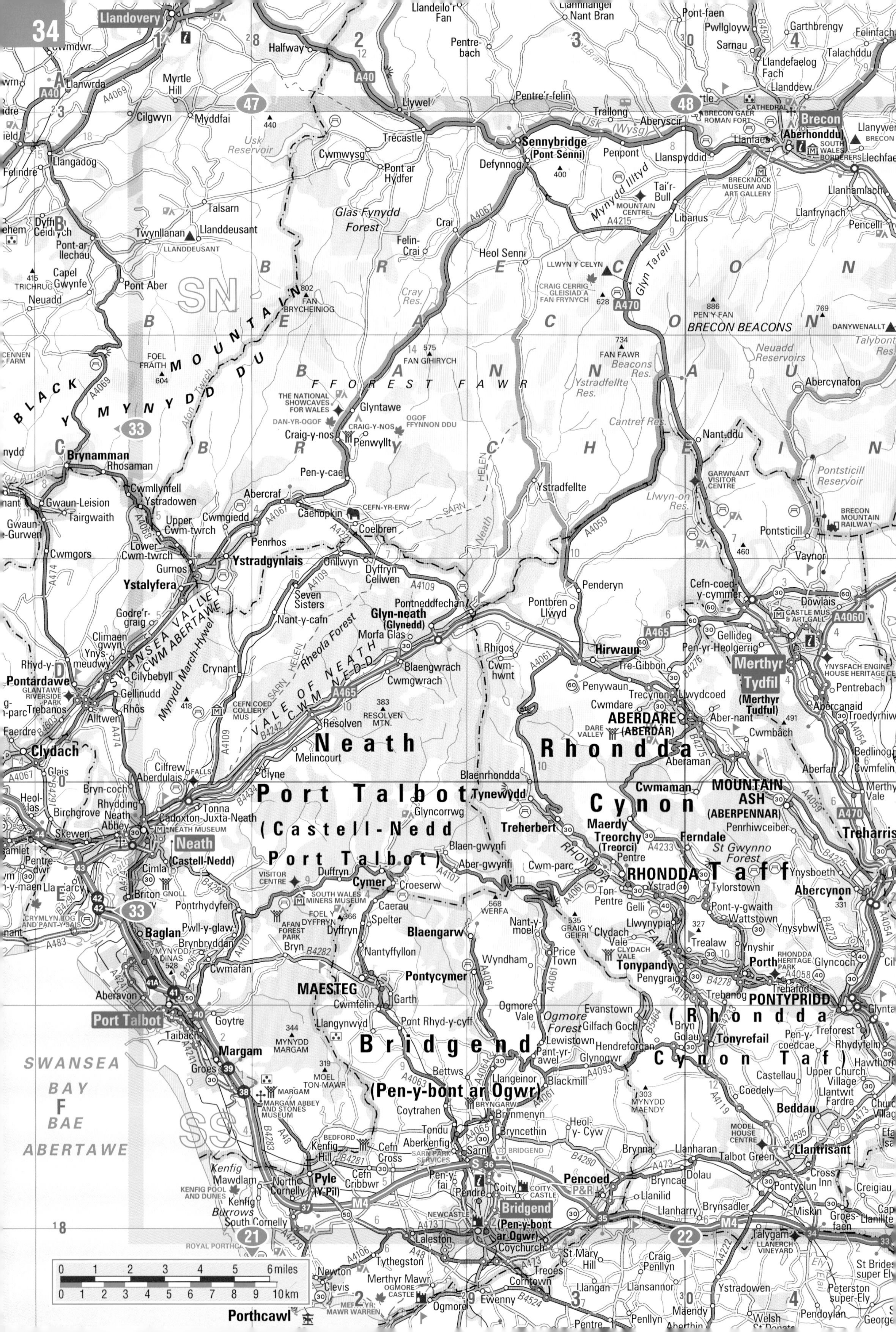

Llandovery
Halfway
Llandeilo'r Fan
Nant Bran
Pont-faen
Pwllgloyw
Garthbrengy
Felinfach
Sarnau
Talachddu
Llandefaelog Fach
Llanddew
Myrtle Hill
Llywel
Pentre-bach
Pentre'r-felin
Trallong
Aberyscir
BRECON GAER ROMAN FORT
CATHEDRAL
Brecon
(Aberhonddu)
Llanywern
Cilgwyn
Myddfai
Usk Reservoir
Trecastle
Sennybridge
(Pont Senni)
Defynnog
Penpont
Llanspyddid
Llanfaes
Llechfaen
Llangadog
Cwmwysg
Pont ar Hydfer
BRECKNOCK MUSEUM AND ART GALLERY
Llanhamlach
Felindre
Talsarn
Glas Fynydd Forest
Crai
Mynydd Illtyd
Tai'r-Bull
MOUNTAIN CENTRE
Libanus
Llanfrynach
Pencelli
Twynllanan
Llanddeusant
Felin-Crai
Heol Senni
LLWYN Y CELYN
Glyn Tarell
Pont-ar-llechau
Capel Gwynfe
TRICHRUG
Pont Aber
Neuadd
FAN BRYCHEINIOG
CRAIG CERRIG GLEISIAD A FAN FRYNYCH
Cray Res.
PEN Y FAN
BRECON BEACONS
DANYWENALLT
Talybont Res.
Neuadd Reservoirs
FAN FAWR
Beacons Res.
Ystradfellte Res.
FAN GIHIRYCH
FOEL FRAITH
BLACK MOUNTAIN
Y MYNYDD DU
FFOREST FAWR
THE NATIONAL SHOWCASES FOR WALES
DAN-YR-OGOF
Glyntawe
CRAIG-Y-NOS
OGOF FFYNNON DDU
Craig-y-nos
Penwyllt
Abercynafon
Cantref Res.
Nant-ddu
Brynamman
Rhosaman
Pen-y-cae
Ystradfellte
GARWNANT VISITOR CENTRE
Llwyn-on Res.
Pontsticill Reservoir
Cwmllynfell
Ystradowen
Abercraf
Caehopkin
CEFN-YR-ERW
Gwaun-Leision
Tairgwaith
Gwaun-Cae-Gurwen
Upper Cwm-twrch
Cwmgiedd
Coelbren
BRECON MOUNTAIN RAILWAY
Pontsticill
Penrhos
Cwmgors
Lower Cwm-twrch
Ystradgynlais
Onllwyn
Dyffryn Cellwen
Vaynor
Gurnos
Penderyn
Cefn-coed-y-cymmer
Ystalyfera
Seven Sisters
Pontneddfechan
Pontbren Llwyd
Dowlais
CASTLE MUS. & ART GALL.
Godre'r-graig
Nant-y-cafn
Glyn-neath
(Glynedd)
Morfa Glas
Hirwaun
Gellideg
Pen-yr-Heolgerrig
Climaen gwyn
Ynys-meudwy
SWANSEA VALLEY
CWM ABERTAWE
Mynydd March-Hywel
Rheola Forest
Rhigos
Cwm-hwnt
Tre-Gibbon
Merthyr Tydfil
(Merthyr Tudful)
YNYSFACH ENGINE HOUSE HERITAGE CENTRE
Rhyd-y-fro
Pontardawe
GLANTAWE RIVERSIDE PARK
Trebanos
Cilybebyll
Gellinudd
Crynant
Blaengwrach
Cwmgwrach
VALE OF NEATH
CWM NEDD
Penywaun
Trecynon
Llwydcoed
Pentrebach
Abercanaid
Troedyrhiw
Rhôs
Alltwen
CEFN COED COLLIERY MUS
Resolven
RESOLVEN MTN.
Cwmdare
ABERDARE
(ABERDÂR)
Aber-nant
DARE VALLEY
Cwmbach
Clydach
Neath
Melincourt
Rhondda
Aberaman
Bedlinog
Glais
Cilfrew
Aberdulais
FALLS
Clyne
Aberfan
Cwmfelin
Bryn-coch
Blaenrhondda
Tynewydd
Cwmaman
MOUNTAIN ASH
(ABERPENNAR)
Heol-las
Rhydding
Birchgrove
Neath Abbey
Tonna
Port Talbot
Cynon
Merthyr Vale
Cadoxton-Juxta-Neath
Glyncorrwg
Treherbert
Maerdy
Skewen
NEATH MUSEUM
Neath
(Castell-Nedd)
(Castell-Nedd Port Talbot)
Treorchy
(Treorci)
Ferndale
Penrhiwceiber
Treharris
Pentre-dwr
Cimla
Blaen-gwynfi
Aber-gwynfi
Cwm-parc
Pentre
St Gwynno Forest
Llansamlet
Duffryn
Cymer
Croeserw
RHONDDA
Ystrad
Taff
Ynysboeth
Briton Ferry
GNOLL
VISITOR CENTRE
SOUTH WALES MINERS MUSEUM
Ton-Pentre
Tylorstown
Abercynon
Pontrhydyfen
Caerau
WERFA
Gelli
Pont-y-gwaith
Llwynypia
Wattstown
CRYMLYN BOG AND PANT-Y-SAIS
Baglan
Pwll-y-glaw
AFAN FOREST PARK
FOEL Y DYFFRYN
Spelter
Dyffryn
Nant-y-moel
GRAIG Y GEIFRI
Clydach Vale
Ynysybwl
Brynbryddan
Bryn
Blaengarw
Trealaw
Ynyshir
MYNYDD DINAS
Nantyffyllon
Wyndham
Price Town
CLYDACH VALE
Porth
RHONDDA HERITAGE PARK
Glyncoch
Cwmafan
Tonypandy
Penygraig
Trehafod
MAESTEG
Pontycymer
Trebanog
PONTYPRIDD
Aberavon
Garth
Cwmfelin
Ogmore Vale
Evanstown
Glyntaff
Port Talbot
Goytre
Llangynwyd
Pont Rhyd-y-cyff
Ogmore Forest
Gilfach Goch
Bryn Golau
Tonyrefail
Treforest
Taibach
MYNYDD MARGAM
Bridgend
Lewistown
Hendreforgan
Pen-y-coedcae
Rhydyfelin
Margam
SWANSEA BAY
BAE ABERTAWE
Pant-yr-awel
Glynogwr
Hawthorn
Groes
MOEL TON-MAWR
Bettws
Llangeinor
Blackmill
Castellau
Upper Church Village
(Pen-y-bont ar Ogwr)
MARGAM
MARGAM ABBEY AND STONES MUSEUM
Coedely
Llantwit Fardre
BRYNGARW
MYNYDD MAENDY
Beddau
Coytrahen
Brynmenyn
Heol-y-Cyw
Tondu
Aberkenfig
Bryncethin
MODEL HOUSE CENTRE
BEDFORD
Kenfig Hill
Cefn Cross
SARN PARK SERVICES
Sarn
BRIDGEND
Brynna
Llanharan
Talbot Green
Llantrisant
Kenfig
Mawdlam
North Cornelly
Pyle
(Y Pîl)
Cefn Cribbwr
Pen-y-fai
Coity
COITY CASTLE
Pencoed
Bryncae
Dolau
Cross Inn
Pontyclun
Creigiau
KENFIG POOL AND DUNES
Kenfig Burrows
Pendre
P&R
Llanilid
NEWCASTLE
Bridgend
(Pen-y-bont ar Ogwr)
Llanharry
Brynsadler
Miskin
Groes-faen
South Cornelly
Laleston
Coychurch
Talygarn
LLANERCH VINEYARD
ROYAL PORTHCAWL
Tythegston
Treoes
St Mary Hill
Craig Penllyn
St Brides super Ely
Newton
Merthyr Mawr
Corntown
Llangan
Llansannor
Ystradowen
Peterston super-Ely
Clevis
OGMORE CASTLE
Ewenny
Maendy
Porthcawl
MERTHYR MAWR WARREN
Ogmore
Pendoylan
Welsh St Donats
Penllyn
Aberthin
George
A40
A4069
A4067
A470
A4059
A4109
A465
A4061
A4060
A4054
A4233
A4058
A4119
A4107
A4063
A4064
A4093
A4061
A48
A4065
B4281
A4229
A473
A4106
B4524
A4222
B4595
B4280
M4
47
48
33
21
22
SN
SS
0 1 2 3 4 5 6 miles
0 1 2 3 4 5 6 7 8 9 10 km

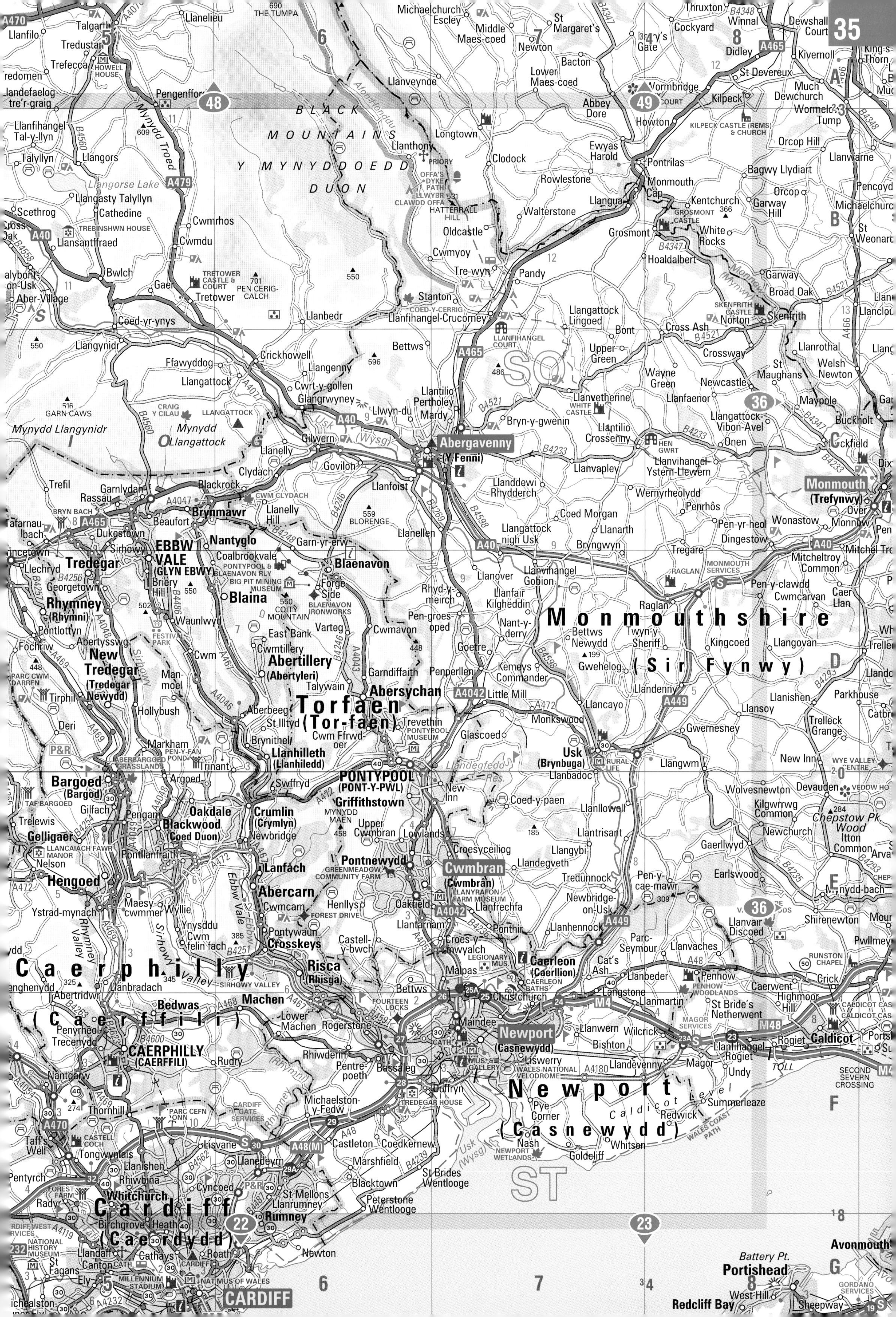
BLACK MOUNTAINS
Y MYNYDDOEDD DUON
Talgarth
Llangors
Llangorse Lake
Crickhowell
Abergavenny
(Y Fenni)
Monmouth
(Trefynwy)
Monmouthshire
(Sir Fynwy)
Torfaen
(Tor-faen)
Blaenavon
Abertillery
(Abertyleri)
Abersychan
Blaina
Brynmawr
EBBW VALE
(GLYN EBWY)
Tredegar
Rhymney
(Rhymni)
New Tredegar
(Tredegar Newydd)
Bargoed
(Bargod)
Blackwood
(Coed Duon)
Oakdale
Crumlin
(Crymlyn)
PONTYPOOL
(PONT-Y-PWL)
Griffithstown
Pontnewydd
Cwmbran
(Cwmbrân)
Usk
(Brynbuga)
Raglan
Abercarn
Crosskeys
Risca
(Rhisga)
Caerleon
(Caerllion)
Newport
(Casnewydd)
Caerphilly
(Caerffili)
CAERPHILLY
(CAERFFILI)
Bedwas
Machen
Hengoed
Gelligaer
Caldicot
Chepstow Pk. Wood
Portishead
Avonmouth
Battery Pt.
Redcliff Bay
Cardiff
(Caerdydd)
CARDIFF
Whitchurch
Rumney
Llandaff
SO
ST
Caldicot Level
SECOND SEVERN CROSSING
A40
A465
A4042
A449
A48
M4
M48
48
49
36
22
23

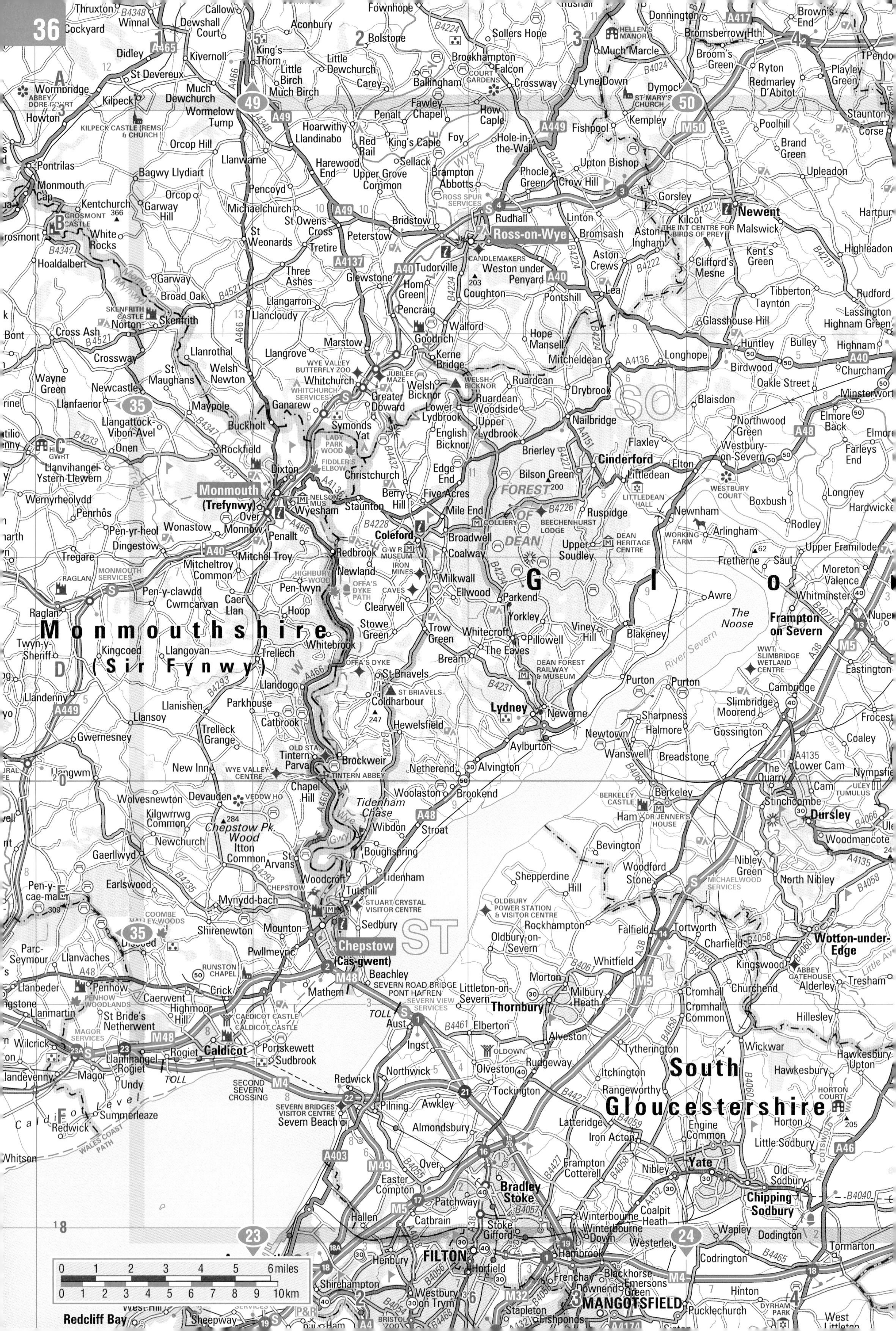
Monmouthshire
(Sir Fynwy)
Gloucestershire
South
Gloucestershire
Monmouth
(Trefynwy)
Chepstow
(Cas-gwent)
Ross-on-Wye
Coleford
Cinderford
Lydney
Newent
Caldicot
Thornbury
Yate
Chipping
Sodbury
Dursley
Wotton-under-
Edge
Bradley
Stoke
FILTON
MANGOTSFIELD
Frampton
on Severn
FOREST OF DEAN
River Severn
The
Noose
Raglan
Tintern
Parva
Newnham
Blakeney
Berkeley
Severn Beach
Portskewett
Magor
Redcliff Bay
SO
ST
0 1 2 3 4 5 6 miles
0 1 2 3 4 5 6 7 8 9 10 km

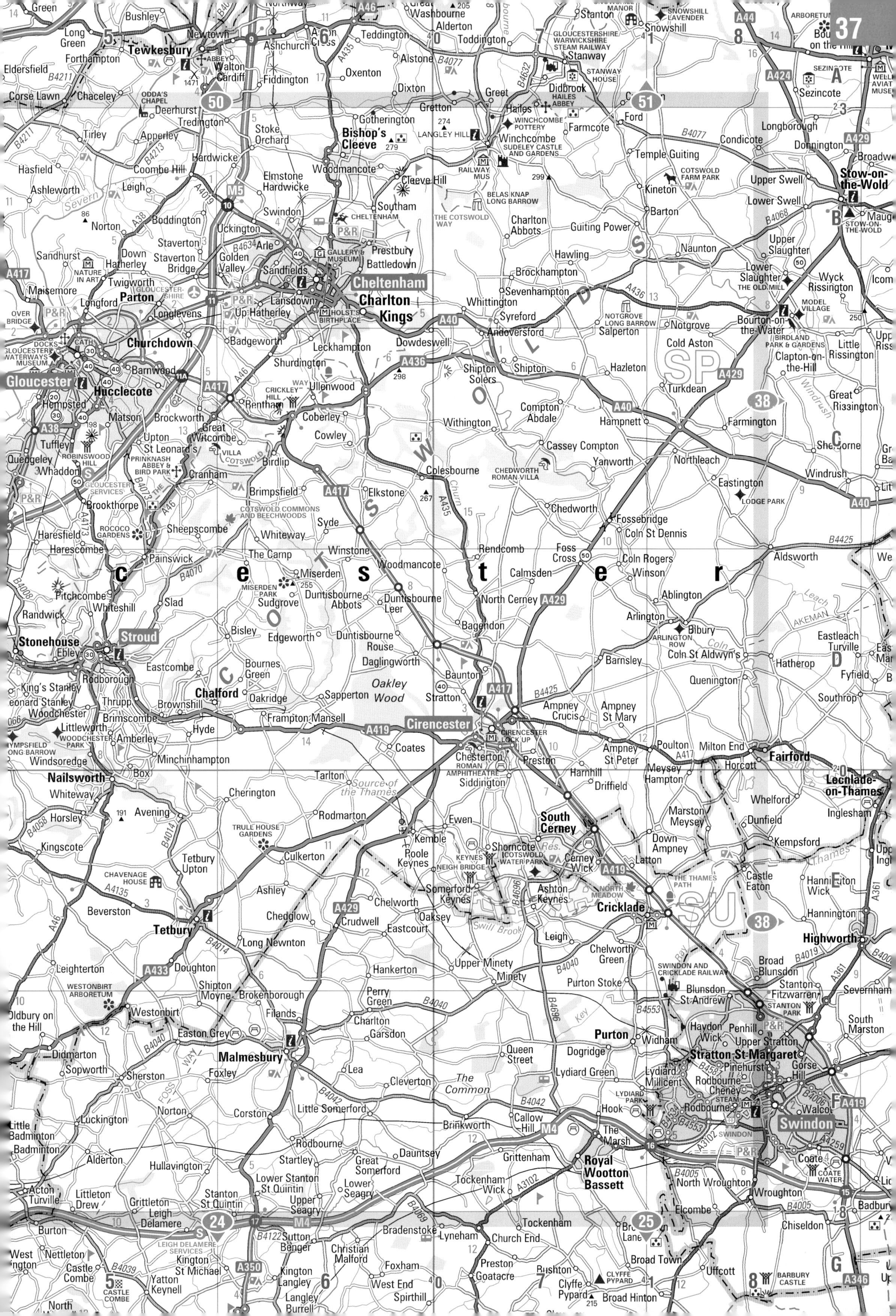

Green
Bushley
Long Green
Tewkesbury
Newtown
Ashchurch
Aston Cross
Teddington
Washbourne
Alderton
Toddington
Stanton
Snowshill
SNOWSHILL LAVENDER
GLOUCESTERSHIRE WARWICKSHIRE STEAM RAILWAY
Stanway
STANWAY HOUSE
ARBORETUM
Bourton-on-the-Hill
SEZINCOTE
Sezincote
Forthampton
Eldersfield
ABBEY
Walton Cardiff
Fiddington
Alstone
Oxenton
Dixton
Corse Lawn
Chaceley
ODDA'S CHAPEL
Deerhurst
Tredington
Gretton
Greet
Didbrook
HAILES ABBEY
Hailes
WINCHCOMBE POTTERY
Farmcote
Ford
Longborough
Condicote
Donnington
Tirley
Apperley
Stoke Orchard
Gotherington
Bishop's Cleeve
LANGLEY HILL
Winchcombe
SUDELEY CASTLE AND GARDENS
Temple Guiting
Hasfield
Coombe Hill
Hardwicke
Woodmancote
RAILWAY MUS
Cleeve Hill
COTSWOLD FARM PARK
Kineton
Upper Swell
Stow-on-the-Wold
Broadwell
Ashleworth
Leigh
Severn
Elmstone Hardwicke
BELAS KNAP LONG BARROW
Lower Swell
Norton
Boddington
Swindon
Southam
CHELTENHAM
THE COTSWOLD WAY
Charlton Abbots
Guiting Power
Barton
STOW-ON-THE-WOLD
Maugersbury
Uckington
Staverton
Sandhurst
Down Hatherley
Staverton Bridge
Golden Valley
Arle
GALLERY & MUSEUM
Prestbury
Battledown
Hawling
Naunton
Upper Slaughter
Lower Slaughter
THE OLD MILL
Wyck Rissington
Icomb
NATURE IN ART
Twigworth
Maisemore
Parton
GLOUCESTERSHIRE
Sandfields
Cheltenham
Lansdown
Charlton Kings
HOLST'S BIRTHPLACE
Brockhampton
Sevenhampton
Whittington
Syreford
NOTGROVE LONG BARROW
Notgrove
Salperton
Bourton-on-the-Water
MODEL VILLAGE
BIRDLAND PARK & GARDENS
Clapton-on-the-Hill
Little Rissington
Upper Rissington
OVER BRIDGE
Longford
Longlevens
Up Hatherley
DOCKS
CATH
GLOUCESTER WATERWAYS MUSEUM
Churchdown
Badgeworth
Leckhampton
Dowdeswell
Andoversford
Cold Aston
Gloucester
Barnwood
Hucclecote
Shurdington
Ullenwood
CRICKLEY HILL
Shipton Solers
Shipton
Hazleton
Turkdean
Great Rissington
Windrush
Hempsted
Matson
Brockworth
Bentham
Coberley
Compton Abdale
Hampnett
Farmington
Tuffley
Upton St Leonard's
Great Witcombe
Cowley
Withington
Cassey Compton
Yanworth
Northleach
Sherborne
Quedgeley
ROBINSWOOD HILL
PRINKNASH ABBEY & BIRD PARK
VILLA
COTSWOLD
Birdlip
Whaddon
Cranham
Colesbourne
CHEDWORTH ROMAN VILLA
Eastington
Windrush
GLOUCESTER SERVICES
Brimpsfield
Elkstone
Churn
LODGE PARK
Brookthorpe
COTSWOLD COMMONS AND BEECHWOODS
Chedworth
Fossebridge
Coln St Dennis
Haresfield
ROCOCO GARDENS
Sheepscombe
Whiteway
Syde
Harescombe
Painswick
The Camp
Winstone
Rendcomb
Foss Cross
Coln Rogers
Winson
Aldsworth
Woodmancote
Miserden
Calmsden
MISERDEN PARK
Duntisbourne Abbots
Duntisbourne Leer
North Cerney
Ablington
Pitchcombe
Whiteshill
Slad
Sudgrove
Bagendon
Arlington
Bibury
ARLINGTON ROW
Coln St Aldwyn's
Leach
AKEMAN
Eastleach Turville
Randwick
Bisley
Edgeworth
Duntisbourne Rouse
Stonehouse
Stroud
Ebley
Eastcombe
Bournes Green
Daglingworth
Barnsley
Hatherop
Fyfield
Quenington
Rodborough
Oakley Wood
Baunton
King's Stanley
Leonard Stanley
Chalford
Oakridge
Sapperton
Stratton
Ampney Crucis
Ampney St Mary
Southrop
Thrupp
Woodchester
Brownshill
Brimscombe
Frampton Mansell
Cirencester
CIRENCESTER LOCK UP
Littleworth
WOODCHESTER PARK
Amberley
Hyde
Coates
Chesterton
ROMAN AMPHITHEATRE
Preston
Ampney St Peter
Poulton
Milton End
Fairford
NYMPSFIELD LONG BARROW
Windsoredge
Minchinhampton
Horcott
Nailsworth
Box
Tarlton
Source of the Thames
Siddington
Harnhill
Driffield
Meysey Hampton
Lechlade-on-Thames
Whiteway
Cherington
Whelford
Inglesham
Horsley
Avening
Rodmarton
Ewen
South Cerney
Marston Meysey
Dunfield
Kingscote
TRULL HOUSE GARDENS
Kemble
Shorncote
KEYNES
COTSWOLD WATER PARK
Res.
Down Ampney
Kempsford
Tetbury Upton
Culkerton
Poole Keynes
NEIGH BRIDGE
Cerney Wick
Latton
Thames
CHAVENAGE HOUSE
Ashley
Somerford Keynes
Ashton Keynes
NORTH MEADOW
THE THAMES PATH
Castle Eaton
Hannington Wick
Beverston
Chelworth
Oaksey
Cricklade
Hannington
Tetbury
Chedglow
Crudwell
Eastcourt
Swill Brook
Leigh
Highworth
Long Newton
Chelworth Green
Ray
Doughton
Leighterton
Hankerton
Upper Minety
Minety
Purton Stoke
SWINDON AND CRICKLADE RAILWAY
Broad Blunsdon
Stanton Fitzwarren
Severnhampton
WESTONBIRT ARBORETUM
Shipton Moyne
Brokenborough
Perry Green
Blunsdon St Andrew
STANTON PARK
Oldbury on the Hill
Westonbirt
Filands
Charlton
Garsdon
Key
Haydon Wick
Penhill
South Marston
Easton Grey
Purton
Widham
Upper Stratton
Didmarton
Malmesbury
Queen Street
Dogridge
Stratton St Margaret
Pinehurst
Sopworth
Sherston
Foxley
Lea
Lydiard Green
Lydiard Millicent
Rodbourne Cheney
Gorse Hill
FOSS WAY
Cleverton
The Common
LYDIARD PARK
Hook
Rodbourne
STEAM
Walcot
Little Badminton
Luckington
Norton
Corston
Little Somerford
Brinkworth
Callow Hill
The Marsh
Swindon
Badminton
Alderton
Rodbourne
SWINDON
Coate
COATE WATER
Hullavington
Startley
Dauntsey
Great Somerford
Grittenham
Royal Wootton Bassett
North Wroughton
Acton Turville
Littleton Drew
Lower Stanton St Quintin
Lower Seagry
Tockenham Wick
Wroughton
Grittleton
Leigh Delamere
Stanton St Quintin
Upper Seagry
Elcombe
Badbury
Burton
LEIGH DELAMERE SERVICES
Sutton Benger
Bradenstoke
Lyneham
Tockenham
Church End
Broad Town Lane
Chiseldon
West Kington
Nettleton
Castle Combe
CASTLE COMBE
Kington St Michael
Kington Langley
Christian Malford
Foxham
Preston
Goatacre
Bushton
CLYFFE PYPARD
Broad Town
Uffcott
BARBURY CASTLE
Yatton Keynell
Langley Burrell
West End
Spirthill
Clyffe Pypard
Broad Hinton
North
C o t s w o l d s
C o t s w o l d s
SP
SU

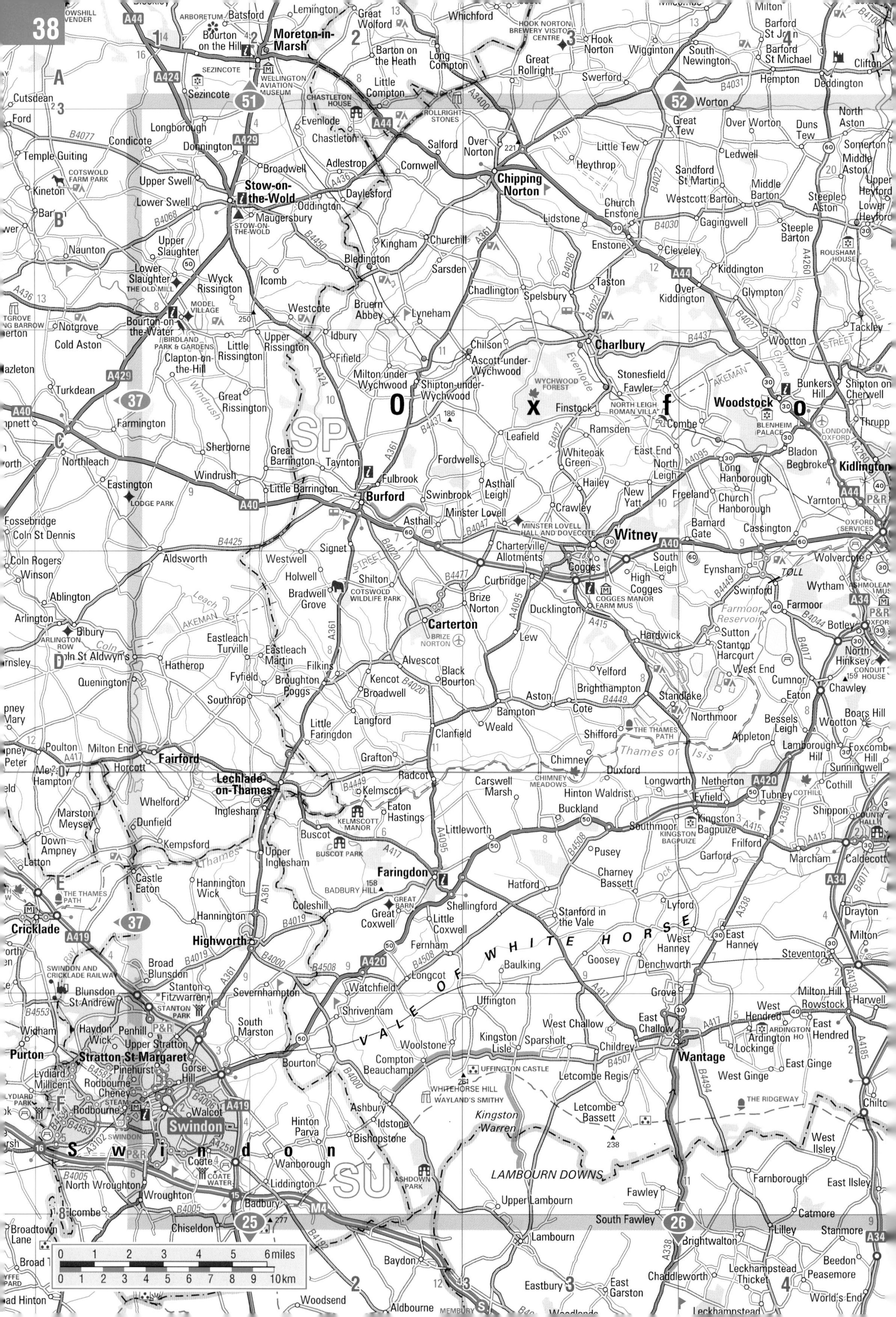
Moreton-in-Marsh
Stow-on-the-Wold
Chipping Norton
Charlbury
Woodstock
Kidlington
Witney
Burford
Carterton
Lechlade-on-Thames
Fairford
Faringdon
Highworth
Cricklade
Swindon
Wantage
Stratton St Margaret
Northleach
Bourton-on-the-Water
Batsford
Bourton on the Hill
Sezincote
Longborough
Condicote
Donnington
Broadwell
Upper Swell
Lower Swell
Maugersbury
Upper Slaughter
Lower Slaughter
Naunton
Wyck Rissington
Little Rissington
Great Rissington
Clapton-on-the-Hill
Cold Aston
Notgrove
Turkdean
Farmington
Sherborne
Windrush
Great Barrington
Little Barrington
Taynton
Fulbrook
Eastington
Aldsworth
Bibury
Coln St Aldwyn's
Hatherop
Quenington
Southrop
Eastleach Turville
Eastleach Martin
Fyfield
Filkins
Broughton Poggs
Kencot
Broadwell
Alvescot
Black Bourton
Langford
Little Faringdon
Clanfield
Grafton
Kelmscot
Eaton Hastings
Buscot
Inglesham
Upper Inglesham
Whelford
Dunfield
Kempsford
Castle Eaton
Hannington Wick
Hannington
Coleshill
Great Coxwell
Little Coxwell
Shellingford
Fernham
Longcot
Watchfield
Shrivenham
Uffington
Woolstone
Compton Beauchamp
Ashbury
Idstone
Bishopstone
Wanborough
Liddington
Badbury
Chiseldon
Hinton Parva
Bourton
South Marston
Stanton Fitzwarren
Blunsdon St Andrew
Broad Blunsdon
Sevenhampton
Kingston Lisle
Sparsholt
Childrey
Letcombe Regis
Letcombe Bassett
West Challow
East Challow
Grove
Denchworth
Goosey
Baulking
Stanford in the Vale
Hatford
Charney Bassett
Pusey
Buckland
Longworth
Hinton Waldrist
Carswell Marsh
Littleworth
Bampton
Aston
Cote
Weald
Shifford
Chimney
Duxford
Brize Norton
Curbridge
Ducklington
Lew
Yelford
Brighthampton
Standlake
Hardwick
Northmoor
Stanton Harcourt
Sutton
Eynsham
Swinford
Cassington
Yarnton
Wolvercote
Wytham
Farmoor
Botley
North Hinksey
Cumnor
Eaton
Appleton
Bessels Leigh
Wootton
Boars Hill
Chawley
Tubney
Fyfield
Kingston Bagpuize
Southmoor
Frilford
Garford
Marcham
Lyford
West Hanney
East Hanney
Steventon
Milton
Drayton
Ardington
East Hendred
West Hendred
Harwell
Rowstock
Lockinge
East Ginge
West Ginge
Farnborough
West Ilsley
East Ilsley
Catmore
Lilley
Brightwalton
Chaddleworth
Leckhampstead Thicket
Peasemore
Beedon
Stanmore
Fawley
South Fawley
Lambourn
Upper Lambourn
Eastbury
East Garston
Baydon
Aldbourne
Woodsend
Wroughton
North Wroughton
Coate
Purton
Lydiard Millicent
Haydon Wick
Penhill
Upper Stratton
Pinehurst
Gorse Hill
Rodbourne
Rodbourne Cheney
Walcot
Fossebridge
Coln St Dennis
Coln Rogers
Winson
Ablington
Arlington
Poulton
Milton End
Horcott
Meysey Hampton
Marston Meysey
Down Ampney
Latton
Cutsdean
Ford
Temple Guiting
Kineton
Longborough
Evenlode
Chastleton
Adlestrop
Oddington
Daylesford
Cornwell
Salford
Little Compton
Long Compton
Barton on the Heath
Great Wolford
Lemington
Whichford
Great Rollright
Hook Norton
Swerford
Wigginton
South Newington
Barford St John
Barford St Michael
Hempton
Deddington
Clifton
Milton
Worton
Over Worton
Great Tew
Little Tew
Duns Tew
North Aston
Middle Aston
Somerton
Upper Heyford
Lower Heyford
Steeple Aston
Middle Barton
Westcott Barton
Sandford St Martin
Ledwell
Heythrop
Over Norton
Church Enstone
Enstone
Lidstone
Gagingwell
Cleveley
Steeple Barton
Kiddington
Over Kiddington
Glympton
Tackley
Wootton
Taston
Spelsbury
Chadlington
Sarsden
Churchill
Kingham
Bledington
Icomb
Westcote
Idbury
Fifield
Bruern Abbey
Lyneham
Chilson
Ascott-under-Wychwood
Shipton-under-Wychwood
Milton under Wychwood
Leafield
Finstock
Stonesfield
Fawler
Ramsden
Combe
Whiteoak Green
East End
North Leigh
Hailey
Crawley
New Yatt
Freeland
Long Hanborough
Church Hanborough
Barnard Gate
Bladon
Begbroke
Bunkers Hill
Shipton on Cherwell
Thrupp
Fordwells
Asthall
Asthall Leigh
Swinbrook
Minster Lovell
Signet
Westwell
Holwell
Shilton
Bradwell Grove
Charterville Allotments
Cogges
High Cogges
South Leigh
VALE OF WHITE HORSE
LAMBOURN DOWNS
Kingston Warren
Thames or Isis
Farmoor Reservoir
Wychwood Forest
SP
SU
Oxford
0 1 2 3 4 5 6 miles
0 1 2 3 4 5 6 7 8 9 10 km

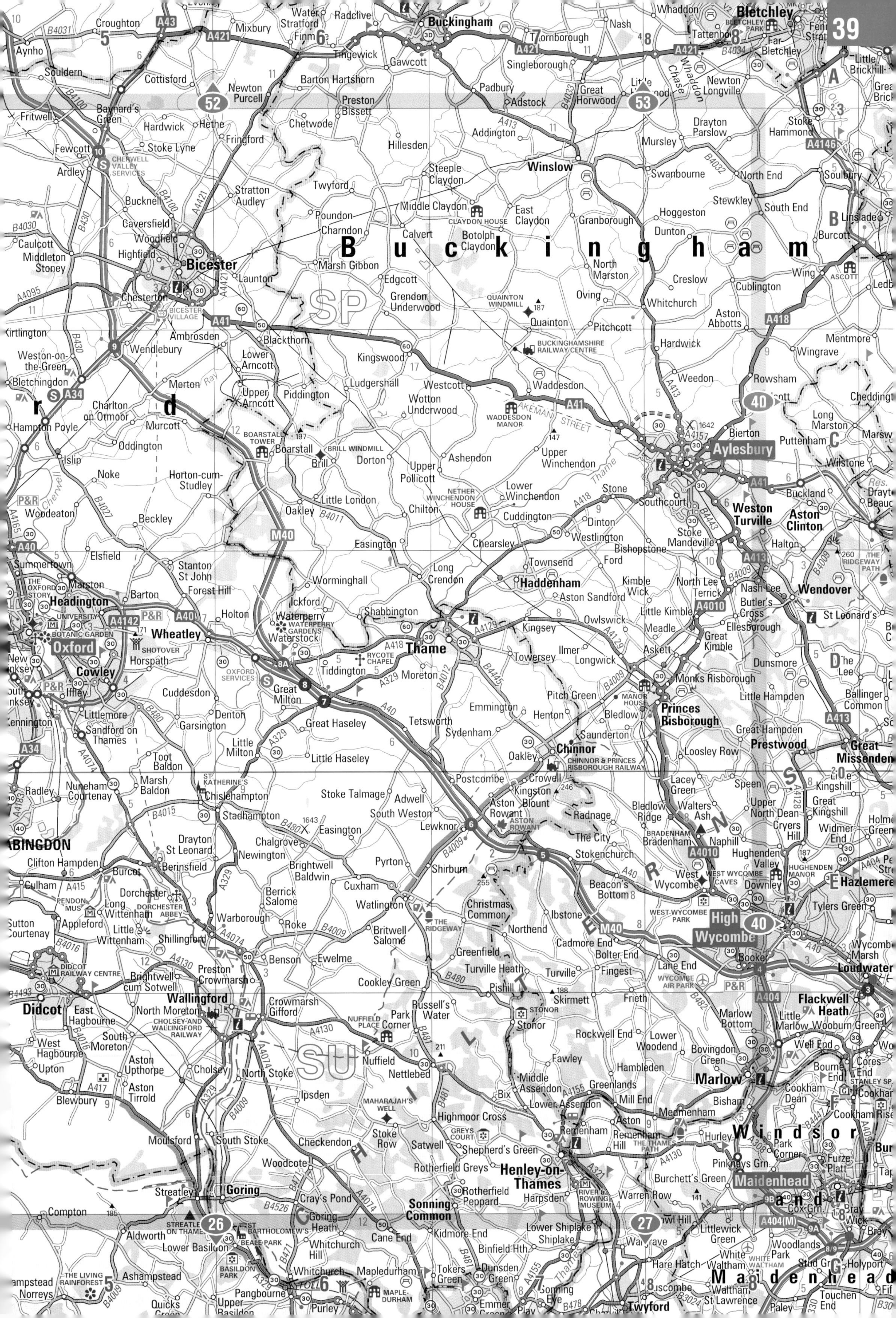
Buckingham
Bicester
Oxford
Aylesbury
Thame
Wheatley
Headington
Cowley
Winslow
Bletchley
Princes Risborough
Wendover
High Wycombe
Marlow
Henley-on-Thames
Wallingford
Didcot
Goring
Maidenhead
Windsor
Twyford
ABINGDON
Haddenham
Chinnor
Watlington
Loudwater
Great Missenden
Prestwood
Buckland
Weston Turville
Aston Clinton
Stoke Mandeville
Waddesdon
Quainton
Brill
Boarstall
Long Crendon
Chearsley
Cuddington
Great Milton
Tetsworth
Chalgrove
Benson
Nettlebed
Nuffield
Stoke Row
Sonning Common
Whitchurch
Pangbourne
Streatley
Cholsey
Blewbury
Kidlington
Islip
Woodeaton
Marston
Horspath
Garsington
Cuddesdon
Sandford on Thames
Kennington
Radley
Nuneham Courtenay
Dorchester
Berinsfield
Culham
Clifton Hampden
Sutton Courtenay
Appleford
Marsh Gibbon
Steeple Claydon
Middle Claydon
East Claydon
Botolph Claydon
Calvert
Charndon
Twyford
Poundon
Stratton Audley
Caversfield
Bucknell
Ardley
Fewcott
Fritwell
Souldern
Aynho
Croughton
Mixbury
Cottisford
Hardwick
Hethe
Fringford
Newton Purcell
Tingewick
Gawcott
Radclive
Water Stratford
Finmere
Barton Hartshorn
Preston Bissett
Chetwode
Hillesden
Padbury
Adstock
Addington
Thornborough
Singleborough
Nash
Whaddon
Great Horwood
Little Horwood
Mursley
Swanbourne
Drayton Parslow
Newton Longville
Stoke Hammond
Soulbury
Granborough
Hoggeston
Dunton
North Marston
Oving
Creslow
Whitchurch
Cublington
Wing
Aston Abbotts
Pitchcott
Hardwick
Weedon
Rowsham
Wingrave
Bierton
Puttenham
Long Marston
Wilstone
Halton
Stone
Dinton
Westlington
Ford
Bishopstone
Kimble Wick
North Lee
Terrick
Little Kimble
Great Kimble
Askett
Meadle
Owlswick
Kingsey
Towersey
Ilmer
Longwick
Monks Risborough
Saunderton
Bledlow
Henton
Emmington
Sydenham
Oakley
Crowell
Kingston Blount
Aston Rowant
Postcombe
Lewknor
Radnage
The City
Stokenchurch
Shirburn
Pyrton
Cuxham
Christmas Common
Northend
Ibstone
Turville
Turville Heath
Fingest
Skirmett
Frieth
Cadmore End
Bolter End
Lane End
Booker
Piddington
Ludgershall
Kingswood
Westcott
Wotton Underwood
Ashendon
Upper Pollicott
Dorton
Chilton
Oakley
Easington
Worminghall
Ickford
Shabbington
Waterperry
Waterstock
Tiddington
Moreton
Little Milton
Great Haseley
Little Haseley
Stadhampton
Chislehampton
Drayton St Leonard
Newington
Warborough
Shillingford
Brightwell Baldwin
Berrick Salome
Britwell Salome
Ewelme
Crowmarsh Gifford
North Stoke
South Stoke
Ipsden
Checkendon
Woodcote
Moulsford
Aston Tirrold
Aston Upthorpe
East Hagbourne
West Hagbourne
Upton
Compton
Aldworth
Ashampstead
Lower Basildon
Upper Basildon
Purley
Mapledurham
Caversham
Binfield Heath
Shiplake
Lower Shiplake
Harpsden
Remenham
Remenham Hill
Wargrave
Hurley
Medmenham
Bisham
Cookham
Cookham Dean
Bourne End
Wooburn Green
Flackwell Heath
Little Marlow
Hambleden
Fawley
Middle Assendon
Lower Assendon
Bix
Highmoor Cross
Rotherfield Greys
Rotherfield Peppard
Kidmore End
Cane End
Tokers Green
Dunsden Green
Sonning Eye
Pinkneys Green
Burchett's Green
Littlewick Green
White Waltham
Waltham St Lawrence
Hare Hatch
Holyport
Cox Green
Bray
Hughenden Valley
Naphill
Walters Ash
Lacey Green
Speen
Bradenham
Bledlow Ridge
Loosley Row
Great Hampden
Little Hampden
Dunsmore
Ellesborough
Butler's Cross
Nash Lee
St Leonard's
Ballinger Common
Kingshill
Cryers Hill
Widmer End
Downley
Tylers Green
Hazlemere
Holmer Green
Stanton St John
Forest Hill
Holton
Elsfield
Beckley
Noke
Horton-cum-Studley
Oddington
Charlton on Otmoor
Murcott
Merton
Ambrosden
Blackthorn
Lower Arncott
Upper Arncott
Wendlebury
Chesterton
Launton
Weston-on-the-Green
Bletchingdon
Hampton Poyle
Middleton Stoney
Caulcott
Kirtlington
Woodfield
Highfield
Edgcott
Grendon Underwood
Littlemore
Iffley
Toot Baldon
Marsh Baldon
Denton
Long Wittenham
Little Wittenham
Preston Crowmarsh
Brightwell-cum-Sotwell
North Moreton
South Moreton
Cray's Pond
Goring Heath
Whitchurch Hill
Cookley Green
Russell's Water
Park Corner
Greenfield
Pishill
Stonor
Rockwell End
Lower Woodend
Bovingdon Green
Warren Row
Woodlands Park
Touchen End
Paley Street
Little Brickhill
Fenny Stratford
Far Bletchley
Tattenhoe
North End
Stewkley
South End
Linslade
Burcott
Mentmore
Cheddington
Marsworth
Drayton Beauchamp
Townsend
Aston Sandford
Bletchley Park
Cherwell Valley Services
Oxford Services
Bicester Village
Claydon House
Quainton Windmill
Buckinghamshire Railway Centre
Waddesdon Manor
Boarstall Tower
Brill Windmill
Nether Winchendon House
Rycote Chapel
Waterperry Gardens
Shotover
Botanic Garden
University
Dorchester Abbey
Pendon Mus
Didcot Railway Centre
Cholsey and Wallingford Railway
Nuffield Place
Maharajah's Well
Greys Court
River & Rowing Museum
Basildon Park
Beale Park
The Living Rainforest
Chinnor & Princes Risborough Railway
Hughenden Manor
West Wycombe Caves
West Wycombe Park
Wycombe Air Park
Stonor
Ascott
The Ridgeway
The Thames Path
Aston Rowant
Akeman Street
Whaddon Chase
Buckingham
SP
SU
Chiltern Hills

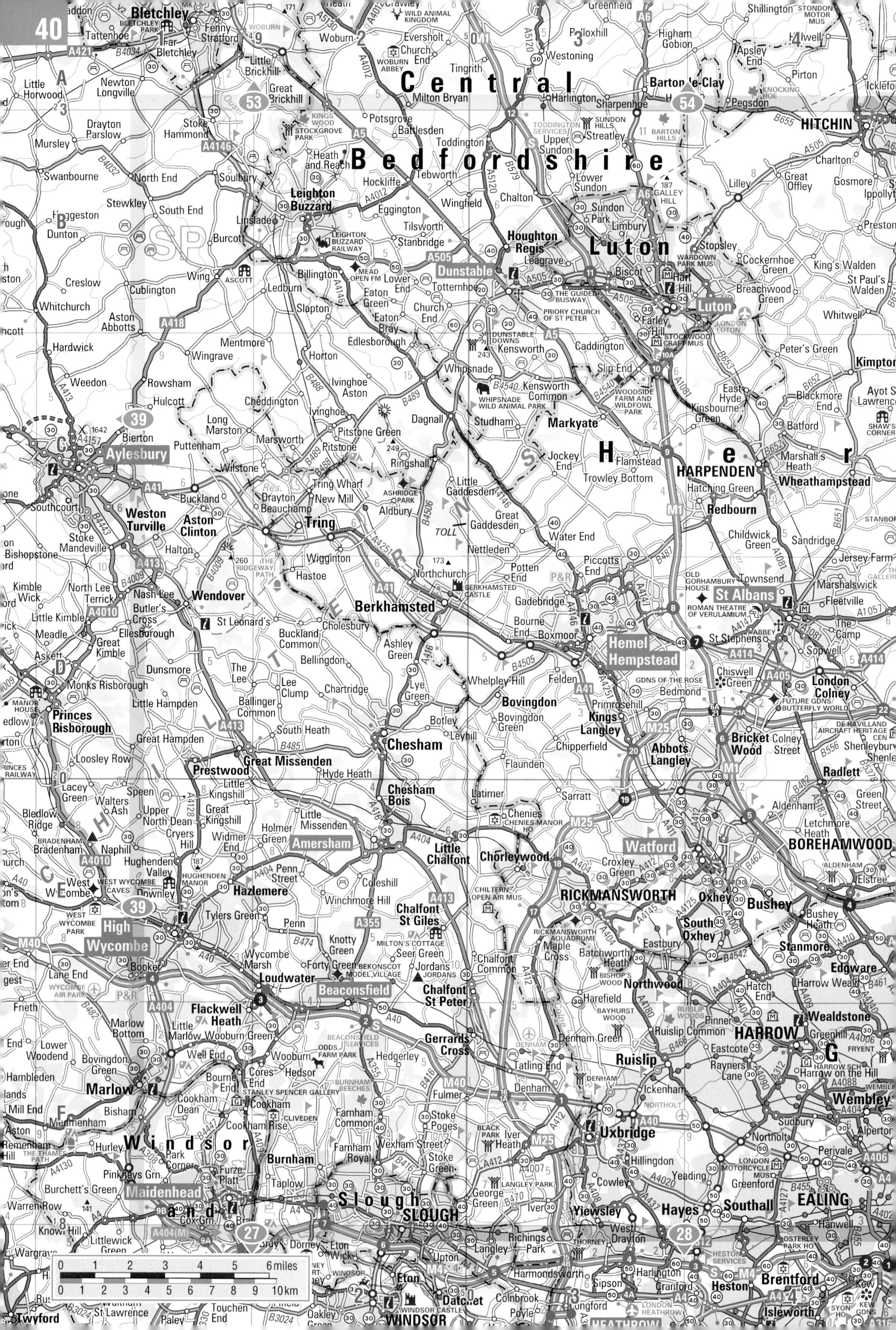

Bletchley
Fenny Stratford
Tattenhoe
Far Bletchley
Woburn
Eversholt
Church End
Woburn Abbey
Westoning
Pulloxhill
Higham Gobion
Shillington
Apsley End
Pirton
Ickleford
Little Horwood
Newton Longville
Little Brickhill
Great Brickhill
Tingrith
Central
Milton Bryan
Harlington
Sharpenhoe
Barton-le-Clay
Pegsdon
HITCHIN
Drayton Parslow
Stoke Hammond
Mursley
Potsgrove
Battlesden
Toddington
Toddington Services
Sundon Hills
Streatley
Barton Hills
Upper Sundon
Charlton
Swanbourne
Heath and Reach
Bedfordshire
Tebworth
Lower Sundon
Lilley
Great Offley
Gosmore
Ippollitts
North End
Soulbury
Hockliffe
Chalton
Galley Hill
Stewkley
South End
Leighton Buzzard
Linslade
Eggington
Wingfield
Sundon Park
Limbury
Hoggeston
Dunton
Burcott
Leighton Buzzard Railway
Tilsworth
Stanbridge
Houghton Regis
Luton
Stopsley
Preston
Wardown Park Mus
Cockernhoe Green
King's Walden
St Paul's Walden
Creslow
Wing
Ascott
Billington
Ledburn
Mead Open Fm
Dunstable
Leagrave
Biscot
Hart Hill
Breachwood Green
Cublington
Whitchurch
Lower End
Totternhoe
The Guided Busway
Priory Church of St Peter
Slapton
Eaton Green
Eaton Bray
Church End
Farley Hill
Stockwood Craft Mus
Luton
London Luton
Whitwell
Aston Abbotts
Dunstable Downs
Kensworth
Caddington
Hardwick
Mentmore
Edlesborough
Horton
Wingrave
Whipsnade
Slip End
Peter's Green
Kimpton
Weedon
Rowsham
Ivinghoe Aston
Kensworth Common
Woodside Farm and Wildfowl Park
East Hyde
Ayot St Lawrence
Blackmore End
Hulcott
Cheddington
Whipsnade Wild Animal Park
Kinsbourne Green
Long Marston
Ivinghoe
Dagnall
Studham
Markyate
Batford
Shaw's Corner
Bierton
Aylesbury
Puttenham
Marsworth
Pitstone Green
Pitstone
Ringshall
Jockey End
Flamstead
HARPENDEN
Marshall's Heath
Wheathampstead
Wilstone
Trowley Bottom
Southcourt
Buckland
Drayton Beauchamp
Tring Wharf
New Mill
Ashridge Park
Little Gaddesden
Hatching Green
Weston Turville
Aston Clinton
Tring
Aldbury
Great Gaddesden
Redbourn
Stoke Mandeville
Halton
Water End
Childwick Green
Sandridge
Bishopstone
Wigginton
Nettleden
Jersey Farm
The Ridgeway Path
Hastoe
Northchurch
Potten End
Piccotts End
Old Gorhambury House
Townsend
Kimble Wick
North Lee
Terrick
Nash Lee
Wendover
Berkhamsted Castle
Roman Theatre of Verulamium
St Albans
Marshalswick
Fleetville
Butler's Cross
Berkhamsted
Gadebridge
Little Kimble
Ellesborough
St Leonard's
Cholesbury
Buckland Common
Bourne End
Boxmoor
St Stephens
The Camp
Meadle
Great Kimble
Ashley Green
Hemel Hempstead
Sopwell
Askett
Dunsmore
The Lee
Bellingdon
Whelpley Hill
Felden
Gdns of the Rose
Chiswell Green
London Colney
Monks Risborough
Lee Clump
Chartridge
Lye Green
Bovingdon
Bedmond
Manor House
Princes Risborough
Little Hampden
Ballinger Common
Primrose Hill
Future Gdns/ Butterfly World
Bovingdon Green
Kings Langley
Botley
South Heath
Leyhill
Abbots Langley
Bricket Wood
Colney Street
De Havilland Aircraft Heritage Centre
Shenleybury
Great Hampden
Chesham
Chipperfield
Loosley Row
Prestwood
Great Missenden
Hyde Heath
Flaunden
Radlett
Lacey Green
Speen
Little Kingshill
Chesham Bois
Latimer
Sarratt
Green Street
Walters Ash
Upper North Dean
Great Kingshill
Little Missenden
Chenies
Chenies Manor Ho
Aldenham
Bledlow Ridge
Cryers Hill
Widmer End
Holmer Green
Amersham
Little Chalfont
Chorleywood
Croxley Green
Watford
Letchmore Heath
BOREHAMWOOD
Bradenham
Naphill
Hughenden Valley
Hughenden Manor
Penn Street
Coleshill
Elstree
West Wycombe
West Wycombe Caves
Downley
Hazlemere
Winchmore Hill
Chiltern Open Air Mus
RICKMANSWORTH
Oxhey
Bushey
Bushey Heath
Tylers Green
Chalfont St Giles
Rickmansworth Aquadrome
South Oxhey
High Wycombe
Penn
Milton's Cottage
Eastbury
Stanmore
Knotty Green
Seer Green
Maple Cross
Batchworth Heath
Edgware
Lane End
Wycombe Air Park
Booker
Wycombe Marsh
Forty Green
Bekonscot Model Village
Jordans
Chalfont Common
Bishop's Wood
Northwood
Hatch End
Harrow Weald
Loudwater
Beaconsfield
Chalfont St Peter
Harefield
Frieth
Flackwell Heath
Marlow Bottom
Little Marlow
Wooburn Green
Beaconsfield Services
Gerrards Cross
Bayhurst Wood
Ruislip Woods
Pinner
Wealdstone
Odds Farm Park
Hedgerley
Denham Green
Ruislip Common
HARROW
Greenhill
Lower Woodend
Bovingdon Green
Well End
Wooburn
Hedsor
Denham
Eastcote
Rayners Lane
Fryent
Hambleden
Marlow
Bourne End
Cores End
Burnham Beeches
Tatling End
Ruislip
Harrow on the Hill
Harrow Sch
Mill End
Cookham Dean
Stanley Spencer Gallery
Cookham
Fulmer
Ickenham
Northolt
Wembley
Medmenham
Bisham
Cliveden
Farnham Common
Stoke Poges
Black Park
Iver Heath
Uxbridge
Sudbury
Aston
Remenham Hill
The Thames Path
Hurley
Windsor
Cookham Rise
Burnham
Farnham Royal
Wexham Street
Stoke Green
Hillingdon
Northolt
Alperton
Perivale
Pinkneys Grn.
Park Corner
Furze Platt
Taplow
Langley Park
Yeading
London Motorcycle Mus
Greenford
Burchett's Green
Maidenhead
Slough
George Green
Cowley
Southall
EALING
Warren Row
and
Cox Grn.
SLOUGH
Iver
Yiewsley
Hayes
Hanwell
Knowl Hill
Littlewick Green
Bray
Dorney
Eton Wick
Langley
Richings Park
West Drayton
Thorney
Osterley Park Ho
Wargrave
Eton
Upton
Harmondsworth
Heston Services
Sipson
Harlington
Cranford
Heston
Brentford
Kew
Windsor Castle
Datchet
Colnbrook
Poyle
Longford
London Heathrow
Isleworth
Syon Ho
Kew Gdns
Twyford
St Lawrence
Touchen End
Oakley Green
WINDSOR
0 1 2 3 4 5 6 miles
0 1 2 3 4 5 6 7 8 9 10 km

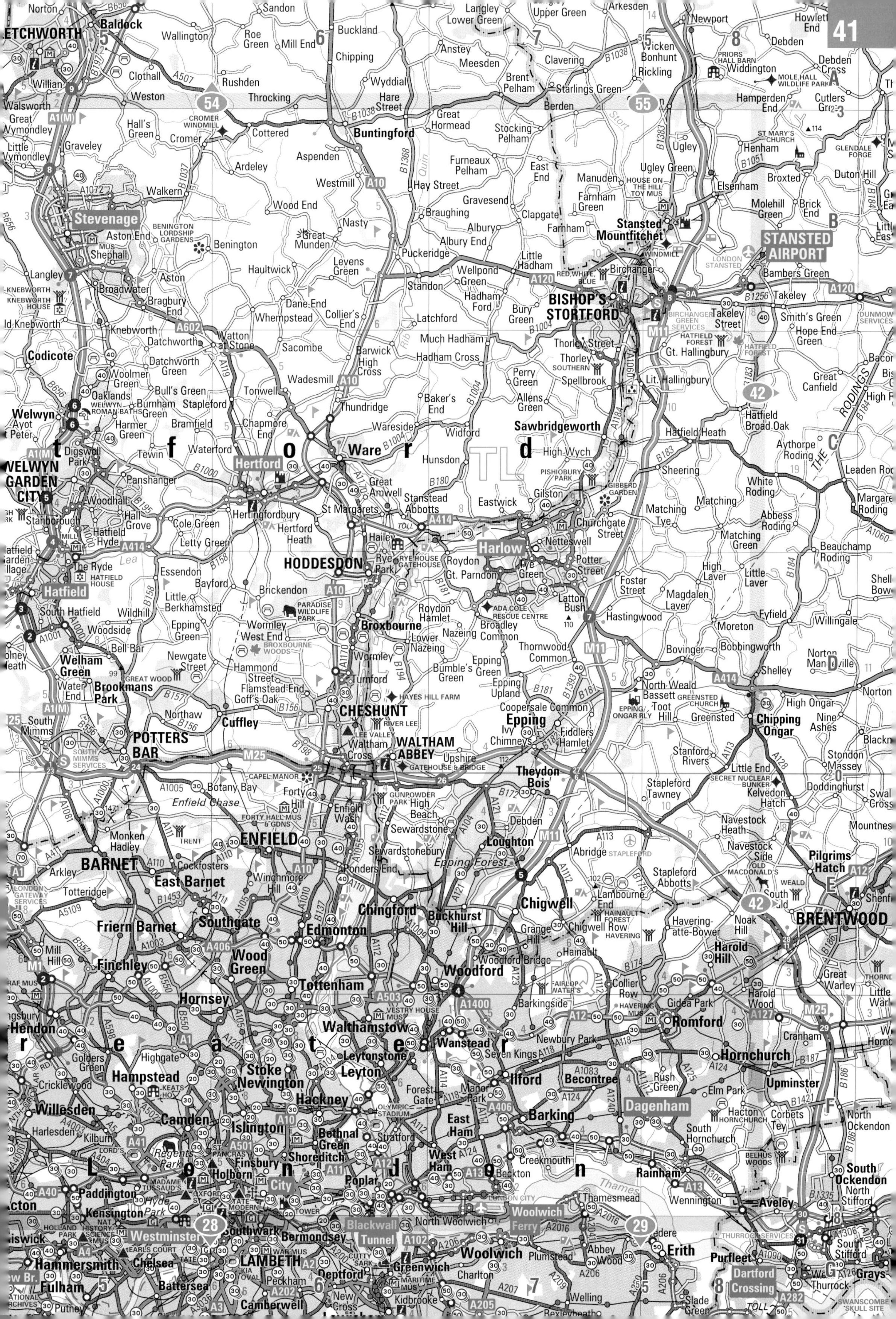

Baldock
Letchworth
Royston
Buckland
Chipping
Buntingford
Newport
Wicken Bonhunt
Rickling
Debden
Widdington
Clavering
Brent Pelham
Starlings Green
Berden
Stocking Pelham
Furneaux Pelham
Great Hormead
Hare Street
Wyddial
Throcking
Cottered
Cromer
Ardeley
Walkern
Stevenage
Benington
Aston
Shephall
Knebworth
Codicote
Welwyn
Welwyn Garden City
Hatfield
Hertford
Ware
Hoddesdon
Broxbourne
Cheshunt
Waltham Abbey
Waltham Cross
Epping
Harlow
Sawbridgeworth
Bishop's Stortford
Stansted Mountfitchet
Stansted Airport
Takeley
Great Canfield
Hatfield Heath
Matching
Chipping Ongar
High Ongar
Brentwood
Romford
Hornchurch
Upminster
Dagenham
Rainham
Barking
Ilford
Woodford
Chigwell
Loughton
Theydon Bois
Enfield
Potters Bar
Barnet
East Barnet
Southgate
Edmonton
Chingford
Tottenham
Walthamstow
Wood Green
Hornsey
Finchley
Hendon
Hampstead
Willesden
Camden
Islington
Stoke Newington
Hackney
Leyton
Leytonstone
Wanstead
Stratford
West Ham
East Ham
Poplar
Paddington
Kensington
Westminster
Hammersmith
Fulham
Chelsea
Battersea
Lambeth
Southwark
Bermondsey
Deptford
Greenwich
Woolwich
Erith
Purfleet
Grays
Aveley
South Ockendon
Thamesmead
Dartford Crossing
Blackwall Tunnel
Woolwich Ferry
Epping Forest
Enfield Chase
M1
M11
M25
A1(M)
A10
A120
A414
A12
A13
28
29
42
54
55

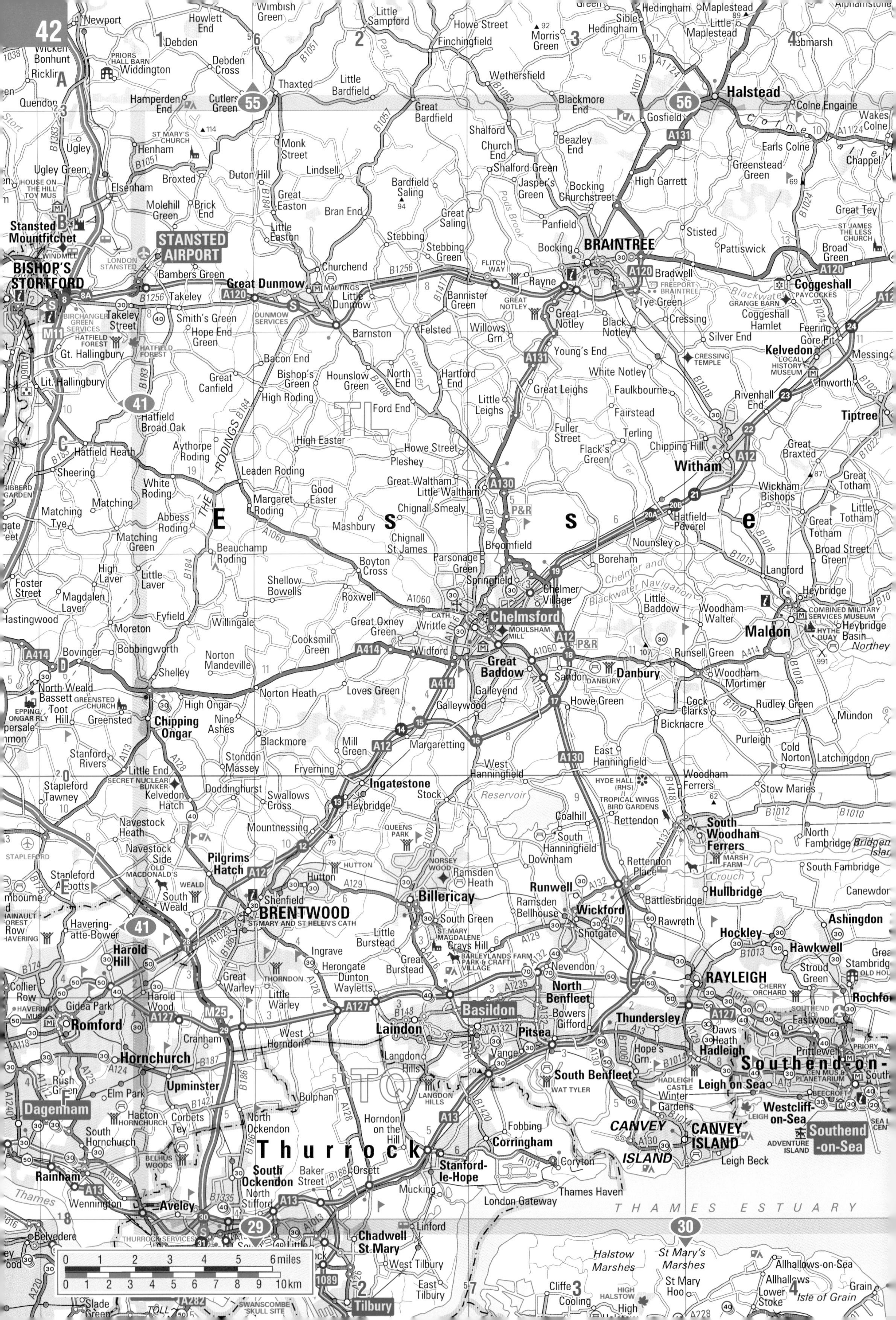
Newport
Wicken Bonhunt
Rickling
Quendon
Howlett End
Debden
Priors Hall Barn
Widdington
Debden Cross
Wimbish Green
Little Sampford
Howe Street
Finchingfield
Morris Green
Sible Hedingham
Hedingham
Maplestead
Little Maplestead
Pebmarsh
Alphamstone
Thaxted
Little Bardfield
Wethersfield
Hamperden End
Cutlers Green
Great Bardfield
Blackmore End
Gosfield
Halstead
Colne Engaine
Wakes Colne
Earls Colne
Chappel
Colne Valley
Ugley
Henham
St Mary's Church
Monk Street
Shalford
Church End
Beazley End
Greenstead Green
Ugley Green
Elsenham
House on the Hill Toy Mus
Broxted
Duton Hill
Lindsell
Shalford Green
Jasper's Green
High Garrett
Bocking Churchstreet
Molehill Green
Brick End
Great Easton
Bardfield Saling
Bran End
Great Saling
Panfield
Stisted
Great Tey
Stansted Mountfitchet
Stansted Airport
Little Easton
Stebbing
Stebbing Green
Bocking
Braintree
Pattiswick
St James the Less Church
Broad Green
Windmill
London Stansted
Bishop's Stortford
Churchend
Flitch Way
Rayne
Bradwell
Freeport Braintree
Coggeshall
Paycockes
Bambers Green
Great Dunmow
Maltings
Little Dunmow
Bannister Green
Great Notley
Tye Green
Grange Barn
Coggeshall Hamlet
Birchanger Green Services
Takeley
Takeley Street
Smith's Green
Hope End Green
Dunmow Services
Barnston
Felsted
Willows Grn.
Black Notley
Cressing
Feering
Hatfield Forest
Gt. Hallingbury
Silver End
Gore Pit
Kelvedon
Messing
Cressing Temple
Local History Museum
Young's End
Bacon End
Great Canfield
Bishop's Green
Hounslow Green
North End
Hartford End
White Notley
Faulkbourne
Inworth
Lit. Hallingbury
High Roding
Little Leighs
Great Leighs
Rivenhall End
Tiptree
Hatfield Broad Oak
Ford End
Fairstead
Aythorpe Roding
High Easter
Fuller Street
Terling
Chipping Hill
Flack's Green
Great Braxted
Hatfield Heath
Howe Street
Pleshey
Witham
Great Totham
Sheering
The Rodings
Leaden Roding
Great Waltham
Little Waltham
Wickham Bishops
White Roding
Good Easter
Matching Tye
Matching
Margaret Roding
Chignall Smealy
Little Totham
Abbess Roding
Mashbury
Essex
Hatfield Peverel
Great Totham
Matching Green
Chignall St James
Broomfield
Nounsley
Broad Street Green
Beauchamp Roding
Boyton Cross
Parsonage Green
Boreham
Langford
High Laver
Little Laver
Springfield
Chelmer Village
Chelmer and Blackwater Navigation
Heybridge
Foster Street
Magdalen Laver
Shellow Bowells
Roxwell
Little Baddow
Woodham Walter
Combined Military Services Museum
Hastingwood
Fyfield
Willingale
Chelmsford
Cath.
Writtle
Great Oxney Green
Moulsham Mill
Maldon
Hythe Quay
Heybridge Basin
Moreton
Cooksmill Green
Northey
Bovinger
Bobbingworth
Norton Mandeville
Widford
Great Baddow
Sandon
Danbury
Runsell Green
Woodham Mortimer
North Weald Bassett
Shelley
Norton Heath
Loves Green
Galleyend
Howe Green
Cock Clarks
Rudley Green
Mundon
Epping Ongar Rly
Toot Hill
Greensted Church
Greensted
Chipping Ongar
High Ongar
Nine Ashes
Blackmore
Galleywood
Bicknacre
Purleigh
Margaretting
Mill Green
Cold Norton
Latchingdon
Stanford Rivers
Little End
Stondon Massey
Fryerning
West Hanningfield
East Hanningfield
Woodham Ferrers
Stapleford Tawney
Secret Nuclear Bunker
Kelvedon Hatch
Doddinghurst
Swallows Cross
Ingatestone
Stock
Reservoir
Hyde Hall (RHS)
Tropical Wings Bird Gardens
Stow Maries
Heybridge
Coalhill
Rettendon
South Woodham Ferrers
North Fambridge
Navestock Heath
Mountnessing
Queens Park
South Hanningfield
Stapleford
Navestock Side
Old Macdonald's
Pilgrims Hatch
Hutton
Norsey Wood
Ramsden Heath
Downham
Rettendon Place
Marsh Farm
South Fambridge
Stapleford Abbotts
Weald
South Weald
Shenfield
Brentwood
St Mary and St Helen's Cath
Billericay
Runwell
Battlesbridge
Hullbridge
Canewdon
Havering-atte-Bower
Ramsden Bellhouse
Wickford
Rawreth
Ashingdon
South Green
Shotgate
Hockley
Harold Hill
Ingrave
Little Burstead
St Mary Magdalene
Crays Hill
Hawkwell
Great Stambridge
Herongate
Dunton Wayletts
Great Burstead
Barleylands Farm Park & Craft Village
Nevendon
Stroud Green
Rayleigh
Collier Row
Great Warley
Thorndon
Little Warley
Harold Wood
North Benfleet
Bowers Gifford
Cherry Orchard
Rochford
Gidea Park
Havering Mus
Romford
Cranham
Basildon
Laindon
Pitsea
Thundersley
Southend
Eastwood
West Horndon
Vange
Hope's Grn.
Daws Heath
Hadleigh
Prittlewell
Priory
Hornchurch
Langdon Hills
South Benfleet
Wat Tyler
Hadleigh Castle
Southend-on-Sea
Cen Mus & Planetarium
Rush Green
Upminster
Leigh on Sea
Elm Park
Bulphan
Winter Gardens
Beecroft
Westcliff-on-Sea
Dagenham
Hacton
Hornchurch
Corbets Tey
North Ockendon
Horndon on the Hill
Fobbing
Canvey
Canvey Island
Leigh
South Hornchurch
Corringham
Adventure Island
Belhus Woods
Thurrock
Stanford-le-Hope
Coryton
Leigh Beck
South Ockendon
Baker Street
Orsett
Rainham
North Stifford
Mucking
Thames Haven
London Gateway
Thames
Wennington
Aveley
Thames Estuary
Belvedere
Thurrock Services
Linford
Chadwell St Mary
Halstow Marshes
St Mary's Marshes
Allhallows-on-Sea
West Tilbury
St Mary Hoo
Allhallows
Cliffe
East Tilbury
High Halstow
Lower Stoke
Isle of Grain
Grain
Cooling
Tilbury
Slade Green
Swanscombe Skull Site
TL
TQ
0 1 2 3 4 5 6 miles
0 1 2 3 4 5 6 7 8 9 10km

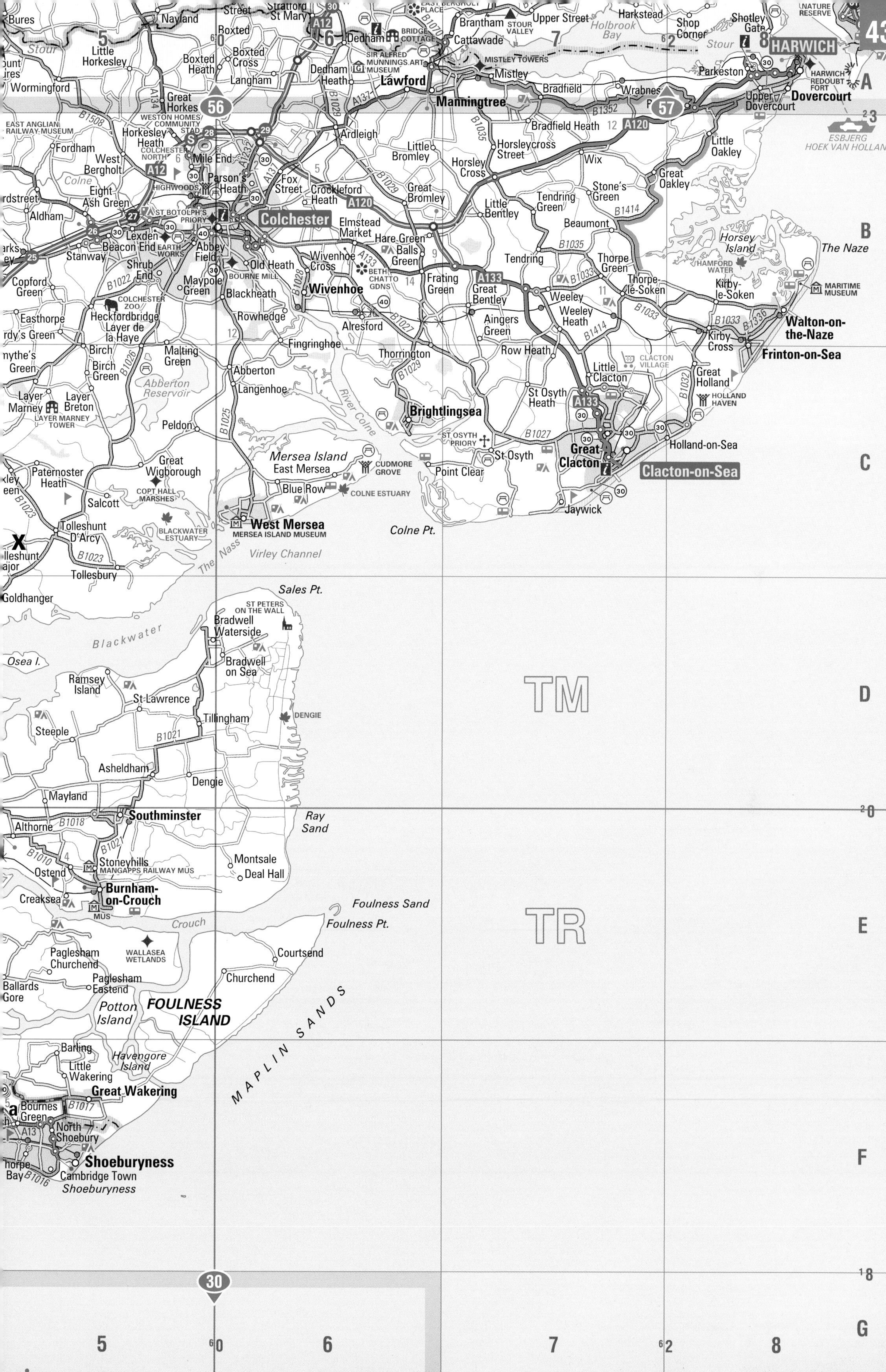
Bures
Nayland
Stratford St Mary
Boxted
Little Horkesley
Boxted Heath
Boxted Cross
Langham
Wormingford
Stour
Dedham
BRIDGE COTTAGE
SIR ALFRED MUNNINGS ART MUSEUM
Dedham Heath
Lawford
EAST BERGHOLT PLACE
Brantham
STOUR VALLEY
Cattawade
Upper Street
Holbrook Bay
Harkstead
Shop Corner
Shotley Gate
NATURE RESERVE
HARWICH
MISTLEY TOWERS
Mistley
Manningtree
Bradfield
Wrabness
Parkeston
HARWICH REDOUBT FORT
Dovercourt
Upper Dovercourt
Great Horkesley
WESTON HOMES COMMUNITY STAD.
EAST ANGLIAN RAILWAY MUSEUM
Horkesley Heath
COLCHESTER NORTH
Fordham
West Bergholt
Colne
Eight Ash Green
Aldham
HIGHWOODS
Mile End
Parson's Heath
Fox Street
Crockleford Heath
Ardleigh
Little Bromley
Great Bromley
Horsley Cross
Horsleycross Street
Bradfield Heath
Wix
Little Oakley
Great Oakley
ESBJERG HOEK VAN HOLLAND
Stone's Green
Tendring Green
Little Bentley
Beaumont
Colchester
ST BOTOLPH'S PRIORY
Lexden
Beacon End
EARTH WORKS
Stanway
Abbey Field
Old Heath
BOURNE MILL
Elmstead Market
Hare Green
Balls Green
Wivenhoe Cross
BETH CHATTO GDNS
Wivenhoe
Tendring
Thorpe Green
Thorpe-le-Soken
Horsey Island
HAMFORD WATER
The Naze
Kirby-le-Soken
MARITIME MUSEUM
Copford Green
Shrub End
Maypole Green
Blackheath
Rowhedge
Frating Green
Great Bentley
Weeley
Weeley Heath
Aingers Green
Walton-on-the-Naze
Kirby Cross
Frinton-on-Sea
Easthorpe
Heckfordbridge
COLCHESTER ZOO
Layer de la Haye
Alresford
Fingringhoe
Thorrington
Row Heath
Little Clacton
CLACTON VILLAGE
Great Holland
HOLLAND HAVEN
Birch
Birch Green
Malting Green
Abberton
Abberton Reservoir
Langenhoe
River Colne
Brightlingsea
St Osyth Heath
Layer Marney
Layer Breton
LAYER MARNEY TOWER
Peldon
ST OSYTH PRIORY
St Osyth
Great Clacton
Holland-on-Sea
Clacton-on-Sea
Mersea Island
East Mersea
CUDMORE GROVE
Point Clear
Great Wigborough
Paternoster Heath
Salcott
COPT HALL MARSHES
Blue Row
COLNE ESTUARY
Jaywick
Tolleshunt D'Arcy
BLACKWATER ESTUARY
West Mersea
MERSEA ISLAND MUSEUM
Colne Pt.
Virley Channel
The Nass
Tollesbury
Goldhanger
Sales Pt.
ST PETERS ON THE WALL
Bradwell Waterside
Bradwell on Sea
Blackwater
Osea I.
Ramsey Island
St Lawrence
Tillingham
DENGIE
Steeple
Asheldham
Dengie
Mayland
TM
Southminster
Althorne
Ray Sand
Stoneyhills
MANGAPPS RAILWAY MUS
Ostend
Montsale
Deal Hall
Burnham-on-Crouch
Creeksea
MUS
Foulness Sand
Foulness Pt.
Crouch
TR
Paglesham Churchend
WALLASEA WETLANDS
Courtsend
Ballards Gore
Paglesham Eastend
Churchend
Potton Island
FOULNESS ISLAND
MAPLIN SANDS
Barling
Little Wakering
Havengore Island
Great Wakering
Bournes Green
North Shoebury
Shoeburyness
Cambridge Town
Shoeburyness
A12
A120
A133
A137
A134
A1232
A13
B1508
B1029
B1035
B1352
B1414
B1033
B1336
B1032
B1027
B1028
B1022
B1026
B1025
B1023
B1021
B1018
B1010
B1017
B1016
56
57
30
5
6
7
8
A
B
C
D
E
F
G
60
62
23
20
18

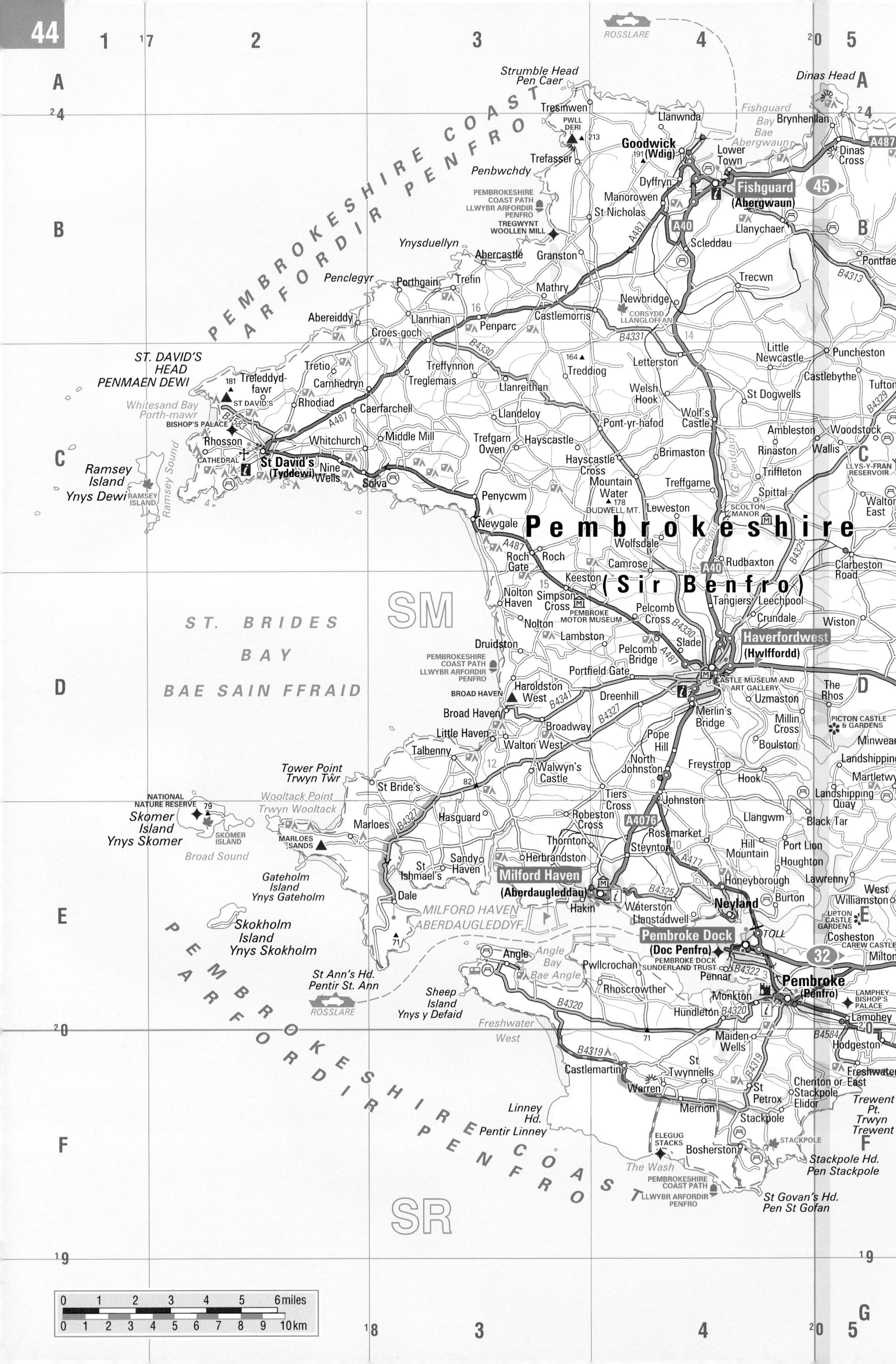
1
2
3
4
5
A
B
C
D
E
F
G
ROSSLARE
Strumble Head
Pen Caer
Dinas Head
PEMBROKESHIRE COAST
ARFORDIR PENFRO
Tresinwen
Llanwnda
Fishguard Bay
Bae Abergwaun
Brynhenllan
PWLL DERI
Goodwick
(Wdig)
Lower Town
Dinas Cross
A487
Trefasser
Penbwchdy
Dyffryn
Fishguard
(Abergwaun)
45
Manorowen
PEMBROKESHIRE COAST PATH
LLWYBR ARFORDIR PENFRO
St Nicholas
A40
Llanychaer
TREGWYNT WOOLLEN MILL
Scleddau
Ynysduellyn
Abercastle
Granston
Pontfaen
B4313
Penclegyr
Porthgain
Trefin
Mathry
Trecwn
Newbridge
CORSYDD LLANGLOFFAN
Abereiddy
Llanrhian
Penparc
Castlemorris
Croes-goch
B4331
B4330
Little Newcastle
Puncheston
ST. DAVID'S HEAD
PENMAEN DEWI
Tretio
Treffynnon
Treglemais
Letterston
Treddiog
Treleddyd-fawr
Carnhedryn
Llanreithan
Castlebythe
Tufton
Welsh Hook
St Dogwells
Whitesand Bay
Porth-mawr
ST DAVID'S
Rhodiad
Caerfarchell
Llandeloy
Wolf's Castle
BISHOP'S PALACE
B4583
A487
Pont-yr-hafod
Ambleston
Woodstock
Rhosson
Whitchurch
Middle Mill
Trefgarn Owen
Hayscastle
Rinaston
Wallis
CATHEDRAL
St David's
(Tyddewi)
Nine Wells
Solva
Brimaston
Hayscastle Cross
Triffleton
LLYS-Y-FRAN RESERVOIR
Ramsey Island
Ynys Dewi
RAMSEY ISLAND
Ramsey Sound
Mountain Water
Treffgarne
Spittal
Penycwm
DUDWELL MT.
Leweston
SCOLTON MANOR
Walton East
Newgale
Pembrokeshire
Wolfsdale
Roch Gate
Roch
Camrose
Rudbaxton
Clarbeston Road
Keeston
(Sir Benfro)
SM
Nolton Haven
Simpson Cross
PEMBROKE MOTOR MUSEUM
Tangiers
Leechpool
Pelcomb Cross
Crundale
Wiston
ST. BRIDES BAY
BAE SAIN FFRAID
Nolton
Lambston
Haverfordwest
(Hwlffordd)
Druidston
Slade
Pelcomb Bridge
Portfield Gate
CASTLE MUSEUM AND ART GALLERY
The Rhos
Haroldston West
BROAD HAVEN
Dreenhill
Uzmaston
B4341
B4327
Broad Haven
Merlin's Bridge
Millin Cross
PICTON CASTLE & GARDENS
Broadway
Pope Hill
Little Haven
Walton West
Boulston
Minwear
Talbenny
Walwyn's Castle
North Johnston
Freystrop
Landshipping
Tower Point
Trwyn Twr
St Bride's
Hook
Martletwy
NATIONAL NATURE RESERVE
Wooltack Point
Trwyn Wooltack
Tiers Cross
Johnston
Landshipping Quay
Skomer Island
Ynys Skomer
SKOMER ISLAND
Marloes
Hasguard
Robeston Cross
A4076
Llangwm
Black Tar
MARLOES SANDS
Rosemarket
Broad Sound
Thornton
Steynton
Hill Mountain
Port Lion
Herbrandston
A477
Houghton
Gateholm Island
Ynys Gateholm
St Ishmael's
Sandy Haven
Milford Haven
(Aberdaugleddau)
Honeyborough
Lawrenny
B4325
West Williamston
Dale
Hakin
Waterston
Neyland
Burton
MILFORD HAVEN
ABERDAUGLEDDYF
Llanstadwell
UPTON CASTLE GARDENS
Skokholm Island
Ynys Skokholm
Pembroke Dock
(Doc Penfro)
TOLL
Cosheston
CAREW CASTLE
Angle
Angle Bay
Bae Angle
PEMBROKE DOCK SUNDERLAND TRUST
32
Milton
Pwllcrochan
Pennar
B4322
St Ann's Hd.
Pentir St. Ann
Rhoscrowther
Pembroke
(Penfro)
Sheep Island
Ynys y Defaid
Monkton
LAMPHEY BISHOP'S PALACE
B4320
Hundleton
Lamphey
Freshwater West
Maiden Wells
B4584
Hodgeston
B4319
St Twynnells
Castlemartin
Freshwater East
Warren
St Petrox
Cheriton or Stackpole Elidor
Trewent Pt.
Trwyn Trewent
Merrion
Linney Hd.
Pentir Linney
Stackpole
ELEGUG STACKS
Bosherston
STACKPOLE
Stackpole Hd.
Pen Stackpole
The Wash
St Govan's Hd.
Pen St Gofan
SR
0 1 2 3 4 5 6 miles
0 1 2 3 4 5 6 7 8 9 10 km

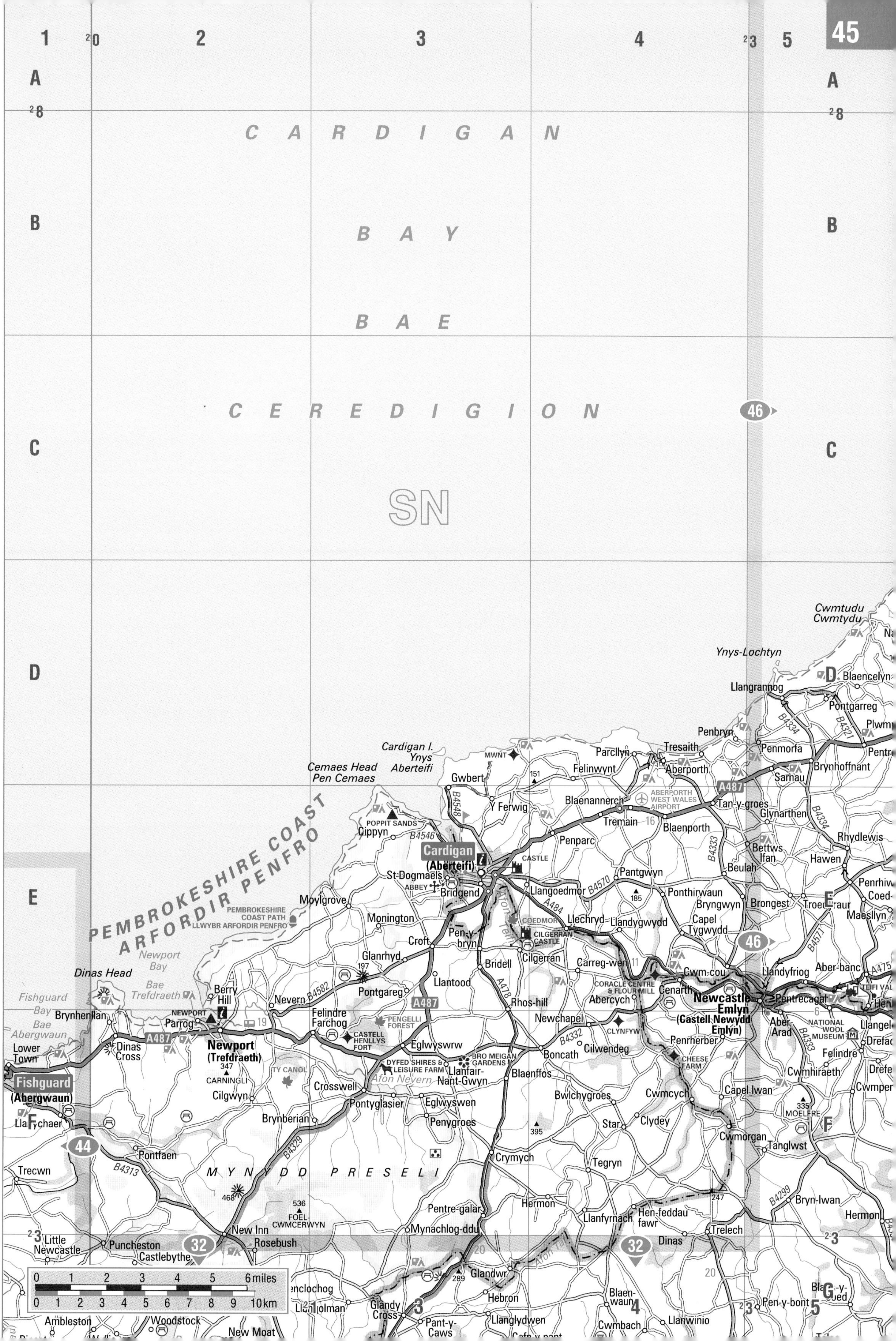

1	2	3	4	5
A				A
B				B
C				C
D				D
E				E
F				F
G				G

C A R D I G A N

B A Y

B A E

C E R E D I G I O N

SN

46

Cwmtudu
Cwmtydu
Ynys-Lochtyn
Llangrannog · D · Blaencelyn
Pontgarreg
Plwm
B4334

Cardigan I.
Ynys
Aberteifi
Cemaes Head
Pen Cemaes
Penbryn
Parcllyn
Tresaith
Penmorfa
Brynhoffnant
Pentre
MWNT
Felinwynt
Aberporth
A487
Sarnau
Gwbert
151
Blaenannerch
Tan-y-groes
Glynarthen
B4334
POPPIT SANDS
Y Ferwig
ABERPORTH
WEST WALES
AIRPORT
Blaenporth
Rhydlewis
Cippyn
B4548
Tremain
16
B4333
Bettws
Ifan
Hawen
B4546
Cardigan
(Aberteifi)
CASTLE
Penparc
Pantgwyn
Beulah
St-Dogmaels
ABBEY
Bridgend
Llangoedmor
B4570
Ponthirwaun
Brongest
Penrhiw-
Troed-yraur
Coed-
Moylgrove
Llechryd
185
Bryngwyn
Capel
Tygwydd
Maesllyn
Monington
A484
COEDMOR
Llandygwydd
46
Pen-y-bryn
CILGERRAN
CASTLE
Carreg-wen
11
Llandyfriog
Aber-banc
A475
Croft
Cilgerran
CORACLE CENTRE
& FLOUR MILL
Cwm-cou
TEIFI VAL
Glanrhyd
197
Bridell
A478
Cenarth
Newcastle
Emlyn
(Castell Newydd
Emlyn)
Pentrecagal
6
Llangel
Llantood
Abercych
Aber-
Arad
NATIONAL
WOOL
MUSEUM
Nevern
B4582
Pontgareg
A487
Rhos-hill
Newchapel
CLYNFYW
Penrherber
Drefac
Felindre
Farchog
PENGELLI
FOREST
Newchapel
B4332
Cilwendeg
CHEESE
FARM
Capel Iwan
Felindre
NEWPORT
Parrog
19
CASTELL
HENLLYS FORT
Eglwyswrw
Bro Meigan
Gardens
Boncath
Penrherber
Cwmhiraeth
Drefe
Newport
(Trefdraeth)
347
CARNINGLI
DYFED SHIRES &
LEISURE FARM
TY CANOL
Llanfair-
Nant-Gwyn
Blaenffos
Bwlchygroes
Cwmcych
Cwmper
Cilgwyn
Crosswell
Crymych
Star
Clydey
335
MOELFRE
Brynberian
Eglwyswen
Penygroes
Cwmorgan
Tanglwst
Pontyglasier
395
F
Llaffchaer
Pontfaen
B4329
M Y N Y D D   P R E S E L I
Crymych
Tegryn
247
B4299
Bryn-Iwan
Trecwn
B4313
468
Pentre-galar
Hermon
Llanfyrnach
Hen-feddau
fawr
Dinas
Hermon
Little
Newcastle
Puncheston
Castlebythe
32
Rosebush
New Inn
536
FOEL-
CWMCERWYN
Mynachlog-ddu
20
Glandwr
32
20
Glandy
Cross
Hebron
Blaen-
waun
Pen-y-bont
Bla-y-
gued
Ambleston
Woodstock
New Moat
nclochog
Glandy
Cross
Pant-y-
Caws
Llanglydwen
Cwmbach
Llanwinio

PEMBROKESHIRE COAST
ARFORDIR PENFRO
PEMBROKESHIRE
COAST PATH
LLWYBR ARFORDIR PENFRO

Dinas Head
Newport
Bay
Fishguard
Bay
Bae
Abergwaun
Brynhenllan
Dinas
Cross
NEWPORT
Berry
Hill
A487
Lower
Town
Fishguard
(Abergwaun)

| 0 | 1 | 2 | 3 | 4 | 5 | 6 miles |
| 0 | 1 | 2 | 3 | 4 | 5 | 6 | 7 | 8 | 9 | 10 km |

44

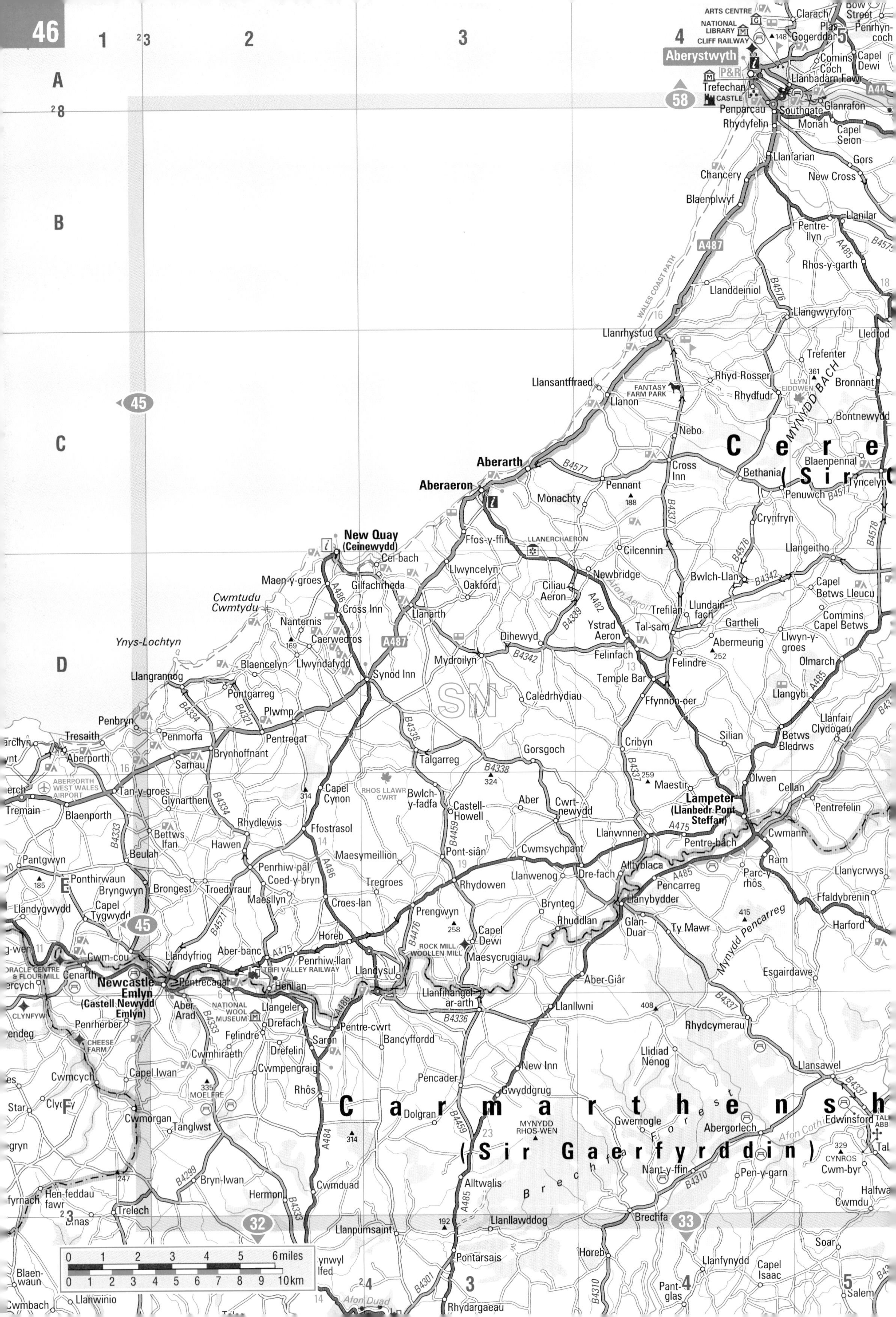

Aberystwyth
ARTS CENTRE
NATIONAL LIBRARY
CLIFF RAILWAY
CASTLE
Clarach
Plas Gogerddan
Bow Street
Penrhyn-coch
Comins Coch
Capel Dewi
Llanbadarn Fawr
Trefechan
Penparcau
Southgate
Glanrafon
Rhydyfelin
Moriah
Capel Seion
Llanfarian
Gors
Chancery
New Cross
Blaenplwyf
Llanilar
Pentre-llyn
Rhos-y-garth
Llanddeiniol
Llangwyryfon
WALES COAST PATH
Llanrhystud
Lledrod
Trefenter
Llansantffraed
FANTASY FARM PARK
Llanon
Rhyd-Rosser
Rhydfudr
LLYN EIDDWEN
MYNYDD BACH
Bronnant
Bontnewydd
Nebo
Aberarth
Aberaeron
Cross Inn
Pennant
Monachty
Bethania
Blaenpennal
Penuwch
Tyncelyn
Ceredigion (Sir Ceredigion)
Crynfryn
Ffos-y-ffin
LLANERCHAERON
Cilcennin
New Quay (Ceinewydd)
Cei-bach
Llangeitho
Maen-y-groes
Gilfachrheda
Llwyncelyn
Oakford
Newbridge
Ciliau Aeron
Bwlch-Llan
Capel Betws Lleucu
Cwmtudu Cwmtydu
Cross Inn
Nanternis
Llanarth
Trefilan
Llundain-fach
Afon Aeron
Commins Capel Betws
Caerwedros
Ystrad Aeron
Tal-sarn
Gartheli
Llwyn-y-groes
Ynys-Lochtyn
Dihewyd
Abermeurig
Blaencelyn
Llwyndafydd
Mydroilyn
Felinfach
Felindre
Olmarch
Llangrannog
Synod Inn
Temple Bar
Pontgarreg
Caledrhydiau
Ffynnon-oer
Llangybi
SN
Plwmp
Penbryn
Tresaith
Penmorfa
Pentregat
Silian
Llanfair Clydogau
Aberporth
Sarnau
Brynhoffnant
Cribyn
Betws Bledrws
Talgarreg
Gorsgoch
ABERPORTH WEST WALES AIRPORT
Tan-y-groes
Glynarthen
Capel Cynon
RHOS LLAWR CWRT
Bwlch-y-fadfa
Castell-Howell
Aber
Cwrt-newydd
Maestir
Olwen
Cellan
Lampeter (Llanbedr Pont Steffan)
Tremain
Blaenporth
Pentrefelin
Rhydlewis
Ffostrasol
Llanwnnen
Cwmann
Bettws Ifan
Hawen
Pont-siân
Cwmsychpant
Pentre-bach
Beulah
Maesymeillion
Ram
Pantgwyn
Ponthirwaun
Penrhiw-pâl
Alltyblaca
Dre-fach
Llanwenog
Llanycrwys
Bryngwyn
Brongest
Troedyraur
Coed-y-bryn
Pencarreg
Parc-y-rhôs
Tregroes
Rhydowen
Capel Tygwydd
Maesllyn
Croes-lan
Llanybydder
Ffaldybrenin
Llandygwydd
Prengwyn
Brynteg
Mynydd Pencarreg
Rhuddlan
Glan-Duar
Ty Mawr
Harford
Horeb
Capel Dewi
Cwm-cou
Llandyfriog
Aber-banc
ROCK MILL WOOLLEN MILL
Maesycrugiau
Penrhiw-llan
Esgairdawe
TEIFI VALLEY RAILWAY
Llandysul
Cenarth
Newcastle Emlyn (Castell Newydd Emlyn)
Pentrecagal
Henllan
Aber-Giâr
Llanfihangel-ar-arth
Llanllwni
Aber-Arad
NATIONAL WOOL MUSEUM
Llangeler
Drefach
Pentre-cwrt
Rhydcymerau
CLYNFYW
Penrherber
Felindre
Saron
Bancyffordd
Llidiad Nenog
CHEESE FARM
Cwmhiraeth
Drefelin
Llansawel
Cwmcych
Capel Iwan
Cwmpengraig
New Inn
Pencader
Rhôs
Gwyddgrug
MOELFRE
Cwmorgan
Tanglwst
Carmarthenshire (Sir Gaerfyrddin)
Dolgran
MYNYDD RHOS-WEN
Gwernogle
Forest
Abergorlech
Edwinsford
Afon Cothi
CYNROS
Cwm-byr
Nant-y-ffin
Pen-y-garn
Brechfa
Bryn-Iwan
Alltwalis
Hermon
Cwmduad
Halfway
Cwmdu
Hen-feddau fawr
Trelech
Llanllawddog
Brechfa
Llanpumsaint
Soar
Pontarsais
Horeb
Llanfynydd
Capel Isaac
Pant-glas
Salem
Llanwinio
Afon Duad
Rhydargaeau
A487
A485
A482
A486
A475
A484
B4575
B4576
B4577
B4578
B4337
B4342
B4339
B4338
B4334
B4321
B4333
B4571
B4459
B4476
B4336
B4299
B4310
B4301
58
45
32
33
0 1 2 3 4 5 6 miles
0 1 2 3 4 5 6 7 8 9 10 km

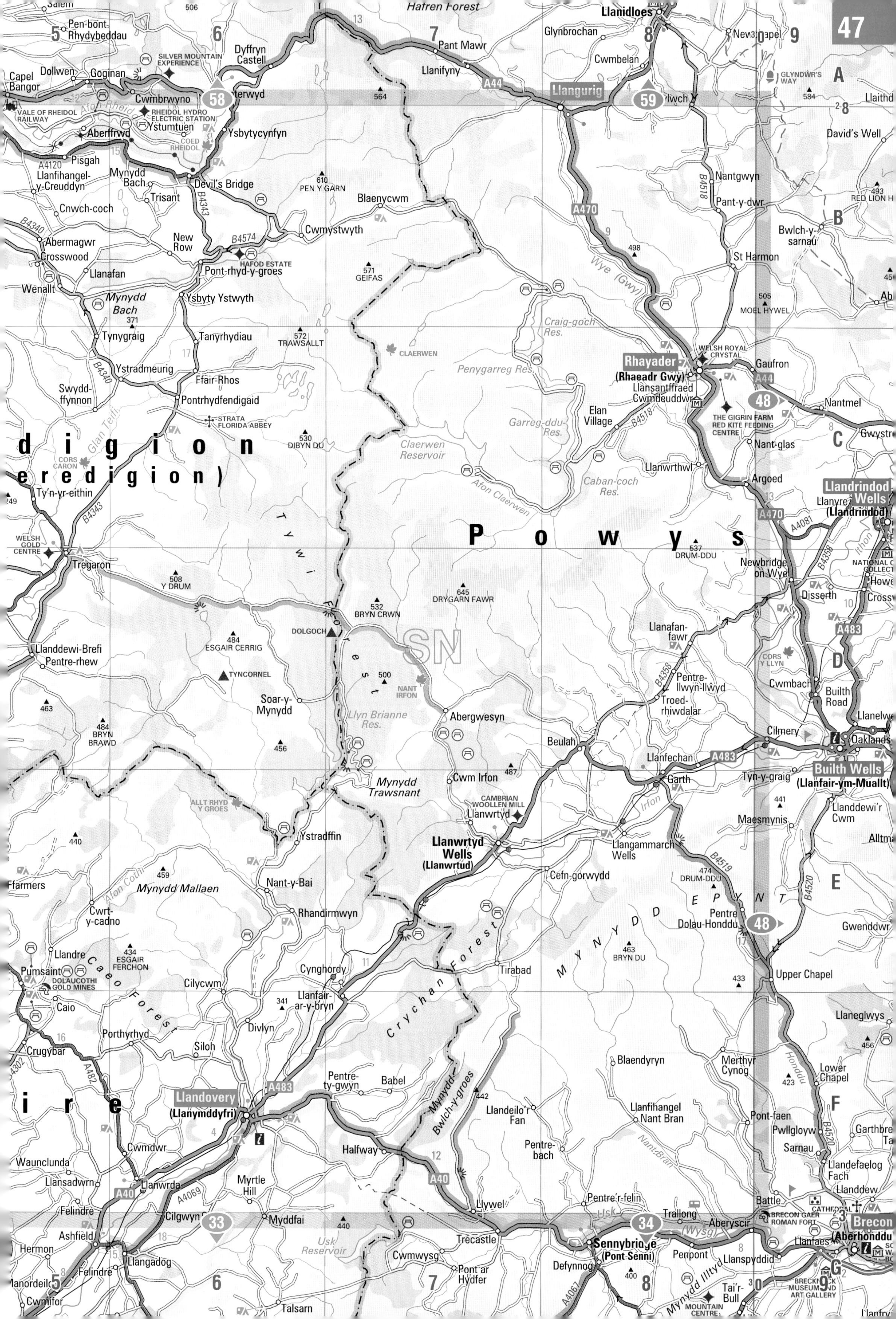

Hafren Forest
Llanidloes
Pen-bont Rhydybeddau
Glynbrochan
Newchapel
Glyndŵr's Way
Dyffryn Castell
Pant Mawr
Cwmbelan
Silver Mountain Experience
Capel Bangor
Dollwen
Goginan
Llanifyny
Llangurig
Cwmbrwyno
Vale of Rheidol Railway
Rheidol Hydro Electric Station
Aberffrwd
Ystumtuen
Coed Rheidol
Ysbytycynfyn
Pisgah
Llanfihangel-y-Creuddyn
Mynydd Bach
Trisant
Devil's Bridge
Pen y Garn
Nantgwyn
Pant-y-dwr
Red Lion H
Cnwch-coch
Blaenycwm
Abermagwr
Crosswood
New Row
Cwmystwyth
Hafod Estate
Pont-rhyd-y-groes
Llanafan
Geifas
St Harmon
Bwlch-y-sarnau
Wye (Gwy)
Wenallt
Mynydd Bach
Ysbyty Ystwyth
Moel Hywel
Craig-goch Res.
Tynygraig
Tanyrhydiau
Trawsallt
Claerwen
Welsh Royal Crystal
Rhayader (Rhaeadr Gwy)
Gaufron
Ystradmeurig
Ffair-Rhos
Penygarreg Res.
Swydd-ffynnon
Pontrhydfendigaid
Llansantffraed Cwmdeuddwr
Nantmel
Strata Florida Abbey
Elan Village
Garreg-ddu Res.
The Gigrin Farm Red Kite Feeding Centre
Glan Teifi
Dibyn Du
Claerwen Reservoir
Nant-glas
Gwystre
digion
(Ceredigion)
Cors Caron
Llanwrthwl
Argoed
Afon Claerwen
Caban-coch Res.
Ty'n-yr-eithin
Llandrindod Wells (Llandrindod)
Llanyre
Tywi Forest
Powys
Welsh Gold Centre
Drum-ddu
Tregaron
Newbridge on Wye
National Collection
Y Drum
Drygarn Fawr
Disserth
Howey
Crossgates
Bryn Crwn
Dolgoch
Esgair Cerrig
SN
Llanafan-fawr
Llanddewi-Brefi
Pentre-rhew
Tyncornel
Cors y Llyn
Nant Irfon
Pentre-llwyn-llwyd
Cwmbach
Builth Road
Soar-y-Mynydd
Llyn Brianne Res.
Troed-rhiwdalar
Abergwesyn
Bryn Brawd
Llanelwedd
Cilmery
Beulah
Oaklands
Llanfechan
Garth
Builth Wells (Llanfair-ym-Muallt)
Tyn-y-graig
Cwm Irfon
Mynydd Trawsnant
Allt Rhyd y Groes
Cambrian Woollen Mill
Llanwrtyd
Irfon
Llanddewi'r Cwm
Maesmynis
Ystradffin
Llanwrtyd Wells (Llanwrtud)
Llangammarch Wells
Allt-mawr
Cefn-gorwydd
Drum-ddu
Ffarmers
Mynydd Mallaen
Afon Cothi
Nant-y-Bai
Mynydd Epynt
Cwrt-y-cadno
Rhandirmwyn
Pentre Dolau-Honddu
Gwenddwr
Llandre
Esgair Ferchon
Caeo Forest
Bryn Du
Crychan Forest
Pumsaint
Dolaucothi Gold Mines
Cynghordy
Tirabad
Upper Chapel
Cilycwm
Llanfair-ar-y-bryn
Caio
Divlyn
Llaneglwys
Porthyrhyd
Siloh
Crugybar
Blaendyryn
Merthyr Cynog
Honddu
Lower Chapel
Pentre-ty-gwyn
Babel
Mynydd Bwlch-y-groes
ire
Llandovery (Llanymddyfri)
Llandeilo'r Fan
Llanfihangel Nant Bran
Pont-faen
Garthbrengy
Pwllgloyw
Cwmdwr
Halfway
Pentre-bach
Sarnau
Wauncluda
Nant Bran
Llandefaelog Fach
Llansadwrn
Llanwrda
Myrtle Hill
Llandew
Felindre
Llywel
Pentre'r-felin
Battle
Cilgwyn
Myddfai
Usk
Trallong
Aberyscir
Brecon Gaer Roman Fort
Cathedral
Brecon (Aberhonddu)
Ashfield
Usk Reservoir
Trecastle
Sennybridge (Pont Senni)
Penpont
Llanspyddid
Llanfaes
Hermon
Llangadog
Cwmwysg
Pont ar Hydfer
Defynnog
Mynydd Illtyd
Brecknock Museum and Art Gallery
Felindre
Tai'r-Bull
Cwmifor
Talsarn
Mountain Centre
Llanfrynach

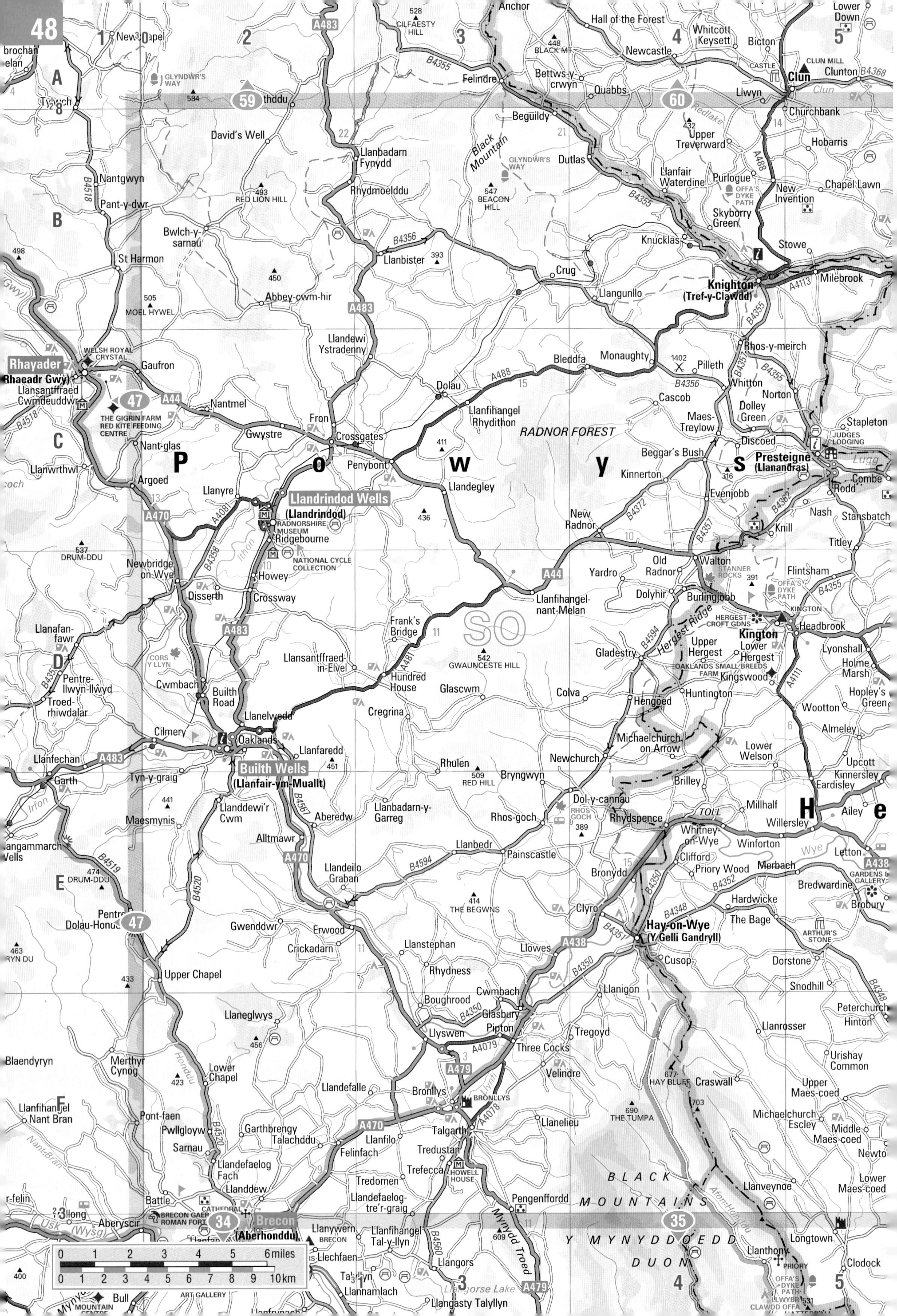

Anchor
Hall of the Forest
CILFAESTY HILL
BLACK MT
Newcastle
Whitcott Keysett
Bicton
Lower Down
Clun
CLUN MILL
Clunton
Felindre
Bettws-y-crwyn
Quabbs
Llwyn
Churchbank
New Chapel
GLYNDWR'S WAY
Tylwch
David's Well
Llanbadarn Fynydd
Beguildy
Black Mountain
Upper Treverward
Hobarris
Nantgwyn
Pant-y-dwr
RED LION HILL
Rhydmoelddu
BEACON HILL
Dutlas
Llanfair Waterdine
Purlogue
OFFA'S DYKE PATH
New Invention
Chapel Lawn
Skyborry Green
Bwlch-y-sarnau
Knucklas
Stowe
St Harmon
Llanbister
Crug
Knighton (Tref-y-Clawdd)
Milebrook
MOEL HYWEL
Abbey-cwm-hir
Llangunllo
Llandewi Ystradenny
WELSH ROYAL CRYSTAL
Rhayader
Rhaeadr Gwy
Llansantffraed Cwmdeuddwr
Gaufron
THE GIGRIN FARM RED KITE FEEDING CENTRE
Nantmel
Bleddfa
Monaughty
Pilleth
Rhos-y-meirch
Whitton
Norton
Dolau
Llanfihangel Rhydithon
Cascob
Dolley Green
Stapleton
Fron
Gwystre
Crossgates
RADNOR FOREST
Maes-Treylow
Discoed
JUDGES LODGING
Nant-glas
Llanwrthwl
Argoed
Penybont
Beggar's Bush
Presteigne (Llanandras)
Combe
Rodd
Powys
Llanyre
Llandegley
Kinnerton
Evenjobb
Llandrindod Wells (Llandrindod)
RADNORSHIRE MUSEUM
Ridgebourne
NATIONAL CYCLE COLLECTION
New Radnor
Nash
Stansbatch
Knill
Titley
DRUM-DDU
Newbridge-on-Wye
Howey
Yardro
Old Radnor
Walton
STANNER ROCKS
Flintsham
Disserth
Crossway
Llanfihangel-nant-Melan
Dolyhir
Burlingjobb
Llanafan-fawr
Frank's Bridge
SO
HERGEST CROFT GDNS
Kington
Headbrook
Hergest Ridge
Upper Hergest
Lower Hergest
Lyonshall
CORS Y LLYN
Llansantffraed-in-Elvel
GWAUNCESTE HILL
Gladestry
OAKLANDS SMALL BREEDS FARM
Kingswood
Holme Marsh
Pentre-llwyn-llwyd
Troed-rhiwdalar
Cwmbach
Builth Road
Hundred House
Glascwm
Colva
Hengoed
Huntington
Hopley's Green
Wootton
Cregrina
Almeley
Llanelwedd
Cilmery
Oaklands
Llanfaredd
Michaelchurch-on-Arrow
Lower Welson
Llanfechan
Builth Wells (Llanfair-ym-Muallt)
Rhulen
Newchurch
Upcott
Kinnersley
Garth
Tyn-y-graig
RED HILL
Bryngwyn
Brilley
Eardisley
Llanddewi'r Cwm
Dol-y-cannau
Millhalf
Maesmynis
Aberedw
Llanbadarn-y-Garreg
Rhos-goch
RHOS GOCH
Rhydspence
TOLL
Willersley
Ailey
Llangammarch Wells
Alltmawr
Whitney-on-Wye
Winforton
Letton
Llanbedr
Painscastle
Clifford
Priory Wood
Merbach
Llandeilo Graban
Bronydd
Bredwardine
GARDENS & GALLERY
DRUM-DDU
THE BEGWNS
Hardwicke
Brobury
Clyro
The Bage
Pentre Dolau-Honddu
Hay-on-Wye (Y Gelli Gandryll)
ARTHUR'S STONE
Gwenddwr
Erwood
Crickadarn
Llanstephan
Llowes
Cusop
Dorstone
Rhydness
Upper Chapel
Snodhill
Llanigon
Boughrood
Cwmbach
Glasbury
Peterchurch
Hinton
Llaneglwys
Pipton
Llanrosser
Llyswen
Tregoyd
Three Cocks
Urishay Common
Blaendyryn
Merthyr Cynog
Lower Chapel
Velindre
HAY BLUFF
Craswall
Upper Maes-coed
Llandefalle
Bronllys
BRONLLYS
THE TUMPA
Llanfihangel Nant Bran
Pont-faen
Michaelchurch Escley
Middle Maes-coed
Llanelieu
Pwllgloyw
Garthbrengy
Talachddu
Llanfilo
Talgarth
Sarnau
Felinfach
Trefecca
Tredustan
Newton
HOWELL HOUSE
Llandefaelog Fach
Llanddew
Tredomen
BLACK MOUNTAINS
Llanveynoe
Lower Maes-coed
Battle
CATHEDRAL
Llandefaelog-tre'r-graig
Pengenffordd
Aberyscir
BRECON GAER ROMAN FORT
Brecon (Aberhonddu)
Y MYNYDDOEDD DUON
Llanywern
BRECON
Llanfihangel Tal-y-llyn
Mynydd Troed
Llanthony
PRIORY
Longtown
Llechfaen
Llangors
Clodock
Llanhamlach
Llangorse Lake
Llangasty Talyllyn
OFFA'S DYKE PATH
LLWYBR CLAWDD OFFA
ART GALLERY
MOUNTAIN CENTRE
Bull
A483
B4355
A488
B4356
A44
A4113
B4357
B4372
A4081
B4358
A470
A4111
B4594
A481
B4567
B4519
B4520
B4350
B4352
B4348
A438
B4351
A4079
A479
A4078
B4560
B4518
B4362
B4368
59
60
47
34
35
0 1 2 3 4 5 6 miles
0 1 2 3 4 5 6 7 8 9 10 km

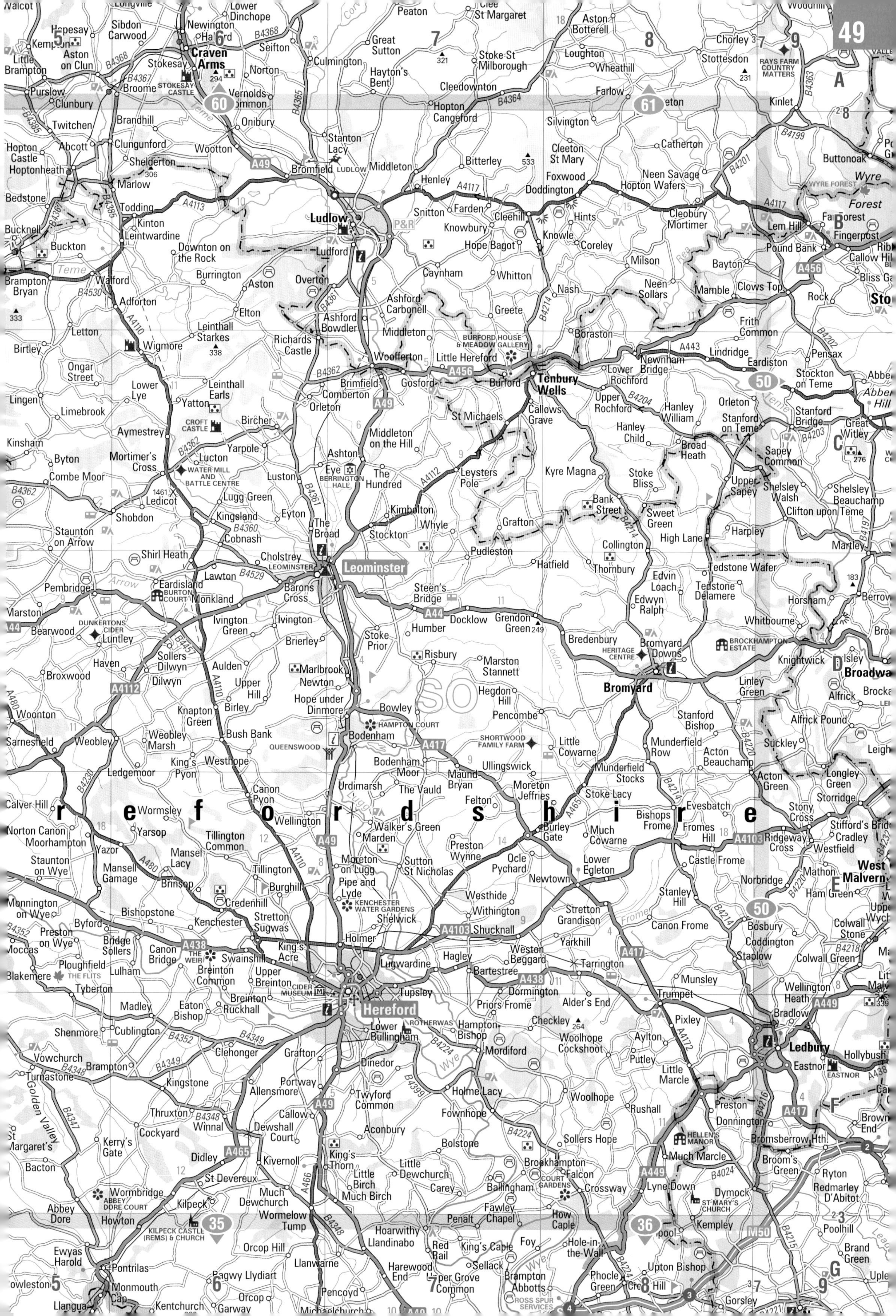

Craven Arms
Stokesay
STOKESAY CASTLE
Newington
Halford
Sibdon Carwood
Hopesay
Kempton
Aston on Clun
Little Brampton
Purslow
Clunbury
Broome
Twitchen
Brandhill
Onibury
Vernolds Common
Norton
Seifton
Culmington
Peaton
Great Sutton
Hayton's Bent
Cleedownton
Clee St Margaret
Stoke St Milborough
Hopton Cangeford
Aston Botterell
Loughton
Wheathill
Farlow
Chorley
Stottesdon
RAYS FARM COUNTRY MATTERS
Kinlet
Silvington
Catherton
Cleeton St Mary
Buttonoak
Wyre Forest
WYRE FOREST
Hopton Castle
Hoptonheath
Abcott
Clungunford
Shelderton
Wootton
Stanton Lacy
Bromfield
LUDLOW
Middleton
Bitterley
Henley
Neen Savage
Hopton Wafers
Foxwood
Doddington
Bedstone
Marlow
Todding
Kinton
Leintwardine
Bucknell
Buckton
Downton on the Rock
Ludlow
Ludford
P&R
Snitton
Farden
Knowbury
Cleehill
Hope Bagot
Hints
Knowle
Coreley
Cleobury Mortimer
Lem Hill
Far Forest
Fingerpost
Pound Bank
Callow Hill
Bliss Gate
Rock
Bayton
Milson
Neen Sollars
Mamble
Clows Top
Brampton Bryan
Walford
Adforton
Burrington
Aston
Overton
Caynham
Whitton
Nash
Elton
Ashford Carbonell
Ashford Bowdler
Greete
Boraston
Frith Common
Pensax
Letton
Birtley
Wigmore
Leinthall Starkes
Richards Castle
Middleton
BURFORD HOUSE & MEADOW GALLERY
Little Hereford
Woofferton
Lindridge
Eardiston
Newnham Bridge
Lower Rochford
Ongar Street
Lingen
Lower Lye
Leinthall Earls
Yatton
Limebrook
Brimfield
Comberton
Orleton
Gosford
Burford
Tenbury Wells
Upper Rochford
Hanley William
Hanley Child
Orleton
Stanford on Teme
Stockton on Teme
Stanford Bridge
Great Witley
Kinsham
Byton
Aymestrey
CROFT CASTLE
Bircher
Callows Grave
St Michaels
Middleton on the Hill
Broad Heath
Sapey Common
Mortimer's Cross
Combe Moor
WATER MILL AND BATTLE CENTRE
Lucton
Yarpole
Ashton
Eye
BERRINGTON HALL
The Hundred
Leysters Pole
Kyre Magna
Stoke Bliss
Upper Sapey
Shelsley Walsh
Shelsley Beauchamp
Clifton upon Teme
Ledicot
Shobdon
Luston
Lugg Green
Kingsland
Eyton
Kimbolton
Bank Street
Sweet Green
Staunton on Arrow
Cobnash
The Broad
Stockton
Whyle
Grafton
High Lane
Harpley
Martley
Shirl Heath
Cholstrey
LEOMINSTER
Leominster
Pudleston
Hatfield
Collington
Thornbury
Tedstone Wafer
Edvin Loach
Tedstone Delamere
Pembridge
Eardisland
BURTON COURT
Lawton
Monkland
Barons Cross
Steen's Bridge
Docklow
Grendon Green
Edwyn Ralph
Horsham
Marston
Bearwood
DUNKERTONS CIDER
Luntley
Ivington Green
Ivington
Stoke Prior
Humber
Bredenbury
HERITAGE CENTRE
Bromyard Downs
BROCKHAMPTON ESTATE
Whitbourne
Knightwick
Isley
Broadwas
Haven
Sollers Dilwyn
Dilwyn
Aulden
Brierley
Risbury
Marston Stannett
Bromyard
Broxwood
Upper Hill
Marlbrook
Newton
Hegdon Hill
Linley Green
Alfrick
Woonton
Knapton Green
Birley
Hope under Dinmore
Bowley
Pencombe
Stanford Bishop
Alfrick Pound
HAMPTON COURT
Sarnesfield
Weobley
Weobley Marsh
Bush Bank
QUEENSWOOD
Bodenham
SHORTWOOD FAMILY FARM
Little Cowarne
Munderfield Row
Suckley
Ledgemoor
King's Pyon
Westhope
Bodenham Moor
Maund Bryan
Ullingswick
Munderfield Stocks
Acton Beauchamp
Acton Green
Longley Green
Storridge
Canon Pyon
Urdimarsh
The Vauld
Moreton Jeffries
Felton
Stoke Lacy
Calver Hill
Wormsley
Wellington
Walker's Green
Burley Gate
Bishops Frome
Evesbatch
Stony Cross
Norton Canon
Moorhampton
Yarsop
Tillington Common
Marden
Preston Wynne
Much Cowarne
Fromes Hill
Ridgeway Cross
Cradley
Westfield
Staunton on Wye
Yazor
Mansel Lacy
Mansell Gamage
Tillington
Brinsop
Moreton on Lugg
Sutton St Nicholas
Ocle Pychard
Lower Egleton
Newtown
Castle Frome
Mathon
West Malvern
Norbridge
Ham Green
Monnington on Wye
Byford
Bishopstone
Credenhill
Burghill
Pipe and Lyde
KENCHESTER WATER GARDENS
Westhide
Withington
Stretton Grandison
Stanley Hill
Canon Frome
Bosbury
Coddington
Colwall Stone
Colwall Green
Preston on Wye
Moccas
Bridge Sollers
Kenchester
Stretton Sugwas
Shelwick
Shucknall
Yarkhill
Staplow
Canon Bridge
THE WEIR
Swainshill
King's Acre
Holmer
Weston Beggard
Tarrington
Ploughfield
Blakemere
THE FLITS
Lulham
Breinton Common
Upper Breinton
CIDER MUSEUM
Lugwardine
Hagley
Bartestree
Munsley
Wellington Heath
Tyberton
Breinton
Tupsley
Dormington
Alder's End
Trumpet
Bradlow
Madley
Eaton Bishop
Ruckhall
Hereford
Priors Frome
Checkley
Pixley
Ledbury
Hollybush
Shenmore
Cublington
Lower Bullingham
ROTHERWAS
Hampton Bishop
Mordiford
Woolhope Cockshoot
Aylton
Eastnor
EASTNOR
Vowchurch
Turnastone
Brampton
Clehonger
Grafton
Dinedor
Putley
Little Marcle
Golden Valley
Kingstone
Allensmore
Portway
Twyford Common
Holme Lacy
Woolhope
Rushall
Preston
Donnington
Thruxton
Winnal
Callow
Dewshall Court
Fownhope
Cockyard
Aconbury
Sollers Hope
HELLEN'S MANOR
Bromsberrow Hth.
Brown End
St Margaret's
Kerry's Gate
Didley
Kivernoll
King's Thorn
Bolstone
Brockhampton
Much Marcle
Broom's Green
Ryton
Bacton
St Devereux
Little Birch
Little Dewchurch
Falcon
COURT GARDENS
Crossway
Lyne Down
Dymock
Redmarley D'Abitot
Wormbridge
ABBEY DORE COURT
Much Birch
Carey
Ballingham
ST MARY'S CHURCH
Abbey Dore
Howton
Kilpeck
KILPECK CASTLE (REMS) & CHURCH
Much Dewchurch
Wormelow Tump
Penalt
Fawley Chapel
How Caple
Kempley
Poolhill
Ewyas Harold
Orcop Hill
Hoarwithy
Llandinabo
Red Rail
King's Caple
Foy
Hole-in-the-Wall
Brand Green
Pontrilas
Llanwarne
Harewood End
Upper Grove Common
Sellack
Brampton Abbotts
Upton Bishop
Phocle Green
Rowlestone
Monmouth Cap
Bagwy Llydiart
Pencoyd
Orcop
ROSS SPUR SERVICES
Gorsley
Llangua
Kentchurch
Garway
Michaelchurch
Teme
Arrow
Lugg
Lodon
Frome
Wye
Rea
SO
Herefordshire
A49
A456
A4117
A443
A44
A4112
A417
A4103
A438
A465
A480
A4110
A449
A466
A4172
M50
B4368
B4367
B4365
B4364
B4363
B4385
B4367
B4530
B4362
B4361
B4360
B4529
B4457
B4230
B4214
B4204
B4203
B4197
B4220
B4218
B4224
B4399
B4348
B4349
B4352
B4347
B4216
B4215
B4024
B4221
B4201
B4202
B4199
B4113

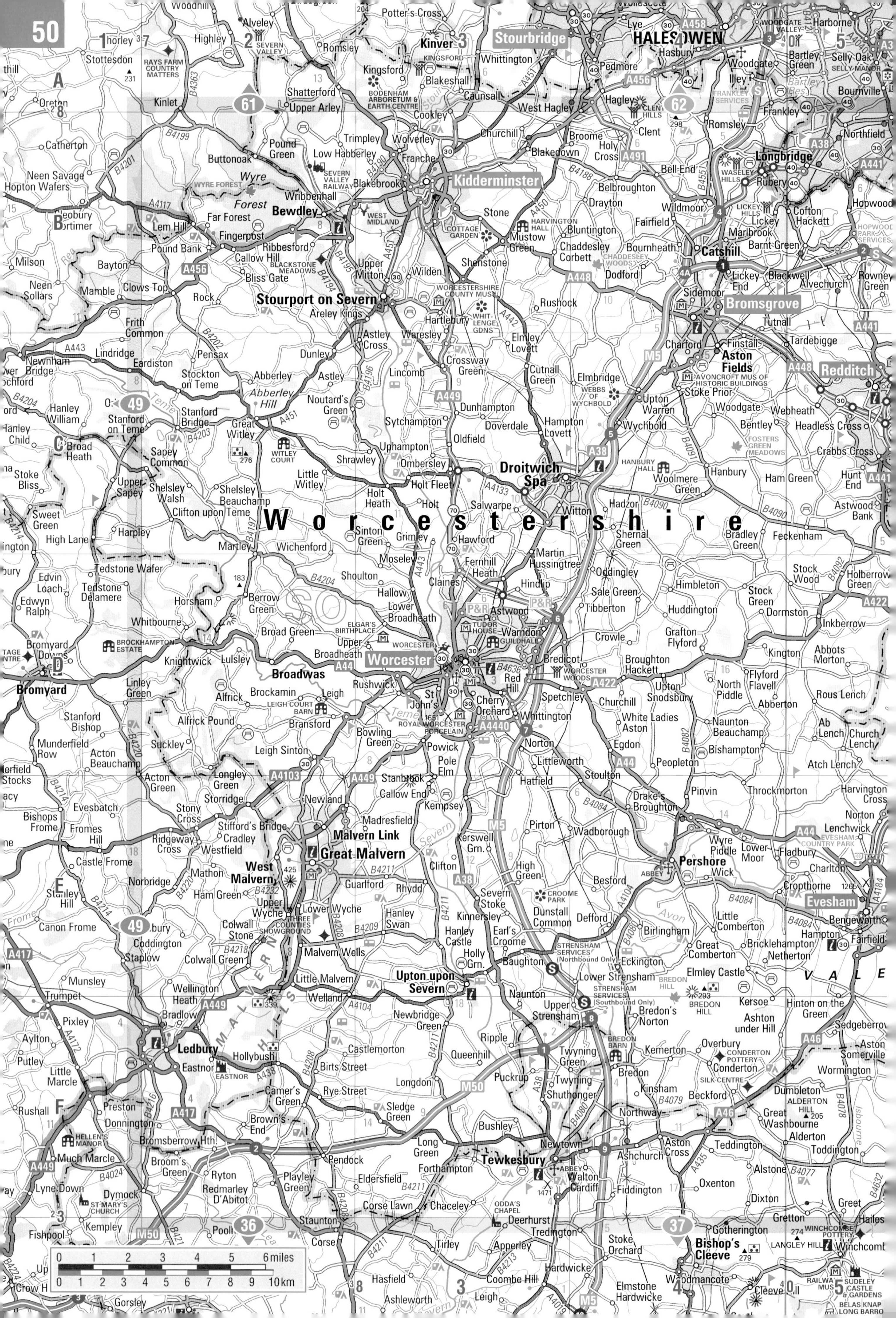

Worcestershire
Stourbridge
Halesowen
Kidderminster
Bewdley
Wyre Forest
Stourport on Severn
Bromsgrove
Redditch
Droitwich Spa
Worcester
Great Malvern
Malvern Link
West Malvern
Malvern Wells
Malvern Hills
Upton upon Severn
Pershore
Evesham
Vale
Tewkesbury
Bishop's Cleeve
Ledbury
Bromyard
Broadwas
Kinver
Hagley
Longbridge
Rubery
Catshill
Aston Fields
Alvechurch
Cleobury Mortimer
Abberley Hill
Ombersley
Fernhill Heath
Martin Hussingtree
Powick
Kempsey
Severn Stoke
Twyning Green
Bredon
Kemerton
Overbury
Beckford
Winchcombe
Deerhurst
Apperley
Hardwicke
Coombe Hill
Ashleworth
Hasfield
Tirley
Corse
Staunton
Eldersfield
Longdon
Much Marcle
Dymock
Kempley
Fishpool
Trumpet
Pixley
Aylton
Putley
Little Marcle
Colwall Stone
Colwall Green
Wellington Heath
Bradlow
Eastnor
Hollybush
Castlemorton
Birts Street
Welland
Little Malvern
Hanley Castle
Hanley Swan
Guarlford
Rhydd
Clifton
Earl's Croome
Croome Park
Defford
Eckington
Birlingham
Great Comberton
Little Comberton
Elmley Castle
Bredon Hill
Ashton under Hill
Kersoe
Hinton on the Green
Sedgeberrow
Aston Somerville
Wormington
Dumbleton
Alderton
Great Washbourne
Teddington
Toddington
Aston Cross
Ashchurch
Walton Cardiff
Fiddington
Oxenton
Dixton
Gretton
Greet
Gotherington
Woodmancote
Cleeve Hill
Stoke Orchard
Elmstone Hardwicke
Tredington
Leigh
Chaceley
Forthampton
Bushley
Ripple
Queenhill
Pendock
Sledge Green
Brown's End
Bromsberrow Hth.
Ryton
Redmarley D'Abitot
Playley Green
Broom's Green
Preston
Donnington
Rushall
Lyne Down
Pixley
Munsley
Coddington
Staplow
Canon Frome
Stanley Hill
Castle Frome
Fromes Hill
Bishops Frome
Evesbatch
Acton Beauchamp
Munderfield Row
Stanford Bishop
Linley Green
Knightwick
Lulsley
Alfrick
Alfrick Pound
Suckley
Longley Green
Storridge
Cradley
Stifford's Bridge
Mathon
Ridgeway Cross
Westfield
Leigh Sinton
Bransford
Brockamin
Leigh
Rushwick
St John's
Bowling Green
Newland
Madresfield
Stanbrook
Callow End
Pole Elm
Broadheath
Upper Broadheath
Lower Broadheath
Hallow
Claines
Grimley
Sinton Green
Holt Heath
Holt Fleet
Shoulton
Moseley
Wichenford
Martley
Berrow Green
Horsham
Whitbourne
Tedstone Wafer
Tedstone Delamere
Edvin Loach
Edwyn Ralph
Bromyard Downs
Harpley
High Lane
Sweet Green
Stoke Bliss
Hanley Child
Hanley William
Broad Heath
Upper Sapey
Sapey Common
Shelsley Walsh
Shelsley Beauchamp
Clifton upon Teme
Stanford on Teme
Stanford Bridge
Stockton on Teme
Great Witley
Little Witley
Witley Court
Shrawley
Astley
Astley Cross
Abberley
Pensax
Eardiston
Lindridge
Newnham Bridge
Frith Common
Mamble
Bayton
Clows Top
Rock
Far Forest
Callow Hill
Bliss Gate
Ribbesford
Lem Hill
Pound Bank
Fingerpost
Neen Sollars
Milson
Neen Savage
Hopton Wafers
Catherton
Oreton
Kinlet
Stottesdon
Highley
Alveley
Buttonoak
Pound Green
Shatterford
Upper Arley
Low Habberley
Trimpley
Wribbenhall
Blakebrook
Franche
Wolverley
Cookley
Kingsford
Blakeshall
Caunsall
Whittington
Romsley
Potter's Cross
Churchill
Blakedown
West Hagley
Broome
Holy Cross
Clent
Clent Hills
Romsley
Frankley
Bell End
Belbroughton
Drayton
Fairfield
Wildmoor
Stone
Harvington Hall
Mustow Green
Bluntington
Chaddesley Corbett
Bournheath
Dodford
Shenstone
Upper Mitton
Wilden
Hartlebury
Waresley
Whitlenge Gdns
Worcestershire County Museum
Elmley Lovett
Rushock
Crossway Green
Lincomb
Cutnall Green
Elmbridge
Webbs of Wychbold
Upton Warren
Wychbold
Stoke Prior
Avoncroft Mus of Historic Buildings
Charford
Finstall
Tardebigge
Tutnall
Sidemoor
Lickey End
Blackwell
Lickey
Lickey Hills
Marlbrook
Barnt Green
Cofton Hackett
Hopwood
Rowney Green
Dunhampton
Doverdale
Hampton Lovett
Sytchampton
Uphampton
Oldfield
Noutard's Green
Salwarpe
Hawford
Witton
Hadzor
Hanbury
Hanbury Hall
Woolmere Green
Bentley
Woodgate
Webheath
Headless Cross
Crabbs Cross
Ham Green
Hunt End
Astwood Bank
Feckenham
Bradley Green
Shernal Green
Oddingley
Hindlip
Himbleton
Sale Green
Tibberton
Huddington
Stock Wood
Stock Green
Dormston
Holberrow Green
Inkberrow
Crowle
Grafton Flyford
Broughton Hackett
Kington
Abbots Morton
Flyford Flavell
North Piddle
Rous Lench
Abberton
Upton Snodsbury
Churchill
White Ladies Aston
Naunton Beauchamp
Bishampton
Ab Lench
Church Lench
Atch Lench
Spetchley
Bredicot
Warndon
Astwood
Red Hill
Cherry Orchard
Whittington
Norton
Littleworth
Hatfield
Stoulton
Egdon
Peopleton
Pinvin
Throckmorton
Harvington Cross
Norton
Lenchwick
Evesham Country Park
Fladbury
Lower Moor
Wyre Piddle
Charlton
Cropthorne
Drake's Broughton
Wadborough
Pirton
Kerswell Grn.
High Green
Besford
Dunstall Common
Kinnersley
Baughton
Holly Grn.
Naunton
Upper Strensham
Lower Strensham
Strensham Services
Bredon's Norton
Bredon Barn
Kinsham
Northway
Shuthonger
Twyning
Puckrup
Mitton
Newtown
Bengeworth
Hampton
Bricklehampton
Netherton
Fairfield
Charlton
Tudor House
Guildhall
Worcester Woods
Royal Worcester Porcelain
Three Counties Showground
Leigh Court Barn
Brockhampton Estate
Elgar's Birthplace
Hellen's Manor
St Mary's Church
Odda's Chapel
Abbey
Winchcombe Pottery
Langley Hill
Sudeley Castle & Gardens
Railway Mus
Belas Knap Long Barrow
Conderton Pottery
Silk Centre
Conderton
Gotherington
Bodenham Arboretum & Earth Centre
Severn Valley Railway
West Midland
Rays Farm Country Matters
Cottage Garden
Fosters Green Meadows
Blackstone Meadows
M5
M50
A38
A44
A46
A449
A456
A448
A441
A442
A443
A4103
A417
A438
A4104
A4440
A422
A4133
A451
A491
A458
0 1 2 3 4 5 6 miles
0 1 2 3 4 5 6 7 8 9 10 km

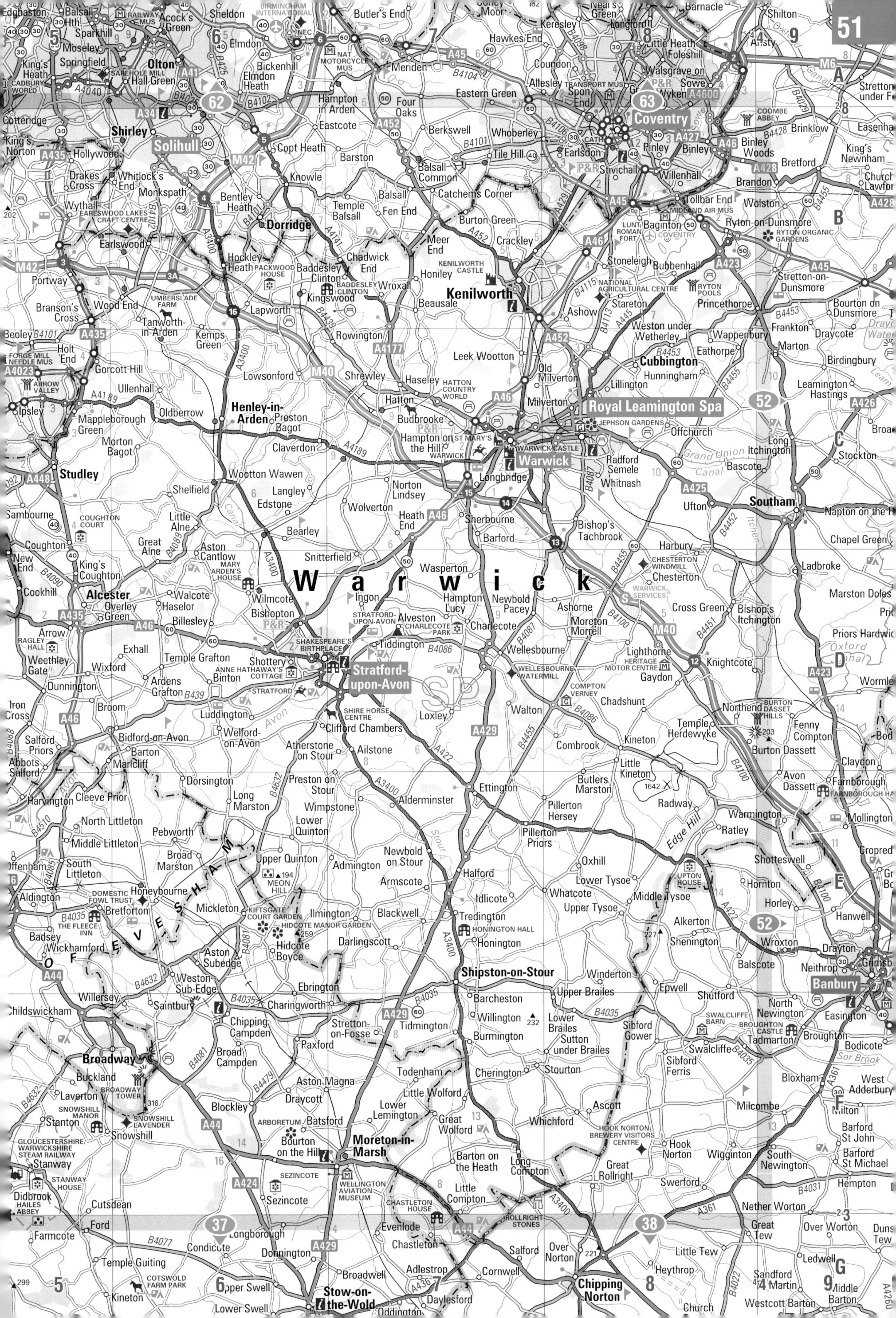
Warwick
Edgbaston
Balsall Hth
Sparkhill
Moseley
Springfield
King's Heath
Olton
Acock's Green
Sheldon
Birmingham International
NEC
Elmdon
Bickenhill
Elmdon Heath
Hall Green
Sarehole Mill
Cadbury World
Cotteridge
King's Norton
Shirley
Solihull
Hollywood
Drakes Cross
Whitlock's End
Monkspath
Wythall
Earlswood Lakes Craft Centre
Earlswood
Portway
Branson's Cross
Wood End
Beoley
Forge Mill Needle Mus
Holt End
Gorcott Hill
Arrow Valley
Ipsley
Mappleborough Green
Morton Bagot
Studley
Sambourne
Coughton Court
Coughton
New End
King's Coughton
Cookhill
Alcester
Overley Green
Arrow
Ragley Hall
Weethley Gate
Wixford
Exhall
Dunnington
Iron Cross
Broom
Salford Priors
Abbots Salford
Marlcliff
Barton
Bidford-on-Avon
Harvington
Cleeve Prior
North Littleton
Middle Littleton
South Littleton
Offenham
Aldington
Badsey
Wickhamford
Bretforton
Domestic Fowl Trust
Honeybourne
The Fleece Inn
Pebworth
Broad Marston
Vale of Evesham
Mickleton
Long Marston
Dorsington
Upper Quinton
Meon Hill
Kiftsgate Court Garden
Hidcote Manor Garden
Hidcote Boyce
Ilmington
Aston Subedge
Weston-Sub-Edge
Willersey
Saintbury
Childswickham
Broadway
Buckland
Laverton
Broadway Tower
Snowshill Manor
Snowshill Lavender
Stanton
Snowshill
Gloucestershire Warwickshire Steam Railway
Stanway
Stanway House
Didbrook
Hailes Abbey
Cutsdean
Ford
Farmcote
Temple Guiting
Cotswold Farm Park
Kineton
Upper Swell
Lower Swell
Stow-on-the-Wold
Longborough
Condicote
Donnington
Broadwell
Adlestrop
Daylesford
Oddington
Evenlode
Chastleton
Chastleton House
Rollright Stones
Salford
Over Norton
Chipping Norton
Cornwell
Heythrop
Little Tew
Great Tew
Chipping Campden
Broad Campden
Ebrington
Charingworth
Paxford
Blockley
Aston Magna
Draycott
Batsford
Arboretum
Bourton on the Hill
Sezincote
Moreton-in-Marsh
Wellington Aviation Museum
Stretton-on-Fosse
Tidmington
Todenham
Little Wolford
Great Wolford
Lower Lemington
Barton on the Heath
Long Compton
Little Compton
Shipston-on-Stour
Barcheston
Willington
Burmington
Cherington
Stourton
Whichford
Ascott
Long Compton
Great Rollright
Hook Norton
Hook Norton Brewery Visitors Centre
Wigginton
Swerford
Nether Worton
Over Worton
Ledwell
Sandford St Martin
Westcott Barton
Middle Barton
South Newington
Barford St John
Barford St Michael
Hempton
Milcombe
Milton
Bloxham
West Adderbury
Bodicote
Broughton
Broughton Castle
North Newington
Tadmarton
Swalcliffe
Swalcliffe Barn
Sibford Gower
Sibford Ferris
Shutford
Epwell
Winderton
Upper Brailes
Lower Brailes
Sutton under Brailes
Banbury
Neithrop
Drayton
Wroxton
Balscote
Easington
Grimsbury
Hanwell
Horley
Hornton
Shotteswell
Alkerton
Shenington
Upton House
Middle Tysoe
Upper Tysoe
Lower Tysoe
Whatcote
Oxhill
Idlicote
Tredington
Honington
Honington Hall
Halford
Armscote
Newbold on Stour
Admington
Blackwell
Darlingscott
Wimpstone
Lower Quinton
Preston on Stour
Alderminster
Atherstone on Stour
Ailstone
Clifford Chambers
Shire Horse Centre
Ettington
Pillerton Hersey
Pillerton Priors
Butlers Marston
Radway
Edge Hill
Ratley
Warmington
Mollington
Cropredy
Farnborough
Farnborough Hall
Avon Dassett
Claydon
Burton Dassett
Burton Dasset Hills
Fenny Compton
Temple Herdewyke
Northend
Little Kineton
Kineton
Combrook
Walton
Loxley
Compton Verney
Chadshunt
Gaydon
Heritage Motor Centre
Lighthorne
Wellesbourne
Wellesbourne Watermill
Moreton Morrell
Ashorne
Charlecote
Charlecote Park
Hampton Lucy
Newbold Pacey
Wasperton
Alveston
Tiddington
Stratford-upon-Avon
Shakespeare's Birthplace
Anne Hathaway's Cottage
Shottery
Binton
Temple Grafton
Ardens Grafton
Luddington
Welford-on-Avon
Bishopton
Wilmcote
Mary Arden's House
Aston Cantlow
Great Alne
Little Alne
Walcote
Haselor
Billesley
Snitterfield
Bearley
Wolverton
Langley
Edstone
Shelfield
Wootton Wawen
Henley-in-Arden
Preston Bagot
Claverdon
Oldberrow
Ullenhall
Tanworth-in-Arden
Umberslade Farm
Kemps Green
Lowsonford
Lapworth
Hockley Heath
Packwood House
Dorridge
Bentley Heath
Knowle
Copt Heath
Hampton in Arden
Eastcote
Barston
Temple Balsall
Balsall Common
Berkswell
Four Oaks
Meriden
Nat Motorcycle Mus
Butler's End
Hawkes End
Keresley
Coundon
Allesley
Eastern Green
Whoberley
Tile Hill
Earlsdon
Coventry
Spon End
Transport Mus
Little Heath
Foleshill
Longford
Walsgrave on Sowe
Wyken
Coombe Abbey
Brinklow
Stretton under Fosse
Ansty
Shilton
Barnacle
Binley
Binley Woods
Pinley
Stivichall
Willenhall
Bretford
King's Newnham
Church Lawford
Brandon
Wolston
Tollbar End
Midland Air Mus
Baginton
Lunt Roman Fort
Ryton-on-Dunsmore
Ryton Organic Gardens
Ryton Pools
Stoneleigh
Bubbenhall
National Agricultural Centre
Stretton-on-Dunsmore
Bourton on Dunsmore
Princethorpe
Frankton
Draycote
Draycote Water
Marton
Birdingbury
Wappenbury
Eathorpe
Weston under Wetherley
Stareton
Ashow
Cubbington
Hunningham
Lillington
Leamington Hastings
Royal Leamington Spa
Jephson Gardens
Offchurch
Long Itchington
Bascote
Stockton
Southam
Napton on the Hill
Ufton
Radford Semele
Whitnash
Harbury
Chesterton
Chesterton Windmill
Warwick Services
Ladbroke
Chapel Green
Marston Doles
Bishop's Itchington
Cross Green
Knightcote
Priors Hardwick
Wormleighton
Bishop's Tachbrook
Barford
Sherbourne
Longbridge
Warwick
Warwick Castle
St Mary's
Hampton on the Hill
Budbrooke
Hatton
Hatton Country World
Haseley
Shrewley
Rowington
Norton Lindsey
Heath End
Milverton
Old Milverton
Leek Wootton
Kenilworth
Kenilworth Castle
Beausale
Honiley
Wroxall
Baddesley Clinton
Kingswood
Chadwick End
Fen End
Balsall
Meer End
Burton Green
Crackley
Catchems Corner
Grand Union Canal
Oxford Canal

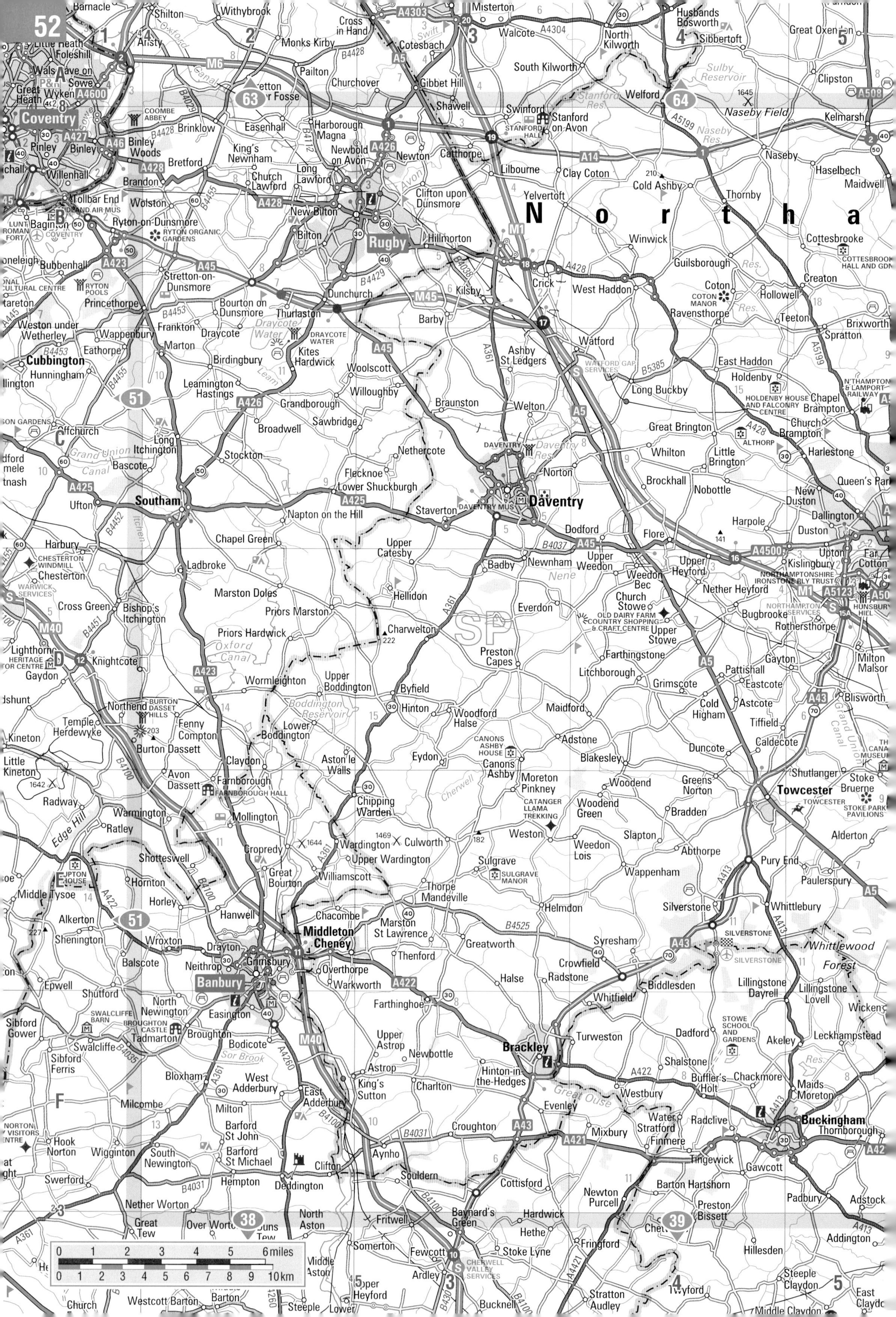

Barnacle
Shilton
Withybrook
Cross in Hand
Misterton
Husbands Bosworth
Great Oxendon
Ansty
Monks Kirby
Cotesbach
Walcote
North Kilworth
Sibbertoft
Little Heath
Foleshill
M6
Pailton
South Kilworth
Walsgrave on Sowe
Great Heath
Wyken
A4600
Churchover
Gibbet Hill
Sulby Reservoir
Clipston
Shawell
Welford
Naseby Field
Kelmarsh
Coventry
Coombe Abbey
Brinklow
Easenhall
Harborough Magna
Swinford
Stanford on Avon
Stanford Hall
Stanford Res.
Naseby Res.
Pinley
Binley
Binley Woods
King's Newnham
Newbold on Avon
Newton
Catthorpe
A14
Naseby
Haselbech
Willenhall
Bretford
Church Lawford
Long Lawford
Lilbourne
Clay Coton
Cold Ashby
Maidwell
Brandon
A428
Clifton upon Dunsmore
Yelvertoft
Thornby
Tollbar End
Wolston
Midland Air Mus
New Bilton
Northa
Baginton
Lunt Roman Fort
Coventry
Ryton-on-Dunsmore
Ryton Organic Gardens
Bilton
Rugby
Hillmorton
Winwick
Cottesbrooke
Cottesbrooke Hall and Gdns
Bubbenhall
A423
A45
Stretton-on-Dunsmore
Ryton Pools
B4429
B4038
Crick
West Haddon
Guilsborough
Creaton
Princethorpe
Bourton on Dunsmore
Thurlaston
Dunchurch
M45
Kilsby
Coton
Coton Manor
Hollowell
Weston under Wetherley
Wappenbury
Frankton
Draycote
Draycote Water
Kites Hardwick
Barby
Watford
Ravensthorpe
Teeton
Brixworth
Spratton
Eathorpe
Marton
Ashby St Ledgers
Watford Gap Services
East Haddon
Cubbington
Hunningham
Birdingbury
Woolscott
A361
B5385
Holdenby
Leamington Hastings
Willoughby
Long Buckby
Holdenby House and Falconry Centre
Chapel Brampton
N'hampton & Lamport Railway
Grandborough
Braunston
Welton
A426
Broadwell
Sawbridge
Great Brington
Church Brampton
Offchurch
Long Itchington
Grand Union Canal
Nethercote
Daventry
Daventry Res.
Whilton
Little Brington
Althorp
Harlestone
Bascote
Stockton
Norton
Brockhall
Nobottle
Queen's Park
A425
Southam
Flecknoe
Lower Shuckburgh
New Duston
Ufton
Napton on the Hill
Staverton
Daventry Mus
Dallington
Harpole
Dodford
Flore
Duston
Harbury
Chapel Green
Upper Catesby
B4037
Upper Weedon
Upper Heyford
A4500
Upton
Chesterton Windmill
Chesterton
Ladbroke
Badby
Newnham
Kislingbury
Far Cotton
Warwick Services
Nene
Weedon Bec
Northamptonshire Ironstone Rly Trust
Marston Doles
Hellidon
Church Stowe
Nether Heyford
M1
A5123
Cross Green
Bishop's Itchington
Priors Marston
Everdon
Old Dairy Farm Country Shopping & Craft Centre
Northampton Services
Hunsbury Hill
Bugbrooke
M40
Priors Hardwick
Charwelton
SP
Upper Stowe
Rothersthorpe
Oxford Canal
Preston Capes
Farthingstone
Gayton
Milton Malsor
Lighthorne Heritage Centre
Knightcote
Gaydon
Wormleighton
Upper Boddington
Litchborough
Pattishall
Eastcote
Byfield
Grimscote
Blisworth
Northend
Burton Dasset Hills
Boddington Reservoir
Hinton
Woodford Halse
Maidford
Cold Higham
Astcote
Temple Herdewyke
Fenny Compton
Lower Boddington
Tiffield
Kineton
Burton Dassett
Canons Ashby House
Adstone
Caldecote
Little Kineton
Claydon
Aston le Walls
Eydon
Canons Ashby
Blakesley
Duncote
Avon Dassett
Farnborough
Farnborough Hall
Moreton Pinkney
Woodend
Greens Norton
Shutlanger
Stoke Bruerne
Radway
Chipping Warden
Cherwell
Catanger Llama Trekking
Woodend Green
Bradden
Towcester
Stoke Park Pavilions
Edge Hill
Warmington
Ratley
Mollington
Wardington
Culworth
Upper Wardington
Weston
Weedon Lois
Slapton
Abthorpe
Alderton
Upton House
Shotteswell
Cropredy
Great Bourton
Williamscott
Sulgrave
Sulgrave Manor
Wappenham
Pury End
Paulerspury
Hornton
Thorpe Mandeville
Middle Tysoe
Horley
Alkerton
Hanwell
Chacombe
Marston St Lawrence
Helmdon
Silverstone
Whittlebury
Shenington
Middleton Cheney
Greatworth
B4525
Syresham
Silverstone
Whittlewood Forest
Wroxton
Drayton
Grimsbury
Balscote
Neithrop
Overthorpe
Thenford
Crowfield
Radstone
Halse
Lillingstone Dayrell
Lillingstone Lovell
Banbury
Epwell
Shutford
Warkworth
A422
Biddlesden
Whitfield
Wicken
North Newington
Farthinghoe
Easington
Swalcliffe Barn
Broughton Castle
Broughton
Tadmarton
Sibford Gower
Swalcliffe
B4035
Bodicote
Sor Brook
Upper Astrop
Newbottle
Brackley
Turweston
Stowe School and Gardens
Dadford
Akeley
Leckhampstead
Shalstone
Sibford Ferris
Bloxham
West Adderbury
Astrop
King's Sutton
Charlton
Hinton-in-the-Hedges
Great Ouse
Westbury
Buffler's Holt
Chackmore
Maids Moreton
Milcombe
Milton
East Adderbury
Evenley
Water Stratford
Radclive
Buckingham
Thornborough
Barford St John
B4031
Croughton
Mixbury
Finmere
Hook Norton
Wigginton
South Newington
Barford St Michael
Aynho
Clifton
Tingewick
Gawcott
Swerford
B4031
Hempton
Deddington
Souldern
Cottisford
Newton Purcell
Barton Hartshorn
Padbury
Adstock
Nether Worton
Preston Bissett
Great Tew
Over Worton
North Aston
Fritwell
Baynard's Green
Hardwick
Hethe
Fringford
Hillesden
Addington
Somerton
Fewcott
Stoke Lyne
Cherwell Valley Services
Middle Aston
Upper Heyford
Ardley
Stratton Audley
Twyford
Steeple Claydon
East Claydon
Church
Westcott Barton
Steeple
Bucknell
Middle Claydon
0 1 2 3 4 5 6 miles
0 1 2 3 4 5 6 7 8 9 10 km

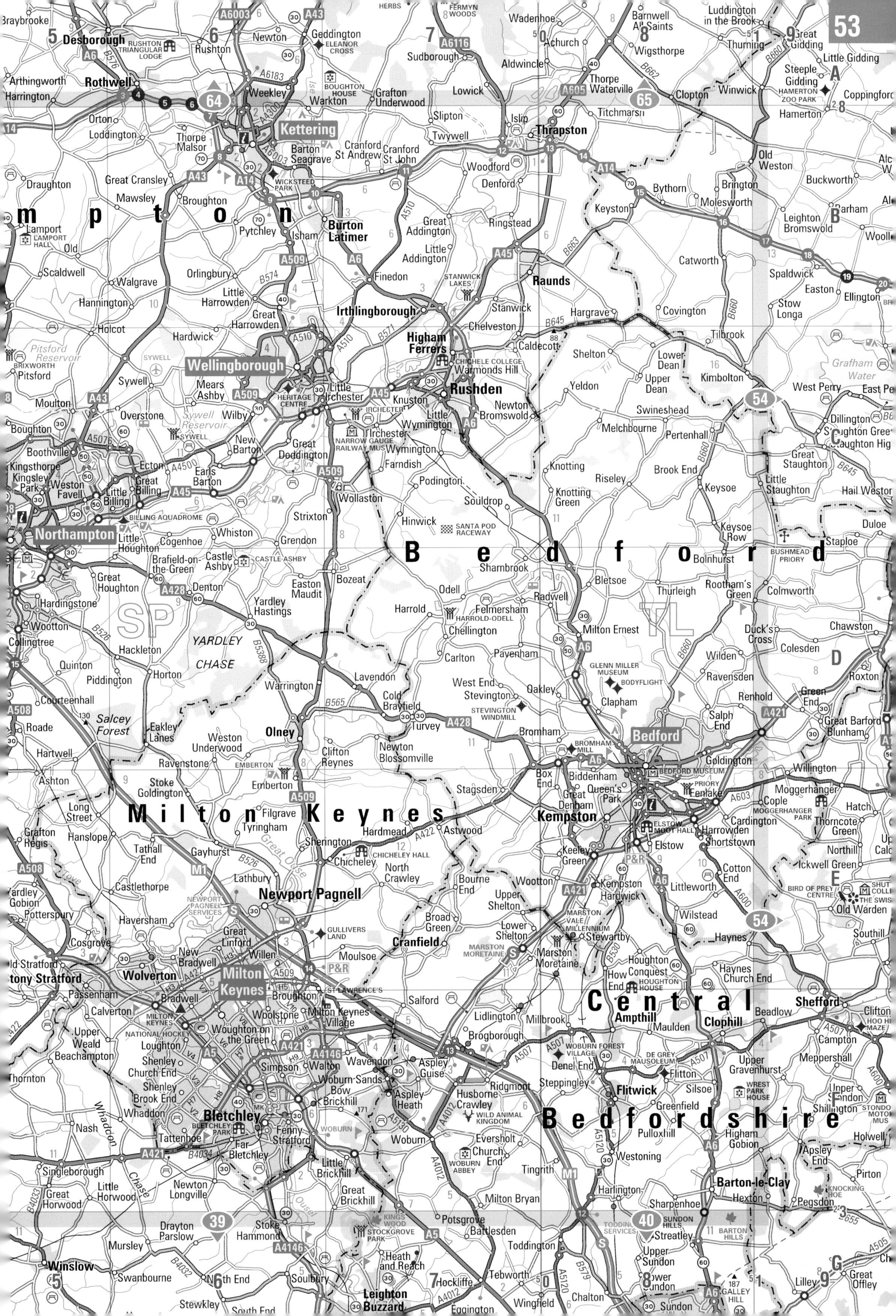
Braybrooke
Desborough
RUSHTON TRIANGULAR LODGE
Rushton
Newton
Geddington
ELEANOR CROSS
HERBS
FERMYN WOODS
Sudborough
Wadenhoe
Achurch
Barnwell
All Saints
Wigsthorpe
Luddington in the Brook
Thurning
Great Gidding
Little Gidding
Arthingworth
Rothwell
Harrington
Weekley
BOUGHTON HOUSE
Warkton
Grafton Underwood
Lowick
Aldwincle
Thorpe Waterville
Clopton
Winwick
Steeple Gidding
HAMERTON ZOO PARK
Coppingford
Hamerton
Orton
Loddington
Thorpe Malsor
Kettering
Barton Seagrave
Cranford St Andrew
Cranford St John
Slipton
Twywell
Islip
Thrapston
Titchmarsh
Old Weston
Draughton
Great Cransley
Mawsley
Broughton
WICKSTEED PARK
Woodford
Denford
Bythorn
Brington
Molesworth
Buckworth
Keyston
Lamport
LAMPORT HALL
Old
Pytchley
Isham
Burton Latimer
Great Addington
Little Addington
Ringstead
Leighton Bromswold
Barham
Scaldwell
Walgrave
Orlingbury
Little Harrowden
Great Harrowden
Finedon
Irthlingborough
STANWICK LAKES
Raunds
Stanwick
Catworth
Spaldwick
Easton
Ellington
Stow Longa
Hannington
Holcot
Hardwick
Pitsford Reservoir
BRIXWORTH
Pitsford
SYWELL
Sywell
Wellingborough
Higham Ferrers
CHICHELE COLLEGE
Chelveston
Caldecott
Hargrave
Covington
Tilbrook
Shelton
Lower Dean
Upper Dean
Kimbolton
Grafham Water
West Perry
East Perry
Mears Ashby
HERITAGE CENTRE
Little Irchester
Knuston
Rushden
Warmonds Hill
Newton Bromswold
Yeldon
Swineshead
Melchbourne
Pertenhall
Dillington
Moulton
Overstone
Sywell Reservoir
Wilby
IRCHESTER
Irchester
NARROW GAUGE RAILWAY MUS
Little Wymington
Wymington
Great Staughton
Boughton
Boothville
Ecton
New Barton
Great Doddington
Farndish
Podington
Knotting
Riseley
Brook End
Keysoe
Little Staughton
Hail Weston
Kingsthorpe
Kingsley Park
Weston Favell
Great Billing
Little Billing
Earls Barton
BILLING AQUADROME
Wollaston
Souldrop
Knotting Green
Northampton
Strixton
Hinwick
SANTA POD RACEWAY
Keysoe Row
Duloe
Staploe
Little Houghton
Cogenhoe
Whiston
Grendon
Bedford
BUSHMEAD PRIORY
Bolnhurst
Brafield-on-the-Green
Castle Ashby
CASTLE ASHBY
Bozeat
Sharnbrook
Great Houghton
Denton
Easton Maudit
Odell
Bletsoe
Thurleigh
Rootham's Green
Colmworth
Hardingstone
SP
Yardley Hastings
Harrold
HARROLD-ODELL
Felmersham
Radwell
TL
Wootton
Collingtree
YARDLEY CHASE
Hackleton
Chellington
Milton Ernest
Duck's Cross
Chawston
Colesden
Quinton
Piddington
Horton
Carlton
Pavenham
GLENN MILLER MUSEUM
BODYFLIGHT
Wilden
Ravensden
Roxton
Courteenhall
Warrington
Lavendon
West End
Stevington
Oakley
Clapham
Renhold
Green End
Roade
Salcey Forest
Eakley Lanes
Weston Underwood
Olney
Cold Brayfield
Turvey
STEVINGTON WINDMILL
Salph End
Great Barford
Blunham
Hartwell
Clifton Reynes
Newton Blossomville
Bromham
BROMHAM MILL
Goldington
Ravenstone
EMBERTON
Emberton
Stoke Goldington
Ashton
Box End
Biddenham
Great Denham
Queen's Park
BEDFORD MUSEUM
PRIORY
Fenlake
Willington
Moggerhanger
MOGGERHANGER PARK
Cople
Hatch
Long Street
Milton Keynes
Filgrave
Tyringham
Stagsden
Hardmead
Astwood
Kempston
ELSTOW MOOT HALL
Harrowden
Cardington
Thorncote Green
Grafton Regis
Hanslope
Tathall End
Gayhurst
Great Ouse
Sherington
CHICHELEY HALL
Chicheley
North Crawley
Keeley Green
Elstow
Shortstown
Northill
Ickwell Green
Cotton End
Yardley Gobion
Potterspury
Castlethorpe
Lathbury
NEWPORT PAGNELL SERVICES
Newport Pagnell
Bourne End
Wootton
Kempston Hardwick
Littleworth
BIRD OF PREY CENTRE
THE SWISS
Old Warden
Haversham
Great Linford
GULLIVERS LAND
Broad Green
Upper Shelton
Lower Shelton
MARSTON VALE MILLENNIUM
Wilstead
Stewartby
Haynes
Southill
Cosgrove
Old Stratford
Stony Stratford
New Bradwell
Willen
Moulsoe
Cranfield
MARSTON MORETAINE
Marston Moretaine
Houghton Conquest
How End
HOUGHTON HOUSE
Haynes Church End
Wolverton
Milton Keynes
Broughton
ST LAWRENCE'S
Passenham
Bradwell
Woolstone
Milton Keynes Village
Salford
Central
Lidlington
Millbrook
Ampthill
Maulden
Clophill
Beadlow
Shefford
Clifton
Calverton
MILTON KEYNES
NATIONAL HOCKEY
Woughton on the Green
Brogborough
WOBURN FOREST VILLAGE
DE GREY MAUSOLEUM
Campton
Upper Weald
Loughton
Shenley Church End
Simpson
Walton
Wavendon
Aspley Guise
Denel End
Flitton
Upper Gravenhurst
Meppershall
Beachampton
Thornton
Shenley Brook End
Woburn Sands
Bow Brickhill
Aspley Heath
Husborne Crawley
Ridgmont
Steppingley
Flitwick
Silsoe
WREST PARK HOUSE
Whaddon
Bletchley
BLETCHLEY PARK
Fenny Stratford
WOBURN
WILD ANIMAL KINGDOM
Greenfield
Bedfordshire
Upper Stondon
Shillington
Nash
Tattenhoe
Far Bletchley
Woburn
Eversholt
WOBURN ABBEY
Church End
Pulloxhill
Higham Gobion
Holwell
Singleborough
Little Brickhill
Tingrith
Westoning
Apsley End
Pirton
Great Horwood
Little Horwood
Newton Longville
Great Brickhill
Milton Bryan
Harlington
Barton-le-Clay
Hexton
KNOCKING HOE
Pegsdon
Sharpenhoe
Drayton Parslow
Stoke Hammond
KINGS WOOD
STOCKGROVE PARK
Potsgrove
Battlesden
TODDINGTON SERVICES
SUNDON HOUSE
Streatley
BARTON HILLS
Mursley
Toddington
Upper Sundon
Winslow
Swanbourne
Mursley
Heath and Reach
Hockliffe
Tebworth
Lower Sundon
GALLEY HILL
Lilley
Great Offley
Stewkley
Sixth End
Soulbury
Leighton Buzzard
Eggington
Wingfield
Chalton
Sundon
South End
A6003
A43
A6116
A605
A6
A14
A509
A510
A45
A4500
A5076
A428
A508
A422
A421
A4146
A5
A507
A600
A603
A4012
A5120
A5130
A505
B576
B662
B660
B663
B574
B571
B645
B526
B5388
B565
B530
B4034
B4033
B4032
B579
B655
M1
64
65
54
39
40

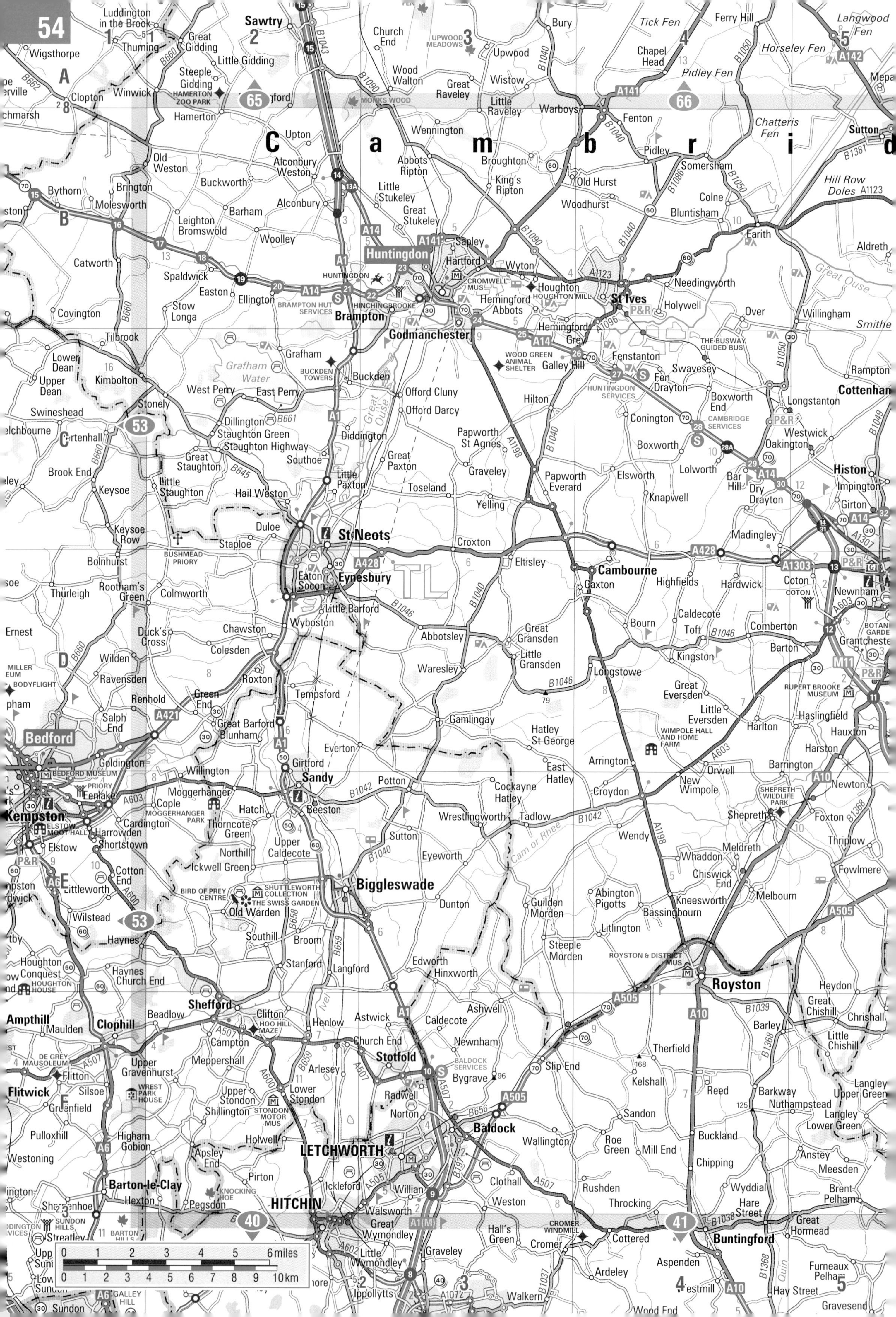
Cambridgeshire
TL
Luddington in the Brook
Sawtry
Church End
Upwood Meadows
Bury
Tick Fen
Ferry Hill
Langwood Fen
Thurning
Great Gidding
Little Gidding
Wigsthorpe
Upwood
Chapel Head
Horseley Fen
Pidley Fen
Steeple Gidding
Hamerton Zoo Park
Wood Walton
Great Raveley
Wistow
Clopton
Winwick
Monks Wood
Little Raveley
Warboys
Fenton
Chatteris Fen
Sutton
Hamerton
Upton
Wennington
Abbots Ripton
Broughton
Pidley
Somersham
Old Weston
Alconbury Weston
King's Ripton
Old Hurst
Hill Row Doles
Bythorn
Brington
Buckworth
Little Stukeley
Woodhurst
Colne
Bluntisham
Molesworth
Barham
Alconbury
Great Stukeley
Leighton Bromswold
Earith
Aldreth
Woolley
Sapley
Huntingdon
Hartford
Wyton
Catworth
Spaldwick
Easton
Ellington
Cromwell Mus
Houghton
Houghton Mill
St Ives
Needingworth
Great Ouse
Brampton Hut Services
Hinchingbrooke
Brampton
Hemingford Abbots
Holywell
Over
Willingham
Smithe
Covington
Tilbrook
Godmanchester
Hemingford Grey
The Busway Guided Bus
Grafham
Grafham Water
Wood Green Animal Shelter
Galley Hill
Fenstanton
Swavesey
Rampton
Lower Dean
Upper Dean
Kimbolton
Buckden Towers
Buckden
Fen Drayton
Cottenham
West Perry
East Perry
Offord Cluny
Hilton
Huntingdon Services
Boxworth End
Longstanton
Swineshead
Stonely
Dillington
Offord Darcy
Conington
Cambridge Services
Staughton Green
Staughton Highway
Diddington
Papworth St Agnes
Westwick
Oakington
Pertenhall
Great Staughton
Southoe
Great Paxton
Boxworth
Brook End
Little Staughton
Little Paxton
Graveley
Papworth Everard
Elsworth
Lolworth
Bar Hill
Dry Drayton
Histon
Impington
Keysoe
Hail Weston
Toseland
Knapwell
Yelling
Girton
Keysoe Row
Duloe
St Neots
Madingley
Staploe
Croxton
Bushmead Priory
Bolnhurst
Eltisley
Cambourne
Eaton Socon
Eynesbury
Caxton
Highfields
Hardwick
Coton
Newnham
Thurleigh
Roxton's Green
Colmworth
Little Barford
Caldecote
Ernest
Chawston
Wyboston
Abbotsley
Great Gransden
Bourn
Toft
Comberton
Grantchester
Duck's Cross
Colesden
Little Gransden
Kingston
Barton
Wilden
Waresley
Longstowe
Ravensden
Roxton
Miller Mus
Bodyflight
Renhold
Green End
Tempsford
Great Eversden
Little Eversden
Rupert Brooke Museum
Salph End
Gamlingay
Haslingfield
Hatley St George
Harlton
Hauxton
Bedford
Great Barford
Blunham
Wimpole Hall and Home Farm
Harston
Goldington
Everton
Girtford
Arrington
Barrington
Bedford Museum
Willington
Sandy
East Hatley
Orwell
Newton
Priory
Fenlake
Moggerhanger
Potton
Cockayne Hatley
New Wimpole
Croydon
Shepreth Wildlife Park
Kempston
Cople
Hatch
Beeston
Moggerhanger Park
Cardington
Thorncote Green
Wrestlingworth
Tadlow
Shepreth
Foxton
Elstow Moot Hall
Harrowden
Elstow
Shortstown
Sutton
Wendy
Cam or Rhee
Thriplow
Northill
Upper Caldecote
Meldreth
Cotton End
Ickwell Green
Eyeworth
Whaddon
Fowlmere
Chiswick End
Littleworth
Bird of Prey Centre
Shuttleworth Collection
The Swiss Garden
Old Warden
Biggleswade
Guilden Morden
Abington Pigotts
Kneesworth
Melbourn
Bassingbourn
Dunton
Wilstead
Southill
Litlington
Broom
Steeple Morden
Haynes
Royston & District Mus
Houghton Conquest
Houghton House
Haynes Church End
Stanford
Langford
Edworth
Hinxworth
Royston
Heydon
Ampthill
Maulden
Clophill
Beadlow
Shefford
Clifton
Ashwell
Great Chishill
Chrishall
Hoo Hill Maze
Henlow
Astwick
Caldecote
Barley
Campton
Church End
Newnham
Little Chishill
De Grey Mausoleum
Flitton
Upper Gravenhurst
Meppershall
Stotfold
Therfield
Arlesey
Baldock Services
Bygrave
Slip End
Flitwick
Silsoe
Wrest Park House
Upper Stondon
Lower Stondon
Radwell
Kelshall
Reed
Barkway
Langley Upper Green
Greenfield
Shillington
Stondon Motor Mus
Norton
Nuthampstead
Langley Lower Green
Baldock
Sandon
Pulloxhill
Higham Gobion
Holwell
Wallington
Roe Green
Mill End
Buckland
Westoning
Letchworth
Apsley End
Chipping
Anstey
Meesden
Pirton
Clothall
Barton-le-Clay
Ickleford
William
Rushden
Wyddial
Brent Pelham
Knocking Hoe
Hexton
Pegsdon
Hitchin
Weston
Throcking
Hare Street
Sharpenhoe
Sundon Hills
Walsworth
Great Wymondley
Hall's Green
Cromer Windmill
Cottered
Buntingford
Great Hormead
Streatley
Barton Hills
Little Wymondley
Graveley
Cromer
Aspenden
Furneaux Pelham
Ardeley
Ippollytts
Walkern
Westmill
Hay Street
Gravesend
Galley Hill
Sundon
Wood End
0 1 2 3 4 5 6 miles
0 1 2 3 4 5 6 7 8 9 10 km

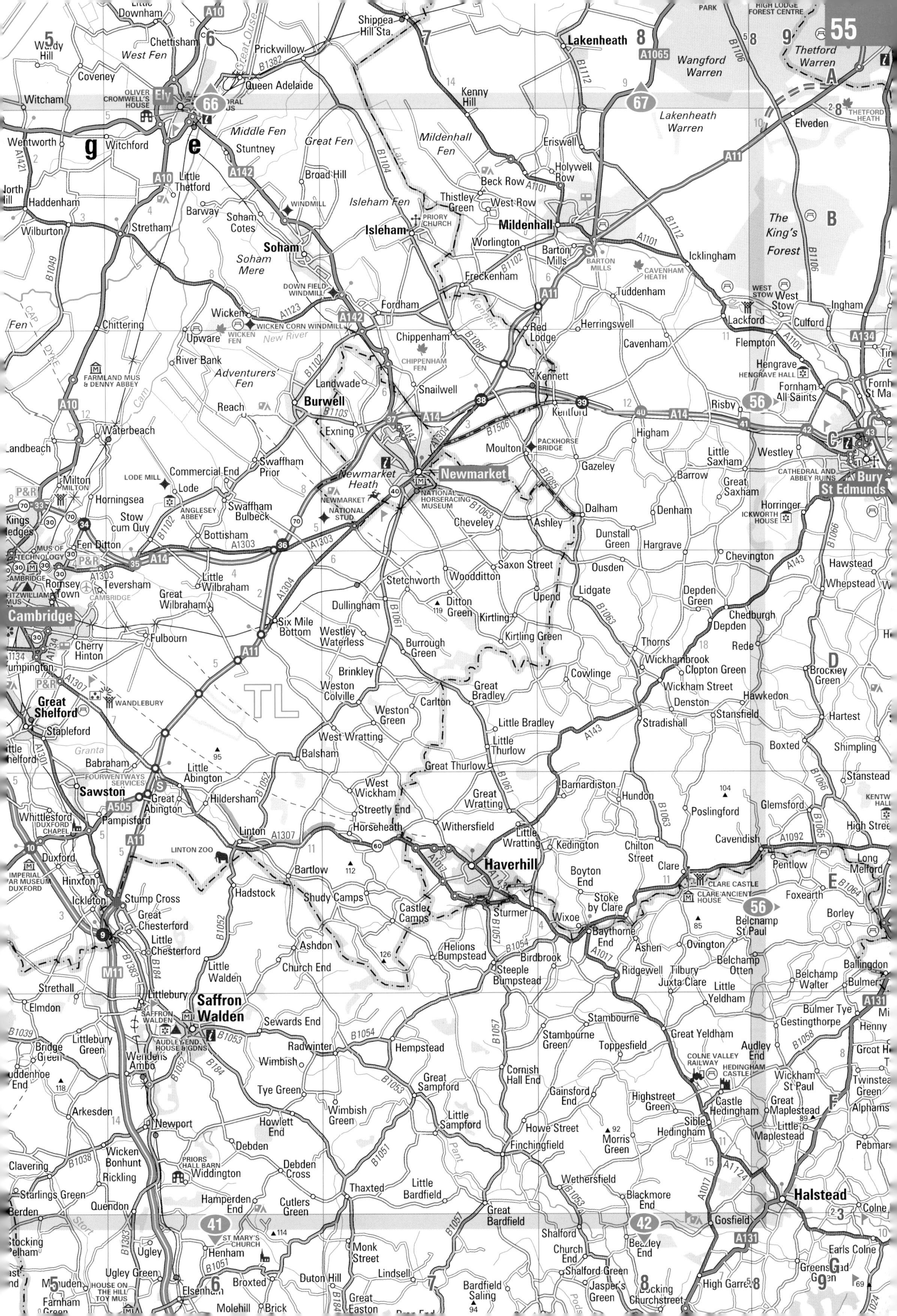
Little Downham
Chettisham
Witchy Hill
West Fen
Coveney
Witcham
Ely
OLIVER CROMWELL'S HOUSE
Prickwillow
Queen Adelaide
Shippea Hill Sta.
Lakenheath
Wangford Warren
Thetford Warren
HIGH LODGE FOREST CENTRE
Kenny Hill
Lakenheath Warren
Elveden
THETFORD HEATH
Wentworth
Witchford
Middle Fen
Great Fen
Stuntney
Mildenhall Fen
Eriswell
Holywell Row
Beck Row
Thistley Green
West Row
Mildenhall
Little Thetford
Haddenham
Wilburton
Stretham
Barway
Soham Cotes
Soham
Soham Mere
Broad Hill
Isleham Fen
Isleham
PRIORY CHURCH
Worlington
Barton Mills
Freckenham
Icklingham
CAVENHAM HEATH
The King's Forest
Tuddenham
West Stow
Ingham
Culford
Lackford
Flempton
Hengrave
HENGRAVE HALL
Fornham All Saints
Fornham St Martin
DOWN FIELD WINDMILL
WINDMILL
Wicken
WICKEN CORN WINDMILL
WICKEN FEN
Upware
New River
Fordham
Chippenham
CHIPPENHAM FEN
Red Lodge
Herringswell
Cavenham
Kennett
Chittering
Fen
CAR DYKE
River Bank
Adventurers' Fen
FARMLAND MUS & DENNY ABBEY
Landwade
Snailwell
Burwell
Reach
Exning
Kentford
Risby
Higham
Moulton
PACKHORSE BRIDGE
Gazeley
Little Saxham
Great Saxham
Barrow
Westley
CATHEDRAL AND ABBEY RUINS
Bury St Edmunds
Waterbeach
Landbeach
Swaffham Prior
Commercial End
Lode
LODE MILL
Milton
Horningsea
Stow cum Quy
ANGLESEY ABBEY
Swaffham Bulbeck
Bottisham
Newmarket Heath
Newmarket
NEWMARKET
NATIONAL STUD
NATIONAL HORSERACING MUSEUM
Cheveley
Ashley
Dalham
Denham
Horringer
ICKWORTH HOUSE
Kings Hedges
Fen Ditton
MUS OF TECHNOLOGY
CAMBRIDGE
Romsey Town
Teversham
FITZWILLIAM MUS
Cambridge
Little Wilbraham
Great Wilbraham
Stetchworth
Woodditton
Saxon Street
Dunstall Green
Hargrave
Ousden
Chevington
Hawstead
Whepstead
Dullingham
Ditton Green
Kirtling
Upend
Lidgate
Depden Green
Chedburgh
Depden
Six Mile Bottom
Westley Waterless
Burrough Green
Kirtling Green
Cherry Hinton
Fulbourn
Trumpington
Thorns
Rede
Wickhambrook
Clopton Green
Wickham Street
Brinkley
Cowlinge
Weston Colville
Great Bradley
Brockley Green
Hawkedon
WANDLEBURY
Great Shelford
Stapleford
Carlton
Weston Green
Denston
Stansfield
Stradishall
Little Bradley
Hartest
West Wratting
Little Thurlow
Balsham
Boxted
Shimpling
Babraham
Great Thurlow
FOURWENTWAYS SERVICES
Sawston
Little Abington
Great Abington
Hildersham
West Wickham
Great Wratting
Barnardiston
Hundon
Poslingford
Glemsford
Stanstead
Streetly End
Whittlesford
DUXFORD CHAPEL
Pampisford
Horseheath
Withersfield
Little Wratting
Kedington
Chilton Street
Cavendish
Linton
LINTON ZOO
Duxford
IMPERIAL WAR MUSEUM DUXFORD
Bartlow
Haverhill
Boyton End
Clare
CLARE CASTLE
CLARE ANCIENT HOUSE
Pentlow
Long Melford
Hinxton
Hadstock
Shudy Camps
Stoke by Clare
Foxearth
Ickleton
Stump Cross
Great Chesterford
Castle Camps
Sturmer
Wixoe
Baythorne End
Belchamp St Paul
Borley
Little Chesterford
Ashdon
Helions Bumpstead
Birdbrook
Ashen
Ovington
Steeple Bumpstead
Church End
Little Walden
Ridgewell
Tilbury Juxta Clare
Belchamp Otten
Belchamp Walter
Ballingdon
Bulmer
Strethall
Littlebury
Saffron Walden
SAFFRON WALDEN
Little Yeldham
Elmdon
Sewards End
Stambourne
Bulmer Tye
Gestingthorpe
Henny
Radwinter
Stambourne Green
Toppesfield
Great Yeldham
Audley End
Bridge Green
Littlebury Green
AUDLEY END HOUSE & GDNS
Wendens Ambo
Hempstead
Wimbish
COLNE VALLEY RAILWAY
HEDINGHAM CASTLE
Great Henny
Duddenhoe End
Great Sampford
Cornish Hall End
Wickham St Paul
Twinstead Green
Tye Green
Gainsford End
Highstreet Green
Castle Hedingham
Great Maplestead
Alphamstone
Arkesden
Wimbish Green
Little Sampford
Sible Hedingham
Little Maplestead
Newport
Howlett End
Howe Street
Morris Green
Wicken Bonhunt
Debden
Finchingfield
Pebmarsh
Clavering
PRIORS HALL BARN
Widdington
Debden Cross
Rickling
Wethersfield
Halstead
Starlings Green
Thaxted
Little Bardfield
Blackmore End
Quendon
Hamperden End
Cutlers Green
Colne
Berden
Great Bardfield
Gosfield
Stocking Pelham
ST MARY'S CHURCH
Henham
Shalford
Beazley End
Ugley
Monk Street
Church End
Earls Colne
Shalford Green
Ugley Green
Duton Hill
Lindsell
Bardfield Saling
Jasper's Green
Cocking Churchstreet
High Garrett
Greenstead Green
Manuden
HOUSE ON THE HILL TOY MUS
Elsenham
Broxted
Farnham Green
Molehill Green
Brick End
Great Easton
TL
A10
A142
A1101
A1065
A11
A1123
A14
A1303
A1304
A1307
A505
A143
A1017
A1124
A131
A1092
A134
M11
B1382
B1104
B1102
B1085
B1506
B1063
B1061
B1052
B1054
B1057
B1053
B1051
B1383
B1038
B1039
B1184
B1066
B1065
B1064
B1058
B1106
B1112
B1049
A1421
A1134
A1301
Great Ouse
Lark
Kennett
Cam
Granta
Stort
Pant

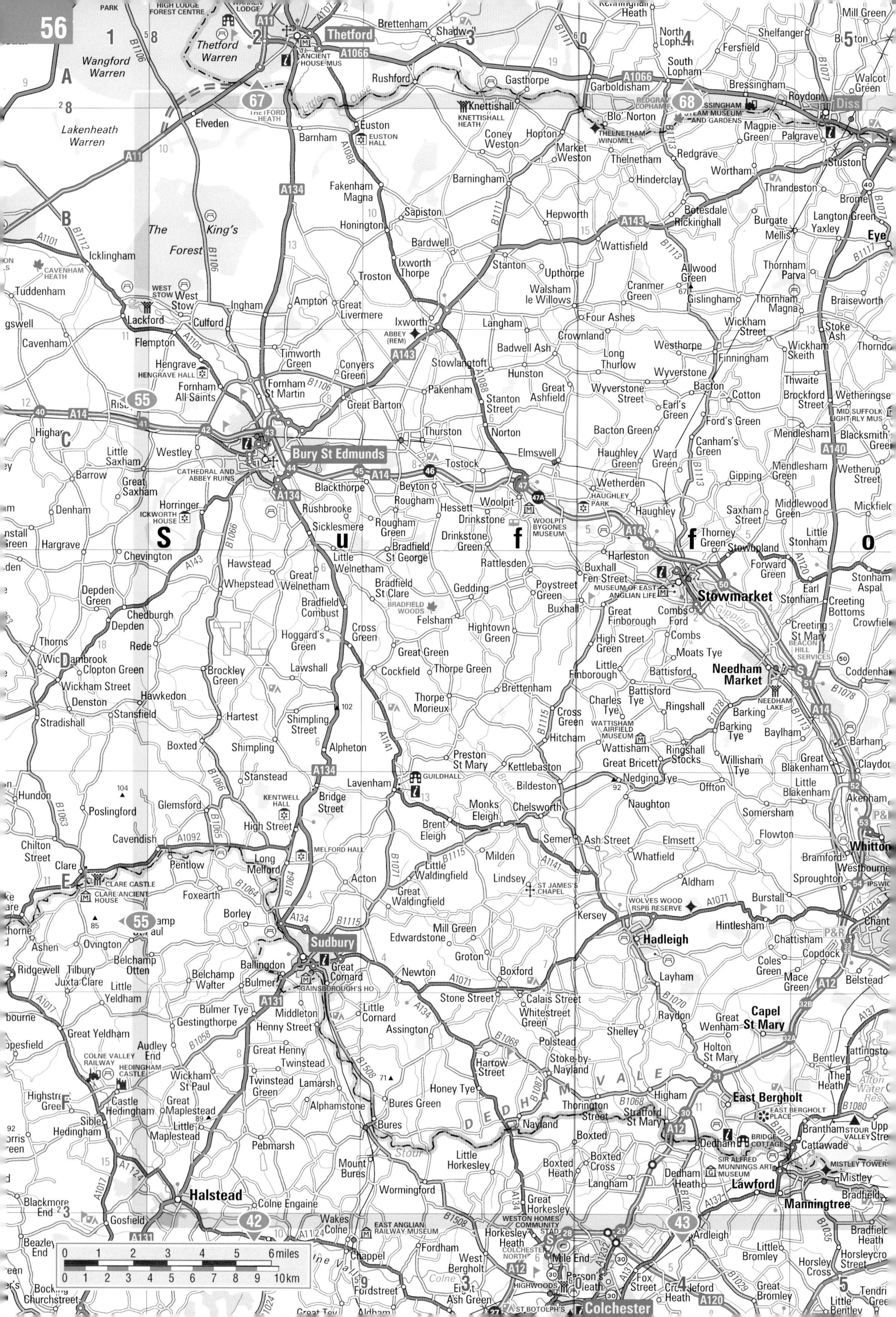
Thetford
Thetford Warren
Wangford Warren
Lakenheath Warren
Brettenham
Shadwell
Rushford
Gasthorpe
Garboldisham
North Lopham
South Lopham
Fersfield
Shelfanger
Mill Green
Bressingham
Roydon
Diss
Walcot Green
Elveden
Euston
Barnham
Knettishall
Coney Weston
Hopton
Blo' Norton
Market Weston
Thelnetham
Redgrave
Palgrave
Magpie Green
Wortham
Stuston
Hinderclay
Thrandeston
Brome
Fakenham Magna
Barningham
Sapiston
Honington
Hepworth
Botesdale
Rickinghall
Burgate
Mellis
Langton Green
Yaxley
Eye
The King's Forest
Icklingham
Cavenham Heath
Tuddenham
Bardwell
Ixworth Thorpe
Troston
Stanton
Upthorpe
Wattisfield
Walsham le Willows
Cranmer Green
Allwood Green
Gislingham
Thornham Parva
Thornham Magna
Braiseworth
West Stow
Lackford
Culford
Ingham
Ampton
Great Livermere
Ixworth
Langham
Four Ashes
Crownland
Wickham Street
Stoke Ash
Cavenham
Flempton
Timworth Green
Conyers Green
Stowlangtoft
Badwell Ash
Long Thurlow
Westhorpe
Finningham
Wickham Skeith
Hengrave
Fornham All Saints
Fornham St Martin
Pakenham
Hunston
Wyverstone
Thwaite
Great Barton
Stanton Street
Great Ashfield
Wyverstone Street
Bacton
Cotton
Brockford Street
Wetheringsett
Risby
Higham
Westley
Little Saxham
Bury St Edmunds
Thurston
Norton
Earl's Green
Bacton Green
Ford's Green
Mendlesham
Barrow
Great Saxham
Blackthorpe
Beyton
Tostock
Elmswell
Haughley Green
Ward Green
Canham's Green
Mendlesham Green
Wetherup Street
Denham
Horringer
Ickworth House
Rushbrooke
Rougham
Hessett
Woolpit
Drinkstone
Wetherden
Haughley
Gipping
Saxham Street
Middlewood Green
Mickfield
Hargrave
Chevington
Sicklesmere
Rougham Green
Drinkstone Green
Thorney Green
Stowupland
Little Stonham
Stonham Aspal
Hawstead
Great Welnetham
Little Welnetham
Bradfield St George
Rattlesden
Harleston
Buxhall Fen Street
Forward Green
Earl Stonham
Depden Green
Whepstead
Bradfield St Clare
Gedding
Poystreet Green
Stowmarket
Creeting Bottoms
Chedburgh
Depden
Bradfield Combust
Felsham
Buxhall
Great Finborough
Combs Ford
Combs
Creeting St Mary
Crowfield
Thorns
Rede
Hoggard's Green
Cross Green
Hightown Green
High Street Green
Moats Tye
Wickhambrook
Clopton Green
Brockley Green
Lawshall
Great Green
Cockfield
Thorpe Green
Little Finborough
Battisford
Needham Market
Coddenham
Wickham Street
Hawkedon
Denston
Stansfield
Hartest
Thorpe Morieux
Brettenham
Battisford Tye
Charles Tye
Ringshall
Barking
Stradishall
Shimpling Street
Alpheton
Cross Green
Hitcham
Wattisham
Barking Tye
Baylham
Barham
Boxted
Shimpling
Preston St Mary
Kettlebaston
Great Bricett
Ringshall Stocks
Willisham Tye
Great Blakenham
Claydon
Stanstead
Lavenham
Bildeston
Nedging Tye
Offton
Little Blakenham
Hundon
Poslingford
Glemsford
Bridge Street
Kentwell Hall
Monks Eleigh
Chelsworth
Naughton
Akenham
Somersham
High Street
Brent Eleigh
Semer
Ash Street
Elmsett
Flowton
Whitton
Chilton Street
Cavendish
Pentlow
Long Melford
Melford Hall
Milden
Whatfield
Bramford
Westbourne
Clare
Little Waldingfield
Great Waldingfield
Acton
Lindsey
Aldham
Sproughton
Ipswich
Foxearth
Borley
Kersey
Burstall
Chantry
Hintlesham
Mill Green
Edwardstone
Hadleigh
Chattisham
Copdock
Ashen
Ovington
Belchamp Otten
Sudbury
Groton
Boxford
Layham
Coles Green
Ridgewell
Tilbury Juxta Clare
Belchamp Walter
Ballingdon
Bulmer
Great Cornard
Newton
Mace Green
Belstead
Little Yeldham
Stone Street
Calais Street
Whitestreet Green
Bulmer Tye
Middleton
Little Cornard
Assington
Raydon
Capel St Mary
Great Wenham
Great Yeldham
Gestingthorpe
Henny Street
Shelley
Polstead
Holton St Mary
Audley End
Great Henny
Twinstead
Harrow Street
Stoke-by-Nayland
Bentley
Tattingstone
Wickham St Paul
Twinstead Green
Lamarsh
Honey Tye
Higham
East Bergholt
The Heath
Castle Hedingham
Great Maplestead
Alphamstone
Bures Green
Dedham Vale
Thorington Street
Stratford St Mary
Sible Hedingham
Little Maplestead
Bures
Nayland
Boxted
Dedham
Brantham
Cattawade
Pebmarsh
Mount Bures
Little Horkesley
Boxted Cross
Boxted Heath
Langham
Dedham Heath
Lawford
Mistley
Manningtree
Bradfield
Halstead
Colne Engaine
Wormingford
Great Horkesley
Gosfield
Blackmore End
Wakes Colne
Chappel
Fordham
Horkesley Heath
Ardleigh
Bradfield Heath
Little Bromley
Horsley Cross
Beazley End
West Bergholt
Mile End
Colchester
Fox Street
Crockleford Heath
Great Bromley
Little Bentley
Eight Ash Green
Fordstreet
0 1 2 3 4 5 6 miles
0 1 2 3 4 5 6 7 8 9 10km

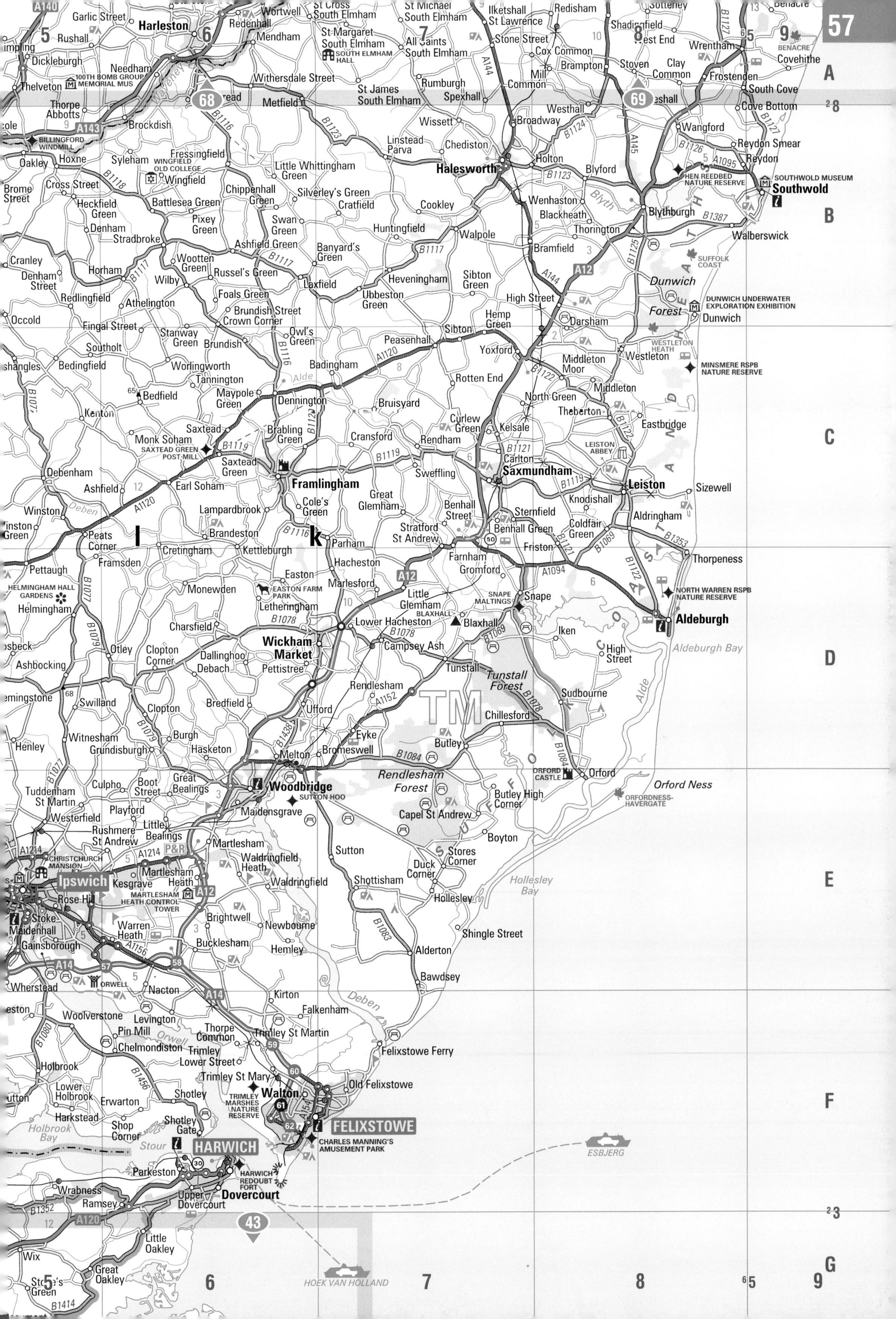

A140
Garlic Street
Harleston
Redenhall
Wortwell
St Cross South Elmham
St Michael South Elmham
Ilketshall St Lawrence
Redisham
Sotterley
Benacre
Rushall
Mendham
St Margaret South Elmham
SOUTH ELMHAM HALL
All Saints South Elmham
Stone Street
Cox Common
Shadingfield
West End
Wrentham
BENACRE
Covehithe
Dickleburgh
Needham
100TH BOMB GROUP MEMORIAL MUS
Withersdale Street
Rumburgh
Brampton
Mill Common
Stoven
Clay Common
Frostenden
South Cove
Thelveton
St James South Elmham
Spexhall
Westhall
Cove Bottom
Thorpe Abbotts
Metfield
68
69
A143
Brockdish
Wissett
Broadway
B1124
A145
Wangford
Reydon Smear
Reydon
B1126
A1095
B1127
Billingford Windmill
Oakley
Hoxne
Syleham
Fressingfield
B1116
B1123
Linstead Parva
Chediston
Halesworth
Holton
Blyford
Wingfield Old College
Wingfield
Little Whittingham Green
HEN REEDBED NATURE RESERVE
SOUTHWOLD MUSEUM
Southwold
Brome Street
Cross Street
B1118
Chippenhall Green
Silverley's Green
Cratfield
Cookley
Wenhaston
Blythburgh
Blackheath
B1387
Walberswick
Heckfield Green
Battlesea Green
Pixey Green
Swan Green
Huntingfield
Walpole
Thorington
Denham
Stradbroke
Ashfield Green
Banyard's Green
B1117
Bramfield
B1125
Blyth
Cranley
Denham Street
Horham
Wootten Green
Russel's Green
Laxfield
Heveningham
Sibton Green
A144
A12
SUFFOLK COAST
Dunwich
Wilby
Foals Green
Ubbeston Green
High Street
Forest
DUNWICH UNDERWATER EXPLORATION EXHIBITION
Dunwich
Redlingfield
Athelington
Brundish Street
Crown Corner
Hemp Green
Darsham
Occold
Fingal Street
Stanway Green
Brundish
Owl's Green
Sibton
Peasenhall
Yoxford
WESTLETON HEATH
Westleton
MINSMERE RSPB NATURE RESERVE
Southolt
Worlingworth
Middleton Moor
Bedingfield
Badingham
A1120
Tannington
Rotten End
B1122
Middleton
Alde
Bedfield
Maypole Green
Dennington
Bruisyard
North Green
Theberton
Eastbridge
Kenton
Curlew Green
Kelsale
Saxtead
Brabling Green
B1120
Cransford
Rendham
LEISTON ABBEY
Monk Soham
SAXTEAD GREEN POST MILL
B1119
B1121
Carlton
Saxtead Green
Framlingham
Sweffling
Saxmundham
Leiston
Sizewell
Debenham
Ashfield
Earl Soham
Great Glemham
Benhall Street
Knodishall
Aldringham
Winston
Deben
Lampardbrook
Cole's Green
Sternfield
Coldfair Green
B1353
Winston Green
Peats Corner
Brandeston
B1116
Parham
Stratford St Andrew
Benhall Green
B1069
Thorpeness
Pettaugh
Cretingham
Kettleburgh
Hacheston
Friston
Framsden
Farnham
Gromford
A1094
Easton
EASTON FARM PARK
Marlesford
HELMINGHAM HALL GARDENS
Monewden
Little Glemham
SNAPE MALTINGS
Snape
NORTH WARREN RSPB NATURE RESERVE
Helmingham
Letheringham
BLAXHALL
Blaxhall
Aldeburgh
B1077
B1078
Charsfield
Lower Hacheston
B1079
Otley
Wickham Market
Campsey Ash
Iken
Ashbocking
Clopton Corner
Dallinghoo
Debach
Pettistree
High Street
Aldeburgh Bay
Tunstall
Tunstall Forest
Rendlesham
Sudbourne
Swilland
Bredfield
TM
Ufford
A1152
Chillesford
Clopton
Witnesham
Grundisburgh
Burgh
Hasketon
B1438
Eyke
Bromeswell
Butley
Henley
Melton
B1084
Orford
ORFORD CASTLE
Tuddenham St Martin
Culpho
Boot Street
Great Bealings
Woodbridge
SUTTON HOO
Rendlesham Forest
Butley High Corner
Orford Ness
ORFORDNESS-HAVERGATE
Playford
Westerfield
Maidensgrave
Capel St Andrew
Little Bealings
Rushmere St Andrew
Boyton
A1214
CHRISTCHURCH MANSION
Martlesham
P&R
Waldringfield Heath
Sutton
Stores Corner
Ipswich
Kesgrave
Martlesham Heath
Waldringfield
Duck Corner
Shottisham
Hollesley Bay
Rose Hill
MARTLESHAM HEATH CONTROL TOWER
Hollesley
Stoke
Brightwell
Newbourne
B1083
Maidenhall
Warren Heath
Bucklesham
Shingle Street
Gainsborough
A1156
Hemley
Alderton
A14
57
58
ORWELL
Bawdsey
Wherstead
Nacton
Kirton
Woolverstone
Levington
Falkenham
Deben
Pin Mill
Orwell
Thorpe Common
Trimley St Martin
B1080
Chelmondiston
Trimley Lower Street
59
Felixstowe Ferry
Holbrook
B1456
Trimley St Mary
60
Walton
Old Felixstowe
Lower Holbrook
Erwarton
Shotley
TRIMLEY MARSHES NATURE RESERVE
61
A154
Harkstead
Shotley Gate
62
FELIXSTOWE
Holbrook Bay
Shop Corner
Stour
HARWICH
CHARLES MANNING'S AMUSEMENT PARK
ESBJERG
Parkeston
HARWICH REDOUBT FORT
30
Wrabness
Ramsey
Upper Dovercourt
Dovercourt
B1352
A120
43
Little Oakley
Wix
Great Oakley
HOEK VAN HOLLAND
B1414
A
B
C
D
E
F
G
5
6
7
8
9

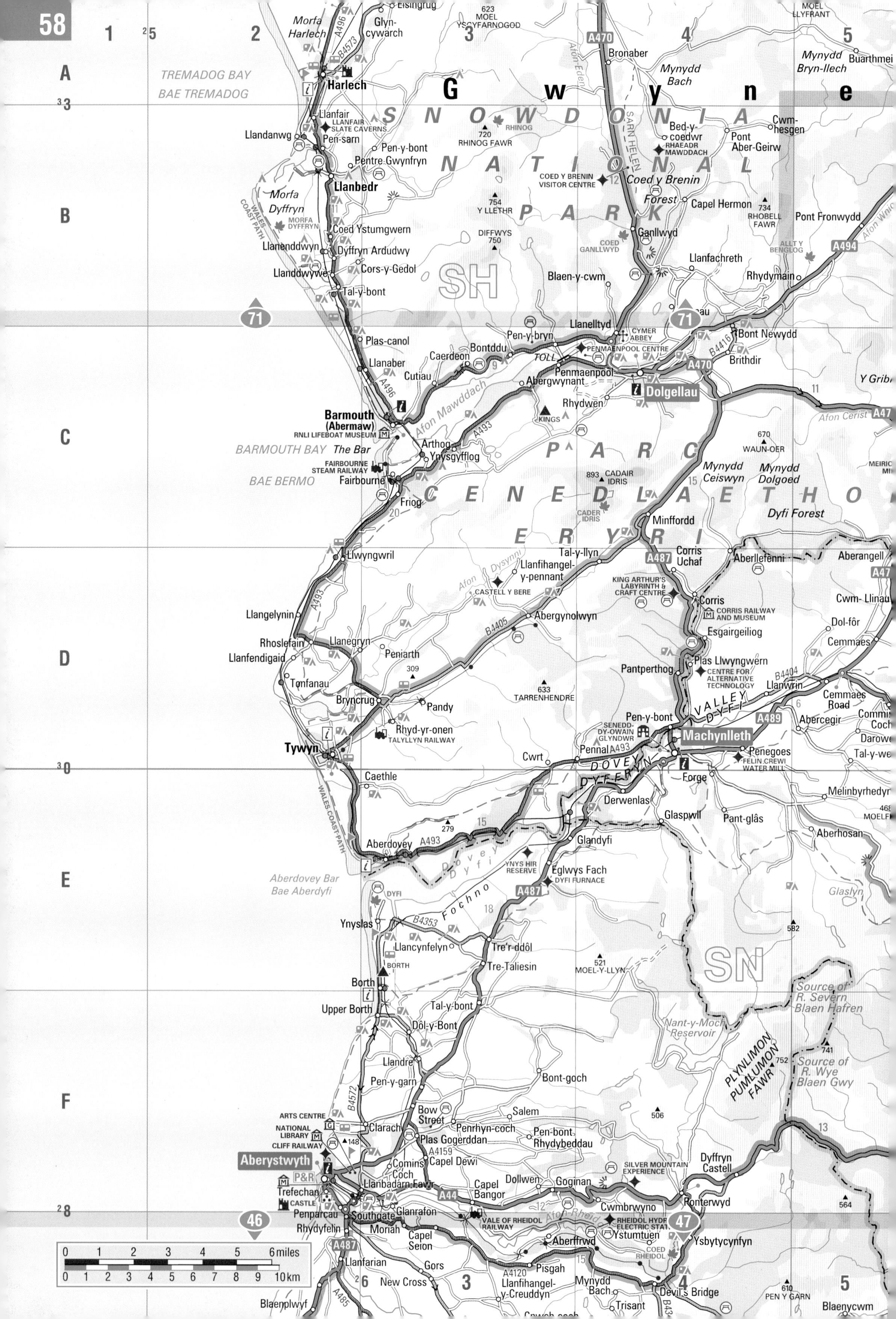

1
2
3
4
5
A
B
C
D
E
F
Morfa Harlech
Glyn-cywarch
Eisingrug
623 MOEL YSGYFARNOGOD
MOEL LLYFRANT
A470
Bronaber
Mynydd Bach
Mynydd Bryn-llech
Buarthmei
TREMADOG BAY
BAE TREMADOG
Harlech
G w y n e
S N O W D O N I A
N A T I O N A L
P A R K
Llanfair
LLANFAIR SLATE CAVERNS
Llandanwg
Pen-sarn
Pen-y-bont
Pentre Gwynfryn
720 RHINOG FAWR
RHINOG
Bed-y-coedwr
RHAEADR MAWDDACH
Cwm-hesgen
Pont Aber-Geirw
SARN HELEN
COED Y BRENIN VISITOR CENTRE
Coed y Brenin Forest
Capel Hermon
734 RHOBELL FAWR
Pont Fronwydd
Llanbedr
Morfa Dyffryn
MORFA DYFFRYN
WALES COAST PATH
754 Y LLETHR
Coed Ystumgwern
DIFFWYS 750
Ganllwyd
COED GANLLWYD
ALLT Y BENGLOG
A494
Llanenddwyn
Dyffryn Ardudwy
Cors-y-Gedol
Llanddwywe
Llanfachreth
Rhydymain
Tal-y-bont
SH
Blaen-y-cwm
71
Plas-canol
Llanelltyd
CYMER ABBEY
Pen-y-bryn
Bont Newydd
Bontddu
Caerdeon
TOLL
PENMAENPOOL CENTRE
B4416
Brithdir
Llanaber
Cutiau
Penmaenpool
A470
Abergwynant
Dolgellau
Y Gribi
A496
Barmouth (Abermaw)
RNLI LIFEBOAT MUSEUM
Afon Mawddach
Rhydwen
KINGS
Afon Cerist
A47
670 WAUN-OER
BARMOUTH BAY
The Bar
Arthog
A493
Ynysgyfflog
P A R C
C E N E D L A E T H O
E R Y R I
FAIRBOURNE STEAM RAILWAY
Fairbourne
BAE BERMO
893 CADAIR IDRIS
Mynydd Ceiswyn
Mynydd Dolgoed
Friog
CADER IDRIS
Dyfi Forest
Minffordd
Tal-y-llyn
Corris Uchaf
A487
Aberllefenni
Aberangell
Llwyngwril
Llanfihangel-y-pennant
Afon Dysynni
KING ARTHUR'S LABYRINTH & CRAFT CENTRE
CASTELL Y BERE
Corris
CORRIS RAILWAY AND MUSEUM
Cwm-Llinau
Llangelynin
Abergynolwyn
Dol-fôr
B4405
Esgairgeiliog
Cemmaes
Rhoslefain
Llanegryn
Llanfendigaid
Peniarth
Plas Llwyngwern
CENTRE FOR ALTERNATIVE TECHNOLOGY
Pantperthog
309
Tonfanau
633 TARRENHENDRE
B4404
Llanwrin
Cemmaes Road
Bryncrug
Pandy
VALLEY DYFI
Pen-y-bont
A489
Abercegir
SENEDD-DY-OWAIN GLYNDWR
Rhyd-yr-onen
TALYLLYN RAILWAY
Machynlleth
Penegoes
FELIN CREWI WATER MILL
Tywyn
Pennal
A493
Cwrt
DOVEY
DYFFRYN
Forge
Tal-y-we
Caethle
Derwenlas
Melinbyrhedyn
Glaspwll
Pant-glâs
279
Aberdovey
Glandyfi
Aberhosan
Dovey
Dyfi
YNYS HIR RESERVE
Aberdovey Bar
Bae Aberdyfi
Eglwys Fach
DYFI FURNACE
A487
DYFI
Fochno
Glaslyn
Ynyslas
B4353
18
582
Llancynfelyn
Tre'r-ddôl
BORTH
521 MOEL-Y-LLYN
SN
Tre-Taliesin
Borth
Source of R. Severn Blaen Hafren
Upper Borth
Tal-y-bont
Dôl-y-Bont
Nant-y-Moch Reservoir
741
Llandre
PLYNLIMON PUMLUMON FAWR
752
Source of R. Wye Blaen Gwy
Pen-y-garn
Bont-goch
B4572
ARTS CENTRE
NATIONAL LIBRARY
CLIFF RAILWAY
Bow Street
Salem
506
Clarach
Penrhyn-coch
148
Pen-bont Rhydybeddau
Plas Gogerddan
Aberystwyth
A4159
Dyffryn Castell
P&R
Comins Coch
Capel Dewi
SILVER MOUNTAIN EXPERIENCE
Trefechan
Llanbadarn Fawr
Capel Bangor
Dollwen
Goginan
CASTLE
A44
Cwmbrwyno
Ponterwyd
564
Penparcau
Southgate
Glanrafon
VALE OF RHEIDOL RAILWAY
Afon Rheidol
RHEIDOL HYDRO ELECTRIC STATION
46
47
Rhydyfelin
Moriah
Capel Seion
Ystumtuen
A487
Aberffrwd
COED RHEIDOL
Ysbytycynfyn
Llanfarian
Gors
Pisgah
A4120
New Cross
Llanfihangel-y-Creuddyn
Mynydd Bach
Devil's Bridge
610 PEN Y GARN
Trisant
Blaenplwyf
A485
Blaenycwm
0 1 2 3 4 5 6 miles
0 1 2 3 4 5 6 7 8 9 10 km

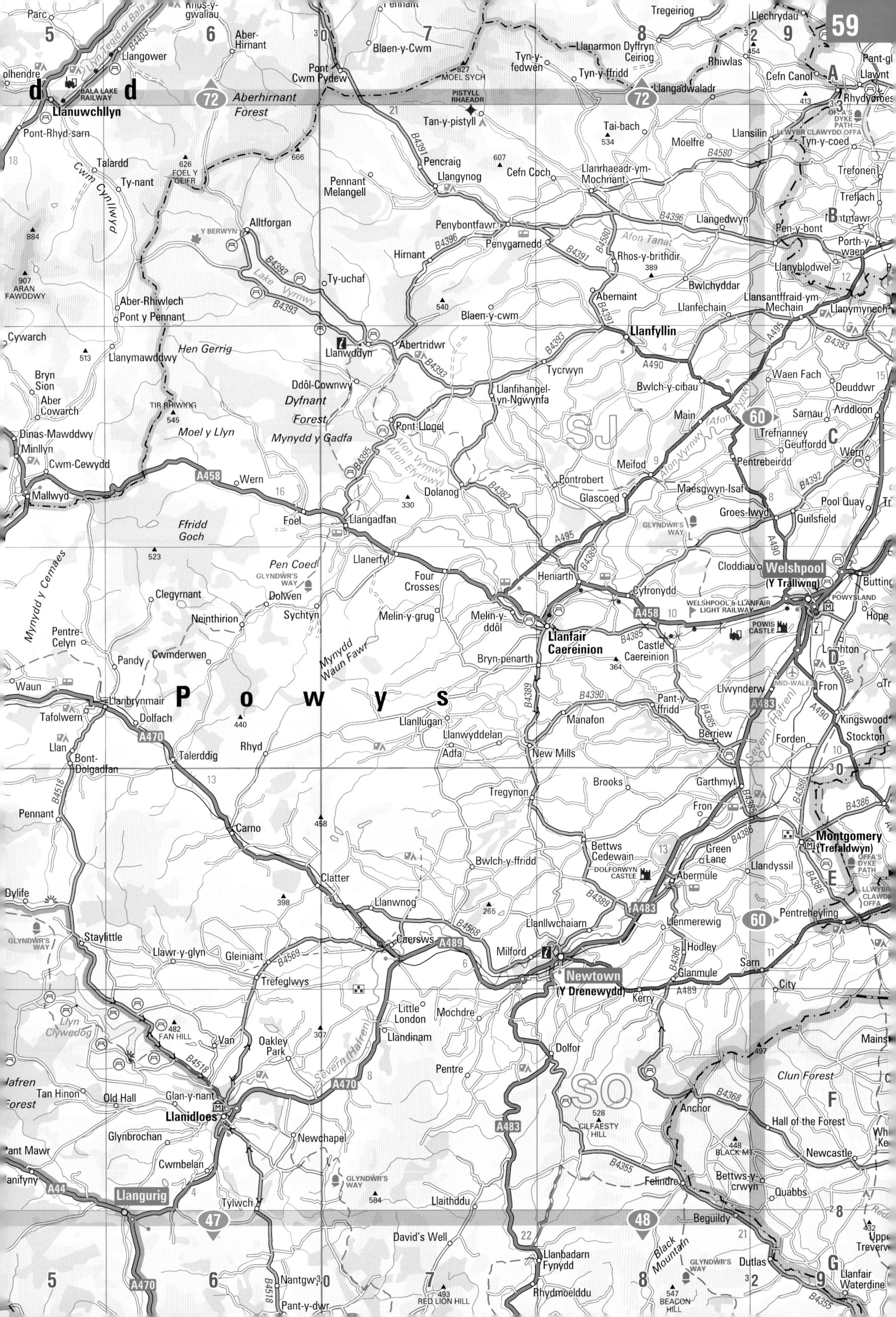
Parc
Rhos-y-gwaliau
Aber-Hirnant
Blaen-y-Cwm
Tregeiriog
Llechrydau
Llangower
Pont Cwm Pydew
827 MOEL SYCH
Tyn-y-fedwen
Llanarmon Dyffryn Ceiriog
Tyn-y-ffridd
Rhiwlas
Cefn Canol
Pant-gl
Llawnt
Rhydycroes
BALA LAKE RAILWAY
Llanuwchllyn
Aberhirnant Forest
PISTYLL RHAEADR
Tan-y-pistyll
Llangadwaladr
Tai-bach
534
Llansilin
Moelfre
OFFA'S DYKE PATH
LLWYBR CLAWDD OFFA
Tyn-y-coed
Pont-Rhyd-sarn
Llyn Tegid or Bala
Talardd
626 FOEL Y GEIFR
666
Pencraig
Llangynog
607
Cefn Coch
Llanrhaeadr-ym-Mochnant
B4580
Trefonen
Ty-nant
Cwm Cynllwyd
Pennant Melangell
Treflach
Llangedwyn
Nantmawr
Y BERWYN
Alltforgan
Penybontfawr
Penygarnedd
Afon Tanat
Pen-y-bont
Porth-y-waen
884
Hirnant
Rhos-y-brithdir
389
Llanyblodwel
907 ARAN FAWDDWY
Lake Vyrnwy
Ty-uchaf
Bwlchyddar
Abernaint
540
Aber-Rhiwlech
Pont y Pennant
Blaen-y-cwm
Llanfechain
Llansantffraid-ym-Mechain
Llanymynech
Cywarch
513
Llanymawddwy
Hen Gerrig
Llanwddyn
Abertridwr
Llanfyllin
A490
A495
Tycrwyn
Waen Fach
Bryn Sion
Ddôl-Cownwy
Llanfihangel-yn-Ngwynfa
Bwlch-y-cibau
Deuddwr
Aber Cowarch
Dyfnant Forest
TIR RHIWIOG
545
SJ
Main
Afon Efyrnwy
Sarnau
Arddleen
Dinas-Mawddwy
Moel y Llyn
Mynydd y Gadfa
Pont-Llogel
Trefnanney
Geuffordd
Minllyn
Afon Vyrnwy
Meifod
Pentrebeirdd
Wern
Cwm-Cewydd
A458
Wern
Dolanog
Pontrobert
Maesgwyn-Isaf
B4392
Mallwyd
16
330
B4382
Glascoed
Pool Quay
Foel
Llangadfan
Groes-lwyd
Guilsfield
Ffridd Goch
GLYNDWR'S WAY
523
Llanerfyl
Pen Coed
Four Crosses
Heniarth
Cloddiau
Welshpool (Y Trallwng)
Buttington
Mynydd y Cemaes
Clegyrnant
Dolwen
Cyfronydd
POWYSLAND
Neinthirion
Sychtyn
Melin-y-grug
Melin-y-ddôl
WELSHPOOL & LLANFAIR LIGHT RAILWAY
Hope
Pentre-Celyn
Mynydd Waun Fawr
Llanfair Caereinion
Castle Caereinion
POWIS CASTLE
Leighton
Pandy
Cwmderwen
Bryn-penarth
364
Waun
MID-WALES
Fron
Llanbrynmair
P o w y s
B4390
Llwynderw
Pant-y-ffridd
A483
Kingswood
Tafolwern
Dolfach
440
Llanllugan
Manafon
Stockton
Llan
A470
Rhyd
Llanwyddelan
Berriew
Forden
Bont-Dolgadfan
Talerddig
Adfa
New Mills
Severn (Hafren)
13
Brooks
Garthmyl
B4518
Tregynon
Fron
B4386
Pennant
Carno
458
Montgomery (Trefaldwyn)
Bettws Cedewain
Green Lane
Llandyssil
Bwlch-y-ffridd
DOLFORWYN CASTLE
Abermule
Dylife
Clatter
Pentreheyling
398
Llanwnog
265
B4389
Llenmerewig
Staylittle
Caersws
A489
Llanllwchaiarn
B4568
Llawr-y-glyn
Gleiniant
B4569
Milford
Hodley
Newtown (Y Drenewydd)
Sarn
Trefeglwys
Glanmule
City
Kerry
Little London
Mochdre
Llyn Clywedog
482 FAN HILL
307
Llandinam
Mainstone
Van
Oakley Park
Dolfor
497
B4518
Severn (Hafren)
Pentre
Clun Forest
Hafren Forest
Tan Hinon
Old Hall
Glan-y-nant
A470
SO
Anchor
B4368
Llanidloes
528 CILFAESTY HILL
Hall of the Forest
Glynbrochan
Newchapel
A483
448 BLACK MT
Newcastle
Pant Mawr
Cwmbelan
B4355
Bettws-y-crwyn
Quabbs
Llanifyny
A44
Llangurig
Tylwch
584
Llaithddu
Felindre
Beguildy
David's Well
Black Mountain
432
Upper Treverward
Llanbadarn Fynydd
Dutlas
Llanfair Waterdine
Nantgwyn
493 RED LION HILL
547 BEACON HILL
Rhydmoelddu
Pant-y-dwr
72
60
47
48

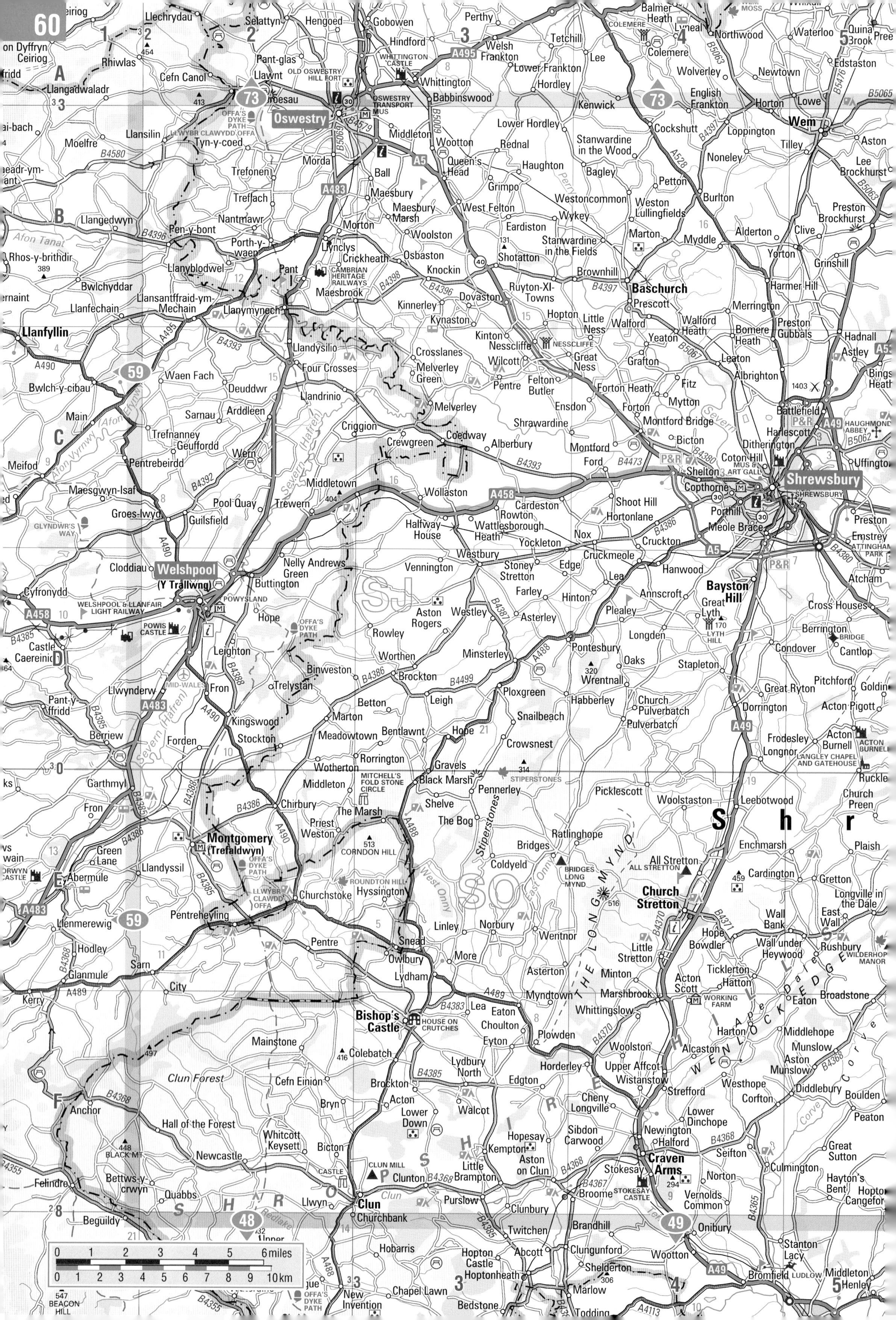

Llechrydau
Selattyn
Hengoed
Gobowen
Perthy
Tetchill
Balmer Heath
Lyneal
Northwood
Waterloo
Quina Brook
Preston Dyffryn Ceiriog
Rhiwlas
454
Pant-glas
Hindford
Whittington Castle
Old Oswestry Hill Fort
Welsh Frankton
Lower Frankton
Lee
Colemere
Wolverley
Newtown
Edstaston
Llangadwaladr
Cefn Canol
Llawnt
Whittington
Hordley
English Frankton
Horton
Lowe
413
Gobowen
Oswestry Transport Mus
Babbinswood
Kenwick
Wem
Offa's Dyke Path
Oswestry
Middleton
Lower Hordley
Cockshutt
Loppington
Aston
Llansilin
Llwybr Clawdd Offa
Tyn-y-coed
Wootton
Rednal
Stanwardine in the Wood
Noneley
Tilley
Moelfre
Queen's Head
Haughton
Lee Brockhurst
Trefonen
Morda
Ball
Bagley
Petton
Maesbury
Grimpo
Burlton
Treflach
Maesbury Marsh
West Felton
Westoncommon
Weston Lullingfields
Preston Brockhurst
Llangedwyn
Nantmawr
Wykey
Pen-y-bont
Morton
Eardiston
Marton
Alderton
Clive
Afon Tanat
Woolston
Stanwardine in the Fields
Myddle
Rhos-y-brithdir
389
Porth-y-waen
Lynclys
Crickheath
Osbaston
131
Shotatton
Yorton
Llanyblodwel
Knockin
Grinshill
Bwlchyddar
Pant
Cambrian Heritage Railways
Brownhill
Baschurch
Harmer Hill
Maesbrook
Ruyton-XI-Towns
Dovaston
Prescott
Llansantffraid-ym-Mechain
Llanfechain
Llanymynech
Kinnerley
Hopton
Little Ness
Walford
Merrington
Kynaston
Walford Heath
Preston Gubbals
Llanfyllin
Llandysilio
Kinton
Nesscliffe
Yeaton
Bomere Heath
Hadnall
Crosslanes
Great Ness
Grafton
Leaton
Astley
Four Crosses
Melverley Green
Wilcott
Waen Fach
Albrighton
Bings Heath
Pentre
Felton Butler
Forton Heath
Fitz
Bwlch-y-cibau
Deuddwr
Llandrinio
1403
Mytton
Forton
Melverley
Ensdon
Battlefield
Sarnau
Arddleen
Main
Afon Efyrnwy
Criggion
Shrawardine
Montford Bridge
Harlescott
Haughmond Abbey
Trefnanney
Geuffordd
Crewgreen
Coedway
Alberbury
Bicton
Ditherington
Wern
Montford
Coton Hill
Uffington
Meifod
Afon Vyrnwy
Pentrebeirdd
Ford
Mus & Art Gall
Shelton
Shrewsbury
Maesgwyn-Isaf
Middletown
Wollaston
Copthorne
404
Trewern
Cardeston
Shoot Hill
Pool Quay
Glyndŵr's Way
Groes-lwyd
Guilsfield
Halfway House
Rowton
Wattlesborough Heath
Hortonlane
Porthill
Preston
Yockleton
Nox
Meole Brace
Emstrey
Attingham Park
Cruckton
Cruckmeole
Westbury
Cloddiau
Welshpool (Y Trallwng)
Nelly Andrews Green
Vennington
Stoney Stretton
Edge
Hanwood
Atcham
Buttington
Lea
Bayston Hill
Cyfronydd
Farley
Annscroft
Powysland
Aston Rogers
Westley
Hinton
Great Lyth
Welshpool & Llanfair Light Railway
Hope
Asterley
Pleasley
Cross Houses
Offa's Dyke Path
Rowley
170
Lyth Hill
Berrington
Powis Castle
Longden
Bridge
Castle Caereinion
Leighton
Worthen
Minsterley
Pontesbury
Condover
Cantlop
Oaks
Stapleton
Binweston
320
Wrentnall
Trelystan
Brockton
Pitchford
Llwynderw
Fron
Mid-Wales
Leigh
Ploxgreen
Habberley
Great Ryton
Golding
Church Pulverbach
Dorrington
Acton Pigott
Pant-y-ffridd
Betton
Pulverbach
Marton
Snailbeach
Kingswood
Bentlawnt
Acton Burnell
Acton Burnell
Berriew
Stockton
Meadowtown
Hope
Frodesley
Forden
Crowsnest
Longnor
Langley Chapel and Gatehouse
Rorrington
314
Gravels
Stiperstones
Ruckley
Garthmyl
Wotherton
Mitchell's Fold Stone Circle
Black Marsh
Middleton
Pennerley
Picklescott
Church Preen
Fron
Chirbury
Shelve
Woolstaston
Leebotwood
The Marsh
Priest Weston
The Bog
Shropshire
Montgomery (Trefaldwyn)
Ratlinghope
513
Corndon Hill
Bridges
Enchmarsh
Plaish
Green Lane
Stiperstones
Coldyeld
Bridges Long Mynd
All Stretton
All Stretton
Llandyssil
Cardington
459
Gretton
Abermule
Roundton Hill
West Onny
East Onny
Hyssington
The Long Mynd
516
Church Stretton
Longville in the Dale
Churchstoke
Llwybr Clawdd Offa
Llanmerewig
Pentreheyling
Linley
Norbury
Wentnor
Wall Bank
East Wall
Hope Bowdler
Rushbury
Snead
Pentre
Little Stretton
Wall under Heywood
Wilderhope Manor
Hodley
Owlbury
More
Asterton
Sarn
Lydham
Ticklerton
Minton
Hatton
Acton Scott
Glanmule
City
Kerry
B4383
Lea
Eaton
Myndtown
Marshbrook
Working Farm
Eaton
Broadstone
Bishop's Castle
House on Crutches
Choulton
Whittingslow
Ape Dale
Wenlock Edge
Harton
Middlehope
Plowden
Eyton
Woolston
Alcaston
Munslow
Mainstone
416
Colebatch
Lydbury North
Upper Affcot
Aston Munslow
Wistanstow
497
Clun Forest
Cefn Einion
Horderley
Edgton
Westhope
Diddlebury
Brockton
Strefford
Corfton
Boulden
Anchor
Bryn
Acton
Walcot
Cheny Longville
Corve
Lower Down
Lower Dinchope
Peaton
Hall of the Forest
Sibdon Carwood
Newington
Halford
448
Black Mt
Whitcott Keysett
Hopesay
Great Sutton
Kempton
Seifton
Newcastle
Bicton
Craven Arms
Aston on Clun
Clun Mill
Clunton
Stokesay
Culmington
Castle
Little Brampton
294
Norton
Felindre
Bettws-y-crwyn
Hayton's Bent
Hopton Cangeford
Broome
Stokesay Castle
Vernolds Common
Quabbs
Llwyn
Purslow
Clun
Clunbury
Beguildy
Redlake
Churchbank
Twitchen
Brandhill
Onibury
Upper
Hobarris
Hopton Castle
Clungunford
Wootton
Stanton Lacy
Shelderton
306
Hoptonheath
Bromfield
Ludlow
Middleton
Henley
Chapel Lawn
Marlow
Offa's Dyke Path
New Invention
Bedstone
Todding
547
Beacon Hill
SJ
SO
0 1 2 3 4 5 6 miles
0 1 2 3 4 5 6 7 8 9 10 km
59
73
48
49

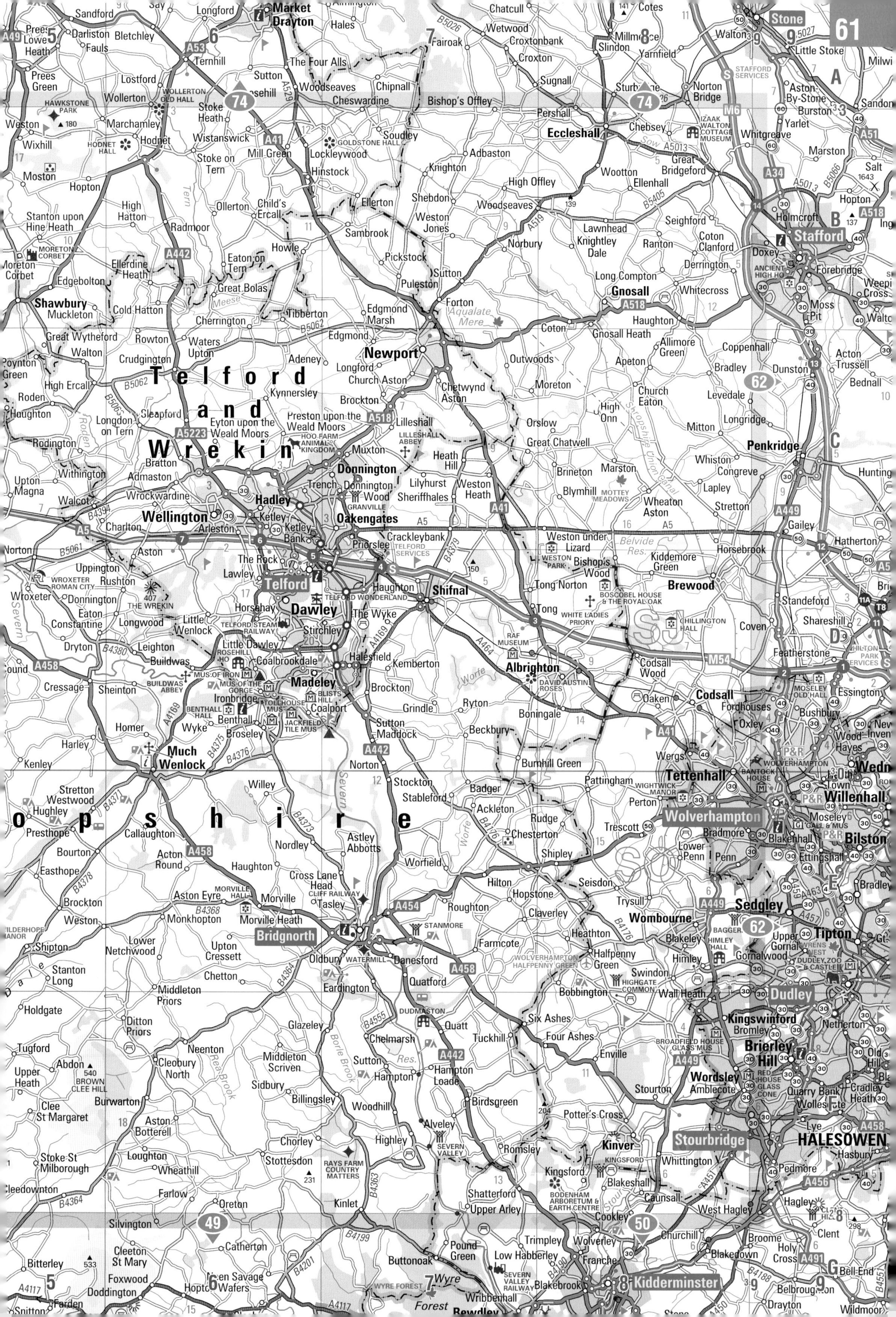
61
Market Drayton
Sandford
Longford
Hales
Prees
Lowe
Heath
Darliston
Fauls
Bletchley
Ternhill
Prees Green
Lostford
Wollerton
Hawkstone Park
Wollerton Old Hall
Sutton
Rosehill
Woodseaves
Chipnall
Cheswardine
Bishop's Offley
The Four Alls
Fairoak
Chatcull
Wetwood
Croxtonbank
Croxton
Sugnall
Pershall
Eccleshall
Cotes
Millmeece
Slindon
Yarnfield
Sturbridge
Norton Bridge
Chebsey
Izaak Walton Cottage Museum
Great Bridgeford
Stone
Walton
Little Stoke
Stafford Services
Aston-By-Stone
Burston
Yarlet
Sandon
Whitgreave
Marston
Salt
Milwich
Weston
Wixhill
Marchamley
Hodnet
Hodnet Hall
Stoke Heath
Wistanswick
Stoke on Tern
Mill Green
Goldstone Hall
Lockleywood
Soudley
Hinstock
Adbaston
Knighton
High Offley
Wootton
Ellenhall
Moston
Hopton
High Hatton
Stanton upon Hine Heath
Moreton Corbet
Ollerton
Child's Ercall
Radmoor
Ellerton
Shebdon
Weston Jones
Woodseaves
Norbury
Lawnhead
Knightley Dale
Ranton
Seighford
Coton Clanford
Doxey
Stafford
Holmcroft
Hopton
Derrington
Ancient High House
Forebridge
Weeping Cross
Moss Pit
Walton
Howle
Eaton upon Tern
Sambrook
Pickstock
Sutton
Puleston
Ellerdine Heath
Edgebolton
Great Bolas
Shawbury
Muckleton
Cold Hatton
Cherrington
Tibberton
Edgmond Marsh
Forton
Aqualate Mere
Long Compton
Gnosall
Whitecross
Haughton
Coton
Gnosall Heath
Great Wytheford
Rowton
Waters Upton
Walton
Edgmond
Crudgington
Adeney
Newport
Outwoods
Allimore Green
Apeton
Coppenhall
Acton Trussell
Dunston
Bradley
Bednall
Poynton Green
Roden
High Ercall
Telford and Wrekin
Longford
Church Aston
Kynnersley
Chetwynd Aston
Moreton
Church Eaton
Levedale
Brockton
Sleapford
Eyton upon the Weald Moors
Preston upon the Weald Moors
Lilleshall
Lilleshall Abbey
Longdon on Tern
High Onn
Orslow
Mitton
Longridge
Haughton
Rodington
Hoo Farm Animal Kingdom
Muxton
Great Chatwell
Penkridge
Withington
Bratton
Admaston
Donnington
Heath Hill
Brineton
Marston
Whiston
Congreve
Upton Magna
Wrockwardine
Trench
Donnington Wood
Lilyhurst
Sheriffhales
Weston Heath
Blymhill
Mottey Meadows
Lapley
Hunting
Walcot
Hadley
Granville
Wheaton Aston
Stretton
Wellington
Ketley
Oakengates
Gailey
Charlton
Arleston
Ketley Bank
Crackleybank
Weston under Lizard
Weston Park
Belvide Res.
Hatherton
Norton
Aston
Priorslee
Telford Services
Kiddemore Green
Horsebrook
Uppington
The Rock
Lawley
Bishop's Wood
Wroxeter Roman City
Rushton
Telford
Haughton
Shifnal
Tong Norton
Brewood
Wroxeter
Donnington
The Wrekin
Telford Wonderland
Boscobel House & The Royal Oak
Eaton Constantine
Horsehay
Dawley
Tong
Standeford
Longwood
Little Wenlock
Telford Steam Railway
The Wyke
White Ladies Priory
Chillington Hall
Shareshill
Coven
Dryton
Leighton
Little Dawley
Stirchley
RAF Museum
Rosehill
Coalbrookdale
Halesfield
Kemberton
Featherstone
Hilton Park Services
Buildwas
Mus. of Iron
Mus. of the Gorge
Albrighton
Codsall Wood
Cressage
Sheinton
Buildwas Abbey
Ironbridge
Madeley
Blists Hill
Brockton
David Austin Roses
Codsall
Moseley Old Hall
Essington
Tollhouse Mus.
Coalport
Grindle
Ryton
Oaken
Fordhouses
Bushbury
Benthall Hall
Benthall
Jackfield Tile Mus.
Sutton Maddock
Boningale
Oxley
Homer
Wyke
Broseley
Beckbury
Wood Hayes
Harley
Much Wenlock
Wergs
Wolverhampton
Kenley
Norton
Burnhill Green
Tettenhall
Bantock House
Wednesfield
Willey
Stockton
Stableford
Badger
Pattingham
Wightwick Manor
Perton
Old Town
Willenhall
Stretton Westwood
Hughley
Ackleton
Shropshire
Presthope
Callaughton
Astley Abbotts
Rudge
Chesterton
Trescott
Wolverhampton
Bradmore
Blakenhall
Moseley
Bilston
Bourton
Acton Round
Nordley
Shipley
Lower Penn
Penn
Ettingshall
Easthope
Haughton
Worfield
Cross Lane Head
Hilton
Seisdon
Trysull
Bradley
Brockton
Aston Eyre
Morville Hall
Morville
Cliff Railway
Tasley
Hopstone
Roughton
Sedgley
Weston
Monkhopton
Morville Heath
Claverley
Stanmore
Wombourne
Bagger.
Tipton
Wilderhope Manor
Bridgnorth
Heathton
Upper Gornal
Wrens Nest
Shipton
Lower Netchwood
Upton Cressett
Farmcote
Blakeley
Himley Hall
Gornalwood
Stanton Long
Oldbury
Watermill
Danesford
Wolverhampton Halfpenny Green
Halfpenny Green
Himley
Dudley Zoo & Castle
Chetton
Quatford
Swindon
Highgate Common
Eardington
Bobbington
Wall Heath
Dudley
Middleton Priors
Dudmaston
Kingswinford
Holdgate
Glazeley
Quatt
Six Ashes
Bromley
Netherton
Ditton Priors
Chelmarsh
Tuckhill
Four Ashes
Broadfield House Glass Mus.
Brierley Hill
Old Hill
Tugford
Neenton
Sutton
Enville
Abdon
Cleobury North
Middleton Scriven
Res.
Hampton
Hampton Loade
Red House Glass Cone
Wordsley
Amblecote
Upper Heath
Brown Clee Hill
Sidbury
Borle Brook
Rea Brook
Stourton
Quarry Bank
Cradley Heath
Clee St Margaret
Burwarton
Billingsley
Woodhill
Birdsgreen
Wollescote
Aston Botterell
Alveley
Potter's Cross
Lye
Chorley
Highley
Severn Valley
Stourbridge
Halesowen
Stoke St Milborough
Loughton
Rays Farm Country Matters
Romsley
Kinver
Hasbury
Wheathill
Stottesdon
Kingsford
Whittington
Cleedownton
Kingsford
Blakeshall
Pedmore
Farlow
Kinlet
Bodenham Arboretum & Earth Centre
Caunsall
Hagley
Oreton
Shatterford
Upper Arley
Cookley
West Hagley
Silvington
Trimpley
Wolverley
Churchill
Broome
Clent
Catherton
Pound Green
Low Habberley
Holy Cross
Cleeton St Mary
Bitterley
Buttonoak
Severn Valley Railway
Franche
Blakedown
Foxwood
Neen Savage
Wafers
Hopton
Doddington
Wyre Forest
Wribbenhall
Blakebrook
Kidderminster
Belbroughton
Bell End
Farden
Snitton
Bewdley
Drayton
Wildmoor
Severn
Meese
Roden
Tern
Worfe
Sow
Stour
Shropshire Union Canal
Dale

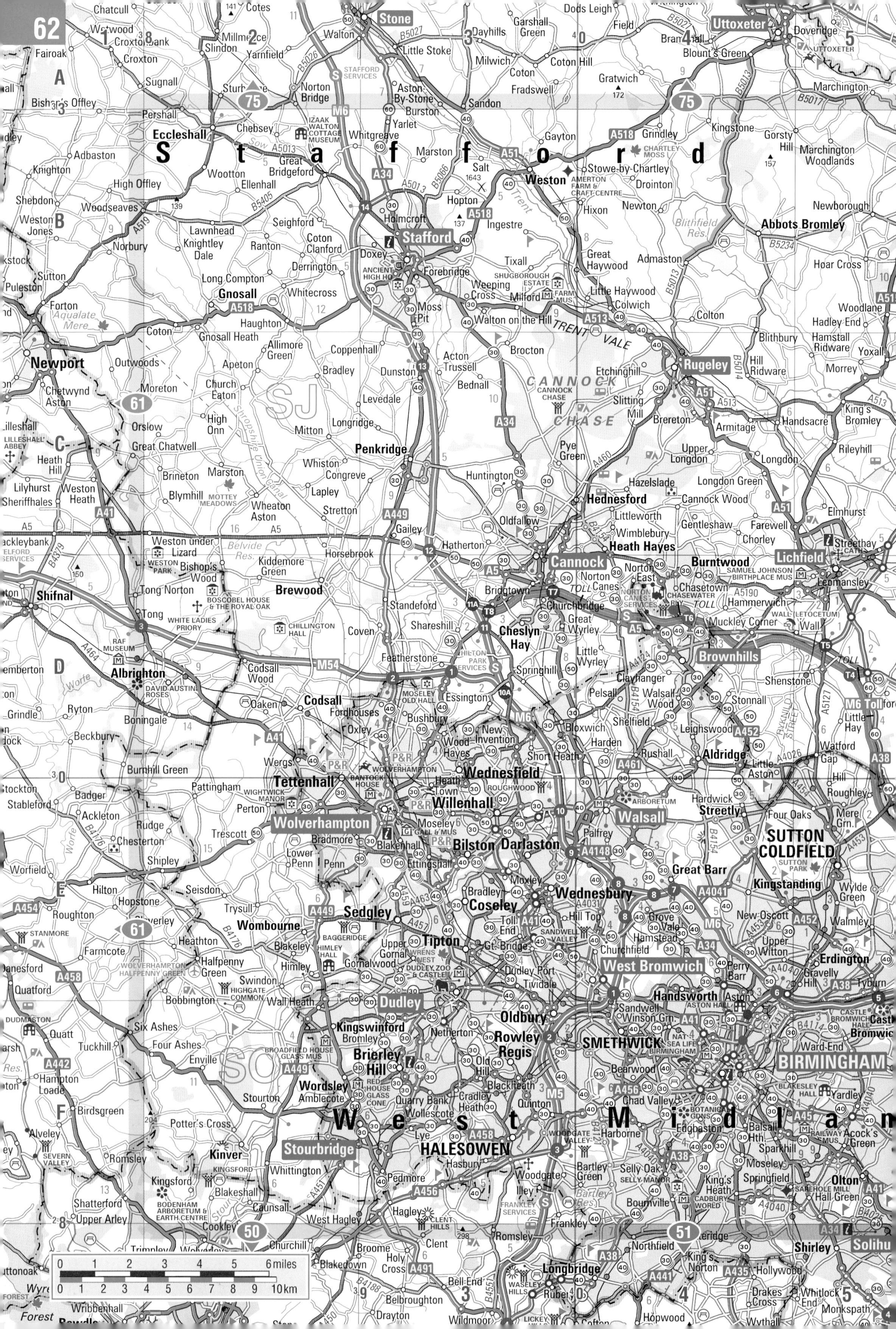
Stafford
West Midlands
Stone
Uttoxeter
Eccleshall
Stafford
Abbots Bromley
Rugeley
Newport
Penkridge
Cannock Chase
Hednesford
Cannock
Heath Hayes
Lichfield
Burntwood
Brownhills
Shifnal
Albrighton
Codsall
Brewood
Cheslyn Hay
Tettenhall
Wolverhampton
Wednesfield
Willenhall
Walsall
Aldridge
Streetly
Sutton Coldfield
Bilston
Darlaston
Wednesbury
Sedgley
Coseley
Tipton
West Bromwich
Dudley
Oldbury
Smethwick
Birmingham
Kingswinford
Brierley Hill
Rowley Regis
Wordsley
Stourbridge
Halesowen
Kinver
Erdington
Kingstanding
Handsworth
Shirley
Longbridge
Solihull
Gnosall
Tong
Wombourne
M6
M54
M5
M6 Toll
A5
A34
A41
A449
A518
A51
0 1 2 3 4 5 6 miles
0 1 2 3 4 5 6 7 8 9 10km

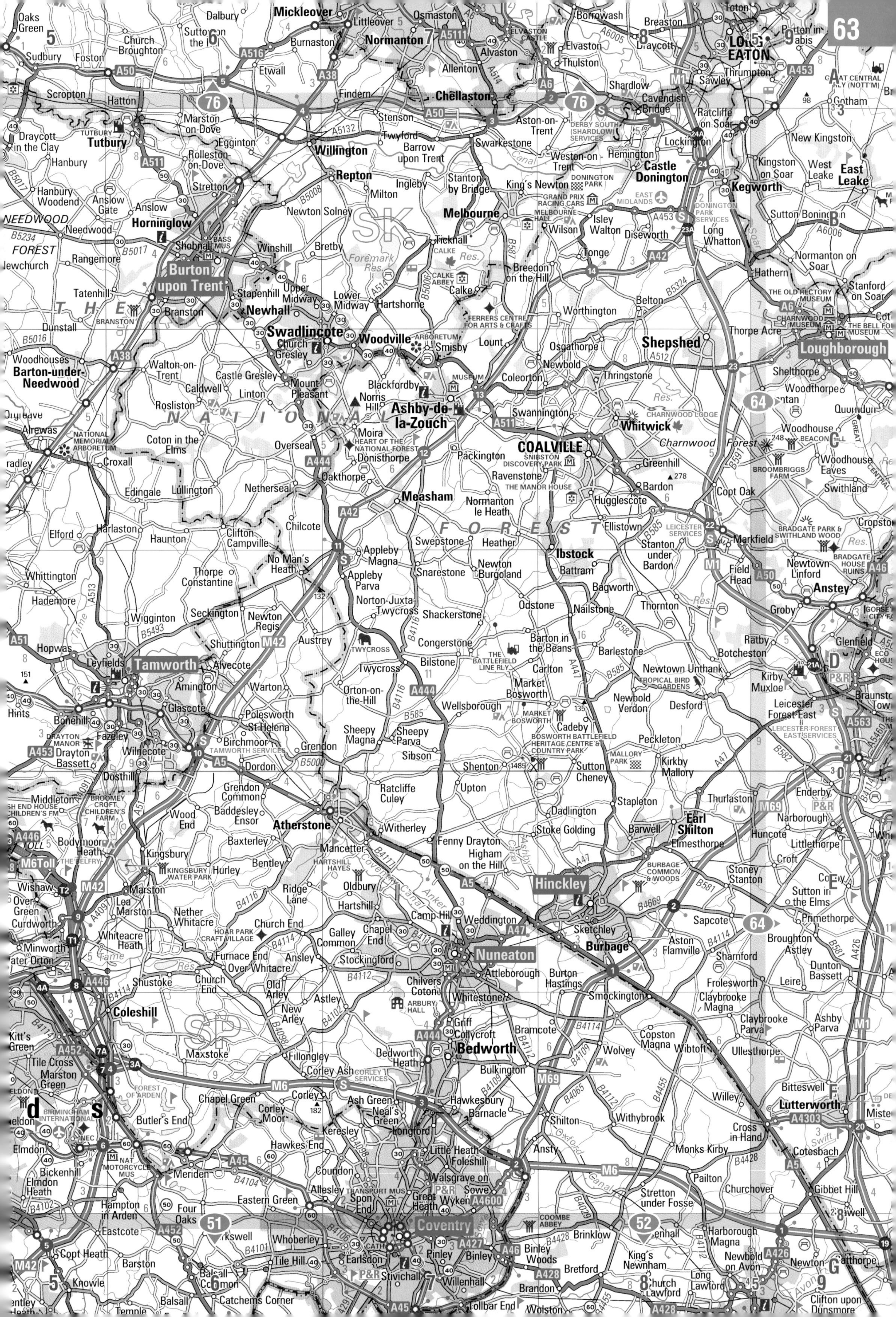
Mickleover
Littleover
Normanton
Osmaston
Borrowash
Breaston
Toton
Long Eaton
Dalbury
Sutton on the Hill
Church Broughton
Burnaston
Alvaston
Elvaston
Thulston
Draycott
Sawley
Thrumpton
Sudbury
Foston
Etwall
Allenton
Shardlow
Cavendish Bridge
Scropton
Hatton
Findern
Chellaston
Stenson
Aston-on-Trent
Ratcliffe on Soar
Gotham
Draycott in the Clay
Tutbury
Marston on Dove
Egginton
Willington
Twyford
Barrow upon Trent
Swarkestone
Weston-on-Trent
Hemington
Lockington
New Kingston
Hanbury
Rolleston-on-Dove
Castle Donington
Kingston on Soar
West Leake
East Leake
Hanbury Woodend
Anslow Gate
Anslow
Stretton
Repton
Milton
Ingleby
Stanton by Bridge
King's Newton
Donington Park
Kegworth
Needwood
Horninglow
Newton Solney
Melbourne
Isley Walton
Diseworth
Long Whatton
Sutton Bonington
Forest
Rangemore
Shobnall
Winshill
Bretby
Ticknall
Tonge
Normanton on Soar
Burton upon Trent
Foremark Res.
Calke
Breedon on the Hill
Hathern
Stanford on Soar
Tatenhill
Stapenhill
Upper Midway
Lower Midway
Hartshorne
Belton
Branston
Newhall
Swadlincote
Woodville
Smisby
Lount
Worthington
Thorpe Acre
Dunstall
Church Gresley
Osgathorpe
Shepshed
Loughborough
Woodhouses
Barton-under-Needwood
Walton-on-Trent
Castle Gresley
Mount Pleasant
Blackfordby
Coleorton
Newbold
Thringstone
Shelthorpe
Woodthorpe
Caldwell
Linton
Norris Hill
Ashby-de-la-Zouch
Swannington
Whitwick
Quorndon
Rosliston
Alrewas
National Memorial Arboretum
Coton in the Elms
Overseal
Moira
Donisthorpe
Charnwood Forest
Woodhouse
Croxall
Packington
Coalville
Greenhill
Woodhouse Eaves
Edingale
Lullington
Netherseal
Oakthorpe
Ravenstone
Bardon
Measham
Normanton le Heath
Hugglescote
Copt Oak
Swithland
Harlaston
Haunton
Clifton Campville
Chilcote
Ellistown
Markfield
Elford
No Man's Heath
Appleby Magna
Swepstone
Heather
Ibstock
Stanton under Bardon
Whittington
Thorpe Constantine
Appleby Parva
Snarestone
Newton Burgoland
Battram
Field Head
Newtown Linford
Anstey
Hademore
Norton-Juxta-Twycross
Bagworth
Odstone
Nailstone
Thornton
Groby
Wigginton
Seckington
Newton Regis
Shackerstone
Ratby
Hopwas
Shuttington
Austrey
Twycross
Congerstone
Barton in the Beans
Barlestone
Botcheston
Glenfield
Tamworth
Leyfields
Alvecote
Bilstone
Carlton
Newtown Unthank
Kirby Muxloe
Amington
Warton
Orton-on-the-Hill
Market Bosworth
Newbold Verdon
Desford
Leicester Forest East
Hints
Glascote
Polesworth
St Helena
Wellsborough
Cadeby
Bonehill
Fazeley
Sheepy Magna
Sheepy Parva
Birchmoor
Grendon
Sibson
Peckleton
Drayton Bassett
Wilnecote
Dordon
Shenton
Sutton Cheney
Kirkby Mallory
Dosthill
Grendon Common
Ratcliffe Culey
Upton
Enderby
Middleton
Wood End
Baddesley Ensor
Atherstone
Witherley
Dadlington
Stapleton
Thurlaston
Earl Shilton
Narborough
Bodymoor Heath
Baxterley
Mancetter
Fenny Drayton
Higham on the Hill
Stoke Golding
Barwell
Elmesthorpe
Huncote
Littlethorpe
Kingsbury
Bentley
Hurley
Hinckley
Croft
Wishaw
Marston
Oldbury
Ridge Lane
Hartshill
Stoney Stanton
Cosby
Over Green
Lea Marston
Nether Whitacre
Camp Hill
Weddington
Sutton in the Elms
Curdworth
Church End
Galley Common
Chapel End
Sketchley
Sapcote
Primethorpe
Whiteacre Heath
Burbage
Aston Flamville
Broughton Astley
Minworth
Water Orton
Furnace End
Over Whitacre
Ansley
Stockingford
Nuneaton
Sharnford
Dunton Bassett
Shustoke
Old Arley
Attleborough
Burton Hastings
Frolesworth
Leire
Astley
Chilvers Coton
Whitestone
Smockington
Claybrooke Magna
Coleshill
New Arley
Arbury Hall
Griff
Collycroft
Bramcote
Claybrooke Parva
Ashby Parva
Kitt's Green
Maxstoke
Fillongley
Bedworth Heath
Bedworth
Copston Magna
Wibtoft
Wolvey
Ullesthorpe
Tile Cross
Marston Green
Corley Ash
Bulkington
Bitteswell
Corley
Ash Green
Hawkesbury
Willey
Lutterworth
Chapel Green
Corley Moor
Neal's Green
Barnacle
Shilton
Withybrook
Cross in Hand
Misterton
Butler's End
Keresley
Longford
Monks Kirby
Cotesbach
Elmdon
Hawkes End
Little Heath
Foleshill
Ansty
Bickenhill
Elmdon Heath
Meriden
Coundon
Walsgrove on Sowe
Pailton
Churchover
Gibbet Hill
Hampton in Arden
Allesley
Eastern Green
Spon End
Great Heath
Wyken
Stretton under Fosse
Four Oaks
Coventry
Bewell
Eastcote
Berkswell
Whoberley
Binley Woods
Brinklow
Harborough Magna
Copt Heath
Tile Hill
Earlsdon
Pinley
Binley
King's Newnham
Newbold on Avon
Newton
Catthorpe
Barston
Stivichall
Willenhall
Bretford
Long Lawford
Knowle
Balsall Common
Catchems Corner
Balsall
Tollbar End
Brandon
Wolston
Church Lawford
Clifton upon Dunsmore
Temple
Bentley Heath
Birmingham International

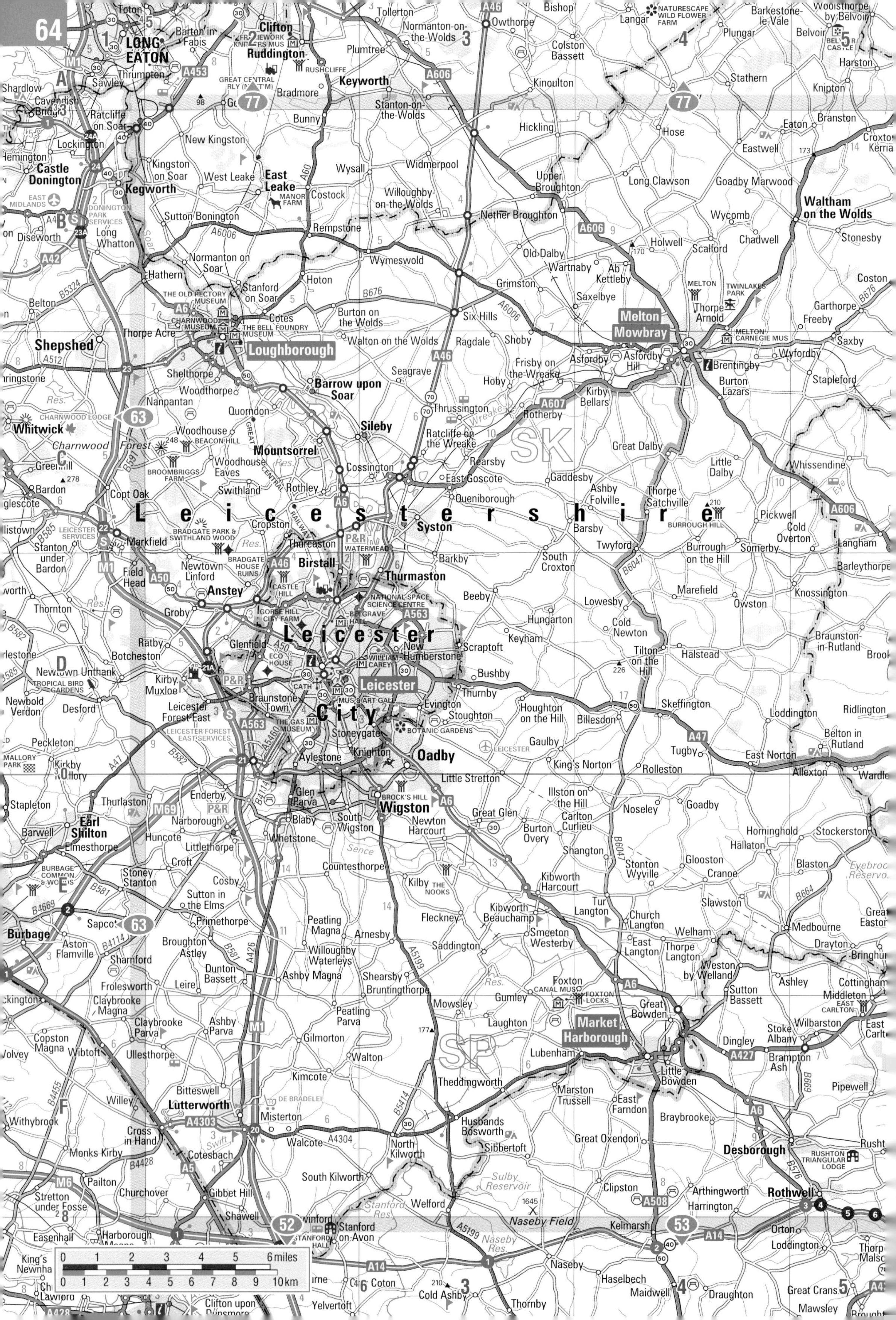
LONG EATON
Toton
Barton in Fabis
Clifton
Ruddington
Tollerton
Normanton-on-the-Wolds
Owthorpe
Bishop
Langar
NATURESCAPE WILD FLOWER FARM
Barkestone-le-Vale
Woolsthorpe by Belvoir
Plungar
Belvoir
Thrumpton
Sawley
Plumtree
Colston Bassett
Harston
Shardlow
Cavendish Bridge
GREAT CENTRAL RLY (N'T'M)
Bradmore
Keyworth
Kinoulton
Stathern
Knipton
Ratcliffe on Soar
Gotham
Bunny
Stanton-on-the-Wolds
Lockington
New Kingston
Hickling
Hose
Eaton
Branston
Croxton Kerrial
Hemington
Castle Donington
Kingston on Soar
West Leake
East Leake
Wysall
Widmerpool
Upper Broughton
Long Clawson
Eastwell
Goadby Marwood
Kegworth
EAST MIDLANDS
Costock
MANOR FARM
Willoughby-on-the-Wolds
Waltham on the Wolds
Sutton Bonington
Nether Broughton
Wycomb
Diseworth
DONINGTON PARK SERVICES
Long Whatton
Rempstone
Holwell
Scalford
Chadwell
Stonesby
Normanton on Soar
Wymeswold
Old Dalby
Wartnaby
Ab Kettleby
Hathern
Hoton
Grimston
Coston
Belton
THE OLD RECTORY MUSEUM
Stanford on Soar
Saxelbye
MELTON
TWINLAKES PARK
Thorpe Arnold
Garthorpe
Cotes
Burton on the Wolds
Six Hills
Melton Mowbray
Freeby
CHARNWOOD MUSEUM
THE BELL FOUNDRY MUSEUM
Thorpe Acre
Shepshed
Loughborough
Walton on the Wolds
Ragdale
Shoby
MELTON CARNEGIE MUS
Saxby
Asfordby
Asfordby Hill
Brentingby
Wyfordby
Frisby on the Wreake
Hoby
Seagrave
Shelthorpe
Burton Lazars
Stapleford
Woodthorpe
Barrow upon Soar
Kirby Bellars
Nanpantan
Quorndon
Thrussington
Rotherby
CHARNWOOD LODGE
Whitwick
Woodhouse
BEACON HILL
Sileby
Ratcliffe on the Wreake
Charnwood Forest
Mountsorrel
Great Dalby
Greenhill
Woodhouse Eaves
Cossington
Rearsby
Little Dalby
Whissendine
BROOMBRIGGS FARM
Gaddesby
Bardon
East Goscote
Ashby Folville
Thorpe Satchville
Copt Oak
Swithland
Rothley
Queniborough
Coalville
Leicestershire
BURROUGH HILL
Pickwell
Cold Overton
Syston
Barsby
LEICESTER SERVICES
Markfield
Cropston
BRADGATE PARK & SWITHLAND WOOD
Thurcaston
WATERMEAD
Twyford
South Croxton
Burrough on the Hill
Somerby
Langham
Stanton under Bardon
Barkby
Field Head
Newtown Linford
BRADGATE HOUSE RUINS
Birstall
Thurmaston
Barleythorpe
CASTLE HILL
Anstey
Marefield
Owston
Knossington
NATIONAL SPACE SCIENCE CENTRE
Beeby
Lowesby
Thornton
Groby
GORSE HILL CITY FARM
BELGRAVE HALL
Hungarton
Cold Newton
Leicester
Ratby
Glenfield
Keyham
Braunston-in-Rutland
Scraptoft
New Humberstone
Tilton on the Hill
Halstead
Botcheston
ECO HOUSE
WILLIAM CAREY
Newtown Unthank
TROPICAL BIRD GARDENS
Kirby Muxloe
Bushby
CATH
Leicester City
Thurnby
Skeffington
Newbold Verdon
Desford
Leicester Forest East
Braunstone Town
THE GAS MUSEUM
MUS & ART GALL
Evington
Houghton on the Hill
Stoughton
Billesdon
Loddington
Ridlington
LEICESTER FOREST EAST SERVICES
BOTANIC GARDENS
Stoneygate
Gaulby
Belton in Rutland
Peckleton
Aylestone
Knighton
Oadby
LEICESTER
Tugby
King's Norton
East Norton
MALLORY PARK
Kirkby Mallory
Rolleston
Allexton
Wardley
Little Stretton
Glen Parva
Enderby
BROCK'S HILL
Wigston
Illston on the Hill
Stapleton
Thurlaston
Noseley
Goadby
Blaby
South Wigston
Newton Harcourt
Great Glen
Carlton Curlieu
Earl Shilton
Narborough
Burton Overy
Barwell
Huncote
Whetstone
Horninghold
Stockerston
Hallaton
Elmesthorpe
Littlethorpe
Shangton
Sence
Croft
Countesthorpe
Stonton Wyville
Gloosten
Blaston
Eyebrook Reservoir
BURBAGE COMMON & WOODS
Stoney Stanton
Cosby
Kilby
THE NOOKS
Kibworth Harcourt
Cranoe
Sutton in the Elms
Slawston
Tur Langton
Fleckney
Kibworth Beauchamp
Church Langton
Great Easton
Sapcote
Primethorpe
Peatling Magna
Medbourne
Burbage
Broughton Astley
Arnesby
Smeeton Westerby
Welham
Aston Flamville
Saddington
East Langton
Thorpe Langton
Drayton
Sharnford
Willoughby Waterleys
Weston by Welland
Bringhurst
Dunton Bassett
Ashby Magna
Shearsby
Foxton
Ashley
Cottingham
Frolesworth
Leire
Bruntingthorpe
CANAL MUS
FOXTON LOCKS
Gumley
Sutton Bassett
Middleton
Hinckley
Claybrooke Magna
Mowsley
Great Bowden
EAST CARLTON
Peatling Parva
Laughton
Market Harborough
Wilbarston
Claybrooke Parva
Ashby Parva
Stoke Albany
East Carlton
Copston Magna
Gilmorton
Lubenham
Dingley
Wolvey
Wibtoft
Ullesthorpe
Brampton Ash
Walton
Little Bowden
Kimcote
Theddingworth
Pipewell
Bitteswell
Marston Trussell
DE BRADELEI
East Farndon
Willey
Lutterworth
Braybrooke
Withybrook
Misterton
Husbands Bosworth
Cross in Hand
Walcote
North Kilworth
Great Oxendon
Desborough
Rushton
Monks Kirby
Sibbertoft
RUSHTON TRIANGULAR LODGE
Cotesbach
South Kilworth
Sulby Reservoir
Clipston
Pailton
Churchover
Gibbet Hill
Welford
Arthingworth
Rothwell
Stretton under Fosse
Stanford Res.
Harrington
Shawell
Swinford
Stanford on Avon
STANFORD HALL
Naseby Field
Kelmarsh
Orton
Easenhall
Harborough Magna
Naseby Res.
Loddington
Thorpe Malsor
King's Newnham
Naseby
Coton
Haselbech
Cold Ashby
Maidwell
Draughton
Great Cransley
Clifton upon Dunsmore
Yelvertoft
Thornby
Mawsley
SK
SP
0 1 2 3 4 5 6 miles
0 1 2 3 4 5 6 7 8 9 10 km

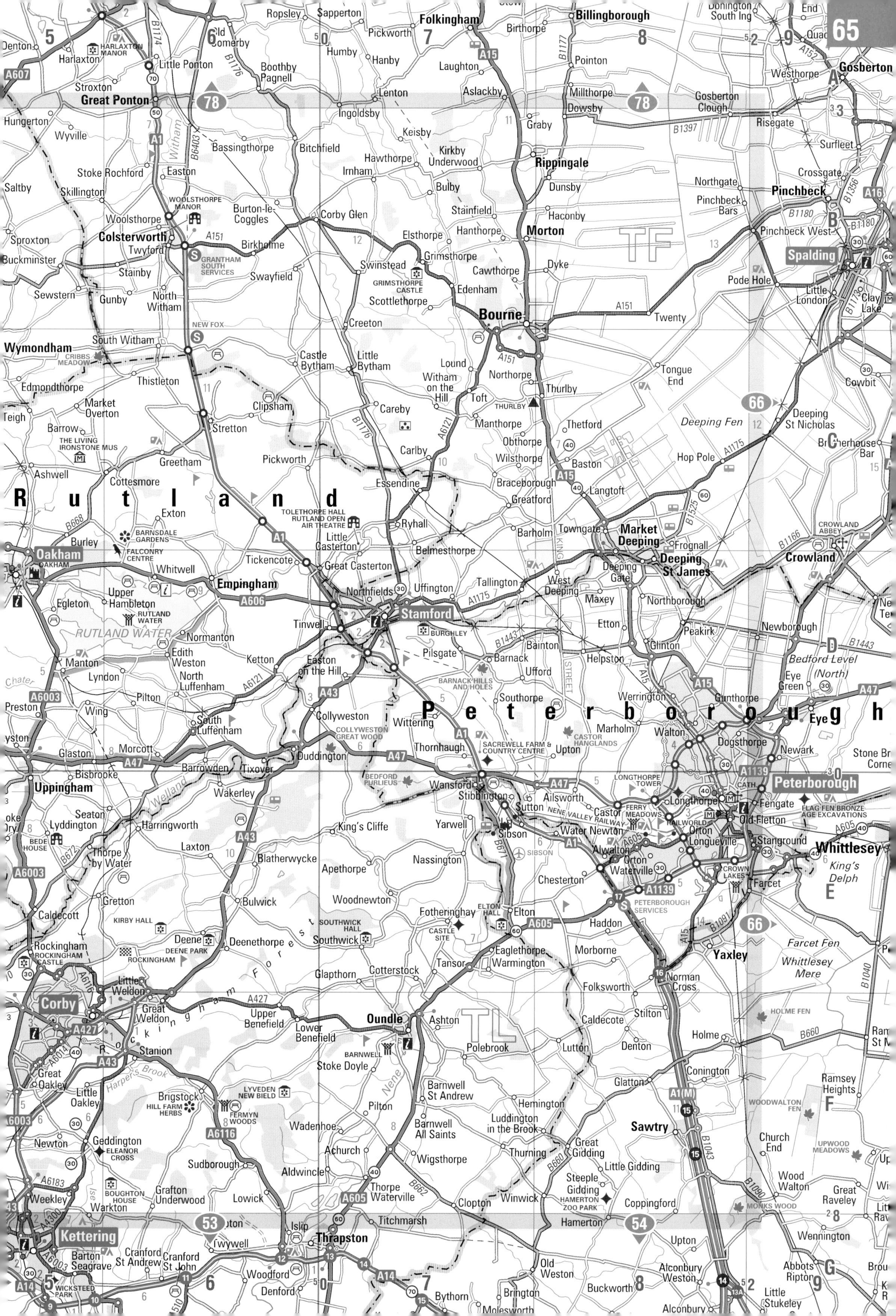
Denton
Harlaxton
HARLAXTON MANOR
Little Ponton
Stroxton
Great Ponton
Hungerton
Wyville
Stoke Rochford
Easton
Saltby
Skillington
Sproxton
Woolsthorpe
WOOLSTHORPE MANOR
Colsterworth
Twyford
Buckminster
Stainby
GRANTHAM SOUTH SERVICES
Sewstern
Gunby
North Witham
NEW FOX
Wymondham
South Witham
CRIBBS MEADOW
Edmondthorpe
Thistleton
Market Overton
Teigh
Barrow
Stretton
THE LIVING IRONSTONE MUS
Greetham
Ashwell
Cottesmore
Rutland
Exton
Burley
BARNSDALE GARDENS
FALCONRY CENTRE
Oakham
OAKHAM
Whitwell
Empingham
Upper Hambleton
Egleton
RUTLAND WATER
Normanton
Edith Weston
Manton
Lyndon
North Luffenham
Pilton
Wing
Preston
South Luffenham
Glaston
Morcott
Bisbrooke
Uppingham
Seaton
Lyddington
BEDE HOUSE
Thorpe by Water
Gretton
Caldecott
Rockingham
ROCKINGHAM CASTLE
KIRBY HALL
Corby
Great Oakley
Little Oakley
Newton
Geddington
ELEANOR CROSS
Weekley
Kettering
Barton Seagrave
Cranford St Andrew
Cranford St John
WICKSTEED PARK
Ropsley
Sapperton
Folkingham
Pickworth
Humby
Hanby
Boothby Pagnell
Old Somerby
Lenton
Ingoldsby
Bassingthorpe
Bitchfield
Keisby
Hawthorpe
Irnham
Burton-le-Coggles
Corby Glen
Birkholme
Swayfield
Swinstead
GRIMSTHORPE CASTLE
Scottlethorpe
Creeton
Castle Bytham
Little Bytham
Clipsham
Pickworth
Careby
Carlby
Essendine
TOLETHORPE HALL RUTLAND OPEN AIR THEATRE
Ryhall
Little Casterton
Tickencote
Great Casterton
Belmesthorpe
Northfields
Uffington
Stamford
Tinwell
BURGHLEY
Ketton
Easton on the Hill
Pilsgate
Collyweston
COLLYWESTON GREAT WOOD
Duddington
Tixover
Barrowden
Wakerley
Harringworth
Laxton
Blatherwycke
King's Cliffe
Apethorpe
Bulwick
Woodnewton
SOUTHWICK HALL
Southwick
Deene
DEENE PARK
Deenethorpe
ROCKINGHAM
Little Weldon
Great Weldon
Upper Benefield
Lower Benefield
Stanion
Brigstock
HILL FARM HERBS
LYVEDEN NEW BIELD
FERMYN WOODS
Sudborough
Grafton Underwood
BOUGHTON HOUSE
Warkton
Lowick
Twywell
Islip
Thrapston
Woodford
Denford
Titchmarsh
Thorpe Waterville
Aldwincle
Achurch
Wadenhoe
Pilton
Stoke Doyle
BARNWELL
Oundle
Glapthorn
Cotterstock
Laughton
Aslackby
Birthorpe
Billingborough
Pointon
Millthorpe
Dowsby
Graby
Kirkby Underwood
Rippingale
Dunsby
Bulby
Stainfield
Haconby
Hanthorpe
Morton
Elsthorpe
Grimsthorpe
Cawthorpe
Dyke
Edenham
Bourne
Twenty
Lound
Witham on the Hill
Northorpe
Toft
Thurlby
THURLBY
Manthorpe
Obthorpe
Wilsthorpe
Thetford
Baston
Braceborough
Greatford
Langtoft
Barholm
Towngate
Market Deeping
Frogmall
Deeping St James
Deeping Gate
Tallington
West Deeping
Maxey
Northborough
Etton
Peakirk
Glinton
Bainton
Barnack
BARNACK HILLS AND HOLES
Ufford
Helpston
Southorpe
Peterborough
Wittering
Thornhaugh
SACREWELL FARM & COUNTRY CENTRE
CASTOR HANGLANDS
Upton
Marholm
Werrington
Walton
Gunthorpe
Dogsthorpe
Newark
BEDFORD PURLIEUS
Wansford
Stibbington
Sutton
Ailsworth
NENE VALLEY RAILWAY
Castor
FERRY MEADOWS
LONGTHORPE TOWER
Longthorpe
Yarwell
Sibson
SIBSON
Water Newton
Alwalton
Orton Waterville
Orton Longueville
RAILWORLD
Nassington
Chesterton
PETERBOROUGH SERVICES
Fotheringhay
CASTLE SITE
ELTON HALL
Elton
Haddon
Tansor
Eaglethorpe
Warmington
Morborne
Folksworth
Norman Cross
Ashton
Polebrook
Caldecote
Stilton
Lutton
Denton
Barnwell St Andrew
Barnwell All Saints
Hemington
Luddington in the Brook
Glatton
Conington
Holme
Sawtry
Thurning
Great Gidding
Little Gidding
Steeple Gidding
HAMERTON ZOO PARK
Coppingford
Wigsthorpe
Clopton
Winwick
Hamerton
Upton
Old Weston
Brington
Bythorn
Molesworth
Buckworth
Alconbury Weston
Alconbury
Donington South Ing
Quadring
Westhorpe
Gosberton
Gosberton Clough
Risegate
Surfleet
Crossgate
Northgate
Pinchbeck
Pinchbeck Bars
Pinchbeck West
Spalding
Pode Hole
Little London
Clay Lake
Tongue End
Cowbit
Deeping Fen
Deeping St Nicholas
Hop Pole
Brotherhouse Bar
CROWLAND ABBEY
Crowland
Newborough
Bedford Level (North)
Eye Green
Eye
Stone Bridge Corner
Peterborough
Fengate
FLAG FEN BRONZE AGE EXCAVATIONS
Old Fletton
Stanground
Whittlesey
King's Delph
CROWN LAKES
Farcet
Farcet Fen
Yaxley
Whittlesey Mere
HOLME FEN
Ramsey Heights
WOODWALTON FEN
Church End
UPWOOD MEADOWS
Wood Walton
Great Raveley
MONKS WOOD
Wennington
Abbots Ripton
Little Stukeley
TF
TL
A607
A1
A151
A15
A606
A6121
A1175
A47
A43
A6003
A427
A6116
A605
A14
A16
A1139
A1(M)
B1176
B1174
B6403
B1177
B1397
B1180
B668
B672
B1443
B1166
B1525
B1091
B1040
B660
B662
B1043
B1090
Witham
Welland
Chater
Nene
Harper's Brook
Ise
Rockingham Forest
78
66
53
54

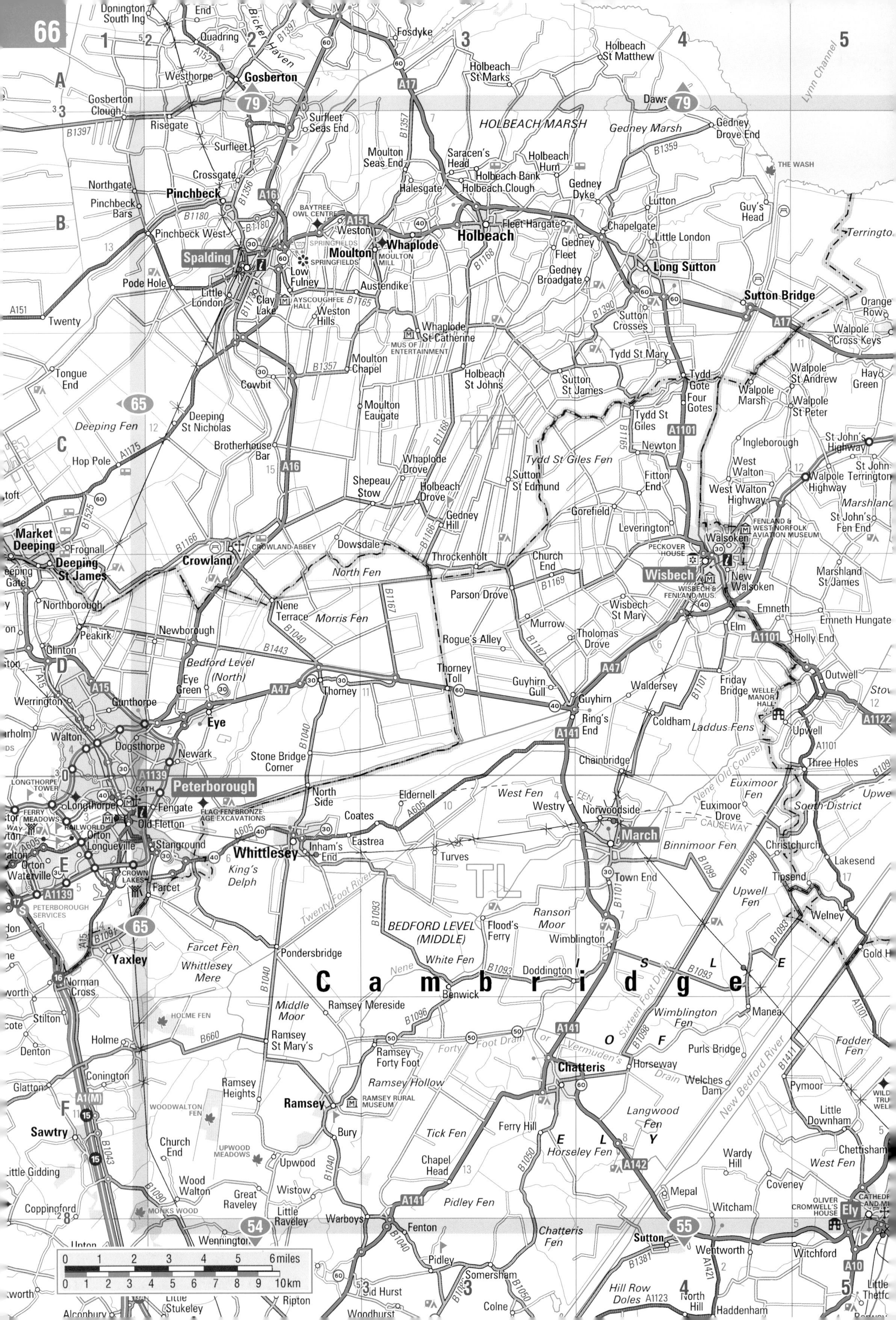
Donington South Ing
End
Quadring
Bicker Haven
Fosdyke
Holbeach St Matthew
Westhorpe
Gosberton
Holbeach St Marks
79
Gosberton Clough
Daws
Lynn Channel
Risegate
Surfleet Seas End
HOLBEACH MARSH
Gedney Marsh
Gedney Drove End
Surfleet
Moulton Seas End
Saracen's Head
Holbeach Hurn
THE WASH
Crossgate
Holbeach Bank
Northgate
Halesgate
Holbeach Clough
Gedney Dyke
Pinchbeck
Lutton
Pinchbeck Bars
BAYTREE OWL CENTRE
Guy's Head
Fleet Hargate
Chapelgate
Pinchbeck West
Weston
Holbeach
Little London
Terrington
SPRINGFIELDS
Moulton
Whaplode
Gedney Fleet
Spalding
Long Sutton
Low Fulney
Gedney Broadgate
Pode Hole
Austendike
Sutton Bridge
Little London
Clay Lake
AYSCOUGHFEE HALL
Weston Hills
Sutton Crosses
Orange Row
Twenty
Whaplode St Catherine
Walpole Cross Keys
MUS OF ENTERTAINMENT
Tydd St Mary
Moulton Chapel
Tydd Gote
Walpole St Andrew
Hay Green
Tongue End
Cowbit
Holbeach St Johns
Sutton St James
Walpole Marsh
Four Gotes
Walpole St Peter
65
Moulton Eaugate
Tydd St Giles
Deeping Fen
Deeping St Nicholas
Newton
Ingleborough
St John's Highway
Hop Pole
Brotherhouse Bar
Tydd St Giles Fen
West Walton
St John's Terrington
Whaplode Drove
Fitton End
Shepeau Stow
Holbeach Drove
Sutton St Edmund
West Walton Highway
Walpole Highway
Marshland
Gedney Hill
Gorefield
St John's Fen End
Market Deeping
Leverington
FENLAND & WEST NORFOLK AVIATION MUSEUM
Frognall
CROWLAND ABBEY
Dowsdale
Walsoken
Deeping St James
Crowland
Throckenholt
Church End
PECKOVER HOUSE
Deeping Gate
North Fen
Wisbech
WISBECH & FENLAND MUS
New Walsoken
Marshland St James
Northborough
Nene Terrace
Morris Fen
Parson Drove
Wisbech St Mary
Emneth
Emneth Hungate
Peakirk
Newborough
Murrow
Tholomas Drove
Elm
Glinton
Rogue's Alley
Holly End
Bedford Level (North)
Thorney Toll
Friday Bridge
Outwell
Werrington
Eye Green
Thorney
Guyhirn Gull
Waldersey
WELLE MANOR HALL
Gunthorpe
Eye
Guyhirn
Ring's End
Coldham
Laddus Fens
Upwell
Walton
Dogsthorpe
Newark
Stone Bridge Corner
Chainbridge
Three Holes
LONGTHORPE TOWER
Peterborough
Nene (Old Course)
Euximoor Fen
Upwell
North Side
Eldernell
West Fen
Longthorpe
Fengate
FLAG FEN BRONZE AGE EXCAVATIONS
Westry
Norwoodside
Euximoor Drove
South District
FERRY MEADOWS
RAILWORLD
Old Fletton
Coates
CAUSEWAY
Orton Longueville
Stanground
Whittlesey
Inham's End
Eastrea
Turves
March
Binnimoor Fen
Christchurch
Orton Waterville
CROWN LAKES
King's Delph
Lakesend
Farcet
TL
Town End
Tipsend
PETERBOROUGH SERVICES
Twenty Foot River
Upwell Fen
Ranson Moor
Welney
Flood's Ferry
BEDFORD LEVEL (MIDDLE)
Wimblington
Yaxley
Pondersbridge
Farcet Fen
White Fen
Gold Hill
Whittlesey Mere
Doddington
Norman Cross
Cambridge
ISLE
Benwick
Manea
Middle Moor
Ramsey Mereside
Stilton
HOLME FEN
Wimblington Fen
Sixteen Foot Drain
Holme
Ramsey St Mary's
Fodder Fen
Denton
Forty Foot Drain
OF
Purls Bridge
Vermuden's Drain
Ramsey Forty Foot
Conington
Chatteris
Horseway
Glatton
Ramsey Hollow
Welches Dam
Pymoor
Ramsey Heights
New Bedford River
Ramsey
RAMSEY RURAL MUSEUM
WOODWALTON FEN
Little Downham
Sawtry
Bury
Ferry Hill
Tick Fen
Langwood Fen
Church End
ELY
Horseley Fen
Chettisham
Little Gidding
UPWOOD MEADOWS
Upwood
Chapel Head
Wardy Hill
West Fen
Wood Walton
Coveney
Great Raveley
Mepal
Wistow
Pidley Fen
Witcham
OLIVER CROMWELL'S HOUSE
Ely
Coppingford
MONKS WOOD
Little Raveley
Warboys
Fenton
Chatteris Fen
Sutton
Wentworth
Witchford
Wennington
54
55
Pidley
Somersham
Hill Row
Doles
Little Stukeley
Ripton
Old Hurst
Colne
North Hill
Haddenham
Little Thetford
Alconbury
Woodhurst
0 1 2 3 4 5 6 miles
0 1 2 3 4 5 6 7 8 9 10km

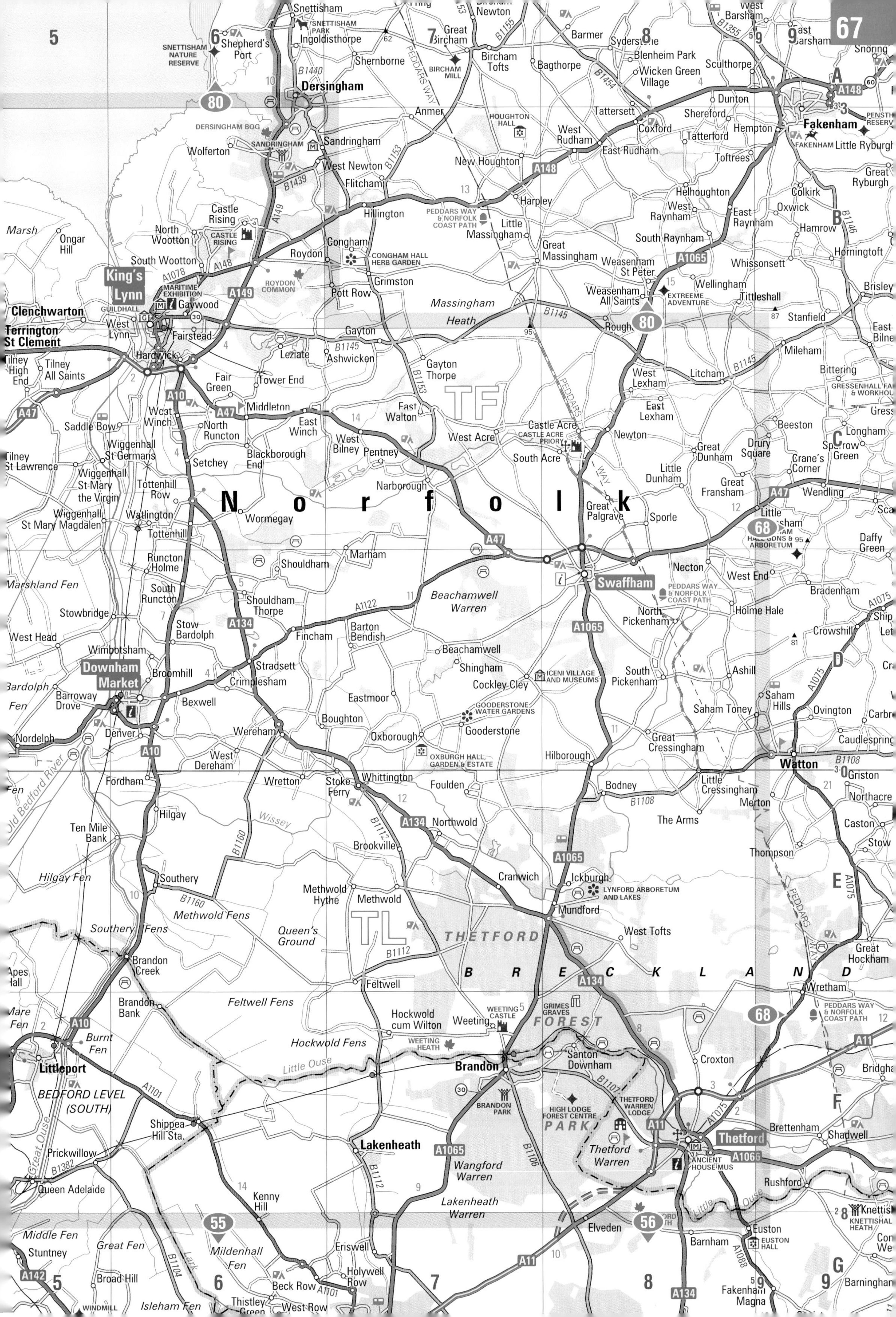
Snettisham
Snettisham Park
Ingoldisthorpe
Snettisham Nature Reserve
Shepherd's Port
Shernborne
Great Bircham
Bircham Mill
Bircham Tofts
Newton
Barmer
Bagthorpe
Syderstone
Blenheim Park
Sculthorpe
Wicken Green Village
West Barsham
East Barsham
Snoring
Dersingham
Dersingham Bog
Sandringham
Wolferton
West Newton
Flitcham
Anmer
Houghton Hall
New Houghton
West Rudham
East Rudham
Tattersett
Coxford
Dunton
Shereford
Tatterford
Hempton
Toftrees
Fakenham
Little Ryburgh
Great Ryburgh
Colkirk
Oxwick
Hamrow
Horningtoft
Helhoughton
West Raynham
East Raynham
South Raynham
Whissonsett
Wellingham
Tittleshall
Brisley
Stanfield
Weasenham St Peter
Weasenham All Saints
Extreme Adventure
Rougham
Peddars Way
Pedders Way & Norfolk Coast Path
Little Massingham
Great Massingham
Harpley
Hillington
Castle Rising
North Wootton
South Wootton
Ongar Hill
Marsh
Congham
Congham Hall Herb Garden
Roydon
Roydon Common
Grimston
Pott Row
Massingham Heath
King's Lynn
Maritime Exhibition
Guildhall
Gaywood
Fairstead
Clenchwarton
Terrington St Clement
West Lynn
Hardwick
Gayton
Leziate
Ashwicken
Gayton Thorpe
Mileham
East Bilney
Litcham
West Lexham
East Lexham
Bittering
Gressenhall Farm & Workhouse
Tilney High End
Tilney All Saints
Fair Green
Tower End
Middleton
East Winch
West Winch
North Runcton
Saddle Bow
Wiggenhall St Germans
Wiggenhall St Mary the Virgin
Wiggenhall St Mary Magdalen
Tilney St Lawrence
Setchey
Blackborough End
West Bilney
Pentney
East Walton
Narborough
West Acre
Castle Acre
Castle Acre Priory
South Acre
Newton
Great Dunham
Little Dunham
Drury Square
Beeston
Longham
Sparrow Green
Crane's Corner
Great Fransham
Wendling
Little Fransham
Hall Gdns & Arboretum
Daffy Green
Norfolk
Tottenhill Row
Watlington
Tottenhill
Wormegay
Great Palgrave
Sporle
Swaffham
Necton
West End
Bradenham
Holme Hale
North Pickenham
Peddars Way & Norfolk Coast Path
Marshland Fen
Runcton Holme
South Runcton
Shouldham
Shouldham Thorpe
Marham
Beachamwell Warren
Stowbridge
West Head
Stow Bardolph
Wimbotsham
Downham Market
Barroway Drove
Bardolph Fen
Fincham
Barton Bendish
Beachamwell
Shingham
Cockley Cley
Iceni Village and Museums
South Pickenham
Ashill
Crowshill
Saham Hills
Saham Toney
Ovington
Carbrooke
Caudlesprings
Stradsett
Crimplesham
Bexwell
Broomhill
Eastmoor
Boughton
Gooderstone Water Gardens
Gooderstone
Nordelph
Denver
Wereham
West Dereham
Oxborough
Oxburgh Hall, Garden & Estate
Hilborough
Great Cressingham
Little Cressingham
Watton
Griston
Fordham
Wretton
Stoke Ferry
Whittington
Foulden
Bodney
Merton
Northacre
Caston
Stow
Old Bedford River
Hilgay
Wissey
Ten Mile Bank
Northwold
Brookville
The Arms
Thompson
Hilgay Fen
Southery
Methwold Hythe
Methwold
Cranwich
Ickburgh
Lynford Arboretum and Lakes
Mundford
Methwold Fens
Southery Fens
Queen's Ground
Thetford
Breckland
West Tofts
Great Hockham
Brandon Creek
Feltwell
Wretham
Apes Hall
Brandon Bank
Feltwell Fens
Hockwold cum Wilton
Weeting
Weeting Castle
Grimes Graves
Forest
Peddars Way & Norfolk Coast Path
Mare Fen
Burnt Fen
Littleport
Hockwold Fens
Weeting Heath
Brandon
Santon Downham
Croxton
Bridgham
Little Ouse
Bedford Level (South)
Brandon Park
High Lodge Forest Centre
Thetford Warren Lodge
Park
Brettenham
Shadwell
Shippea Hill Sta.
Prickwillow
Great Ouse
Lakenheath
Thetford Warren
Ancient House Mus
Rushford
Queen Adelaide
Wangford Warren
Kenny Hill
Lakenheath Warren
Knettishall
Knettishall Heath
Middle Fen
Stuntney
Great Fen
Mildenhall Fen
Lark
Eriswell
Elveden
Euston
Euston Hall
Barnham
Broad Hill
Beck Row
Holywell Row
Fakenham Magna
Barningham
Windmill
Isleham Fen
Thistley Green
West Row
TF
TL

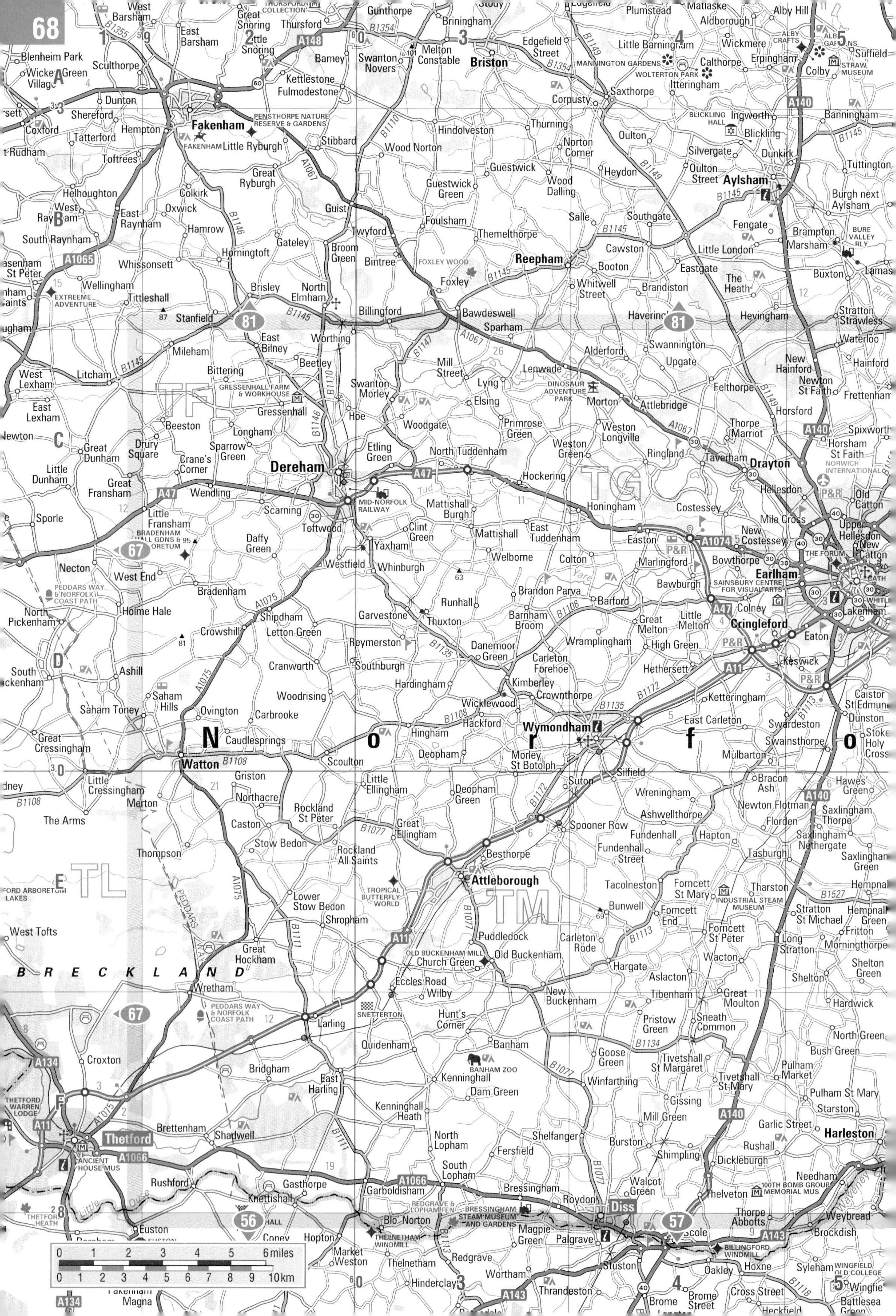

West Barsham
Great Snoring
Thursford
Gunthorpe
Briningham
Plumstead
Matlaske
Alby Hill
East Barsham
Little Snoring
A148
B1354
Melton Constable
Briston
Edgefield Street
Little Barningham
Aldborough
Wickmere
Erpingham
Suffield
Blenheim Park
Sculthorpe
Barney
Swanton Novers
Kettlestone
Fulmodestone
MANNINGTON GARDENS
WOLTERTON PARK
Calthorpe
Itteringham
Colby
STRAW MUSEUM
Wicken Green Village
Dunton
Saxthorpe
Corpusty
A140
Shereford
Fakenham
PENSTHORPE NATURE RESERVE & GARDENS
Stibbard
Hindolveston
Thurning
BLICKLING HALL
Ingworth
Banningham
Coxford
Tatterford
Hempton
FAKENHAM
Little Ryburgh
Wood Norton
Norton Corner
Oulton
Blickling
B1145
East Rudham
Toftrees
Guestwick
Silvergate
Dunkirk
Great Ryburgh
Guestwick Green
Wood Dalling
Heydon
Oulton Street
Aylsham
Tuttington
Helhoughton
Colkirk
B1149
Burgh next Aylsham
West Raynham
East Raynham
Oxwick
Guist
Foulsham
Salle
Southgate
Fengate
South Raynham
Hamrow
Twyford
Themelthorpe
Cawston
Little London
Brampton
Marsham
BURE VALLEY RLY
A1065
Whissonsett
Horningtoft
Gateley
Broom Green
Bintree
FOXLEY WOOD
Reepham
Booton
Eastgate
Buxton
Lamas
Helhoughton
Wellingham
B1146
Brisley
North Elmham
Foxley
Whitwell Street
Brandiston
The Heath
EXTREME ADVENTURE
Tittleshall
Stanfield
Billingford
Bawdeswell
Sparham
Haveringland
Hevingham
Stratton Strawless
81
Mileham
East Bilney
Worthing
A1067
Alderford
Swannington
Waterloo
Beetley
B1147
Mill Street
Upgate
New Hainford
Hainford
West Lexham
Litcham
Bittering
Swanton Morley
Lyng
Lenwade
Newton St Faith
Frettenham
GRESSENHALL FARM & WORKHOUSE
DINOSAUR ADVENTURE PARK
Morton
Felthorpe
East Lexham
Gressenhall
Hoe
Elsing
Attlebridge
Horsford
Beeston
Longham
Woodgate
Primrose Green
Weston Longville
Thorpe Marriot
Spixworth
Newton
Great Dunham
Drury Square
Sparrow Green
Crane's Corner
Etling Green
North Tuddenham
Weston Green
Ringland
Taverham
Drayton
Horsham St Faith
NORWICH INTERNATIONAL
Little Dunham
Great Fransham
Dereham
A47
Hockering
TG
Hellesdon
Old Catton
Wendling
MID-NORFOLK RAILWAY
Tud
Mattishall Burgh
Honingham
Costessey
Sporle
Little Fransham
Scarning
Toftwood
Clint Green
Mattishall
East Tuddenham
Mile Cross
Upper Hellesdon
New Costessey
BRADENHAM HALL GDNS & ARBORETUM
Daffy Green
Yaxham
Easton
A1074
New Catton
THE FORUM
67
Westfield
Whinburgh
Welborne
Colton
Marlingford
Bowthorpe
Earlham
Necton
West End
SAINSBURY CENTRE FOR VISUAL ARTS
Bawburgh
CATH
PEDDARS WAY & NORFOLK COAST PATH
Bradenham
A1075
Runhall
Brandon Parva
Yare
Barford
North Pickenham
Holme Hale
Shipdham
Garvestone
Thuxton
Barnham Broom
B1108
Great Melton
Little Melton
Colney
Lakenham
Crowshill
Letton Green
Cringleford
Eaton
Reymerston
B1135
Danemoor Green
Wramplingham
High Green
South Pickenham
Ashill
Cranworth
Southburgh
Carleton Forehoe
Hethersett
A11
Keswick
Saham Hills
Hardingham
Kimberley
Woodrising
Crownthorpe
B1172
Ketteringham
Caistor St Edmund
Saham Toney
Ovington
Carbrooke
Wicklewood
Dunston
Hackford
Wymondham
East Carleton
Swardeston
Stoke Holy Cross
Great Cressingham
N
Caudlesprings
Hingham
o
r
f
o
Swainsthorpe
Mulbarton
Deopham
Morley St Botolph
Watton
Scoulton
Griston
Silfield
Bracon Ash
Hawes' Green
Little Cressingham
Little Ellingham
Suton
Merton
Northacre
Deopham Green
Wreningham
A140
Newton Flotman
Saxlingham Thorpe
Rockland St Peter
Ashwellthorpe
Florden
The Arms
Caston
Great Ellingham
Spooner Row
Fundenhall
Hapton
Saxlingham Nethergate
Thompson
Stow Bedon
B1077
Rockland All Saints
Besthorpe
Fundenhall Street
Tasburgh
Saxlingham Green
TL
Attleborough
TM
Tacolneston
Forncett St Mary
Tharston
Hempnall
E
INDUSTRIAL STEAM MUSEUM
B1527
PEDDARS WAY
TROPICAL BUTTERFLY WORLD
Lower Stow Bedon
Bunwell
Forncett End
Stratton St Michael
Hempnall Green
Shropham
Fritton
West Tofts
B1111
Puddledock
Carleton Rode
B1113
Forncett St Peter
Long Stratton
Morningthorpe
Great Hockham
OLD BUCKENHAM MILL
Church Green
Old Buckenham
Hargate
Wacton
Shelton Green
B R E C K L A N D
Eccles Road
Aslacton
Shelton
Wilby
New Buckenham
Tibenham
Great Moulton
Wretham
SNETTERTON
Hunt's Corner
Pristow Green
Sneath Common
Hardwick
Larling
Quidenham
Banham
B1134
North Green
Croxton
BANHAM ZOO
Goose Green
Tivetshall St Margaret
Bush Green
A134
Bridgham
Kenninghall
Winfarthing
Pulham Market
East Harling
Dam Green
Tivetshall St Mary
Pulham St Mary
THETFORD WARREN LODGE
Kenninghall Heath
Gissing
Starston
Mill Green
Garlic Street
Brettenham
Shadwell
Thetford
North Lopham
Shelfanger
Burston
Harleston
A1066
ANCIENT HOUSE MUS
Fersfield
Shimpling
Rushall
South Lopham
Dickleburgh
Rushford
Gasthorpe
Garboldisham
Bressingham
Walcot Green
Needham
100TH BOMB GROUP MEMORIAL MUS
Knettishall
Roydon
Thelveton
REDGRAVE & LOPHAM FEN
BRESSINGHAM STEAM MUSEUM AND GARDENS
Diss
Thorpe Abbotts
Weybread
THETFORD HEATH
Little Ouse
56
Blo' Norton
57
Scole
Brockdish
Euston
THELNETHAM WINDMILL
Magpie Green
Palgrave
A143
BILLINGFORD WINDMILL
Coney Weston
Hopton
Market Weston
Redgrave
Stuston
Oakley
Hoxne
Syleham
WINGFIELD OLD COLLEGE
Thelnetham
Wortham
Thrandeston
Cross Street
B1118
Wingfie
Hinderclay
Brome
Brome Street
Battlesea Green
Fakenham Magna
Hoxne
Heckfield
0 1 2 3 4 5 6 miles
0 1 2 3 4 5 6 7 8 9 10 km

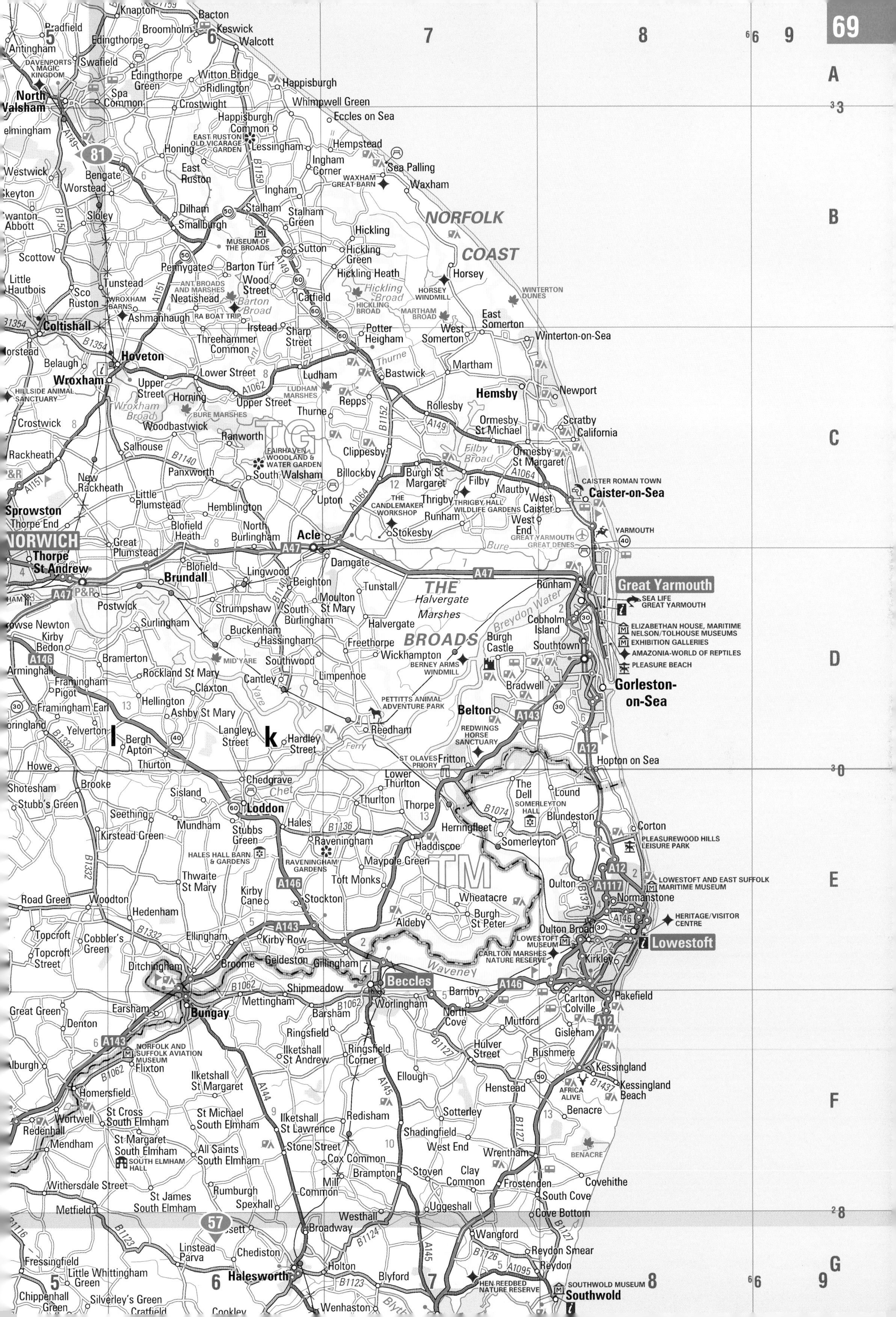

NORFOLK
COAST
THE
BROADS
Halvergate
Marshes
Knapton
Bacton
Bradfield
Broomholm
Keswick
Walcott
Antingham
Edingthorpe
DAVENPORTS MAGIC KINGDOM
Swafield
Edingthorpe Green
Witton Bridge
Happisburgh
North Walsham
Spa Common
Ridlington
Crostwight
Whimpwell Green
Eccles on Sea
Happisburgh Common
EAST RUSTON OLD VICARAGE GARDEN
Lessingham
Hempstead
Honing
Ingham Corner
Sea Palling
Westwick
Bengate
East Ruston
WAXHAM GREAT BARN
Waxham
Worstead
Ingham
Dilham
Stalham
Stalham Green
Swanton Abbott
Sloley
Smallburgh
Hickling
MUSEUM OF THE BROADS
Sutton
Hickling Green
Scottow
Pennygate
Barton Turf
Hickling Heath
Horsey
Little Hautbois
Tunstead
ANT BROADS AND MARSHES
Wood Street
Hickling Broad
HORSEY WINDMILL
WINTERTON DUNES
Sco Ruston
WROXHAM BARNS
Neatishead
Catfield
Barton Broad
HICKLING BROAD
MARTHAM BROAD
East Somerton
Ashmanhaugh
RA BOAT TRIP
Coltishall
Irstead
Sharp Street
Potter Heigham
West Somerton
Winterton-on-Sea
Threehammer Common
Horstead
Belaugh
Hoveton
Thurne
Bastwick
Martham
Wroxham
Lower Street
Ludham
LUDHAM MARSHES
Hemsby
Newport
HILLSIDE ANIMAL SANCTUARY
Upper Street
Horning
Upper Street
Repps
Rollesby
Wroxham Broad
BURE MARSHES
Thurne
Crostwick
Woodbastwick
Ormesby St Michael
Scratby
California
Ranworth
Rackheath
Salhouse
FAIRHAVEN WOODLAND & WATER GARDEN
Clippesby
Filby Broad
Ormesby St Margaret
New Rackheath
Panxworth
South Walsham
Billockby
Burgh St Margaret
Filby
CAISTER ROMAN TOWN
Caister-on-Sea
Mautby
Little Plumstead
Upton
THE CANDLEMAKER WORKSHOP
Thrigby
THRIGBY HALL WILDLIFE GARDENS
West Caister
Sprowston
Thorpe End
Hemblington
Runham
West End
Blofield Heath
North Burlingham
Acle
Stokesby
GREAT YARMOUTH GREAT DENES
YARMOUTH
NORWICH
Great Plumstead
Bure
Thorpe St Andrew
Blofield
Damgate
Brundall
Lingwood
Beighton
Tunstall
Runham
Great Yarmouth
Postwick
Moulton St Mary
SEA LIFE GREAT YARMOUTH
Strumpshaw
South Burlingham
Breydon Water
Cobholm Island
Trowse Newton
Surlingham
Halvergate
ELIZABETHAN HOUSE, MARITIME NELSON/TOLHOUSE MUSEUMS
Kirby Bedon
Buckenham
Burgh Castle
EXHIBITION GALLERIES
Hassingham
Freethorpe
Southtown
AMAZONIA-WORLD OF REPTILES
Bramerton
MID YARE
Southwood
Wickhampton
BERNEY ARMS WINDMILL
PLEASURE BEACH
Arminghall
Rockland St Mary
Limpenhoe
Bradwell
Gorleston-on-Sea
Framingham Pigot
Cantley
Claxton
Framingham Earl
Hellington
Yare
PETTITTS ANIMAL ADVENTURE PARK
Belton
Ashby St Mary
Reedham
REDWINGS HORSE SANCTUARY
Poringland
Yelverton
Bergh Apton
Langley Street
Hardley Street
Ferry
Howe
Thurton
ST OLAVES PRIORY
Fritton
Hopton on Sea
Chedgrave
Lower Thurlton
Shotesham
Brooke
Sisland
Chet
The Dell
Lound
SOMERLEYTON HALL
Stubb's Green
Loddon
Thurlton
Thorpe
Seething
Blundeston
Mundham
Hales
Herringfleet
Corton
Kirstead Green
Stubbs Green
Raveningham
Haddiscoe
Somerleyton
PLEASUREWOOD HILLS LEISURE PARK
HALES HALL BARN & GARDENS
RAVENINGHAM GARDENS
Maypole Green
Thwaite St Mary
Toft Monks
Oulton
LOWESTOFT AND EAST SUFFOLK MARITIME MUSEUM
Road Green
Woodton
Kirby Cane
Stockton
Wheatacre
Normanstone
Hedenham
Burgh St Peter
HERITAGE/VISITOR CENTRE
Aldeby
Oulton Broad
Topcroft
Cobbler's Green
Ellingham
Kirby Row
LOWESTOFT MUSEUM
Lowestoft
Topcroft Street
CARLTON MARSHES NATURE RESERVE
Kirkley
Ditchingham
Broome
Geldeston
Gillingham
Waveney
Beccles
Shipmeadow
Barnby
Carlton Colville
Pakefield
Great Green
Earsham
Mettingham
Worlingham
North Cove
Bungay
Barsham
Mutford
Denton
Gisleham
Ringsfield
NORFOLK AND SUFFOLK AVIATION MUSEUM
Hulver Street
Rushmere
Ilketshall St Andrew
Ringsfield Corner
Kessingland
Alburgh
Flixton
Ilketshall St Margaret
Ellough
Henstead
AFRICA ALIVE
Kessingland Beach
Homersfield
St Cross South Elmham
St Michael South Elmham
Ilketshall St Lawrence
Redisham
Sotterley
Benacre
Wortwell
Redenhall
St Margaret South Elmham
Shadingfield
Mendham
Stone Street
West End
Wrentham
BENACRE
SOUTH ELMHAM HALL
All Saints South Elmham
Cox Common
Brampton
Stoven
Clay Common
Withersdale Street
Mill Common
Frostenden
Covehithe
Rumburgh
South Cove
St James South Elmham
Spexhall
Uggeshall
Metfield
Westhall
Cove Bottom
Broadway
Wangford
Linstead Parva
Chediston
Reydon Smear
Fressingfield
Holton
Reydon
Little Whittingham Green
Halesworth
Blyford
HEN REEDBED NATURE RESERVE
SOUTHWOLD MUSEUM
Chippenhall Green
Silverley's Green
Cratfield
Cookley
Wenhaston
Southwold
A149
A1151
A1062
A1064
A47
A146
A143
A12
A1117
A144
A145
A1095
B1150
B1159
B1354
B1140
B1152
B1332
B1136
B1074
B1062
B1127
B1437
B1375
B1123
B1124
B1126
B1116
TG
TM
81
57
5
6
7
8
9
A
B
C
D
E
F
G

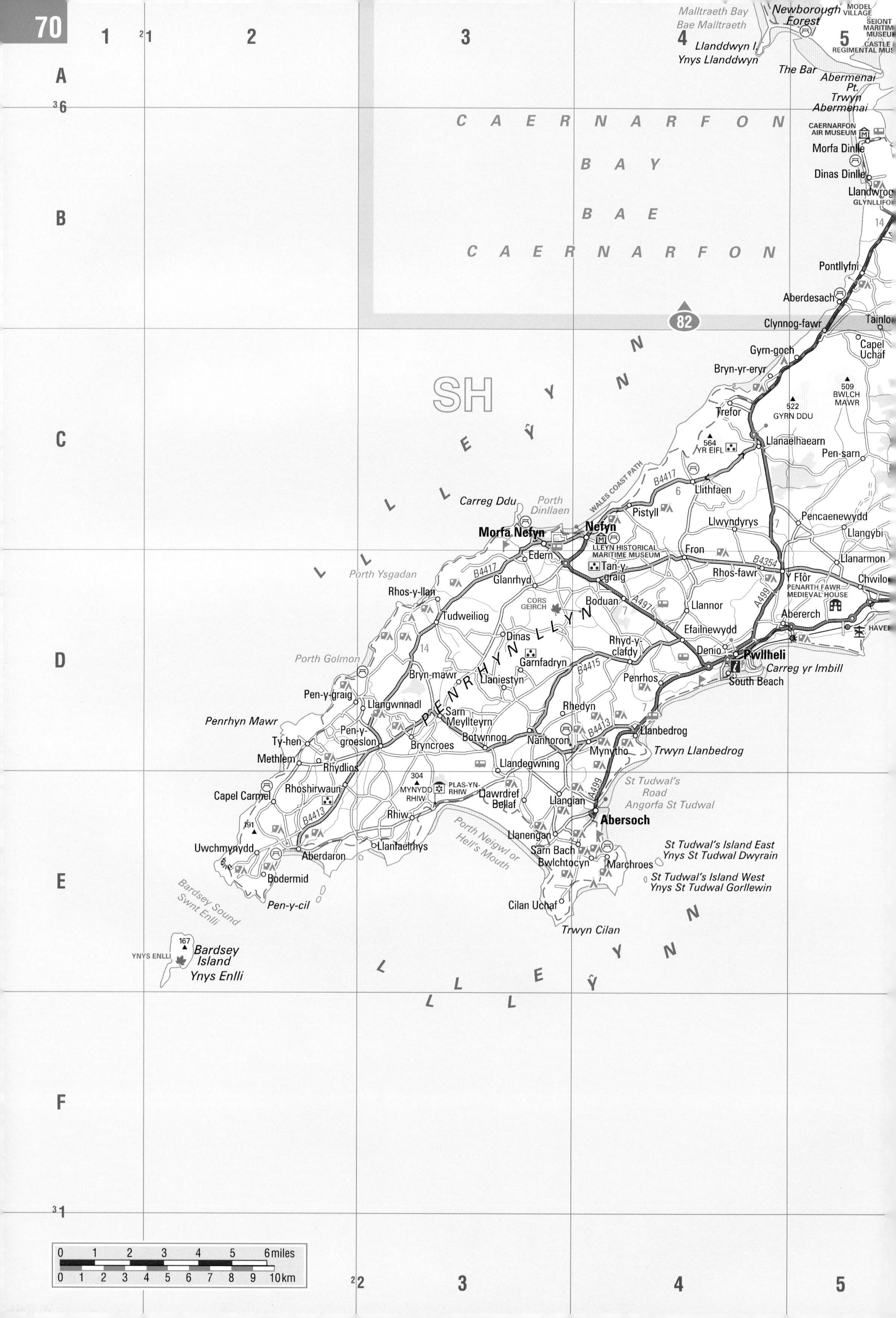

1 1 2 3 4 5

A

B

C

D

E

F

CAERNARFON

BAY

BAE

CAERNARFON

SH

Malltraeth Bay
Bae Malltraeth

Newborough
Forest

MODEL
VILLAGE

Llanddwyn I.
Ynys Llanddwyn

SEIONT
MARITIME
MUSEUM
CASTLE
REGIMENTAL MUS

The Bar

Abermenai
Pt.
Trwyn
Abermenai

CAERNARFON
AIR MUSEUM

Morfa Dinlle

Dinas Dinlle

Llandwrog
GLYNLLIFO

14

Pontllyfni

Aberdesach

82

Clynnog-fawr

Tainlo

Capel
Uchaf

Gyrn-goch

Bryn-yr-eryr

509
BWLCH
MAWR

522
GYRN DDU

Trefor

564
YR EIFL

Llanaelhaearn

Pen-sarn

Llithfaen

B4417 6

Pistyll

Pencaenewydd

Llwyndyrys

Llangybi

WALES COAST PATH

Carreg Ddu

Porth
Dinllaen

Porth Ysgadan

Morfa Nefyn

Nefyn

LLEYN HISTORICAL
MARITIME MUSEUM

Edern

Tan-y-
graig

Fron

B4354

Rhos-fawr

Llanarmon

Y Ffôr

Chwilo

Glanrhyd

B4417

Rhos-y-llan

CORS
GEIRCH

Boduan

A497

Llannor

PENARTH FAWR
MEDIEVAL HOUSE

Tudweiliog

Dinas

Garnfadryn

Llaniestyn

Efailnewydd

Abererch

HAVE

Porth Golmon

Bryn-mawr

14

Rhyd-y-
clafdy

Denio

Pwllheli

PENRHYN LLŶN

B4415

Penrhos

South Beach

Carreg yr Imbill

Pen-y-graig

Llangwnnadl

Rhedyn

Penrhyn Mawr

Sarn
Meyllteyrn

B4413

Llanbedrog

Pen-y-
groeslon

Botwnnog

Nanhoron

Mynytho

Trwyn Llanbedrog

Ty-hen

Bryncroes

Methlem

Llandegwning

St Tudwal's
Road
Angorfa St Tudwal

Rhydlios

A499

Rhoshirwaun

304
MYNYDD
RHIW

PLAS-YN-
RHIW

Llawrdref
Bellaf

Llangian

Capel Carmel

191

Rhiw

Abersoch

B4413

St Tudwal's Island East
Ynys St Tudwal Dwyrain

Porth Neigwl or
Hell's Mouth

Llanengan

Sarn Bach

Uwchmynydd

Aberdaron

Llanfaelrhys

Bwlchtocyn

Marchroes

St Tudwal's Island West
Ynys St Tudwal Gorllewin

Bodermid

Cilan Uchaf

Pen-y-cil

Bardsey Sound
Swnt Enlli

Trwyn Cilan

LLEYN

167

YNYS ENLLI

Bardsey
Island
Ynys Enlli

0 1 2 3 4 5 6 miles
0 1 2 3 4 5 6 7 8 9 10km

2 3 4 5

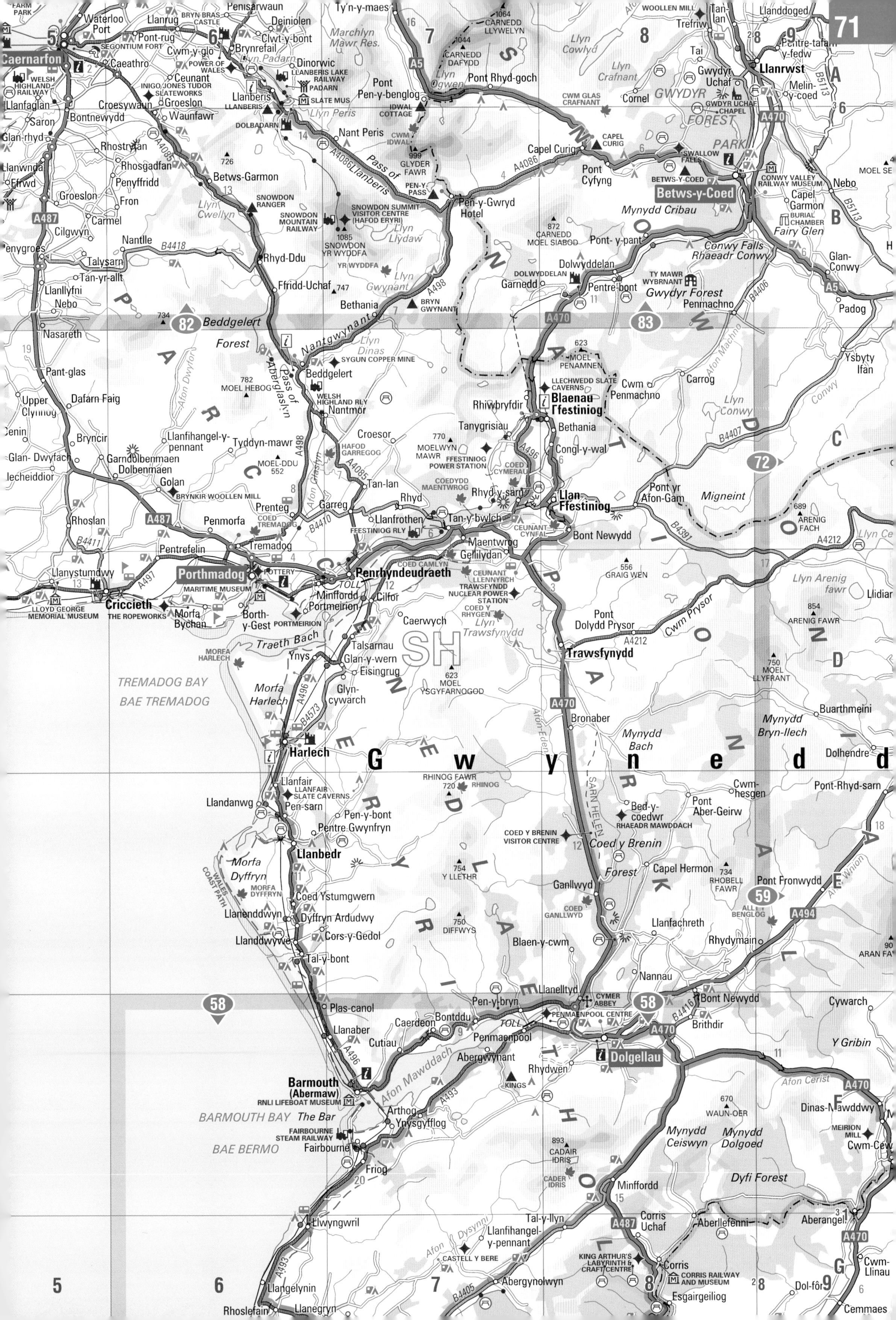
Caernarfon
Waterloo Port
Llanrug
Bryn Bras Castle
Penisarwaun
Deiniolen
Ty'n-y-maes
Marchlyn Mawr Res.
1064 Carnedd Llywelyn
1044 Carnedd Dafydd
Woollen Mill
Trefriw
Tan-lan
Llanddoged
Pentre-tafarn-y-fedw
Llanrwst
Segontium Fort
Pont-rug
Cwm-y-glo
Clwt-y-bont
Brynrefail
Llyn Padarn
Caeathro
Power of Wales
Dinorwic
Llanberis Lake Railway
Padarn
Slate Mus
Welsh Highland Railway
Inigo Jones Tudor Slateworks
Ceunant
Llanberis
Llanfaglan
Croesywaun
Groeslon
Bontnewydd
Saron
Waunfawr
Dolbadarn
Glan-rhyd
Rhostryfan
Rhosgadfan
Llanwnda
Efrwd
Groeslon
Penyffridd
Fron
Carmel
Cilgwyn
Betws-Garmon
Llyn Cwellyn
Snowdon Ranger
Snowdon Mountain Railway
Snowdon Summit Visitor Centre (Hafod Eryri)
1085 Snowdon Yr Wyddfa
Yr Wyddfa
Llyn Llydaw
Nantlle
Penygroes
Talysarn
Tan-yr-allt
Llanllyfni
Nebo
Rhyd-Ddu
Ffridd-Uchaf
747
Llyn Gwynant
Bethania
Bryn Gwynant
Pont Pen-y-benglog
Idwal Cottage
Llyn Ogwen
Cwm Idwal
999 Glyder Fawr
Pen-y-Pass
Nant Peris
Llyn Peris
Pass of Llanberis
Pen-y-Gwryd Hotel
Pont Rhyd-goch
Capel Curig
Llyn Cowlyd
Llyn Crafnant
Cwm Glas Crafnant
Cornel
Gwydyr Forest
Gwydyr Uchaf
Gwydyr Uchaf Chapel
Tai
Melin-y-coed
Swallow Falls
Betws-y-Coed
Conwy Valley Railway Museum
Pont Cyfyng
Mynydd Cribau
Capel Garmon
Burial Chamber
Fairy Glen
Nebo
Moel Se
872 Carnedd Moel Siabod
Pont-y-pant
Conwy Falls Rhaeadr Conwy
Glan-Conwy
Dolwyddelan
Pentre-bont
Garnedd
Ty Mawr Wybrnant
Gwydyr Forest
Penmachno
Padog
734
82
Beddgelert Forest
83
Nasareth
Pant-glas
Upper Clynnog
Dafarn Faig
782 Moel Hebog
Pass of Aberglaslyn
Nantgwynant
Llyn Dinas
Sygun Copper Mine
Beddgelert
Welsh Highland Rly
Nantmor
623 Moel Penamnen
Llechwedd Slate Caverns
Blaenau Ffestiniog
Cwm Penmachno
Carrog
Ysbyty Ifan
Llyn Conwy
Rhiwbryfdir
Tanygrisiau
Bethania
Bryncir
Llanfihangel-y-pennant
Tyddyn-mawr
Garndolbenmaen
Dolbenmaen
Glan-Dwyfach
Moel-Ddu 552
Golan
Brynkir Woollen Mill
Croesor
Hafod Garregog
770 Moelwyn Mawr
Ffestiniog Power Station
Coed Cymerau
Congl-y-wal
Coedydd Maentwrog
Rhyd-y-sarn
Llan Ffestiniog
Pont yr Afon-Gam
Migneint
72
689 Arenig Fach
Rhoslan
Prenteg
Penmorfa
Coed Tremadog
Tan-lan
Garreg
Rhyd
Llanfrothen
Tan-y-bwlch
Ceunant Cynfal
Bont Newydd
Llyn Celyn
Tremadog
Ffestiniog Rly
Maentwrog
Gellilydan
Pentrefelin
Llanystumdwy
Porthmadog
Pottery
Maritime Museum
Coed Camlyn
Penrhyndeudraeth
Ceunant Llennyrch
Trawsfynydd Nuclear Power Station
556 Graig Wen
Llyn Arenig fawr
Llidiar
Criccieth
Lloyd George Memorial Museum
The Ropeworks
Morfa Bychan
Borth-y-Gest
Minffordd
Portmeirion
Cilfor
Caerwych
Coed y Rhygen
Llyn Trawsfynydd
Pont Dolydd Prysor
Cwm Prysor
854 Arenig Fawr
Morfa Harlech
Traeth Bach
Ynys
Talsarnau
Glan-y-wern
Eisingrug
SH
Trawsfynydd
750 Moel Llyfrant
Tremadog Bay
Bae Tremadog
Morfa Harlech
Glyn-cywarch
623 Moel Ysgyfarnogod
Bronaber
Mynydd Bach
Buarthmeini
Mynydd Bryn-llech
Harlech
Gwynedd
Dolhendre
Llanfair
Llanfair Slate Caverns
Rhinog Fawr 720
Rhinog
Cwm-hesgen
Pont-Rhyd-sarn
Llandanwg
Pen-sarn
Pen-y-bont
Bed-y-coedwr
Rhaeadr Mawddach
Pont Aber-Geirw
Pentre Gwynfryn
Coed y Brenin Visitor Centre
Coed y Brenin Forest
Morfa Dyffryn
Llanbedr
Wales Coast Path
754 Y Llethr
Capel Hermon
734 Rhobell Fawr
Pont Fronwydd
59
Morfa Dyffryn
Coed Ystumgwern
Ganllwyd
Coed Ganllwyd
Allt y Benglog
Llanenddwyn
Dyffryn Ardudwy
750 Diffwys
Llanfachreth
Cors-y-Gedol
Llanddwywe
Blaen-y-cwm
Rhydymain
Aran Fa
Tal-y-bont
Nannau
58
Llanelltyd
Cymer Abbey
Bont Newydd
Cywarch
Plas-canol
Pen-y-bryn
Penmaenpool Centre
Bontddu
Caerdeon
Toll
Penmaenpool
Brithdir
Llanaber
Cutiau
Y Gribin
Abergwynant
Rhydwen
Dolgellau
Barmouth (Abermaw)
Afon Mawddach
Kings
RNLI Lifeboat Museum
670 Waun-Oer
Dinas-Mawddwy
Barmouth Bay
The Bar
Arthog
Ynysgyfflog
Meirion Mill
Cwm-Cew
Fairbourne Steam Railway
Fairbourne
893 Cadair Idris
Mynydd Ceiswyn
Mynydd Dolgoed
Bae Bermo
Friog
Cader Idris
Dyfi Forest
Minffordd
Llwyngwril
Tal-y-llyn
Corris Uchaf
Aberllefenni
Aberangell
Llanfihangel-y-pennant
Castell y Bere
King Arthur's Labyrinth & Craft Centre
Corris
Corris Railway and Museum
Cwm-Llinau
Llangelynin
Abergynolwyn
Esgairgeiliog
Dol-fôr
Cemmaes
Rhoslefain
Llanegryn
A5
A487
A4085
A4086
A498
A470
A496
A497
A4212
A4416
A494
A493
A4086
B4418
B4410
B4411
B4573
B4391
B4407
B4406
B5113
B4405
5
6
7
8
9
A
B
C
D
E
F
G

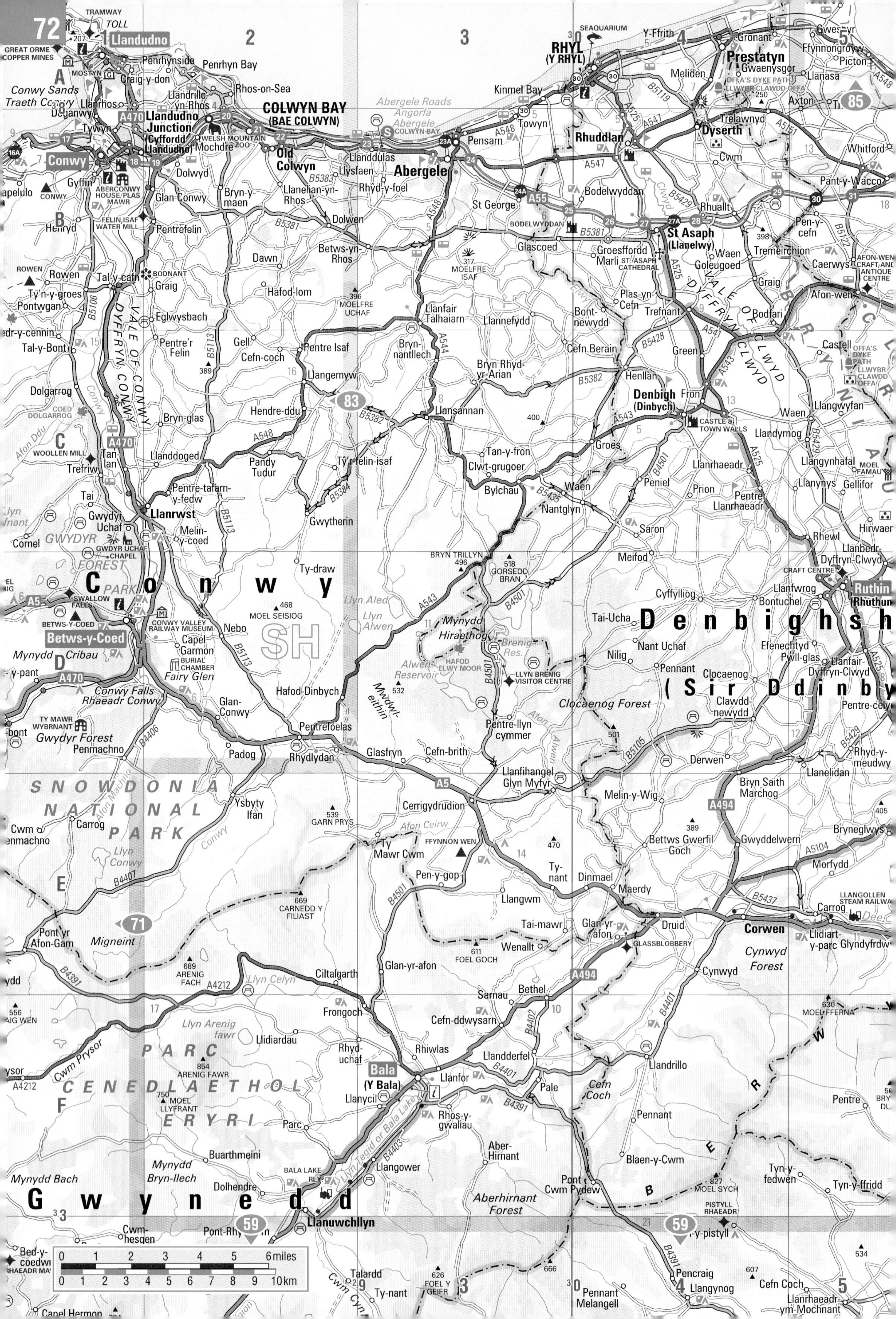
Llandudno
GREAT ORME COPPER MINES
TRAMWAY
TOLL
Conwy Sands
Traeth Conwy
Penrhynside
Penrhyn Bay
Craig-y-don
Rhos-on-Sea
Llandrillo-yn-Rhos
Llanrhos
Deganwy
Llandudno Junction (Cyffordd Llandudno)
COLWYN BAY (BAE COLWYN)
WELSH MOUNTAIN ZOO
Mochdre
Old Colwyn
Abergele Roads
Angorfa Abergele
Llanddulas
Llysfaen
Abergele
Rhyd-y-foel
Pensarn
Towyn
Kinmel Bay
SEAQUARIUM
RHYL (Y RHYL)
Y-Ffrith
Gronant
Gwespyr
Ffynnongroyw
Picton
Prestatyn
Gwaenysgor
Llanasa
Meliden
OFFA'S DYKE PATH
LLWYBR CLAWDD OFFA
Axton
Trelawnyd
Dyserth
Rhuddlan
Whitford
Cwm
Conwy
Tywyn
Gyffin
ABERCONWY HOUSE/PLAS MAWR
CONWY
Dolwyd
Bryn-y-maen
Glan Conwy
Llanelian-yn-Rhos
Dolwen
Betws-yn-Rhos
Bodelwyddan
St George
BODELWYDDAN
Glascoed
St Asaph (Llanelwy)
ST ASAPH CATHEDRAL
Groesffordd Marli
Rhuallt
Pen-y-cefn
Tremeirchion
Waen
Goleugoed
Caerwys
AFON-WEN CRAFT AND ANTIQUE CENTRE
Pant-y-Wacco
Henryd
FELIN ISAF WATER MILL
Pentrefelin
Dawn
MOELFRE ISAF
ROWEN
Rowen
Ty'n-y-groes
Pontwgan
Tal-y-cafn
BODNANT
Graig
Hafod-lom
MOELFRE UCHAF
Llanfair Talhaiarn
Llannefydd
Bont-newydd
Plas-yn-Cefn
Trefnant
VALE OF CLWYD
DYFFRYN CLWYD
Bodfari
Afon-wen
Graig
Tal-y-Bont
Eglwysbach
Pentre'r Felin
Gell
Cefn-coch
Pentre Isaf
Bryn-nantllech
Cefn Berain
Bryn Rhyd-yr-Arian
Henllan
Green
Castell
OFFA'S DYKE PATH
LLWYBR CLAWDD OFFA
VALE OF CONWY
DYFFRYN CONWY
Dolgarrog
COED DOLGARROG
Llangernyw
Hendre-ddu
Llansannan
Denbigh (Dinbych)
Fron
CASTLE & TOWN WALLS
Waen
Llangwyfan
Bryn-glas
Llanddoged
Pandy Tudur
Tan-y-fron
Groes
Llandyrnog
WOOLLEN MILL
Trefriw
Tan-lan
Tŷ'r-felin-isaf
Clwt-grugoer
Llanrhaeadr
Llangynhafal
MOEL FAMAU
Bylchau
Peniel
Prion
Pentre Llanrhaeadr
Llanynys
Gellifor
Tai
Pentre-tafarn-y-fedw
Llanrwst
Gwytherin
Waen
Nantglyn
Saron
Gwydyr Uchaf
GWYDYR UCHAF CHAPEL
GWYDYR FOREST PARK
Melin-y-coed
Cornel
Rhewl
Hirwaer
Ty-draw
BRYN TRILLYN
GORSEDD BRAN
Meifod
Llanbedr-Dyffryn-Clwyd
CRAFT CENTRE
Ruthin (Rhuthun)
Llanfwrog
Bontuchel
Cyffylliog
Conwy
SWALLOW FALLS
BETWS-Y-COED
Betws-y-Coed
CONWY VALLEY RAILWAY MUSEUM
MOEL SEISIOG
Nebo
SH
Llyn Aled
Llyn Alwen
Mynydd Hiraethog
Tai-Ucha
Denbighshire
Capel Garmon
BURIAL CHAMBER
Fairy Glen
Mynydd Cribau
Brenig Res.
HAFOD ELWY MOOR
Nant Uchaf
Nilig
Efenechtyd
Pwll-glas
Alwen Reservoir
LLYN BRENIG VISITOR CENTRE
Pennant
Clocaenog
Llanfair-Dyffryn-Clwyd
Conwy Falls
Rhaeadr Conwy
Glan-Conwy
Hafod-Dinbych
Mwdwl-eithin
(Sir Ddinbych)
Clocaenog Forest
Clawdd-newydd
Pentre-celyn
TY MAWR WYBRNANT
Gwydyr Forest
Penmachno
Pentrefoelas
Pentre-llyn cymmer
Padog
Rhydlydan
Glasfryn
Cefn-brith
Derwen
Rhyd-y-meudwy
Llanelidan
Llanfihangel Glyn Myfyr
SNOWDONIA NATIONAL PARK
Ysbyty Ifan
Cerrigydrudion
Melin-y-Wig
Bryn Saith Marchog
Cwm Penmachno
Carrog
GARN PRYS
Afon Ceirw
Llyn Conwy
Ty Mawr Cwm
FFYNNON WEN
Bettws Gwerfil Goch
Gwyddelwern
Bryneglwys
Pen-y-gop
Ty-nant
Dinmael
Maerdy
Morfydd
Llangwm
LLANGOLLEN STEAM RAILWAY
Carrog
CARNEDD Y FILIAST
Tai-mawr
Glan-yr-afon
Druid
Corwen
Llidiart-y-parc
Glyndyfrdwy
Pont yr Afon-Gam
Migneint
FOEL GOCH
Wenallt
GLASSBLOBBERY
Cynwyd Forest
Cynwyd
ARENIG FACH
Llyn Celyn
Ciltalgarth
Glan-yr-afon
Sarnau
Bethel
Frongoch
Cefn-ddwysarn
MOEL FFERNA
AIG WEN
Llyn Arenig fawr
Llidiardau
Rhyd-uchaf
Rhiwlas
Llandderfel
Llandrillo
PARC CENEDLAETHOL ERYRI
ARENIG FAWR
Cwm Prysor
Bala (Y Bala)
Llanfor
Pale
Cefn Coch
Llanycil
MOEL LLYFRANT
Rhos-y-gwaliau
Pennant
Pentre
BERWYN
Parc
Llyn Tegid or Bala Lake
Aber-Hirnant
Buarthmeini
Mynydd Bryn-llech
Llangower
Blaen-y-Cwm
Tyn-y-fedwen
Tyn-y-ffridd
Mynydd Bach
BALA LAKE RLY
Dolhendre
Pont Cwm Pydew
MOEL SYCH
Aberhirnant Forest
Gwynedd
PISTYLL RHAEADR
Llanuwchllyn
Cwm-hesgen
Pont-Rhyd...
Bed-y-coedwr
RHAEADR MAWDDACH
Talardd
Ty-nant
FOEL Y GEIFR
Pennant Melangell
Pencraig
Llangynog
Cefn Coch
Llanrhaeadr-ym-Mochnant
Capel Hermon
0 1 2 3 4 5 6 miles
0 1 2 3 4 5 6 7 8 9 10 km

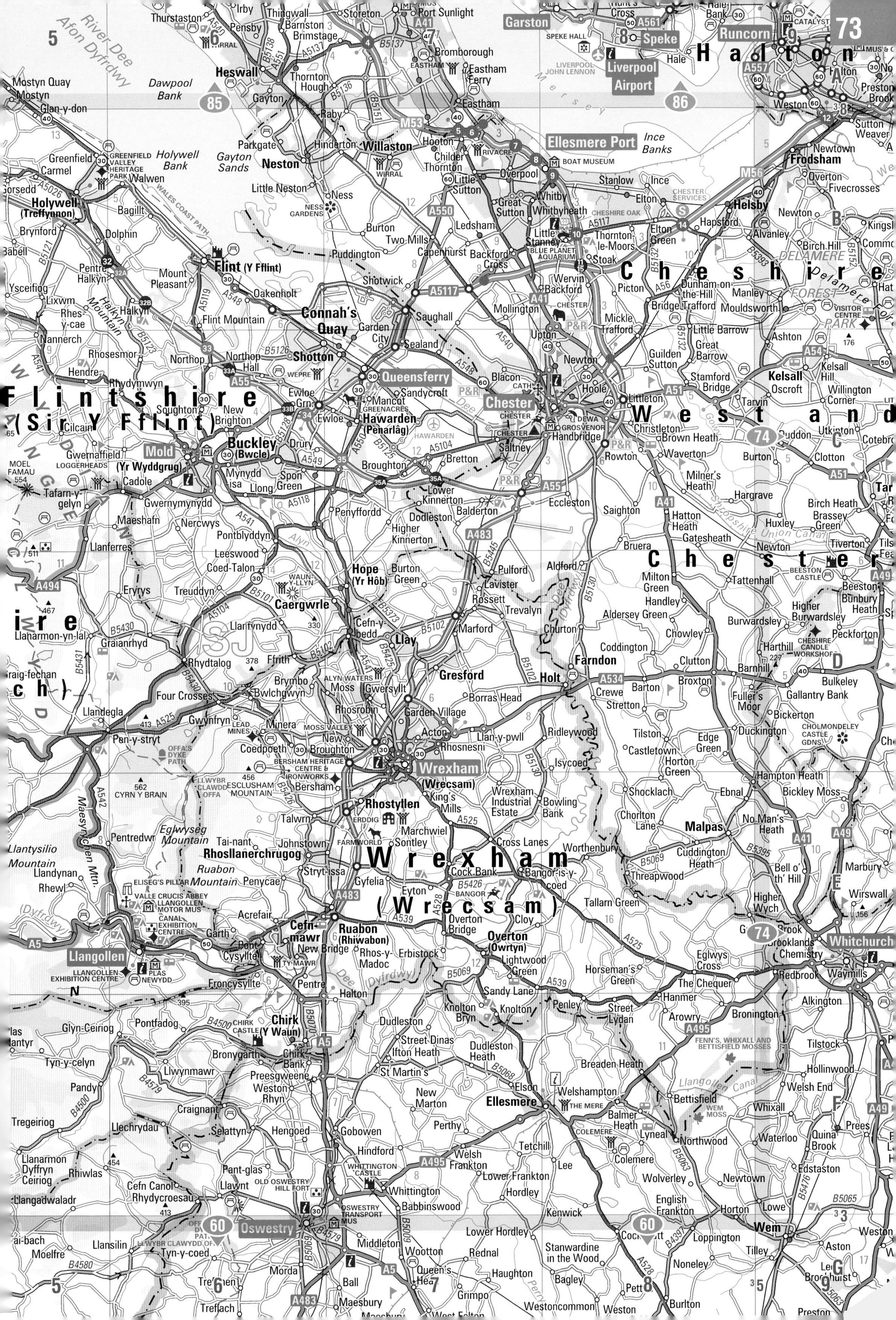
Halton
Cheshire
West and Chester
Flintshire
(Sir Y Fflint)
Wrexham
(Wrecsam)
Garston
Speke
Runcorn
Liverpool John Lennon Airport
Speke Hall
Hale
Thurstaston
Irby
Thingwall
Storeton
Port Sunlight
Pensby
Barnston
Brimstage
Bromborough
Eastham
Eastham Ferry
Heswall
Thornton Hough
Dawpool Bank
River Dee
Afon Dyfrdwy
Mostyn Quay
Mostyn
Glan-y-don
Gayton
Raby
Greenfield
Carmel
Greenfield Valley Heritage Park
Holywell Bank
Gayton Sands
Parkgate
Neston
Hinderton
Willaston
Hooton
Childer Thornton
Ellesmere Port
Boat Museum
Ince Banks
Overpool
Little Sutton
Great Sutton
Whitby
Whitbyheath
Stanlow
Ince
Elton
Frodsham
Newtown
Overton
Fivecrosses
Helsby
Gorsedd
Holywell (Treffynnon)
Walwen
Bagillt
Little Neston
Ness
Ness Gardens
Wales Coast Path
Brynford
Dolphin
Burton
Two Mills
Ledsham
Capenhurst
Puddington
Backford Cross
Little Stanney
Blue Planet Aquarium
Thornton-le-Moors
Elton Green
Hapsford
Dunham-on-the-Hill
Alvanley
Manley
Mouldsworth
Delamere Forest Park
Birch Hill
Newton
Babell
Pentre Halkyn
Mount Pleasant
Flint (Y Fflint)
Oakenholt
Shotwick
Ysceifiog
Lixwm
Rhes-y-cae
Halkyn
Halkyn Mountain
Flint Mountain
Connah's Quay
Garden City
Saughall
Mollington
Chester Services
Cheshire Oak
Stoak
Picton
Wervin
Backford
Upton
Mickle Trafford
Bridge Trafford
Little Barrow
Great Barrow
Ashton
Nannerch
Rhosesmor
Northop
Northop Hall
Shotton
Sealand
Queensferry
Blacon
Chester
Newton
Hoole
Guilden Sutton
Stamford Bridge
Kelsall
Kelsall Hill
Oscroft
Willington Corner
Tarvin
Hendre
Rhydymwyn
Soughton
New Brighton
Ewloe
Ewloe Grn
Mancot
Sandycroft
Hawarden (Penarlâg)
Greenacres
Hawarden
Littleton
Christleton
Brown Heath
Duddon
Utkinton
Cotebrook
Cilcain
Buckley (Bwcle)
Drury
Broughton
Bretton
Saltney
Handbridge
Grosvenor
Rowton
Waverton
Burton
Clotton
Gwernaffield
Loggerheads
Mold (Yr Wyddgrug)
Moel Famau
Mynydd Isa
Spon Green
Llong
Lower Kinnerton
Eccleston
Saighton
Milner's Heath
Hargrave
Tarporley
Tafarn-y-gelyn
Cadole
Gwernymynydd
Penyffordd
Dodleston
Balderton
Hatton Heath
Gatesheath
Huxley
Birch Heath
Brassey Green
Maeshafn
Nercwys
Pontblyddyn
Higher Kinnerton
Shropshire Union Canal
Llanferres
Leeswood
Coed-Talon
Bruera
Newton
Tiverton
Beeston Castle
Hope (Yr Hôb)
Burton Green
Pulford
Aldford
Tattenhall
Beeston
Waun-y-Llyn
Lavister
Milton Green
Handley
Bunbury
Higher Burwardsley
Eryrys
Treuddyn
Caergwrle
Rossett
Trevalyn
Aldersey Green
Burwardsley
Peckforton
Llanarmon-yn-Ial
Llanfynydd
Cefn-y-bedd
Marford
Churton
Chowley
Graianrhyd
Llay
Coddington
Harthill
Cheshire Candle Workshop
Rhydtalog
Ffrith
Farndon
Clutton
Barnhill
Bulkeley
Craig-fechan
Brymbo
Alyn Waters
Gresford
Holt
Crewe
Barton
Broxton
Gallantry Bank
Fuller's Moor
Bickerton
Four Crosses
Bwlchgwyn
Moss
Gwersyllt
Borras Head
Stretton
Llandegla
Gwynfryn
Rhosrobin
Garden Village
Ridleywood
Tilston
Duckington
Cholmondeley Castle Gdns
Pen-y-stryt
Offa's Dyke Path
Lead Mines
Minera
Moss Valley
New Broughton
Acton
Rhosnesni
Llan-y-pwll
Castletown
Edge Green
Coedpoeth
Bersham Heritage Centre & Ironworks
Wrexham (Wrecsam)
Isycoed
Horton Green
Cyrn y Brain
Esclusham Mountain
Llwybr Clawdd Offa
Bersham
King's Mills
Wrexham Industrial Estate
Bowling Bank
Shocklach
Ebnal
Hampton Heath
Bickley Moss
Maesyrychen Mtn.
Rhostyllen
Erddig
Chorlton Lane
Malpas
No Man's Heath
Llantysilio Mountain
Pentredwr
Eglwyseg Mountain
Tai-nant
Talwrn
Marchwiel
Farmworld
Sontley
Cross Lanes
Worthenbury
Cuddington Heath
Llandynan
Rhosllanerchrugog
Johnstown
Threapwood
Bell o' th' Hill
Marbury
Rhewl
Ruabon Mountain
Stryt-issa
Cock Bank
Bangor-is-y-coed
Wirswall
Eliseg's Pillar
Valle Crucis Abbey
Llangollen Motor Mus
Penycae
Gyfelia
Eyton
Bangor
Tallarn Green
Higher Wych
Canal Exhibition Centre
Acrefair
Cefn-mawr
Ruabon (Rhiwabon)
Overton Bridge
Cloy
Overton (Owrtyn)
Brook
Whitchurch
Garth
Pont Cysyllte
Ty Mawr
New Bridge
Rhos-y-Madoc
Erbistock
Lightwood Green
Eglwys Cross
Brooklands
Chemistry
Llangollen
Llangollen Exhibition Centre
Plas Newydd
Froncysyllte
Pentre
Halton
Horseman's Green
The Chequer
Redbrook
Waymills
Sandy Lane
Penley
Hanmer
Alkington
Glyn-Ceiriog
Pontfadog
Chirk Castle
Chirk (Y Waun)
Knolton Bryn
Knolton
Street Lydan
Arowry
Bronington
Tyn-y-celyn
Bronygarth
Chirk Bank
Dudleston
Street Dinas
Ifton Heath
Dudleston Heath
Fenn's, Whixall and Bettisfield Mosses
Tilstock
Llwynmawr
Preesgweene
Weston Rhyn
St Martin's
Breaden Heath
Hollinwood
Pandy
Llangollen Canal
Welsh End
Craignant
New Marton
Elson
Welshampton
Bettisfield
Whixall
Tregeiriog
Llechrydau
Selattyn
Hengoed
Gobowen
Perthy
Ellesmere
The Mere
Balmer Heath
Wem Moss
Prees
Llanarmon Dyffryn Ceiriog
Rhiwlas
Pant-glas
Hindford
Whittington Castle
Welsh Frankton
Tetchill
Colemere
Lyneal
Northwood
Waterloo
Quina Brook
Llawnt
Old Oswestry Hill Fort
Lower Frankton
Lee
Edstaston
Cefn Canol
Rhydycroesau
Whittington
Hordley
Wolverley
Newtown
Llangadwaladr
Oswestry Transport Mus
Babbinswood
English Frankton
Lowe
Oswestry
Kenwick
Horton
Cockshutt
Wem
Llansilin
Llwybr Clawdd Offa
Tyn-y-coed
Middleton
Lower Hordley
Loppington
Weston
Moelfre
Wootton
Rednal
Stanwardine in the Wood
Tilley
Aston
Morda
Queen's Head
Haughton
Bagley
Noneley
Lee Brockhurst
Trefonen
Ball
Grimpo
Pett
Treflach
Maesbury
Westoncommon
Weston
Burlton
Preston
Weston
Runcorn
Sutton Weaver
Preston Brook
Halton
Kingsley
Crowton
M53
M56
A41
A55
A483
A5
A494
A525
A534
A539
A495
A49
A51
A54
A550
A5117
A548
A540
A5104
A5026
A542
A5118
A541
85
86
74
60

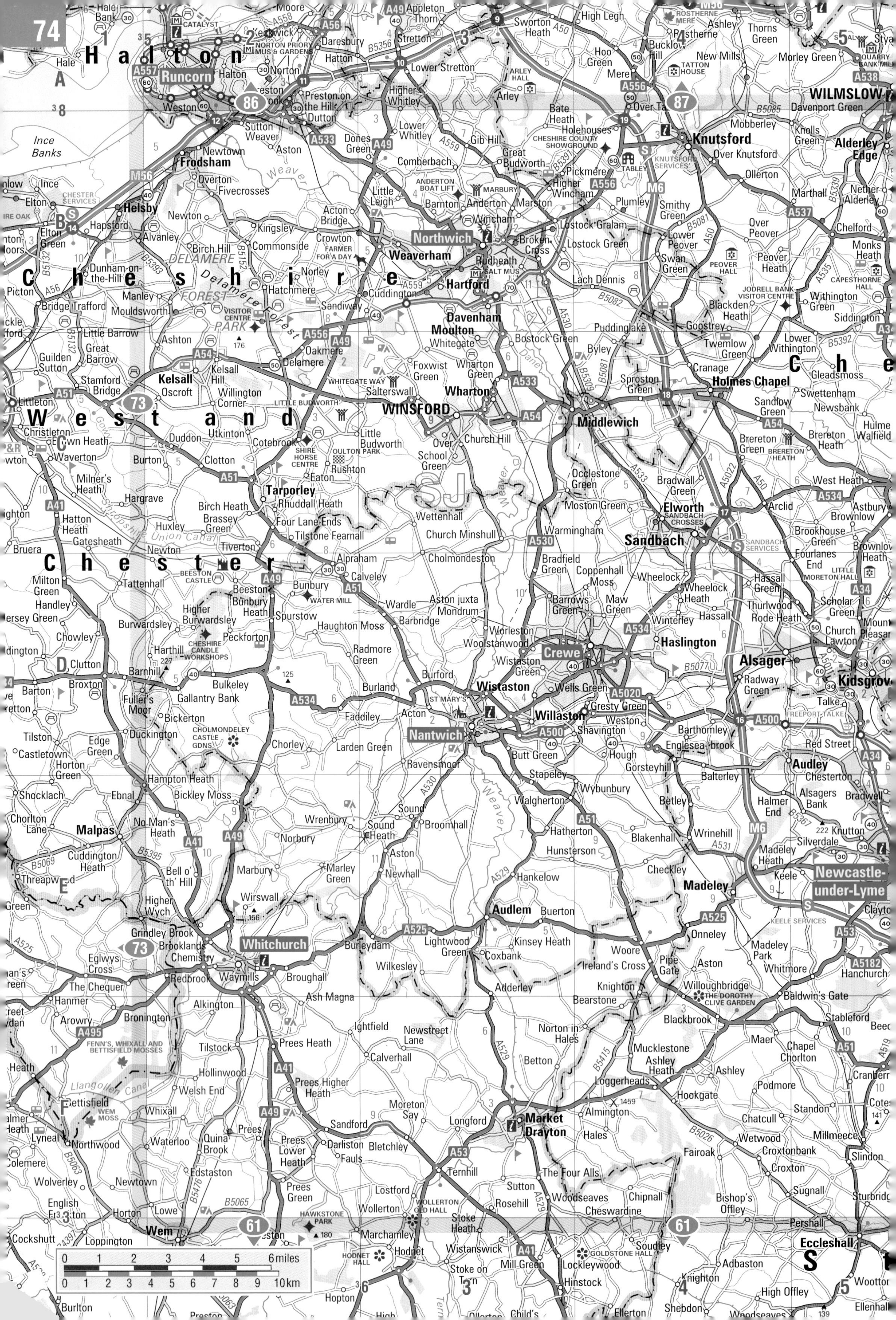
Halton
Runcorn
Cheshire
West and
Chester
Frodsham
Helsby
Northwich
Weaverham
Hartford
Davenham
Moulton
Kelsall
WINSFORD
Middlewich
Knutsford
WILMSLOW
Alderley Edge
Holmes Chapel
Tarporley
Elworth
Sandbach
Crewe
Haslington
Alsager
Kidsgrove
Wistaston
Willaston
Nantwich
Audley
Malpas
Madeley
Newcastle-under-Lyme
Audlem
Whitchurch
Market Drayton
Wem
Eccleshall
DELAMERE FOREST
SJ
86
87
73
61
0 1 2 3 4 5 6 miles
0 1 2 3 4 5 6 7 8 9 10 km

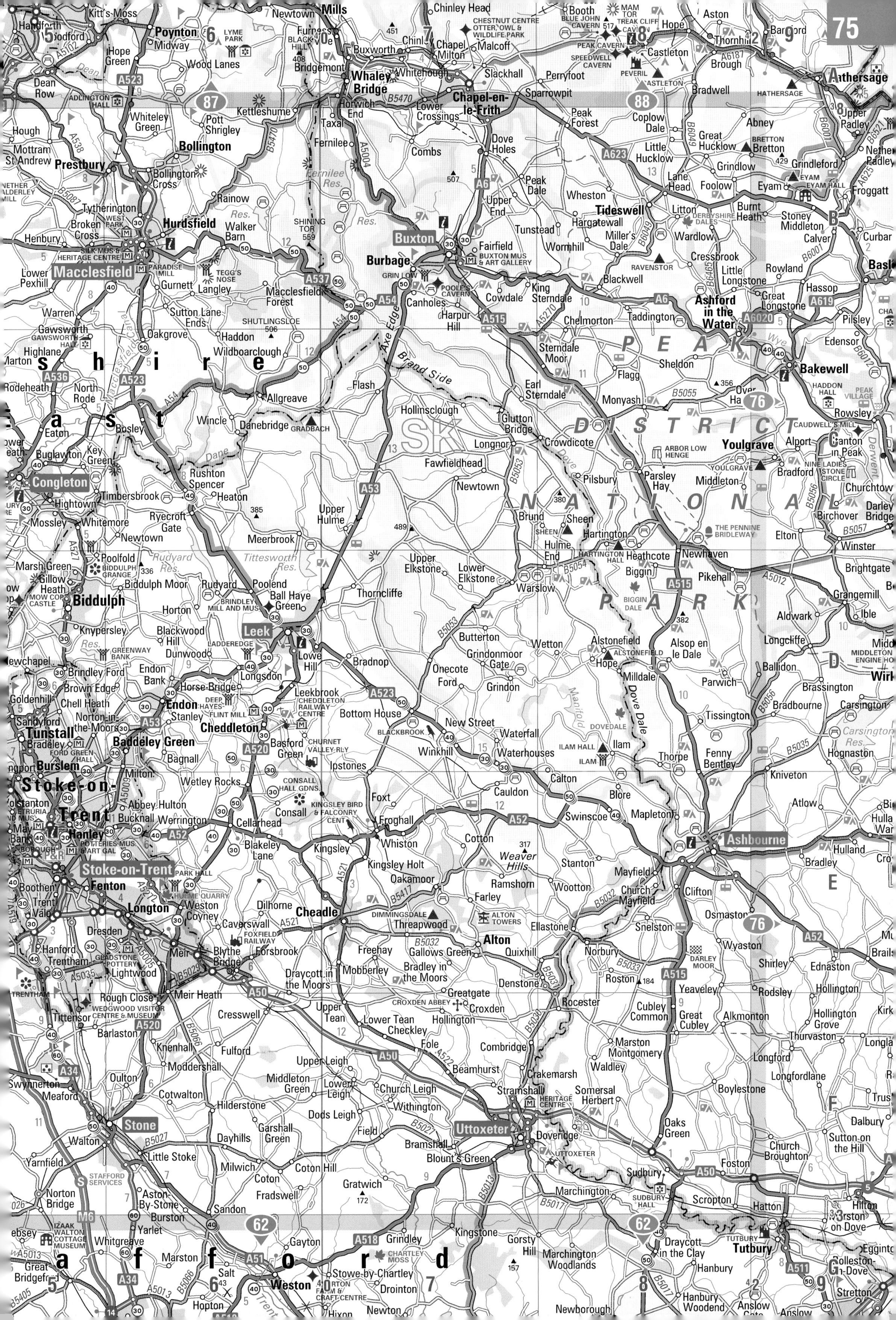
Handforth
Kitt's Moss
Poynton
Midway
Newtown
Mills
Chinley Head
Booth
Mam Tor
Aston
Hope
Bamford
Lyme Park
Furness Vale
Black Hill
Chestnut Centre Otter, Owl & Wildlife Park
Blue John Cavern
Treak Cliff Cavern
Peak Cavern
Speedwell Cavern
Castleton
Thornhill
Brough
Hope Green
Wood Lanes
Buxworth
Bridgemont
Chinley
Chapel Milton
Malcoff
Whaley Bridge
Whitehough
Slackhall
Perryfoot
Peveril
Dean Row
Adlington Hall
Kettleshume
Horwich End
Chapel-en-le-Frith
Sparrowpit
Bradwell
Hathersage
Whiteley Green
Pott Shrigley
Taxal
Lower Crossings
Peak Forest
Coplow Dale
Abney
Upper Padley
Hough
Bollington
Fernilee
Combs
Dove Holes
Little Hucklow
Great Hucklow
Bretton
Nether Padley
Mottram St Andrew
Prestbury
Bollington Cross
Fernilee Res.
Peak Dale
Lane Head
Grindlow
Grindleford
Nether Alderley
Rainow
Upper End
Wheston
Foolow
Eyam
Eyam Hall
Froggatt
Tytherington
Hurdsfield
Walker Barn
Shining Tor
Tideswell
Litton
Derbyshire Heath
Burnt Heath
Stoney Middleton
Henbury
Broken Cross
Heritage Centre
Silk Mus.
Paradise Mill
Buxton
Tunstead
Hargatewall
Miller's Dale
Wardlow
Calver
Curbar
Macclesfield
Burbage
Fairfield
Buxton Mus & Art Gallery
Wormhill
Cressbrook
Rowland
Baslow
Lower Pexhill
Gurnett
Tegg's Nose
Langley
Macclesfield Forest
Grin Low
Poole's Cavern
Ravenstor
Little Longstone
Hassop
Canholes
King Sterndale
Blackwell
Ashford in the Water
Great Longstone
Warren
Sutton Lane Ends
Harpur Hill
Cowdale
Taddington
Gawsworth
Gawsworth Hall
Oakgrove
Haddon
Shutlingsloe
Axe Edge
Chelmorton
Pilsley
Highlane
Marton
Wildboarclough
Sterndale Moor
Sheldon
Edensor
Bakewell
Flash
Allgreave
Earl Sterndale
Flagg
Monyash
Over Haddon
Haddon Hall
Peak Village
Rowsley
Rodeheath
North Rode
Eaton
Bosley
Wincle
Danebridge
Gradbach
Hollinsclough
Glutton Bridge
Longnor
Crowdicote
Arbor Low Henge
Youlgrave
Alport
Stanton in Peak
Caudwell's Mill
Nine Ladies Stone Circle
Buglawton
Key Green
Fawfieldhead
Pilsbury
Parsley Hay
Middleton
Bradford
Churchtown
Congleton
Rushton Spencer
Newtown
Timbersbrook
Heaton
Hightown
Mossley
Whitemore
Ryecroft Gate
Upper Hulme
Brund
Sheen
Hartington
Heathcote
The Pennine Bridleway
Birchover
Darley Bridge
Elton
Winster
Newtown
Meerbrook
Hulme End
Hartington Hall
Newhaven
Biggin
Pikehall
Brightgate
Poolfold
Rudyard Res.
Tittesworth Res.
Upper Elkstone
Lower Elkstone
Warslow
Biddulph Grange
Marsh Green
Gillow Heath
Biddulph Moor
Rudyard
Poolend
Mow Cop Castle
Biddulph
Brindley Mill and Mus.
Ball Haye Green
Thorncliffe
Biggin Dale
Grangemill
Horton
Aldwark
Ible
Knypersley
Blackwood Hill
Leek
Butterton
Wetton
Alstonefield
Alsop en le Dale
Longcliffe
Middleton
Greenway Bank
Ladderedge
Lowe Hill
Bradnop
Grindonmoor Gate
Hope
Ballidon
Newchapel
Brindley Ford
Dunwood
Endon Bank
Onecote
Milldale
Parwich
Wirksworth
Goldenhill
Brown Edge
Longsdon
Leekbrook
Cheddleton Railway Centre
Ford
Grindon
Bassington
Dove Dale
Chell Heath
Horse Bridge
Deep Hayes
Flint Mill
Endon
Stanley
Bottom House
Tissington
Bradbourne
Carsington
Sandyford
Norton-in-the-Moors
Cheddleton
Blackbrook
New Street
Waterfall
Dovedale
Carsington Res.
Tunstall
Bradeley
Baddeley Green
Basford Green
Churnet Valley Rly
Winkhill
Ilam Hall
Ilam
Thorpe
Fenny Bentley
Hognaston
Ford Green Hall
Burslem
Bagnall
Ipstones
Waterhouses
Calton
Kniveton
Stoke-on-Trent
Milton
Wetley Rocks
Consall Hall Gdns.
Cauldon
Blore
Atlow
Abbey Hulton
Foxt
Mapleton
Etruria
Bucknall
Werrington
Cellarhead
Consall
Kingsley Bird & Falcony Cent
Froghall
Swinscoe
Hanley
Potteries Mus. & Art Gal
Whiston
Cotton
Ashbourne
Hulland
Blakeley Lane
Kingsley
Weaver Hills
Stanton
Mayfield
Bradley
Park Hall
Kingsley Holt
Oakamoor
Ramshorn
Church Mayfield
Clifton
Boothen
Fenton
Wootton
Trent Vale
Longton
Weston Coyney
Dilhorne
Cheadle
Farley
Dimmingsdale
Threapwood
Alton Towers
Ellastone
Snelston
Osmaston
Caverswall
Foxfield Railway
Dresden
Alton
Norbury
Wyaston
Hanford
Trentham
Meir
Blythe Bridge
Forsbrook
Freehay
Gallows Green
Quixhill
Darley Moor
Shirley
Ednaston
Gladstone Pottery
Lightwood
Draycott in the Moors
Mobberley
Bradley in the Moors
Denstone
Roston
Yeaveley
Rodsley
Hollington
Trentham
Rough Close
Meir Heath
Greatgate
Croxden Abbey
Croxden
Rocester
Cubley Common
Alkmonton
Hollington Grove
Wedgwood Visitor Centre & Museum
Tittensor
Barlaston
Cresswell
Upper Tean
Lower Tean
Checkley
Hollington
Great Cubley
Thurvaston
Longlane
Knenhall
Fulford
Fole
Combridge
Marston Montgomery
Longford
Moddershall
Upper Leigh
Beamhurst
Crakemarsh
Waldley
Longfordlane
Oulton
Middleton Green
Lower Leigh
Church Leigh
Stramshall
Heritage Centre
Somersal Herbert
Boylestone
Swynnerton
Meaford
Cotwalton
Hilderstone
Withington
Trusley
Stone
Dods Leigh
Garshall Green
Field
Uttoxeter
Oaks Green
Dalbury
Walton
Dayhills
Bramshall
Doveridge
Church Broughton
Sutton on the Hill
Yarnfield
Little Stoke
Blount's Green
Uttoxeter
Milwich
Coton
Coton Hill
Sudbury
Foston
Stafford Services
Aston-By-Stone
Gratwich
Marchington
Sudbury Hall
Scropton
Hatton
Hilton
Norton Bridge
Fradswell
Sandon
Burston
Yarlet
Kingstone
Gorsty Hill
Marchington Woodlands
Draycott in the Clay
Tutbury
Marston on Dove
Izaak Walton Cottage Museum
Whitgreave
Gayton
Grindley
Chartley Moss
Marston
Salt
Weston
Stowe-by-Chartley
Drointon
Hanbury
Egginton
Rolleston-on-Dove
Great Bridgeford
Norton Farm & Craft Centre
Hopton
Hixon
Newton
Newborough
Hanbury Woodend
Anslow
Stretton
Peak District National Park
Cheshire
East
Stafford

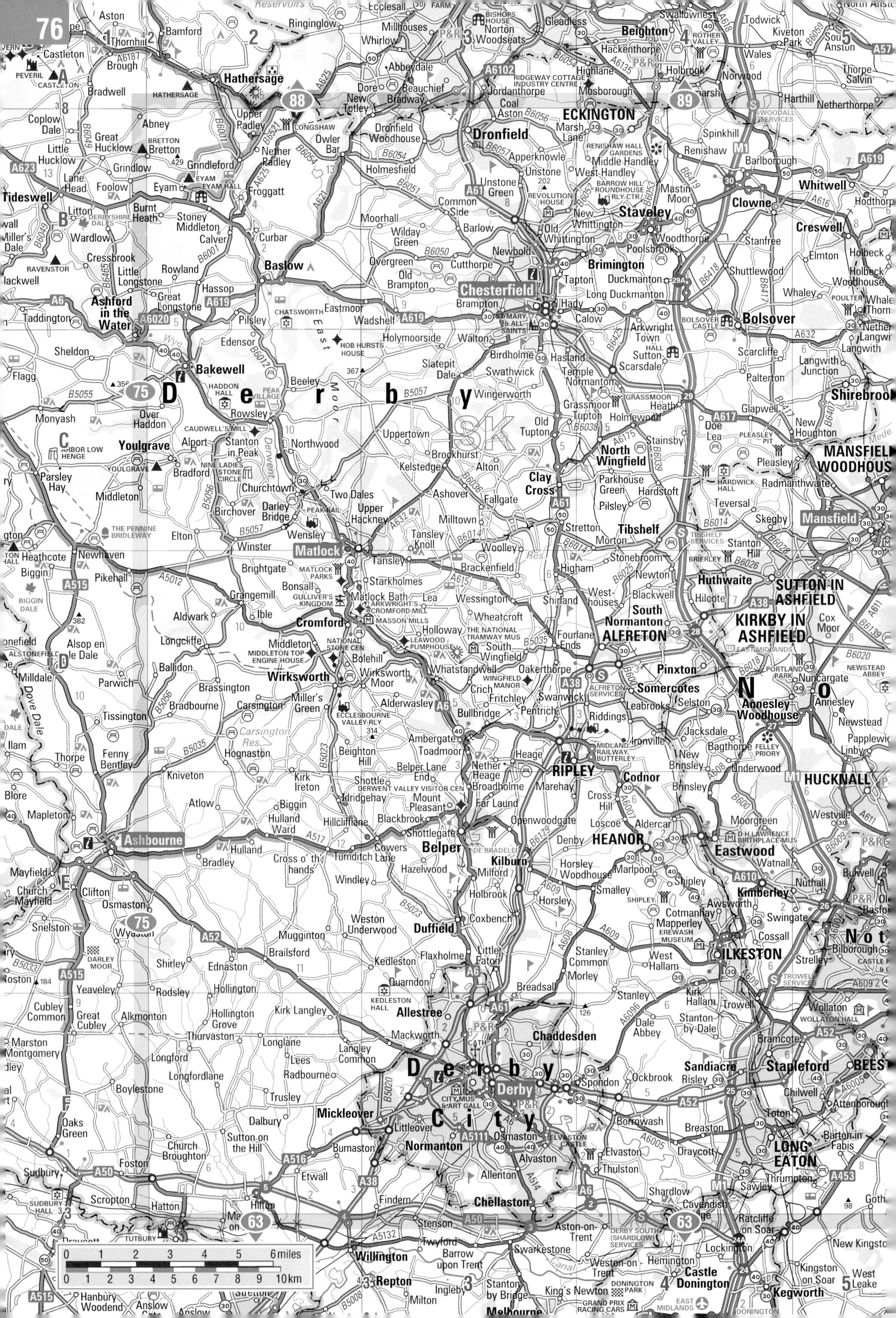

Aston
Bamford
Ringinglow
Ecclesall
Millhouses
Whirlow
Abbeydale
Bishops House
Norton
Woodseats
Gleadless
Beighton
Swallownest
Todwick
Kiveton Park
Rother Valley
Wales
Hackenthorpe
Highlane
Holbrook
Norwood
Thorpe Salvin
Castleton
Peveril
Thornhill
Hope
Brough
Hathersage
Bradwell
Dore
Beauchief
Bradway
Jordanthorpe
Ridgeway Cottage Industry Centre
Mosborough
Harthill
Netherthorpe
Coplow Dale
Abney
Upper Padley
New Totley
Longshaw
Owler Bar
Dronfield Woodhouse
Coal Aston
Dronfield
Eckington
Marsh Lane
Renishaw Hall Gardens
Spinkhill
Woodall Services
Renishaw
Little Hucklow
Great Hucklow
Bretton
Grindleford
Nether Padley
Holmesfield
Apperknowle
Middle Handley
West Handley
Unstone
Unstone Green
Barlborough
Whitwell
Tideswell
Grindlow
Lane Head
Foolow
Eyam
Eyam Hall
Froggatt
Barrow Hill Roundhouse Rly Ctr
Revolution House
Mastin Moor
Clowne
Hodthorpe
Litton
Burnt Heath
Stoney Middleton
Calver
Curbar
Moorhall
Wilday Green
Common Side
Barlow
New Whittington
Old Whittington
Staveley
Woodthorpe
Poolsbrook
Creswell
Stanfree
Elmton
Holbeck
Holbeck Woodhouse
Miller's Dale
Wardlow
Derbyshire Dales
Cressbrook
Ravenstor
Blackwell
Little Longstone
Rowland
Hassop
Baslow
Overgreen
Old Brampton
Cutthorpe
Newbold
Brimington
Tapton
Duckmanton
Long Duckmanton
Shuttlewood
Whaley
Poulter
Whaley Thorns
Ashford in the Water
Great Longstone
Taddington
Pilsley
Chatsworth
Eastmoor
Wadshelf
Brampton
Chesterfield
St Mary & All Saints
Hady
Calow
Arkwright Town
Bolsover
Bolsover Castle
Nether Langwith
Langwith
Sheldon
Edensor
Hob Hursts House
Holymoorside
Walton
Birdholme
Hasland
Sutton Hall
Sutton Scarsdale
Scarcliffe
Langwith Junction
Flagg
Bakewell
Slatepit Dale
Swathwick
Temple Normanton
Palterton
Haddon Hall
Peak Village
Beeley
East Moor
Wingerworth
Grassmoor
Grassmoor Heath
Shirebrook
Derby
Monyash
Over Haddon
Rowsley
Caudwell's Mill
Old Tupton
Tupton
Holmewood
Glapwell
Doe Lea
New Houghton
Arbor Low Henge
Youlgrave
Alport
Stanton in Peak
Northwood
Uppertown
Brockhurst
Alton
Stainsby
North Wingfield
Pleasley Pit
Mansfield Woodhouse
Parsley Hay
Bradford
Nine Ladies Stone Circle
Kelstedge
Clay Cross
Parkhouse Green
Hardstoft
Pleasley
Radmanthwaite
Hardwick Hall
Churchtown
Two Dales
Ashover
Fallgate
Middleton
Darley Bridge
Peak Rail
Upper Hackney
Pilsley
Teverstal
Skegby
Mansfield
Birchover
Milltown
Stretton
Tibshelf
Tibshelf Services
The Pennine Bridleway
Elton
Wensley
Tansley Knoll
Woolley
Morton
Stanton Hill
Heathcote
Newhaven
Winster
Matlock
Tansley
Brackenfield
Higham
Stonebroom
Brierley
Biggin
Pikehall
Brightgate
Matlock Parks
Starkholmes
Newton
Huthwaite
Sutton in Ashfield
Grangemill
Bonsall
Gulliver's Kingdom
Matlock Bath
Lea
Wessington
Shirland
Westhouses
Blackwell
Hilcote
Kirkby in Ashfield
Biggin Dale
Aldwark
Ible
Arkwright's Cromford Mill
Masson Mills
Wheatcroft
South Normanton
Cox Moor
Cromford
Holloway
The National Tramway Mus
Fourlane Ends
Alfreton
Longcliffe
Alsop en le Dale
Middleton
National Stone Cen
Leawood Pumphouse
South Wingfield
Middleton Top Engine House
Bolehill
East Midlands
Newstead Abbey
Alstonefield
Ballidon
Wirksworth
Wirksworth Moor
Whatstandwell
Oakerthorpe
Pinxton
Portland Park
Nuncargate
Milldale
Parwich
Brassington
Miller's Green
Wingfield Manor
Crich
Alfreton Services
Somercotes
Dove Dale
Bradbourne
Carsington
Alderwasley
Fritchley
Swanwick
Leabrooks
Selston
Annesley Woodhouse
Annesley
Tissington
Ecclesbourne Valley Rly
Bullbridge
Pentrich
Riddings
Jacksdale
Newstead
Ilam
Carsington Res.
Ambergate
Ironville
Bagthorpe
Felley Priory
Papplewick
Linby
Thorpe
Fenny Bentley
Hognaston
Beighton Hill
Toadmoor
Heage
Midland Railway Butterley
New Brinsley
Underwood
Kniveton
Belper Lane End
Nether Heage
Ripley
Codnor
Hucknall
Blore
Kirk Ireton
Shottle
Derwent Valley Visitor Cen
Broadholme
Marehay
Brinsley
Idridgehay
Mount Pleasant
Far Laund
Cross Hill
Mapleton
Atlow
Biggin
Hulland Ward
Hillcliffane
Blackbrook
Shottlegate
Openwoodgate
Loscoe
Aldercar
Moorgreen
D H Lawrence Birthplace Mus
Westville
Ashbourne
Hulland
Cross o' th' hands
Turnditch
Cowers Lane
Belper
De Bradelei
Denby
Heanor
Eastwood
Bulwell
Mayfield
Bradley
Hazelwood
Kilburn
Milford
Horsley Woodhouse
Marlpool
Watnall
Church Mayfield
Clifton
Windley
Holbrook
Smalley
Shipley
Kimberley
Nuthall
Osmaston
Horsley
Awsworth
Swingate
Basford
Snelston
Wyaston
Weston Underwood
Duffield
Coxbench
Cotmanhay
Mapperley
Erewash Museum
Cossall
Not
Bilborough
Mugginton
Brailsford
Little Eaton
Stanley Common
West Hallam
Ilkeston
Strelley
Darley Moor
Shirley
Ednaston
Kedleston
Flaxholme
Morley
Trowell Services
Roston
Yeaveley
Rodsley
Hollington
Quarndon
Kedleston Hall
Breadsall
Stanley
Kirk Hallam
Trowell
Cubley Common
Great Cubley
Alkmonton
Hollington Grove
Kirk Langley
Allestree
Dale Abbey
Stanton-by-Dale
Wollaton
Wollaton Hall
Marston Montgomery
Thurvaston
Longlane
Langley Common
Mackworth
Chaddesden
Bramcote
Longford
Lees
Radbourne
Derby
Spondon
Ockbrook
Sandiacre
Risley
Stapleford
Beest
Longfordlane
Boylestone
Trusley
Mickleover
City Mus & Art Gall
Chilwell
Attenborough
Oaks Green
Dalbury
Littleover
Derby City
Borrowash
Breaston
Toton
Long Eaton
Barton in Fabis
Church Broughton
Sutton on the Hill
Burnaston
Normanton
Osmaston
Elvaston Castle
Elvaston
Draycott
Sudbury
Foston
Etwall
Alvaston
Thulston
Thrumpton
Allenton
Shardlow
Sawley
Sudbury Hall
Scropton
Hatton
Hilton
Findern
Chellaston
Cavendish Bridge
Gotham
Tutbury
Stenson
Aston-on-Trent
Ratcliffe on Soar
Derby South (Shardlow) Services
Twyford
Swarkestone
Willington
Barrow upon Trent
Weston-on-Trent
Lockington
Hemington
New Kingston
Repton
Ingleby
Stanton by Bridge
King's Newton
Donington Park
Castle Donington
Kingston on Soar
West Leake
Hanbury Woodend
Anslow
Milton
Melbourne
Grand Prix Racing Cars
East Midlands
Kegworth
0 1 2 3 4 5 6 miles
0 1 2 3 4 5 6 7 8 9 10 km
SK
88
89
75
63

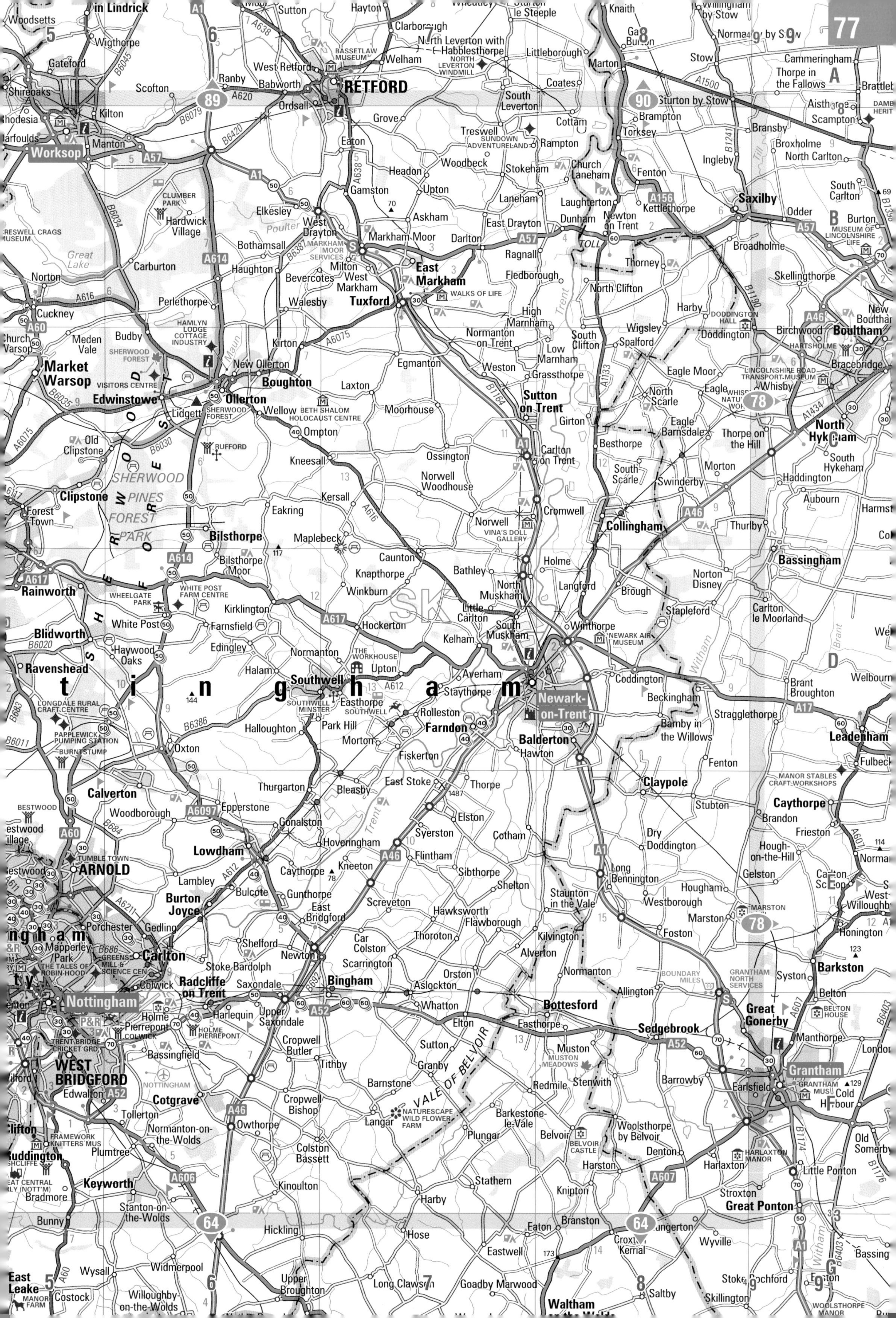

Woodsetts
Wigthorpe
Gateford
Shireoaks
Worksop
Manton
Kilton
Scofton
Ranby
Babworth
West Retford
Ordsall
RETFORD
BASSETLAW MUSEUM
Welham
Clarborough
North Leverton with Habblesthorpe
NORTH LEVERTON WINDMILL
Littleborough
South Leverton
Coates
Cottam
Treswell
SUNDOWN ADVENTURELAND
Rampton
Grove
Eaton
Headon
Woodbeck
Stokeham
Church Laneham
Laneham
Gamston
Upton
Askham
Elkesley
West Drayton
Markham Moor
Darlton
East Drayton
Dunham
Laughterton
Newton on Trent
Kettlethorpe
Ragnall
Fledborough
Thorney
North Clifton
Bothamsall
Haughton
Milton
West Markham
East Markham
Bevercotes
WALKS OF LIFE
Tuxford
Walesby
High Marnham
Normanton on Trent
South Clifton
Low Marnham
Wigsley
Spalford
Harby
DODDINGTON HALL
Doddington
Kirton
Egmanton
Weston
Grassthorpe
Sutton on Trent
Girton
Eagle Moor
Eagle
North Scarle
Eagle Barnsdale
Thorpe on the Hill
Boughton
New Ollerton
Ollerton
Wellow
BETH SHALOM HOLOCAUST CENTRE
Laxton
Moorhouse
Ompton
Kneesall
Ossington
Carlton on Trent
Besthorpe
South Scarle
Swinderby
Morton
Norwell Woodhouse
Cromwell
Norwell
VINA'S DOLL GALLERY
Collingham
Thurlby
Kersall
Eakring
Maplebeck
Caunton
Knapthorpe
Winkburn
Bathley
Holme
North Muskham
Langford
Brough
Norton Disney
Bassingham
Little Carlton
South Muskham
Kelham
Winthorpe
NEWARK AIR MUSEUM
Stapleford
Carlton le Moorland
Kirklington
Hockerton
Normanton
THE WORKHOUSE
Upton
Averham
Staythorpe
Southwell
SOUTHWELL MINSTER
Easthorpe
Rolleston
Farndon
Newark-on-Trent
Coddington
Beckingham
Brant Broughton
Balderton
Hawton
Barnby in the Willows
Stragglethorpe
Halam
Edingley
Farnsfield
Halloughton
Park Hill
Morton
Fiskerton
Fenton
Claypole
Thurgarton
Bleasby
East Stoke
Thorpe
Elston
Stubton
Caythorpe
Epperstone
Gonalston
Hoveringham
Syerston
Cotham
Dry Doddington
Long Bennington
Flintham
Sibthorpe
Shelton
Kneeton
Caythorpe
Gunthorpe
East Bridgford
Screveton
Hawksworth
Flawborough
Staunton in the Vale
Westborough
Hougham
Marston
Foston
Thoroton
Kilvington
Alverton
Car Colston
Scarrington
Orston
Normanton
Allington
Shelford
Newton
Bingham
Aslockton
Whatton
Bottesford
Sedgebrook
Elton
Easthorpe
Muston
MUSTON MEADOWS
Redmile
Stenwith
Barrowby
Saxondale
Upper Saxondale
Cropwell Butler
Tithby
Sutton
Granby
Barnstone
Langar
NATURESCAPE WILD FLOWER FARM
Cropwell Bishop
Colston Bassett
Plungar
Barkestone-le-Vale
Belvoir
BELVOIR CASTLE
Woolsthorpe by Belvoir
Denton
Harlaxton
HARLAXTON MANOR
Harston
Knipton
Stathern
Kinoulton
Harby
Hickling
Hose
Eaton
Branston
Eastwell
Croxton Kerrial
Long Clawson
Goadby Marwood
Waltham
Saltby
Upper Broughton
Stroxton
Great Ponton
Wyville
Skillington
Stoke Rochford
VALE OF BELVOIR
Knaith
Gate Burton
Marton
Stow
Normanby by Stow
Cammeringham
Thorpe in the Fallows
Brattleby
Sturton by Stow
Aisthorpe
Scampton
Brampton
Torksey
Bransby
Broxholme
North Carlton
Ingleby
Fenton
Saxilby
Odder
South Carlton
Burton
MUSEUM OF LINCOLNSHIRE LIFE
Broadholme
Skellingthorpe
Birchwood
Boultham
HARTSHOLME
LINCOLNSHIRE ROAD TRANSPORT MUSEUM
Bracebridge
Whisby
North Hykeham
South Hykeham
Haddington
Aubourn
Welbourn
Leadenham
Fulbeck
MANOR STABLES CRAFT WORKSHOPS
Brandon
Frieston
Hough-on-the-Hill
Gelston
Carlton Scroop
West Willoughby
Honington
Barkston
Syston
BOUNDARY MILLS
GRANTHAM NORTH SERVICES
Belton
BELTON HOUSE
Great Gonerby
Manthorpe
Grantham
Earlsfield
GRANTHAM MUS
Harrowby
Old Somerby
Little Ponton
Bassingham
Colsterworth
WOOLSTHORPE MANOR
Cold Harbour
Harmston
Boothby Graffoe
Carburton
Great Lake
CRESWELL CRAGS MUSEUM
CLUMBER PARK
Hardwick Village
Norton
Cuckney
Church Warsop
Meden Vale
Budby
HAMLYN LODGE COTTAGE INDUSTRY
SHERWOOD FOREST VISITORS CENTRE
Market Warsop
Edwinstowe
Perlethorpe
Lidgett
SHERWOOD FOREST
Old Clipstone
RUFFORD
SHERWOOD PINES FOREST PARK
Clipstone
Forest Town
Bilsthorpe
Bilsthorpe Moor
WHITE POST FARM CENTRE
WHEELGATE PARK
Rainworth
White Post
Blidworth
Haywood Oaks
Ravenshead
LONGDALE RURAL CRAFT CENTRE
PAPPLEWICK PUMPING STATION
BURNTSTUMP
Oxton
Calverton
Woodborough
Lowdham
BESTWOOD
Bestwood Village
TUMBLE TOWN
ARNOLD
Lambley
Burton Joyce
Bulcote
Porchester
Gedling
Mapperley Park
GREENS MILL & SCIENCE CEN
THE TALES OF ROBIN HOOD
Carlton
Colwick
Stoke Bardolph
Radcliffe on Trent
Nottingham
Holme Pierrepont
HOLME PIERREPONT
Harlequin
TRENT BRIDGE CRICKET GRD
COLWICK
Bassingfield
WEST BRIDGFORD
Edwalton
NOTTINGHAM
Cotgrave
Tollerton
Clifton
Ruddington
FRAMEWORK KNITTERS MUS
Normanton-on-the-Wolds
Plumtree
Owthorpe
Keyworth
Bradmore
Stanton-on-the-Wolds
Bunny
Widmerpool
Wysall
East Leake
Costock
Willoughby-on-the-Wolds
Nottingham
SK

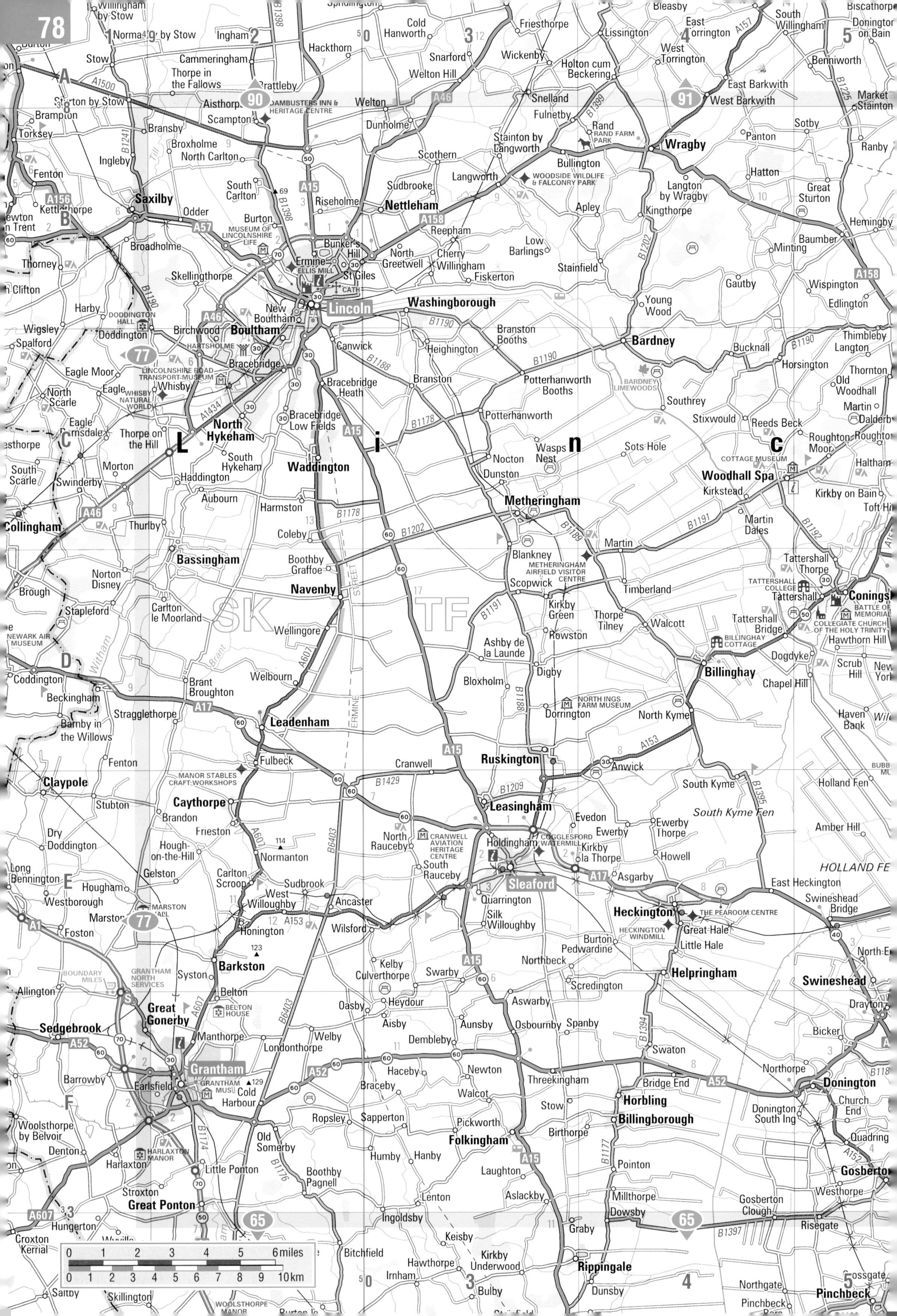
Willingham by Stow
Normanby by Stow
Ingham
Spridlington
Cold Hanworth
Friesthorpe
Bleasby
East Torrington
South Willingham
Biscathorpe
Donington on Bain
Burton
Stow
Cammeringham
Hackthorn
Snarford
Wickenby
Lissington
West Torrington
Benniworth
Thorpe in the Fallows
Brattleby
Welton Hill
Holton cum Beckering
East Barkwith
West Barkwith
Market Stainton
Sturton by Stow
Brampton
Aisthorpe
Scampton
DAMBUSTERS INN & HERITAGE CENTRE
Welton
Dunholme
Snelland
Fulnetby
Rand
RAND FARM PARK
Sotby
Panton
Ranby
Torksey
Bransby
Broxholme
North Carlton
Scothern
Stainton by Langworth
Wragby
Ingleby
Bullington
Fenton
South Carlton
Sudbrooke
Langworth
WOODSIDE WILDLIFE & FALCONRY PARK
Hatton
Langton by Wragby
Great Sturton
Saxilby
Kettlethorpe
Odder
Riseholme
Nettleham
Apley
Kingthorpe
Newton on Trent
Burton
MUSEUM OF LINCOLNSHIRE LIFE
Reepham
Hemingby
Broadholme
Bunker's Hill
Low Barlings
Baumber
Minting
Thorney
Ermine
ELLIS MILL
North Greetwell
Cherry Willingham
Stainfield
Skellingthorpe
St Giles
CATH
Fiskerton
Gautby
Wispington
Clifton
Lincoln
Washingborough
Young Wood
Edlington
Harby
DODDINGTON HALL
Doddington
New Boultham
Wigsley
Birchwood
Boultham
Branston Booths
Bardney
Thimbleby
Spalford
HARTSHOLME
Canwick
Heighington
Bucknall
Langton
Horsington
Eagle Moor
LINCOLNSHIRE ROAD TRANSPORT MUSEUM
Bracebridge
Branston
Potterhanworth Booths
Thornton
Eagle
WHISBY NATURAL WORLD
Whisby
Bracebridge Heath
BARDNEY LIMEWOODS
Old Woodhall
North Scarle
Southrey
Martin
Bracebridge Low Fields
Potterhanworth
Stixwould
Reeds Beck
Dalderby
Eagle Barnsdale
Thorpe on the Hill
North Hykeham
Roughton Moor
Roughton
Besthorpe
South Hykeham
Wasps Nest
Sots Hole
COTTAGE MUSEUM
South Scarle
Morton
Haddington
Waddington
Nocton
Halthar
Woodhall Spa
Swinderby
Dunston
Kirkstead
Kirkby on Bain
Aubourn
Metheringham
Tofl Hill
Collingham
Thurlby
Harmston
Martin Dales
Coleby
Blankney
Martin
Tattershall Thorpe
Bassingham
Boothby Graffoe
METHERINGHAM AIRFIELD VISITOR CENTRE
Timberland
TATTERSHALL COLLEGE
Tattershall
Coningsby
Norton Disney
Brough
Navenby
Scopwick
Kirkby Green
Thorpe Tilney
Walcott
Tattershall Bridge
BATTLE OF BRITAIN MEMORIAL
Stapleford
Carlton le Moorland
COLLEGIATE CHURCH OF THE HOLY TRINITY
Wellingore
Rowston
BILLINGHAY COTTAGE
Hawthorn Hill
NEWARK AIR MUSEUM
Ashby de la Launde
Dogdyke
Scrub Hill
New York
Billinghay
Coddington
Bloxholm
Digby
Chapel Hill
Brant Broughton
Welbourn
Beckingham
NORTH INGS FARM MUSEUM
Dorrington
Stragglethorpe
North Kyme
Haven Bank
Leadenham
Barnby in the Willows
Cranwell
Ruskington
Anwick
Fenton
Fulbeck
MANOR STABLES CRAFT WORKSHOPS
Claypole
South Kyme
Holland Fen
Caythorpe
Leasingham
Stubton
Brandon
Evedon
Everby Thorpe
South Kyme Fen
Frieston
Ewerby
Amber Hill
Dry Doddington
North Rauceby
CRANWELL AVIATION HERITAGE CENTRE
Holdingham
COGGLESFORD WATERMILL
Kirkby la Thorpe
Hough-on-the-Hill
Normanton
Howell
Long Bennington
Gelston
Carlton Scroop
South Rauceby
Sleaford
Asgarby
HOLLAND FEN
Hougham
Sudbrook
East Heckington
Westborough
West Willoughby
Ancaster
Quarrington
Heckington
THE PEAROOM CENTRE
Swineshead Bridge
MARSTON HALL
Marston
Silk Willoughby
Foston
Honington
Wilsford
HECKINGTON WINDMILL
Great Hale
Little Hale
Burton Pedwardine
North End
BOUNDARY MILL
GRANTHAM NORTH SERVICES
Syston
Barkston
Kelby
Culverthorpe
Swarby
Northbeck
Scredington
Helpringham
Swineshead
Allington
Belton
BELTON HOUSE
Heydour
Aswarby
Drayton
Sedgebrook
Great Gonerby
Oasby
Aisby
Aunsby
Osbournby
Spanby
Manthorpe
Welby
Dembleby
Bicker
Londonthorpe
Swaton
Grantham
Haceby
Newton
Threekingham
Northorpe
Barrowby
Earlsfield
GRANTHAM MUS
Cold Harbour
Braceby
Walcot
Bridge End
Donington
Horbling
Church End
Woolsthorpe by Belvoir
Ropsley
Sapperton
Stow
Billingborough
Donington South Ing
Pickworth
Birthorpe
Denton
HARLAXTON MANOR
Harlaxton
Old Somerby
Folkingham
Quadring
Humby
Hanby
Pointon
Gosberton
Little Ponton
Boothby Pagnell
Laughton
Stroxton
Millthorpe
Westhorpe
Great Ponton
Lenton
Aslackby
Gosberton Clough
Dowsby
Hungerton
Ingoldsby
Risegate
Croxton Kerrial
Graby
Keisby
Bitchfield
Kirkby Underwood
Hawthorpe
Rippingale
Irnham
Northgate
Pinchbeck
Bulby
Dunsby
Saltby
Skillington
WOOLSTHORPE MANOR
Pinchbeck
0 1 2 3 4 5 6 miles
0 1 2 3 4 5 6 7 8 9 10 km
SK
TF
L i n c
ERMINE STREET
Witham
Brant
Till

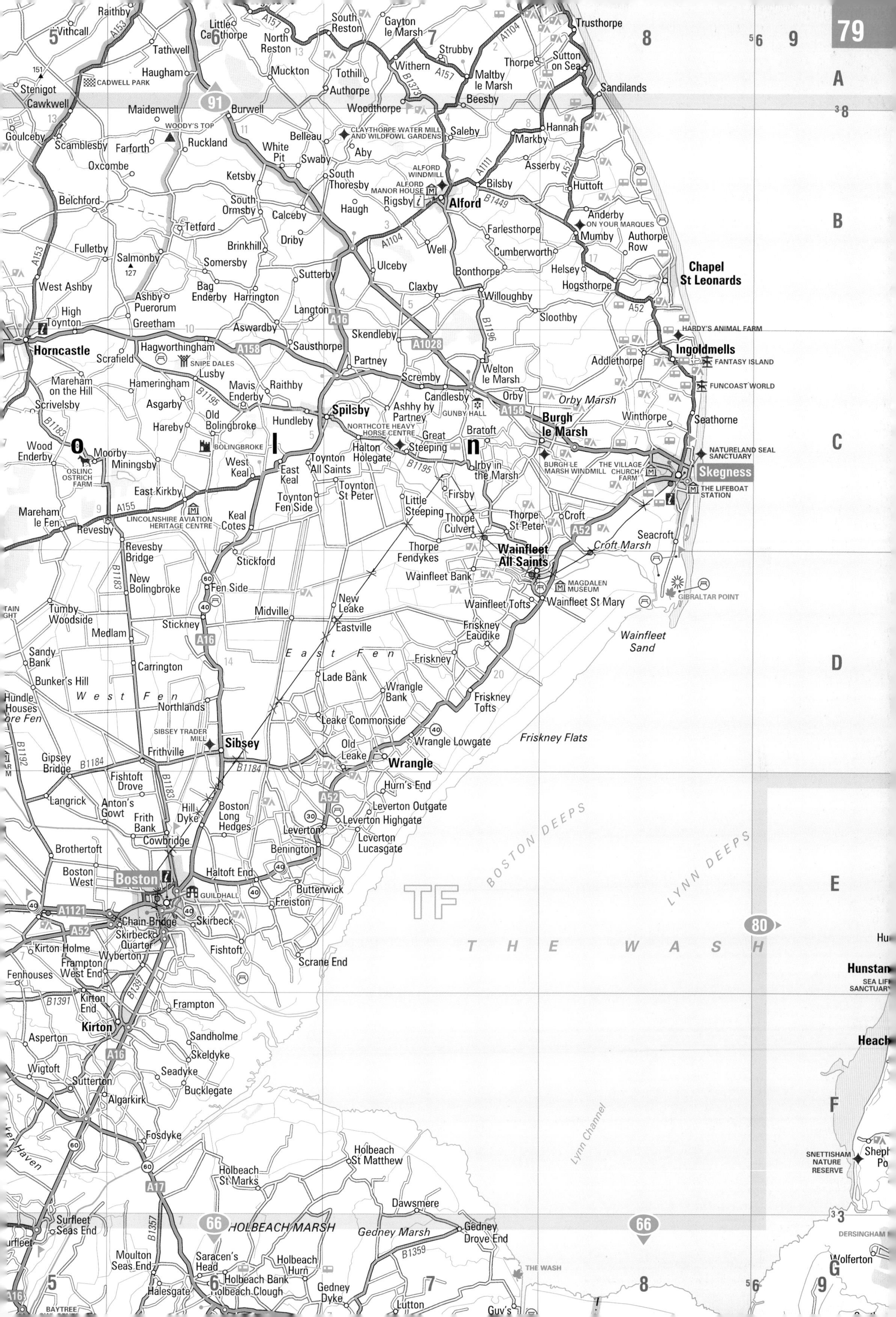

Raithby
Vithcall
Little Cawthorpe
Tathwell
Haugham
CADWELL PARK
Stenigot
Cawkwell
Maidenwell
Burwell
WOODY'S TOP
Goulceby
Scamblesby
Farforth
Ruckland
Oxcombe
Belchford
Tetford
Fulletby
Salmonby
West Ashby
Ashby Puerorum
High Toynton
Greetham
Horncastle
Scrafield
Hagworthingham
SNIPE DALES
Mareham on the Hill
Hameringham
Lusby
Scrivelsby
Asgarby
Hareby
Old Bolingbroke
BOLINGBROKE
Wood Enderby
Moorby
Miningsby
OSLINC OSTRICH FARM
East Kirkby
Mareham le Fen
Revesby
LINCOLNSHIRE AVIATION HERITAGE CENTRE
Revesby Bridge
New Bolingbroke
Tumby Woodside
Medlam
Sandy Bank
Bunker's Hill
West Fen
Hundle Houses
Carrington
Northlands
SIBSEY TRADER MILL
Sibsey
Frithville
Gipsey Bridge
Fishtoft Drove
Langrick
Anton's Gowt
Frith Bank
Hill Dyke
Cowbridge
Brothertoft
Boston West
Boston
GUILDHALL
Chain Bridge
Skirbeck
Skirbeck Quarter
Kirton Holme
Wyberton
Frampton West End
Fenhouses
Kirton End
Kirton
Frampton
Asperton
Wigtoft
Sutterton
Algarkirk
Fosdyke
Surfleet Seas End
Moulton Seas End
Halesgate
South Reston
North Reston
Gayton le Marsh
Mucklon
Tothill
Withern
Strubby
Authorpe
Woodthorpe
Maltby le Marsh
Beesby
CLAYTHORPE WATER MILL AND WILDFOWL GARDENS
Belleau
Aby
Saleby
White Pit
Swaby
South Thoresby
ALFORD WINDMILL
ALFORD MANOR HOUSE
Rigsby
Alford
Ketsby
South Ormsby
Calceby
Haugh
Driby
Brinkhill
Somersby
Bag Enderby
Harrington
Sutterby
Ulceby
Well
Langton
Aswardby
Skendleby
Claxby
Sausthorpe
Partney
Scremby
Candlesby
Mavis Enderby
Raithby
Ashby by Partney
GUNBY HALL
Spilsby
Hundleby
NORTHCOTE HEAVY HORSE CENTRE
Great Steeping
Halton Holegate
Toynton All Saints
West Keal
East Keal
Toynton St Peter
Toynton Fen Side
Keal Cotes
Little Steeping
Firsby
Irby in the Marsh
Bratoft
Stickford
Thorpe Culvert
Thorpe Fendykes
Fen Side
Stickney
Midville
New Leake
Eastville
East Fen
Lade Bank
Leake Commonside
Old Leake
Wrangle
Wrangle Bank
Boston Long Hedges
Leverton
Benington
Haltoft End
Butterwick
Freiston
Fishtoft
Scrane End
Sandholme
Skeldyke
Seadyke
Bucklegate
Holbeach St Marks
Holbeach St Matthew
HOLBEACH MARSH
Gedney Marsh
Dawsmere
Gedney Drove End
Saracen's Head
Holbeach Hurn
Holbeach Bank
Holbeach Clough
Gedney Dyke
Lutton
Guy's Head
THE WASH
Trusthorpe
Thorpe
Sutton on Sea
Sandilands
Hannah
Markby
Asserby
Bilsby
Huttoft
Anderby
ON YOUR MARQUES
Mumby
Authorpe Row
Farlesthorpe
Cumberworth
Bonthorpe
Helsey
Hogsthorpe
Chapel St Leonards
Willoughby
Sloothby
HARDY'S ANIMAL FARM
Ingoldmells
FANTASY ISLAND
FUNCOAST WORLD
Addlethorpe
Welton le Marsh
Orby
Orby Marsh
Burgh le Marsh
Winthorpe
Seathorne
BURGH LE MARSH WINDMILL
THE VILLAGE CHURCH FARM
NATURELAND SEAL SANCTUARY
Skegness
THE LIFEBOAT STATION
Croft
Thorpe St Peter
Seacroft
Croft Marsh
Wainfleet All Saints
Wainfleet Bank
MAGDALEN MUSEUM
Wainfleet Tofts
Wainfleet St Mary
GIBRALTAR POINT
Wainfleet Sand
Friskney Eaudike
Friskney
Friskney Tofts
Friskney Flats
Wrangle Lowgate
Hurn's End
Leverton Outgate
Leverton Highgate
Leverton Lucasgate
BOSTON DEEPS
LYNN DEEPS
TF
THE WASH
Lynn Channel
Hunstanton
SEA LIFE SANCTUARY
Heacham
SNETTISHAM NATURE RESERVE
DERSINGHAM
Wolferton
A
B
C
D
E
F
G
5
6
7
8
9

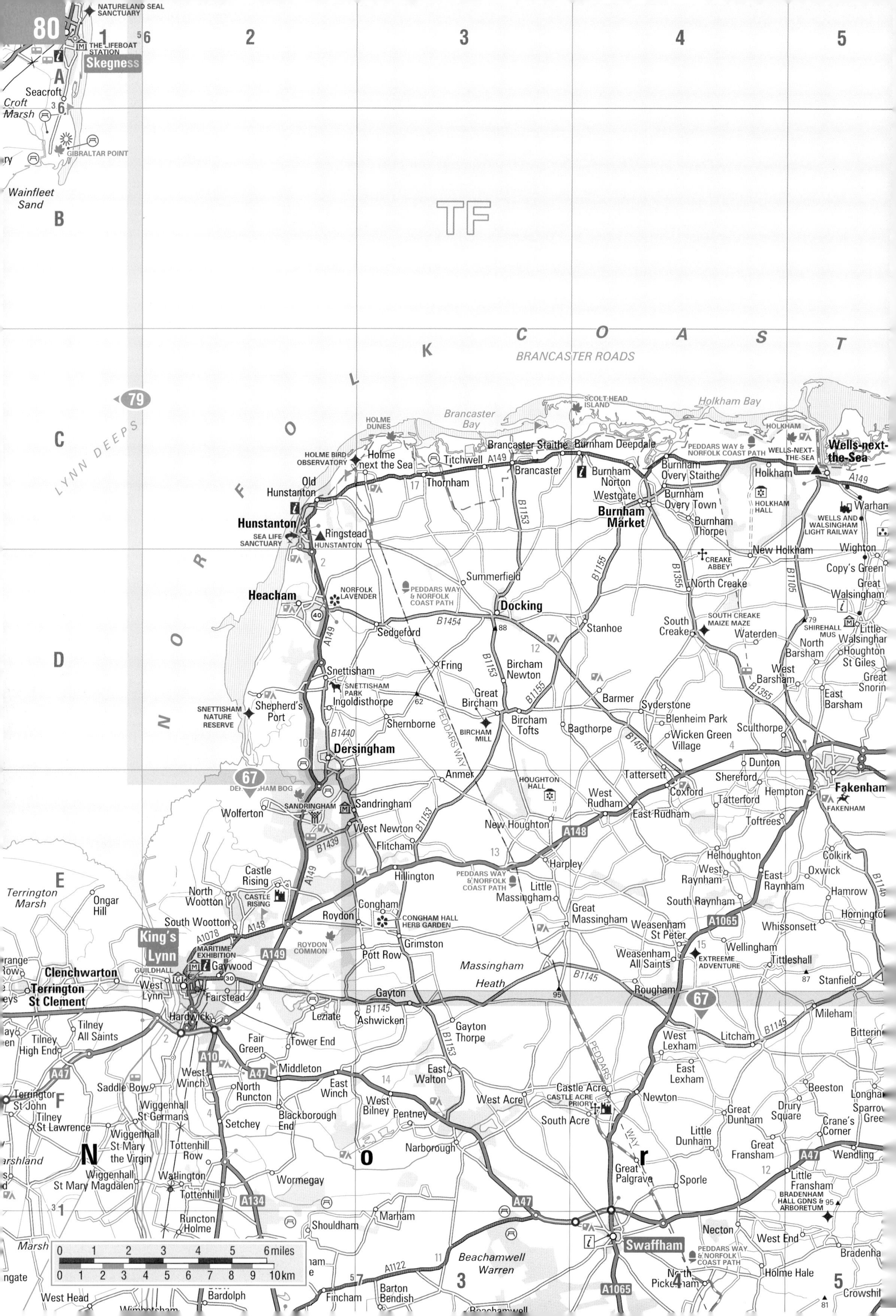

1
2
3
4
5
A
B
C
D
E
F
TF
NATURELAND SEAL SANCTUARY
THE LIFEBOAT STATION
Skegness
Seacroft
Croft Marsh
GIBRALTAR POINT
Wainfleet Sand
LYNN DEEPS
79
NORFOLK COAST
BRANCASTER ROADS
Brancaster Bay
SCOLT HEAD ISLAND
Holkham Bay
HOLME DUNES
HOLME BIRD OBSERVATORY
Holme next the Sea
Titchwell
Brancaster Staithe
Burnham Deepdale
PEDDARS WAY & NORFOLK COAST PATH
HOLKHAM
WELLS-NEXT-THE-SEA
Wells-next-the-Sea
Brancaster
Thornham
Old Hunstanton
Burnham Norton
Burnham Overy Staithe
Holkham
A149
Westgate
Burnham Overy Town
HOLKHAM HALL
Warham
Burnham Market
Burnham Thorpe
WELLS AND WALSINGHAM LIGHT RAILWAY
Hunstanton
SEA LIFE SANCTUARY
Ringstead
HUNSTANTON
CREAKE ABBEY
New Holkham
Wighton
Copy's Green
Great Walsingham
B1153
B1155
B1355
B1105
Summerfield
North Creake
Heacham
NORFOLK LAVENDER
PEDDARS WAY & NORFOLK COAST PATH
Docking
South Creake
SOUTH CREAKE MAIZE MAZE
SHIREHALL MUS
Little Walsingham
B1454
Sedgeford
Stanhoe
Waterden
North Barsham
Houghton St Giles
Fring
Bircham Newton
West Barsham
Great Snoring
Snettisham
SNETTISHAM PARK
Great Bircham
Barmer
East Barsham
SNETTISHAM NATURE RESERVE
Shepherd's Port
Ingoldisthorpe
Syderstone
Blenheim Park
Shernborne
BIRCHAM MILL
Bircham Tofts
Bagthorpe
Wicken Green Village
Sculthorpe
B1440
Dersingham
PEDDARS WAY
Dunton
67
DERSINGHAM BOG
Anmer
HOUGHTON HALL
Tattersett
Shereford
Fakenham
Wolferton
SANDRINGHAM
Sandringham
West Rudham
Coxford
Hempton
Tattersford
FAKENHAM
East Rudham
West Newton
New Houghton
Toftrees
B1439
Flitcham
A148
Helhoughton
Colkirk
Castle Rising
Hillington
Harpley
West Raynham
Oxwick
East Raynham
Terrington Marsh
Ongar Hill
North Wootton
CASTLE RISING
PEDDARS WAY & NORFOLK COAST PATH
Little Massingham
South Raynham
Hamrow
B1146
Congham
Horningtoft
South Wootton
Roydon
CONGHAM HALL HERB GARDEN
Great Massingham
Weasenham St Peter
A1065
Whissonsett
King's Lynn
A1078
MARITIME EXHIBITION
ROYDON COMMON
Grimston
Weasenham All Saints
Wellingham
GUILDHALL
Gaywood
A149
Pott Row
Massingham Heath
EXTREME ADVENTURE
Tittleshall
Clenchwarton
Stanfield
B1145
Terrington St Clement
West Lynn
Fairstead
Gayton
Rougham
Hardwick
Leziate
Ashwicken
Mileham
Gayton Thorpe
Bittering
Tilney All Saints
Fair Green
Tower End
West Lexham
Litcham
Tilney High End
A10
PEDDARS WAY
A47
West Winch
Middleton
East Walton
East Lexham
Saddle Bow
East Winch
North Runcton
Castle Acre
CASTLE ACRE PRIORY
Beeston
Longham
Terrington St John
Tilney St Lawrence
Wiggenhall St Germans
West Bilney
Pentney
West Acre
Newton
Great Dunham
Drury Square
Sparrow Green
Setchey
Blackborough End
South Acre
Crane's Corner
Wiggenhall St Mary the Virgin
Tottenhill Row
Little Dunham
Great Fransham
Narborough
Marshland
Wendling
Wiggenhall St Mary Magdalen
Watlington
Wormegay
Great Palgrave
Sporle
Little Fransham
Tottenhill
BRADENHAM HALL GDNS & ARBORETUM
A134
Marham
Runcton Holme
Shouldham
Necton
West End
Marsh
Swaffham
PEDDARS WAY & NORFOLK COAST PATH
Bradenham
0 1 2 3 4 5 6 miles
0 1 2 3 4 5 6 7 8 9 10 km
A1122
Beachamwell Warren
North Pickenham
Holme Hale
Fincham
Barton Bendish
West Head
Bardolph
A1065
Crownthorpe

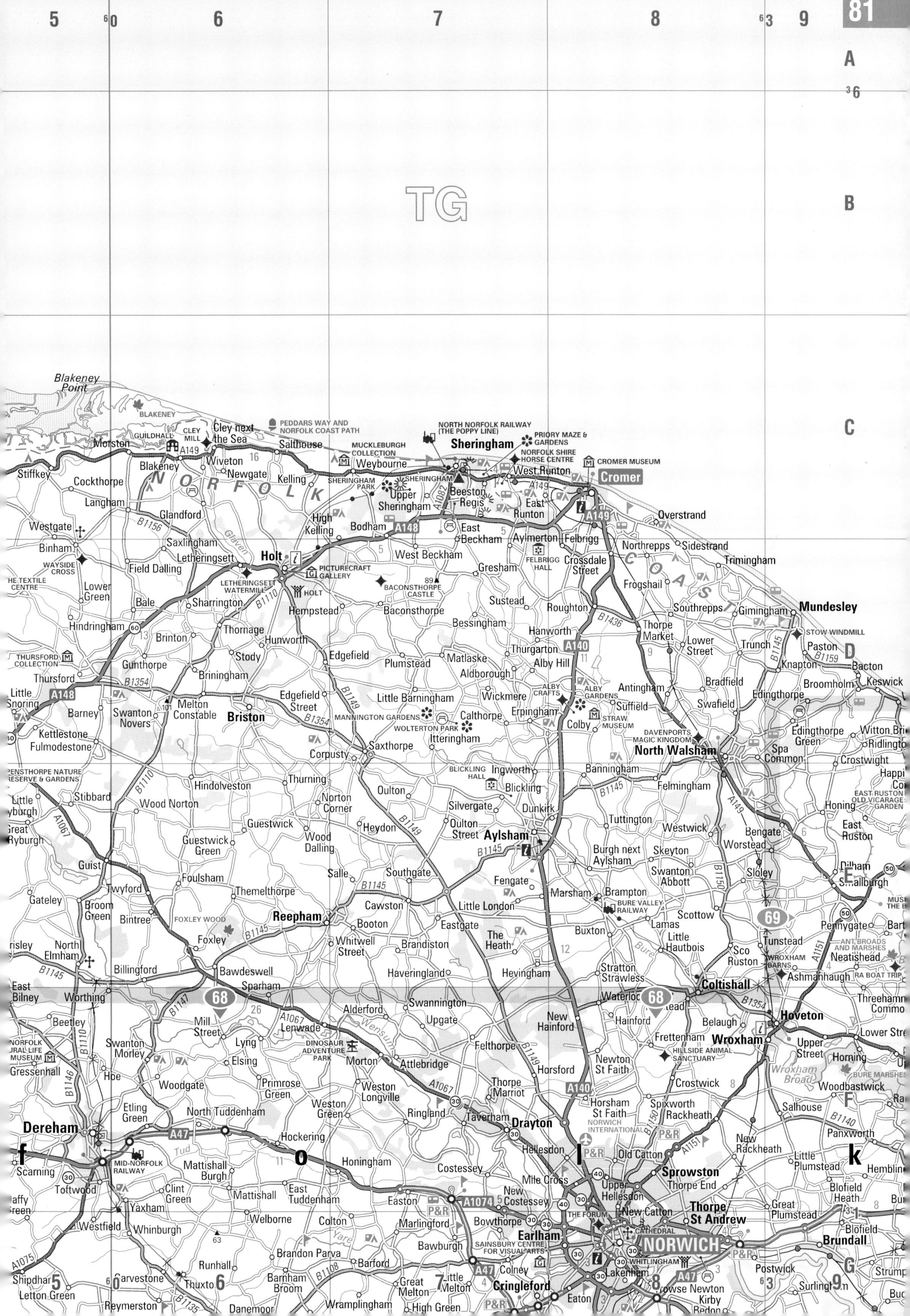
5
60
6
7
8
63
9
A
36
B
C
D
E
F
G
TG
Blakeney Point
BLAKENEY
CLEY MILL
Cley next the Sea
GUILDHALL
Morston
A149
Stiffkey
Blakeney
Wiveton
Newgate
Salthouse
Kelling
NORFOLK
PEDDARS WAY AND NORFOLK COAST PATH
MUCKLEBURGH COLLECTION
Weybourne
NORTH NORFOLK RAILWAY (THE POPPY LINE)
Sheringham
PRIORY MAZE & GARDENS
NORFOLK SHIRE HORSE CENTRE
CROMER MUSEUM
West Runton
Cromer
SHERINGHAM PARK
SHERINGHAM
Upper Sheringham
Beeston Regis
East Runton
A1082
Cockthorpe
Langham
Glandford
High Kelling
Bodham
A148
East Beckham
Aylmerton
Felbrigg
A149
Overstrand
Westgate
Binham
B1156
Saxlingham
Letheringsett
Holt
West Beckham
FELBRIGG HALL
Crossdale Street
Northrepps
Sidestrand
Trimingham
COAST
WAYSIDE CROSS
Field Dalling
THE TEXTILE CENTRE
LETHERINGSETT WATERMILL
PICTURECRAFT GALLERY
BACONSTHORPE CASTLE
Gresham
Frogshall
Lower Green
Bale
Sharrington
HOLT
Hempstead
Baconsthorpe
Sustead
Roughton
Southrepps
Gimingham
Mundesley
B1110
Hindringham
Brinton
Thornage
Hunworth
Bessingham
Hanworth
B1436
Thorpe Market
STOW WINDMILL
Lower Street
Trunch
Paston
THURSFORD COLLECTION
Gunthorpe
Stody
Edgefield
Plumstead
Matlaske
Thurgarton
A140
Alby Hill
Knapton
B1159
Bacton
B1145
Thursford
Briningham
Aldborough
Bradfield
Broomholm
Keswick
Little Snoring
A148
B1354
Edgefield Street
B1149
Little Barningham
Wickmere
ALBY CRAFTS
ALBY GARDENS
Antingham
Edingthorpe
Barney
Swanton Novers
Melton Constable
Briston
Suffield
Swafield
MANNINGTON GARDENS
Calthorpe
Erpingham
Colby
STRAW MUSEUM
WOLTERTON PARK
Itteringham
Kettlestone
Fulmodestone
Saxthorpe
DAVENPORTS MAGIC KINGDOM
North Walsham
Edingthorpe Green
Witton Bridge
Ridlington
Spa Common
Corpusty
Crostwight
PENSTHORPE NATURE RESERVE & GARDENS
BLICKLING HALL
Ingworth
Banningham
Little Ryburgh
Stibbard
Hindolveston
Thurning
Blickling
Felmingham
Oulton
EAST RUSTON OLD VICARAGE GARDEN
Wood Norton
Norton Corner
Silvergate
Dunkirk
Honing
Great Ryburgh
A1067
Guestwick
Heydon
Oulton Street
Aylsham
Tuttington
Westwick
Bengate
East Ruston
Guestwick Green
Wood Dalling
B1145
Burgh next Aylsham
Skeyton
Worstead
Guist
Salle
Southgate
Swanton Abbott
B1150
Sloley
Dilham
Smallburgh
Twyford
Foulsham
Themelthorpe
B1145
Fengate
Marsham
Brampton
Gateley
Broom Green
Bintree
FOXLEY WOOD
Reepham
Cawston
Little London
BURE VALLEY RAILWAY
Scottow
69
Pennygate
Booton
Eastgate
Lamas
Foxley
Whitwell Street
Brandiston
The Heath
Buxton
Little Hautbois
Sco Ruston
Tunstead
ANT BROADS AND MARSHES
Neatishead
North Elmham
Billingford
Bure
WROXHAM BARNS
Ashmanhaugh
B1145
Bawdeswell
Haveringland
Heyhoe
Hevingham
Stratton Strawless
Coltishall
East Bilney
Worthing
68
Sparham
Waterloo
68
Threehammer Common
B1141
Alderford
Swannington
B1354
Beetley
Mill Street
26
A1067
Lenwade
Wensum
Upgate
New Hainford
Hainford
Belaugh
Hoveton
NORFOLK RURAL LIFE MUSEUM
Swanton Morley
Lyng
DINOSAUR ADVENTURE PARK
Felthorpe
Frettenham
Wroxham
Lower Street
Upper Street
Horning
Gressenhall
Elsing
Morton
Attlebridge
B1149
HILLSIDE ANIMAL SANCTUARY
Hoe
B1146
Woodgate
Primrose Green
Weston Longville
Horsford
Newton St Faith
Crostwick
Wroxham Broad
BURE MARSHES
Woodbastwick
Etling Green
A1067
Thorpe Marriot
A140
Salhouse
North Tuddenham
Weston Green
Ringland
Taverham
Drayton
Horsham St Faith
Spixworth
Rackheath
NORWICH INTERNATIONAL
B1140
Panxworth
Dereham
A47
Hockering
B1150
P&R
New Rackheath
Tud
Hellesdon
Old Catton
A1151
MID-NORFOLK RAILWAY
Mattishall Burgh
Honingham
Costessey
Sprowston
Little Plumstead
Hemblington
Scarning
Toftwood
Clint Green
East Tuddenham
Mile Cross
Thorpe End
Blofield Heath
Mattishall
Easton
A1074
New Costessey
Upper Hellesdon
Great Plumstead
Yaxham
Welborne
P&R
THE FORUM
New Catton
Thorpe St Andrew
Westfield
Whinburgh
Colton
Marlingford
Bowthorpe
CATHEDRAL
Blofield
Earlham
Yare
NORWICH
Brundall
Bawburgh
SAINSBURY CENTRE FOR VISUAL ARTS
A1075
Runhall
Brandon Parva
Barford
WHITLINGHAM
P&R
Shipdham
Garvestone
Thuxton
Barnham Broom
B1108
Great Melton
Little Melton
A47
Colney
Cringleford
Lakenham
A47
Postwick
Strumpshaw
Letton Green
Eaton
Trowse Newton
Kirby Bedon
Surlingham
Reymerston
B1135
Danemoor
Wramplingham
High Green
P&R

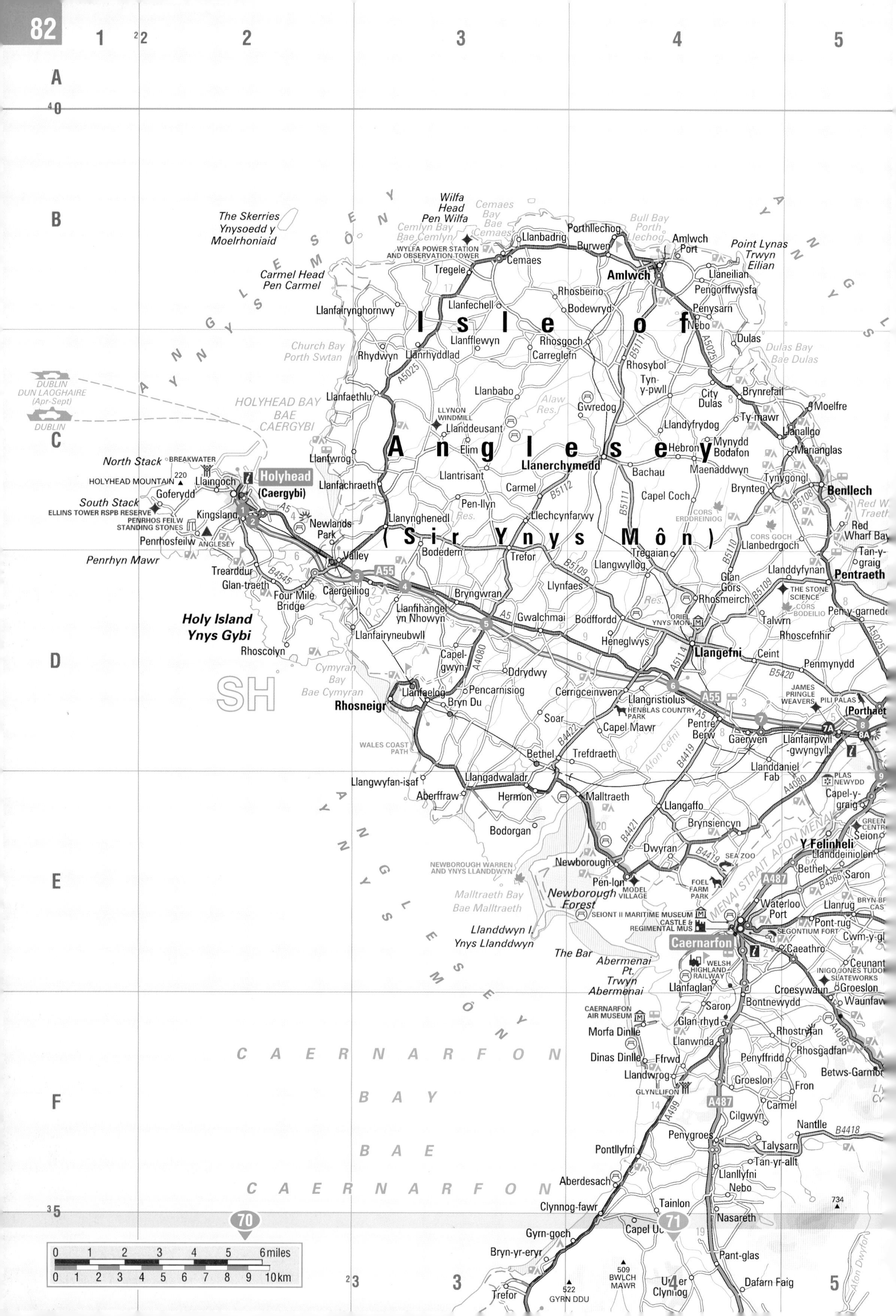
1
2
3
4
5
A
B
C
D
E
F
Isle of Anglesey
(Sir Ynys Môn)
The Skerries
Ynysoedd y Moelrhoniaid
Carmel Head
Pen Carmel
Wilfa Head
Pen Wilfa
Cemlyn Bay
Bae Cemlyn
Cemaes Bay
Bae Cemaes
WYLFA POWER STATION AND OBSERVATION TOWER
Llanbadrig
Porthllechog
Bull Bay
Porth Llechog
Burwen
Amlwch Port
Amlwch
Point Lynas
Trwyn Eilian
Llaneilian
Pengorffwysfa
Penysarn
Nebo
Cemaes
Tregele
Rhosbeirio
Bodewryd
Llanfechell
Llanfairynghornwy
Llanfflewyn
Rhosgoch
Carreglefn
Church Bay
Porth Swtan
Rhydwyn
Llanrhyddlad
Dulas
Dulas Bay
Bae Dulas
Rhosybol
Tyn-y-pwll
City Dulas
Brynrefail
Moelfre
Ty-mawr
Llanallgo
Llanbabo
Alaw Res.
Gwredog
Llanfaethlu
HOLYHEAD BAY
BAE CAERGYBI
LLYNON WINDMILL
Llanddeusant
Llandyfrydog
Mynydd Bodafon
Hebron
Marianglas
DUBLIN
DUN LAOGHAIRE
(Apr-Sept)
Elim
Llanerchymedd
Bachau
Maenaddwyn
Tynygongl
Benllech
North Stack
BREAKWATER
HOLYHEAD MOUNTAIN
220
Llaingoch
Holyhead
(Caergybi)
Llanfwrog
Llantrisant
Carmel
Capel Coch
Brynteg
Red Wharf Bay
Goferydd
South Stack
ELLINS TOWER RSPB RESERVE
PENRHOS FEILW STANDING STONES
Kingsland
Llanfachraeth
Newlands Park
Pen-llyn
Llechcynfarwy
CORS ERDDREINIOG
CORS GOCH
Llanbedrgoch
Penrhosfeilw
ANGLESEY
Llanynghenedl
Bodedern
Trefor
Tregaian
Tan-y-graig
Penrhyn Mawr
Trearddur
Valley
Llangwyllog
Llanddyfnan
Pentraeth
Glan-traeth
Four Mile Bridge
Caergeiliog
Bryngwran
Llynfaes
Glan Gors
Rhosmeirch
THE STONE SCIENCE
CORS BODEILIO
Pen-y-garnedd
Holy Island
Ynys Gybi
Llanfihangel yn Nhowyn
Gwalchmai
Bodffordd
ORIEL YNYS MÔN
Talwrn
Rhoscefnhir
Rhoscolyn
Llanfairyneubwll
Heneglwys
Llangefni
Ceint
Penmynydd
SH
Cymyran Bay
Bae Cymyran
Capel-gwyn
Ddrydwy
Rhosneigr
Llanfaelog
Pencarnisiog
Bryn Du
Cerrigceinwen
Llangristiolus
HENBLAS COUNTRY PARK
JAMES PRINGLE WEAVERS
PILI PALAS
Soar
Capel Mawr
Pentre Berw
Gaerwen
Llanfairpwll-gwyngyll
WALES COAST PATH
Bethel
Trefdraeth
Llanddaniel Fab
PLAS NEWYDD
Capel-y-graig
Llangwyfan-isaf
Llangadwaladr
Aberffraw
Hermon
Malltraeth
Llangaffo
Brynsiencyn
Bodorgan
Dwyran
SEA ZOO
MENAI STRAIT AFON MENAI
Y Felinheli
Llanddeiniolen
Bethel
Saron
NEWBOROUGH WARREN AND YNYS LLANDDWYN
Newborough
Pen-lon
MODEL VILLAGE
FOEL FARM PARK
Malltraeth Bay
Bae Malltraeth
Newborough Forest
SEIONT II MARITIME MUSEUM
CASTLE & REGIMENTAL MUS
Waterloo Port
Llanrug
Pont-rug
SEGONTIUM FORT
Llanddwyn I.
Ynys Llanddwyn
The Bar
Caernarfon
Caeathro
Cwm-y-glo
Abermenai Pt.
Trwyn Abermenai
WELSH HIGHLAND RAILWAY
Llanfaglan
Ceunant
INIGO JONES TUDOR SLATEWORKS
Groeslon
Croesywaun
Saron
Bontnewydd
Waunfawr
CAERNARFON AIR MUSEUM
Morfa Dinlle
Glan-rhyd
Llanwnda
Rhostryfan
Rhosgadfan
CAERNARFON BAY
BAE CAERNARFON
Dinas Dinlle
Ffrwd
Llandwrog
Penyffridd
Betws-Garmon
GLYNLLIFON
Groeslon
Fron
Carmel
Cilgwyn
Nantlle
Penygroes
Talysarn
Pontllyfni
Tan-yr-allt
Llanllyfni
Nebo
Aberdesach
Tainlon
Clynnog-fawr
Nasareth
734
Gyrn-goch
Capel Uchaf
Bryn-yr-eryr
Pant-glas
509
BWLCH MAWR
522
GYRN DDU
Trefor
Uwchmynydd
Clynnog
Dafarn Faig
70
71
A55
A5
A5025
A487
A499
A4080
A4085
B5111
B5112
B5109
B5110
B5108
B5420
B4545
B4422
B4419
B4421
B4366
B4418
0 1 2 3 4 5 6 miles
0 1 2 3 4 5 6 7 8 9 10 km

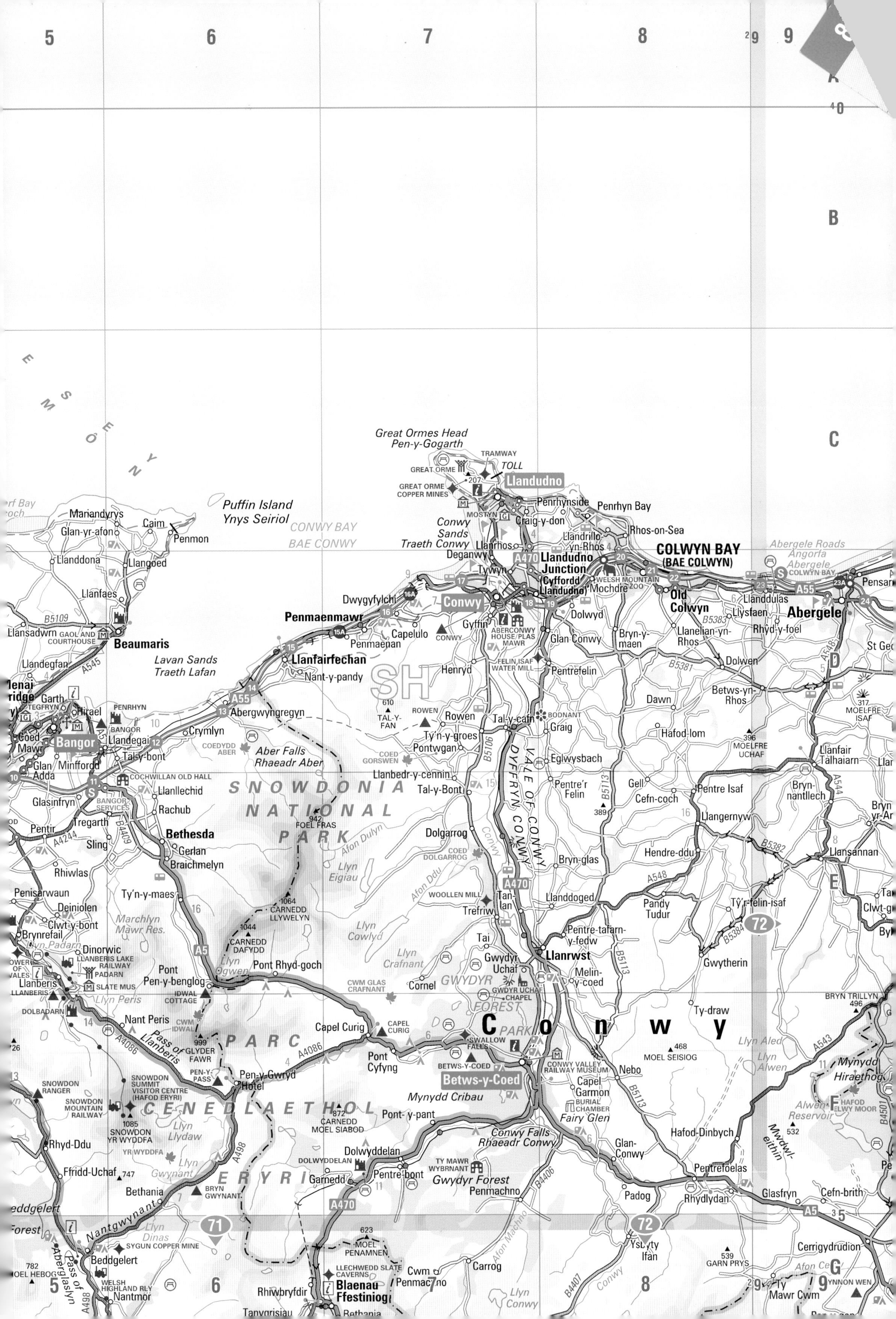

5
6
7
8
9
A
B
C
D
E
F
G
Great Ormes Head
Pen-y-Gogarth
TRAMWAY
TOLL
GREAT ORME
GREAT ORME COPPER MINES
Llandudno
MOSTYN
Penrhynside
Penrhyn Bay
Craig-y-don
Llandrillo-yn-Rhos
Rhos-on-Sea
Llanrhos
Conwy Sands
Traeth Conwy
Deganwy
Tywyn
A470
Llandudno Junction
(Cyffordd Llandudno)
COLWYN BAY
(BAE COLWYN)
Abergele Roads
Angorfa Abergele
WELSH MOUNTAIN ZOO
Mochdre
Old Colwyn
Llanddulas
Abergele
Pensar
Puffin Island
Ynys Seiriol
CONWY BAY
BAE CONWY
Mariandyrys
Glan-yr-afon
Caim
Penmon
Llanddona
Llangoed
Llanfaes
B5109
Llansadwrn
GAOL AND COURTHOUSE
Beaumaris
Lavan Sands
Traeth Lafan
Llandegfan
A545
Dwygyfylchi
Penmaenmawr
Conwy
Capelulo
Penmaenan
Gyffin
CONWY
ABERCONWY HOUSE/PLAS MAWR
Glan Conwy
Dolwyd
Bryn-y-maen
Llysfaen
B5383
Llanelian-yn-Rhos
Rhyd-y-foel
St Ge
Llanfairfechan
Nant-y-pandy
SH
Henryd
FELIN ISAF WATER MILL
Pentrefelin
B5381
Dolwen
Betws-yn-Rhos
Dawn
A548
A55
Garth
Hirael
PENRHYN
TEGFRYN
Bangor
BANGOR
Llandegai
Abergwyngregyn
Crymlyn
610 TAL-Y-FAN
ROWEN
Rowen
Tal-y-cafn
BODNANT
Graig
Hafod-lom
396 MOELFRE UCHAF
317 MOELFRE ISAF
Llanfair Talhaiarn
Coed Mawr
Glan Adda
Minffordd
Tal-y-bont
COEDYDD ABER
Aber Falls
Rhaeadr Aber
COED GORSWEN
Ty'n-y-groes
Pontwgan
B5106
VALE OF CONWY
DYFFRYN CONWY
Eglwysbach
COCHWILLAN OLD HALL
Llanllechid
SNOWDONIA NATIONAL PARK
Llanbedr-y-cennin
Tal-y-Bont
Pentre'r Felin
B5113
389
Gell
Cefn-coch
Pentre Isaf
Bryn-nantllech
A544
Glasinfryn
BANGOR SERVICES
Rachub
942 FOEL FRAS
Tregarth
Pentir
Sling
A4244
B4409
Bethesda
Gerlan
Braichmelyn
Rhiwlas
Afon Dulyn
Llyn Eigiau
Dolgarrog
COED DOLGARROG
Conwy
Bryn-glas
Hendre-ddu
Llangernyw
B5382
Llansannan
Bryn-yr-Ar
Penisarwaun
Deiniolen
Ty'n-y-maes
Clwt-y-bont
Brynrefail
Marchlyn Mawr Res.
1064 CARNEDD LLYWELYN
Afon Ddu
WOOLLEN MILL
Trefriw
Tan-lan
A470
Llanddoged
Pandy Tudur
Tŷ'r-felin-isaf
72
B5384
Clwt-y-g
Llyn Padarn
Dinorwic
LLANBERIS LAKE RAILWAY
PADARN
SLATE MUS
Llanberis
1044 CARNEDD DAFYDD
Llyn Cowlyd
Tai
Pentre-tafarn-y-fedw
Llanrwst
Gwydyr Uchaf
B5113
Gwytherin
A5
Pont Pen-y-benglog
Llyn Ogwen
Pont Rhyd-goch
Llyn Crafnant
CWM GLAS CRAFNANT
Cornel
GWYDYR
GWYDYR UCHAF CHAPEL
Melin-y-coed
FOREST PARK
Ty-draw
BRYN TRILLYN 496
DOLBADARN
LLANBERIS
Llyn Peris
IDWAL COTTAGE
CWM IDWAL
Nant Peris
A4086
Pass of Llanberis
999 GLYDER FAWR
PARC
Capel Curig
CAPEL CURIG
Pont Cyfyng
SWALLOW FALLS
BETWS-Y-COED
Betws-y-Coed
Conwy
468 MOEL SEISIOG
Nebo
CONWY VALLEY RAILWAY MUSEUM
Capel Garmon
BURIAL CHAMBER
Fairy Glen
Llyn Aled
Llyn Alwen
A543
Mynydd Hiraethog
Alwen Reservoir
HAFOD ELWY MOOR
532
B4501
SNOWDON RANGER
PEN-Y-PASS
Pen-y-Gwryd Hotel
SNOWDON SUMMIT VISITOR CENTRE (HAFOD ERYRI)
SNOWDON MOUNTAIN RAILWAY
1085 SNOWDON YR WYDDFA
CENEDLAETHOL
Llyn Llydaw
Mynydd Cribau
872 CARNEDD MOEL SIABOD
Pont-y-pant
Conwy Falls
Rhaeadr Conwy
Glan-Conwy
Hafod-Dinbych
Mwdwl-eithin
Rhyd-Ddu
YR WYDDFA
A498
Llyn Gwynant
Ffridd-Uchaf 747
Bethania
BRYN GWYNANT
ERYRI
DOLWYDDELAN
Dolwyddelan
Garnedd
Pentre-bont
TY MAWR WYBRNANT
Gwydyr Forest
Penmachno
B4406
Padog
Pentrefoelas
Rhydlydan
Glasfryn
Cefn-brith
A5
Beddgelert
Forest
Nantgwynant
Llyn Dinas
71
A470
623 MOEL PENAMNEN
Afon Machno
72
Ysbyty Ifan
539 GARN PRYS
Cerrigydrudion
Afon Ce
SYGUN COPPER MINE
782 MOEL HEBOG
Pass of Aberglaslyn
WELSH HIGHLAND RLY
Nantmor
Rhiwbryfdir
LLECHWEDD SLATE CAVERNS
Blaenau Ffestiniog
Cwm Penmachno
Carrog
B4407
Conwy
Llyn Conwy
Ty Mawr Cwm
YNNON WEN
Tanygrisiau
Bethania

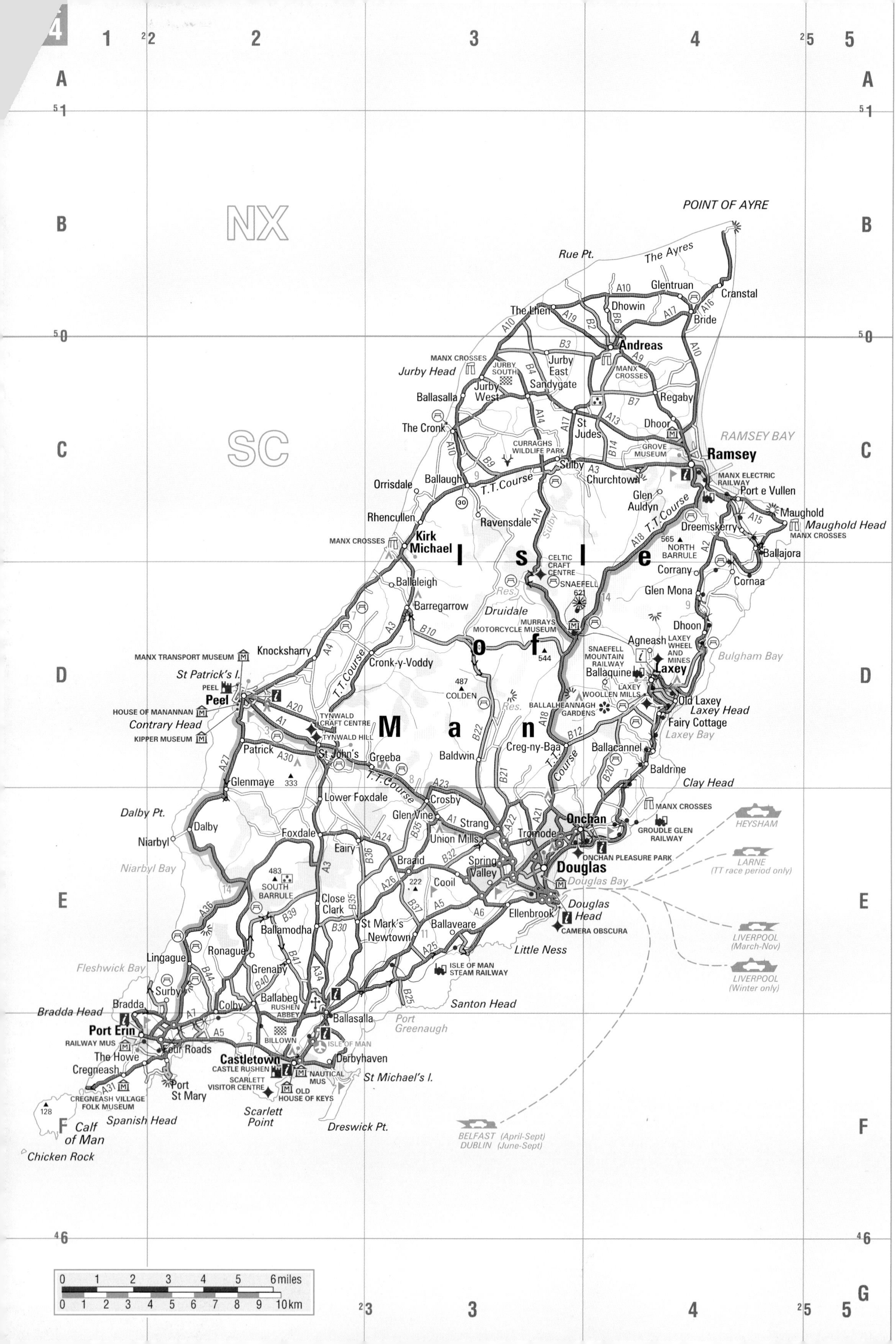
NX
SC
Isle of Man
POINT OF AYRE
The Ayres
Rue Pt.
Glentruan
Cranstal
Dhowin
Bride
The Lhen
Andreas
Jurby Head
MANX CROSSES
JURBY SOUTH
Jurby East
Sandygate
Jurby West
Ballasalla
Regaby
The Cronk
St Judes
Dhoor
GROVE MUSEUM
CURRAGHS WILDLIFE PARK
RAMSEY BAY
Ramsey
Sulby
Churchtown
MANX ELECTRIC RAILWAY
Orrisdale
Ballaugh
T.T.Course
Port e Vullen
Glen Auldyn
Maughold
Maughold Head
Rhencullen
Ravensdale
Dreemskerry
Kirk Michael
565 NORTH BARRULE
Ballajora
CELTIC CRAFT CENTRE
Corrany
Cornaa
Ballaleigh
SNAEFELL 621
Glen Mona
Barregarrow
Druidale
Dhoon
MURRAYS MOTORCYCLE MUSEUM
Knocksharry
MANX TRANSPORT MUSEUM
Agneash
LAXEY WHEEL AND MINES
SNAEFELL MOUNTAIN RAILWAY
Bulgham Bay
Cronk-y-Voddy
544
St Patrick's I.
PEEL
Peel
HOUSE OF MANANNAN
Contrary Head
KIPPER MUSEUM
Ballaquine
Laxey
487 COLDEN
WOOLLEN MILLS
Old Laxey
Laxey Head
BALLALHEANNAGH GARDENS
Fairy Cottage
TYNWALD CRAFT CENTRE
TYNWALD HILL
Laxey Bay
Patrick
St John's
Greeba
Baldwin
Creg-ny-Baa
Ballacannel
Baldrine
Glenmaye
333
Clay Head
Lower Foxdale
Crosby
Dalby Pt.
Glen Vine
Strang
Onchan
HEYSHAM
GROUDLE GLEN RAILWAY
Dalby
Niarbyl
Foxdale
Union Mills
Tromode
ONCHAN PLEASURE PARK
Eairy
LARNE (TT race period only)
Niarbyl Bay
Braaid
Spring Valley
Douglas
483 SOUTH BARRULE
222
Cooil
Douglas Bay
Close Clark
Ellenbrook
Douglas Head
Ballamodha
St Mark's
Newtown
Ballaveare
CAMERA OBSCURA
LIVERPOOL (March-Nov)
Ronague
Little Ness
Lingague
Fleshwick Bay
Grenaby
ISLE OF MAN STEAM RAILWAY
LIVERPOOL (Winter only)
Surby
Bradda
Ballabeg
RUSHEN ABBEY
Santon Head
Bradda Head
Colby
Ballasalla
Port Greenaugh
Port Erin
BILLOWN
RAILWAY MUS
Four Roads
ISLE OF MAN
The Howe
Castletown
CASTLE RUSHEN
NAUTICAL MUS
Derbyhaven
Cregneash
SCARLETT VISITOR CENTRE
OLD HOUSE OF KEYS
St Michael's I.
Port St Mary
CREGNEASH VILLAGE FOLK MUSEUM
128
Calf of Man
Spanish Head
Scarlett Point
Dreswick Pt.
BELFAST (April-Sept)
DUBLIN (June-Sept)
Chicken Rock
0 1 2 3 4 5 6 miles
0 1 2 3 4 5 6 7 8 9 10 km

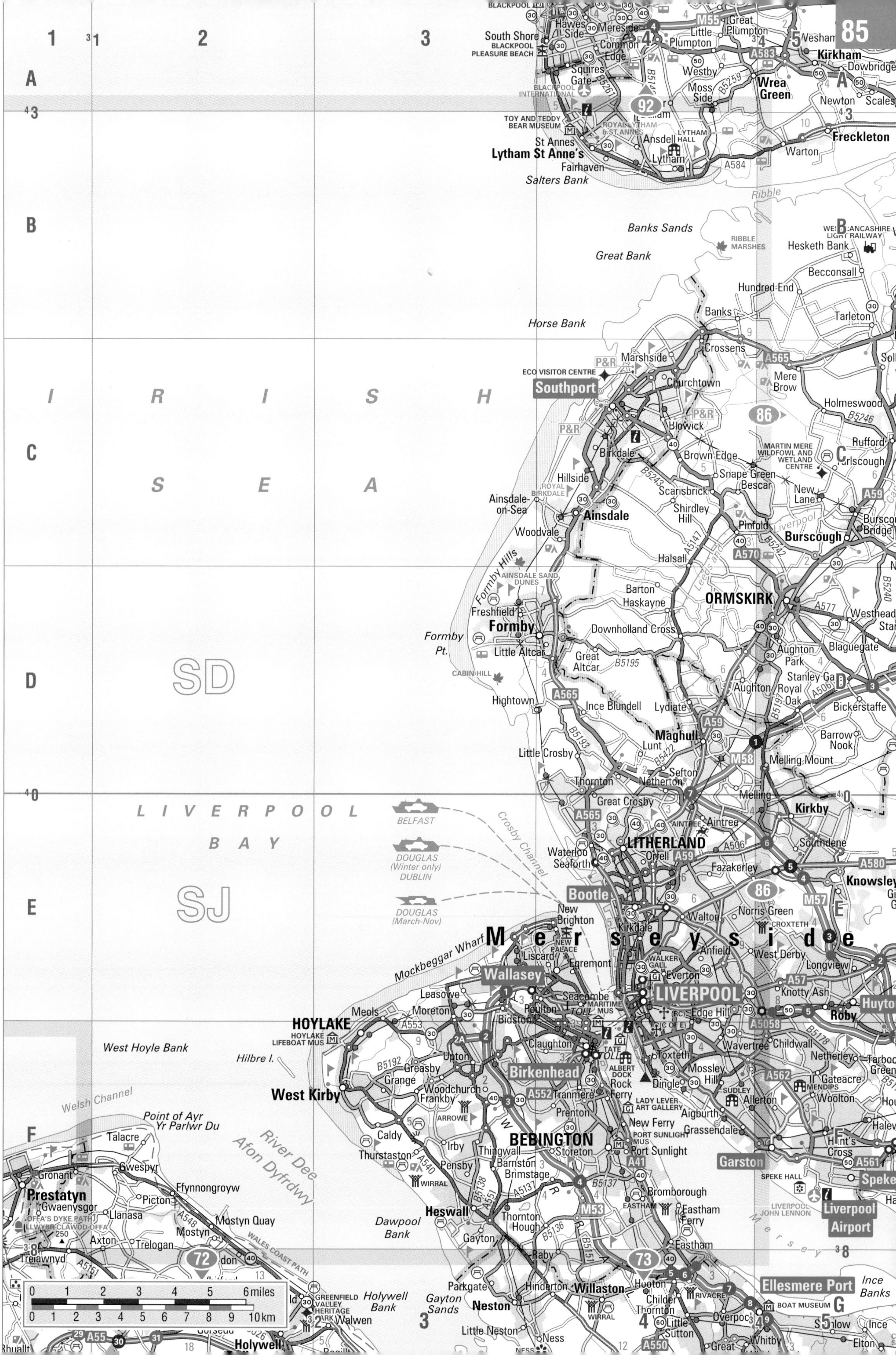

IRISH SEA
LIVERPOOL BAY
SD
SJ
Merseyside
BLACKPOOL
South Shore
BLACKPOOL PLEASURE BEACH
Hawes Side
Mereside
Common Edge
Squires Gate
BLACKPOOL INTERNATIONAL
TOY AND TEDDY BEAR MUSEUM
ROYAL LYTHAM & ST ANNES
St Annes
Lytham St Anne's
Fairhaven
Salters Bank
Ansdell
LYTHAM HALL
Lytham
Great Plumpton
Little Plumpton
Westby
Moss Side
Wrea Green
Wesham
Kirkham
Dowbridge
Newton
Scales
Freckleton
Warton
Ribble
Banks Sands
Great Bank
RIBBLE MARSHES
WEST LANCASHIRE LIGHT RAILWAY
Hesketh Bank
Becconsall
Hundred End
Tarleton
Horse Bank
Banks
Crossens
Marshside
ECO VISITOR CENTRE
Southport
Churchtown
Mere Brow
Holmeswood
Rufford
Blowick
Birkdale
Brown Edge
MARTIN MERE WILDFOWL AND WETLAND CENTRE
Snape Green
Bescar
Hillside
ROYAL BIRKDALE
Scarisbrick
New Lane
Ainsdale-on-Sea
Ainsdale
Shirdley Hill
Woodvale
Pinfold
Burscough
Burscough Bridge
Halsall
Formby Hills
AINSDALE SAND DUNES
Barton
Haskayne
ORMSKIRK
Westhead
Freshfield
Formby
Downholland Cross
Formby Pt.
Little Altcar
Great Altcar
Aughton Park
Blaguegate
CABIN HILL
Stanley Gate
Aughton
Royal Oak
Bickerstaffe
Hightown
Ince Blundell
Lydiate
Barrow Nook
Maghull
Lunt
Little Crosby
Melling Mount
Sefton
Thornton
Netherton
Melling
Kirkby
Great Crosby
BELFAST
Crosby Channel
AINTREE
Aintree
DOUGLAS (Winter only) DUBLIN
Waterloo
Seaforth
LITHERLAND
Orrell
Southdene
Fazakerley
Knowsley
Bootle
DOUGLAS (March-Nov)
New Brighton
Walton
Norris Green
CROXTETH
Kirkdale
Mockbeggar Wharf
NEW PALACE
Liscard
Anfield
West Derby
Egremont
Wallasey
WALKER GALL
Everton
Longview
Leasowe
Seacombe
LIVERPOOL
Knotty Ash
Huyton
Meols
Moreton
Poulton
MARITIME MUS
Edge Hill
Roby
HOYLAKE
HOYLAKE LIFEBOAT MUS
Bidston
Wavertree
Childwall
Claughton
TATE
West Hoyle Bank
Hilbre I.
Upton
Toxteth
Netherley
Tarbock Green
Greasby
Birkenhead
ALBERT DOCK
Mossley Hill
Gateacre
Grange
Rock
Dingle
MENDIPS
Woodchurch
Tranmere
Ferry
SUDLEY
Allerton
Woolton
Welsh Channel
West Kirby
Frankby
ARROWE
LADY LEVER ART GALLERY
Aigburth
Point of Ayr
Yr Parlwr Du
Prenton
New Ferry
River Dee
Afon Dyfrdwy
Caldy
BEBINGTON
PORT SUNLIGHT MUS
Grassendale
Hunt's Cross
Talacre
Thurstaston
Irby
Thingwall
Storeton
Port Sunlight
Garston
Gronant
Gwespyr
Pensby
Barnston
Brimstage
SPEKE HALL
Speke
Prestatyn
WIRRAL
Ffynnongroyw
Bromborough
Gwaenysgor
Picton
EASTHAM
Eastham Ferry
LIVERPOOL JOHN LENNON
Liverpool Airport
OFFA'S DYKE PATH
LLWYBR CLAWDD OFFA
Llanasa
Heswall
Thornton Hough
Dawpool Bank
Mostyn Quay
Mostyn
Axton
Trelogan
Gayton
Eastham
Mersey
Trelawnyd
WALES COAST PATH
Raby
Parkgate
Hinderton
Willaston
Hooton
Ellesmere Port
Ince Banks
GREENFIELD VALLEY HERITAGE PARK
Holywell Bank
Gayton Sands
Neston
WIRRAL
Childer Thornton
RIVACRE
BOAT MUSEUM
Walwen
Little Sutton
Overpool
Stanlow
Ince
Gorsedd
Holywell
Little Neston
Ness
Whitby
Great
Elton
Bhuallt
0 1 2 3 4 5 6 miles
0 1 2 3 4 5 6 7 8 9 10 km

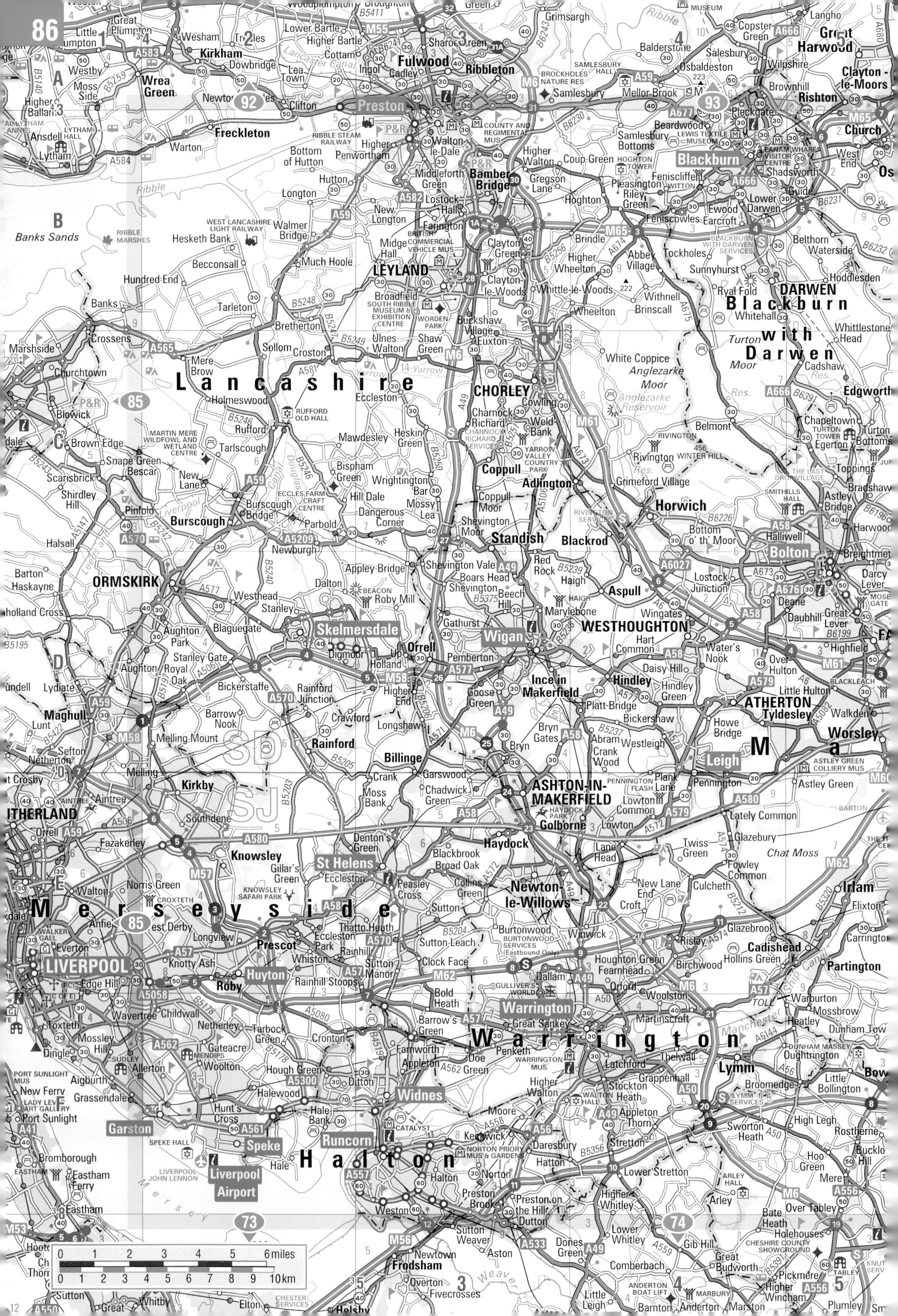

Lancashire
Merseyside
Warrington
Halton
Blackburn with Darwen
Preston
Blackburn
Bolton
Wigan
St Helens
Skelmersdale
Leigh
Huyton
LIVERPOOL
Widnes
Runcorn
Speke
Garston
Liverpool Airport
Fulwood
Ribbleton
Kirkham
Wrea Green
Freckleton
Lytham
Ansdell
Warton
Longton
Hesketh Bank
Banks Sands
Tarleton
Bretherton
LEYLAND
CHORLEY
Coppull
Adlington
Horwich
Standish
ORMSKIRK
Burscough
Rufford
Parbold
Orrell
Rainford
Billinge
Kirkby
Maghull
Knowsley
Prescot
ASHTON-IN-MAKERFIELD
Golborne
Haydock
Newton-le-Willows
Hindley
WESTHOUGHTON
ATHERTON
Tyldesley
Worsley
Irlam
Cadishead
Lymm
Frodsham
DARWEN
Bamber Bridge
Penwortham
Ince in Makerfield
Walton-le-Dale
Samlesbury
Rishton
Clayton-le-Moors
Great Harwood
Church
Edgworth
Turton Moor
Anglezarke Moor
Chat Moss
Banks
Crossens
Churchtown
Marshside
Scarisbrick
Halsall
Aughton
Lydiate
Melling
Aintree
Fazakerley
Walton
Everton
Roby
Woolton
Hale
Halewood
Daresbury
Moore
Preston Brook
Sutton Weaver
Grappenhall
Thelwall
Culcheth
Glazebury
Partington
Carrington
Flixton
0 1 2 3 4 5 6 miles
0 1 2 3 4 5 6 7 8 9 10 km
92
93
85
73
74

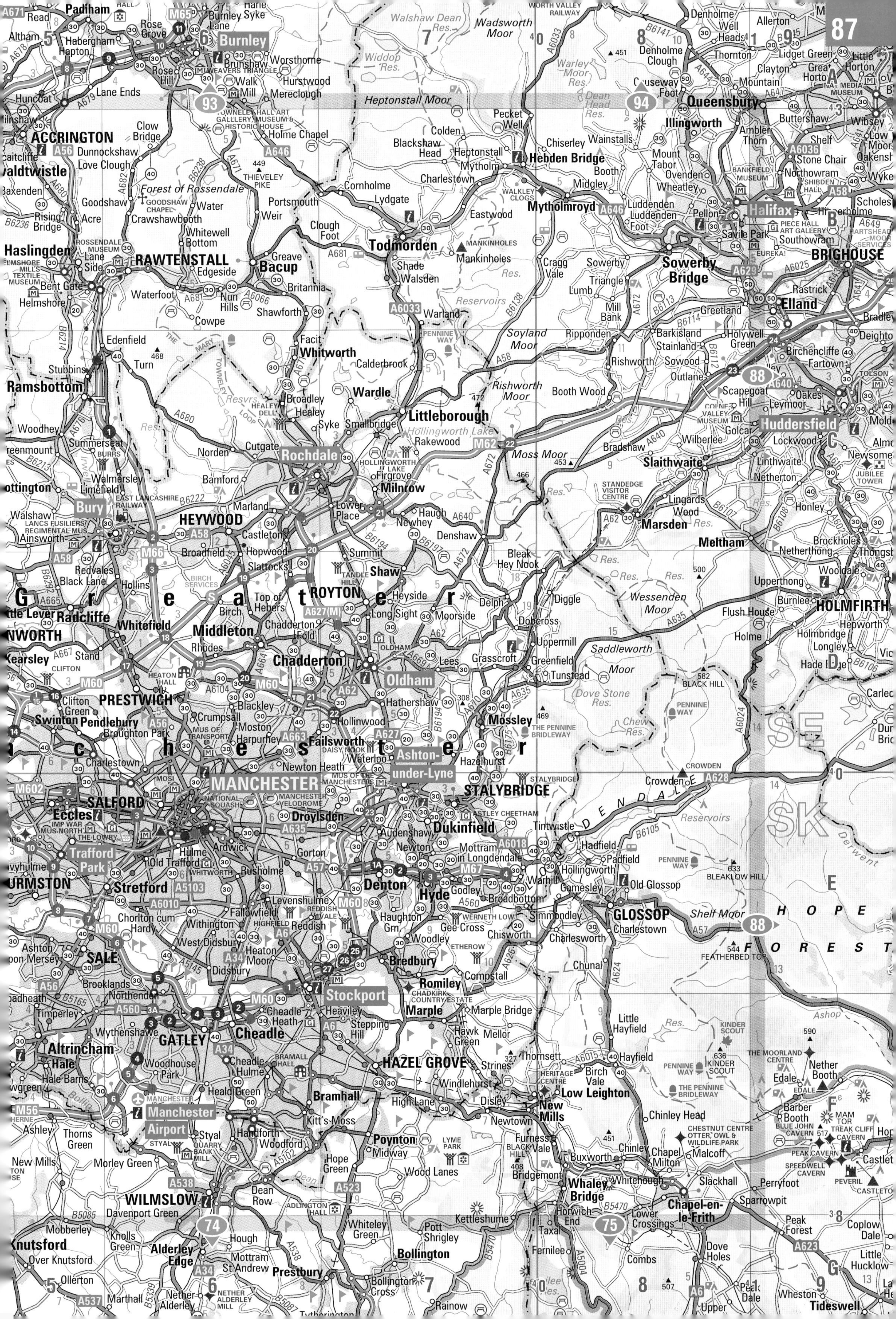
Padiham
Burnley
Accrington
Oswaldtwistle
Haslingden
Rawtenstall
Bacup
Todmorden
Hebden Bridge
Mytholmroyd
Heptonstall Moor
Queensbury
Halifax
Brighouse
Sowerby Bridge
Elland
Huddersfield
Whitworth
Ramsbottom
Bury
Heywood
Rochdale
Littleborough
Milnrow
Marsden
Slaithwaite
Meltham
Holmfirth
Royton
Shaw
Middleton
Radcliffe
Prestwich
Chadderton
Oldham
Mossley
Ashton-under-Lyne
Stalybridge
Dukinfield
Droylsden
Manchester
Salford
Eccles
Trafford Park
Urmston
Stretford
Sale
Denton
Hyde
Glossop
Stockport
Bredbury
Romiley
Marple
Cheadle
Gatley
Altrincham
Hale
Hazel Grove
Bramhall
Manchester Airport
Poynton
Wilmslow
New Mills
Low Leighton
Whaley Bridge
Chapel-en-le-Frith
Knutsford
Alderley Edge
Prestbury
Bollington
Tideswell
Edale
Hope Forest
Longdendale
Saddleworth Moor
Greater Manchester

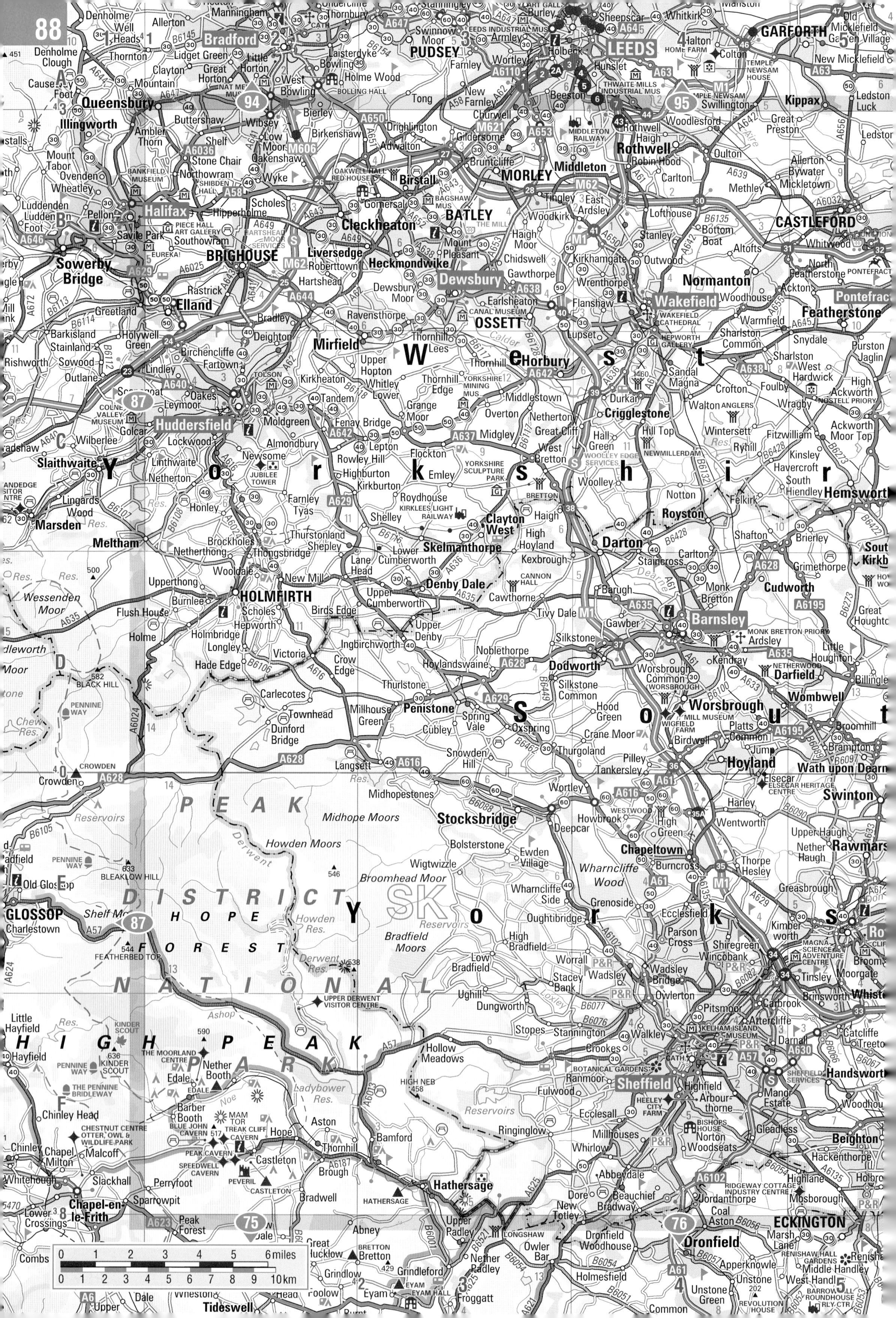
Bradford
LEEDS
PUDSEY
GARFORTH
Queensbury
Halifax
BRIGHOUSE
Cleckheaton
BATLEY
MORLEY
Rothwell
CASTLEFORD
Dewsbury
OSSETT
Wakefield
Normanton
Featherstone
Sowerby Bridge
Elland
Huddersfield
Mirfield
Horbury
Slaithwaite
Marsden
Meltham
HOLMFIRTH
Skelmanthorpe
Denby Dale
Darton
Barnsley
Hemsworth
Cudworth
Darfield
Wombwell
Worsbrough
Penistone
Stocksbridge
Chapeltown
Hoyland
Sheffield
Rotherham
GLOSSOP
Chapel-en-le-Frith
Castleton
Hathersage
Dronfield
ECKINGTON
West Yorkshire
South Yorkshire
PEAK DISTRICT NATIONAL PARK
HOPE FOREST
HIGH PEAK
SK
0 1 2 3 4 5 6 miles
0 1 2 3 4 5 6 7 8 9 10 km

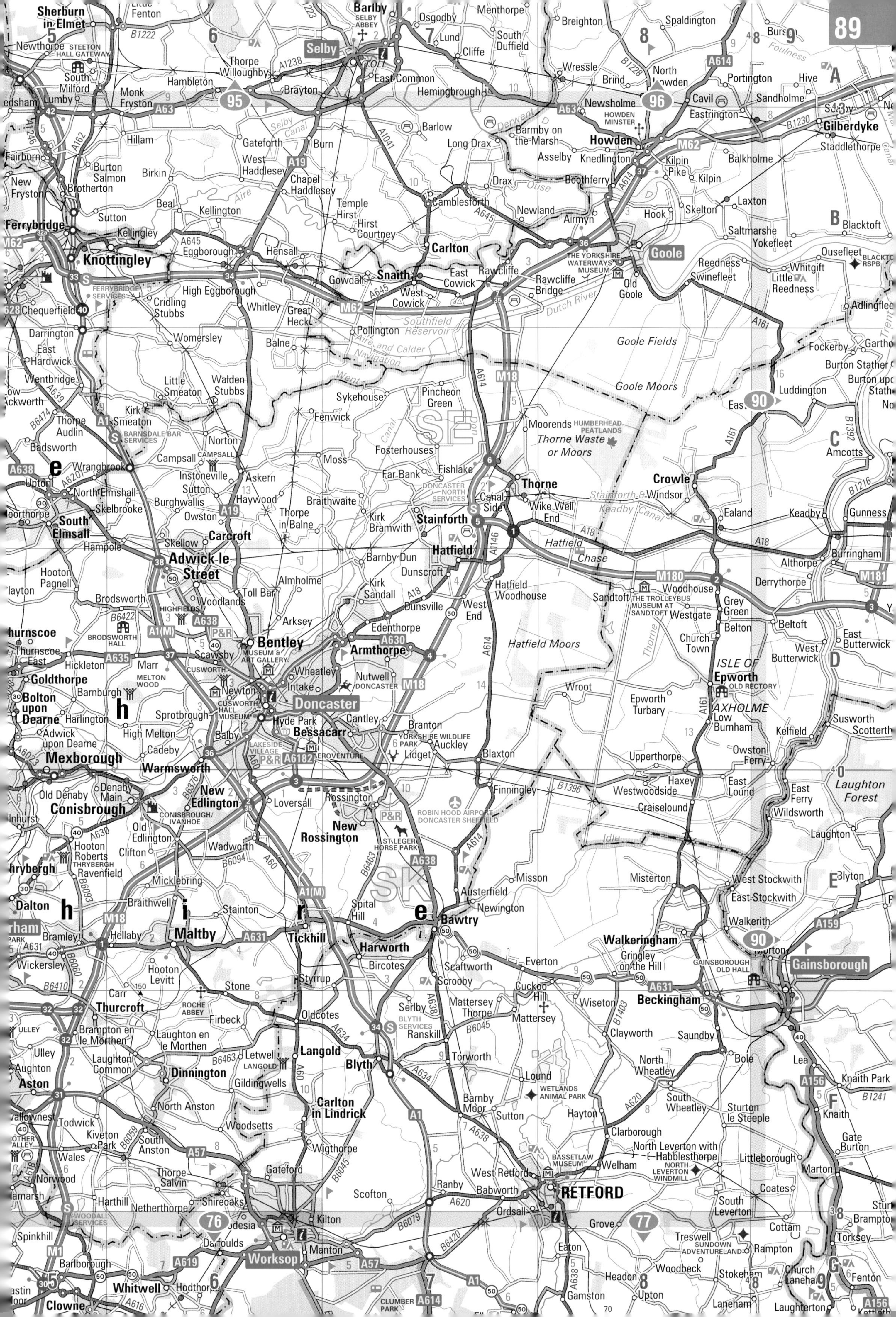

Sherburn in Elmet
Fenton
Barlby
Selby Abbey
Osgodby
Menthorpe
Breighton
Spaldington
Newthorpe
Steeton Hall Gateway
Selby
Thorpe Willoughby
Lund
Cliffe
South Duffield
Wressle
North Howden
Portington
Hive
South Milford
Hambleton
East Common
Hemingbrough
Brind
Monk Fryston
Lumby
Brayton
Newsholme
Howden Minster
Cavil
Sandholme
Eastrington
Gilberdyke
Staddlethorpe
Hillam
Gateforth
Burn
Barlow
Barmby on the Marsh
Long Drax
Asselby
Howden
Knedlington
Kilpin Pike
Kilpin
Balkholme
Fairburn
Burton Salmon
Birkin
West Haddlesey
Chapel Haddlesey
Drax
Boothferry
New Fryston
Brotherton
Beal
Kellington
Temple Hirst
Camblesforth
Newland
Airmyn
Hook
Skelton
Laxton
Sutton
Hirst Courtney
Ferrybridge
Kellingley
Eggborough
Hensall
Carlton
The Yorkshire Waterways Museum
Goole
Saltmarshe
Yokefleet
Blacktoft
Knottingley
Snaith
East Cowick
Rawcliffe
Rawcliffe Bridge
Old Goole
Reedness
Swinefleet
Ousefleet
Whitgift
Little Reedness
Gowdall
West Cowick
High Eggborough
Ferrybridge Services
Cridling Stubbs
Whitley
Great Heck
Southfield Reservoir
Dutch River
Chequerfield
Pollington
Aire and Calder Navigation
Adlingfleet
Darrington
East Hardwick
Womersley
Balne
Goole Fields
Fockerby
Garthorpe
Burton Stather
Went
Wentbridge
Little Smeaton
Walden Stubbs
Goole Moors
Luddington
Ackworth
Sykehouse
Pincheon Green
Kirk Smeaton
Thorpe Audlin
Fenwick
Moorends
Humberhead Peatlands
Thorne Waste or Moors
Amcotts
Barnsdale Bar Services
Norton
Badsworth
Fosterhouses
Wrangbrook
Campsall
Moss
Fishlake
Upton
Instoneville
Askern
Far Bank
Doncaster North Services
Thorne
Crowle
North Elmshall
Sutton
Canal Side
Stainforth & Keadby Canal
Windsor
Skelbrooke
Burghwallis
Haywood
Braithwaite
Wike Well End
Moorthorpe
South Elmsall
Owston
Thorpe in Balne
Kirk Bramwith
Stainforth
Ealand
Keadby
Gunness
Carcroft
Hampole
Skellow
Hatfield
Hatfield Chase
Burringham
Adwick le Street
Barnby Dun
Dunscroft
Althorpe
Hooton Pagnell
Clayton
Almholme
Kirk Sandall
Hatfield Woodhouse
Woodhouse
Derrythorpe
Brodsworth
Woodlands
Toll Bar
Dunsville
West End
Sandtoft
The Trolleybus Museum at Sandtoft
Westgate
Grey Green
Highfields
Arksey
Edenthorpe
Belton
Beltoft
Thurnscoe
Brodsworth Hall
Bentley
Armthorpe
Hatfield Moors
Church Town
East Butterwick
West Butterwick
Thurnscoe East
Hickleton
Marr
Scawsby
Museum & Art Gallery
Nutwell
Doncaster
Isle of Axholme
Epworth
Old Rectory
Goldthorpe
Melton Wood
Cusworth
Wheatley
Intake
Wroot
Epworth Turbary
Bolton upon Dearne
Barnburgh
Newton
Cusworth Hall Museum
Cantley
Low Burnham
Kelfield
Susworth
Scotterthorpe
Harlington
Sprotbrough
Hyde Park
Branton
Yorkshire Wildlife Park
Adwick upon Dearne
High Melton
Balby
Bessacarr
Auckley
Cadeby
Lakeside Village
Lidget
Blaxton
Upperthorpe
Owston Ferry
Mexborough
Warmsworth
Aeroventure
Haxey
East Lound
Laughton Forest
Old Denaby
Denaby Main
New Edlington
Loversall
Rossington
Finningley
Westwoodside
East Ferry
Conisbrough
Conisbrough Ivanhoe
Robin Hood Airport Doncaster Sheffield
Craiselound
Wildsworth
Old Edlington
New Rossington
Laughton
Hooton Roberts
Wadworth
St Leger Horse Park
Idle
Thrybergh
Ravenfield
Clifton
Misson
Misterton
West Stockwith
Blyton
Micklebring
Austerfield
East Stockwith
Dalton
Braithwell
Stainton
Spital Hill
Newington
Walkerith
Bramley
Hellaby
Maltby
Tickhill
Bawtry
Walkeringham
Morton
Wickersley
Harworth
Bircotes
Scaftworth
Everton
Gringley on the Hill
Gainsborough Old Hall
Gainsborough
Hooton Levitt
Styrrup
Scrooby
Carr
Stone
Cuckoo Hill
Wiseton
Beckingham
Thurcroft
Roche Abbey
Serlby
Mattersey Thorpe
Mattersey
Firbeck
Oldcotes
Blyth Services
Brampton en le Morthen
Laughton en le Morthen
Ranskill
Clayworth
Saundby
Ulley
Letwell
Langold
Torworth
Bole
Laughton Common
Dinnington
Blyth
North Wheatley
Lea
Aughton
Aston
Gildingwells
Lound
Wetlands Animal Park
Knaith Park
South Wheatley
Sturton le Steeple
North Anston
Carlton in Lindrick
Barnby Moor
Sutton
Hayton
Knaith
Swallownest
Todwick
Woodsetts
Kiveton Park
South Anston
Clarborough
Gate Burton
Wales
Wigthorpe
Bassetlaw Museum
North Leverton with Habblesthorpe
North Leverton Windmill
Littleborough
Welham
Marton
Thorpe Salvin
Gateford
West Retford
Norwood
Harthill
Shireoaks
Netherthorpe
Scofton
Ranby
Babworth
Retford
Coates
Woodall Services
Kilton
Ordsall
South Leverton
Sturton
Brampton
Spinkhill
Rhodesia
Darfoulds
Grove
Treswell
Sundown Adventureland
Rampton
Cottam
Torksey
Worksop
Manton
Eaton
Barlborough
Whitwell
Hodthorpe
Woodbeck
Stokeham
Church Laneham
Fenton
Headon
Upton
Gamston
Laneham
Laughterton
Clowne
Clumber Park
Ketlethorpe

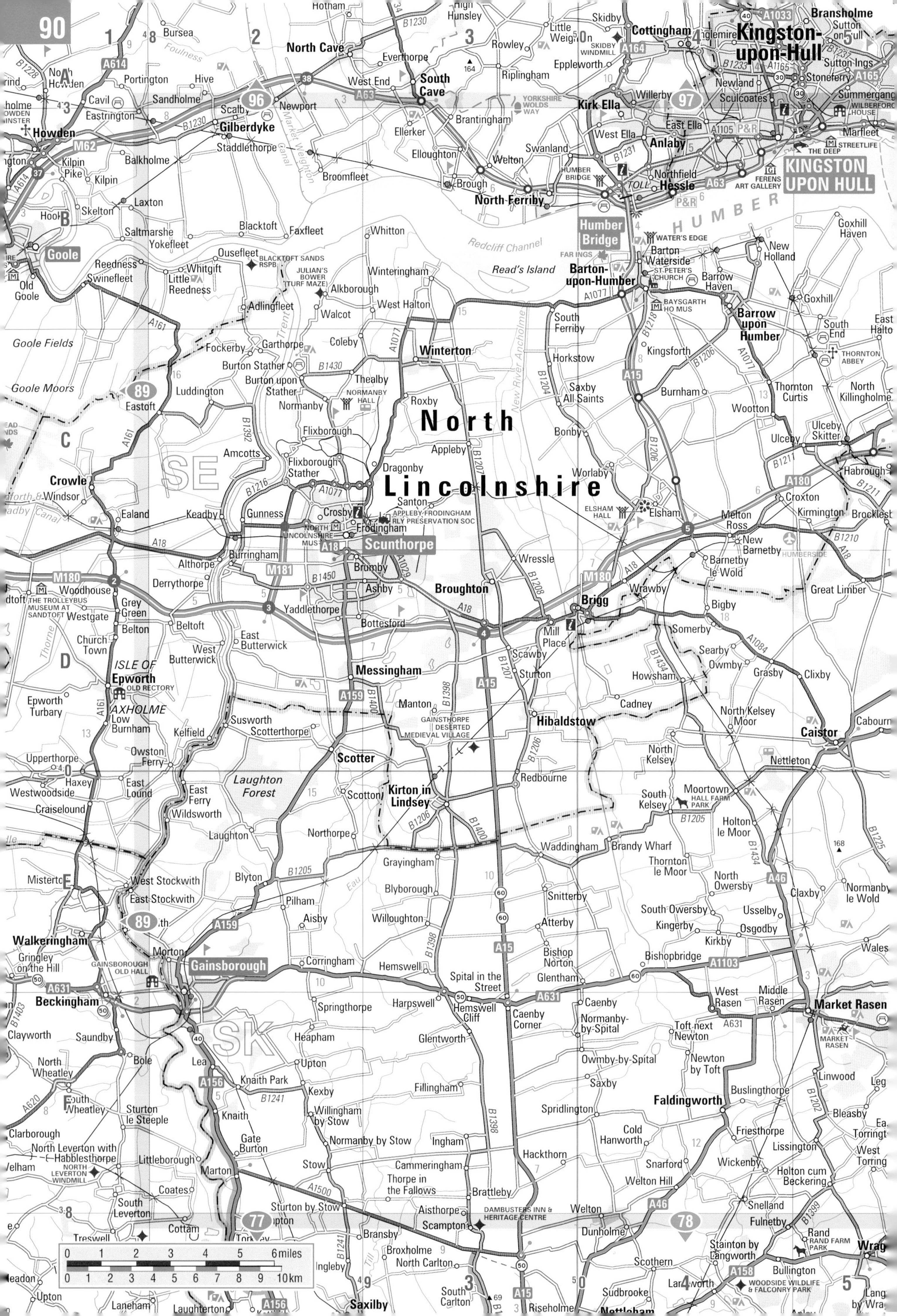
North Lincolnshire
Kingston-upon-Hull
KINGSTON UPON HULL
HUMBER
Humber Bridge
Scunthorpe
Goole
Gainsborough
Hotham
High Hunsley
Skidby
Cottingham
Bransholme
Sutton-on-Hull
Bursea
Foulness
North Cave
Little Weighton
SKIDBY WINDMILL
Rowley
Everthorpe
Eppleworth
Riplingham
Portington
Hive
West End
South Cave
Sutton Ings
Stoneferry
Newland
Summergangs
Sculcoates
WILBERFORCE HOUSE
Cavil
Sandholme
Newport
YORKSHIRE WOLDS WAY
Kirk Ella
Willerby
Eastrington
Scalby
Gilberdyke
Ellerker
Brantingham
East Ella
Marfleet
Howden
Staddlethorpe
Market Weighton Canal
West Ella
Anlaby
THE DEEP
STREETLIFE
Kilpin Pike
Balkholme
Kilpin
Elloughton
Swanland
Welton
Broomfleet
Brough
HUMBER BRIDGE
Northfield
Hessle
FERENS ART GALLERY
North Ferriby
Laxton
Skelton
Hook
Saltmarshe
Yokefleet
Blacktoft
Faxfleet
Whitton
Redcliff Channel
Goxhill Haven
WATER'S EDGE
Barton Waterside
New Holland
Ousefleet
BLACKTOFT SANDS RSPB
FAR INGS
Read's Island
Barton-upon-Humber
ST PETER'S CHURCH
Barrow Haven
Reedness
Whitgift
Little Reedness
JULIAN'S BOWER (TURF MAZE)
Winteringham
Old Goole
Swinefleet
Alkborough
Goxhill
BAYSGARTH HO MUS
Adlingfleet
Walcot
West Halton
South Ferriby
Barrow upon Humber
East Halton
South End
Goole Fields
Fockerby
Garthorpe
Coleby
Winterton
Kingsforth
Trent
New River Ancholme
Burton Stather
Horkstow
THORNTON ABBEY
Thealby
Burton upon Stather
Luddington
NORMANBY HALL
Goole Moors
Eastoft
Normanby
Roxby
Saxby All Saints
Burnham
Thornton Curtis
North Killingholme
Wootton
Flixborough
Bonby
Ulceby Skitter
Ulceby
Crowle
Amcotts
Appleby
Flixborough Stather
Worlaby
Habrough
Dragonby
Lincolnshire
Stainforth & Keadby Canal
Windsor
Santon
Croxton
Ealand
Keadby
Gunness
Crosby
APPLEBY-FRODINGHAM RLY PRESERVATION SOC
ELSHAM HALL
Elsham
Melton Ross
Kirmington
Brocklesby
NORTH LINCOLNSHIRE MUS
Frodingham
New Barnetby
HUMBERSIDE
Burringham
Brumby
Wressle
Barnetby le Wold
Althorpe
Derrythorpe
Ashby
Broughton
Wrawby
Great Limber
Woodhouse
Grey Green
THE TROLLEYBUS MUSEUM AT SANDTOFT
Westgate
Yaddlethorpe
Brigg
Bigby
Belton
Beltoft
Bottesford
Mill Place
Somerby
Church Town
East Butterwick
West Butterwick
Scawby
Searby
Owmby
Thorne
ISLE OF AXHOLME
Epworth
OLD RECTORY
Messingham
Sturton
Howsham
Grasby
Clixby
Epworth Turbary
Manton
Cadney
Low Burnham
GAINSTHORPE DESERTED MEDIEVAL VILLAGE
Hibaldstow
North Kelsey Moor
Susworth
Scotterthorpe
Kelfield
Caistor
Cabourne
Owston Ferry
Scotter
North Kelsey
Nettleton
Upperthorpe
Haxey
Laughton Forest
Redbourne
Westwoodside
East Lound
East Ferry
Scotton
Kirton in Lindsey
South Kelsey
Moortown
HALL FARM PARK
Craiselound
Wildsworth
Holton le Moor
Laughton
Northorpe
Waddingham
Brandy Wharf
Grayingham
Thornton le Moor
Misterton
West Stockwith
Blyton
Eau
North Owersby
Normanby le Wold
East Stockwith
Blyborough
Snitterby
Claxby
Pilham
Aisby
South Owersby
Usselby
Willoughton
Atterby
Kingerby
Osgodby
Walkeringham
Morton
Kirkby
Bishop Norton
Wales
Gringley on the Hill
GAINSBOROUGH OLD HALL
Corringham
Bishopbridge
Hemswell
Glentham
Beckingham
Spital in the Street
West Rasen
Middle Rasen
Market Rasen
Springthorpe
Harpswell
Hemswell Cliff
Caenby
Caenby Corner
Normanby-by-Spital
Toft next Newton
MARKET RASEN
Clayworth
Saundby
Heapham
Glentworth
Bole
Lea
Upton
Owmby-by-Spital
Newton by Toft
North Wheatley
Knaith Park
Kexby
Saxby
Linwood
South Wheatley
Sturton le Steeple
Knaith
Willingham by Stow
Fillingham
Faldingworth
Buslingthorpe
Leg
Spridlington
Bleasby
Clarborough
Gate Burton
Cold Hanworth
Friesthorpe
East Torrington
North Leverton with Habblesthorpe
Normanby by Stow
Ingham
Hackthorn
Lissington
West Torrington
NORTH LEVERTON WINDMILL
Littleborough
Stow
Cammeringham
Snarford
Wickenby
Holton cum Beckering
Marton
Thorpe in the Fallows
Welton Hill
Coates
South Leverton
Sturton by Stow
Brattleby
Snelland
Aisthorpe
DAMBUSTERS INN & HERITAGE CENTRE
Welton
Scampton
Dunholme
Fulnetby
Cottam
Treswell
Bransby
Rand
RAND FARM PARK
Stainton by Langworth
Wragby
Broxholme
North Carlton
Scothern
Ingleby
Bullington
Larworth
WOODSIDE WILDLIFE & FALCONRY PARK
Saxilby
South Carlton
Sudbrooke
Lang by Wragby
Laneham
Laughterton
Riseholme
Nettleham
SE
SK
M62
M180
M181
A614
A63
A1033
A164
A165
A1165
A1105
A161
A1077
A15
A18
A1029
A159
A180
A1084
A46
A1103
A631
A156
A620
A1500
A158
B1228
B1230
B1231
B1237
B1233
B1430
B1216
B1392
B1450
B1207
B1204
B1206
B1218
B1211
B1210
B1208
B1434
B1400
B1398
B1205
B1241
B1403
B1225
B1202
B1399
96
97
89
77
78
0 1 2 3 4 5 6 miles
0 1 2 3 4 5 6 7 8 9 10 km

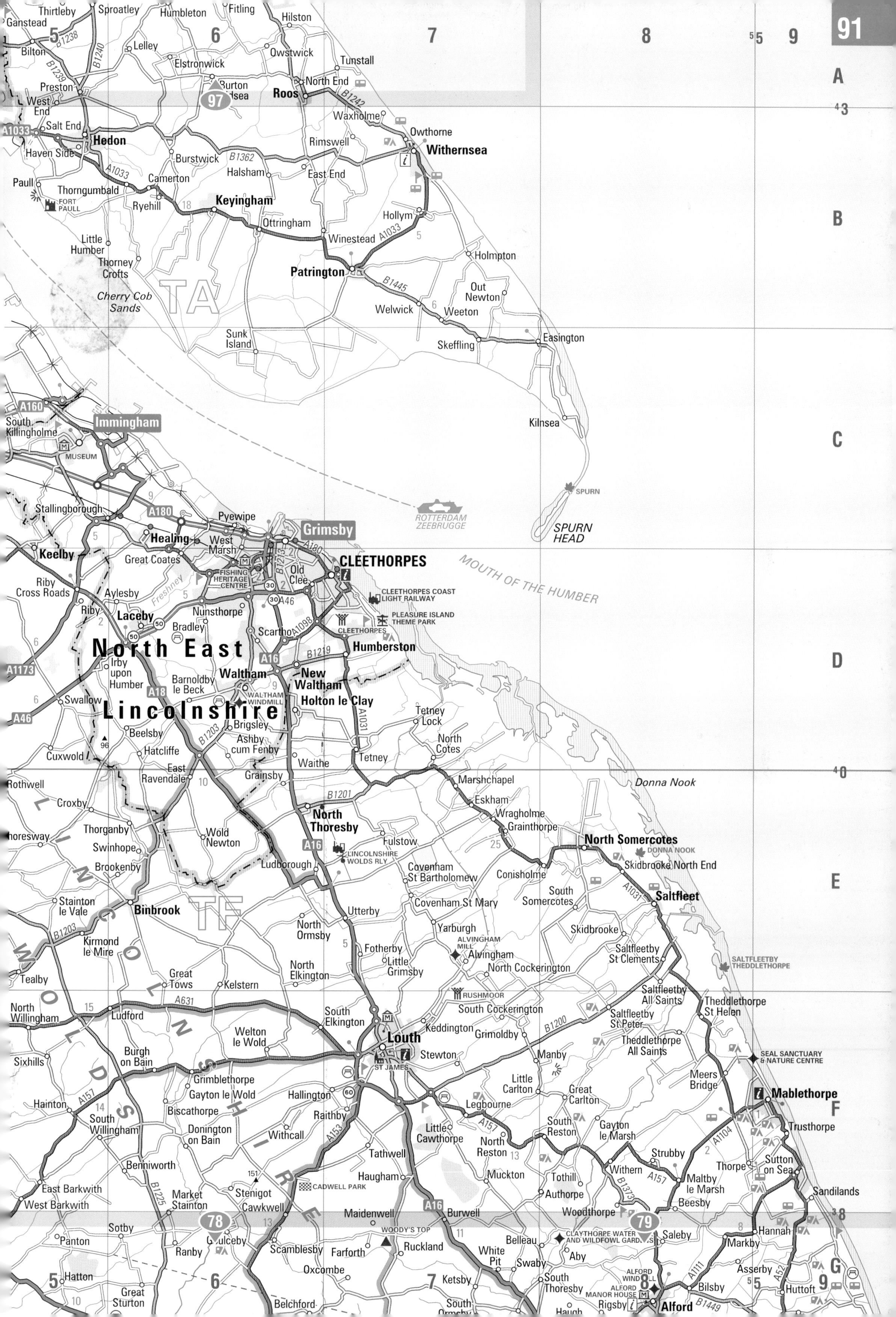
5
6
7
8
9
A
B
C
D
E
F
G
Thirtleby
Sproatley
Humbleton
Fitling
Hilston
Ganstead
Bilton
Lelley
Owstwick
Tunstall
Elstronwick
Preston
Burton Pidsea
North End
Roos
97
West End
Waxholme
Salt End
A1033
Hedon
Owthorne
Rimswell
Withernsea
Haven Side
Burstwick
B1362
Halsham
East End
Paull
Camerton
Thorngumbald
FORT PAULL
Ryehill
Keyingham
Hollym
Ottringham
Little Humber
Winestead
A1033
Holmpton
Thorney Crofts
Patrington
B1445
Out Newton
Cherry Cob Sands
TA
Welwick
Weeton
Sunk Island
Skeffling
Easington
A160
South Killingholme
Immingham
MUSEUM
Kilnsea
SPURN
Stallingborough
A180
Pyewipe
ROTTERDAM ZEEBRUGGE
Grimsby
SPURN HEAD
Healing
West Marsh
Keelby
Great Coates
CLEETHORPES
MOUTH OF THE HUMBER
FISHING HERITAGE CENTRE
Old Clee
Riby Cross Roads
Aylesby
Freshney
CLEETHORPES COAST LIGHT RAILWAY
Riby
Laceby
Nunsthorpe
A46
PLEASURE ISLAND THEME PARK
Bradley
Scartho
A1098
CLEETHORPES
North East
Humberston
A1173
Irby upon Humber
A16
B1219
Waltham
New Waltham
Barnoldby le Beck
A18
WALTHAM WINDMILL
Holton le Clay
Swallow
Lincolnshire
A46
Brigsley
A1031
Tetney Lock
Beelsby
B1203
Ashby cum Fenby
North Cotes
Cuxwold
Hatcliffe
Tetney
Waithe
East Ravendale
Grainsby
Rothwell
Donna Nook
Marshchapel
B1201
Croxby
Eskham
North Thoresby
Wragholme
Thorganby
Wold Newton
Grainthorpe
North Somercotes
Swinhope
Fulstow
DONNA NOOK
A16
LINCOLNSHIRE WOLDS RLY
Skidbrooke North End
Ludborough
Covenham St Bartholomew
Conisholme
Brookenby
A1031
South Somercotes
Saltfleet
Stainton le Vale
Binbrook
TF
Covenham St Mary
Utterby
Skidbrooke
B1203
North Ormsby
Yarburgh
Fotherby
ALVINGHAM MILL
Alvingham
Saltfleetby St Clements
SALTFLEETBY THEDDLETHORPE
Kirmond le Mire
Little Grimsby
Tealby
North Elkington
North Cockerington
Great Tows
Kelstern
Saltfleetby All Saints
A631
RUSHMOOR
Theddlethorpe St Helen
North Willingham
Ludford
South Elkington
South Cockerington
Saltfleetby St Peter
Welton le Wold
Keddington
B1200
Louth
Grimoldby
Theddlethorpe All Saints
Burgh on Bain
Sixhills
Stewton
Manby
SEAL SANCTUARY & NATURE CENTRE
ST JAMES
Grimblethorpe
Meers Bridge
Little Carlton
Gayton le Wold
Hallington
Great Carlton
Mablethorpe
Hainton
A157
Biscathorpe
Raithby
Legbourne
South Willingham
A157
South Reston
Gayton le Marsh
Trusthorpe
Donington on Bain
Witchcall
A153
Little Cawthorpe
A1104
North Reston
Strubby
Sutton on Sea
Tathwell
Thorpe
Benniworth
Withern
A157
Haugham
Muckton
Tothill
Maltby le Marsh
East Barkwith
Stenigot
CADWELL PARK
B1373
Sandilands
Market Stainton
Authorpe
West Barkwith
Cawkwell
B1225
Beesby
Woodthorpe
Maidenwell
A16
Burwell
78
79
Sotby
WOODY'S TOP
CLAYTHORPE WATER AND WILDFOWL GARDENS
Saleby
Hannah
Panton
Goulceby
Ruckland
Belleau
Markby
Ranby
Scamblesby
Farforth
White Pit
Aby
Swaby
A1111
Asserby
Oxcombe
Hatton
Ketsby
South Thoresby
ALFORD WINDMILL
A52
Bilsby
Great Sturton
Belchford
South Ormsby
ALFORD MANOR HOUSE
Huttoft
Haugh
Rigsby
Alford
B1449

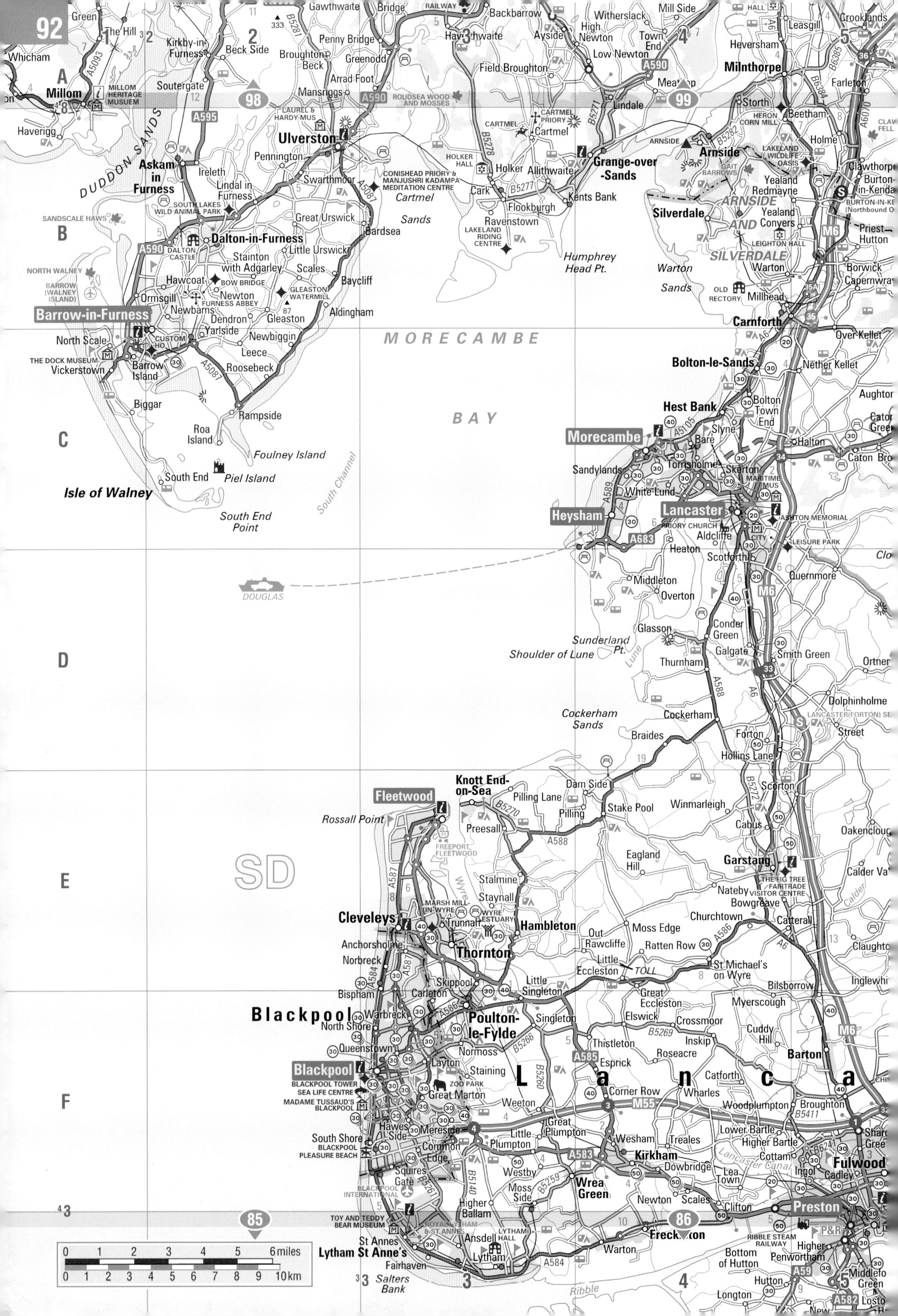

Green
The Hill
Whicham
Millom
MILLOM HERITAGE MUSEUM
Haverigg
DUDDON SANDS
Kirkby-in-Furness
Beck Side
Soutergate
Askam in Furness
Ireleth
Lindal in Furness
SOUTH LAKES WILD ANIMAL PARK
SANDSCALE HAWS
Dalton-in-Furness
DALTON CASTLE
NORTH WALNEY
BARROW (WALNEY ISLAND)
Hawcoat
BOW BRIDGE
Ormsgill
Newton
FURNESS ABBEY
Newbarns
Barrow-in-Furness
Dendron
Yarlside
North Scale
CUSTOM HO
THE DOCK MUSEUM
Vickerstown
Barrow Island
Biggar
Roa Island
Rampside
Foulney Island
Piel Island
South End
Isle of Walney
South End Point
South Channel
Gawthwaite
Bridge
RAILWAY
Penny Bridge
Broughton Beck
Greenodd
Arrad Foot
Mansriggs
LAUREL & HARDY MUS
ROUDSEA WOOD AND MOSSES
Ulverston
Pennington
Swarthmoor
CONISHEAD PRIORY & MANJUSHRI KADAMPA MEDITATION CENTRE
Cartmel Sands
Great Urswick
Little Urswick
Bardsea
Stainton with Adgarley
Scales
Baycliff
GLEASTON WATERMILL
Gleaston
Aldingham
Newbiggin
Leece
Roosebeck
MORECAMBE
BAY
Backbarrow
Haverthwaite
Ayside
High Newton
Witherslack
Low Newton
Field Broughton
Town End
Mill Side
Meathop
Lindale
CARTMEL
CARTMEL PRIORY
Cartmel
HOLKER HALL
Holker
Cark
Allithwaite
Flookburgh
Grange-over-Sands
Kents Bank
Ravenstown
LAKELAND RIDING CENTRE
Humphrey Head Pt.
HALL
Leasgill
Crooklands
Heversham
Milnthorpe
Farleton
Storth
Beetham
HERON CORN MILL
Holme
Arnside
LAKELAND WILDLIFE OASIS
GAIT BARROWS
Clawthorpe
Burton-in-Kendal
Yealand Redmayne
ARNSIDE AND SILVERDALE
Silverdale
Yealand Conyers
BURTON-IN-KENDAL (Northbound Only)
Priest Hutton
LEIGHTON HALL
Warton
Warton Sands
Borwick
Capernwray
OLD RECTORY
Millhead
Carnforth
Over Kellet
Bolton-le-Sands
Nether Kellet
Aughton
Hest Bank
Bolton Town End
Slyne
Morecambe
Bare
Halton
Caton
Torrisholme
Skerton
MARITIME MUS
Sandylands
White Lund
Heysham
Lancaster
ASHTON MEMORIAL
PRIORY CHURCH
Aldcliffe
CITY
LEISURE PARK
Heaton
Scotforth
Quernmore
DOUGLAS
Middleton
Overton
Conder Green
Glasson
Sunderland Pt.
Shoulder of Lune
Lune
Thurnham
Galgate
Smith Green
Cockerham Sands
Cockerham
Dolphinholme
LANCASTER (FORTON) SERVICES
Braides
Forton
Street
Hollins Lane
Knott End-on-Sea
Fleetwood
Rossall Point
Dam Side
Pilling Lane
Pilling
Stake Pool
Winmarleigh
Scorton
Preesall
FREEPORT FLEETWOOD
Cabus
Oakenclough
Eagland Hill
Garstang
THE FIG TREE FAIRTRADE VISITOR CENTRE
Calder Vale
SD
Stalmine
Staynall
Nateby
Bowgreave
Wyre
MARSH MILL IN-WYRE
WYRE ESTUARY
Cleveleys
Trunnah
Hambleton
Churchtown
Catterall
Moss Edge
Out Rawcliffe
Ratten Row
Claughton
Anchorsholme
Thornton
Norbreck
Little Eccleston
TOLL
St Michael's on Wyre
Inglewhite
Skippool
Little Singleton
Bilsborrow
Bispham
Carleton
Great Eccleston
Myerscough
Blackpool
Warbreck
Poulton-le-Fylde
Singleton
Elswick
Crossmoor
North Shore
Thistleton
Inskip
Cuddy Hill
Queenstown
Normoss
Esprick
Roseacre
Barton
Blackpool
BLACKPOOL TOWER
SEA LIFE CENTRE
MADAME TUSSAUD'S BLACKPOOL
Layton
Staining
Lancashire
Catforth
Corner Row
Wharles
ZOO PARK
Great Marton
Weeton
Woodplumpton
Broughton
Hawes Side
Mereside
Great Plumpton
Little Plumpton
South Shore
BLACKPOOL PLEASURE BEACH
Common Edge
Wesham
Treales
Lower Bartle
Higher Bartle
Kirkham
Cottam
Fulwood
Lancaster Canal
Ingol
Cadley
Westby
Dowbridge
Lea Town
Squires Gate
Moss Side
Wrea Green
BLACKPOOL INTERNATIONAL
Higher Ballam
Newton
Scales
Clifton
Preston
TOY AND TEDDY BEAR MUSEUM
ROYAL LYTHAM & ST ANNES
LYTHAM HALL
Freckleton
RIBBLE STEAM RAILWAY
P&R
St Annes
Lytham St Anne's
Ansdell
Lytham
Warton
Bottom of Hutton
Higher Penwortham
Fairhaven
Salters Bank
Ribble
Hutton
Longton
Middleforth Green
Lostock
98
99
85
86
A
B
C
D
E
F
0 1 2 3 4 5 6 miles
0 1 2 3 4 5 6 7 8 9 10 km

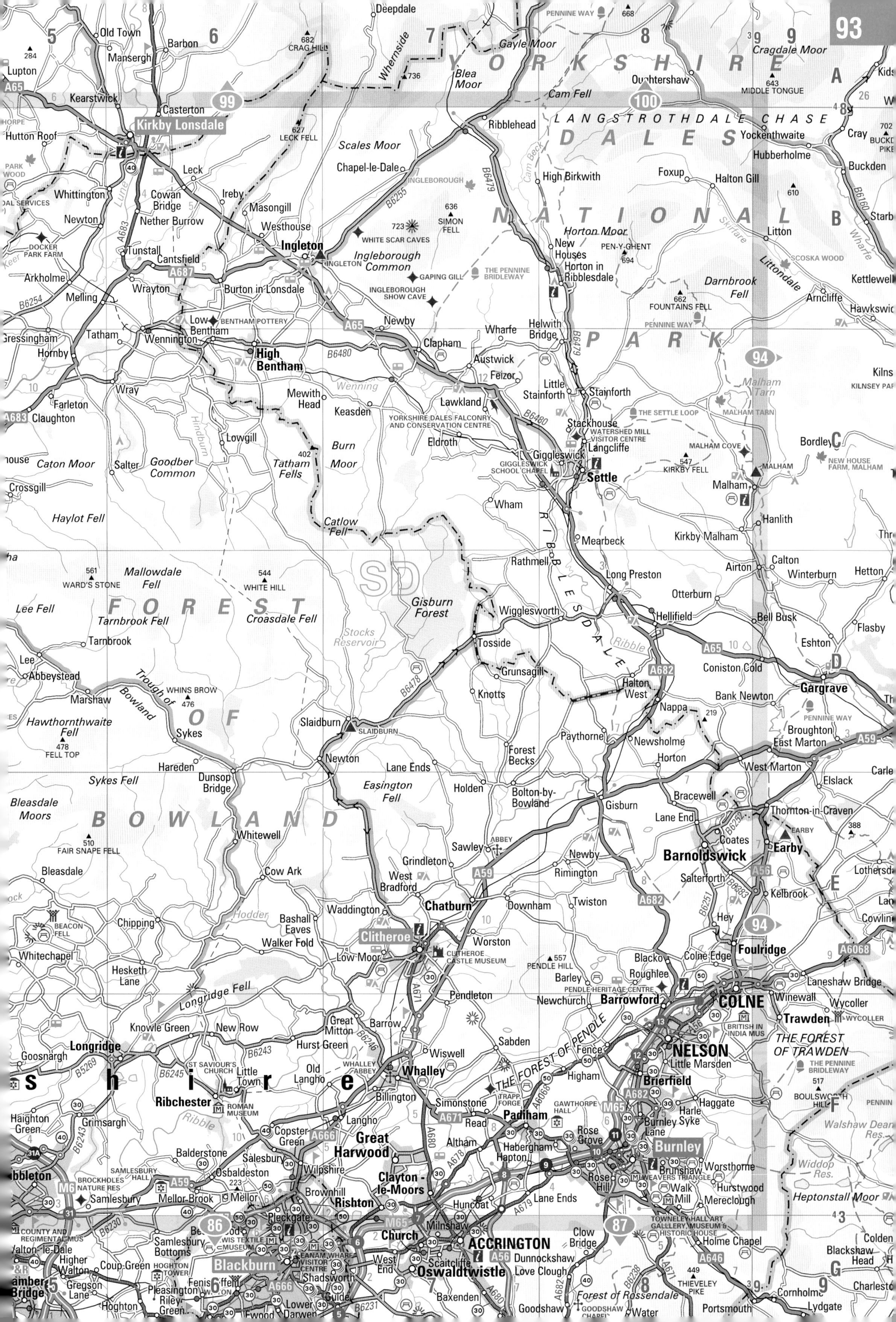
Deepdale
PENNINE WAY
668
Old Town
682
CRAG HILL
Whernside
Gayle Moor
Cragdale Moor
Barbon
Mansergh
284
Lupton
YORKSHIRE
736
Blea Moor
Oughtershaw
643
MIDDLE TONGUE
Kidstones
A65
Kearstwick
Casterton
99
Cam Fell
100
Kirkby Lonsdale
627
LECK FELL
Ribblehead
LANGSTROTHDALE CHASE
DALES
Yockenthwaite
Cray
702
BUCKDEN PIKE
Hutton Roof
Scales Moor
Hubberholme
PARK WOOD
Leck
Chapel-le-Dale
INGLEBOROUGH
Cam Beck
High Birkwith
Foxup
Halton Gill
Buckden
Whittington
Cowan Bridge
Ireby
B6255
B6479
610
Newton
Nether Burrow
Masongill
636
SIMON FELL
NATIONAL
Litton
Starbotton
DOCKER PARK FARM
Westhouse
723
WHITE SCAR CAVES
Horton Moor
New Houses
PEN-Y-GHENT
694
Skirfare
Tunstall
Cantsfield
Ingleton
INGLETON
Ingleborough Common
THE PENNINE BRIDLEWAY
Horton in Ribblesdale
SCOSKA WOOD
Littondale
Wharfe
Arkholme
A687
GAPING GILL
Darnbrook Fell
Kettlewell
Wrayton
Burton in Lonsdale
INGLEBOROUGH SHOW CAVE
662
FOUNTAINS FELL
Arncliffe
Hawkswick
Melling
B6254
Low Bentham
BENTHAM POTTERY
Newby
A65
PENNINE WAY
Gressingham
Tatham
Wennington
Wharfe
Helwith Bridge
PARK
Hornby
High Bentham
B6480
Clapham
94
Austwick
Feizor
Kilnsey
KILNSEY PARK
Wray
Wenning
Little Stainforth
Stainforth
Malham Tarn
10
Farleton
Mewith Head
Lawkland
B6480
Claughton
A683
Keasden
YORKSHIRE DALES FALCONRY AND CONSERVATION CENTRE
THE SETTLE LOOP
MALHAM TARN
Hindburn
Lowgill
Burn Moor
Eldroth
Stackhouse
WATERSHED MILL VISITOR CENTRE
Langcliffe
Bordley
Caton Moor
Salter
Goodber Common
402
Tatham Fells
Giggleswick
GIGGLESWICK SCHOOL CHAPEL
Settle
MALHAM COVE
547
KIRKBY FELL
MALHAM
NEW HOUSE FARM, MALHAM
Crossgill
Malham
Wham
Haylot Fell
Catlow Fell
Hanlith
Kirkby Malham
Mearbeck
SD
RIBBLESDALE
Rathmell
Airton
Calton
Winterburn
Hetton
561
WARD'S STONE
Mallowdale Fell
544
WHITE HILL
Long Preston
Otterburn
Lee Fell
FOREST
Gisburn Forest
Wigglesworth
Hellifield
Bell Busk
Tarnbrook Fell
Croasdale Fell
Flasby
Tarnbrook
Stocks Reservoir
Tosside
Ribble
A65
Eshton
Lee
Abbeystead
Grunsagill
A682
Coniston Cold
Marshaw
Trough of Bowland
WHINS BROW
476
B6478
Knotts
Halton West
Bank Newton
Gargrave
Hawthornthwaite Fell
OF
Slaidburn
SLAIDBURN
Nappa
219
PENNINE WAY
478
FELL TOP
Sykes
Paythorne
Broughton
Newsholme
East Marton
A59
Hareden
Newton
Forest Becks
Horton
Sykes Fell
Dunsop Bridge
Lane Ends
West Marton
Carleton
Easington Fell
Holden
Bolton-by-Bowland
Bracewell
Elslack
Bleasdale Moors
BOWLAND
Gisburn
Lane End
Thornton-in-Craven
Whitewell
B6252
Coates
388
EARBY
510
FAIR SNAPE FELL
ABBEY
Sawley
Barnoldswick
Earby
Newby
Bleasdale
Cow Ark
Grindleton
West Bradford
A59
Rimington
Lothersdale
Salterforth
A56
B6383
Kelbrook
Twiston
Hodder
Bashall Eaves
Waddington
Chatburn
Downham
A682
B6251
BEACON FELL
Chipping
Clitheroe
Worston
Hey
94
Cowling
Walker Fold
Whitechapel
Low Moor
CLITHEROE CASTLE MUSEUM
557
PENDLE HILL
Blacko
Colne Edge
Foulridge
A6068
Hesketh Lane
Barley
Roughlee
PENDLE HERITAGE CENTRE
Laneshaw Bridge
A671
Longridge Fell
Pendleton
Newchurch
Barrowford
COLNE
Winewall
Wycoller
WYCOLLER
Great Mitton
Barrow
Trawden
Knowle Green
New Row
BRITISH IN INDIA MUS
THE FOREST OF TRAWDEN
Longridge
B6243
Hurst Green
B6246
Wiswell
Sabden
THE FOREST OF PENDLE
Fence
NELSON
Goosnargh
ST SAVIOUR'S CHURCH
Little Town
WHALLEY ABBEY
Whalley
Little Marsden
THE PENNINE BRIDLEWAY
B5269
B6245
Old Langho
Higham
Brierfield
517
BOULSWORTH HILL
Lancashire
Ribchester
ROMAN MUSEUM
Billington
TRAPP FORGE
GAWTHORPE HALL
A682
Haggate
PENNINE
Haighton Green
Grimsargh
Simonstone
A6068
Padiham
M65
Harle Syke
Ribble
B6243
Langho
A671
Read
Burnley Lane
Walshaw Dean Res.
Copster Green
A666
Great Harwood
A680
Altham
Habergham
Rose Grove
Balderstone
Salesbury
Hapton
Burnley
Ribbleton
SAMLESBURY HALL
A59
Osbaldeston
Wilpshire
A678
Worsthorne
Widdop Res.
M6
BROCKHOLES NATURE RES
223
Mellor
Brownhill
Clayton-le-Moors
Rose Hill
Brunshaw
WEAVERS TRIANGLE
Hurstwood
Samlesbury
Mellor Brook
Rishton
Huncoat
A679
Lane Ends
Walk Mill
Mereclough
Heptonstall Moor
B6230
Pleckgate
M65
Milnshaw
TOWNELEY HALL ART GALLERY MUSEUM & HISTORIC HOUSE
COUNTY AND REGIMENTAL MUS
86
87
Church
ACCRINGTON
Clow Bridge
Holme Chapel
Colden
Walton-le-Dale
Samlesbury Bottoms
LEWIS TEXTILE MUSEUM
A56
Dunnockshaw
Blackshaw Head
Higher Walton
Coup Green
HOGHTON TOWER
Blackburn
EANAM WHARF VISITOR CENTRE
West End
Scaitcliffe
Oswaldtwistle
Love Clough
A646
Bamber Bridge
Gregson Lane
Feniscowles
Pleasington
A666
Shadsworth
B6238
449
THIEVELEY PIKE
Charlestown
Hoghton
Riley Green
Guide
Lower Darwen
B6231
Baxenden
A680
A682
Forest of Rossendale
Goodshaw
GOODSHAW CHAPEL
Water
Portsmouth
Cornholme
Lydgate
Ewood

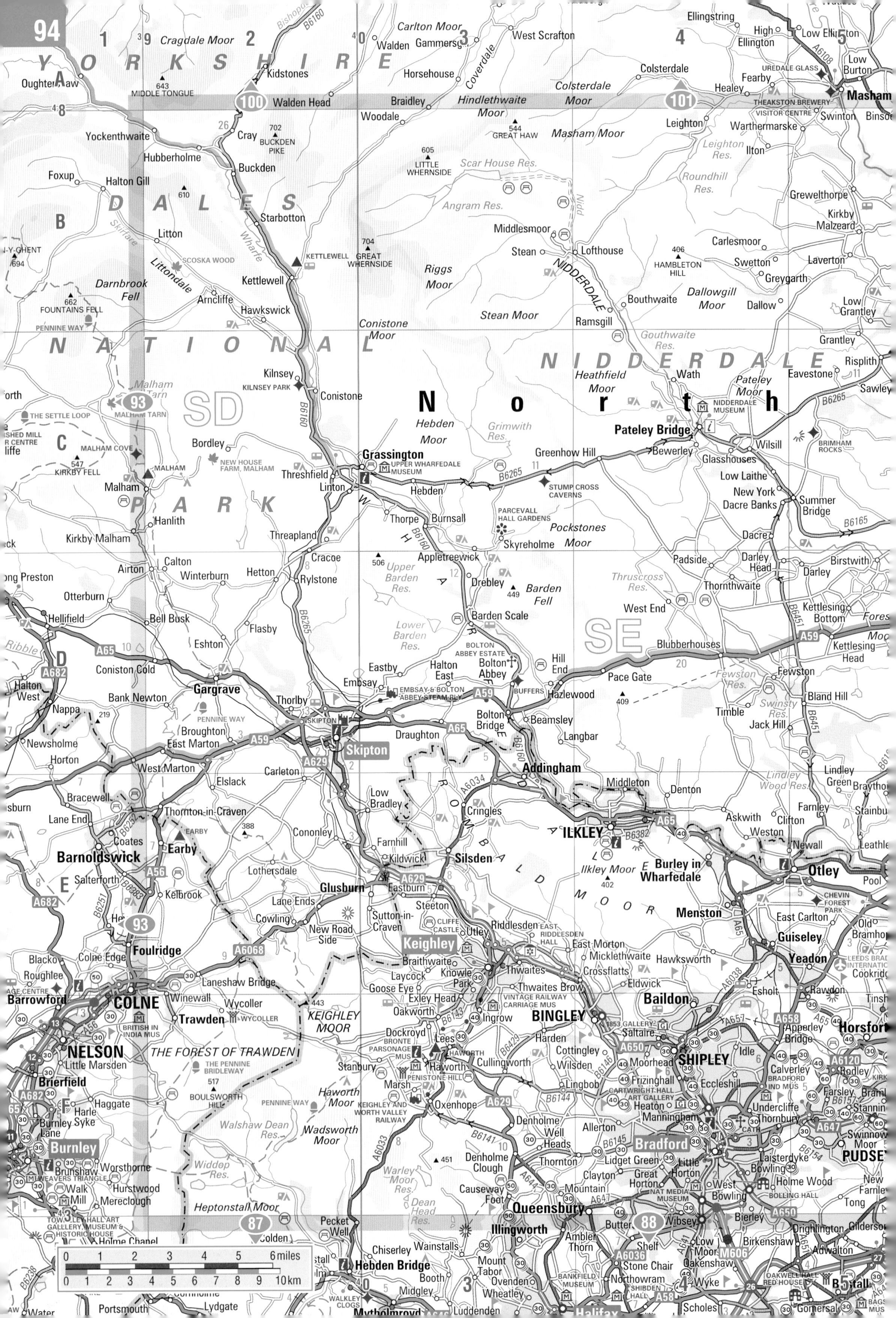
YORKSHIRE
DALES
NATIONAL
PARK
NIDDERDALE
North
SD
SE
Cragdale Moor
Oughtershaw
MIDDLE TONGUE
Kidstones
Walden Head
Carlton Moor
Walden
Gammersgill
West Scrafton
Horsehouse
Coverdale
Braidley
Woodale
Hindlethwaite Moor
Colsterdale
Colsterdale Moor
Ellingstring
High Ellington
Low Ellington
Fearby
Healey
Masham
THEAKSTON BREWERY VISITOR CENTRE
Swinton
Low Burton
Leighton
Warthermarske
Ilton
Leighton Res.
Roundhill Res.
Yockenthwaite
Hubberholme
Cray
BUCKDEN PIKE
Buckden
GREAT HAW
Masham Moor
LITTLE WHERNSIDE
Scar House Res.
Angram Res.
Foxup
Halton Gill
Starbotton
Litton
Littondale
SCOSKA WOOD
Wharfe
KETTLEWELL
GREAT WHERNSIDE
Kettlewell
Riggs Moor
Middlesmoor
Stean
Lofthouse
HAMBLETON HILL
Grewelthorpe
Kirkby Malzeard
Carlesmoor
Swetton
Greygarth
Laverton
Dallowgill Moor
Dallow
Low Grantley
Grantley
Bouthwaite
Ramsgill
Stean Moor
Darnbrook Fell
FOUNTAINS FELL
Arncliffe
Hawkswick
PENNINE WAY
Conistone Moor
Gouthwaite Res.
Heathfield Moor
Wath
Pateley Moor
Eavestone
Risplith
Sawley
Kilnsey
KILNSEY PARK
Conistone
Malham Tarn
MALHAM TARN
THE SETTLE LOOP
MALHAM COVE
KIRKBY FELL
MALHAM
Malham
Bordley
NEW HOUSE FARM, MALHAM
Threshfield
Grassington
UPPER WHARFEDALE MUSEUM
Linton
Hebden
Hebden Moor
Grimwith Res.
Greenhow Hill
STUMP CROSS CAVERNS
Pateley Bridge
NIDDERDALE MUSEUM
Bewerley
Glasshouses
Wilsill
BRIMHAM ROCKS
Low Laithe
New York
Dacre Banks
Summer Bridge
Hanlith
Kirkby Malham
Thorpe
Burnsall
PARCEVALL HALL GARDENS
Pockstones Moor
Skyreholme
Dacre
Threapland
Cracoe
Upper Barden Res.
Appletreewick
Drebley
Barden Fell
Padside
Darley Head
Darley
Birstwith
Thornthwaite
Thruscross Res.
Airton
Calton
Winterburn
Hetton
Rylstone
Long Preston
Otterburn
Hellifield
Bell Busk
Flasby
Eshton
Barden Scale
Lower Barden Res.
West End
Kettlesing Bottom
BOLTON ABBEY ESTATE
Bolton Abbey
Hill End
Blubberhouses
Kettlesing Head
Coniston Cold
Halton West
Gargrave
Eastby
Halton East
Embsay
EMBSAY & BOLTON ABBEY STEAM RLY
BUFFERS
Hazlewood
Pace Gate
Fewston Res.
Fewston
Bland Hill
Bank Newton
Nappa
Newsholme
Broughton
East Marton
Thorlby
SKIPTON
Skipton
Draughton
Bolton Bridge
Beamsley
Langbar
Timble
Swinsty Res.
Jack Hill
Horton
West Marton
Elslack
Carleton
Addingham
Middleton
Denton
Lindley Wood Res.
Lindley Green
Bracewell
Thornton-in-Craven
Low Bradley
RO MBALD MOOR
Cringles
ILKLEY
Ilkley Moor
Askwith
Clifton
Farnley
Weston
Newall
Otley
Lane End
Coates
EARBY
Earby
Barnoldswick
Cononley
Farnhill
Kildwick
Silsden
Burley in Wharfedale
Salterforth
Kelbrook
Lothersdale
Glusburn
Eastburn
Steeton
Menston
CHEVIN FOREST PARK
East Carlton
Lane Ends
Cowling
New Road Side
Sutton-in-Craven
CLIFFE CASTLE
Utley
Riddlesden
EAST RIDDLESDEN HALL
Guiseley
Yeadon
Foulridge
Colne Edge
Keighley
East Morton
Micklethwaite
Hawksworth
Blacko
Roughlee
Barrowford
COLNE
Laneshaw Bridge
Braithwaite
Laycock
Knowle Park
Thwaites
Crossflatts
Eldwick
Thwaites Brow
Winewall
Wycoller
WYCOLLER
Goose Eye
Exley Head
Oakworth
VINTAGE RAILWAY CARRIAGE MUS
Ingrow
BINGLEY
Baildon
Esholt
Rawdon
Trawden
KEIGHLEY MOOR
BRITISH IN INDIA MUS
NELSON
Little Marsden
THE FOREST OF TRAWDEN
THE PENNINE BRIDLEWAY
Dockroyd
BRONTE PARSONAGE MUS
Lees
HAWORTH
Haworth
PENISTONE HILL
Cullingworth
Harden
Cottingley
Wilsden
1853 GALLERY
Saltaire
Moorhead
SHIPLEY
Idle
Apperley Bridge
Horsforth
Calverley
Rodley
Brierfield
BOULSWORTH HILL
Stanbury
Marsh
Haworth Moor
KEIGHLEY AND WORTH VALLEY RAILWAY
Oxenhope
Lingbob
Frizinghall
CARTWRIGHT HALL ART GALLERY
Heaton
Manningham
Eccleshill
BRADFORD IND MUS
Farsley
Undercliffe
Thornbury
Stanningley
Haggate
Harle Syke
Burnley Lane
Walshaw Dean Res.
Wadsworth Moor
Denholme
Well Heads
Allerton
Bradford
Swinnow Moor
PUDSEY
Burnley
Brunshaw
Worsthorne
WEAVERS TRIANGLE
Walk Mill
Hurstwood
Mereclough
Widdop Res.
Denholme Clough
Thornton
Lidget Green
Little Horton
Laisterdyke
Bowling
Holme Wood
Clayton
Great Horton
West Bowling
BOLLING HALL
Tong
Warley Moor Res.
Dean Head Res.
Causeway Foot
Mountain
NAT MEDIA MUSEUM
TOWNELEY HALL ART GALLERY, MUSEUM & HISTORIC HOUSE
Holme Chapel
Heptonstall Moor
Queensbury
Illingworth
Wibsey
Bierley
Drighlington
Gildersome
Colden
Pecket Well
Chiserley
Wainstalls
Ambler Thorn
Shelf
Low Moor
Birkenshaw
Adwalton
Hebden Bridge
Mount Tabor
Ovenden
Stone Chair
Oakenshaw
Northowram
Wyke
OAKWELL HALL
RED HOUSE
BANKFIELD MUSEUM
SHIBDEN HALL
Booth
Wheatley
Midgley
WALKLEY CLOGS
Mytholmroyd
Luddenden
Scholes
Gomersal
Birstall
Portsmouth
Lydgate
Water
0 1 2 3 4 5 6 miles
0 1 2 3 4 5 6 7 8 9 10 km

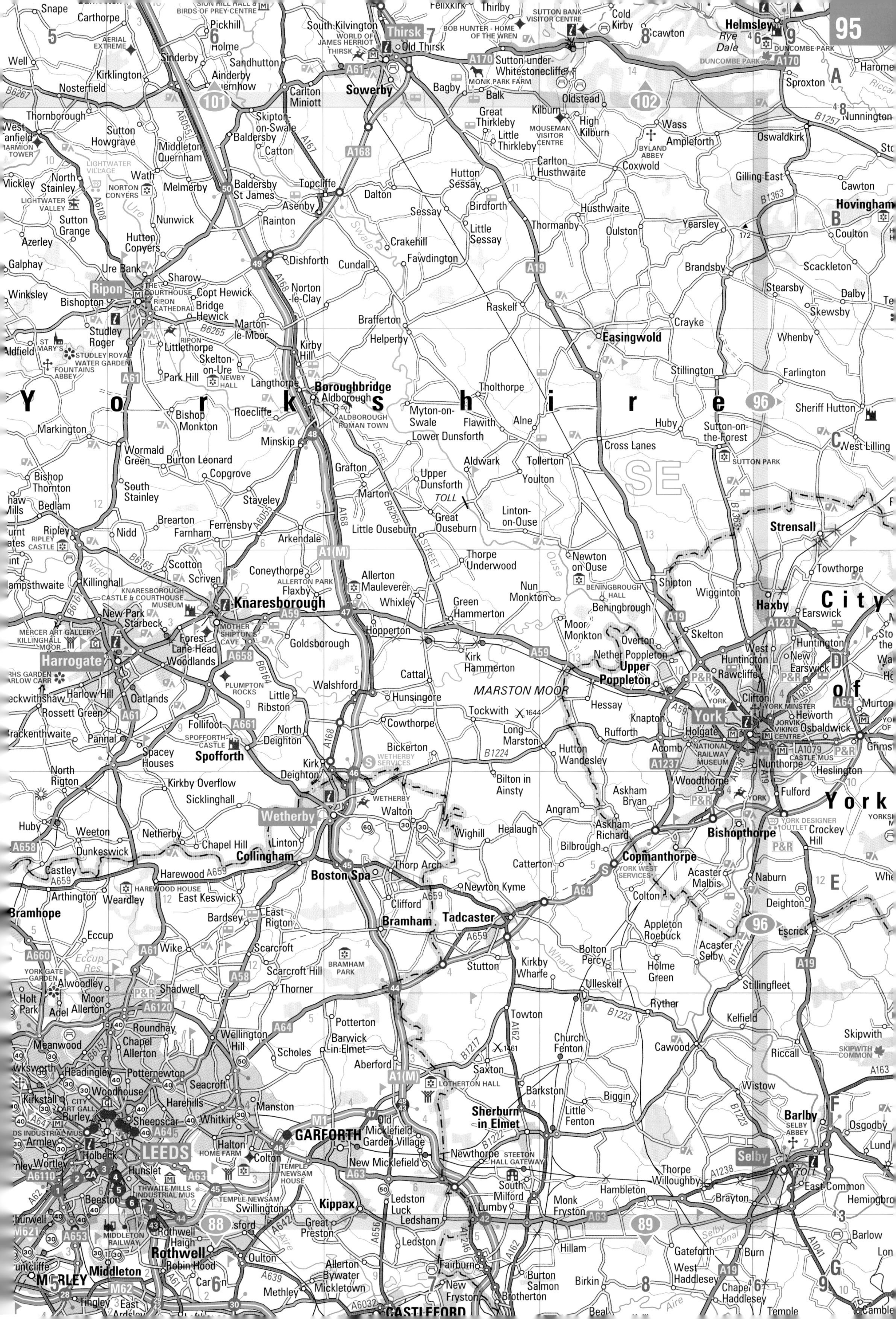
Snape
Carthorpe
Pickhill
Holme
Sinderby
Sandhutton
Ainderby
Quernhow
Kirklington
Nosterfield
Well
AERIAL EXTREME
Thornborough
Sutton Howgrave
Middleton Quernham
Skipton-on-Swale
Baldersby
Catton
Carlton Miniott
South Kilvington
WORLD OF JAMES HERRIOT
Thirsk
Old Thirsk
Sowerby
BOB HUNTER - HOME OF THE WREN
Felixkirk
Thirlby
SUTTON BANK VISITOR CENTRE
Cold Kirby
Scawton
Helmsley
Rye Dale
DUNCOMBE PARK
Harome
Sproxton
Sutton-under-Whitestonecliffe
MONK PARK FARM
Bagby
Balk
Great Thirkleby
Little Thirkleby
Kilburn
MOUSEMAN VISITOR CENTRE
Oldstead
High Kilburn
Wass
Ampleforth
BYLAND ABBEY
Oswaldkirk
Nunnington
Carlton Husthwaite
Coxwold
Gilling East
Cawton
Hovingham
Coulton
North Stainley
LIGHTWATER VILLAGE
NORTON CONYERS
Wath
Melmerby
Baldersby St James
Topcliffe
Asenby
Dalton
Hutton Sessay
Birdforth
Sessay
Husthwaite
Thormanby
Oulston
Yearsley
Brandsby
Scackleton
Mickley
Sutton Grange
Azerley
Nunwick
Hutton Conyers
Rainton
Dishforth
Cundall
Crakehill
Fawdington
Little Sessay
Raskelf
Stearsby
Dalby
Skewsby
Galphay
Ure Bank
Ripon
Sharow
THE COURTHOUSE
RIPON CATHEDRAL
Copt Hewick
Bridge Hewick
Norton-le-Clay
Winksley
Bishopton
Studley Roger
ST MARY'S
STUDLEY ROYAL WATER GARDEN
FOUNTAINS ABBEY
Aldfield
Littlethorpe
Marton-le-Moor
Brafferton
Helperby
Crayke
Easingwold
Whenby
Skelton-on-Ure
NEWBY HALL
Park Hill
Kirby Hill
Langthorpe
Boroughbridge
Aldborough
ALDBOROUGH ROMAN TOWN
Tholthorpe
Stillington
Farlington
Yorkshire
Markington
Bishop Monkton
Roecliffe
Myton-on-Swale
Flawith
Alne
Huby
Sutton-on-the-Forest
Sheriff Hutton
West Lilling
SUTTON PARK
Lower Dunsforth
Cross Lanes
Minskip
Wormald Green
Burton Leonard
Copgrove
Grafton
Aldwark
Tollerton
Youlton
SE
Bishop Thornton
South Stainley
Upper Dunsforth
Marton
TOLL
Staveley
Great Ouseburn
Linton-on-Ouse
Bedlam
Brearton
Ferrensby
Farnham
Ripley
RIPLEY CASTLE
Nidd
Little Ouseburn
Arkendale
Strensall
Thorpe Underwood
Newton on Ouse
Towthorpe
Scotton
Scriven
Coneythorpe
ALLERTON PARK
Allerton Mauleverer
Whixley
BENINGBROUGH HALL
Nun Monkton
Shipton
Wigginton
Haxby
Earswick
City of York
Killinghall
KNARESBOROUGH CASTLE & COURTHOUSE MUSEUM
Knaresborough
New Park
Starbeck
MERCER ART GALLERY
KILLINGHALL MOOR
Forest Lane Head
MOTHER SHIPTON'S CAVE
Goldsborough
Green Hammerton
Hopperton
Beningbrough
Moor Monkton
Overton
Skelton
Huntington
West Huntington
New Earswick
Harrogate
Woodlands
Kirk Hammerton
Nether Poppleton
Upper Poppleton
Rawcliffe
Stockton on the Forest
RHS GARDEN HARLOW CARR
Harlow Hill
Oatlands
PLUMPTON ROCKS
Little Ribston
Walshford
Cattal
Hunsingore
MARSTON MOOR
Hessay
Knapton
Clifton
YORK MINSTER
JORVIK VIKING CENTRE
Heworth
Osbaldwick
Murton
Rossett Green
Follifoot
SPOFFORTH CASTLE
Spofforth
North Deighton
Cowthorpe
Tockwith
Long Marston
Rufforth
York
Holgate
NATIONAL RAILWAY MUSEUM
Acomb
CASTLE MUS
Nunthorpe
Heslington
Pannal
Spacey Houses
Bickerton
WETHERBY SERVICES
Kirk Deighton
Hutton Wandesley
North Rigton
Kirkby Overflow
Sicklinghall
Bilton in Ainsty
Askham Bryan
Woodthorpe
Fulford
WETHERBY
Wetherby
Walton
Angram
Huby
Weeton
Netherby
Dunkeswick
Chapel Hill
Linton
Collingham
Wighill
Healaugh
Askham Richard
Bilbrough
Bishopthorpe
YORK DESIGNER OUTLET
Crockey Hill
Copmanthorpe
Catterton
YORK WEST SERVICES
Thorp Arch
Boston Spa
Harewood
HAREWOOD HOUSE
Castley
Arthington
Weardley
East Keswick
Newton Kyme
Acaster Malbis
Naburn
Deighton
Colton
Clifford
Bramham
Tadcaster
Bramhope
Bardsey
East Rigton
Appleton Roebuck
Escrick
Eccup
Wike
Scarcroft
BRAMHAM PARK
Stutton
Bolton Percy
Acaster Selby
Kirkby Wharfe
Holme Green
YORK GATE GARDEN
Alwoodley
Scarcroft Hill
Thorner
Ulleskelf
Stillingfleet
Holt Park
Adel
Moor Allerton
Shadwell
Rawdon
Roundhay
Towton
Rither
Kelfield
Potterton
Barwick in Elmet
Wellington Hill
Scholes
Church Fenton
Cawood
Skipwith
SKIPWITH COMMON
Meanwood
Chapel Allerton
Riccall
Potternewton
Aberford
Saxton
Headingley
Seacroft
LOTHERTON HALL
Barkston
Biggin
Wistow
Woodhouse
Kirkstall
Harehills
Manston
Sherburn in Elmet
Little Fenton
Barlby
SELBY ABBEY
Osgodby
Burley
Sheepscar
Whitkirk
GARFORTH
Micklefield
Garden Village
Armley
Halton
HOME FARM
Colton
TEMPLE NEWSAM HOUSE
New Micklefield
Newthorpe
STEETON HALL GATEWAY
Thorpe Willoughby
Selby
Lund
Holbeck
LEEDS
Wortley
Hunslet
THWAITE MILLS INDUSTRIAL MUS
South Milford
Hambleton
East Common
Hemingbrough
Beeston
TEMPLE NEWSAM
Swillington
Kippax
Ledston Luck
Ledsham
Lumby
Monk Fryston
Brayton
Great Preston
MIDDLETON RAILWAY
Rothwell
Rothwell Haigh
Ledston
Hillam
Gateforth
Burn
Barlow
Robin Hood
Oulton
Allerton Bywater
Fairburn
Burton Salmon
Birkin
West Haddlesey
Chapel Haddlesey
Middleton
MORLEY
Carlton
Methley
Mickletown
New Fryston
Brotherton
Tingley
East Ardsley
CASTLEFORD
Beal
Temple
Camblesforth
A1(M)
A19
A59
A64
A61
A168
A170
A658
A659
A162
A63
B1224
B1223
B6265
Ouse
Wharfe
Aire
Selby Canal

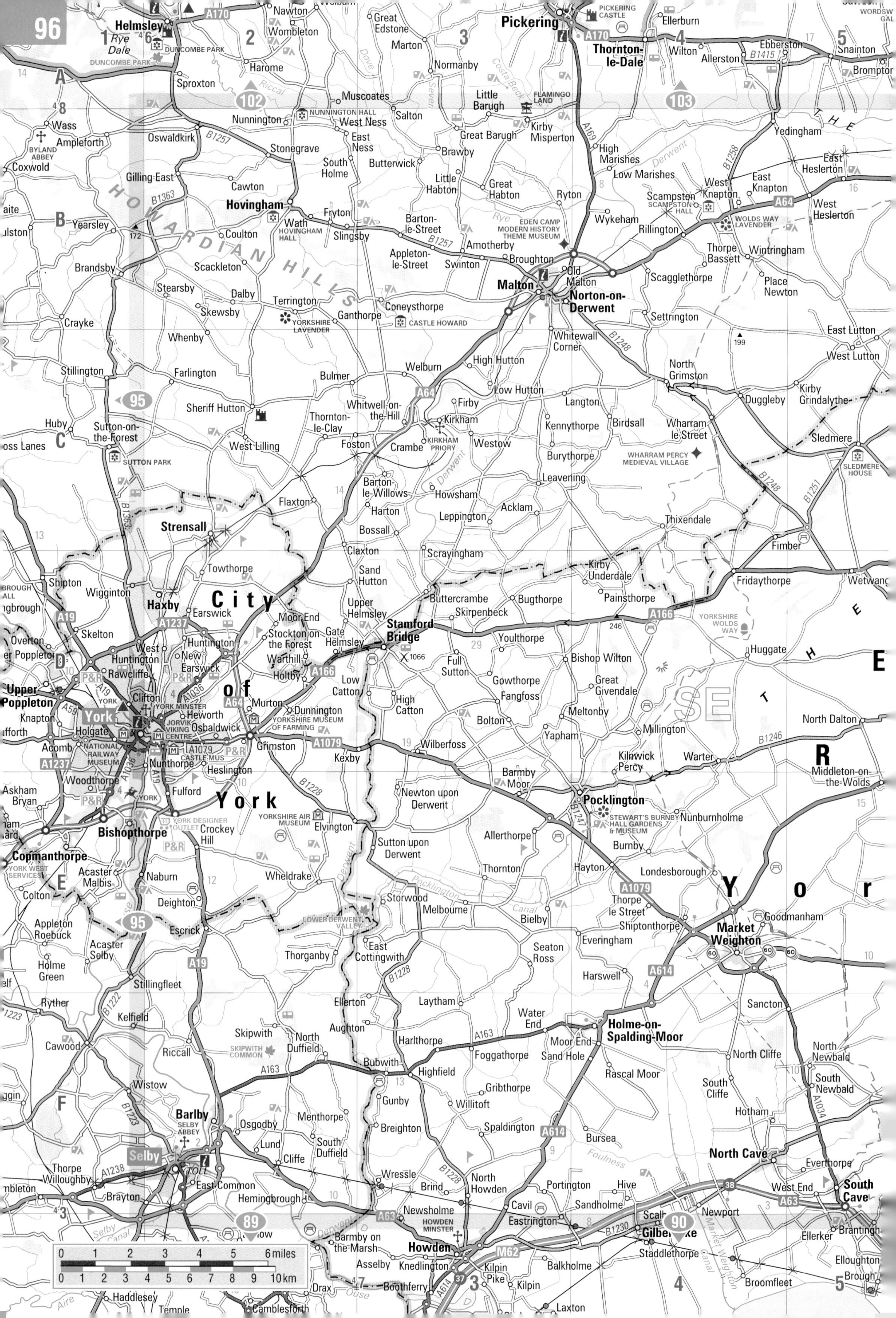
Helmsley
Rye Dale
Duncombe Park
Nawton
Wombleton
A170
Great Edstone
Marton
Pickering
Pickering Castle
Ellerburn
Thornton-le-Dale
Wilton
Allerston
Ebberston
Snainton
Brompton
B1415
Harome
Sproxton
Normanby
102
103
Riccal
Muscoates
Little Barugh
Flamingo Land
Nunnington
Nunnington Hall
West Ness
Salton
Kirby Misperton
Great Barugh
Wass
Ampleforth
Byland Abbey
Coxwold
Oswaldkirk
B1257
East Ness
Stonegrave
Brawby
A169
High Marishes
Derwent
Yedingham
East Heslerton
South Holme
Butterwick
Low Marishes
Gilling East
Cawton
Little Habton
Great Habton
Ryton
West Knapton
East Knapton
B1258
Scampston
Scampston Hall
A64
West Heslerton
Howardian Hills
B1363
Hovingham
Fryton
Barton-le-Street
Eden Camp Modern History Theme Museum
Wykeham
Rillington
Wolds Way Lavender
Yearsley
Wath
Hovingham Hall
Slingsby
Coulton
Amotherby
Thorpe Bassett
Wintringham
Appleton-le-Street
Swinton
Broughton
Brandsby
Scackleton
Malton
Old Malton
Norton-on-Derwent
Scagglethorpe
Place Newton
Stearsby
Dalby
Terrington
Skewsby
Yorkshire Lavender
Ganthorpe
Coneysthorpe
Castle Howard
Settrington
Crayke
Whenby
Whitewall Corner
B1248
East Lutton
West Lutton
Stillington
Farlington
Bulmer
Welburn
High Hutton
North Grimston
95
Sheriff Hutton
Whitwell-on-the-Hill
Low Hutton
Firby
Langton
Duggleby
Kirby Grindalythe
Huby
Sutton-on-the-Forest
Thornton-le-Clay
Kirkham
Kennythorpe
Birdsall
Wharram le Street
Sledmere
Sutton Park
West Lilling
Foston
Crambe
Kirkham Priory
Westow
Burythorpe
Wharram Percy Medieval Village
Sledmere House
Leavening
Barton-le-Willows
Howsham
Flaxton
Harton
Acklam
Leppington
Thixendale
B1251
Strensall
Bossall
Claxton
Scrayingham
Fimber
Towthorpe
Sand Hutton
Kirby Underdale
Fridaythorpe
Wetwang
Shipton
Wigginton
Haxby
City of York
Upper Helmsley
Buttercrambe
Bugthorpe
Painsthorpe
Skirpenbeck
Earswick
Moor End
Stamford Bridge
A166
Yorkshire Wolds Way
A19
A1237
Skelton
Stockton on the Forest
Gate Helmsley
Youlthorpe
Huggate
Overton
Huntington
West Huntington
New Earswick
Warthill
1066
Full Sutton
Bishop Wilton
Rawcliffe
Holtby
Low Catton
Gowthorpe
Great Givendale
Upper Poppleton
A59
Clifton
York Minster
A1036
High Catton
Fangfoss
Murton
Dunnington
Yorkshire Museum of Farming
Meltonby
Knapton
Holgate
Jorvik Viking Centre
Heworth
Osbaldwick
Bolton
Millington
North Dalton
Acomb
National Railway Museum
A1079
Castle Mus
Grimston
Kexby
Wilberfoss
Yapham
B1246
Nunthorpe
Heslington
Kilnwick Percy
Warter
Middleton-on-the-Wolds
Woodthorpe
Fulford
B1228
Newton upon Derwent
Barmby Moor
Pocklington
Askham Bryan
Bishopthorpe
York Designer Outlet
Crockey Hill
Yorkshire Air Museum
Elvington
B1247
Stewart's Burnby Hall Gardens & Museum
Nunburnholme
Allerthorpe
Copmanthorpe
York West Services
Sutton upon Derwent
Burnby
Acaster Malbis
Naburn
Wheldrake
Thornton
Hayton
Londesborough
Colton
Deighton
Storwood
Pocklington Canal
Melbourne
Thorpe le Street
Goodmanham
Bielby
Appleton Roebuck
Escrick
Lower Derwent Valley
Shiptonthorpe
Market Weighton
Acaster Selby
Thorganby
East Cottingwith
Everingham
Seaton Ross
A614
Holme Green
Harswell
Stillingfleet
Rythe
Kelfield
B1222
Ellerton
Laytham
Sancton
Water End
Holme-on-Spalding-Moor
Aughton
Skipwith
Skipwith Common
North Duffield
A163
Harlthorpe
Foggathorpe
Moor End
Sand Hole
North Cliffe
North Newbald
Cawood
Riccall
Bubwith
Highfield
Rascal Moor
South Cliffe
South Newbald
Wistow
Gribthorpe
Gunby
Willitoft
Hotham
A1034
B1223
Barlby
Selby Abbey
Osgodby
Menthorpe
Breighton
Spaldington
Bursea
North Cave
Selby
Lund
South Duffield
Everthorpe
Thorpe Willoughby
A1238
Cliffe
Foulness
Wressle
Brind
North Howden
Portington
Hive
West End
South Cave
East Common
Brayton
Hemingbrough
A63
Newsholme
Howden Minster
Cavil
Sandholme
Eastrington
Newport
Scalby
Gilberdyke
Brantingham
89
90
M62
B1230
Barmby on the Marsh
Howden
Ellerker
Staddlethorpe
Market Weighton Canal
Asselby
Knedlington
Kilpin Pike
Balkholme
Ellaughton
Brough
Broomfleet
Kilpin
Drax
Boothferry
Ouse
Haddlesey
Temple
Camblesforth
Laxton
Selby Canal
Aire
0 1 2 3 4 5 6 miles
0 1 2 3 4 5 6 7 8 9 10 km

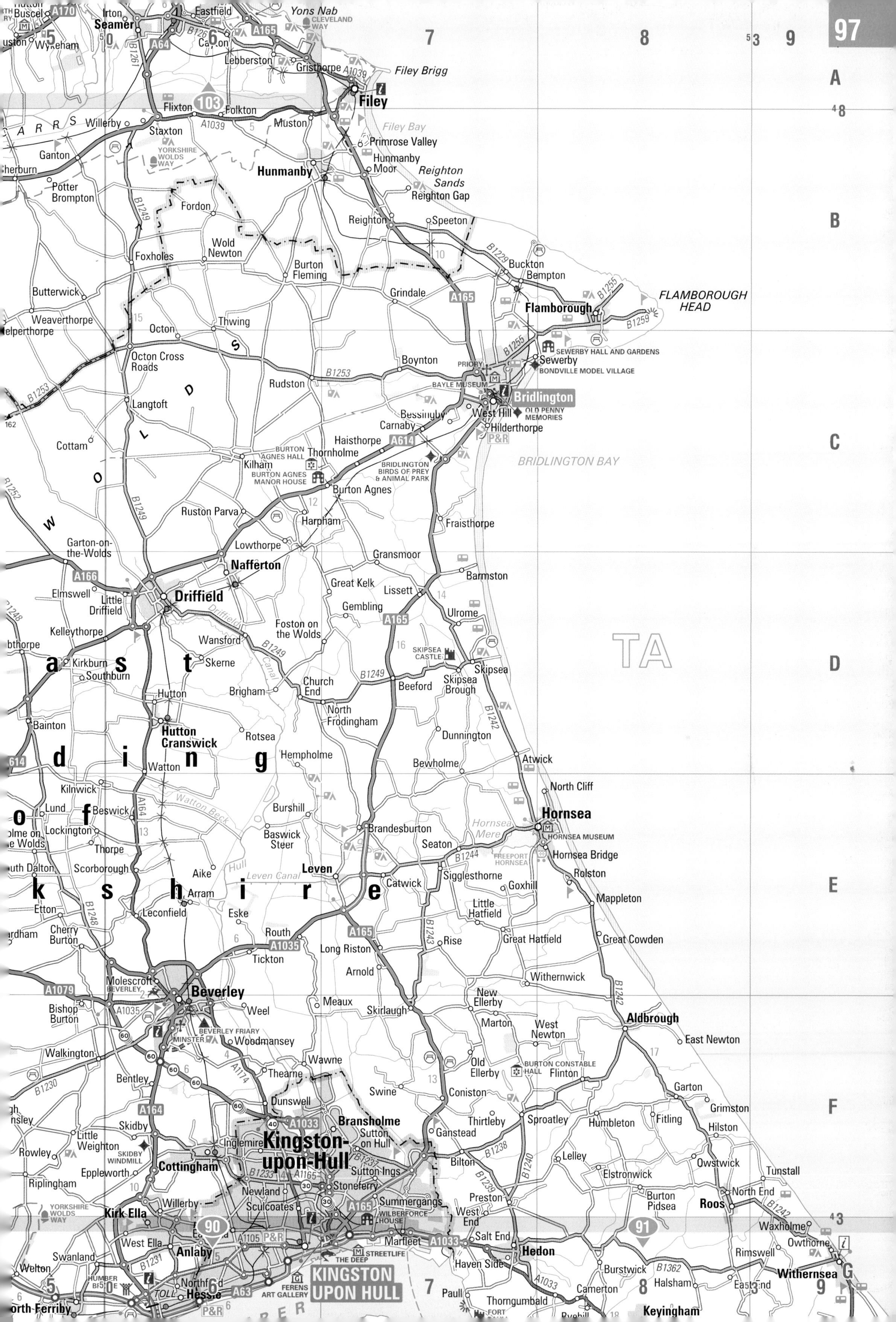
Yons Nab
CLEVELAND WAY
Seamer
Irton
Eastfield
Cayton
Wykeham
Lebberston
Gristhorpe
Filey Brigg
Filey
Flixton
Folkton
Staxton
Willerby
Muston
Filey Bay
Primrose Valley
Ganton
YORKSHIRE WOLDS WAY
Hunmanby
Hunmanby Moor
Reighton Sands
Reighton Gap
Potter Brompton
Fordon
Reighton
Speeton
Wold Newton
Foxholes
Burton Fleming
Buckton
Bempton
Butterwick
Grindale
FLAMBOROUGH HEAD
Flamborough
Weaverthorpe
Thwing
Octon
Octon Cross Roads
Boynton
SEWERBY HALL AND GARDENS
Sewerby
BONDVILLE MODEL VILLAGE
PRIORY
BAYLE MUSEUM
Bridlington
Rudston
Langtoft
Bessingby
Carnaby
West Hill
OLD PENNY MEMORIES
Hilderthorpe
Cottam
Haisthorpe
BURTON AGNES HALL
Thornholme
BRIDLINGTON BAY
Kilham
BURTON AGNES MANOR HOUSE
BRIDLINGTON BIRDS OF PREY & ANIMAL PARK
Burton Agnes
Ruston Parva
Harpham
Fraisthorpe
Garton-on-the-Wolds
Lowthorpe
Gransmoor
Nafferton
Barmston
Elmswell
Little Driffield
Driffield
Great Kelk
Lissett
Gembling
Ulrome
Kelleythorpe
Foston on the Wolds
Wansford
TA
Kirkburn
Southburn
Skerne
SKIPSEA CASTLE
Skipsea
Church End
Beeford
Skipsea Brough
Brigham
Hutton
North Frodingham
Bainton
Hutton Cranswick
Rotsea
Dunnington
Hempholme
Atwick
Watton
Bewholme
Kilnwick
North Cliff
Lund
Beswick
Burshill
Hornsea
Lockington
Baswick Steer
Brandesburton
Hornsea Mere
HORNSEA MUSEUM
Thorpe
Seaton
FREEPORT HORNSEA
Hornsea Bridge
Scorborough
Leven Canal
Leven
Sigglesthorpe
Rolston
Aike
Catwick
Goxhill
Arram
Mappleton
Etton
Little Hatfield
Leconfield
Eske
Cherry Burton
Routh
Rise
Great Hatfield
Great Cowden
Tickton
Long Riston
Molescroft
Arnold
Withernwick
Beverley
Bishop Burton
Weel
Meaux
Skirlaugh
New Ellerby
Marton
West Newton
Aldbrough
BEVERLEY FRIARY
MINSTER
Woodmansey
East Newton
Walkington
Wawne
Old Ellerby
BURTON CONSTABLE HALL
Flinton
Bentley
Thearne
Coniston
Garton
Swine
Dunswell
Thirtleby
Sproatley
Humbleton
Fitling
Grimston
Hilston
Skidby
Bransholme
Ganstead
Little Weighton
SKIDBY WINDMILL
Inglemire
Kingston-upon-Hull
Sutton on Hull
Rowley
Bilton
Lelley
Owstwick
Tunstall
Cottingham
Sutton Ings
Elstronwick
Epplewoth
Riplingham
Newland
Stoneferry
North End
Burton Pidsea
Roos
Willerby
Summergangs
Preston
Sculcoates
WILBERFORCE HOUSE
West End
Waxholme
Kirk Ella
Owthorne
Marfleet
Salt End
West Ella
Hedon
Rimswell
Anlaby
STREETLIFE
Swanland
THE DEEP
Haven Side
Burstwick
Halsham
Withernsea
Welton
HUMBER BRIDGE
Northfield
Hessle
FERENS ART GALLERY
KINGSTON UPON HULL
Paull
Camerton
East End
Thorngumbald
North Ferriby
Keyingham
A170
A165
A64
A1039
B1261
B1249
B1229
B1255
B1259
A165
B1253
B1252
A166
A614
B1248
B1249
A164
B1244
B1242
B1243
A1035
A1079
A1174
B1230
A1033
B1237
B1233
B1238
B1239
B1240
B1231
A1105
A63
B1362
A1033
B1242
103
90
91
P&R
Driffield Canal
Watton Beck
Hull
W O L D S
E a s t R i d i n g o f Y o r k s h i r e
Y A R R S
5
6
7
8
9
A
B
C
D
E
F
G

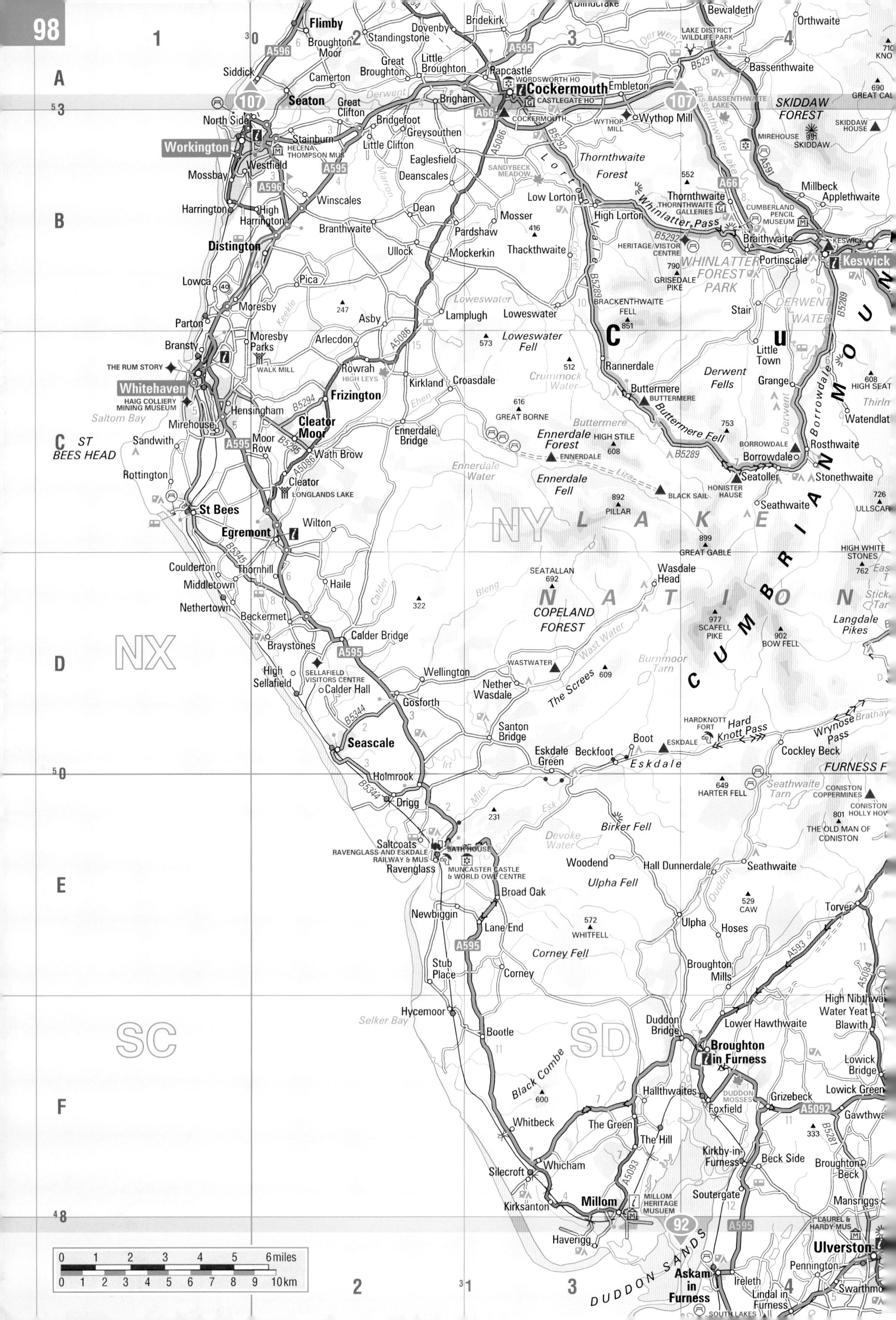
1
2
3
4
A
B
C
D
E
F
Flimby
Broughton Moor
Dovenby
Bridekirk
Standingstone
Bewaldeth
Orthwaite
LAKE DISTRICT WILDLIFE PARK
Great Broughton
Little Broughton
Papcastle
Camerton
Siddick
Seaton
Great Clifton
Brigham
WORDSWORTH HO
Cockermouth
Embleton
CASTLEGATE HO
COCKERMOUTH
Wythop Mill
WYTHOP MILL
Bassenthwaite
BASSENTHWAITE LAKE
SKIDDAW FOREST
SKIDDAW HOUSE
GREAT CAL
690
931
SKIDDAW
MIREHOUSE
North Side
Workington
HELENA THOMPSON MUS
Stainburn
Bridgefoot
Greysouthen
Little Clifton
Eaglesfield
Deanscales
SANDYBECK MEADOW
Thornthwaite Forest
Westfield
Mossbay
Winscales
Harrington
High Harrington
Dean
Branthwaite
Low Lorton
High Lorton
Mosser
Pardshaw
Thornthwaite
THORNTHWAITE GALLERIES
CUMBERLAND PENCIL MUSEUM
Millbeck
Applethwaite
Whinlatter Pass
Braithwaite
Portinscale
Keswick
KESWICK
Distington
Ullock
Mockerkin
Thackthwaite
416
552
HERITAGE/VISITOR CENTRE
790
GRISEDALE PIKE
WHINLATTER FOREST PARK
Lorton Vale
Lowca
Pica
Moresby
247
Asby
Lamplugh
Loweswater
BRACKENTHWAITE FELL
851
Stair
DERWENT WATER
Parton
Bransty
Moresby Parks
Arlecdon
573
Loweswater Fell
Little Town
THE RUM STORY
WALK MILL
Rowrah
HIGH LEYS
Kirkland
Croasdale
512
Rannerdale
Crummock Water
Derwent Fells
Grange
Whitehaven
HAIG COLLIERY MINING MUSEUM
Frizington
Buttermere
BUTTERMERE
Borrowdale
HIGH SEAT
608
Watendlath
Saltom Bay
Hensingham
Mirehouse
Cleator Moor
616
GREAT BORNE
Ennerdale Bridge
Buttermere Fell
753
ST BEES HEAD
Sandwith
Moor Row
Ennerdale Forest
HIGH STILE
608
ENNERDALE
BORROWDALE
Rosthwaite
Wath Brow
Rottington
Cleator
LONGLANDS LAKE
Ennerdale Water
Ennerdale Fell
Seatoller
Stonethwaite
HONISTER HAUSE
BLACK SAIL
Seathwaite
726
ULLSCAR
St Bees
Egremont
Wilton
892
PILLAR
NY
LAKE
899
GREAT GABLE
CUMBRIAN MOUNTAINS
HIGH WHITE STONES
762
Coulderton
Thornhill
Middletown
Haile
SEATALLAN
692
Wasdale Head
NATIONAL
Nethertown
Beckermet
322
COPELAND FOREST
977
SCAFELL PIKE
902
BOW FELL
Langdale Pikes
Stickle Tarn
NX
Braystones
Calder Bridge
Wast Water
Burnmoor Tarn
High Sellafield
SELLAFIELD VISITORS CENTRE
Calder Hall
Wellington
WASTWATER
Nether Wasdale
609
The Screes
Gosforth
Santon Bridge
HARDKNOTT FORT
Hard Knott Pass
Wrynose Pass
Seascale
Eskdale Green
Beckfoot
Boot
ESKDALE
Eskdale
Cockley Beck
FURNESS F
Holmrook
649
HARTER FELL
Seathwaite Tarn
CONISTON COPPERMINES
CONISTON
Drigg
231
801
HOLLY HOW
THE OLD MAN OF CONISTON
Birker Fell
Devoke Water
Saltcoats
RAVENGLASS AND ESKDALE RAILWAY & MUS
BATH HOUSE
Ravenglass
MUNCASTER CASTLE & WORLD OWL CENTRE
Woodend
Hall Dunnerdale
Seathwaite
Ulpha Fell
Broad Oak
529
CAW
Torver
Newbiggin
572
WHITFELL
Ulpha
Hoses
Lane End
Corney Fell
Stub Place
Corney
Broughton Mills
High Nibthwaite
Water Yeat
Blawith
Hycemoor
Selker Bay
Bootle
Duddon Bridge
Lower Hawthwaite
SC
SD
Broughton in Furness
Lowick Bridge
Black Combe
600
Hallthwaites
DUDDON MOSSES
Foxfield
Grizebeck
Lowick Green
Gawthwaite
333
Whitbeck
The Green
The Hill
Kirkby-in-Furness
Beck Side
Broughton Beck
Silecroft
Whicham
Kirksanton
Millom
MILLOM HERITAGE MUSEUM
Soutergate
Mansriggs
LAUREL & HARDY MUS
Haverigg
Ulverston
Pennington
DUDDON SANDS
Askam in Furness
Ireleth
Lindal in Furness
Swarthmoor
SOUTH LAKES
A596
A595
A66
A5086
B5292
B5291
A591
B5289
B5294
B5295
B5345
B5344
A5093
A593
A5084
A5092
B5281
107
92
40
0 1 2 3 4 5 6 miles
0 1 2 3 4 5 6 7 8 9 10 km

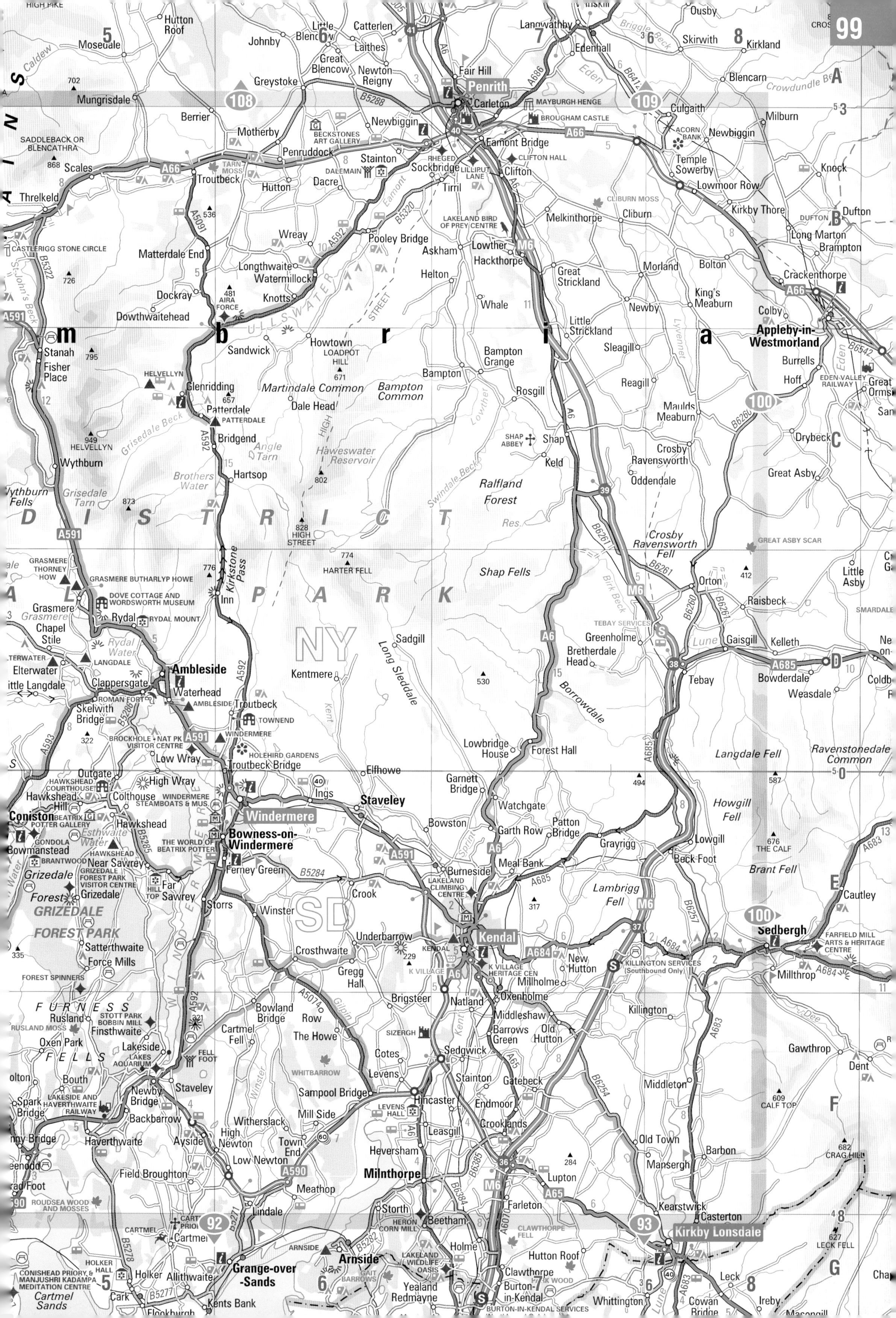

High Pike
Hutton Roof
Mosedale
Little Blencow
Catterlen
Langwathby
Ousby
Skirwith
Kirkland
Johnby
Laithes
Edenhall
Great Blencow
Newton Reigny
Fair Hill
Blencarn
Crowdundle Beck
Greystoke
Penrith
Mungrisdale
Carleton
Mayburgh Henge
Culgaith
Berrier
Newbiggin
Brougham Castle
Milburn
Motherby
Beckstones Art Gallery
Acorn Bank
Saddleback or Blencathra
Penruddock
Eamont Bridge
Temple Sowerby
Stainton
Rheged
Clifton Hall
Knock
Scales
Tarn Moss
Dalemain
Sockbridge
Lilliput Lane
Clifton
Lowmoor Row
Threlkeld
Troutbeck
Hutton
Dacre
Tirril
Kirkby Thore
Cliburn Moss
Cliburn
Dufton
Melkinthorpe
Lakeland Bird of Prey Centre
Long Marton
Wreay
Castlerigg Stone Circle
Pooley Bridge
Askham
Lowther
Brampton
Matterdale End
Hackthorpe
Morland
Bolton
Longthwaite
Great Strickland
Crackenthorpe
Watermillock
Helton
King's Meaburn
Dockray
Aira Force
Knotts
Whale
Newby
Colby
Dowthwaitehead
Little Strickland
Appleby-in-Westmorland
Ullswater
Stanah
Sandwick
Howtown
Loadpot Hill
Bampton Grange
Sleagill
Burrells
Fisher Place
Helvellyn
Glenridding
Bampton
Hoff
Eden Valley Railway
Great Ormside
Martindale Common
Bampton Common
Rosgill
Reagill
Dale Head
Patterdale
Maulds Meaburn
Bridgend
Shap Abbey
Shap
Drybeck
Grisedale Beck
Angle Tarn
Haweswater Reservoir
Crosby Ravensworth
Wythburn
Keld
Hartsop
Great Asby
Brothers Water
Oddendale
Ralfland Forest
Wythburn Fells
Grisedale Tarn
Lake District National Park
High Street
Crosby Ravensworth Fell
Great Asby Scar
Harter Fell
Grasmere
Thorney How
Grasmere Butharlyp Howe
Kirkstone Pass
Shap Fells
Orton
Little Asby
Dove Cottage and Wordsworth Museum
Inn
Raisbeck
Smardale
Rydal
Rydal Mount
Tebay Services
Chapel Stile
Rydal Water
Sadgill
Greenholme
Gaisgill
Kelleth
Elterwater
Langdale
Ambleside
Bretherdale Head
Lune
Tebay
Bowderdale
Little Langdale
Clappersgate
Waterhead
Kentmere
Long Sleddale
Weasdale
Skelwith Bridge
Roman Fort
Troutbeck
Townend
Borrowdale
Brockhole - Nat Pk Visitor Centre
Windermere
Lowbridge House
Forest Hall
Langdale Fell
Ravenstonedale Common
Low Wray
Holehird Gardens
Troutbeck Bridge
Outgate
Elfhowe
Garnett Bridge
Hawkshead Courthouse
High Wray
Ings
Staveley
Howgill Fell
Hawkshead Hill
Colthouse
Windermere Steamboats & Mus.
Watchgate
Coniston
Beatrix Potter Gallery
Hawkshead
Bowston
Patton Bridge
Lowgill
The Calf
Gondola
Esthwaite Water
The World of Beatrix Potter
Bowness-on-Windermere
Garth Row
Grayrigg
Bowmanstead
Brantwood
Near Sawrey
Ferney Green
Burneside
Meal Bank
Beck Foot
Brant Fell
Grizedale Forest Park Visitor Centre
Far Sawrey
Lakeland Climbing Centre
Lambrigg Fell
Cautley
Grizedale
Storrs
Winster
Crook
Kendal
Sedbergh
Farfield Mill Arts & Heritage Centre
Underbarrow
New Hutton
Killington Services (Southbound Only)
Satterthwaite
Crosthwaite
K Village Heritage Cen
Force Mills
Gregg Hall
Millholme
Millthrop
Forest Spinners
Brigsteer
Natland
Oxenholme
Furness Fells
Stott Park Bobbin Mill
Bowland Bridge
Row
Middleshaw
Killington
Rusland
Rusland Moss
Finsthwaite
Cartmel Fell
Sizergh
Barrows Green
Old Hutton
Oxen Park
The Howe
Lakeside
Lakes Aquarium
Fell Foot
Cotes
Sedgwick
Gawthrop
Dent
Whitbarrow
Levens
Stainton
Gatebeck
Bouth
Staveley
Newby Bridge
Sampool Bridge
Hincaster
Middleton
Lakeside and Haverthwaite Railway
Levens Hall
Endmoor
Calf Top
Backbarrow
Witherslack
Mill Side
Crooklands
Haverthwaite
Ayside
High Newton
Town End
Leasgill
Old Town
Barbon
Crag Hill
Heversham
Mansergh
Low Newton
Lupton
Field Broughton
Milnthorpe
Meathop
Roudsea Wood and Mosses
Storth
Farleton
Kearstwick
Casterton
Lindale
Heron Corn Mill
Beetham
Cartmel Priory
Cartmel
Clawthorpe Fell
Kirkby Lonsdale
Leck Fell
Arnside
Holme
Holker Hall
Hutton Roof
Conishead Priory & Manjushri Kadampa Meditation Centre
Holker
Allithwaite
Grange-over-Sands
Lakeland Wildlife Oasis
Clawthorpe
Gait Barrows
Yealand Redmayne
Burton-in-Kendal
Leck
Cartmel Sands
Cark
Whittington
Cowan Bridge
Ireby
Kents Bank
Flookburgh
Burton-in-Kendal Services

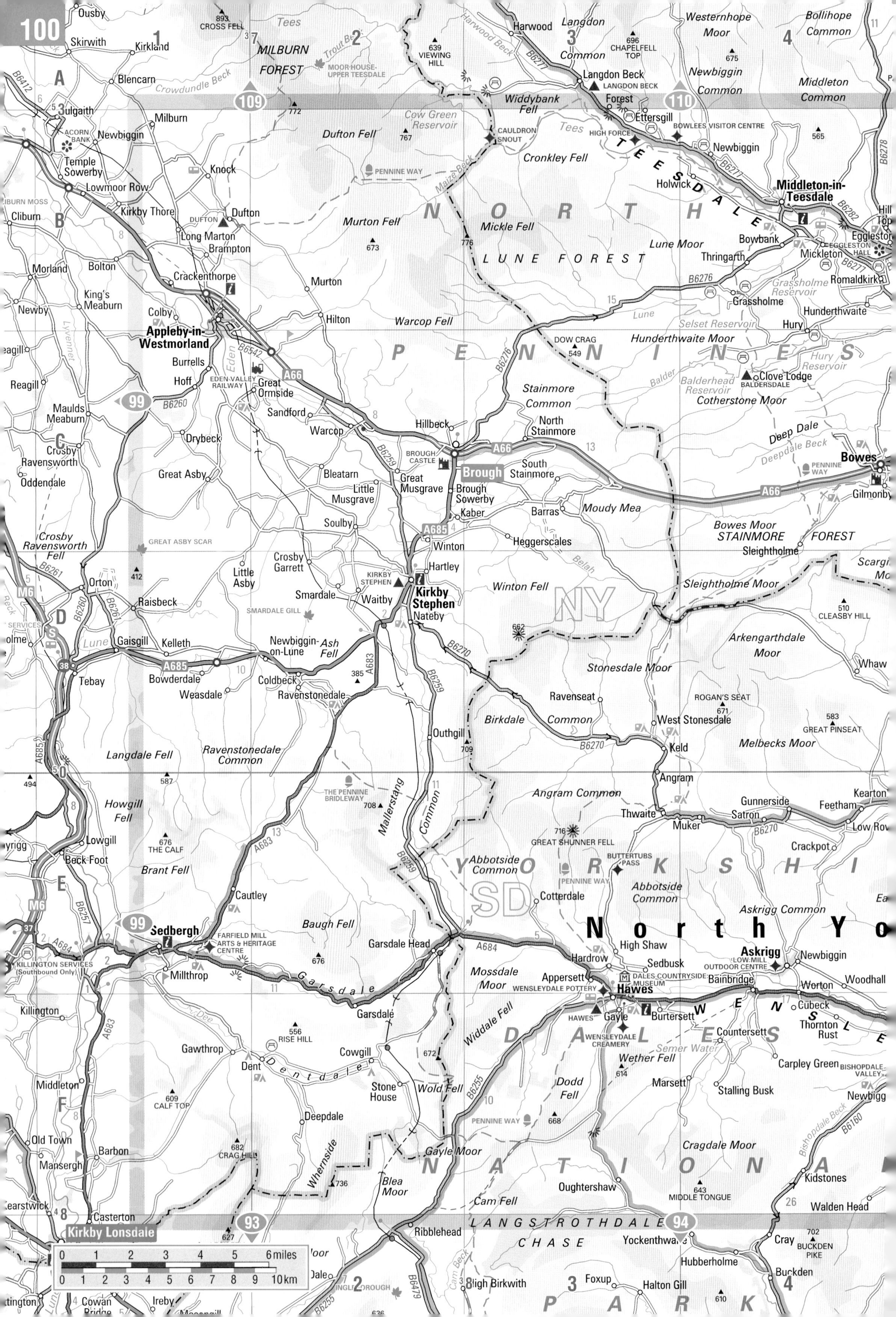

Ousby
893 CROSS FELL
Tees
MILBURN FOREST
Trout Beck
MOOR HOUSE-UPPER TEESDALE
Skirwith
Kirkland
Blencarn
Crowdundle Beck
Culgaith
Milburn
ACORN BANK
Newbiggin
Temple Sowerby
Lowmoor Row
Kirkby Thore
Knock
DUFTON
Dufton
Long Marton
Brampton
Cliburn
Morland
Bolton
King's Meaburn
Newby
Crackenthorpe
Colby
Appleby-in-Westmorland
Burrells
Hoff
Reagill
EDEN VALLEY RAILWAY
Great Ormside
Sandford
Warcop
Maulds Meaburn
Drybeck
Crosby Ravensworth
Oddendale
Great Asby
GREAT ASBY SCAR
Crosby Ravensworth Fell
Orton
Raisbeck
Little Asby
Crosby Garrett
Smardale
SMARDALE GILL
Waitby
Gaisgill
Kelleth
Newbiggin-on-Lune
Ash Fell
Tebay
Bowderdale
Weasdale
Coldbeck
Ravenstonedale
Langdale Fell
Ravenstonedale Common
Howgill Fell
676 THE CALF
Brant Fell
Lowgill
Beck Foot
Cautley
Sedbergh
FARFIELD MILL ARTS & HERITAGE CENTRE
KILLINGTON SERVICES (Southbound Only)
Millthrop
Killington
Garsdale
Baugh Fell
Garsdale Head
Gawthrop
Dent
Dentdale
556 RISE HILL
Cowgill
Stone House
Middleton
609 CALF TOP
Deepdale
Whernside
Old Town
Barbon
682 CRAG HILL
Mansergh
Casterton
Kirkby Lonsdale
Cowan Bridge
Ireby
639 VIEWING HILL
Cow Green Reservoir
Dufton Fell
CAULDRON SNOUT
PENNINE WAY
Murton Fell
Murton
Hilton
Warcop Fell
Mickle Fell
LUNE FOREST
NORTH PENNINES
Harwood
Harwood Beck
Langdon Common
696 CHAPELFELL TOP
Langdon Beck
LANGDON BECK
Widdybank Fell
Forest
Ettersgill
HIGH FORCE
BOWLEES VISITOR CENTRE
Newbiggin
Cronkley Fell
TEESDALE
Holwick
Westernhope Moor
Newbiggin Common
Bollihope Common
Middleton Common
Middleton-in-Teesdale
Lune Moor
Bowbank
Mickleton
Eggleston
EGGLESTON HALL
Thringarth
Romaldkirk
Grassholme Reservoir
Grassholme
Hunderthwaite
Lune
Selset Reservoir
Hury
DOW CRAG
Hunderthwaite Moor
Hury Reservoir
Balderhead Reservoir
Clove Lodge
BALDERSDALE
Cotherstone Moor
Stainmore Common
North Stainmore
Hillbeck
BROUGH CASTLE
Brough
South Stainmore
Deep Dale
Deepdale Beck
Bowes
Gilmonby
Bleatarn
Great Musgrave
Little Musgrave
Brough Sowerby
Kaber
Barras
Moody Mea
Soulby
Winton
Heggerscales
Bowes Moor
STAINMORE FOREST
Sleightholme
Hartley
KIRKBY STEPHEN
Kirkby Stephen
Nateby
Winton Fell
NY
Sleightholme Moor
510 CLEASBY HILL
Arkengarthdale Moor
Stonesdale Moor
Whaw
Ravenseat
ROGAN'S SEAT
Birkdale
Common
West Stonesdale
583 GREAT PINSEAT
Outhgill
Keld
Melbecks Moor
Angram
Angram Common
THE PENNINE BRIDLEWAY
Mallerstang Common
Thwaite
Muker
Gunnerside
Satron
Feetham
Kearton
Low Row
716 GREAT SHUNNER FELL
BUTTERTUBS PASS
Crackpot
Abbotside Common
YORKSHIRE
SD
Cotterdale
Askrigg Common
North Yorkshire
High Shaw
Askrigg
LOW MILL OUTDOOR CENTRE
Newbiggin
Hardrow
Sedbusk
DALES COUNTRYSIDE MUSEUM
Bainbridge
Mossdale Moor
Appersett
WENSLEYDALE POTTERY
Hawes
Worton
Woodhall
Gayle
Burtersett
Cubeck
Thornton Rust
Widdale Fell
WENSLEYDALE CREAMERY
WENSLEYDALE
Countersett
Semer Water
Wether Fell
Carpley Green
BISHOPDALE VALLEY
Marsett
Stalling Busk
Newbigg
Wold Fell
Dodd Fell
Cragdale Moor
Bishopdale Beck
Gayle Moor
YORKSHIRE DALES NATIONAL PARK
Blea Moor
Oughtershaw
643 MIDDLE TONGUE
Kidstones
Cam Fell
Walden Head
Ribblehead
LANGSTROTHDALE CHASE
Yockenthwaite
Cray
702 BUCKDEN PIKE
Hubberholme
Buckden
High Birkwith
Foxup
Halton Gill
Cam Beck
INGLEBOROUGH
A66
A685
A683
A684
B6259
B6270
B6276
B6277
B6260
B6261
B6542
B6255
B6479
B6160
M6
0 1 2 3 4 5 6 miles
0 1 2 3 4 5 6 7 8 9 10 km
109
110
99
93
94

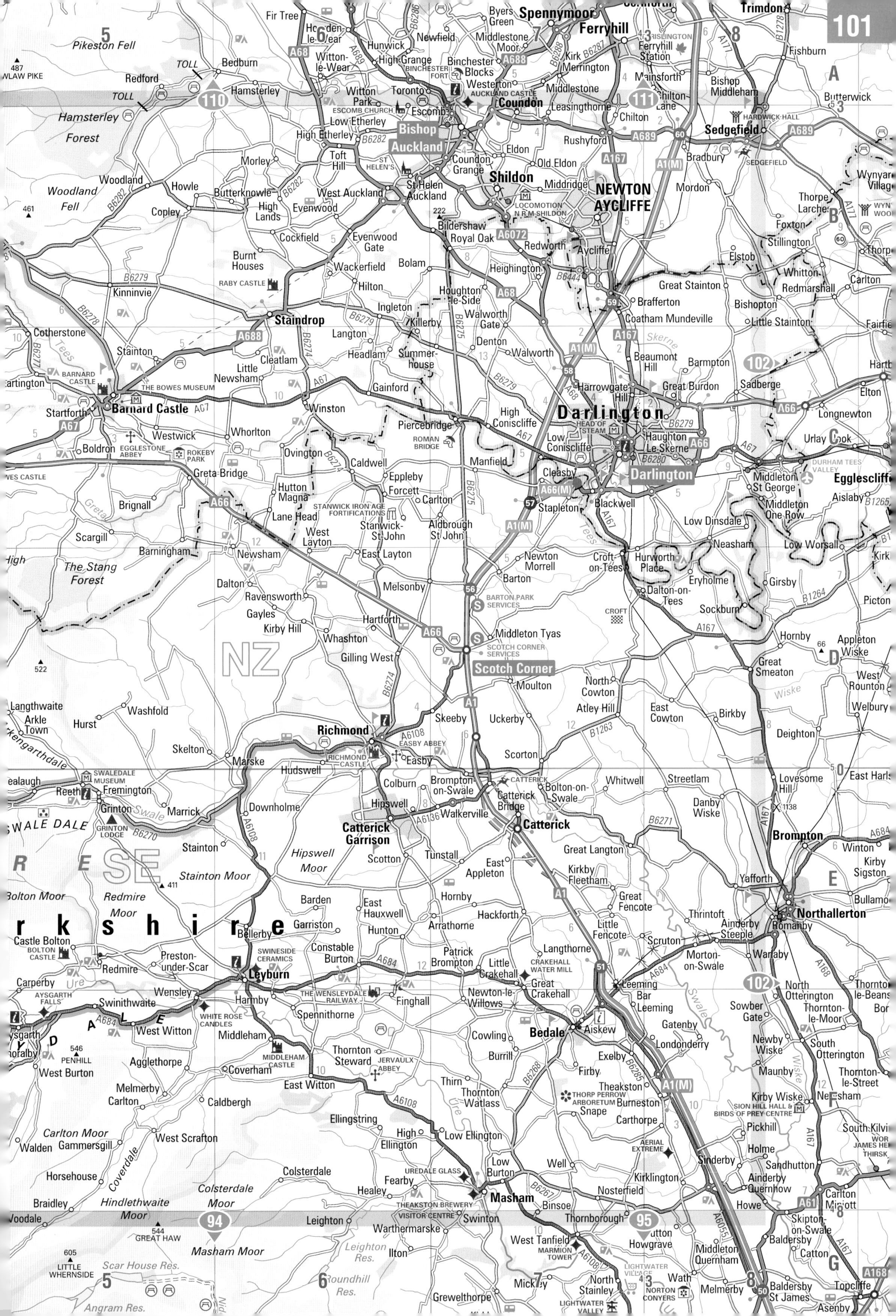
Pikeston Fell
Bedburn
Redford
TOLL
Hamsterley
110
Hamsterley Forest
Woodland Fell
Woodland
Howle
Copley
Butterknowle
High Lands
Evenwood
Morley
Toft Hill
Fir Tree
Howden-le-Wear
Witton-le-Wear
Hunwick
Newfield
High Grange
Witton Park
Toronto
Escomb
ESCOMB CHURCH
Low Etherley
High Etherley
Bishop Auckland
BINCHESTER FORT
Binchester Blocks
Westerton
AUCKLAND CASTLE
Coundon
Coundon Grange
Eldon
Shildon
Old Eldon
Middlestone
Middlestone Moor
Byers Green
Spennymoor
Ferryhill
Ferryhill Station
Kirk Merrington
Leasingthorne
Chilton
Rushyford
Mainsforth
Bishop Middleham
Fishburn
Trimdon
111
Sedgefield
HARDWICK HALL
Butterwick
Bradbury
Mordon
NEWTON AYCLIFFE
LOCOMOTION N.R.M. SHILDON
Middridge
ST HELEN'S
St Helen Auckland
West Auckland
Cockfield
Evenwood Gate
Bildershaw
Royal Oak
Redworth
Aycliffe
Heighington
Burnt Houses
RABY CASTLE
Wackerfield
Bolam
Hilton
Kinninvie
Staindrop
Ingleton
Houghton-le-Side
Walworth Gate
Killerby
Langton
Headlam
Summerhouse
Denton
Walworth
Gainford
Cotherstone
Stainton
Cleatham
Little Newsham
BARNARD CASTLE
THE BOWES MUSEUM
Barnard Castle
Startforth
Westwick
Whorlton
Winston
Piercebridge
ROMAN BRIDGE
High Coniscliffe
Low Coniscliffe
Boldron
EGGLESTONE ABBEY
ROKEBY PARK
Greta Bridge
Ovington
Caldwell
Eppleby
Forcett
Carlton
Manfield
Hutton Magna
Lane Head
STANWICK IRON AGE FORTIFICATIONS
Stanwick-St-John
Aldbrough St John
Brignall
Scargill
Barningham
West Layton
East Layton
Newsham
The Stang Forest
Dalton
Ravensworth
Gayles
Kirby Hill
Melsonby
Hartforth
Whashton
Gilling West
Middleton Tyas
SCOTCH CORNER SERVICES
Scotch Corner
BARTON PARK SERVICES
Barton
Newton Morrell
NZ
Darlington
HEAD OF STEAM
Haughton Le Skerne
Harrowgate Hill
Great Burdon
Cleasby
Stapleton
Blackwell
Beaumont Hill
Barmpton
Brafferton
Coatham Mundeville
Great Stainton
Elstob
Bishopton
Little Stainton
Redmarshall
Whitton
Stillington
Foxton
Thorpe Larches
Carlton
Sadberge
Longnewton
Elton
Urlay Nook
DURHAM TEES VALLEY
Middleton St George
Middleton One Row
Egglescliffe
Aislaby
Low Dinsdale
Neasham
Low Worsall
Hurworth Place
Croft-on-Tees
Eryholme
Dalton-on-Tees
Sockburn
Girsby
CROFT
Picton
Hornby
Appleton Wiske
Great Smeaton
West Rounton
Welbury
Deighton
North Cowton
Moulton
Atley Hill
East Cowton
Birkby
Uckerby
Skeeby
Scorton
Langthwaite
Arkle Town
Hurst
Washfold
Arkengarthdale
Skelton
Marske
Richmond
EASBY ABBEY
Easby
RICHMOND CASTLE
Hudswell
SWALEDALE MUSEUM
Reeth
Fremington
Grinton
Healaugh
Marrick
GRINTON LODGE
SWALE DALE
Downholme
Colburn
Brompton-on-Swale
CATTERICK
Catterick Bridge
Bolton-on-Swale
Whitwell
Streetlam
Danby Wiske
Lovesome Hill
Hipswell
Walkerville
Catterick Garrison
Catterick
Stainton
Hipswell Moor
Scotton
Tunstall
Great Langton
East Appleton
Kirkby Fleetham
Brompton
Winton
Kirby Sigston
Yafforth
Northallerton
Romanby
Bullamoor
Stainton Moor
Bolton Moor
Redmire Moor
SE
Yorkshire
Barden
East Hauxwell
Hornby
Hackforth
Great Fencote
Little Fencote
Thrintoft
Ainderby Steeple
Scruton
Langthorne
Bellerby
Garriston
Hunton
Arrathorne
Castle Bolton
BOLTON CASTLE
Redmire
Preston-under-Scar
SWINESIDE CERAMICS
Constable Burton
Patrick Brompton
Little Crakehall
CRAKEHALL WATER MILL
Great Crakehall
Leeming
Leeming Bar
Morton-on-Swale
Warlaby
North Otterington
Thornton-le-Beans
Carperby
AYSGARTH FALLS
Swinithwaite
Wensley
Leyburn
Harmby
THE WENSLEYDALE RAILWAY
Finghall
Spennithorne
Newton-le-Willows
Bedale
Aiskew
Sowber Gate
Thornton-le-Moor
WHITE ROSE CANDLES
West Witton
Middleham
MIDDLEHAM CASTLE
Thornton Steward
JERVAULX ABBEY
Cowling
Burrill
Gatenby
Londonderry
Exelby
Firby
Newby Wiske
South Otterington
Aysgarth
Thoralby
PENHILL
West Burton
Agglethorpe
Coverham
East Witton
Thirn
Thornton Watlass
THORP PERROW ARBORETUM
Snape
Theakston
Burneston
Carthorpe
Maunby
Thornton-le-Street
Kirby Wiske
SION HILL HALL & BIRDS OF PREY CENTRE
Newsham
Melmerby
Carlton
Caldbergh
Ellingstring
High Ellington
Low Ellington
Pickhill
South Kilvington
Carlton Moor
Walden
Gammersgill
West Scrafton
Coverdale
AERIAL EXTREME
Sinderby
Holme
Sandhutton
Horsehouse
Colsterdale
Fearby
Healey
UREDALE GLASS
Low Burton
Masham
Well
Kirklington
Ainderby Quernhow
Carlton Miniott
Braidley
Hindlethwaite Moor
Colsterdale Moor
THEAKSTON BREWERY VISITOR CENTRE
Binsoe
Nosterfield
Howe
Woodale
94
GREAT HAW
Leighton
Swinton
Thornborough
95
Sutton Howgrave
Skipton-on-Swale
Baldersby
Catton
Warthermarske
West Tanfield
MARMION TOWER
Middleton Quernham
LITTLE WHERNSIDE
Scar House Res.
Masham Moor
Leighton Res.
Ilton
Roundhill Res.
Grewelthorpe
Mickley
North Stainley
LIGHTWATER VILLAGE
LIGHTWATER VALLEY
NORTON CONYERS
Wath
Melmerby
Baldersby St James
Topcliffe
Asenby
Angram Res.
102
A1(M)
A66
A68
A688
A689
A167
A6072
A67
A66(M)
A6108
A6136
A684
A61
A168
A19
B6282
B6279
B6278
B6274
B6275
B6280
B6444
B6271
B6270
B6267
B6268
B6285
B1263
B1264
A1
A177

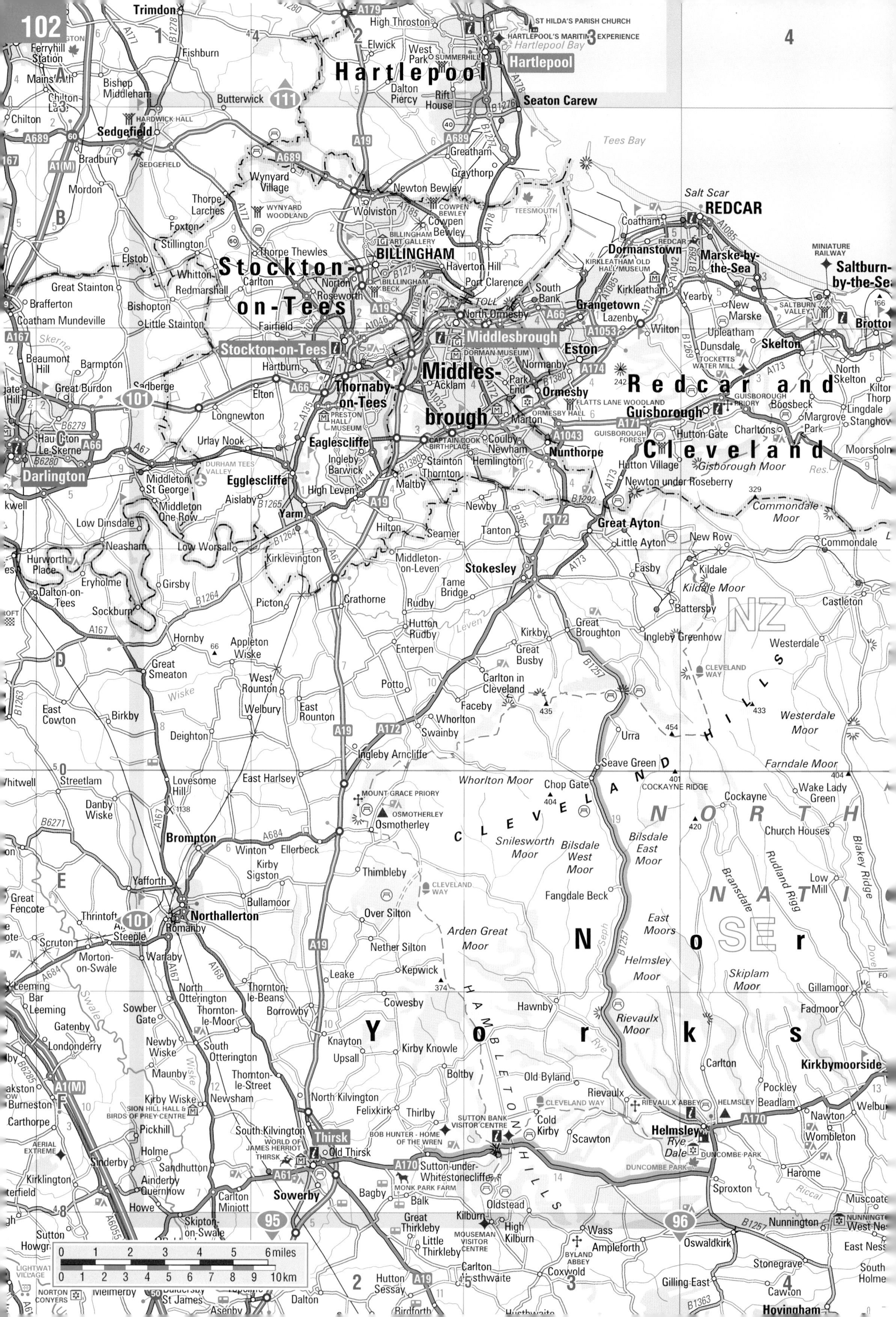
Trimdon
A179
High Throston
Elwick
West Park
Summerhill
St Hilda's Parish Church
Hartlepool's Maritime Experience
Hartlepool Bay
Hartlepool
Ferryhill Station
Fishburn
Mainsforth
Bishop Middleham
Chilton
Dalton Piercy
Rift House
Seaton Carew
Butterwick
111
Hardwick Hall
Sedgefield
A689
A1(M)
Bradbury
Greatham
Graythorp
Tees Bay
Mordon
Wynyard Village
Newton Bewley
Thorpe Larches
Wynyard Woodland
Wolviston
Cowpen Bewley
Teesmouth
Salt Scar
REDCAR
Coatham
Foxton
Stillington
Billingham Art Gallery
BILLINGHAM
Dormanstown
Marske-by-the-Sea
Miniature Railway
Saltburn-by-the-Sea
Elstob
Thorpe Thewles
Haverton Hill
Kirkleatham Old Hall Museum
Great Stainton
Whitton
Stockton-on-Tees
Carlton
Norton
Port Clarence
South Bank
Kirkleatham
Yearby
New Marske
Saltburn Valley
Brotton
Brafferton
Redmarshall
Billingham Beck
Roseworth
Grangetown
Lazenby
Bishopton
Coatham Mundeville
Little Stainton
Toll
North Ormesby
A66
Wilton
Upleatham
Fairfield
Middlesbrough
A1053
Dunsdale
Skelton
Skerne
Stockton-on-Tees
Dorman Museum
Eston
Tocketts Water Mill
Beaumont Hill
Barmpton
Hartburn
Middles-brough
Normanby
Redcar and Cleveland
North Skelton
Great Burdon
Sadberge
Elton
Thornaby-on-Tees
Acklam
Park End
Ormesby
Guisborough Priory
Kilton Thorpe
101
Longnewton
Preston Hall Museum
Flatts Lane Woodland
Guisborough
Boosbeck
Lingdale
Marton
Ormesby Hall
Margrove Park
Stanghow
Haughton-le-Skerne
Urlay Nook
Eaglescliffe
Captain Cook Birthplace
Coulby Newham
Nunthorpe
Guisborough Forest
Hutton Gate
Charltons
Cleveland
Moorsholm
Darlington
A67
Middleton St George
Durham Tees Valley
Egglescliffe
Ingleby Barwick
Stainton
Thornton
Hemlington
Hutton Village
Gisborough Moor
Res.
Maltby
High Leven
Newton under Roseberry
Middleton One Row
Aislaby
Yarm
Newby
Commondale Moor
Low Dinsdale
Hilton
Seamer
Tanton
Great Ayton
New Row
Neasham
Low Worsall
Little Ayton
Commondale
Hurworth Place
Kirklevington
Middleton-on-Leven
Stokesley
Easby
Kildale
Eryholme
Girsby
Kildale Moor
Dalton-on-Tees
Tame Bridge
Castleton
Sockburn
Picton
Crathorne
Rudby
Battersby
NZ
Hutton Rudby
Leven
Hornby
Appleton Wiske
Kirkby
Great Broughton
Ingleby Greenhow
Westerdale
Great Smeaton
Great Busby
Enterpen
Cleveland Way
West Rounton
Carlton in Cleveland
Potto
Wiske
East Cowton
Birkby
Welbury
East Rounton
Faceby
Whorlton
Westerdale Moor
Deighton
Swainby
Urra
Ingleby Arncliffe
Seave Green
Farndale Moor
Whitwell
Streetlam
Lovesome Hill
East Harlsey
Whorlton Moor
Chop Gate
Cockayne Ridge
Wake Lady Green
Danby Wiske
Mount Grace Priory
Osmotherley
Cockayne
North
Church Houses
Brompton
Winton
Ellerbeck
Snilesworth Moor
Bilsdale West Moor
Bilsdale East Moor
Cleveland
Kirby Sigston
Thimbleby
Rudland Rigg
Blakey Ridge
Bransdale
Yafforth
Fangdale Beck
Low Mill
Great Fencote
National
Bullamoor
Thrintoft
Northallerton
Over Silton
Romanby
Ainderby Steeple
East Moors
Arden Great Moor
Scruton
Nether Silton
Morton-on-Swale
Warlaby
Helmsley Moor
Skiplam Moor
Park
Leeming Bar
Leeming
North Otterington
Thornton-le-Beans
Kepwick
Leake
Cowesby
Gillamoor
Borrowby
Sowerby Gate
Thornton-le-Moor
Hawnby
Fadmoor
Gatenby
Swale
Rievaulx Moor
Londonderry
Newby Wiske
South Otterington
Knayton
Upsall
Kirby Knowle
Hambleton Hills
Yorkshire
Carlton
Kirkbymoorside
Maunby
Thornton-le-Street
Boltby
Old Byland
Kirby Wiske
Newsham
North Kilvington
Rievaulx
Pockley
Sion Hill Hall & Birds of Prey Centre
Felixkirk
Thirlby
Rievaulx Abbey
Helmsley
Beadlam
Welburn
Burneston
Carthorpe
Pickhill
South Kilvington
Sutton Bank Visitor Centre
Cold Kirby
Helmsley
A170
Nawton
Wombleton
Aerial Extreme
World of James Herriot
Thirsk
Bob Hunter - Home of the Wren
Scawton
Rye Dale
Duncombe Park
Holme
Old Thirsk
Sinderby
Sandhutton
Sutton-under-Whitestonecliffe
Kirklington
Ainderby Quernhow
Monk Park Farm
Harome
Carlton Miniott
Sowerby
Bagby
Balk
Oldstead
Sproxton
Riccal
Muscoates
Howe
Skipton-on-Swale
95
Great Thirkleby
Kilburn
High Kilburn
96
Nunnington
Nunnington Hall
West Ness
Sutton
Mouseman Visitor Centre
Little Thirkleby
Wass
Ampleforth
Oswaldkirk
East Ness
Byland Abbey
Coxwold
Stonegrave
Carlton Husthwaite
Gilling East
South Holme
Lightwater Valley
Hutton Sessay
Cawton
Norton Conyers
St James
Dalton
Birdforth
Asenby
Hovingham
0 1 2 3 4 5 6 miles
0 1 2 3 4 5 6 7 8 9 10 km

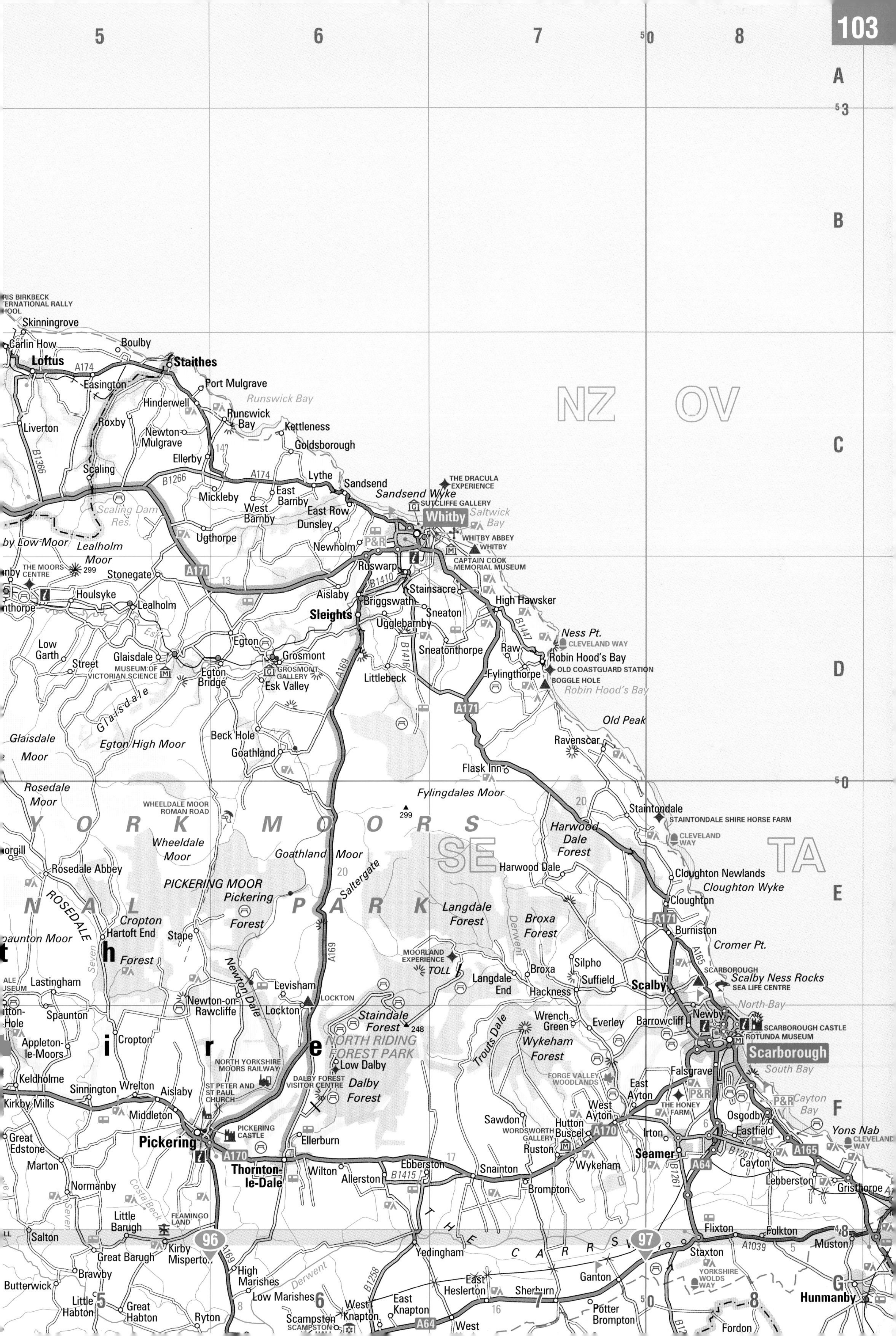

5
6
7
8
A
B
C
D
E
F
G
NZ
OV
SE
TA
Skinningrove
Carlin How
Boulby
Loftus
A174
Staithes
Easington
Port Mulgrave
Runswick Bay
Hinderwell
Runswick Bay
Kettleness
Liverton
Roxby
Newton Mulgrave
Goldsborough
B1366
Ellerby
Scaling
A174
Lythe
B1266
Sandsend
THE DRACULA EXPERIENCE
Mickleby
East Barnby
Sandsend Wyke
SUTCLIFFE GALLERY
Scaling Dam Res.
West Barnby
East Row
Whitby
Saltwick Bay
Dunsley
Ugthorpe
WHITBY ABBEY
Lealholm Moor
Newholm
P&R
WHITBY
CAPTAIN COOK MEMORIAL MUSEUM
THE MOORS CENTRE
299
Stonegate
A171
Ruswarp
B1410
Houlsyke
Aislaby
Stainsacre
Lealholm
Briggswath
High Hawsker
Sleights
Sneaton
Ugglebarnby
B1447
Ness Pt.
CLEVELAND WAY
Low Garth
Egton
Raw
Robin Hood's Bay
Glaisdale
Street
Grosmont
B1416
Sneatonthorpe
OLD COASTGUARD STATION
MUSEUM OF VICTORIAN SCIENCE
Egton Bridge
GROSMONT GALLERY
Esk Valley
A169
Littlebeck
Fylingthorpe
BOGGLE HOLE
Robin Hood's Bay
Glaisdale
A171
Old Peak
Glaisdale Moor
Egton High Moor
Beck Hole
Goathland
Ravenscar
Flask Inn
Rosedale Moor
Fylingdales Moor
WHEELDALE MOOR ROMAN ROAD
299
Staintondale
STAINTONDALE SHIRE HORSE FARM
YORK MOORS
Harwood Dale Forest
CLEVELAND WAY
Wheeldale Moor
Goathland Moor
Rosedale Abbey
Harwood Dale
Cloughton Newlands
PICKERING MOOR
Saltergate
Cloughton Wyke
NAL PARK
Pickering Forest
Cloughton
ROSEDALE
Cropton
Langdale Forest
Broxa Forest
A171
Hartoft End
Stape
Derwent
Burniston
Cromer Pt.
MOORLAND EXPERIENCE
TOLL
A169
Silpho
A165
Forest
Newton Dale
Broxa
Suffield
SCARBOROUGH SEA LIFE CENTRE
Scalby Ness Rocks
Lastingham
Levisham
Langdale End
Hackness
Scalby
Newton-on-Rawcliffe
LOCKTON
North Bay
Spaunton
Lockton
Staindale Forest
Wrench Green
Everley
Barrowcliff
Newby
SCARBOROUGH CASTLE
248
Trouts Dale
ROTUNDA MUSEUM
Appleton-le-Moors
Cropton
NORTH RIDING FOREST PARK
Wykeham Forest
Scarborough
NORTH YORKSHIRE MOORS RAILWAY
Low Dalby
South Bay
Keldholme
Sinnington
Wrelton
Aislaby
ST PETER AND ST PAUL CHURCH
DALBY FOREST VISITOR CENTRE
Dalby Forest
FORGE VALLEY WOODLANDS
Falsgrave
East Ayton
Kirkby Mills
P&R
Middleton
West Ayton
THE HONEY FARM
Cayton Bay
Sawdon
Osgodby
Great Edstone
Pickering
PICKERING CASTLE
Ellerburn
Hutton Buscel
Irton
Yons Nab
A170
WORDSWORTH GALLERY
A170
Eastfield
CLEVELAND WAY
Ruston
Seamer
B1261
A165
Marton
Thornton-le-Dale
Wilton
Ebberston
17
Snainton
Wykeham
A64
Cayton
Allerston
B1415
B1261
Normanby
Brompton
Lebberston
Gristhorpe
Costa Beck
Little Barugh
FLAMINGO LAND
THE CARRS
Flixton
Folkton
Salton
96
97
A1039
Muston
Great Barugh
Kirby Misperton
A169
Yedingham
Staxton
Brawby
High Marishes
Derwent
B1258
East Heslerton
Ganton
YORKSHIRE WOLDS WAY
Butterwick
Low Marishes
Sherburn
Hunmanby
Little Habton
Great Habton
West Knapton
East Knapton
16
Potter Brompton
Ryton
Scampston
SCAMPSTON
A64
West
Fordon

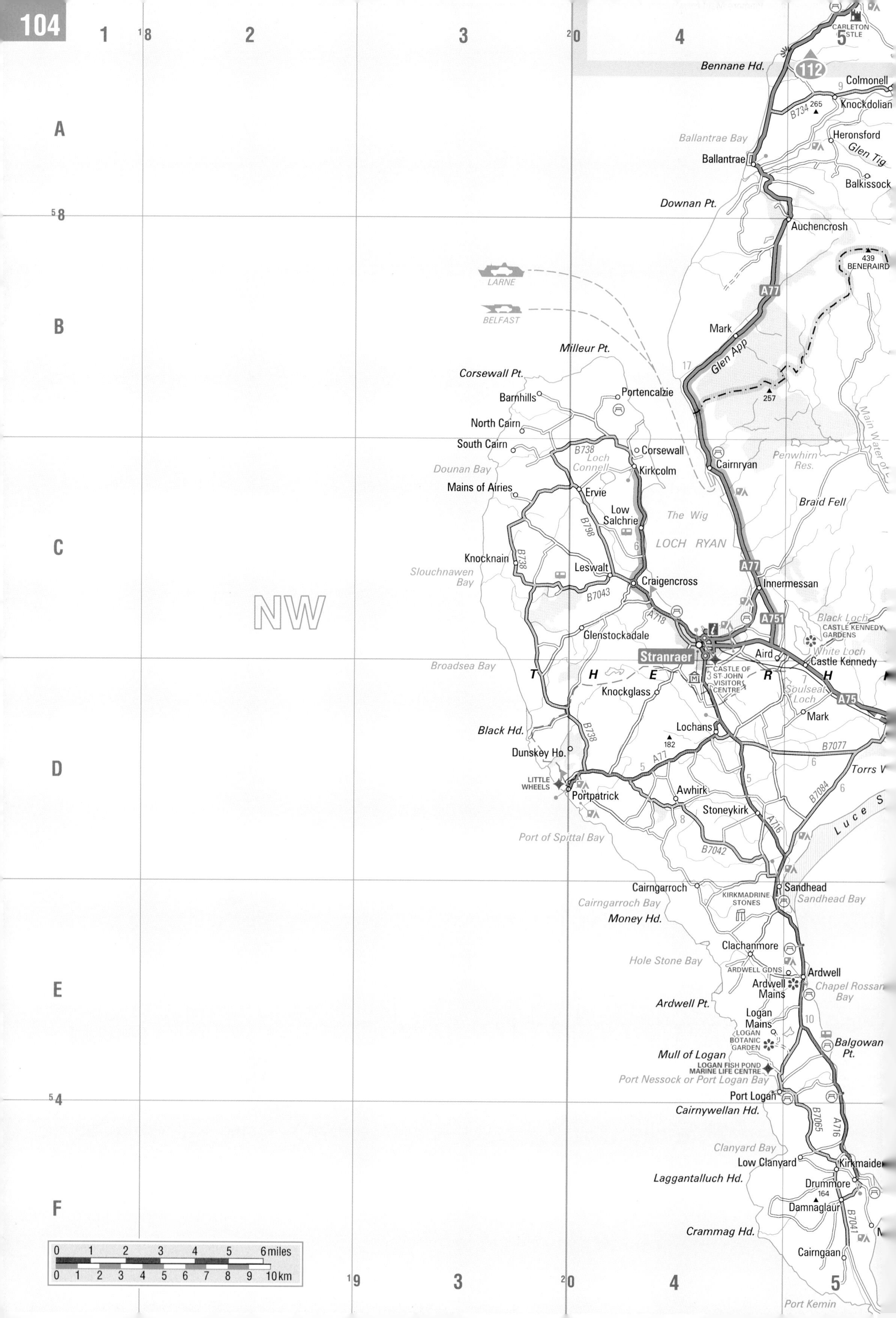

1   18   2   3   20   4   5

A

58

B

LARNE

BELFAST

Milleur Pt.

Corsewall Pt.

Barnhills

North Cairn

South Cairn   B738   Corsewall

Dounan Bay   *Loch Connell*   Kirkcolm

Mains of Airies   Ervie

Low Salchrie

B798

C

Knocknain   Leswalt

Slouchnawen Bay   B738   Craigencross

B7043

A718

Glenstockadale

Broadsea Bay   T H E   R H

Stranraer

CASTLE OF ST. JOHN VISITOR CENTRE

Knockglass

Black Hd.

B738   Lochans

Dunskey Ho.   182

A77

LITTLE WHEELS   Awhirk

Portpatrick   5

Stoneykirk   A716

Port of Spittal Bay   8   B7042

Cairngarroch   KIRKMADRINE STONES   Sandhead

Cairngarroch Bay   *Sandhead Bay*

Money Hd.

Clachanmore

Hole Stone Bay   ARDWELL GDNS   Ardwell

Ardwell Mains   *Chapel Rossan Bay*

E   *Ardwell Pt.*   Logan Mains   10

LOGAN BOTANIC GARDEN

Mull of Logan   Balgowan Pt.

LOGAN FISH POND MARINE LIFE CENTRE

Port Nessock or Port Logan Bay

54   Port Logan

Cairnywellan Hd.   B7065   A716

Clanyard Bay   Kirkmaiden

Low Clanyard

Laggantalluch Hd.   Drummore
164

F   Damnaglaur   B7041

Crammag Hd.

Cairngaan

Port Kemin

CARLETON STLE   5

Bennane Hd.   112

Colmonell
9
B734   265   Knockdolian

Heronsford   *Glen Tig*

Ballantrae   Balkissock

Downan Pt.   Auchencrosh

439 BENERAIRD

A77

Mark

17   *Glen App*   257

Main Water of

Cairnryan   *Penwhirn Res.*

Braid Fell

LOCH RYAN   A77

Innermessan   *Black Loch*

A751   CASTLE KENNEDY GARDENS

White Loch

Aird   Castle Kennedy

Soulseat Loch   A75

Mark

B7077

6

Torrs V

5   B7084   6

Luce S

Scale

0 1 2 3 4 5 6 miles

0 1 2 3 4 5 6 7 8 9 10km

19   3   20   4   5

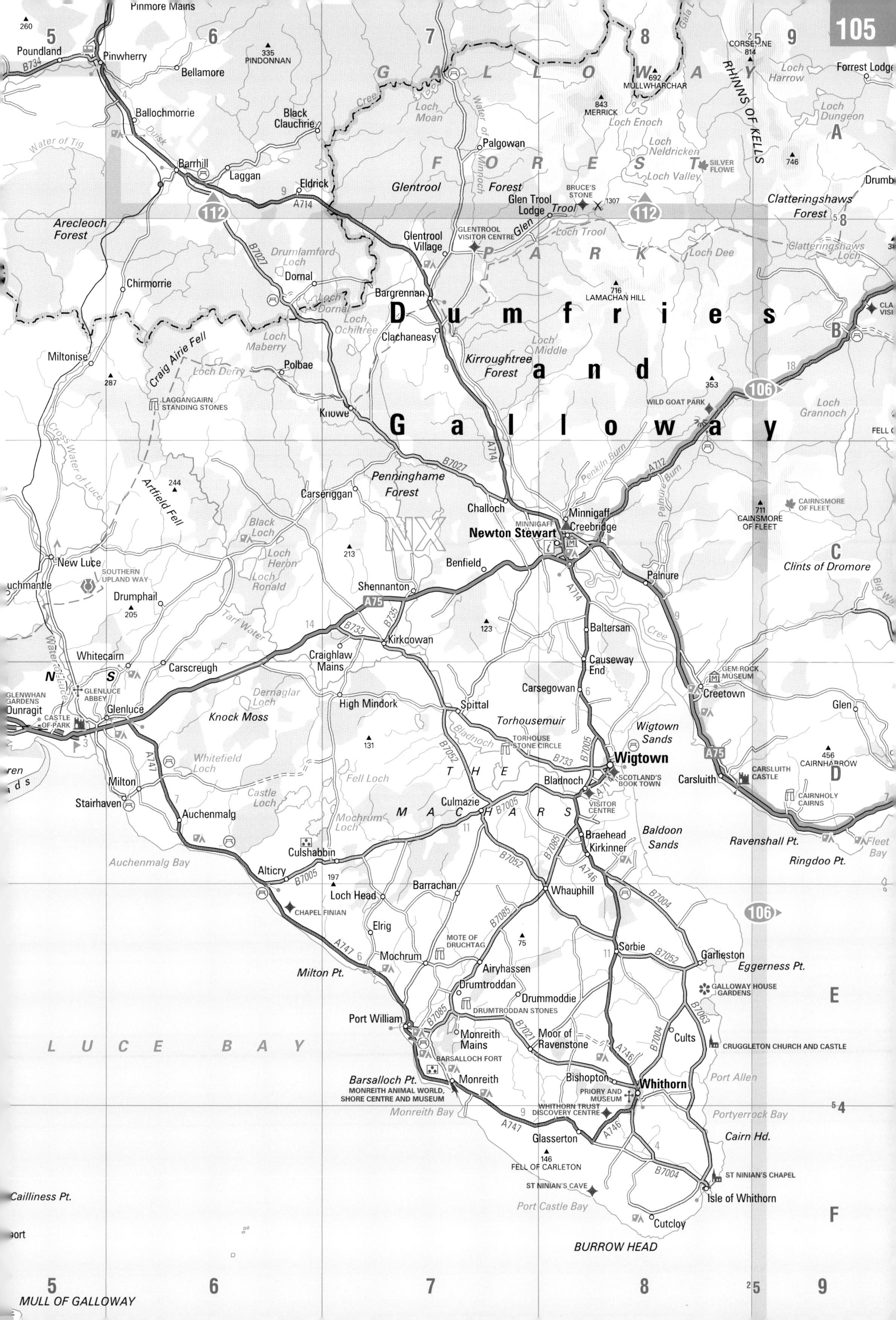
Dumfries and Galloway
GALLOWAY FOREST PARK
Pinmore Mains
Poundland
Pinwherry
Bellamore
PINDONNAN
Ballochmorrie
Black Clauchrie
Barrhill
Laggan
Eldrick
Water of Tig
Arecleoch Forest
Drumlamford Loch
Dornal
Loch Dornal
Loch Ochiltree
Chirmorrie
Miltonise
Craig Airie Fell
Loch Maberry
Loch Derry
Polbae
LAGGANGAIRN STANDING STONES
Knowe
Cross Water of Luce
Artfield Fell
Carseriggan
Penninghame Forest
Black Loch
Loch Heron
Loch Ronald
New Luce
SOUTHERN UPLAND WAY
Drumphail
Tarf Water
Whitecairn
Carscreugh
GLENLUCE ABBEY
GLENWHAN GARDENS
Dunragit
CASTLE OF PARK
Glenluce
Dernaglar Loch
Knock Moss
Whitefield Loch
Milton
Stairhaven
Castle Loch
Auchenmalg
Auchenmalg Bay
Mochrum Loch
Culshabbin
Alticry
CHAPEL FINIAN
Loch Head
Elrig
Barrachan
Mochrum
Milton Pt.
MOTE OF DRUCHTAG
Airyhassen
Drumtroddan
Drummoddie
DRUMTRODDAN STONES
Port William
Monreith Mains
BARSALLOCH FORT
Barsalloch Pt.
Monreith
MONREITH ANIMAL WORLD, SHORE CENTRE AND MUSEUM
Monreith Bay
LUCE BAY
Cailliness Pt.
MULL OF GALLOWAY
Glasserton
FELL OF CARLETON
ST NINIAN'S CAVE
Port Castle Bay
BURROW HEAD
Cutcloy
Isle of Whithorn
ST NINIAN'S CHAPEL
Cairn Hd.
Portyerrock Bay
Port Allen
Whithorn
PRIORY AND MUSEUM
WHITHORN TRUST DISCOVERY CENTRE
Bishopton
Moor of Ravenstone
Cults
CRUGGLETON CHURCH AND CASTLE
GALLOWAY HOUSE GARDENS
Garlieston
Eggerness Pt.
Sorbie
Whauphill
Kirkinner
Braehead
Baldoon Sands
VISITOR CENTRE
Bladnoch
Wigtown
SCOTLAND'S BOOK TOWN
Wigtown Sands
Culmazie
THE MACHARS
TORHOUSE STONE CIRCLE
Torhousemuir
Spittal
High Mindork
Craighlaw Mains
Kirkcowan
Shennanton
Fell Loch
Benfield
Carsegowan
Causeway End
Baltersan
Newton Stewart
MINNIGAFF
Minnigaff
Creebridge
Challoch
Palnure
Clachaneasy
Bargrennan
Glentrool Village
GLENTROOL VISITOR CENTRE
Glentrool
Glen Trool Lodge
BRUCE'S STONE
Loch Trool
Palgowan
Water of Minnoch
Loch Moan
Forest
Kirroughtree Forest
Loch Middle
LAMACHAN HILL
WILD GOAT PARK
Penkiln Burn
Palnure Burn
CAIRNSMORE OF FLEET
CAINSMORE OF FLEET
Clints of Dromore
Loch Grannoch
GEM ROCK MUSEUM
Creetown
Carsluith
CARSLUITH CASTLE
CAIRNHOLY CAIRNS
CAIRNHARROW
Glen
Ravenshall Pt.
Ringdoo Pt.
Fleet Bay
MULLWHARCHAR
MERRICK
Loch Enoch
Loch Neldricken
Loch Valley
SILVER FLOWE
RHINNS OF KELLS
CORSERINE
Loch Harrow
Forrest Lodge
Loch Dungeon
Clatteringshaws Forest
Clatteringshaws Loch
Loch Dee
NX
A75
A714
A712
A747
A746
B7027
B733
B735
B7005
B7052
B7085
B7004
B7021
B7063
B734
112
106

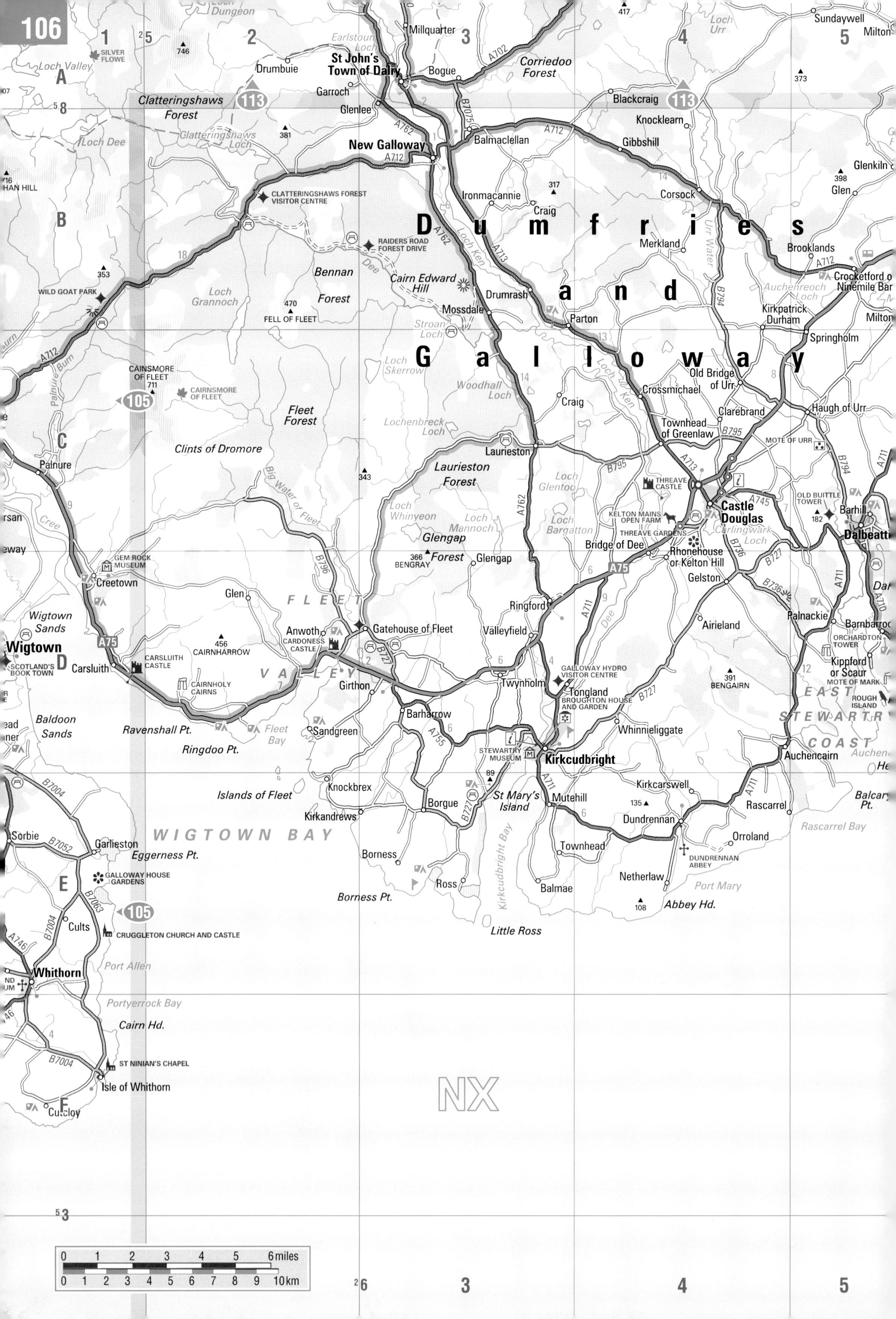
Dumfries and Galloway
Dungeon
Millquarter
417
Loch Urr
Sundaywell
Milton
1
2
3
4
5
SILVER FLOWE
746
Earlstoun Loch
St John's Town of Dalry
A702
Corriedoo Forest
373
Loch Valley
Drumbuie
Bogue
A
Garroch
Clatteringshaws Forest
113
Blackcraig
Glenlee
B7075
Knocklearn
381
A762
A712
Clatteringshaws Loch
Loch Dee
New Galloway
Balmaclellan
Gibbshill
Glenkiln
HAN HILL
398
Glen
CLATTERINGSHAWS FOREST VISITOR CENTRE
Ironmacannie
317
Craig
Corsock
B
RAIDERS ROAD FOREST DRIVE
Loch Ken
A713
Merkland
Urr Water
Brooklands
18
Dee
353
Bennan Forest
Cairn Edward Hill
A712
Crocketford or Ninemile Bar
WILD GOAT PARK
Loch Grannoch
Drumrash
Auchenreoch Loch
470
FELL OF FLEET
Mossdale
Parton
B794
Kirkpatrick Durham
Milton
Stroan Loch
Springholm
A712
Loch Skerrow
Old Bridge of Urr
CAINSMORE OF FLEET
711
CAIRNSMORE OF FLEET
105
Woodhall Loch
Craig
Crossmichael
Palnure Burn
Fleet Forest
Clarebrand
Haugh of Urr
Lochenbreck Loch
Townhead of Greenlaw
B795
C
Clints of Dromore
Laurieston
MOTE OF URR
Palnure
Laurieston Forest
B795
Loch Glentoo
THREAVE CASTLE
A713
343
Big Water of Fleet
Castle Douglas
A745
OLD BUITTLE TOWER
Barhill
Cree
Loch Whinyeon
Loch Mannoch
KELTON MAINS OPEN FARM
Loch Bargatton
182
Dalbeattie
A762
THREAVE GARDENS
Carlingwark Loch
Glengap
Bridge of Dee
Rhonehouse or Kelton Hill
B736
GEM ROCK MUSEUM
366 BENGRAY
Forest
Glengap
A75
B727
A711
Creetown
B796
Gelston
Glen
FLEET
B736
Wigtown Sands
Ringford
A711
Dee
Palnackie
Barnbarroch
Anwoth
Gatehouse of Fleet
Valleyfield
Airieland
A75
CARDONESS CASTLE
456 CAIRNHARROW
B727
ORCHARDTON TOWER
Wigtown
D
SCOTLAND'S BOOK TOWN
Carsluith
CARSLUITH CASTLE
VALLEY
Kippford or Scaur
Girthon
Twynholm
GALLOWAY HYDRO VISITOR CENTRE
391 BENGAIRN
MOTE OF MARK
CAIRNHOLY CAIRNS
Tongland
BROUGHTON HOUSE AND GARDEN
B727
EAST
ROUGH ISLAND
Barharrow
STEWARTRY
Baldoon Sands
Ravenshall Pt.
Fleet Bay
Sandgreen
A755
Whinnieliggate
Ringdoo Pt.
STEWARTRY MUSEUM
Kirkcudbright
COAST
Auchencairn
B7004
Islands of Fleet
Knockbrex
89
St Mary's Isle
Mutehill
A711
Kirkcarswell
Balcary Pt.
Kirkandrews
Borgue
B727
135
Dundrennan
Rascarrel
Rascarrel Bay
Sorbie
B7052
Garlieston
WIGTOWN BAY
Kirkcudbright Bay
Townhead
Orroland
Eggerness Pt.
Borness
DUNDRENNAN ABBEY
GALLOWAY HOUSE GARDENS
E
Ross
Netherlaw
Port Mary
Balmae
B7063
Borness Pt.
108
Abbey Hd.
B7004
105
Cults
CRUGGLETON CHURCH AND CASTLE
Little Ross
A746
Port Allen
Whithorn
Portyerrock Bay
Cairn Hd.
B7004
ST NINIAN'S CHAPEL
Isle of Whithorn
F
Cutcloy
NX
0 1 2 3 4 5 6 miles
0 1 2 3 4 5 6 7 8 9 10 km
6
3
4
5

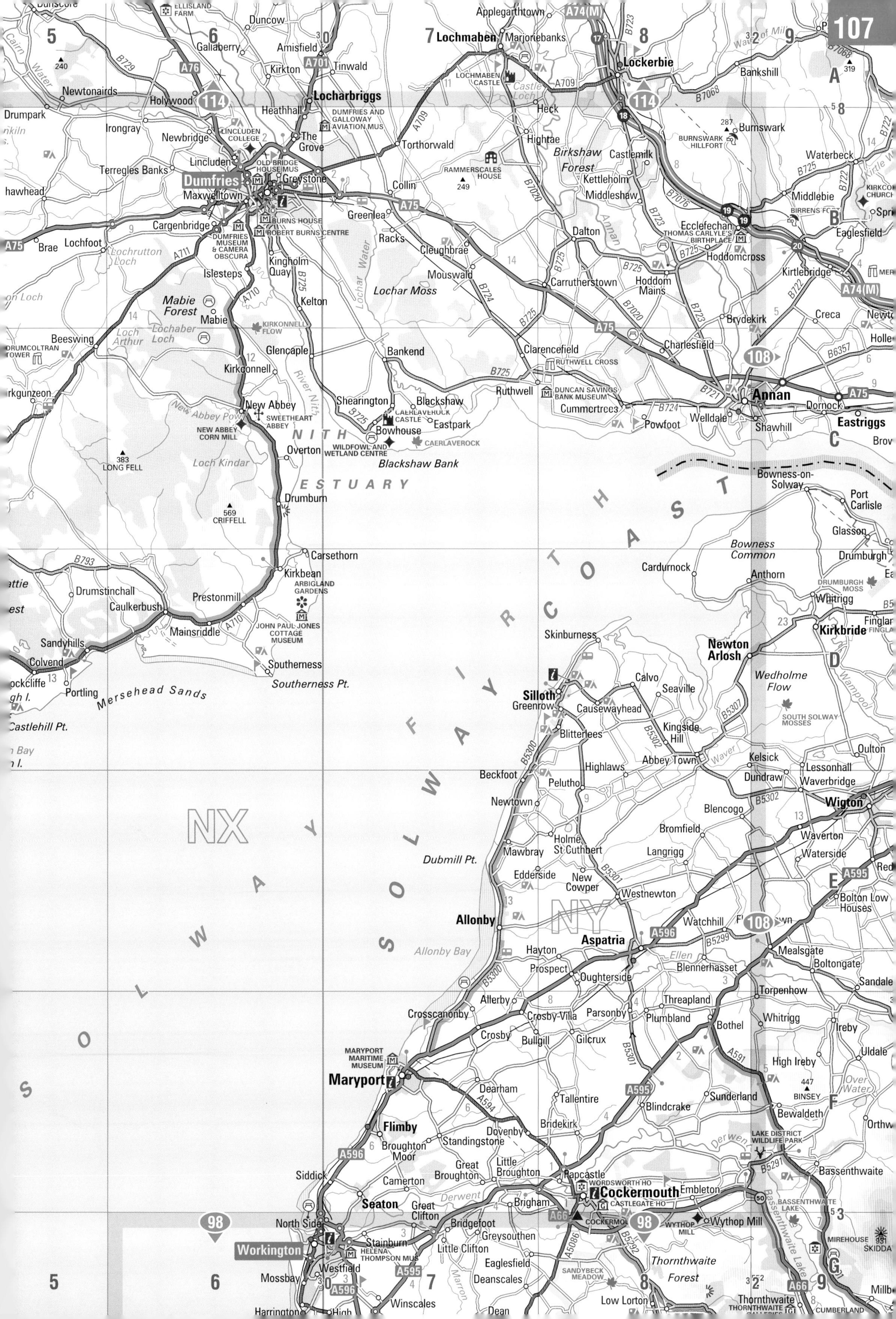
Lochmaben
Marjoriebanks
Applegarthtown
A74(M)
Lockerbie
Bankshill
Duncow
Amisfield
Tinwald
Kirkton
Gallaberry
ELLISLAND FARM
Newtonairds
Holywood
Locharbriggs
Heathhall
DUMFRIES AND GALLOWAY AVIATION MUS
Drumpark
Irongray
Newbridge
LINCLUDEN COLLEGE
The Grove
Torthorwald
LOCHMABEN CASTLE
Castle Loch
Heck
Hightae
Birkshaw Forest
Castlemilk
Burnswark
BURNSWARK HILLFORT
Waterbeck
Lincluden
Terregles Banks
OLD BRIDGE HOUSE MUS
Greystone
RAMMERSCALES HOUSE
Kettleholm
Middleshaw
Middlebie
KIRKCONNEL CHURCH
Dumfries
Maxwelltown
hawhead
Collin
Greenlea
Cargenbridge
BURNS HOUSE
ROBERT BURNS CENTRE
DUMFRIES MUSEUM & CAMERA OBSCURA
Brae
Lochfoot
Lochrutton Loch
Racks
Cleughbrae
Dalton
Ecclefechan
THOMAS CARLYLE'S BIRTHPLACE
Hoddomcross
Eaglesfield
BIRRENS FORT
Kingholm Quay
Islesteps
Mouswald
Carrutherstown
Hoddom Mains
Kirtlebridge
Lochar Moss
Mabie Forest
Mabie
Kelton
Lochar Water
Brydekirk
Creca
Beeswing
Loch Arthur
Lochaber Loch
KIRKCONNELL FLOW
Glencaple
Bankend
Clarencefield
RUTHWELL CROSS
Charlesfield
DRUMCOLTRAN TOWER
Kirkconnell
River Nith
Ruthwell
DUNCAN SAVINGS BANK MUSEUM
Cummertrees
Annan
Dornock
Eastriggs
rkgunzeon
New Abbey
SWEETHEART ABBEY
New Abbey Pow
NEW ABBEY CORN MILL
Shearington
Blackshaw
CAERLAVEROCK CASTLE
Eastpark
Bowhouse
CAERLAVEROCK
Powfoot
Welldale
Shawhill
383 LONG FELL
Loch Kindar
NITH
Overton
WILDFOWL AND WETLAND CENTRE
Blackshaw Bank
ESTUARY
Drumburn
569 CRIFFELL
Bowness-on-Solway
Port Carlisle
Glasson
Bowness Common
Drumburgh
Carsethorn
Kirkbean
ARBIGLAND GARDENS
Cardurnock
Anthorn
DRUMBURGH MOSS
Drumstinchall
Caulkerbush
Prestonmill
Whitrigg
Mainsriddle
JOHN PAUL JONES COTTAGE MUSEUM
Skinburness
Kirkbride
Sandyhills
Colvend
Southerness
Southerness Pt.
Newton Arlosh
Wedholme Flow
Portling
Mersehead Sands
Silloth
Greenrow
Calvo
Seaville
Causewayhead
Kingside Hill
SOUTH SOLWAY MOSSES
Castlehill Pt.
Blitterlees
Abbey Town
Waver
Kelsick
Oulton
Highlaws
Beckfoot
Pelutho
Dundraw
Lessonhall
Waverbridge
Newtown
Blencogo
Wigton
NX
Bromfield
Waverton
Holme St Cuthbert
Mawbray
Langrigg
Waterside
Dubmill Pt.
Edderside
New Cowper
Westnewton
Bolton Low Houses
Allonby
NY
Watchhill
Aspatria
Allonby Bay
Hayton
Ellen
Blennerhasset
Mealsgate
Boltongate
Prospect
Oughterside
Sandale
Torpenhow
Allerby
Threapland
Crosscanonby
Crosby Villa
Parsonby
Plumbland
Whitrigg
Ireby
Crosby
Bullgill
Gilcrux
Bothel
MARYPORT MARITIME MUSEUM
Maryport
High Ireby
Uldale
447 BINSEY
Over Water
Dearham
Tallentire
Sunderland
Blindcrake
Bewaldeth
Flimby
Bridekirk
Dovenby
Orthwaite
Broughton Moor
Standingstone
Derwent
LAKE DISTRICT WILDLIFE PARK
Great Broughton
Little Broughton
Bassenthwaite
Siddick
Camerton
Papcastle
WORDSWORTH HO
Cockermouth
Embleton
Seaton
Great Clifton
Brigham
CASTLEGATE HO
BASSENTHWAITE LAKE
North Side
Bridgefoot
Greysouthen
COCKERMOUTH
WYTHOP MILL
Wythop Mill
MIREHOUSE
SKIDDAW
Workington
Stainburn
HELENA THOMPSON MUS
Little Clifton
Eaglesfield
Thornthwaite Forest
Westfield
SANDYBECK MEADOW
Mossbay
Deanscales
Marron
Winscales
Low Lorton
Thornthwaite
Bassenthwaite Lake
Harrington
High
Dean
CUMBERLAND
SOLWAY FIRTH
SOLWAY COAST
A75
A76
A701
A709
A711
A710
B729
B725
B724
B7020
B723
B7076
B7068
B722
B721
B6357
B793
B5300
B5302
B5307
B5301
B5299
A596
A595
A594
A591
A66
A5086
B5292
B5291
114
108
98
50

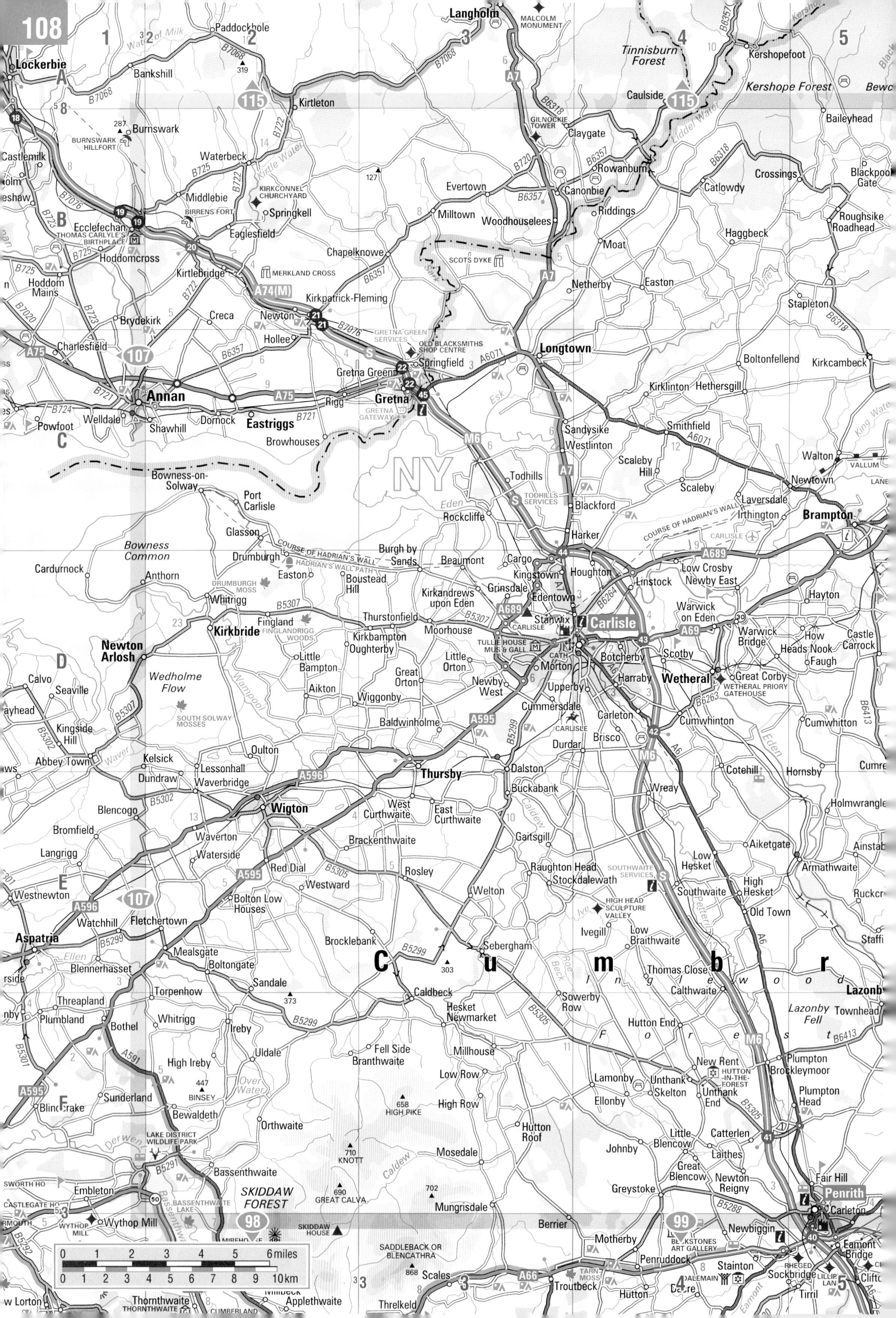
Lockerbie
Paddockhole
Water of Milk
Bankshill
Langholm
Malcolm Monument
Tinnisburn Forest
Kershopefoot
Kershope Forest
Kirtleton
Caulside
Burnswark
Burnswark Hillfort
Gilnockie Tower
Claygate
Baileyhead
Castlemilk
Waterbeck
Kirtle Water
Rowanburn
Canonbie
Catlowdy
Crossings
Blackpool Gate
Middlebie
Kirkconnel Churchyard
Evertown
Birrens Fort
Springkell
Milltown
Woodhouselees
Riddings
Roughsike
Roadhead
Ecclefechan
Thomas Carlyle's Birthplace
Eaglesfield
Haggbeck
Moat
Chapelknowe
Scots Dyke
Hoddomcross
Kirtlebridge
Merkland Cross
Netherby
Easton
Hoddom Mains
Kirkpatrick-Fleming
Stapleton
Brydekirk
Creca
Newton
Gretna Green Services
Old Blacksmiths Shop Centre
Charlesfield
Hollee
Springfield
Longtown
Boltonfellend
Kirkcambeck
Gretna Green
Kirklinton
Hethersgill
Annan
Gretna
Rigg
Gretna Gateway
Powfoot
Welldale
Shawhill
Dornock
Eastriggs
Browhouses
Sandysike
Westlinton
Smithfield
Scaleby Hill
Walton
Vallum
Bowness-on-Solway
NY
Todhills
Todhills Services
Newtown
Port Carlisle
Blackford
Scaleby
Laversdale
Irthington
Brampton
Eden
Rockcliffe
Course of Hadrian's Wall
Glasson
Bowness Common
Harker
Carlisle
Drumburgh
Burgh by Sands
Beaumont
Cargo
Hadrian's Wall Path
Cardurnock
Anthorn
Easton
Boustead Hill
Kingstown
Houghton
Low Crosby
Newby East
Drumburgh Moss
Grinsdale
Linstock
Kirkandrews upon Eden
Edentown
Hayton
Whitrigg
Thurstonfield
Stanwix
Warwick on Eden
Fingland
Finglandrigg Woods
Kirkbride
Moorhouse
Kirkbampton
Tullie House Mus & Gall
Warwick Bridge
How
Castle Carrock
Newton Arlosh
Oughterby
Cath
Botcherby
Scotby
Heads Nook
Little Bampton
Little Orton
Morton
Faugh
Calvo
Seaville
Wedholme Flow
Great Orton
Newby West
Harraby
Wetheral
Great Corby
Wetheral Priory Gatehouse
Aikton
Wiggonby
Upperby
Kingside Hill
South Solway Mosses
Wampool
Cummersdale
Carleton
Cumwhinton
Cumwhitton
Baldwinholme
Brisco
Abbey Town
Waver
Kelsick
Oulton
Durdar
Cotehill
Hornsby
Dundraw
Lessonhall
Waverbridge
Thursby
Dalston
Buckabank
Wreay
Holmwrangle
Blencogo
Wigton
West Curthwaite
East Curthwaite
Caldew
Bromfield
Waverton
Gaitsgill
Aiketgate
Brackenthwaite
Langrigg
Waterside
Red Dial
Raughton Head
Southwaite Services
Low Hesket
Armathwaite
Rosley
Stockdalewath
Westward
High Hesket
Westnewton
Bolton Low Houses
Welton
Southwaite
Old Town
High Head Sculpture Valley
Watchhill
Fletchertown
Aspatria
Ivegill
Low Braithwaite
Brocklebank
Sebergham
Mealsgate
Ellen
Blennerhasset
Boltongate
Cumbria
Inglewood Forest
Thomas Close
Lazonby
Sandale
Caldbeck
Calthwaite
Torpenhow
Threapland
Hesket Newmarket
Sowerby Row
Lazonby Fell
Townhead
Plumbland
Bothel
Whitrigg
Ireby
Hutton End
Fell Side
Branthwaite
Uldale
High Ireby
Millhouse
New Rent
Hutton-in-the-Forest
Plumpton
Brockleymoor
Binsey
Over Water
Low Row
Lamonby
Unthank
Skelton
Unthank End
Plumpton Head
Blindcrake
Sunderland
High Row
Ellonby
High Pike
Bewaldeth
Orthwaite
Hutton Roof
Little Blencow
Catterlen
Lake District Wildlife Park
Derwent
Knott
Mosedale
Johnby
Laithes
Great Blencow
Newton Reigny
Fair Hill
Bassenthwaite
Embleton
Skiddaw Forest
Great Calva
Greystoke
Penrith
Bassenthwaite Lake
Mungrisdale
Carleton
Wythop Mill
Berrier
Newbiggin
Skiddaw House
Motherby
Blakestones Art Gallery
Eamont Bridge
Saddleback or Blencathra
Penruddock
Stainton
Rheged
Scales
Tarn Moss
Troutbeck
Sockbridge
Lillipan
Clifton
Dalemain
Hutton
Dacre
Tirril
Thornthwaite
Applethwaite
Threlkeld
Low Lorton
Millbeck
Cumberland
Eamont
0 1 2 3 4 5 6 miles
0 1 2 3 4 5 6 7 8 9 10 km
A7
A74(M)
A75
A6071
M6
A689
A69
A6
A595
A596
A591
A66
B7068
B722
B725
B723
B7020
B7076
B6357
B721
B724
B5307
B5302
B5299
B5305
B6263
B6264
B6413
B6318
B720
B5291
B5292
B5288
115
107
98
99

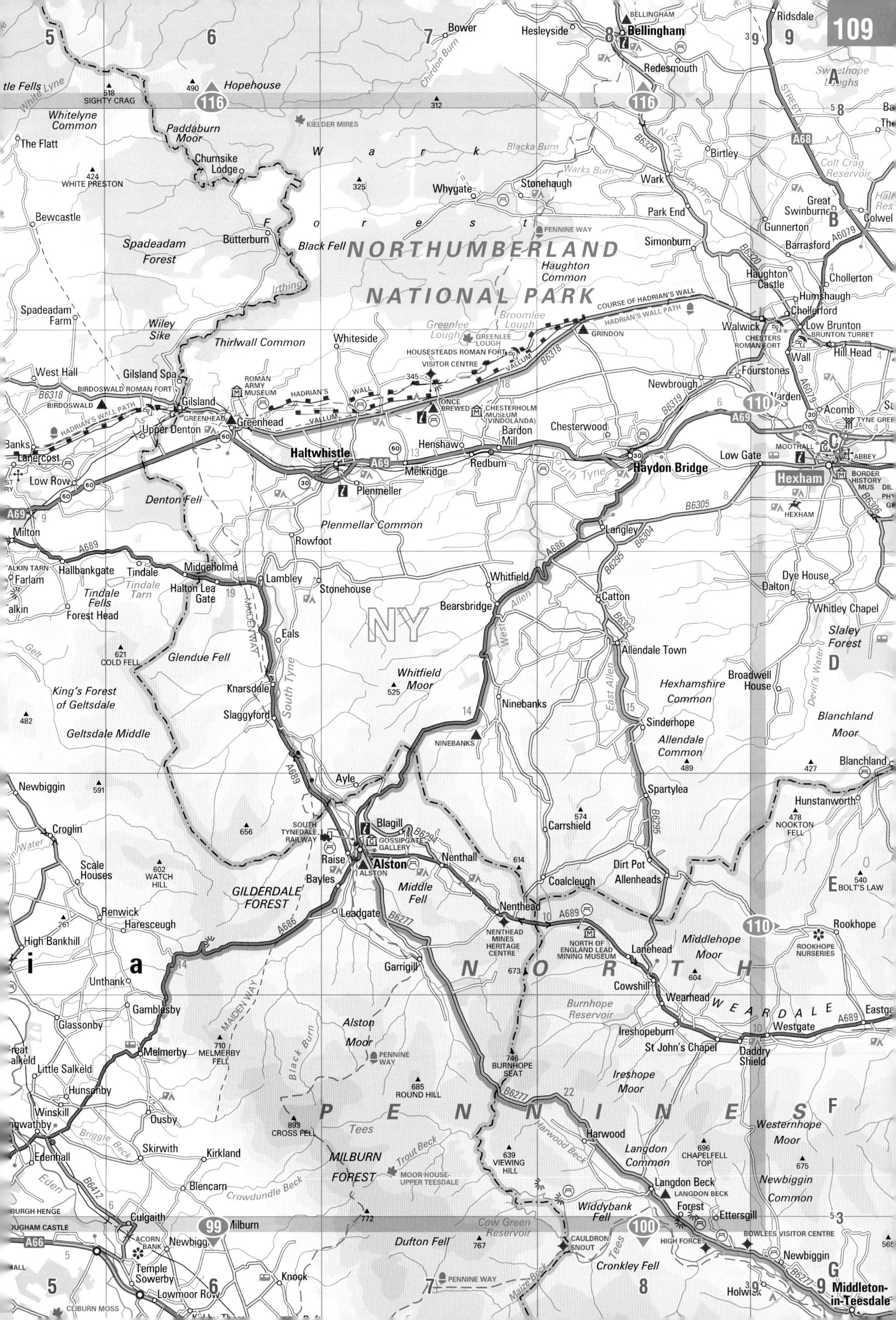
NORTHUMBERLAND NATIONAL PARK
NORTH PENNINES
NY
Wark Forest
Bellingham
Redesmouth
Hesleyside
Bower
Ridsdale
Sweethope Loughs
Hopehouse
Sighty Crag
Whitelyne Common
Paddaburn Moor
Kielder Mires
The Flatt
Churnsike Lodge
White Preston
Blacka Burn
Warks Burn
Whygate
Stonehaugh
Wark
Birtley
Colt Crag Reservoir
Park End
Great Swinburne
Gunnerton
Colwell
Barrasford
Bewcastle
Spadeadam Forest
Butterburn
Black Fell
Pennine Way
Simonburn
Haughton Common
Haughton Castle
Chollerton
Humshaugh
Chollerford
Irthing
Spadeadam Farm
Wiley Sike
Thirlwall Common
Whiteside
Greenlee Lough
Broomlee Lough
Course of Hadrian's Wall
Hadrian's Wall Path
Grindon
Walwick
Chesters Roman Fort
Low Brunton
Brunton Turret
Wall
Hill Head
West Hall
Gilsland Spa
Birdoswald Roman Fort
Birdoswald
Roman Army Museum
Housesteads Roman Fort
Visitor Centre
Vallum
Fourstones
Newbrough
Warden
Acomb
Gilsland
Greenhead
Upper Denton
Once Brewed
Chesterholm Museum (Vindolanda)
Chesterwood
Tyne Green
Banks
Lanercost
Henshaw
Bardon Mill
Moothall
Abbey
Haltwhistle
Melkridge
Redburn
Haydon Bridge
Low Gate
Hexham
Border History Mus
Low Row
Plenmeller
South Tyne
Denton Fell
Plenmellar Common
Langley
Milton
Rowfoot
Tindale
Midgeholme
Hallbankgate
Talkin Tarn
Farlam
Tindale Tarn
Tindale Fells
Halton Lea Gate
Lambley
Stonehouse
Maiden Way
Whitfield
Catton
Dye House
Dalton
Whitley Chapel
Forest Head
Bearsbridge
West Allen
Slaley Forest
Eals
Cold Fell
Glendue Fell
Allendale Town
Broadwell House
Whitfield Moor
Hexhamshire Common
Devil's Water
King's Forest of Geltsdale
Knarsdale
Slaggyford
Ninebanks
East Allen
Sinderhope
Blanchland Moor
Geltsdale Middle
Allendale Common
Blanchland
Newbiggin
Ayle
Spartylea
Hunstanworth
Nookton Fell
Croglin
South Tynedale Railway
Blagill
Gossipgate Gallery
Carrshield
Raise
Alston
Nenthall
Dirt Pot
Allenheads
Scale Houses
Watch Hill
Bayles
Middle Fell
Coalcleugh
Bolt's Law
Gilderdale Forest
Nenthead
Nenthead Mines Heritage Centre
North of England Lead Mining Museum
Renwick
Harescugh
Leadgate
Rookhope
Rookhope Nurseries
High Bankhill
Garrigill
Lanehead
Middlehope Moor
Unthank
Cowshill
Wearhead
Burnhope Reservoir
Weardale
Eastgate
Gamblesby
Glassonby
Alston Moor
Ireshopeburn
Westgate
Melmerby
Melmerby Fell
St John's Chapel
Daddry Shield
Little Salkeld
Black Burn
Burnhope Seat
Ireshope Moor
Hunsonby
Round Hill
Winskill
Ousby
Pennines
Langwathby
Briggle Beck
Cross Fell
Tees
Harwood
Westernhope Moor
Edenhall
Skirwith
Kirkland
Milburn Forest
Trout Beck
Viewing Hill
Harwood Beck
Langdon Common
Chapelfell Top
Eden
Moor House-Upper Teesdale
Newbiggin Common
Blencarn
Crowdundle Beck
Langdon Beck
Forest
Ettersgill
Widdybank Fell
Culgaith
Milburn
Cow Green Reservoir
Bowlees Visitor Centre
Acorn Bank
Newbiggin
Dufton Fell
Cauldron Snout
High Force
Temple Sowerby
Cronkley Fell
Knock
Maize Beck
Holwick
Middleton-in-Teesdale
Lowmoor Row
Cliburn Moss
Brougham Castle
A69
A689
A686
A68
A6079
B6318
B6319
B6320
B6305
B6304
B6295
B6303
B6294
B6277
B6412
A66
116
110
99
100

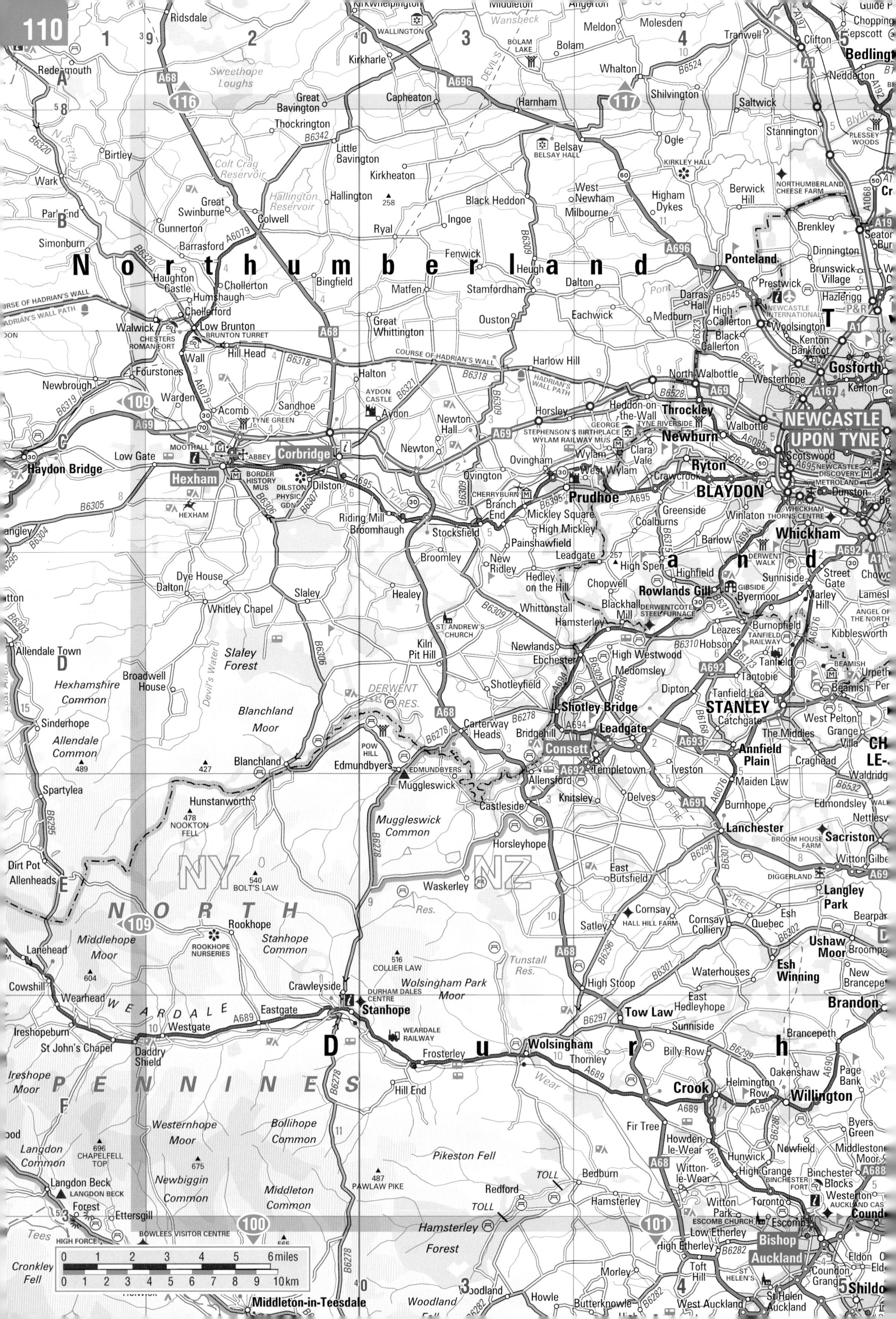
Northumberland
Durham
NORTH PENNINES
NEWCASTLE UPON TYNE
Hexham
Corbridge
Consett
Bishop Auckland
Redesmouth
Ridsdale
Sweethope Loughs
Great Bavington
Thockrington
Little Bavington
Kirkharle
WALLINGTON
Capheaton
Kirkheaton
Colt Crag Reservoir
Hallington Reservoir
Hallington
Birtley
Wark
Park End
Simonburn
Great Swinburne
Gunnerton
Colwell
Barrasford
Ryal
Ingoe
Black Heddon
Fenwick
Belsay
BELSAY HALL
Harnham
Bolam
BOLAM LAKE
Meldon
Molesden
Whalton
Tranwell
Clifton
Bedlington
Shilvington
Saltwick
Stannington
Ogle
KIRKLEY HALL
West Newham
Milbourne
Higham Dykes
Berwick Hill
NORTHUMBERLAND CHEESE FARM
Brenkley
Dinnington
Ponteland
Prestwick
Brunswick Village
Hazlerigg
NEWCASTLE INTERNATIONAL
Woolsington
Kenton Bankfoot
Gosforth
Kenton
Darras Hall
High Callerton
Black Callerton
Medburn
Eachwick
Dalton
Heugh
Stamfordham
Matfen
Bingfield
Haughton Castle
Chollerton
Humshaugh
Chollerford
Walwick
Low Brunton
BRUNTON TURRET
CHESTERS ROMAN FORT
COURSE OF HADRIAN'S WALL
HADRIAN'S WALL PATH
Wall
Hill Head
Great Whittington
Ouston
Harlow Hill
Halton
Fourstones
Newbrough
Warden
Acomb
Sandhoe
TYNE GREEN
AYDON CASTLE
Aydon
Newton Hall
Newton
Horsley
Heddon-on-the-Wall
North Walbottle
Westerhope
Throckley
Walbottle
Newburn
TYNE RIVERSIDE
GEORGE STEPHENSON'S BIRTHPLACE
WYLAM RAILWAY MUS
Wylam
Clara Vale
Ryton
Crawcrook
West Wylam
Ovingham
Ovington
Prudhoe
CHERRYBURN
Branch End
Mickley Square
High Mickley
BLAYDON
Scotswood
NEWCASTLE DISCOVERY
METROLAND
Dunston
WHICKHAM THORNS CENTRE
Whickham
Winlaton
Greenside
Coalburns
Barlow
Haydon Bridge
Low Gate
MOOTHALL
ABBEY
BORDER HISTORY MUS
DILSTON PHYSIC GDN
Dilston
Riding Mill
Broomhaugh
Stocksfield
Broomley
New Ridley
Painshawfield
Leadgate
High Spen
Highfield
DERWENT WALK
Sunniside
Street Gate
Rowlands Gill
GIBSIDE
Byermoor
Marley Hill
Lamesley
ANGEL OF THE NORTH
Kibblesworth
Chopwell
Hedley on the Hill
Blackhall Mill
DERWENTCOTE STEEL FURNACE
Whittonstall
Hamsterley
Burnopfield
Leazes
TANFIELD RAILWAY
Hobson
Tanfield
BEAMISH
Beamish
Urpeth
Tantobie
Tanfield Lea
STANLEY
Catchgate
West Pelton
Grange Villa
The Middles
Annfield Plain
Craghead
Waldridge
HEXHAM
Dye House
Dalton
Slaley
Healey
Whitley Chapel
ST ANDREW'S CHURCH
Kiln Pit Hill
Newlands
Ebchester
High Westwood
Medomsley
Dipton
Shotleyfield
Allendale Town
Slaley Forest
Broadwell House
Hexhamshire Common
Sinderhope
Allendale Common
Blanchland Moor
DERWENT RES.
Carterway Heads
Bridgehill
Shotley Bridge
Leadgate
Templetown
Iveston
Maiden Law
Blanchland
POW HILL
Edmundbyers
EDMUNDBYERS
Muggleswick
Castleside
Allensford
Knitsley
Delves
Burnhope
Edmondsley
Nettlesworth
Lanchester
BROOM HOUSE FARM
Sacriston
Spartylea
Hunstanworth
NOOKTON FELL
Muggleswick Common
Horsleyhope
Witton Gilbert
DIGGERLAND
Langley Park
East Butsfield
Dirt Pot
Allenheads
NY
NZ
BOLT'S LAW
Waskerley
Cornsay
HALL HILL FARM
Satley
Cornsay Colliery
Quebec
Esh
Bearpark
Ushaw Moor
Broompark
Esh Winning
New Brancepeth
Brandon
Lanehead
Middlehope Moor
Rookhope
ROOKHOPE NURSERIES
Stanhope Common
COLLIER LAW
Tunstall Res.
Waterhouses
High Stoop
Cowshill
Crawleyside
Wolsingham Park Moor
DURHAM DALES CENTRE
Stanhope
Wearhead
WEARDALE
Eastgate
Westgate
Ireshopeburn
St John's Chapel
Daddry Shield
WEARDALE RAILWAY
Frosterley
Wolsingham
Thornley
Tow Law
East Hedleyhope
Sunniside
Billy Row
Brancepeth
Oakenshaw
Page Bank
Ireshope Moor
Hill End
Crook
Helmington Row
Willington
Byers Green
Fir Tree
Howden-le-Wear
Hunwick
Newfield
Middlestone Moor
Westernhope Moor
Bollihope Common
Langdon Common
CHAPELFELL TOP
Pikeston Fell
Witton-le-Wear
High Grange
Binchester
BINCHESTER FORT
Blocks
Newbiggin Common
PAWLAW PIKE
Bedburn
Langdon Beck
LANGDON BECK
Middleton Common
Redford
Hamsterley
Witton Park
Toronto
Westerton
AUCKLAND CASTLE
Coundon
Forest
Ettersgill
TOLL
ESCOMB CHURCH
Escomb
HIGH FORCE
BOWLEES VISITOR CENTRE
Tees
Hamsterley Forest
Low Etherley
High Etherley
Eldon
Cronkley Fell
Toft Hill
ST HELEN'S
Coundon Grange
Shildon
Morley
Middleton-in-Teesdale
Woodland
Howle
Butterknowle
West Auckland
St Helen Auckland
0 1 2 3 4 5 6 miles
0 1 2 3 4 5 6 7 8 9 10 km

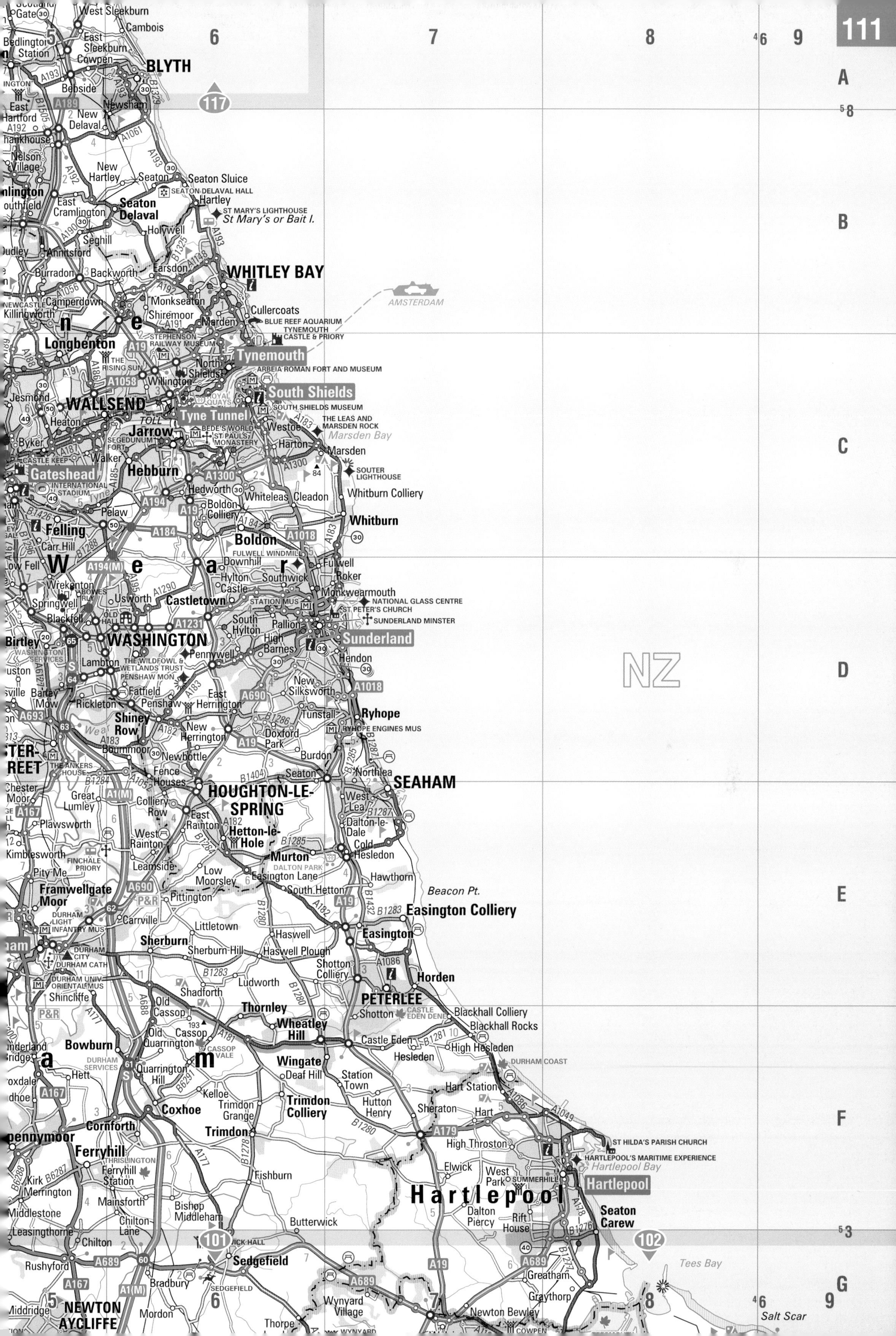

6
7
8
9
A
B
C
D
E
F
G
BLYTH
West Sleekburn
Cambois
East Sleekburn
Cowpen
Bedlington Station
Bebside
Newsham
East Hartford
New Delaval
New Hartley
Seaton
Seaton Sluice
SEATON DELAVAL HALL
Hartley
ST MARY'S LIGHTHOUSE
St Mary's or Bait I.
East Cramlington
Seaton Delaval
Holywell
Seghill
Annitsford
Burradon
Backworth
Earsdon
WHITLEY BAY
AMSTERDAM
Camperdown
Killingworth
Monkseaton
Shiremoor
Marden
Cullercoats
BLUE REEF AQUARIUM
TYNEMOUTH CASTLE & PRIORY
Longbenton
STEPHENSON RAILWAY MUSEUM
Tynemouth
North Shields
ARBEIA ROMAN FORT AND MUSEUM
South Shields
THE RISING SUN
Willington
Jesmond
WALLSEND
Heaton
Tyne Tunnel
SOUTH SHIELDS MUSEUM
THE LEAS AND MARSDEN ROCK
Marsden Bay
Westoe
Jarrow
BEDE'S WORLD
ST PAUL'S MONASTERY
SEGEDUNUM FORT
Byker
Harton
Marsden
Walker
CASTLE KEEP
Gateshead
Hebburn
SOUTER LIGHTHOUSE
INTERNATIONAL STADIUM
Hedworth
Whiteleas
Cleadon
Whitburn Colliery
Boldon Colliery
Pelaw
Felling
Whitburn
Carr Hill
Boldon
FULWELL WINDMILL
Downhill
Fulwell
Roker
Hylton Castle
Southwick
Wrekenton
Springwell
Usworth
Castletown
Monkwearmouth
STATION MUS
NATIONAL GLASS CENTRE
ST PETER'S CHURCH
SUNDERLAND MINSTER
Blackfell
South Hylton
Pallion
Sunderland
Birtley
WASHINGTON
Pennywell
High Barnes
Hendon
WASHINGTON SERVICES
Lambton
THE WILDFOWL & WETLANDS TRUST
PENSHAW MON
NZ
New Silksworth
Fatfield
East Herrington
Rickleton
Penshaw
Tunstall
Ryhope
RYHOPE ENGINES MUS
Shiney Row
New Herrington
Doxford Park
Bournmoor
Newbottle
Burdon
THE ANKERS HOUSE
Fence Houses
Seaton
Northlea
SEAHAM
Chester Moor
Great Lumley
HOUGHTON-LE-SPRING
Colliery Row
East Rainton
West Lea
Dalton-le-Dale
Plawsworth
West Rainton
Hetton-le-Hole
Cold Hesledon
Kimblesworth
FINCHALE PRIORY
Leamside
Murton
DALTON PARK
Pity Me
Low Moorsley
Easington Lane
Hawthorn
South Hetton
Beacon Pt.
Framwellgate Moor
Pittington
Easington Colliery
DURHAM LIGHT INFANTRY MUS
Carrville
Littletown
Haswell
Easington
Sherburn
Sherburn Hill
Haswell Plough
DURHAM CITY
DURHAM CATH
Shotton Colliery
Horden
DURHAM UNIV ORIENTAL MUS
Shincliffe
Ludworth
Shadforth
PETERLEE
Old Cassop
Thornley
Shotton
CASTLE EDEN DENE
Blackhall Colliery
Blackhall Rocks
Cassop
Wheatley Hill
Old Quarrington
Castle Eden
Bowburn
CASSOP VALE
High Hesleden
DURHAM SERVICES
Quarrington Hill
Wingate
Hesleden
DURHAM COAST
Hett
Deaf Hill
Station Town
Hart Station
Kelloe
Trimdon Grange
Trimdon Colliery
Hutton Henry
Coxhoe
Sheraton
Hart
Cornforth
Trimdon
High Throston
ST HILDA'S PARISH CHURCH
HARTLEPOOL'S MARITIME EXPERIENCE
Hartlepool Bay
Ferryhill
THRISLINGTON
Ferryhill Station
Elwick
West Park
SUMMERHILL
Hartlepool
Kirk Merrington
Fishburn
Mainsforth
Bishop Middleham
Hartlepool
Seaton Carew
Middlestone
Chilton Lane
Butterwick
Dalton Piercy
Rift House
Leasingthorne
Chilton
Sedgefield
Tees Bay
Rushyford
Bradbury
SEDGEFIELD
Greatham
Graythorp
Wynyard Village
Newton Bewley
Middridge
NEWTON AYCLIFFE
Mordon
Thorpe
Salt Scar
117
101
102

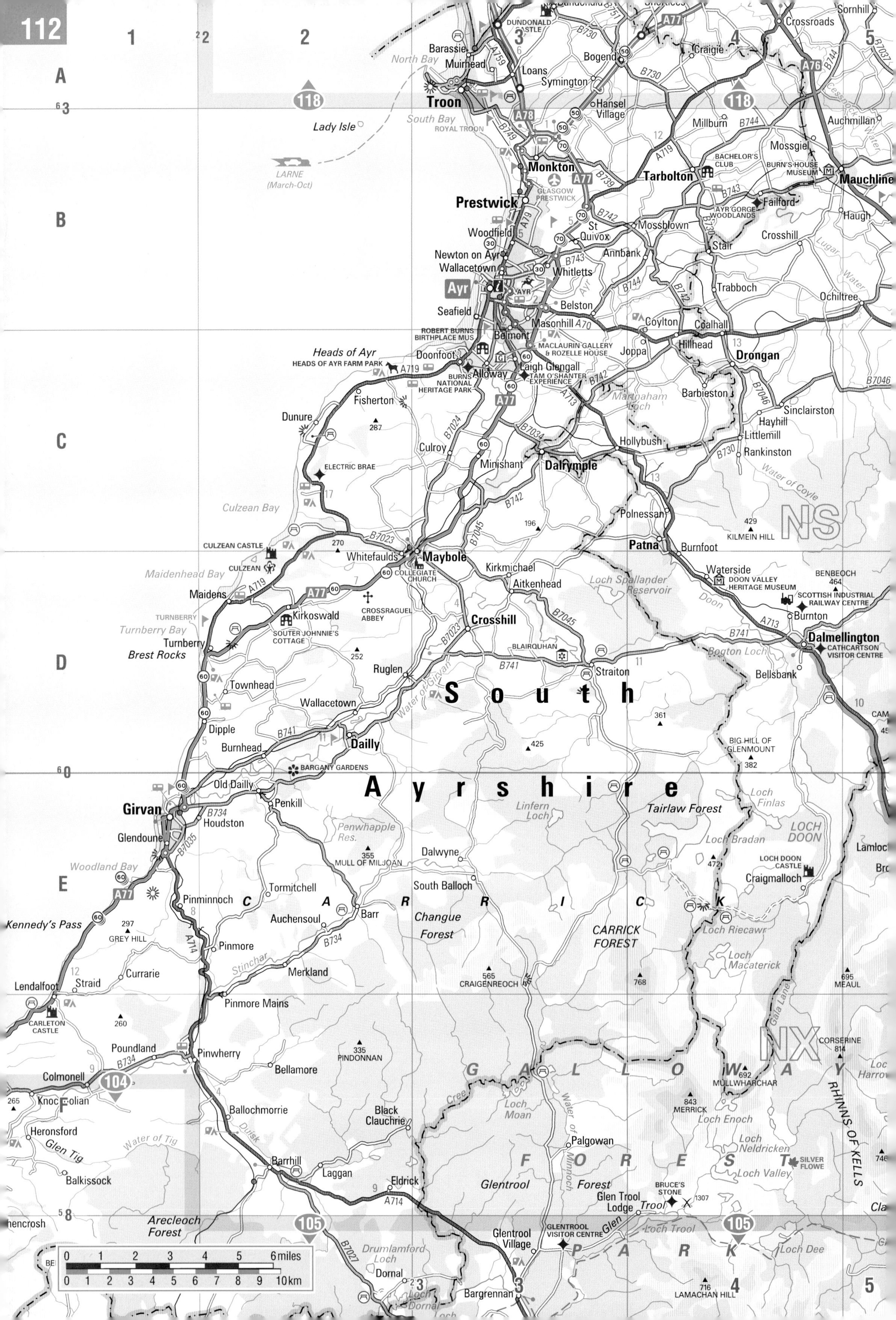
South Ayrshire
GALLOWAY FOREST PARK
CARRICK
CARRICK FOREST
Troon
Barassie
Muirhead
North Bay
Loans
Symington
Bogend
Craigie
Crossroads
Sornhill
Hansel Village
South Bay
ROYAL TROON
Lady Isle
LARNE
(March-Oct)
Millburn
Auchmillan
Mossgiel
BACHELOR'S CLUB
BURN'S HOUSE MUSEUM
Mauchline
Monkton
GLASGOW PRESTWICK
Tarbolton
Prestwick
AYR GORGE WOODLANDS
Failford
Haugh
Woodfield
St Quivox
Mossblown
Crosshill
Stair
Annbank
Newton on Ayr
Wallacetown
Whitletts
Ayr
Trabboch
Ochiltree
Seafield
Belston
Coylton
Coalhall
Masonhill
ROBERT BURNS BIRTHPLACE MUS
Belmont
MACLAURIN GALLERY & ROZELLE HOUSE
Hillhead
Drongan
Heads of Ayr
HEADS OF AYR FARM PARK
Doonfoot
Joppa
Alloway
Laigh Glengall
BURNS NATIONAL HERITAGE PARK
TAM O'SHANTER EXPERIENCE
Martnaham Loch
Barbieston
Fisherton
Sinclairston
Hayhill
Dunure
Littlemill
Hollybush
Rankinston
Culroy
Minishant
Dalrymple
ELECTRIC BRAE
Water of Coyle
Culzean Bay
Polnessan
KILMEIN HILL
NS
CULZEAN CASTLE
Whitefaulds
Maybole
Patna
Burnfoot
COLLEGIATE CHURCH
Kirkmichael
Waterside
DOON VALLEY HERITAGE MUSEUM
Maidenhead Bay
CULZEAN
Aitkenhead
Loch Spallander Reservoir
BENBEOCH
Maidens
SCOTTISH INDUSTRIAL RAILWAY CENTRE
TURNBERRY
Kirkoswald
CROSSRAGUEL ABBEY
Burnton
Turnberry Bay
SOUTER JOHNNIE'S COTTAGE
Crosshill
Turnberry
Dalmellington
CATHCARTSON VISITOR CENTRE
Brest Rocks
BLAIRQUHAN
Bogton Loch
Straiton
Bellsbank
Ruglen
Townhead
Wallacetown
Water of Girvan
Dipple
BIG HILL OF GLENMOUNT
Burnhead
Dailly
BARGANY GARDENS
Old Dailly
Girvan
Penkill
Linfern Loch
Loch Finlas
Tairlaw Forest
Houdston
Glendoune
Penwhapple Res.
LOCH DOON
Loch Bradan
Lamloch
MULL OF MILJOAN
Dalwyne
Woodland Bay
LOCH DOON CASTLE
Craigmalloch
South Balloch
Tormitchell
Pinminnoch
Kennedy's Pass
Auchensoul
Barr
Changue Forest
GREY HILL
Loch Riecawr
Pinmore
Loch Macaterick
Currarie
Stinchar
Merkland
CRAIGENREOCH
MEAUL
Straid
Lendalfoot
Pinmore Mains
Gala Lane
CARLETON CASTLE
PINDONNAN
NX
CORSERINE
Poundland
Pinwherry
Colmonell
Bellamore
MULLWHARCHAR
RHINNS OF KELLS
Knockdolian
Cree
Loch Moan
MERRICK
Loch Enoch
Ballochmorrie
Black Clauchrie
Heronsford
Glen Tig
Water of Tig
Duisk
Palgowan
Loch Neldricken
Water of Minnoch
SILVER FLOWE
Barrhill
Laggan
Loch Valley
Balkissock
Eldrick
Glentrool
Forest
BRUCE'S STONE
Glen Trool Lodge
Trool
Arecleoch Forest
Glentrool Village
GLENTROOL VISITOR CENTRE
Glen
Loch Trool
Drumlamford Loch
Loch Dee
Dornal
Bargrennan
LAMACHAN HILL
Loch Dornal
0 1 2 3 4 5 6 miles
0 1 2 3 4 5 6 7 8 9 10 km
118
104
105

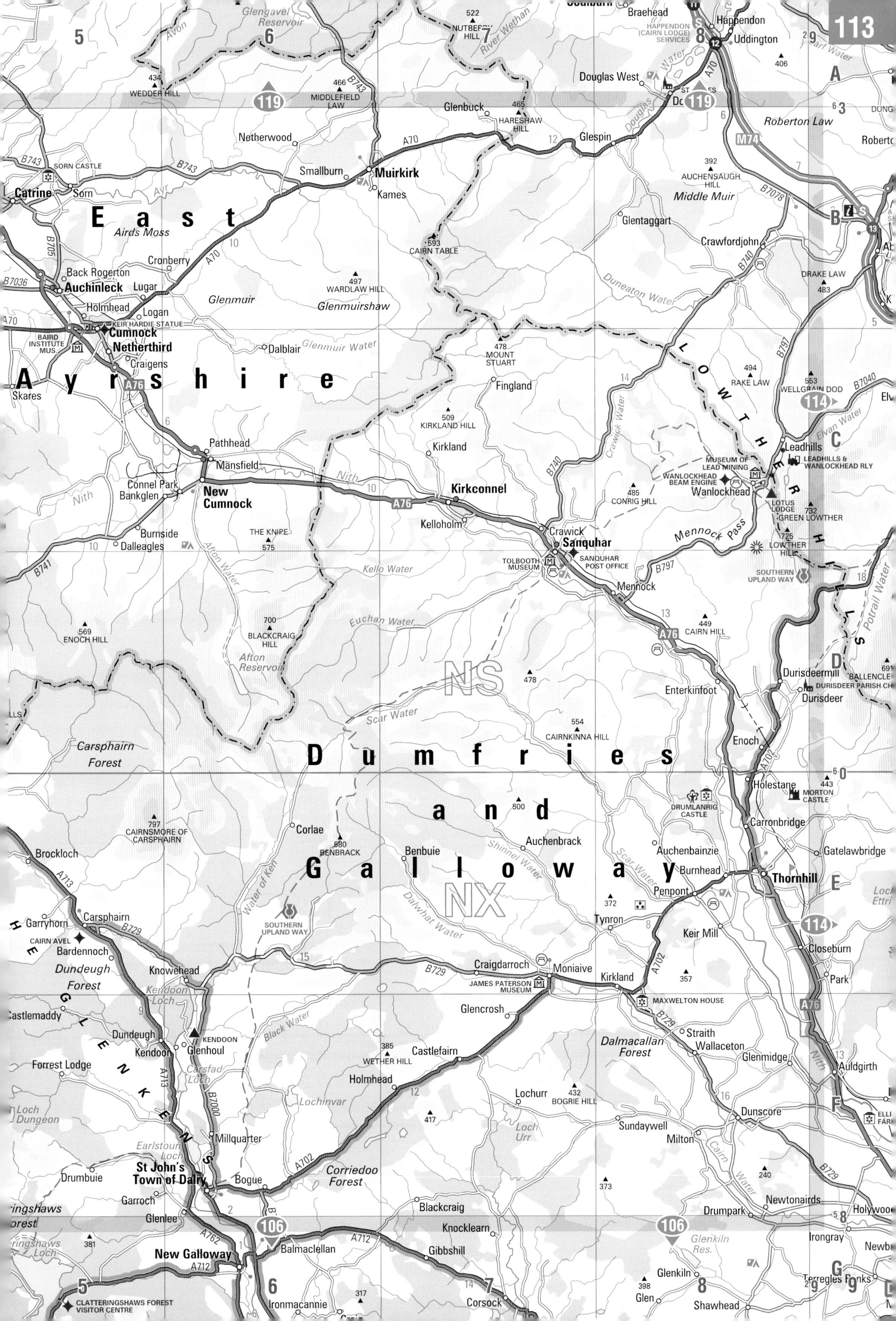
East Ayrshire
Dumfries and Galloway
LOWTHER HILLS
THE GLENKENS
NS
NX
Glengavel Reservoir
522 NUTBERRY HILL
River Wethan
Braehead
HAPPENDON (CAIRN LODGE) SERVICES
Happendon
Uddington
406
434 WEDDER HILL
466 MIDDLEFIELD LAW
Douglas West
Douglas Water
Glenbuck
465 HARESHAW HILL
Robertson Law
Robertson
Netherwood
Glespin
392 AUCHENSAUGH HILL
Middle Muir
SORN CASTLE
Catrine
Sorn
Smallburn
Muirkirk
Kames
Glentaggart
Airds Moss
593 CAIRN TABLE
Crawfordjohn
Cronberry
Back Rogerton
Auchinleck
Lugar
497 WARDLAW HILL
DRAKE LAW 483
Glenmuir
Glenmuirshaw
Duneaton Water
Holmhead
Logan
KEIR HARDIE STATUE
Cumnock
BAIRD INSTITUTE MUS.
Netherthird
Dalblair
Glenmuir Water
478 MOUNT STUART
Craigens
Skares
Fingland
494 RAKE LAW
553 WELLGRAIN DOD
509 KIRKLAND HILL
Elvan Water
Pathhead
Kirkland
Leadhills
LEADHILLS & WANLOCKHEAD RLY
Mansfield
Connel Park
Bankglen
New Cumnock
Nith
Kirkconnel
MUSEUM OF LEAD MINING
WANLOCKHEAD BEAM ENGINE
Wanlockhead
485 CONRIG HILL
LOTUS LODGE
732 GREEN LOWTHER
Kelloholm
Crawick Water
Burnside
Dalleagles
THE KNIPE 575
Crawick
Sanquhar
TOLBOOTH MUSEUM
SANQUHAR POST OFFICE
Mennock Pass
725 LOWTHER HILL
Kello Water
B797
Mennock
SOUTHERN UPLAND WAY
Afton Water
Euchan Water
569 ENOCH HILL
700 BLACKCRAIG HILL
449 CAIRN HILL
Potrail Water
Afton Reservoir
478
Durisdeermill
DURISDEER PARISH CH.
691 BALLENCLEUCH
Durisdeer
Enterkinfoot
Scar Water
554 CAIRNKINNA HILL
Enoch
Carsphairn Forest
443 MORTON CASTLE
Holestane
500
DRUMLANRIG CASTLE
Carronbridge
797 CAIRNSMORE OF CARSPHAIRN
Corlae
580 BENBRACK
Auchenbrack
Auchenbainzie
Brockloch
Benbuie
Shinnel Water
Gatelawbridge
Burnhead
Thornhill
Penpont
372
Garryhorn
Carsphairn
Dalwhat Water
Tynron
SOUTHERN UPLAND WAY
Water of Ken
CAIRN AVEL
Bardennoch
Keir Mill
Closeburn
Dundeugh Forest
Knowehead
Craigdarroch
Moniaive
JAMES PATERSON MUSEUM
Kirkland
357
Park
Kendoon Loch
MAXWELTON HOUSE
Castlemaddy
Glencrosh
Black Water
Dundeugh
KENDOON
Glenhoul
Kendoon
385 WETHER HILL
Castlefairn
Straith
Wallaceton
Dalmacallan Forest
Glenmidge
Auldgirth
Forrest Lodge
Carsfad Loch
Holmhead
Loch Dungeon
Lochinvar
417
Lochurr
432 BOGRIE HILL
Dunscore
ELLISLAND FARM
Sundaywell
Loch Urr
Milton
Cairn Water
Earlstoun Loch
Millquarter
Drumbuie
St John's Town of Dalry
Bogue
Corriedoo Forest
240
373
Garroch
Blackcraig
Newtonairds
Drumpark
Holywood
Glenlee
Knocklearn
Irongray
Clatteringshaws Loch
381
Balmaclellan
Gibbshill
Glenkiln Res.
Newbridge
New Galloway
Glenkiln
398
Terregles Banks
Glen
Shawhead
CLATTERINGSHAWS FOREST VISITOR CENTRE
Ironmacannie
317
Corsock
A70
A76
A702
A713
A712
A762
B729
B740
B743
B705
B7036
B741
B7000
B7078
B797
B7040
M74
119
114
106

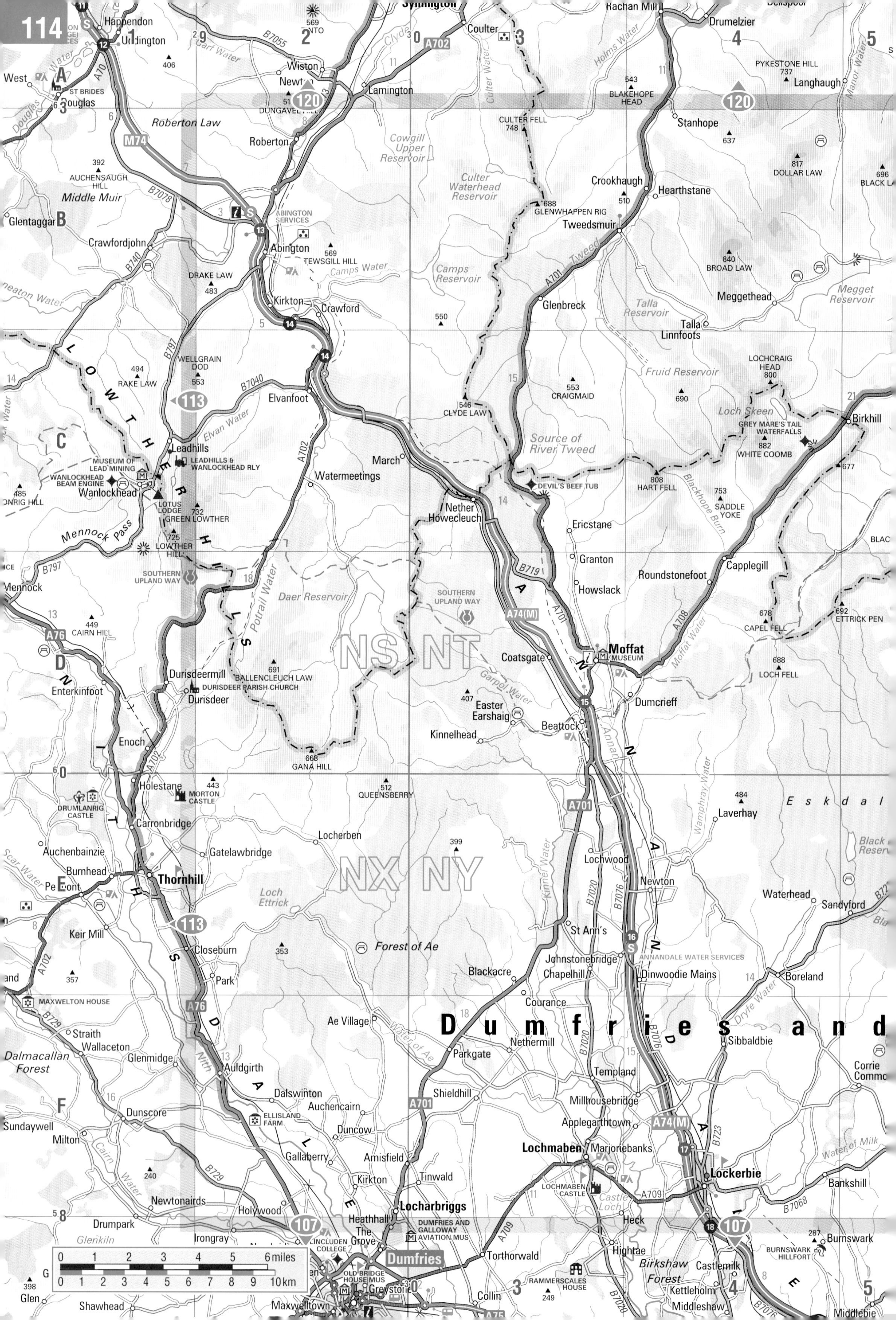
Happendon
Uddington
Douglas
ST BRIDES
West
Roberton Law
M74
AUCHENSAUGH HILL
392
Middle Muir
B7078
Glentaggar
Crawfordjohn
B740
DRAKE LAW
483
B7055
Wiston
Newton
DUNGAVEL HILL
120
Roberton
Lamington
Coulter
A702
Clyde
Culter Water
Cowgill Upper Reservoir
Culter Waterhead Reservoir
CULTER FELL
748
ABINGTON SERVICES
Abington
TEWSGILL HILL
569
Camps Water
Camps Reservoir
Kirkton
Crawford
550
688
GLENWHAPPEN RIG
Rachan Mill
Drumelzier
PYKESTONE HILL
737
Langhaugh
Manor Water
Holms Water
543
BLAKEHOPE HEAD
Stanhope
637
817
DOLLAR LAW
696
Crookhaugh
510
Hearthstone
Tweedsmuir
Tweed
A701
840
BROAD LAW
Meggethead
Megget Reservoir
Glenbreck
Talla Reservoir
Talla
Linnfoots
Fruid Reservoir
LOCHCRAIG HEAD
800
690
Loch Skeen
GREY MARE'S TAIL WATERFALLS
882
WHITE COOMB
Birkhill
677
WELLGRAIN DOD
553
494
RAKE LAW
B797
B7040
Elvanfoot
113
Elvan Water
Leadhills
MUSEUM OF LEAD MINING
LEADHILLS & WANLOCKHEAD RLY
WANLOCKHEAD BEAM ENGINE
Wanlockhead
485
LOTUS LODGE
732
GREEN LOWTHER
725
LOWTHER HILL
Mennock Pass
SOUTHERN UPLAND WAY
Mennock
LOWTHER HILLS
546
CLYDE LAW
553
CRAIGMAID
Source of River Tweed
March
Watermeetings
A702
Nether Howecleuch
DEVIL'S BEEF TUB
808
HART FELL
Blackhope Burn
753
SADDLE YOKE
Ericstane
Granton
Howslack
B719
Roundstonefoot
Capplegill
A708
Potrail Water
Daer Reservoir
SOUTHERN UPLAND WAY
A74(M)
NS NT
Coatsgate
Moffat
MUSEUM
Moffat Water
678
CAPEL FELL
692
ETTRICK PEN
688
LOCH FELL
449
CAIRN HILL
A76
Durisdeermill
Enterkinfoot
Durisdeer
DURISDEER PARISH CHURCH
691
BALLENCLEUCH LAW
Garpol Water
407
Easter Earshaig
Beattock
Dumcrieff
Kinnelhead
Annan
Enoch
668
GANA HILL
Holestane
443
MORTON CASTLE
512
QUEENSBERRY
DRUMLANRIG CASTLE
Carronbridge
A701
484
Laverhay
Eskdale
Wamphray Water
Black Reservoir
Locherben
399
Auchenbainzie
Gatelawbridge
Lochwood
Kinnel Water
Scar Water
Burnhead
Penpont
Thornhill
NX NY
Newton
B7020
B7076
Waterhead
Sandyford
Loch Ettrick
Keir Mill
Closeburn
353
Forest of Ae
St Ann's
ANNANDALE WATER SERVICES
Johnstonebridge
Chapelhill
Dinwoodie Mains
Boreland
Dryfe Water
A702
357
Park
Blackacre
Courance
MAXWELTON HOUSE
A76
B729
Straith
Wallaceton
Ae Village
Water of Ae
Dumfries and Galloway
Nethermill
Sibbaldbie
Dalmacallan Forest
Glenmidge
Auldgirth
Nith
Parkgate
Templand
Corrie Common
Dalswinton
Shieldhill
Millhousebridge
Auchencairn
Sundaywell
Dunscore
ELLISLAND FARM
A701
Applegarthtown
A74(M)
Milton
Duncow
Cairn Water
Gallaberry
Amisfield
Lochmaben
Marjoriebanks
B723
Water of Milk
240
B729
Kirkton
Tinwald
LOCHMABEN CASTLE
Castle Loch
A709
Lockerbie
Bankshill
Newtonairds
Holywood
Locharbriggs
B7068
Drumpark
Heathhall
DUMFRIES AND GALLOWAY AVIATION MUS
Heck
107
287
Burnswark
BURNSWARK HILLFORT
Glenkiln
Irongray
The Grove
LINCLUDEN COLLEGE
A709
Torthorwald
Hightae
Birkshaw Forest
Castlemilk
Dumfries
OLD BRIDGE HOUSE MUS
Greystone
RAMMERSCALES HOUSE
249
Kettleholm
Middleshaw
398
Glen
Shawhead
Maxwelltown
Collin
A75
B7020
Middlebie
0 1 2 3 4 5 6 miles
0 1 2 3 4 5 6 7 8 9 10 km
NITHSDALE
ANNANDALE

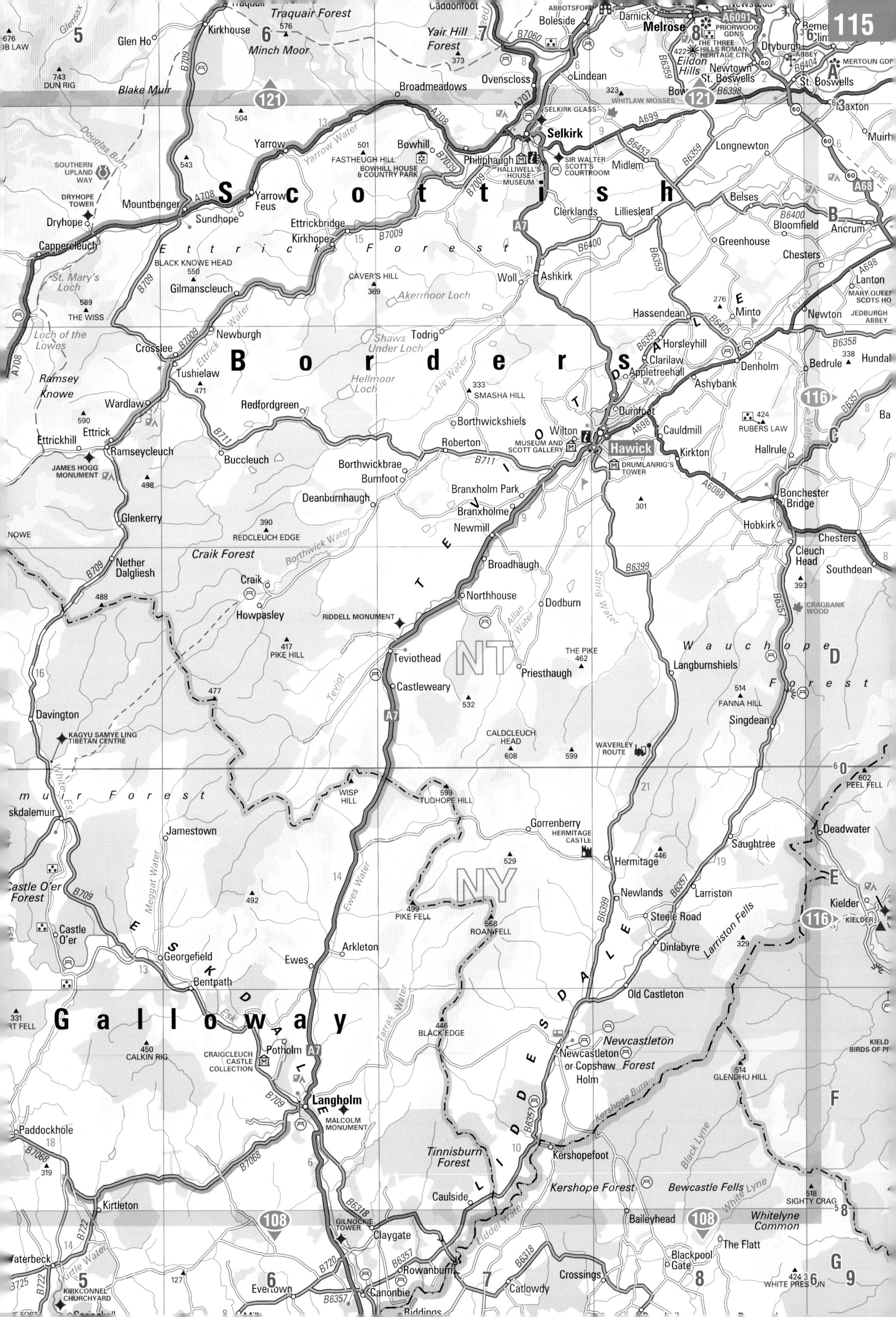
Traquair Forest
576
Caddonfoot
ABBOTSFORD
Boleside
Darnick
Melrose
A6091
PRIORWOOD GDNS
THE THREE HILLS ROMAN HERITAGE CTR
Eildon Hills
Newtown St. Boswells
Dryburgh
ABBEY
MERTOUN GDN
St. Boswells
Bemersyde
Kirkhouse
Glen Ho
Minch Moor
Yair Hill Forest
373
Tweed
B7060
676
LAW
743
DUN RIG
Blake Muir
121
504
Broadmeadows
Ovenscloss
Lindean
323
WHITLAW MOSSES
Bowden
B6398
Maxton
Muirhouse
SELKIRK GLASS
Selkirk
A699
A708
A707
Yarrow
Yarrow Water
501
FASTHEUGH HILL
Bowhill
BOWHILL HOUSE & COUNTRY PARK
B7039
Philiphaugh
HALLIWELL'S HOUSE MUSEUM
SIR WALTER SCOTT'S COURTROOM
Midlem
B6453
B6359
Longnewton
A68
Douglas Burn
SOUTHERN UPLAND WAY
543
B709
DRYHOPE TOWER
Dryhope
Mountbenger
Yarrow Feus
Sundhope
Scottish
Ettrickbridge
Kirkhope
B7009
Clerklands
Lilliesleaf
Belses
B6400
Bloomfield
Ancrum
Cappercleuch
Ettrick Forest
A7
B6400
Greenhouse
Chesters
BLACK KNOWE HEAD
550
St. Mary's Loch
CAVER'S HILL
369
Akermoor Loch
Woll
Ashkirk
A698
Lanton
MARY QUEEN OF SCOTS HO
JEDBURGH ABBEY
Gilmanscleuch
589
THE WISS
276
Minto
Newton
Hassendean
B6405
Teviot
Loch of the Lowes
Crosslee
Newburgh
Ettrick Water
Shaws Under Loch
Todrig
Horsleyhill
Clarilaw
B6358
338
Hundalee
Bedrule
Denholm
A708
Tushielaw
471
Borders
Hellmoor Loch
Ale Water
Appletreehall
Ashybank
Ramsey Knowe
Wardlaw
Redfordgreen
333
SMASHA HILL
116
B6357
590
Ettrick
Ettrickhill
B711
Borthwickshiels
Burnfoot
Cauldmill
424
RUBERS LAW
Wilton
MUSEUM AND SCOTT GALLERY
Hawick
Kirkton
Hallrule
Ramseycleuch
JAMES HOGG MONUMENT
Buccleuch
Roberton
B711
DRUMLANRIG'S TOWER
Borthwickbrae
Burnfoot
498
Deanburnhaugh
Branxholm Park
Branxholme
A6088
301
Bonchester Bridge
TEVIOTDALE
Glenkerry
Newmill
Hobkirk
Chesters
Cleuch Head
390
REDCLEUCH EDGE
Borthwick Water
Craik Forest
Broadhaugh
Southdean
B709
Nether Dalgliesh
Craik
B6399
393
CRAGBANK WOOD
Northhouse
Dodburn
Slitrig Water
Howpasley
RIDDELL MONUMENT
Allan Water
488
Wauchope Forest
417
PIKE HILL
NT
THE PIKE
462
Teviothead
Priesthaugh
Langburnshiels
Castleweary
532
514
FANNA HILL
477
Teviot
Davington
Singdean
KAGYU SAMYE LING TIBETAN CENTRE
CALDCLEUCH HEAD
608
599
WAVERLEY ROUTE
White Esk
WISP HILL
599
TUDHOPE HILL
602
PEEL FELL
Eskdalemuir Forest
Eskdalemuir
Jamestown
Gorrenberry
HERMITAGE CASTLE
Deadwater
Saughtree
21
446
Hermitage
529
Castle O'er Forest
B709
Meggat Water
492
Ewes Water
NY
499
PIKE FELL
Newlands
B6357
Larriston
Kielder
Steele Road
KIELDER
568
ROAN FELL
Castle O'er
ESKDALE
Arkleton
B6399
329
Dinlabyre
Larriston Fells
Georgefield
Ewes
Bentpath
Old Castleton
Tarras Water
331
FELL
Galloway
LIDDESDALE
446
BLACK EDGE
Newcastleton
450
CALKIN RIG
CRAIGCLEUCH CASTLE COLLECTION
Potholm
A7
Newcastleton or Copshaw Holm
Forest
KIELDER BIRDS OF PREY
514
GLENDHU HILL
B709
Langholm
MALCOLM MONUMENT
Kershope Burn
Paddockhole
B7068
B6357
B7068
Tinnisburn Forest
Kershopefoot
Black Lyne
319
Kirtleton
Caulside
Kershope Forest
Bewcastle Fells
White Lyne
518
SIGHTY CRAG
B722
108
GILNOCKIE TOWER
Claygate
Liddel Water
Baileyhead
Whitelyne Common
B6318
The Flatt
Waterbeck
Kirtle Water
127
B720
B6357
Rowanburn
B6318
Crossings
Blackpool Gate
424
WHITE PRESTON
KIRKCONNEL CHURCHYARD
Evertown
Canonbie
Catlowdy
B6357
Riddings
B725
B722

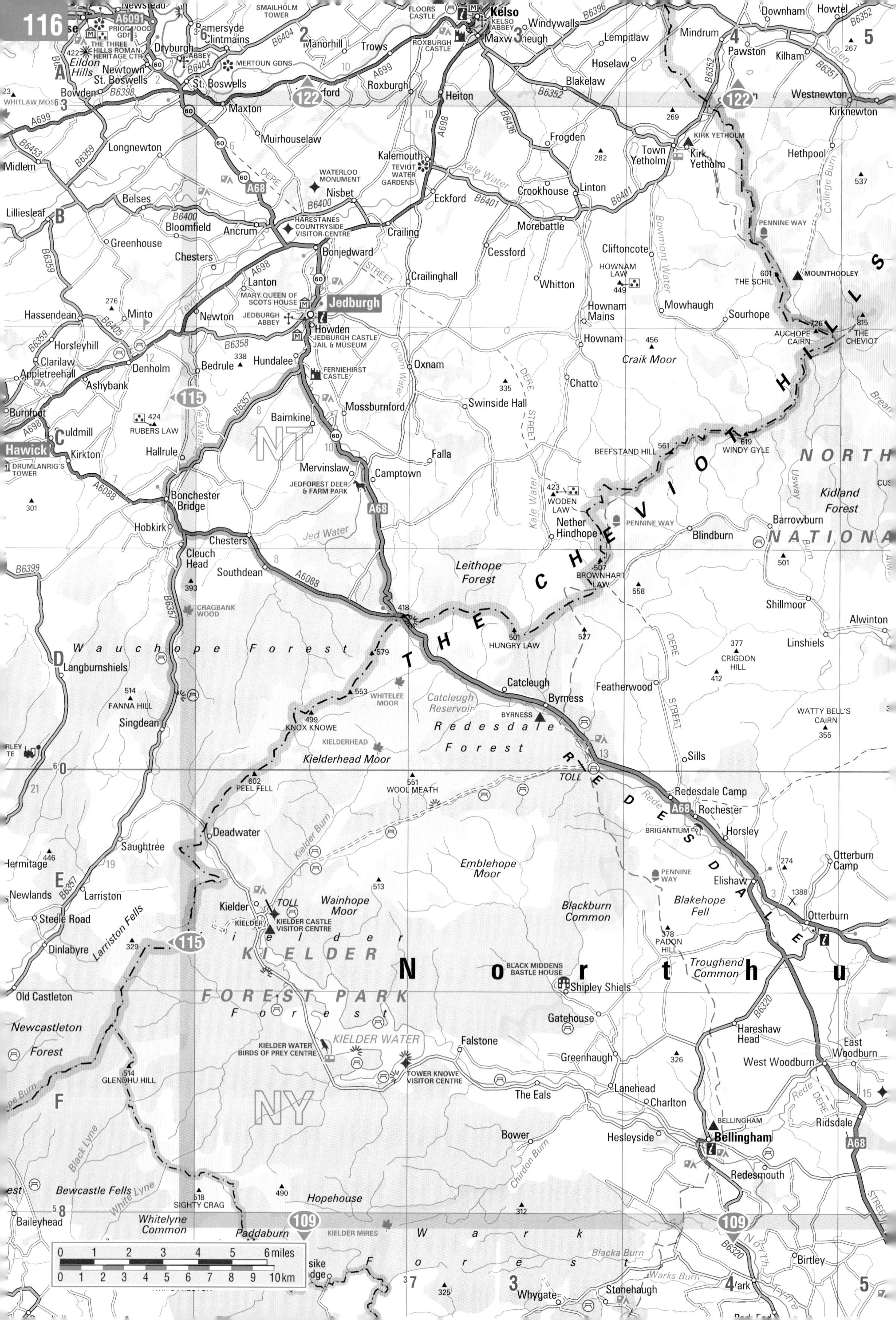
Kelso
Floors Castle
Smailholm Tower
Dryburgh
Dryburgh Abbey
Mertoun Gdns
Newtown St. Boswells
St. Boswells
Eildon Hills
Bowden
Maxton
Manorhill
Trows
Roxburgh
Roxburgh Castle
Kelso Abbey
Windywalls
Lempitlaw
Hoselaw
Blakelaw
Mindrum
Downham
Howtel
Pawston
Kilham
Westnewton
Kirknewton
Heiton
Kalemouth
Teviot Water Gardens
Frogden
Town Yetholm
Kirk Yetholm
Hethpool
Waterloo Monument
Nisbet
Eckford
Crookhouse
Linton
Longnewton
Muirhouselaw
Midlem
Lilliesleaf
Belses
Bloomfield
Ancrum
Harestanes Countryside Visitor Centre
Crailing
Morebattle
Cliftoncote
Greenhouse
Chesters
Bonjedward
Cessford
Hownam Law
Pennine Way
Lanton
Crailinghall
Whitton
The Schil
Mounthooley
Mary Queen of Scots House
Jedburgh
Jedburgh Abbey
Newton
Minto
Hassendean
Howden
Jedburgh Castle Jail & Museum
Hownam Mains
Mowhaugh
Sourhope
Auchope Cairn
The Cheviot
Horsleyhill
Clarilaw
Appletreehall
Denholm
Bedrule
Hundalee
Oxnam
Hownam
Craik Moor
Ferniehirst Castle
Ashybank
Chatto
Swinside Hall
Burnfoot
Hawick
Rubers Law
Bairnkine
Mossburnford
Culdmill
Kirkton
Hallrule
Falla
Beefstand Hill
Windy Gyle
North
Drumlanrig's Tower
Mervinslaw
Camptown
Jedforest Deer & Farm Park
Woden Law
Kidland Forest
Bonchester Bridge
Hobkirk
Chesters
Nether Hindhope
Pennine Way
Blindburn
Barrowburn
National
Cleuch Head
Southdean
Leithope Forest
Brownhart Law
Shillmoor
Cragbank Wood
The Cheviot Hills
Alwinton
Wauchope Forest
Hungry Law
Linshiels
Langburnshiels
Crigdon Hill
Catcleugh
Byrness
Featherwood
Fanna Hill
Whitelee Moor
Catcleugh Reservoir
Watty Bell's Cairn
Singdean
Knox Knowe
Redesdale Forest
Kielderhead
Kielderhead Moor
Sills
Peel Fell
Wool Meath
Toll
Redesdale Camp
Rochester
Redesdale
Bremenium
Horsley
Deadwater
Saughtree
Hermitage
Kielder Burn
Emblehope Moor
Otterburn Camp
Pennine Way
Elishaw
Newlands
Larriston
Larriston Fells
Kielder
Kielder Castle Visitor Centre
Wainhope Moor
Blackburn Common
Blakehope Fell
Otterburn
Steele Road
Dinlabyre
Padon Hill
Kielder Forest Park
Black Middens Bastle House
Shipley Shiels
Troughend Common
Northumberland
Old Castleton
Newcastleton Forest
Gatehouse
Hareshaw Head
Kielder Water
Kielder Water Birds of Prey Centre
Falstone
East Woodburn
West Woodburn
Greenhaugh
Glendhu Hill
Tower Knowe Visitor Centre
The Eals
Lanehead
Charlton
Ridsdale
Bellingham
Hesleyside
Bower
Black Lyne
White Lyne
Chirdon Burn
Bewcastle Fells
Redesmouth
Sighty Crag
Hopehouse
Baileyhead
Whitelyne Common
Paddaburn
Kielder Mires
Wark Forest
Blacka Burn
Birtley
Warks Burn
Stonehaugh
Whygate
Wark
North Tyne
0 1 2 3 4 5 6 miles
0 1 2 3 4 5 6 7 8 9 10 km
NT
NY
A68
A698
A699
A6088
A6091
B6357
B6352
B6320
109
115
122

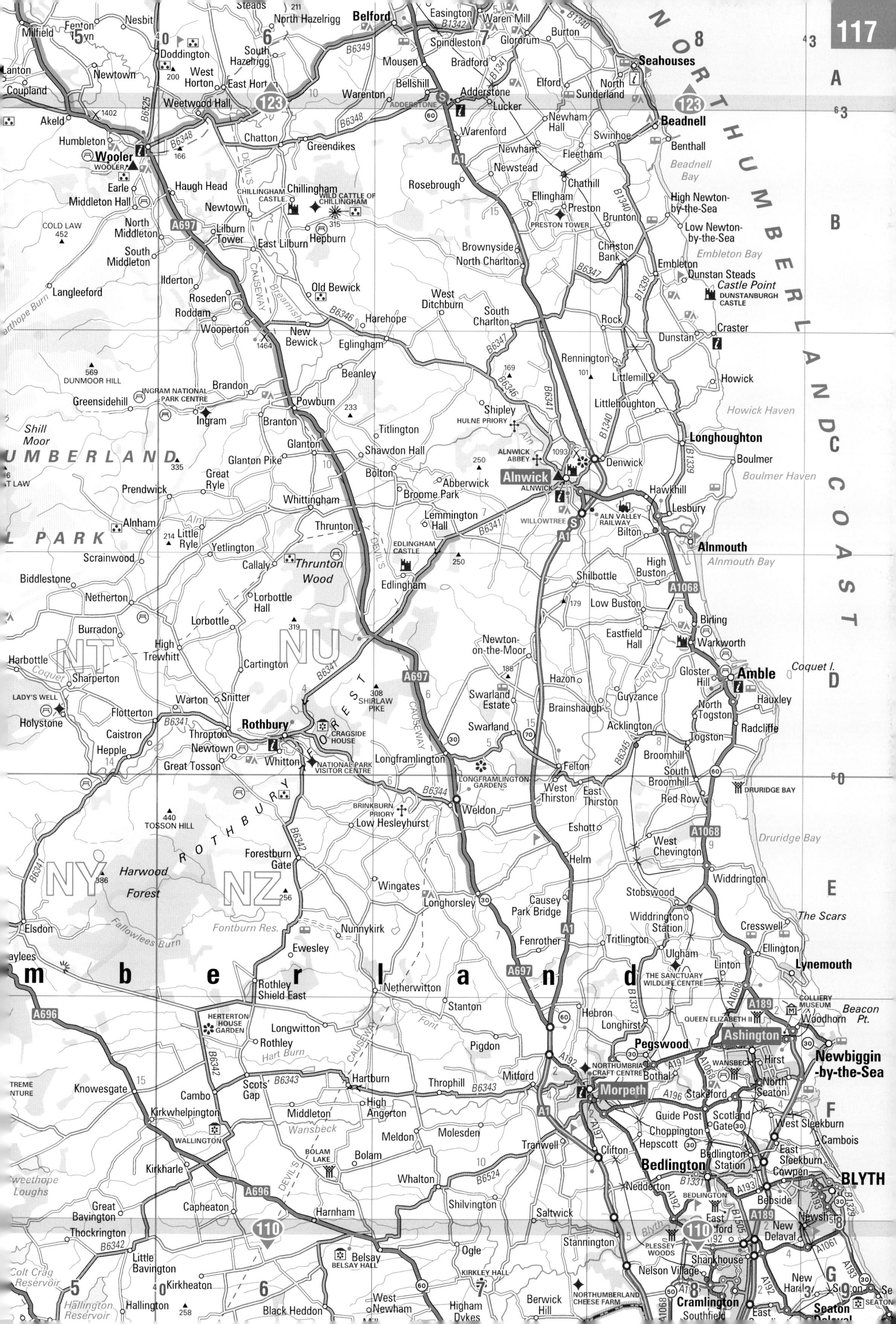
NORTHUMBERLAND COAST
Northumberland
Milfield
Fenton
Nesbit
Doddington
North Hazelrigg
Belford
Easington
Waren Mill
Spindlestone
Glororum
Burton
Seahouses
Lanton
Coupland
Newtown
West Horton
South Hazelrigg
East Horton
Mousen
Bradford
Bellshill
Warenton
Adderstone
Lucker
Elford
North Sunderland
Beadnell
Akeld
Weetwood Hall
Humbleton
Wooler
Earle
Middleton Hall
Chatton
Greendikes
Warenford
Newham Hall
Swinhoe
Benthall
Newham
Fleetham
Newstead
Beadnell Bay
Haugh Head
Chillingham
Chillingham Castle
Wild Cattle of Chillingham
Rosebrough
Chathill
Ellingham
Preston
Preston Tower
High Newton-by-the-Sea
Low Newton-by-the-Sea
Embleton Bay
Brunton
Christon Bank
Cold Law
North Middleton
South Middleton
Lilburn Tower
East Lilburn
Hepburn
Brownyside
North Charlton
Embleton
Dunstan Steads
Castle Point
Dunstanburgh Castle
Langleeford
Ilderton
Roseden
Roddam
Wooperton
Old Bewick
New Bewick
Harehope
Eglingham
West Ditchburn
South Charlton
Rock
Dunstan
Craster
Dunmoor Hill
Beanley
Rennington
Littlemill
Howick
Brandon
Greensidehill
Ingram National Park Centre
Ingram
Powburn
Branton
Shipley
Hulne Priory
Littlehoughton
Howick Haven
Longhoughton
Shill Moor
Titlington
Glanton
Glanton Pike
Shawdon Hall
Alnwick Abbey
Alnwick
Denwick
Boulmer
Boulmer Haven
Great Ryle
Bolton
Abberwick
Prendwick
Broome Park
Whittingham
Hawkhill
Lesbury
Alnham
Lemmington Hall
Willowtree
Aln Valley Railway
Bilton
Alnmouth
Alnmouth Bay
Little Ryle
Thrunton
Yetlington
Edlingham Castle
Scrainwood
Callaly
Thrunton Wood
Edlingham
High Buston
Shilbottle
Biddlestone
Netherton
Lorbottle Hall
Low Buston
Birling
Burradon
Lorbottle
Eastfield Hall
Warkworth
Newton-on-the-Moor
High Trewhitt
Harbottle
Sharperton
Cartington
Gloster Hill
Amble
Coquet I.
Hazon
Hauxley
Lady's Well
Holystone
Warton
Snitter
Shirlaw Pike
Swarland Estate
Guyzance
Brainshaugh
North Togston
Flotterton
Rothbury
Cragside House
Swarland
Acklington
Radcliffe
Caistron
Thropton
Newtown
Togston
Hepple
Great Tosson
Whitton
National Park Visitor Centre
Longframlington
Felton
Broomhill
South Broomhill
Druridge Bay
Longframlington Gardens
West Thirston
East Thirston
Red Row
Rothbury Forest
Brinkburn Priory
Low Hesleyhurst
Weldon
Tosson Hill
Eshott
West Chevington
Druridge Bay
Forestburn Gate
Helm
Widdrington
Harwood Forest
Wingates
Stobswood
Longhorsley
Causey Park Bridge
Widdrington Station
The Scars
Elsdon
Fontburn Res.
Nunnykirk
Cresswell
Fallowlees Burn
Fenrother
Tritlington
Ellington
Ewesley
Ulgham
Linton
Lynemouth
The Sanctuary Wildlife Centre
Rothley Shield East
Netherwitton
Colliery Museum
Beacon Pt.
Stanton
Hebron
Queen Elizabeth II
Woodhorn
Herterton House Garden
Longhirst
Ashington
Longwitton
Pigdon
Pegswood
Newbiggin-by-the-Sea
Rothley
Hart Burn
Northumbria Craft Centre
Hirst
Wansbeck
Bothal
Knowesgate
Scots' Gap
Hartburn
Throphill
Mitford
Morpeth
North Seaton
Cambo
High Angerton
Stakeford
Kirkwhelpington
Middleton
Guide Post
Scotland Gate
Wansbeck
Choppington
West Sleekburn
Wallington
Meldon
Molesden
Hepscott
Cambois
Bolam Lake
Bolam
Tranwell
Clifton
Bedlington
Bedlington Station
East Sleekburn
Kirkharle
Whalton
Cowpen
Blyth
Sweethope Loughs
Nedderton
Bebside
Great Bavington
Capheaton
Shilvington
Saltwick
Thockrington
Harnham
Blyth
Plessey Woods
East Cramlington
New Delaval
Stannington
Newsham
Little Bavington
Belsay
Belsay Hall
Ogle
Shankhouse
Colt Crag Reservoir
Kirkheaton
Kirkley Hall
Nelson Village
New Hartley
Hallington Reservoir
Hallington
Black Heddon
West Newham
Higham Dykes
Berwick Hill
Northumberland Cheese Farm
Cramlington
Seaton Delaval
Southfield
A1
A697
A696
A1068
A189
A192
A193
A197
A196
B6525
B6348
B6349
B1342
B1340
B1341
B1339
B6347
B6346
B6341
B6344
B6345
B6342
B6343
B6524
B1337
B1331
B1505
B1329
A1061
123
110
NT
NU
NY
NZ
Devil's Causeway

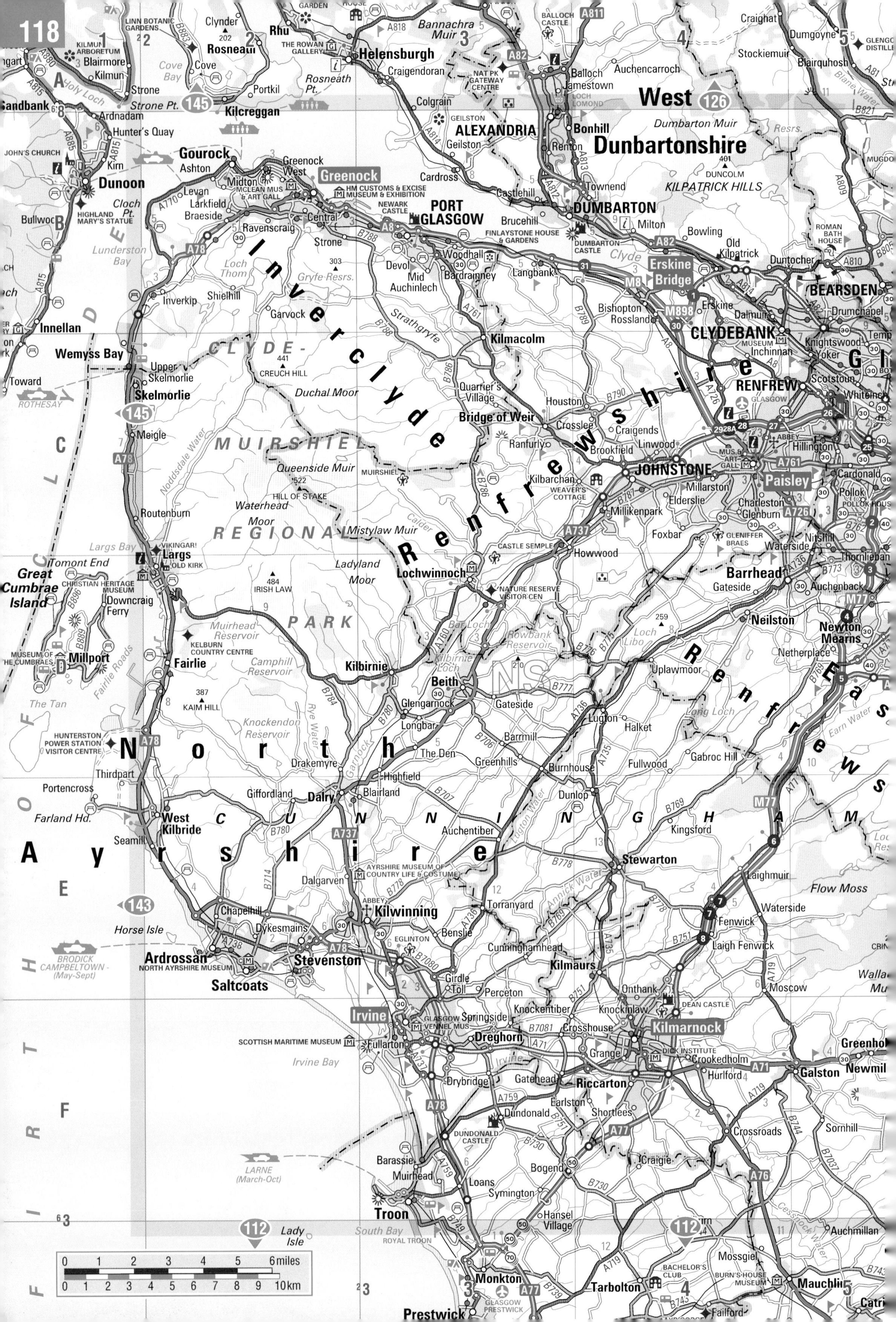
Helensburgh
Rhu
Rosneath
Kilcreggan
Dunoon
Gourock
Greenock
Port Glasgow
Alexandria
Dumbarton
West Dunbartonshire
Dunbartonshire
KILPATRICK HILLS
Erskine Bridge
Clydebank
Bearsden
Renfrew
Glasgow
Paisley
Johnstone
Inverclyde
Renfrewshire
East Renfrewshire
Kilmacolm
Bridge of Weir
Lochwinnoch
Barrhead
Neilston
Newton Mearns
Wemyss Bay
Skelmorlie
Largs
Great Cumbrae Island
Millport
Fairlie
CLYDE-MUIRSHIEL REGIONAL PARK
Kilbirnie
Beith
Dalry
North Ayrshire
West Kilbride
Ardrossan
Saltcoats
Stevenston
Kilwinning
Irvine
Kilmarnock
Stewarton
Kilmaurs
Fenwick
Galston
Troon
Prestwick
Tarbolton
Mauchline
FIRTH OF CLYDE
CUNNINGHAME
Irvine Bay
South Bay
Lady Isle
Horse Isle
0 1 2 3 4 5 6 miles
0 1 2 3 4 5 6 7 8 9 10km

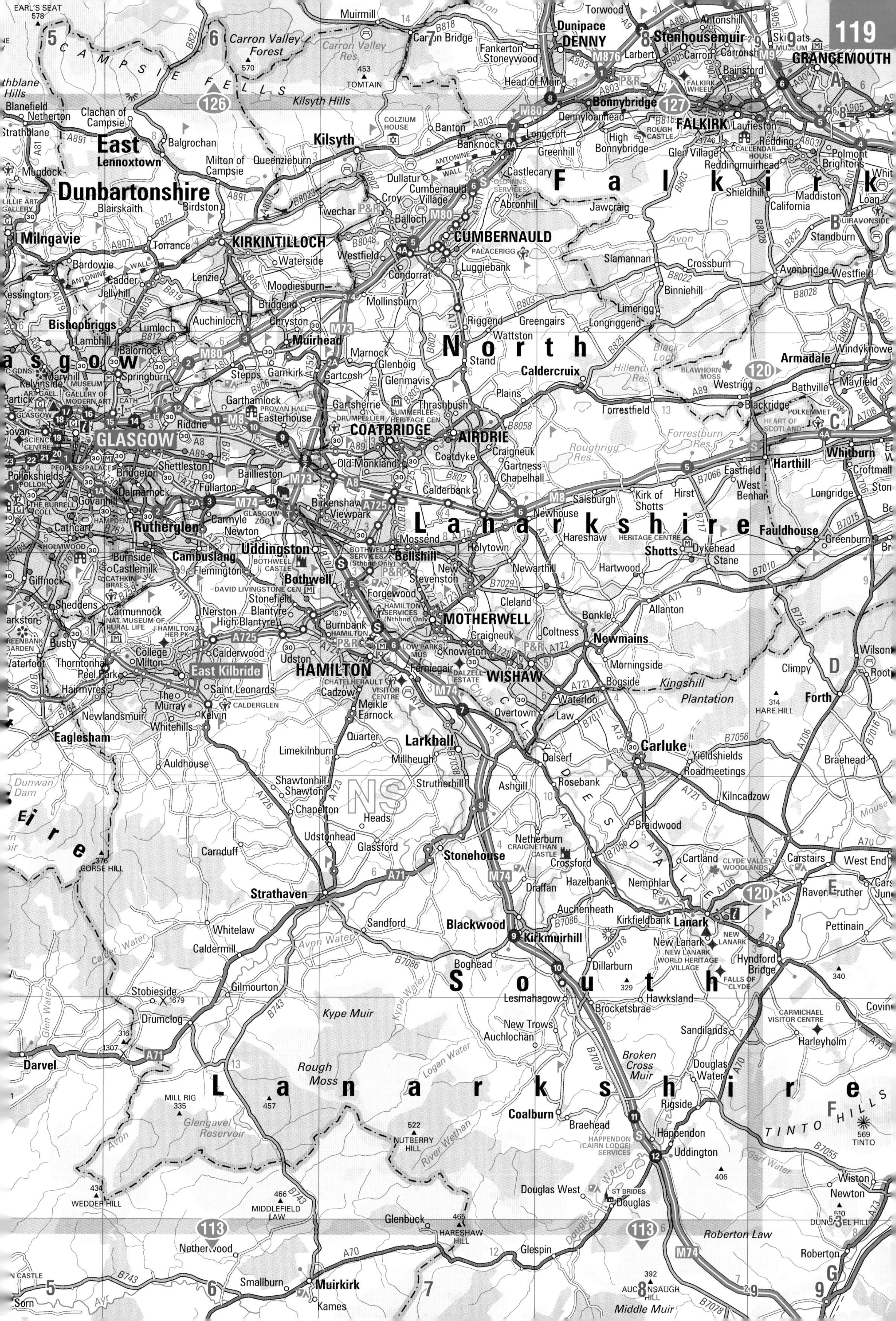
East Dunbartonshire
Falkirk
North Lanarkshire
South Lanarkshire
GLASGOW
GRANGEMOUTH
FALKIRK
DENNY
Dunipace
Stenhousemuir
Larbert
Bonnybridge
Kilsyth
Kilsyth Hills
Campsie Fells
Carron Valley Forest
Carron Valley Res.
Carron Bridge
Lennoxtown
Milngavie
Bishopbriggs
KIRKINTILLOCH
CUMBERNAULD
COATBRIDGE
AIRDRIE
Muirhead
Stepps
Caldercruix
Armadale
Whitburn
Harthill
Shotts
Fauldhouse
Bellshill
Uddingston
Bothwell
MOTHERWELL
WISHAW
Newmains
HAMILTON
East Kilbride
Rutherglen
Cambuslang
Blantyre
Larkhall
Carluke
Lanark
Carstairs
Forth
Strathaven
Stonehouse
Blackwood
Kirkmuirhill
Lesmahagow
Coalburn
Douglas
Douglas West
Muirkirk
Glespin
Darvel
Eaglesham
Busby
Clydesdale
Kingshill Plantation
Kype Muir
Rough Moss
Tinto Hills
Glengavel Reservoir
Broken Cross Muir
Roberton Law
Middle Muir
NS

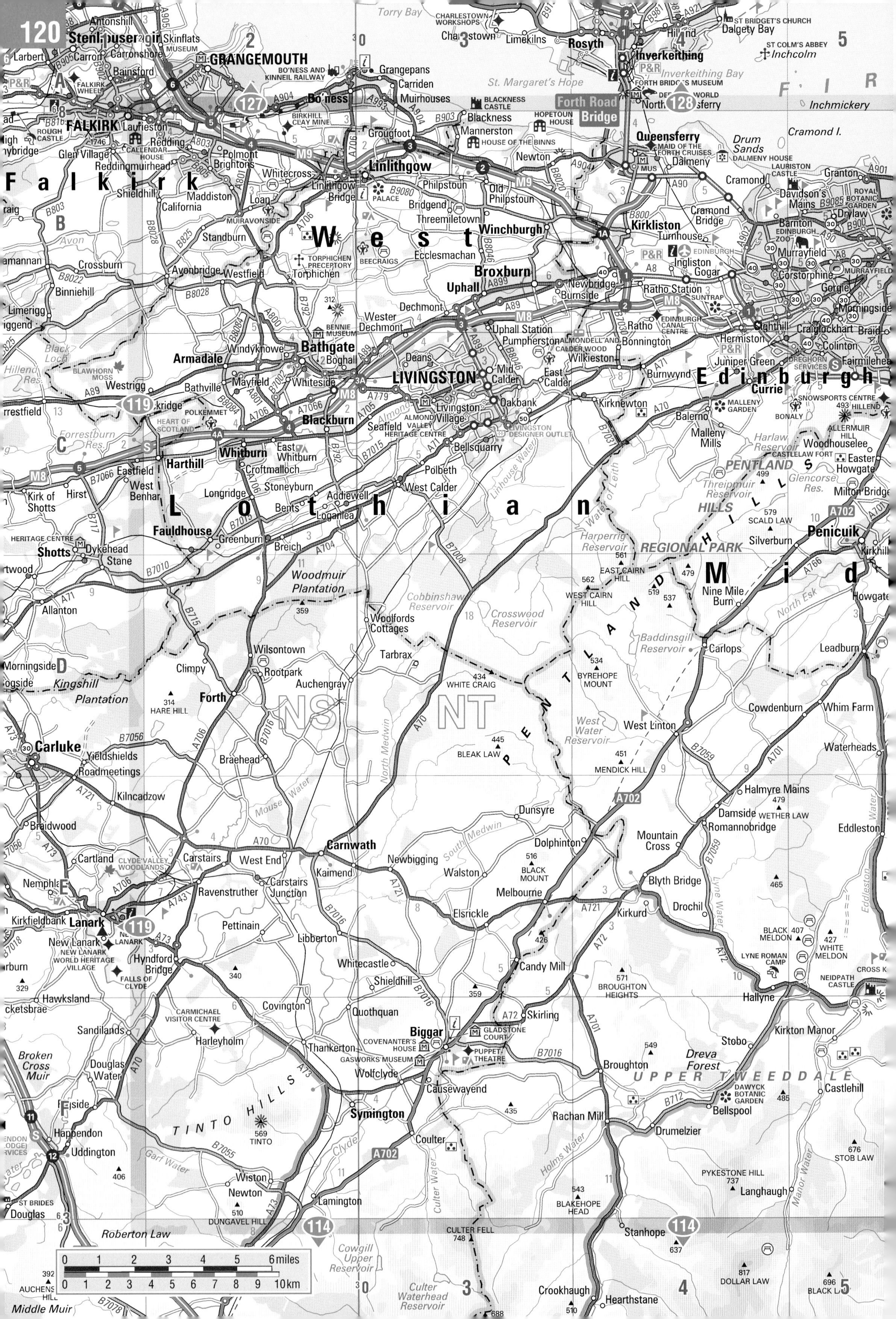
Falkirk
West Lothian
Edinburgh
Mid
PENTLAND HILLS REGIONAL PARK
PENTLAND
UPPER TWEEDDALE
TINTO HILLS
GRANGEMOUTH
FALKIRK
Stenhousemuir
Larbert
Carron
Carronshore
Bainsford
Skinflats
Laurieston
Redding
Polmont
Brightons
Reddingmuirhead
Glen Village
Shieldhill
California
Maddiston
Whitecross
Bo'ness
Grangepans
Carriden
Muirhouses
Blackness
Mannerston
Grougfoot
Linlithgow
Linlithgow Bridge
Philpstoun
Old Philpstoun
Bridgend
Threemiletown
Winchburgh
Ecclesmachan
Broxburn
Uphall
Dechmont
Wester Dechmont
Uphall Station
Pumpherston
Bathgate
Boghall
Armadale
Windyknowe
Westrigg
Bathville
Mayfield
Whiteside
Blackburn
Seafield
LIVINGSTON
Deans
Livingston Village
Mid Calder
East Calder
Oakbank
Bellsquarry
Polbeth
West Calder
Addiewell
Loganlea
Stoneyburn
Bents
Longridge
Whitburn
East Whitburn
Croftmalloch
Harthill
Eastfield
West Benhar
Fauldhouse
Greenburn
Breich
Shotts
Dykehead
Stane
Kirk of Shotts
Hirst
Torphichen
Westfield
Avonbridge
Standburn
Crossburn
Binniehill
Limerigg
Allanton
Charlestown
Limekilns
Rosyth
Inverkeithing
Hillend
Dalgety Bay
Inchcolm
Inchmickery
North Queensferry
Queensferry
Dalmeny
Newton
Kirkliston
Turnhouse
Ingliston
Gogar
Ratho Station
Ratho
Newbridge
Burnside
Bonnington
Wilkieston
Kirknewton
Hermiston
Juniper Green
Currie
Balerno
Malleny Mills
Burnwynd
Cramond
Cramond Bridge
Cramond I.
Granton
Davidson's Mains
Barnton
Drylaw
Murrayfield
Corstorphine
Gorgie
Morningside
Sighthill
Craiglockhart
Colinton
Fairmilehead
Woodhouselee
Easter Howgate
Milton Bridge
Penicuik
Silverburn
Nine Mile Burn
Carlops
Howgate
Leadburn
Cowdenburn
Whim Farm
Waterheads
West Linton
Halmyre Mains
Damside
Romannobridge
Mountain Cross
Eddleston
Blyth Bridge
Drochil
Kirkurd
Dolphinton
Dunsyre
Newbigging
Walston
Melbourne
Elsrickle
Candy Mill
Skirling
Broughton
Biggar
Stobo
Kirkton Manor
Hallyne
Dreva Forest
Bellspool
Drumelzier
Rachan Mill
Castlehill
Langhaugh
Stanhope
Crookhaugh
Hearthstane
Woolfords Cottages
Tarbrax
Wilsontown
Rootpark
Auchengray
Climpy
Forth
Braehead
Carluke
Yieldshields
Roadmeetings
Kilncadzow
Braidwood
Cartland
Carstairs
Carstairs Junction
West End
Carnwath
Kaimend
Ravenstruther
Pettinain
Libberton
Whitecastle
Shieldhill
Quothquan
Covington
Thankerton
Wolfclyde
Causewayend
Symington
Coulter
Lamington
Wiston
Newton
Nemphlar
Lanark
Kirkfieldbank
New Lanark
Hyndford Bridge
Hawksland
Sandilands
Harleyholm
Douglas Water
Happendon
Uddington
Douglas
Roberton Law
Middle Muir
Woodmuir Plantation
Kingshill Plantation
Morningside
Cobbinshaw Reservoir
Crosswood Reservoir
Harperrig Reservoir
Baddinsgill Reservoir
West Water Reservoir
Threipmuir Reservoir
Harlaw Reservoir
Glencorse Res.
Cowgill Upper Reservoir
Culter Waterhead Reservoir
Forth Road Bridge
M9
M8
A70
A702
A72
A721
A73
A706
127
128
119
114
0 1 2 3 4 5 6 miles
0 1 2 3 4 5 6 7 8 9 10 km
NS
NT

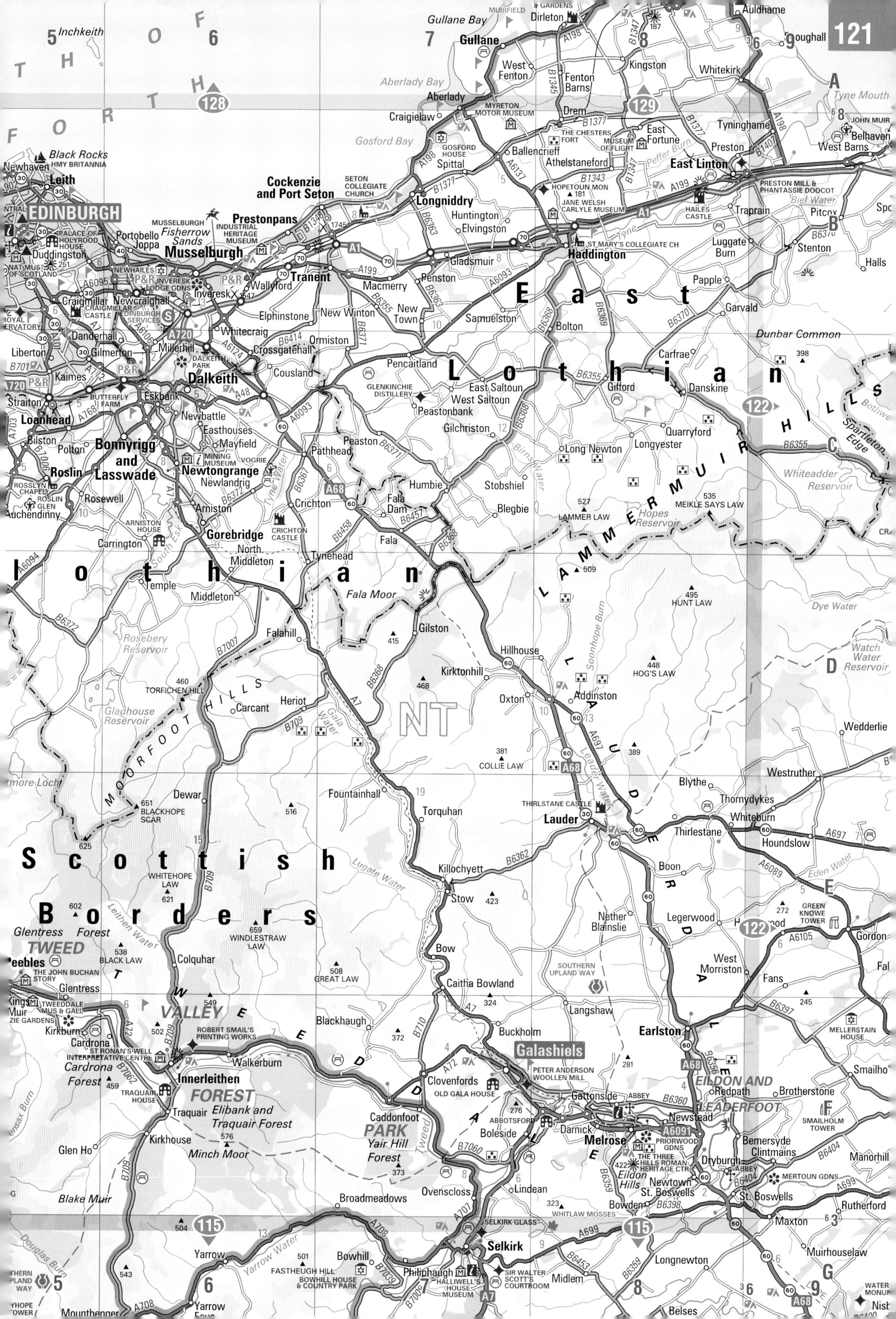
FIRTH OF FORTH
Inchkeith
Gullane Bay
Aberlady Bay
Gosford Bay
Dirleton
Gullane
West Fenton
Fenton Barns
Kingston
Whitekirk
Auldhame
Tyne Mouth
Aberlady
Craigielaw
MYRETON MOTOR MUSEUM
Drem
THE CHESTERS FORT
MUSEUM OF FLIGHT
East Fortune
Tyninghame
JOHN MUIR
Belhaven
West Barns
GOSFORD HOUSE
Spittal
Ballencrieff
Athelstaneford
Peffer Burn
Preston
East Linton
HOPETOUN MON
JANE WELSH CARLYLE MUSEUM
PRESTON MILL & PHANTASSIE DOOCOT
Biel Water
HAILES CASTLE
Traprain
Pitcox
Black Rocks
Newhaven
HMY BRITANNIA
Leith
EDINBURGH
Cockenzie and Port Seton
SETON COLLEGIATE CHURCH
Longniddry
Huntington
Elvington
Prestonpans
MUSSELBURGH
Fisherrow Sands
INDUSTRIAL HERITAGE MUSEUM
Portobello
Joppa
Musselburgh
PALACE OF HOLYROOD HOUSE
Duddingston
NAT MUS OF SCOTLAND
Haddington
ST MARY'S COLLEGIATE CH
Luggate Burn
Stenton
Halls
Gladsmuir
NEWHAILES
INVERESK LODGE GDNS
Inveresk
Wallyford
Tranent
Macmerry
Penston
Papple
Craigmillar
Newcraighall
CRAIGMILLAR CASTLE
EDINBURGH SERVICES
Elphinstone
New Winton
New Town
Samuelston
Garvald
East Lothian
Whitecraig
Danderhall
Liberton
Gilmerton
Millerhill
Ormiston
Crossgatehall
Bolton
Dunbar Common
Carfrae
Pencaitland
Cousland
DALKEITH PARK
Dalkeith
Kaimes
Straiton
BUTTERFLY FARM
Eskbank
GLENKINCHIE DISTILLERY
East Saltoun
West Saltoun
Gifford
Danskine
Loanhead
Peastonbank
Newbattle
Easthouses
Mayfield
Gilchriston
Quarryford
Longyester
Bilston
Polton
Bonnyrigg and Lasswade
MINING MUSEUM
VOGRIE
Newtongrange
Newlandrig
Peaston
Pathhead
Long Newton
Roslin
ROSSLYN CHAPEL
ROSLIN GLEN
Rosewell
Auchendinny
Arniston
Crichton
Humbie
Fala Dam
Stobshiel
Blegbie
LAMMERMUIR HILLS
Whiteadder Reservoir
Spartleton Edge
Hopes Reservoir
LAMMER LAW
MEIKLE SAYS LAW
ARNISTON HOUSE
Carrington
Gorebridge
CRICHTON CASTLE
Fala
Tynehead
North Middleton
Lothian
Temple
Middleton
Fala Moor
HUNT LAW
Dye Water
Rosebery Reservoir
Falahill
Gilston
Hillhouse
Watch Water Reservoir
Kirktonhill
HOG'S LAW
TORFICHEN HILL
MOORFOOT HILLS
Carcant
Heriot
Gala Water
Oxton
Addinston
Soonhope Burn
Gladhouse Reservoir
NT
Wedderlie
COLLIE LAW
Leader Water
LAUDERDALE
Westruther
Blythe
Thornydykes
Dewar
Fountainhall
Torquhan
THIRLSTANE CASTLE
Lauder
Whiteburn
Thirlestane
Houndslow
BLACKHOPE SCAR
Scottish Borders
Lugate Water
Killochyett
Boon
Eden Water
WHITEHOPE LAW
Stow
Nether Blainslie
Legerwood
GREEN KNOWE TOWER
Gordon
Glentress Forest
TWEED
Leithen Water
WINDLESTRAW LAW
Peebles
BLACK LAW
THE JOHN BUCHAN STORY
Colquhar
GREAT LAW
Bow
SOUTHERN UPLAND WAY
West Morriston
Fans
Glentress
Kings Muir
TWEEDDALE MUS & GALL
TWEED VALLEY
Caitha Bowland
Langshaw
Kirkburn
Cardrona
ROBERT SMAIL'S PRINTING WORKS
Blackhaugh
Buckholm
Earlston
MELLERSTAIN HOUSE
ST RONAN'S WELL INTERPRETATIVE CENTRE
Cardrona Forest
Walkerburn
Galashiels
PETER ANDERSON WOOLLEN MILL
EILDON AND LEADERFOOT
Smailholm
Innerleithen
Clovenfords
OLD GALA HOUSE
Gattonside
ABBEY
Redpath
Brotherstone
TRAQUAIR HOUSE
FOREST
Traquair
Elibank and Traquair Forest
Caddonfoot
TWEED PARK
Yair Hill Forest
ABBOTSFORD
Boleside
Darnick
Newstead
SMAILHOLM TOWER
Melrose
PRIORWOOD GDNS
THE THREE HILLS ROMAN HERITAGE CTR
Bemersyde
Clintmains
Kirkhouse
Minch Moor
Glen Ho
Eildon Hills
Dryburgh
ABBEY
Manorhill
MERTOUN GDNS
Newtown St. Boswells
St. Boswells
Rutherford
Blake Muir
Broadmeadows
Ovenscloss
Lindean
Bowden
WHITLAW MOSSES
Maxton
SELKIRK GLASS
Selkirk
Muirhouselaw
Douglas Burn
Yarrow
Yarrow Water
FASTHEUGH HILL
Bowhill
BOWHILL HOUSE & COUNTRY PARK
Philiphaugh
HALLIWELL'S HOUSE MUSEUM
SIR WALTER SCOTT'S COURTROOM
Midlem
Longnewton
SOUTHERN UPLAND WAY
Mounthenger
Belses
WATER MONUM
Nisbet

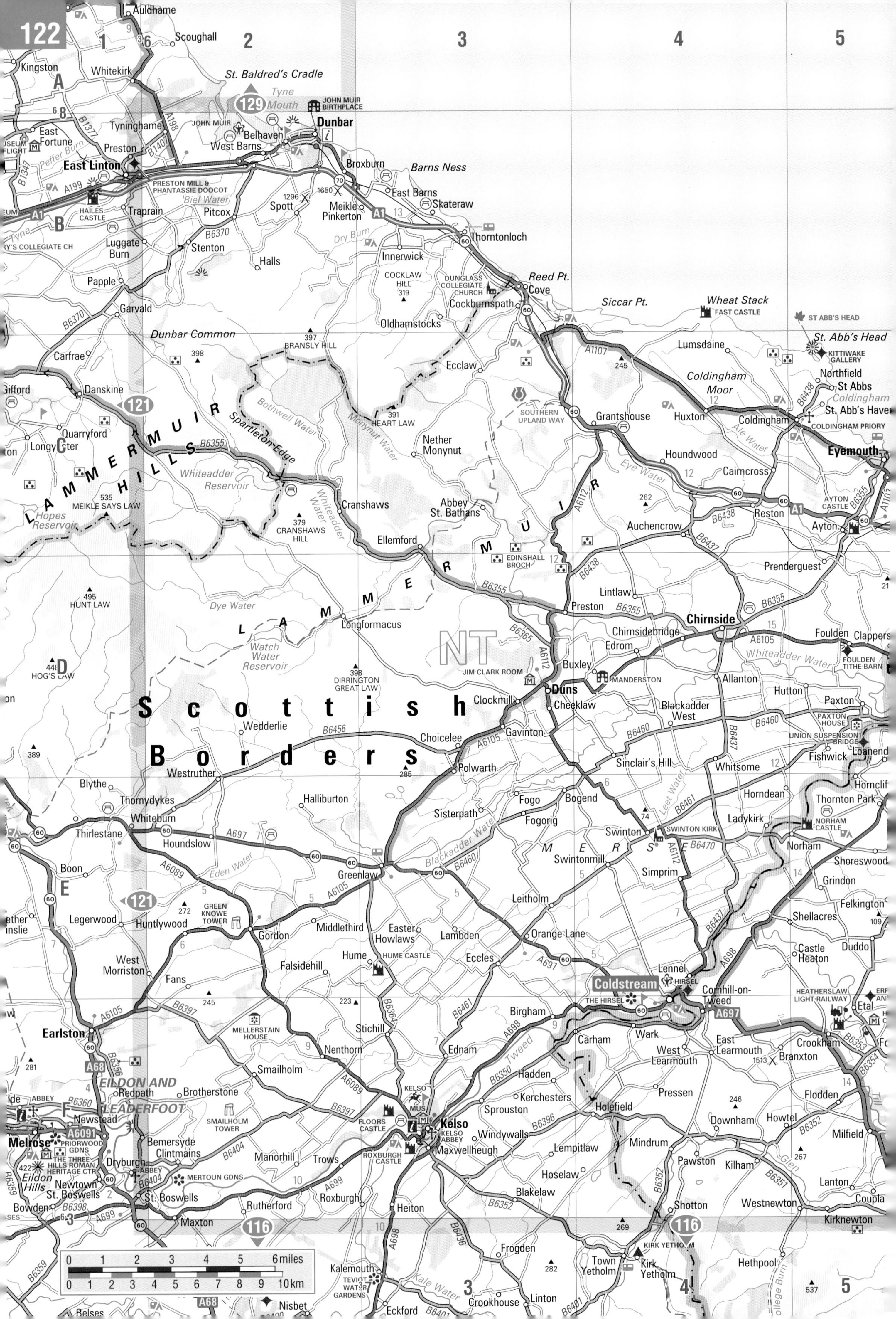

Auldhame
Scoughall
1
2
3
4
5
Kingston
Whitekirk
A
St. Baldred's Cradle
Tyne Mouth
129
JOHN MUIR BIRTHPLACE
Dunbar
East Fortune
Tyninghame
JOHN MUIR
Belhaven
West Barns
Preston
Peffer Burn
East Linton
Broxburn
Barns Ness
PRESTON MILL & PHANTASSIE DOOCOT
Biel Water
East Barns
Skateraw
Spott
Meikle Pinkerton
HAILES CASTLE
Traprain
Pitcox
B
Thorntonloch
Luggate Burn
Stenton
Dry Burn
Innerwick
Halls
COCKLAW HILL 319
DUNGLASS COLLEGIATE CHURCH
Reed Pt.
Cove
Papple
Cockburnspath
Siccar Pt.
Wheat Stack
FAST CASTLE
ST ABB'S HEAD
Garvald
Oldhamstocks
Dunbar Common
397 BRANSLY HILL
St. Abb's Head
Lumsdaine
KITTIWAKE GALLERY
Carfrae
398
Ecclaw
245
Coldingham Moor
Northfield
St Abbs
Coldingham
Gifford
Danskine
121
Bothwell Water
Monynut Water
391 HEART LAW
SOUTHERN UPLAND WAY
Grantshouse
Huxton
Coldingham
St. Abb's Haven
COLDINGHAM PRIORY
Quarryford
C
Longyester
LAMMERMUIR
HILLS
Spartleton Edge
B6355
Nether Monynut
Ale Water
Houndwood
Eyemouth
Whiteadder Reservoir
Eye Water
Cairncross
535 MEIKLE SAYS LAW
Hopes Reservoir
Cranshaws
Whiteadder Water
Abbey St. Bathans
262
AYTON CASTLE
Auchencrow
Reston
Ayton
379 CRANSHAWS HILL
Ellemford
EDINSHALL BROCH
Prenderguest
495 HUNT LAW
Dye Water
LAMMERMUIR
Lintlaw
Preston
Chirnside
Longformacus
Watch Water Reservoir
NT
Chirnsidebridge
Edrom
Foulden
Clappers
Whiteadder Water
FOULDEN TITHE BARN
448
D
HOG'S LAW
398 DIRRINGTON GREAT LAW
JIM CLARK ROOM
Buxley
MANDERSTON
Allanton
Duns
Cheeklaw
Clockmill
Hutton
Paxton
Scottish Borders
Blackadder West
Wedderlie
PAXTON HOUSE
UNION SUSPENSION BRIDGE
Choicelee
Gavinton
389
285
Polwarth
Sinclair's Hill
Fishwick
Loanend
Westruther
Whitsome
Blythe
Horncliffe
Halliburton
Horndean
Thornydykes
Thornton Park
Fogo
Bogend
Sisterpath
Fogorig
Ladykirk
Whiteburn
74
Leet Water
NORHAM CASTLE
Thirlestane
Houndslow
Swinton
SWINTON KIRK
Blackadder Water
MERSE
Norham
Swintonmill
Shoreswood
Boon
Eden Water
Greenlaw
Simprim
Grindon
E
121
272
GREEN KNOWE TOWER
Leitholm
Felkington
Shellacres
109
Legerwood
Huntlywood
Gordon
Middlethird
Easter Howlaws
Lambden
Orange Lane
Duddo
West Morriston
Hume
HUME CASTLE
Eccles
Castle Heaton
Falsidehill
Lennel
Fans
Coldstream
HIRSEL
Cornhill-on-Tweed
245
223
THE HIRSEL
HEATHERSLAW LIGHT RAILWAY
Etal
Earlston
MELLERSTAIN HOUSE
Stichill
Birgham
Carham
Wark
East Learmouth
West Learmouth
Crookham
Nenthorn
Ednam
1513
Branxton
281
Smailholm
Hadden
Tweed
EILDON AND LEADERFOOT
Redpath
Brotherstone
Kerchesters
Pressen
Flodden
KELSO MUS
Sprouston
Holefield
246
Howtel
Newstead
SMAILHOLM TOWER
FLOORS CASTLE
Kelso
KELSO ABBEY
Downham
Milfield
Melrose
PRIORWOOD GDNS
THE THREE HILLS ROMAN HERITAGE CTR
Bemersyde
Clintmains
Windywalls
Mindrum
267
Eildon Hills
Dryburgh
ABBEY
Manorhill
Trows
ROXBURGH CASTLE
Maxwellheugh
Lempitlaw
Pawston
Kilham
Glen
Newtown St. Boswells
MERTOUN GDNS
Roxburgh
Hoselaw
Lanton
St. Boswells
Rutherford
Blakelaw
Shotton
Westnewton
Coupland
Bowden
Heiton
Maxton
116
269
116
Kirknewton
Frogden
KIRK YETHOLM
Kalemouth
282
Town Yetholm
Kirk Yetholm
Hethpool
TEVIOT WATER GARDENS
Kale Water
3
4
5
Crookhouse
Linton
537
Nisbet
Belses
Eckford
0 1 2 3 4 5 6 miles
0 1 2 3 4 5 6 7 8 9 10 km

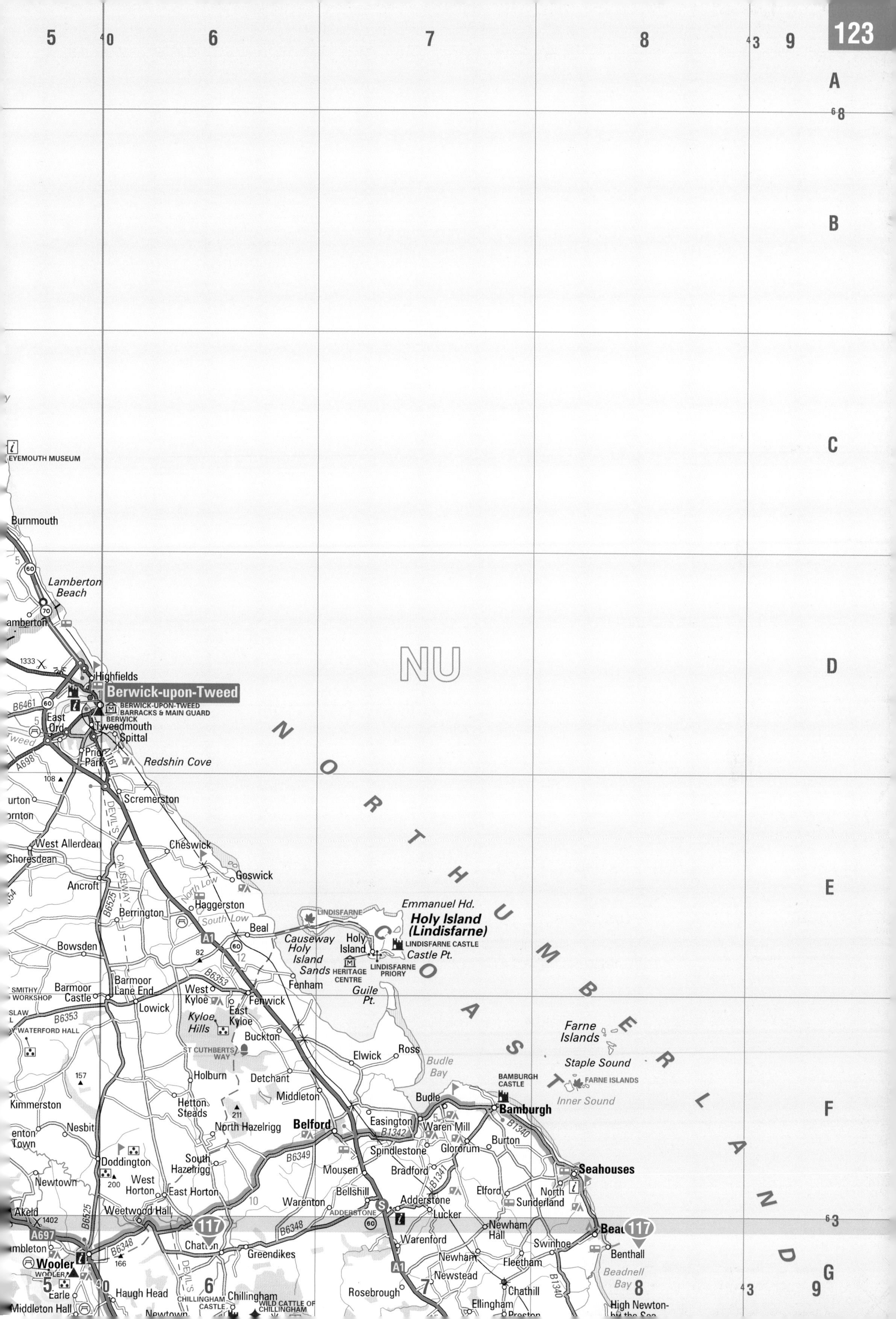
NU
NORTHUMBERLAND COAST
EYEMOUTH MUSEUM
Burnmouth
Lamberton Beach
Highfields
Berwick-upon-Tweed
BERWICK-UPON-TWEED BARRACKS & MAIN GUARD
BERWICK
East Ord
Tweedmouth
Spittal
Prior Park
Redshin Cove
A698
A1167
B6461
Scremerston
DEVIL'S CAUSEWAY
West Allerdean
Shoresdean
Cheswick
Goswick
Ancroft
North Low
South Low
Haggerston
Berrington
B6525
Beal
A1
Bowsden
LINDISFARNE
Emmanuel Hd.
Holy Island (Lindisfarne)
Causeway
Holy Island Sands
Holy Island
LINDISFARNE CASTLE
Castle Pt.
HERITAGE CENTRE
LINDISFARNE PRIORY
Fenham
Guile Pt.
SMITHY WORKSHOP
Barmoor Castle
Barmoor Lane End
B6353
Lowick
West Kyloe
East Kyloe
Fenwick
Kyloe Hills
WATERFORD HALL
Buckton
ST CUTHBERTS WAY
Elwick
Ross
Budle Bay
Farne Islands
Staple Sound
FARNE ISLANDS
BAMBURGH CASTLE
Inner Sound
Holburn
Detchant
Middleton
Kimmerston
Hetton Steads
North Hazelrigg
Belford
Budle
Bamburgh
Easington
Waren Mill
B1340
B1342
Nesbit
Spindlestone
Glororum
Burton
Doddington
South Hazelrigg
B6349
Mousen
Bradford
B1341
Seahouses
Newtown
West Horton
East Horton
Bellshill
Elford
North Sunderland
Warenton
Adderstone
ADDERSTONE
Weetwood Hall
Lucker
Akeld
A697
Chatton
B6348
Warenford
Newham Hall
Swinhoe
Beadnell
Benthall
Wooler
Greendikes
Newham
Fleetham
Earle
Haugh Head
Newstead
Beadnell Bay
Chillingham
CHILLINGHAM CASTLE
WILD CATTLE OF CHILLINGHAM
Rosebrough
Chathill
Middleton Hall
Ellingham
High Newton-by-the-Sea
117
A B C D E F G
5 6 7 8 9

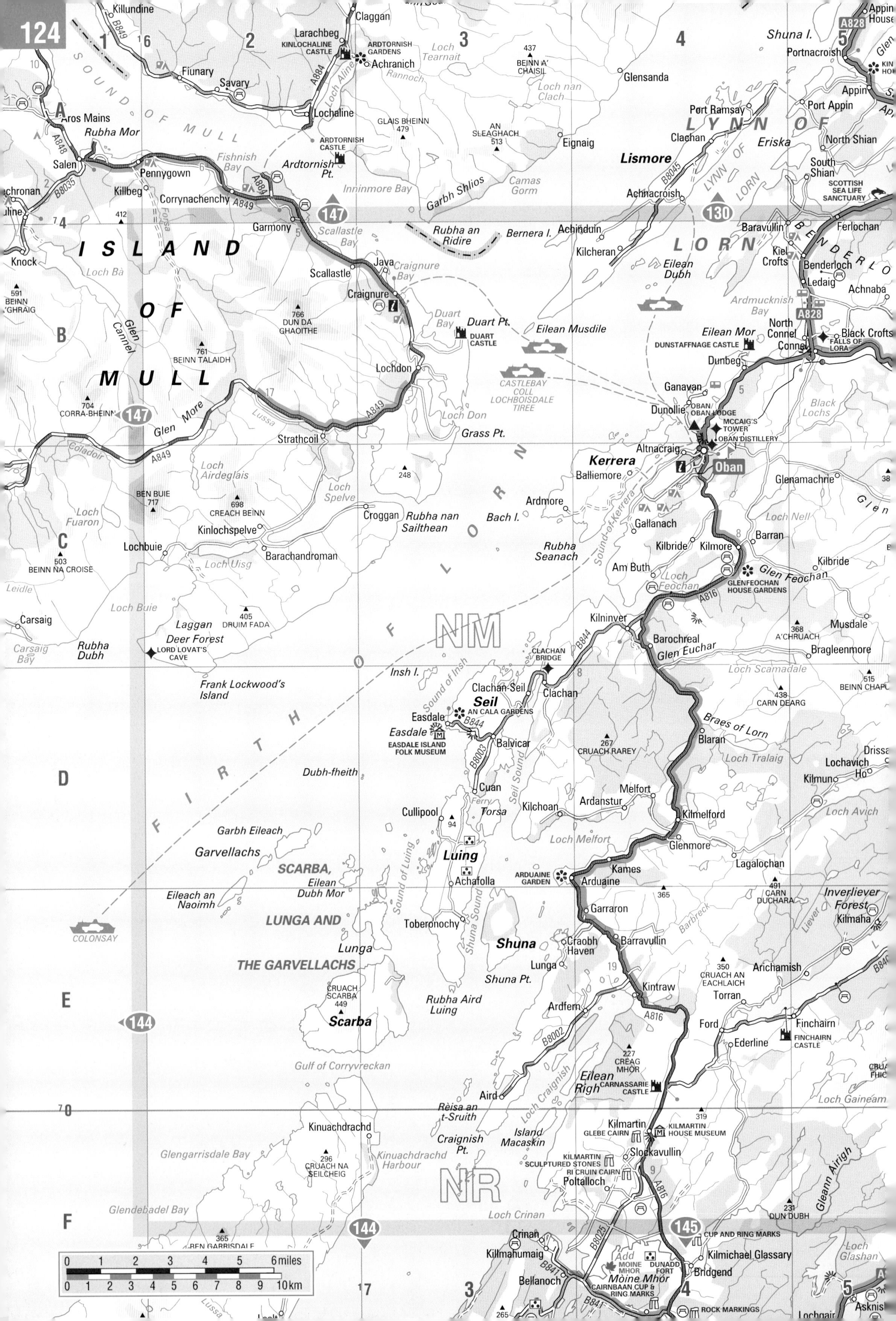

1 16 2 3 4 5

A

B

C

D

E

F

SOUND OF MULL

ISLAND

OF

MULL

Killundine
Claggan
B849
Larachbeg
KINLOCHALINE CASTLE
ARDTORNISH GARDENS
Achranich
Fiunary
Savary
A884
Loch Aline
Loch Tearnait
437
BEINN A' CHAISIL
Glensanda
Shuna I.
A828
Appin House
Portnacroish

Aros Mains
Rubha Mor
A848
Salen
chronan
B8035
aline
Killbeg
Pennygown
Corrynachenchy
A849
412
Garmony
147
Scallastle Bay
Java
Craignure Bay
Scallastle
Craignure
DUN DA GHAOITHE
766
Loch Bà
761
BEINN TALAIDH
Glen Cannel
591
BEINN 'GHRAIG

Lochaline
GLAIS BHEINN
479
Ardtornish Gardens
ARDTORNISH CASTLE
Ardtornish Pt.
Fishnish Bay
Inninmore Bay
Garbh Shlios
Camas Gorm
Rubha an Ridire
147
LYNN OF LORN
AN SLEAGHACH
513
Eignaig
Bernera I.
Rubha an Ridire
Achinduin
Kilcheran
Lismore
Port Ramsay
Clachan
Eriska
Achnacroish
130

MULL

Knock
704
CORRA-BHEINN
147
Coladoir
A849
Glen More
Lussa
BEN BUIE
717
698
CREACH BEINN
Lochdon
Loch Don
17
A849
Strathcoil
Loch Airdeglais
Loch Spelve
Croggan
Rubha nan Sailthean
Duart Bay
Duart Pt.
DUART CASTLE
Grass Pt.
Eilean Musdile
CASTLEBAY COLL LOCHBOISDALE TIREE
Bach I.
248
Ardmore
Rubha Seanach
Am Buth
LYNN OF LORN
Achinduin
Dunollie
Ganavan
Dunbeg
DUNSTAFFNAGE CASTLE
Eilean Mor
Eilean Dubh
Ardmucknish Bay
Baravullin
Kiel Crofts
Benderloch
Ledaig
Connel
North Connel
FALLS OF LORA
Achnaba
Black Crofts
Port Appin
North Shian
South Shian
SCOTTISH SEA LIFE SANCTUARY
Ferlochan
A828
A828

Loch Fuaron
503
BEINN NA CROISE
Leidle
Lochbuie
Barachandroman
Loch Uisg
Carsaig
Carsaig Bay
Rubha Dubh
Laggan Deer Forest
405
DRUIM FADA
LORD LOVAT'S CAVE
Frank Lockwood's Island
Insh I.
Sound of Insh
NM
Kinlochspelve
CLACHAN BRIDGE
Clachan
Clachan-Seil
Seil
AN CALA GARDENS
B844
8
Barochreal
Glen Euchar
Loch Scamadale
Kilninver
Kerrera
Balliemore
Ardmore
Sound of Kerrera
Gallanach
Kilbride
Kilmore
Am Buth
Loch Feochan
GLENFEOCHAN HOUSE GARDENS
Glen Feochan
Kilbride
A816
8
Barran
Oban
OBAN LODGE
MCCAIG'S TOWER
OBAN DISTILLERY
Altnacraig
Glenamachrie
Loch Nell
368
A'CHRUACH
Musdale
Bragleenmore
515
BEINN CHAPL

FIRTH

Garbh Eileach
Garvellachs
Eileach an Naoimh
SCARBA,
Eilean Dubh Mor
LUNGA AND
THE GARVELLACHS
Lunga
CRUACH SCARBA
449
Scarba
COLONSAY
144
Dubh-fheith
Easdale
Easdale
EASDALE ISLAND FOLK MUSEUM
Balvicar
Cuan
Cullipool
94
Torsa
Luing
Achafolla
Toberonochy
Shuna Sound
Shuna
Lunga
Shuna Pt.
Rubha Aird Luing
Sound of Luing
Kilchoan
Ferry
Melfort
267
CRUACH RAREY
Ardanstur
Loch Melfort
Glenmore
ARDUAINE GARDEN
Kames
Arduaine
Garraron
365
Craobh Haven
Barravullin
Kilmelford
Lagalochan
491
CARN DUCHARA
Braes of Lorn
Blaran
438
CARN DEARG
Loch Tralaig
Drissa
Lochavich Ho
Kilmun
Loch Avich
Inverliever Forest
Kilmaha
Arichamish
350
CRUACH AN EACHLAICH
Torran
B841

Gulf of Corryvreckan
Kinuachdrachd
Glengarrisdale Bay
296
CRUACH NA SEILCHEIG
Kinuachdrachd Harbour
Rèisa an t-Sruith
Craignish Pt.
Island Macaskin
Aird
Eilean Righ
227
CREAG MHOR
CARNASSARIE CASTLE
NR
Ardfern
B8002
Kintraw
Ford
Ederline
Torran
A816
Finchairn
FINCHAIRN CASTLE
144
Kilmartin
GLEBE CAIRN
KILMARTIN HOUSE MUSEUM
319
Slockavullin
KILMARTIN SCULPTURED STONES
RI CRUIN CAIRN
Poltalloch
145
Crinan
Killmahumaig
GLEN GARRISDALE
365
Glendebadel Bay
Bellanoch
Crinan
B8025
MOINE MHOR
DUNADD FORT
Mòine Mhór
CAIRNBAAN CUP & RING MARKS
ROCK MARKINGS
Kilmichael Glassary
Bridgend
A841
CUP AND RING MARKS
Kilmichael Glassary
231
DUN DUBH
Loch Glashan
Gleann Airigh
A816
9

0 7 3 4 5

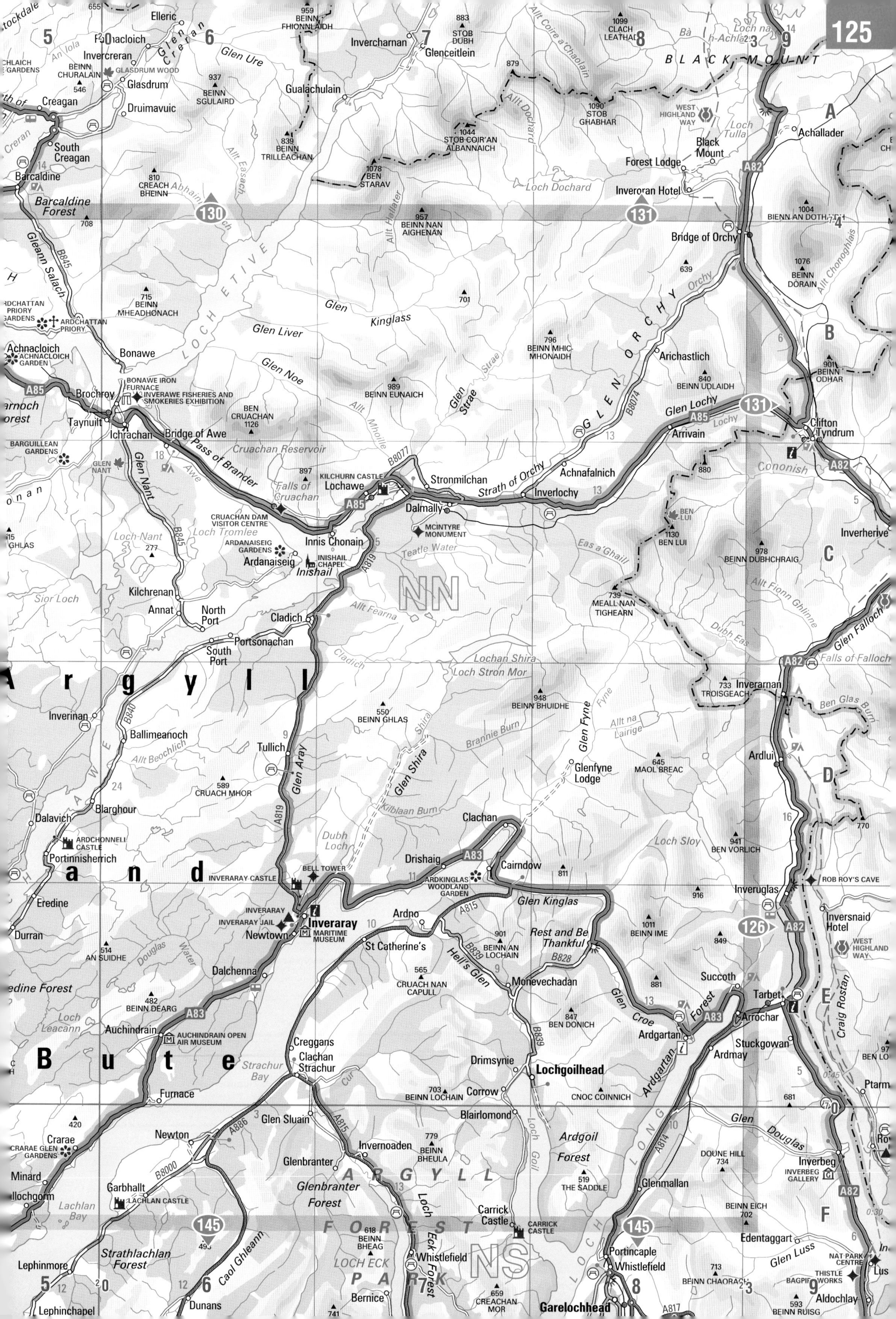
Elleric
Inverlochy
Glen Creran
Glen Ure
Invercreran
Glasdrum
Glasdrum Wood
Creagan
Druimavuic
South Creagan
Barcaldine
Barcaldine Forest
Gleann Salach
Beinn Churalain
Beinn Sgulaird
Creach Bheinn
Beinn Fhionnlaidh
Inverchamnan
Glenceitlein
Gualachulain
Beinn Trilleachan
Ben Starav
Stob Dubh
Stob Coir'an Albannaich
Clach Leathad
Stob Ghabhar
Black Mount
West Highland Way
Loch Tulla
Achallader
Forest Lodge
Loch Dochard
Inveroran Hotel
Bridge of Orchy
Beinn an Dothaidh
Beinn Dorain
Allt Chonoghlais
Beinn nan Aighenan
Allt Hallater
Loch Etive
Beinn Mheadhonach
Ardchattan Priory Gardens
Ardchattan Priory
Achnacloich
Achnacloich Garden
Bonawe
Glen Liver
Glen Kinglass
Glen Noe
Beinn Eunaich
Beinn Mhic-Mhonaidh
Glen Strae
Glen Orchy
Arichastlich
Beinn Udlaidh
Beinn Odhar
Bonawe Iron Furnace
Inverawe Fisheries and Smokeries Exhibition
Brochroy
Taynuilt
Ichrachan
Bridge of Awe
Pass of Brander
Ben Cruachan
Cruachan Reservoir
Barguillean Gardens
Glen Nant
Falls of Cruachan
Kilchurn Castle
Lochawe
Stronmilchan
Strath of Orchy
Achnafalnich
Inverlochy
Dalmally
Glen Lochy
Arrivain
Clifton
Tyndrum
Cononish
Ben Lui
Inverherive
McIntyre Monument
Cruachan Dam Visitor Centre
Loch Tromlee
Loch Nant
Ardanaiseig Gardens
Ardanaiseig
Innis Chonain
Inishail Chapel
Inishail
Teatle Water
Eas a'Ghaill
Beinn Dubhchraig
Allt Fionn Ghlinne
NN
Kilchrenan
Annat
North Port
Sior Loch
Cladich
Allt Fearna
Meall nan Tighearn
Dubh Eas
Glen Falloch
Falls of Falloch
Portsonachan
South Port
Lochan Shira
Loch Stron Mor
Argyll and Bute
Beinn Bhuidhe
Inverarnan
Troisgeach
Ben Glas Burn
Inverinan
Ballimeanoch
Allt Beochlich
Beinn Ghlas
Glen Shira
Brannie Burn
Glen Fyne
Allt na Lairige
Tullich
Glen Aray
Glenfyne Lodge
Maol Breac
Ardlui
Cruach Mhor
Kilblaan Burn
Loch Awe
Dalavich
Blarghour
Clachan
Ardchonnell Castle
Portinnisherrich
Dubh Loch
Loch Sloy
Ben Vorlich
Drishaig
Bell Tower
Inveraray Castle
Cairndow
Ardkinglas Woodland Garden
Rob Roy's Cave
Eredine
Glen Kinglas
Inveruglas
Inversnaid Hotel
Inveraray
Inveraray Jail
Newtown
Maritime Museum
Ardno
Durran
An Suidhe
Douglas Water
St Catherine's
Beinn an Lochain
Rest and Be Thankful
Beinn Ime
West Highland Way
Dalchenna
Eredine Forest
Cruach nan Capull
Hell's Glen
Monevechadan
Succoth
Tarbet
Craig Rostan
Beinn Dearg
Loch Leacann
Auchindrain
Auchindrain Open Air Museum
Glen Croe
Ardgartan Forest
Arrochar
Ben Donich
Ardgartan
Stuckgowan
Ardmay
Creggans
Clachan Strachur
Strachur Bay
Drimsynie
Lochgoilhead
Furnace
Beinn Lochain
Corrow
Cnoc Coinnich
Ptarmigan
Ben Lomond
Glen Sluain
Blairlomond
Loch Long
Glen Douglas
Crarae
Crarae Glen Gardens
Newton
Invernoaden
Beinn Bheula
Ardgoil Forest
Doune Hill
Inverbeg
Inverbeg Gallery
Minard
Glenbranter
Argyll Forest Park
Glenbranter Forest
Loch Goil
The Saddle
Glenmallan
Lochgair
Garbhallt
Lachlan Castle
Lachlan Bay
Loch Eck
Carrick Castle
Beinn Eich
Strathlachlan Forest
Beinn Bheag
Edentaggart
Glen Luss
Lephinmore
Caol Ghleann
Whistlefield
Eck Forest
NS
Portincaple
Whistlefield
Nat Park Centre
Luss
Thistle Bagpipe Works
Beinn Chaorach
Lephinchapel
Dunans
Bernice
Creachan Mor
Garelochhead
Aldochlay
Beinn Ruisg
130
131
126
145

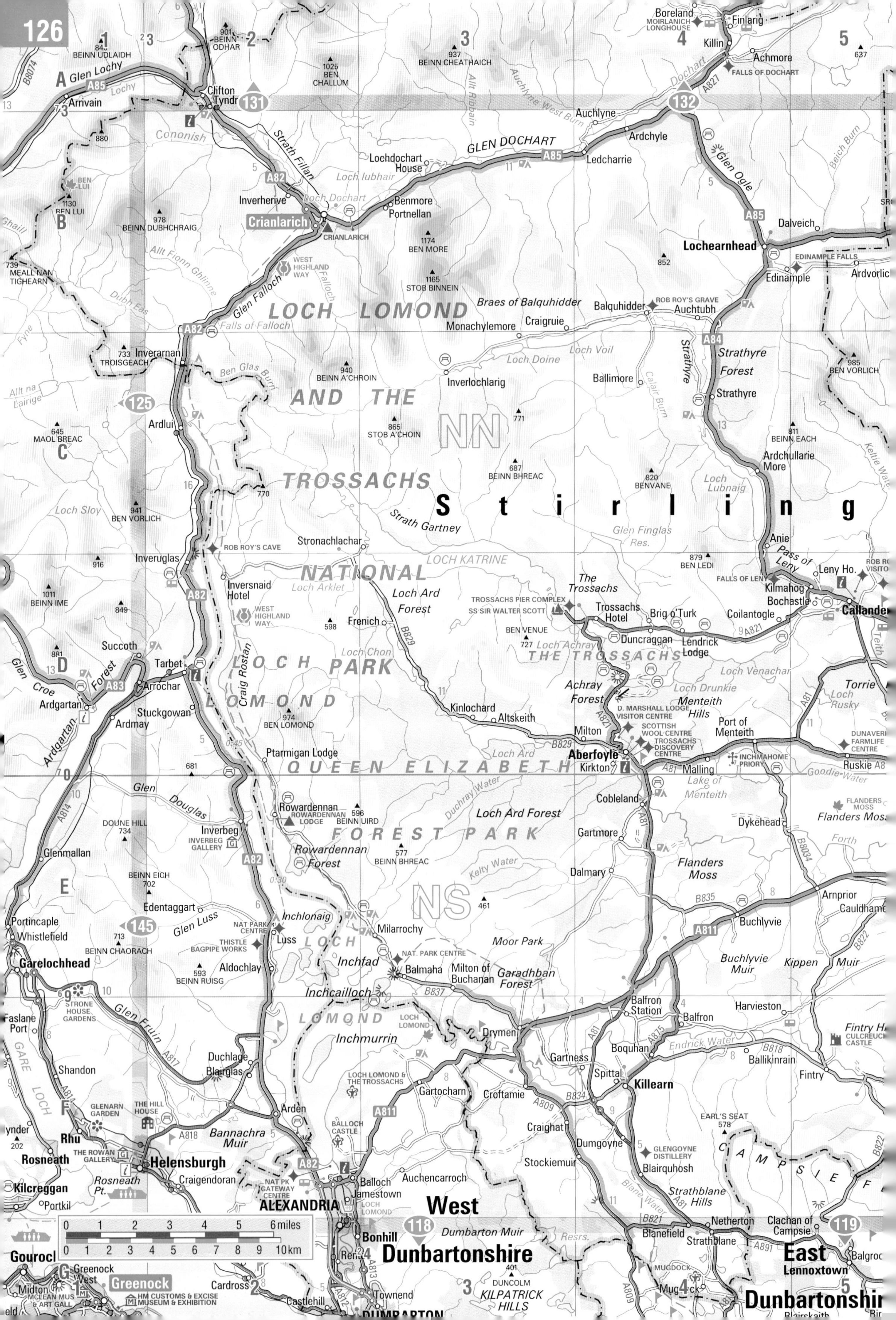

BEINN UDLAIDH
BEINN ODHAR
BEN CHALLUM
BEINN CHEATHAICH
Boreland
MOIRLANICH LONGHOUSE
Finlarig
Killin
Achmore
FALLS OF DOCHART
Glen Lochy
Arrivain
Clifton
Tyndrum
131
132
Cononish
Strath Fillan
Auchlyne
Ardchyle
GLEN DOCHART
Ledcharrie
Glen Ogle
Lochdochart House
Loch Iubhair
BEN LUI
Inverherive
Loch Dochart
Benmore
Portnellan
Crianlarich
CRIANLARICH
BEINN DUBHCHRAIG
BEN MORE
STOB BINNEIN
Dalveich
Lochearnhead
EDINAMPLE FALLS
Edinample
Ardvorlich
MEALL NAN TIGHEARN
Allt Fionn Ghlinne
WEST HIGHLAND WAY
Glen Falloch
LOCH LOMOND
Braes of Balquhidder
Balquhidder
ROB ROY'S GRAVE
Auchtubh
Monachylemore
Craigruie
Falls of Falloch
Inverarnan
TROISGEACH
Ben Glas Burn
Loch Doine
Loch Voil
Strathyre Forest
Strathyre
BEINN A'CHROIN
Inverlochlarig
Ballimore
BEN VORLICH
125
AND THE
MAOL BREAC
Ardlui
STOB A'CHOIN
NN
BEINN EACH
Ardchullarie More
BEINN BHREAC
BENVANE
Loch Lubnaig
TROSSACHS
Loch Sloy
BEN VORLICH
Strath Gartney
Stirling
Glen Finglas Res.
Anie
Pass of Leny
ROB ROY'S CAVE
Stronachlachar
Inveruglas
NATIONAL
LOCH KATRINE
BEN LEDI
Leny Ho.
FALLS OF LENY
Kilmahog
Bochastle
Callander
BEINN IME
Inversnaid Hotel
Loch Arklet
Loch Ard Forest
The Trossachs
TROSSACHS PIER COMPLEX
SS SIR WALTER SCOTT
Trossachs Hotel
Brig o'Turk
Coilantogle
Frenich
BEN VENUE
Duncraggan
Lendrick Lodge
Loch Achray
THE TROSSACHS
Loch Venachar
Succoth
Loch Chon
PARK
Tarbet
Arrochar
Glen Croe
Forest
Ardgartan
Craig Rostan
LOCH LOMOND
Achray Forest
Loch Drunkie
Menteith Hills
Torrie
Loch Rusky
Stuckgowan
Ardmay
BEN LOMOND
Kinlochard
Altskeith
D. MARSHALL LODGE VISITOR CENTRE
SCOTTISH WOOL CENTRE
TROSSACHS DISCOVERY CENTRE
Milton
Aberfoyle
Kirkton
Port of Menteith
DUNAVERIG FARMLIFE CENTRE
Ptarmigan Lodge
Loch Ard
QUEEN ELIZABETH
INCHMAHOME PRIORY
Malling
Lake of Menteith
Ruskie
Goodie Water
Glen Douglas
Rowardennan
ROWARDENNAN LODGE
BEINN UIRD
Duchray Water
Cobleland
Loch Ard Forest
FLANDERS MOSS
Flanders Moss
DOUNE HILL
Inverbeg
INVERBEG GALLERY
FOREST PARK
Gartmore
Dykehead
Forth
Glenmallan
Rowardennan Forest
BEINN BHREAC
Kelty Water
Flanders Moss
Dalmary
BEINN EICH
NS
Arnprior
Cauldhame
Edentaggart
B835
Portincaple
Whistlefield
145
Glen Luss
Inchlonaig
Milarrochy
NAT PARK CENTRE
THISTLE BAGPIPE WORKS
Luss
LOCH
BEINN CHAORACH
Moor Park
Buchlyvie
Garelochhead
NAT. PARK CENTRE
Inchfad
Balmaha
Milton of Buchanan
Garadhban Forest
Buchlyvie Muir
Kippen
Muir
Aldochlay
BEINN RUISG
Inchcailloch
STRONE HOUSE GARDENS
Glen Fruin
LOMOND
LOCH LOMOND
Balfron Station
Balfron
Harvieston
Faslane Port
Inchmurrin
Drymen
Fintry Hills
CULCREUCH CASTLE
GARE LOCH
Endrick Water
Boquhan
Ballikinrain
Duchlage
Blairglas
Gartness
Shandon
LOCH LOMOND & THE TROSSACHS
Spittal
Killearn
Fintry
Gartocharn
Croftamie
GLENARN GARDEN
THE HILL HOUSE
Arden
EARL'S SEAT
Rhu
Bannachra Muir
BALLOCH CASTLE
Craighat
Dumgoyne
CAMPSIE FELLS
Rosneath
THE ROWAN GALLERY
Helensburgh
Stockiemuir
GLENGOYNE DISTILLERY
Blairquhosh
Kilcreggan
Rosneath Pt.
Craigendoran
NAT PK GATEWAY CENTRE
Balloch
Auchencarroch
Portkil
ALEXANDRIA
Jamestown
LOCH LOMOND
West
Strathblane Hills
Blane Water
Netherton
Clachan of Campsie
118
119
Bonhill
Dumbarton Muir
Resrs.
Blanefield
Strathblane
East
Gourock
Renton
Dunbartonshire
Lennoxtown
Balgrochan
Greenock West
Greenock
DUNCOLM
MUGDOCK
Midton
MCLEAN MUS & ART GALL
HM CUSTOMS & EXCISE MUSEUM & EXHIBITION
Cardross
Castlehill
Townend
KILPATRICK HILLS
Mugdock
Dunbartonshire
DUMBARTON
A85
A82
A83
A814
A817
A818
A811
A81
A821
A84
A827
A809
A875
A891
A813
A812
B8074
B829
B837
B834
B8034
B818
B821
B822
0 1 2 3 4 5 6 miles
0 1 2 3 4 5 6 7 8 9 10 km

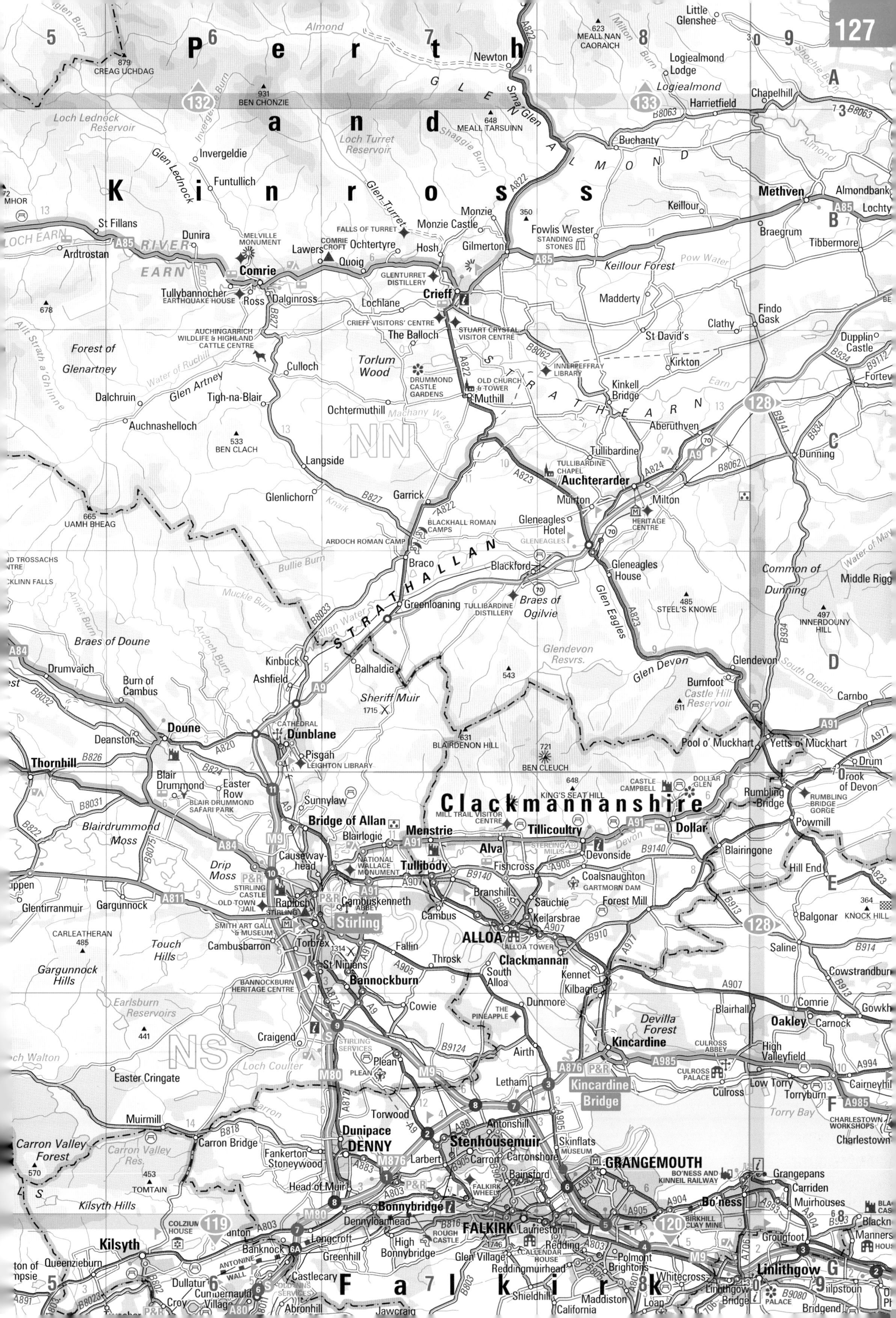
Perth and Kinross
Clackmannanshire
Falkirk
NN
NS
GLEN ALMOND
STRATHEARN
STRATHALLAN
RIVER EARN
132
133
128
119
120
Almond
CREAG UCHDAG
BEN CHONZIE
Loch Lednock Reservoir
Invergeldie
Glen Lednock
Funtullich
Newton
Sma' Glen
MEALL TARSUINN
Loch Turret Reservoir
Glen Turret
MEALL NAN CAORAICH
Little Glenshee
Logiealmond Lodge
Logiealmond
Chapelhill
Harrietfield
Buchanty
Methven
Almondbank
Lochty
Keillour
Braegrum
Tibbermore
Monzie
Monzie Castle
Fowlis Wester
STANDING STONES
Keillour Forest
Pow Water
Gilmerton
Hosh
FALLS OF TURRET
Ochtertyre
COMRIE CROFT
Lawers
Quoig
MELVILLE MONUMENT
St Fillans
Dunira
Ardtrostan
LOCH EARN
MHOR
Comrie
Tullybannocher
EARTHQUAKE HOUSE
Ross
Dalginross
GLENTURRET DISTILLERY
Crieff
Lochlane
CRIEFF VISITORS' CENTRE
STUART CRYSTAL VISITOR CENTRE
The Balloch
Madderty
Clathy
Findo Gask
St David's
Dupplin Castle
AUCHINGARRICH WILDLIFE & HIGHLAND CATTLE CENTRE
Forest of Glenartney
Water of Ruchill
Culloch
Torlum Wood
DRUMMOND CASTLE GARDENS
OLD CHURCH & TOWER
Muthill
INNERPEFFRAY LIBRARY
Kirkton
Kinkell Bridge
Forteviot
Glen Artney
Dalchruin
Tigh-na-Blair
Auchnashelloch
Ochtermuthill
Machany Water
Aberuthven
BEN CLACH
Langside
Tullibardine
TULLIBARDINE CHAPEL
Auchterarder
Dunning
Glenlichorn
Garrick
Knaik
Muirton
Milton
HERITAGE CENTRE
UAMH BHEAG
BLACKHALL ROMAN CAMPS
ARDOCH ROMAN CAMP
Gleneagles Hotel
GLENEAGLES
Braco
Blackford
Gleneagles House
Common of Dunning
Water of May
Middle Rigg
Bullie Burn
Muckle Burn
Greenloaning
TULLIBARDINE DISTILLERY
Braes of Ogilvie
Glen Eagles
STEEL'S KNOWE
INNERDOUNY HILL
Allan Water
Braes of Doune
Glendevon Resvrs.
Kinbuck
Ashfield
Balhaldie
Glen Devon
Glendevon
Burnfoot
Castle Hill Reservoir
South Queich
Carnbo
Drumvaich
Burn of Cambus
Sheriff Muir
CATHEDRAL
Dunblane
Doune
Deanston
BLAIRDENON HILL
BEN CLEUCH
Pool o' Muckhart
Yetts o' Muckhart
Drum
Crook of Devon
Thornhill
Pisgah
LEIGHTON LIBRARY
Blair Drummond
Easter Row
BLAIR DRUMMOND SAFARI PARK
KING'S SEAT HILL
CASTLE CAMPBELL
DOLLAR GLEN
Rumbling Bridge
RUMBLING BRIDGE GORGE
Sunnylaw
MILL TRAIL VISITOR CENTRE
Blairdrummond Moss
Bridge of Allan
Menstrie
Tillicoultry
Dollar
Powmill
Blairlogie
Alva
Devonside
STERLING MILLS
Causewayhead
NATIONAL WALLACE MONUMENT
Tullibody
Fishcross
Blairingone
Hill End
Drip Moss
Coalsnaughton
GARTMORN DAM
STIRLING CASTLE
OLD TOWN JAIL
Raploch
Cambuskenneth
ABBEY
Branshill
Sauchie
Forest Mill
Glentirranmuir
Gargunnock
Stirling
Cambus
Keilarsbrae
Balgonar
KNOCK HILL
SMITH ART GALL & MUSEUM
CARLEATHERAN
Touch Hills
Cambusbarron
Torbrex
ALLOA
ALLOA TOWER
Saline
Fallin
Throsk
Clackmannan
St Ninians
Gargunnock Hills
Bannockburn
BANNOCKBURN HERITAGE CENTRE
South Alloa
Kennet
Kilbagie
Cowstrandburn
Earlsburn Reservoirs
Cowie
THE PINEAPPLE
Dunmore
Comrie
Gowkhall
Blairhall
Oakley
Carnock
Devilla Forest
Craigend
STIRLING SERVICES
Kincardine
CULROSS ABBEY
High Valleyfield
Loch Walton
Plean
PLEAN
Airth
CULROSS PALACE
Easter Cringate
Loch Coulter
Letham
Kincardine Bridge
Low Torry
Torryburn
Cairneyhill
Culross
Torry Bay
CHARLESTOWN WORKSHOPS
Charlestown
Muirmill
Torwood
Antonshill
Carron
Carron Valley Forest
Carron Bridge
Carron Valley Res.
Dunipace
DENNY
Stenhousemuir
Skinflats
Fankerton
Stoneywood
Larbert
Carronshore
MUSEUM
GRANGEMOUTH
BO'NESS AND KINNEIL RAILWAY
Grangepans
Carriden
TOMTAIN
Kilsyth Hills
Head of Muir
FALKIRK WHEEL
Bainsford
Muirhouses
Bonnybridge
Bo'ness
Dennyloanhead
ROUGH CASTLE
BIRKHILL CLAY MINE
COLZIUM HOUSE
Banton
Longcroft
FALKIRK
Laurieston
Blackness
Manners
Kilsyth
Queenzieburn
Banknock
ANTONINE WALL
High Bonnybridge
Greenhill
Glen Village
CALLENDAR HOUSE
Redding
Polmont
Brightons
Reddingmuirhead
Grougfoot
Linlithgow
Linlithgow Bridge
Whitecross
PALACE
Philpstoun
Bridgend
Dullatur
Cumbernauld Village
Castlecary
Croy
Abronhill
Jawcraig
Shieldhill
Maddiston
California
Loan
A822
A85
A9
A823
A824
A91
A820
A84
M9
A811
A907
A908
A977
B9140
A905
A876
A985
M80
M876
A883
A803
A88
A904
A994
A706
A872
B827
B8033
B8062
B8063
B934
B9141
B826
B824
B8031
B822
B8075
B8032
B9124
B818
B910
B913
B914
B905
B816
B803
B8028
B9080

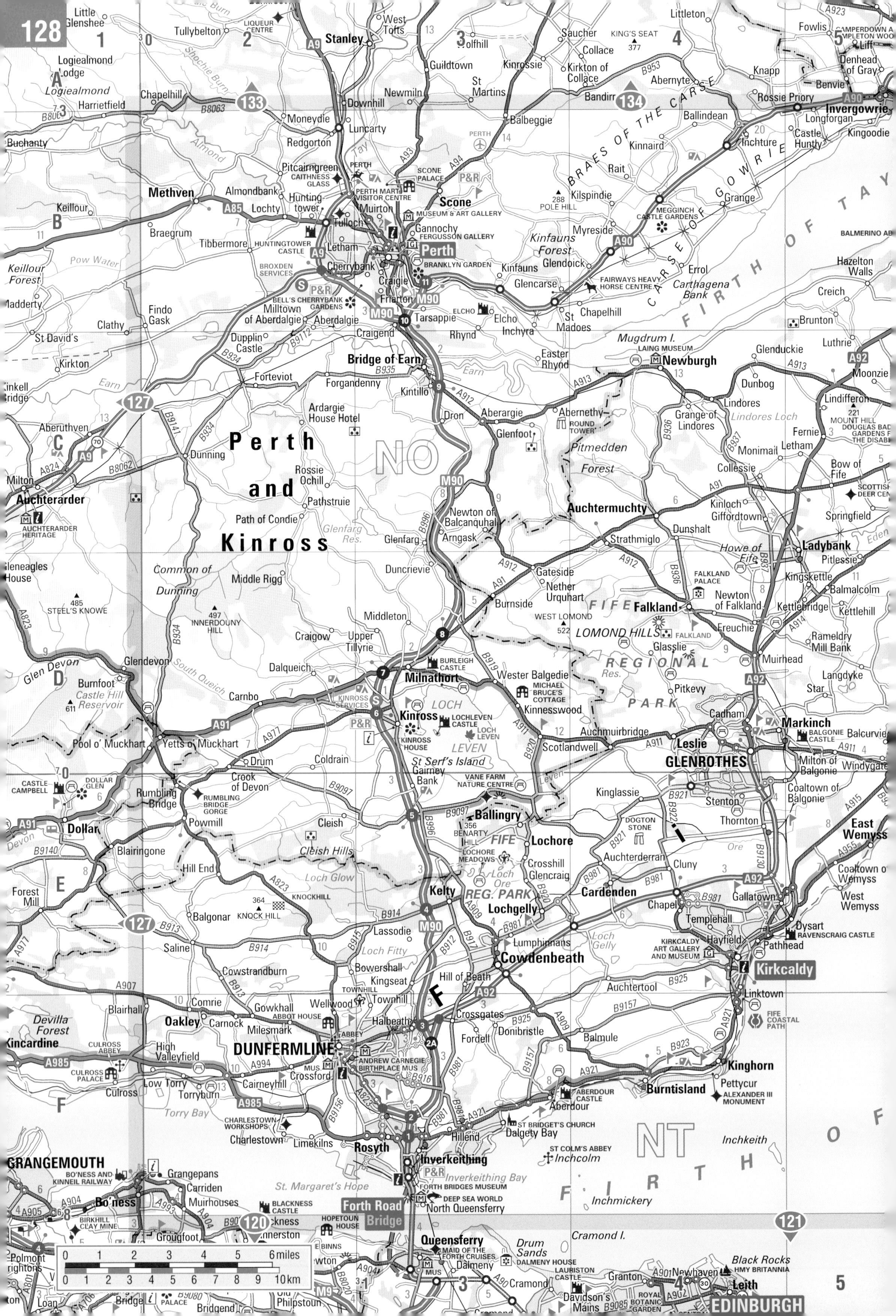

Perth and Kinross
FIFE
NO
NT
FIRTH OF TAY
FIRTH OF FORTH
BRAES OF THE CARSE
CARSE OF GOWRIE
LOMOND HILLS REGIONAL PARK
Stanley
West Tofts
Saucher
Littleton
Fowlis
Little Glenshee
Tullybelton
LIQUEUR CENTRE
Wolfhill
KING'S SEAT
Collace
Kirkton of Collace
Kinrossie
Guildtown
St Martins
Logiealmond Lodge
Logiealmond
Harrietfield
Chapelhill
Downhill
Newmiln
Balbeggie
Bandirran
Abernyte
Knapp
Rossie Priory
Benvie
Invergowrie
Longforgan
Kingoodie
Castle Huntly
Inchture
Ballindean
Kinnaird
Rait
Moneydie
Luncarty
Redgorton
Buchanty
Pitcairngreen
CAITHNESS GLASS
PERTH
SCONE PALACE
Scone
PERTH MART VISITOR CENTRE
Methven
Almondbank
Hunting tower
Lochty
Keillour
Braegrum
Tibbermore
HUNTINGTOWER CASTLE
Tulloch
Muirton
MUSEUM & ART GALLERY
Gannochy
FERGUSSON GALLERY
Perth
Letham
BRANKLYN GARDEN
Cherrybank
BROXDEN SERVICES
Craigie
Friarton
Keillour Forest
Pow Water
Kilspindie
POLE HILL
Myreside
Kinfauns Forest
Glendoick
Kinfauns
Glencarse
MEGGINCH CASTLE GARDENS
Grange
Errol
FAIRWAYS HEAVY HORSE CENTRE
Carthagena Bank
Chapelhill
St Madoes
Elcho
ELCHO
Inchyra
Rhynd
Tarsappie
Madderty
Findo Gask
Clathy
St David's
BELL'S CHERRYBANK GARDENS
Milltown of Aberdalgie
Aberdalgie
Dupplin Castle
Craigend
Kirkton
Bridge of Earn
Easter Rhynd
Mugdrum I.
LAING MUSEUM
Newburgh
Glenduckie
Luthrie
Creich
Brunton
Hazelton Walls
BALMERINO ABBEY
Forteviot
Forgandenny
Kintillo
Kinkell Bridge
Earn
Dunbog
Lindores
Grange of Lindores
Lindores Loch
Moonzie
Lindifferon
MOUNT HILL
Aberargie
Abernethy
ROUND TOWER
Dron
Ardargie House Hotel
Glenfoot
Aberuthven
Dunning
Pitmedden Forest
Monimail
Letham
Fernie
Collessie
Bow of Fife
Milton
Auchterarder
AUCHTERARDER HERITAGE
Rossie Ochil
Pathstruie
Path of Condie
Glenfarg Res.
Glenfarg
Newton of Balcanquhal
Arngask
Auchtermuchty
Kinloch
Giffordtown
Springfield
SCOTTISH DEER CENTRE
Dunshalt
Strathmiglo
Ladybank
Howe of Fife
Pitlessie
Kingskettle
Gleneagles House
Common of Dunning
Middle Rigg
Duncrievie
Gateside
Nether Urquhart
FALKLAND PALACE
Newton of Falkland
Balmalcolm
Kettlebridge
Kettlehill
STEEL'S KNOWE
INNERDOUNY HILL
Burnside
WEST LOMOND
Falkland
Freuchie
Rameldry Mill Bank
Middleton
Craigow
Upper Tillyrie
Glasslie
Muirhead
Langdyke
Star
Glen Devon
Glendevon
South Queich
Dalqueich
BURLEIGH CASTLE
Milnathort
Wester Balgedie
MICHAEL BRUCE'S COTTAGE
Kinnesswood
Pitkevy
Cadham
Markinch
BALGONIE CASTLE
Balcurvie
Burnfoot
Castle Hill Reservoir
Carnbo
KINROSS SERVICES
Kinross
LOCH LEVEN
LOCHLEVEN CASTLE
KINROSS HOUSE
Auchmuirbridge
Leslie
GLENROTHES
Milton of Balgonie
Windygates
Pool o' Muckhart
Yetts o' Muckhart
Drum
Coldrain
St Serf's Island
Gairney Bank
Scotlandwell
CASTLE CAMPBELL
DOLLAR GLEN
Crook of Devon
Rumbling Bridge
RUMBLING BRIDGE GORGE
VANE FARM NATURE CENTRE
Kinglassie
Stenton
Coaltown of Balgonie
Dollar
Powmill
Cleish
Ballingry
BENARTY HILL
DOGTON STONE
Thornton
East Wemyss
Devon
Blairingone
Cleish Hills
Lochore
LOCHORE MEADOWS
Crosshill
Glencraig
Auchterderran
Cluny
Ore
Coaltown of Wemyss
Forest Mill
Hill End
Loch Glow
KNOCKHILL
Kelty
REG. PARK
Cardenden
Chapel
Gallatown
West Wemyss
Balgonar
KNOCK HILL
Lochgelly
Templehall
Dysart
RAVENSCRAIG CASTLE
Saline
Lassodie
Loch Fitty
Lumphinnans
Loch Gelly
KIRKCALDY ART GALLERY AND MUSEUM
Hayfield
Pathhead
Cowdenbeath
Kirkcaldy
Cowstrandburn
Bowershall
Kingseat
Hill of Beath
Auchtertool
Linktown
TOWNHILL
Townhill
Comrie
Blairhall
Gowkhall
Wellwood
ABBOT HOUSE
Crossgates
FIFE COASTAL PATH
Devilla Forest
Oakley
Carnock
Milesmark
Halbeath
Donibristle
Fordell
Balmule
Kincardine
CULROSS ABBEY
High Valleyfield
DUNFERMLINE
ABBEY
ANDREW CARNEGIE BIRTHPLACE MUS
Kinghorn
Pettycur
ALEXANDER III MONUMENT
Burntisland
CULROSS PALACE
Culross
Low Torry
Torryburn
Cairneyhill
Crossford
ABERDOUR CASTLE
Aberdour
Torry Bay
CHARLESTOWN WORKSHOPS
Charlestown
Limekilns
Rosyth
Hillend
ST BRIDGET'S CHURCH
Dalgety Bay
ST COLM'S ABBEY
Inchcolm
Inchkeith
GRANGEMOUTH
BO'NESS AND KINNEIL RAILWAY
Grangepans
Carriden
Bo'ness
Muirhouses
BLACKNESS CASTLE
Blackness
Inverkeithing
Inverkeithing Bay
FORTH BRIDGES MUSEUM
DEEP SEA WORLD
North Queensferry
Inchmickery
St. Margaret's Hope
Forth Road Bridge
HOPETOUN HOUSE
BIRKHILL CLAY MINE
Grougfoot
Queensferry
MAID OF THE FORTH CRUISES
Dalmeny
Drum Sands
DALMENY HOUSE
Cramond I.
Cramond
LAURISTON CASTLE
Granton
Newhaven
Black Rocks
HMY BRITANNIA
Leith
EDINBURGH
Davidson's Mains
ROYAL BOTANIC GARDEN
Polmont
Brightons
Loan
Bridgend
Philpstoun
miles
km

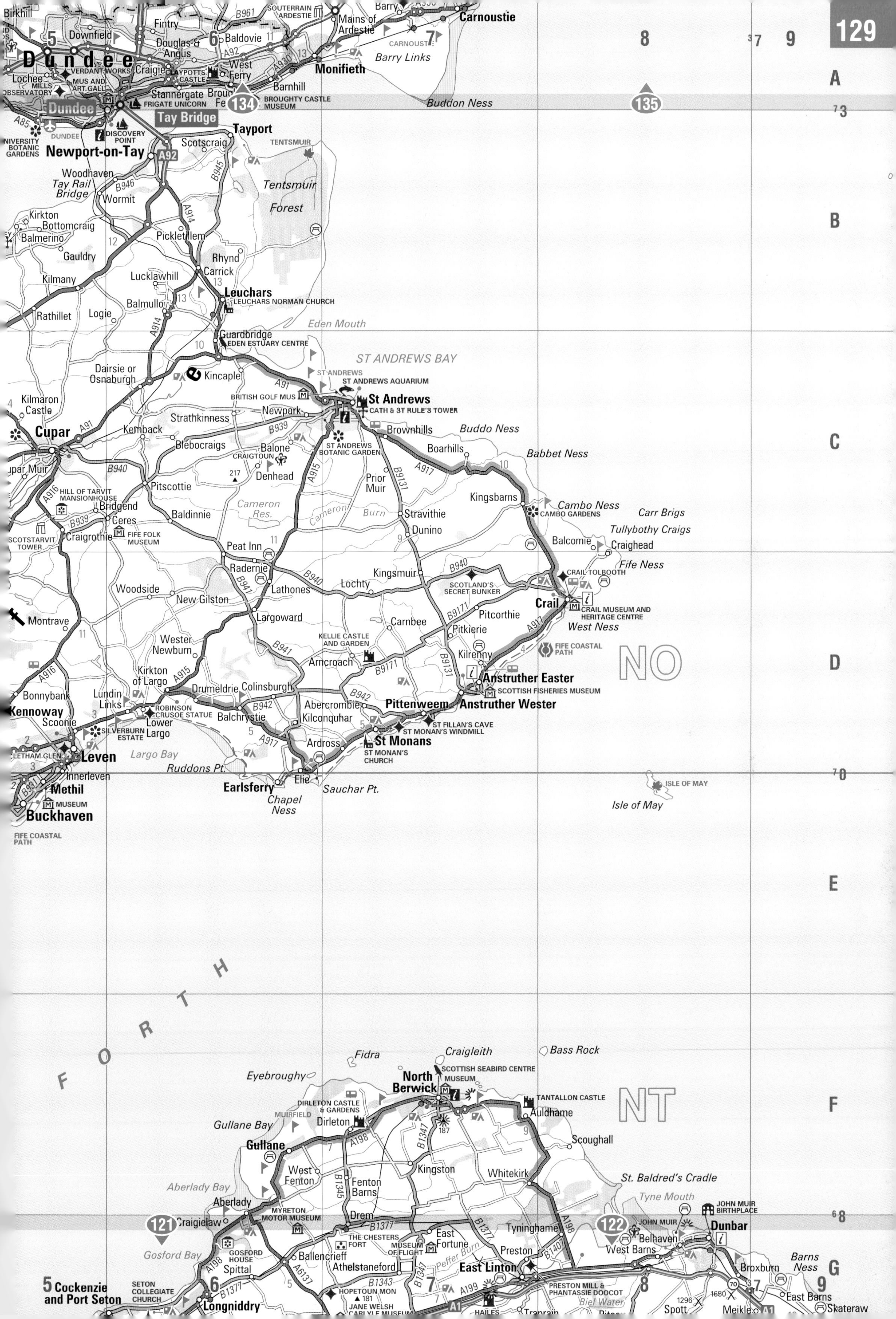

8
9
A
B
C
D
E
F
G
NO
NT
Dundee
Newport-on-Tay
Tay Bridge
Tay Rail Bridge
Broughty Castle Museum
Frigate Unicorn
Discovery Point
Verdant Works
Mus and Art Gall
Mills Observatory
Botanic Gardens
Birkhill
Downfield
Fintry
Douglas & Angus
Baldovie
Lochee
Craigie
West Ferry
Stannergate
Monifieth
Barnhill
Carnoustie
Barry Links
Buddon Ness
Mains of Ardestie
Souterrain Ardestie
Tayport
Scotscraig
Tentsmuir
Tentsmuir Forest
Woodhaven
Wormit
Kirkton
Bottomcraig
Balmerino
Gauldry
Kilmany
Pickletillem
Rhynd
Carrick
Lucklawhill
Balmullo
Leuchars
Leuchars Norman Church
Rathillet
Logie
Guardbridge
Eden Estuary Centre
Eden Mouth
St Andrews Bay
Dairsie or Osnaburgh
Kincaple
Kilmaron Castle
Cupar
British Golf Mus
St Andrews Aquarium
St Andrews
Cath & St Rule's Tower
Strathkinness
Newpark
Kemback
Blebocraigs
Brownhills
Buddo Ness
Boarhills
Babbet Ness
Balone
Craigtoun
Denhead
St Andrews Botanic Garden
Prior Muir
Pitscottie
Hill of Tarvit Mansionhouse
Bridgend
Ceres
Craigrothie
Fife Folk Museum
Scotstarvit Tower
Baldinnie
Cameron Res.
Cameron Burn
Stravithie
Dunino
Kingsbarns
Cambo Ness
Cambo Gardens
Carr Brigs
Tullybothy Craigs
Balcomie
Craighead
Fife Ness
Crail Tolbooth
Peat Inn
Radernie
Lathones
Lochty
Kingsmuir
Scotland's Secret Bunker
Crail
Crail Museum and Heritage Centre
West Ness
Woodside
New Gilston
Montrave
Largoward
Carnbee
Pitcorthie
Pitkierie
Kellie Castle and Garden
Kilrenny
Fife Coastal Path
Wester Newburn
Arncroach
Anstruther Easter
Scottish Fisheries Museum
Anstruther Wester
Pittenweem
St Fillan's Cave
St Monan's Windmill
St Monans
St Monan's Church
Kirkton of Largo
Drumeldrie
Colinsburgh
Abercrombie
Kilconquhar
Bonnybank
Lundin Links
Robinson Crusoe Statue
Lower Largo
Balchrystie
Kennoway
Scoonie
Silverburn Estate
Leven
Largo Bay
Ruddons Pt.
Ardross
Elie
Earlsferry
Chapel Ness
Sauchar Pt.
Isle of May
Innerleven
Methil
Museum
Buckhaven
Letham Glen
F O R T H
Fidra
Craigleith
Bass Rock
Eyebroughy
North Berwick
Scottish Seabird Centre
Museum
Tantallon Castle
Auldhame
Scoughall
Dirleton Castle & Gardens
Dirleton
Muirfield
Gullane Bay
Gullane
West Fenton
Fenton Barns
Kingston
Whitekirk
St. Baldred's Cradle
Tyne Mouth
Aberlady Bay
Aberlady
Myreton Motor Museum
Drem
Craigielaw
The Chesters Fort
East Fortune
Museum of Flight
Tyninghame
Preston
John Muir Birthplace
John Muir
Dunbar
Belhaven
West Barns
Gosford Bay
Gosford House
Spittal
Ballencrieff
Athelstaneford
Peffer Burn
East Linton
Preston Mill & Phantassie Doocot
Biel Water
Broxburn
Barns Ness
East Barns
Skateraw
Cockenzie and Port Seton
Seton Collegiate Church
Longniddry
Hopetoun Mon
Jane Welsh Carlyle Museum
Hailes
Traprain
Spott
Meikle
134
135
121
122

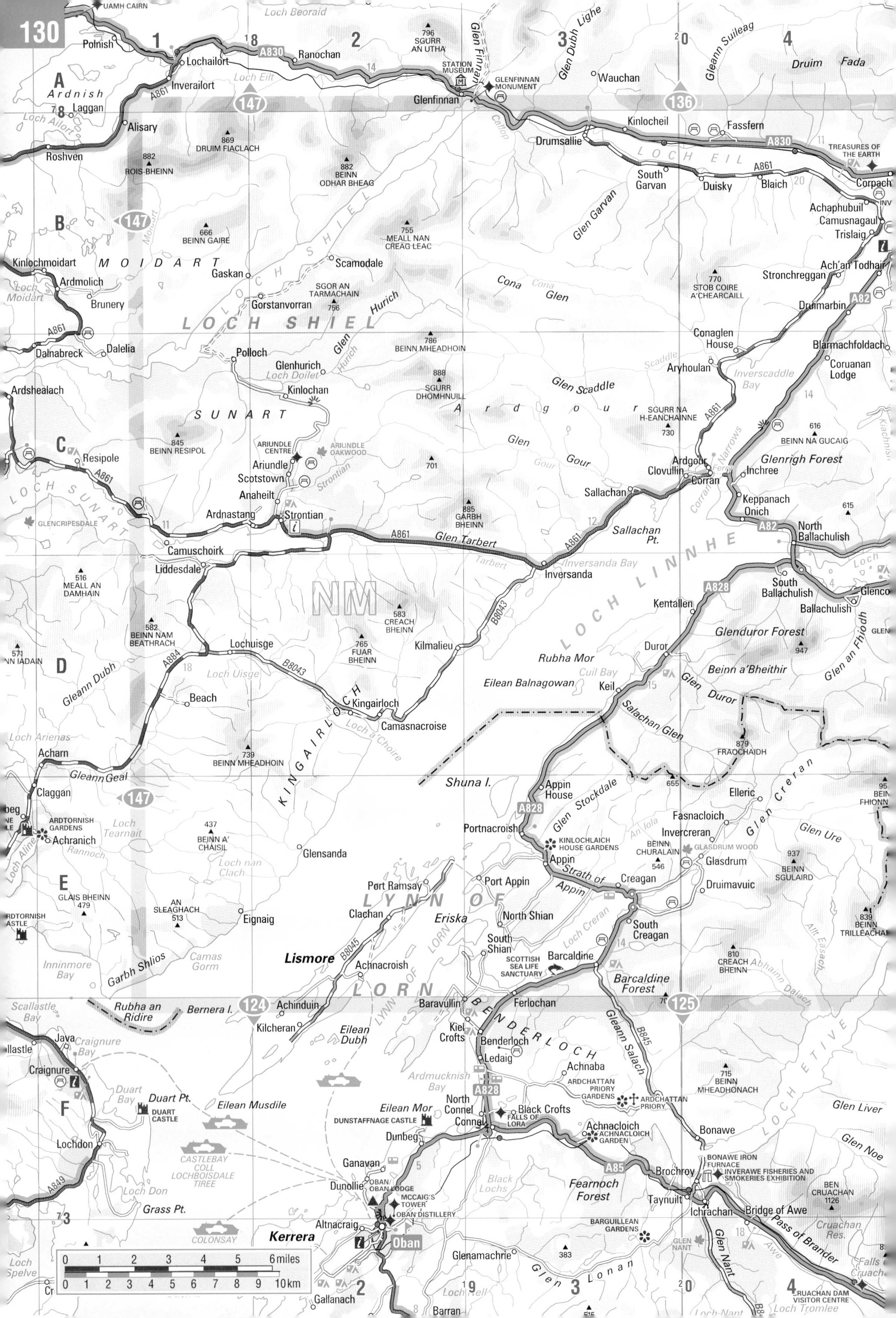

UAMH CAIRN
Loch Beoraid
Polnish
Lochailort
A830
Ranochan
796 SGURR AN UTHA
Glen Finnan
Glen Dubh Lighe
Gleann Suileag
Druim Fada
Ardnish
Inverailort
Loch Eilt
147
STATION MUSEUM
GLENFINNAN MONUMENT
Wauchan
Glenfinnan
136
Laggan
Loch Ailort
A861
Alisary
869 DRUIM FIACLACH
Callop
Kinlocheil
Fassfern
Drumsallie
LOCH EIL
TREASURES OF THE EARTH
Corpach
Roshven
882 ROIS-BHEINN
882 BEINN ODHAR BHEAG
South Garvan
Duisky
Blaich
Achaphubuil
Camusnagaul
Trislaig
Glen Garvan
666 BEINN GAIRE
755 MEALL NAN CREAG LEAC
LOCH SHIEL
Moidart
Kinlochmoidart
MOIDART
Scamodale
Cona
Cona Glen
Ach'an Todhair
Stronchreggan
770 STOB COIRE A'CHEARCAILL
Gaskan
Ardmolich
Loch Moidart
Brunery
SGOR AN TARMACHAIN 756
Gorstanvorran
Glen Hurich
Druimarbin
A82
A861
Dalnabreck
Dalelia
Polloch
786 BEINN MHEADHOIN
Conaglen House
Blarmachfoldach
Glenhurich
Loch Doilet
Aryhoulan
Coruanan Lodge
Inverscaddle Bay
Scaddle
Kinlochan
888 SGURR DHOMHNUILL
Glen Scaddle
Ardshealach
SUNART
Ardgour
SGURR NA H-EANCHAINNE 730
845 BEINN RESIPOL
ARIUNDLE CENTRE
ARIUNDLE OAKWOOD
Glen Gour
616 BEINN NA GUCAIG
Glenrigh Forest
Resipole
Ariundle
Scotstown
Strontian
701
Ardgour
Clovullin
Corran
Corran Narrows
Inchree
LOCH SUNART
Anaheilt
Sallachan
Keppanach
Onich
615
GLENCRIPESDALE
Ardnastang
Strontian
885 GARBH BHEINN
Sallachan Pt.
North Ballachulish
Camuschoirk
A861
Glen Tarbert
Tarbert
Inversanda Bay
Inversanda
LOCH LINNHE
Liddesdale
516 MEALL AN DAMHAIN
NM
583 CREACH BHEINN
B8043
South Ballachulish
Glencoe
Ballachulish
Kentallen
A828
582 BEINN NAM BEATHRACH
Glenduror Forest
571
Lochuisge
765 FUAR BHEINN
Kilmalieu
Rubha Mor
Duror
947
Glen an Fhiodh
Loch Uisge
B8043
A884
Beinn a'Bheithir
Gleann Dubh
Cuil Bay
Eilean Balnagowan
Keil
Glen Duror
Beach
Kingairloch
Camasnacroise
Salachan Glen
Loch a'Choire
Loch Arienas
Acharn
739 BEINN MHEADHOIN
KINGAIRLOCH
879 FRAOCHAIDH
Gleann Geal
Claggan
Shuna I.
Appin House
655
Elleric
Glen Creran
ARDTORNISH GARDENS
Achranich
Loch Tearnait
Rannoch
437 BEINN A' CHAISIL
Glen Stockdale
Portnacroish
Fasnacloich
Invercreran
Glen Ure
KINLOCHLAICH HOUSE GARDENS
BEINN CHURALAIN 546
GLASDRUM WOOD
Glasdrum
937 BEINN SGULAIRD
Loch Aline
Glensanda
Loch nan Clach
Appin
Strath of Appin
Port Ramsay
Port Appin
Creagan
Druimavuic
GLAIS BHEINN 479
AN SLEAGHACH 513
Eignaig
LYNN OF LORN
Clachan
Eriska
North Shian
South Creagan
839 BEINN TRILLEACHAN
South Shian
Loch Creran
Lismore
B8045
Achnacroish
SCOTTISH SEA LIFE SANCTUARY
Barcaldine
810 CREACH BHEINN
Allt Easach
Innimore Bay
Garbh Shlios
Camas Gorm
Barcaldine Forest
Abhainn Dalach
LORN
Scallastle Bay
Rubha an Ridire
Bernera I.
124
Achinduin
Baravullin
BENDERLOCH
Ferlochan
125
LOCH ETIVE
Kilcheran
Lynn of Lorn
Eilean Dubh
Kiel Crofts
Benderloch
Java
Craignure Bay
Craignure
Ledaig
Gleann Salach
B845
Achnaba
715 BEINN MHEADHONACH
Ardmucknish Bay
Duart Bay
Duart Pt.
DUART CASTLE
Eilean Musdile
A828
ARDCHATTAN PRIORY GARDENS
ARDCHATTAN PRIORY
Glen Liver
North Connel
Eilean Mor
DUNSTAFFNAGE CASTLE
Connel
Black Crofts
FALLS OF LORA
Achnacloich
ACHNACLOICH GARDEN
Bonawe
Glen Noe
Lochdon
Dunbeg
CASTLEBAY COLL LOCHBOISDALE TIREE
Ganavan
Black Lochs
A85
BONAWE IRON FURNACE
INVERAWE FISHERIES AND SMOKERIES EXHIBITION
Brochroy
Fearnoch Forest
A849
Loch Don
Dunollie
OBAN LODGE
MCCAIG'S TOWER
OBAN DISTILLERY
Taynuilt
BEN CRUACHAN 1126
Grass Pt.
Ichrachan
Bridge of Awe
Pass of Brander
Altnacraig
Kerrera
BARGUILLEAN GARDENS
GLEN NANT
Glen Nant
Cruachan Res.
Oban
COLONSAY
Glenamachrie
383
Glen Lonan
Awe
Falls of Cruachan
Loch Spelve
Gallanach
Loch Nell
CRUACHAN DAM VISITOR CENTRE
Barran
Loch Tromlee
0 1 2 3 4 5 6 miles
0 1 2 3 4 5 6 7 8 9 10 km

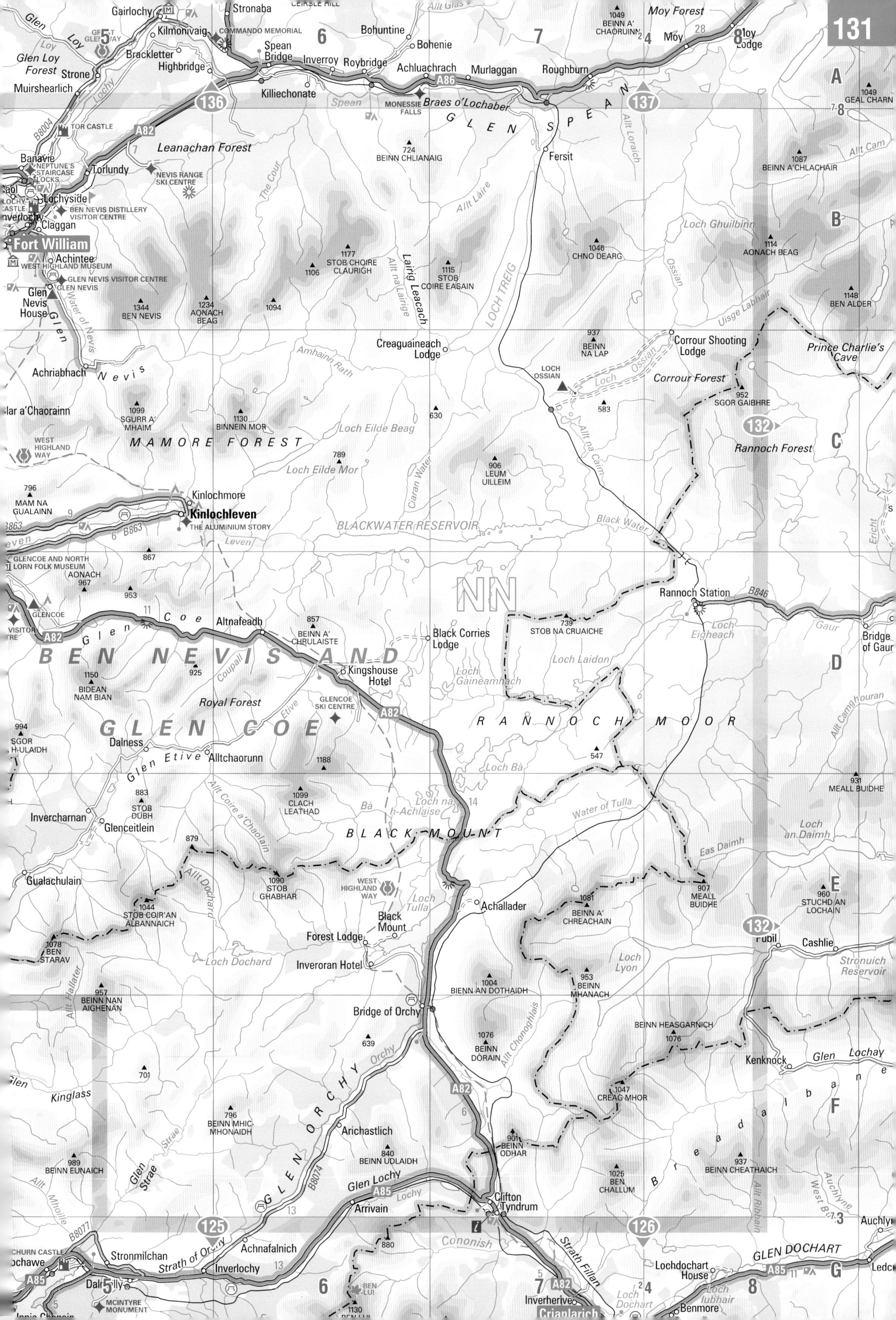
Gairlochy
Stronaba
Glen Loy
Kilmonivaig
COMMANDO MEMORIAL
Bohuntine
Bohenie
1049
BEINN A' CHAORUINN
Moy Forest
Moy
Moy Lodge
Glen Loy Forest
Brackletter
Spean Bridge
Highbridge
Inverroy
Roybridge
Achluachrach
Murlaggan
Roughburn
A86
Strone
Muirshearlich
Killiechonate
Spean
MONESSIE FALLS
Braes o'Lochaber
GLEN SPEAN
136
137
1049
GEAL CHARN
B8004
TOR CASTLE
A82
Leanachan Forest
724
BEINN CHLIANAIG
Fersit
Allt Loraich
Banavie
NEPTUNE'S STAIRCASE LOCKS
Torlundy
NEVIS RANGE SKI CENTRE
The Cour
1087
BEINN A'CHLACHAIR
Allt Cam
Lochyside
BEN NEVIS DISTILLERY VISITOR CENTRE
Allt Làire
Claggan
Fort William
Achintee
WEST HIGHLAND MUSEUM
GLEN NEVIS VISITOR CENTRE
GLEN NEVIS
Loch Ghuilbinn
1114
AONACH BEAG
1177
STOB CHOIRE CLAURIGH
1106
Allt na Lairige
Lairig Leacach
1115
STOB COIRE EASAIN
1046
CHNO DEARG
LOCH TREIG
Ossian
Glen Nevis House
Water of Nevis
1344
BEN NEVIS
1234
AONACH BEAG
1094
1148
BEN ALDER
Uisge Labhair
937
BEINN NA LAP
Corrour Shooting Lodge
Prince Charlie's Cave
Creaguaineach Lodge
Amhainn Rath
Achriabhach
Nevis
LOCH OSSIAN
Loch Ossian
Corrour Forest
952
SGOR GAIBHRE
583
630
1099
SGURR A' MHAIM
1130
BINNEIN MOR
Loch Eilde Beag
132
Rannoch Forest
Allt na Cairn
WEST HIGHLAND WAY
MAMORE FOREST
789
Loch Eilde Mor
Ciaran Water
906
LEUM UILLEIM
796
MAM NA GUALAINN
Kinlochmore
Kinlochleven
THE ALUMINIUM STORY
B863
BLACKWATER RESERVOIR
Black Water
Ericht
Leven
867
GLENCOE AND NORTH LORN FOLK MUSEUM
AONACH
967
953
NN
Rannoch Station
B846
GLENCOE
Coe
Altnafeadh
857
BEINN A' CHRULAISTE
Black Corries Lodge
739
STOB NA CRUAICHE
Loch Eigheach
Gaur
Bridge of Gaur
Glen
BEN NEVIS AND
925
Coupall
Kingshouse Hotel
Loch Laidon
1150
BIDEAN NAM BIAN
Loch Gaineamhach
Royal Forest
Etive
GLENCOE SKI CENTRE
A82
GLEN COE
RANNOCH MOOR
Allt Camghouran
994
SGOR H-ULAIDH
Dalness
Glen Etive
Alltchaorunn
1188
547
Loch Bà
883
STOB DUBH
Allt Coire a' Chaolain
1099
CLACH LEATHAD
Loch na h-Achlaise
Bà
Water of Tulla
931
MEALL BUIDHE
Inverchamnan
Glenceitlein
879
BLACK MOUNT
Loch an Daimh
Eas Daimh
Allt Dochard
1090
STOB GHABHAR
WEST HIGHLAND WAY
907
MEALL BUIDHE
960
STUCHD AN LOCHAIN
Gualachulain
1044
STOB COIR'AN ALBANNAICH
Loch Tulla
Achallader
1081
BEINN A' CHREACHAIN
Black Mount
Forest Lodge
132
Fubil
Cashlie
1078
BEN STARAV
Loch Dochard
Inveroran Hotel
Loch Lyon
Stronuich Reservoir
Allt Hallater
957
BEINN NAN AIGHENAN
1004
BIENN AN DOTHAIDH
953
BEINN MHANACH
Bridge of Orchy
BEINN HEASGARNICH
1076
639
1076
BEINN DORAIN
Allt Chonoghlais
Kenknock
Glen Lochay
701
Glen Kinglass
Orchy
A82
1047
CREAG MHOR
796
BEINN MHIC-MHONAIDH
GLEN ORCHY
Breadalbane
Arichastlich
Strae
901
BEINN ODHAR
989
BEINN EUNAICH
Glen Strae
840
BEINN UDLAIDH
937
BEINN CHEATHAICH
1026
BEN CHALLUM
Allt Mhoille
B8074
Glen Lochy
A85
Lochy
Clifton
Tyndrum
Arrivain
Allt Ribhain
West Burn
Auchlyne
Auchlyne
125
126
B8077
CHURN CASTLE
Lochawe
Stronmilchan
Strath of Orchy
Achnafalnich
880
Cononish
Strath Fillan
GLEN DOCHART
A85
Lochdochart House
Ledc
Inverlochy
A85
Dalmally
MCINTYRE MONUMENT
BEN LUI
1130
BEN LUI
A82
Inverherive
Loch Dochart
Loch Iubhair
Benmore
Crianlarich

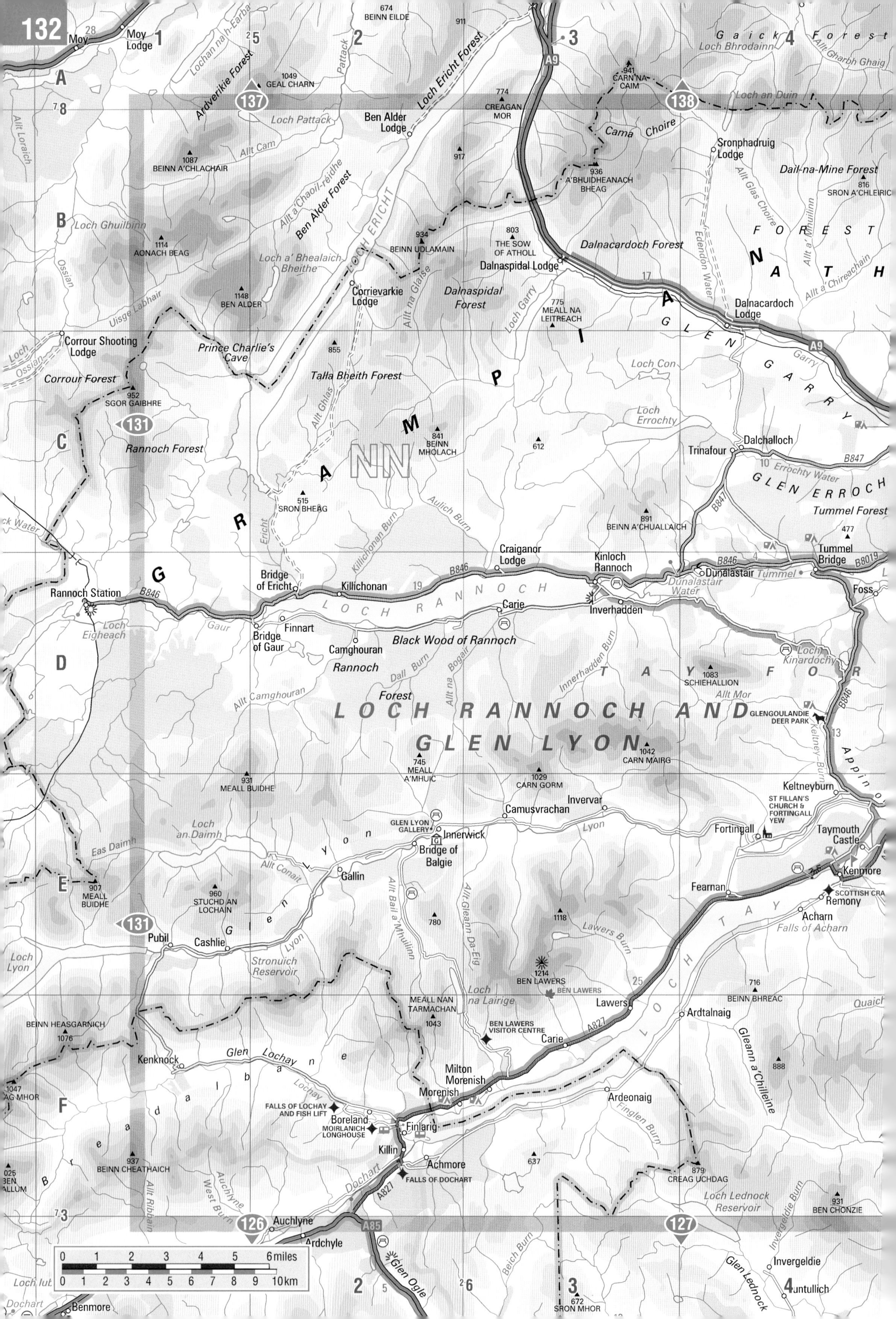

Moy
Moy Lodge
Lochan na h-Earba
Ardverikie Forest
674 BEINN EILDE
911
Pattack
Loch Ericht Forest
1049 GEAL CHARN
137
Loch Pattack
Ben Alder Lodge
774 CREAGAN MOR
A9
941 CARN NA CAIM
138
Gaick Forest
Loch Bhrodainn
Allt Gharbh Ghaig
Loch an Duin
Cama Choire
Sronphadruig Lodge
Allt Loraich
1087 BEINN A'CHLACHAIR
Allt Cam
917
936 A'BHUIDHEANACH BHEAG
Dail-na-Mine Forest
816 SRON A'CHLEIRICH
Allt a'Chaoil-reidhe
Ben Alder Forest
LOCH ERICHT
Allt Glas Choire
Loch Ghuilbinn
1114 AONACH BEAG
934 BEINN UDLAMAIN
803 THE SOW OF ATHOLL
Dalnacardoch Forest
FOREST
Loch a' Bhealaich Bheithe
Dalnaspidal Lodge
Edendon Water
Allt a'Mhuilinn
Ossian
1148 BEN ALDER
Corrievarkie Lodge
Allt na Glaise
Dalnaspidal Forest
Loch Garry
775 MEALL NA LEITREACH
17
Dalnacardoch Lodge
Allt a'Chireachain
Uisge Labhair
NATH
Loch Ossian
Corrour Shooting Lodge
Prince Charlie's Cave
855
GLEN GARRY
Garry
Corrour Forest
Talla Bheith Forest
Loch Con
952 SGOR GAIBHRE
131
GRAMPIAN
Loch Errochty
Rannoch Forest
Allt Ghlas
841 BEINN MHOLACH
612
Dalchalloch
Trinafour
B847
10
Errochty Water
GLEN ERROCHT
515 SRON BHEAG
Aulich Burn
891 BEINN A'CHUALLAICH
Tummel Forest
477
Water
Ericht
Killichonan Burn
B846
Craiganor Lodge
Kinloch Rannoch
Tummel Bridge
B8019
Rannoch Station
Bridge of Ericht
Killichonan
19
LOCH RANNOCH
Dunalastair
Dunalastair Water
Tummel
Foss
Loch Eigheach
Gaur
Bridge of Gaur
Finnart
Carie
Inverhadden
Camghouran
Black Wood of Rannoch
Loch Kinardochy
Rannoch
Dall Burn
Allt na Bogair
Innerhadden Burn
1083 SCHIEHALLION
Allt Camghouran
Forest
Allt Mor
TAY FOREST
LOCH RANNOCH AND GLEN LYON
GLENGOULANDIE DEER PARK
Keltney Burn
13
1042 CARN MAIRG
Appin of
745 MEALL A'MHUIC
931 MEALL BUIDHE
1029 CARN GORM
Keltneyburn
Invervar
Camusvrachan
ST FILLAN'S CHURCH & FORTINGALL YEW
Loch an Daimh
Lyon
GLEN LYON GALLERY
Innerwick
Fortingall
Taymouth Castle
Eas Daimh
Bridge of Balgie
Allt Conait
Glen Lyon
Kenmore
Gallin
Fearnan
SCOTTISH CRA
907 MEALL BUIDHE
960 STUCHD AN LOCHAIN
Allt Bail a'Mhuilinn
Allt Gleann Da-Eig
Remony
780
1118
Acharn
Falls of Acharn
LOCH TAY
Lawers Burn
Pubil
Cashlie
Loch Lyon
Stronuich Reservoir
1214 BEN LAWERS
BEN LAWERS
25
716 BEINN BHREAC
Loch na Lairige
Quaich
MEALL NAN TARMACHAN
Lawers
Ardtalnaig
1043
BEINN HEASGARNICH 1076
BEN LAWERS VISITOR CENTRE
Carie
A827
Gleann a'Chilleine
Glen Lochay
Kenknock
888
Milton Morenish
1047 AG MHOR
Morenish
Ardeonaig
Lochay
FALLS OF LOCHAY AND FISH LIFT
Boreland
Finglen Burn
MOIRLANICH LONGHOUSE
Finlarig
Glen Dochart
Killin
637
Achmore
879 CREAG UCHDAG
937 BEINN CHEATHAICH
Dochart
FALLS OF DOCHART
025 BEN ALLUM
Allt Ribhain
Auchlyne West Burn
Loch Lednock Reservoir
931 BEN CHONZIE
Invergeldie Burn
126
Auchlyne
Ardchyle
A85
127
Glen Ogle
Beich Burn
Glen Lednock
Invergeldie
Comrie... Funtullich
0 1 2 3 4 5 6 miles
0 1 2 3 4 5 6 7 8 9 10 km
Loch Iubhair
Dochart
Benmore
672 SRON MHOR
A B C D E F
1 2 3 4 5 6 7 8

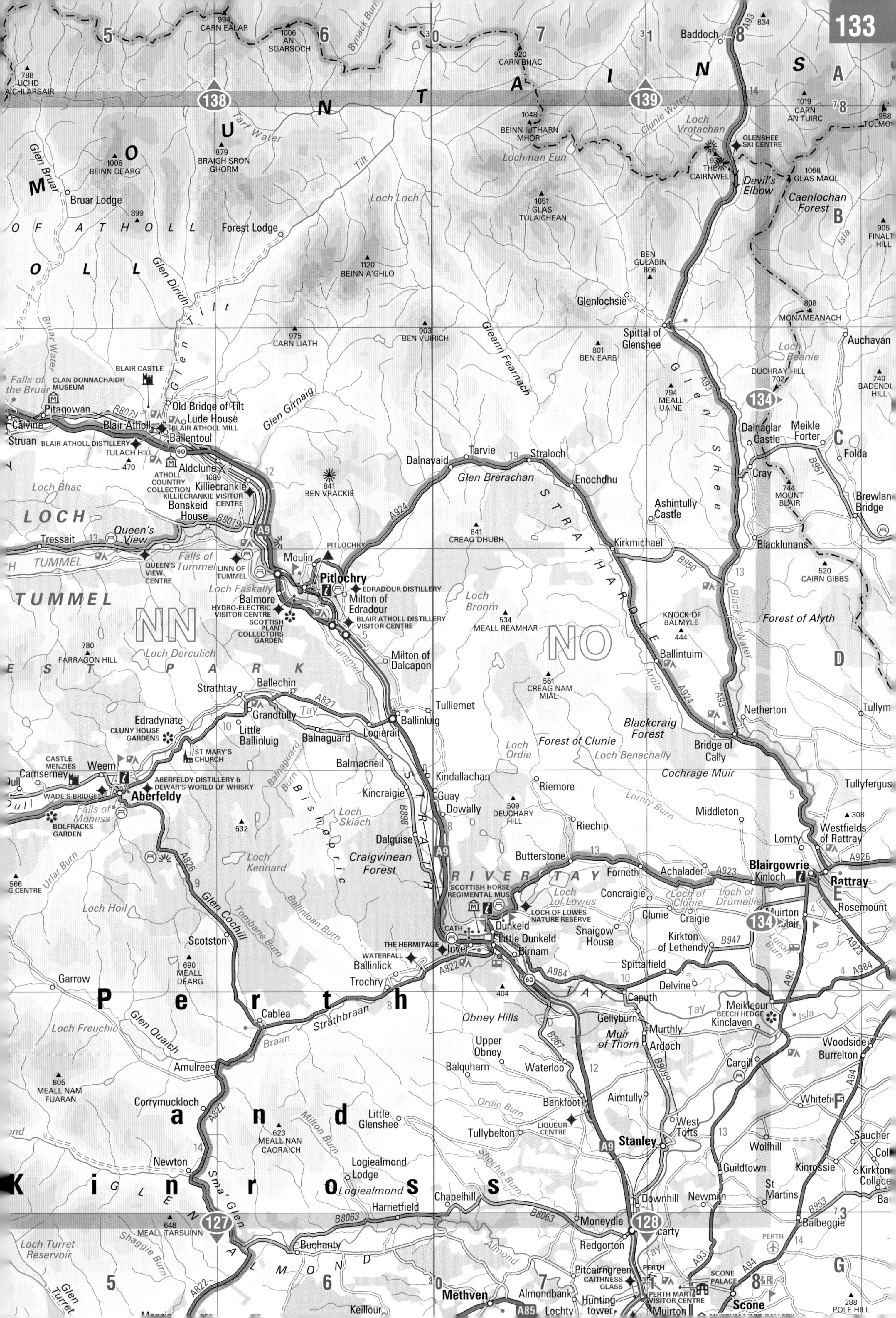
MOUNTAINS
FOREST OF ATHOLL
LOCH TUMMEL
TUMMEL FOREST PARK
NN
NO
RIVER TAY
STRATHARDLE
STRATH TAY
Perth and Kinross
GLEN ALMOND
CARN EALAR
AN SGARSOCH
CARN BHAC
UCHD ACHLARSAIR
BEINN DEARG
BRAIGH SRON GHORM
BEINN IUTHARN MHOR
Loch nan Eun
Loch Vrotachan
GLENSHEE SKI CENTRE
THE CAIRNWELL
Devil's Elbow
GLAS MAOL
Caenlochan Forest
CARN AN TUIRC
Bruar Lodge
Forest Lodge
Loch Loch
GLAS TULAICHEAN
BEINN A'GHLO
BEN GULABIN
Glenlochsie
Spittal of Glenshee
MONAMEANACH
Auchavan
Loch Beanie
DUCHRAY HILL
BADENDUN HILL
FINALTY HILL
CARN LIATH
BEN VUIRICH
Gleann Fearnach
BEN EARB
MEALL UAINE
Glen Shee
Glen Bruar
Glen Tilt
Glen Diridh
Tarf Water
Bruar Water
Clunie Water
Falls of the Bruar
CLAN DONNACHAIDH MUSEUM
BLAIR CASTLE
Pitagowan
Calvine
Struan
Blair Atholl
BLAIR ATHOLL MILL
Old Bridge of Tilt
Lude House
Ballentoul
BLAIR ATHOLL DISTILLERY
TULACH HILL
ATHOLL COUNTRY COLLECTION
Aldclune
Killiecrankie
KILLIECRANKIE VISITOR CENTRE
Bonskeid House
Loch Bhac
Glen Girnaig
BEN VRACKIE
Dalnavaid
Tarvie
Straloch
Glen Brerachan
Enochdhu
Ashintully Castle
Kirkmichael
Dalnaglar Castle
Meikle Forter
Cray
Folda
MOUNT BLAIR
Brewlands Bridge
Blacklunans
CAIRN GIBBS
Forest of Alyth
Black Water
Tressait
Queen's View
QUEEN'S VIEW CENTRE
Falls of Tummel
LINN OF TUMMEL
Moulin
PITLOCHRY
Pitlochry
CREAG DHUBH
EDRADOUR DISTILLERY
Milton of Edradour
BLAIR ATHOLL DISTILLERY VISITOR CENTRE
Loch Faskally
Balmore
HYDRO-ELECTRIC VISITOR CENTRE
SCOTTISH PLANT COLLECTORS GARDEN
Loch Broom
MEALL REAMHAR
KNOCK OF BALMYLE
Ballintuim
FARRAGON HILL
Loch Derculich
Milton of Dalcapon
CREAG NAM MIAL
Strathtay
Ballechin
Grandtully
Edradynate
CLUNY HOUSE GARDENS
Little Ballinluig
Tulliemet
Ballinluig
Logierait
Balnaguard
ST MARY'S CHURCH
Netherton
Tullymet
Blackcraig Forest
Forest of Clunie
Loch Ordie
Loch Benachally
Bridge of Cally
Cochrage Muir
CASTLE MENZIES
Camserney
Weem
ABERFELDY DISTILLERY & DEWAR'S WORLD OF WHISKY
WADE'S BRIDGE
Aberfeldy
Falls of Moness
BOLFRACKS GARDEN
Balmacneil
Kindallachan
Kincraigie
Guay
Dowally
Loch Skiach
Bishopric
DEUCHARY HILL
Riemore
Lornty Burn
Riechip
Middleton
Tullyfergus
Lornty
Westfields of Rattray
Dalguise
Craigvinean Forest
Loch Kennard
Butterstone
Forneth
Achalader
Blairgowrie
Kinloch
Rattray
Rosemount
SCOTTISH HORSE REGIMENTAL MUS
Loch of Lowes
LOCH OF LOWES NATURE RESERVE
Concraigie
Loch of Clunie
Loch of Drumellie
Clunie
Craigie
Muirton of Ballochblair
Loch Hoil
Glen Cochill
Tombane Burn
Ballinloan Burn
Urlar Burn
Scotston
CATH
Dunkeld
Little Dunkeld
Birnam
THE HERMITAGE
Inver
WATERFALL
Ballinlick
Trochry
Snaigow House
Kirkton of Lethendy
Spittalfield
Delvine
MEALL DEARG
Garrow
Cablea
Strathbraan
Braan
Caputh
Meikleour
BEECH HEDGE
Kinclaven
Isla
Loch Freuchie
Glen Quaich
Obney Hills
Upper Obney
Gellyburn
Murthly
Muir of Thorn
Ardoch
Woodside
Burrelton
Amulree
Balquharn
Waterloo
Cargill
MEALL NAM FUARAN
Corrymuckloch
Little Glenshee
Ordie Burn
Bankfoot
Aimtully
LIQUEUR CENTRE
Whitefield
MEALL NAN CAORAICH
Milton Burn
Tullybelton
West Tofts
Stanley
Wolfhill
Saucher
Newton
Logiealmond Lodge
Logiealmond
Shochie Burn
Guildtown
Kinrossie
Kirkton of Collace
Sma' Glen
Chapelhill
Downhill
Newmill
St Martins
MEALL TARSUINN
Harrietfield
Moneydie
Balbeggie
Loch Turret Reservoir
Shaggie Burn
Buchanty
Almond
Redgorton
PERTH
Glen Turret
Pitcairngreen
CAITHNESS GLASS
PERTH MART VISITOR CENTRE
SCONE PALACE
Methven
Almondbank
Huntingtower
Keillour
Lochty
Scone
POLE HILL
A9
A93
A924
A827
A822
A826
A923
A926
A984
A94
A85
B8079
B8019
B950
B951
B898
B947
B867
B9099
B953
B8063
138
139
134
127
128

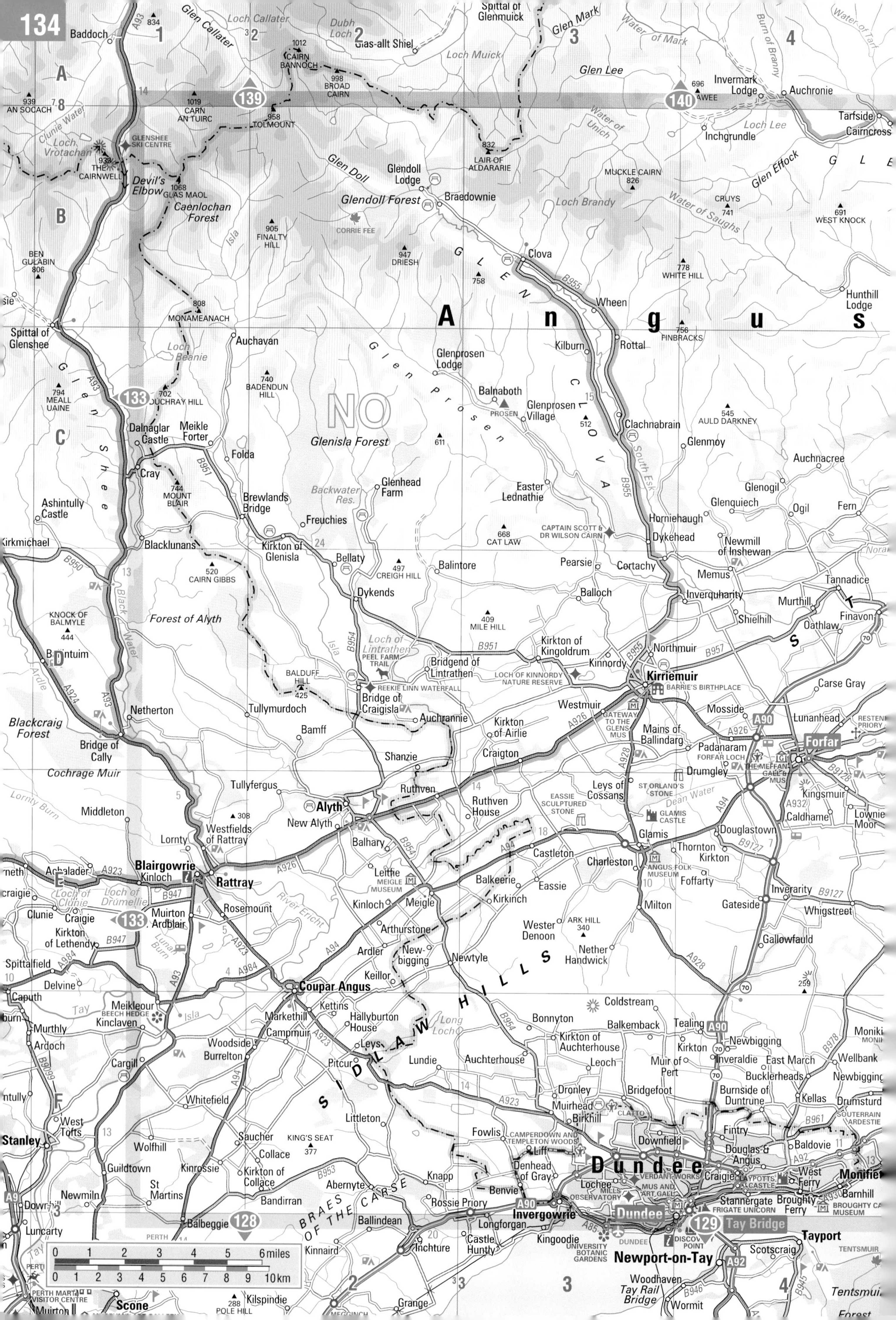
Baddoch
Glen Callater
Loch Callater
Dubh Loch
Glas-allt Shiel
Spittal of Glenmuick
Glen Mark
Water of Mark
Loch Muick
Glen Lee
Burn of Branny
Water of Tarf
Invermark Lodge
Auchronie
Tarfside
Cairncross
Loch Lee
Inchgrundle
Glen Effock
CAIRN BANNOCH
BROAD CAIRN
CARN AN TUIRC
TOLMOUNT
AN SOCACH
Clunie Water
Loch Vrotachan
GLENSHEE SKI CENTRE
THE CAIRNWELL
Devil's Elbow
GLAS MAOL
Caenlochan Forest
LAIR OF ALDARARIE
Water of Unich
MUCKLE CAIRN
Glen Doll
Glendoll Lodge
Glendoll Forest
Braedownie
CORRIE FEE
FINALTY HILL
DRIESH
Loch Brandy
Water of Saughs
CRUYS
WEST KNOCK
Clova
WHITE HILL
Hunthill Lodge
BEN GULABIN
MONAMEANACH
Wheen
Angus
Spittal of Glenshee
Auchavan
Loch Beanie
Kilburn
Rottal
FINBRACKS
Glen Prosen
Glenprosen Lodge
Balnaboth
Glenprosen Village
Glen Clova
MEALL UAINE
BADENDUN HILL
DUCHRAY HILL
NO
PROSEN
Clachnabrain
AULD DARKNEY
Glenmoy
Glen Shee
Dalnaglar Castle
Meikle Forter
Glenisla Forest
South Esk
Auchnacree
Folda
Cray
MOUNT BLAIR
Glenhead Farm
Backwater Res.
Easter Lednathie
Glenogil
Ashintully Castle
Brewlands Bridge
Freuchies
Glenquiech
Ogil
Fern
Horniehaugh
Dykehead
CAPTAIN SCOTT & DR WILSON CAIRN
CAT LAW
Newmill of Inshewan
Kirkmichael
Blacklunans
Kirkton of Glenisla
Bellaty
CREIGH HILL
Balintore
Pearsie
Cortachy
Memus
Tannadice
CAIRN GIBBS
Dykends
Balloch
Inverquharity
Murthill
Finavon
KNOCK OF BALMYLE
Forest of Alyth
Black Water
MILE HILL
Shielhill
Oathlaw
Loch of Lintrathen
PEEL FARM TRAIL
Kirkton of Kingoldrum
Northmuir
Ballintuim
BALDUFF HILL
Bridgend of Lintrathen
LOCH OF KINNORDY NATURE RESERVE
Kinnordy
Kirriemuir
BARRIE'S BIRTHPLACE
REEKIE LINN WATERFALL
Bridge of Craigisla
Carse Gray
Netherton
Tullymurdoch
Auchrannie
Westmuir
GATEWAY TO THE GLENS MUS
Mosside
Blackcraig Forest
Bamff
Kirkton of Airlie
Mains of Ballindarg
Lunanhead
RESTENNETH PRIORY
Bridge of Cally
Forfar
Padanaram
FORFAR LOCH
Cochrage Muir
Shanzie
Craigton
THE MEFFAN GALL & MUS
Drumgley
Lornty Burn
Tullyfergus
Ruthven
Leys of Cossans
ST ORLAND'S STONE
Kingsmuir
Middleton
Alyth
Ruthven House
EASSIE SCULPTURED STONE
Dean Water
Caldhame
Lownie Moor
New Alyth
Westfields of Rattray
GLAMIS CASTLE
Douglastown
Lornty
Balhary
Glamis
Thornton
Kirkton
Achalader
Blairgowrie
Kinloch
Rattray
Castleton
Charleston
ANGUS FOLK MUSEUM
Foffarty
Leitfie
MEIGLE MUSEUM
Balkeerie
Eassie
Inverarity
Loch of Clunie
Loch of Drumellie
Kinloch
Meigle
Kirkinch
Milton
Gateside
Whigstreet
Clunie
Craigie
Muirton
Ardblair
Rosemount
River Ericht
Arthurstone
Wester Denoon
ARK HILL
Kirkton of Lethendy
Lunan Burn
Ardler
Newbigging
Nether Handwick
Gallowfauld
Spittalfield
Delvine
Keillor
Newtyle
SIDLAW HILLS
Caputh
Meikleour
BEECH HEDGE
Coupar Angus
Kettins
Coldstream
Tay
Isla
Kinclaven
Markethill
Hallyburton House
Long Loch
Bonnyton
Murthly
Campmuir
Kirkton of Auchterhouse
Balkemback
Tealing
Ardoch
Woodside
Burrelton
Leys
Lundie
Auchterhouse
Leoch
Muir of Pert
Newbigging
Inveraldie
East March
Wellbank
Cargill
Pitcur
Bucklerheads
Newbigging
Whitefield
Dronley
Bridgefoot
Burnside of Duntrune
Kellas
Drumsturdy
Muirhead
Birkhill
CLATTO
Fintry
SOUTERRAIN ARDESTIE
West Tofts
Littleton
Stanley
Saucher
KING'S SEAT
Fowlis
CAMPERDOWN AND TEMPLETON WOODS
Downfield
Douglas & Angus
Baldovie
Wolfhill
Collace
Liff
Guildtown
Kinrossie
Kirkton of Collace
Denhead of Gray
Dundee
VERDANT WORKS
Craigie
CLAYPOTTS CASTLE
West Ferry
Monifieth
Barnhill
Newmiln
St Martins
Abernyte
Knapp
Benvie
Lochee
MUS AND ART GALL
MILLS OBSERVATORY
Broughty Ferry
BROUGHTY CASTLE MUSEUM
Stannergate
FRIGATE UNICORN
BRAES OF THE CARSE
Bandirran
Rossie Priory
Invergowrie
Balbeggie
Ballindean
Longforgan
Kingoodie
Tay Bridge
Tayport
Luncarty
Castle Huntly
Inchture
UNIVERSITY BOTANIC GARDENS
DUNDEE
DISCOVERY POINT
Newport-on-Tay
Scotscraig
TENTSMUIR
Kinnaird
PERTH MART VISITOR CENTRE
Woodhaven
Tay Rail Bridge
Wormit
Tentsmuir Forest
Scone
POLE HILL
Kilspindie
Grange
Muirton
0 1 2 3 4 5 6 miles
0 1 2 3 4 5 6 7 8 9 10 km

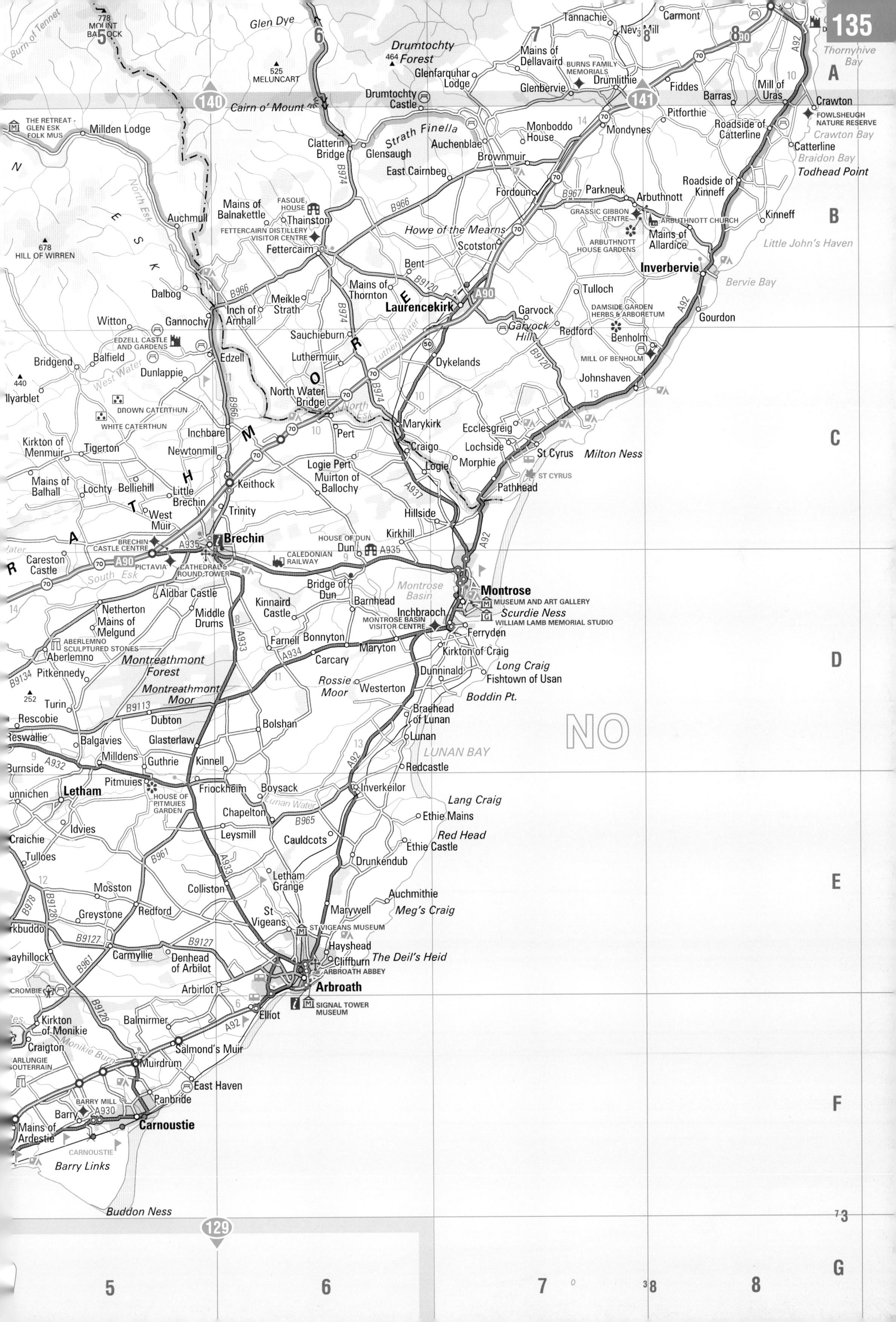
778
MOUNT
BATTOCK
Burn of Tennet
Glen Dye
Drumtochty
Forest
464
525
MELUNCART
Tannachie
Carmont
Nether Mill
Mains of
Dellavaird
BURNS FAMILY
MEMORIALS
Drumlithie
Glenbervie
Glenfarquhar
Lodge
Drumtochty
Castle
Cairn o' Mount
140
141
90
70
Fiddes
Barras
Mill of
Uras
Crawton
Thornyhive
Bay
FOWLSHEUGH
NATURE RESERVE
Crawton Bay
Catterline
Braidon Bay
Todhead Point
Pitforthie
Roadside of
Catterline
Mondynes
Monboddo
House
THE RETREAT -
GLEN ESK
FOLK MUS
Millden Lodge
Clatterin
Bridge
Strath Finella
Glensaugh
Auchenblae
Brownmuir
East Cairnbeg
B974
Fordoun
B967
Parkneuk
Arbuthnott
Roadside of
Kinneff
Kinneff
North Esk
Mains of
Balnakettle
FASQUE
HOUSE
Thainston
FETTERCAIRN DISTILLERY
VISITOR CENTRE
Fettercairn
B966
Howe of the Mearns
Scotston
GRASSIC GIBBON
CENTRE
ARBUTHNOTT CHURCH
ARBUTHNOTT
HOUSE GARDENS
Mains of
Allardice
Little John's Haven
Auchmull
678
HILL OF WIRREN
Bent
B9120
Mains of
Thornton
Inverbervie
Bervie Bay
Dalbog
Meikle
Strath
Inch of
Arnhall
Laurencekirk
A90
Tulloch
DAMSIDE GARDEN
HERBS & ARBORETUM
Garvock
Garvock
Hill
Redford
Benholm
Gourdon
A92
Witton
Gannochy
EDZELL CASTLE
AND GARDENS
Edzell
Sauchieburn
Luthermuir
Luther Water
Dykelands
MILL OF BENHOLM
Johnshaven
Bridgend
Balfield
West Water
Dunlappie
440
Illyarblet
BROWN CATERTHUN
WHITE CATERTHUN
B966
North Water
Bridge
North Esk
Marykirk
Ecclesgreig
Lochside
St Cyrus
Milton Ness
ST CYRUS
Kirkton of
Menmuir
Tigerton
Inchbare
Newtonmill
Pert
Craigo
Logie Pert
Logie
Morphie
Muirton of
Ballochy
Mains of
Balhall
Lochty
Belliehill
Little
Brechin
Keithock
Pathhead
A937
West
Muir
Trinity
Hillside
Kirkhill
BRECHIN
CASTLE CENTRE
A935
Brechin
HOUSE OF DUN
Dun
CALEDONIAN
RAILWAY
Careston
Castle
PICTAVIA
CATHEDRAL &
ROUND TOWER
South Esk
Bridge of
Dun
Montrose
Basin
Montrose
MUSEUM AND ART GALLERY
Scurdie Ness
WILLIAM LAMB MEMORIAL STUDIO
Aldbar Castle
Netherton
Mains of
Melgund
Middle
Drums
Kinnaird
Castle
Barnhead
Inchbraoch
MONTROSE BASIN
VISITOR CENTRE
Ferryden
ABERLEMNO
SCULPTURED STONES
Aberlemno
A933
Farnell
Bonnyton
A934
Maryton
Kirkton of Craig
Montreathmont
Forest
Carcary
Dunninald
Long Craig
Fishtown of Usan
B9134
Pitkennedy
Rossie
Moor
Westerton
Boddin Pt.
252
Turin
Montreathmont
Moor
B9113
Braehead
of Lunan
Rescobie
Dubton
Bolshan
NO
Lunan
LUNAN BAY
Reswallie
Balgavies
Glasterlaw
Millden
Guthrie
Kinnell
A932
Burnside
Redcastle
Letham
Pitmuies
HOUSE OF
PITMUIES
GARDEN
Friockheim
Boysack
Lunan Water
Inverkeilor
Lang Craig
Dunnichen
Chapelton
B965
Ethie Mains
Idvies
Leysmill
Cauldcots
Red Head
Ethie Castle
Craichie
B961
Tulloes
Drunkendub
Letham
Grange
Mosston
Colliston
Auchmithie
B978
B9128
Greystone
Redford
Marywell
Meg's Craig
St
Vigeans
ST VIGEANS MUSEUM
Kirkbuddo
B9127
B9127
Hayshead
Carmyllie
Denhead
of Arbilot
Cliffburn
The Deil's Heid
Gallowhillock
ARBROATH ABBEY
Arbroath
CROMBIE
Arbirlot
SIGNAL TOWER
MUSEUM
Elliot
B9128
Kirkton
of Monikie
Balmirmer
A92
Salmond's Muir
Craigton
Monikie Burn
CARLUNGIE
SOUTERRAIN
Muirdrum
East Haven
BARRY MILL
Panbride
Barry
A930
Carnoustie
Mains of
Ardestie
CARNOUSTIE
Barry Links
Buddon Ness
129
A
B
C
D
E
F
G
5
6
7
8
3
73
38

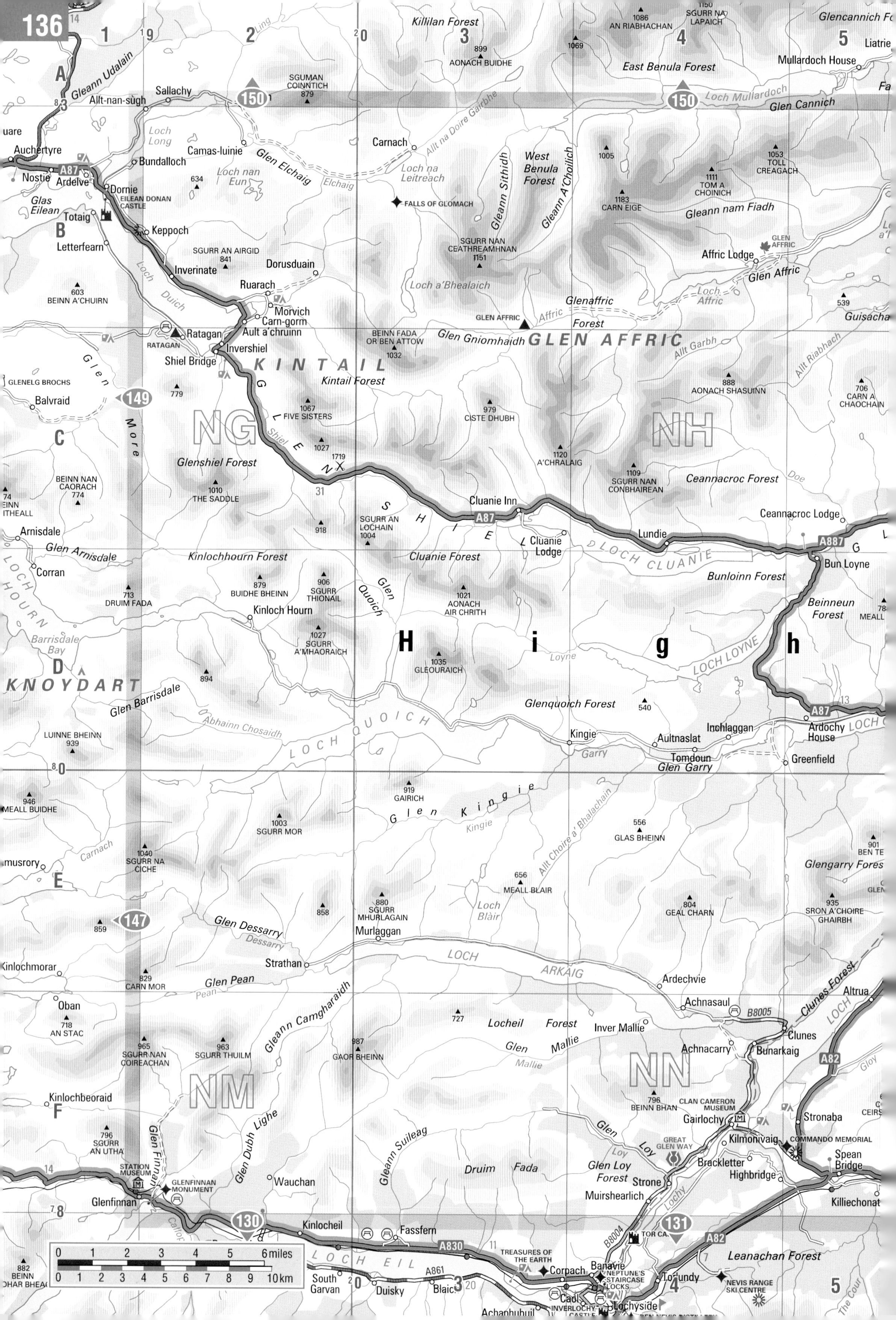
Killilan Forest
899
AONACH BUIDHE
1086
AN RIABHACHAN
1150
SGURR NA LAPAICH
1069
Glencannich Fo
Liatrie
Mullardoch House
East Benula Forest
Loch Mullardoch
Glen Cannich
Gleann Udalain
Sallachy
Allt-nan-sùgh
SGUMAN COINNTICH
879
150
Loch Long
Camas-luinie
Carnach
Allt na Doire Gairbhe
Glen Elchaig
Elchaig
Loch na Leitreach
Auchertyre
Bundalloch
Loch nan Eun
634
A87
Nostie
Ardelve
Dornie
EILEAN DONAN CASTLE
Glas Eilean
Totaig
FALLS OF GLOMACH
West Benula Forest
Gleann Sithidh
Gleann A'Choilich
1005
1053
TOLL CREAGACH
1111
TOM A CHOINICH
1183
CARN EIGE
Gleann nam Fiadh
Keppoch
Letterfearn
SGURR AN AIRGID
841
Inverinate
Dorusduain
SGURR NAN CEATHREAMHNAN
1151
GLEN AFFRIC
Affric Lodge
Glen Affric
Loch Affric
603
BEINN A'CHUIRN
Loch Duich
Ruarach
Morvich
Carn-gorm
Ault a'chruinn
Loch a'Bhealaich
Glenaffric Forest
GLEN AFFRIC
Affric
539
Guisachan
Ratagan
RATAGAN
Invershiel
Shiel Bridge
BEINN FADA OR BEN ATTOW
1032
Glen Gniomhaidh
KINTAIL
Kintail Forest
Allt Garbh
Allt Riabhach
GLENELG BROCHS
Glen More
149
Balvraid
779
1067
FIVE SISTERS
979
CISTE DHUBH
888
AONACH SHASUINN
706
CARN A CHAOCHAIN
NG
NH
GLEN SHIEL
Shiel
1027
1719
C
Glenshiel Forest
1120
A'CHRALAIG
1109
SGURR NAN CONBHAIREAN
Ceannacroc Forest
Doe
BEINN NAN CAORACH
774
1010
THE SADDLE
31
Cluanie Inn
A87
Ceannacroc Lodge
SGURR AN LOCHAIN
1004
918
Cluanie Lodge
Lundie
LOCH CLUANIE
A887
Arnisdale
Glen Arnisdale
Kinlochhourn Forest
Cluanie Forest
Bun Loyne
Corran
LOCH HOURN
879
BUIDHE BHEINN
906
SGURR THIONAIL
Glen Quoich
1021
AONACH AIR CHRITH
Bunloinn Forest
713
DRUIM FADA
Kinloch Hourn
Beinneun Forest
MEALL
Barrisdale Bay
1027
SGURR A'MHAORAICH
H
i
g
h
1035
GLEOURAICH
Loyne
LOCH LOYNE
D
KNOYDART
894
Glen Barrisdale
Glenquoich Forest
540
A87
Abhainn Chosaidh
LOCH QUOICH
Kingie
Aultnaslat
Inchlaggan
Ardochy House
LOCH GARRY
LUINNE BHEINN
939
Garry
Tomdoun
Glen Garry
Greenfield
946
MEALL BUIDHE
919
GAIRICH
Glen Kingie
Kingie
Allt Choire a' Bhalachain
1003
SGURR MOR
556
GLAS BHEINN
Carnach
1040
SGURR NA CICHE
901
BEN TEE
Glengarry Forest
E
656
MEALL BLAIR
Loch Blàir
880
SGURR MHURLAGAIN
858
804
GEAL CHARN
935
SRON A'CHOIRE GHAIRBH
859
147
Glen Dessarry
Dessarry
Murlaggan
Kinlochmorar
Strathan
LOCH ARKAIG
829
CARN MOR
Glen Pean
Pean
Ardechvie
Oban
718
AN STAC
Gleann Camgharaidh
727
Achnasaul
B8005
Clunes Forest
Altrua
Locheil Forest
Inver Mallie
Clunes
965
SGURR NAN COIREACHAN
963
SGURR THUILM
987
GAOR BHEINN
Glen Mallie
Mallie
Achnacarry
Bunarkaig
A82
Gloy
NM
NN
Kinlochbeoraid
F
796
SGURR AN UTHA
Glen Finnan
Glen Dubh Lighe
Gleann Suileag
796
BEINN BHAN
CLAN CAMERON MUSEUM
Gairlochy
Stronaba
Glen Loy
Loy
GREAT GLEN WAY
Kilmonivaig
COMMANDO MEMORIAL
STATION MUSEUM
GLENFINNAN MONUMENT
Wauchan
Druim Fada
Glen Loy Forest
Strone
Brackletter
Highbridge
Spean Bridge
Glenfinnan
Muirshearlich
Lochy
Killiechonat
130
Kinlocheil
Fassfern
131
TOR CA.
B8004
A82
Leanachan Forest
0 1 2 3 4 5 6 miles
0 1 2 3 4 5 6 7 8 9 10 km
LOCH EIL
A830
TREASURES OF THE EARTH
A861
Corpach
Banavie
NEPTUNE'S STAIRCASE LOCKS
Torlundy
NEVIS RANGE SKI CENTRE
882
BEINN ODHAR BHEAG
South Garvan
Duisky
Blaich
Caol
Lochyside
INVERLOCHY CASTLE
Achaphubuil
1
2
3
4
5
A
B
D
19
20
80
78
14
11
13
7

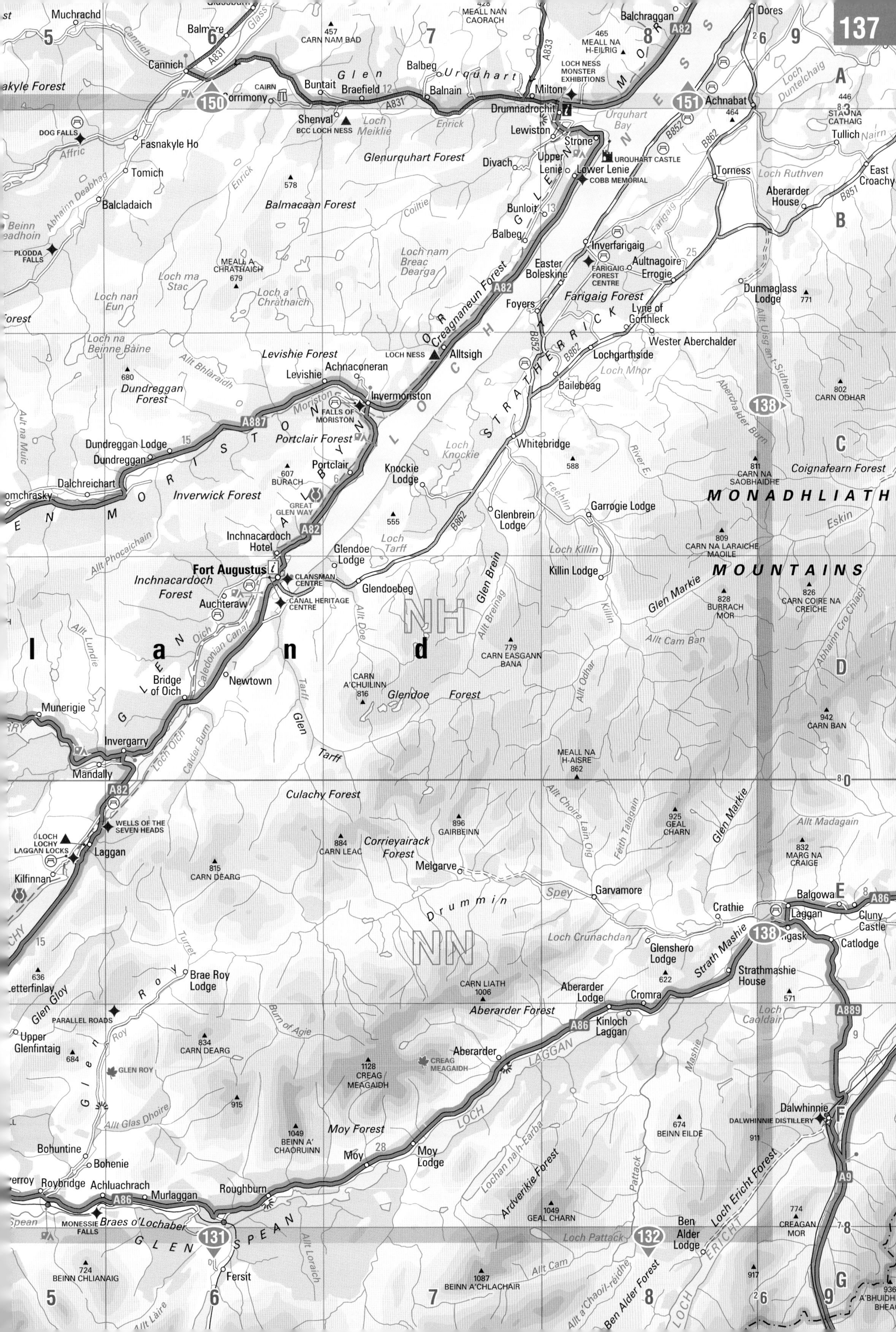

Muchrachd
Balmore
Glass
457
CARN NAM BAD
428
MEALL NAN CAORACH
Balchraggan
465
MEALL NA H-EILRIG
LOCH NESS MONSTER EXHIBITIONS
Dores
A82
A831
A833
Cannich
Guisachan
Fasnakyle Forest
CAIRN
Corrimony
150
Buntait
Glen Urquhart
Braefield
Balbeg
Balnain
Milton
Drumnadrochit
151
Achnabat
446
STAC NA CATHAIG
Loch Duntelchaig
Shenval
BCC LOCH NESS
Loch Meiklie
Enrick
Lewiston
Urquhart Bay
464
B852
B862
DOG FALLS
Affric
Fasnakyle Ho
Glenurquhart Forest
Strone
URQUHART CASTLE
Tullich
Nairn
Tomich
Divach
Upper Lenie
Lower Lenie
COBB MEMORIAL
Torness
Loch Ruthven
East Croachy
Abhainn Deabhag
578
Balcladaich
Balmacaan Forest
Coiltie
Bunloit
Aberarder House
B851
Beinn Mheadhoin
Balbeg
Inverfarigaig
Farigaig
PLODDA FALLS
MEALL A' CHRATHAICH
679
Loch nam Breac Dearga
Easter Boleskine
FARIGAIG FOREST CENTRE
Aultnagoire
Errogie
Loch ma Stac
Loch a' Chràthaich
Loch nan Eun
Creagnaneun Forest
Farigaig Forest
Foyers
Dunmaglass Lodge
771
Lyne of Gorthleck
Wester Aberchalder
Loch na Beinne Bàine
Allt Bhlàraidh
Levishie Forest
LOCH NESS
Alltsigh
Lochgarthside
Loch Mhor
680
Dundreggan Forest
Levishie
Achnaconeran
Bailebeag
Allt Uisg an t-Sidhein
802
CARN ODHAR
138
Invermoriston
FALLS OF MORISTON
Moriston
A887
Portclair Forest
Dundreggan Lodge
Dundreggan
Whitebridge
Loch Knockie
Aberchalder Burn
River E
Allt na Muic
Portclair
607
BURACH
GREAT GLEN WAY
Knockie Lodge
588
811
CARN NA SAOBHAIDHE
Coignafearn Forest
Dalchreichart
Inverwick Forest
Feehlin
Glenbrein Lodge
Garrogie Lodge
MONADHLIATH
Ceannacroc
Glen Moriston
Loch Ness
Strath Errick
555
Allt Phocaichain
Inchnacardoch Hotel
Loch Tarff
809
CARN NA LARAICHE MAOILE
Eskin
Loch Killin
Fort Augustus
CLANSMAN CENTRE
Glendoe Lodge
Glendoebeg
Killin Lodge
MOUNTAINS
Inchnacardoch Forest
CANAL HERITAGE CENTRE
Glen Brein
Allt Breinag
Glen Markie
828
BURRACH MOR
826
CARN COIRE NA CREICHE
Auchteraw
Allt Doe
Killin
Abhainn Cro Chlach
Allt Lundie
NH
Oich
Caledonian Canal
779
CARN EASGANN BANA
Allt Cam Ban
Highland
Allt Odhar
Bridge of Oich
Newtown
Tarff
CARN A'CHUILINN
816
Glendoe Forest
Glen Tarff
Munerigie
942
CARN BAN
Glen Garry
Invergarry
Loch Oich
Calder Burn
MEALL NA H-AISRE
862
Mandally
Culachy Forest
Allt Choire Lain Oig
Feith Talagain
Allt Madagain
896
GAIRBEINN
925
GEAL CHARN
LOCH LOCHY
WELLS OF THE SEVEN HEADS
884
CARN LEAC
Corrieyairack Forest
832
MARG NA CRAIGE
LAGGAN LOCKS
Laggan
815
CARN DEARG
Melgarve
Kilfinnan
Spey
Garvamore
Crathie
Balgowan
Laggan
A86
Cluny Castle
Drummin
Loch Crunachdan
Glenshero Lodge
Strath Mashie
Catlodge
Loch Lochy
NN
Turret
636
Letterfinlay
Brae Roy Lodge
Glen Roy
622
Strathmashie House
CARN LIATH
1006
Aberarder Lodge
Cromra
571
Glen Gloy
PARALLEL ROADS
Aberarder Forest
Kinloch Laggan
Loch Caoldair
A889
Burn of Agie
Upper Glenfintaig
684
834
CARN DEARG
Aberarder
Loch Laggan
Mashie
GLEN ROY
1128
CREAG MEAGAIDH
CREAG MEAGAIDH
915
Allt Glas Dhoire
Dalwhinnie
DALWHINNIE DISTILLERY
674
BEINN EILDE
1049
BEINN A' CHAORUINN
Moy Forest
Lochan na h-Earba
Ardverikie Forest
Bohuntine
Bohenie
Moy
Moy Lodge
Pattack
911
Loch Ericht Forest
Inverroy
Roybridge
Achluachrach
Murlaggan
Roughburn
A9
1049
GEAL CHARN
774
CREAGAN MOR
MONESSIE FALLS
Braes o'Lochaber
Spean
131
Glen Spean
Allt Loraich
Loch Pattack
132
Ben Alder Lodge
Loch Ericht
724
BEINN CHLIANAIG
Fersit
1087
BEINN A'CHLACHAIR
Allt Cam
Allt a' Choil-reidhe
Ben Alder Forest
917
936
A'BHUIDHEANACH BHEAG
Allt Laire

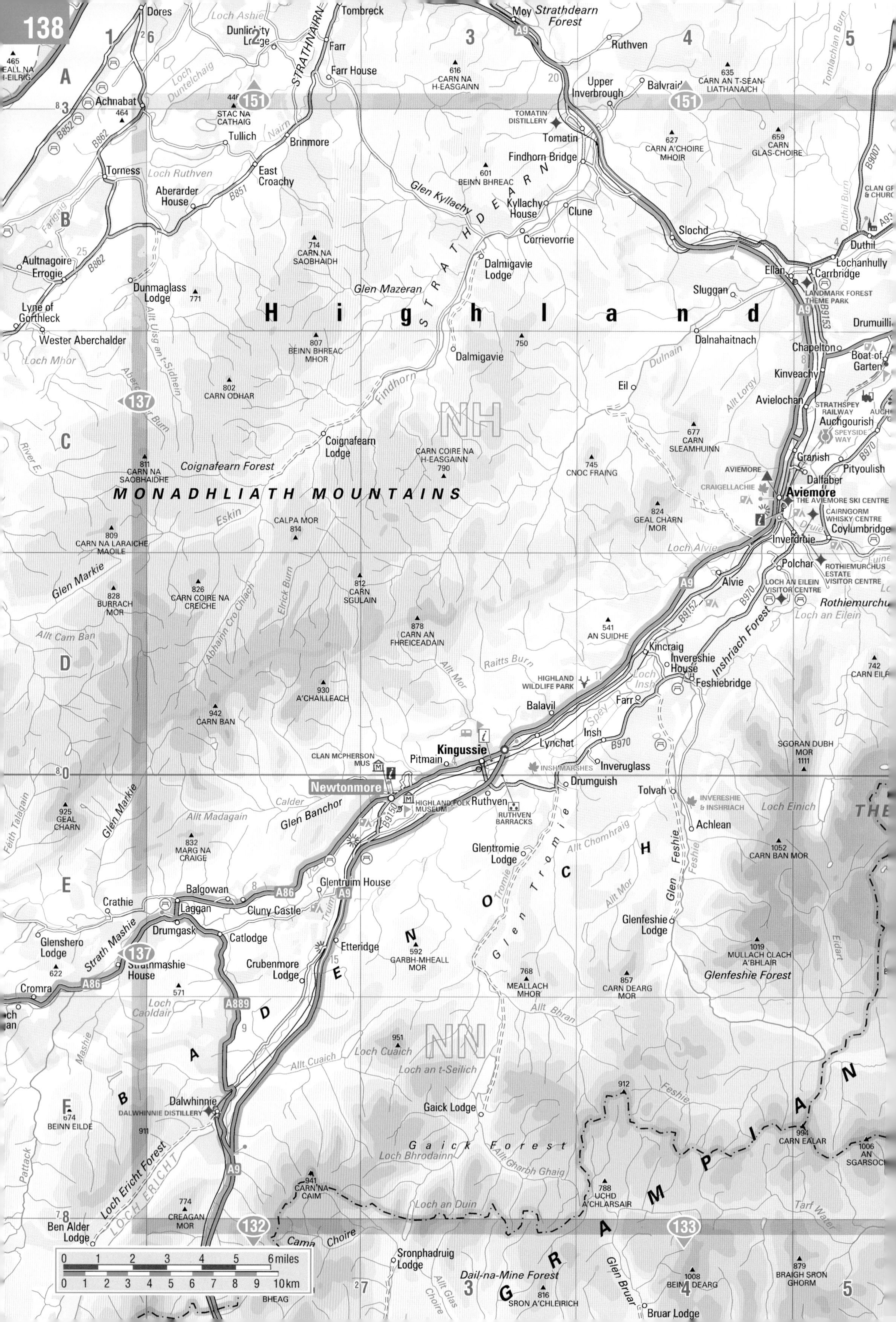

Dores
Loch Ashie
Dunlichity Lodge
STRATHNAIRN
Tombreck
Farr
Farr House
Moy
Strathdearn Forest
A9
Ruthven
616 CARN NA H-EASGAINN
635 CARN AN T-SEAN-LIATHANAICH
Tomatlan Burn
465 EALL NA I-EILRIG
Achnabat
464
B852
B862
Loch Duntelchaig
446 STAC NA CATHAIG
151
Upper Inverbrough
Balvraid
TOMATIN DISTILLERY
Tomatin
Tullich
Nairn
Brinmore
627 CARN A'CHOIRE MHOIR
659 CARN GLAS-CHOIRE
B9007
Torness
Loch Ruthven
East Croachy
Findhorn Bridge
601 BEINN BHREAC
Aberarder House
B851
Glen Kyllachy
Kyllachy House
Clune
STRATHDEARN
CLAN GRANT & CHURCH
Farigaig
Corrievorrie
Slochd
Duthil Burn
A938
Duthil
714 CARN NA SAOBHAIDH
Aultnagoire
Errogie
Dalmigavie Lodge
Ellan
Lochanhully
Carrbridge
LANDMARK FOREST THEME PARK
Dunmaglass Lodge
771
Glen Mazeran
Sluggan
Lyne of Gorthleck
Highland
B9153
Drumuillie
Wester Aberchalder
807 BEINN BHREAC MHOR
750
Dalnahaitnach
Chapelton
Boat of Garten
Loch Mhor
Allt Uisg an t-Sidhein
Dalmigavie
Dulnain
802 CARN ODHAR
Kinveachy
Findhorn
Eil
Allt Lorgy
Avielochan
137
NH
STRATHSPEY RAILWAY
Auchgourish
SPEYSIDE WAY
River E.
Coignafearn Lodge
CARN COIRE NA H-EASGAINN 790
677 CARN SLEAMHUINN
Granish
B970
Pityoulish
811 CARN NA SAOBHAIDHE
Coignafearn Forest
745 CNOC FRAING
AVIEMORE
Dalfaber
MONADHLIATH MOUNTAINS
CRAIGELLACHIE
Aviemore
THE AVIEMORE SKI CENTRE
Eskin
824 GEAL CHARN MOR
CAIRNGORM WHISKY CENTRE
809 CARN NA LARAICHE MAOILE
CALPA MOR 814
Inverdruie
Coylumbridge
Loch Alvie
Polchar
ROTHIEMURCHUS ESTATE VISITOR CENTRE
Glen Markie
826 CARN COIRE NA CREICHE
Abhainn Cro Chlach
Elrick Burn
812 CARN SGULAIN
Alvie
B9152
LOCH AN EILEIN VISITOR CENTRE
Rothiemurchus
828 BURRACH MOR
878 CARN AN FHREICEADAIN
541 AN SUIDHE
Loch an Eilein
Allt Cam Ban
Kincraig
Inshriach Forest
Invereshie House
Feshiebridge
Raitts Burn
742 CARN EILRIG
Allt Mor
HIGHLAND WILDLIFE PARK
Loch Insh
930 A'CHAILLEACH
Balavil
Farr
942 CARN BAN
Spey
Insh
Lynchat
B970
SGORAN DUBH MOR 1111
CLAN MCPHERSON MUS
Pitmain
Kingussie
Inveruglass
INSH MARSHES
Drumguish
Newtonmore
Tolvah
925 GEAL CHARN
Glen Markie
Calder
HIGHLAND FOLK MUSEUM
Ruthven
RUTHVEN BARRACKS
INVERESHIE & INSHRIACH
Loch Einich
Feith Talagain
Allt Madagain
Glen Banchor
B9150
Achlean
Allt Chomhraig
832 MARG NA CRAIGE
Glentromie Lodge
1052 CARN BAN MOR
Glen Tromie
Tromie
Glen Feshie
Feshie
MONADHLIATH
Glentruim House
Allt Mor
Balgowan
A86
A9
Crathie
Laggan
Cluny Castle
Truim
Glenfeshie Lodge
Drumgask
Catlodge
Glenshero Lodge
Strath Mashie
Etteridge
592 GARBH-MHEALL MOR
1019 MULLACH CLACH A'BHLAIR
Eidart
622
Strathmashie House
Crubenmore Lodge
768 MEALLACH MHOR
857 CARN DEARG MOR
Glenfeshie Forest
Cromra
571
A889
Loch Caoldair
Allt Bhran
Mashie
951
NN
Loch Cuaich
Allt Cuaich
Loch an t-Seilich
912
Dalwhinnie
DALWHINNIE DISTILLERY
674 BEINN EILDE
Gaick Lodge
Gaick Forest
994 CARN EALAR
1006 AN SGARSOCH
911
Loch Bhrodainn
Allt Gharbh Ghaig
Pattack
Loch Ericht Forest
LOCH ERICHT
941 CARN NA CAIM
788 UCHD A'CHLARSAIR
Loch an Duin
Tarf Water
774 CREAGAN MOR
Ben Alder Lodge
132
133
Cama Choire
GRAMPIAN
Sronphadruig Lodge
Dail-na-Mine Forest
879 BRAIGH SRON GHORM
Glen Bruar
1008 BEINN DEARG
816 SRON A'CHLEIRICH
Allt Glas
BHEAG
Bruar Lodge
0 1 2 3 4 5 6 miles
0 1 2 3 4 5 6 7 8 9 10 km

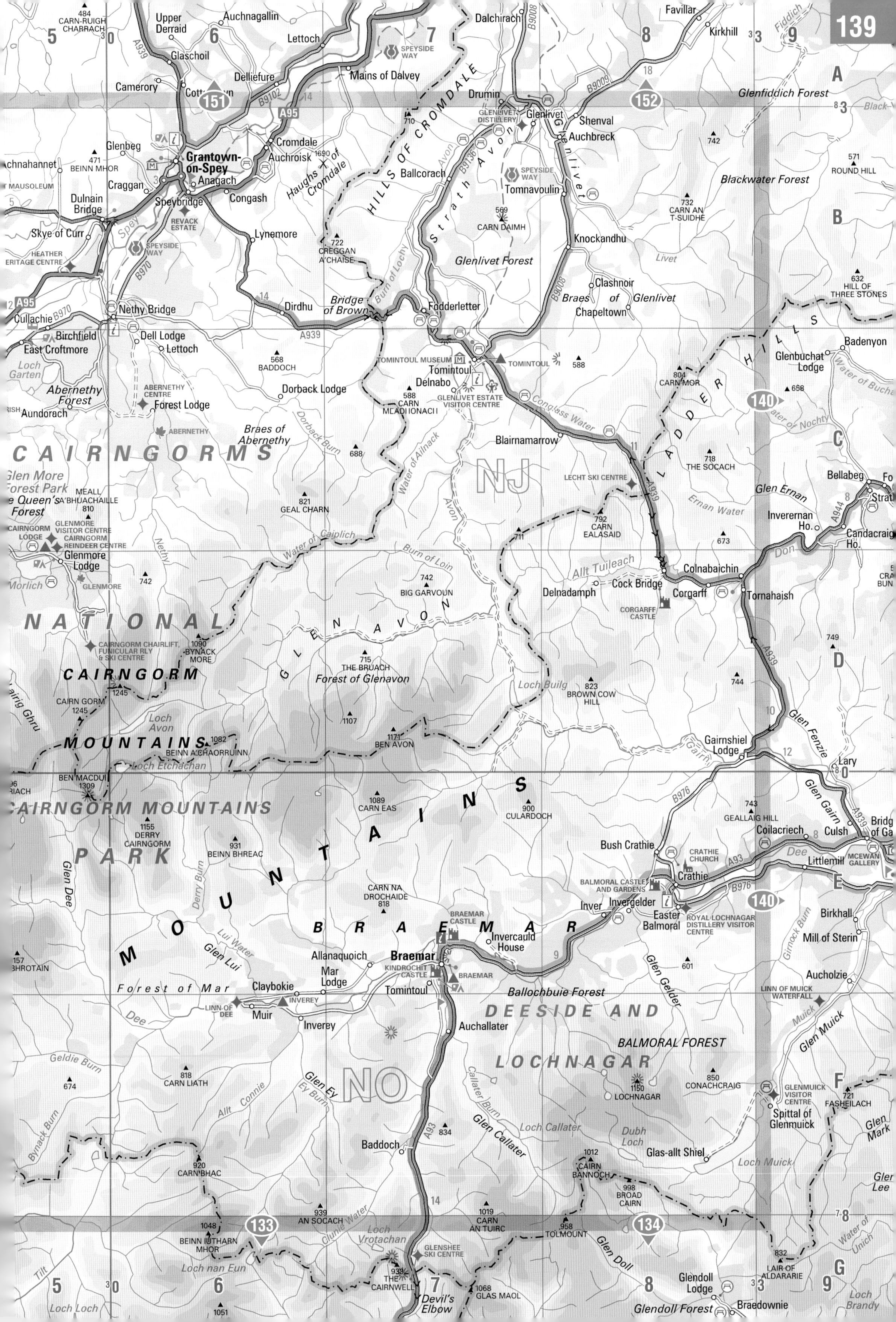

Upper Derraid
Auchnagallin
Lettoch
Glaschoil
Dellefure
Mains of Dalvey
Camerory
SPEYSIDE WAY
HILLS OF CROMDALE
Dalchirach
Drumin
GLENLIVET DISTILLERY
Glenlivet
Shenval
Auchbreck
Favillar
Kirkhill
Glenfiddich Forest
Blackwater Forest
571 ROUND HILL
742
732 CARN AN T-SUIDHE
Glenbeg
471 BEINN MHOR
Grantown-on-Spey
Cromdale
Auchroisk
Haughs of Cromdale
Ballcorach
Craggan
Anagach
Congash
Dulnain Bridge
Speybridge
REVACK ESTATE
Skye of Curr
Lynemore
Strath Avon
Tomnavoulin
569 CARN DAIMH
Knockandhu
Livet
HEATHER HERITAGE CENTRE
722 CREGGAN A'CHAISE
Glenlivet Forest
Clashnoir
Braes of Glenlivet
Chapeltown
632 HILL OF THREE STONES
Cullachie
Nethy Bridge
Dirdhu
Bridge of Brown
Fodderletter
Birchfield
East Croftmore
Dell Lodge
Lettoch
Loch Garten
568 BADDOCH
TOMINTOUL MUSEUM
Tomintoul
TOMINTOUL
588
Delnabo
GLENLIVET ESTATE VISITOR CENTRE
588 CARN MEADHONACH
Abernethy Forest
ABERNETHY CENTRE
Forest Lodge
Dorback Lodge
Aundorach
ABERNETHY
Braes of Abernethy
Dorback Burn
Conglass Water
Blairnamarrow
LADDER HILLS
804 CARN MOR
Badenyon
Glenbuchat Lodge
656
Water of Nochty
718 THE SOCACH
CAIRNGORMS
Glen More Forest Park
Queen's Forest
MEALL A'BHUACHAILLE 810
GLENMORE VISITOR CENTRE
CAIRNGORM LODGE
CAIRNGORM REINDEER CENTRE
Glenmore Lodge
Morlich
GLENMORE
742
688
Water of Ailnack
NJ
LECHT SKI CENTRE
821 GEAL CHARN
792 CARN EALASAID
Bellabeg
Glen Ernan
Ernan Water
Inverernan Ho.
Candacraig Ho.
673
711
Water of Caiplich
Burn of Loin
742 BIG GARVOUN
Allt Tuileach
Delnadamph
Cock Bridge
Colnabaichin
Corgarff
Tornahaish
CORGARFF CASTLE
Don
NATIONAL
CAIRNGORM CHAIRLIFT, FUNICULAR RLY & SKI CENTRE
1090 BYNACK MORE
GLEN AVON
715 THE BRUACH
Forest of Glenavon
749
CAIRNGORM
1245
CAIRN GORM 1245
Loch Builg
823 BROWN COW HILL
744
Lairig Ghru
Loch Avon
1107
1171 BEN AVON
Glen Fenzie
MOUNTAINS
1082 BEINN A'CHAORRUINN
Loch Etchachan
Gairnshiel Lodge
Gairn
Lary
BEN MACDUI 1309
1089 CARN EAS
900 CULARDOCH
743 GEALLAIG HILL
Glen Gairn
CAIRNGORM MOUNTAINS
MOUNTAINS
1155 DERRY CAIRNGORM
931 BEINN BHREAC
Bush Crathie
CRATHIE CHURCH
Coilacriech
Culsh
Bridge of Gairn
PARK
Glen Dee
Derry Burn
Crathie
Dee
Littlemill
MCEWAN GALLERY
CARN NA DROCHAIDE 818
BALMORAL CASTLE AND GARDENS
Inver
Invergelder
Easter Balmoral
ROYAL LOCHNAGAR DISTILLERY VISITOR CENTRE
Birkhall
Mill of Sterin
BRAEMAR
BRAEMAR CASTLE
Invercauld House
Lui Water
Glen Lui
Allanaquoich
Braemar
Mar Lodge
KINDROCHIT CASTLE
Glen Gelder
601
Aucholzie
Forest of Mar
Claybokie
INVEREY
Tomintoul
Ballochbuie Forest
LINN OF MUICK WATERFALL
LINN OF DEE
Muir
Inverey
Auchallater
DEESIDE AND LOCHNAGAR
Glen Muick
BALMORAL FOREST
Geldie Burn
818 CARN LIATH
674
Glen Ey
Ey Burn
NO
1150 LOCHNAGAR
850 CONACHCRAIG
GLENMUICK VISITOR CENTRE
Spittal of Glenmuick
721 FASHEILACH
Allt Connie
Callater Burn
Glen Callater
Loch Callater
Dubh Loch
Glen Mark
Bynack Burn
834
Baddoch
Glas-allt Shiel
Loch Muick
920 CARN BHAC
1012 CAIRN BANNOCH
998 BROAD CAIRN
Glen Lee
939 AN SOCACH
Clunie Water
1019 CARN AN TUIRC
958 TOLMOUNT
1048 BEINN IUTHARN MHOR
Loch Vrotachan
GLENSHEE SKI CENTRE
Glen Doll
832 LAIR OF ALDARARIE
Water of Unich
Tilt
Loch nan Eun
939 THE CAIRNWELL
1068 GLAS MAOL
Glendoll Lodge
Loch Brandy
Loch Loch
1051
Devil's Elbow
Glendoll Forest
Braedownie
151
152
133
134
140
A95
A939
A93
A944
B970
B9102
B9136
B9008
B9009
B976

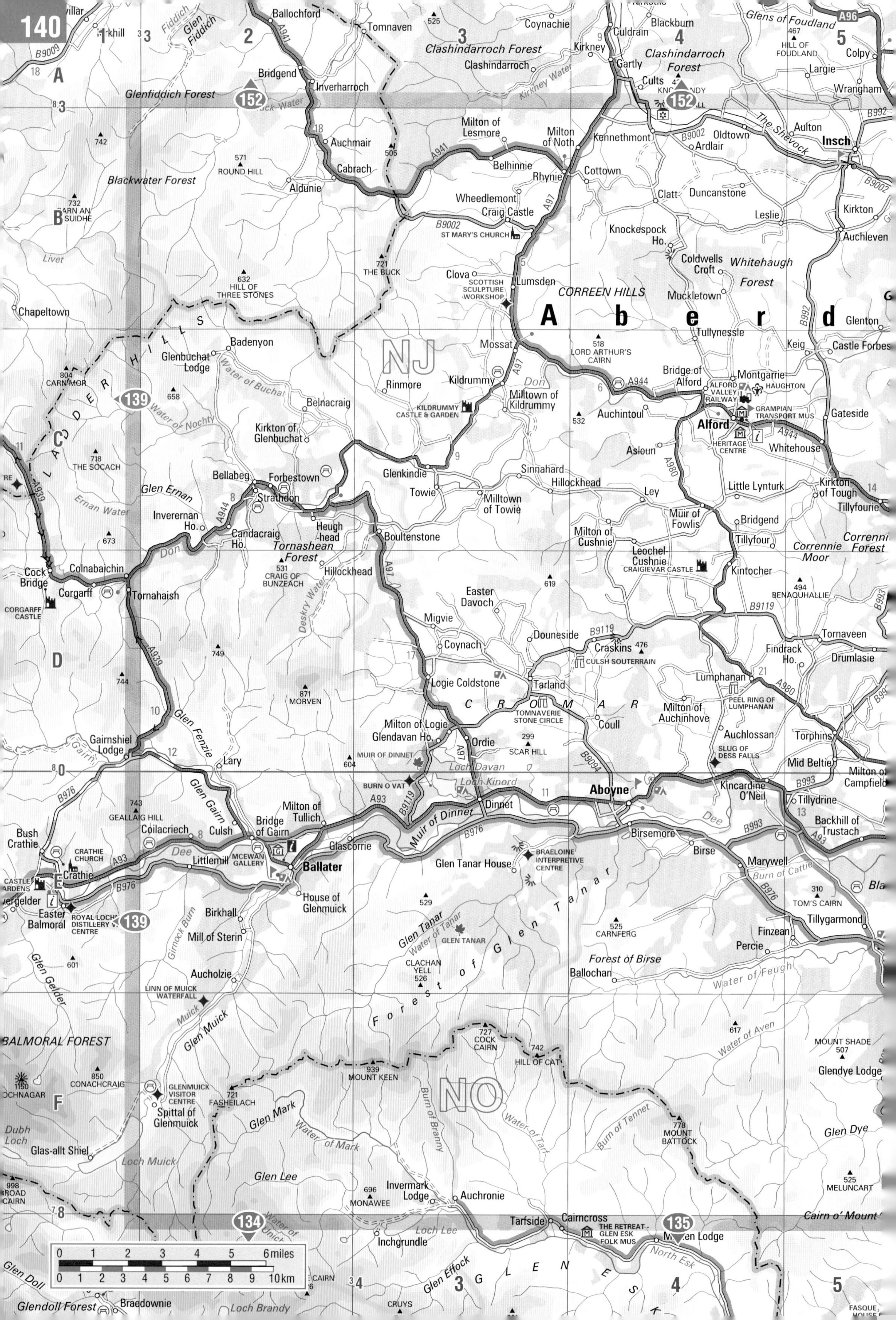
Ballochford
Tomnaven
Coynachie
Culdrain
Blackburn
Glens of Foudland
A96
Glen Fiddich
Fiddich
A941
525
Clashindarroch Forest
Kirkney
Clashindarroch Forest
467
HILL OF FOUDLAND
Colpy
B9009
Clashindarroch
Gartly
Largie
Bridgend
Kirkney Water
Cults
Inverharroch
152
Glenfiddich Forest
Wrangham
B992
742
Auchmair
Milton of Lesmore
Milton of Noth
Kennethmont
B9002
Oldtown
Aulton
The Shevock
Insch
505
571
ROUND HILL
Ardlair
Cabrach
Belhinnie
Cottown
Blackwater Forest
Aldunie
Rhynie
B9002
732
CARN AN SUIDHE
Wheedlemont
Clatt
Duncanstone
Kirkton
Craig Castle
Leslie
A97
B9002
ST MARY'S CHURCH
Knockespock Ho.
Auchleven
Livet
Coldwells Croft
Whitehaugh Forest
721
THE BUCK
Clova
632
HILL OF THREE STONES
SCOTTISH SCULPTURE WORKSHOP
Lumsden
CORREEN HILLS
Muckletown
Chapeltown
A b e r d
Glenton
B992
Tullynessle
Mossat
518
LORD ARTHUR'S CAIRN
Keig
Castle Forbes
Badenyon
NJ
Glenbuchat Lodge
Water of Buchat
804
CARN MOR
L A D D E R H I L L S
139
658
Rinmore
Kildrummy
Don
Milltown of Kildrummy
A944
Bridge of Alford
Montgarrie
ALFORD VALLEY RAILWAY
HAUGHTON
Belnacraig
KILDRUMMY CASTLE & GARDEN
532
Auchintoul
GRAMPIAN TRANSPORT MUS
Gateside
Water of Nochty
Kirkton of Glenbuchat
Alford
HERITAGE CENTRE
A944
Whitehouse
718
THE SOCACH
Asloun
A980
A939
Bellabeg
Forbestown
Glenkindie
Sinnahard
Hillockhead
Little Lynturk
Kirkton of Tough
Glen Ernan
Strathdon
Towie
Milltown of Towie
Ley
Tillyfourie
Ernan Water
Inverernan Ho.
A944
Heugh -head
Muir of Fowlis
Bridgend
Candacraig Ho.
Tornashean Forest
Boultenstone
Milton of Cushnie
Tillyfour
Correnie Forest
673
Leochel-Cushnie
Correnie Moor
Don
Colnabaichin
531
CRAIG OF BUNZEACH
Hillockhead
CRAIGIEVAR CASTLE
Kintocher
Cock Bridge
Corgarff
Tornahaish
Deskry Water
619
494
BENAQUHALLIE
CORGARFF CASTLE
Easter Davoch
B9119
B993
Migvie
Douneside
B9119
Tornaveen
A939
749
Coynach
Craskins
476
Findrack Ho.
Drumlasie
CULSH SOUTERRAIN
D
744
Lumphanan
A980
Tarland
Logie Coldstone
871
MORVEN
C R O M A R
PEEL RING OF LUMPHANAN
TOMNAVERIE STONE CIRCLE
Milton of Auchinhove
Glen Fenzie
Milton of Logie
Coull
Gairnshiel Lodge
Glendavan Ho.
Ordie
299
SCAR HILL
Auchlossan
Torphins
SLUG OF DESS FALLS
Lary
MUIR OF DINNET
B9094
Mid Beltie
604
Loch Davan
A97
Milton of Campfield
B976
Glen Gairn
BURN O VAT
Loch Kinord
Aboyne
Kincardine O'Neil
B993
743
GEALLAIG HILL
A93
Dinnet
Tillydrine
Milton of Tullich
B9119
Muir of Dinnet
Backhill of Trustach
Bush Crathie
Coilacriech
Culsh
Bridge of Gairn
B976
Dee
Birsemore
B993
A93
CRATHIE CHURCH
Glascorrie
BRAELOINE INTERPRETIVE CENTRE
Birse
Crathie
Dee
Littlemill
MCEWAN GALLERY
Ballater
Glen Tanar House
Marywell
Burn of Cattie
CASTLE GARDENS
A93
B976
House of Glenmuick
B976
310
TOM'S CAIRN
Easter Balmoral
ROYAL LOCHNAGAR DISTILLERY VISITOR CENTRE
139
Girnock Burn
Birkhall
529
G l e n T a n a r
Tillygarmond
Mill of Sterin
Glen Tanar
Water of Tanar
GLEN TANAR
525
CARNFERG
Finzean
Percie
Glen Gelder
601
Aucholzie
CLACHAN YELL 526
Forest of Birse
Ballochan
Water of Feugh
LINN OF MUICK WATERFALL
Muick
Glen Muick
F o r e s t o f G l e n T a n a r
617
Water of Aven
MOUNT SHADE 507
BALMORAL FOREST
727
COCK CAIRN
742
HILL OF CAT
Glendye Lodge
850
CONACHCRAIG
939
MOUNT KEEN
1150 LOCHNAGAR
GLENMUICK VISITOR CENTRE
721
FASHEILACH
NO
F
Spittal of Glenmuick
Glen Mark
Burn of Branny
Water of Tarf
Burn of Tennet
778
MOUNT BATTOCK
Glen Dye
Dubh Loch
Water of Mark
Glas-allt Shiel
Loch Muick
Glen Lee
998 BROAD CAIRN
696
MONAWEE
Invermark Lodge
Auchronie
525
MELUNCART
Tarfside
Cairncross
Cairn o' Mount
134
Water of Unich
Loch Lee
THE RETREAT - GLEN ESK FOLK MUS
135
Millden Lodge
North Esk
Inchgrundle
0 1 2 3 4 5 6 miles
0 1 2 3 4 5 6 7 8 9 10km
Glen Doll
CAIRN
Glen Effock
G L E N E S K
Glendoll Forest
Braedownie
Loch Brandy
CRUYS
FASQUE HOUSE
A B C D F
1 2 3 4 5

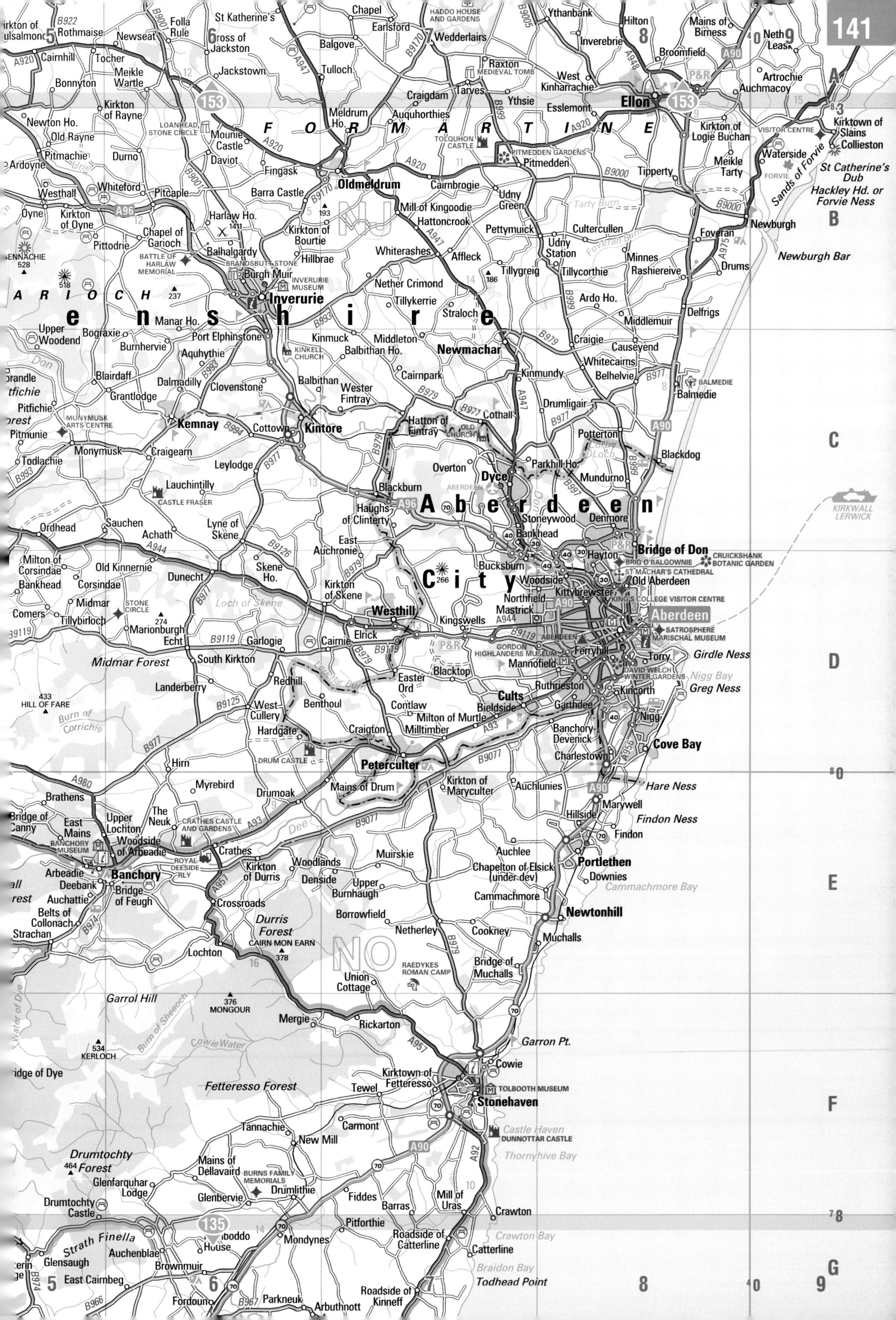

Chapel
Earlsford
HADDO HOUSE AND GARDENS
Wedderlairs
Ythanbank
Hilton
Mains of Birness
Neth Leask
St Katherine's
Folla Rule
Rothmaise
Newseat
Cross of Jackston
Balgove
Tulloch
Raxton
MEDIEVAL TOMB
Inverebrie
Broomfield
West Kinharrachie
Artrochie
Auchmacoy
Cairnhill
Tocher
Meikle Wartle
Bonnyton
Jackstown
Craigdam
Tarves
Ythsie
Esslemont
Ellon
Kirkton of Rayne
Newton Ho.
Old Rayne
Meldrum Ho.
Auquhorthies
Kirkton of Logie Buchan
Kirktown of Slains
Collieston
VISITOR CENTRE
LOANHEAD STONE CIRCLE
Mounie Castle
F O R M A R T I N E
TOLQUHON CASTLE
Pitmachie
Durno
Daviot
Fingask
PITMEDDEN GARDENS
Pitmedden
Waterside
FORVIE
Sands of Forvie
St Catherine's Dub
Hackley Hd. or Forvie Ness
Ardoyne
Whiteford
Pitcaple
Barra Castle
Oldmeldrum
Cairnbrogie
Udny Green
Tipperty
Meikle Tarty
Westhall
Oyne
Kirkton of Oyne
Chapel of Garioch
Pittodrie
Harlaw Ho.
Mill of Kingoodie
Hattoncrook
Pettymuick
Tarty Burn
Cultercullen
Foveran Burn
Udny Station
Foveran
Newburgh
Newburgh Bar
BENNACHIE 528
BATTLE OF HARLAW MEMORIAL
Balhalgardy
BRANDSBUTT STONE
Burgh Muir
Kirkton of Bourtie
Hillbrae
Whiterashes
Affleck
Tillygreig
Tillycorthie
Minnes
Rashierieve
Drums
INVERURIE MUSEUM
Inverurie
Nether Crimond
Tillykerrie
Straloch
Ardo Ho.
Delfrigs
G A R I O C H
A b e r d e e n s h i r e
Upper Woodend
Bograxie
Manar Ho.
Port Elphinstone
Burnhervie
Kinmuck
Middleton
Balbithan Ho.
KINKELL CHURCH
Newmachar
Middlemuir
Craigie
Causeyend
Whitecairns
Belhelvie
BALMEDIE
Balmedie
Don
Brandle
Pitfichie
Aquhythie
Blairdaff
Grantlodge
Dalmadilly
Clovenstone
Balbithan
Wester Fintray
Cairnpark
Kinmundy
Drumligair
Pitfichie
MUNYMUSK ARTS CENTRE
Kemnay
Cottown
Kintore
Hatton of Fintray
OLD CHURCH
Cothall
Potterton
Corby Loch
Blackdog
Pitmunie
Monymusk
Craigearn
Todlachie
Leylodge
Overton
Dyce
Parkhill Ho.
Mundurno
Lauchintilly
CASTLE FRASER
Blackburn
ABERDEEN
Haughs of Clinterty
A b e r d e e n C i t y
Stoneywood
Denmore
KIRKWALL LERWICK
Ordhead
Sauchen
Achath
Lyne of Skene
Bankhead
East Auchronie
Hayton
Bridge of Don
CRUICKSHANK BOTANIC GARDEN
Milton of Corsindae
Old Kinnernie
Skene Ho.
BRIG O' BALGOWNIE
ST MACHAR'S CATHEDRAL
Bucksburn
Woodside
Old Aberdeen
Bankhead
Corsindae
Dunecht
Kirkton of Skene
Kittybrewster
KING'S COLLEGE VISITOR CENTRE
Midmar
STONE CIRCLE
Loch of Skene
Northfield
Mastrick
Aberdeen
Comers
Tillybirloch
Marionburgh
Westhill
Kingswells
SATROSPHERE
MARISCHAL MUSEUM
Echt
Garlogie
Cairnie
Elrick
GORDON HIGHLANDERS MUSEUM
Ferryhill
Torry
Girdle Ness
Midmar Forest
South Kirkton
Mannofield
Nigg Bay
DAVID WELCH WINTER GARDENS
Greg Ness
Landerberry
Redhill
Easter Ord
Blacktop
Ruthrieston
Kincorth
HILL OF FARE 433
Leuchar Burn
Cults
Bieldside
Garthdee
Burn of Corrichie
West Cullery
Benthoul
Contlaw
Milton of Murtle
Milltimber
Hardgate
Craigton
Banchory-Devenick
Nigg
Cove Bay
DRUM CASTLE
Hirn
Peterculter
Charlestown
Kirkton of Maryculter
Auchlunies
Hare Ness
Myrebird
Drumoak
Mains of Drum
Brathens
The Neuk
Marywell
Hillside
Findon Ness
Bridge of Canny
East Mains
Upper Lochton
CRATHES CASTLE AND GARDENS
Dee
Findon
Woodside of Arbeadie
BANCHORY MUSEUM
Crathes
Auchlee
Arbeadie
Banchory
ROYAL DEESIDE RLY
Kirkton of Durris
Woodlands
Muirskie
Chapelton of Elsick (under dev)
Portlethen
Deebank
Bridge of Feugh
Denside
Upper Burnhaugh
Downies
Cammachmore Bay
Auchattie
Crossroads
Cammachmore
Belts of Collonach
Durris Forest
Borrowfield
Newtonhill
Strachan
Netherley
Cookney
Muchalls
Lochton
CAIRN MON EARN 378
NO
RAEDYKES ROMAN CAMP
Bridge of Muchalls
Union Cottage
Garrol Hill
376 MONGOUR
Water of Dye
Burn of Sheeoch
Mergie
Rickarton
Garron Pt.
Cowie Water
534 KERLOCH
Cowie
Bridge of Dye
Fetteresso Forest
Kirktown of Fetteresso
Tewel
TOLBOOTH MUSEUM
Stonehaven
Tannachie
Carmont
Castle Haven
DUNNOTTAR CASTLE
New Mill
Drumtochty Forest 464
Mains of Dellavaird
BURNS FAMILY MEMORIALS
Thornyhive Bay
Glenfarquhar Lodge
Drumlithie
Glenbervie
Fiddes
Mill of Uras
Barras
Drumtochty Castle
Crawton
Strath Finella
Pitforthie
Mondynes
Roadside of Catterline
Crawton Bay
Auchenblae
Catterline
Glensaugh
Brownmuir
Braidon Bay
East Cairnbeg
Roadside of Kinneff
Todhead Point
Fordoun
Parkneuk
Arbuthnott

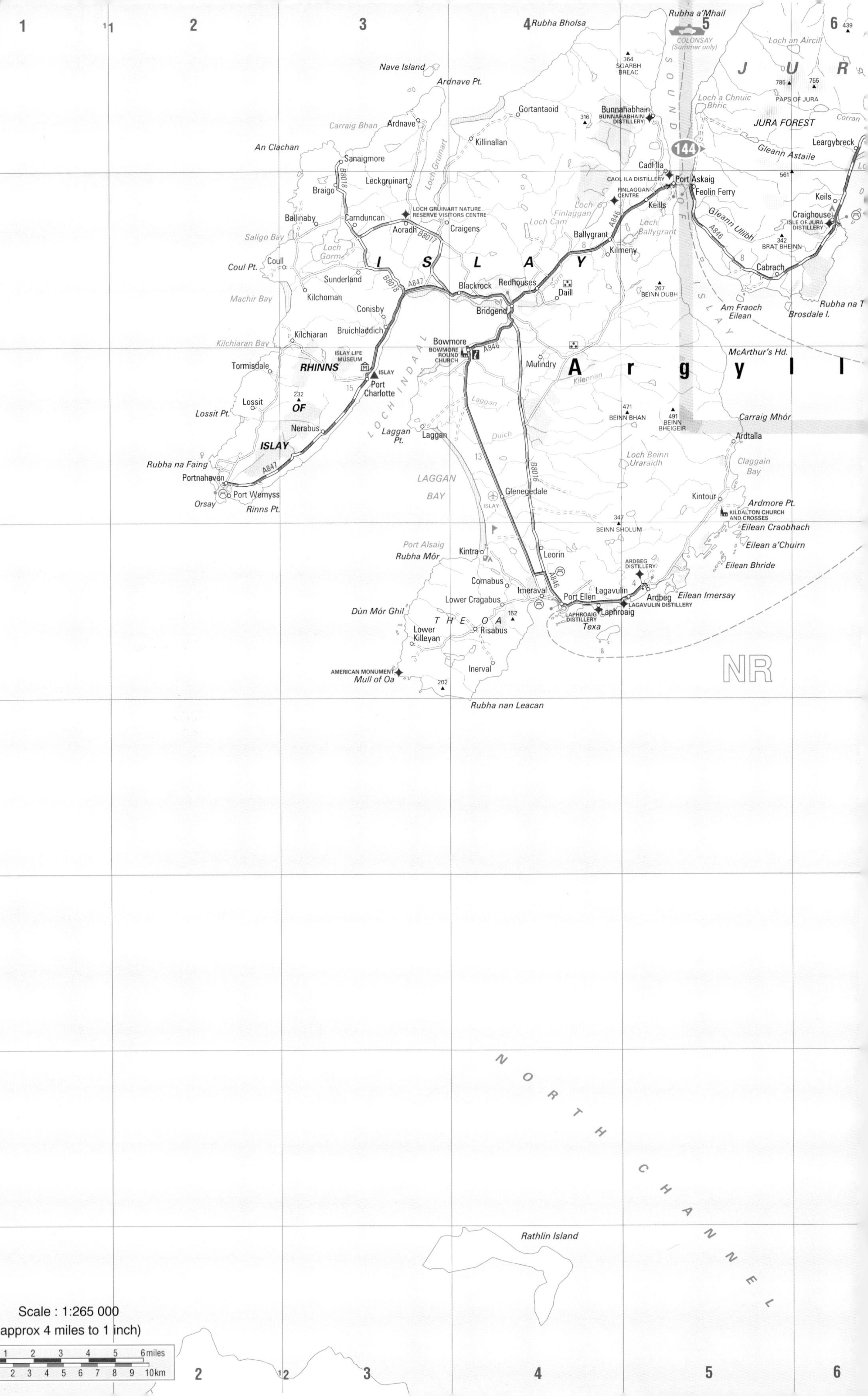

1   1   2   3   4   Rubha Bholsa   5   Rubha a'Mhail   6   439

Nave Island
Ardnave Pt.

COLONSAY
(Summer only)

Loch an Aircill

J   U   R

364
SGARBH
BREAC

785   755
PAPS OF JURA

Gortantaoid

Loch a Chnuic
Bhric

JURA FOREST

Corran

An Clachan

Carraig Bhan   Ardnave

Killinallan

316

Bunnahabhain
BUNNAHABHAIN
DISTILLERY

144

Leargybreck

Gleann Astaile

A   Sanaigmore

561

7   Braigo
B8018   Leckgruinart

Caol Ila
CAOL ILA DISTILLERY

Port Askaig

Keils

Ballinaby   Carnduncan   LOCH GRUINART NATURE
RESERVE VISITORS CENTRE

FINLAGGAN
CENTRE   Keills

Feolin Ferry

Craighouse
ISLE OF JURA
DISTILLERY

342
BRAT BHEINN

Coull   Aoradh   B8017   Craigens   I   S   L   A   Y

Loch Cam

A846

Gleann Ullibh

A846

Coul Pt.   Loch
Gorm   Ballygrant   Cabrach

8

Saligo Bay   B8018   A847   Blackrock   Redhouses
Kilmeny

B   Sunderland   Loch
Ballygrant

Machir Bay   Kilchoman   Conisby   Bridgend   Daill   267
BEINN DUBH   Am Fraoch
Eilean

Rubha na T

Brosdale I.

Kilchiaran   Bruichladdich   Bowmore
BOWMORE
ROUND
CHURCH

Mulindry   McArthur's Hd.

Kilchiaran Bay   Kilchiaran   ISLAY LIFE
MUSEUM

Tormisdale   RHINNS   Port
Charlotte   A   r   g   y   l   l

232   15   Kilennan

471
BEINN BHAN   491
BEINN
BHEIGEIR   Carraig Mhòr

C   Lossit   OF   Laggan
Pt.   13   Ardtalla

Lossit Pt.   Lossit   Duich   Loch Beinn
Uraraidh   Claggain
Bay

Nerabus   ISLAY   Laggan

Rubha na Faing   A847   LAGGAN   Kintour
Ardmore Pt.

Portnahaven   BAY   Glenegedale   347
BEINN SHOLUM   KILDALTON CHURCH
AND CROSSES

Orsay   Port Wemyss   ISLAY   Eilean Craobhach

Rinns Pt.   Eilean a'Chuirn

Port Alsaig   Eilean Bhride

Rubha Mòr   Kintra   ARDBEG
DISTILLERY

D   Dùn Mòr Ghil   Cornabus   Leorin   Ardbeg
Laphroaig   Lagavulin   Ardbeg   Eilean Imersay

Lower Cragabus   Imeraval   Port Ellen   LAGAVULIN DISTILLERY

T   H   E   O   A   152   Risabus   LAPHROAIG
DISTILLERY   Laphroaig

Lower
Killeyan   Texa

AMERICAN MONUMENT   Inerval
Mull of Oa   202   NR

Rubha nan Leacan

E

F

N   O   R   T   H

G   C   H   A   N   N   E   L

Rathlin Island

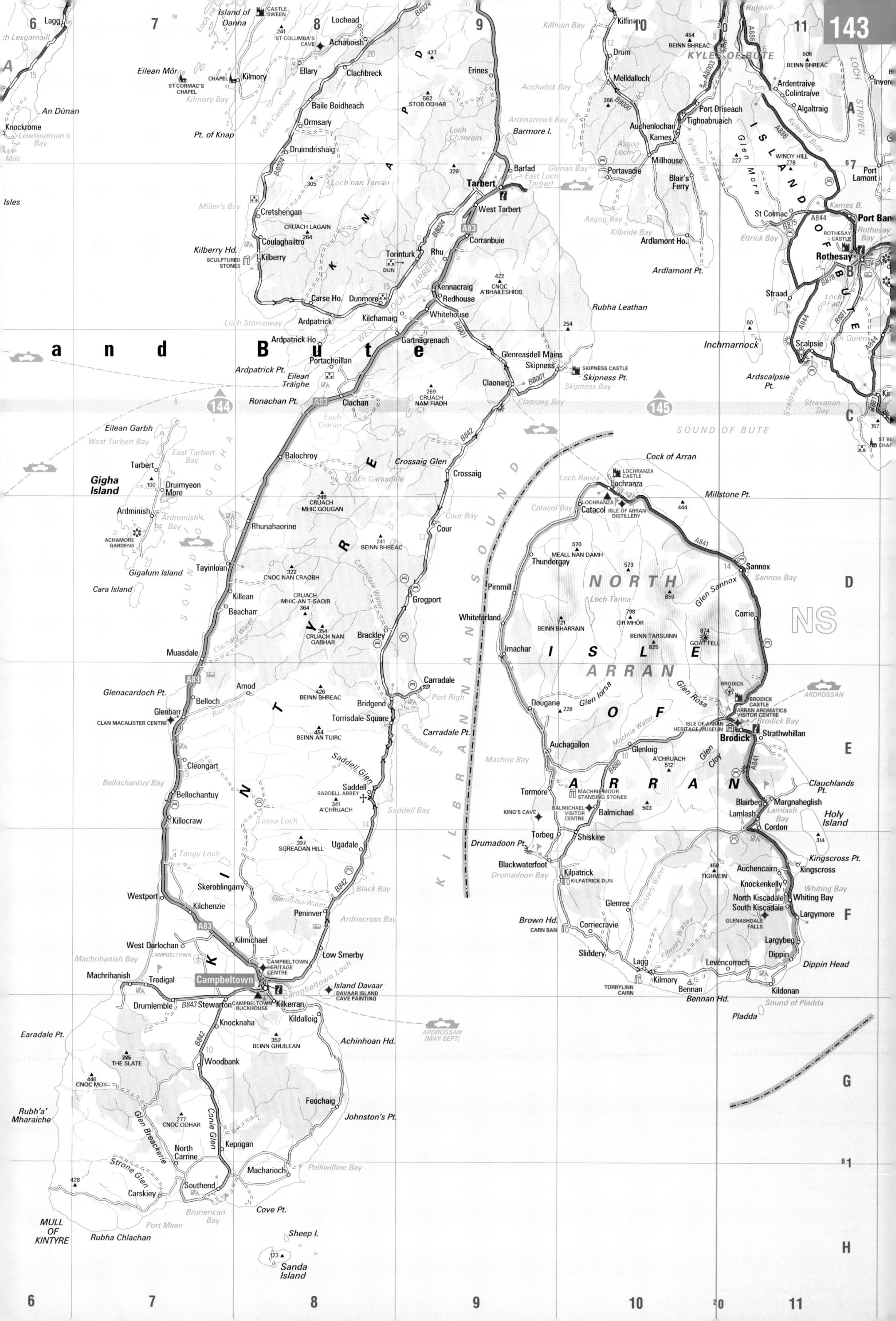

Lagg
Island of Danna
Castle Sween
Lochead
St Columba's Cave
Achahoish
Eilean Mòr
St Cormac's Chapel
Kilmory
Kilmory Bay
Ellary
Clachbreck
Erines
Kilfinan Bay
Kilfinan
Drum
Melldalloch
Beinn Bhreac
Kyles of Bute
Ardentraive
Colintraive
Algaltraig
Loch Striven
An Dùnan
Knockrome
Lowlandman's Bay
Baile Boidheach
Ormsary
Stob Odhar
Auchalick Bay
Ardmarnock Bay
Barmore I.
Pt. of Knap
Loch Chaorain
Auchenlochan
Port Driseach
Tighnabruaich
Kames
Glen More
Island of Bute
Windy Hill
Port Lamont
Druimdrishaig
Asgog Loch
Millhouse
Portavadie
Glenan Bay
Barfad
Tarbert
East Loch Tarbert
West Tarbert
Loch nan Torran
Blair's Ferry
Kames B.
Port Bannatyne
Isles
Miller's Bay
Cretshengan
Cruach Lagain
Coulaghailtro
Kilberry Hd.
Sculptured Stones
Kilberry
Torinturk
Dun
Rhu
Corranbuie
Asgog Bay
Kilbride Bay
Ardlamont Ho.
Ardlamont Pt.
St Colmac
Ettrick Bay
Rothesay Castle
Rothesay
Rothesay Bay
Kennacraig
Redhouse
Cnoc A'Bhaileshios
Carse Ho.
Dunmore
Kilchamaig
Whitehouse
West Loch Tarbert
Loch Stornoway
Ardpatrick
Rubha Leathan
Straad
Loch Fad
Inchmarnock
Scalpsie
Loch Quien
Ardpatrick Ho.
Gartnagrenach
and Bute
Portachoillan
Glenreasdell Mains
Skipness
Skipness Castle
Skipness Pt.
Skipness Bay
Ardpatrick Pt.
Eilean Traighe
Claonaig
Claonaig Bay
Ardscalpsie Pt.
Scalpsie Bay
Stravanan Bay
Ronachan Pt.
Clachan
Cruach nam Fiadh
144
145
Loch Ciaran
Sound of Bute
Eilean Garbh
West Tarbert Bay
East Tarbert Bay
Tarbert
Gigha Island
Druimyeon More
Sound of Gigha
Balochroy
Crossaig Glen
Crossaig
Loch Garasdale
Cock of Arran
Lochranza Castle
Lochranza
Loch Ranza
Millstone Pt.
Ardminish
Ardminish Bay
Achamore Gardens
Cruach Mhic Gougan
Catacol
Catacol Bay
Isle of Arran Distillery
Cour Bay
Cour
Rhunahaorine
Beinn Bhreac
Meall nan Damh
Thundergay
Sannox
Sannox Bay
Gigalum Island
Tayinloan
Cnoc nan Craobh
Cara Island
Killean
Beacharr
Cruach Mhic-an T-Saoir
Grogport
Pirnmill
North
Glen Sannox
Loch Tanna
Cir Mhòr
Corrie
NS
Whitefarland
Beinn Bharrain
Beinn Tarsuinn
Goat Fell
Imachar
Isle
Arran
Muasdale
Clachaig Water
Cruach nan Gabhar
Brackley
Kintyre
Carradale
Port Righ
Amod
Belloch
Barr Water
Glenacardoch Pt.
Glenbarr
Clan Macalister Centre
Beinn Bhreac
Bridgend
Torrisdale-Square
Beinn an Tuirc
Carradale Pt.
Carradale Bay
Kilbrannan Sound
Dougarie
Glen Iorsa
of
Glen Rosa
Brodick
Brodick Castle
Arran Aromatics Visitor Centre
Brodick Bay
Isle of Arran Heritage Museum
Strathwhillan
Ardrossan
Auchagallon
Machrie Water
Glenloig
Glen Cloy
A'Chruach
Machrie Bay
Cleongart
Saddell Glen
Saddell
Saddell Abbey
A'Chruach
Bellochantuy Bay
Bellochantuy
Tormore
Machrie Moor Standing Stones
Clauchlands Pt.
Killocraw
Lussa Loch
Saddell Bay
King's Cave
Balmichael Visitor Centre
Balmichael
Blairbeg
Margnaheglish
Lamlash
Lamlash Bay
Holy Island
Cordon
Tangy Loch
Sgreadan Hill
Ugadale
Torbeg
Shiskine
Drumadoon Pt.
Blackwaterfoot
Drumadoon Bay
Kilpatrick
Kilpatrick Dun
Kingscross Pt.
Kingscross
Auchencairn
Tighvein
Knockenkelly
Whiting Bay
Westport
Skeroblingarry
Kilchenzie
Black Bay
Glenlussa Water
Peninver
Ardnacross Bay
Sliddery Water
Glenree
North Kiscadale
South Kiscadale
Glenashdale Falls
Largymore
Brown Hd.
Carn Ban
Corriecravie
Kilmory Water
Kilmichael
West Darlochan
Campbeltown
Low Smerby
Sliddery
Largybeg
Dippin
Dippin Head
Machrihanish Bay
Campbeltown Heritage Centre
Machrihanish
Trodigal
Campbeltown Loch
Island Davaar
Davaar Island Cave Painting
Lagg
Kilmory
Levencorroch
Torrylinn Cairn
Bennan
Bennan Hd.
Kildonan
Sound of Pladda
Pladda
Drumlemble
Stewarton
Campbeltown Buckhouse
Kilkerran
Kildalloig
Ardrossan (May-Sept)
Knocknaha
Eeradale Pt.
Beinn Ghuilean
Achinhoan Hd.
The Slate
Woodbank
Cnoc Moy
Feochaig
Rubh'a' Mharaiche
Glen Breackerie
Cnoc Odhar
Conie Glen
Johnston's Pt.
North Carrine
Keprigan
Strone Glen
Macharioch
Polliwilline Bay
Southend
Carskiey
Cove Pt.
Brunerican Bay
Port Mean
Mull of Kintyre
Rubha Chlachan
Sheep I.
Sanda Island

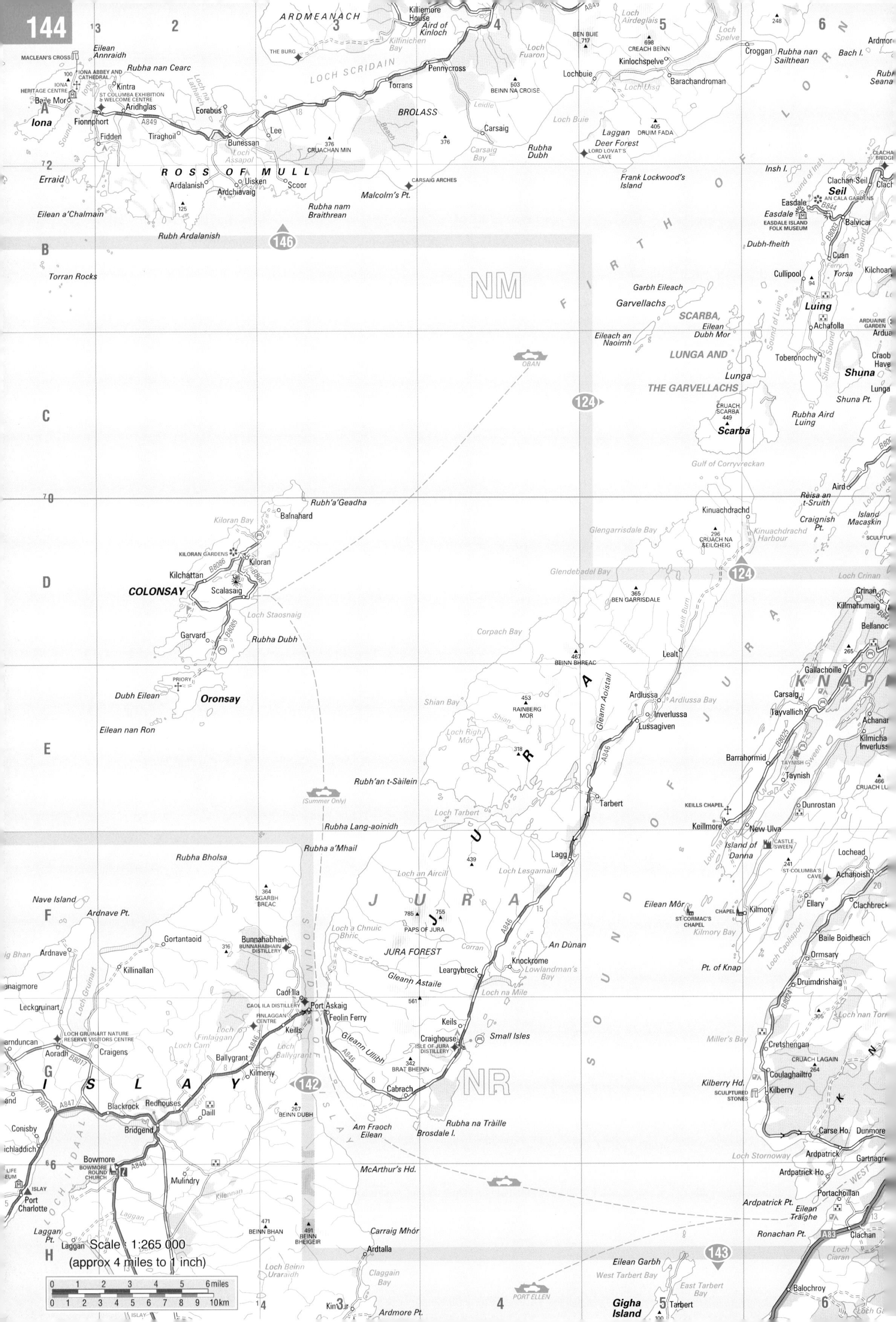

ARDMEANACH
Killiemore House
Aird of Kinloch
Kilfinichen Bay
THE BURG
LOCH SCRIDAIN
Pennycross
Torrans
Loch Airdeglais
Loch Spelve
Croggan
Rubha nan Sailthean
Bach I.
Ardmor
BEN BUIE 717
698 CREACH BEINN
Kinlochspelve
Barachandroman
Lochbuie
Loch Uisg
Loch Fuaron
503 BEINN NA CROISE
BROLASS
Leidle
Carsaig
Carsaig Bay
Rubha Dubh
Loch Buie
Laggan Deer Forest
405 DRUIM FADA
LORD LOVAT'S CAVE
MACLEAN'S CROSS
Eilean Annraidh
IONA ABBEY AND CATHEDRAL
Rubha nan Cearc
IONA HERITAGE CENTRE
ST COLUMBA EXHIBITION & WELCOME CENTRE
Kintra
Baile Mor
Iona
Sound of Iona
Fionnphort
Aridhglas
Fidden
Tiraghoil
Loch na Lathaich
Eorabus
Bunessan
Loch Assapol
Lee
376 CRUACHAN MIN
376
ROSS OF MULL
Erraid
Ardalanish
Uisken
Ardchiavaig
Scoor
CARSAIG ARCHES
Malcolm's Pt.
Rubha nam Braithrean
125
Eilean a'Chalmain
Rubh Ardalanish
146
Frank Lockwood's Island
Insh I.
Sound of Insh
Clachan-Seil
Seil
Easdale
AN CALA GARDENS
Easdale
EASDALE ISLAND FOLK MUSEUM
Balvicar
Dubh-fheith
Cuan
Seil Sound
Cullipool
94
Torsa
Kilchoan
Luing
Achafolla
ARDUAINE GARDEN
Sound of Luing
Garbh Eileach
Garvellachs
SCARBA, Eilean Dubh Mor
LUNGA AND THE GARVELLACHS
Eileach an Naoimh
Toberonochy
Shuna Sound
Craobh Haven
Shuna
Lunga
Shuna Pt.
Rubha Aird Luing
CRUACH SCARBA 449
Scarba
Gulf of Corryvreckan
FIRTH OF LORN
NM
B
Torran Rocks
OBAN
124
Aird
Rèisa an t-Sruith
Craignish Pt.
Island Macaskin
Loch Craignish
Kinuachdrachd
Kinuachdrachd Harbour
296 CRUACH NA SEILCHEIG
Glengarrisdale Bay
Glendebadel Bay
124
Loch Crinan
Crinan
Kilmahumaig
Bellanoch
Rubh'a'Geadha
Balnahard
Kiloran Bay
KILORAN GARDENS
Kiloran
Kilchattan
COLONSAY
Scalasaig
Loch Staosnaig
Garvard
Rubha Dubh
365 BEN GARRISDALE
Corpach Bay
Lussa
Lealt Burn
Lealt
467 BEINN BHREAC
265
Gallachoille
KNAPDALE
Carsaig
Tayvallich
PRIORY
Dubh Eilean
Oronsay
Eilean nan Ron
Shian Bay
453 RAINBERG MOR
Loch Righ Mòr
Gleann Aoistail
Ardlussa
Ardlussa Bay
Inverlussa
Lussagiven
318
Achanar
Kilmichael Inverlussa
Barrahormid
TAYNISH
Taynish
Loch Sween
466 CRUACH LU
(Summer Only)
Rubh'an t-Sàilein
Tarbert
Loch Tarbert
KEILLS CHAPEL
Dunrostan
Keillmore
New Ulva
Rubha Lang-aoinidh
Rubha a'Mhail
Rubha Bholsa
439
Loch an Aircill
Lagg
Loch Lesgamaill
Island of Danna
CASTLE SWEEN
Lochead
241 ST COLUMBA'S CAVE
Achahoish
Nave Island
Ardnave Pt.
364 SGARBH BREAC
JURA
785
755
PAPS OF JURA
15
Eilean Mòr
ST CORMAC'S CHAPEL
CHAPEL
Kilmory
Kilmory Bay
Ellary
Clachbreck
Gortantaoid
Ardnave
316
Bunnahabhain
BUNNAHABHAIN DISTILLERY
Loch a Chnuic Bhric
JURA FOREST
Corran
An Dùnan
Knockrome
Lowlandman's Bay
Baile Boidheach
Ormsary
Killinallan
Loch Gruinart
Gleann Astaile
Leargybreck
Loch na Mile
Pt. of Knap
Loch Caolisport
Druimdrishaig
Caol Ila
CAOL ILA DISTILLERY
Port Askaig
Feolin Ferry
561
Leckgruinart
FINLAGGAN CENTRE
Keills
Loch Finlaggan
Gleann Ullibh
Keils
Craighouse
ISLE OF JURA DISTILLERY
Small Isles
306
Loch nan Torr
LOCH GRUINART NATURE RESERVE VISITORS CENTRE
Aoradh
Craigens
Loch Carn
Loch Ballygrant
Ballygrant
Miller's Bay
Cretshengan
CRUACH LAGAIN 264
ISLAY
Kilmeny
142
342 BRAT BHEINN
Cabrach
NR
Kilberry Hd.
SCULPTURED STONES
Coulaghailtro
Kilberry
Blackrock
Redhouses
Daill
267 BEINN DUBH
SOUND OF ISLAY
Conisby
Bridgend
Am Fraoch Eilean
Brosdale I.
Rubha na Tràille
Carse Ho.
Dunmore
Bowmore
BOWMORE ROUND CHURCH
LOCH INDAAL
Mulindry
McArthur's Hd.
Loch Stornoway
Ardpatrick
Gartnagrenach
Ardpatrick Ho.
WEST LOCH TARBERT
Port Charlotte
Kilennan
Portachoillan
Ardpatrick Pt.
Eilean Traighe
Laggan Pt.
Laggan
471 BEINN BHAN
491 BEINN BHEIGEIR
Carraig Mhór
Ronachan Pt.
Clachan
Scale 1:265 000
(approx 4 miles to 1 inch)
0 1 2 3 4 5 6 miles
0 1 2 3 4 5 6 7 8 9 10 km
Ardtalla
143
Eilean Garbh
Loch Beinn Uraraidh
Claggain Bay
West Tarbert Bay
East Tarbert Bay
PORT ELLEN
Gigha Island
Tarbert
Balochroy
Kintour
Ardmore Pt.
A849
A846
A847
A83
B8086
B8087
B8085
B8017
B8018
B8002
B844
B8025
B8024

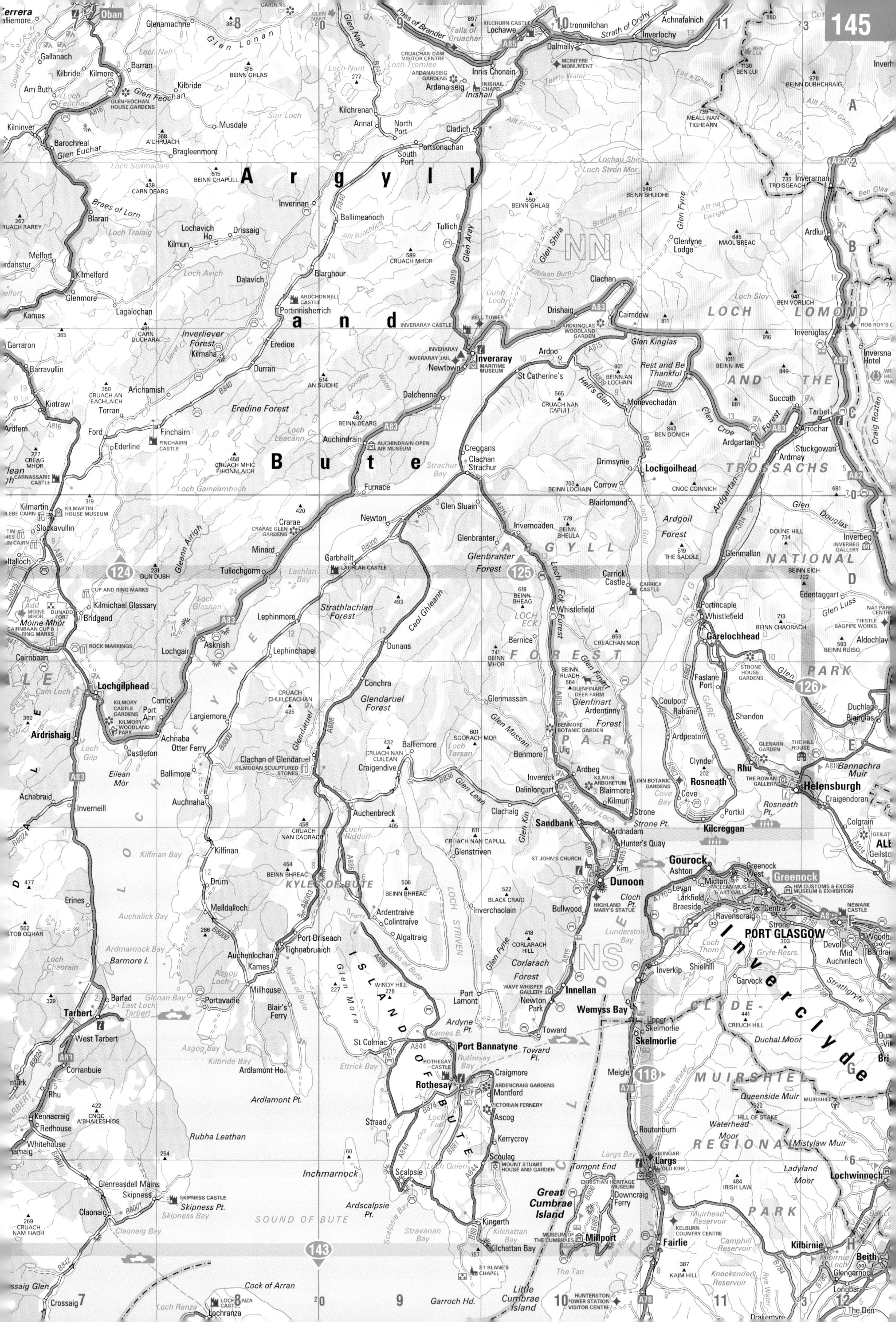
Argyll
and
Bute
ARGYLL
FOREST
PARK
LOCH LOMOND
AND THE
TROSSACHS
NATIONAL
PARK
Inverclyde
CLYDE
MUIRSHIEL
REGIONAL
PARK
NN
NS
Oban
Kerrera
Glenamachrie
Glen Lonan
Gallanach
Kilbride
Kilmore
Barran
Am Buth
Glen Feochan
Glenfeochan House Gardens
Kilninver
Barochreal
Glen Euchar
Bragleenmore
Musdale
A'Chruach
Braes of Lorn
Blaran
Loch Tralaig
Lochavich Ho
Drissaig
Kilmun
Loch Avich
Melfort
Kilmelford
Glenmore
Kames
Lagalochan
Dalavich
Carn Duchara
Inverliever Forest
Kilmaha
Eredine
Durran
Arichamish
Cruach an Eachlaich
Torran
Kintraw
Ford
Ederline
Finchairn
Finchairn Castle
Eredine Forest
Cruach Mhic Fhionnlaich
Loch Gaineamhach
Kilmartin
Kilmartin House Museum
Slockavullin
Cup and Ring Marks
Kilmichael Glassary
Dunadd Fort
Moine Mhor
Bridgend
Rock Markings
Cairnbaan
Lochgilphead
Kilmory Castle Gardens
Kilmory Woodland Park
Ardrishaig
Crinan Canal
Loch Gilp
Achabraid
Inverneill
Erines
Stob Odhar
Barmore I.
Loch Chaorain
Barfad
Tarbert
West Tarbert
East Loch Tarbert
Corranbuie
Rhu
Kennacraig
Redhouse
Whitehouse
Cnoc a'Bhaileshios
Glenreasdell Mains
Skipness
Skipness Castle
Skipness Pt.
Skipness Bay
Claonaig
Claonaig Bay
Cruach nam Fiadh
Crossaig
Lochranza
Loch Ranza
Cock of Arran
Sound of Bute
Inchmarnock
Rubha Leathan
Ardlamont Pt.
Ardlamont Ho.
Kilbride Bay
Asgog Bay
Portavadie
Millhouse
Kames
Tighnabruaich
Auchenlochan
Melldalloch
Drum
Kilfinan
Kilfinan Bay
Auchalick Bay
Ardmarnock Bay
Glenan Bay
Blair's Ferry
Auchnaha
Ballimore
Otter Ferry
Achnaba
Castleton
Eilean Mòr
Largiemore
Loch Fyne
Port Ann
Carrick
Lochgair
Asknish
Lephinmore
Lephinchapel
Minard
Tullochgorm
Crarae
Crarae Glen Gardens
Furnace
Auchindrain
Auchindrain Open Air Museum
Dalchenna
Inveraray
Inveraray Castle
Inveraray Jail
Newtown
Maritime Museum
Bell Tower
Ardchonnell Castle
Portinnisherrich
Blarghour
Cruach Mhor
Ballimeanoch
Inverinan
Loch Awe
South Port
Portsonachan
North Port
Annat
Kilchrenan
Cladich
Innis Chonain
Ardanaiseig Gardens
Ardanaiseig
Inishail Chapel
Cruachan Dam Visitor Centre
Loch Tromlee
Glen Nant
Falls of Cruachan
Pass of Brander
Kilchurn Castle
Lochawe
Dalmally
McIntyre Monument
Tyndrum
Strath of Orchy
Inverlochy
Achnafalnich
Ben Lui
Beinn Dubhchraig
Meall nan Tighearn
Glen Fyne
Glenfyne Lodge
Maol Breac
Beinn Bhuidhe
Beinn Ghlas
Brannie Burn
Glen Shira
Lochan Shira
Loch Stron Mor
Tullich
Glen Aray
Dubh Loch
Clachan
Drishaig
Cairndow
Ardkinglas Woodland Garden
Glen Kinglas
Rest and Be Thankful
Hell's Glen
Beinn an Lochain
Ardno
St Catherine's
Cruach nan Capull
Mnevechadan
Glen Croe
Beinn Donich
Ardgartan
Arrochar
Tarbet
Succoth
Loch Sloy
Ben Vorlich
Inveruglas
Beinn Ime
Inverarnan
Troisgeach
Ardlui
Rob Roy's Cave
Inversnaid Hotel
Craig Rostan
Stuckgowan
Ardmay
Glen Douglas
Doune Hill
Inverbeg
Beinn Eich
Edentaggart
Glen Luss
Beinn Chaorach
Aldochlay
Beinn Ruisg
Glen Fruin
Strachur
Clachan Strachur
Creggans
Strachur Bay
Glen Sluain
Newton
Garbhallt
Lachlan Castle
Lachlan Bay
Strathlachlan Forest
Caol Ghleann
Dunans
Conchra
Glendaruel Forest
Glendaruel
Clachan of Glendaruel
Kilmodan Sculptured Stones
Cruach Chuilceachan
Balliemore
Cruach nan Cuilean
Craigendive
Glen Lean
Auchenbreck
Cruach nan Caorach
Loch Riddon
Kyles of Bute
Beinn Bhreac
Ardentraive
Colintraive
Algaltraig
Port Driseach
Glen More
Island of Bute
Windy Hill
Ardyne Pt.
Port Lamont
Kames B.
St Colmac
Port Bannatyne
Ettrick Bay
Rothesay
Rothesay Castle
Rothesay Bay
Craigmore
Ardencraig Gardens
Montford
Victorian Fernery
Ascog
Kerrycroy
Scoulag
Mount Stuart House and Garden
Straad
Loch Fad
Loch Quien
Scalpsie
Scalpsie Bay
Ardscalpsie Pt.
Stravanan Bay
Kingarth
Kilchattan Bay
St Blane's Chapel
Garroch Hd.
Glenbranter
Glenbranter Forest
Invernoaden
Beinn Bheula
Drimsynie
Lochgoilhead
Corrow
Beinn Lochain
Cnoc Coinnich
Blairlomond
Loch Goil
Ardgoil Forest
The Saddle
Carrick Castle
Loch Eck
Whistlefield
Beinn Bheag
Bernice
Beinn Mhor
Creachan Mor
Glen Finart
Glenfinart Deer Farm
Beinn Ruadh
Ardentinny
Glenmassan
Glen Massan
Sgorach Mor
Loch Tarsan
Benmore
Benmore Botanic Garden
Uig
Ardbeg
Kilmun Arboretum
Inverechaig
Dalinlongart
Blairmore
Kilmun
Strone
Strone Pt.
Holy Loch
Clachaig
Sandbank
Ardnadam
Hunter's Quay
Kirn
Dunoon
St John's Church
Highland Mary's Statue
Cloch Pt.
Bullwood
Loch Striven
Glenstriven
Black Craig
Inverchaolain
Corlarach Hill
Corlarach Forest
Wave Whisper Gallery
Newton Park
Innellan
Toward
Toward Pt.
Wemyss Bay
Lunderston Bay
Glen Kin
Portincaple
Whistlefield
Garelochhead
Faslane Port
Coulport
Rahane
Gare Loch
Loch Long
Ardpeaton
Clynder
Rosneath
Cove
Portkil
Kilcreggan
Rosneath Pt.
Shandon
Strone House Gardens
Glenarn Garden
The Hill House
Rhu
The Rowan Gallery
Helensburgh
Craigendoran
Colgrain
Duchlage
Blairglas
Bannachra Muir
Gourock
Ashton
Greenock
Greenock West
Midton
McLean Mus & Art Gall
HM Customs & Excise Museum & Exhibition
Newark Castle
Port Glasgow
Levan
Larkfield
Braeside
Ravenscraig
Central
Strone
Loch Thom
Gryfe Resrs.
Devol
Mid Auchinlech
Inverkip
Shielhill
Garvock
Strathgryfe
Upper Skelmorlie
Skelmorlie
Creuch Hill
Duchal Moor
Meigle
Queenside Muir
Hill of Stake
Muirshiel
Waterhead Moor
Mistylaw Muir
Routenburn
Largs
Largs Bay
Vikingar! Old Kirk
Ladyland Moor
Lochwinnoch
Irish Law
Great Cumbrae Island
Christian Heritage Museum
Tomont End
Downcraig Ferry
Millport
Museum of the Cumbraes
Fairlie
Fairlie Roads
Kelburn Country Centre
Muirhead Reservoir
Camphill Reservoir
Kilbirnie
Kilbirnie Loch
Beith
Glengarnock
Kaim Hill
Knockendon Reservoir
Little Cumbrae Island
The Tan
Hunterston Power Station Visitor Centre
124
125
126
118
143

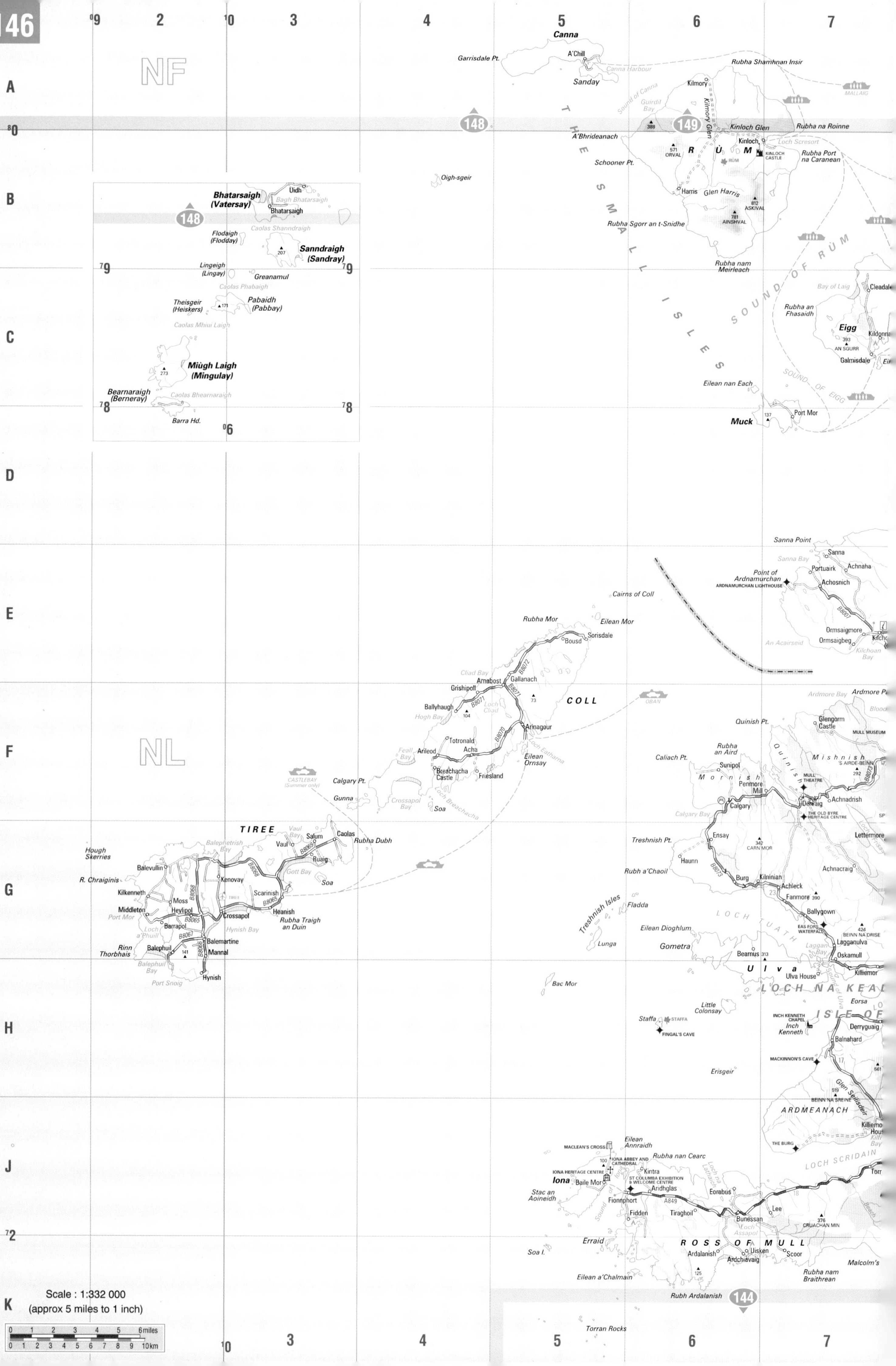

NF

Canna
Garrisdale Pt.
A'Chill
Sanday
Canna Harbour
Rubha Shamhnan Insir
Kilmory
MALLAIG
Guirdil Bay
A'Bhrideanach
Kinloch Glen
Rubha na Roinne
Kinloch
Loch Scresort
571 ORVAL
RÙM
RÙM
KINLOCH CASTLE
Rubha Port na Caranean
Schooner Pt.
Harris
Glen Harris
Rubha Sgorr an t-Snidhe
812 ASKIVAL
781 AINSHVAL
Rubha nam Meirleach
SOUND OF RÙM

THE SMALL ISLES

Oigh-sgeir

Bhatarsaigh (Vatersay)
Bagh Bhatarsaigh
Uidh
Bhatarsaigh
Flodaigh (Flodday)
Caolas Shanndraigh
79
Sanndraigh (Sandray)
79
207
Lingeigh (Lingay)
Greanamul
Theisgeir (Heiskers)
171
Pabaidh (Pabbay)
Caolas Phabaigh
Caolas Mhiui Laigh
273
Miùgh Laigh (Mingulay)
Bearnaraigh (Berneray)
Caolas Bhearnaraigh
78
78
Barra Hd.
06

Bay of Laig
Cleadale
Rubha an Fhasaidh
Eigg
393
Kildonna
AN SGURR
Galmisdale
Eil
SOUND OF EIGG
Eilean nan Each
Muck
137
Port Mor

NL

Sanna Point
Sanna Bay
Sanna
Achnaha
Point of Ardnamurchan
Portuairk
ARDNAMURCHAN LIGHTHOUSE
Achosnich
B8007
Cairns of Coll
Rubha Mor
Eilean Mor
Sorisdale
Bousd
An Acairseid
Ormsaigmore
Kilcho
Ormsaigbeg
Kilchoan Bay
Cliad Bay
Amabost
Gallanach
Grishipoll
B8072
B8071
COLL
Ballyhaugh
104
73
OBAN
Loch Chad
Ardmore Bay
Ardmore Pt
Hogh Bay
Arinagour
Blood
Totronald
Acha
Arileod
B8070
Loch Eatharna
Eilean Ornsay
Caliach Pt.
Rubha an Aird
Quinish Pt.
Glengorm Castle
MULL MUSEUM
Feall Bay
Breachacha Castle
Friesland
Sunipol
Mornish
Penmore Mill
Mishnish
S AIRDE-BEINN
292
CASTLEBAY (Summer only)
Calgary Pt.
Gunna
Crossapol Bay
Soa
Loch Breachacha
Calgary Bay
Dervaig
MULL THEATRE
Achnadrish
THE OLD BYRE HERITAGE CENTRE
Lettermore
SP
TIREE
Vaul Bay
Balephetrish Bay
Salum
Caolas
Rubha Dubh
Calgary
Ensay
342
CARN MOR
Hough Skerries
Balevullin
Vaul
B8068
Ruaig
Gott Bay
Soa
Treshnish Pt.
Haunn
B8073
Burg
Kilninian
231
Achleck
R. Chraiginis
Kenovay
TIREE
Scarinish
B8065
Heanish
Rubh a'Chaoil
Fanmore
390
Kilkenneth
B8066
Moss
B8065
Crossapol
Rubha Traigh an Duin
Treshnish Isles
Fladda
LOCH TUATH
Ballygown
EAS FORS WATERFALL
424
BEINN NA DRISE
Middleton
Heylipol
Barrapol
Balemartine
B8067
Hynish Bay
Eilean Dioghlum
Lunga
Eilean Dioghlum
Gometra
Bearnus
313
Lagganulva
Laggan
Oskamull
Rinn Thorbhais
Balephuil
141
Mannal
Bac Mor
ULVA
Ulva House
Killiemor
Balephuil Bay
Hynish
Port Snoig
Ulva Ho.
LOCH NA KEAL
ISLE OF
Eorsa
Staffa
STAFFA
Little Colonsay
INCH KENNETH CHAPEL
Inch Kenneth
Derryguaig
FINGAL'S CAVE
Balnahard
MACKINNON'S CAVE
Erisgeir
17
561
ARDMEANACH
599
BEINN NA SREINE
Glen Seilisdeir
Killiemor Hous
THE BURG
MACLEAN'S CROSS
Eilean Annraidh
Rubha nan Cearc
LOCH SCRIDAIN
100
IONA ABBEY AND CATHEDRAL
Kintra
St COLUMBA EXHIBITION & WELCOME CENTRE
Ardnaglas
IONA HERITAGE CENTRE
Iona
Baile Mor
Eorabus
Torr
Stac an Aoineadh
Fionnphort
A849
Lee
Fidden
Tiraghoil
Bunessan
376
CRUACHAN MIN
72
Erraid
ROSS OF MULL
Uisken
Scoor
Soa I.
Ardalanish
125
Ardchiavaig
Malcolm's
Eilean a'Chalmain
Rubha nam Braithrean
Rubh Ardalanish
Torran Rocks

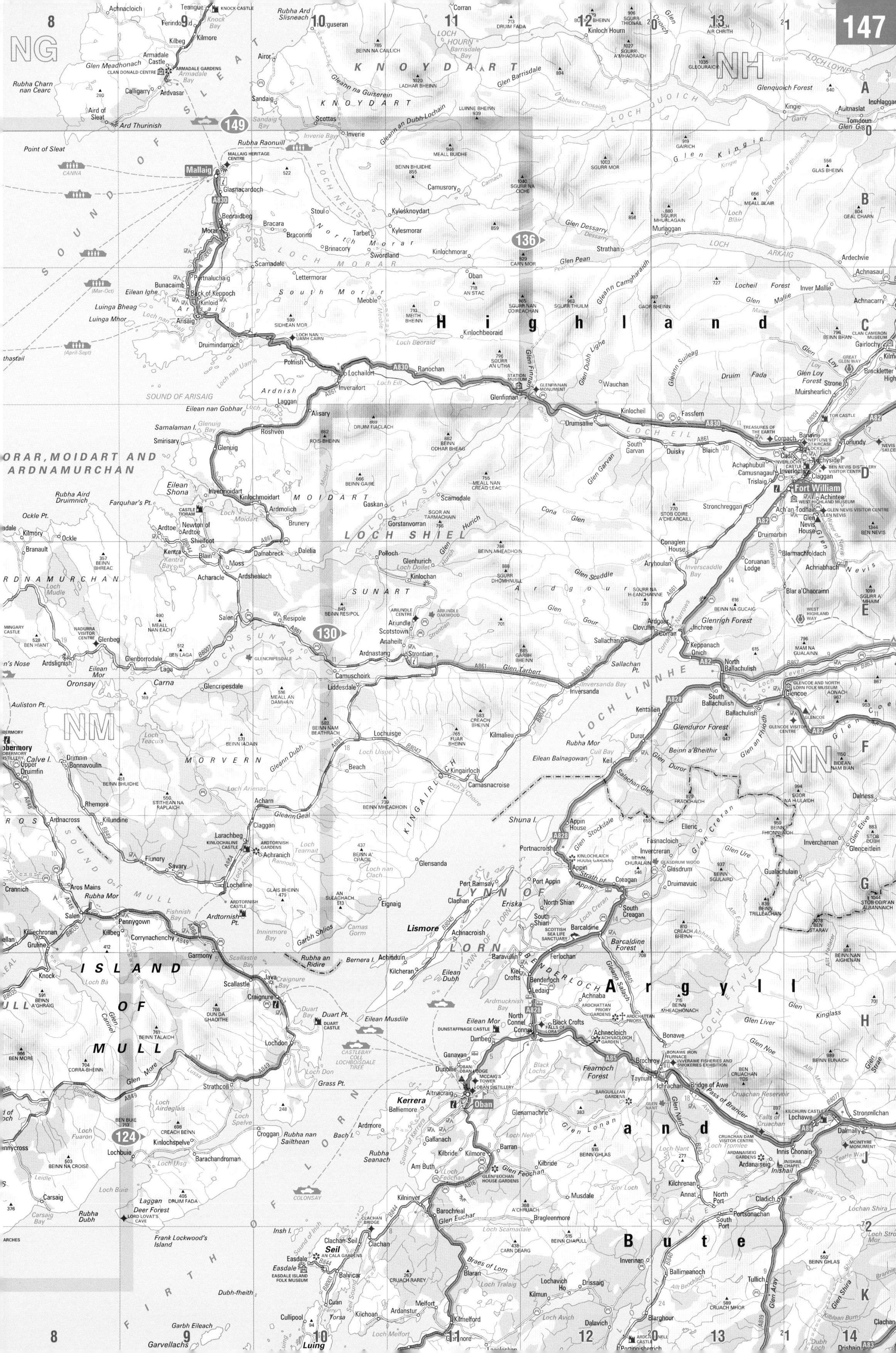
NG
NH
NM
NN
Highland
Argyll and Bute
KNOYDART
MORAR, MOIDART AND ARDNAMURCHAN
MOIDART
SUNART
MORVERN
ISLAND OF MULL
LORN
BENDERLOCH
SOUND OF SLEAT
SOUND OF ARISAIG
SOUND OF MULL
FIRTH OF LORN
LOCH LINNHE
LOCH SHIEL
LOCH SUNART
LOCH EIL
LOCH ARKAIG
LOCH QUOICH
LOCH MORAR
LOCH NEVIS
LOCH HOURN
LOCH ETIVE
LYNN OF LORN
Mallaig
Fort William
Oban
Armadale
Ardvasar
Inverie
Arisaig
Glenfinnan
Lochailort
Acharacle
Salen
Strontian
Kilchoan
Tobermory
Craignure
Lochaline
Corran
Ardgour
Kentallen
Ballachulish
Glencoe
Appin
Lismore
Kerrera
Connel
Taynuilt
Dalmally
Inveraray
Kilmelford
Seil
Easdale
Luing
Garvellachs
Lochbuie
Kilninver
Ben Nevis
Banavie
Corpach
Spean Bridge
A830
A861
A82
A828
A85
A816
A849
A884
B8043
136
130
149
124

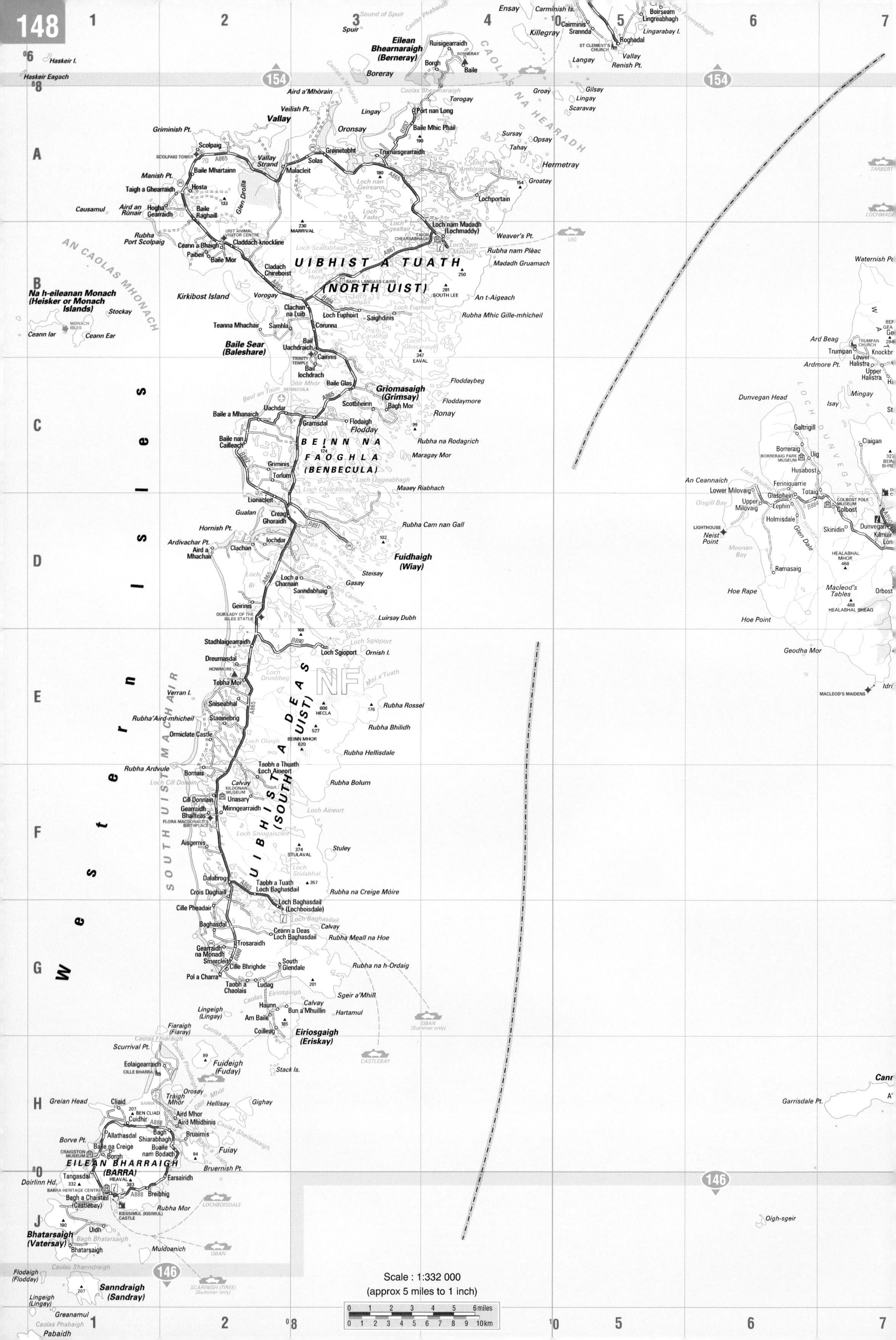

Eilean Bhearnaraigh (Berneray)
Ruisigearraidh
Borgh
Baile
Boreray
Sound of Spuir
Spuir
Ensay
Carminish Is.
Killegray
Cairminis
Srannda
Boirseam
Lingreabhagh
Lingarabay I.
Roghadal
ST CLEMENT'S CHURCH
Langay
Vallay
Renish Pt.
Haskeir I.
Haskeir Eagach
154
Aird a'Mhòrain
Caolas Bhearnaraigh
Groay
Gilsay
Lingay
Scaravay
Torogay
Port nan Long
Baile Mhic Phail
Veilish Pt.
Vallay
Lingay
Oronsay
CAOLAS NA HEARADH
Sursay
Tahay
Opsay
Hermetray
Griminish Pt.
Scolpaig
SCOLPAIG TOWER
Vallay Strand
Solas
Greinetobht
Trumaisgearraidh
Malacleit
Loch nan Geireann
Groatay
Lochportain
Baile Mhartainn
Manish Pt.
Taigh a Ghearraidh
Hosta
Glen Drolla
Aird an Runair
Hogha Gearraidh
Baile Raghaill
Causamul
Loch Fada
230 MARRIVAL
Loch nam Madadh (Lochmaddy)
TAIGH CHEARSABHAGH
Weaver's Pt.
UIG
Rubha Port Scolpaig
UIST ANIMAL VISITOR CENTRE
Claddach-knockline
Ceann a Bhaigh
Paibeil
Baile Mor
Loch Scadabhagh
Rubha nam Plèac
Madadh Gruamach
AN CAOLAS MHONACH
UIBHIST A TUATH (NORTH UIST)
Cladach Chireboist
BARPA LANGASS CAIRN
250
281 SOUTH LEE
Na h-eileanan Monach (Heisker or Monach Islands)
Kirkibost Island
Vorogay
An t-Aigeach
Stockay
MONACH ISLES
Ceann Iar
Ceann Ear
Clachan na Luib
Loch Euphoirt
Saighdinis
Rubha Mhic Gille-mhicheil
Teanna Mhachair
Samhla
Corunna
Baile Sear (Baleshare)
Bail Uachdrach
Cairinis
TRINITY TEMPLE
347 EAVAL
Bail Iochdrach
Oitir Mhòr
Baile Glas
Floddaybeg
Griomasaigh (Grimsay)
Floddaymore
Beul an Toim
BENBECULA
Scotbheinn
Bagh Mor
Ronay
Uachdar
Baile a Mhanaich
Gramsdal
Flodaigh
Flodday
BEINN NA FAOGHLA (BENBECULA)
Baile nan Cailleach
Rubha na Rodagrich
Maragay Mor
Griminis
Torlum
Loch Uisgeabhagh
Loch Chiorabhagh
Maaey Riabhach
Lionacleit
Gualan
Creag Ghoraidh
Rubha Cam nan Gall
Hornish Pt.
Iochdar
Ardivachar Pt.
Aird a Mhachair
Clachan
Bagh nam Faoileann
Fuidhaigh (Wiay)
Loch Bi
Steisay
Loch a Charnain
Gasay
Sanndabhaig
Geirinis
OUR LADY OF THE ISLES STATUE
Luirsay Dubh
Stadhlaigearraidh
Loch Sgioport
Ornish I.
Dreumasdal
HOWMORE
Loch Druidibeg
Mol a Tuath
Tobha Mor
NF
Verran I.
Sniseabhal
Staoinebrig
606 HECLA
Rubha Rossel
Rubha'Aird-mhicheil
Ormiclate Castle
527
Rubha Bhilidh
BEINN MHOR 620
Loch Olaigh
Rubha Hellisdale
UIBHIST A DEAS (SOUTH UIST)
Rubha Ardvule
Bornais
Taobh a Tuath Loch Aineort
Loch Cill Donnain
Rubha Bolum
Calvay
KILDONAN MUSEUM
Cill Donnain
Unasary
Gearraidh Bhailteas
Minngearraidh
Loch Aineort
FLORA MACDONALD'S BIRTHPLACE
Loch Sniogaisclett
Aisgernis
374 STULAVAL
Stuley
SOUTH UIST MACHAIR
Western Isles
Dalabrog
Taobh a Tuath Loch Baghasdail
357
Crois Dughaill
Rubha na Creige Móire
Cille Pheadair
Loch Baghasdail (Lochboisdale)
Baghasdal
Calvay
Ceann a Deas Loch Baghasdail
Rubha Meall na Hoe
Trosaraidh
Gearraidh na Monadh
Smercleit
Cille Bhrighde
South Glendale
Rubha na h-Ordaig
Pol a Charra
Taobh a Chaolais
Ludag
201
Sgeir a'Mhill
Lingeigh (Lingay)
Caolas Eiriosgaigh
Haunn
Calvay
Bun a'Mhuillin
Hartamul
Am Baile
OBAN (Summer only)
Coilleag
185
Eiriosgaigh (Eriskay)
Fiaraigh (Fiaray)
Caolas Fhiaraigh
Caolas Bharraigh
CASTLEBAY
Scurrival Pt.
89
Fuideigh (Fuday)
Eolaigearraidh
CILLE BHARRA
Stack Is.
Orosay
Greian Head
Traigh Mhor
Hellisay
Gighay
Cliaid
207 BEN CLIAD
Aird Mhor
Cuidhir
Aird Mhidhinis
Caolas Sheileasaigh
Allathasdal
Bagh Shiarabhagh
Bruairnis
Borve Pt.
CRAIGSTON MUSEUM
Baile na Creige
Buaile nam Bodach
Fuiay
Borgh
EILEAN BHARRAIGH (BARRA)
94
Bruernish Pt.
HEAVAL 383
Doirlinn Hd.
Tangasdal
332
Eorsairidh
BARRA HERITAGE CENTRE
A888
Breibhig
Bagh a Chaisteil (Castlebay)
KIESSIMUL (KISIMUL) CASTLE
Rubha Mor
LOCHBOISDALE
190
Uidh
Bhatarsaigh (Vatersay)
Bagh Bhatarsaigh
Bhatarsaigh
Muldoanich
OBAN
Caolas Shanndraigh
Flodaigh (Flodday)
146
SCARINISH (TIREE) (Summer only)
207
Sanndraigh (Sandray)
Lingeigh (Lingay)
Greanamul
Caolas Phabaigh
Pabaidh
Scale : 1:332 000 (approx 5 miles to 1 inch)
0 1 2 3 4 5 6 miles
0 1 2 3 4 5 6 7 8 9 10 km
Loch Fionnsbhagh
TARBERT
LOCHMADDY
Waternish Pt.
Ard Beag
Trumpan
TRUMPAN CHURCH
Knockbr
Ardmore Pt.
Lower Halistra
Upper Halistra
Dunvegan Head
Mingay
Isay
LOCH DUNVEGAN
Galtrigill
Claigan
Borreraig
BORRERAIG PARK MUSEUM
Uig
Husabost
An Ceannaich
Lower Milovaig
Feriniquarrie
Totaig
Oisgill Bay
Upper Milovaig
Glaspheinn
Lephin
COLBOST FOLK MUSEUM
Colbost
Holmisdale
LIGHTHOUSE
Neist Point
Skinidin
Dunvegan
Kilmuir
Glen Dale
Moonen Bay
HEALABHAL MHOR 468
Ramasaig
Macleod's Tables
Hoe Rape
488 HEALABHAL BHEAG
Orbost
Hoe Point
Geodha Mor
MACLEOD'S MAIDENS
Idri
Garrisdale Pt.
Canr
Oigh-sgeir
A B C D E F G H J
1 2 3 4 5 6 7
A865 A867 B894 B892 B891 B890 B888 A888 B883 B884

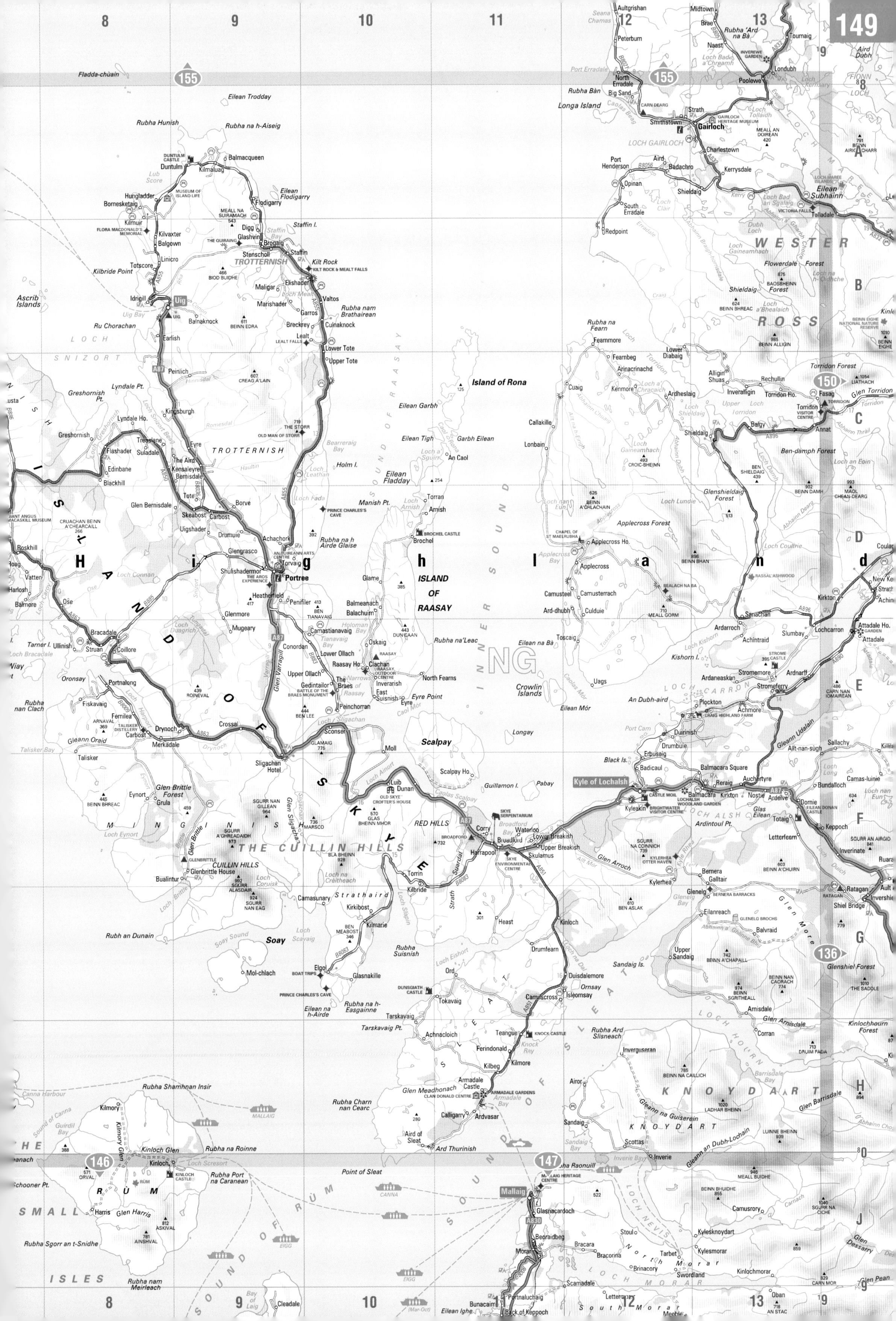
8
9
10
11
12
13
19
155
155
Fladda-chùain
Eilean Trodday
Rubha Hunish
Rubha na h-Aiseig
Duntulm Castle
Duntulm
Balmacqueen
Kilmaluag
Lub Score
Hungladder
Museum of Island Life
Borneskeitag
Kilmuir
Flora MacDonald's Memorial
Eilean Flodigarry
Flodigarry
Meall na Suiramach
Digg
Staffin I.
Staffin Bay
Kilvaxter
Balgown
The Quiraing
Glashvin
Brogaig
Staffin
Stenscholl
TROTTERNISH
Linicro
Kilt Rock
Kilt Rock & Mealt Falls
Totscore
Kilbride Point
Biod Buidhe
Elishader
Maligar
Loch Mealt
Valtos
Ascrib Islands
Idrigill
Uig
Uig Bay
Marishader
Rubha nam Brathairean
Garros
Balnaknock
Beinn Edra
Ru Chorachan
Breckrey
Culnaknock
Lealt
Lealt Falls
Lower Tote
Upper Tote
Earlish
LOCH
SNIZORT
Peinlich
Creag a'Lain
Greshornish Pt.
Lyndale Pt.
Kingsburgh
Lyndale Ho.
The Storr
Old Man of Storr
Greshornish
Treaslane
Suladale
Eyre
TROTTERNISH
Flashader
The Aird
Kensaleyre
Bernisdale
Edinbane
Blackhill
Glen Bernisdale
Tote
Borve
Skeabost
Carbost
Uigshader
Drumuie
Achachork
Glengrasco
Giant Angus MacAskill Museum
Cruachan Beinn a'Chearcaill
Roskhill
Roag
Vatten
Harlosh
Balmore
Ose
Loch Connan
Shulishadermor
The Aros Experience
Torvaig
Portree
Heatherfield
An Tuireann Arts Centre
Glenmore
Mugeary
Loch Duagrich
Bracadale
Ullinish
Struan
Coillore
Tarner I.
Loch Bracadale
Wiay
Oronsay
Portnalong
Roineval
Rubha nan Clach
Fiskavaig
Fernilea
Arnaval
Talisker Distillery
Carbost
Drynoch
Crossal
Gleann Oraid
Merkadale
Talisker Bay
Talisker
Sligachan Hotel
Glen Varragill
Penifiler
Ben Tianavaig
Camastianavaig
Tianavaig Bay
Conordan
Lower Ollach
Upper Ollach
Gedintailor
Battle of the Braes Monument
The Braes
Peinchorran
Ben Lee
Loch Sligachan
Sconser
Glamaig
Eynort
Glen Brittle Forest
Grula
Beinn Bhreac
Loch Eynort
MINGINISH
Sgurr nan Gillean
Glen Sligachan
Marsco
Sgurr a'Ghreadaidh
Glenbrittle
CUILLIN HILLS
THE CUILLIN HILLS
Glenbrittle House
Bualintur
Sgurr Alasdair
Sgurr nan Eag
Loch Coruisk
Loch Brittle
Bla Bheinn
Loch na Creitheach
Camasunary
Strathaird
Kirkibost
Rubh an Dunain
Soay Sound
Soay
Loch Scavaig
Ben Meabost
Kilmarie
Mol-chlach
Elgol
Boat Trips
Prince Charles's Cave
Glasnakille
Rubha na h-Easgainne
Eilean na h-Airde
Island of Rona
Eilean Garbh
Eilean Tigh
Garbh Eilean
An Caol
Holm I.
Eilean Fladday
Torran
Arnish
Manish Pt.
Prince Charles's Cave
Rubha na h Airde Glaise
Brochel Castle
Brochel
Glame
ISLAND OF RAASAY
Balmeanach
Balachuirn
Dun Caan
Oskaig
Raasay Ho
Clachan
Raasay Outdoor Centre
Inverarish
East Suisnish
Eyre
Eyre Point
North Fearns
Rubha na'Leac
SOUND OF RAASAY
INNER SOUND
Moll
Scalpay
Scalpay Ho.
Luib
Dunan
Old Skye Crofter's House
Glas Bheinn Mhor
Loch Ainort
RED HILLS
Caolas Scalpay
Guillamon I.
Pabay
Skye Serpentarium
Broadford Bay
Corry
Waterloo
Broadford
Harrapool
Skye Environmental Centre
Lower Breakish
Upper Breakish
Skulamus
Torrin
Kilbride
Strath Suardal
Loch Slapin
Rubha Suisnish
Heast
Kinloch
Drumfearn
Loch Eishort
Ord
Dunsgiath Castle
Tokavaig
Tarskavaig
Tarskavaig Pt.
Duisdalemore
Ornsay
Camuscross
Isleornsay
Achnacloich
Teangue
Knock Castle
Knock Bay
Ferindonald
Kilbeg
Kilmore
Armadale Castle
Armadale Gardens
Clan Donald Centre
Glen Meadhonach
Armadale Bay
Calligarry
Ardvasar
Aird of Sleat
Ard Thurinish
Rubha Charn nan Cearc
SLEAT
SOUND OF SLEAT
Point of Sleat
Mallaig
Mallaig Heritage Centre
Glasnacardoch
Beoraidbeg
Morar
Bunacaimb
Portnaluchaig
Back of Keppoch
Eilean Ighe
Bay of Laig
Cleadale
Eigg
Canna
Rubha Shamhnan Insir
Canna Harbour
Sound of Canna
Kilmory
Guirdil Bay
Kilmory Glen
Kinloch Glen
Rubha na Roinne
Kinloch
Kinloch Castle
Loch Scresort
Orval
RÙM
Rubha Port na Caranean
Schooner Pt.
SMALL ISLES
Harris
Glen Harris
Askival
Ainshval
Rubha Sgorr an t-Snidhe
Rubha nam Meirleach
SOUND OF RÙM
SOUND OF EIGG
146
147
Seana Chamas
Aultgrishan
Midtown
Brae
Rubha 'Ard na Bà
Naast
Tournaig
Inverewe Garden
Peterburn
Loch Bad a'Chreamh
Port Erradale
North Erradale
Londubh
Poolewe
Rubha Bàn
Big Sand
Longa Island
Caolas Beag
Carn Dearg
Strath
Gairloch Heritage Museum
Smithstown
Gairloch
Loch Tollaidh
LOCH GAIRLOCH
Meall an Doirein
Charlestown
Port Henderson
Aird
Badachro
Kerrysdale
Opinan
Shieldaig
South Erradale
Loch Bad an Sgalaig
Victoria Falls
Talladale
Eilean Subhainn
Redpoint
Dubh Loch
Loch Gaineamhach
WESTER
Flowerdale
Forest
Baosbheinn
Shieldaig Forest
Beinn Bhreac
Loch a'Bhealaich
ROSS
Beinn Eighe National Nature Reserve
Beinn Alligin
Rubha na Fearn
Fearnmore
Fearnbeg
Arinacrinachd
Lower Diabaig
Loch Torridon
Alligin Shuas
Rechullin
Torridon Forest
Liathach
Inveralligin
Torridon Ho.
Fasag
Glen Torridon
Torridon Visitor Centre
Cuaig
Kenmore
Ardheslaig
Loch Shieldaig
Balgy
Annat
Callakille
Lonbain
Shieldaig
Ben-damph Forest
Loch Gaineamhach
Croic-bheinn
Ben Shieldaig
Loch Damh
Beinn Damh
Maol Chean-dearg
Glenshieldaig Forest
Loch Lundie
Beinn a'Chlachain
Applecross Forest
Chapel of St Maelrubha
Applecross Ho.
Applecross Bay
Applecross
Beinn Bhan
Loch Coultrie
Rassal Ashwood
Coulags
New Kelso
Strathcarron
Achintee
Camusteel
Camusterrach
Bealach na Ba
Kirkton
Ard-dhubh
Culduie
Meall Gorm
Sanachan
Loch Kishorn
Ardarroch
Achintraid
Slumbay
Lochcarron
Attadale Ho.
Attadale Gardens
Attadale
Toscaig
Eilean na Bà
Kishorn I.
Strome Castle
Ardnarff
Crowlin Islands
Caolas Mòr
Uags
Ardaneaskan
Stromemore
Stromeferry
Carn nan Iomairean
LOCH CARRON
An Dubh-aird
Eilean Mòr
Plockton
Achmore
Craig Highland Farm
Port Cam
Duirinish
Drumbuie
Gleann Udalain
Longay
Allt-nan-sugh
Sallachy
Erbusaig
Black Is.
Badicaul
Balmacara Square
Auchtertyre
Camas-luinie
Kyle of Lochalsh
Reraig
Castle Moil
Kyleakin
Brightwater Visitor Centre
Lochalsh Woodland Garden
Balmacara
Kirkton
Nostie
Ardelve
Dornie
Eilean Donan Castle
Bundalloch
Loch Long
LOCH ALSH
Glas Eilean
Ardintoul Pt.
Totaig
Keppoch
Letterfearn
Sgurr an Airgid
Inverinate
Sgurr na Coinnich
Kylerhea Otter Haven
Glen Arroch
Kylerhea
Kyle Rhea
Beinn a'Chuirn
Bernera
Galltair
Glenelg
Bernera Barracks
Glenelg Bay
Ratagan
Shiel Bridge
Ben Aslak
Eilanreach
Glenelg Brochs
Balvraid
Glen More
Upper Sandaig
Beinn a'Chapaill
Sandaig Is.
Glenshiel Forest
136
Beinn nan Caorach
Beinn Sgritheall
The Saddle
Arnisdale
Glen Arnisdale
Kinlochhourn Forest
Corran
LOCH HOURN
Rubha Ard Slisneach
Inverguseran
Druim Fada
Beinn na Caillich
Airor
KNOYDART
Barrisdale Bay
Glen Barrisdale
Ladhar Bheinn
Gleann na Guiserein
Sandaig
Sandaig Bay
Scottas
Inverie Bay
Inverie
Gleann an Dubh-Lochain
Luinne Bheinn
Rubha Raonuill
Meall Buidhe
Beinn Bhuidhe
Camusrory
Sgurr na Ciche
LOCH NEVIS
Carnach
Stoul
Bracara
Bracorina
Brinacory
Tarbet
Kyleknoydart
Kylesmorar
North Morar
Swordland
Kinlochmorar
LOCH MORAR
Glen Dessarry
Carn Mor
Scamadale
Letterneurn
South Morar
Oban
An Stac
Meoble
Glen Pean
A855
A87
A850
A863
B885
A851
B883
B8083
A830
A832
A896
A890
B8021
B8056
A B C D E F G H J
Highland
ISLE OF SKYE

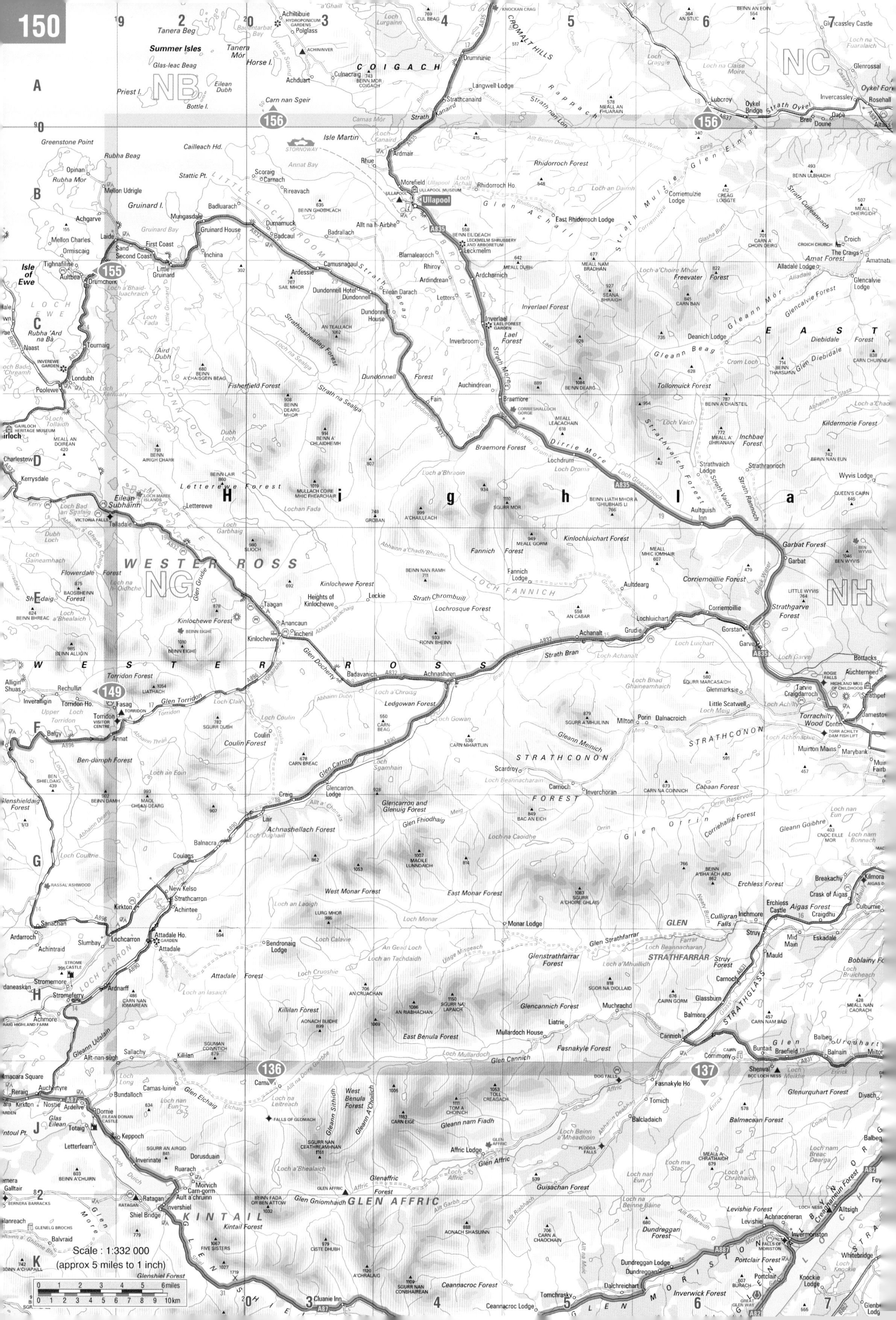
Summer Isles
Tanera Beg
Tanera Mór
Horse I.
Glas-leac Beag
Priest I.
Eilean Dubh
Bottle I.
Achiltibuie
Polglass
Achduart
Culnacraig
COIGACH
Carn nan Sgeir
Isle Martin
Cailleach Hd.
Greenstone Point
Rubha Beag
Opinan
Rubha Mor
Mellon Udrigle
Stattic Pt.
Scoraig
Carnach
Rireavach
Annat Bay
Gruinard I.
Achgarve
Mungasdale
Badluarach
Gruinard Bay
Gruinard House
Dumnamuck
Badcaul
Laide
Sand
First Coast
Second Coast
Mellon Charles
Ormiscaig
Inchina
Tighnafiline
Aultbea
Drumchork
Little Gruinard
Isle of Ewe
LOCH EWE
Rubha 'Ard na Bà
Naast
Tournaig
INVEREWE GARDEN
Londubh
Poolewe
Ullapool
ULLAPOOL MUSEUM
Rhue
Ardmair
Morefield
Rhidorroch Ho.
Rhidorroch Forest
East Rhidorroch Lodge
Glen Achall
LOCH BROOM
Allt na h-Airbhe
Badrallach
Blarnalearoch
Rhiroy
Ardindrean
Letters
Leckmelm
Ardcharnich
Inverlael
Inverlael Forest
Lael Forest
Inverbroom
Strath More
Braemore
CORRIESHALLOCH GORGE
Auchindrean
Camusnagaul
Ardessie
Dundonnell Hotel
Dundonnell
Eilean Darach
Dundonnell House
Dundonnell Forest
Fain
Strathnasheallag Forest
AN TEALLACH
Strath na Sealga
Fisherfield Forest
FIONN LOCH
Letterewe Forest
Letterewe
Dubh Loch
Lochan Fada
Braemore Forest
Dirrie More
Lochdrum
Loch Droma
Loch Glascarnoch
Loch a'Bhraoin
Drumrunie
Langwell Lodge
Strathcanaird
Strath Kanaird
Strath nan Lon
Rappach
CROMALT HILLS
KNOCKAN CRAG
NC
NB
NG
NH
Lubcroy
Oykel Bridge
Strath Oykel
Invercassley
Rosehall
Glencassley Castle
Glenrossal
Oykel Forest
Brae
Doune
Altass
Glen Einig
Strath Mulzie
Corriemulzie Lodge
Strath Cuileannach
Croich
The Craigs
Amat Forest
Alladale Lodge
Freevater Forest
Glencalvie Lodge
Glencalvie Forest
Gleann Mór
Deanich Lodge
Gleann Beag
Diebidale
Tollomuick Forest
Kildermorie Forest
Strathvaich Forest
Strathvaich Lodge
Strath Vaich
Strath Rannoch
Strathrannoch
Wyvis Lodge
Aultguish Inn
Inchbae Forest
Garbat Forest
Garbat
BEN WYVIS
Corriemoillie Forest
Strathgarve Forest
Kinlochluichart Forest
Fannich Forest
LOCH FANNICH
Fannich Lodge
Highland
WESTER ROSS
Loch Maree
Eilean Subhainn
Talladale
VICTORIA FALLS
Gairloch
GAIRLOCH HERITAGE MUSEUM
Charlestown
Kerrysdale
Loch Bad an Sgalaig
Flowerdale Forest
Shieldaig
Kinlochewe Forest
Kinlochewe
Taagan
Anancaun
Incheril
Heights of Kinlochewe
Leckie
Strath Chrombuill
Lochrosque Forest
Glen Docherty
Badavanich
Achnasheen
Achanalt
Strath Bran
Grudie
Lochluichart
Aultdearg
Corriemoillie
Gorstan
Garve
Loch Luichart
Loch Garve
Bottacks
Auchterneed
ROGIE FALLS
Tarvie
Craigdarroch
Strathpeffer
Jamestown
Contin
Torrachilty Wood
Marybank
Muirton Mains
WESTER ROSS
Torridon Forest
Torridon
Fasag
Glen Torridon
Alligin Shuas
Inveralligin
Rechullin
Torridon Ho.
Upper Loch Torridon
Balgy
Annat
Ben-damph Forest
Coulin Forest
Coulin
Ledgowan Forest
Loch Gowan
Glen Carron
Loch Sgamhain
Craig
Glencarron Lodge
Glencarron and Glenuig Forest
Lair
Achnashellach Forest
Balnacra
Coulags
Loch Dughaill
Loch Coultrie
Shieldaig Forest
New Kelso
Strathcarron
Achintee
Kirkton
Sanachan
Ardarroch
Achintraid
Slumbay
Lochcarron
Attadale Ho.
Attadale
LOCH CARRON
STROME CASTLE
Stromemore
Stromeferry
Ardnarff
Achmore
Plockton
Duirinish
Attadale Forest
West Monar Forest
East Monar Forest
Loch Monar
Monar Lodge
Bendronaig Lodge
Loch Calavie
An Gead Loch
Loch an Tachdaidh
Loch Cruoshie
Killilan Forest
East Benula Forest
Glen Fhiodhaig
Glen Orrin
Orrin Reservoir
Corriehallie Forest
Gleann Goibhre
STRATHCONON
Strathconon Forest
Scardroy
Carnoch
Inverchoran
Gleann Meinich
Milton
Porin
Dalnacroich
Little Scatwell
Glenmarksie
Cabaan Forest
Erchless Forest
Erchless Castle
Aigas Forest
Breakachy
Crask of Aigas
Kilmorack
Culburnie
Craigdhu
Eskadale
Culligran Falls
Inchmore
Struy
Mid Main
Mauld
Glen Strathfarrar
STRATHFARRAR
Glenstrathfarrar Forest
Struy Forest
Carnoch
Glassburn
Balmore
STRATHGLASS
Glencannich Forest
Muchrachd
Liatrie
Mullardoch House
Loch Mullardoch
Glen Cannich
Fasnakyle Forest
Cannich
Cormmony
Buntait
Glen Urquhart
Shenval
Braefield
Balbeg
Balnain
Milton
Glenurquhart Forest
Divach
Fasnakyle Ho
Tomich
Balcladaich
DOG FALLS
PLODDA FALLS
Balmacaan Forest
Loch Ness
Sallachy
Allt-nan-sùgh
Killilan
Gleann Udalain
Camas-luinie
Glen Elchaig
Carnach
FALLS OF GLOMACH
West Benula Forest
Gleann Sithidh
Gleann a'Choilich
Gleann nam Fiadh
Affric Lodge
Glen Affric
Loch Affric
Loch Beinn a'Mheadhoin
Guisachan Forest
Loch a'Bhealaich
Glenaffric Forest
GLEN AFFRIC
Glen Gniomhaidh
KINTAIL
Kintail Forest
GLEN SHIEL
Glenshiel Forest
Cluanie Inn
Ceannacroc Forest
Ceannacroc Lodge
Dundreggan Forest
Dundreggan Lodge
Dundreggan
Dalchreichart
Tomchrasky
GLEN MORISTON
Invermoriston
Levishie Forest
Levishie
Achnaconeran
Alltsigh
Portclair Forest
Portclair
Inverwick Forest
Knockie Lodge
Whitebridge
Glenbeg Lodge
Kyle of Lochalsh
Balmacara Square
Reraig
Auchertyre
Nostie
Ardelve
Dornie
EILEAN DONAN CASTLE
Kirkton
Glas Eilean
Totaig
Keppoch
Letterfearn
Inverinate
Dorusduain
Ruarach
Morvich
Camgorm
Ault a'chruinn
Invershiel
Shiel Bridge
Ratagan
Loch Duich
Glen More
Balvraid
Glenelg
GLENELG BROCHS
BERNERA BARRACKS
Scale : 1:332 000
(approx 5 miles to 1 inch)
0 1 2 3 4 5 6 miles
0 1 2 3 4 5 6 7 8 9 10 km
155
156
149
136
137
A835
A832
A896
A890
A87
A887
A831
A82
A837

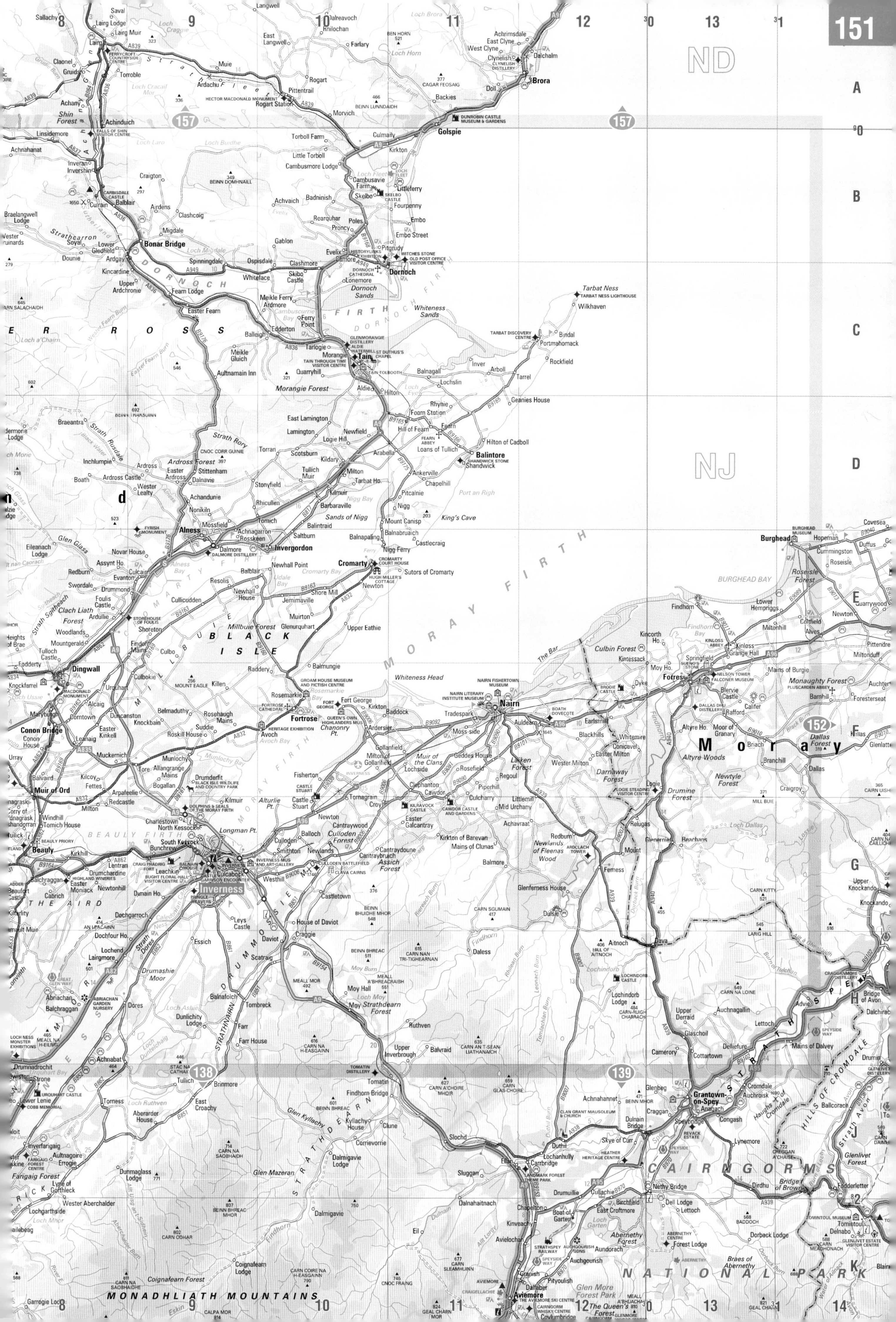

ND
NJ
Lairg
Lairg Lodge
Lairg Muir
Saval
Sallachy
Langwell
East Langwell
Dalreavoch
Rhilochan
Farlary
Loch Brora
Achrimsdale
East Clyne
West Clyne
Clynelish
Dalchalm
Brora
Doll
Backies
Golspie
Dunrobin Castle Museum & Gardens
Rogart
Rogart Station
Pittentrail
Muie
Ardachu
Strath Fleet
Morvich
Achany
Shin Forest
Achinduich
Falls of Shin Visitor Centre
Linsidemore
Achnahanat
Invershin
Culrain
Carbisdale Castle
Balblair
Braelangwell Lodge
Strathcarron
Soyal
Dounie
Lower Gledfield
Ardgay
Bonar Bridge
Kincardine
Upper Ardchronie
Fearn Lodge
Migdale
Clashcoig
Airdens
Craigton
Torboll Farm
Little Torboll
Cambusmore Lodge
Culmaily
Kirkton
Loch Fleet
Cambusavie Farm
Skelbo
Skelbo Castle
Littleferry
Fourpenny
Embo
Embo Street
Achvaich
Badninish
Rearquhar
Poles
Proncy
Gablon
Evelix
Pitgrudy
Camore
Dornoch
Dornoch Cathedral
Lonemore
Dornoch Sands
Spinningdale
Ospisdale
Clashmore
Skibo Castle
Whiteface
Meikle Ferry
Ardmore
Dornoch Firth
Whiteness Sands
Easter Fearn
Edderton
Ferry Point
Balleigh
Tarlogie
Morangie
Tain
Glenmorangie Distillery
Tain Through Time Visitor Centre
Quarryhill
Morangie Forest
Meikle Gluich
Aultnamain Inn
Ross
Tarbat Ness
Tarbat Ness Lighthouse
Wilkhaven
Tarbat Discovery Centre
Bindal
Portmahomack
Rockfield
Inver
Arboll
Tarrel
Balnagall
Lochslin
Aldie
Hilton
Geanies House
Rhynie
Fearn Station
Hill of Fearn
Fearn
Fearn Abbey
Loans of Tullich
Hilton of Cadboll
Balintore
Shandwick
Shandwick Stone
East Lamington
Lamington
Newfield
Logie Hill
Arabella
Kildary
Scotsburn
Torran
Tullich Muir
Milton
Tarbat Ho.
Ankerville
Chapelhill
Pitcalnie
Port an Righ
Nigg
Nigg Bay
Sands of Nigg
Mount Canisp
King's Cave
Balnapaling
Balnabruaich
Castlecraig
Nigg Ferry
Strath Rory
Ardross Forest
Ardross
Easter Ardross
Stittenham
Dalnavie
Ardross Castle
Inchlumpie
Braeantra
Strath Rusdale
Boath
Western Lealty
Stonyfield
Kilmuir
Barbaraville
Rhicullen
Achandunie
Nonikiln
Mossfield
Tomich
Balintraid
Saltburn
Alness
Achnagarron
Rosskeen
Dalmore
Dalmore Distillery
Invergordon
Fyrish Monument
Glen Glass
Eileanach Lodge
Novar House
Assynt Ho.
Redburn
Culcairn
Evanton
Swordale
Drummond
Foulis Castle
Clach Liath
Ardullie
Woodlands
Mountgerald
Tulloch Castle
Dingwall
Fodderty
Knockfarrel
Cromarty Firth
Balblair
Newhall Point
Resolis
Newhall House
Cullicudden
Jemimaville
Shore Mill
Cromarty
Cromarty Court House
Hugh Miller's Cottage
Sutors of Cromarty
Newton
Cromarty Bay
Udale Bay
Muirton
Glenurquhart
Upper Eathie
Millbuie Forest
Black Isle
Storehouse of Foulis
Shoreton
Findon Mains
Culbo
Culbokie
Urquhart
Raddery
Balmungie
Moray Firth
Whiteness Head
Mount Eagle
Killen
Rosemarkie
Groam House Museum and Pictish Centre
Fortrose
Fortrose Cathedral
Fort George
Chanonry Pt.
Kirkton
Baddock
Ardersier
Alcaig
Conon Bridge
Conon House
Maryburgh
Duncanston
Knockbain
Belmaduthy
Rosehaugh Mains
Suddie
Easter Kinkell
Roskill House
Avoch
Avoch Bay
Leanaig
Muckernich
Munlochy
Munlochy Bay
Allangrange Mains
Tore
Bogallan
Drumderfit
Black Isle Wildlife and Country Park
Urray
Balvaird
Kilcoy
Fettes
Muir of Ord
Arpafeelie
Redcastle
Milton
Kilmuir
Alturlie Pt.
Windhill
Tomich House
Charlestown
North Kessock
South Kessock
Longman Pt.
Beauly Firth
Beauly
Beauly Priory
Kirkhill
Bunchrew
Craig Phadrig
Leachkin
Balnain House
Inverness
Inverness Castle
Culcabock
Inverness Mus and Art Gallery
Balchraggan
Easter Moniack
Newtonhill
Dunain Ho.
The Aird
Dochgarroch
Dochfour Ho.
Lochend
Laimgore
Abriachan
Balchraggan
Dores
Drumashie Moor
Strath Dores
Essich
Leys Castle
Daviot
Scatraig
Balnafoich
Tombreck
Dunlichity Lodge
Loch Ness Monster Exhibitions
Drumnadrochit
Lewiston
Strone
Urquhart Castle
Lower Lenie
Achnabat
Farr
Farr House
Strathnairn
Tullich
Brinmore
Torness
Aberarder House
East Croachy
Inverfarigaig
Aultnagoire
Errogie
Farigaig Forest
Dunmaglass Lodge
Lyne of Gorthleck
Wester Aberchalder
Lochgarthside
Coignafearn Lodge
Coignafearn Forest
Monadhliath Mountains
Garrogie Lodge
Castle Stuart
Tornagrain
Croy
Newton
Cantraywood
Culloden
Culloden Forest
Balloch
Smithton
Newlands
Culloden Battlefield
Clava Cairns
Cantraybruich
Cantraydoune
Westhill
Castletown
House of Daviot
Craggie
Assich Forest
Fisherton
Gollanfield
Milton of Gollanfield
Muir of the Clans
Lochside
Clephanton
Cawdor
Cawdor Castle and Gardens
Kilravock Castle
Easter Galcantray
Geddes House
Rosefield
Culcharry
Piperhill
Regoul
Littlemill
Mid Urchany
Achavraat
Kirkton of Barevan
Mains of Clunas
Balmore
Tradespark
Moss-side
Nairn
Nairn Fishertown Museum
Nairn Literary Institute Museum
Auldearn
Boath Dovecote
Laiken Forest
The Bar
Culbin Forest
Kintessack
Kincorth Ho.
Moy Ho.
Dyke
Brodie Castle
Earlsmill
Blackhills
Whitemire
Conicavel
Easter Milton
Wester Milton
Darnaway Forest
Logie
Logie Steading Visitor Centre
Relugas
Redburn
Ardclach Tower
Newlands of Fleenas Wood
Mount
Ferness
Glenferness House
Dulsie
Findhorn
Findhorn Bay
Kinloss
Kinloss Abbey
Springfield
Sueno's Stone
Forres
Nelson Tower
Falconer Museum
Grange Hall
Burghead
Burghead Museum
Burghead Bay
Hopeman
Cummingston
Roseisle
Roseisle Forest
Duffus
Covesea
Lower Hempriggs
Miltonhill
Coltfield
Alves
Newton
Quarrywood
Pittendrich
Miltonduff
Mains of Burgie
Monaughty Forest
Pluscarden Abbey
Barnhill
Blervie Castle
Califer
Rafford
Dallas Dhu Distillery
Altyre Ho.
Moor of Granary
Briach
Branchill
Altyre Woods
Moray
Dallas Forest
Dallas
Newtyle Forest
Drumine Forest
Craigroy
Glenernie
Beachans
Loch Dallas
Aitnoch
Hill of Aitnoch
Dava
Daless
Lochindorb
Lochindorb Castle
Lochindorb Lodge
Carn-ruigh Charrach
Moy Hall
Loch Moy
Moy
Strathdearn Forest
Ruthven
Upper Inverbrough
Balvraid
Tomatin
Tomatin Distillery
Findhorn Bridge
Glen Kyllachy
Kyllachy House
Clune
Corrievorrie
Dalmigavie Lodge
Dalmigavie
Slochd
Sluggan
Glen Mazeran
Strathdearn
Achnahannet
Clan Grant Mausoleum & Church
Dulnain Bridge
Skye of Curr
Heather Heritage Centre
Duthil
Lochanhully
Carrbridge
Landmark Forest Theme Park
Ellan
Drumuillie
Dalnahaitnach
Chapelton
Boat of Garten
Kinveachy
Avielochan
Eil
Strathspey Railway
Loch Garten
Abernethy Forest
Aundorach
Auchgourish
Granish
Pityoulish
Dalfaber
Aviemore
The Aviemore Ski Centre
Craigellachie
Glen More Forest Park
The Queen's Forest
Coylumbridge
Cairngorm Whisky Centre
Cairngorms National Park
Nethy Bridge
Birchfield
East Croftmore
Dell Lodge
Lettoch
Forest Lodge
Abernethy Centre
Braes of Abernethy
Grantown-on-Spey
Anagach
Craggan
Glenbeg
Speybridge
Revack Estate
Congash
Cromdale
Auchroisk
Haughs of Cromdale
Hills of Cromdale
Lynemore
Dirdhu
Bridge of Brown
Fodderletter
Tomintoul
Tomintoul Museum
Glenlivet Estate Visitor Centre
Delnabo
Dorback Lodge
Glenlivet Forest
Strath Avon
Strath Spey
Upper Derraid
Glaschoil
Cottartown
Camerory
Auchnagallin
Lettoch
Delliefure
Mains of Dalvey
Advie
Bridge of Avon
Dalchirach
Cragganmore Distillery
Speyside Way
Upper Knockando
Knockando
Larig Hill
Carn Kitty
Drumin
Blairn
Dorback Burn
Burn of Tulchan

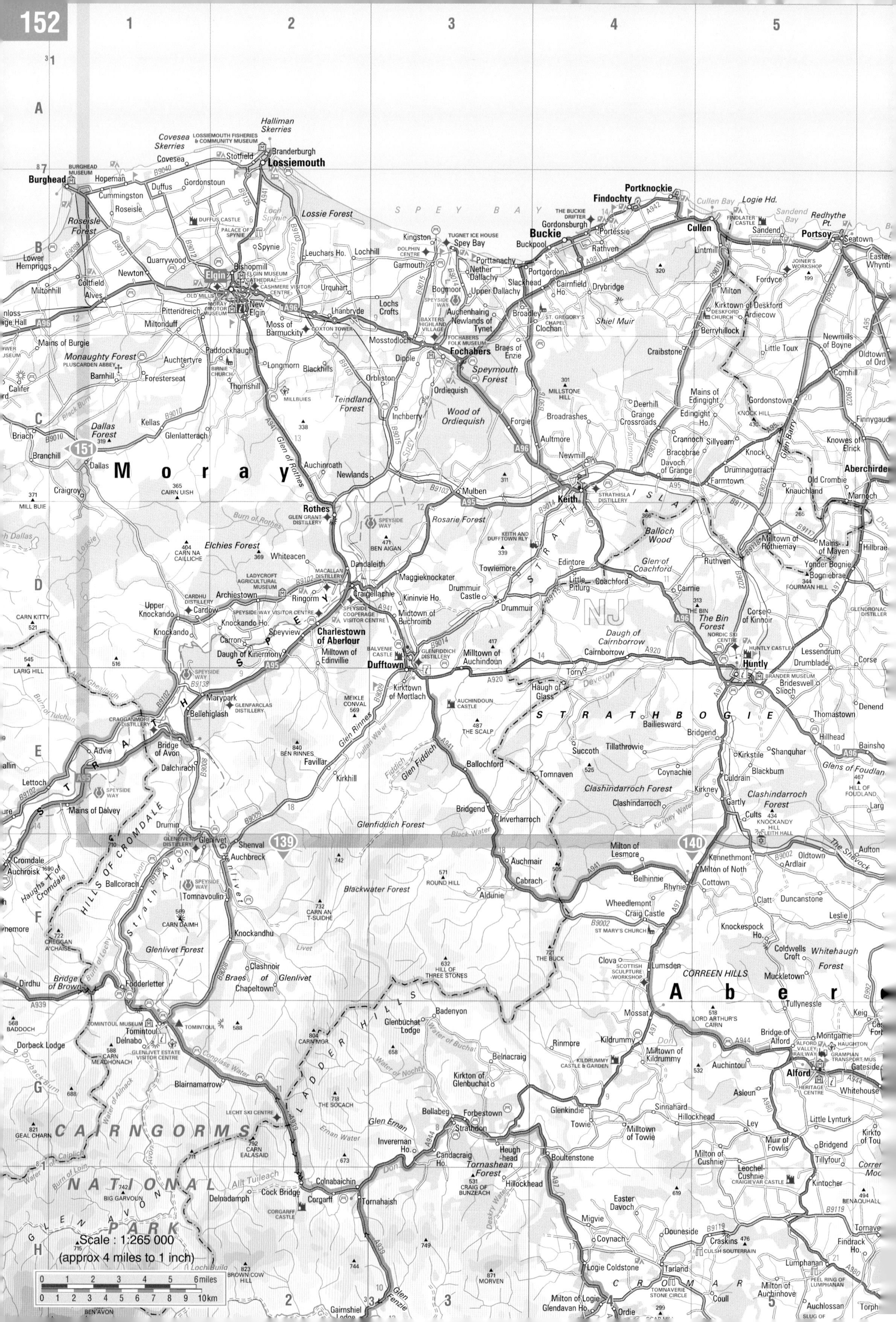
1
2
3
4
5
A
B
C
D
E
F
G
H
Halliman Skerries
Covesea Skerries
LOSSIEMOUTH FISHERIES & COMMUNITY MUSEUM
Covesea
Stotfield
Branderburgh
Lossiemouth
Burghead
BURGHEAD MUSEUM
Hopeman
Duffus
Gordonstoun
Cummingston
Roseisle
Roseisle Forest
DUFFUS CASTLE
PALACE OF SPYNIE
Loch Spynie
Lossie Forest
Spynie
Lower Hempriggs
Quarrywood
Bishopmill
Elgin
ELGIN MUSEUM
CATHEDRAL
CASHMERE VISITOR CENTRE
OLD MILLS
MORAY MOTOR MUSEUM
New Elgin
Newton
Coltfield
Alves
Miltonhill
Pittendreich
Miltonduff
Mains of Burgie
Monaughty Forest
PLUSCARDEN ABBEY
Auchtertyre
Paddockhaugh
BIRNIE CHURCH
Barnhill
Foresterseat
Thornshill
Califer
Kellas
Dallas Forest
Glenlatterach
Briach
Branchill
151
Dallas
Moray
Craigroy
MILL BUIE
CAIRN UISH
Longmorn
Blackhills
MILLBUIES
Moss of Barmuckity
COXTON TOWER
Lhanbryde
Urquhart
Leuchars Ho.
Lochhill
Kingston
DOLPHIN CENTRE
TUGNET ICE HOUSE
Spey Bay
SPEY BAY
Garmouth
Portgordon
Porttannachy
Nether Dallachy
Upper Dallachy
Bogmoor
SPEYSIDE WAY
Auchenhalrig
Newlands of Tynet
BAXTERS HIGHLAND VILLAGE
Lochs Crofts
Mosstodloch
FOCHABERS FOLK MUSEUM
Fochabers
Speymouth Forest
Dipple
Orbliston
Teindland Forest
Ordiequish
Wood of Ordiequish
Inchberry
Glen of Rothes
Auchinroath
Newlands
Rothes
GLEN GRANT DISTILLERY
Burn of Rothes
Elchies Forest
CARN NA CAILLICHE
Whiteacen
BEN AIGAN
Dandaleith
MACALLAN DISTILLERY
LADYCROFT AGRICULTURAL MUSEUM
Archiestown
Ringorm
Craigellachie
SPEYSIDE COOPERAGE VISITOR CENTRE
CARDHU DISTILLERY
Cardow
Upper Knockando
Knockando
Knockando Ho.
Carron
Daugh of Kinermony
Speyview
Charlestown of Aberlour
Milltown of Edinvillie
CARN KITTY
LARIG HILL
SPEYSIDE WAY
Marypark
Bellehiglash
GLENFARCLAS DISTILLERY
CRAGGANMORE DISTILLERY
Advie
Bridge of Avon
Dalchirach
Lettoch
Mains of Dalvey
STRATH SPEY
Cromdale
Auchroisk
Haughs of Cromdale
HILLS OF CROMDALE
Ballcorach
Drumin
GLENLIVET DISTILLERY
Glenlivet
Auchbreck
Shenval
139
Tomnavoulin
CARN DAIMH
Glenlivet Forest
Knockandhu
Clashnoir
Braes of Glenlivet
Chapeltown
CREGGAN A'CHAISE
Fodderletter
Bridge of Brown
Dirdhu
BADDOCH
TOMINTOUL MUSEUM
Tomintoul
Delnabo
Dorback Lodge
CARN MEADHONACH
GLENLIVET ESTATE VISITOR CENTRE
Conglass Water
Blairnamarrow
LECHT SKI CENTRE
CAIRNGORMS NATIONAL PARK
GEAL CHARN
CARN EALASAID
Allt Tuileach
BIG GARVOUN
Delnadamph
Cock Bridge
CORGARFF CASTLE
Corgarff
Colnabaichin
Tornahaish
GLEN AVON
Loch Builg
BROWN COW HILL
BEN AVON
Gairnshiel Lodge
Glen Gairn
Scale : 1:265 000
(approx 4 miles to 1 inch)
0 1 2 3 4 5 6 miles
0 1 2 3 4 5 6 7 8 9 10 km
LADDER HILLS
CARN MOR
THE SOCACH
Glenbuchat Lodge
Badenyon
Water of Buchat
Kirkton of Glenbuchat
Belnacraig
Glen Ernan
Inverernan Ho.
Bellabeg
Forbestown
Strathdon
Candacraig Ho.
Tornashean Forest
Heugh-head
CRAIG OF BUNZEACH
Hillockhead
Boultenstone
Deskry Water
MORVEN
Glenkindie
Towie
Milltown of Towie
Sinnahard
Hillockhead
Easter Davoch
Migvie
Coynach
Logie Coldstone
Douneside
Tarland
CULSH SOUTERRAIN
Craskins
TOMNAVERIE STONE CIRCLE
Coull
Milton of Logie
Glendavan Ho.
Ordie
CROMAR
Blackwater Forest
ROUND HILL
Aldunie
CARN AN T-SUIDHE
Glenfiddich Forest
HILL OF THREE STONES
Livet
Cabrach
Auchmair
Inverharroch
Bridgend
Ballochford
Glen Fiddich
THE SCALP
AUCHINDOUN CASTLE
Kirktown of Mortlach
Dufftown
BALVENIE CASTLE
GLENFIDDICH DISTILLERY
Milltown of Auchindoun
MEIKLE CONVAL
Glen Rinnes
BEN RINNES
Favillar
Kirkhill
Mulben
Rosarie Forest
KEITH AND DUFFTOWN RLY
Towiemore
Maggieknockater
Kininvie Ho.
Midtown of Buchromb
Drummuir Castle
Drummuir
Keith
STRATHISLA DISTILLERY
STRATH ISLA
Edintore
Little Pitlurg
Coachford
Balloch Wood
Glen of Coachford
Daugh of Cairnborrow
Cairnborrow
Torry
Haugh of Glass
Deveron
STRATHBOGIE
Bailiesward
Bridgend
Tillathrowie
Succoth
Tomnaven
Coynachie
Clashindarroch Forest
Clashindarroch
Kirkney Water
Black Water
Milton of Lesmore
Belhinnie
Rhynie
Wheedlemont
Craig Castle
ST MARY'S CHURCH
THE BUCK
Clova
SCOTTISH SCULPTURE WORKSHOP
Lumsden
CORREEN HILLS
Aber
Mossat
Kildrummy
KILDRUMMY CASTLE & GARDEN
Milltown of Kildrummy
Rinmore
Findochty
Portknockie
Buckie
THE BUCKIE DRIFTER
Gordonsburgh
Portessie
Buckpool
Rathven
Cullen
Cullen Bay
Logie Hd.
FINDLATER CASTLE
Sandend
Sandend Bay
Redhythe Pt.
Portsoy
Seatown
Easter Whyntie
Slackhead
Cairnfield Ho.
Drybridge
Broadley
ST. GREGORY'S CHAPEL
Clochan
Shiel Muir
Braes of Enzie
Lintmill
Milton
Fordyce
JOINER'S WORKSHOP
Kirktown of Deskford
DESKFORD CHURCH
Ardiecow
Berryhillock
Craibstone
Little Toux
Newmills of Boyne
Oldtown of Ord
Cornhill
MILLSTONE HILL
Deerhill
Grange Crossroads
Broadrashes
Forgie
Aultmore
Newmill
Mains of Edingight
Edingight Ho.
Gordonstown
KNOCK HILL
Glen Barry
Crannoch
Sillyearn
Bracobrae
Davoch of Grange
Knock
Drumnagorrach
Farmtown
Finnygaud
Knowes of Elrick
Aberchirder
Old Crombie
Knauchland
Marnoch
Milltown of Rothiemay
Mains of Mayen
Hillbrae
Yonder Bognie
Bogniebrae
FOURMAN HILL
Ruthven
Cairnie
THE BIN
The Bin Forest
Corse of Kinnoir
GLENDRONACH DISTILLERY
NORDIC SKI CENTRE
HUNTLY CASTLE
Huntly
BRANDER MUSEUM
Lessendrum
Drumblade
Corse
Brideswell
Slioch
Denend
Thomastown
Hillhead
Bainshole
Kirkstile
Shanquhar
Glens of Foudland
HILL OF FOUDLAND
Blackburn
Culdrain
Kirkney
Gartly
Clashindarroch Forest
Cults
KNOCKANDY HILL
LEITH HALL
Largue
140
Kennethmont
Oldtown
Ardlair
Aulton
The Shevock
Milton of Noth
Cottown
Clatt
Duncanstone
Leslie
Knockespock Ho.
Coldwells Croft
Whitehaugh Forest
Muckletown
Tullynessle
Keig
LORD ARTHUR'S CAIRN
Bridge of Alford
Montgarrie
ALFORD VALLEY RAILWAY
HAUGHTON
GRAMPIAN TRANSPORT MUS
Auchintoul
Alford
HERITAGE CENTRE
Gateside
Whitehouse
Asloun
Little Lynturk
Ley
Hillockhead
Muir of Fowlis
Bridgend
Tillyfour
Milton of Cushnie
Leochel Cushnie
CRAIGIEVAR CASTLE
Kintocher
BENAQUHALLIE
Tornaveen
Findrack Ho.
Lumphanan
PEEL RING OF LUMPHANAN
Milton of Auchinhove
Auchlossan
Torphins
NJ

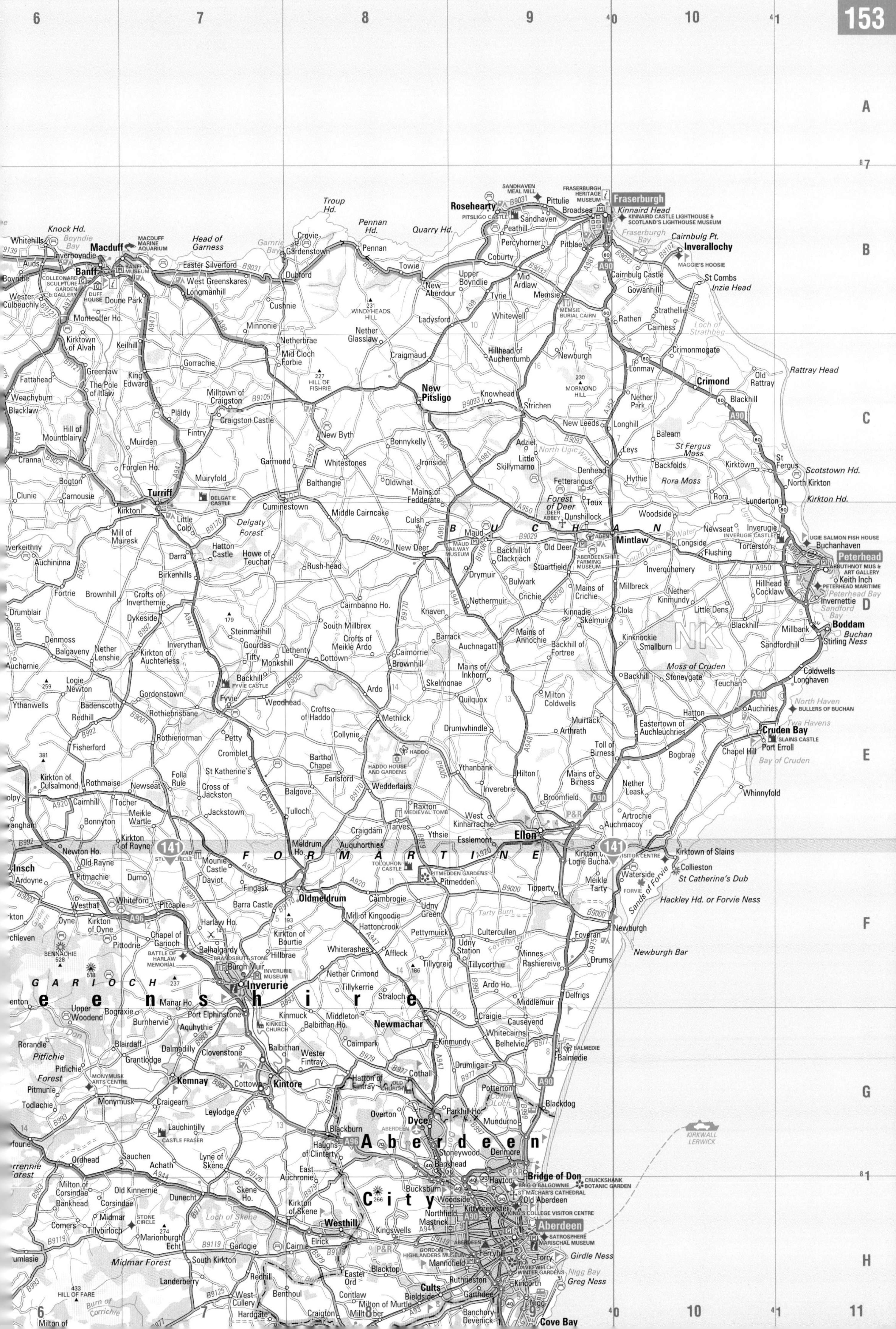

Fraserburgh
Peterhead
Aberdeen
Aberdeen City
Aberdeenshire
B U C H A N
F O R M A R T I N E
G A R I O C H
Rosehearty
Pittulie
Sandhaven
Kinnaird Head
Kinnaird Castle Lighthouse & Scotland's Lighthouse Museum
Fraserburgh Bay
Cairnbulg Pt.
Inverallochy
Maggie's Hoosie
St Combs
Inzie Head
Cairnbulg Castle
Rathen
Loch of Strathbeg
Crimonmogate
Rattray Head
Old Rattray
Crimond
Lonmay
Troup Hd.
Pennan Hd.
Quarry Hd.
Pennan
Crovie
Gardenstown
Gamrie Bay
Head of Garness
Knock Hd.
Whitehills
Boyndie Bay
Macduff
Macduff Marine Aquarium
Banff
Banff Museum
Inverboyndie
Duff House
Doune Park
Colleonard Sculpture Garden & Gallery
Easter Silverford
West Greenskares
Longmanhill
Dubford
Cushnie
Towie
New Aberdour
Upper Boyndlie
Coburty
Percyhorner
Peathill
Pitblae
Mid Ardlaw
Tyrie
Memsie
Memsie Burial Cairn
Whitewell
Ladysford
Windyheads Hill
Nether Glasslaw
Netherbrae
Mid Cloch Forbie
Minnonie
Craigmaud
Hill of Fishrie
Hillhead of Auchentumb
Newburgh
Mormond Hill
Strichen
Knowhead
New Pitsligo
New Leeds
Longhill
Nether Park
Blackhill
Montcoffer Ho.
Kirktown of Alvah
Keilhill
Gorrachie
Greenlaw
King Edward
The Pole of Itlaw
Fattahead
Weachyburn
Blacklaw
Hill of Mountblairy
Milltown of Craigston
Craigston Castle
Plaidy
Fintry
Muirden
New Byth
Bonnykelly
Forglen Ho.
Cranna
Bogton
Clunie
Carnousie
Turriff
Delgatie Castle
Muiryfold
Garmond
Whitestones
Ironside
Oldwhat
Balthangie
Mains of Fedderate
Cuminestown
Middle Cairncake
Culsh
Adziel
Little Skillymarno
North Ugie Water
Denhead
Fetterangus
Forest of Deer
Deer Abbey
Dunshillock
Toux
Balearn
Leys
St Fergus Moss
Backfolds
Rora Moss
Hythie
Rora
Kirktown
St Fergus
Scotstown Hd.
North Kirkton
Kirkton Hd.
Lunderton
Woodside
Newseat
Inverugie
Inverugie Castle
Torterston
Ugie Salmon Fish House
Buchanhaven
Longside
Flushing
Mintlaw
Aden
Aberdeenshire Farming Museum
Old Deer
Stuartfield
Maud
Maud Railway Museum
Backhill of Clackriach
Drymuir
Bulwark
Crichie
Mains of Crichie
New Deer
Rush-head
Kirkton
Little Colp
Delgaty Forest
Mill of Muiresk
Hatton Castle
Howe of Teuchar
Darra
Birkenhills
Auchininna
Inverkeithny
Fortrie
Brownhill
Crofts of Inverthernie
Dykeside
Drumblair
Denmoss
Balgaveny
Nether Lenshie
Kirkton of Auchterless
Inverythan
Gourdas
Tifty
Steinmanhill
Lethenty
Monkshill
Cottown
South Millbrex
Crofts of Meikle Ardo
Cairnbanno Ho.
Knaven
Nethermuir
Barrack
Auchnagatt
Cairnorrie
Brownhill
Mains of Annochie
Backhill of Fortree
Kinnadie
Skelmuir
Clola
Millbreck
Nether Kinmundy
Inverquhomery
Hillhead of Cocklaw
Peterhead Bay
Keith Inch
Peterhead Maritime
Arbuthnot Mus & Art Gallery
Invernettie
Sandford Bay
Little Dens
Blackhill
Millbank
Boddam
Buchan Ness
Stirling
Sandfordhill
Kinknockie
Smallburn
Moss of Cruden
Backhill
Stoneygate
Teuchan
Coldwells
Longhaven
North Haven
Bullers of Buchan
Auchiries
Hatton
Cruden Bay
Slains Castle
Port Erroll
Two Havens
Bay of Cruden
Chapel Hill
Eastertown of Auchleuchries
Bogbrae
Whinnyfold
Nether Leask
Artrochie
Auchmacoy
Muirtack
Arthrath
Toll of Birness
Mains of Birness
Milton of Coldwells
Hilton
Broomfield
Ellon
Esslemont
Ythsie
Skelmonae
Quilquox
Mains of Inkhorn
Drumwhindle
Ythanbank
Inverebrie
West Kinharrachie
Tarves
Raxton
Medieval Tomb
Haddo
Haddo House and Gardens
Methlick
Ardo
Crofts of Haddo
Woodhead
Fyvie
Fyvie Castle
Backhill
Gordonstown
Logie Newton
Badenscoth
Rothiebrisbane
Ythanwells
Aucharnie
Redhill
Fisherford
Rothienorman
Petty
Cromblet
St Katherine's
Collynie
Barthol Chapel
Earlsford
Wedderlairs
Folla Rule
Cross of Jackston
Jackstown
Balgove
Tulloch
Craigdam
Kirkton of Culsalmond
Rothmaise
Newseat
Tocher
Meikle Wartle
Cairnhill
Bonnyton
Kirkton of Rayne
Newton Ho.
Old Rayne
Insch
Ardoyne
Pitmachie
Durno
Mounie Castle
Daviot
Fingask
Meldrum Ho.
Auquhorthies
Tolquhon Castle
Pitmedden Gardens
Pitmedden
Oldmeldrum
Barra Castle
Cairnbrogie
Udny Green
Tipperty
Kirkton of Logie Buchan
Visitor Centre
Kirktown of Slains
Collieston
St Catherine's Dub
Waterside
Forvie
Sands of Forvie
Hackley Hd. or Forvie Ness
Meikle Tarty
Newburgh
Newburgh Bar
Foveran
Drums
Westhall
Whiteford
Pitcaple
Oyne
Kirkton of Oyne
Pitcaple
Harlaw Ho.
Chapel of Garioch
Pittodrie
Battle of Harlaw Memorial
Balhalgardy
Brandsbutt Stone
Bennachie
Burgh Muir
Inverurie
Inverurie Museum
Hillbrae
Kirkton of Bourtie
Mill of Kingoodie
Hattoncrook
Whiterashes
Affleck
Pettymuick
Udny Station
Cultercullen
Tillygreig
Tillycorthie
Minnes
Rashiereive
Nether Crimond
Tillykerrie
Straloch
Ardo Ho.
Middlemuir
Delfrigs
Manar Ho.
Upper Woodend
Bograxie
Port Elphinstone
Burnhervie
Aquhythie
Kinmuck
Kinkell Church
Middleton
Balbithan Ho.
Newmachar
Craigie
Causeyend
Whitecairns
Belhelvie
Balmedie
Blairdaff
Dalmadilly
Clovenstone
Balbithan
Wester Fintray
Cairnpark
Kinmundy
Drumligair
Pitfichie Forest
Monymusk Arts Centre
Grantlodge
Kemnay
Cottown
Kintore
Hatton of Fintray
Old Church
Cothall
Potterton
Corby Loch
Blackdog
Monymusk
Craigearn
Leylodge
Todlachie
Lauchintilly
Castle Fraser
Overton
Dyce
Aberdeen Airport
Parkhill Ho.
Mundurno
Blackburn
Haughs of Clinterty
Stoneywood
Denmore
Kirkwall Lerwick
Ordhead
Sauchen
Achath
Lyne of Skene
Bankhead
Bridge of Don
Cruickshank Botanic Garden
East Auchronie
Bucksburn
Hayton
Brig o' Balgownie
St Machar's Cathedral
Old Aberdeen
King's College Visitor Centre
Milton of Corsindae
Bankhead
Old Kinnernie
Corsindae
Dunecht
Skene Ho.
Kirkton of Skene
Woodside
Kittybrewster
Northfield
Mastrick
Midmar
Comers
Tillybirloch
Stone Circle
Marionburgh
Echt
Loch of Skene
Westhill
Kingswells
Satrosphere
Marischal Museum
Garlogie
Cairnie
Elrick
Gordon Highlanders Museum
Mannofield
Ferryhill
Torry
Girdle Ness
Midmar Forest
South Kirkton
Landerberry
Redhill
Blacktop
Ruthrieston
David Welch Winter Gardens
Nigg Bay
Greg Ness
Kincorth
Hill of Fare
Burn of Corrichie
West Cullerly
Hardgate
Benthoul
Easter Ord
Contlaw
Craigton
Milltimber
Milton of Murtle
Bieldside
Cults
Garthdee
Banchory Devenick
Nigg
Cove Bay
Milton of
NK
A90 A96 A97 A98 A920 A944 A947 A948 A950 A952 A975 A981 A93 A952
B9031 B9105 B9093 B9170 B9170 B9005 B9001 B9002 B9000 B9027 B9029 B9030 B9032 B9033 B9107 B9025 B9024 B992 B9119 B9125 B9126 B9139 B977 B979 B993 B994 B999 B9108 B9040
141
6 7 8 9 10 11
A B C D E F G H

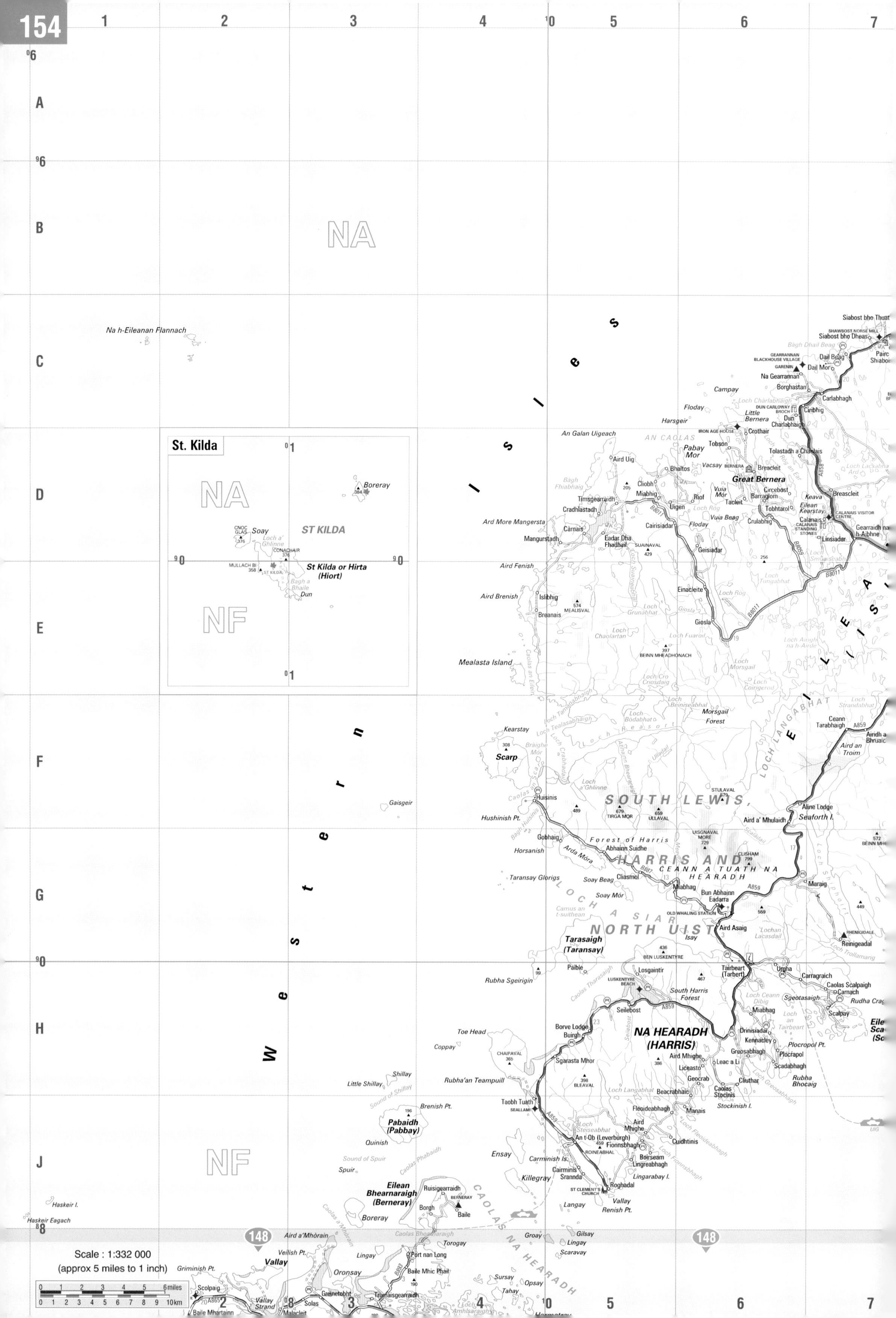
NA
St. Kilda
Boreray
Soay
ST KILDA
CONACHAIR
St Kilda or Hirta
(Hiort)
Bagh a Bhaile
Dun
NF
Na h-Eileanan Flannach
Western Isles
Great Bernera
Little Bernera
Mealasta Island
Scarp
Kearstay
Gaisgeir
SOUTH LEWIS, HARRIS AND
CEANN A TUATH NA HEARADH
Forest of Harris
LOCH SIAR
NORTH UIST
Tarasaigh
(Taransay)
NA HEARADH
(HARRIS)
Tairbeart
(Tarbert)
An t-Ob (Leverburgh)
Roghadal
Pabaidh
(Pabbay)
Eilean
Bhearnaraigh
(Berneray)
CAOLAS NA HEARADH
Valley
Scalpay
Morsgail
Forest
Loch Langabhat
Loch Seaforth
Calanais
Carlabhagh
Uig
Huisinis
Hushinish Pt.
Toe Head
Shillay
Haskeir I.
Haskeir Eagach
Scale : 1:332 000
(approx 5 miles to 1 inch)
148
148

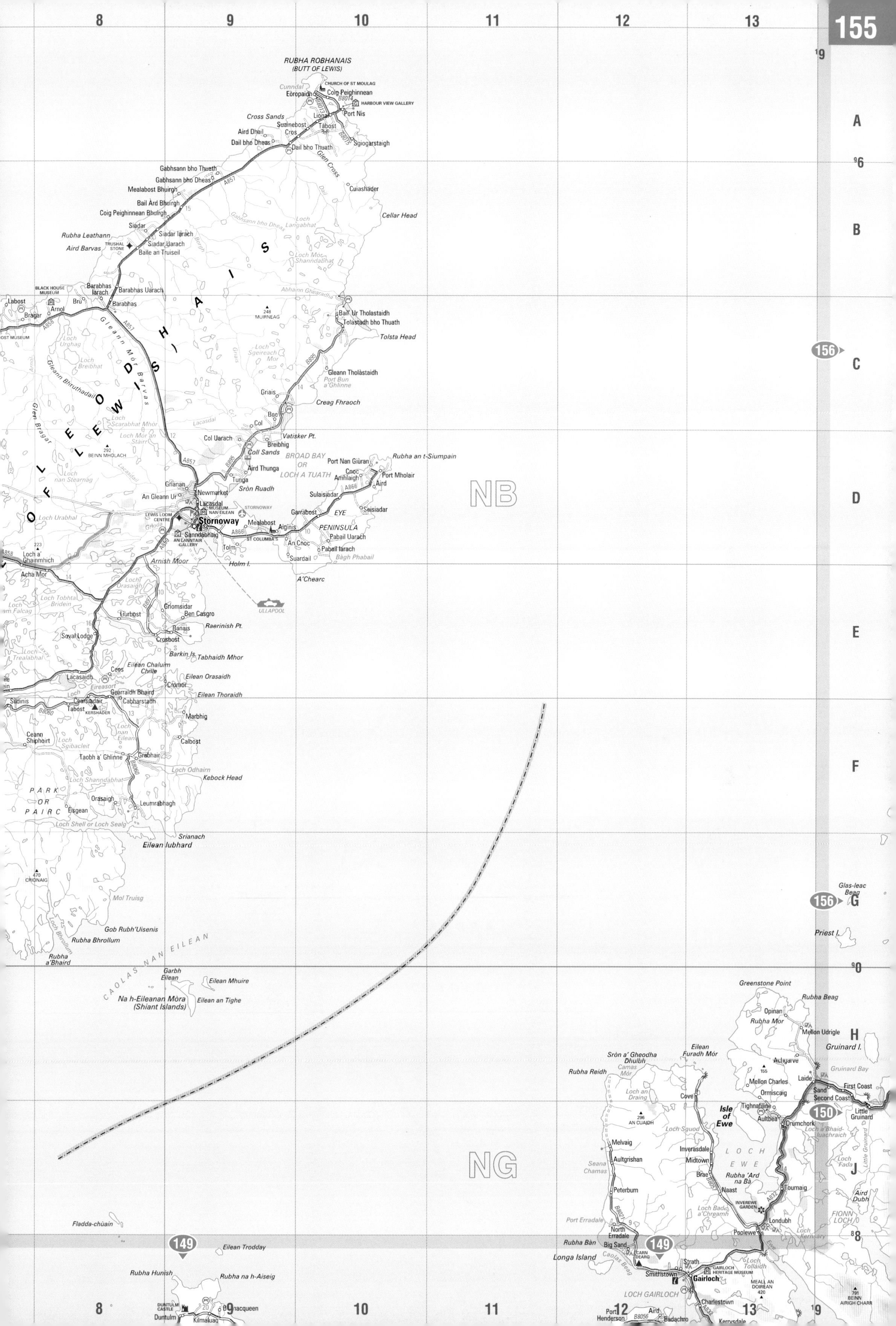
RUBHA ROBHANAIS
(BUTT OF LEWIS)
CHURCH OF ST MOULAG
Cunndal
Eòropaidh
Coig Peighinnean
HARBOUR VIEW GALLERY
Lional
Port Nis
Cross Sands
Suainebost
Tabost
Aird Dhail
Cros
Dail bho Dheas
Dail bho Thuath
Sgiogarstaigh
Glen Cross
Gabhsann bho Thuath
Gabhsann bho Dheas
Cuiashader
Mealabost Bhuirgh
Bail Àrd Bhuirgh
Coig Peighinnean Bhuirgh
Cellar Head
Loch Langabhat
Siadar
Rubha Leathann
Siadar Iarach
TRUSHAL STONE
Siadar Uarach
Aird Barvas
Baile an Truiseil
Loch Mor Shanndabhat
BLACK HOUSE MUSEUM
Barabhas Iarach
Barabhas Uarach
Labost
Brù
Arnol
Barabhas
Bragar
Abhainn Ghearadha
Baile Ur Tholastaidh
Tolastadh bho Thuath
248 MUIRNEAG
Tolsta Head
Gleann Mòr Barvas
Loch Urghag
Loch Breibhat
Gleann Bhruthadail
Loch Sgeireach Mor
Gleann Tholàstaidh
Port Bun a' Ghlinne
Glen Bragar
Griais
Creag Fhraoch
Loch Scarabhat Mhòr
Lacasdal
Bac
Col
Loch Mòr an Stàirr
Col Uarach
Vatisker Pt.
292 BEINN MHOLACH
Breibhig
Coll Sands
BROAD BAY OR LOCH A TUATH
Port Nan Giùran
Rubha an t-Siumpain
Aird Thunga
Loch nan Stearnag
Tunga
Cnoc Amhlaigh
Port Mholair
Aird
Sròn Ruadh
Griannan
Newmarket
Sulaisiadar
NB
An Gleann Ur
Lacasdal
MUSEUM NAN EILEAN
STORNOWAY
Seisiadar
LEWIS LOOM CENTRE
Garrabost
EYE
Loch Urabhal
Stornoway
Mealabost
Aiginis
PENINSULA
Sanndabhaig
ST COLUMBA'S
AN LANNTAIR GALLERY
Pabail Uarach
An Cnoc
223
Loch a' Ghainmhich
Tolm
Pabail Iarach
Suardail
Bàgh Phabail
Arnish Moor
Holm I.
Acha Mor
A' Chearc
Loch Orasaigh
Loch Tobhtal Bridein
Gromsidar
ULLAPOOL
Liurbost
Ben Casgro
Ranais
Raerinish Pt.
Soval Lodge
Crosbost
Loch Trealabhal
Barkin Is.
Tabhaidh Mhor
Eilean Chaluim Chille
Ceos
Lacasaidh
Eilean Orasaidh
Eireasort
Cromor
Gearraidh Bhaird
Eilean Thoraidh
Cearsiadair
Cabharstadh
Tabost
KERSHADER
Marbhig
Loch nan Eilean
Ceann Shiphoirt
Loch Sgibacleit
Calbost
Taobh a' Ghlinne
Grabhair
Loch Odhairn
Loch Shanndabhat
Kebock Head
PARK OR PAIRC
Orasaigh
Eisgean
Leumrabhagh
Loch Shell or Loch Sealg
Srianach
Eilean Iubhard
470 CRIONAIG
Mol Truisg
Gob Rubh' Uisenis
Loch Bhrollum
Rubha Bhrollum
Rubha a' Bhaird
CAOLAS NAN EILEAN
Garbh Eilean
Eilean Mhuire
Na h-Eileanan Mòra (Shiant Islands)
Eilean an Tighe
Glas-leac Beag
156
Priest I.
Greenstone Point
Rubha Beag
Opinan
Rubha Mor
Mellon Udrigle
Gruinard I.
Eilean Furadh Mòr
Sròn a' Gheodha Dhulbh
Camas Mòr
Rubha Reidh
Achgarve
Gruinard Bay
155
Laide
First Coast
Mellon Charles
Sand
Second Coast
Loch an Draing
Ormiscaig
Cove
Isle of Ewe
Tighnafiline
Aultbea
150
Little Gruinard
296 AN CUAIDH
Drumchork
Loch a' Bhaid-luachraich
Loch Sguod
Melvaig
Inverasdale
LOCH EWE
Loch Fada
Aultgrishan
Midtown
Seana Chamas
NG
Brae
Rubha 'Ard na Bà
Tournaig
Peterburn
Naast
Aird Dubh
INVEREWE GARDEN
Loch Bad a' Chreamh
FIONN LOCH
Port Erradale
Londubh
North Erradale
Poolewe
Loch Kernsary
Fladda-chùain
149
Eilean Trodday
Rubha Bàn
Big Sand
CARN DEARG
Longa Island
Caolas Beag
Strath
Loch Tollaidh
Smithstown
Gairloch
GAIRLOCH HERITAGE MUSEUM
MEALL AN DOIREAN 420
Rubha Hunish
Rubha na h-Aiseig
LOCH GAIRLOCH
791 BEINN AIRIGH CHARR
DUNTULM CASTLE
Bornacqueen
Duntulm
Kilmaluag
Port Henderson
Aird
Badachro
Charlestown
Kerrysdale
A857
A858
A851
B895
A866
A859
B897
B8014
B8015
B8060
B8021
B8056
A832

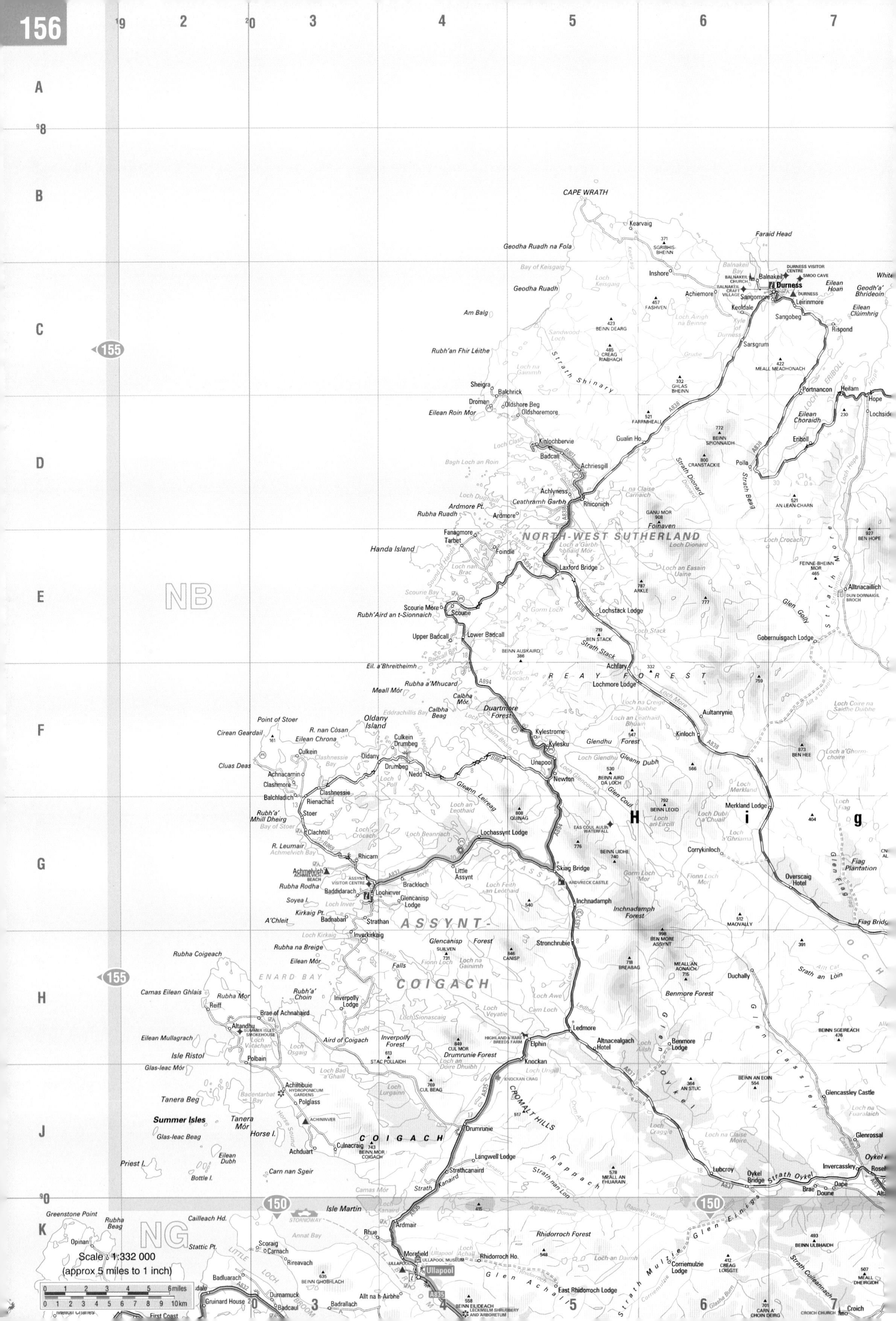
CAPE WRATH
Kearvaig
Faraid Head
Geodha Ruadh na Fola
Bay of Keisgaig
Inshore
Balnakeil
Durness
Sangomore
Geodha Ruadh
Achiemore
Keoldale
Leirinmore
Sangobeg
Rispond
Eilean Hoan
Geodh'a' Bhrideoin
Eilean Clùimhrig
Am Balg
Rubh'an Fhir Léithe
Sarsgrum
Strath Shinary
Sandwood Loch
Sheigra
Balchrick
Droman
Oldshore Beg
Oldshoremore
Eilean Roin Mor
Portnancon
Heilam
Hope
Lochside
Eilean Choraidh
Eriboll
Loch Eriboll
Kinlochbervie
Badcall
Achriesgill
Gualin Ho.
Polla
Strath Beag
Strath Dionard
Bagh Loch an Roin
Achlyness
Ceathramh Garbh
Rhiconich
Ardmore Pt.
Rubha Ruadh
Ardmore
Foinaven
NORTH-WEST SUTHERLAND
Loch Dionard
Loch Crocach
BEN HOPE
Fanagmore
Tarbet
Foindle
Handa Island
Laxford Bridge
NB
Arkle
Scourie More
Scourie
Rubh'Aird an t-Sionnaich
Lochstack Lodge
Alltnacaillich
Glen Golly
Upper Badcall
Lower Badcall
Gobernuisgach Lodge
Strath Stack
Eil. a'Bhreitheimh
Achfary
REAY FOREST
Rubha a'Mhucard
Lochmore Lodge
Meall Mór
Calbha Mór
Calbha Beag
Duartmore Forest
Eddrachillis Bay
Oldany Island
Aultanrynie
Point of Stoer
Cirean Geardail
R. nan Còsan
Eilean Chrona
Culkein Drumbeg
Kylestrome
Kylesku
Glendhu Forest
Kinloch
BEN HEE
Cluas Deas
Culkein
Oldany
Drumbeg
Nedd
Unapool
Gleann Dubh
Newton
Achnacarnin
Clashmore
Clashnessie
Balchladich
Rienachait
Gleann Leireag
Loch Merkland
Merkland Lodge
Rubh'a' Mhill Dheirg
Stoer
Clachtoll
Bay of Stoer
QUINAG
Lochassynt Lodge
Corrykinloch
Flag Plantation
R. Leumair
Achmelvich Bay
Rhicarn
Achmelvich
Little Assynt
Loch Assynt
Skiag Bridge
Ardvreck Castle
Overscaig Hotel
Rubha Rodha
Brackloch
Baddidarach
Lochinver
Glencanisp Lodge
Inchnadamph
Inchnadamph Forest
Soyea I.
Kirkaig Pt.
Badnaban
Strathan
ASSYNT-
A'Chleit
Inverkirkaig
Fiag Bridge
BEN MORE ASSYNT
Rubha Coigeach
Rubha na Breige
Glencanisp Forest
Suilven
Stronchrubie
Eilean Mór
CANISP
BREABAG
Falls
ENARD BAY
COIGACH
Duchally
Camas Eilean Ghlais
Rubha Mor
Rubh'a' Choin
Inverpolly Lodge
Benmore Forest
Reiff
Brae of Achnahaird
Altandhu
Loch Sionascaig
Ledmore
Eilean Mullagrach
Aird of Coigach
Inverpolly Forest
Altnacealgach Hotel
Benmore Lodge
Isle Ristol
Polbain
CUL MOR
Drumrunie Forest
Elphin
Knockan
Glas-leac Mór
STAC POLLAIDH
Achiltibuie
Glen Oykel
CUL BEAG
Tanera Beg
Badentarbat Bay
Polglass
CROMALT HILLS
Glencassley Castle
Summer Isles
Tanera Mór
Glas-leac Beag
Horse I.
Drumrunie
COIGACH
Glenrossal
Culnacraig
Achduart
Langwell Lodge
Priest I.
Eilean Dubh
Oykel
Invercassley
Carn nan Sgeir
Strathcanaird
Rappach
Lubcroy
Oykel Bridge
Strath Oykel
Bottle I.
Strath Kanaird
Brae
Doune
Oape
Rosehall
Isle Martin
Greenstone Point
Rubha Beag
Cailleach Hd.
NG
Ardmair
Glen Einig
Opinan
Rhue
Rhidorroch Forest
Stattic Pt.
Scoraig
Carnach
Annat Bay
Scale 1:332 000
(approx 5 miles to 1 inch)
Morefield
Ullapool
Rhidorroch Ho.
Strath Mulzie
Corriemulzie Lodge
Rireavach
Loch an Daimh
Strath Cuileannach
Badluarach
Glen Achall
East Rhidorroch Lodge
Little Loch Broom
Loch Broom
Gruinard House
Dumamuck
Badcaul
Badrallach
Altnaharrie
First Coast
Croich
155
150

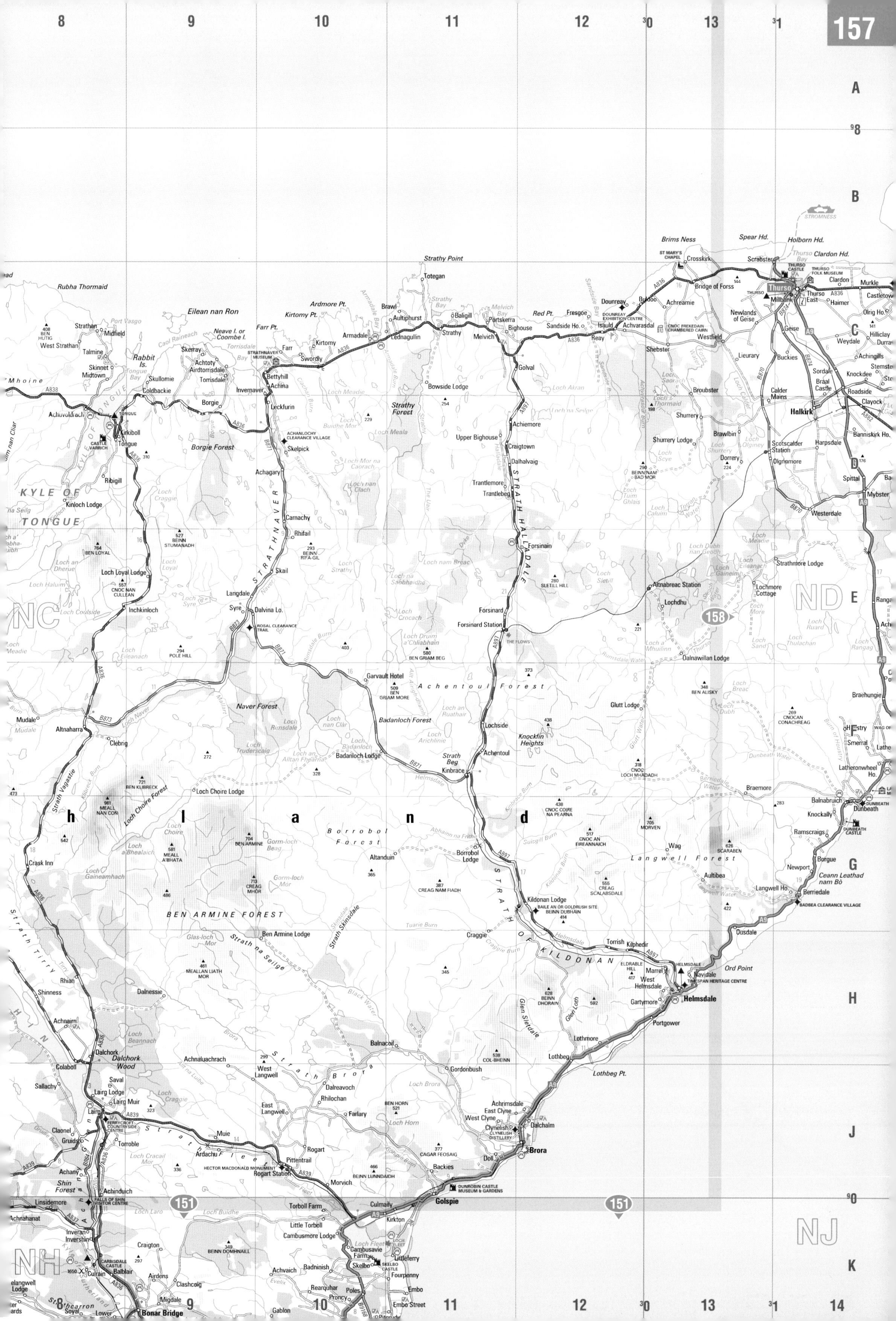
Strathy Point
Rubha Thormaid
Eilean nan Ron
Ardmore Pt.
Kirtomy Pt.
Farr Pt.
Brims Ness
Spear Hd.
Holborn Hd.
Clardon Hd.
Thurso
Scrabster
Crosskirk
Bridge of Forss
Dounreay
Reay
Melvich
Portskerra
Bighouse
Strathy
Armadale
Bettyhill
Farr
Tongue
KYLE OF TONGUE
Borgie Forest
Strathy Forest
STRATHNAVER
STRATH HALLADALE
Forsinard
Forsinard Station
Altnabreac Station
Achentoul Forest
Naver Forest
Badanloch Forest
Knockfin Heights
Kinbrace
Loch Choire Lodge
Borrobol Forest
BEN ARMINE FOREST
Langwell Forest
STRATH OF KILDONAN
Helmsdale
Ord Point
Dunbeath
Berriedale
Lothbeg Pt.
Brora
Golspie
Strath Brora
Strath Fleet
Lairg
Rogart Station
Altnaharra
Crask Inn
Halkirk
Spittal
Westerdale
Bonar Bridge
NC
ND
NH
NJ
158
151
h
l
a
n
d

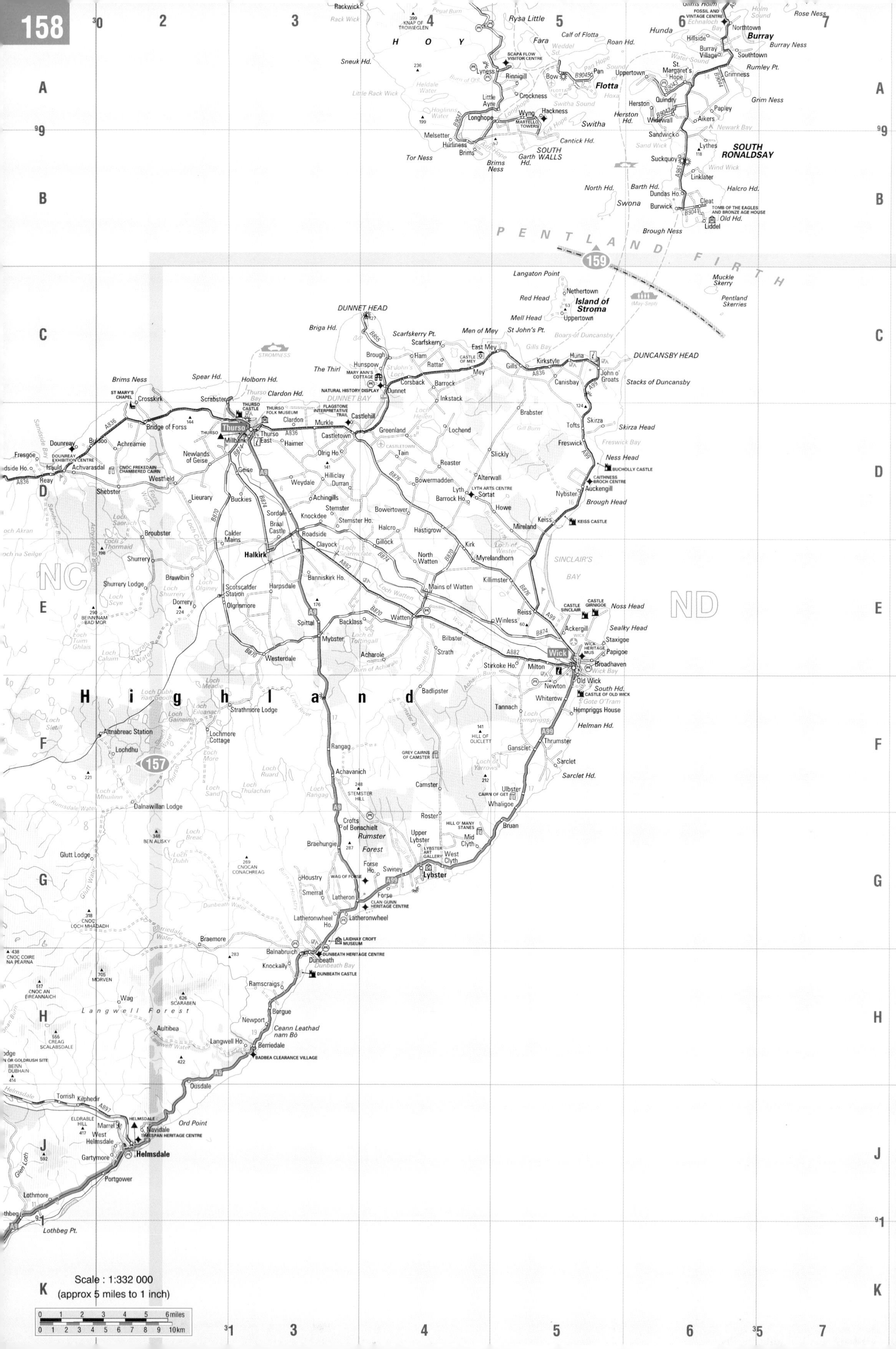
HOY
Flotta
Burray
SOUTH RONALDSAY
Swona
SOUTH WALLS
PENTLAND FIRTH
Island of Stroma
DUNNET HEAD
DUNCANSBY HEAD
Stacks of Duncansby
John o' Groats
Dunnet
Castletown
Thurso
Scrabster
Halkirk
Wick
Keiss
Reiss
Watten
Spittal
Mybster
Lybster
Latheron
Latheronwheel
Dunbeath
Berriedale
Helmsdale
Navidale
Portgower
Lothbeg Pt.
Dounreay
Reay
Westfield
Shebster
Altnabreac Station
Dalnawillan Lodge
Glutt Lodge
Braemore
MORVEN
SCARABEN
Langwell Forest
Rumster Forest
SINCLAIR'S BAY
Noss Head
Sarclet Hd.
Thrumster
Ulbster
Highland
NC
ND
Scale : 1:332 000
(approx 5 miles to 1 inch)
0 1 2 3 4 5 6 miles
0 1 2 3 4 5 6 7 8 9 10 km

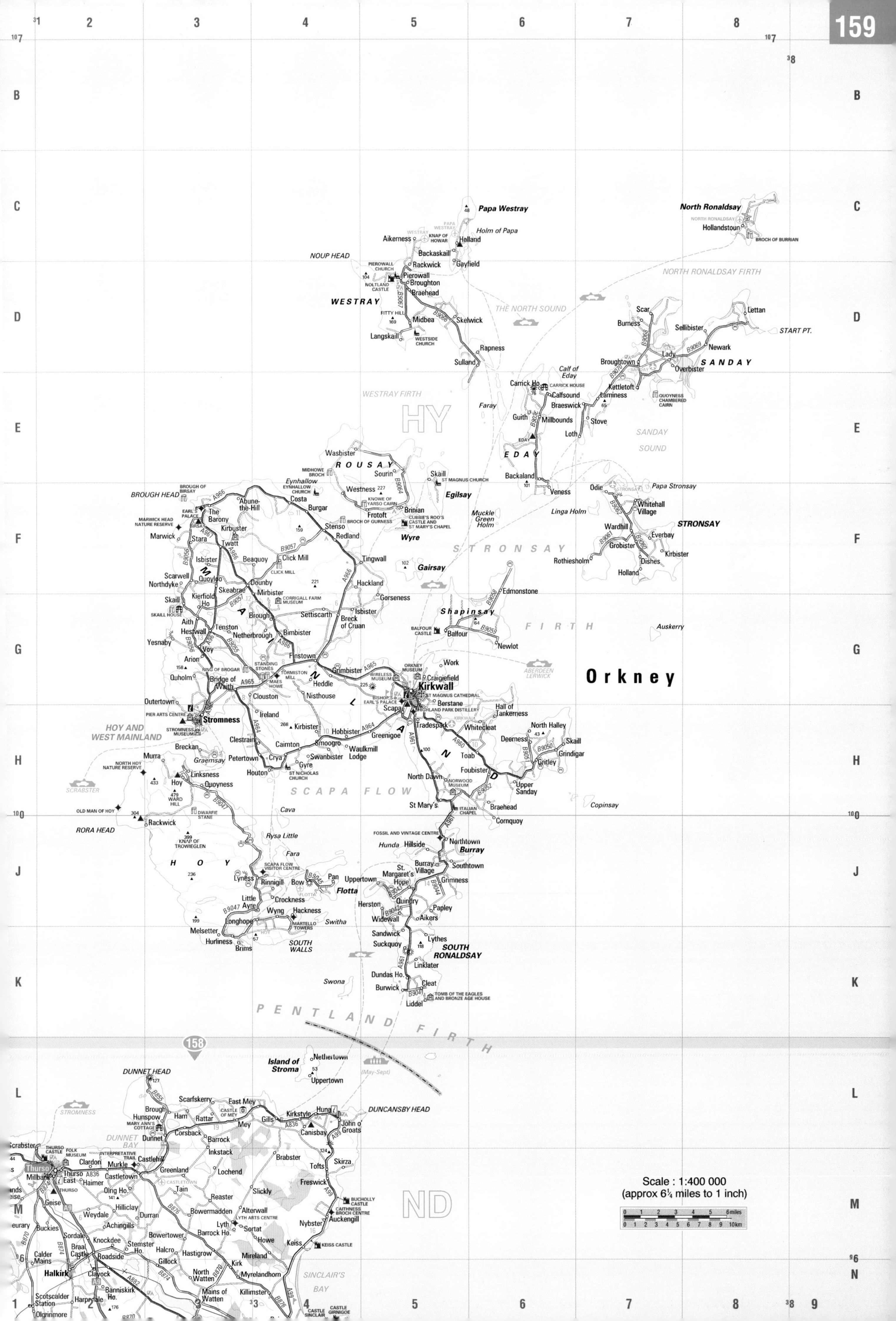

Papa Westray
Holm of Papa
Aikerness
Holland
Backaskaill
Gayfield
NOUP HEAD
Rackwick
Pierowall
Broughton
Braehead
WESTRAY
Skelwick
Midbea
Langskaill
Rapness
Sulland
North Ronaldsay
Hollandstoun
BROCH OF BURRIAN
NORTH RONALDSAY FIRTH
THE NORTH SOUND
Scar
Burness
Lettan
Sellibister
START PT.
Newark
Lady
SANDAY
Broughtown
Overbister
Calf of Eday
Carrick Ho.
CARRICK HOUSE
Calfsound
Kettletoft
Laminess
QUOYNESS CHAMBERED CAIRN
Braeswick
Faray
Guith
Millbounds
Stove
Loth
SANDAY SOUND
WESTRAY FIRTH
HY
Wasbister
EDAY
ROUSAY
Sourin
Skaill
ST MAGNUS CHURCH
Backaland
Veness
Odie
Papa Stronsay
Westness
Egilsay
Whitehall Village
Eynhallow
BROUGH HEAD
Costa
Abune-the-Hill
Burgar
Brinian
Frotoft
Linga Holm
STRONSAY
The Barony
Kirbuster
Muckle Green Holm
Wyre
Wardhill
Everbay
Marwick
Stara
Stenso
Redland
Twatt
Grobister
Kirbister
Rothiesholm
Dishes
Holland
S T R O N S A Y
Isbister
Beaquoy
Click Mill
Tingwall
Gairsay
Scarwell
Northdyke
Quoyloo
Dounby
Hackland
Edmonstone
Skaill
Kierfiold Ho
Skeabrae
Mirbister
Gorseness
Shapinsay
Aith
Hestwall
Tenston
Netherbrough
Brough
Settiscarth
Isbister
Breck of Cruan
Balfour
F I R T H
Auskerry
Yesnaby
Bimbister
Newlot
Voy
Arion
Finstown
Work
Quholm
Bridge of Waith
Grimbister
Heddle
Craigiefield
Kirkwall
Orkney
Outertown
Clouston
Nisthouse
Scapa
Berstane
Hall of Tankerness
Stromness
Ireland
Kirbister
Hobbister
Tradespark
Whitecleat
North Halley
HOY AND WEST MAINLAND
Clestrain
Cairnton
Smoogro
Greenigoe
Deerness
Skaill
Grindigar
Breckan
Graemsay
Waulkmill Lodge
Toab
Gritley
Murra
Petertown
Crya
Swanbister
Gyre
Foubister
Linksness
Houton
North Dawn
Hoy
Quoyness
S C A P A   F L O W
Upper Sanday
Braehead
Copinsay
OLD MAN OF HOY
Rackwick
St Mary's
Cornquoy
RORA HEAD
Cava
Rysa Little
Northtown
Hunda
Hillside
Burray
Fara
H O Y
St. Margaret's Hope
Burray Village
Southtown
Lyness
Rinnigill
Bow
Pan
Uppertown
Grimness
Flotta
Little Ayre
Crockness
Herston
Quindry
Papley
Wyng
Hackness
Widewall
Aikers
Switha
Longhope
Melsetter
Hurliness
Brims
SOUTH WALLS
Sandwick
Suckquoy
Lythes
SOUTH RONALDSAY
Linklater
Swona
Dundas Ho.
Cleat
Burwick
TOMB OF THE EAGLES AND BRONZE AGE HOUSE
Liddel
P E N T L A N D   F I R T H
158
Island of Stroma
Nethertown
Uppertown
(May-Sept)
DUNNET HEAD
DUNCANSBY HEAD
Scarfskerry
East Mey
Brough
Ham
Rattar
CASTLE OF MEY
Mey
Gills
Kirkstyle
Huna
John o' Groats
Hunspow
MARY ANN'S COTTAGE
Dunnet
Corsback
Canisbay
DUNNET BAY
Barrock
Scrabster
THURSO CASTLE
FOLK MUSEUM
Clardon
Inkstack
Brabster
Skirza
Thurso
Murkle
Castlehill
Greenland
Lochend
Tofts
Millbank
East
Castletown
Haimer
Tain
Olrig Ho.
Freswick
Slickly
Scale : 1:400 000
(approx 6¼ miles to 1 inch)
Geise
Hilliclay
Reaster
ND
BUCHOLLY CASTLE
CAIRNESS BROCH CENTRE
Weydale
Durran
Bowermadden
Alterwall
Auckengill
Achingills
Lyth
LYTH ARTS CENTRE
Nybster
Buckies
Sordale
Knockdee
Bowertower
Barrock Ho.
Sortat
Braal Castle
Stemster Ho.
Halcro
Howe
Keiss
KEISS CASTLE
Calder Mains
Roadside
Hastigrow
Mireland
Halkirk
Gillock
Kirk
Clayock
North Watten
Myrelandhorn
SINCLAIR'S BAY
Banniskirk Ho.
Scotscalder Station
Harpsdale
Mains of Watten
Killimster
CASTLE SINCLAIR
CASTLE GIRNIGOE
Olgrinmore

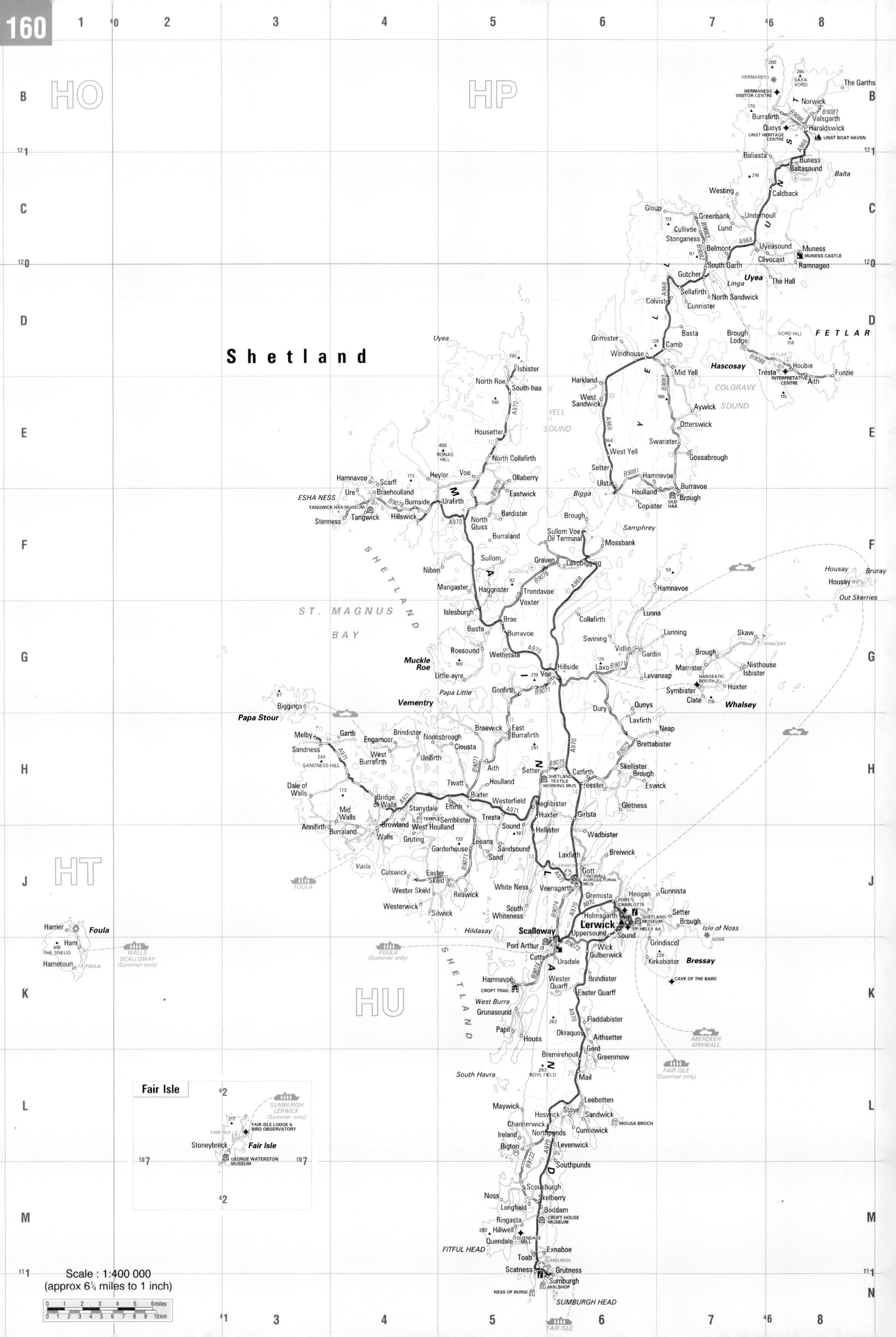
Shetland
HO
HP
HT
HU
Unst
Yell
Mainland
Fetlar
Whalsay
Bressay
Foula
Papa Stour
Muckle Roe
Vementry
St. Magnus Bay
Shetland
Yell Sound
Colgrave Sound
Hermaness Visitor Centre
Unst Heritage Centre
Unst Boat Haven
Muness Castle
Haroldswick
Baltasound
Uyeasound
Belmont
Gutcher
Mid Yell
Burravoe
Old Haa
Sullom Voe Oil Terminal
Brae
Voe
Hanseatic Booth
Shetland Textile Working Mus
Tingwall Agricultural Mus
Lerwick
Fort Charlotte
Shetland Museum
Up Helly Aa
Isle of Noss
Cave of the Bard
Scalloway
Croft Trail
Sandwick
Mousa Broch
Croft House Museum
Quendale Mill
Jarlshof
Sumburgh
Sumburgh Head
Fitful Head
Ness of Burgi
Foula (Summer only)
Walls Scalloway (Summer only)
Aberdeen Kirkwall
Fair Isle (Summer only)
Fair Isle
Fair Isle Lodge & Bird Observatory
George Waterston Museum
Stoneybreck
Sumburgh Lerwick (Summer only)
Scale : 1:400 000
(approx 6¼ miles to 1 inch)
6 miles
10 km

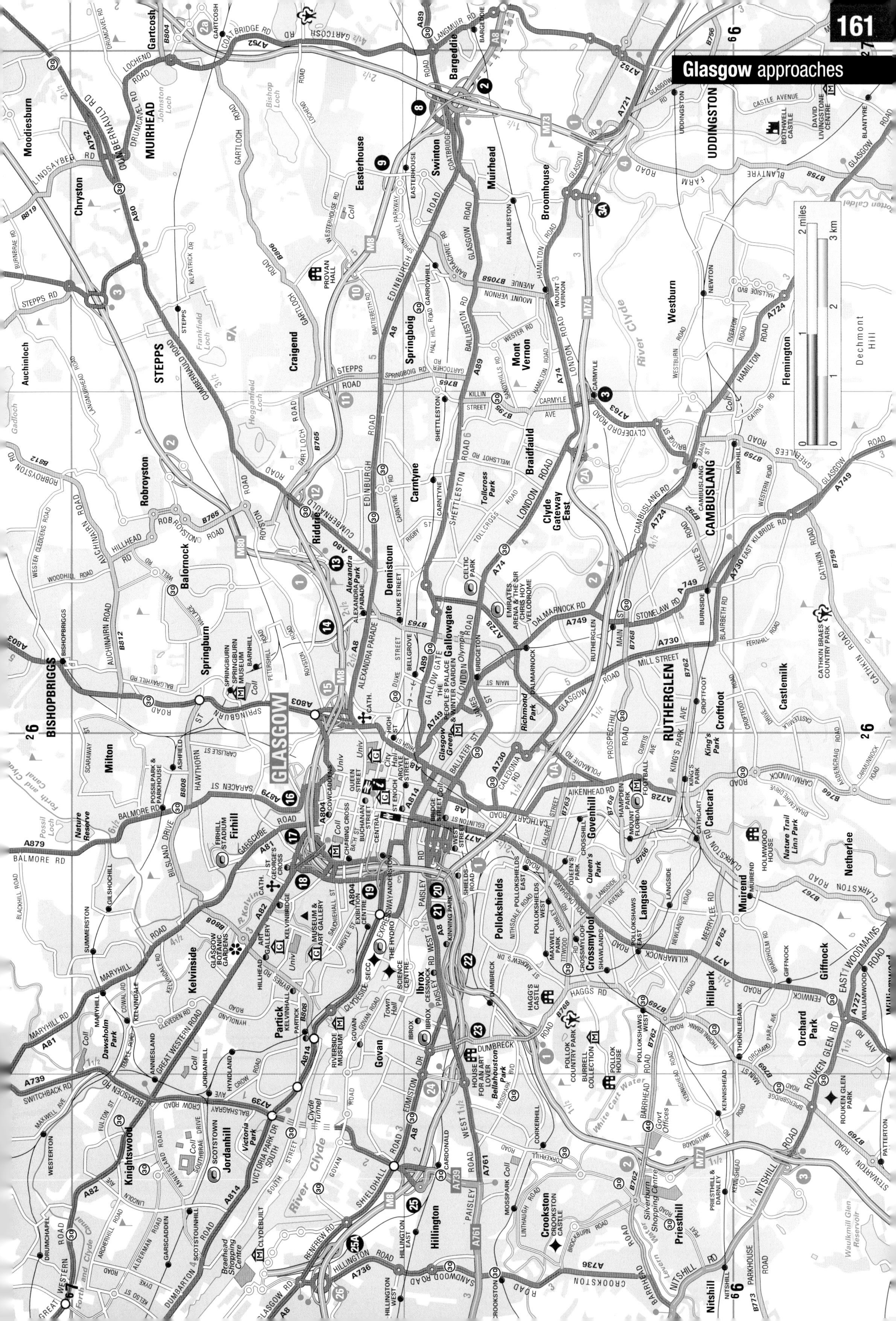
GLASGOW
Bishopbriggs
Muirhead
Moodiesburn
Chryston
Stepps
Auchinloch
Robroyston
Balornock
Springburn
Milton
Craigend
Easterhouse
Swinton
Bargeddie
Gartcosh
Springboig
Riddrie
Carntyne
Dennistoun
Gallowgate
Mont Vernon
Braidfauld
Broomhouse
Uddingston
Westburn
Flemington
Cambuslang
Rutherglen
Croftfoot
Castlemilk
Cathcart
Govanhill
Crossmyloof
Langside
Muirend
Netherlee
Giffnock
Hillpark
Orchard Park
Priesthill
Nitshill
Crookston
Hillington
Pollokshields
Ibrox
Govan
Partick
Kelvinside
Jordanhill
Knightswood
Firhill
River Clyde
Celtic Park
Hampden Park
Pollok Country Park
Burrell Collection
Rouken Glen Park
Linn Park
Bellahouston Park
Glasgow Botanic Gardens
Provan Hall
Haggs Castle
Crookston Castle
Bothwell Castle
Cathkin Braes Country Park
Dechmont Hill
Clyde Gateway East
Tollcross Park
Alexandra Park
Victoria Park
Dawsholm Park
Richmond Park
Glasgow Green
2 miles
3 km

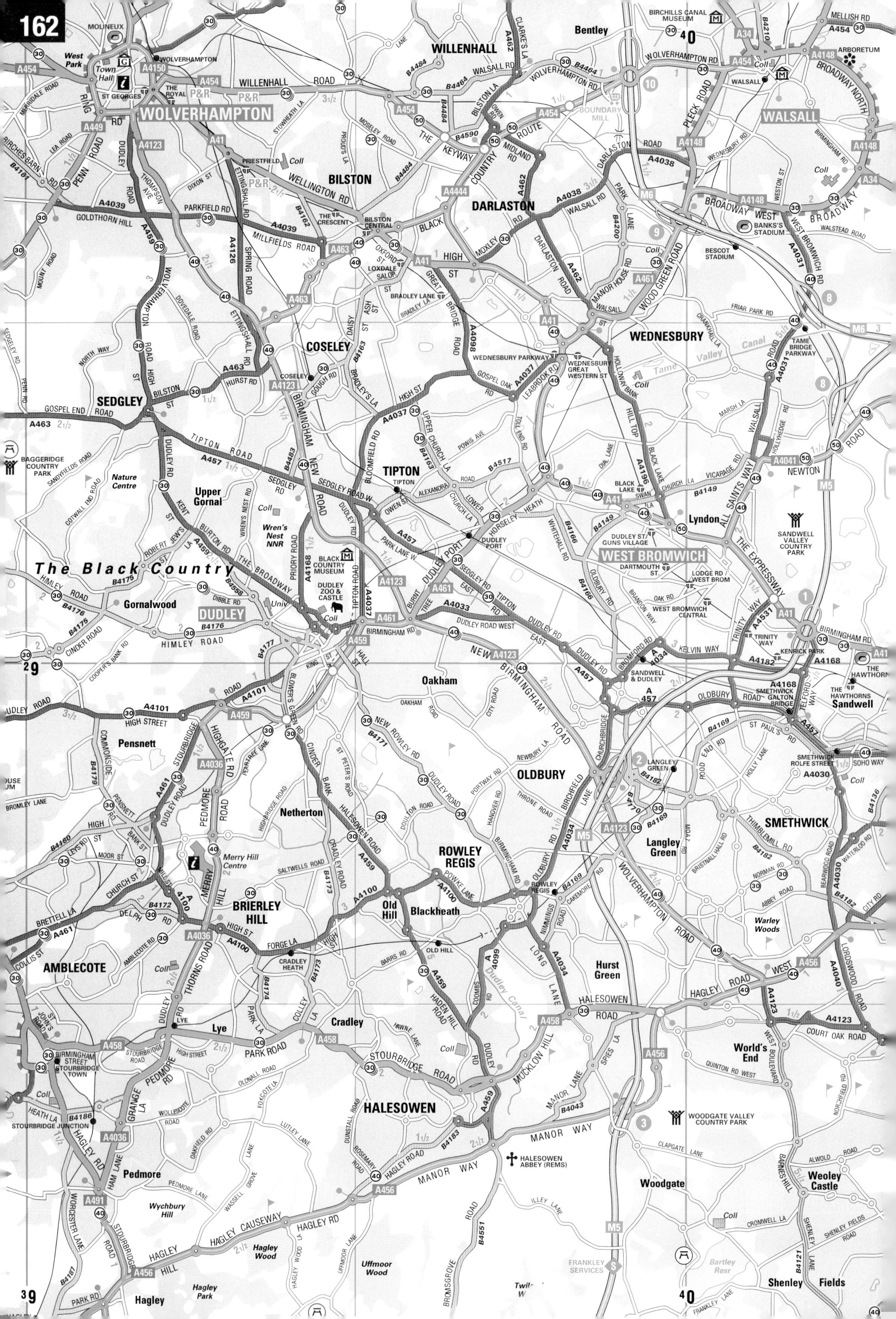
WOLVERHAMPTON
MOLINEUX
West Park
Town Hall
ST GEORGES
THE ROYAL
WILLENHALL
Bentley
BIRCHILLS CANAL MUSEUM
WALSALL
ARBORETUM
BILSTON
BILSTON CENTRAL
THE CRESCENT
PRIESTFIELD
DARLASTON
BOUNDARY MILL
BESCOT STADIUM
BANKS'S STADIUM
WEDNESBURY
WEDNESBURY PARKWAY
WEDNESBURY GREAT WESTERN ST
TAME BRIDGE PARKWAY
COSELEY
SEDGLEY
BAGGERIDGE COUNTRY PARK
Nature Centre
Upper Gornal
TIPTON
Wren's Nest NNR
BLACK COUNTRY MUSEUM
DUDLEY ZOO & CASTLE
DUDLEY PORT
Black Lake
DUDLEY ST GUNS VILLAGE
WEST BROMWICH
DARTMOUTH ST.
LODGE RD / WEST BROM
WEST BROMWICH CENTRAL
Lyndon
SANDWELL VALLEY COUNTRY PARK
NEWTON
The Black Country
Gornalwood
DUDLEY
Oakham
SANDWELL & DUDLEY
THE HAWTHORNS
Sandwell
SMETHWICK GALTON BRIDGE
SMETHWICK ROLFE STREET
Pensnett
Netherton
OLDBURY
LANGLEY GREEN
Langley Green
SMETHWICK
Merry Hill Centre
ROWLEY REGIS
BRIERLEY HILL
Old Hill
Blackheath
OLD HILL
CRADLEY HEATH
AMBLECOTE
Hurst Green
Warley Woods
Lye
Cradley
World's End
STOURBRIDGE TOWN
STOURBRIDGE JUNCTION
HALESOWEN
HALESOWEN ABBEY (REMS)
WOODGATE VALLEY COUNTRY PARK
Woodgate
Weoley Castle
Pedmore
Wychbury Hill
Hagley Wood
Uffmoor Wood
FRANKLEY SERVICES
Bartley Resr
Hagley
Hagley Park
Shenley Fields
M5
M6
A41
A454
A4123
A459
A461
A4037
A4036
A4100
A458
A456
A457
A4034
A4030
A4040
A491

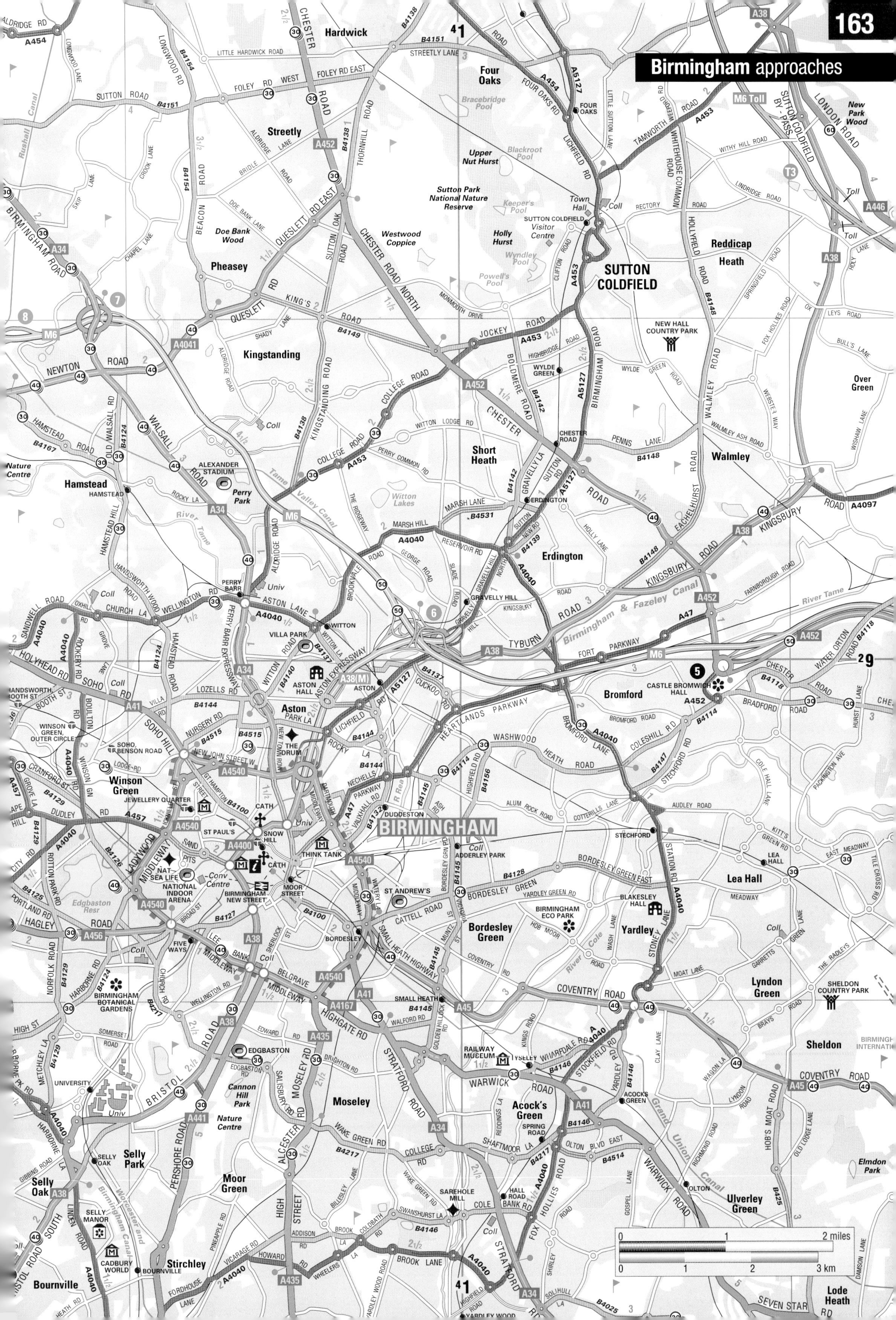
Hardwick
Four Oaks
Streetly
Bracebridge Pool
Blackroot Pool
Upper Nut Hurst
Sutton Park National Nature Reserve
Keeper's Pool
Town Hall
Coll
SUTTON COLDFIELD
Visitor Centre
Holly Hurst
Wyndley Pool
Powell's Pool
Doe Bank Wood
Westwood Coppice
Pheasey
SUTTON COLDFIELD
Reddicap Heath
New Park Wood
NEW HALL COUNTRY PARK
Kingstanding
Over Green
Walmley
Short Heath
Witton Lakes
ERDINGTON
Erdington
Hamstead
Nature Centre
ALEXANDER STADIUM
Perry Park
River Tame
Tame Valley Canal
PERRY BARR
Univ
GRAVELLY HILL
Birmingham & Fazeley Canal
VILLA PARK
WITTON
ASTON HALL
ASTON
Aston
Bromford
CASTLE BROMWICH HALL
THE DRUM
Winson Green
WINSON GREEN, OUTER CIRCLE
SOHO, BENSON ROAD
JEWELLERY QUARTER
CATH
ST PAUL'S
SNOW HILL
BIRMINGHAM
DUDDESTON
THINK TANK
Coll
ADDERLEY PARK
STECHFORD
LEA HALL
Lea Hall
NAT SEA LIFE
NATIONAL INDOOR ARENA
Conv Centre
BIRMINGHAM NEW STREET
MOOR STREET
ST ANDREW'S
Bordesley Green
BIRMINGHAM ECO PARK
BLAKESLEY HALL
Yardley
Edgbaston Resr
FIVE WAYS
BORDESLEY
BIRMINGHAM BOTANICAL GARDENS
SMALL HEATH
Lyndon Green
SHELDON COUNTRY PARK
EDGBASTON
RAILWAY MUSEUM
TYSELEY
Sheldon
UNIVERSITY
Univ
Cannon Hill Park
Nature Centre
Moseley
Acock's Green
ACOCKS GREEN
SPRING ROAD
Selly Park
SELLY OAK
Selly Oak
Moor Green
SAREHOLE MILL
HALL GREEN
OLTON
Ulverley Green
Elmdon Park
SELLY MANOR
CADBURY WORLD
BOURNVILLE
Stirchley
Bournville
Lode Heath
Grand Union Canal
Worcester and Birmingham Canal
River Cole
River Rea
M6
M6 Toll
A38
A452
A453
A5127
A34
A4040
A4540
A41
A45
A435
A441
0 1 2 miles
0 1 2 3 km

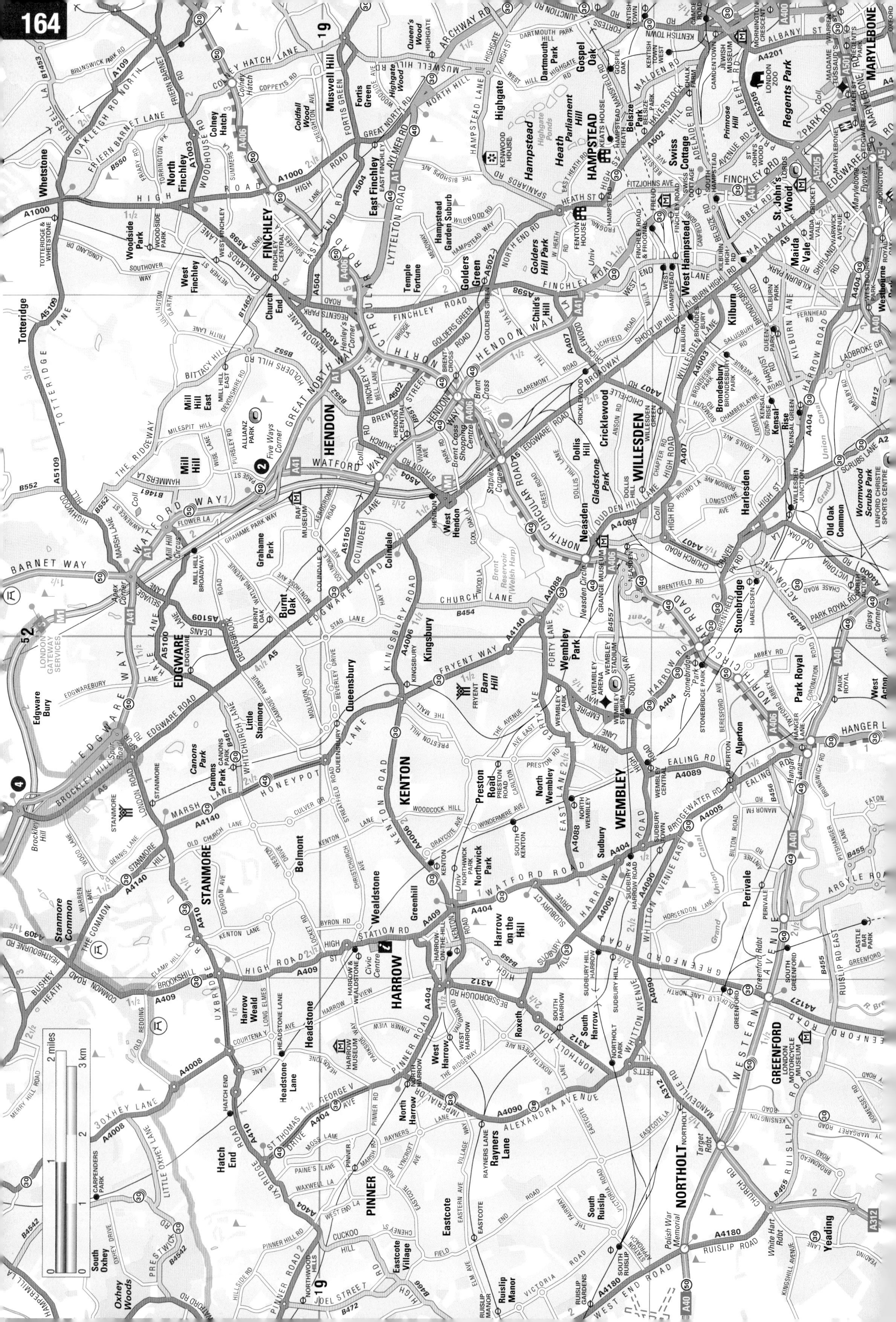

Whetstone
North Finchley
Colney Hatch
Finchley
Muswell Hill
Fortis Green
East Finchley
Highgate
Hampstead
Hampstead Heath
Parliament Hill
Gospel Oak
Dartmouth Park
Belsize Park
Swiss Cottage
Primrose Hill
Regents Park
London Zoo
Marylebone
St. John's Wood
Maida Vale
Kilburn
West Hampstead
Golders Green
Golders Hill Park
Child's Hill
Hampstead Garden Suburb
Temple Fortune
West Finchley
Woodside Park
Totteridge
Church End
Mill Hill
Mill Hill East
Hendon
West Hendon
Colindale
Cricklewood
Dollis Hill
Gladstone Park
Willesden
Brondesbury
Kensal Rise
Harlesden
Neasden
Grahame Park
Burnt Oak
Edgware
Edgware Bury
Kingsbury
Queensbury
Wembley
Wembley Park
Wembley Stadium
North Wembley
Sudbury
Alperton
Stonebridge
Park Royal
West Acton
Old Oak Common
Wormwood Scrubs Park
Kenton
Preston Road
Northwick Park
Belmont
Little Stanmore
Canons Park
Stanmore
Stanmore Common
Harrow Weald
Wealdstone
Greenhill
Harrow
Harrow on the Hill
Headstone
Headstone Lane
Hatch End
West Harrow
North Harrow
Roxeth
South Harrow
Rayners Lane
Pinner
Eastcote
Eastcote Village
Ruislip Manor
South Ruislip
Northolt
Greenford
Perivale
Yeading
South Oxhey
Oxhey Woods
Brockley Hill
Brent Cross
Staples Corner
Five Ways Corner
Apex Corner
North Circular Road
Edgware Road
Watford Way
Great North Way
Western Avenue
2 miles
3 km

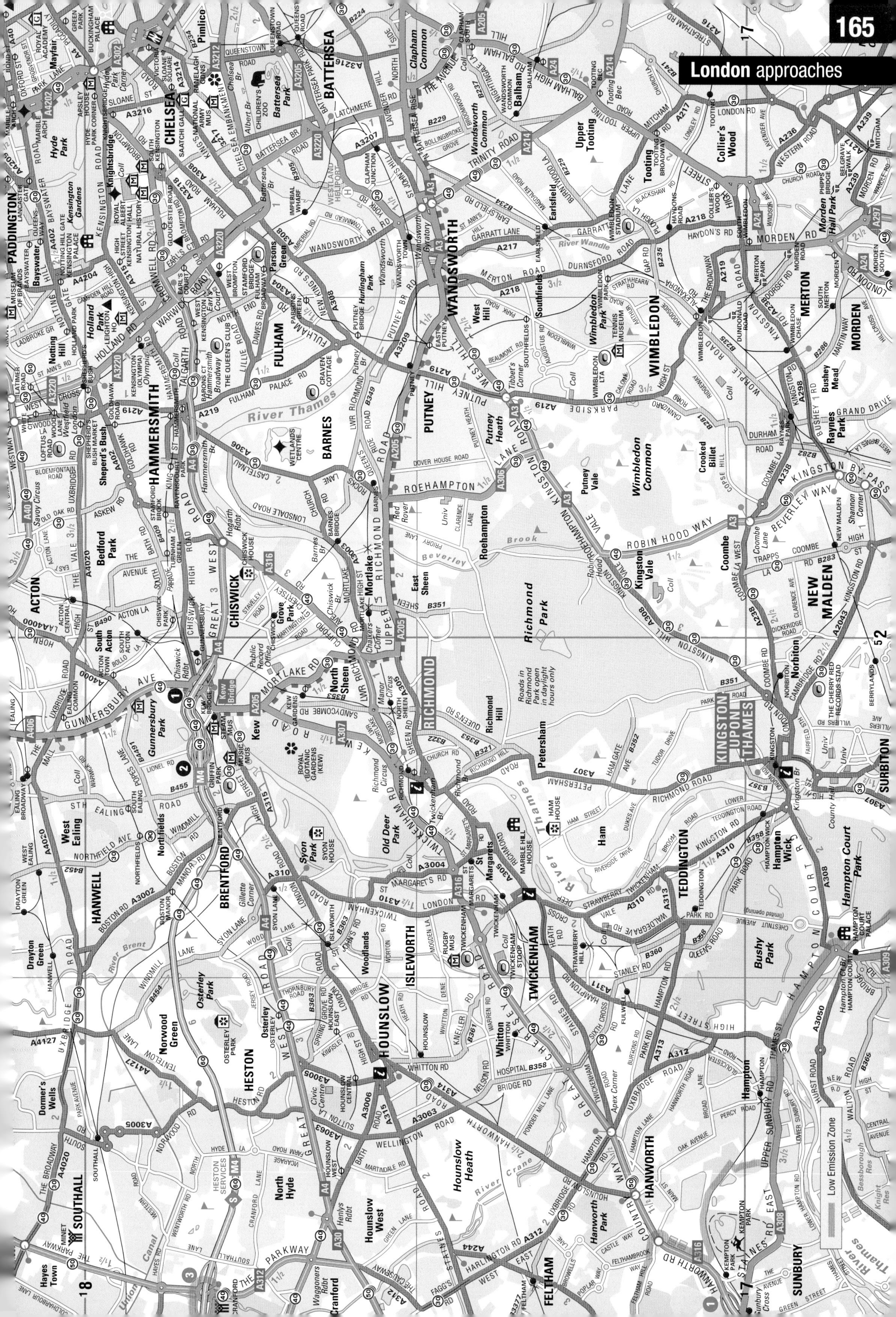
PADDINGTON
Bayswater
Mayfair
Hyde Park
Kensington Gardens
Knightsbridge
CHELSEA
Pimlico
BATTERSEA
Battersea Park
Clapham Common
Balham
Tooting Bec
Upper Tooting
Tooting
Collier's Wood
Wandsworth Common
Earlsfield
WANDSWORTH
Parsons Green
Hurlingham Park
FULHAM
Holland Park
Notting Hill
HAMMERSMITH
Shepherd's Bush
Southfields
West Hill
Wimbledon Park
WIMBLEDON
MERTON
MORDEN
Morden Hall Park
PUTNEY
Putney Heath
BARNES
River Thames
Roehampton
Putney Vale
Wimbledon Common
Crooked Billet
Raynes Park
Bushey Mead
Coombe
NEW MALDEN
Kingston Vale
Richmond Park
Bedford Park
ACTON
South Acton
CHISWICK
Grove Park
Mortlake
East Sheen
North Sheen
RICHMOND
Richmond Hill
Petersham
Ham
KINGSTON UPON THAMES
Norbiton
SURBITON
Gunnersbury Park
Kew
Royal Botanic Gardens (Kew)
Old Deer Park
Syon Park
West Ealing
Northfields
BRENTFORD
HANWELL
Drayton Green
Osterley Park
Norwood Green
HESTON
Osterley
ISLEWORTH
Woodlands
HOUNSLOW
Whitton
TWICKENHAM
St Margarets
TEDDINGTON
Hampton Wick
Hampton Court Park
Bushy Park
Hampton
Hounslow Heath
Hounslow West
North Hyde
Dormer's Wells
SOUTHALL
Hayes Town
Cranford
HANWORTH
Hanworth Park
FELTHAM
SUNBURY
Low Emission Zone

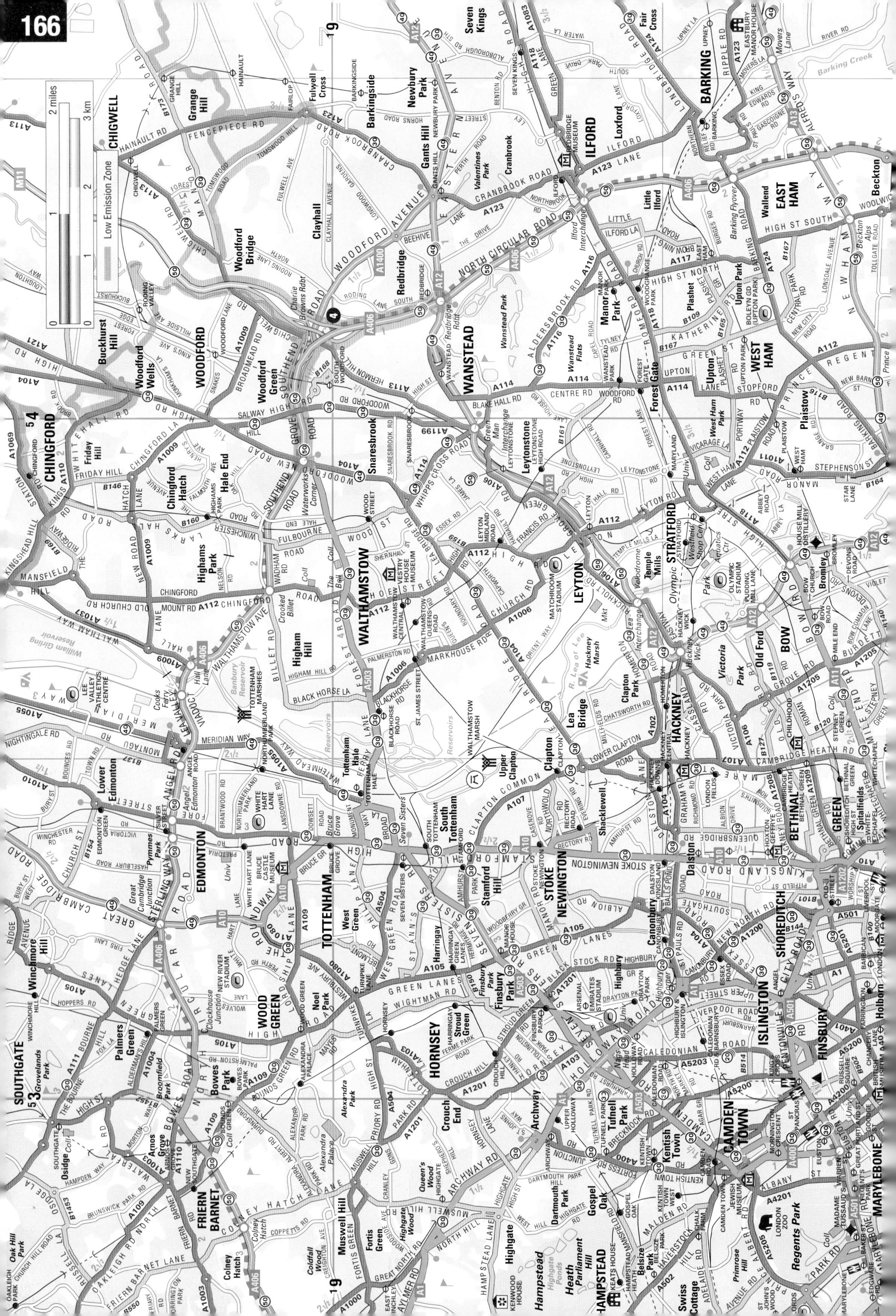
CHIGWELL
Grange Hill
Buckhurst Hill
Woodford Wells
WOODFORD
Woodford Bridge
Woodford Green
CHINGFORD
Friday Hill
Chingford Hatch
Hale End
Highams Park
Clayhall
Barkingside
Fulwell Cross
Newbury Park
Gants Hill
Seven Kings
Redbridge
Cranbrook
ILFORD
Loxford
Fair Cross
BARKING
WANSTEAD
Snaresbrook
Leytonstone
Forest Gate
Manor Park
Little Ilford
Plashet
Upton Park
EAST HAM
Wallend
Beckton
WEST HAM
Upton
Plaistow
WALTHAMSTOW
Higham Hill
LEYTON
STRATFORD
Temple Mills
Lower Edmonton
EDMONTON
Pymmes Park
TOTTENHAM
South Tottenham
Tottenham Hale
Upper Clapton
Clapton
Lea Bridge
Clapton Park
HACKNEY
Victoria Park
Old Ford
BOW
Bromley
BETHNAL GREEN
Winchmore Hill
SOUTHGATE
Palmers Green
WOOD GREEN
Noel Park
West Green
Harringay
Stamford Hill
STOKE NEWINGTON
Shacklewell
Dalston
Canonbury
SHOREDITCH
Highbury
Finsbury Park
HORNSEY
Stroud Green
Crouch End
Bowes Park
Arnos Grove
Osidge
FRIERN BARNET
Colney Hatch
Muswell Hill
Fortis Green
Highgate
Archway
Tufnell Park
Kentish Town
CAMDEN TOWN
ISLINGTON
FINSBURY
Holborn
MARYLEBONE
Regents Park
Gospel Oak
Dartmouth Park
HAMPSTEAD
Belsize Park
Swiss Cottage
Primrose Hill
Hampstead Heath
Low Emission Zone
2 miles
3 km

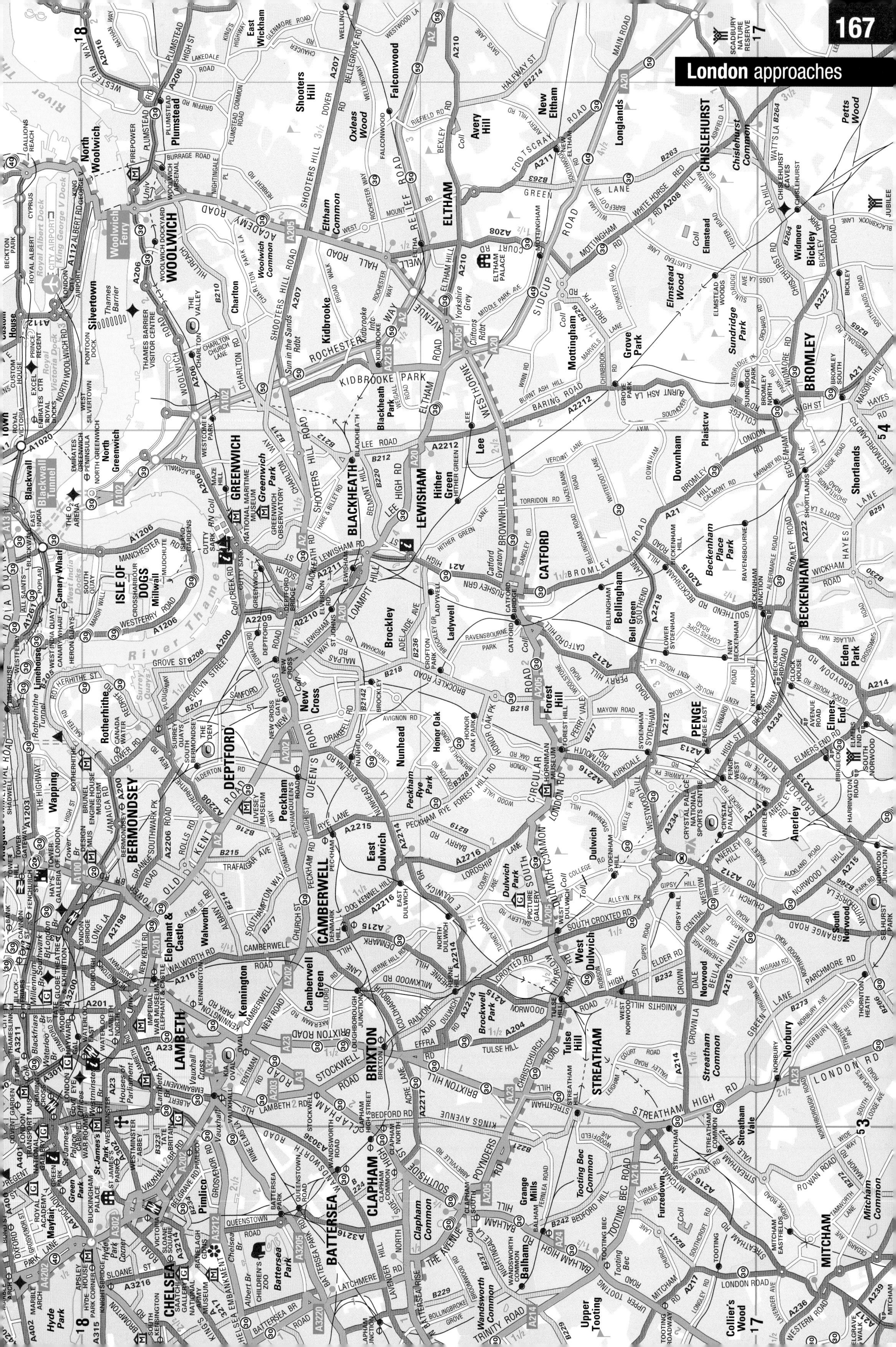
Plumstead
North Woolwich
Woolwich Ferry
WOOLWICH
Shooters Hill
Falconwood
East Wickham
Oxleas Wood
Avery Hill
New Eltham
Longlands
CHISLEHURST
Chislehurst Common
Petts Wood
ELTHAM
Eltham Common
Woolwich Common
Charlton
Kidbrooke
Silvertown
Thames Barrier
ELTHAM PALACE
SIDCUP
Mottingham
Grove Park
Elmstead Wood
Sundridge Park
Widmore
Bickley
BROMLEY
North Greenwich
GREENWICH
Greenwich Park
Blackheath Park
BLACKHEATH
LEWISHAM
Hither Green
Lee
Downham
Plaistow
Shortlands
Blackwall
Canary Wharf
ISLE OF DOGS
Millwall
CATFORD
Beckenham Place Park
Bellingham
Bell Green
BECKENHAM
Eden Park
Brockley
Ladywell
Limehouse
Rotherhithe
New Cross
DEPTFORD
Forest Hill
PENGE
Elmers End
Nunhead
Honor Oak
Peckham Rye Park
Wapping
BERMONDSEY
Peckham
East Dulwich
Dulwich
Anerley
CAMBERWELL
Walworth
Elephant & Castle
Kennington
Camberwell Green
South Norwood
Dulwich Park
West Dulwich
Norwood
LAMBETH
BRIXTON
Brockwell Park
Tulse Hill
STREATHAM
Streatham Common
Norbury
Vauxhall
Houses of Parliament
Pimlico
CLAPHAM
BATTERSEA
Battersea Park
Clapham Common
Grange Mills
Tooting Bec Common
Streatham Vale
Mitcham Common
MITCHAM
Green Park
Mayfair
Hyde Park
CHELSEA
Furzedown
Balham
Tooting Bec
Wandsworth Common
Upper Tooting
Collier's Wood
River Thames

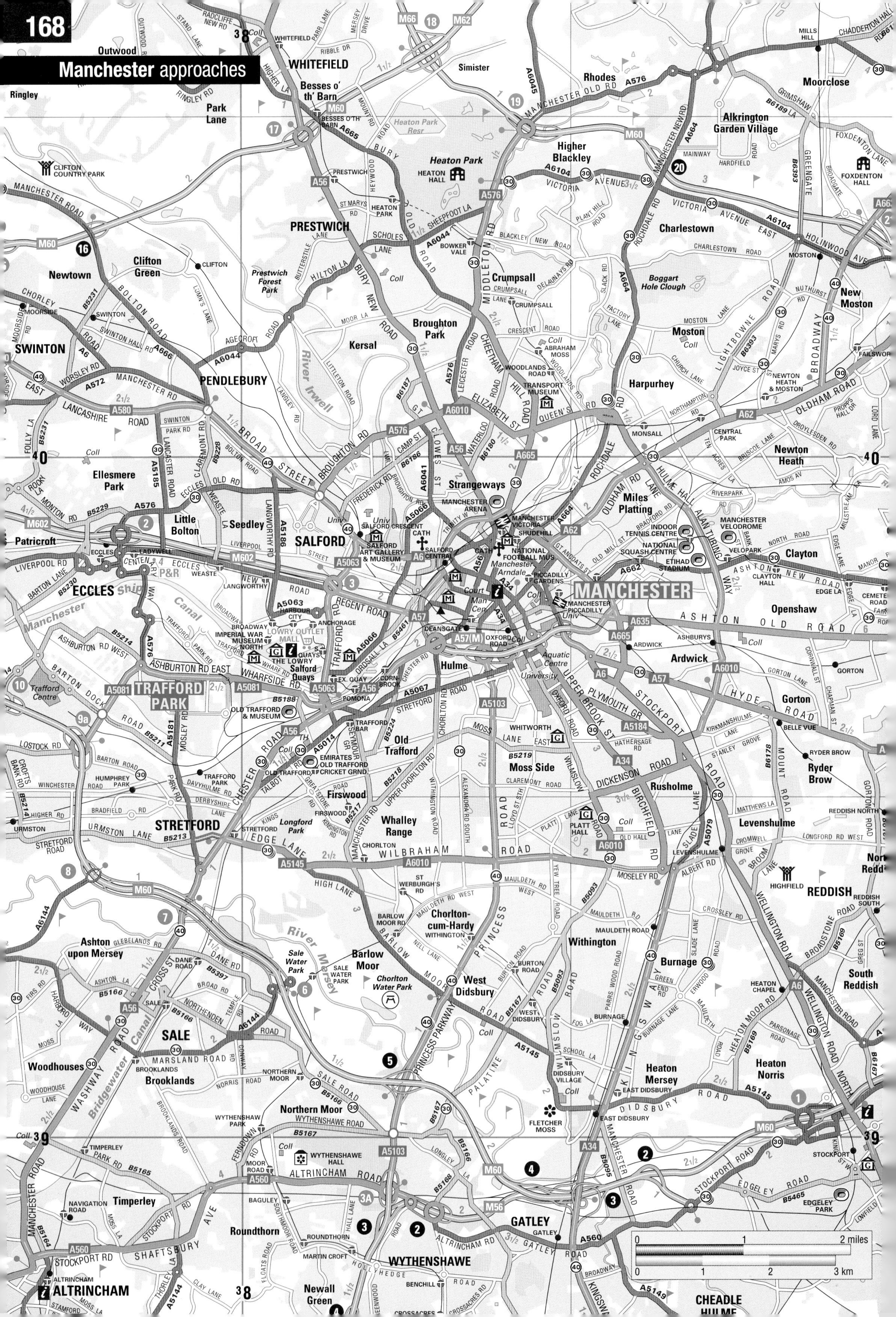
WHITEFIELD
Besses o' th' Barn
Simister
Rhodes
Moorclose
Alkrington Garden Village
Outwood
Ringley
Park Lane
Heaton Park
Higher Blackley
Charlestown
PRESTWICH
Clifton Green
Newtown
SWINTON
Crumpsall
Boggart Hole Clough
New Moston
Prestwich Forest Park
Kersal
Broughton Park
Moston
PENDLEBURY
Harpurhey
River Irwell
Ellesmere Park
Newton Heath
Miles Platting
Strangeways
Little Bolton
Seedley
Patricroft
SALFORD
Clayton
ECCLES
MANCHESTER
Openshaw
Manchester Ship Canal
Ardwick
TRAFFORD PARK
Hulme
Gorton
Old Trafford
Moss Side
Ryder Brow
Rusholme
STRETFORD
Firswood
Whalley Range
Levenshulme
Longford Park
REDDISH
Chorlton-cum-Hardy
Withington
Ashton upon Mersey
River Mersey
Barlow Moor
West Didsbury
Burnage
South Reddish
Sale Water Park
Chorlton Water Park
SALE
Woodhouses
Brooklands
Heaton Mersey
Heaton Norris
Northern Moor
Timperley
Roundthorn
GATLEY
WYTHENSHAWE
ALTRINCHAM
Newall Green
CHEADLE HULME
0 1 2 miles
0 1 2 3 km

Town plan symbols

Motorway
Primary route – dual, single carriageway
A road – dual, single carriageway
B road – dual, single carriageway

Minor through road
One-way street
Pedestrian roads
Shopping streets

Railway with station
Tramway with station
Underground or Metro station

H Hospital
P Parking
Police, Post Office
Shopmobility
Youth hostel

Bus or railway station building
Shopping precinct or retail park
Park
Congestion charge zone

✝ Abbey or cathedral
Ancient monument
Aquarium
Art gallery
Bird collection or aviary
Building of interest
Castle
Church of interest
Cinema
Garden
Historic ship
House
House and garden
Museum
Preserved railway
Roman antiquity
Safari park
Theatre
Tourist information centre
Zoo
✦ Other place of interest

Aberdeen

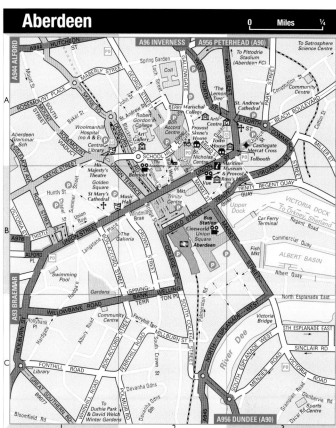

Birmingham

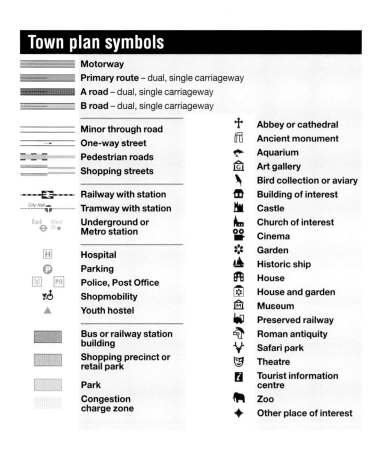

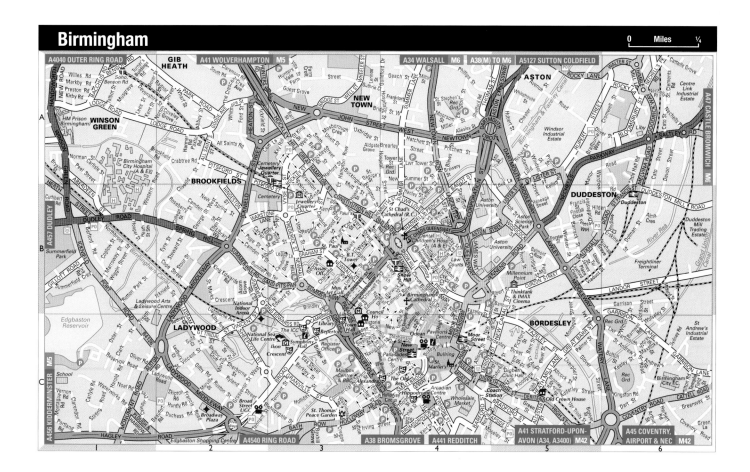

Bath

0 Miles ¼

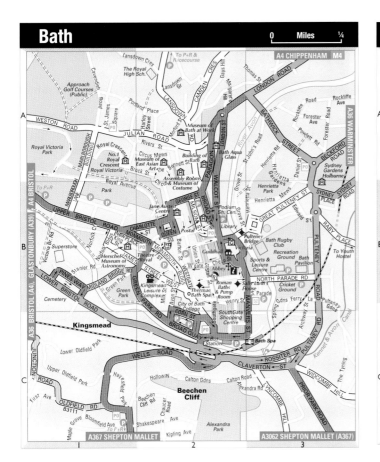

Bradford

0 Miles ¼

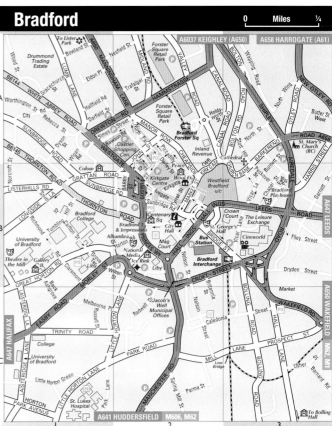

Bristol

0 Miles ¼

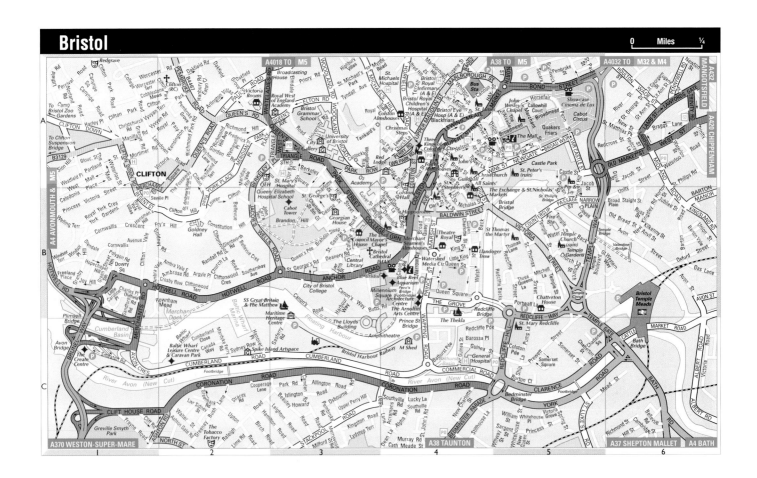

Cambridge

0 Miles ¼

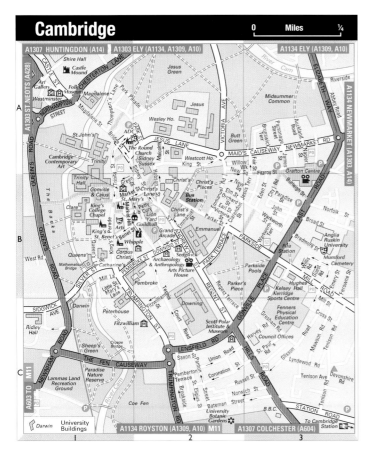

Cardiff / Caerdydd

0 Miles ¼

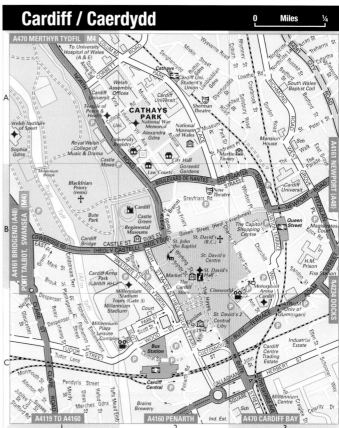

Coventry

0 Miles ¼

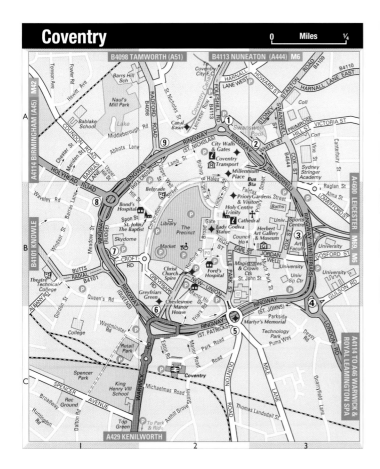

Derby

0 Miles ¼

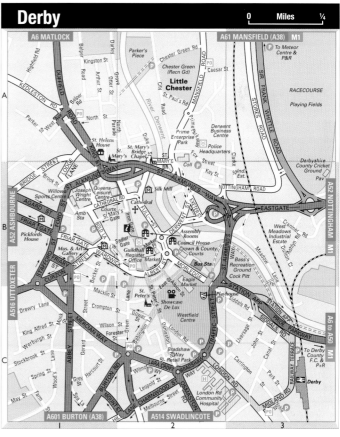

Edinburgh

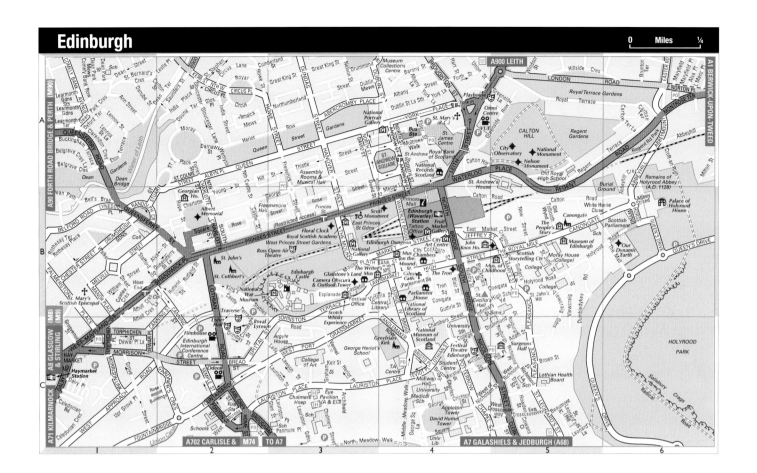

Glasgow

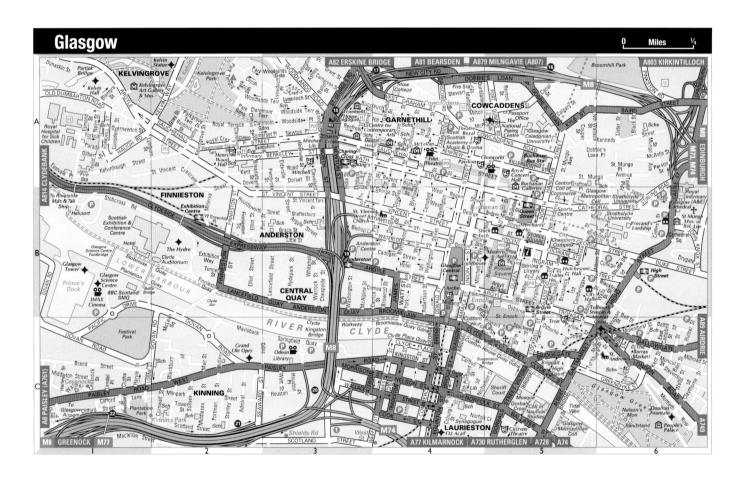

Gloucester

0 Miles ¼

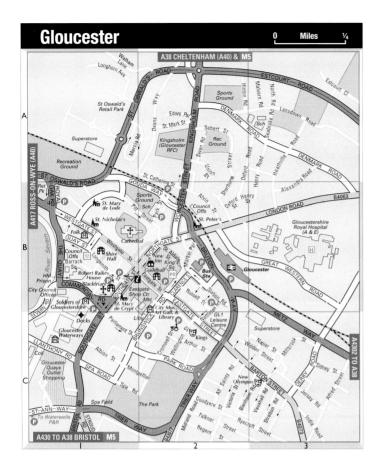

Hull

0 Miles ¼

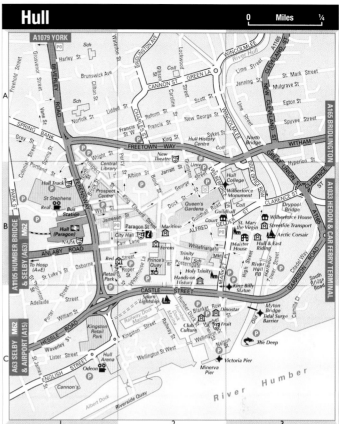

Leeds

0 Miles ¼

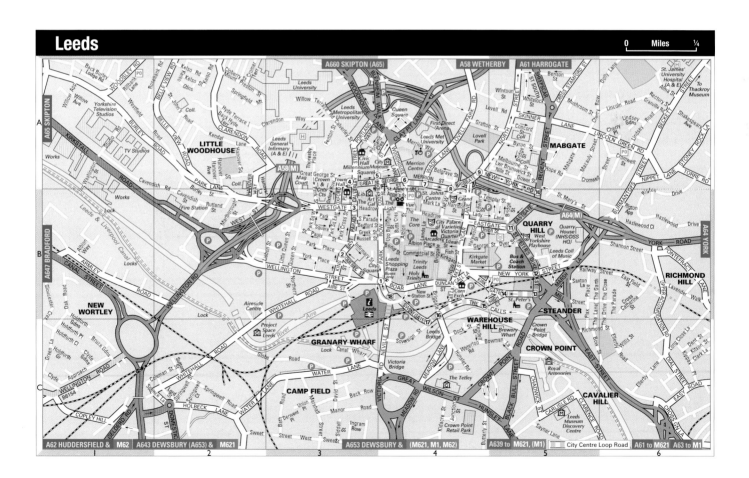

REGENT'S PARK
REGENT'S PARK
SOMERS TOWN
FITZROVIA
BLOOMSBURY
SOHO
MAYFAIR
ST. JAMES'S
HYDE PARK
GREEN PARK
ST. JAMES'S PARK
WESTMINSTER
BELGRAVIA
Euston
St. Pancras International
King's Cross
British Library
British Museum
University of London
University College
Regent's College
Open Air Theatre
Queen Mary's Gardens
Madame Tussaud's
Marble Arch
Speakers' Corner
Wellington Arch
Apsley House
Buckingham Palace
Buckingham Palace Gardens
St James's Palace
Clarence House
Piccadilly Circus
Oxford Circus
Trafalgar Square
Nelson's Column
National Gallery
National Portrait Gallery
Charing Cross
Covent Garden
Royal Opera House
London Transport Museum
Houses of Parliament
Westminster Abbey
Big Ben
Westminster Bridge
Lambeth Bridge
London Eye Millennium Pier
London Aquarium
Victoria
Victoria Coach Sta
Westminster Cathedral (RC)
Westminster Pier
Lambeth Pier
Embankment Pier
Cleopatra's Needle
Royal Acad of Arts
Wallace Collection
British Telecom Tower
Royal Acad of Dramatic Art
Coram's Fields (Children's Playground)
The Foundling Museum
Miles
0
½
1
2
3
4
A
B
C
D
E

FINSBURY
CLERKENWELL
HOLBORN
HOXTON
SHOREDITCH
THE CITY
SOUTHWARK
LAMBETH
RIVER THAMES
London Docklands
STEPNEY
POPLAR
CANNING TOWN
WAPPING
ROTHERHITHE
BERMONDSEY
MILLWALL
ISLE OF DOGS
DEPTFORD
GREENWICH
Congestion Charging Zone
0 Miles 1

Liverpool

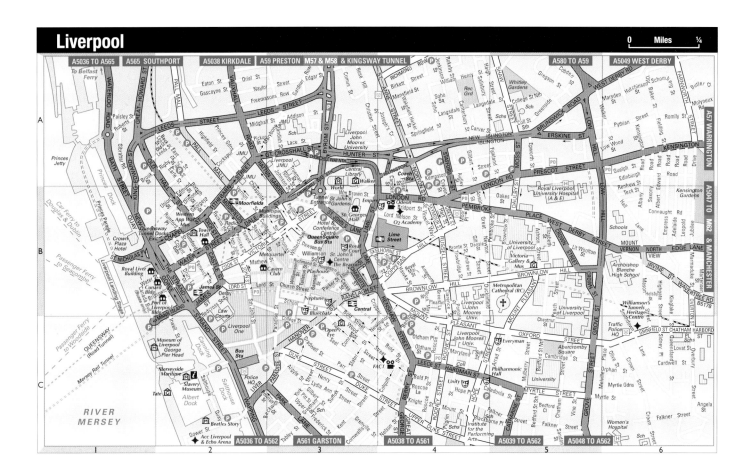

Manchester

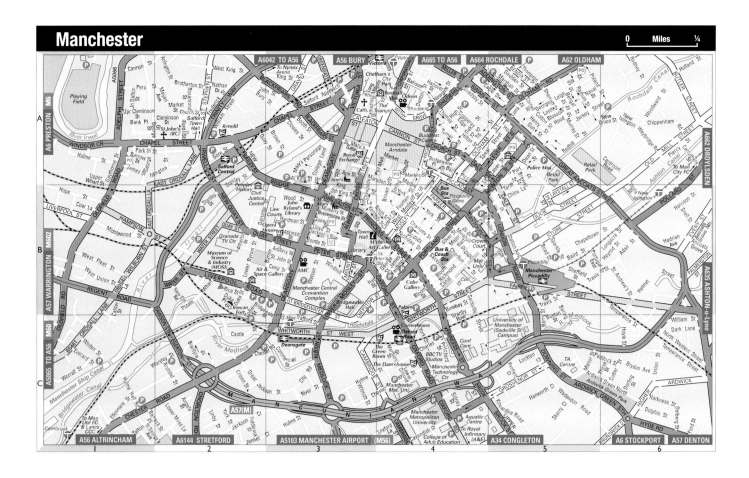

Leicester

0 Miles ¼

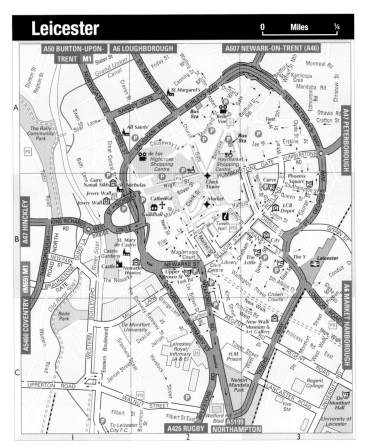

Middlesbrough

0 Miles ¼

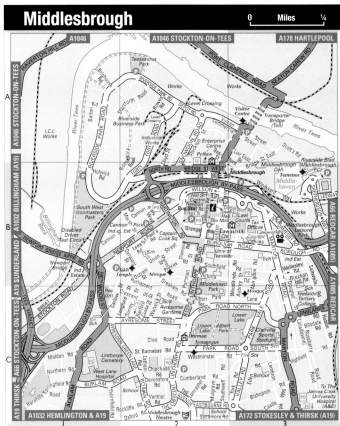

Newcastle upon Tyne

0 Miles ¼

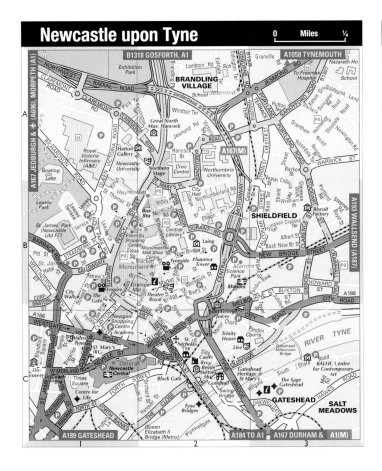

Norwich

0 Miles ¼

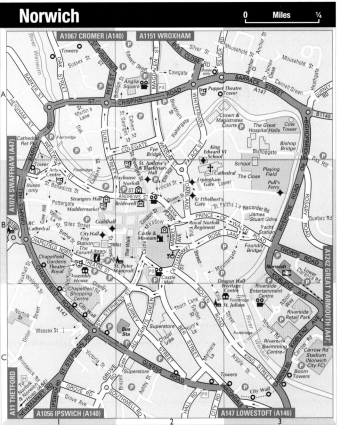

Nottingham

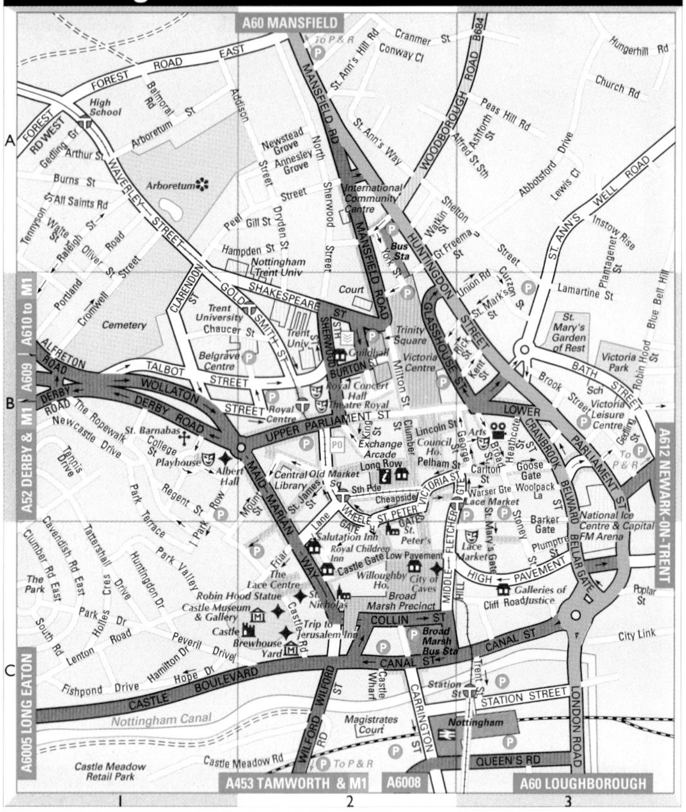

Oxford

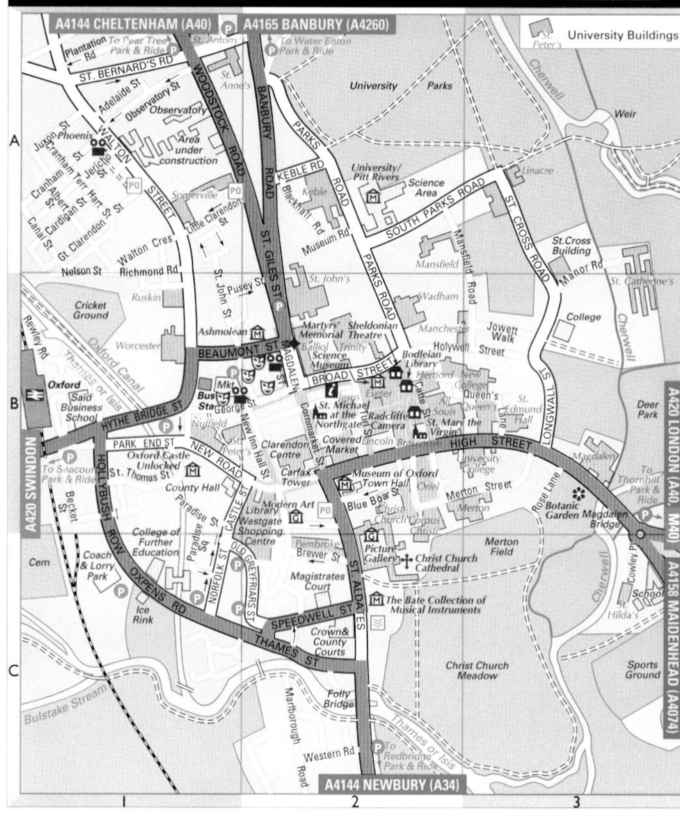

Plymouth

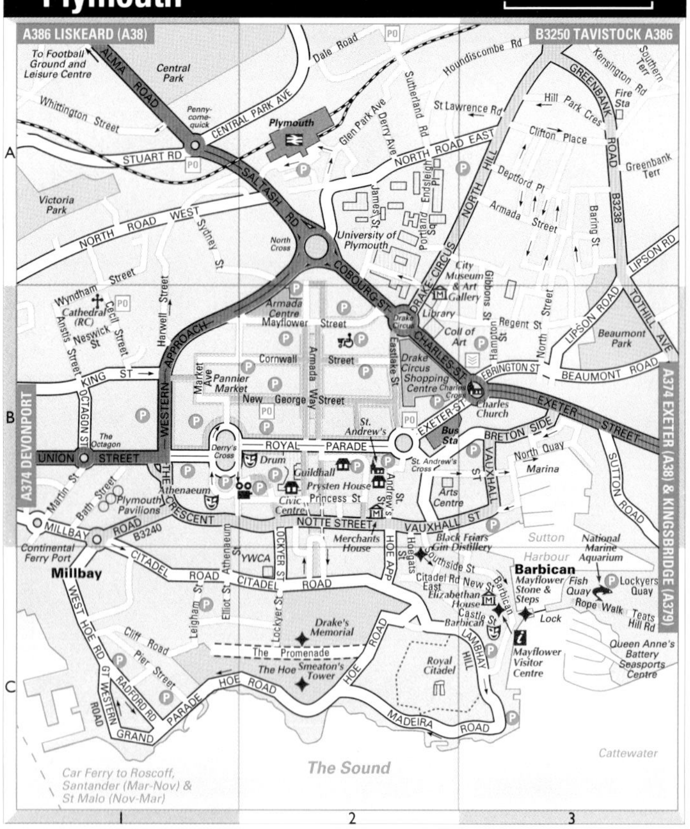

Portsmouth

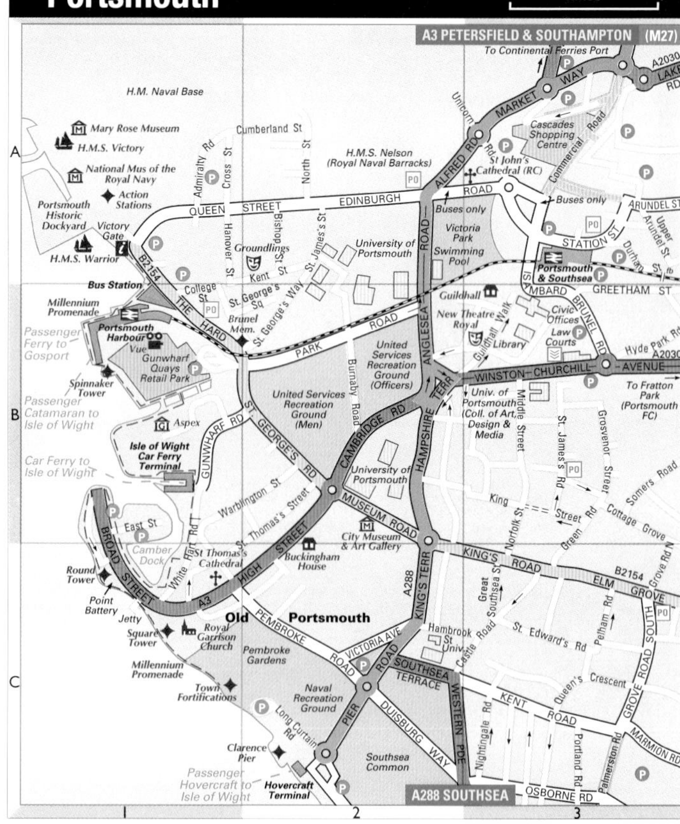

Reading

0 Miles ¼

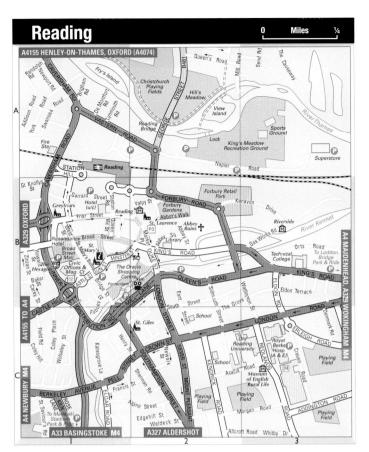

Southampton

0 Miles ¼

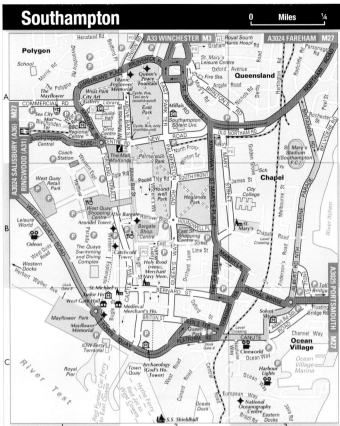

Sheffield

0 Miles ¼

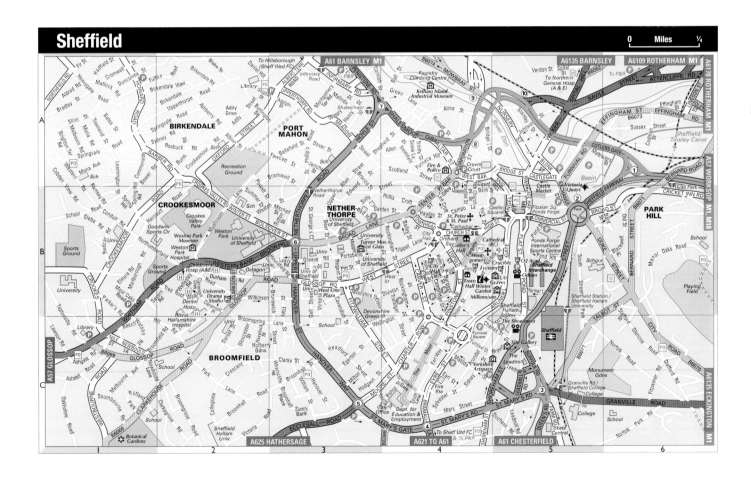

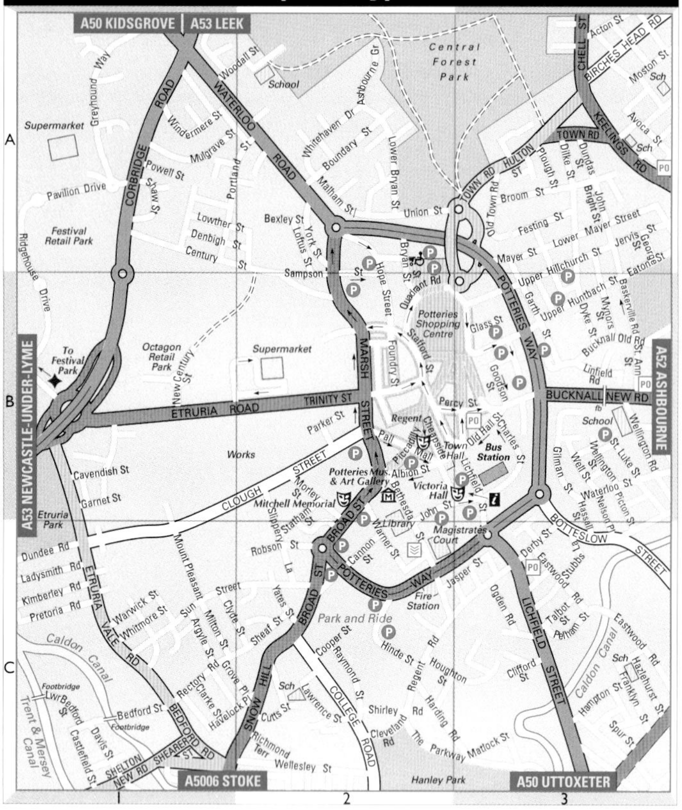

Stoke-on-Trent (Hanley)

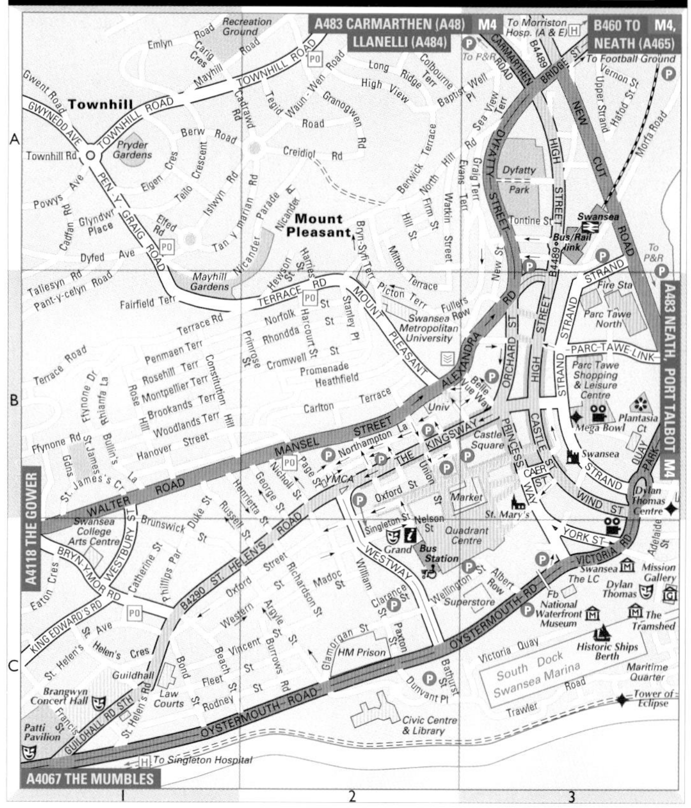

Swansea / Abertawe

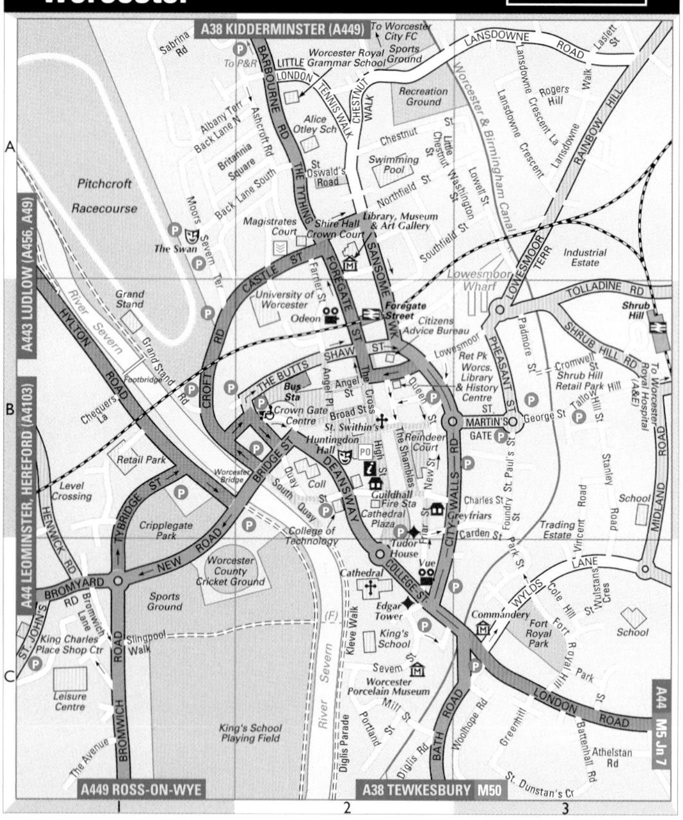

Worcester

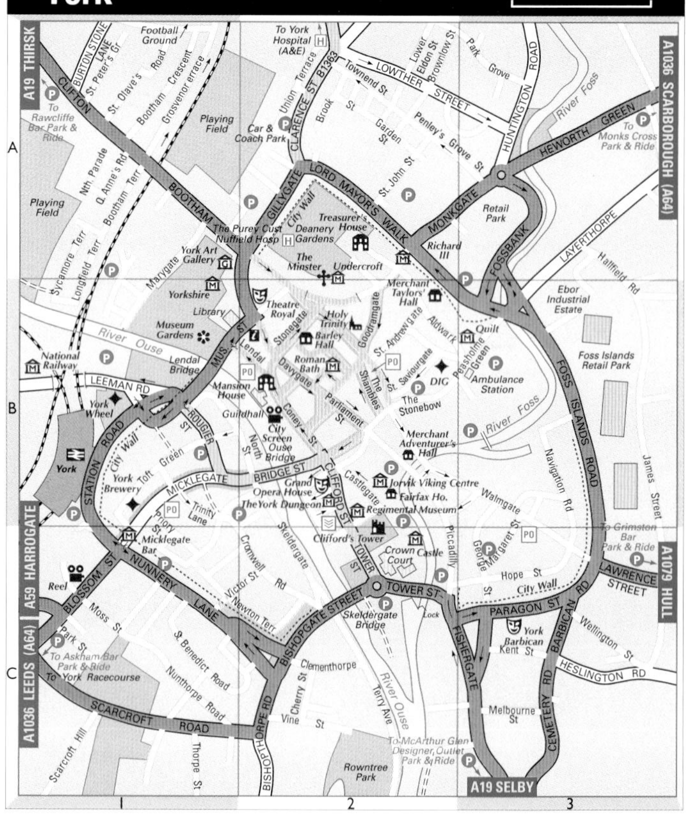

York

Index to road maps of Britain

Abbreviations used in the index

Aberdeen	Aberdeen City
Aberds	Aberdeenshire
Ald	Alderney
Anglesey	Isle of Anglesey
Angus	Angus
Argyll	Argyll and Bute
Bath	Bath and North East Somerset
Bedford	Bedford
Bl Gwent	Blaenau Gwent
Blackburn	Blackburn with Darwen
Blackpool	Blackpool
Bmouth	Bournemouth
Borders	Scottish Borders
Brack	Bracknell
Bridgend	Bridgend
Brighton	City of Brighton and Hove
Bristol	City and County of Bristol
Bucks	Buckinghamshire
C Beds	Central Bedfordshire
Caerph	Caerphilly
Cambs	Cambridgeshire
Cardiff	Cardiff
Carms	Carmarthenshire
Ceredig	Ceredigion
Ches E	Cheshire East
Ches W	Cheshire West and Chester
Clack	Clackmannanshire
Conwy	Conwy
Corn	Cornwall
Cumb	Cumbria
Darl	Darlington
Denb	Denbighshire
Derby	City of Derby
Derbys	Derbyshire
Devon	Devon
Dorset	Dorset
Dumfries	Dumfries and Galloway
Dundee	Dundee City
Durham	Durham
E Ayrs	East Ayrshire
E Dunb	East Dunbartonshire
E Loth	East Lothian
E Renf	East Renfrewshire
E Sus	East Sussex
E Yorks	East Riding of Yorkshire
Edin	City of Edinburgh
Essex	Essex
Falk	Falkirk
Fife	Fife
Flint	Flintshire
Glasgow	City of Glasgow
Glos	Gloucestershire
Gtr Man	Greater Manchester
Guern	Guernsey
Gwyn	Gwynedd
Halton	Halton
Hants	Hampshire
Hereford	Herefordshire
Herts	Hertfordshire
Highld	Highland
Hrtlpl	Hartlepool
Hull	Hull
IoM	Isle of Man
IoW	Isle of Wight
Invclyd	Inverclyde
Jersey	Jersey
Kent	Kent
Lancs	Lancashire
Leicester	City of Leicester
Leics	Leicestershire
Lincs	Lincolnshire
London	Greater London
Luton	Luton
M Keynes	Milton Keynes
M Tydf	Merthyr Tydfil
Mbro	Middlesbrough
Medway	Medway
Mers	Merseyside
Midloth	Midlothian
Mon	Monmouthshire
Moray	Moray
N Ayrs	North Ayrshire
N Lincs	North Lincolnshire
N Lanark	North Lanarkshire
N Som	North Somerset
N Yorks	North Yorkshire
NE Lincs	North East Lincolnshire
Neath	Neath Port Talbot
Newport	City and County of Newport
Norf	Norfolk
Northants	Northamptonshire
Northumb	Northumberland
Nottingham	City of Nottingham
Notts	Nottinghamshire
Orkney	Orkney
Oxon	Oxfordshire
Pboro	Peterborough
Pembs	Pembrokeshire
Perth	Perth and Kinross
Plym	Plymouth
Poole	Poole
Powys	Powys
Ptsmth	Portsmouth
Reading	Reading
Redcar	Redcar and Cleveland
Renfs	Renfrewshire
Rhondda	Rhondda Cynon Taff
Rutland	Rutland
S Ayrs	South Ayrshire
S Glos	South Gloucestershire
S Lanark	South Lanarkshire
S Yorks	South Yorkshire
Scilly	Scilly
Shetland	Shetland
Shrops	Shropshire
Slough	Slough
Som	Somerset
Soton	Southampton
Staffs	Staffordshire
Southend	Southend-on-Sea
Stirling	Stirling
Stockton	Stockton-on-Tees
Stoke	Stoke-on-Trent
Suff	Suffolk
Sur	Surrey
Swansea	Swansea
Swindon	Swindon
T&W	Tyne and Wear
Telford	Telford and Wrekin
Thurrock	Thurrock
Torbay	Torbay
Torf	Torfaen
V Glam	The Vale of Glamorgan
W Berks	West Berkshire
W Dunb	West Dunbartonshire
W Isles	Western Isles
W Loth	West Lothian
W Mid	West Midlands
W Sus	West Sussex
W Yorks	West Yorkshire
Warks	Warwickshire
Warr	Warrington
Wilts	Wiltshire
Windsor	Windsor and Maidenhead
Wokingham	Wokingham
Worcs	Worcestershire
Wrex	Wrexham
York	City of York

How to use the index

Example

Trudoxhill Som **24** E2

- grid square
- page number
- county or unitary authority

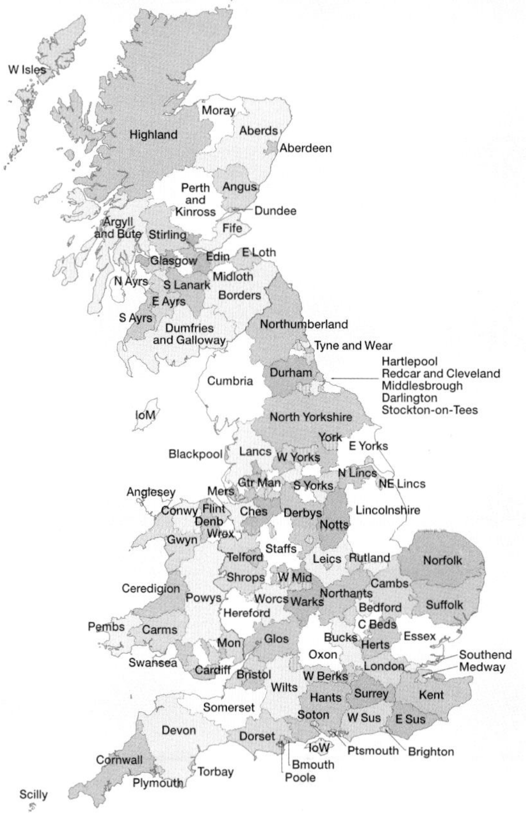

A

Baulking Oxon 38 E3
Baumber Lincs 78 B5
Baunton Glos 37 D7
Baverstock Wilts 24 F5
Bawburgh Norf 68 D4
Bawdeswell Norf 81 E6
Bawdrip Som 22 F5
Bawdsey Suff 57 E7
Bawtry S Yorks 89 E7
Baxenden Lancs 87 B5
Baxterley Warks 63 E6
Baybridge Hants 15 B6
Baycliff Cumb 92 B2
Baydon Wilts 25 B7
Bayford Herts 41 D6
Bayford Som 12 B5
Bayles Cumb 109 E7
Baylham Suff 56 D5
Baynard's Green Oxon 39 B5
Bayston Hill Shrops 60 D4
Baythorn End Essex 55 E8
Bayton Worcs 49 B8
Beach Highld 130 D1
Beachampton Bucks 53 F5
Beachamwell Norf 67 D7
Beachans Moray 151 G13
Beacharr Argyll 143 D7
Beachborough Kent 19 B8
Beachley Glos 36 E2
Beacon Devon 11 D6
Beacon End Essex 43 B5
Beacon Hill Sur 27 F6
Beacon's Bottom Bucks 39 E7
Beaconsfield Bucks 40 F2
Beacrabhaic W Isles 154 H6
Beadlam N Yorks 102 F4
Beadlow C Beds 54 F2
Beadnell Northumb 117 B8
Beaford Devon 9 C7
Beal N Yorks 89 B6
Beal Northumb 123 E6
Beamhurst Staffs 75 F7
Beaminster Dorset 12 D2
Beamish Durham 110 D5
Beamsley N Yorks 94 D3
Bean Kent 29 B6
Beanacre Wilts 24 C4
Beanley Northumb 117 C6
Beaquoy Orkney 159 F4
Bear Cross Bmouth 13 E8
Beardwood Blackburn 86 B4
Beare Green Sur 28 E2
Bearley Warks 51 C6
Bearnus Argyll 146 G6
Bearpark Durham 110 E5
Bearsbridge Northumb 109 D7
Bearsden E Dunb 118 B5
Bearsted Kent 29 D8
Bearstone Shrops 74 F4
Bearwood Hereford 49 D5
Bearwood Poole 13 E8
Bearwood W Mid 62 F4
Beattock Dumfries 114 D3
Beauchamp Roding Essex 42 C1
Beauchief S Yorks 88 F4
Beaufort Bl Gwent 35 C5
Beaufort Castle Highld 151 G8
Beaulieu Hants 14 D4
Beauly Highld 151 G8
Beaumaris Anglesey 83 D6
Beaumont Cumb 108 D3
Beaumont Essex 43 B7
Beaumont Hill Darl 101 C7
Beausale Warks 51 B7
Beauworth Hants 15 B6
Beaworthy Devon 9 E6
Beazley End Essex 42 B3
Bebington Mers 85 F4
Bebside Northumb 117 F8
Beccles Suff 69 E7
Becconsall Lancs 86 B2
Beck Foot Cumb 99 E8
Beck Hole N Yorks 103 D6
Beck Row Suff 55 B7
Beck Side Cumb 98 F4
Beckbury Shrops 61 D7
Beckenham London 28 C4
Beckermet Cumb 98 D2
Beckfoot Cumb 98 D3
Beckfoot Cumb 107 E7
Beckford Worcs 50 F4
Beckhampton Wilts 25 C5
Beckingham Lincs 77 D8
Beckingham Notts 89 F8
Beckington Som 24 D3
Beckley E Sus 19 C5
Beckley Hants 14 E3
Beckley Oxon 39 C5
Beckton London 41 F7
Beckwithshaw N Yorks 95 D5
Becontree London 41 F7
Bed-y-coedwr Gwyn 71 E8
Bedale N Yorks 101 F7
Bedburn Durham 110 F4
Bedchester Dorset 13 C6
Beddau Rhondda 34 F4
Beddgelert Gwyn 71 C6
Beddingham E Sus 17 D8
Beddington London 28 C4
Bedfield Suff 57 C6
Bedford Bedford 53 E8
Bedham W Sus 16 B4
Bedhampton Hants 15 D8
Bedingfield Suff 57 C5
Bedlam N Yorks 95 C5
Bedlington Northumb 117 F8
Bedlington Station Northumb 117 F8
Bedlinog M Tydf 34 D4
Bedminster Bristol 23 B7
Bedmond Herts 40 D3
Bednall Staffs 62 C3
Bedrule Borders 116 C2
Bedstone Shrops 49 B5
Bedwas Caerph 35 F5
Bedworth Warks 63 F7
Bedworth Heath Warks 63 F7
Beeby Leics 64 D3
Beech Hants 26 F4
Beech Staffs 75 F5
Beech Hill Gtr Man 86 D3
Beech Hill W Berks 26 C4
Beechingstoke Wilts 25 D5
Beedon W Berks 26 B2
Beeford E Yorks 97 D7
Beeley Derbys 76 C2
Beelsby NE Lincs 91 D6
Beenham W Berks 26 C3
Beeny Corn 8 E3
Beer Devon 11 F7
Beer Hackett Dorset 12 C3
Beercrocombe Som 11 B8
Beesands Devon 7 E6
Beesby Lincs 91 F8
Beeson Devon 7 E6
Beeston C Beds 54 E2
Beeston Ches W 74 D2
Beeston Norf 68 C2
Beeston Notts 76 F5
Beeston W Yorks 95 F5
Beeston Regis Norf 81 C7
Beeswing Dumfries 107 C5
Beetham Cumb 92 B4
Beetley Norf 68 C2
Begbroke Oxon 38 C4
Begelly Pembs 32 D2
Beggar's Bush Powys 48 C4
Beguildy Powys 48 B3
Beighton Norf 69 D6
Beighton S Yorks 88 F5
Beighton Hill Derbys 76 D2
Beith N Ayrs 118 D3
Bekesbourne Kent 31 D5
Belaugh Norf 69 C5
Belbroughton Worcs 50 B4
Belchamp Otten Essex 56 E2
Belchamp St Paul Essex 55 E8
Belchamp Walter Essex 56 E2
Belchford Lincs 79 B5
Belford Northumb 123 F7
Belhaven E Loth 122 B2
Belhelvie Aberds 141 C8
Belhinnie Aberds 140 B3
Bell Bar Herts 41 D5
Bell Busk N Yorks 94 D2
Bell End Worcs 50 B4
Bell o'th'Hill Ches W 74 E2
Bellabeg Aberds 140 C2
Bellamore S Ayrs 112 F2
Bellanoch Argyll 144 D6
Bellaty Angus 134 D2
Belleau Lincs 79 B7
Bellehiglash Moray 152 E1
Bellerby N Yorks 101 E6
Bellever Devon 6 B4
Belliehill Angus 135 C5
Bellingdon Bucks 40 D2
Bellingham Northumb 116 F4
Belloch Argyll 143 E7
Bellochantuy Argyll 143 E7
Bells Yew Green E Sus 18 B3
Bellsbank E Ayrs 112 D4
Bellshill N Lanark 119 C7
Bellshill Northumb 123 F7
Bellspool Borders 120 F4
Bellsquarry W Loth 120 C3
Belmaduthy Highld 151 F9
Belmesthorpe Rutland 65 C7
Belmont Blackburn 86 C4
Belmont London 28 C3
Belmont S Ayrs 112 B3
Belmont Shetland 160 C7
Belnacraig Aberds 140 C2
Belowda Corn 4 C4
Belper Derbys 76 E3
Belper Lane End Derbys 76 E3
Belsay Northumb 110 B4
Belses Borders 115 B8
Belsford Devon 7 D5
Belstead Suff 56 E5
Belston S Ayrs 112 B3
Belstone Devon 9 E8
Belthorn Blackburn 86 B5
Beltinge Kent 31 C5
Beltoft N Lincs 90 D2
Belton Leics 63 B8
Belton Lincs 78 F2
Belton N Lincs 89 D8
Belton Norf 69 D7
Belton in Rutland Rutland 64 D5
Beltring Kent 29 E7
Belts of Collonach Aberds 141 E5
Belvedere London 29 B5
Belvoir Leics 77 F8
Bembridge IoW 15 F7
Bemersyde Borders 121 F8
Bemerton Wilts 25 F6
Bempton E Yorks 97 B7
Ben Alder Lodge Highld 132 B2
Ben Armine Lodge Highld 157 H10
Ben Casgro W Isles 155 E9
Benacre Suff 69 F8
Benbuie Dumfries 113 E7
Benderloch Argyll 124 B5
Bendronaig Lodge Highld 150 H3
Benenden Kent 18 B5
Benfield Dumfries 105 C7
Bengate Norf 69 B6
Bengeworth Worcs 50 E5
Benhall Green Suff 57 C7
Benhall Street Suff 57 C7
Benholm Aberds 135 C8
Beningbrough N Yorks 95 D8
Benington Herts 41 B5
Benington Lincs 79 E6
Benllech Anglesey 82 C5
Benmore Argyll 145 E10
Benmore Stirling 126 B3
Benmore Lodge Highld 156 H6
Bennacott Corn 8 E4
Bennan N Ayrs 143 F10
Benniworth Lincs 91 F6
Benover Kent 29 E8
Bensham T&W 110 C5
Benslie N Ayrs 118 E3
Benson Oxon 39 E6
Bent Aberds 135 B6
Bent Gate Lancs 87 B5
Benthall Northumb 117 B8
Benthall Shrops 61 D6
Bentham Glos 37 C6
Benthoul Aberdeen 141 D7
Bentlawnt Shrops 60 D3
Bentley E Yorks 97 F6
Bentley Hants 27 E5
Bentley S Yorks 89 D6
Bentley Suff 56 F5
Bentley Warks 63 E6
Bentley Worcs 50 C4
Bentley Heath W Mid 51 B6
Benton Devon 21 F5
Bentpath Dumfries 115 E6
Bents W Loth 120 C2
Bentworth Hants 26 E4
Benvie Dundee 134 F3
Benwick Cambs 66 E3
Beoley Worcs 51 C5
Beoraidbeg Highld 147 B9
Bepton W Sus 16 C2
Berden Essex 41 B7
Bere Alston Devon 6 C2
Bere Ferrers Devon 6 C2
Bere Regis Dorset 13 E6
Berepper Corn 3 D5
Bergh Apton Norf 69 D6
Berinsfield Oxon 39 E5
Berkeley Glos 36 E3
Berkhamsted Herts 40 D2
Berkley Som 24 E3
Berkswell W Mid 51 B7
Bermondsey London 28 B4
Bernera Highld 149 F13
Bernice Argyll 145 D10
Bernisdale Highld 149 C9
Berrick Salome Oxon 39 E6
Berriedale Highld 158 H3
Berrier Cumb 99 B5
Berriew Powys 59 D8
Berrington Northumb 123 E6
Berrington Shrops 60 D5
Berrow Som 22 D5
Berrow Green Worcs 50 D2
Berry Down Cross Devon 20 E4
Berry Hill Glos 36 C2
Berry Hill Pembs 45 E2
Berry Pomeroy Devon 7 C6
Berryhillock Moray 152 B5
Berrynarbor Devon 20 E4
Bersham Wrex 73 E7
Berstane Orkney 159 G5
Berwick E Sus 18 E2
Berwick Bassett Wilts 25 B5
Berwick Hill Northumb 110 B4
Berwick St James Wilts 25 F5
Berwick St John Wilts 13 B7
Berwick St Leonard Wilts 24 F4
Berwick-upon-Tweed Northumb 123 D5
Bescar Lancs 85 C4
Besford Worcs 50 E4
Bessacarr S Yorks 89 D7
Bessels Leigh Oxon 38 D4
Bessingby E Yorks 97 C7
Bessingham Norf 81 D7
Bestbeech Hill E Sus 18 B3
Besthorpe Norf 68 E3
Besthorpe Notts 77 C8
Bestwood Nottingham 77 E5
Bestwood Village Notts 77 E5
Beswick E Yorks 97 E6
Betchworth Sur 28 E3
Bethania Ceredig 46 C4
Bethania Gwyn 71 C8
Bethania Gwyn 83 F6
Bethel Anglesey 82 D3
Bethel Gwyn 72 F3
Bethel Gwyn 82 E5
Bethersden Kent 30 E3
Bethesda Gwyn 83 E6
Bethesda Pembs 32 C1
Bethlehem Carms 33 B7
Bethnal Green London 41 F6
Betley Staffs 74 E4
Betsham Kent 29 B7
Betteshanger Kent 31 D7
Bettiscombe Dorset 11 E8
Bettisfield Wrex 73 F8
Betton Shrops 60 D3
Betton Shrops 74 F3
Bettws Bridgend 34 F3
Bettws Mon 35 C6
Bettws Newport 35 E6
Bettws Cedewain Powys 59 E8
Bettws Gwerfil Goch Denb 72 E4
Bettws Ifan Ceredig 46 E2
Bettws Newydd Mon 35 D7
Bettws-y-crwyn Shrops 60 F2
Bettyhill Highld 157 C10
Betws Carms 33 C7
Betws Bledrws Ceredig 46 D4
Betws-Garmon Gwyn 82 F5
Betws-y-Coed Conwy 83 F7
Betws-yn-Rhos Conwy 72 B3
Beulah Ceredig 45 E4
Beulah Powys 47 D8
Bevendean Brighton 17 D7
Bevercotes Notts 77 B6
Beverley E Yorks 97 F6
Beverston Glos 37 E5
Bevington Glos 36 E3
Bewaldeth Cumb 108 F2
Bewcastle Cumb 109 B5
Bewdley Worcs 50 B2
Bewerley N Yorks 94 C4
Bewholme E Yorks 97 D7
Bexhill E Sus 18 E4
Bexley London 29 B5
Bexleyheath London 29 B5
Bexwell Norf 67 D6
Beyton Suff 56 C3
Bhaltos W Isles 154 D5
Bhatarsaigh W Isles 148 J1
Bibury Glos 37 D8
Bicester Oxon 39 B5
Bickenhall Som 11 C7
Bickenhill W Mid 63 F5
Bicker Lincs 78 F5
Bickershaw Gtr Man 86 D4
Bickerstaffe Lancs 86 D2
Bickerton Ches E 74 D2
Bickerton N Yorks 95 D7
Bickington Devon 7 B5
Bickington Devon 20 F4
Bickleigh Devon 6 C3
Bickleigh Devon 10 D4
Bickleton Devon 20 F4
Bickley London 28 C5
Bickley Moss Ches W 74 E2
Bicknacre Essex 42 D3
Bicknoller Som 22 F3
Bicknor Kent 30 D2
Bickton Hants 14 C2
Bicton Shrops 60 C4
Bicton Shrops 60 F2
Bidborough Kent 29 E6
Biddenden Kent 19 B5
Biddenham Bedford 53 E8
Biddestone Wilts 24 B3
Biddisham Som 23 D5
Biddlesden Bucks 52 E4
Biddlestone Northumb 117 D5
Biddulph Staffs 75 D5
Biddulph Moor Staffs 75 D6
Bideford Devon 9 B6
Bidford-on-Avon Warks 51 D6
Bidston Mers 85 E3
Bielby E Yorks 96 E3
Bieldside Aberdeen 141 D7
Bierley IoW 15 G6
Bierley W Yorks 94 F4
Bierton Bucks 39 C8
Big Sand Highld 149 A12
Bigbury Devon 6 E4
Bigbury on Sea Devon 6 E4
Bigby Lincs 90 D4
Biggar Cumb 92 C1
Biggar S Lanark 120 F3
Biggin Derbys 75 D8
Biggin Derbys 76 E2
Biggin N Yorks 95 F8
Biggin Hill London 28 D5
Biggings Shetland 160 G3
Biggleswade C Beds 54 E2
Bighouse Highld 157 C11
Bighton Hants 26 F4
Bignor W Sus 16 C3
Bigton Shetland 160 L5
Bilberry Corn 4 C5
Bilborough Nottingham 76 E5
Bilbrook Som 22 E2
Bilbrough N Yorks 95 E8
Bilbster Highld 158 E4
Bildershaw Durham 101 B7
Bildeston Suff 56 E3
Billericay Essex 42 E2
Billesdon Leics 64 D4
Billesley Warks 51 D6
Billingborough Lincs 78 F4
Billinge Mers 86 D3
Billingford Norf 81 E6
Billingham Stockton 102 B2
Billinghay Lincs 78 D4
Billingley S Yorks 88 D5
Billingshurst W Sus 16 B4
Billingsley Shrops 61 F7
Billington C Beds 40 B2
Billington Lancs 93 F7
Billockby Norf 69 C7
Billy Row Durham 110 F4
Bilsborrow Lancs 92 F5
Bilsby Lincs 79 B7
Bilsham W Sus 16 D3
Bilsington Kent 19 B7
Bilson Green Glos 36 C3
Bilsthorpe Notts 77 C6
Bilsthorpe Moor Notts 77 D6
Bilston Midloth 121 C5
Bilston W Mid 62 E3
Bilstone Leics 63 D7
Bilting Kent 30 E4
Bilton E Yorks 97 F7
Bilton Northumb 117 C8
Bilton Warks 52 B2
Bilton in Ainsty N Yorks 95 E7
Bimbister Orkney 159 G4
Binbrook Lincs 91 E6
Binchester Blocks Durham 110 F5
Bincombe Dorset 12 F4
Bindal Highld 151 C12
Binegar Som 23 E8
Binfield Brack 27 B6
Binfield Heath Oxon 26 B5
Bingfield Northumb 110 B2
Bingham Notts 77 F7
Bingley W Yorks 94 F4
Bings Heath Shrops 60 C5
Binham Norf 81 D5
Binley Hants 26 D2
Binley W Mid 51 B8
Binley Woods Warks 51 B8
Binniehill Falk 119 B8
Binsoe N Yorks 94 B5
Binstead IoW 15 E6
Binsted Hants 27 E5
Binton Warks 51 D6
Bintree Norf 81 E6
Binweston Shrops 60 D3
Birch Essex 43 C5
Birch Gtr Man 87 D6
Birch Green Essex 43 C5
Birch Heath Ches W 74 C2
Birch Hill Ches W 74 B2
Birch Vale Derbys 87 F8
Bircham Newton Norf 80 D3
Bircham Tofts Norf 80 D3
Birchanger Essex 41 B8
Birchencliffe W Yorks 88 C2
Bircher Hereford 49 C6
Birchgrove Cardiff 22 B3
Birchgrove Swansea 33 E8
Birchington Kent 31 C6
Birchmoor Warks 63 D6
Birchover Derbys 76 C2
Birchwood Lincs 78 C2
Birchwood Warr 86 E4
Bircotes Notts 89 E7
Birdbrook Essex 55 E8
Birdforth N Yorks 95 B7
Birdham W Sus 16 E2
Birdholme Derbys 76 C3
Birdingbury Warks 52 C2
Birdlip Glos 37 C6
Birds Edge W Yorks 88 D3
Birdsall N Yorks 96 C4
Birdsgreen Shrops 61 F7
Birdsmoor Gate Dorset 11 D8
Birdston E Dunb 119 B6
Birdwell S Yorks 88 D4
Birdwood Glos 36 C4
Birgham Borders 122 F3
Birkby N Yorks 101 D8
Birkdale Mers 85 C4
Birkenhead Mers 85 F4
Birkenhills Aberds 153 D7
Birkenshaw N Lanark 119 C6
Birkenshaw W Yorks 88 B3
Birkhall Aberds 140 E2
Birkhill Angus 134 F3
Birkhill Borders 114 C5
Birkholme Lincs 65 B6
Birkin N Yorks 89 B6
Birley Hereford 49 D6
Birling Kent 29 C7
Birling Northumb 117 D8
Birling Gap E Sus 18 F2
Birlingham Worcs 50 E4
Birmingham W Mid 62 F4
Birnam Perth 133 E7
Birse Aberds 140 E4
Birsemore Aberds 140 E4
Birstall Leics 64 D2
Birstall W Yorks 88 B3
Birstwith N Yorks 94 D5
Birthorpe Lincs 78 F4
Birtley Hereford 49 C5
Birtley Northumb 109 B8
Birtley T&W 111 D5
Birts Street Worcs 50 F2
Bisbrooke Rutland 65 E5
Biscathorpe Lincs 91 F6
Biscot Luton 40 B3
Bish Mill Devon 10 B2
Bisham Windsor 39 F8
Bishampton Worcs 50 D4
Bishop Auckland Durham 101 B7
Bishop Burton E Yorks 97 F5
Bishop Middleham Durham 111 F6
Bishop Monkton N Yorks 95 C6
Bishop Norton Lincs 90 E3
Bishop Sutton Bath 23 D7
Bishop Thornton N Yorks 95 C5
Bishop Wilton E Yorks 96 D3
Bishopbridge Lincs 90 E4
Bishopbriggs E Dunb 119 C6
Bishopmill Moray 152 B2
Bishops Cannings Wilts 24 C5
Bishop's Castle Shrops 60 F3
Bishop's Caundle Dorset 12 C4
Bishop's Cleeve Glos 37 B6
Bishops Frome Hereford 49 E8
Bishop's Green Essex 42 C2
Bishop's Hull Som 11 B7
Bishop's Itchington Warks 51 D8
Bishops Lydeard Som 11 B6
Bishops Nympton Devon 10 B2
Bishop's Offley Staffs 61 B7
Bishop's Stortford Herts 41 B7
Bishop's Sutton Hants 26 F4
Bishop's Tachbrook Warks 51 C8
Bishops Tawton Devon 20 F4
Bishop's Waltham Hants 15 C6
Bishop's Wood Staffs 62 D2
Bishopsbourne Kent 31 D5
Bishopsteignton Devon 7 B7
Bishopstoke Hants 15 C5
Bishopston Swansea 33 F6
Bishopstone Bucks 39 C8
Bishopstone E Sus 17 D8
Bishopstone Hereford 49 E6
Bishopstone Swindon 38 F2
Bishopstone Wilts 13 B8
Bishopstrow Wilts 24 E3
Bishopswood Som 11 C7
Bishopsworth Bristol 23 C7
Bishopthorpe York 95 E8
Bishopton Darl 102 B1
Bishopton Dumfries 105 E8
Bishopton N Yorks 95 B5
Bishopton Renfs 118 B4
Bishopton Warks 51 D6
Bishton Newport 35 F7
Bisley Glos 37 D6
Bisley Sur 27 D7
Bispham Blackpool 92 E3
Bispham Green Lancs 86 C2
Bissoe Corn 3 B6
Bisterne Close Hants 14 D3
Bitchfield Lincs 65 B6
Bittadon Devon 20 E4
Bittaford Devon 6 D4
Bittering Norf 68 C2
Bitterley Shrops 49 B7
Bitterne Soton 15 C5
Bitteswell Leics 64 F2
Bitton S Glos 23 C8
Bix Oxon 39 F7
Bixter Shetland 160 H5
Blaby Leics 64 E2
Black Bourton Oxon 38 D2
Black Callerton T&W 110 C4
Black Clauchrie S Ayrs 112 F2
Black Corries Lodge Highld 131 D6
Black Crofts Argyll 124 B5
Black Dog Devon 10 D3
Black Heddon Northumb 110 B3
Black Lane Gtr Man 87 D5
Black Marsh Shrops 60 E3
Black Mount Argyll 131 E6
Black Notley Essex 42 B3
Black Pill Swansea 33 E7
Black Tar Pembs 44 E4
Black Torrington Devon 9 D6
Blackacre Dumfries 114 E3
Blackadder West Borders 122 D4
Blackawton Devon 7 D6
Blackborough Devon 11 D5
Blackborough End Norf 67 C6
Blackboys E Sus 18 C2
Blackbrook Derbys 76 E3
Blackbrook Mers 86 E3
Blackbrook Staffs 74 F4
Blackburn Aberds 141 C7
Blackburn Aberds 152 E5
Blackburn Blackburn 86 B4
Blackburn W Loth 120 C2
Blackcraig Dumfries 113 F7
Blackden Heath Ches E 74 B4
Blackdog Aberds 141 C8
Blackfell T&W 111 D5
Blackfield Hants 14 D5
Blackford Cumb 108 C3
Blackford Perth 127 D7
Blackford Som 12 B4
Blackford Som 23 E6
Blackfordby Leics 63 C7
Blackgang IoW 15 G5
Blackhall Colliery Durham 111 F7
Blackhall Mill T&W 110 D4
Blackhall Rocks Durham 111 F7
Blackham E Sus 29 F5
Blackhaugh Borders 121 F7
Blackheath Essex 43 B6
Blackheath Suff 57 B8
Blackheath Sur 27 E8
Blackheath W Mid 62 F3
Blackhill Aberds 153 C10
Blackhill Aberds 153 D10
Blackhill Highld 149 C8
Blackhills Highld 151 F12
Blackhills Moray 152 C2
Blackhorse S Glos 23 B8
Blackland Wilts 24 C5
Blacklaw Aberds 153 C6
Blackley Gtr Man 87 D6
Blacklunans Perth 134 C1
Blackmill Bridgend 34 F3
Blackmoor Hants 27 F5
Blackmoor Gate Devon 21 E5
Blackmore Essex 42 D2
Blackmore End Essex 55 F8
Blackmore End Herts 40 C4
Blackness Falk 120 B3
Blacknest Hants 27 E5
Blacko Lancs 93 E8
Blackpool Blackpool 92 F3
Blackpool Devon 7 E6
Blackpool Pembs 32 C1
Blackpool Gate Cumb 108 B5
Blackridge W Loth 119 C8
Blackrock Argyll 142 B4
Blackrock Mon 35 C6
Blackrod Gtr Man 86 C4
Blackshaw Dumfries 107 C7
Blackshaw Head W Yorks 87 B7
Blacksmith's Green Suff 56 C5
Blackstone W Sus 17 C6
Blackthorn Oxon 39 C6
Blackthorpe Suff 56 C3
Blacktoft E Yorks 90 B2
Blacktop Aberdeen 141 D7
Blacktown Newport 35 F6
Blackwall Tunnel London 41 F6
Blackwater Corn 3 B6
Blackwater Hants 27 D6
Blackwater IoW 15 F6
Blackwaterfoot N Ayrs 143 F9
Blackwell Darl 101 C7
Blackwell Derbys 75 B8
Blackwell Derbys 76 D4
Blackwell W Sus 28 F4
Blackwell Warks 51 E7
Blackwell Worcs 50 B4
Blackwood = Coed Duon Caerph 35 E5
Blackwood S Lanark 119 E7
Blackwood Hill Staffs 75 D6
Blacon Ches W 73 C7
Bladnoch Dumfries 105 D8
Bladon Oxon 38 C4
Blaen-gwynfi Neath 34 E2
Blaen-waun Carms 32 B3
Blaen-y-coed Carms 32 B4
Blaen-y-Cwm Denb 72 F4
Blaen-y-cwm Gwyn 71 E8
Blaen-y-cwm Powys 59 B7
Blaenannerch Ceredig 45 E4
Blaenau Ffestiniog Gwyn 71 C8
Blaenavon Torf 35 D6
Blaencelyn Ceredig 46 D2
Blaendyryn Powys 47 F8
Blaenffos Pembs 45 F3
Blaengarw Bridgend 34 E3
Blaengwrach Neath 34 D2
Blaenpennal Ceredig 46 C5
Blaenplwyf Ceredig 46 B4
Blaenporth Ceredig 45 E4
Blaenrhondda Rhondda 34 D3
Blaenycwm Ceredig 47 B7
Blagdon N Som 23 D7
Blagdon Torbay 7 C6
Blagdon Hill Som 11 C7
Blagill Cumb 109 E7
Blaguegate Lancs 86 D2
Blaich Highld 130 B4
Blain Highld 147 E9
Blaina Bl Gwent 35 D6
Blair Atholl Perth 133 C5
Blair Drummond Stirling 127 E6
Blairbeg N Ayrs 143 E11
Blairdaff Aberds 141 C5
Blairglas Argyll 126 F2
Blairgowrie Perth 134 E1
Blairhall Fife 128 F2
Blairingone Perth 127 E8
Blairland N Ayrs 118 E3
Blairlogie Stirling 127 E7
Blairlomond Argyll 125 F7
Blairmore Argyll 145 E10
Blairnamarrow Moray 139 C8
Blairquhosh Stirling 126 F4
Blair's Ferry Argyll 145 G8
Blairskaith E Dunb 119 B5
Blaisdon Glos 36 C4
Blakebrook Worcs 50 B3
Blakedown Worcs 50 B3
Blakelaw Borders 122 F3
Blakeley Staffs 62 E2
Blakeley Lane Staffs 75 E6
Blakemere Hereford 49 E5
Blakeney Glos 36 D3
Blakeney Norf 81 C6
Blakenhall Ches E 74 E4
Blakenhall W Mid 62 E3
Blakeshall Worcs 62 F2
Blakesley Northants 52 D4
Blanchland Northumb 110 D2
Bland Hill N Yorks 94 D5
Blandford Forum Dorset 13 D6
Blandford St Mary Dorset 13 D6
Blanefield Stirling 119 B5
Blankney Lincs 78 C3
Blantyre S Lanark 119 D6
Blar a'Chaorainn Highld 131 C5
Blaran Argyll 124 D4
Blarghour Argyll 125 D5
Blarmachfoldach Highld 130 C4
Blarnalearoch Highld 150 B4
Blashford Hants 14 D2
Blaston Leics 64 E5
Blatherwycke Northants 65 E6
Blawith Cumb 98 F4
Blaxhall Suff 57 D7
Blaxton S Yorks 89 D7
Blaydon T&W 110 C4
Bleadon N Som 22 D5
Bleak Hey Nook Gtr Man 87 D8
Blean Kent 30 C5
Bleasby Lincs 90 F5
Bleasby Notts 77 E7
Bleasdale Lancs 93 E5
Bleatarn Cumb 100 C2
Blebocraigs Fife 129 C6
Bleddfa Powys 48 C4
Bledington Glos 38 B2
Bledlow Bucks 39 D7
Bledlow Ridge Bucks 39 E7
Blegbie E Loth 121 C7
Blencarn Cumb 109 F6
Blencogo Cumb 107 E8
Blendworth Hants 15 C8
Blenheim Park Norf 80 D4
Blennerhasset Cumb 107 E8
Blervie Castle Moray 151 F13
Bletchingdon Oxon 39 C5
Bletchingley Sur 28 D4
Bletchley M Keynes 53 F6
Bletchley Shrops 74 F3
Bletherston Pembs 32 B1
Bletsoe Bedford 53 D8
Blewbury Oxon 39 F5
Blickling Norf 81 E7
Blidworth Notts 77 D5
Blindburn Northumb 116 C4
Blindcrake Cumb 107 F8
Blindley Heath Sur 28 E4
Blisland Corn 5 B6
Bliss Gate Worcs 50 B2
Blissford Hants 14 C2
Blisworth Northants 52 D5
Blithbury Staffs 62 B4
Blitterlees Cumb 107 D8
Blockley Glos 51 F6
Blofield Norf 69 D6
Blofield Heath Norf 69 C6
Blo' Norton Norf 56 B4
Bloomfield Borders 115 B8
Blore Staffs 75 E8
Blount's Green Staffs 75 F7
Blowick Mers 85 C4
Bloxham Oxon 52 F2
Bloxholm Lincs 78 D3
Bloxwich W Mid 62 D3
Bloxworth Dorset 13 E6
Blubberhouses N Yorks 94 D4
Blue Anchor Som 22 E2
Blue Anchor Swansea 33 E6
Blue Row Essex 43 C6
Blundeston Suff 69 E8
Blunham C Beds 54 D2
Blunsdon St Andrew Swindon 37 F8
Bluntington Worcs 50 B3
Bluntisham Cambs 54 B4
Blunts Corn 5 C8
Blyborough Lincs 90 E3
Blyford Suff 57 B8
Blymhill Staffs 62 C2
Blyth Northumb 117 F9
Blyth Notts 89 F7
Blyth Bridge Borders 120 E4
Blythburgh Suff 57 B8
Blythe Borders 121 E8
Blythe Bridge Staffs 75 E6
Blyton Lincs 90 E2
Boarhills Fife 129 C7
Boarhunt Hants 15 D7
Boar's Head Gtr Man 86 D3
Boars Hill Oxon 38 D4
Boarshead E Sus 18 B2
Boarstall Bucks 39 C6
Boasley Cross Devon 9 E6
Boat of Garten Highld 138 C5
Boath Highld 151 D8
Bobbing Kent 30 C2
Bobbington Staffs 62 E2
Bobbingworth Essex 41 D8
Bocaddon Corn 5 D6
Bochastle Stirling 126 D5
Bocking Essex 42 B3
Bocking Churchstreet Essex 42 B3
Boddam Aberds 153 D11
Boddam Shetland 160 M5
Boddington Glos 37 B5
Bodedern Anglesey 82 C3
Bodelwyddan Denb 72 B4
Bodenham Hereford 49 D7
Bodenham Wilts 14 B2
Bodenham Moor Hereford 49 D7
Bodermid Gwyn 70 E2
Bodewryd Anglesey 82 B3
Bodfari Denb 72 B4
Bodffordd Anglesey 82 D4
Bodham Norf 81 C7
Bodiam E Sus 18 C4
Bodicote Oxon 52 F2
Bodieve Corn 4 B4
Bodinnick Corn 5 D6
Bodle Street Green E Sus 18 D3
Bodmin Corn 5 C5
Bodney Norf 67 E8
Bodorgan Anglesey 82 E3
Bodsham Kent 30 E5
Boduan Gwyn 70 D4
Bodymoor Heath Warks 63 E5
Bogallan Highld 151 F9
Bogbrae Aberds 153 E10
Bogend Borders 122 E3
Bogend S Ayrs 118 F3
Boghall W Loth 120 C2
Boghead S Lanark 119 E7
Bogmoor Moray 152 B3
Bogniebrae Aberds 152 D5
Bognor Regis W Sus 16 E3
Bograxie Aberds 141 C6
Bogside N Lanark 119 D8
Bogton Aberds 153 C6
Bogue Dumfries 113 F6
Bohenie Highld 137 F5
Bohortha Corn 3 C7
Bohuntine Highld 137 F5
Boirseam W Isles 154 J5
Bojewyan Corn 2 C2
Bolam Durham 101 B6
Bolam Northumb 117 F6
Bolberry Devon 6 F4
Bold Heath Mers 86 F3
Boldon T&W 111 C6
Boldon Colliery T&W 111 C6
Boldre Hants 14 E4
Boldron Durham 101 C5
Bole Notts 89 F8
Bolehill Derbys 76 D2
Boleside Borders 121 F7
Bolham Devon 10 C4
Bolham Water Devon 11 C6
Bolingey Corn 4 D2
Bollington Ches E 75 B6
Bollington Cross Ches E 75 B6
Bolney W Sus 17 B6
Bolnhurst Bedford 53 D8
Bolshan Angus 135 D6
Bolsover Derbys 76 B4
Bolsterstone S Yorks 88 E3
Bolstone Hereford 49 F7
Boltby N Yorks 102 F2
Bolter End Bucks 39 E7
Bolton Cumb 99 B8
Bolton E Loth 121 B8
Bolton E Yorks 96 D3
Bolton Gtr Man 86 D5
Bolton Northumb 117 C7
Bolton Abbey N Yorks 94 D3
Bolton Bridge N Yorks 94 D3
Bolton-by-Bowland Lancs 93 E7
Bolton-le-Sands Lancs 92 C4
Bolton Low Houses Cumb 108 E2
Bolton-on-Swale N Yorks 101 E7
Bolton Percy N Yorks 95 E8
Bolton Town End Lancs 92 C4
Bolton upon Dearne S Yorks 89 D5
Boltonfellend Cumb 108 C4
Boltongate Cumb 108 E2
Bolventor Corn 5 B6
Bomere Heath Shrops 60 C4
Bon-y-maen Swansea 33 E7
Bonar Bridge Highld 151 B9
Bonawe Argyll 125 B6
Bonby N Lincs 90 C4
Boncath Pembs 45 F4
Bonchester Bridge Borders 115 C8
Bonchurch IoW 15 G6
Bondleigh Devon 9 D8
Bonehill Devon 6 B5
Bonehill Staffs 63 D5
Bo'ness Falk 127 F8
Bonhill W Dunb 118 B3
Boningale Shrops 62 D2
Bonjedward Borders 116 B2
Bonkle N Lanark 119 D8
Bonnavoulin Highld 147 F8
Bonnington Edin 120 C4
Bonnington Kent 19 B7
Bonnybank Fife 129 D5
Bonnybridge Falk 127 F7
Bonnykelly Aberds 153 C8
Bonnyrigg and Lasswade Midloth 121 C6
Bonnyton Aberds 153 E6
Bonnyton Angus 134 F3
Bonnyton Angus 135 D6
Bonsall Derbys 76 D2
Bonskeid House Perth 133 C5
Bont Mon 35 C7
Bont-Dolgadfan Powys 59 D5
Bont-goch Ceredig 58 F3
Bont-newydd Conwy 72 B4
Bont Newydd Gwyn 71 C8
Bont Newydd Gwyn 71 E8
Bontddu Gwyn 58 C3
Bonthorpe Lincs 79 B7
Bontnewydd Ceredig 46 C5
Bontnewydd Gwyn 82 F4
Bontuchel Denb 72 D4
Bonvilston V Glam 22 B2
Booker Bucks 39 E8
Boon Borders 121 E8
Boosbeck Redcar 102 C4
Boot Cumb 98 D3
Boot Street Suff 57 E6
Booth W Yorks 87 B8
Booth Wood W Yorks 87 C8
Boothby Graffoe Lincs 78 D2
Boothby Pagnell Lincs 78 F2
Boothen Stoke 75 E5
Boothferry E Yorks 89 B8
Boothville Northants 53 C5
Bootle Cumb 98 F3
Bootle Mers 85 E4
Booton Norf 81 E7
Boquhan Stirling 126 F4
Boraston Shrops 49 B8
Borden Kent 30 C2
Borden W Sus 16 B2
Bordley N Yorks 94 C2
Bordon Hants 27 F6
Bordon Camp Hants 27 F5
Boreham Essex 42 D3
Boreham Wilts 24 E3
Boreham Street E Sus 18 D3
Borehamwood Herts 40 E4
Boreland Dumfries 114 E4
Boreland Stirling 132 F2
Borgh W Isles 148 H1
Borgh W Isles 154 J4
Borghastan W Isles 154 C7
Borgie Highld 157 D9
Borgue Dumfries 106 E3
Borgue Highld 158 H3
Borley Essex 56 E2
Bornais W Isles 148 F2
Bornesketaig Highld 149 A8
Borness Dumfries 106 E3
Borough Green Kent 29 D7
Boroughbridge N Yorks 95 C6
Borras Head Wrex 73 D7
Borreraig Highld 148 C6
Borrobol Lodge Highld 157 G11
Borrowash Derbys 76 F4
Borrowby N Yorks 102 F2
Borrowdale Cumb 98 C4
Borrowfield Aberds 141 E7
Borth Ceredig 58 E3
Borth-y-Gest Gwyn 71 D6
Borthwickbrae Borders 115 C7
Borthwickshiels Borders 115 C7
Borve Highld 149 D9
Borve Lodge W Isles 154 H5
Borwick Lancs 92 B5
Bosavern Corn 2 C2
Bosbury Hereford 49 E8
Boscastle Corn 8 E3
Boscombe Bmouth 14 E2
Boscombe Wilts 25 F7
Boscoppa Corn 4 D5
Bosham W Sus 16 D2
Bosherston Pembs 44 F4
Boskenna Corn 2 D3
Bosley Ches E 75 C6
Bossall N Yorks 96 C3
Bossiney Corn 8 F2
Bossingham Kent 31 E5
Bossington Som 21 E7
Bostock Green Ches W 74 C3
Boston Lincs 79 E6
Boston Long Hedges Lincs 79 E6
Boston Spa W Yorks 95 E7
Boston West Lincs 79 E5
Boswinger Corn 3 B8
Botallack Corn 2 C2
Botany Bay London 41 E5
Botcherby Cumb 108 D4
Botcheston Leics 63 D8
Botesdale Suff 56 B4
Bothal Northumb 117 F8
Bothamsall Notts 77 B6
Bothel Cumb 107 F8
Bothenhampton Dorset 12 E2
Bothwell S Lanark 119 D7
Botley Bucks 40 D2
Botley Hants 15 C6
Botley Oxon 38 D4
Botolph Claydon Bucks 39 B7
Botolphs W Sus 17 D5
Bottacks Highld 150 E7
Bottesford Leics 77 F8
Bottesford N Lincs 90 D2
Bottisham Cambs 55 C6
Bottlesford Wilts 25 D6
Bottom Boat W Yorks 88 B4
Bottom House Staffs 75 D7
Bottom o'th'Moor Gtr Man 86 C4
Bottom of Hutton Lancs 86 B2
Bottomcraig Fife 129 B5
Botusfleming Corn 6 C2
Botwnnog Gwyn 70 D3
Bough Beech Kent 29 E5
Boughrood Powys 48 F3
Boughspring Glos 36 E2
Boughton Norf 67 D6
Boughton Northants 53 C5
Boughton Notts 77 C6
Boughton Aluph Kent 30 E4
Boughton Lees Kent 30 E4
Boughton Malherbe Kent 30 E2
Boughton Monchelsea Kent 29 D8
Boughton Street Kent 30 D4
Boulby Redcar 103 C5
Boulden Shrops 60 F5
Boulmer Northumb 117 C8
Boulston Pembs 44 D4
Boultenstone Aberds 140 C3
Boultham Lincs 78 C2
Bourn Cambs 54 D4
Bourne Lincs 65 B7
Bourne End Bucks 40 F1
Bourne End C Beds 53 E7
Bourne End Herts 40 D3
Bournemouth Bmouth 13 E8
Bournes Green Glos 37 D6
Bournes Green Southend 43 F5
Bournheath Worcs 50 B4
Bournmoor Durham 111 D6
Bournville W Mid 62 F4
Bourton Dorset 24 F2
Bourton N Som 23 C5
Bourton Oxon 38 F2
Bourton Shrops 61 E5
Bourton on Dunsmore Warks 52 B2
Bourton on the Hill Glos 51 F6
Bourton-on-the-Water Glos 38 B1
Bousd Argyll 146 E5
Boustead Hill Cumb 108 D2
Bouth Cumb 99 F5
Bouthwaite N Yorks 94 B4
Boveney Bucks 27 B7
Boverton V Glam 21 C8
Bovey Tracey Devon 7 B6
Bovingdon Herts 40 D3
Bovingdon Green Bucks 39 F8
Bovingdon Green Herts 40 D3
Bovinger Essex 41 D8
Bovington Camp Dorset 13 F6
Bow Borders 121 E7
Bow Devon 10 D2
Bow Orkney 159 J4
Bow Brickhill M Keynes 53 F7
Bow of Fife Fife 128 C5
Bow Street Ceredig 58 F3
Bowbank Durham 100 B4
Bowburn Durham 111 F6
Bowcombe IoW 15 F5
Bowd Devon 11 E6
Bowden Borders 121 F8
Bowden Devon 7 E6
Bowden Hill Wilts 24 C4
Bowderdale Cumb 100 D1
Bowdon Gtr Man 87 F5
Bower Northumb 116 F3
Bower Hinton Som 12 C2
Bowerchalke Wilts 13 B8
Bowerhill Wilts 24 C4
Bowermadden Highld 158 D4
Bowers Gifford Essex 42 F3
Bowershall Fife 128 E2
Bowertower Highld 158 D4
Bowes Durham 100 C4
Bowgreave Lancs 92 E4
Bowgreen Gtr Man 87 F5
Bowhill Borders 115 B7
Bowhouse Dumfries 107 C7
Bowland Bridge Cumb 99 F6
Bowley Hereford 49 D7
Bowlhead Green Sur 27 F7
Bowling W Dunb 118 B4
Bowling W Yorks 94 F4
Bowling Bank Wrex 73 E7
Bowling Green Worcs 50 D3
Bowmanstead Cumb 99 E5
Bowmore Argyll 142 C4
Bowness-on-Solway Cumb 108 C2
Bowness-on-Windermere Cumb 99 E6
Bowsden Northumb 123 E5
Bowside Lodge Highld 157 C11
Bowston Cumb 99 E6
Bowthorpe Norf 68 D4
Box Glos 37 D5
Box Wilts 24 C3
Box End Bedford 53 E8
Boxbush Glos 36 C4
Boxford Suff 56 E3
Boxford W Berks 26 B2
Boxgrove W Sus 16 D3
Boxley Kent 29 D8
Boxmoor Herts 40 D3
Boxted Essex 56 F4
Boxted Suff 56 D2
Boxted Cross Essex 56 F4
Boxted Heath Essex 56 F4
Boxworth Cambs 54 C4
Boxworth End Cambs 54 C4
Boyden Gate Kent 31 C6
Boylestone Derbys 75 F8
Boyndie Aberds 153 B6
Boynton E Yorks 97 C7
Boysack Angus 135 E6
Boyton Corn 8 E5
Boyton Suff 57 E7
Boyton Wilts 24 F4
Boyton Cross Essex 42 D2
Boyton End Suff 55 E8
Bozeat Northants 53 D7

Churchtown Mers 85 C4
Churnsike Lodge Northumb 109 B6
Churston Ferrers Torbay 7 D7
Churt Sur 27 F6
Churton Ches W 73 D8
Churwell W Yorks 88 B3
Chute Standen Wilts 25 D8
Chwilog Gwyn 70 D5
Chyandour Corn 2 C3
Cilan Uchaf Gwyn 70 E3
Cilcain Flint 73 C5
Cilcennin Ceredig 46 C4
Cilfor Gwyn 71 D7
Cilfrew Neath 34 D1
Cilfynydd Rhondda 34 E4
Cilgerran Pembs 45 E3
Cilgwyn Carms 33 B8
Cilgwyn Gwyn 82 F4
Cilgwyn Pembs 45 F2
Ciliau Aeron Ceredig 46 D3
Cill Donnain W Isles 148 F2
Cille Bhrighde W Isles 148 G2
Cille Pheadair W Isles 148 G2
Cilmery Powys 48 D2
Cilsan Carms 33 B6
Ciltalgarth Gwyn 72 E2
Cilwendeg Pembs 45 F4
Cilybebyll Neath 33 D8
Cilycwm Carms 47 F6
Cimla Neath 34 E1
Cinderford Glos 36 C3
Cippyn Pembs 45 E3
Circebost W Isles 154 D6
Cirencester Glos 37 D7
Ciribhig W Isles 154 C6
City London 41 F6
City Powys 60 F2
City Dulas Anglesey 82 C4
Clachaig Argyll 145 E10
Clachan Argyll 124 D3
Clachan Argyll 125 D7
Clachan Argyll 130 E2
Clachan Argyll 144 H6
Clachan Highld 149 E10
Clachan W Isles 148 D2
Clachan na Luib W Isles 148 B3
Clachan of Campsie E Dunb 119 B6
Clachan of Glendaruel Argyll 145 E8
Clachan-Seil Argyll 124 D3
Clachan Strachur Argyll 125 E6
Clachaneasy Dumfries 105 B7
Clachanmore Dumfries 104 E4
Clachbreck Argyll 144 F6
Clachnabrain Angus 134 C3
Clachtoll Highld 156 G3
Clackmannan Clack 127 E8
Clacton-on-Sea Essex 43 C7
Cladach Chireboist W Isles 148 B2
Claddach-knockline W Isles 148 B2
Cladich Argyll 125 C6
Claggan Highld 131 B5
Claggan Highld 147 G9
Claigan Highld 148 C7
Claines Worcs 50 D3
Clandown Bath 23 D8
Clanfield Hants 15 C7
Clanfield Oxon 38 D2
Clanville Hants 25 E8
Claonaig Argyll 145 H7
Claonel Highld 157 J8
Clap Hill Kent 19 B7
Clapgate Dorset 13 D8
Clapgate Herts 41 B7
Clapham Bedford 53 D8
Clapham London 28 B3
Clapham N Yorks 93 C7
Clapham W Sus 16 D4
Clappers Borders 122 D5
Clappersgate Cumb 99 D5
Clapton Som 12 D2
Clapton-in-Gordano N Som 23 B6
Clapton-on-the-Hill Glos 38 C1
Clapworthy Devon 9 B8
Clara Vale T&W 110 C4
Clarach Ceredig 58 F3
Clarbeston Pembs 32 B1
Clarbeston Road Pembs 32 B1
Clarborough Notts 89 F8
Clardon Highld 158 D3
Clare Suff 55 E8
Clarebrand Dumfries 106 C4
Clarencefield Dumfries 107 C7
Clarilaw Borders 115 C8
Clark's Green Sur 28 F2
Clarkston E Renf 119 D5
Clashandorran Highld 151 G8
Clashcoig Highld 151 B9
Clashindarroch Aberds 152 E4
Clashmore Highld 151 C10
Clashmore Highld 156 F3
Clashnessie Highld 156 F3
Clashnoir Moray 139 B8
Clate Shetland 160 G7
Clathy Perth 127 C8
Clatt Aberds 140 B4
Clatter Powys 59 E6
Clatterford IoW 15 F5
Clatterin Bridge Aberds 135 B6
Clatworthy Som 22 F2
Claughton Lancs 92 E5
Claughton Lancs 93 C5
Claughton Mers 85 F4
Claverdon Warks 51 C6
Claverham N Som 23 C6
Clavering Essex 55 F5
Claverley Shrops 61 E7
Claverton Bath 24 C2
Clawdd-newydd Denb 72 D4
Clawthorpe Cumb 92 B5
Clawton Devon 9 E5
Claxby Lincs 79 B7
Claxby Lincs 90 E5
Claxton N Yorks 96 C2
Claxton Norf 69 D6
Clay Common Suff 69 F7
Clay Coton Northants 52 B3
Clay Cross Derbys 76 C3
Clay Hill W Berks 26 B3
Clay Lake Lincs 66 B2
Claybokie Aberds 139 E6
Claybrooke Magna Leics 63 F8
Claybrooke Parva Leics 63 F8
Claydon Oxon 52 D2
Claydon Suff 56 D5
Claygate Dumfries 108 B3
Claygate Kent 29 E8
Claygate Sur 28 C2
Claygate Cross Kent 29 D7
Clayhanger Devon 10 B5
Clayhanger W Mid 62 D4
Clayhidon Devon 11 C6
Clayhill E Sus 18 C5
Clayhill Hants 14 D4
Clayock Highld 158 E3
Claypole Lincs 77 E8
Clayton S Yorks 89 D5
Clayton Staffs 75 E5
Clayton W Sus 17 C6
Clayton W Yorks 94 F4
Clayton Green Lancs 86 B3
Clayton-le-Moors Lancs 93 F7
Clayton-le-Woods Lancs 86 B3
Clayton West W Yorks 88 C3
Clayworth Notts 89 F8
Cleadale Highld 146 C7
Cleadon T&W 111 C6
Clearbrook Devon 6 C3
Clearwell Glos 36 D2
Cleasby N Yorks 101 C7
Cleat Orkney 159 K5
Cleatlam Durham 101 C6
Cleator Cumb 98 C2
Cleator Moor Cumb 98 C2
Clebrig Highld 157 F8
Cleckheaton W Yorks 88 B2
Clee St Margaret Shrops 61 F5
Cleedownton Shrops 61 F5
Cleehill Shrops 49 B7
Cleethorpes NE Lincs 91 D7
Cleeton St Mary Shrops 49 B8
Cleeve N Som 23 C6
Cleeve Hill Glos 37 B6
Cleeve Prior Worcs 51 E5
Clegyrnant Powys 59 D6
Clehonger Hereford 49 F6
Cleish Perth 128 E2
Cleland N Lanark 119 D8
Clench Common Wilts 25 C6
Clenchwarton Norf 67 B5
Clent Worcs 50 B4
Cleobury Mortimer Shrops 49 B8
Cleobury North Shrops 61 F6
Cleongart Argyll 143 E7
Clephanton Highld 151 F11
Clerklands Borders 115 B8
Clestrain Orkney 159 H4
Cleuch Head Borders 115 C8
Cleughbrae Dumfries 107 B7
Clevancy Wilts 25 B5
Clevedon N Som 23 B6
Cleveley Oxon 38 B3
Cleveleys Lancs 92 E3
Cleverton Wilts 37 F6
Clevis Bridgend 21 B7
Clewer Som 23 D6
Cley next the Sea Norf 81 C6
Cliaid W Isles 148 H1
Cliasmol W Isles 154 G5
Cliburn Cumb 99 B7
Click Mill Orkney 159 F4
Cliddesden Hants 26 E4
Cliff End E Sus 19 D5
Cliffburn Angus 135 E6
Cliffe Medway 29 B8
Cliffe N Yorks 96 F2
Cliffe Woods Medway 29 B8
Clifford Hereford 48 E4
Clifford W Yorks 95 E7
Clifford Chambers Warks 51 D6
Clifford's Mesne Glos 36 B4
Cliffsend Kent 31 C7
Clifton Bristol 23 B7
Clifton C Beds 54 F2
Clifton Cumb 99 B7
Clifton Derbys 75 E8
Clifton Lancs 92 F4
Clifton N Yorks 94 E4
Clifton Northumb 117 F8
Clifton Nottingham 77 F5
Clifton Oxon 52 F2
Clifton S Yorks 89 E6
Clifton Stirling 131 F7
Clifton Worcs 50 E3
Clifton York 95 D8
Clifton Campville Staffs 63 C6
Clifton Green Gtr Man 87 D5
Clifton Hampden Oxon 39 E5
Clifton Reynes M Keynes 53 D7
Clifton upon Dunsmore Warks 52 B3
Clifton upon Teme Worcs 50 C2
Cliftoncote Borders 116 B4
Cliftonville Kent 31 B7
Climaen gwyn Neath 33 D8
Climping W Sus 16 D4
Climpy S Lanark 120 D2
Clink Som 24 E2
Clint N Yorks 95 D5
Clint Green Norf 68 C3
Clintmains Borders 122 F2
Cliobh W Isles 154 D5
Clippesby Norf 69 C7
Clipsham Rutland 65 C6
Clipston Northants 64 F4
Clipstone Notts 77 C5
Clitheroe Lancs 93 E7
Cliuthar W Isles 154 H6
Clive Shrops 60 B5
Clivocast Shetland 160 C8
Clixby Lincs 90 D5
Clocaenog Denb 72 D4
Clochan Moray 152 B4
Clock Face Mers 86 E3
Clockmill Borders 122 D3
Cloddiau Powys 60 D2
Clodock Hereford 35 B7
Clola Aberds 153 D10
Clophill C Beds 53 F8
Clopton Northants 65 F7
Clopton Suff 57 D6
Clopton Corner Suff 57 D6
Clopton Green Suff 55 D8
Close Clark IoM 84 E2
Closeburn Dumfries 113 E8
Closworth Som 12 C3
Clothall Herts 54 F3
Clotton Ches W 74 C2
Clough Foot W Yorks 87 B7
Cloughton N Yorks 103 E8
Cloughton Newlands N Yorks 103 E8
Clousta Shetland 160 H5
Clouston Orkney 159 G3
Clova Aberds 140 B3
Clova Angus 134 B3
Clove Lodge Durham 100 C4
Clovelly Devon 8 B5
Clovenfords Borders 121 F7
Clovenstone Aberds 141 C6
Clovullin Highld 130 C4
Clow Bridge Lancs 87 B6
Clowne Derbys 76 B4
Clows Top Worcs 50 B2
Cloy Wrex 73 E7
Cluanie Inn Highld 136 C3
Cluanie Lodge Highld 136 C3
Clun Shrops 60 F3
Clunbury Shrops 60 F3
Clunderwen Carms 32 C2
Clune Highld 138 B3
Clunes Highld 136 F5
Clungunford Shrops 49 B5
Clunie Aberds 153 C6
Clunie Perth 133 E8
Clunton Shrops 60 F3
Cluny Fife 128 E4
Cluny Castle Highld 138 E2
Clutton Bath 23 D8
Clutton Ches W 73 D8
Clwt-grugoer Conwy 72 C3
Clwt-y-bont Gwyn 83 E5
Clydach Mon 35 C6
Clydach Swansea 33 D7
Clydach Vale Rhondda 34 E3
Clydebank W Dunb 118 B4
Clydey Pembs 45 F4
Clyffe Pypard Wilts 25 B5
Clynder Argyll 145 E11
Clyne Neath 34 D2
Clynelish Highld 157 J11
Clynnog-fawr Gwyn 82 F4
Clyro Powys 48 E4
Clyst Honiton Devon 10 E4
Clyst Hydon Devon 10 D5
Clyst St George Devon 10 F4
Clyst St Lawrence Devon 10 D5
Clyst St Mary Devon 10 E4
Cnoc Amhlaigh W Isles 155 D10
Cnwch-coch Ceredig 47 B5
Coachford Aberds 152 D4
Coad's Green Corn 5 B7
Coal Aston Derbys 76 B3
Coalbrookdale Telford 61 D6
Coalbrookvale Bl Gwent 35 D5
Coalburn S Lanark 119 F8
Coalburns T&W 110 C4
Coalcleugh Northumb 109 E8
Coaley Glos 36 D4
Coalhall E Ayrs 112 C4
Coalhill Essex 42 E3
Coalpit Heath S Glos 36 F3
Coalport Telford 61 D6
Coalsnaughton Clack 127 E8
Coaltown of Balgonie Fife 128 E4
Coaltown of Wemyss Fife 128 E5
Coalville Leics 63 C8
Coalway Glos 36 C2
Coat Som 12 B2
Coatbridge N Lanark 119 C7
Coatdyke N Lanark 119 C7
Coate Swindon 38 F1
Coate Wilts 24 C5
Coates Cambs 66 E3
Coates Glos 37 D6
Coates Lancs 93 E8
Coates Notts 90 F2
Coates W Sus 16 C3
Coatham Redcar 102 B3
Coatham Mundeville Darl 101 B7
Coatsgate Dumfries 114 D3
Cobbaton Devon 9 B8
Cobbler's Green Norf 69 E5
Coberley Glos 37 C6
Cobham Kent 29 C7
Cobham Sur 28 C2
Cobholm Island Norf 69 D8
Cobleland Stirling 126 E4
Cobnash Hereford 49 C6
Coburty Aberds 153 B9
Cock Bank Wrex 73 E7
Cock Bridge Aberds 139 D8
Cock Clarks Essex 42 D4
Cockayne N Yorks 102 E4
Cockayne Hatley Cambs 54 E3
Cockburnspath Borders 122 B3
Cockenzie and Port Seton E Loth 121 B7
Cockerham Lancs 92 D4
Cockermouth Cumb 107 F8
Cockernhoe Green Herts 40 B4
Cockfield Durham 101 B6
Cockfield Suff 56 D3
Cockfosters London 41 E5
Cocking W Sus 16 C2
Cockington Torbay 7 C6
Cocklake Som 23 E6
Cockley Beck Cumb 98 D4
Cockley Cley Norf 67 D7
Cockshutt Shrops 60 B4
Cockthorpe Norf 81 C5
Cockwood Devon 10 F4
Cockyard Hereford 49 F6
Codda Corn 5 B6
Coddenham Suff 56 D5
Coddington Ches W 73 D8
Coddington Hereford 50 E2
Coddington Notts 77 D8
Codford St Mary Wilts 24 F4
Codford St Peter Wilts 24 F4
Codicote Herts 41 C5
Codmore Hill W Sus 16 B4
Codnor Derbys 76 E4
Codrington S Glos 24 B2
Codsall Staffs 62 D2
Codsall Wood Staffs 62 D2
Coed Duon = Blackwood Caerph 35 E5
Coed Mawr Gwyn 83 D5
Coed Morgan Mon 35 C7
Coed-Talon Flint 73 D6
Coed-y-bryn Ceredig 46 E2
Coed-y-paen Mon 35 E7
Coed-yr-ynys Powys 35 B5
Coed Ystumgwern Gwyn 71 E6
Coedely Rhondda 34 F4
Coedkernew Newport 35 F6
Coedpoeth Wrex 73 D6
Coedway Powys 60 C3
Coelbren Powys 34 C2
Coffinswell Devon 7 C6
Cofton Hackett Worcs 50 B5
Cogan V Glam 22 B3
Cogenhoe Northants 53 C6
Cogges Oxon 38 D3
Coggeshall Essex 42 B4
Coggeshall Hamlet Essex 42 B4
Coggins Mill E Sus 18 C2
Coig Peighinnean W Isles 155 A10
Coig Peighinnean Bhuirgh W Isles 155 B9
Coignafearn Lodge Highld 138 C2
Coilacriech Aberds 140 E2
Coilantogle Stirling 126 D4
Coilleag W Isles 148 G2
Coillore Highld 149 E8
Coity Bridgend 34 F3
Col W Isles 155 C9
Col Uarach W Isles 155 D9
Colaboll Highld 157 H8
Colan Corn 4 C3
Colaton Raleigh Devon 11 F5
Colbost Highld 148 D7
Colburn N Yorks 101 E6
Colby Cumb 100 B1
Colby IoM 84 E2
Colby Norf 81 D8
Colchester Essex 43 B6
Colcot V Glam 22 C3
Cold Ash W Berks 26 C3
Cold Ashby Northants 52 B4
Cold Ashton S Glos 24 B2
Cold Aston Glos 37 C8
Cold Blow Pembs 32 C2
Cold Brayfield M Keynes 53 D7
Cold Hanworth Lincs 90 F4
Cold Harbour Lincs 78 F2
Cold Hatton Telford 61 B6
Cold Hesledon Durham 111 E7
Cold Higham Northants 52 D4
Cold Kirby N Yorks 102 F3
Cold Newton Leics 64 D4
Cold Northcott Corn 8 F4
Cold Norton Essex 42 D4
Cold Overton Leics 64 C5
Coldbackie Highld 157 D9
Coldbeck Cumb 100 D2
Coldblow London 29 B6
Coldean Brighton 17 D7
Coldeast Devon 7 B6
Colden W Yorks 87 B7
Colden Common Hants 15 B5
Coldfair Green Suff 57 C8
Coldham Cambs 66 D4
Coldharbour Glos 36 D2
Coldharbour Kent 29 D6
Coldharbour Sur 28 E2
Coldingham Borders 122 C5
Coldrain Perth 128 D2
Coldred Kent 31 E6
Coldridge Devon 9 D8
Coldstream Angus 134 F3
Coldstream Borders 122 F4
Coldwaltham W Sus 16 C4
Coldwells Aberds 153 D11
Coldwells Croft Aberds 140 B4
Coldyeld Shrops 60 E3
Cole Som 23 F8
Cole Green Herts 41 C5
Cole Henley Hants 26 D2
Colebatch Shrops 60 F3
Colebrook Devon 10 D5
Colebrooke Devon 10 E2
Coleby Lincs 78 C2
Coleby N Lincs 90 C2
Coleford Devon 10 D2
Coleford Glos 36 C2
Coleford Som 23 E8
Colehill Dorset 13 D8
Coleman's Hatch E Sus 29 F5
Colemere Shrops 73 F8
Colemore Hants 26 F5
Coleorton Leics 63 C8
Colerne Wilts 24 B3
Cole's Green Suff 57 C6
Coles Green Suff 56 E4
Colesbourne Glos 37 C6
Colesden Bedford 54 D2
Coleshill Bucks 40 E2
Coleshill Oxon 38 E2
Coleshill Warks 63 F6
Colestocks Devon 11 D5
Colgate W Sus 28 F3
Colgrain Argyll 126 F2
Colinsburgh Fife 129 D6
Colinton Edin 120 C5
Colintraive Argyll 145 F9
Colkirk Norf 80 E5
Collace Perth 134 F2
Collafirth Shetland 160 G6
Collaton St Mary Torbay 7 D6
College Milton S Lanark 119 D6
Collessie Fife 128 C4
Collier Row London 41 E8
Collier Street Kent 29 E8
Collier's End Herts 41 B6
Collier's Green Kent 18 B4
Colliery Row T&W 111 E6
Collieston Aberds 141 B9
Collin Dumfries 107 B7
Collingbourne Ducis Wilts 25 D7
Collingbourne Kingston Wilts 25 D7
Collingham Notts 77 C8
Collingham W Yorks 95 E6
Collington Hereford 49 C8
Collingtree Northants 53 D5
Collins Green Warr 86 E3
Colliston Angus 135 E6
Collycroft Warks 63 F7
Collynie Aberds 153 E8
Collyweston Northants 65 D6
Colmonell S Ayrs 104 A5
Colmworth Bedford 54 D2
Coln Rogers Glos 37 D7
Coln St Aldwyn's Glos 37 D8
Coln St Dennis Glos 37 C7
Colnabaichin Aberds 139 D8
Colnbrook Slough 27 B8
Colne Cambs 54 B4
Colne Lancs 93 E8
Colne Edge Lancs 93 E8
Colne Engaine Essex 56 F2
Colney Norf 68 D4
Colney Heath Herts 41 D5
Colney Street Herts 40 D4
Colpy Aberds 153 E6
Colquhar Borders 121 E6
Colsterdale N Yorks 101 F6
Colsterworth Lincs 65 B6
Colston Bassett Notts 77 F6
Coltfield Moray 151 E14
Colthouse Cumb 99 E5
Coltishall Norf 69 C5
Coltness N Lanark 119 D8
Colton Cumb 99 F5
Colton N Yorks 95 E8
Colton Norf 68 D4
Colton Staffs 62 B4
Colton W Yorks 95 F6
Colva Powys 48 D4
Colvend Dumfries 107 D5
Colvister Shetland 160 D7
Colwall Green Hereford 50 E2
Colwall Stone Hereford 50 E2
Colwell Northumb 110 B2
Colwich Staffs 62 B4
Colwick Notts 77 E6
Colwinston V Glam 21 B8
Colworth W Sus 16 D3
Colwyn Bay = Bae Colwyn Conwy 83 D8
Colyford Devon 11 E7
Colyton Devon 11 E7
Combe Hereford 48 C5
Combe Oxon 38 C4
Combe W Berks 25 C8
Combe Common Sur 27 F7
Combe Down Bath 24 C2
Combe Florey Som 22 F3
Combe Hay Bath 24 D2
Combe Martin Devon 20 E4
Combe Moor Hereford 49 C5
Combe Raleigh Devon 11 D6
Combe St Nicholas Som 11 C8
Combeinteignhead Devon 7 B7
Comberbach Ches W 74 B3
Comberton Cambs 54 D4
Comberton Hereford 49 C6
Combpyne Devon 11 E7
Combridge Staffs 75 F7
Combrook Warks 51 D8
Combs Derbys 75 B7
Combs Suff 56 D4
Combs Ford Suff 56 D4
Combwich Som 22 E4
Comers Aberds 141 D5
Comins Coch Ceredig 58 F3
Commercial End Cambs 55 C6
Commins Capel Betws Ceredig 46 D5
Commins Coch Powys 58 D5
Common Edge Blackpool 92 F3
Common Side Derbys 76 B3
Commondale N Yorks 102 C4
Commonmoor Corn 5 C7
Commonside Ches W 74 B2
Compstall Gtr Man 87 E7
Compton Devon 7 C6
Compton Hants 15 B5
Compton Sur 27 E6
Compton Sur 27 E7
Compton W Berks 26 B3
Compton W Sus 15 C8
Compton Wilts 25 D6
Compton Abbas Dorset 13 C6
Compton Abdale Glos 37 C7
Compton Bassett Wilts 24 B5
Compton Beauchamp Oxon 38 F2
Compton Bishop Som 23 D5
Compton Chamberlayne Wilts 13 B8
Compton Dando Bath 23 C8
Compton Dundon Som 23 F6
Compton Martin Bath 23 D7
Compton Pauncefoot Som 12 B4
Compton Valence Dorset 12 E3
Comrie Fife 128 F2
Comrie Perth 127 B6
Conaglen House Highld 130 C4
Conchra Argyll 145 E9
Concraigie Perth 133 E8
Conder Green Lancs 92 D4
Conderton Worcs 50 F4
Condicote Glos 38 B1
Condorrat N Lanark 119 B7
Condover Shrops 60 D4
Coney Weston Suff 56 B3
Coneyhurst W Sus 16 B5
Coneysthorpe N Yorks 96 B3
Coneythorpe N Yorks 95 D6
Conford Hants 27 F6
Congash Highld 139 B6
Congdon's Shop Corn 5 B7
Congerstone Leics 63 D7
Congham Norf 80 E3
Congl-y-wal Gwyn 71 C8
Congleton Ches E 75 C5
Congresbury N Som 23 C6
Congreve Staffs 62 C3
Conicavel Moray 151 F12
Coningsby Lincs 78 D5
Conington Cambs 54 C4
Conington Cambs 65 F8
Conisbrough S Yorks 89 E6
Conisby Argyll 142 B3
Conisholme Lincs 91 E8
Coniston Cumb 99 E5
Coniston E Yorks 97 F7
Coniston Cold N Yorks 94 D2
Conistone N Yorks 94 C2
Connah's Quay Flint 73 C6
Connel Argyll 124 B5
Connel Park E Ayrs 113 C6
Connor Downs Corn 2 C4
Conon Bridge Highld 151 F8
Conon House Highld 151 F8
Cononley N Yorks 94 E2
Conordan Highld 149 E10
Consall Staffs 75 E6
Consett Durham 110 D4
Constable Burton N Yorks 101 E6
Constantine Corn 3 D6
Constantine Bay Corn 4 B3
Contin Highld 150 F7
Contlaw Aberdeen 141 D7
Conwy Conwy 83 D7
Conyer Kent 30 C3
Conyers Green Suff 56 C2
Cooden E Sus 18 E4
Cooil IoM 84 E3
Cookbury Devon 9 D6
Cookham Windsor 40 F1
Cookham Dean Windsor 40 F1
Cookham Rise Windsor 40 F1
Cookhill Worcs 51 D5
Cookley Suff 57 B7
Cookley Worcs 62 F2
Cookley Green Oxon 39 E6
Cookney Aberds 141 E7
Cookridge W Yorks 95 E5
Cooksbridge E Sus 17 C8
Cooksmill Green Essex 42 D2
Coolham W Sus 16 B5
Cooling Medway 29 B8
Coombe Corn 4 D4
Coombe Corn 8 C4
Coombe Hants 15 B7
Coombe Wilts 25 D6
Coombe Bissett Wilts 14 B2
Coombe Hill Glos 37 B5
Coombe Keynes Dorset 13 F6
Coombes W Sus 17 D5
Coopersale Common Essex 41 D7
Cootham W Sus 16 C4
Copdock Suff 56 E5
Copford Green Essex 43 B5
Copgrove N Yorks 95 C6
Copister Shetland 160 F6
Cople Bedford 54 E2
Copley Durham 101 B5
Coplow Dale Derbys 75 B8
Copmanthorpe York 95 E8
Coppathorne Corn 8 D4
Coppenhall Staffs 62 C3
Coppenhall Moss Ches E 74 D4
Copperhouse Corn 2 C4
Coppingford Cambs 65 F8
Copplestone Devon 10 D2
Coppull Lancs 86 C3
Coppull Moor Lancs 86 C3
Copsale W Sus 17 B5
Copster Green Lancs 93 F6
Copston Magna Warks 63 F8
Copt Heath W Mid 51 B6
Copt Hewick N Yorks 95 B6
Copt Oak Leics 63 C8
Copthorne Shrops 60 C4
Copthorne Sur 28 F4
Copy's Green Norf 80 D5
Copythorne Hants 14 C4
Corbets Tey London 42 F1
Corbridge Northumb 110 C2
Corby Northants 65 F5
Corby Glen Lincs 65 B6
Cordon N Ayrs 143 E11
Coreley Shrops 49 B8
Cores End Bucks 40 F2
Corfe Som 11 C7
Corfe Castle Dorset 13 F7
Corfe Mullen Dorset 13 E7
Corfton Shrops 60 F4
Corgarff Aberds 139 D8
Corhampton Hants 15 B7
Corlae Dumfries 113 E6
Corley Warks 63 F7
Corley Ash Warks 63 F6
Corley Moor Warks 63 F6
Cornaa IoM 84 D4
Cornabus Argyll 142 D4
Cornel Conwy 83 E7
Corner Row Lancs 92 F4
Corney Cumb 98 E3
Cornforth Durham 111 F6
Cornhill Aberds 152 C5
Cornhill-on-Tweed Northumb 122 F4
Cornholme W Yorks 87 B7
Cornish Hall End Essex 55 F7
Cornquoy Orkney 159 J6
Cornsay Durham 110 E4
Cornsay Colliery Durham 110 E4
Corntown Highld 151 F8
Corntown V Glam 21 B8
Cornwell Oxon 38 B2
Cornwood Devon 6 D4
Cornworthy Devon 7 D6
Corpach Highld 130 B4
Corpusty Norf 81 D7
Corran Highld 130 C4
Corran Highld 149 H13
Corranbuie Argyll 145 G7
Corrany IoM 84 D4
Corrie N Ayrs 143 D11
Corrie Common Dumfries 114 F5
Corriecravie N Ayrs 143 F10
Corriemoillie Highld 150 E6
Corriemulzie Lodge Highld 150 B6
Corrievarkie Lodge Perth 132 B2
Corrievorrie Highld 138 B3
Corrimony Highld 150 H6
Corringham Lincs 90 E2
Corringham Thurrock 42 F3
Corris Gwyn 58 D4
Corris Uchaf Gwyn 58 D4
Corrour Shooting Lodge Highld 131 C8
Corrow Argyll 125 E7
Corry Highld 149 F11
Corry of Ardnagrask Highld 151 G8
Corrykinloch Highld 156 G6
Corrymuckloch Perth 133 F5
Corrynachenchy Argyll 147 G9
Cors-y-Gedol Gwyn 71 E6
Corsback Highld 158 C4
Corscombe Dorset 12 D3
Corse Aberds 152 D6
Corse Glos 36 B4
Corse Lawn Worcs 50 F3
Corse of Kinnoir Aberds 152 D5
Corsewall Dumfries 104 C4
Corsham Wilts 24 B3
Corsindae Aberds 141 D5
Corsley Wilts 24 E3
Corsley Heath Wilts 24 E3
Corsock Dumfries 106 B4
Corston Bath 23 C8
Corston Wilts 37 F6
Corstorphine Edin 120 B4
Cortachy Angus 134 D3
Corton Suff 69 E8
Corton Wilts 24 E4
Corton Denham Som 12 B4
Coruanan Lodge Highld 130 C4
Corunna W Isles 148 B3
Corwen Denb 72 E4
Coryton Devon 9 F6
Coryton Thurrock 42 F3
Cosby Leics 64 E2
Coseley W Mid 62 E3
Cosgrove Northants 53 E5
Cosham Ptsmth 15 D7
Cosheston Pembs 32 D1
Cossall Notts 76 E4
Cossington Leics 64 C3
Cossington Som 23 E5
Costa Orkney 159 F4
Costessey Norf 68 C4
Costock Notts 64 B2
Coston Leics 64 B5
Cote Oxon 38 D3
Cotebrook Ches W 74 C2
Cotehill Cumb 108 D4
Cotes Cumb 99 F6
Cotes Leics 64 B2
Cotes Staffs 74 F5
Cotesbach Leics 64 F2
Cotgrave Notts 77 F6
Cothall Aberds 141 C7
Cotham Notts 77 E7
Cothelstone Som 22 F3
Cotherstone Durham 101 C5
Cothill Oxon 38 E4
Cotleigh Devon 11 D7
Cotmanhay Derbys 76 E4
Cotmaton Devon 11 F6
Coton Cambs 54 D5
Coton Northants 52 B4
Coton Staffs 62 B2
Coton Staffs 75 F6
Coton Clanford Staffs 62 B2
Coton Hill Shrops 60 C4
Coton Hill Staffs 75 F6
Coton in the Elms Derbys 63 C6
Cott Devon 7 C5
Cottam E Yorks 97 C5
Cottam Lancs 92 F5
Cottam Notts 77 B8
Cottartown Highld 151 H13
Cottenham Cambs 54 C5
Cotterdale N Yorks 100 E3
Cottered Herts 41 B6
Cotteridge W Mid 50 B5
Cotterstock Northants 65 E7
Cottesbrooke Northants 52 B5
Cottesmore Rutland 65 C6
Cotteylands Devon 10 C4
Cottingham E Yorks 97 F6
Cottingham Northants 64 E5
Cottingley W Yorks 94 F4
Cottisford Oxon 52 F3
Cotton Staffs 75 E7
Cotton Suff 56 C4
Cotton End Bedford 53 E8
Cottown Aberds 140 B4
Cottown Aberds 141 C6
Cottown Aberds 153 D8
Cotwalton Staffs 75 F6
Couch's Mill Corn 5 D6
Coughton Hereford 36 B2
Coughton Warks 51 C5
Coulaghailtro Argyll 144 G6
Coulags Highld 150 G2
Coulby Newham Mbro 102 C3
Coulderton Cumb 98 D1
Coulin Highld 150 F3
Coull Aberds 140 D4
Coull Argyll 142 B3
Coulport Argyll 145 E11
Coulsdon London 28 D3
Coulston Wilts 24 D4
Coulter S Lanark 120 F3
Coulton N Yorks 96 B2
Cound Shrops 61 D5
Coundon Durham 101 B7
Coundon W Mid 63 F7
Coundon Grange Durham 101 B7
Countersett N Yorks 100 F4
Countess Wilts 25 E6
Countess Wear Devon 10 F4
Countesthorpe Leics 64 E2
Countisbury Devon 21 E6
County Oak W Sus 28 F3
Coup Green Lancs 86 B3
Coupar Angus Perth 134 E2
Coupland Northumb 122 F5
Cour Argyll 143 D9
Courance Dumfries 114 E3
Court-at-Street Kent 19 B7
Court Henry Carms 33 B6
Courteenhall Northants 53 D5
Courtsend Essex 43 E6
Courtway Som 22 F4
Cousland Midloth 121 C6
Cousley Wood E Sus 18 B3
Cove Argyll 145 E11
Cove Borders 122 B3
Cove Devon 10 C4
Cove Hants 27 D6
Cove Highld 155 H13
Cove Bay Aberdeen 141 D8
Cove Bottom Suff 57 B8
Covehithe Suff 69 F8
Coven Staffs 62 D3
Coveney Cambs 66 F4
Covenham St Bartholomew Lincs 91 E7
Covenham St Mary Lincs 91 E7
Coventry W Mid 51 B8
Coverack Corn 3 E6
Coverham N Yorks 101 F6
Covesea Moray 152 A1
Covington Cambs 53 B8
Covington S Lanark 120 F2
Cow Ark Lancs 93 E6
Cowan Bridge Lancs 93 B6
Cowbeech E Sus 18 D3
Cowbit Lincs 66 C2
Cowbridge Lincs 79 E6
Cowbridge Som 21 E8
Cowbridge = Y Bont-Faen V Glam 21 B8
Cowdale Derbys 75 B7
Cowden Kent 29 E5
Cowdenbeath Fife 128 E3
Cowdenburn Borders 120 D5
Cowers Lane Derbys 76 E3
Cowes IoW 15 E5
Cowesby N Yorks 102 F2
Cowfold W Sus 17 B6
Cowgill Cumb 100 F2
Cowie Aberds 141 F7
Cowie Stirling 127 F7
Cowley Devon 10 E4
Cowley Glos 37 C6
Cowley London 40 F3
Cowley Oxon 39 D5
Cowleymoor Devon 10 C4
Cowling Lancs 86 C3
Cowling N Yorks 94 E2
Cowling N Yorks 101 F7
Cowlinge Suff 55 D8
Cowpe Lancs 87 B6
Cowpen Northumb 117 F8
Cowpen Bewley Stockton 102 B2
Cowplain Hants 15 C7
Cowshill Durham 109 E8
Cowslip Green N Som 23 C6
Cowstrandburn Fife 128 E2
Cowthorpe N Yorks 95 D7
Cox Common Suff 69 F6
Cox Green Windsor 27 B6
Cox Moor Notts 76 D5
Coxbank Ches E 74 E3
Coxbench Derbys 76 E3
Coxford Norf 80 E4
Coxford Soton 14 C4
Coxheath Kent 29 D8
Coxhill Kent 31 E6
Coxhoe Durham 111 F6
Coxley Som 23 E7
Coxwold N Yorks 95 B8
Coychurch Bridgend 21 B8
Coylton S Ayrs 112 B4
Coylumbridge Highld 138 C5
Coynach Aberds 140 D3
Coynachie Aberds 152 E4
Coytrahen Bridgend 34 F2
Crabadon Devon 7 D5
Crabbs Cross Worcs 50 C5
Crabtree W Sus 17 B6
Crackenthorpe Cumb 100 B1
Crackington Haven Corn 8 E3
Crackley Warks 51 B7
Crackleybank Shrops 61 C7
Crackpot N Yorks 100 E4
Cracoe N Yorks 94 C2
Craddock Devon 11 C5
Cradhlastadh W Isles 154 D5
Cradley Hereford 50 E2
Cradley Heath W Mid 62 F3
Crafthole Corn 5 D8
Cragg Vale W Yorks 87 B8
Craggan Highld 139 B6
Craggie Highld 151 H10
Craggie Highld 157 H11
Craghead Durham 110 D5
Crai Powys 34 B2
Craibstone Moray 152 C4
Craichie Angus 135 E5
Craig Dumfries 106 B3
Craig Dumfries 106 C3
Craig Highld 150 G3
Craig Castle Aberds 140 B3
Craig-cefn-parc Swansea 33 D7
Craig Penllyn V Glam 21 B8
Craig-y-don Conwy 83 C7
Craig-y-nos Powys 34 C2
Craiganor Lodge Perth 132 D3
Craigdam Aberds 153 E8
Craigdarroch Dumfries 113 E7
Craigdarroch Highld 150 F7
Craigdhu Highld 150 G7
Craigearn Aberds 141 C6
Craigellachie Moray 152 D2
Craigencross Dumfries 104 C4
Craigend Perth 128 B3
Craigend Stirling 127 F6
Craigendive Argyll 145 E9
Craigendoran Argyll 126 F2
Craigends Renfs 118 C4
Craigens Argyll 142 B3
Craigens E Ayrs 113 C5
Craighat Stirling 126 F3
Craighead Fife 129 D8
Craighlaw Mains Dumfries 105 C7
Craighouse Argyll 144 G4
Craigie Aberds 141 C8
Craigie Dundee 134 F4
Craigie Perth 128 B3
Craigie Perth 133 E8
Craigie S Ayrs 118 F4
Craigiefield Orkney 159 G5
Craigielaw E Loth 121 B7
Craiglockhart Edin 120 B5
Craigmalloch E Ayrs 112 E4
Craigmaud Aberds 153 C8
Craigmillar Edin 121 B5
Craigmore Argyll 145 G10
Craignant Shrops 73 F6
Craigneuk N Lanark 119 C7
Craigneuk N Lanark 119 D7
Craignure Argyll 124 B3
Craigo Angus 135 C6
Craigow Perth 128 D2
Craigrothie Fife 129 C5
Craigroy Moray 151 F14
Craigruie Stirling 126 B3
Craigston Castle Aberds 153 C7
Craigton Aberdeen 141 D7
Craigton Angus 134 D3
Craigton Angus 135 F5
Craigton Highld 151 B9
Craigtown Highld 157 D11
Craik Borders 115 D6
Crail Fife 129 D8
Crailing Borders 116 B2
Crailinghall Borders 116 B2
Craiselound N Lincs 89 E8
Crakehill N Yorks 95 B7
Crakemarsh Staffs 75 F7
Crambe N Yorks 96 C3
Cramlington Northumb 111 B5
Cramond Edin 120 B4
Cramond Bridge Edin 120 B4
Cranage Ches E 74 C4
Cranberry Staffs 74 F5
Cranborne Dorset 13 C8
Cranbourne Brack 27 B7
Cranbrook, Devon 10 E5
Cranbrook Kent 18 B4
Cranbrook Common Kent 18 B4
Crane Moor S Yorks 88 D4
Crane's Corner Norf 68 C2
Cranfield C Beds 53 E7
Cranford London 28 B2
Cranford St Andrew Northants 53 B7
Cranford St John Northants 53 B7
Cranham Glos 37 C5
Cranham London 42 F1
Crank Mers 86 E3
Crank Wood Gtr Man 86 D4
Cranleigh Sur 27 F8
Cranley Suff 57 B5
Cranmer Green Suff 56 B4
Cranmore IoW 14 F4
Cranna Aberds 153 C6
Crannich Argyll 147 G8
Crannoch Moray 152 C4
Cranoe Leics 64 E4
Cransford Suff 57 C7
Cranshaws Borders 122 C2
Cranstal IoM 84 B4
Crantock Corn 4 C2
Cranwell Lincs 78 E3
Cranwich Norf 67 E7
Cranworth Norf 68 D2
Craobh Haven Argyll 124 E3
Crapstone Devon 6 C3
Crarae Argyll 125 F5
Crask Inn Highld 157 G8
Crask of Aigas Highld 150 G7
Craskins Aberds 140 D4
Craster Northumb 117 C8
Craswall Hereford 48 F4
Cratfield Suff 57 B7
Crathes Aberds 141 E6
Crathie Aberds 139 E8
Crathie Highld 137 E8
Crathorne N Yorks 102 D2
Craven Arms Shrops 60 F4
Crawcrook T&W 110 C4
Crawford Lancs 86 D2
Crawford S Lanark 114 B2
Crawfordjohn S Lanark 113 B8
Crawick Dumfries 113 C7
Crawley Hants 26 F2
Crawley Oxon 38 C3
Crawley W Sus 28 F3
Crawley Down W Sus 28 F4
Crawleyside Durham 110 E2
Crawshawbooth Lancs 87 B6
Crawton Aberds 135 B8
Cray N Yorks 94 B2
Cray Perth 133 C8
Crayford London 29 B6
Crayke N Yorks 95 B8
Crays Hill Essex 42 E3
Cray's Pond Oxon 39 F6
Creacombe Devon 10 C3
Creag Ghoraidh W Isles 148 D2
Creagan Argyll 130 E3
Creaguaineach Lodge Highld 131 C7
Creaksea Essex 43 E5
Creaton Northants 52 B5
Creca Dumfries 108 B2
Credenhill Hereford 49 E6
Crediton Devon 10 D3
Creebridge Dumfries 105 C8
Creech Heathfield Som 11 B7
Creech St Michael Som 11 B7
Creed Corn 3 B8
Creekmouth London 41 F7
Creeting Bottoms Suff 56 D5
Creeting St Mary Suff 56 D4
Creeton Lincs 65 B7
Creetown Dumfries 105 D8
Creg-ny-Baa IoM 84 D3
Creggans Argyll 125 E6
Cregneash IoM 84 F
Cregrina Powys 48 D3
Creich Fife 128 B5
Creigiau Cardiff 34 F4
Cremyll Corn 6 D2
Creslow Bucks 39 B8
Cressage Shrops 61 D5
Cressbrook Derbys 75 B8
Cresselly Pembs 32 D1
Cressing Essex 42 B3
Cresswell Northumb 117 E8
Cresswell Staffs 75 F6
Cresswell Quay Pembs 32 D1
Creswell Derbys 76 B5
Cretingham Suff 57 C6
Cretshengan Argyll 144 G6
Crewe Ches E 74 D4
Crewe Ches W 73 D8
Crewgreen Powys 60 C3
Crewkerne Som 12 D2
Crianlarich Stirling 126 B
Cribyn Ceredig 46 D
Criccieth Gwyn 71 D5
Crich Derbys 76 D
Crichie Aberds 153 D
Crichton Midloth 121 C
Crick Mon 36 E
Crick Northants 52 B
Crickadarn Powys 48 E
Cricket Malherbie Som 11 C
Cricket St Thomas Som 11 D
Crickheath Shrops 60 B
Crickhowell Powys 35 C
Cricklade Wilts 37 E
Cricklewood London 41 F
Cridling Stubbs N Yorks 89 B
Crieff Perth 127 B
Criggion Powys 60 C
Crigglestone W Yorks 88 C
Crimond Aberds 153 C
Crimonmogate Aberds 153 C
Crimplesham Norf 67 D
Crinan Argyll 144 D
Cringleford Norf 68 D
Cringles W Yorks 94
Crinow Pembs 32
Cripplesease Corn 2
Cripplestyle Dorset 13
Cripp's Corner E Sus 18
Croasdale Cumb 98
Crock Street Som 11
Crockenhill Kent 29
Crockernwell Devon 10
Crockerton Wilts 24
Crocketford or Ninemile Bar Dumfries 106
Crockey Hill York 96
Crockham Hill Kent 28
Crockleford Heath Essex 43
Crockness Orkney 159
Croes-goch Pembs 44
Croes-lan Ceredig 46
Croes-y-mwyalch Torf 35
Croeserw Neath 34
Croesor Gwyn 71
Croesyceiliog Carms 33
Croesyceiliog Torf 35
Croesywaun Gwyn 82
Croft Leics 64
Croft Lincs 79
Croft Pembs 45
Croft Warr 86
Croft-on-Tees N Yorks 101
Croftamie Stirling 126
Croftmalloch W Loth 120
Crofton W Yorks 88

Golden Hill Hants 14 E3
Golden Pot Hants 26 E5
Golden Valley Glos 37 B6
Goldenhill Stoke 75 D5
Golders Green London 41 F5
Goldhanger Essex 43 D5
Golding Shrops 60 D5
Goldington Bedford 53 D8
Goldsborough N Yorks 95 D6
Goldsborough N Yorks 103 C6
Goldsithney Corn 2 C4
Goldsworthy Devon 9 B5
Goldthorpe S Yorks 89 D5
Gollanfield Highld 151 F11
Golspie Highld 157 J11
Golval Highld 157 C11
Gomeldon Wilts 25 F6
Gomersal W Yorks 88 B3
Gomshall Sur 27 E8
Gonalston Notts 77 E6
Gonfirth Shetland 160 G5
Good Easter Essex 42 C2
Gooderstone Norf 67 D7
Goodleigh Devon 20 F5
Goodmanham E Yorks 96 E4
Goodnestone Kent 30 C4
Goodnestone Kent 31 D6
Goodrich Hereford 36 C2
Goodrington Torbay 7 D6
Goodshaw Lancs 87 B6
Goodwick = Wdig Pembs 44 B4
Goodworth Clatford Hants 25 E8
Goole E Yorks 89 B8
Goonbell Corn 3 B6
Goonhavern Corn 4 D2
Goose Eye W Yorks 94 E3
Goose Green Gtr Man 86 D3
Goose Green Norf 68 F4
Goose Green W Sus 16 C5
Gooseham Corn 8 C4
Goosey Oxon 38 E3
Goosnargh Lancs 93 F5
Goostrey Ches E 74 B4
Gorcott Hill Warks 51 C5
Gord Shetland 160 L6
Gordon Borders 122 E2
Gordonbush Highld 157 J11
Gordonsburgh Moray 152 B4
Gordonstoun Moray 152 B1
Gordonstown Aberds 152 C5
Gordonstown Aberds 153 E7
Gore Kent 31 D7
Gore Cross Wilts 24 D5
Gore Pit Essex 42 C4
Gorebridge Midloth 121 C6
Gorefield Cambs 66 C4
Gorey Jersey 17
Gorgie Edin 120 B5
Goring Oxon 39 F6
Goring-by-Sea W Sus 16 D5
Goring Heath Oxon 26 B4
Gorleston-on-Sea Norf 69 D8
Gornalwood W Mid 62 E3
Gorrachie Aberds 153 C7
Gorran Churchtown Corn 3 B8
Gorran Haven Corn 3 B9
Gorrenberry Borders 115 E7
Gors Ceredig 46 B5
Gorse Hill Swindon 38 F1
Gorsedd Flint 73 B5
Gorseinon Swansea 33 E6
Gorseness Orkney 159 G5
Gorsgoch Ceredig 46 D3
Gorslas Carms 33 C6
Gorsley Glos 36 B3
Gorstan Highld 150 E6
Gorstanvorran Highld 130 B2
Gorsteyhill Staffs 74 D4
Gorsty Hill Staffs 62 B5
Gortantaoid Argyll 142 A4
Gorton Gtr Man 87 E6
Gosbeck Suff 57 D5
Gosberton Lincs 78 F5
Gosberton Clough Lincs 65 B8
Gosfield Essex 42 B3
Gosford Hereford 49 C7
Gosforth Cumb 98 D2
Gosforth T&W 110 C5
Gosmore Herts 40 B4
Gosport Hants 15 E7
Gossabrough Shetland 160 E7
Gossington Glos 36 D4
Goswick Northumb 123 E6
Gotham Notts 76 F5
Gotherington Glos 37 B6
Gott Shetland 160 J6
Goudhurst Kent 18 B4
Goulceby Lincs 79 B5
Gourdas Aberds 153 D7
Gourdon Aberds 135 B8
Gourock Invclyd 118 B2
Govan Glasgow 119 C5
Govanhill Glasgow 119 C5
Goveton Devon 7 E5
Govilon Mon 35 C6
Gowanhill Aberds 153 B10
Gowdall E Yorks 89 B7
Gowerton Swansea 33 E6
Gowkhall Fife 128 F2
Gowthorpe E Yorks 96 D3
Goxhill E Yorks 97 E7
Goxhill N Lincs 90 B5
Goxhill Haven N Lincs 90 B5
Goytre Neath 34 F1
Grabhair W Isles 155 F8
Graby Lincs 65 B7
Grade Corn 3 E6
Graffham W Sus 16 C3
Grafham Cambs 54 C2
Grafham Sur 27 E8
Grafton Hereford 49 F6
Grafton N Yorks 95 C7
Grafton Oxon 38 D2
Grafton Shrops 60 C4
Grafton Worcs 49 C7
Grafton Flyford Worcs 50 D4
Grafton Regis Northants 53 E5
Grafton Underwood Northants 65 F6
Grafty Green Kent 30 E2
Graianrhyd Denb 73 D6
Graig Conwy 83 D8
Graig Denb 72 B4
Graig-fechan Denb 72 D5
Grain Medway 30 B2
Grainsby Lincs 91 E6
Grainthorpe Lincs 91 E7
Grampound Corn 3 B8
Grampound Road Corn 4 D4
Gramsdal W Isles 148 C3
Granborough Bucks 39 B7
Granby Notts 77 F7
Grandborough Warks 52 C2
Grandtully Perth 133 D6
Grange Cumb 98 C4
Grange E Ayrs 118 F4
Grange Medway 29 C8
Grange Mers 85 F3
Grange Perth 128 B4
Grange Crossroads Moray 152 C4
Grange Hall Moray 151 E13
Grange Hill Essex 41 E7
Grange Moor W Yorks 88 C3
Grange of Lindores Fife 128 C4
Grange-over-Sands Cumb 92 B4
Grange Villa Durham 110 D5
Grangemill Derbys 76 D2
Grangemouth Falk 127 F8
Grangepans Falk 128 F2
Grangetown Cardiff 22 B3
Grangetown Redcar 102 B3
Granish Highld 138 C5
Gransmoor E Yorks 97 D7
Granston Pembs 44 B3
Grantchester Cambs 54 D5
Grantham Lincs 78 F2
Grantley N Yorks 94 C5
Grantlodge Aberds 141 C6
Granton Dumfries 114 D3
Granton Edin 120 B5
Grantown-on-Spey Highld 139 B6
Grantshouse Borders 122 C4
Grappenhall Warr 86 F4
Grasby Lincs 90 D4
Grasmere Cumb 99 D5
Grasscroft Gtr Man 87 D7
Grassendale Mers 85 F4
Grassholme Durham 100 B4
Grassington N Yorks 94 C3
Grassmoor Derbys 76 C4
Grassthorpe Notts 77 C7
Grateley Hants 25 E7
Gratwich Staffs 75 F7
Graveley Cambs 54 C3
Graveley Herts 41 B5
Gravelly Hill W Mid 62 E5
Gravels Shrops 60 D3
Graven Shetland 160 F6
Graveney Kent 30 C4
Gravesend Herts 41 B7
Gravesend Kent 29 B7
Grayingham Lincs 90 E3
Grayrigg Cumb 99 E7
Grays Thurrock 29 B7
Grayshott Hants 27 F6
Grayswood Sur 27 F7
Graythorp Hrtlpl 102 B3
Grazeley Wokingham 26 C4
Greasbrough S Yorks 88 E5
Greasby Mers 85 F3
Great Abington Cambs 55 E6
Great Addington Northants 53 B7
Great Alne Warks 51 D6
Great Altcar Lancs 85 D4
Great Amwell Herts 41 C6
Great Asby Cumb 100 C1
Great Ashfield Suff 56 C3
Great Ayton N Yorks 102 C3
Great Baddow Essex 42 D3
Great Bardfield Essex 55 F7
Great Barford Bedford 54 D2
Great Barr W Mid 62 E4
Great Barrington Glos 38 C2
Great Barrow Ches W 73 C8
Great Barton Suff 56 C2
Great Barugh N Yorks 96 B3
Great Bavington Northumb 117 F5
Great Bealings Suff 57 E6
Great Bedwyn Wilts 25 C7
Great Bentley Essex 43 B7
Great Billing Northants 53 C6
Great Bircham Norf 80 D3
Great Blakenham Suff 56 D5
Great Blencow Cumb 108 F4
Great Bolas Telford 61 B6
Great Bookham Sur 28 D2
Great Bourton Oxon 52 E2
Great Bowden Leics 64 F4
Great Bradley Suff 55 D7
Great Braxted Essex 42 C4
Great Bricett Suff 56 D4
Great Brickhill Bucks 53 F7
Great Bridge W Mid 62 E3
Great Bridgeford Staffs 62 B2
Great Brington Northants 52 C4
Great Bromley Essex 43 B6
Great Broughton Cumb 107 F7
Great Broughton N Yorks 102 D3
Great Budworth Ches W 74 B3
Great Burdon Darl 101 C8
Great Burgh Sur 28 D3
Great Burstead Essex 42 E2
Great Busby N Yorks 102 D3
Great Canfield Essex 42 C1
Great Carlton Lincs 91 F8
Great Casterton Rutland 65 D7
Great Chart Kent 30 E3
Great Chatwell Staffs 61 C7
Great Chesterford Essex 55 E6
Great Cheverell Wilts 24 D4
Great Chishill Cambs 54 F5
Great Clacton Essex 43 C7
Great Cliff W Yorks 88 C4
Great Clifton Cumb 98 B2
Great Coates NE Lincs 91 D6
Great Comberton Worcs 50 E4
Great Corby Cumb 108 D4
Great Cornard Suff 56 E2
Great Cowden E Yorks 97 E8
Great Coxwell Oxon 38 E2
Great Crakehall N Yorks 101 E7
Great Cransley Northants 53 B6
Great Cressingham Norf 67 D8
Great Crosby Mers 85 E4
Great Cubley Derbys 75 F8
Great Dalby Leics 64 C4
Great Denham Bedford 53 E8
Great Doddington Northants 53 C6
Great Dunham Norf 67 C8
Great Dunmow Essex 42 B2
Great Durnford Wilts 25 F6
Great Easton Essex 42 B2
Great Easton Leics 64 E5
Great Eccleston Lancs 92 E4
Great Edstone N Yorks 103 F5
Great Ellingham Norf 68 E3
Great Elm Som 24 E2
Great Eversden Cambs 54 D4
Great Fencote N Yorks 101 E7
Great Finborough Suff 56 D4
Great Fransham Norf 67 C8
Great Gaddesden Herts 40 C3
Great Gidding Cambs 65 F8
Great Givendale E Yorks 96 D4
Great Glemham Suff 57 C7
Great Glen Leics 64 E3
Great Gonerby Lincs 77 F8
Great Gransden Cambs 54 D3
Great Green Norf 69 F5
Great Green Suff 56 D3
Great Habton N Yorks 96 B3
Great Hale Lincs 78 E4
Great Hallingbury Essex 41 C8
Great Hampden Bucks 39 D8
Great Harrowden Northants 53 B6
Great Harwood Lancs 93 F7
Great Haseley Oxon 39 D6
Great Hatfield E Yorks 97 E7
Great Haywood Staffs 62 B4
Great Heath W Mid 63 F7
Great Heck N Yorks 89 B6
Great Henny Essex 56 F2
Great Hinton Wilts 24 D4
Great Hockham Norf 68 E2
Great Holland Essex 43 C8
Great Horkesley Essex 56 F3
Great Hormead Herts 41 B6
Great Horton W Yorks 94 F4
Great Horwood Bucks 53 F5
Great Houghton Northants 53 D5
Great Houghton S Yorks 88 D5
Great Hucklow Derbys 75 B8
Great Kelk E Yorks 97 D7
Great Kimble Bucks 39 D8
Great Kingshill Bucks 40 E1
Great Langton N Yorks 101 E7
Great Leighs Essex 42 C3
Great Lever Gtr Man 86 D5
Great Limber Lincs 90 D5
Great Linford M Keynes 53 E6
Great Livermere Suff 56 B2
Great Longstone Derbys 76 B2
Great Lumley Durham 111 E5
Great Lyth Shrops 60 D4
Great Malvern Worcs 50 E2
Great Maplestead Essex 56 F2
Great Marton Blackpool 92 F3
Great Massingham Norf 80 E3
Great Melton Norf 68 D4
Great Milton Oxon 39 D6
Great Missenden Bucks 40 D1
Great Mitton Lancs 93 F7
Great Mongeham Kent 31 D7
Great Moulton Norf 68 E4
Great Munden Herts 41 B6
Great Musgrave Cumb 100 C2
Great Ness Shrops 60 C3
Great Notley Essex 42 B3
Great Oakley Essex 43 B7
Great Oakley Northants 65 F5
Great Offley Herts 40 B4
Great Ormside Cumb 100 C2
Great Orton Cumb 108 D3
Great Ouseburn N Yorks 95 C7
Great Oxendon Northants 64 F4
Great Oxney Green Essex 42 D2
Great Palgrave Norf 67 C8
Great Parndon Essex 41 D7
Great Paxton Cambs 54 C3
Great Plumpton Lancs 92 F3
Great Plumstead Norf 69 C6
Great Ponton Lincs 78 F2
Great Preston W Yorks 88 B5
Great Raveley Cambs 66 F2
Great Rissington Glos 38 C1
Great Rollright Oxon 51 F8
Great Ryburgh Norf 81 E5
Great Ryle Northumb 117 C6
Great Ryton Shrops 60 D4
Great Saling Essex 42 B3
Great Salkeld Cumb 109 F5
Great Sampford Essex 55 F7
Great Sankey Warr 86 F3
Great Saxham Suff 55 C8
Great Shefford W Berks 25 B8
Great Shelford Cambs 55 D5
Great Smeaton N Yorks 101 D8
Great Snoring Norf 80 D5
Great Somerford Wilts 37 F6
Great Stainton Darl 101 B8
Great Stambridge Essex 42 E4
Great Staughton Cambs 54 C2
Great Steeping Lincs 79 C7
Great Stonar Kent 31 D7
Great Strickland Cumb 99 B7
Great Stukeley Cambs 54 B3
Great Sturton Lincs 78 B5
Great Sutton Ches W 73 B7
Great Sutton Shrops 60 F5
Great Swinburne Northumb 110 B2
Great Tew Oxon 38 B3
Great Tey Essex 42 B4
Great Thurkleby N Yorks 95 B7
Great Thurlow Suff 55 D7
Great Torrington Devon 9 C6
Great Tosson Northumb 117 D6
Great Totham Essex 42 C4
Great Totham Essex 42 C4
Great Tows Lincs 91 E6
Great Urswick Cumb 92 B2
Great Wakering Essex 43 F5
Great Waldingfield Suff 56 E3
Great Walsingham Norf 80 D5
Great Waltham Essex 42 C2
Great Warley Essex 42 E1
Great Washbourne Glos 50 F4
Great Weldon Northants 65 F6
Great Welnetham Suff 56 D2
Great Wenham Suff 56 F4
Great Whittington Northumb 110 B3
Great Wigborough Essex 43 C5
Great Wilbraham Cambs 55 D6
Great Wishford Wilts 25 F5
Great Witcombe Glos 37 C6
Great Witley Worcs 50 C2
Great Wolford Warks 51 F7
Great Wratting Suff 55 E7
Great Wymondley Herts 41 B5
Great Wyrley Staffs 62 D3
Great Wytheford Shrops 61 C5
Great Yarmouth Norf 69 D8
Great Yeldham Essex 55 F8
Greater Doward Hereford 36 C2
Greatford Lincs 65 C7
Greatgate Staffs 75 E7
Greatham Hants 27 F5
Greatham Hrtlpl 102 B2
Greatham W Sus 16 C4
Greatstone on Sea Kent 19 C7
Greatworth Northants 52 E3
Greave Lancs 87 B6
Greeba IoM 84 D3
Green Denb 72 C4
Green End Bedford 54 D2
Green Hammerton N Yorks 95 D7
Green Lane Powys 59 E8
Green Ore Som 23 D7
Green St Green London 29 C5
Green Street Herts 40 E4
Greenbank Shetland 160 C7
Greenburn W Loth 120 C2
Greendikes Northumb 117 B6
Greenfield C Beds 53 F8
Greenfield Flint 73 B5
Greenfield Gtr Man 87 D7
Greenfield Highld 136 D5
Greenfield Oxon 39 E7
Greenford London 40 F4
Greengairs N Lanark 119 B7
Greenham W Berks 26 C2
Greenhaugh Northumb 116 F3
Greenhead Northumb 109 C6
Greenhill Falk 119 B8
Greenhill Kent 31 C5
Greenhill Leics 63 C8
Greenhill London 40 F4
Greenhills N Ayrs 118 D3
Greenhithe Kent 29 B6
Greenholm E Ayrs 118 F5
Greenholme Cumb 99 D7
Greenhouse Borders 115 B8
Greenhow Hill N Yorks 94 C4
Greenigoe Orkney 159 H5
Greenland Highld 158 D4
Greenlands Bucks 39 F7
Greenlaw Aberds 153 C6
Greenlaw Borders 122 E3
Greenlea Dumfries 107 B7
Greenloaning Perth 127 D7
Greenmount Gtr Man 87 C5
Greenmow Shetland 160 L6
Greenock Invclyd 118 B2
Greenock West Invclyd 118 B2
Greenodd Cumb 99 F5
Greenrow Cumb 107 D8
Greens Norton Northants 52 E4
Greenside T&W 110 C4
Greensidehill Northumb 117 C5
Greenstead Green Essex 42 B4
Greensted Essex 41 D8
Greenwich London 28 B4
Greet Glos 50 F5
Greete Shrops 49 B7
Greetham Lincs 79 B6
Greetham Rutland 65 C6
Greetland W Yorks 87 B8
Gregg Hall Cumb 99 E6
Gregson Lane Lancs 86 B3
Greinetobht W Isles 148 A3
Greinton Som 23 F6
Gremista Shetland 160 J6
Grenaby IoM 84 E2
Grendon Northants 53 C6
Grendon Warks 63 D6
Grendon Common Warks 63 E6
Grendon Green Hereford 49 D7
Grendon Underwood Bucks 39 B6
Grenofen Devon 6 B2
Grenoside S Yorks 88 E4
Greosabhagh W Isles 154 H6
Gresford Wrex 73 D7
Gresham Norf 81 D7
Greshornish Highld 149 C8
Gressenhall Norf 68 C2
Gressingham Lancs 93 C5
Gresty Green Ches E 74 D4
Greta Bridge Durham 101 C5
Gretna Dumfries 108 C3
Gretna Green Dumfries 108 C3
Gretton Glos 50 F5
Gretton Northants 65 E5
Gretton Shrops 60 E5
Grewelthorpe N Yorks 94 B5
Grey Green N Lincs 89 D8
Greygarth N Yorks 94 B4
Greynor Carms 33 D6
Greysouthen Cumb 98 B2
Greystoke Cumb 108 F4
Greystone Angus 135 E5
Greystone Dumfries 107 B6
Greywell Hants 26 D5
Griais W Isles 155 C9
Grianan W Isles 155 D9
Gribthorpe E Yorks 96 F3
Gridley Corner Devon 9 E5
Griff Warks 63 F7
Griffithstown Torf 35 E6
Grimbister Orkney 159 G4
Grimblethorpe Lincs 91 F6
Grimeford Village Lancs 86 C4
Grimethorpe S Yorks 88 D5
Griminis W Isles 148 C2
Grimister Shetland 160 D6
Grimley Worcs 50 C3
Grimness Orkney 159 J5
Grimoldby Lincs 91 F7
Grimpo Shrops 60 B3
Grimsargh Lancs 93 F5
Grimsbury Oxon 52 E2
Grimsby NE Lincs 91 C6
Grimscote Northants 52 D4
Grimscott Corn 8 D4
Grimsthorpe Lincs 65 B7
Grimston E Yorks 97 F8
Grimston Leics 64 B3
Grimston Norf 80 E3
Grimston York 96 D2
Grimstone Dorset 12 E4
Grinacombe Moor Devon 9 E6
Grindale E Yorks 97 B7
Grindigar Orkney 159 H6
Grindiscol Shetland 160 K6
Grindle Shrops 61 D7
Grindleford Derbys 76 B2
Grindleton Lancs 93 E7
Grindley Staffs 62 B4
Grindley Brook Shrops 74 E2
Grindlow Derbys 75 B8
Grindon Northumb 122 E5
Grindon Staffs 75 D7
Grindonmoor Gate Staffs 75 D7
Gringley on the Hill Notts 89 E8
Grinsdale Cumb 108 D3
Grinshill Shrops 60 B5
Grinton N Yorks 101 E5
Griomsidar W Isles 155 E8
Grishipoll Argyll 146 F4
Grisling Common E Sus 17 B8
Gristhorpe N Yorks 103 F8
Griston Norf 68 E2
Gritley Orkney 159 H6
Grittenham Wilts 37 F7
Grittleton Wilts 37 F5
Grizebeck Cumb 98 F4
Grizedale Cumb 99 E5
Grobister Orkney 159 F7
Groby Leics 64 D2
Groes Conwy 72 C4
Groes Neath 34 F1
Groes-faen Rhondda 34 F4
Groes-lwyd Powys 60 C2
Groesffordd Marli Denb 72 B4
Groeslon Gwyn 82 E5
Groeslon Gwyn 82 F4
Grogport Argyll 143 D9
Gromford Suff 57 D7
Gronant Flint 72 A4
Groombridge E Sus 18 B2
Grosmont Mon 35 B8
Grosmont N Yorks 103 D6
Groton Suff 56 E3
Grougfoot Falk 120 B3
Grouville Jersey 17
Grove Dorset 12 G5
Grove Kent 31 C6
Grove Notts 77 B7
Grove Oxon 38 E4
Grove Park London 28 B5
Grove Vale W Mid 62 E4
Grovesend Swansea 33 D6
Grudie Highld 150 E6
Gruids Highld 157 J8
Gruinard House Highld 150 B2
Grula Highld 149 F8
Gruline Argyll 147 G8
Grunasound Shetland 160 K5
Grundisburgh Suff 57 D6
Grunsagill Lancs 93 D7
Gruting Shetland 160 J4
Grutness Shetland 160 N6
Gualachulain Highld 131 E5
Gualin Ho. Highld 156 D6
Guardbridge Fife 129 C6
Guarlford Worcs 50 E3
Guay Perth 133 E7
Guestling Green E Sus 19 D5
Guestling Thorn E Sus 18 D5
Guestwick Norf 81 E6
Guestwick Green Norf 81 E6
Guide Blackburn 86 B5
Guide Post Northumb 117 F8
Guilden Morden Cambs 54 E3
Guilden Sutton Ches W 73 C8
Guildford Sur 27 E7
Guildtown Perth 133 F8
Guilsborough Northants 52 B4
Guilsfield Powys 60 C2
Guilton Kent 31 D6
Guineaford Devon 20 F4
Guisborough Redcar 102 C4
Guiseley W Yorks 94 E4
Guist Norf 81 E5
Guith Orkney 159 E6
Guiting Power Glos 37 B7
Gulberwick Shetland 160 K6
Gullane E Loth 129 F6
Gulval Corn 2 C3
Gulworthy Devon 6 B2
Gumfreston Pembs 32 D2
Gumley Leics 64 E3
Gummow's Shop Corn 4 D3
Gun Hill E Sus 18 D2
Gunby E Yorks 96 F3
Gunby Lincs 65 B6
Gundleton Hants 26 F4
Gunn Devon 20 F5
Gunnerside N Yorks 100 E4
Gunnerton Northumb 110 B2
Gunness N Lincs 90 C2
Gunnislake Corn 6 B2
Gunnista Shetland 160 J7
Gunthorpe Norf 81 D6
Gunthorpe Notts 77 E6
Gunthorpe Pboro 65 D8
Gunville IoW 15 F5
Gunwalloe Corn 3 D5
Gurnard IoW 15 E5
Gurnett Ches E 75 B6
Gurney Slade Som 23 E8
Gurnos Powys 34 D1
Gussage All Saints Dorset 13 C8
Gussage St Michael Dorset 13 C7
Guston Kent 31 E7
Gutcher Shetland 160 D7
Guthrie Angus 135 D5
Guyhirn Cambs 66 D3
Guyhirn Gull Cambs 66 D3
Guy's Head Lincs 66 B4
Guy's Marsh Dorset 13 B6
Guyzance Northumb 117 D8
Gwaenysgor Flint 72 A4
Gwalchmai Anglesey 82 D3
Gwaun-Cae-Gurwen Neath 33 C8
Gwaun-Leision Neath 33 C8
Gwbert Ceredig 45 E3
Gweek Corn 3 D6
Gwehelog Mon 35 D7
Gwenddwr Powys 48 E2
Gwennap Corn 3 C6
Gwenter Corn 3 E6
Gwernaffield Flint 73 C6
Gwernesney Mon 35 D8
Gwernogle Carms 46 F4
Gwernymynydd Flint 73 C6
Gwersyllt Wrex 73 D7
Gwespyr Flint 85 F2
Gwithian Corn 2 B4
Gwredog Anglesey 82 C4
Gwyddelwern Denb 72 E4
Gwyddgrug Carms 46 F3
Gwydyr Uchaf Conwy 83 E7
Gwynfryn Wrex 73 D6
Gwystre Powys 48 C2
Gwytherin Conwy 83 E8
Gyfelia Wrex 73 E7
Gyffin Conwy 83 D7
Gyre Orkney 159 H4
Gyrn-goch Gwyn 70 C5

H

Habberley Shrops 60 D3
Habergham Lancs 93 F8
Habrough NE Lincs 90 C5
Haceby Lincs 78 F3
Hacheston Suff 57 D7
Hackbridge London 28 C3
Hackenthorpe S Yorks 88 F5
Hackford Norf 68 D3
Hackforth N Yorks 101 E7
Hackland Orkney 159 F4
Hackleton Northants 53 D6
Hackness N Yorks 103 E7
Hackness Orkney 159 J4
Hackney London 41 F6
Hackthorn Lincs 90 F3
Hackthorpe Cumb 99 B7
Haconby Lincs 65 B8
Hacton London 41 F8
Hadden Borders 122 F3
Haddenham Bucks 39 D7
Haddenham Cambs 55 B5
Haddington E Loth 121 B8
Haddington Lincs 78 C2
Haddiscoe Norf 69 E7
Haddon Cambs 65 E8
Haddon Ches E 75 C6
Hade Edge W Yorks 88 D2
Hademore Staffs 63 D5
Hadfield Derbys 87 E8
Hadham Cross Herts 41 C7
Hadham Ford Herts 41 B7
Hadleigh Essex 42 F4
Hadleigh Suff 56 E4
Hadley Telford 61 C6
Hadley End Staffs 62 B5
Hadlow Kent 29 E7
Hadlow Down E Sus 18 C2
Hadnall Shrops 60 C5
Hadstock Essex 55 E6
Hady Derbys 76 B3
Hadzor Worcs 50 C4
Haffenden Quarter Kent 30 E2
Hafod-Dinbych Conwy 83 F8
Hafod-Iom Conwy 83 D8
Haggate Lancs 93 F8
Haggbeck Cumb 108 B4
Haggerston Northumb 123 E6
Haggrister Shetland 160 F5
Hagley Hereford 49 E7
Hagley Worcs 62 F3
Hagworthingham Lincs 79 C6
Haigh Gtr Man 86 D4
Haigh S Yorks 88 C3
Haigh Moor W Yorks 88 B3
Haighton Green Lancs 93 F5
Hail Weston Cambs 54 C2
Haile Cumb 98 D2
Hailes Glos 50 F5
Hailey Herts 41 C6
Hailey Oxon 38 C3
Hailsham E Sus 18 E2
Haimer Highld 158 D3
Hainault London 41 E7
Hainford Norf 68 C5
Hainton Lincs 91 F5
Hairmyres S Lanark 119 D6
Haisthorpe E Yorks 97 C7
Hakin Pembs 44 E3
Halam Notts 77 D6
Halbeath Fife 128 F3
Halberton Devon 10 C5
Halcro Highld 158 D4
Hale Gtr Man 87 F5
Hale Halton 86 F2
Hale Hants 14 C2
Hale Bank Halton 86 F2
Hale Street Kent 29 E7
Halebarns Gtr Man 87 F5
Hales Norf 69 E6
Hales Staffs 74 F4
Hales Place Kent 30 D5
Halesfield Telford 61 D7
Halesgate Lincs 66 B3
Halesowen W Mid 62 F3
Halesworth Suff 57 B7
Halewood Mers 86 F2
Halford Shrops 60 F4
Halford Warks 51 E7
Halfpenny Furze Carms 32 C3
Halfpenny Green Staffs 62 E2
Halfway Carms 46 F5
Halfway Carms 47 F7
Halfway W Berks 26 C2
Halfway Bridge W Sus 16 B3
Halfway House Shrops 60 C3
Halfway Houses Kent 30 B3
Halifax W Yorks 87 B8
Halket E Ayrs 118 D4
Halkirk Highld 158 E3
Halkyn Flint 73 B6
Hall Dunnerdale Cumb 98 E4
Hall Green W Mid 62 F5
Hall Green W Yorks 88 C4
Hall Grove Herts 41 C5
Hall of Tankerness Orkney 159 H6
Hall of the Forest Shrops 60 F2
Halland E Sus 18 D2
Hallaton Leics 64 E4
Hallatrow Bath 23 D8
Hallbankgate Cumb 109 D5
Hallen S Glos 36 F2
Halliburton Borders 122 E2
Hallin Highld 148 C7
Halling Medway 29 C8
Hallington Lincs 91 F7
Hallington Northumb 110 B2
Halliwell Gtr Man 86 C5
Halloughton Notts 77 D6
Hallow Worcs 50 D3
Hallrule Borders 115 C8
Halls E Loth 122 B2
Hall's Green Herts 41 B5
Hallsands Devon 7 F6
Hallthwaites Cumb 98 F3
Hallworthy Corn 8 F3
Hallyburton House Perth 134 F2
Hallyne Borders 120 E4
Halmer End Staffs 74 E4
Halmore Glos 36 D3
Halmyre Mains Borders 120 E4
Halnaker W Sus 16 D3
Halsall Lancs 85 C4
Halse Northants 52 E3
Halse Som 11 B6
Halsetown Corn 2 C4
Halsham E Yorks 91 B6
Halsinger Devon 20 F4
Halstead Essex 56 F2
Halstead Kent 29 C5
Halstead Leics 64 D4
Halstock Dorset 12 D3
Haltham Lincs 78 C5
Haltoft End Lincs 79 E6
Halton Bucks 40 C1
Halton Halton 86 F3
Halton Lancs 92 C5
Halton Northumb 110 C2
Halton W Yorks 95 F6
Halton Wrex 73 F7
Halton East N Yorks 94 D3
Halton Gill N Yorks 93 B8
Halton Holegate Lincs 79 C7
Halton Lea Gate Northumb 109 D6
Halton West N Yorks 93 D8
Haltwhistle Northumb 109 C7
Halvergate Norf 69 D7
Halwell Devon 7 D5
Halwill Devon 9 E6
Halwill Junction Devon 9 D6
Ham Devon 11 D7
Ham Glos 36 E3
Ham Highld 158 C4
Ham Kent 31 D7
Ham London 28 B2
Ham Shetland 160 K1
Ham Wilts 25 C8
Ham Common Dorset 13 B6
Ham Green Hereford 50 E2
Ham Green Kent 19 C5
Ham Green Kent 30 C2
Ham Green N Som 23 B7
Ham Green Worcs 50 C5
Ham Street Som 23 F7
Hamble-le-Rice Hants 15 D5
Hambleden Bucks 39 F7
Hambledon Hants 15 C7
Hambledon Sur 27 F7
Hambleton Lancs 92 E3
Hambleton N Yorks 95 F8
Hambridge Som 11 B8
Hambrook S Glos 23 B8
Hambrook W Sus 15 D8
Hameringham Lincs 79 C6
Hamerton Cambs 54 B2
Hametoun Shetland 160 K1
Hamilton S Lanark 119 D7
Hammer W Sus 27 F6
Hammerpot W Sus 16 D4
Hammersmith London 28 B3
Hammerwich Staffs 62 D4
Hammerwood E Sus 28 F5
Hammond Street Herts 41 D6
Hammoon Dorset 13 C6
Hamnavoe Shetland 160 E4
Hamnavoe Shetland 160 E6
Hamnavoe Shetland 160 F6
Hamnavoe Shetland 160 K5
Hampden Park E Sus 18 E3
Hamperden End Essex 55 F6
Hampnett Glos 37 C7
Hampole S Yorks 89 C6
Hampreston Dorset 13 E8
Hampstead London 41 F5
Hampstead Norreys W Berks 26 B3
Hampsthwaite N Yorks 95 D5
Hampton London 28 C2
Hampton Shrops 61 F7
Hampton Worcs 50 E5
Hampton Bishop Hereford 49 F7
Hampton Heath Ches W 73 E8
Hampton in Arden W Mid 63 F6
Hampton Loade Shrops 61 F7
Hampton Lovett Worcs 50 C3
Hampton Lucy Warks 51 D7
Hampton on the Hill Warks 51 C7
Hampton Poyle Oxon 39 C5
Hamrow Norf 80 E5
Hamsey E Sus 17 C8
Hamsey Green London 28 D4
Hamstall Ridware Staffs 62 C5
Hamstead IoW 14 E5
Hamstead W Mid 62 E4
Hamstead Marshall W Berks 26 C2
Hamsterley Durham 110 D4
Hamsterley Durham 110 F4
Hamstreet Kent 19 B7
Hamworthy Poole 13 E7
Hanbury Staffs 63 B5
Hanbury Worcs 50 C4
Hanbury Woodend Staffs 63 B5
Hanby Lincs 78 F3
Hanchurch Staffs 74 E5
Handbridge Ches W 73 C8
Handcross W Sus 17 B6
Handforth Ches E 87 F6
Handley Ches W 73 D8
Handsacre Staffs 62 C4
Handsworth S Yorks 88 F5
Handsworth W Mid 62 E4
Handy Cross Devon 9 B6
Hanford Stoke 75 E5
Hanging Langford Wilts 24 F5
Hangleton W Sus 16 D4
Hanham S Glos 23 B8
Hankelow Ches E 74 E3
Hankerton Wilts 37 E6
Hankham E Sus 18 E3
Hanley Stoke 75 E5
Hanley Castle Worcs 50 E3
Hanley Child Worcs 49 C8
Hanley Swan Worcs 50 E3
Hanley William Worcs 49 C8
Hanlith N Yorks 94 C2
Hanmer Wrex 73 F8
Hannah Lincs 79 B8
Hannington Hants 26 D3
Hannington Northants 53 B6
Hannington Swindon 38 E1
Hannington Wick Swindon 38 E1
Hansel Village S Ayrs 118 F3
Hanslope M Keynes 53 E6
Hanthorpe Lincs 65 B7
Hanwell London 40 F4
Hanwell Oxon 52 E2
Hanwood Shrops 60 D4
Hanworth London 28 B2
Hanworth Norf 81 D7
Happendon S Lanark 119 F8
Happisburgh Norf 69 A6
Happisburgh Common Norf 69 B6
Hapsford Ches W 73 B8
Hapton Lancs 93 F7
Hapton Norf 68 E4
Harberton Devon 7 D5
Harbertonford Devon 7 D5
Harbledown Kent 30 D5
Harborne W Mid 62 F4
Harborough Magna Warks 52 B2
Harbottle Northumb 117 D5
Harbury Warks 51 D8
Harby Leics 77 F7
Harby Notts 77 B8
Harcombe Devon 11 E6
Harden W Mid 62 D4
Harden W Yorks 94 F3
Hardenhuish Wilts 24 B4
Hardgate Aberds 141 D6
Hardham W Sus 16 C4
Hardingham Norf 68 D3
Hardingstone Northants 53 D5
Hardington Som 24 D2
Hardington Mandeville Som 12 C3
Hardington Marsh Som 12 D3
Hardley Hants 14 D5
Hardley Street Norf 69 D6
Hardmead M Keynes 53 E7
Hardrow N Yorks 100 E3
Hardstoft Derbys 76 C4
Hardway Hants 15 D7
Hardway Som 24 F2
Hardwick Bucks 39 C8
Hardwick Cambs 54 D4
Hardwick Norf 67 C6
Hardwick Norf 68 F5
Hardwick Northants 53 C6
Hardwick Notts 77 B6
Hardwick Oxon 38 D3
Hardwick Oxon 39 B5
Hardwick W Mid 62 E4
Hardwicke Glos 36 C4
Hardwicke Glos 37 B6
Hardwicke Hereford 48 E4
Hardy's Green Essex 43 B5
Hare Green Essex 43 B6
Hare Hatch Wokingham 27 B6
Hare Street Herts 41 B6
Hareby Lincs 79 C6
Hareden Lancs 93 D6
Harefield London 40 E3
Harehills W Yorks 95 F6
Harehope Northumb 117 B6
Haresceugh Cumb 109 E6
Harescombe Glos 37 C5
Haresfield Glos 37 C5
Hareshaw N Lanark 119 C8
Hareshaw Head Northumb 116 F4
Harewood W Yorks 95 E6
Harewood End Hereford 36 B2
Harford Carms 46 E5
Harford Devon 6 D4
Hargate Norf 68 E4
Hargatewall Derbys 75 B8
Hargrave Ches W 73 C8
Hargrave Northants 53 B8
Hargrave Suff 55 D8
Harker Cumb 108 C3
Harkland Shetland 160 E6
Harkstead Suff 57 F5
Harlaston Staffs 63 C6
Harlaw Ho. Aberds 141 B6
Harlaxton Lincs 77 F8
Harle Syke Lancs 93 F8
Harlech Gwyn 71 D6
Harlequin Notts 77 F6
Harlescott Shrops 60 C5
Harlesden London 41 F5
Harleston Devon 7 E5
Harleston Norf 68 F5
Harleston Suff 56 D4
Harlestone Northants 52 C5
Harley S Yorks 88 E4
Harley Shrops 61 D5
Harleyholm S Lanark 120 F2
Harlington C Beds 53 F8
Harlington London 27 B8
Harlington S Yorks 89 D5
Harlosh Highld 149 D7
Harlow Essex 41 C7
Harlow Hill N Yorks 95 D5
Harlow Hill Northumb 110 C3
Harlthorpe E Yorks 96 F3
Harlton Cambs 54 D4
Harman's Cross Dorset 13 F7
Harmby N Yorks 101 F6
Harmer Green Herts 41 C5
Harmer Hill Shrops 60 B4
Harmondsworth London 27 B8
Harmston Lincs 78 C2
Harnham Northumb 110 B3
Harnhill Glos 37 D7
Harold Hill London 41 E8
Harold Wood London 41 E8
Haroldston West Pembs 44 D3
Haroldswick Shetland 160 B8
Harome N Yorks 102 F4
Harpenden Herts 40 C4
Harpford Devon 11 E5
Harpham E Yorks 97 C6
Harpley Norf 80 E3
Harpley Worcs 49 C8
Harpole Northants 52 C4
Harpsdale Highld 158 E3
Harpsden Oxon 39 F7
Harpswell Lincs 90 F3
Harpur Hill Derbys 75 B7
Harpurhey Gtr Man 87 D6
Harraby Cumb 108 D4
Harrapool Highld 149 F11
Harrier Shetland 160 J1
Harrietfield Perth 127 B8
Harrietsham Kent 30 D2
Harrington Cumb 98 B1
Harrington Lincs 79 B6
Harrington Northants 64 F4
Harringworth Northants 65 E6
Harris Highld 146 B6
Harrogate N Yorks 95 D6
Harrold Bedford 53 D7
Harrow London 40 F4
Harrow on the Hill London 40 F4
Harrow Street Suff 56 F3
Harrow Weald London 40 E4
Harrowbarrow Corn 5 C8
Harrowden Bedford 53 E8
Harrowgate Hill Darl 101 C7
Harston Cambs 54 D5
Harston Leics 77 F8
Harswell E Yorks 96 E4
Hart Hrtlpl 111 F7
Hart Common Gtr Man 86 D4
Hart Hill Luton 40 B4
Hart Station Hrtlpl 111 F7
Hartburn Northumb 117 F6
Hartburn Stockton 102 C2
Hartest Suff 56 D2
Hartfield E Sus 29 F5
Hartford Cambs 54 B3
Hartford Ches W 74 B3
Hartford End Essex 42 C2
Hartfordbridge Hants 27 D5
Hartforth N Yorks 101 D6
Harthill Ches W 74 D2
Harthill N Lanark 120 C2
Harthill S Yorks 89 F5
Hartington Derbys 75 C8
Hartland Devon 8 B4
Hartlebury Worcs 50 B3
Hartlepool Hrtlpl 111 F8
Hartley Cumb 100 D2
Hartley Kent 18 B4
Hartley Kent 29 C7
Hartley Northumb 111 B6
Hartley Westpall Hants 26 D4
Hartley Wintney Hants 27 D5
Hartlip Kent 30 C2
Hartoft End N Yorks 103 E5
Harton N Yorks 96 C3
Harton Shrops 60 F4
Harton T&W 111 C6
Hartpury Glos 36 B4
Hartshead W Yorks 88 B2
Hartshill Warks 63 E7
Hartshorne Derbys 63 B7
Hartsop Cumb 99 C6
Hartwell Northants 53 D5
Hartwood N Lanark 119 D8
Harvieston Stirling 126 F4
Harvington Worcs 51 E5
Harvington Cross Worcs 51 E5
Harwell Oxon 38 F4
Harwich Essex 57 F6
Harwood Durham 109 F8
Harwood Gtr Man 86 C5
Harwood Dale N Yorks 103 E7
Harworth Notts 89 E7
Hasbury W Mid 62 F3
Hascombe Sur 27 E7
Haselbech Northants 52 B5
Haselbury Plucknett Som 12 C2
Haseley Warks 51 C7
Haselor Warks 51 D6
Hasfield Glos 37 B5
Hasguard Pembs 44 E3
Haskayne Lancs 85 D4
Hasketon Suff 57 D6
Hasland Derbys 76 C3
Haslemere Sur 27 F7
Haslingden Lancs 87 B5
Haslingfield Cambs 54 D5
Haslington Ches E 74 D4
Hassall Ches E 74 D4
Hassall Green Ches E 74 D4
Hassell Street Kent 30 E4
Hassendean Borders 115 B8
Hassingham Norf 69 D6
Hassocks W Sus 17 C6
Hassop Derbys 76 B2
Hastigrow Highld 158 D4
Hastingleigh Kent 30 E4
Hastings E Sus 18 E5
Hastingwood Essex 41 D7
Hastoe Herts 40 D2
Haswell Durham 111 E6
Haswell Plough Durham 111 E6
Hatch C Beds 54 E2
Hatch Hants 26 D4
Hatch Wilts 13 B7
Hatch Beauchamp Som 11 B8
Hatch End London 40 E4
Hatch Green Som 11 C8
Hatchet Gate Hants 14 D4
Hatching Green Herts 40 C4
Hatchmere Ches W 74 B2
Hatcliffe NE Lincs 91 D6
Hatfield Hereford 49 D7
Hatfield Herts 41 D5
Hatfield S Yorks 89 D7
Hatfield Worcs 50 D3
Hatfield Broad Oak Essex 41 C8
Hatfield Garden Village Herts 41 D5
Hatfield Heath Essex 41 C8
Hatfield Hyde Herts 41 C5
Hatfield Peverel Essex 42 C3
Hatfield Woodhouse S Yorks 89 D7
Hatford Oxon 38 E3
Hatherden Hants 25 D8
Hatherleigh Devon 9 D7
Hathern Leics 63 B8
Hatherop Glos 38 D1
Hathersage Derbys 88 F3
Hathershaw Gtr Man 87 D7

Hatherton Ches E 74 E3
Hatherton Staffs 62 C3
Hatley St George Cambs 54 D3
Hatt Corn 5 C8
Hattingley Hants 26 F4
Hatton Aberds 153 E10
Hatton Derbys 63 B6
Hatton Lincs 78 B4
Hatton Shrops 60 E4
Hatton Warks 51 C7
Hatton Warr 86 F3
Hatton Castle Aberds 153 D7
Hatton Heath Ches W 73 C8
Hatton of Fintray Aberds 141 C7
Hattoncrook Aberds 141 B7
Haugh E Ayrs 112 B4
Haugh Gtr Man 87 C7
Haugh Lincs 79 B7
Haugh Head Northumb 117 B6
Haugh of Glass Moray 152 E4
Haugh of Urr Dumfries 106 C5
Haugham Lincs 91 F7
Haughley Suff 56 C4
Haughley Green Suff 56 C4
Haughs of Clinterty Aberdeen 141 C7
Haughton Notts 77 B6
Haughton Shrops 60 B3
Haughton Shrops 61 C5
Haughton Shrops 61 D7
Haughton Shrops 61 E6
Haughton Staffs 62 B2
Haughton Castle Northumb 110 B2
Haughton Green Gtr Man 87 E7
Haughton Moss Ches E 74 D2
Haultwick Herts 41 B6
Haunn Argyll 146 G6
Haunn W Isles 148 G2
Haunton Staffs 63 C6
Hauxley Northumb 117 D8
Hauxton Cambs 54 D5
Havant Hants 15 D8
Haven Hereford 49 D6
Haven Bank Lincs 78 D5
Haven Side E Yorks 91 B5
Havenstreet IoW 15 E6
Havercroft W Yorks 88 C4
Haverfordwest = Hwlffordd Pembs 44 D4
Haverhill Suff 55 E7
Haverigg Cumb 92 B1
Havering-atte-Bower London 41 E8
Haveringland Norf 81 E7
Haversham M Keynes 53 E6
Haverthwaite Cumb 99 F5
Haverton Hill Stockton 102 B2
Hawarden = Penarlâg Flint 73 C7
Hawcoat Cumb 92 B2
Hawen Ceredig 46 E2
Hawes N Yorks 100 F3
Hawes' Green Norf 68 E5
Hawes Side Blackpool 92 F3
Hawford Worcs 50 C3
Hawick Borders 115 C8
Hawk Green Gtr Man 87 F7
Hawkchurch Devon 11 D8
Hawkedon Suff 55 D8
Hawkenbury Kent 18 B2
Hawkenbury Kent 30 E2
Hawkeridge Wilts 24 D3
Hawkerland Devon 11 F5
Hawkes End W Mid 63 F7
Hawkesbury S Glos 36 F4
Hawkesbury Warks 63 F7
Hawkesbury Upton S Glos 36 F4
Hawkhill Northumb 117 C8
Hawkhurst Kent 18 B4
Hawkinge Kent 31 F6
Hawkley Hants 15 B8
Hawkridge Som 21 F7
Hawkshead Cumb 99 E5
Hawkshead Hill Cumb 99 E5
Hawksland S Lanark 119 F8
Hawkswick N Yorks 94 B2
Hawksworth Notts 77 E7
Hawksworth W Yorks 94 E4
Hawksworth W Yorks 95 F5
Hawkwell Essex 42 E4
Hawley Hants 27 D6
Hawley Kent 29 B6
Hawling Glos 37 B7
Hawnby N Yorks 102 F3
Haworth W Yorks 94 F3
Hawstead Suff 56 D2
Hawthorn Durham 111 E7
Hawthorn Rhondda 35 F5
Hawthorn Wilts 24 C3
Hawthorn Hill Brack 27 B6
Hawthorn Hill Lincs 78 D5
Hawthorpe Lincs 65 B7
Hawton Notts 77 D7
Haxby York 96 D2
Haxey N Lincs 89 D8
Hay Green Norf 66 C5
Hay-on-Wye = Y Gelli Gandryll Powys 48 E4
Hay Street Herts 41 B6
Haydock Mers 86 E3
Haydon Dorset 12 C4
Haydon Bridge Northumb 109 C8
Haydon Wick Swindon 37 F8
Haye Corn 5 C8
Hayes London 28 C5
Hayes London 40 F4
Hayfield Derbys 87 F8
Hayfield Fife 128 E4
Hayhill E Ayrs 112 C4
Hayhillock Angus 135 E5
Hayle Corn 2 C4
Haynes C Beds 53 E8
Haynes Church End C Beds 53 E8
Hayscastle Pembs 44 C3
Hayscastle Cross Pembs 44 C4
Hayshead Angus 135 E6
Hayton Aberdeen 141 D8
Hayton Cumb 107 E8
Hayton Cumb 108 D5
Hayton E Yorks 96 E4
Hayton Notts 89 F8
Hayton's Bent Shrops 60 F5
Haytor Vale Devon 7 B5
Haywards Heath W Sus 17 B7
Haywood S Yorks 89 C6
Haywood Oaks Notts 77 D6
Hazel Grove Gtr Man 87 F7
Hazel Street Kent 18 B3
Hazelbank S Lanark 119 E8
Hazelbury Bryan Dorset 12 D5
Hazeley Hants 26 D5
Hazelhurst Gtr Man 87 D7
Hazelslade Staffs 62 C4
Hazelton Glos 37 C7
Hazelton Walls Fife 128 B5
Hazelwood Derbys 76 E3
Hazlemere Bucks 40 E1
Hazlerigg T&W 110 B5
Hazlewood N Yorks 94 D3
Hazon Northumb 117 D7
Heacham Norf 80 D2
Head of Muir Falk 127 F7
Headbourne Worthy Hants 26 F2
Headbrook Hereford 48 D5
Headcorn Kent 30 E2
Headingley W Yorks 95 F5
Headington Oxon 39 D5
Headlam Durham 101 C6
Headless Cross Worcs 50 C5
Headley Hants 26 C3
Headley Hants 27 F6
Headley Sur 28 D3
Headon Notts 77 B7
Heads S Lanark 119 E7
Heads Nook Cumb 108 D4
Heage Derbys 76 D3
Healaugh N Yorks 95 E7
Healaugh N Yorks 101 E5
Heald Green Gtr Man 87 F6
Heale Devon 20 E5
Heale Som 23 E8
Healey Gtr Man 87 C6
Healey N Yorks 101 F6
Healey Northumb 110 D3
Healing NE Lincs 91 C6
Heamoor Corn 2 C3
Heanish Argyll 146 G3
Heanor Derbys 76 E4
Heanton Punchardon Devon 20 F4
Heapham Lincs 90 F2
Hearthstane Borders 114 B4
Heasley Mill Devon 21 F6
Heast Highld 149 G11
Heath Cardiff 22 B3
Heath Derbys 76 C4
Heath and Reach C Beds 40 B2
Heath End Hants 26 C3
Heath End Sur 27 E6
Heath End Warks 51 C7
Heath Hayes Staffs 62 C4
Heath Hill Shrops 61 C7
Heath House Som 23 E6
Heath Town W Mid 62 E3
Heathcote Derbys 75 C8
Heather Leics 63 C7
Heatherfield Highld 149 D9
Heathfield Devon 7 B6
Heathfield E Sus 18 C2
Heathfield Som 11 B6
Heathhall Dumfries 107 B6
Heathrow Airport London 27 B8
Heathstock Devon 11 D7
Heathton Shrops 62 E2
Heatley Warr 86 F5
Heaton Lancs 92 C4
Heaton Staffs 75 C6
Heaton T&W 111 C5
Heaton W Yorks 94 F4
Heaton Moor Gtr Man 87 E6
Heaverham Kent 29 D6
Heaviley Gtr Man 87 F7
Heavitree Devon 10 E4
Hebburn T&W 111 C6
Hebden N Yorks 94 C3
Hebden Bridge W Yorks 87 B7
Hebron Anglesey 82 C4
Hebron Carms 32 B2
Hebron Northumb 117 F7
Heck Dumfries 114 F3
Heckfield Hants 26 C5
Heckfield Green Suff 57 B5
Heckfordbridge Essex 43 B5
Heckington Lincs 78 E4
Heckmondwike W Yorks 88 B3
Heddington Wilts 24 C4
Heddle Orkney 159 G4
Heddon-on-the-Wall Northumb 110 C4
Hedenham Norf 69 E6
Hedge End Hants 15 C5
Hedgerley Bucks 40 F2
Hedging Som 11 B8
Hedley on the Hill Northumb 110 D3
Hednesford Staffs 62 C4
Hedon E Yorks 91 B5
Hedsor Bucks 40 F2
Hedworth T&W 111 C6
Hegdon Hill Hereford 49 D7
Heggerscales Cumb 100 C3
Heglibister Shetland 160 H5
Heighington Darl 101 B7
Heighington Lincs 78 C3
Heights of Brae Highld 151 E8
Heights of Kinlochewe Highld 150 E3
Heilam Highld 156 C7
Heiton Borders 122 F3
Hele Devon 10 D4
Hele Devon 20 E4
Helensburgh Argyll 145 E11
Helford Corn 3 D6
Helford Passage Corn 3 D6
Helhoughton Norf 80 E4
Helions Bumpstead Essex 55 E7
Hellaby S Yorks 89 E6
Helland Corn 5 B5
Hellesdon Norf 68 C5
Hellidon Northants 52 D3
Hellifield N Yorks 93 D8
Hellingly E Sus 18 D2
Hellington Norf 69 D6
Hellister Shetland 160 J5
Helm Northumb 117 E7
Helmdon Northants 52 E3
Helmingham Suff 57 D5
Helmington Row Durham 110 F4
Helmsdale Highld 157 H13
Helmshore Lancs 87 B5
Helmsley N Yorks 102 F4
Helperby N Yorks 95 C7
Helperthorpe N Yorks 97 B5
Helpringham Lincs 78 E4
Helpston Pboro 65 D8
Helsby Ches W 73 B8
Helsey Lincs 79 B8
Helston Corn 3 D5
Helstone Corn 8 F2
Helton Cumb 99 B7
Helwith Bridge N Yorks 93 C8
Hemblington Norf 69 C6
Hemel Hempstead Herts 40 D3
Hemingbrough N Yorks 96 F2
Hemingby Lincs 78 B5
Hemingford Abbots Cambs 54 B3
Hemingford Grey Cambs 54 B3
Hemingstone Suff 57 D5
Hemington Leics 63 B8
Hemington Northants 65 F7
Hemington Som 24 D2
Hemley Suff 57 E6
Hemlington Mbro 102 C3
Hemp Green Suff 57 C7
Hempholme E Yorks 97 D6
Hempnall Norf 68 E5
Hempnall Green Norf 68 E5
Hempriggs House Highld 158 F5
Hempstead Essex 55 F7
Hempstead Medway 29 C8
Hempstead Norf 69 B7
Hempstead Norf 81 D7
Hempsted Glos 37 C5
Hempton Norf 80 E5
Hempton Oxon 52 F2
Hemsby Norf 69 C7
Hemswell Lincs 90 E3
Hemswell Cliff Lincs 90 F3
Hemsworth W Yorks 88 C5
Hemyock Devon 11 C6
Hen-feddau fawr Pembs 45 F4
Henbury Bristol 23 B7
Henbury Ches E 75 B5
Hendon London 41 F5
Hendon T&W 111 D7
Hendre Flint 73 C5
Hendre-ddu Conwy 83 E8
Hendreforgan Rhondda 34 F3
Hendy Carms 33 D6
Heneglwys Anglesey 82 D4
Henfield W Sus 17 C6
Henford Devon 9 E5
Henghurst Kent 19 B6
Hengoed Caerph 35 E5
Hengoed Powys 48 D4
Hengoed Shrops 73 F6
Hengrave Suff 56 C2
Henham Essex 41 B8
Heniarth Powys 59 D8
Henlade Som 11 B7
Henley Shrops 49 B7
Henley Som 23 F6
Henley Suff 57 D5
Henley W Sus 16 B2
Henley-in-Arden Warks 51 C6
Henley-on-Thames Oxon 39 F7
Henley's Down E Sus 18 D4
Henllan Ceredig 46 E2
Henllan Denb 72 C4
Henllan Amgoed Carms 32 B2
Henllys Torf 35 E6
Henlow C Beds 54 F2
Hennock Devon 10 F3
Henny Street Essex 56 F2
Henryd Conwy 83 D7
Henry's Moat Pembs 32 B1
Hensall N Yorks 89 B6
Henshaw Northumb 109 C7
Hensingham Cumb 98 C1
Henstead Suff 69 F7
Henstridge Som 12 C5
Henstridge Ash Som 12 B5
Henstridge Marsh Som 12 B5
Henton Oxon 39 D7
Henton Som 23 E6
Henwood Corn 5 B7
Heogan Shetland 160 J6
Heol-las Swansea 33 E7
Heol Senni Powys 34 B3
Heol-y-Cyw Bridgend 34 F3
Hepburn Northumb 117 B6
Hepple Northumb 117 D5
Hepscott Northumb 117 F8
Heptonstall W Yorks 87 B7
Hepworth Suff 56 B3
Hepworth W Yorks 88 D2
Herbrandston Pembs 44 E3
Hereford Hereford 49 E7
Heriot Borders 121 D6
Hermiston Edin 120 B4
Hermitage Borders 115 E8
Hermitage Dorset 12 D4
Hermitage W Berks 26 B3
Hermitage W Sus 15 D8
Hermon Anglesey 82 E3
Hermon Carms 33 B7
Hermon Carms 46 F2
Hermon Pembs 45 F4
Herne Kent 31 C5
Herne Bay Kent 31 C5
Herner Devon 9 B7
Hernhill Kent 30 C4
Herodsfoot Corn 5 C7
Herongate Essex 42 E2
Heronsford S Ayrs 104 A5
Herriard Hants 26 E4
Herringfleet Suff 69 E7
Herringswell Suff 55 B8
Hersden Kent 31 C6
Hersham Corn 8 D4
Hersham Sur 28 C2
Herstmonceux E Sus 18 D3
Herston Orkney 159 J5
Hertford Herts 41 C6
Hertford Heath Herts 41 C6
Hertingfordbury Herts 41 C6
Hesket Newmarket Cumb 108 F3
Hesketh Bank Lancs 86 B2
Hesketh Lane Lancs 93 E6
Heskin Green Lancs 86 C3
Hesleden Durham 111 F7
Hesleyside Northumb 116 F4
Heslington York 96 D2
Hessay York 95 D8
Hessenford Corn 5 D8
Hessett Suff 56 C3
Hessle E Yorks 90 B4
Hest Bank Lancs 92 C4
Heston London 28 B2
Hestwall Orkney 159 G3
Heswall Mers 85 F3
Hethe Oxon 39 B5
Hethersett Norf 68 D4
Hethersgill Cumb 108 C4
Hethpool Northumb 116 B4
Hett Durham 111 F5
Hetton N Yorks 94 D2
Hetton-le-Hole T&W 111 E6
Hetton Steads Northumb 123 F6
Heugh Northumb 110 B3
Heugh-head Aberds 140 C2
Heveningham Suff 57 B7
Hever Kent 29 E5
Heversham Cumb 99 F6
Hevingham Norf 81 E7
Hewas Water Corn 3 B8
Hewelsfield Glos 36 D2
Hewish N Som 23 C6
Hewish Som 12 D2
Heworth York 96 D2
Hexham Northumb 110 C2
Hextable Kent 29 B6
Hexton Herts 54 F2
Hexworthy Devon 6 B4
Hey Lancs 93 E8
Heybridge Essex 42 D4
Heybridge Essex 42 E2
Heybridge Basin Essex 42 D4
Heybrook Bay Devon 6 E3
Heydon Cambs 54 E5
Heydon Norf 81 E7
Heydour Lincs 78 F3
Heylipol Argyll 146 G2
Heylor Shetland 160 E4
Heysham Lancs 92 C4
Heyshott W Sus 16 C2
Heyside Gtr Man 87 D7
Heytesbury Wilts 24 E4
Heythrop Oxon 38 B3
Heywood Gtr Man 87 C6
Heywood Wilts 24 D3
Hibaldstow N Lincs 90 D3
Hickleton S Yorks 89 D5
Hickling Norf 69 B7
Hickling Notts 64 B3
Hickling Green Norf 69 B7
Hickling Heath Norf 69 B7
Hickstead W Sus 17 B6
Hidcote Boyce Glos 51 E6
High Ackworth W Yorks 88 C5
High Angerton Northumb 117 F6
High Bankhill Cumb 109 E5
High Barnes T&W 111 D6
High Beach Essex 41 E7
High Bentham N Yorks 93 C6
High Bickington Devon 9 B8
High Birkwith N Yorks 93 B7
High Blantyre S Lanark 119 D6
High Bonnybridge Falk 119 B8
High Bradfield S Yorks 88 E3
High Bray Devon 21 F5
High Brooms Kent 29 E6
High Bullen Devon 9 B7
High Buston Northumb 117 D8
High Callerton Northumb 110 B4
High Catton E Yorks 96 D3
High Cogges Oxon 38 D3
High Coniscliffe Darl 101 C7
High Cross Hants 15 B8
High Cross Herts 41 C6
High Easter Essex 42 C2
High Eggborough N Yorks 89 B6
High Ellington N Yorks 101 F6
High Ercall Telford 61 C5
High Etherley Durham 101 B6
High Garrett Essex 42 B3
High Grange Durham 110 F4
High Green Norf 68 D4
High Green S Yorks 88 E4
High Green Worcs 50 E3
High Halden Kent 19 B5
High Halstow Medway 29 B8
High Ham Som 23 F6
High Harrington Cumb 98 B2
High Hatton Shrops 61 B6
High Hawsker N Yorks 103 D7
High Hesket Cumb 108 E4
High Hesleden Durham 111 F7
High Hoyland S Yorks 88 C3
High Hunsley E Yorks 97 F5
High Hurstwood E Sus 17 B8
High Hutton N Yorks 96 C3
High Ireby Cumb 108 F2
High Kelling Norf 81 C7
High Kilburn N Yorks 95 B8
High Lands Durham 101 B6
High Lane Gtr Man 87 F7
High Lane Worcs 49 C8
High Laver Essex 41 D8
High Legh Ches E 86 F5
High Leven Stockton 102 C2
High Littleton Bath 23 D8
High Lorton Cumb 98 B3
High Marishes N Yorks 96 B4
High Marnham Notts 77 B8
High Melton S Yorks 89 D6
High Mickley Northumb 110 C3
High Mindork Dumfries 105 D7
High Newton Cumb 99 F6
High Newton-by-the-Sea Northumb 117 B8
High Nibthwaite Cumb 98 F4
High Offley Staffs 61 B7
High Ongar Essex 42 D1
High Onn Staffs 62 C2
High Roding Essex 42 C2
High Row Cumb 108 F3
High Salvington W Sus 16 D5
High Sellafield Cumb 98 D2
High Shaw N Yorks 100 E3
High Spen T&W 110 D4
High Stoop Durham 110 E4
High Street Corn 4 D4
High Street Kent 18 B4
High Street Suff 56 E2
High Street Suff 57 B8
High Street Suff 57 D8
High Street Green Suff 56 D4
High Throston Hrtlpl 111 F7
High Toynton Lincs 79 C5
High Trewhitt Northumb 117 D6
High Valleyfield Fife 128 F2
High Westwood Durham 110 D4
High Wray Cumb 99 E5
High Wych Herts 41 C7
High Wycombe Bucks 40 E1
Higham Derbys 76 D3
Higham Kent 29 B8
Higham Lancs 93 F8
Higham Suff 55 C8
Higham Suff 56 F4
Higham Dykes Northumb 110 B4
Higham Ferrers Northants 53 C7
Higham Gobion C Beds 54 F2
Higham on the Hill Leics 63 E7
Higham Wood Kent 29 E6
Highampton Devon 9 D6
Highbridge Highld 136 F4
Highbridge Som 22 E5
Highbrook W Sus 28 F4
Highburton W Yorks 88 C2
Highbury Som 23 E8
Highclere Hants 26 C2
Highcliffe Dorset 14 E3
Higher Ansty Dorset 13 D5
Higher Ashton Devon 10 F3
Higher Ballam Lancs 92 F3
Higher Bartle Lancs 92 F5
Higher Boscaswell Corn 2 C2
Higher Burwardsley Ches W 74 D2
Higher Clovelly Devon 8 B5
Higher End Gtr Man 86 D3
Higher Kinnerton Flint 73 C7
Higher Penwortham Lancs 86 B3
Higher Town Scilly 2 E4
Higher Walreddon Devon 6 B2
Higher Walton Lancs 86 B3
Higher Walton Warr 86 F3
Higher Wheelton Lancs 86 B4
Higher Whitley Ches W 86 F4
Higher Wincham Ches W 74 B3
Higher Wych Ches W 73 E8
Highfield E Yorks 96 F3
Highfield Gtr Man 86 D5
Highfield N Ayrs 118 D3
Highfield Oxon 39 B5
Highfield S Yorks 88 F4
Highfield T&W 110 D4
Highfields Cambs 54 D4
Highfields Northumb 123 D5
Highgate London 41 F5
Highlane Ches E 75 C5
Highlane Derbys 88 F5
Highlaws Cumb 107 E8
Highleadon Glos 36 B4
Highleigh W Sus 16 E2
Highley Shrops 61 F7
Highmoor Cross Oxon 39 F7
Highmoor Hill Mon 36 F1
Highnam Glos 36 C4
Highnam Green Glos 36 B4
Highsted Kent 30 C3
Highstreet Green Essex 55 F8
Hightae Dumfries 107 B7
Hightown Ches E 75 C5
Hightown Mers 85 D4
Hightown Green Suff 56 D3
Highway Wilts 24 B5
Highweek Devon 7 B6
Highworth Swindon 38 E2
Hilborough Norf 67 D8
Hilcote Derbys 76 D4
Hilcott Wilts 25 D6
Hilden Park Kent 29 E6
Hildenborough Kent 29 E6
Hildersham Cambs 55 E6
Hilderstone Staffs 75 F6
Hilderthorpe E Yorks 97 C7
Hilfield Dorset 12 D4
Hilgay Norf 67 E6
Hill Pembs 32 D2
Hill S Glos 36 E3
Hill W Mid 62 E5
Hill Brow W Sus 15 B8
Hill Dale Lancs 86 C2
Hill Dyke Lincs 79 E6
Hill End Durham 110 F3
Hill End Fife 128 E2
Hill End N Yorks 94 D3
Hill Head Hants 15 D6
Hill Head Northumb 110 C2
Hill Mountain Pembs 44 E4
Hill of Beath Fife 128 E3
Hill of Fearn Highld 151 D11
Hill of Mountblairy Aberds 153 C6
Hill Ridware Staffs 62 C4
Hill Top Durham 100 B4
Hill Top Hants 14 D5
Hill Top W Mid 62 E3
Hill Top W Yorks 88 C4
Hill View Dorset 13 E7
Hillam N Yorks 89 B6
Hillbeck Cumb 100 C2
Hillborough Kent 31 C6
Hillbrae Aberds 141 B6
Hillbrae Aberds 152 D6
Hillbutts Dorset 13 D7
Hillclifflane Derbys 76 E2
Hillcommon Som 11 B6
Hillend Fife 128 F3
Hillerton Devon 10 E2
Hillesden Bucks 39 B6
Hillesley Glos 36 F4
Hillfarance Som 11 B6
Hillhead Aberds 152 E5
Hillhead Devon 7 D7
Hillhead S Ayrs 112 C4
Hillhead of Auchentumb Aberds 153 C9
Hillhead of Cocklaw Aberds 153 D10
Hillhouse Borders 121 D8
Hilliclay Highld 158 D3
Hillingdon London 40 F3
Hillington Glasgow 118 C5
Hillington Norf 80 E3
Hillmorton Warks 52 B3
Hillockhead Aberds 140 C3
Hillockhead Aberds 140 D2
Hillside Aberds 141 E8
Hillside Angus 135 C7
Hillside Mers 85 C4
Hillside Orkney 159 J5
Hillside Shetland 160 G6
Hillswick Shetland 160 F4
Hillway IoW 15 F7
Hillwell Shetland 160 M5
Hilmarton Wilts 24 B5
Hilperton Wilts 24 D3
Hilsea Ptsmth 15 D7
Hilston E Yorks 97 F8
Hilton Aberds 153 E9
Hilton Cambs 54 C3
Hilton Cumb 100 B2
Hilton Derbys 76 F2
Hilton Dorset 13 D5
Hilton Durham 101 B6
Hilton Highld 151 C10
Hilton Shrops 61 E7
Hilton Stockton 102 C2
Hilton of Cadboll Highld 151 D11
Himbleton Worcs 50 D4
Himley Staffs 62 E2
Hincaster Cumb 99 F7
Hinckley Leics 63 E8
Hinderclay Suff 56 B4
Hinderton Ches W 73 B7
Hinderwell N Yorks 103 C5
Hindford Shrops 73 F7
Hindhead Sur 27 F6
Hindley Gtr Man 86 D4
Hindley Green Gtr Man 86 D4
Hindlip Worcs 50 D3
Hindolveston Norf 81 E6
Hindon Wilts 24 F4
Hindringham Norf 81 D5
Hingham Norf 68 D3
Hinstock Shrops 61 B6
Hintlesham Suff 56 E4
Hinton Hants 14 E3
Hinton Hereford 48 F5
Hinton Northants 52 D3
Hinton S Glos 24 B2
Hinton Shrops 60 D4
Hinton Ampner Hants 15 B6
Hinton Blewett Bath 23 D7
Hinton Charterhouse Bath 24 D2
Hinton-in-the-Hedges Northants 52 F3
Hinton Martell Dorset 13 D8
Hinton on the Green Worcs 50 E5
Hinton Parva Swindon 38 F2
Hinton St George Som 12 C2
Hinton St Mary Dorset 13 C5
Hinton Waldrist Oxon 38 E3
Hints Shrops 49 B8
Hints Staffs 63 D5
Hinwick Bedford 53 C7
Hinxhill Kent 30 E4
Hinxton Cambs 55 E5
Hinxworth Herts 54 E3
Hipperholme W Yorks 88 B2
Hipswell N Yorks 101 E6
Hirael Gwyn 83 D5
Hiraeth Carms 32 B2
Hirn Aberds 141 D6
Hirnant Powys 59 B7
Hirst N Lanark 119 C8
Hirst Northumb 117 F8
Hirst Courtney N Yorks 89 B7
Hirwaen Denb 72 C5
Hirwaun Rhondda 34 D3
Hiscott Devon 9 B7
Histon Cambs 54 C5
Hitcham Suff 56 D3
Hitchin Herts 40 B4
Hither Green London 28 B4
Hittisleigh Devon 10 E2
Hive E Yorks 96 F4
Hixon Staffs 62 B4
Hoaden Kent 31 D6
Hoaldalbert Mon 35 B7
Hoar Cross Staffs 62 B5
Hoarwithy Hereford 36 B2
Hoath Kent 31 C6
Hobarris Shrops 48 B5
Hobbister Orkney 159 H4
Hobkirk Borders 115 C8
Hobson Durham 110 D4
Hoby Leics 64 C3
Hockering Norf 68 C3
Hockerton Notts 77 D7
Hockley Essex 42 E4
Hockley Heath W Mid 51 B6
Hockliffe C Beds 40 B2
Hockwold cum Wilton Norf 67 F7
Hockworthy Devon 10 C5
Hoddesdon Herts 41 D6
Hoddlesden Blackburn 86 B5
Hoddom Mains Dumfries 107 B8
Hoddomcross Dumfries 107 B8
Hodgeston Pembs 32 E1
Hodley Powys 59 E8
Hodnet Shrops 61 B6
Hodthorpe Derbys 76 B5
Hoe Hants 15 C6
Hoe Norf 68 C2
Hoe Gate Hants 15 C7
Hoff Cumb 100 C1
Hog Patch Sur 27 E6
Hoggard's Green Suff 56 D2
Hoggeston Bucks 39 B8
Hogha Gearraidh W Isles 148 A2
Hoghton Lancs 86 B4
Hognaston Derbys 76 D2
Hogsthorpe Lincs 79 B8
Holbeach Lincs 66 B3
Holbeach Bank Lincs 66 B3
Holbeach Clough Lincs 66 B3
Holbeach Drove Lincs 66 C3
Holbeach Hurn Lincs 66 B3
Holbeach St Johns Lincs 66 C3
Holbeach St Marks Lincs 79 F6
Holbeach St Matthew Lincs 79 F7
Holbeck Notts 76 B5
Holbeck W Yorks 95 F5
Holbeck Woodhouse Notts 76 B5
Holberrow Green Worcs 50 D5
Holbeton Devon 6 D4
Holborn London 41 F6
Holbrook Derbys 76 E3
Holbrook S Yorks 88 F5
Holbrook Suff 57 F5
Holburn Northumb 123 F6
Holbury Hants 14 D5
Holcombe Devon 7 B7
Holcombe Som 23 E8
Holcombe Rogus Devon 11 C5
Holcot Northants 53 C5
Holden Lancs 93 E7
Holdenby Northants 52 C4
Holdenhurst Bmouth 14 E2
Holdgate Shrops 61 F5
Holdingham Lincs 78 E3
Holditch Dorset 11 D8
Hole-in-the-Wall Hereford 36 B3
Holefield Borders 122 F4
Holehouses Ches E 74 B4
Holemoor Devon 9 D6
Holestane Dumfries 113 E8
Holford Som 22 E3
Holgate York 95 D8
Holker Cumb 92 B3
Holkham Norf 80 C4
Hollacombe Devon 9 D5
Holland Orkney 159 C5
Holland Orkney 159 F7
Holland Fen Lincs 78 E5
Holland-on-Sea Essex 43 C8
Hollandstoun Orkney 159 C8
Hollee Dumfries 108 C2
Hollesley Suff 57 E7
Hollicombe Torbay 7 C6
Hollingbourne Kent 30 D2
Hollington Derbys 76 F2
Hollington E Sus 18 D4
Hollington Staffs 75 F7
Hollington Grove Derbys 76 F2
Hollingworth Gtr Man 87 E8
Hollins Gtr Man 87 D6
Hollins Green Warr 86 E4
Hollins Lane Lancs 92 D4
Hollinsclough Staffs 75 C7
Hollinwood Gtr Man 87 D7
Hollinwood Shrops 74 F2
Hollocombe Devon 9 C8
Hollow Meadows S Yorks 88 F3
Holloway Derbys 76 D3
Hollowell Northants 52 B4
Holly End Norf 66 D4
Holly Green Worcs 50 E3
Hollybush Caerph 35 D5
Hollybush E Ayrs 112 C3
Hollybush Worcs 50 F2
Hollym E Yorks 91 B7
Hollywood Worcs 51 B5
Holmbridge W Yorks 88 D2
Holmbury St Mary Sur 28 E2
Holmbush Corn 4 D5
Holmcroft Staffs 62 B3
Holme Cambs 65 F8
Holme Cumb 92 B5
Holme N Yorks 102 F1
Holme Notts 77 D8
Holme W Yorks 88 D2
Holme Chapel Lancs 87 B6
Holme Green N Yorks 95 E8
Holme Hale Norf 67 D8
Holme Lacy Hereford 49 F7
Holme Marsh Hereford 48 D5
Holme next the Sea Norf 80 C3
Holme-on-Spalding-Moor E Yorks 96 F4
Holme on the Wolds E Yorks 97 E5
Holme Pierrepont Notts 77 F6
Holme St Cuthbert Cumb 107 E8
Holme Wood W Yorks 94 F4
Holmer Hereford 49 E7
Holmer Green Bucks 40 E2
Holmes Chapel Ches E 74 C4
Holmesfield Derbys 76 B3
Holmeswood Lancs 86 C2
Holmewood Derbys 76 C4
Holmfirth W Yorks 88 D2
Holmhead Dumfries 113 F7
Holmhead E Ayrs 113 B5
Holmisdale Highld 148 D6
Holmpton E Yorks 91 B7
Holmrook Cumb 98 E2
Holmsgarth Shetland 160 J6
Holmwrangle Cumb 108 E5
Holne Devon 6 C5
Holnest Dorset 12 D4
Holsworthy Devon 8 D5
Holsworthy Beacon Devon 9 D5
Holt Dorset 13 D8
Holt Norf 81 D6
Holt Wilts 24 C3
Holt Worcs 50 C3
Holt Wrex 73 D8
Holt End Hants 26 F4
Holt End Worcs 51 C5
Holt Fleet Worcs 50 C3
Holt Heath Worcs 50 C3
Holt Park W Yorks 95 E5
Holtby York 96 D2
Holton Oxon 39 D6
Holton Som 12 B4
Holton Suff 57 B7
Holton cum Beckering Lincs 90 F5
Holton Heath Dorset 13 E7
Holton le Clay Lincs 91 D6
Holton le Moor Lincs 90 E4
Holton St Mary Suff 56 F4
Holwell Dorset 12 C5
Holwell Herts 54 F2
Holwell Leics 64 B4
Holwell Oxon 38 D2
Holwick Durham 100 B4
Holworth Dorset 13 F5
Holy Cross Worcs 50 B4
Holy Island Northumb 123 E7
Holybourne Hants 26 E5
Holyhead = Caergybi Anglesey 82 C2
Holymoorside Derbys 76 C3
Holyport Windsor 27 B6
Holystone Northumb 117 D5
Holytown N Lanark 119 C7
Holywell Cambs 54 B4
Holywell Corn 4 D2
Holywell Dorset 12 D3
Holywell E Sus 18 F2
Holywell = Treffynnon Flint 73 B5
Holywell Northumb 111 B6
Holywell Green W Yorks 87 C8
Holywell Lake Som 11 B6
Holywell Row Suff 55 B8
Holywood Dumfries 114 F2
Hom Green Hereford 36 B2
Homer Shrops 61 D6
Homersfield Suff 69 F5
Homington Wilts 14 B2
Honey Hill Kent 30 C5
Honey Street Wilts 25 C6
Honey Tye Suff 56 F3
Honeyborough Pembs 44 E4
Honeybourne Worcs 51 E6
Honeychurch Devon 9 D8
Honiley Warks 51 B7
Honing Norf 69 B6
Honingham Norf 68 C4
Honington Lincs 78 E2
Honington Suff 56 B3
Honington Warks 51 E7
Honiton Devon 11 D6
Honley W Yorks 88 C2
Hoo Green Ches E 86 F5
Hoo St Werburgh Medway 29 B8
Hood Green S Yorks 88 D4
Hooe E Sus 18 E3
Hooe Plym 6 D3
Hooe Common E Sus 18 D3
Hook E Yorks 89 B8
Hook Hants 26 D5
Hook London 28 C2
Hook Pembs 44 D4
Hook Wilts 37 F7
Hook Green Kent 18 B3
Hook Green Kent 29 C7
Hook Norton Oxon 51 F8
Hooke Dorset 12 E3
Hookgate Staffs 74 F4
Hookway Devon 10 E3
Hookwood Sur 28 E3
Hoole Ches W 73 C8
Hooley Sur 28 D3
Hoop Mon 36 D2
Hooton Ches W 73 B7
Hooton Levitt S Yorks 89 E6
Hooton Pagnell S Yorks 89 D5
Hooton Roberts S Yorks 89 E5
Hop Pole Lincs 65 C8
Hope Derbys 88 F2
Hope Devon 6 F4
Hope Highld 156 B7
Hope Powys 60 D2
Hope Shrops 60 D3
Hope Staffs 75 D8
Hope = Yr Hôb Flint 73 D7
Hope Bagot Shrops 49 B7
Hope Bowdler Shrops 60 E4
Hope End Green Essex 42 B1
Hope Green Ches E 87 F7
Hope Mansell Hereford 36 C3
Hope under Dinmore Hereford 49 D7
Hopeman Moray 152 B1
Hope's Green Essex 42 F3
Hopesay Shrops 60 F3
Hopley's Green Hereford 48 D5
Hopperton N Yorks 95 D7
Hopstone Shrops 61 E7
Hopton Shrops 60 B3
Hopton Shrops 61 B5
Hopton Staffs 62 B3
Hopton Suff 56 B3
Hopton Cangeford Shrops 60 F5
Hopton Castle Shrops 49 B5
Hopton on Sea Norf 69 D8
Hopton Wafers Shrops 49 B8
Hoptonheath Shrops 49 B5
Hopwas Staffs 63 D5
Hopwood Gtr Man 87 D6
Hopwood Worcs 50 B5
Horam E Sus 18 D2
Horbling Lincs 78 F4
Horbury W Yorks 88 C3
Horcott Glos 38 D1
Horden Durham 111 E7
Horderley Shrops 60 F4
Hordle Hants 14 E3
Hordley Shrops 73 F7
Horeb Carms 33 B6
Horeb Carms 33 D5
Horeb Ceredig 46 E2
Horfield Bristol 23 B8
Horham Suff 57 B6
Horkesley Heath Essex 43 B5
Horkstow N Lincs 90 C3
Horley Oxon 52 E2
Horley Sur 28 E3
Hornblotton Green Som 23 F7
Hornby Lancs 93 C5
Hornby N Yorks 101 E7
Hornby N Yorks 102 D1
Horncastle Lincs 79 C5
Hornchurch London 41 F8
Horncliffe Northumb 122 E5
Horndean Borders 122 E4
Horndean Hants 15 C8
Horndon Devon 6 B3
Horndon on the Hill Thurrock 42 F2
Horne Sur 28 E4
Horniehaugh Angus 134 C4
Horning Norf 69 C6
Horninghold Leics 64 E5
Horninglow Staffs 63 B6
Horningsea Cambs 55 C5
Horningsham Wilts 24 E3
Horningtoft Norf 80 E5
Horns Corner Kent 18 C4
Horns Cross Devon 9 B5
Horns Cross E Sus 18 C5
Hornsby Cumb 108 D5
Hornsea E Yorks 97 E8
Hornsea Bridge E Yorks 97 E8
Hornsey London 41 F6
Hornton Oxon 51 E8
Horrabridge Devon 6 C3
Horringer Suff 56 C2
Horringford IoW 15 F6
Horse Bridge Staffs 75 D6
Horsebridge Devon 6 B2
Horsebridge Hants 25 F8
Horsebrook Staffs 62 C2
Horsehay Telford 61 D6
Horseheath Cambs 55 E7
Horsehouse N Yorks 101 F5
Horsell Sur 27 D7
Horseman's Green Wrex 73 E8
Horseway Cambs 66 F4
Horsey Norf 69 B7
Horsford Norf 68 C4
Horsforth W Yorks 94 F5
Horsham W Sus 28 F2
Horsham Worcs 50 D2
Horsham St Faith Norf 68 C5
Horsington Lincs 78 C4
Horsington Som 12 B5
Horsley Derbys 76 E3
Horsley Glos 37 E5
Horsley Northumb 110 C3
Horsley Northumb 116 E4
Horsley Cross Essex 43 B7
Horsley Woodhouse Derbys 76 E3
Horsleycross Street Essex 43 B7
Horsleyhill Borders 115 C8
Horsleyhope Durham 110 E3
Horsmonden Kent 29 E7
Horspath Oxon 39 D5
Horstead Norf 69 C5
Horsted Keynes W Sus 17 B7
Horton Bucks 40 C2
Horton Dorset 13 D8
Horton Lancs 93 D8
Horton Northants 53 D6
Horton S Glos 36 F4
Horton Shrops 60 B4
Horton Som 11 C8
Horton Staffs 75 D6
Horton Swansea 33 F5
Horton Wilts 25 C5
Horton Windsor 27 B8
Horton-cum-Studley Oxon 39 C5
Horton Green Ches W 73 E8
Horton Heath Hants 15 C5
Horton in Ribblesdale N Yorks 93 B8
Horton Kirby Kent 29 C6
Hortonlane Shrops 60 C4
Horwich Gtr Man 86 C4
Horwich End Derbys 87 F8
Horwood Devon 9 B7
Hose Leics 64 B4
Hoselaw Borders 122 F4
Hoses Cumb 98 E4
Hosh Perth 127 B7
Hosta W Isles 148 A2
Hoswick Shetland 160 L6
Hotham E Yorks 96 F4
Hothfield Kent 30 E3
Hoton Leics 64 B2
Houbie Shetland 160 D8
Houdston S Ayrs 112 E1
Hough Ches E 74 D4
Hough Ches E 75 B5
Hough Green Halton 86 F2
Hough-on-the-Hill Lincs 78 E2
Hougham Lincs 77 E8
Houghton Cambs 54 B3
Houghton Cumb 108 D4
Houghton Hants 25 F8
Houghton Pembs 44 E4
Houghton W Sus 16 C4
Houghton Conquest C Beds 53 E8
Houghton Green E Sus 19 C6
Houghton Green Warr 86 E4
Houghton-le-Side Darl 101 B7
Houghton-Le-Spring T&W 111 E6
Houghton on the Hill Leics 64 D3
Houghton Regis C Beds 40 B3
Houghton St Giles Norf 80 D5
Houlland Shetland 160 F7
Houlland Shetland 160 H5
Houlsyke N Yorks 103 D5
Hound Hants 15 D5
Hound Green Hants 26 D5
Houndslow Borders 122 E2
Houndwood Borders 122 C4
Hounslow London 28 B2
Hounslow Green Essex 42 C2
Housay Shetland 160 F8
House of Daviot Highld 151 G10
House of Glenmuick Aberds 140 E2
Housetter Shetland 160 E5
Houss Shetland 160 K5
Houston Renfs 118 C4
Houstry Highld 158 G3
Houton Orkney 159 H4
Hove Brighton 17 D6
Hoveringham Notts 77 E6
Hoveton Norf 69 C6
Hovingham N Yorks 96 B2
How Cumb 108 D5
How Caple Hereford 49 F8
How End C Beds 53 E8
How Green Kent 29 E5
Howbrook S Yorks 88 E4
Howden Borders 116 B2
Howden E Yorks 89 B8
Howden-le-Wear Durham 110 F4
Howe Highld 158 D5
Howe N Yorks 101 F8
Howe Norf 69 D5
Howe Bridge Gtr Man 86 D4
Howe Green Essex 42 D3
Howe of Teuchar Aberds 153 D7
Howe Street Essex 42 C2
Howe Street Essex 55 F7
Howell Lincs 78 E4
Howey Powys 48 D2
Howgate Midloth 120 D5
Howick Northumb 117 C8
Howle Durham 101 B5
Howle Telford 61 B6
Howlett End Essex 55 F6
Howley Som 11 D7
Hownam Borders 116 C3
Hownam Mains Borders 116 B3
Howpasley Borders 115 D6
Howsham N Lincs 90 D4
Howsham N Yorks 96 C3
Howslack Dumfries 114 D3
Howtel Northumb 122 F4
Howton Hereford 35 B8
Howtown Cumb 99 C6
Howwood Renfs 118 C3
Hoxne Suff 57 B5
Hoy Orkney 159 H3
Hoylake Mers 85 F3
Hoyland S Yorks 88 D4
Hoylandswaine S Yorks 88 D3
Hubberholme N Yorks 94 B2
Hubbert's Bridge Lincs 79 E5
Huby N Yorks 95 C8
Huby N Yorks 95 E5
Hucclecote Glos 37 C5
Hucking Kent 30 D2
Hucknall Notts 76 E5
Huddersfield W Yorks 88 C2
Huddington Worcs 50 D4
Hudswell N Yorks 101 D6
Huggate E Yorks 96 D4
Hugglescote Leics 63 C8
Hugh Town Scilly 2 E4
Hughenden Valley Bucks 40 E1
Hughley Shrops 61 E5
Huish Devon 9 C7
Huish Wilts 25 C6
Huish Champflower Som 11 B5
Huish Episcopi Som 12 B2
Huisinis W Isles 154 F4
Hulcott Bucks 40 C1
Hulland Derbys 76 E2
Hulland Ward Derbys 76 E2
Hullavington Wilts 37 F5
Hullbridge Essex 42 E4
Hulme Gtr Man 87 E6

Hulme End Staffs 75 D8
Hulme Walfield Ches E 74 C5
Hulver Street Suff 69 F7
Hulverstone IoW 14 F4
Humber Hereford 49 D7
Humber Bridge N Lincs 90 B4
Humberston NE Lincs 91 D7
Humbie E Loth 121 C7
Humbleton E Yorks 97 F8
Humbleton Northumb 117 B5
Humby Lincs 78 F3
Hume Borders 122 E3
Humshaugh Northumb 110 B2
Huna Highld 158 C5
Huncoat Lancs 93 F7
Huncote Leics 64 E2
Hundalee Borders 116 C2
Hunderthwaite Durham 100 B4
Hundle Houses Lincs 79 D5
Hundleby Lincs 79 C6
Hundleton Pembs 44 E4
Hundon Suff 55 E8
Hundred Acres Hants 15 C6
Hundred End Lancs 86 B2
Hundred House Powys 48 D3
Hungarton Leics 64 D3
Hungerford Hants 14 C2
Hungerford W Berks 25 C8
Hungerford Newtown W Berks 25 B8
Hungerton Lincs 65 B5
Hungladder Highld 149 A8
Hunmanby N Yorks 97 B6
Hunmanby Moor N Yorks 97 B7
Hunningham Warks 51 C8
Hunny Hill IoW 15 F5
Hunsdon Herts 41 C7
Hunsingore N Yorks 95 D7
Hunslet W Yorks 95 F6
Hunsonby Cumb 109 F5
Hunspow Highld 158 C4
Hunstanton Norf 80 C2
Hunstanworth Durham 110 E2
Hunsterson Ches E 74 E3
Hunston Suff 56 C3
Hunston W Sus 16 D2
Hunstrete Bath 23 C8
Hunt End Worcs 50 C5
Hunter's Quay Argyll 145 F10
Hunthill Lodge Angus 134 B4
Hunting-tower Perth 128 B2
Huntingdon Cambs 54 B3
Huntingfield Suff 57 B7
Huntingford Dorset 24 F3
Huntington E Loth 121 B7
Huntington Hereford 48 D4
Huntington Staffs 62 C3
Huntington York 96 D2
Huntley Glos 36 C4
Huntly Aberds 152 E5
Huntlywood Borders 122 E2
Hunton Kent 29 E8
Hunton N Yorks 101 E6
Hunt's Corner Norf 68 F3
Hunt's Cross Mers 86 F2
Huntsham Devon 10 B5
Huntspill Som 22 E5
Huntworth Som 22 F5
Hunwick Durham 110 F4
Hunworth Norf 81 D6
Hurdsfield Ches E 75 B6
Hurley Warks 63 E6
Hurley Windsor 39 F8
Hurlford E Ayrs 118 F4
Hurliness Orkney 159 K3
Hurn Dorset 14 E2
Hurn's End Lincs 79 E7
Hursley Hants 14 B5
Hurst N Yorks 101 D5
Hurst Som 12 C2
Hurst Wokingham 27 B5
Hurst Green E Sus 18 C4
Hurst Green Lancs 93 F6
Hurst Wickham W Sus 17 C6
Hurstbourne Priors Hants 26 E2
Hurstbourne Tarrant Hants 25 D8
Hurstpierpoint W Sus 17 C6
Hurstwood Lancs 93 F8
Hurtmore Sur 27 E7
Hurworth Place Darl 101 D7
Hury Durham 100 C4
Husabost Highld 148 C7
Husbands Bosworth Leics 64 F3
Husborne Crawley C Beds 53 F7
Husthwaite N Yorks 95 B8
Hutchwns Bridgend 21 B7
Huthwaite Notts 76 D4
Huttoft Lincs 79 B8
Hutton Borders 122 D5
Hutton Cumb 99 B6
Hutton E Yorks 97 D6
Hutton Essex 42 E2
Hutton Lancs 86 B2
Hutton N Som 22 D5
Hutton Buscel N Yorks 103 F7
Hutton Conyers N Yorks 95 B6
Hutton Cranswick E Yorks 97 D6
Hutton End Cumb 108 F4
Hutton Gate Redcar 102 C3
Hutton Henry Durham 111 F7
Hutton-le-Hole N Yorks 103 E5
Hutton Magna Durham 101 C6
Hutton Roof Cumb 93 B5
Hutton Roof Cumb 108 F3
Hutton Rudby N Yorks 102 D2
Hutton Sessay N Yorks 95 B7
Hutton Village Redcar 102 C3
Hutton Wandesley N Yorks 95 D8
Huxley Ches W 74 C2
Huxter Shetland 160 G7
Huxter Shetland 160 H5
Huxton Borders 122 C4
Huyton Mers 86 E2
Hwlffordd = Haverfordwest Pembs 44 D4
Hycemoor Cumb 98 F2
Hyde Glos 37 D5
Hyde Gtr Man 87 E7
Hyde Hants 14 C2
Hyde Heath Bucks 40 D2
Hyde Park S Yorks 89 D6
Hydestile Sur 27 E7
Hylton Castle T&W 111 D6
Hyndford Bridge S Lanark 120 E2
Hynish Argyll 146 H2
Hyssington Powys 60 E3
Hythe Hants 14 D5
Hythe Kent 19 B8
Hythe End Windsor 27 B8
Hythie Aberds 153 C10

I

Ibberton Dorset 13 D5
Ible Derbys 76 D2
Ibsley Hants 14 D2
Ibstock Leics 63 C8
Ibstone Bucks 39 E7
Ibthorpe Hants 25 D8
Ibworth Hants 26 D3
Ichrachan Argyll 125 B6
Ickburgh Norf 67 E8
Ickenham London 40 F3
Ickford Bucks 39 D6
Ickham Kent 31 D6
Ickleford Herts 54 F2
Icklesham E Sus 19 D5
Ickleton Cambs 55 E5
Icklingham Suff 55 B8
Ickwell Green C Beds 54 E2
Icomb Glos 38 B2
Idbury Oxon 38 C2
Iddesleigh Devon 9 D7
Ide Devon 10 E3
Ide Hill Kent 29 D5
Ideford Devon 7 B6
Iden E Sus 19 C6
Iden Green Kent 18 B4
Iden Green Kent 18 B5
Idle W Yorks 94 F4
Idlicote Warks 51 E7
Idmiston Wilts 25 F6
Idole Carms 33 C5
Idridgehay Derbys 76 E2
Idrigill Highld 149 B8
Idstone Oxon 38 F2
Idvies Angus 135 E5
Iffley Oxon 39 D5
Ifield W Sus 28 F3
Ifold W Sus 27 F8
Iford E Sus 17 D8
Ifton Heath Shrops 73 F7
Ightfield Shrops 74 F2
Ightham Kent 29 D6
Iken Suff 57 D8
Ilam Staffs 75 D8
Ilchester Som 12 B3
Ilderton Northumb 117 B6
Ilford London 41 F7
Ilfracombe Devon 20 E4
Ilkeston Derbys 76 E4
Ilketshall St Andrew Suff 69 F6
Ilketshall St Lawrence Suff 69 F6
Ilketshall St Margaret Suff 69 F6
Ilkley W Yorks 94 E4
Illey W Mid 62 F3
Illingworth W Yorks 87 B8
Illogan Corn 3 B5
Illston on the Hill Leics 64 E4
Ilmer Bucks 39 D7
Ilmington Warks 51 E7
Ilminster Som 11 C8
Ilsington Devon 7 B5
Ilston Swansea 33 E6
Ilton N Yorks 94 B4
Ilton Som 11 C8
Imachar N Ayrs 143 D9
Imeraval Argyll 142 D4
Immingham NE Lincs 91 C5
Impington Cambs 54 C5
Ince Ches W 73 B8
Ince Blundell Mers 85 D4
Ince in Makerfield Gtr Man 86 D3
Inch of Arnhall Aberds 135 B6
Inchbare Angus 135 C6
Inchberry Moray 152 C3
Inchbraoch Angus 135 D7
Incheril Highld 150 E3
Inchgrundle Angus 134 B4
Inchina Highld 150 B2
Inchinnan Renfs 118 C4
Inchkinloch Highld 157 E8
Inchlaggan Highld 136 D4
Inchlumpie Highld 151 D8
Inchmore Highld 150 G6
Inchnacardoch Hotel Highld 137 C6
Inchnadamph Highld 156 G5
Inchree Highld 130 C4
Inchture Perth 128 B4
Inchyra Perth 128 B3
Indian Queens Corn 4 D4
Inerval Argyll 142 D4
Ingatestone Essex 42 E2
Ingbirchworth S Yorks 88 D3
Ingestre Staffs 62 B3
Ingham Lincs 90 F3
Ingham Norf 69 B6
Ingham Suff 56 B2
Ingham Corner Norf 69 B6
Ingleborough Norf 66 C4
Ingleby Derbys 63 B7
Ingleby Lincs 77 B8
Ingleby Arncliffe N Yorks 102 D2
Ingleby Barwick Stockton 102 C2
Ingleby Greenhow N Yorks 102 D3
Inglemire Hull 97 F6
Inglesbatch Bath 24 C2
Inglesham Swindon 38 E2
Ingleton Durham 101 B6
Ingleton N Yorks 93 B6
Inglewhite Lancs 92 E5
Ingliston Edin 120 B4
Ingoe Northumb 110 B3
Ingol Lancs 92 F5
Ingoldisthorpe Norf 80 D2
Ingoldmells Lincs 79 C8
Ingoldsby Lincs 78 F3
Ingon Warks 51 D7
Ingram Northumb 117 C6
Ingrow W Yorks 94 F3
Ings Cumb 99 E6
Ingst S Glos 36 F2
Ingworth Norf 81 E7
Inham's End Cambs 66 E2
Inkberrow Worcs 50 D5
Inkpen W Berks 25 C8
Inkstack Highld 158 C4
Inn Cumb 99 D6
Innellan Argyll 145 F10
Innerleithen Borders 121 F6
Innerleven Fife 129 D5
Innermessan Dumfries 104 C4
Innerwick E Loth 122 B3
Innerwick Perth 132 E2
Innis Chonain Argyll 125 C7
Insch Aberds 140 B5
Insh Highld 138 D4
Inshore Highld 156 C6
Inskip Lancs 92 F4
Instoneville S Yorks 89 C6
Instow Devon 20 F3
Intake S Yorks 89 D6
Inver Aberds 139 E8
Inver Highld 151 C11
Inver Perth 133 E7
Inver Mallie Highld 136 F4
Inverailort Highld 147 C10
Inveraldie Angus 134 F4
Inveralligin Highld 149 C13
Inverallochy Aberds 153 B10
Inveran Highld 151 B8
Inveraray Argyll 125 E6
Inverarish Highld 149 E10
Inverarity Angus 134 E4
Inverarnan Stirling 126 C2
Inverasdale Highld 155 J13
Inverbeg Argyll 126 E2
Inverbervie Aberds 135 B8
Inverboyndie Aberds 153 B6
Inverbroom Highld 150 C4
Invercassley Highld 156 J7
Invercauld House Aberds 139 E7
Inverchaolain Argyll 145 F9
Invercharnan Highld 131 E5
Inverchoran Highld 150 F5
Invercreran Argyll 130 E4
Inverdruie Highld 138 C5
Inverebrie Aberds 153 E9
Invereck Argyll 145 E10
Inverernan Ho. Aberds 140 C2
Invereshie House Highld 138 D4
Inveresk E Loth 121 B6
Inverey Aberds 139 F6
Inverfarigaig Highld 137 B8
Invergarry Highld 137 D6
Invergelder Aberds 139 E8
Invergeldie Perth 127 B6
Invergordon Highld 151 E10
Invergowrie Perth 134 F3
Inverguseran Highld 149 H12
Inverhadden Perth 132 D3
Inverharroch Moray 152 E3
Inverherive Stirling 126 B2
Inverie Highld 147 B10
Inverinan Argyll 125 D5
Inverinate Highld 136 B2
Inverkeilor Angus 135 E6
Inverkeithing Fife 128 F3
Inverkeithny Aberds 153 D6
Inverkip Invclyd 118 B2
Inverkirkaig Highld 156 H3
Inverlael Highld 150 C4
Inverlochlarig Stirling 126 C3
Inverlochy Argyll 125 C7
Inverlochy Highld 131 B5
Inverlussa Argyll 144 E5
Invermark Lodge Angus 140 F3
Invermoidart Highld 147 D9
Invermoriston Highld 137 C7
Invernaver Highld 157 C10
Inverneill Argyll 145 E7
Inverness Highld 151 G9
Invernettie Aberds 153 D11
Invernoaden Argyll 125 F7
Inveroran Hotel Argyll 131 E6
Inverpolly Lodge Highld 156 H3
Inverquharity Angus 134 D4
Inverquhomery Aberds 153 D10
Inverroy Highld 137 F5
Inversanda Highld 130 D3
Invershiel Highld 136 C2
Invershin Highld 151 B8
Inversnaid Hotel Stirling 126 D2
Inverugie Aberds 153 D11
Inveruglas Argyll 126 D2
Inveruglass Highld 138 D4
Inverurie Aberds 141 B6
Invervar Perth 132 E3
Inverythan Aberds 153 D7
Inwardleigh Devon 9 E7
Inworth Essex 42 C4
Iochdar W Isles 148 D2
Iping W Sus 16 B2
Ipplepen Devon 7 C6
Ipsden Oxon 39 F6
Ipsley Worcs 51 C5
Ipstones Staffs 75 D7
Ipswich Suff 57 E5
Irby Mers 85 F3
Irby in the Marsh Lincs 79 C7
Irby upon Humber NE Lincs 91 D5
Irchester Northants 53 C7
Ireby Cumb 108 F2
Ireby Lancs 93 B6
Ireland Orkney 159 H4
Ireland Shetland 160 L5
Ireland's Cross Shrops 74 E4
Ireleth Cumb 92 B2
Ireshopeburn Durham 109 F8
Irlam Gtr Man 86 E5
Irnham Lincs 65 B7
Iron Acton S Glos 36 F3
Iron Cross Warks 51 D5
Ironbridge Telford 61 D6
Irongray Dumfries 107 B6
Ironmacannie Dumfries 106 B3
Ironside Aberds 153 C8
Ironville Derbys 76 D4
Irstead Norf 69 B6
Irthington Cumb 108 C4
Irthlingborough Northants 53 B7
Irton N Yorks 103 F8
Irvine N Ayrs 118 F3
Isauld Highld 157 C12
Isbister Orkney 159 F3
Isbister Orkney 159 G4
Isbister Shetland 160 D5
Isbister Shetland 160 G7
Isfield E Sus 17 C8
Isham Northants 53 B6
Isle Abbotts Som 11 B8
Isle Brewers Som 11 B8
Isle of Whithorn Dumfries 105 F8
Isleham Cambs 55 B7
Isleornsay Highld 149 G12
Islesburgh Shetland 160 G5
Islesteps Dumfries 107 B6
Isleworth London 28 B2
Isley Walton Leics 63 B8
Islibhig W Isles 154 E4
Islington London 41 F6
Islip Northants 53 B7
Islip Oxon 39 C5
Istead Rise Kent 29 C7
Isycoed Wrex 73 D8
Itchen Soton 14 C5
Itchen Abbas Hants 26 F3
Itchen Stoke Hants 26 F3
Itchingfield W Sus 16 B5
Itchington S Glos 36 F3
Itteringham Norf 81 D7
Itton Devon 9 E8
Itton Common Mon 36 E1
Ivegill Cumb 108 E4
Iver Bucks 40 F3
Iver Heath Bucks 40 F3
Iveston Durham 110 D4
Ivinghoe Bucks 40 C2
Ivinghoe Aston Bucks 40 C2
Ivington Hereford 49 D6
Ivington Green Hereford 49 D6
Ivy Chimneys Essex 41 D7
Ivy Cross Dorset 13 B6
Ivy Hatch Kent 29 D6
Ivybridge Devon 6 D4
Ivychurch Kent 19 C7
Iwade Kent 30 C3
Iwerne Courtney or Shroton Dorset 13 C6
Iwerne Minster Dorset 13 C6
Ixworth Suff 56 B3
Ixworth Thorpe Suff 56 B3

J

Jack Hill N Yorks 94 D5
Jack in the Green Devon 10 E5
Jacksdale Notts 76 D4
Jackstown Aberds 153 E7
Jacobstow Corn 8 E3
Jacobstowe Devon 9 D7
Jameston Pembs 32 E1
Jamestown Dumfries 115 E6
Jamestown Highld 150 F7
Jamestown W Dunb 126 F2
Jarrow T&W 111 C6
Jarvis Brook E Sus 18 C2
Jasper's Green Essex 42 B3
Java Argyll 124 B3
Jawcraig Falk 119 B8
Jaywick Essex 43 C7
Jealott's Hill Brack 27 B6
Jedburgh Borders 116 B2
Jeffreyston Pembs 32 D1
Jellyhill E Dunb 119 B6
Jemimaville Highld 151 E10
Jersey Farm Herts 40 D4
Jesmond T&W 111 C5
Jevington E Sus 18 E2
Jockey End Herts 40 C3
John o'Groats Highld 158 C5
Johnby Cumb 108 F4
John's Cross E Sus 18 C4
Johnshaven Aberds 135 C7
Johnston Pembs 44 D4
Johnstone Renfs 118 C4
Johnstonebridge Dumfries 114 E3
Johnstown Carms 33 C5
Johnstown Wrex 73 E7
Joppa Edin 121 B6
Joppa S Ayrs 112 C4
Jordans Bucks 40 E2
Jordanthorpe S Yorks 88 F4
Jump S Yorks 88 D4
Jumpers Green Dorset 14 E2
Juniper Green Edin 120 C4
Jurby East IoM 84 C3
Jurby West IoM 84 C3

K

Kaber Cumb 100 C2
Kaimend S Lanark 120 E2
Kaimes Edin 121 C5
Kalemouth Borders 116 B3
Kames Argyll 124 D4
Kames Argyll 145 F8
Kames E Ayrs 113 B6
Kea Corn 3 B7
Keadby N Lincs 90 C2
Keal Cotes Lincs 79 C6
Kearsley Gtr Man 87 D5
Kearstwick Cumb 99 F8
Kearton N Yorks 100 E4
Kearvaig Highld 156 B5
Keasden N Yorks 93 C7
Keckwick Halton 86 F3
Keddington Lincs 91 F7
Kedington Suff 55 E8
Kedleston Derbys 76 E3
Keelby Lincs 91 C5
Keele Staffs 74 E5
Keeley Green Bedford 53 E8
Keeston Pembs 44 D4
Keevil Wilts 24 D4
Kegworth Leics 63 B8
Kehelland Corn 2 B5
Keig Aberds 140 C5
Keighley W Yorks 94 E3
Keil Highld 130 D3
Keilarsbrae Clack 127 E7
Keilhill Aberds 153 C7
Keillmore Argyll 144 E5
Keillor Perth 134 E2
Keillour Perth 127 B8
Keills Argyll 142 B5
Keils Argyll 144 G4
Keinton Mandeville Som 23 F7
Keir Mill Dumfries 113 E8
Keisby Lincs 65 B7
Keiss Highld 158 D5
Keith Moray 152 C4
Keith Inch Aberds 153 D11
Keithock Angus 135 C6
Kelbrook Lancs 94 E2
Kelby Lincs 78 E3
Keld Cumb 99 C7
Keld N Yorks 100 D3
Keldholme N Yorks 103 F5
Kelfield N Lincs 90 D2
Kelfield N Yorks 95 F8
Kelham Notts 77 D7
Kellan Argyll 147 G8
Kellas Angus 134 F4
Kellas Moray 152 C1
Kellaton Devon 7 F6
Kelleth Cumb 100 D1
Kelleythorpe E Yorks 97 D5
Kelling Norf 81 C6
Kellingley N Yorks 89 B6
Kellington N Yorks 89 B6
Kelloe Durham 111 F6
Kelloholm Dumfries 113 C7
Kelly Devon 9 F5
Kelly Bray Corn 5 B8
Kelmarsh Northants 52 B5
Kelmscot Oxon 38 E2
Kelsale Suff 57 C7
Kelsall Ches W 74 C2
Kelsall Hill Ches W 74 C2
Kelshall Herts 54 F4
Kelsick Cumb 107 D8
Kelso Borders 122 F3
Kelstedge Derbys 76 C3
Kelstern Lincs 91 E6
Kelston Bath 24 C2
Keltneyburn Perth 132 E4
Kelton Dumfries 107 B6
Kelty Fife 128 E3
Kelvedon Essex 42 C4
Kelvedon Hatch Essex 42 E1
Kelvin S Lanark 119 D6
Kelvinside Glasgow 119 C5
Kelynack Corn 2 C2
Kemback Fife 129 C6
Kemberton Shrops 61 D7
Kemble Glos 37 E6
Kemerton Worcs 50 F4
Kemeys Commander Mon 35 D7
Kemnay Aberds 141 C6
Kemp Town Brighton 17 D7
Kempley Glos 36 B3
Kemps Green Warks 51 B6
Kempsey Worcs 50 E3
Kempsford Glos 38 E1
Kempshott Hants 26 D4
Kempston Bedford 53 E8
Kempston Hardwick Bedford 53 E8
Kempton Shrops 60 F3
Kemsing Kent 29 D6
Kemsley Kent 30 C3
Kenardington Kent 19 B6
Kenchester Hereford 49 E6
Kencot Oxon 38 D2
Kendal Cumb 99 E7
Kendoon Dumfries 113 F6
Kendray S Yorks 88 D4
Kenfig Bridgend 34 F2
Kenfig Hill Bridgend 34 F2
Kenilworth Warks 51 B7
Kenknock Stirling 132 F1
Kenley London 28 D4
Kenley Shrops 61 D5
Kenmore Highld 149 C12
Kenmore Perth 132 E4
Kenn Devon 10 F4
Kenn N Som 23 C6
Kennacley W Isles 154 H6
Kennacraig Argyll 145 G7
Kennerleigh Devon 10 D3
Kennet Clack 127 E8
Kennethmont Aberds 140 B4
Kennett Cambs 55 C7
Kennford Devon 10 F4
Kenninghall Norf 68 F3
Kenninghall Heath Norf 68 F3
Kennington Kent 30 E4
Kennington Oxon 39 D5
Kennoway Fife 129 D5
Kenny Hill Suff 55 B7
Kennythorpe N Yorks 96 C3
Kenovay Argyll 146 G2
Kensaleyre Highld 149 C9
Kensington London 28 B3
Kensworth C Beds 40 C3
Kensworth Common C Beds 40 C3
Kent's Oak Hants 14 B4
Kent Street E Sus 18 D4
Kent Street Kent 29 D7
Kent Street W Sus 17 B6
Kentallen Highld 130 D4
Kentchurch Hereford 35 B8
Kentford Suff 55 C8
Kentisbeare Devon 11 D5
Kentisbury Devon 20 E5
Kentisbury Ford Devon 20 E5
Kentmere Cumb 99 D6
Kenton Devon 10 F4
Kenton Suff 57 C5
Kenton T&W 110 C5
Kenton Bankfoot T&W 110 C5
Kentra Highld 147 E9
Kents Bank Cumb 92 B3
Kent's Green Glos 36 B4
Kenwick Shrops 73 F8
Kenwyn Corn 3 B7
Keoldale Highld 156 C6
Keppanach Highld 130 C4
Keppoch Highld 136 B2
Keprigan Argyll 143 G7
Kepwick N Yorks 102 E2
Kerchesters Borders 122 F3
Keresley W Mid 63 F7
Kernborough Devon 7 E5
Kerne Bridge Hereford 36 C2
Kerris Corn 2 D3
Kerry Powys 59 F8
Kerrycroy Argyll 145 G10
Kerry's Gate Hereford 49 F5
Kerrysdale Highld 149 A13
Kersall Notts 77 C7
Kersey Suff 56 E4
Kershopefoot Cumb 115 F7
Kersoe Worcs 50 F4
Kerswell Devon 11 D5
Kerswell Green Worcs 50 E3
Kesgrave Suff 57 E6
Kessingland Suff 69 F8
Kessingland Beach Suff 69 F8
Kessington E Dunb 119 B5
Kestle Corn 3 B8
Kestle Mill Corn 4 D3
Keston London 28 C5
Keswick Cumb 98 B4
Keswick Norf 68 D5
Keswick Norf 81 D9
Ketley Telford 61 C6
Ketley Bank Telford 61 C6
Ketsby Lincs 79 B6
Kettering Northants 53 B6
Ketteringham Norf 68 D4
Kettins Perth 134 F2
Kettlebaston Suff 56 D3
Kettlebridge Fife 128 D5
Kettleburgh Suff 57 C6
Kettlehill Fife 128 D5
Kettleholm Dumfries 107 B8
Kettleness N Yorks 103 C6
Kettleshume Ches E 75 B6
Kettlesing Bottom N Yorks 94 D5
Kettlesing Head N Yorks 94 D5
Kettlestone Norf 81 D5
Kettlethorpe Lincs 77 B8
Kettletoft Orkney 159 E7
Kettlewell N Yorks 94 B2
Ketton Rutland 65 D6
Kew London 28 B2
Kew Br. London 28 B2
Kewstoke N Som 22 C5
Kexbrough S Yorks 88 D4
Kexby Lincs 90 F2
Kexby York 96 D3
Key Green Ches E 75 C5
Keyham Leics 64 D3
Keyhaven Hants 14 E4
Keyingham E Yorks 91 B6
Keymer W Sus 17 C7
Keynsham Bath 23 C8
Keysoe Bedford 53 C8
Keysoe Row Bedford 53 C8
Keyston Cambs 53 B8
Keyworth Notts 77 F6
Kibblesworth T&W 110 D5
Kibworth Beauchamp Leics 64 E3
Kibworth Harcourt Leics 64 E3
Kidbrooke London 28 B5
Kiddemore Green Staffs 62 D2
Kidderminster Worcs 50 B3
Kiddington Oxon 38 B4
Kidlington Oxon 38 C4
Kidmore End Oxon 26 B4
Kidsgrove Staffs 74 D5
Kidstones N Yorks 100 F4
Kidwelly = Cydweli Carms 33 D5
Kiel Crofts Argyll 124 B5
Kielder Northumb 116 E2
Kierfiold Ho Orkney 159 G3
Kilbagie Fife 127 F8
Kilbarchan Renfs 118 C4
Kilbeg Highld 149 H11
Kilberry Argyll 144 G6
Kilbirnie N Ayrs 118 D3
Kilbride Argyll 124 C4
Kilbride Argyll 124 C5
Kilbride Highld 149 F10
Kilburn Angus 134 C3
Kilburn Derbys 76 E3
Kilburn London 41 F5
Kilburn N Yorks 95 B8
Kilby Leics 64 E3
Kilchamaig Argyll 145 G7
Kilchattan Argyll 144 D2
Kilchattan Bay Argyll 145 H10
Kilchenzie Argyll 143 F7
Kilcheran Argyll 124 B4
Kilchiaran Argyll 142 B3
Kilchoan Argyll 124 D3
Kilchoan Highld 146 E7
Kilchoman Argyll 142 B3
Kilchrenan Argyll 125 C6
Kilconquhar Fife 129 D6
Kilcot Glos 36 B3
Kilcoy Highld 151 F8
Kilcreggan Argyll 145 E11
Kildale N Yorks 102 D4
Kildalloig Argyll 143 G8
Kildary Highld 151 D10
Kildermorie Lodge Highld 151 D8
Kildonan N Ayrs 143 F11
Kildonan Lodge Highld 157 G12
Kildonnan Highld 146 C7
Kildrummy Aberds 140 C3
Kildwick N Yorks 94 E3
Kilfinan Argyll 145 F8
Kilfinnan Highld 137 E5
Kilgetty Pembs 32 D2
Kilgwrrwg Common Mon 36 E1
Kilham E Yorks 97 C6
Kilham Northumb 122 F4
Kilkenneth Argyll 146 G2
Kilkerran Argyll 143 G8
Kilkhampton Corn 9 E6
Killamarsh Derbys 89 F5
Killay Swansea 33 E7
Killbeg Argyll 147 G9
Killean Argyll 143 D7
Killearn Stirling 126 F4
Killen Highld 151 F9
Killerby Darl 101 C6
Killichonan Perth 132 D2
Killiechonate Highld 136 F5
Killiechronan Argyll 147 G8
Killiecrankie Perth 133 C6
Killiemor Argyll 146 H7
Killiemore House Argyll 146 J7
Killilan Highld 150 H2
Killimster Highld 158 E5
Killin Stirling 132 F2
Killin Lodge Highld 137 D8
Killinallan Argyll 142 A4
Killinghall N Yorks 95 D5
Killington Cumb 99 F8
Killingworth T&W 111 B5
Killmahumaig Argyll 144 D6
Killochyett Borders 121 E7
Killocraw Argyll 143 E7
Killundine Highld 147 G8
Kilmacolm Invclyd 118 C3
Kilmaha Argyll 124 E5
Kilmahog Stirling 126 D5
Kilmalieu Highld 130 D2
Kilmaluag Highld 149 A9
Kilmany Fife 129 B5
Kilmarie Highld 149 G10
Kilmarnock E Ayrs 118 F4
Kilmaron Castle Fife 129 C5
Kilmartin Argyll 124 F4
Kilmaurs E Ayrs 118 E4
Kilmelford Argyll 124 D4
Kilmeny Argyll 142 B4
Kilmersdon Som 23 D8
Kilmeston Hants 15 B6
Kilmichael Argyll 143 F7
Kilmichael Glassary Argyll 145 D7
Kilmichael of Inverlussa Argyll 144 E6
Kilmington Devon 11 E7
Kilmington Wilts 24 F2
Kilmonivaig Highld 136 F4
Kilmorack Highld 150 G7
Kilmore Argyll 124 C4
Kilmore Highld 149 H11
Kilmory Argyll 144 F6
Kilmory Highld 147 D8
Kilmory Highld 149 H8
Kilmory N Ayrs 143 F10
Kilmuir Highld 148 D7
Kilmuir Highld 149 A8
Kilmuir Highld 151 D10
Kilmuir Highld 151 G9
Kilmun Argyll 124 D5
Kilmun Argyll 145 E10
Kiln Pit Hill Northumb 110 D3
Kilncadzow S Lanark 119 E8
Kilndown Kent 18 B4
Kilnhurst S Yorks 89 E5
Kilninian Argyll 146 G6
Kilninver Argyll 124 C4
Kilnsea E Yorks 91 C8
Kilnsey N Yorks 94 C2
Kilnwick E Yorks 97 E5
Kilnwick Percy E Yorks 96 D4
Kiloran Argyll 144 D2
Kilpatrick N Ayrs 143 F10
Kilpeck Hereford 49 F6
Kilphedir Highld 157 H12
Kilpin E Yorks 89 B8
Kilpin Pike E Yorks 89 B8
Kilrenny Fife 129 D7
Kilsby Northants 52 B3
Kilspindie Perth 128 B4
Kilsyth N Lanark 119 B7
Kiltarlity Highld 151 G8
Kilton Notts 77 B5
Kilton Som 22 E3
Kilton Thorpe Redcar 102 C4
Kilvaxter Highld 149 B8
Kilve Som 22 E3
Kilvington Notts 77 E7
Kilwinning N Ayrs 118 E3
Kimber worth S Yorks 88 E5
Kimberley Norf 68 D3
Kimberley Notts 76 E5
Kimble Wick Bucks 39 D8
Kimblesworth Durham 111 E5
Kimbolton Cambs 53 C8
Kimbolton Hereford 49 C7
Kimcote Leics 64 F2
Kimmeridge Dorset 13 G7
Kimmerston Northumb 123 F5
Kimpton Hants 25 E7
Kimpton Herts 40 C4
Kinbrace Highld 157 F11
Kinbuck Stirling 127 D6
Kincaple Fife 129 C6
Kincardine Fife 127 F8
Kincardine Highld 151 C9
Kincardine Bridge Falk 127 F8
Kincardine O'Neil Aberds 140 E4
Kinclaven Perth 134 F1
Kincorth Aberdeen 141 D8
Kincorth Ho. Moray 151 E13
Kincraig Highld 138 D4
Kincraigie Perth 133 E6
Kindallachan Perth 133 E6
Kineton Glos 37 B7
Kineton Warks 51 D8
Kinfauns Perth 128 B3
King Edward Aberds 153 C7
King Sterndale Derbys 75 B7
Kingairloch Highld 130 D2
Kingarth Argyll 145 H9
Kingcoed Mon 35 D8
Kingerby Lincs 90 E4
Kingham Oxon 38 B2
Kingholm Quay Dumfries 107 B6
Kinghorn Fife 128 F4
Kingie Highld 136 D4
Kinglassie Fife 128 E4
Kingoodie Perth 128 B5
King's Acre Hereford 49 E6
King's Bromley Staffs 62 C5
King's Caple Hereford 36 B2
King's Cliffe Northants 65 E7
King's Coughton Warks 51 D5
King's Heath W Mid 62 F4
Kings Hedges Cambs 55 C5
Kings Langley Herts 40 D3
King's Hill Kent 29 D7
King's Lynn Norf 67 B6
King's Meaburn Cumb 99 B8
King's Mills Wrex 73 E7
Kings Muir Borders 121 F5
King's Newnham Warks 52 B2
King's Newton Derbys 63 B7
King's Norton Leics 64 D3
King's Norton W Mid 51 B5
King's Nympton Devon 9 C8
King's Pyon Hereford 49 D6
King's Ripton Cambs 54 B3
King's Somborne Hants 25 F8
King's Stag Dorset 12 C5
King's Stanley Glos 37 D5
King's Sutton Northants 52 F2
King's Thorn Hereford 49 F7
King's Walden Herts 40 B4
Kings Worthy Hants 26 F2
Kingsand Corn 6 D2
Kingsbarns Fife 129 C7
Kingsbridge Devon 6 E5
Kingsbridge Som 21 F8
Kingsburgh Highld 149 C8
Kingsbury London 41 F5
Kingsbury Warks 63 E6
Kingsbury Episcopi Som 12 B2
Kingsclere Hants 26 D3
Kingscote Glos 37 E5
Kingscott Devon 9 C7
Kingscross N Ayrs 143 F11
Kingsdon Som 12 B3
Kingsdown Kent 31 E7
Kingseat Fife 128 E3
Kingsey Bucks 39 D7
Kingsfold W Sus 28 F2
Kingsford E Ayrs 118 E4
Kingsford Worcs 62 F2
Kingsforth N Lincs 90 C4
Kingsgate Kent 31 B7
Kingsheanton Devon 20 F4
Kingshouse Hotel Highld 131 D6
Kingside Hill Cumb 107 D8
Kingskerswell Devon 7 C6
Kingskettle Fife 128 D5
Kingsland Anglesey 82 C2
Kingsland Hereford 49 C6
Kingsley Ches W 74 B2
Kingsley Hants 27 F5
Kingsley Staffs 75 E7
Kingsley Green W Sus 27 F6
Kingsley Holt Staffs 75 E7
Kingsley Park Northants 53 C5
Kingsmuir Angus 134 E4
Kingsmuir Fife 129 D7
Kingsnorth Kent 19 B7
Kingstanding W Mid 62 E4
Kingsteignton Devon 7 B6
Kingsthorpe Northants 53 C5
Kingston Cambs 54 D4
Kingston Devon 6 E4
Kingston Dorset 13 D5
Kingston Dorset 13 G7
Kingston E Loth 129 F7
Kingston Hants 14 D2
Kingston IoW 15 F5
Kingston Kent 31 D5
Kingston Moray 152 B3
Kingston Bagpuize Oxon 38 E4
Kingston Blount Oxon 39 E7
Kingston by Sea W Sus 17 D6
Kingston Deverill Wilts 24 F3
Kingston Gorse W Sus 16 D4
Kingston Lisle Oxon 38 F3
Kingston Maurward Dorset 12 E5
Kingston near Lewes E Sus 17 D7
Kingston on Soar Notts 64 B2
Kingston Russell Dorset 12 E3
Kingston Seymour N Som 23 C6
Kingston St Mary Som 11 B7
Kingston Upon Hull Hull 90 B4
Kingston upon Thames London 28 C2
Kingston Vale London 28 B3
Kingstone Hereford 49 F6
Kingstone Som 11 C8
Kingstone Staffs 62 B4
Kingstown Cumb 108 D3
Kingswear Devon 7 D6
Kingswells Aberdeen 141 D7
Kingswinford W Mid 62 F2
Kingswood Bucks 39 C6
Kingswood Glos 36 E4
Kingswood Hereford 48 D4
Kingswood Kent 30 D2
Kingswood Powys 60 D2
Kingswood S Glos 23 B8
Kingswood Sur 28 D3
Kingswood Warks 51 B6
Kingthorpe Lincs 78 B4
Kington Hereford 48 D4
Kington Worcs 50 D4
Kington Langley Wilts 24 B4
Kington Magna Dorset 13 B5
Kington St Michael Wilts 24 B4
Kingussie Highld 138 D3
Kingweston Som 23 F7
Kininvie Ho. Moray 152 D3
Kinkell Bridge Perth 127 C8
Kinknockie Aberds 153 D10
Kinlet Shrops 61 F7
Kinloch Fife 128 C4
Kinloch Highld 146 B6
Kinloch Highld 149 G11
Kinloch Highld 156 F6
Kinloch Perth 133 E8
Kinloch Perth 134 E2
Kinloch Hourn Highld 136 D2
Kinloch Laggan Highld 137 F8
Kinloch Lodge Highld 157 D8
Kinloch Rannoch Perth 132 D3
Kinlochan Highld 130 C2
Kinlochard Stirling 126 D3
Kinlochbeoraid Highld 147 C11
Kinlochbervie Highld 156 D5
Kinlocheil Highld 130 B3
Kinlochewe Highld 150 E3
Kinlochleven Highld 131 C5
Kinlochmoidart Highld 147 D10
Kinlochmorar Highld 147 B11
Kinlochmore Highld 131 C5
Kinlochspelve Argyll 124 C2
Kinloid Highld 147 C9
Kinloss Moray 151 E13
Kinmel Bay Conwy 72 A3
Kinmuck Aberds 141 C7
Kinmundy Aberds 141 C7
Kinnadie Aberds 153 D9
Kinnaird Perth 128 B4
Kinnaird Castle Angus 135 D6
Kinneff Aberds 135 B8
Kinnelhead Dumfries 114 D3
Kinnell Angus 135 D6
Kinnerley Shrops 60 B3
Kinnersley Hereford 48 E5
Kinnersley Worcs 50 E3
Kinnerton Powys 48 C4
Kinnesswood Perth 128 D3
Kinninvie Durham 101 B5
Kinnordy Angus 134 D3
Kinoulton Notts 77 F6
Kinross Perth 128 D3
Kinrossie Perth 134 F1
Kinsbourne Green Herts 40 C4
Kinsey Heath Ches E 74 E3
Kinsham Hereford 49 C5
Kinsham Worcs 50 F4
Kinsley W Yorks 88 C5
Kinson Bmouth 13 E8
Kintbury W Berks 25 C8
Kintessack Moray 151 E12
Kintillo Perth 128 C3
Kintocher Aberds 140 D4
Kinton Hereford 49 B6
Kinton Shrops 60 C3
Kintore Aberds 141 C6
Kintour Argyll 142 C5
Kintra Argyll 142 D4
Kintra Argyll 146 J6
Kintraw Argyll 124 E4
Kinuachdrachd Argyll 124 F3
Kinveachy Highld 138 C5
Kinver Staffs 62 F2
Kippax W Yorks 95 F7
Kippen Stirling 127 E5
Kippford or Scaur Dumfries 106 D5
Kirbister Orkney 159 F7
Kirbister Orkney 159 H4
Kirbuster Orkney 159 F3
Kirby Bedon Norf 69 D5
Kirby Bellars Leics 64 C4
Kirby Cane Norf 69 E6
Kirby Cross Essex 43 B8
Kirby Grindalythe N Yorks 96 C5
Kirby Hill N Yorks 95 C6
Kirby Hill N Yorks 101 D6
Kirby Knowle N Yorks 102 F2
Kirby-le-Soken Essex 43 B8
Kirby Misperton N Yorks 96 B3
Kirby Muxloe Leics 64 D2
Kirby Row Norf 69 E6
Kirby Sigston N Yorks 102 E2
Kirby Underdale E Yorks 96 D4
Kirby Wiske N Yorks 102 F1
Kirdford W Sus 16 B4
Kirk Highld 158 E4
Kirk Bramwith S Yorks 89 C7
Kirk Deighton N Yorks 95 D6
Kirk Ella E Yorks 90 B4
Kirk Hallam Derbys 76 E4
Kirk Hammerton N Yorks 95 D7
Kirk Ireton Derbys 76 D2
Kirk Langley Derbys 76 F2
Kirk Merrington Durham 111 F5
Kirk Michael IoM 84 C3
Kirk of Shotts N Lanark 119 C8
Kirk Sandall S Yorks 89 D7
Kirk Smeaton N Yorks 89 C6
Kirk Yetholm Borders 116 B4
Kirkabister Shetland 160 K6
Kirkandrews Dumfries 106 E3
Kirkandrews upon Eden Cumb 108 D3
Kirkbampton Cumb 108 D3
Kirkbean Dumfries 107 D6
Kirkbride Cumb 108 D2
Kirkbuddo Angus 135 E5
Kirkburn Borders 121 F5
Kirkburn E Yorks 97 D5
Kirkburton W Yorks 88 C2
Kirkby Lincs 90 E4
Kirkby Mers 86 E2
Kirkby N Yorks 102 D3
Kirkby Fleetham N Yorks 101 E7
Kirkby Green Lincs 78 D3
Kirkby In Ashfield Notts 76 D5
Kirkby-in-Furness Cumb 98 F4
Kirkby la Thorpe Lincs 78 E3
Kirkby Lonsdale Cumb 93 B6
Kirkby Malham N Yorks 93 C8
Kirkby Mallory Leics 63 D8
Kirkby Malzeard N Yorks 94 B5
Kirkby Mills N Yorks 103 F5
Kirkby on Bain Lincs 78 C5
Kirkby Overflow N Yorks 95 E6
Kirkby Stephen Cumb 100 D2
Kirkby Thore Cumb 99 B8
Kirkby Underwood Lincs 65 B7
Kirkby Wharfe N Yorks 95 E8
Kirkbymoorside N Yorks 102 F4
Kirkcaldy Fife 128 E4
Kirkcambeck Cumb 108 C5
Kirkcarswell Dumfries 106 E4
Kirkcolm Dumfries 104 C4
Kirkconnel Dumfries 113 C7
Kirkconnell Dumfries 107 C6
Kirkcowan Dumfries 105 C7
Kirkcudbright Dumfries 106 D3
Kirkdale Mers 85 E4
Kirkfieldbank S Lanark 119 E8
Kirkgunzeon Dumfries 107 C5
Kirkham Lancs 92 F4
Kirkham N Yorks 96 C3
Kirkhamgate W Yorks 88 B3
Kirkharle Northumb 117 F6
Kirkheaton Northumb 110 B3
Kirkheaton W Yorks 88 C2
Kirkhill Angus 135 C6
Kirkhill Highld 151 G8
Kirkhill Midloth 120 C5
Kirkhill Moray 152 E2
Kirkhope Borders 115 B6
Kirkhouse Borders 121 F6
Kirkiboll Highld 157 D8
Kirkibost Highld 149 G10
Kirkinch Angus 134 E3
Kirkinner Dumfries 105 D8
Kirkintilloch E Dunb 119 B6
Kirkland Cumb 98 C2
Kirkland Cumb 109 F6
Kirkland Dumfries 113 C7
Kirkland Dumfries 113 E8
Kirkleatham Redcar 102 B3
Kirklevington Stockton 102 D2
Kirkley Suff 69 E8
Kirklington N Yorks 101 F8
Kirklington Notts 77 D6
Kirklinton Cumb 108 C4
Kirkliston Edin 120 B4
Kirkmaiden Dumfries 104 F5
Kirkmichael Perth 133 D7
Kirkmichael S Ayrs 112 D3
Kirkmuirhill S Lanark 119 E7
Kirknewton Northumb 122 F5
Kirknewton W Loth 120 C4
Kirkney Aberds 152 E5
Kirkoswald Cumb 109 E5
Kirkoswald S Ayrs 112 D2
Kirkpatrick Durham Dumfries 106 B4
Kirkpatrick-Fleming Dumfries 108 B2
Kirksanton Cumb 98 F3
Kirkstall W Yorks 95 F5
Kirkstead Lincs 78 C4
Kirkstile Aberds 152 E5
Kirkstyle Highld 158 C5
Kirkton Aberds 140 B5
Kirkton Aberds 153 D6
Kirkton Angus 134 E4
Kirkton Angus 134 F4
Kirkton Borders 115 C8
Kirkton Dumfries 114 F2
Kirkton Fife 129 B5
Kirkton Highld 149 F1
Kirkton Highld 150 G2
Kirkton Highld 151 B10
Kirkton Highld 151 F10
Kirkton Perth 127 C8
Kirkton S Lanark 114 B2
Kirkton Stirling 126 D4
Kirkton Manor Borders 120 F5
Kirkton of Airlie Angus 134 D

Kirkton of Auchterhouse Angus 134 F3
Kirkton of Auchterless Aberds 153 D7
Kirkton of Barevan Highld 151 G11
Kirkton of Bourtie Aberds 141 B7
Kirkton of Collace Perth 134 F1
Kirkton of Craig Angus 135 D7
Kirkton of Culsalmond Aberds 153 E6
Kirkton of Durris Aberds 141 E6
Kirkton of Glenbuchat Aberds 140 C2
Kirkton of Glenisla Angus 134 C2
Kirkton of Kingoldrum Angus 134 D3
Kirkton of Largo Fife 129 D6
Kirkton of Lethendy Perth 133 E8
Kirkton of Logie Buchan Aberds 141 B8
Kirkton of Maryculter Aberds 141 E7
Kirkton of Menmuir Angus 135 C5
Kirkton of Monikie Angus 135 F5
Kirkton of Oyne Aberds 141 B5
Kirkton of Rayne Aberds 153 F6
Kirkton of Skene Aberds 141 D7
Kirkton of Tough Aberds 140 C5
Kirktonhill Borders 121 D7
Kirktown Aberds 153 C10
Kirktown of Alvah Aberds 153 B6
Kirktown of Deskford Moray 152 B5
Kirktown of Fetteresso Aberds 141 F7
Kirktown of Mortlach Moray 152 E3
Kirktown of Slains Aberds 141 B9
Kirkurd Borders 120 E4
Kirkwall Orkney 159 G5
Kirkwhelpington Northumb 117 F5
Kirmington N Lincs 90 C5
Kirmond le Mire Lincs 91 E5
Kirn Argyll 145 F10
Kirriemuir Angus 134 D3
Kirstead Green Norf 69 E5
Kirtlebridge Dumfries 108 B2
Kirtleton Dumfries 115 F5
Kirtling Cambs 55 D7
Kirtling Green Cambs 55 D7
Kirtlington Oxon 38 C4
Kirtomy Highld 157 C10
Kirton Lincs 79 F6
Kirton Notts 77 C6
Kirton Suff 57 F6
Kirton End Lincs 79 E5
Kirton Holme Lincs 79 E5
Kirton in Lindsey N Lincs 90 E3
Kislingbury Northants 52 D4
Kites Hardwick Warks 52 C2
Kittisford Som 11 B5
Kittle Swansea 33 F6
Kitt's Green W Mid 63 F5
Kitt's Moss Gtr Man 87 F6
Kittybrewster Aberdeen 141 D8
Kitwood Hants 26 F4
Kivernoll Hereford 49 F6
Kiveton Park S Yorks 89 F5
Knaith Lincs 90 F2
Knaith Park Lincs 90 F2
Knap Corner Dorset 13 B6
Knaphill Sur 27 D7
Knapp Perth 134 F2
Knapp Som 11 B8
Knapthorpe Notts 77 D7
Knapton Norf 81 D9
Knapton York 95 D8
Knapton Green Hereford 49 D6
Knapwell Cambs 54 C4
Knaresborough N Yorks 95 D6
Knarsdale Northumb 109 D6
Knauchland Moray 152 C5
Knaven Aberds 153 D8
Knayton N Yorks 102 F2
Knebworth Herts 41 B5
Knedlington E Yorks 89 B8
Kneesall Notts 77 C7
Kneesworth Cambs 54 E4
Kneeton Notts 77 E7
Knelston Swansea 33 F5
Knenhall Staffs 75 F6
Knettishall Suff 68 F2
Knightacott Devon 21 F5
Knightcote Warks 51 D8
Knightley Dale Staffs 62 B2
Knighton Devon 6 E3
Knighton Leicester 64 D2
Knighton = Tref-Y-Clawdd Powys 48 B4
Knighton Staffs 61 B7
Knighton Staffs 74 E4
Knightswood Glasgow 118 C5
Knightwick Worcs 50 D2
Knill Hereford 48 C4
Knipton Leics 77 F8
Knitsley Durham 110 E4
Kniveton Derbys 76 D2
Knock Argyll 147 H8
Knock Cumb 100 B1
Knock Moray 152 C5
Knockally Highld 158 H3
Knockan Highld 156 H5
Knockandhu Moray 139 B8
Knockando Moray 152 D1
Knockando Ho. Moray 152 D2
Knockbain Highld 151 F9
Knockbreck Highld 148 B7
Knockbrex Dumfries 106 E2
Knockdee Highld 158 D3
Knockdolian S Ayrs 104 A5
Knockenkelly N Ayrs 143 F11
Knockentiber E Ayrs 118 F3
Knockespock Ho. Aberds 140 B4
Knockfarrel Highld 151 F8
Knockglass Dumfries 104 D4
Knockholt Kent 29 D5
Knockholt Pound Kent 29 D5
Knockie Lodge Highld 137 C7
Knockin Shrops 60 B3
Knockinlaw E Ayrs 118 F4
Knocklearn Dumfries 106 B4
Knocknaha Argyll 143 G7
Knocknain Dumfries 104 C3
Knockrome Argyll 144 F4
Knocksharry IoM 84 D2
Knodishall Suff 57 C8
Knolls Green Ches E 74 B5
Knolton Wrex 73 F7
Knolton Bryn Wrex 73 F7
Knook Wilts 24 E4
Knossington Leics 64 D5
Knott End-on-Sea Lancs 92 E3
Knotting Bedford 53 C8
Knotting Green Bedford 53 C8
Knottingley W Yorks 89 B6
Knotts Cumb 99 B6
Knotts Lancs 93 D7
Knotty Ash Mers 86 E2
Knotty Green Bucks 40 E2
Knowbury Shrops 49 B7
Knowe Dumfries 105 B7
Knowehead Dumfries 113 E6
Knowes of Elrick Aberds 152 C6
Knowesgate Northumb 117 F5
Knoweton N Lanark 119 D7
Knowhead Aberds 153 C9
Knowl Hill Windsor 27 B6
Knowle Bristol 23 B8
Knowle Devon 10 D2
Knowle Devon 11 F5
Knowle Devon 20 F3
Knowle Shrops 49 B7
Knowle W Mid 51 B6
Knowle Green Lancs 93 F6
Knowle Park W Yorks 94 E3
Knowlton Dorset 13 C8
Knowlton Kent 31 D6
Knowsley Mers 86 E2
Knowstone Devon 10 B3
Knox Bridge Kent 29 E8
Knucklas Powys 48 B4
Knuston Northants 53 C7
Knutsford Ches E 74 B4
Knutton Staffs 74 E5
Knypersley Staffs 75 D5
Kuggar Corn 3 E6
Kyle of Lochalsh Highld 149 F12
Kyleakin Highld 149 F12
Kylerhea Highld 149 F12
Kylesknoydart Highld 147 B11
Kylesku Highld 156 F5
Kylesmorar Highld 147 B11
Kylestrome Highld 156 F5
Kyllachy House Highld 138 B3
Kynaston Shrops 60 B3
Kynnersley Telford 61 C6
Kyre Magna Worcs 49 C8

L

La Fontenelle Guern 16
La Planque Guern 16
Labost W Isles 155 C7
Lacasaidh W Isles 155 E8
Lacasdal W Isles 155 D9
Laceby NE Lincs 91 D6
Lacey Green Bucks 39 E8
Lach Dennis Ches W 74 B4
Lackford Suff 55 B8
Lacock Wilts 24 C4
Ladbroke Warks 52 D2
Laddingford Kent 29 E7
Lade Bank Lincs 79 D6
Ladock Corn 4 D3
Lady Orkney 159 D7
Ladybank Fife 128 C5
Ladykirk Borders 122 E4
Ladysford Aberds 153 B9
Laga Highld 147 E9
Lagalochan Argyll 124 D4
Lagavulin Argyll 142 D5
Lagg Argyll 144 F4
Lagg N Ayrs 143 F10
Laggan Argyll 142 C3
Laggan Highld 137 E5
Laggan Highld 138 E2
Laggan Highld 147 D10
Laggan S Ayrs 112 F2
Lagganulva Argyll 146 G7
Laide Highld 155 H13
Laigh Fenwick E Ayrs 118 E4
Laigh Glengall S Ayrs 112 C3
Laighmuir E Ayrs 118 E4
Laindon Essex 42 F2
Lair Highld 150 G3
Lairg Highld 157 J8
Lairg Lodge Highld 157 J8
Lairg Muir Highld 157 J8
Lairgmore Highld 151 H8
Laisterdyke W Yorks 94 F4
Laithes Cumb 108 F4
Lake IoW 15 F6
Lake Wilts 25 F6
Lakenham Norf 68 D5
Lakenheath Suff 67 F7
Lakesend Norf 66 E5
Lakeside Cumb 99 F5
Laleham Sur 27 C8
Laleston Bridgend 21 B7
Lamarsh Essex 56 F2
Lamas Norf 81 E8
Lambden Borders 122 E3
Lamberhurst Kent 18 B3
Lamberhurst Quarter Kent 18 B3
Lamberton Borders 123 D5
Lambeth London 28 B4
Lambhill Glasgow 119 C5
Lambley Northumb 109 D6
Lambley Notts 77 E6
Lamborough Hill Oxon 38 D4
Lambourn W Berks 25 B8
Lambourne End Essex 41 E7
Lambs Green W Sus 28 F3
Lambston Pembs 44 D4
Lambton T&W 111 D5
Lamerton Devon 6 B2
Lamesley T&W 111 D5
Laminess Orkney 159 E7
Lamington Highld 151 D10
Lamington S Lanark 120 F2
Lamlash N Ayrs 143 E11
Lamloch Dumfries 112 E5
Lamonby Cumb 108 F4
Lamorna Corn 2 D3
Lamorran Corn 3 B7
Lampardbrook Suff 57 C6
Lampeter = Llanbedr Pont Steffan Ceredig 46 E4
Lampeter Velfrey Pembs 32 C2
Lamphey Pembs 32 D1
Lamplugh Cumb 98 B2
Lamport Northants 53 B5
Lamyatt Som 23 F8
Lana Devon 8 E5
Lanark S Lanark 119 E8
Lancaster Lancs 92 C4
Lanchester Durham 110 E4
Lancing W Sus 17 D5
Landbeach Cambs 55 C5
Landcross Devon 9 B6
Landerberry Aberds 141 D6
Landford Wilts 14 C3
Landford Manor Wilts 14 B3
Landimore Swansea 33 E5
Landkey Devon 20 F4
Landore Swansea 33 E7
Landrake Corn 5 C8
Landscove Devon 7 C5
Landshipping Pembs 32 C1
Landshipping Quay Pembs 32 C1
Landulph Corn 6 C2
Landwade Suff 55 C7
Lane Corn 4 C3
Lane End Bucks 39 E8
Lane End Cumb 98 E3
Lane End Dorset 13 E6
Lane End Hants 15 B6
Lane End IoW 15 F7
Lane End Lancs 93 E8
Lane Ends Lancs 93 D7
Lane Ends Lancs 93 F7
Lane Ends N Yorks 94 E2
Lane Head Derbys 75 B8
Lane Head Durham 101 C6
Lane Head Gtr Man 86 E4
Lane Head W Yorks 88 D2
Lane Side Lancs 87 B5
Laneast Corn 8 F4
Laneham Notts 77 B8
Lanehead Durham 109 E8
Lanehead Northumb 116 F3
Lanercost Cumb 109 C5
Laneshaw Bridge Lancs 94 E2
Lanfach Caerph 35 E6
Langar Notts 77 F7
Langbank Renfs 118 B3
Langbar N Yorks 94 D3
Langburnshiels Borders 115 D8
Langcliffe N Yorks 93 C8
Langdale Highld 157 E9
Langdale End N Yorks 103 E7
Langdon Corn 8 F5
Langdon Beck Durham 109 F8
Langdon Hills Essex 42 F2
Langdyke Fife 128 D5
Langenhoe Essex 43 C6
Langford C Beds 54 E2
Langford Devon 10 D5
Langford Essex 42 D4
Langford Notts 77 D8
Langford Oxon 38 D2
Langford Budville Som 11 B6
Langham Essex 56 F4
Langham Norf 81 C6
Langham Rutland 64 C5
Langham Suff 56 C3
Langhaugh Borders 120 F5
Langho Lancs 93 F7
Langholm Dumfries 115 F6
Langleeford Northumb 117 B5
Langley Ches E 75 B6
Langley Hants 14 D5
Langley Herts 41 B5
Langley Kent 30 D2
Langley Northumb 109 C8
Langley Slough 27 B8
Langley W Sus 16 B2
Langley Warks 51 C6
Langley Burrell Wilts 24 B4
Langley Common Derbys 76 F2
Langley Heath Kent 30 D2
Langley Lower Green Essex 54 F5
Langley Marsh Som 11 B5
Langley Park Durham 110 E5
Langley Street Norf 69 D6
Langley Upper Green Essex 54 F5
Langney E Sus 18 E3
Langold Notts 89 F6
Langore Corn 8 F5
Langport Som 12 B2
Langrick Lincs 79 E5
Langridge Bath 24 C2
Langridge Ford Devon 9 B7
Langrigg Cumb 107 E8
Langrish Hants 15 B8
Langsett S Yorks 88 D3
Langshaw Borders 121 F8
Langside Perth 127 C6
Langskaill Orkney 159 D5
Langstone Hants 15 D8
Langstone Newport 35 E7
Langthorne N Yorks 101 E7
Langthorpe N Yorks 95 C6
Langthwaite N Yorks 101 D5
Langtoft E Yorks 97 C6
Langtoft Lincs 65 C8
Langton Durham 101 C6
Langton Lincs 78 C5
Langton Lincs 79 B6
Langton N Yorks 96 C3
Langton by Wragby Lincs 78 B4
Langton Green Kent 18 B2
Langton Green Suff 56 B5
Langton Herring Dorset 12 F4
Langton Matravers Dorset 13 G8
Langtree Devon 9 C6
Langwathby Cumb 109 F5
Langwell Ho. Highld 158 H3
Langwell Lodge Highld 156 J4
Langwith Derbys 76 C5
Langwith Junction Derbys 76 C5
Langworth Lincs 78 B3
Lanivet Corn 4 C5
Lanlivery Corn 5 D5
Lanner Corn 3 C6
Lanreath Corn 5 D6
Lansallos Corn 5 D6
Lansdown Glos 37 B6
Lanteglos Highway Corn 5 D6
Lanton Borders 116 B2
Lanton Northumb 122 F5
Lapford Devon 10 D2
Laphroaig Argyll 142 D4
Lapley Staffs 62 C2
Lapworth Warks 51 B6
Larachbeg Highld 147 G9
Larbert Falk 127 F7
Larden Green Ches E 74 D2
Largie Aberds 152 E6
Largiemore Argyll 145 E8
Largoward Fife 129 D6
Largs N Ayrs 118 D2
Largybeg N Ayrs 143 F11
Largymore N Ayrs 143 F11
Larkfield Invclyd 118 B2
Larkhall S Lanark 119 D7
Larkhill Wilts 25 E6
Larling Norf 68 F2
Larriston Borders 115 E8
Lartington Durham 101 C5
Lary Aberds 140 D2
Lasham Hants 26 E4
Lashenden Kent 30 E2
Lassington Glos 36 B4
Lassodie Fife 128 E3
Lastingham N Yorks 103 E5
Latcham Som 23 E6
Latchford Herts 41 B6
Latchford Warr 86 F4
Latchingdon Essex 42 D4
Latchley Corn 6 B2
Lately Common Warr 86 E4
Lathbury M Keynes 53 E6
Latheron Highld 158 G3
Latheronwheel Highld 158 G3
Latheronwheel Ho. Highld 158 G3
Lathones Fife 129 D6
Latimer Bucks 40 E3
Latteridge S Glos 36 F3
Lattiford Som 12 B4
Latton Wilts 37 E7
Latton Bush Essex 41 D7
Lauchintilly Aberds 141 C6
Lauder Borders 121 E8
Laugharne Carms 32 C4
Laughterton Lincs 77 B8
Laughton E Sus 18 D2
Laughton Leics 64 F3
Laughton Lincs 78 F3
Laughton Lincs 90 E2
Laughton Common S Yorks 89 F6
Laughton en le Morthen S Yorks 89 F6
Launcells Corn 8 D4
Launceston Corn 8 F5
Launton Oxon 39 B6
Laurencekirk Aberds 135 B7
Laurieston Dumfries 106 C3
Laurieston Falk 120 B2
Lavendon M Keynes 53 D7
Lavenham Suff 56 E3
Laverhay Dumfries 114 E4
Laversdale Cumb 108 C4
Laverstock Wilts 25 F6
Laverstoke Hants 26 E2
Laverton Glos 51 F5
Laverton N Yorks 94 B5
Laverton Som 24 D2
Lavister Wrex 73 D7
Law S Lanark 119 D8
Lawers Perth 127 B6
Lawers Perth 132 F3
Lawford Essex 56 F4
Lawhitton Corn 9 F5
Lawkland N Yorks 93 C7
Lawley Telford 61 D6
Lawnhead Staffs 62 B2
Lawrenny Pembs 32 D1
Lawshall Suff 56 D2
Lawton Hereford 49 D6
Laxey IoM 84 D4
Laxfield Suff 57 B6
Laxfirth Shetland 160 H6
Laxfirth Shetland 160 J6
Laxford Bridge Highld 156 E5
Laxo Shetland 160 G6
Laxobigging Shetland 160 F6
Laxton E Yorks 89 B8
Laxton Northants 65 E6
Laxton Notts 77 C7
Laycock W Yorks 94 E3
Layer Breton Essex 43 C5
Layer de la Haye Essex 43 C5
Layer Marney Essex 43 C5
Layham Suff 56 E4
Laylands Green W Berks 25 C8
Laytham E Yorks 96 F3
Layton Blackpool 92 F3
Lazenby Redcar 102 B3
Lazonby Cumb 108 F5
Le Planel Guern 16
Le Skerne Haughton Darl 101 C8
Le Villocq Guern 16
Lea Derbys 76 D3
Lea Hereford 36 B3
Lea Lincs 90 F2
Lea Shrops 60 D4
Lea Shrops 60 F3
Lea Wilts 37 F6
Lea Marston Warks 63 E6
Lea Town Lancs 92 F4
Leabrooks Derbys 76 D4
Leac a Li W Isles 154 H6
Leachkin Highld 151 G9
Leadburn Midloth 120 D5
Leaden Roding Essex 42 C1
Leadenham Lincs 78 D2
Leadgate Cumb 109 E7
Leadgate Durham 110 D4
Leadgate T&W 110 D4
Leadhills S Lanark 113 C8
Leafield Oxon 38 C3
Leagrave Luton 40 B3
Leake N Yorks 102 E2
Leake Commonside Lincs 79 D6
Lealholm N Yorks 103 D5
Lealt Argyll 144 D5
Lealt Highld 149 B10
Leamington Hastings Warks 52 C2
Leamonsley Staffs 62 D5
Leamside Durham 111 E6
Leanaig Highld 151 F8
Leargybreck Argyll 144 F4
Leasgill Cumb 99 F6
Leasingham Lincs 78 E3
Leasingthorne Durham 101 B7
Leasowe Mers 85 E3
Leatherhead Sur 28 D2
Leatherhead Common Sur 28 D2
Leathley N Yorks 94 E5
Leaton Shrops 60 C4
Leaveland Kent 30 D4
Leavening N Yorks 96 C3
Leaves Green London 28 C5
Leazes Durham 110 D4
Lebberston N Yorks 103 F8
Lechlade-on-Thames Glos 38 E2
Leck Lancs 93 B6
Leckford Hants 25 F8
Leckfurin Highld 157 D10
Leckgruinart Argyll 142 B3
Leckhampstead Bucks 52 F5
Leckhampstead W Berks 26 B2
Leckhampstead Thicket W Berks 26 B2
Leckhampton Glos 37 C6
Leckie Highld 150 E3
Leckmelm Highld 150 B4
Leckwith V Glam 22 B3
Leconfield E Yorks 97 E6
Ledaig Argyll 124 B5
Ledburn Bucks 40 B2
Ledbury Hereford 50 F2
Ledcharrie Stirling 126 B4
Ledgemoor Hereford 49 D6
Ledicot Hereford 49 C6
Ledmore Highld 156 H5
Lednagullin Highld 157 C10
Ledsham Ches W 73 B7
Ledsham W Yorks 89 B5
Ledston W Yorks 88 B5
Ledston Luck W Yorks 95 F7
Ledwell Oxon 38 B4
Lee Argyll 146 J7
Lee Devon 20 E3
Lee Hants 14 C4
Lee Lancs 93 D5
Lee Shrops 73 F8
Lee Brockhurst Shrops 60 B5
Lee Clump Bucks 40 D2
Lee Mill Devon 6 D4
Lee Moor Devon 6 C3
Lee-on-the-Solent Hants 15 D6
Leeans Shetland 160 J5
Leebotten Shetland 160 L6
Leebotwood Shrops 60 E4
Leece Cumb 92 C2
Leechpool Pembs 44 D4
Leeds Kent 30 D2
Leeds W Yorks 95 F5
Leedstown Corn 2 C5
Leek Staffs 75 D6
Leek Wootton Warks 51 C7
Leekbrook Staffs 75 D6
Leeming N Yorks 101 F7
Leeming Bar N Yorks 101 E7
Lees Derbys 76 F2
Lees Gtr Man 87 D7
Lees W Yorks 94 F3
Leeswood Flint 73 C6
Legbourne Lincs 91 F7
Legerwood Borders 121 E8
Legsby Lincs 90 F5
Leicester Leicester 64 D2
Leicester Forest East Leics 64 D2
Leigh Dorset 12 D4
Leigh Glos 37 B5
Leigh Gtr Man 86 D4
Leigh Kent 29 E6
Leigh Shrops 60 D3
Leigh Sur 28 E3
Leigh Wilts 37 E7
Leigh Worcs 50 D2
Leigh Beck Essex 42 F4
Leigh Common Som 12 B5
Leigh Delamere Wilts 24 B3
Leigh Green Kent 19 B6
Leigh on Sea Southend 42 F4
Leigh Park Hants 15 D8
Leigh Sinton Worcs 50 D2
Leigh upon Mendip Som 23 E8
Leigh Woods N Som 23 B7
Leighswood W Mid 62 D4
Leighterton Glos 37 E5
Leighton N Yorks 94 B4
Leighton Powys 60 D2
Leighton Shrops 61 D6
Leighton Som 24 E2
Leighton Bromswold Cambs 54 B2
Leighton Buzzard C Beds 40 B2
Leinthall Earls Hereford 49 C6
Leinthall Starkes Hereford 49 C6
Leintwardine Hereford 49 B6
Leire Leics 64 E2
Leirinmore Highld 156 C7
Leiston Suff 57 C8
Leitfie Perth 134 E2
Leith Edin 121 B5
Leitholm Borders 122 E3
Lelant Corn 2 C4
Lelley E Yorks 97 F8
Lem Hill Worcs 50 B2
Lemmington Hall Northumb 117 C7
Lempitlaw Borders 122 F3
Lenchwick Worcs 50 E5
Lendalfoot S Ayrs 112 F1
Lendrick Lodge Stirling 126 D4
Lenham Kent 30 D2
Lenham Heath Kent 30 E3
Lennel Borders 122 E4
Lennoxtown E Dunb 119 B6
Lenton Lincs 78 F3
Lenton Nottingham 77 F5
Lentran Highld 151 G8
Lenwade Norf 68 C3
Leny Ho. Stirling 126 D5
Lenzie E Dunb 119 B6
Leoch Angus 134 F3
Leochel-Cushnie Aberds 140 C4
Leominster Hereford 49 D6
Leonard Stanley Glos 37 D5
Leorin Argyll 142 D4
Lepe Hants 15 E5
Lephin Highld 148 D6
Lephinchapel Argyll 145 D8
Lephinmore Argyll 145 D8
Leppington N Yorks 96 C3
Lepton W Yorks 88 C3
Lerryn Corn 5 D6
Lerwick Shetland 160 J6
Lesbury Northumb 117 C8
Leslie Aberds 140 B4
Leslie Fife 128 D4
Lesmahagow S Lanark 119 F8
Lesnewth Corn 8 E3
Lessendrum Aberds 152 D5
Lessingham Norf 69 B6
Lessonhall Cumb 108 D2
Leswalt Dumfries 104 C4
Letchmore Heath Herts 40 E4
Letchworth Herts 54 F3
Letcombe Bassett Oxon 38 F3
Letcombe Regis Oxon 38 F3
Letham Angus 135 E5
Letham Falk 127 F7
Letham Fife 128 C5
Letham Perth 128 B2
Letham Grange Angus 135 E6
Lethenty Aberds 153 D8
Letheringham Suff 57 D6
Letheringsett Norf 81 D6
Lettaford Devon 10 F2
Lettan Orkney 159 D8
Letterewe Highld 150 D2
Letterfearn Highld 149 F13
Letterfinlay Highld 137 E5
Lettermorar Highld 147 C10
Lettermore Argyll 146 G7
Letters Highld 150 C4
Letterston Pembs 44 C4
Lettoch Highld 139 C6
Lettoch Highld 151 H13
Letton Hereford 48 E5
Letton Hereford 49 B5
Letton Green Norf 68 D2
Letty Green Herts 41 C5
Letwell S Yorks 89 F6
Leuchars Fife 129 B6
Leuchars Ho. Moray 152 B2
Leumrabhagh W Isles 155 F8
Levan Invclyd 118 B2
Levaneap Shetland 160 G6
Levedale Staffs 62 C2
Leven E Yorks 97 E7
Leven Fife 129 D5
Levencorroch N Ayrs 143 F11
Levens Cumb 99 F6
Levens Green Herts 41 B6
Levenshulme Gtr Man 87 E6
Levenwick Shetland 160 L6
Leverburgh = An t-Ob W Isles 154 J5
Leverington Cambs 66 C4
Leverton Lincs 79 E7
Leverton Highgate Lincs 79 E7
Leverton Lucasgate Lincs 79 E7
Leverton Outgate Lincs 79 E7
Levington Suff 57 F6
Levisham N Yorks 103 E6
Levishie Highld 137 C7
Lew Oxon 38 D3
Lewannick Corn 8 F4
Lewdown Devon 9 F6
Lewes E Sus 17 C8
Leweston Pembs 44 C4
Lewisham London 28 B4
Lewiston Highld 137 B8
Lewistown Bridgend 34 F3
Lewknor Oxon 39 E7
Leworthy Devon 8 D5
Leworthy Devon 21 F5
Lewtrenchard Devon 9 F6
Lexden Essex 43 B5
Ley Aberds 140 C4
Ley Corn 5 C6
Leybourne Kent 29 D7
Leyburn N Yorks 101 E6
Leyfields Staffs 63 D6
Leyhill Bucks 40 D2
Leyland Lancs 86 B3
Leylodge Aberds 141 C6
Leymoor W Yorks 88 C2
Leys Aberds 153 C10
Leys Perth 134 F2
Leys Castle Highld 151 G9
Leys of Cossans Angus 134 E3
Leysdown-on-Sea Kent 30 B4
Leysmill Angus 135 E6
Leysters Pole Hereford 49 C7
Leyton London 41 F6
Leytonstone London 41 F6
Lezant Corn 5 B8
Leziate Norf 67 C6
Lhanbryde Moray 152 B2
Liatrie Highld 150 H5
Libanus Powys 34 B3
Libberton S Lanark 120 E2
Liberton Edin 121 C5
Liceasto W Isles 154 H6
Lichfield Staffs 62 D5
Lickey Worcs 50 B4
Lickey End Worcs 50 B4
Lickfold W Sus 16 B3
Liddel Orkney 159 K5
Liddesdale Highld 130 D1
Liddington Swindon 38 F2
Lidgate Suff 55 D8
Lidget S Yorks 89 D7
Lidget Green W Yorks 94 F4
Lidgett Notts 77 C6
Lidlington C Beds 53 F7
Lidstone Oxon 38 B3
Lieurary Highld 158 D2
Liff Angus 134 F3
Lifton Devon 9 F5
Liftondown Devon 9 F5
Lighthorne Warks 51 D8
Lightwater Sur 27 C7
Lightwood Stoke 75 E6
Lightwood Green Ches E 74 E3
Lightwood Green Wrex 73 E7
Lilbourne Northants 52 B3
Lilburn Tower Northumb 117 B6
Lilleshall Telford 61 C7
Lilley Herts 40 B4
Lilley W Berks 26 B2
Lilliesleaf Borders 115 B8
Lillingstone Dayrell Bucks 52 F5
Lillingstone Lovell Bucks 52 E5
Lillington Dorset 12 C4
Lillington Warks 51 C8
Lilliput Poole 13 E8
Lilstock Som 22 E3
Lilyhurst Shrops 61 C7
Limbury Luton 40 B3
Limebrook Hereford 49 C5
Limefield Gtr Man 87 C6
Limekilnburn S Lanark 119 D7
Limekilns Fife 128 F2
Limerigg Falk 119 B8
Limerstone IoW 14 F5
Limington Som 12 B3
Limpenhoe Norf 69 D6
Limpley Stoke Wilts 24 C2
Limpsfield Sur 28 D5
Limpsfield Chart Sur 28 D5
Linby Notts 76 D5
Linchmere W Sus 27 F6
Lincluden Dumfries 107 B6
Lincoln Lincs 78 B2
Lincomb Worcs 50 C3
Lincombe Devon 6 D5
Lindal in Furness Cumb 92 B2
Lindale Cumb 99 F6
Lindean Borders 121 F7
Lindfield W Sus 17 B7
Lindford Hants 27 F6
Lindifferon Fife 128 C5
Lindley W Yorks 88 C2
Lindley Green N Yorks 94 E5
Lindores Fife 128 C4
Lindridge Worcs 49 C8
Lindsell Essex 42 B2
Lindsey Suff 56 E3
Linford Hants 14 D2
Linford Thurrock 29 B7
Lingague IoM 84 E2
Lingards Wood W Yorks 87 C8
Lingbob W Yorks 94 F3
Lingdale Redcar 102 C4
Lingen Hereford 49 C5
Lingfield Sur 28 E4
Lingreabhagh W Isles 154 J5
Lingwood Norf 69 D6
Linicro Highld 149 B8
Linkenholt Hants 25 D8
Linkhill Kent 18 C5
Linkinhorne Corn 5 B8
Linklater Orkney 159 K5
Linksness Orkney 159 H3
Linktown Fife 128 E4
Linley Shrops 60 E3
Linley Green Hereford 49 D8
Linlithgow W Loth 120 B3
Linlithgow Bridge W Loth 120 B2
Linshiels Northumb 116 D4
Linsiadar W Isles 154 D7
Linsidemore Highld 151 B8
Linslade C Beds 40 B2
Linstead Parva Suff 57 B7
Linstock Cumb 108 D4
Linthwaite W Yorks 88 C2
Lintlaw Borders 122 D4
Lintmill Moray 152 B5
Linton Borders 116 B3
Linton Cambs 55 E6
Linton Derbys 63 C6
Linton Hereford 36 B3
Linton Kent 29 E8
Linton N Yorks 94 C2
Linton Northumb 117 E8
Linton W Yorks 95 E6
Linton-on-Ouse N Yorks 95 C7
Linwood Hants 14 D2
Linwood Lincs 90 F5
Linwood Renfs 118 C4
Lionacleit W Isles 148 D2
Lional W Isles 155 A10
Liphook Hants 27 F6
Liscard Mers 85 E4
Liscombe Som 21 F7
Liskeard Corn 5 C7
L'Islet Guern 16
Liss Hants 15 B8
Liss Forest Hants 15 B8
Lissett E Yorks 97 D7
Lissington Lincs 90 F5
Lisvane Cardiff 35 F5
Liswerry Newport 35 F7
Litcham Norf 67 C8
Litchborough Northants 52 D4
Litchfield Hants 26 D2
Litherland Mers 85 E4
Litlington Cambs 54 E4
Litlington E Sus 18 E2
Little Abington Cambs 55 E6
Little Addington Northants 53 B7
Little Alne Warks 51 C6
Little Altcar Mers 85 D4
Little Asby Cumb 100 D1
Little Assynt Highld 156 G4
Little Aston Staffs 62 D4
Little Atherfield IoW 15 F5
Little Ayre Orkney 159 J4
Little-ayre Shetland 160 G5
Little Ayton N Yorks 102 C3
Little Baddow Essex 42 D3
Little Badminton S Glos 37 F5
Little Ballinluig Perth 133 D6
Little Bampton Cumb 108 D2
Little Bardfield Essex 55 F7
Little Barford Bedford 54 D2
Little Barningham Norf 81 D7
Little Barrington Glos 38 C2
Little Barrow Ches W 73 B8
Little Barugh N Yorks 96 B3
Little Bavington Northumb 110 B2
Little Bealings Suff 57 E6
Little Bedwyn Wilts 25 C7
Little Bentley Essex 43 B7
Little Berkhamsted Herts 41 D5
Little Billing Northants 53 C6
Little Birch Hereford 49 F7
Little Blakenham Suff 56 E5
Little Blencow Cumb 108 F4
Little Bollington Ches E 86 F5
Little Bookham Sur 28 D2
Little Bowden Leics 64 F4
Little Bradley Suff 55 D7
Little Brampton Shrops 60 F3
Little Brechin Angus 135 C5
Little Brickhill M Keynes 53 F7
Little Brington Northants 52 C4
Little Bromley Essex 43 B6
Little Broughton Cumb 107 F7
Little Budworth Ches W 74 C2
Little Burstead Essex 42 E2
Little Bytham Lincs 65 C7
Little Carlton Lincs 91 F7
Little Carlton Notts 77 D7
Little Casterton Rutland 65 D7
Little Cawthorpe Lincs 91 F7
Little Chalfont Bucks 40 E2
Little Chart Kent 30 E3
Little Chesterford Essex 55 E6
Little Cheverell Wilts 24 D4
Little Chishill Cambs 54 F5
Little Clacton Essex 43 C7
Little Clifton Cumb 98 B2
Little Colp Aberds 153 D7
Little Comberton Worcs 50 E4
Little Common E Sus 18 E4
Little Compton Warks 51 F7
Little Cornard Suff 56 F2
Little Cowarne Hereford 49 D8
Little Coxwell Oxon 38 E2
Little Crakehall N Yorks 101 E7
Little Cressingham Norf 67 D8
Little Crosby Mers 85 D4
Little Dalby Leics 64 C4
Little Dawley Telford 61 D6
Little Dens Aberds 153 D10
Little Dewchurch Hereford 49 F7
Little Downham Cambs 66 F5
Little Driffield E Yorks 97 D6
Little Dunham Norf 67 C8
Little Dunkeld Perth 133 E7
Little Dunmow Essex 42 B2
Little Easton Essex 42 B2
Little Eaton Derbys 76 E3
Little Eccleston Lancs 92 E4
Little Ellingham Norf 68 E3
Little End Essex 41 D8
Little Eversden Cambs 54 D4
Little Faringdon Oxon 38 D2
Little Fencote N Yorks 101 E7
Little Fenton N Yorks 95 F8
Little Finborough Suff 56 D4
Little Fransham Norf 68 C2
Little Gaddesden Herts 40 C2
Little Gidding Cambs 65 F8
Little Glemham Suff 57 D7
Little Glenshee Perth 133 F6
Little Gransden Cambs 54 D3
Little Green Som 24 E2
Little Grimsby Lincs 91 E7
Little Gruinard Highld 150 C2
Little Habton N Yorks 96 B3
Little Hadham Herts 41 B7
Little Hale Lincs 78 E4
Little Hallingbury Essex 41 C7
Little Hampden Bucks 40 D1
Little Harrowden Northants 53 B6
Little Haseley Oxon 39 D6
Little Hatfield E Yorks 97 E7
Little Hautbois Norf 81 E8
Little Haven Pembs 44 D3
Little Hay Staffs 62 D5
Little Hayfield Derbys 87 F8
Little Haywood Staffs 62 B4
Little Heath W Mid 63 F7
Little Hereford Hereford 49 C7
Little Horkesley Essex 56 F3
Little Horsted E Sus 17 C8
Little Horton W Yorks 94 F4
Little Horwood Bucks 53 F5
Little Houghton Northants 53 D6
Little Houghton S Yorks 88 D5
Little Hucklow Derbys 75 B8
Little Hulton Gtr Man 86 D5
Little Humber E Yorks 91 B5
Little Hungerford W Berks 26 B3
Little Irchester Northants 53 C7
Little Kimble Bucks 39 D8
Little Kineton Warks 51 D8
Little Kingshill Bucks 40 E1
Little Langdale Cumb 99 D5
Little Langford Wilts 25 F5
Little Laver Essex 41 D8
Little Leigh Ches W 74 B3
Little Leighs Essex 42 C3
Little Lever Gtr Man 87 D5
Little London Bucks 39 C6
Little London E Sus 18 D2
Little London Hants 25 E8
Little London Hants 26 D4
Little London Lincs 66 B2
Little London Lincs 66 B4
Little London Norf 81 E7
Little London Powys 59 F7
Little Longstone Derbys 75 B8
Little Lynturk Aberds 140 C4
Little Malvern Worcs 50 E2
Little Maplestead Essex 56 F2
Little Marcle Hereford 49 F8
Little Marlow Bucks 40 F1
Little Marsden Lancs 93 F8
Little Massingham Norf 80 E3
Little Melton Norf 68 D4
Little Mill Mon 35 D7
Little Milton Oxon 39 D6
Little Missenden Bucks 40 E2
Little Musgrave Cumb 100 C2
Little Ness Shrops 60 C4
Little Neston Ches W 73 B6
Little Newcastle Pembs 44 C4
Little Newsham Durham 101 C6
Little Oakley Essex 43 B8
Little Oakley Northants 65 F5
Little Orton Cumb 108 D3
Little Ouseburn N Yorks 95 C7
Little Paxton Cambs 54 C2
Little Petherick Corn 4 B4
Little Pitlurg Moray 152 D4
Little Plumpton Lancs 92 F3
Little Plumstead Norf 69 C6
Little Ponton Lincs 78 F2
Little Raveley Cambs 54 B3
Little Reedness E Yorks 90 B2
Little Ribston N Yorks 95 D6
Little Rissington Glos 38 C1
Little Ryburgh Norf 81 E5
Little Ryle Northumb 117 C6
Little Salkeld Cumb 109 F5
Little Sampford Essex 55 F7
Little Sandhurst Brack 27 C6
Little Saxham Suff 55 C8
Little Scatwell Highld 150 F6
Little Sessay N Yorks 95 B7
Little Shelford Cambs 54 D5
Little Singleton Lancs 92 F3
Little Skillymarno Aberds 153 C9
Little Smeaton N Yorks 89 C6
Little Snoring Norf 81 D5
Little Sodbury S Glos 36 F4
Little Somborne Hants 25 F8
Little Somerford Wilts 37 F6
Little Stainforth N Yorks 93 C8
Little Stainton Darl 101 B8
Little Stanney Ches W 73 B8
Little Staughton Bedford 54 C2
Little Steeping Lincs 79 C7
Little Stoke Staffs 75 F6
Little Stonham Suff 56 C5
Little Stretton Leics 64 D3
Little Stretton Shrops 60 E4
Little Strickland Cumb 99 C7
Little Stukeley Cambs 54 B3
Little Sutton Ches W 73 B7
Little Tew Oxon 38 B3
Little Thetford Cambs 55 B6
Little Thirkleby N Yorks 95 B7
Little Thurlow Suff 55 D7
Little Thurrock Thurrock 29 B7
Little Torboll Highld 151 B10
Little Torrington Devon 9 C6
Little Totham Essex 42 C4
Little Toux Aberds 152 C5
Little Town Cumb 98 C4
Little Town Lancs 93 F6
Little Urswick Cumb 92 B2
Little Wakering Essex 43 F5
Little Walden Essex 55 E6
Little Waldingfield Suff 56 E3
Little Walsingham Norf 80 D5
Little Waltham Essex 42 C3
Little Warley Essex 42 E2
Little Weighton E Yorks 97 F5
Little Weldon Northants 65 F6
Little Welnetham Suff 56 C2
Little Wenlock Telford 61 D6
Little Whittingham Green Suff 57 B6
Little Wilbraham Cambs 55 D6
Little Wishford Wilts 25 F5
Little Witley Worcs 50 C2
Little Wittenham Oxon 39 E5
Little Wolford Warks 51 F7
Little Wratting Suff 55 E7
Little Wymington Bedford 53 C7
Little Wymondley Herts 41 B5
Little Wyrley Staffs 62 D4
Little Yeldham Essex 55 F8
Littlebeck N Yorks 103 D6
Littleborough Gtr Man 87 C7
Littleborough Notts 90 F2
Littlebourne Kent 31 D6
Littlebredy Dorset 12 F3
Littlebury Essex 55 F6
Littlebury Green Essex 55 F5
Littledean Glos 36 C3
Littleferry Highld 151 B11
Littleham Devon 9 B6
Littleham Devon 10 F5
Littlehampton W Sus 16 D4
Littlehempston Devon 7 C6
Littlehoughton Northumb 117 C8
Littlemill Aberds 140 E2
Littlemill E Ayrs 112 C4
Littlemill Highld 151 F12
Littlemill Northumb 117 C8
Littlemoor Dorset 12 F4
Littlemore Oxon 39 D5
Littleover Derby 76 F3
Littleport Cambs 67 F5
Littlestone on Sea Kent 19 C7
Littlethorpe Leics 64 E2
Littlethorpe N Yorks 95 C6
Littleton Ches W 73 C8
Littleton Hants 26 F2
Littleton Perth 134 F2
Littleton Som 23 F6
Littleton Sur 27 C8
Littleton Sur 27 E7
Littleton Drew Wilts 37 F5
Littleton-on-Severn S Glos 36 F2
Littleton Pannell Wilts 24 D5
Littletown Durham 111 E6
Littlewick Green Windsor 27 B6
Littleworth Bedford 53 E8
Littleworth Glos 37 D5
Littleworth Oxon 38 E3
Littleworth Staffs 62 C4
Littleworth Worcs 50 D3
Litton Derbys 75 B8
Litton N Yorks 94 B2
Litton Som 23 D7
Litton Cheney Dorset 12 E3
Liurbost W Isles 155 E8
Liverpool Mers 85 E4
Liverpool Airport Mers 86 F2
Liversedge W Yorks 88 B3
Liverton Devon 7 B6
Liverton Redcar 103 C5
Livingston W Loth 120 C3
Livingston Village W Loth 120 C3
Lixwm Flint 73 B5
Lizard Corn 3 E6
Llaingoch Anglesey 82 C2
Llaithddu Powys 59 F7
Llan Powys 59 D5
Llan Ffestiniog Gwyn 71 C8
Llan-y-pwll Wrex 73 D7
Llanaber Gwyn 58 C3
Llanaelhaearn Gwyn 70 C4
Llanafan Ceredig 47 B5
Llanafan-fawr Powys 47 D8
Llanallgo Anglesey 82 C4
Llanandras = Presteigne Powys 48 C5
Llanarmon Gwyn 70 D5
Llanarmon Dyffryn Ceiriog Wrex 73 F5
Llanarmon-yn-Ial Denb 73 D5
Llanarth Ceredig 46 D3
Llanarth Mon 35 C7
Llanarthne Carms 33 B6
Llanasa Flint 85 F2
Llanbabo Anglesey 82 C3
Llanbadarn Fawr Ceredig 58 F3

Manar Ho. Aberds 141 B6
Manaton Devon 10 F2
Manby Lincs 91 F7
Mancetter Warks 63 E7
Manchester Gtr Man 87 E6
Manchester Airport Gtr Man 87 F6
Mancot Flint 73 C7
Mandally Highld 137 D5
Manea Cambs 66 F4
Manfield N Yorks 101 C7
Mangaster Shetland 160 F5
Mangotsfield S Glos 23 B8
Mangurstadh W Isles 154 D5
Mankinholes W Yorks 87 B7
Manley Ches W 74 B2
Mannal Argyll 146 G2
Mannerston W Loth 120 B3
Manningford Bohune Wilts 25 D6
Manningford Bruce Wilts 25 D6
Manningham W Yorks 94 F4
Mannings Heath W Sus 17 B6
Mannington Dorset 13 D8
Manningtree Essex 56 F4
Mannofield Aberdeen 141 D8
Manor London 41 F7
Manor Estate S Yorks 88 F4
Manorbier Pembs 32 E1
Manordeilo Carms 33 B7
Manorhill Borders 122 F2
Manorowen Pembs 44 B4
Mansel Lacy Hereford 49 E6
Manselfield Swansea 33 F6
Mansell Gamage Hereford 49 E5
Mansergh Cumb 99 F8
Mansfield E Ayrs 113 C6
Mansfield Notts 76 C5
Mansfield Woodhouse Notts 76 C5
Mansriggs Cumb 98 F4
Manston Dorset 13 C6
Manston Kent 31 C7
Manston W Yorks 95 F6
Manswood Dorset 13 D7
Manthorpe Lincs 65 C7
Manthorpe Lincs 78 F2
Manton N Lincs 90 D3
Manton Notts 77 B5
Manton Rutland 65 D5
Manton Wilts 25 C6
Manuden Essex 41 B7
Maperton Som 12 B4
Maple Cross Herts 40 E3
Maplebeck Notts 77 C7
Mapledurham Oxon 26 B4
Mapledurwell Hants 26 D4
Maplehurst W Sus 17 B5
Maplescombe Kent 29 C6
Mapleton Derbys 75 E8
Mapperley Derbys 76 E4
Mapperley Park Nottingham 77 E5
Mapperton Dorset 12 E3
Mappleborough Green Warks 51 C5
Mappleton E Yorks 97 E8
Mappowder Dorset 12 D5
Mar Lodge Aberds 139 E6
Maraig W Isles 154 G6
Marazanvose Corn 4 D3
Marazion Corn 2 C4
Marbhig W Isles 155 F9
Marbury Ches E 74 E2
March Cambs 66 E4
March S Lanark 114 C2
Marcham Oxon 38 E4
Marchamley Shrops 61 B5
Marchington Staffs 75 F8
Marchington Woodlands Staffs 62 B5
Marchroes Gwyn 70 E4
Marchwiel Wrex 73 E7
Marchwood Hants 14 C4
Marcross V Glam 21 C8
Marden Hereford 49 E7
Marden Kent 29 E8
Marden T&W 111 B6
Marden Wilts 25 D5
Marden Beech Kent 29 E8
Marden Thorn Kent 29 E8
Mardy Mon 35 C7
Marefield Leics 64 D4
Mareham le Fen Lincs 79 C5
Mareham on the Hill Lincs 79 C5
Marehay Derbys 76 E3
Marehill W Sus 16 C4
Maresfield E Sus 17 B8
Marfleet Hull 90 B5
Marford Wrex 73 D7
Margam Neath 34 F1
Margaret Marsh Dorset 13 C6
Margaret Roding Essex 42 C1
Margaretting Essex 42 D2
Margate Kent 31 B7
Margnaheglish N Ayrs 143 E11
Margrove Park Redcar 102 C4
Marham Norf 67 C7
Marhamchurch Corn 8 D4
Marholm Pboro 65 D8
Mariandyrys Anglesey 83 C6
Marianglas Anglesey 82 C5
Mariansleigh Devon 10 B2
Marionburgh Aberds 141 D6
Marishader Highld 149 B9
Marjoriebanks Dumfries 114 F3
Mark Dumfries 104 D5
Mark S Ayrs 104 B4
Mark Som 23 E5
Mark Causeway Som 23 E5
Mark Cross E Sus 17 C8
Mark Cross E Sus 18 B2
Markbeech Kent 29 E5
Markby Lincs 79 B7
Market Bosworth Leics 63 D8
Market Deeping Lincs 65 D8
Market Drayton Shrops 74 F3
Market Harborough Leics 64 F4
Market Lavington Wilts 24 D5
Market Overton Rutland 65 C5
Market Rasen Lincs 90 F5
Market Stainton Lincs 78 B5
Market Warsop Notts 77 C5
Market Weighton E Yorks 96 E4
Market Weston Suff 56 B3
Markethill Perth 134 F2
Markfield Leics 63 C8
Markham Caerph 35 D5
Markham Moor Notts 77 B7
Markinch Fife 128 D4
Markington N Yorks 95 C5
Marks Tey Essex 43 B5
Marksbury Bath 23 C8
Markyate Herts 40 C3
Marland Gtr Man 87 C6
Marlborough Wilts 25 C6
Marlbrook Hereford 49 D7
Marlbrook Worcs 50 B4
Marlcliff Warks 51 D5
Marldon Devon 7 C6
Marlesford Suff 57 D7
Marley Green Ches E 74 E2
Marley Hill T&W 110 D5
Marley Mount Hants 14 E3
Marlingford Norf 68 D4
Marloes Pembs 44 E2
Marlow Bucks 39 F8
Marlow Hereford 49 B6
Marlow Bottom Bucks 40 F1
Marlpit Hill Kent 28 E5
Marlpool Derbys 76 E4
Marnhull Dorset 13 C5
Marnoch Aberds 152 C5
Marnock N Lanark 119 C7
Marple Gtr Man 87 F7
Marple Bridge Gtr Man 87 F7
Marr S Yorks 89 D6
Marrel Highld 157 H13
Marrick N Yorks 101 E5
Marrister Shetland 160 G7
Marros Carms 32 D3
Marsden T&W 111 C6
Marsden W Yorks 87 C8
Marsett N Yorks 100 F4
Marsh Devon 11 C7
Marsh W Yorks 94 F3
Marsh Baldon Oxon 39 E5
Marsh Gibbon Bucks 39 B6
Marsh Green Devon 10 E5
Marsh Green Kent 28 E5
Marsh Green Staffs 75 D5
Marsh Lane Derbys 76 B4
Marsh Street Som 21 E8
Marshall's Heath Herts 40 C4
Marshalsea Dorset 11 D8
Marshalswick Herts 40 D4
Marsham Norf 81 E7
Marshaw Lancs 93 D5
Marshborough Kent 31 D7
Marshbrook Shrops 60 F4
Marshchapel Lincs 91 E7
Marshfield Newport 35 F6
Marshfield S Glos 24 B2
Marshgate Corn 8 E3
Marshland St James Norf 66 D5
Marshside Mers 85 C4
Marshwood Dorset 11 E8
Marske N Yorks 101 D6
Marske-by-the-Sea Redcar 102 B4
Marston Ches W 74 B3
Marston Hereford 49 D5
Marston Lincs 77 E8
Marston Oxon 39 D5
Marston Staffs 62 B3
Marston Staffs 62 C2
Marston Warks 63 E6
Marston Wilts 24 D4
Marston Doles Warks 52 D2
Marston Green W Mid 63 F5
Marston Magna Som 12 B3
Marston Meysey Wilts 37 E8
Marston Montgomery Derbys 75 F8
Marston Moretaine C Beds 53 E7
Marston on Dove Derbys 63 B6
Marston St Lawrence Northants 52 E3
Marston Stannett Hereford 49 D7
Marston Trussell Northants 64 F3
Marstow Hereford 36 C2
Marsworth Bucks 40 C2
Marten Wilts 25 D7
Marthall Ches E 74 B5
Martham Norf 69 C7
Martin Hants 13 C8
Martin Kent 31 E7
Martin Lincs 78 C5
Martin Lincs 78 D4
Martin Dales Lincs 78 C4
Martin Drove End Hants 13 B8
Martin Hussingtree Worcs 50 C3
Martin Mill Kent 31 E7
Martinhoe Devon 21 E5
Martinhoe Cross Devon 21 E5
Martinscroft Warr 86 F4
Martinstown Dorset 12 F4
Martlesham Suff 57 E6
Martlesham Heath Suff 57 E6
Martletwy Pembs 32 C1
Martley Worcs 50 D2
Martock Som 12 C2
Marton Ches E 75 C5
Marton E Yorks 97 F7
Marton Lincs 90 F2
Marton Mbro 102 C3
Marton N Yorks 95 C7
Marton N Yorks 103 F5
Marton Shrops 60 B4
Marton Shrops 60 D2
Marton Warks 52 C2
Marton-le-Moor N Yorks 95 B6
Martyr Worthy Hants 26 F3
Martyr's Green Sur 27 D8
Marwick Orkney 159 F3
Marwood Devon 20 F4
Mary Tavy Devon 6 B3
Marybank Highld 150 F7
Maryburgh Highld 151 F8
Maryhill Glasgow 119 C5
Marykirk Aberds 135 C6
Marylebone Gtr Man 86 D3
Marypark Moray 152 E1
Maryport Cumb 107 F7
Maryport Dumfries 104 F5
Maryton Angus 135 D6
Marywell Aberds 140 E4
Marywell Aberds 141 E8
Marywell Angus 135 E6
Masham N Yorks 101 F7
Mashbury Essex 42 C2
Masongill N Yorks 93 B6
Masonhill S Ayrs 112 B3
Mastin Moor Derbys 76 B4
Mastrick Aberdeen 141 D7
Matching Essex 41 C8
Matching Green Essex 41 C8
Matching Tye Essex 41 C8
Matfen Northumb 110 B3
Matfield Kent 29 E7
Mathern Mon 36 E2
Mathon Hereford 50 E2
Mathry Pembs 44 B3
Matlaske Norf 81 D7
Matlock Derbys 76 C2
Matlock Bath Derbys 76 D2
Matson Glos 37 C5
Matterdale End Cumb 99 B5
Mattersey Notts 89 F7
Mattersey Thorpe Notts 89 F7
Mattingley Hants 26 D5
Mattishall Norf 68 C3
Mattishall Burgh Norf 68 C3
Mauchline E Ayrs 112 B4
Maud Aberds 153 D9
Maugersbury Glos 38 B2
Maughold IoM 84 C4
Mauld Highld 150 H7
Maulden C Beds 53 F8
Maulds Meaburn Cumb 99 C8
Maunby N Yorks 102 F1
Maund Bryan Hereford 49 D7
Maundown Som 11 B5
Mautby Norf 69 C7
Mavis Enderby Lincs 79 C6
Maw Green Ches E 74 D4
Mawbray Cumb 107 E7
Mawdesley Lancs 86 C2
Mawdlam Bridgend 34 F2
Mawgan Corn 3 D6
Mawla Corn 3 B6
Mawnan Corn 3 D6
Mawnan Smith Corn 3 D6
Mawsley Northants 53 B6
Maxey Pboro 65 D8
Maxstoke Warks 63 F6
Maxton Borders 122 F2
Maxton Kent 31 E7
Maxwellheugh Borders 122 F3
Maxwelltown Dumfries 107 B6
Maxworthy Corn 8 E4
May Bank Staffs 75 E5
Mayals Swansea 33 E7
Maybole S Ayrs 112 D3
Mayfield E Sus 18 C2
Mayfield Midloth 121 C6
Mayfield Staffs 75 E8
Mayfield W Loth 120 C2
Mayford Sur 27 D7
Mayland Essex 43 D5
Maynard's Green E Sus 18 D2
Maypole Mon 36 C1
Maypole Scilly 2 E4
Maypole Green Essex 43 B5
Maypole Green Norf 69 E7
Maypole Green Suff 57 C6
Maywick Shetland 160 L5
Meadle Bucks 39 D8
Meadowtown Shrops 60 D3
Meaford Staffs 75 F5
Meal Bank Cumb 99 E7
Mealabost W Isles 155 D9
Mealabost Bhuirgh W Isles 155 B9
Mealsgate Cumb 108 E2
Meanwood W Yorks 95 F5
Mearbeck N Yorks 93 C8
Meare Som 23 E6
Meare Green Som 11 B8
Mears Ashby Northants 53 C6
Measham Leics 63 C7
Meath Green Sur 28 E3
Meathop Cumb 99 F6
Meaux E Yorks 97 F6
Meavy Devon 6 C3
Medbourne Leics 64 E4
Medburn Northumb 110 B4
Meddon Devon 8 C4
Meden Vale Notts 77 C5
Medlam Lincs 79 D6
Medmenham Bucks 39 F8
Medomsley Durham 110 D4
Medstead Hants 26 F4
Meer End W Mid 51 B7
Meerbrook Staffs 75 C6
Meers Bridge Lincs 91 F8
Meesden Herts 54 F5
Meeth Devon 9 D7
Meggethead Borders 114 B4
Meidrim Carms 32 B3
Meifod Denb 72 D4
Meifod Powys 59 C8
Meigle N Ayrs 118 C1
Meigle Perth 134 E2
Meikle Earnock S Lanark 119 D7
Meikle Ferry Highld 151 C10
Meikle Forter Angus 134 C1
Meikle Gluich Highld 151 C9
Meikle Pinkerton E Loth 122 B3
Meikle Strath Aberds 135 B6
Meikle Tarty Aberds 141 B8
Meikle Wartle Aberds 153 E7
Meikleour Perth 134 F1
Meinciau Carms 33 C5
Meir Stoke 75 E6
Meir Heath Staffs 75 E6
Melbourn Cambs 54 E4
Melbourne Derbys 63 B7
Melbourne E Yorks 96 E3
Melbourne S Lanark 120 E3
Melbury Abbas Dorset 13 B6
Melbury Bubb Dorset 12 D3
Melbury Osmond Dorset 12 D3
Melbury Sampford Dorset 12 D3
Melby Shetland 160 H3
Melchbourne Bedford 53 C8
Melcombe Bingham Dorset 13 D5
Melcombe Regis Dorset 12 F4
Meldon Devon 9 E7
Meldon Northumb 117 F7
Meldreth Cambs 54 E4
Meldrum Ho. Aberds 141 B7
Melfort Argyll 124 D4
Melgarve Highld 137 E7
Meliden Denb 72 A4
Melin-y-coed Conwy 83 E8
Melin-y-ddôl Powys 59 D7
Melin-y-grug Powys 59 D7
Melin-y-Wig Denb 72 E4
Melinbyrhedyn Powys 58 E5
Melincourt Neath 34 D2
Melkinthorpe Cumb 99 B7
Melkridge Northumb 109 C7
Melksham Wilts 24 C4
Melldalloch Argyll 145 F8
Melling Lancs 93 B5
Melling Mers 85 D4
Melling Mount Mers 86 D2
Mellis Suff 56 B5
Mellon Charles Highld 155 H13
Mellon Udrigle Highld 155 H13
Mellor Gtr Man 87 F7
Mellor Lancs 93 F6
Mellor Brook Lancs 93 F6
Mells Som 24 E2
Melmerby Cumb 109 F6
Melmerby N Yorks 95 B6
Melmerby N Yorks 101 F5
Melplash Dorset 12 E2
Melrose Borders 121 F8
Melsetter Orkney 159 K3
Melsonby N Yorks 101 D6
Meltham W Yorks 88 C2
Melton Suff 57 D6
Melton Constable Norf 81 D6
Melton Mowbray Leics 64 C4
Melton Ross N Lincs 90 C4
Meltonby E Yorks 96 D3
Melvaig Highld 155 J12
Melverley Shrops 60 C3
Melverley Green Shrops 60 C3
Melvich Highld 157 C11
Membury Devon 11 D7
Memsie Aberds 153 B9
Memus Angus 134 D4
Menabilly Corn 5 D5
Menai Bridge = Porthaethwy Anglesey 83 D5
Mendham Suff 69 F5
Mendlesham Suff 56 C5
Mendlesham Green Suff 56 C4
Menheniot Corn 5 C7
Mennock Dumfries 113 D8
Menston W Yorks 94 E4
Menstrie Clack 127 E7
Menthorpe N Yorks 96 F2
Mentmore Bucks 40 C2
Meoble Highld 147 C10
Meole Brace Shrops 60 C4
Meols Mers 85 E3
Meonstoke Hants 15 C7
Meopham Kent 29 C7
Meopham Station Kent 29 C7
Mepal Cambs 66 F4
Meppershall C Beds 54 F2
Merbach Hereford 48 E5
Mere Ches E 86 F5
Mere Wilts 24 F3
Mere Brow Lancs 86 C2
Mere Green W Mid 62 E5
Mereclough Lancs 93 F8
Mereside Blackpool 92 F3
Mereworth Kent 29 D7
Mergie Aberds 141 F6
Meriden W Mid 63 F6
Merkadale Highld 149 E8
Merkland Dumfries 106 B4
Merkland S Ayrs 112 E2
Merkland Lodge Highld 156 G7
Merley Poole 13 E8
Merlin's Bridge Pembs 44 D4
Merrington Shrops 60 B4
Merrion Pembs 44 F4
Merriott Som 12 C2
Merrivale Devon 6 B3
Merrow Sur 27 D8
Merrymeet Corn 5 C7
Mersham Kent 19 B7
Merstham Sur 28 D3
Merston W Sus 16 D2
Merstone IoW 15 F6
Merther Corn 3 B7
Merthyr Carms 32 B4
Merthyr Cynog Powys 47 F8
Merthyr-Dyfan V Glam 22 C3
Merthyr Mawr Bridgend 21 B7
Merthyr Tudful = Merthyr Tydfil M Tydf 34 D4
Merthyr Tydfil = Merthyr Tudful M Tydf 34 D4
Merthyr Vale M Tydf 34 E4
Merton Devon 9 C7
Merton London 28 B3
Merton Norf 68 E2
Merton Oxon 39 C5
Mervinslaw Borders 116 C2
Meshaw Devon 10 C2
Messing Essex 42 C4
Messingham N Lincs 90 D2
Metfield Suff 69 F5
Metheringham Lincs 78 C3
Methil Fife 129 E5
Methlem Gwyn 70 D2
Methley W Yorks 88 B4
Methlick Aberds 153 E8
Methven Perth 128 B2
Methwold Norf 67 E7
Methwold Hythe Norf 67 E7
Mettingham Suff 69 F6
Mevagissey Corn 3 B9
Mewith Head N Yorks 93 C7
Mexborough S Yorks 89 D5
Mey Highld 158 C4
Meysey Hampton Glos 37 E8
Miabhag W Isles 154 G5
Miabhag W Isles 154 H6
Miabhig W Isles 154 D5
Michaelchurch Hereford 36 B2
Michaelchurch Escley Hereford 48 F5
Michaelchurch on Arrow Powys 48 D4
Michaelston-le-Pit V Glam 22 B3
Michaelston-y-Fedw Newport 35 F6
Michaelstow Corn 5 B5
Michealston-super-Ely Cardiff 22 B3
Micheldever Hants 26 F3
Michelmersh Hants 14 B4
Mickfield Suff 56 C5
Mickle Trafford Ches W 73 C8
Micklebring S Yorks 89 E6
Mickleby N Yorks 103 C6
Mickleham Sur 28 D2
Mickleover Derby 76 F3
Micklethwaite W Yorks 94 E4
Mickleton Durham 100 B4
Mickleton Glos 51 E6
Mickletown W Yorks 88 B4
Mickley N Yorks 95 B5
Mickley Square Northumb 110 C3
Mid Ardlaw Aberds 153 B9
Mid Auchinlech Invclyd 118 B3
Mid Beltie Aberds 140 D5
Mid Calder W Loth 120 C3
Mid Cloch Forbie Aberds 153 C7
Mid Clyth Highld 158 G4
Mid Lavant W Sus 16 D2
Mid Main Highld 150 H7
Mid Urchany Highld 151 G11
Mid Walls Shetland 160 H4
Mid Yell Shetland 160 D7
Midbea Orkney 159 D5
Middle Assendon Oxon 39 F7
Middle Aston Oxon 38 B4
Middle Barton Oxon 38 B4
Middle Cairncake Aberds 153 D8
Middle Claydon Bucks 39 B7
Middle Drums Angus 135 D5
Middle Handley Derbys 76 B4
Middle Littleton Worcs 51 E5
Middle Maes-coed Hereford 48 F5
Middle Mill Pembs 44 C3
Middle Rasen Lincs 90 F4
Middle Rigg Perth 128 D2
Middle Tysoe Warks 51 E8
Middle Wallop Hants 25 F7
Middle Winterslow Wilts 25 F7
Middle Woodford Wilts 25 F6
Middlebie Dumfries 108 B2
Middleforth Green Lancs 86 B3
Middleham N Yorks 101 F6
Middlehope Shrops 60 F4
Middlemarsh Dorset 12 D4
Middlemuir Aberds 141 B8
Middlesbrough Mbro 102 B2
Middleshaw Cumb 99 F7
Middleshaw Dumfries 107 B8
Middlesmoor N Yorks 94 B3
Middlestone Durham 111 F5
Middlestone Moor Durham 110 F5
Middlestown W Yorks 88 C3
Middlethird Borders 122 E2
Middleton Aberds 141 C7
Middleton Argyll 146 G2
Middleton Cumb 99 F8
Middleton Derbys 75 C8
Middleton Derbys 76 D2
Middleton Essex 56 F2
Middleton Gtr Man 87 D6
Middleton Hants 26 E2
Middleton Hereford 49 C7
Middleton Lancs 92 D4
Middleton Midloth 121 D6
Middleton N Yorks 94 E4
Middleton N Yorks 103 F5
Middleton Norf 67 C6
Middleton Northants 64 F5
Middleton Northumb 117 F6
Middleton Northumb 123 F7
Middleton Perth 128 D3
Middleton Perth 133 E8
Middleton Shrops 49 B7
Middleton Shrops 60 B3
Middleton Shrops 60 E2
Middleton Suff 57 C8
Middleton Swansea 33 F5
Middleton W Yorks 88 B3
Middleton Warks 63 E5
Middleton Cheney Northants 52 E2
Middleton Green Staffs 75 F6
Middleton Hall Northumb 117 B5
Middleton-in-Teesdale Durham 100 B4
Middleton Moor Suff 57 C8
Middleton-on-Leven N Yorks 102 D2
Middleton-on-Sea W Sus 16 D3
Middleton on the Hill Hereford 49 C7
Middleton-on-the-Wolds E Yorks 96 E5
Middleton One Row Darl 102 C1
Middleton Priors Shrops 61 E6
Middleton Quernham N Yorks 95 B6
Middleton Scriven Shrops 61 F6
Middleton St George Darl 101 C8
Middleton Stoney Oxon 39 B5
Middleton Tyas N Yorks 101 D7
Middletown Cumb 98 D1
Middletown Powys 60 C3
Middlewich Ches E 74 C3
Middlewood Green Suff 56 C4
Middlezoy Som 23 F5
Middridge Durham 101 B7
Midfield Highld 157 C8
Midge Hall Lancs 86 B3
Midgeholme Cumb 109 D6
Midgham W Berks 26 C3
Midgley W Yorks 87 B8
Midgley W Yorks 88 C3
Midhopestones S Yorks 88 E3
Midhurst W Sus 16 B2
Midlem Borders 115 B8
Midmar Aberds 141 D5
Midsomer Norton Bath 23 D8
Midton Invclyd 118 B2
Midtown Highld 155 J13
Midtown Highld 157 C8
Midtown of Buchromb Moray 152 D3
Midville Lincs 79 D6
Midway Ches E 87 F7
Migdale Highld 151 B9
Migvie Aberds 140 D3
Milarrochy Stirling 126 E3
Milborne Port Som 12 C4
Milborne St Andrew Dorset 13 E6
Milborne Wick Som 12 B4
Milbourne Northumb 110 B4
Milburn Cumb 100 B1
Milbury Heath S Glos 36 E3
Milcombe Oxon 52 F2
Milden Suff 56 E3
Mildenhall Suff 55 B8
Mildenhall Wilts 25 C7
Mile Cross Norf 68 C5
Mile Elm Wilts 24 C4
Mile End Essex 43 B5
Mile End Glos 36 C2
Mile Oak Brighton 17 D6
Milebrook Powys 48 B5
Milebush Kent 29 E8
Mileham Norf 68 C2
Milesmark Fife 128 F2
Milfield Northumb 122 F5
Milford Derbys 76 E3
Milford Devon 8 B4
Milford Powys 59 E7
Milford Staffs 62 B3
Milford Sur 27 E7
Milford Wilts 14 B2
Milford Haven = Aberdaugleddau Pembs 44 E4
Milford on Sea Hants 14 E3
Milkwall Glos 36 D2
Milkwell Wilts 13 B7
Mill Bank W Yorks 87 B8
Mill Common Suff 69 F7
Mill End Bucks 39 F7
Mill End Herts 54 F4
Mill Green Essex 42 D2
Mill Green Norf 68 F4
Mill Green Suff 56 E3
Mill Hill London 41 E5
Mill Lane Hants 27 D5
Mill of Kingoodie Aberds 141 B7
Mill of Muiresk Aberds 153 D6
Mill of Sterin Aberds 140 E2
Mill of Uras Aberds 141 F7
Mill Place N Lincs 90 D3
Mill Side Cumb 99 F6
Mill Street Norf 68 C3
Milland W Sus 16 B2
Millarston Renfs 118 C4
Millbank Aberds 153 D11
Millbank Highld 158 D3
Millbeck Cumb 98 B4
Millbounds Orkney 159 E6
Millbreck Aberds 153 D10
Millbridge Sur 27 E6
Millbrook C Beds 53 F8
Millbrook Corn 6 D2
Millbrook Soton 14 C4
Millburn S Ayrs 112 B4
Millcombe Devon 7 E6
Millcorner E Sus 18 C5
Milldale Staffs 75 D8
Millden Lodge Angus 135 B5
Milldens Angus 135 D5
Millerhill Midloth 121 C6
Miller's Dale Derbys 75 B8
Miller's Green Derbys 76 D2
Millgreen Shrops 61 B6
Millhalf Hereford 48 E4
Millhayes Devon 11 D7
Millhead Lancs 92 B4
Millheugh S Lanark 119 D7
Millholme Cumb 99 E7
Millhouse Argyll 145 F8
Millhouse Cumb 108 F3
Millhouse Green S Yorks 88 D3
Millhousebridge Dumfries 114 F4
Millhouses S Yorks 88 F4
Millikenpark Renfs 118 C4
Millin Cross Pembs 44 D4
Millington E Yorks 96 D4
Millmeece Staffs 74 F5
Millom Cumb 98 F3
Millook Corn 8 E3
Millpool Corn 5 B6
Millport N Ayrs 145 H10
Millquarter Dumfries 113 F6
Millthorpe Lincs 78 F4
Millthrop Cumb 100 E1
Milltimber Aberdeen 141 D7
Milltown Corn 5 D6
Milltown Derbys 76 C3
Milltown Devon 20 F4
Milltown Dumfries 108 B3
Milltown of Aberdalgie Perth 128 B2
Milltown of Auchindoun Moray 152 D3
Milltown of Craigston Aberds 153 C7
Milltown of Edinvillie Moray 152 D2
Milltown of Kildrummy Aberds 140 C3
Milltown of Rothiemay Moray 152 D5
Milltown of Towie Aberds 140 C3
Milnathort Perth 128 D3
Milner's Heath Ches W 73 C8
Milngavie E Dunb 119 B5
Milnrow Gtr Man 87 C7
Milnshaw Lancs 87 B5
Milnthorpe Cumb 99 F6
Milo Carms 33 C6
Milson Shrops 49 B8
Milstead Kent 30 D3
Milston Wilts 25 E6
Milton Angus 134 E3
Milton Cambs 55 C5
Milton Cumb 109 C5
Milton Derbys 63 B7
Milton Dumfries 105 D6
Milton Dumfries 106 B5
Milton Dumfries 113 F8
Milton Highld 150 F6
Milton Highld 150 H7
Milton Highld 151 D10
Milton Highld 151 G8
Milton Highld 158 E5
Milton Moray 152 B5
Milton N Som 22 C5
Milton Notts 77 B7
Milton Oxon 38 E4
Milton Oxon 52 F2
Milton Pembs 32 D1
Milton Perth 127 C8
Milton Ptsmth 15 E7
Milton Stirling 126 D4
Milton Stoke 75 D6
Milton W Dunb 118 B4
Milton Abbas Dorset 13 D6
Milton Abbot Devon 6 D2
Milton Bridge Midloth 120 C5
Milton Bryan C Beds 53 F7
Milton Clevedon Som 23 F8
Milton Coldwells Aberds 153 E9
Milton Combe Devon 6 C2
Milton Damerel Devon 9 C5
Milton End Glos 37 D8
Milton Ernest Bedford 53 D8
Milton Green Ches W 73 D8
Milton Hill Oxon 38 E4
Milton Keynes M Keynes 53 F6
Milton Keynes Village M Keynes 53 F6
Milton Lilbourne Wilts 25 C6
Milton Malsor Northants 52 D5
Milton Morenish Perth 132 F3
Milton of Auchinhove Aberds 140 D4
Milton of Balgonie Fife 128 D5
Milton of Buchanan Stirling 126 E3
Milton of Campfield Aberds 140 D5
Milton of Campsie E Dunb 119 B6
Milton of Corsindae Aberds 141 D5
Milton of Cushnie Aberds 140 C4
Milton of Dalcapon Perth 133 D6
Milton of Edradour Perth 133 D6
Milton of Gollanfield Highld 151 F10
Milton of Lesmore Aberds 140 B3
Milton of Logie Aberds 140 D3
Milton of Murtle Aberdeen 141 D7
Milton of Noth Aberds 140 B4
Milton of Tullich Aberds 140 E2
Milton on Stour Dorset 13 B5
Milton Regis Kent 30 C3
Milton under Wychwood Oxon 38 C2
Miltonduff Moray 152 B1
Miltonhill Moray 151 E13
Miltonise Dumfries 105 B5
Milverton Som 11 B6
Milverton Warks 51 C8
Milwich Staffs 75 F6
Minard Argyll 125 F5
Minchinhampton Glos 37 D5
Mindrum Northumb 122 F4
Minehead Som 21 E8
Minera Wrex 73 D6
Minety Wilts 37 E7
Minffordd Gwyn 58 C4
Minffordd Gwyn 71 D6
Minffordd Gwyn 83 D5
Miningsby Lincs 79 C6
Minions Corn 5 B7
Minishant S Ayrs 112 C3
Minllyn Gwyn 59 C5
Minnes Aberds 141 B8
Minngearraidh W Isles 148 F2
Minnigaff Dumfries 105 C8
Minnonie Aberds 153 B7
Minskip N Yorks 95 C6
Minstead Hants 14 C3
Minsted W Sus 16 B2
Minster Kent 30 B3
Minster Kent 31 C7
Minster Lovell Oxon 38 C3
Minsterley Shrops 60 D3
Minsterworth Glos 36 C4
Minterne Magna Dorset 12 D4
Minting Lincs 78 B4
Mintlaw Aberds 153 D9
Minto Borders 115 B8
Minton Shrops 60 E4
Minwear Pembs 32 C1
Minworth W Mid 63 E5
Mirbister Orkney 159 F4
Mirehouse Cumb 98 C1
Mireland Highld 158 D5
Mirfield W Yorks 88 C3
Miserden Glos 37 D6
Miskin Rhondda 34 F4
Misson Notts 89 E7
Misterton Leics 64 F2
Misterton Notts 89 E8
Misterton Som 12 D2
Mistley Essex 56 F5
Mitcham London 28 C3
Mitchel Troy Mon 36 C1
Mitcheldean Glos 36 C3
Mitchell Corn 4 D3
Mitcheltroy Common Mon 36 D1
Mitford Northumb 117 F7
Mithian Corn 4 D2
Mitton Staffs 62 C2
Mixbury Oxon 52 F4
Moat Cumb 108 B4
Moats Tye Suff 56 D4
Mobberley Ches E 74 B4
Mobberley Staffs 75 E7
Moccas Hereford 49 E5
Mochdre Conwy 83 D8
Mochdre Powys 59 F7
Mochrum Dumfries 105 E7
Mockbeggar Hants 14 D2
Mockerkin Cumb 98 B2
Modbury Devon 6 D4
Moddershall Staffs 75 F6
Moelfre Anglesey 82 C5
Moelfre Powys 59 B8
Moffat Dumfries 114 D3
Moggerhanger C Beds 54 E2
Moira Leics 63 C7
Mol-chlach Highld 149 G9
Molash Kent 30 D4
Mold = Yr Wyddgrug Flint 73 C6
Moldgreen W Yorks 88 C2
Molehill Green Essex 42 B1
Molescroft E Yorks 97 E6
Molesden Northumb 117 F7
Molesworth Cambs 53 B8
Moll Highld 149 E10
Molland Devon 10 B3
Mollington Ches W 73 B7
Mollington Oxon 52 E2
Mollinsburn N Lanark 119 B7
Monachty Ceredig 46 C4
Monachylemore Stirling 126 C3
Monar Lodge Highld 150 G5
Monaughty Powys 48 C4
Monboddo House Aberds 135 B7
Mondynes Aberds 135 B7
Monevechadan Argyll 125 E7
Monewden Suff 57 D6
Moneydie Perth 128 B2
Moniaive Dumfries 113 E7
Monifieth Angus 134 F4
Monikie Angus 135 F4
Monimail Fife 128 C4
Monington Pembs 45 E3
Monk Bretton S Yorks 88 D4
Monk Fryston N Yorks 89 B6
Monk Sherborne Hants 26 D4
Monk Soham Suff 57 C6
Monk Street Essex 42 B2
Monken Hadley London 41 E5
Monkhopton Shrops 61 E6
Monkland Hereford 49 D6
Monkleigh Devon 9 B6
Monknash V Glam 21 B8
Monkokehampton Devon 9 D7
Monks Eleigh Suff 56 E3
Monk's Gate W Sus 17 B6
Monks Heath Ches E 74 B5
Monks Kirby Warks 63 F8
Monks Risborough Bucks 39 D8
Monkseaton T&W 111 B6
Monkshill Aberds 153 D7
Monksilver Som 22 F2
Monkspath W Mid 51 B6
Monkswood Mon 35 D7
Monkton Devon 11 D6
Monkton Kent 31 C6
Monkton Pembs 44 E4
Monkton S Ayrs 112 B3
Monkton Combe Bath 24 C2
Monkton Deverill Wilts 24 F3
Monkton Farleigh Wilts 24 C3
Monkton Heathfield Som 11 B7
Monkton Up Wimborne Dorset 13 C8
Monkwearmouth T&W 111 D6
Monkwood Hants 26 F4
Monmouth = Trefynwy Mon 36 C2
Monmouth Cap Mon 35 B7
Monnington on Wye Hereford 49 E5
Monreith Dumfries 105 E7
Monreith Mains Dumfries 105 E7
Mont Saint Guern 16
Montacute Som 12 C2
Montcoffer Ho. Aberds 153 B6
Montford Argyll 145 G10
Montford Shrops 60 C4
Montford Bridge Shrops 60 C4
Montgarrie Aberds 140 C4
Montgomery = Trefaldwyn Powys 60 E2
Montrave Fife 129 D5
Montrose Angus 135 D7
Montsale Essex 43 E6
Monxton Hants 25 E8
Monyash Derbys 75 C8
Monymusk Aberds 141 C5
Monzie Perth 127 B7
Monzie Castle Perth 127 B7
Moodiesburn N Lanark 119 B6
Moonzie Fife 128 C5
Moor Allerton W Yorks 95 F5
Moor Crichel Dorset 13 D7
Moor End E Yorks 96 F4
Moor End York 96 D2
Moor Monkton N Yorks 95 D8
Moor of Granary Moray 151 F13
Moor of Ravenstone Dumfries 105 E7
Moor Row Cumb 98 C2
Moor Street Kent 30 C2
Moorby Lincs 79 C5
Moordown Bmouth 13 E8
Moore Halton 86 F3
Moorend Glos 36 D4
Moorends S Yorks 89 C7
Moorgate S Yorks 88 E5
Moorgreen Notts 76 E4
Moorhall Derbys 76 B3
Moorhampton Hereford 49 E5
Moorhead W Yorks 94 F4
Moorhouse Cumb 108 D3
Moorhouse Notts 77 C7
Moorlinch Som 23 F5
Moorsholm Redcar 102 C4
Moorside Gtr Man 87 D7
Moorthorpe W Yorks 89 C5
Moortown Hants 14 D2
Moortown IoW 14 F5
Moortown Lincs 90 E4
Morangie Highld 151 C10
Morar Highld 147 B9
Morborne Cambs 65 E8
Morchard Bishop Devon 10 D2
Morcombelake Dorset 12 E2
Morcott Rutland 65 D6
Morda Shrops 60 B2
Morden Dorset 13 E7
Morden London 28 C3
Mordiford Hereford 49 F7
Mordon Durham 101 B8
More Shrops 60 E3
Morebath Devon 10 B4
Morebattle Borders 116 B3
Morecambe Lancs 92 C4
Morefield Highld 150 B4
Moreleigh Devon 7 D5
Morenish Perth 132 F2
Moresby Cumb 98 B1
Moresby Parks Cumb 98 C1
Morestead Hants 15 B6
Moreton Dorset 13 F6
Moreton Essex 41 D8
Moreton Mers 85 E3
Moreton Oxon 39 D6
Moreton Staffs 61 C7
Moreton Corbet Shrops 61 B5
Moreton-in-Marsh Glos 51 F7
Moreton Jeffries Hereford 49 E8
Moreton Morrell Warks 51 D8
Moreton on Lugg Hereford 49 E7
Moreton Pinkney Northants 52 E3
Moreton Say Shrops 74 F3
Moreton Valence Glos 36 D4
Moretonhampstead Devon 10 F2
Morfa Carms 33 C6
Morfa Carms 33 E6
Morfa Bach Carms 32 C4
Morfa Bychan Gwyn 71 D6
Morfa Dinlle Gwyn 82 F4
Morfa Glas Neath 34 D2
Morfa Nefyn Gwyn 70 C3
Morfydd Denb 72 E5
Morgan's Vale Wilts 14 B2
Moriah Ceredig 46 B5
Morland Cumb 99 B7
Morley Derbys 76 E3
Morley Durham 101 B6
Morley W Yorks 88 B3
Morley Green Ches E 87 F6
Morley St Botolph Norf 68 E3
Morningside Edin 120 B5
Morningside N Lanark 119 D8
Morningthorpe Norf 68 E5
Morpeth Northumb 117 F8
Morphie Aberds 135 C7
Morrey Staffs 62 C5
Morris Green Essex 55 F8
Morriston Swansea 33 E7
Morston Norf 81 C6
Mortehoe Devon 20 E3
Mortimer W Berks 26 C4
Mortimer West End Hants 26 C4
Mortimer's Cross Hereford 49 C6
Mortlake London 28 B3
Morton Cumb 108 D3
Morton Derbys 76 C4
Morton Lincs 65 B7
Morton Lincs 77 C8
Morton Lincs 90 E2
Morton Norf 68 C4
Morton Notts 77 D7
Morton S Glos 36 E3
Morton Shrops 60 B2
Morton Bagot Warks 51 C6
Morton-on-Swale N Yorks 101 E8
Morvah Corn 2 C3
Morval Corn 5 D7
Morvich Highld 136 B2
Morvich Highld 157 J10
Morville Shrops 61 E6
Morville Heath Shrops 61 E6
Morwenstow Corn 8 C4
Mosborough S Yorks 88 F5
Moscow E Ayrs 118 E4
Mosedale Cumb 108 F3
Moseley W Mid 62 E3
Moseley W Mid 62 F4
Moseley Worcs 50 D3
Moss Argyll 146 G2
Moss Highld 147 E9
Moss S Yorks 89 C6
Moss Wrex 73 D7
Moss Bank Mers 86 E3
Moss Edge Lancs 92 E4
Moss End Brack 27 B6
Moss of Barmuckity Moray 152 B2
Moss Pit Staffs 62 B3
Moss-side Highld 151 F11
Moss Side Lancs 92 F3
Mossat Aberds 140 C3
Mossbank Shetland 160 F6
Mossbay Cumb 98 B1
Mossblown S Ayrs 112 B4
Mossbrow Gtr Man 86 F5
Mossburnford Borders 116 C2
Mossdale Dumfries 106 B3
Mossend N Lanark 119 C7
Mosser Cumb 98 B3
Mossfield Highld 151 D9
Mossgiel E Ayrs 112 B4
Mosside Angus 134 D4
Mossley Ches E 75 C5
Mossley Gtr Man 87 D7
Mossley Hill Mers 85 F4
Mosstodloch Moray 152 B3
Mosston Angus 135 E5
Mossy Lea Lancs 86 C3
Mosterton Dorset 12 D2
Moston Gtr Man 87 D6
Moston Shrops 61 B5
Moston Green Ches E 74 C4
Mostyn Flint 85 F2
Mostyn Quay Flint 85 F2
Motcombe Dorset 13 B6
Mothecombe Devon 6 E4
Motherby Cumb 99 B6
Motherwell N Lanark 119 D7
Mottingham London 28 B5
Mottisfont Hants 14 B4
Mottistone IoW 14 F5
Mottram in Longdendale Gtr Man 87 E7
Mottram St Andrew Ches E 75 B5
Mouilpied Guern 16
Mouldsworth Ches W 74 B2
Moulin Perth 133 D6
Moulsecoomb Brighton 17 D7
Moulsford Oxon 39 F5
Moulsoe M Keynes 53 E7
Moulton Ches W 74 C3
Moulton Lincs 66 B3
Moulton N Yorks 101 D7
Moulton Northants 53 C5
Moulton Suff 55 C7
Moulton V Glam 22 B2
Moulton Chapel Lincs 66 C2
Moulton Eaugate Lincs 66 C3
Moulton Seas End Lincs 66 B3
Moulton St Mary Norf 69 D6
Mounie Castle Aberds 141 B6
Mount Corn 4 D2
Mount Corn 5 C6
Mount Highld 151 G12
Mount Bures Essex 56 F3
Mount Canisp Highld 151 D10
Mount Hawke Corn 3 B6
Mount Pleasant Ches E 74 D5
Mount Pleasant Derbys 63 C6
Mount Pleasant Derbys 76 E3
Mount Pleasant Flint 73 B6
Mount Pleasant Hants 14 E3
Mount Pleasant W Yorks 88 B3
Mount Sorrel Wilts 13 B8
Mount Tabor W Yorks 87 B8
Mountain W Yorks 94 F3
Mountain Ash = Aberpennar Rhondda 34 E4
Mountain Cross Borders 120 E4

196 Mou–Nor

Mountain Water Pembs 44 C4
Mountbenger Borders 115 B6
Mountfield E Sus 18 C4
Mountgerald Highld 151 E8
Mountjoy Corn 4 C3
Mountnessing Essex 42 E2
Mounton Mon 36 E2
Mountsorrel Leics 64 C2
Mousehole Corn 2 D3
Mousen Northumb 123 F7
Mouswald Dumfries 107 B7
Mow Cop Ches E 75 D5
Mowhaugh Borders 116 B4
Mowsley Leics 64 F3
Moxley W Mid 62 E3
Moy Highld 137 F7
Moy Highld 151 H10
Moy Hall Highld 151 H10
Moy Ho. Moray 151 E13
Moy Lodge Highld 137 F7
Moyles Court Hants 14 D2
Moylgrove Pembs 45 E3
Muasdale Argyll 143 D7
Much Birch Hereford 49 F7
Much Cowarne Hereford 49 E8
Much Dewchurch Hereford 49 F6
Much Hadham Herts 41 C7
Much Hoole Lancs 86 B2
Much Marcle Hereford 49 F8
Much Wenlock Shrops 61 D6
Muchalls Aberds 141 E8
Muchelney Som 12 B2
Muchlarnick Corn 5 D7
Muchrachd Highld 150 H5
Muckernich Highld 151 F8
Mucking Thurrock 42 F2
Muckleford Dorset 12 E4
Mucklestone Staffs 74 F4
Muckleton Shrops 61 B5
Muckletown Aberds 140 B4
Muckley Corner Staffs 62 D4
Muckton Lincs 91 F7
Mudale Highld 157 F8
Muddiford Devon 20 F4
Mudeford Dorset 14 E2
Mudford Som 12 C3
Mudgley Som 23 E6
Mugdock Stirling 119 B5
Mugeary Highld 149 E9
Mugginton Derbys 76 E2
Muggleswick Durham 110 E3
Muie Highld 157 J9
Muir Aberds 139 F6
Muir of Fairburn Highld 150 F7
Muir of Fowlis Aberds 140 C4
Muir of Ord Highld 151 F8
Muir of Pert Angus 134 F4
Muirden Aberds 153 C7
Muirdrum Angus 135 F5
Muirhead Angus 134 F3
Muirhead Fife 128 D4
Muirhead N Lanark 119 C6
Muirhead S Ayrs 118 F3
Muirhouselaw Borders 116 B2
Muirhouses Falk 128 F2
Muirkirk E Ayrs 113 B6
Muirmill Stirling 127 F6
Muirshearlich Highld 136 F4
Muirskie Aberds 141 E7
Muirtack Aberds 153 E9
Muirton Highld 151 E10
Muirton Perth 127 C8
Muirton Perth 128 B3
Muirton Mains Highld 150 F7
Muirton of Ardblair Perth 134 E1
Muirton of Ballochy Angus 135 C6
Muiryfold Aberds 153 C7
Muker N Yorks 100 E4
Mulbarton Norf 68 D4
Mulben Moray 152 C3
Mulindry Argyll 142 C4
Mullardoch House Highld 150 H5
Mullion Corn 3 E5
Mullion Cove Corn 3 E5
Mumby Lincs 79 B8
Munderfield Row Hereford 49 D8
Munderfield Stocks Hereford 49 D8
Mundesley Norf 81 D9
Mundford Norf 67 E8
Mundham Norf 69 E6
Mundon Essex 42 D4
Mundurno Aberdeen 141 C8
Munerigie Highld 137 D5
Muness Shetland 160 C8
Mungasdale Highld 150 B2
Mungrisdale Cumb 108 F3
Munlochy Highld 151 F9
Munsley Hereford 49 E8
Munslow Shrops 60 F5
Murchington Devon 9 F8
Murcott Oxon 39 C5
Murkle Highld 158 D3
Murlaggan Highld 136 E3
Murlaggan Highld 137 F6
Murra Orkney 159 H3
Murrayfield Edin 120 B5
Murrow Cambs 66 D3
Mursley Bucks 39 B8
Murthill Angus 134 D4
Murthly Perth 133 F7
Murton Cumb 100 B2
Murton Durham 111 E6
Murton Northumb 123 E5
Murton York 96 D2
Musbury Devon 11 E7
Muscoates N Yorks 102 F4
Musdale Argyll 124 C5
Musselburgh E Loth 121 B6
Muston Leics 77 F8
Muston N Yorks 97 B6
Mustow Green Worcs 50 B3
Mutehill Dumfries 106 E3
Mutford Suff 69 F7
Muthill Perth 127 C7
Mutterton Devon 10 D5
Muxton Telford 61 C7
Mybster Highld 158 E3
Myddfai Carms 34 B1
Myddle Shrops 60 B4
Mydroilyn Ceredig 46 D3
Myerscough Lancs 92 F4
Mylor Bridge Corn 3 C7
Mynachlog-ddu Pembs 45 F3
Myndtown Shrops 60 F3
Mynydd Bach Ceredig 47 B6
Mynydd-bach Mon 36 E1
Mynydd Bodafon Anglesey 82 C4
Mynydd-isa Flint 73 C6
Mynyddygarreg Carms 33 D5
Mynytho Gwyn 70 D4
Myrebird Aberds 141 E6
Myrelandhorn Highld 158 E4
Myreside Perth 128 B4
Myrtle Hill Carms 47 F6
Mytchett Sur 27 D6
Mytholm W Yorks 87 B7
Mytholmroyd W Yorks 87 B8
Myton-on-Swale N Yorks 95 C7
Mytton Shrops 60 C4

N

Na Gearrannan W Isles 154 C6
Naast Highld 155 J13
Naburn York 95 E8
Nackington Kent 31 D5
Nacton Suff 57 E6
Nafferton E Yorks 97 D6
Nailbridge Glos 36 C3
Nailsbourne Som 11 B7
Nailsea N Som 23 B6
Nailstone Leics 63 D8
Nailsworth Glos 37 E5
Nairn Highld 151 F11
Nalderswood Sur 28 E3
Nancegollan Corn 2 C5
Nancledra Corn 2 C3
Nanhoron Gwyn 70 D3
Nannau Gwyn 71 E8
Nannerch Flint 73 C5
Nanpantan Leics 64 C2
Nanpean Corn 4 D4
Nanstallon Corn 4 C5
Nant-ddu Powys 34 C4
Nant-glas Powys 47 C8
Nant Peris Gwyn 83 F6
Nant Uchaf Denb 72 D4
Nant-y-Bai Carms 47 E6
Nant-y-cafn Neath 34 D2
Nant-y-derry Mon 35 D7
Nant-y-ffin Carms 46 F4
Nant-y-moel Bridgend 34 E3
Nant-y-pandy Conwy 83 D6
Nanternis Ceredig 46 D2
Nantgaredig Carms 33 B5
Nantgarw Rhondda 35 F5
Nantglyn Denb 72 C4
Nantgwyn Powys 47 B8
Nantlle Gwyn 82 F5
Nantmawr Shrops 60 B2
Nantmel Powys 48 C2
Nantmor Gwyn 71 C7
Nantwich Ches E 74 D3
Nantycaws Carms 33 C5
Nantyffyllon Bridgend 34 E2
Nantyglo Bl Gwent 35 C5
Naphill Bucks 39 E8
Nappa N Yorks 93 D8
Napton on the Hill Warks 52 C2
Narberth = Arberth Pembs 32 C2
Narborough Leics 64 E2
Narborough Norf 67 C7
Nasareth Gwyn 82 F4
Naseby Northants 52 B4
Nash Bucks 53 F5
Nash Hereford 48 C5
Nash Newport 35 F7
Nash Shrops 49 B8
Nash Lee Bucks 39 D8
Nassington Northants 65 E7
Nasty Herts 41 B6
Nateby Cumb 100 D2
Nateby Lancs 92 E4
Natland Cumb 99 F7
Naughton Suff 56 E4
Naunton Glos 37 B8
Naunton Worcs 50 F3
Naunton Beauchamp Worcs 50 D4
Navenby Lincs 78 D2
Navestock Heath Essex 41 E8
Navestock Side Essex 42 E1
Navidale Highld 157 H13
Nawton N Yorks 102 F4
Nayland Suff 56 F3
Nazeing Essex 41 D7
Neacroft Hants 14 E2
Neal's Green Warks 63 F7
Neap Shetland 160 H7
Near Sawrey Cumb 99 E5
Neasham Darl 101 C8
Neath = Castell-Nedd Neath 33 E8
Neath Abbey Neath 33 E8
Neatishead Norf 69 B6
Nebo Anglesey 82 B4
Nebo Ceredig 46 C4
Nebo Conwy 83 F8
Nebo Gwyn 82 F4
Necton Norf 67 D8
Nedd Highld 156 F4
Nedderton Northumb 117 F8
Nedging Tye Suff 56 E4
Needham Norf 68 F5
Needham Market Suff 56 D4
Needingworth Cambs 54 B4
Needwood Staffs 63 B5
Neen Savage Shrops 49 B8
Neen Sollars Shrops 49 B8
Neenton Shrops 61 F6
Nefyn Gwyn 70 C4
Neilston E Renf 118 D4
Neinthirion Powys 59 D6
Neithrop Oxon 52 E2
Nelly Andrews Green Powys 60 D2
Nelson Caerph 35 E5
Nelson Lancs 93 F8
Nelson Village Northumb 111 B5
Nemphlar S Lanark 119 E8
Nempnett Thrubwell N Som 23 C7
Nene Terrace Lincs 66 D2
Nenthall Cumb 109 E7
Nenthead Cumb 109 E7
Nenthorn Borders 122 F2
Nerabus Argyll 142 C3
Nercwys Flint 73 C6
Nerston S Lanark 119 D6
Nesbit Northumb 123 F5
Ness Ches W 73 B7
Nesscliffe Shrops 60 C3
Neston Ches W 73 B6
Neston Wilts 24 C3
Nether Alderley Ches E 74 B5
Nether Blainslie Borders 121 E8
Nether Booth Derbys 88 F2
Nether Broughton Leics 64 B3
Nether Burrow Lancs 93 B6
Nether Cerne Dorset 12 E4
Nether Compton Dorset 12 C3
Nether Crimond Aberds 141 B7
Nether Dalgliesh Borders 115 D5
Nether Dallachy Moray 152 B3
Nether Exe Devon 10 D4
Nether Glasslaw Aberds 153 C8
Nether Handwick Angus 134 E3
Nether Haugh S Yorks 88 E5
Nether Heage Derbys 76 D3
Nether Heyford Northants 52 D4
Nether Hindhope Borders 116 C3
Nether Howecleuch S Lanark 114 C3
Nether Kellet Lancs 92 C5
Nether Kinmundy Aberds 153 D10
Nether Langwith Notts 76 B5
Nether Leask Aberds 153 E10
Nether Lenshie Aberds 153 D6
Nether Monynut Borders 122 C3
Nether Padley Derbys 76 B2
Nether Park Aberds 153 C10
Nether Poppleton York 95 D8
Nether Silton N Yorks 102 E2
Nether Stowey Som 22 F3
Nether Urquhart Fife 128 D3
Nether Wallop Hants 25 F8
Nether Wasdale Cumb 98 D3
Nether Whitacre Warks 63 E6
Nether Worton Oxon 52 F2
Netheravon Wilts 25 E6
Netherbrae Aberds 153 C7
Netherbrough Orkney 159 G4
Netherburn S Lanark 119 E8
Netherbury Dorset 12 E2
Netherby Cumb 108 B3
Netherby N Yorks 95 E6
Nethercote Warks 52 C3
Nethercott Devon 20 F3
Netherend Glos 36 D2
Netherfield E Sus 18 D4
Netherhampton Wilts 14 B2
Netherlaw Dumfries 106 E4
Netherley Aberds 141 E7
Netherley Mers 86 F2
Nethermill Dumfries 114 F3
Nethermuir Aberds 153 D9
Netherplace E Renf 118 D5
Netherseal Derbys 63 C6
Netherthird E Ayrs 113 C5
Netherthong W Yorks 88 D2
Netherthorpe S Yorks 89 F6
Netherton Angus 135 D5
Netherton Devon 7 B6
Netherton Hants 25 D8
Netherton Mers 85 D4
Netherton Northumb 117 D5
Netherton Oxon 38 E4
Netherton Perth 133 D8
Netherton Stirling 119 B5
Netherton W Mid 62 F3
Netherton W Yorks 88 C2
Netherton W Yorks 88 C3
Netherton Worcs 50 E4
Nethertown Cumb 98 D1
Nethertown Highld 158 C5
Netherwitton Northumb 117 E7
Netherwood E Ayrs 113 B6
Nethy Bridge Highld 139 B6
Netley Hants 15 D5
Netley Marsh Hants 14 C4
Netteswell Essex 41 C7
Nettlebed Oxon 39 F7
Nettlebridge Som 23 E8
Nettlecombe Dorset 12 E3
Nettleden Herts 40 C3
Nettleham Lincs 78 B3
Nettlestead Kent 29 D7
Nettlestead Green Kent 29 D7
Nettlestone IoW 15 E7
Nettlesworth Durham 111 E5
Nettleton Lincs 90 D5
Nettleton Wilts 24 B3
Neuadd Carms 33 B7
Nevendon Essex 42 E3
Nevern Pembs 45 E2
New Abbey Dumfries 107 C6
New Aberdour Aberds 153 B8
New Addington London 28 C4
New Alresford Hants 26 F3
New Alyth Perth 134 E2
New Arley Warks 63 F6
New Ash Green Kent 29 C7
New Barn Kent 29 C7
New Barnetby N Lincs 90 C4
New Barton Northants 53 C6
New Bewick Northumb 117 B6
New-bigging Angus 134 E2
New Bilton Warks 52 B2
New Bolingbroke Lincs 79 D6
New Boultham Lincs 78 B2
New Bradwell M Keynes 53 E6
New Brancepeth Durham 110 E5
New Bridge Wrex 73 E6
New Brighton Flint 73 C6
New Brighton Mers 85 E4
New Brinsley Notts 76 D4
New Broughton Wrex 73 D7
New Buckenham Norf 68 E3
New Byth Aberds 153 C8
New Catton Norf 68 C5
New Cheriton Hants 15 B6
New Costessey Norf 68 C4
New Cowper Cumb 107 E8
New Cross Ceredig 46 B5
New Cross London 28 B4
New Cumnock E Ayrs 113 C6
New Deer Aberds 153 D8
New Delaval Northumb 111 B5
New Duston Northants 52 C5
New Earswick York 96 D2
New Edlington S Yorks 89 E6
New Elgin Moray 152 B2
New Ellerby E Yorks 97 F7
New Eltham London 28 B5
New End Worcs 51 D5
New Farnley W Yorks 94 F5
New Ferry Mers 85 F4
New Fryston W Yorks 89 B5
New Galloway Dumfries 106 B3
New Gilston Fife 129 D6
New Grimsby Scilly 2 E3
New Hainford Norf 68 C5
New Hartley Northumb 111 B6
New Haw Sur 27 C8
New Hedges Pembs 32 D2
New Herrington T&W 111 D6
New Hinksey Oxon 39 D5
New Holkham Norf 80 D4
New Holland N Lincs 90 B4
New Houghton Derbys 76 C4
New Houghton Norf 80 E3
New Houses N Yorks 93 B8
New Humberstone Leicester 64 D3
New Hutton Cumb 99 E7
New Hythe Kent 29 D8
New Inn Carms 46 F3
New Inn Mon 36 D1
New Inn Pembs 45 F2
New Inn Torf 35 E7
New Invention Shrops 48 B4
New Invention W Mid 62 D3
New Kelso Highld 150 G2
New Kingston Notts 64 B2
New Lanark S Lanark 119 E8
New Lane Lancs 86 C2
New Lane End Warr 86 E4
New Leake Lincs 79 D7
New Leeds Aberds 153 C9
New Longton Lancs 86 B3
New Luce Dumfries 105 C5
New Malden London 28 C3
New Marske Redcar 102 B4
New Marton Shrops 73 F7
New Micklefield W Yorks 95 F7
New Mill Aberds 141 F6
New Mill Herts 40 C2
New Mill W Yorks 88 D2
New Mill Wilts 25 C6
New Mills Ches E 87 F5
New Mills Corn 4 D3
New Mills Derbys 87 F7
New Mills Powys 59 D7
New Milton Hants 14 E3
New Moat Pembs 32 B1
New Ollerton Notts 77 C6
New Oscott W Mid 62 E4
New Park N Yorks 95 D5
New Pitsligo Aberds 153 C8
New Polzeath Corn 4 B4
New Quay = Ceinewydd Ceredig 46 D2
New Rackheath Norf 69 C5
New Radnor Powys 48 C4
New Rent Cumb 108 F4
New Ridley Northumb 110 D3
New Road Side N Yorks 94 E2
New Romney Kent 19 C7
New Rossington S Yorks 89 E7
New Row Ceredig 47 B6
New Row Lancs 93 F6
New Row N Yorks 102 C4
New Sarum Wilts 25 F6
New Silksworth T&W 111 D6
New Stevenston N Lanark 119 D7
New Street Staffs 75 D7
New Street Lane Shrops 74 F3
New Swanage Dorset 13 F8
New Totley S Yorks 76 B3
New Town E Loth 121 B7
New Tredegar = Tredegar Newydd Caerph 35 D5
New Trows S Lanark 119 F8
New Ulva Argyll 144 E6
New Walsoken Cambs 66 D4
New Waltham NE Lincs 91 D6
New Whittington Derbys 76 B3
New Wimpole Cambs 54 E4
New Winton E Loth 121 B7
New Yatt Oxon 38 C3
New York Lincs 78 D5
New York N Yorks 94 C4
Newall W Yorks 94 E4
Newark Orkney 159 D8
Newark Pboro 66 D2
Newark-on-Trent Notts 77 D7
Newarthill N Lanark 119 D7
Newbarns Cumb 92 B2
Newbattle Midloth 121 C6
Newbiggin Cumb 92 C2
Newbiggin Cumb 98 E2
Newbiggin Cumb 99 B6
Newbiggin Cumb 99 B8
Newbiggin Cumb 109 E5
Newbiggin Durham 100 B4
Newbiggin N Yorks 100 E4
Newbiggin N Yorks 100 F4
Newbiggin-by-the-Sea Northumb 117 F9
Newbiggin-on-Lune Cumb 100 D2
Newbigging Angus 134 F4
Newbigging Angus 134 F4
Newbigging S Lanark 120 E3
Newbold Derbys 76 B3
Newbold Leics 63 C8
Newbold on Avon Warks 52 B2
Newbold on Stour Warks 51 E7
Newbold Pacey Warks 51 D7
Newbold Verdon Leics 63 D8
Newborough Anglesey 82 E4
Newborough Pboro 66 D2
Newborough Staffs 62 B5
Newbottle Northants 52 F3
Newbottle T&W 111 D6
Newbourne Suff 57 E6
Newbridge Caerph 35 E6
Newbridge Ceredig 46 D4
Newbridge Corn 2 C3
Newbridge Corn 5 C8
Newbridge Dumfries 107 B6
Newbridge Edin 120 B4
Newbridge Hants 14 C3
Newbridge IoW 14 F5
Newbridge Pembs 44 B4
Newbridge Green Worcs 50 F3
Newbridge-on-Usk Mon 35 E7
Newbridge on Wye Powys 48 D2
Newbrough Northumb 109 C8
Newbuildings Devon 10 D2
Newburgh Aberds 141 B8
Newburgh Aberds 153 C9
Newburgh Borders 115 C6
Newburgh Fife 128 C4
Newburgh Lancs 86 C2
Newburn T&W 110 C4
Newbury W Berks 26 C2
Newbury Park London 41 F7
Newby Cumb 99 B7
Newby Lancs 93 E8
Newby N Yorks 93 B7
Newby N Yorks 102 C3
Newby N Yorks 103 E8
Newby Bridge Cumb 99 F5
Newby East Cumb 108 D4
Newby West Cumb 108 D3
Newby Wiske N Yorks 102 F1
Newcastle Mon 35 C8
Newcastle Shrops 60 F2
Newcastle Emlyn = Castell Newydd Emlyn Carms 46 E2
Newcastle-under-Lyme Staffs 74 E5
Newcastle Upon Tyne T&W 110 C5
Newcastleton or Copshaw Holm Borders 115 F7
Newchapel Pembs 45 F4
Newchapel Powys 59 F6
Newchapel Staffs 75 D5
Newchapel Sur 28 E4
Newchurch Carms 32 B4
Newchurch IoW 15 F6
Newchurch Kent 19 B7
Newchurch Lancs 93 F8
Newchurch Mon 36 E1
Newchurch Powys 48 D4
Newchurch Staffs 62 B5
Newcott Devon 11 D7
Newcraighall Edin 121 B6
Newdigate Sur 28 E2
Newell Green Brack 27 B6
Newenden Kent 18 C5
Newent Glos 36 B4
Newerne Glos 36 D3
Newfield Durham 110 F5
Newfield Highld 151 D10
Newford Scilly 2 E4
Newfound Hants 26 D3
Newgale Pembs 44 C3
Newgate Norf 81 C6
Newgate Street Herts 41 D6
Newhall Ches E 74 E3
Newhall Derbys 63 B6
Newhall House Highld 151 E9
Newhall Point Highld 151 E10
Newham Northumb 117 B7
Newham Hall Northumb 117 B7
Newhaven Derbys 75 D8
Newhaven E Sus 17 D8
Newhaven Edin 121 B5
Newhey Gtr Man 87 C7
Newholm N Yorks 103 C6
Newhouse N Lanark 119 C7
Newick E Sus 17 B8
Newingreen Kent 19 B8
Newington Kent 19 B8
Newington Kent 30 C2
Newington Kent 31 C7
Newington Notts 89 E7
Newington Oxon 39 E6
Newington Shrops 60 F4
Newland Glos 36 D2
Newland Hull 97 F6
Newland N Yorks 89 B7
Newland Worcs 50 E2
Newlandrig Midloth 121 C6
Newlands Borders 115 E8
Newlands Highld 151 G10
Newlands Moray 152 C3
Newlands Northumb 110 D3
Newland's Corner Sur 27 E8
Newlands of Geise Highld 158 D2
Newlands of Tynet Moray 152 B3
Newlands Park Anglesey 82 C2
Newlandsmuir S Lanark 119 D6
Newlot Orkney 159 G6
Newlyn Corn 2 D3
Newmachar Aberds 141 C7
Newmains N Lanark 119 D8
Newmarket Suff 55 C7
Newmarket W Isles 155 D9
Newmill Borders 115 C7
Newmill Corn 2 C3
Newmill Moray 152 C4
Newmill of Inshewan Angus 134 C4
Newmills of Boyne Aberds 152 C5
Newmiln Perth 133 F8
Newmilns E Ayrs 118 F5
Newnham Cambs 54 D5
Newnham Glos 36 C3
Newnham Hants 26 D5
Newnham Herts 54 F3
Newnham Kent 30 D3
Newnham Northants 52 D3
Newnham Bridge Worcs 49 C8
Newpark Fife 129 C6
Newport Devon 20 F4
Newport E Yorks 96 F4
Newport Essex 55 F6
Newport Highld 158 H3
Newport IoW 15 F6
Newport = Casnewydd Newport 35 F7
Newport Norf 69 C8
Newport = Trefdraeth Pembs 45 F2
Newport Telford 61 C7
Newport-on-Tay Fife 129 B6
Newport Pagnell M Keynes 53 E6
Newpound Common W Sus 16 B4
Newquay Corn 4 C3
Newsbank Ches E 74 C5
Newseat Aberds 153 D10
Newseat Aberds 153 E7
Newsham N Yorks 101 C6
Newsham N Yorks 102 F1
Newsham Northumb 111 B6
Newsholme E Yorks 89 B8
Newsholme Lancs 93 D8
Newsome W Yorks 88 C2
Newstead Borders 121 F8
Newstead Northumb 117 B7
Newstead Notts 76 D5
Newthorpe N Yorks 95 F7
Newton Argyll 125 F6
Newton Borders 116 B2
Newton Bridgend 21 B7
Newton Cambs 54 E5
Newton Cambs 66 C4
Newton Cardiff 22 B4
Newton Ches W 73 C8
Newton Ches W 74 B2
Newton Ches W 74 D2
Newton Cumb 92 B2
Newton Derbys 76 D4
Newton Dorset 13 C5
Newton Dumfries 108 B2
Newton Dumfries 114 E4
Newton Gtr Man 87 E7
Newton Hereford 48 F5
Newton Hereford 49 D7
Newton Highld 151 E10
Newton Highld 151 G10
Newton Highld 156 F5
Newton Highld 158 F5
Newton Lancs 92 F4
Newton Lancs 93 B5
Newton Lancs 93 D6
Newton Lincs 78 F3
Newton Moray 152 B1
Newton Norf 67 C8
Newton Northants 65 F5
Newton Northumb 110 C3
Newton Notts 77 E6
Newton Perth 133 F5
Newton S Lanark 119 C6
Newton S Lanark 120 F2
Newton S Yorks 89 D6
Newton Staffs 62 B4
Newton Suff 56 E3
Newton Swansea 33 F7
Newton W Loth 120 B3
Newton Warks 52 B3
Newton Wilts 14 B3
Newton Abbot Devon 7 B6
Newton Arlosh Cumb 107 D8
Newton Aycliffe Durham 101 B7
Newton Bewley Hrtlpl 102 B2
Newton Blossomville M Keynes 53 D7
Newton Bromswold Northants 53 C7
Newton Burgoland Leics 63 D7
Newton by Toft Lincs 90 F4
Newton Ferrers Devon 6 E3
Newton Flotman Norf 68 E5
Newton Hall Northumb 110 C3
Newton Harcourt Leics 64 E3
Newton Heath Gtr Man 87 D6
Newton Ho. Aberds 141 B5
Newton Kyme N Yorks 95 E7
Newton-le-Willows Mers 86 E3
Newton-le-Willows N Yorks 101 F7
Newton Longville Bucks 53 F6
Newton Mearns E Renf 118 D5
Newton Morrell N Yorks 101 D7
Newton Mulgrave N Yorks 103 C5
Newton of Ardtoe Highld 147 D9
Newton of Balcanquhal Perth 128 C3
Newton of Falkland Fife 128 D4
Newton on Ayr S Ayrs 112 B3
Newton on Ouse N Yorks 95 D8
Newton-on-Rawcliffe N Yorks 103 E6
Newton-on-the-Moor Northumb 117 D7
Newton on Trent Lincs 77 B8
Newton Park Argyll 145 G10
Newton Poppleford Devon 11 F5
Newton Purcell Oxon 52 F4
Newton Regis Warks 63 D6
Newton Reigny Cumb 108 F4
Newton Solney Derbys 63 B6
Newton St Cyres Devon 10 E3
Newton St Faith Norf 68 C5
Newton St Loe Bath 24 C2
Newton St Petrock Devon 9 C6
Newton Stacey Hants 26 E2
Newton Stewart Dumfries 105 C8
Newton Tony Wilts 25 E7
Newton Tracey Devon 9 B7
Newton under Roseberry Redcar 102 C3
Newton upon Derwent E Yorks 96 E3
Newton Valence Hants 26 F5
Newtonairds Dumfries 113 F8
Newtongrange Midloth 121 C6
Newtonhill Aberds 141 E8
Newtonhill Highld 151 G8
Newtonmill Angus 135 C6
Newtonmore Highld 138 E3
Newtown Argyll 125 E6
Newtown Ches W 74 B2
Newtown Corn 3 D6
Newtown Cumb 107 E7
Newtown Cumb 108 C5
Newtown Derbys 87 F7
Newtown Devon 10 B2
Newtown Glos 36 D3
Newtown Glos 50 F4
Newtown Hants 14 B4
Newtown Hants 14 C3
Newtown Hants 15 C6
Newtown Hants 15 C7
Newtown Hants 15 D5
Newtown Hants 26 C2
Newtown Hereford 49 E8
Newtown Highld 137 D6
Newtown IoM 84 E3
Newtown IoW 14 E5
Newtown Northumb 117 B6
Newtown Northumb 117 D6
Newtown Northumb 123 F5
Newtown Poole 13 E8
Newtown = Y Drenewydd Powys 59 E8
Newtown Shrops 73 F8
Newtown Staffs 75 C6
Newtown Staffs 75 C7
Newtown Wilts 13 B7
Newtown Linford Leics 64 D2
Newtown St Boswells Borders 121 F8
Newtown Unthank Leics 63 D8
Newtyle Angus 134 E2
Neyland Pembs 44 E4
Niarbyl IoM 84 E2
Nibley S Glos 36 F3
Nibley Green Glos 36 E4
Nibon Shetland 160 F5
Nicholashayne Devon 11 C6
Nicholaston Swansea 33 F6
Nidd N Yorks 95 C6
Nigg Aberdeen 141 D8
Nigg Highld 151 D11
Nigg Ferry Highld 151 E10
Nightcott Som 10 B3
Nilig Denb 72 D4
Nine Ashes Essex 42 D1
Nine Mile Burn Midloth 120 D4
Nine Wells Pembs 44 C2
Ninebanks Northumb 109 D7
Ninfield E Sus 18 D4
Ningwood IoW 14 F4
Nisbet Borders 116 B2
Nisthouse Orkney 159 G4
Nisthouse Shetland 160 G7
Niton IoW 15 G6
Nitshill Glasgow 118 C5
No Man's Heath Ches W 74 E2
No Man's Heath Warks 63 D6
Noak Hill London 41 E8
Noblethorpe S Yorks 88 D3
Nobottle Northants 52 C4
Nocton Lincs 78 C3
Noke Oxon 39 C5
Nolton Pembs 44 D3
Nolton Haven Pembs 44 D3
Nomansland Devon 10 C3
Nomansland Wilts 14 C3
Noneley Shrops 60 B4
Nonikiln Highld 151 D9
Nonington Kent 31 D6
Noonsbrough Shetland 160 H4
Norbreck Blackpool 92 E3
Norbridge Hereford 50 E2
Norbury Ches E 74 E2
Norbury Derbys 75 E8
Norbury Shrops 60 E3
Norbury Staffs 61 B7
Nordelph Norf 67 D5
Norden Gtr Man 87 C6
Norden Heath Dorset 13 F7
Nordley Shrops 61 E6
Norham Northumb 122 E5
Norley Ches W 74 B2
Norleywood Hants 14 E4
Norman Cross Cambs 65 E8
Normanby N Lincs 90 C2
Normanby N Yorks 103 F5
Normanby Redcar 102 C3
Normanby-by-Spital Lincs 90 F4
Normanby by Stow Lincs 90 F2
Normanby le Wold Lincs 90 E5
Normandy Sur 27 D7
Norman's Bay E Sus 18 E3
Norman's Green Devon 11 D5
Normanstone Suff 69 E8
Normanton Derby 76 F3
Normanton Leics 77 E8
Normanton Lincs 78 E2
Normanton Notts 77 D7
Normanton Rutland 65 D6
Normanton W Yorks 88 B4
Normanton le Heath Leics 63 C7
Normanton on Soar Notts 64 B2
Normanton-on-the-Wolds Notts 77 F6
Normanton on Trent Notts 77 C7
Normoss Lancs 92 F3
Norney Sur 27 E7
Norrington Common Wilts 24 C3
Norris Green Mers 85 E4
Norris Hill Leics 63 C7
North Anston S Yorks 89 F6
North Aston Oxon 38 B4
North Baddesley Hants 14 C4
North Ballachulish Highld 130 C4
North Barrow Som 12 B4
North Barsham Norf 80 D5
North Benfleet Essex 42 F3
North Bersted W Sus 16 D3
North Berwick E Loth 129 F7
North Boarhunt Hants 15 C7
North Bovey Devon 10 F2
North Bradley Wilts 24 D3
North Brentor Devon 9 F6
North Brewham Som 24 F2
North Buckland Devon 20 E3
North Burlingham Norf 69 C6
North Cadbury Som 12 B4
North Cairn Dumfries 104 B3
North Carlton Lincs 78 B2
North Carrine Argyll 143 H7
North Cave E Yorks 96 F4
North Cerney Glos 37 D7
North Charford Wilts 14 C2
North Charlton Northumb 117 B7
North Cheriton Som 12 B4
North Cliff E Yorks 97 E8
North Cliffe E Yorks 96 F4
North Clifton Notts 77 B8
North Cockerington Lincs 91 E7
North Coker Som 12 C3
North Collafirth Shetland 160 E5
North Common E Sus 17 B7
North Connel Argyll 124 B5
North Cornelly Bridgend 34 F2
North Cotes Lincs 91 D7
North Cove Suff 69 F7
North Cowton N Yorks 101 D7
North Crawley M Keynes 53 E7
North Cray London 29 B5
North Creake Norf 80 D4
North Curry Som 11 B8
North Dalton E Yorks 96 D5
North Dawn Orkney 159 H5
North Deighton N Yorks 95 D6
North Duffield N Yorks 96 F2
North Elkington Lincs 91 E6
North Elmham Norf 81 E5
North Elmshall W Yorks 89 C5
North End Bucks 39 B8
North End E Yorks 97 F8
North End Essex 42 C2
North End Hants 26 C2
North End Lincs 78 E5
North End N Som 23 C6
North End Ptsmth 15 D7
North End Som 11 B7
North End W Sus 16 D5
North Erradale Highld 155 J12
North Fambridge Essex 42 E4
North Fearns Highld 149 E10
North Featherstone W Yorks 88 B5
North Ferriby E Yorks 90 B3
North Frodingham E Yorks 97 D7
North Gluss Shetland 160 F5
North Gorley Hants 14 C2
North Green Norf 68 F5
North Green Suff 57 C7
North Greetwell Lincs 78 B3
North Grimston N Yorks 96 C4
North Halley Orkney 159 H6
North Halling Medway 29 C8
North Hayling Hants 15 D8
North Hazelrigg Northumb 123 F6
North Heasley Devon 21 F6
North Heath W Sus 16 B4
North Hill Cambs 55 B5
North Hill Corn 5 B7
North Hinksey Oxon 38 D4
North Holmwood Sur 28 E2
North Howden E Yorks 96 F3
North Huish Devon 6 D5
North Hykeham Lincs 78 C2
North Johnston Pembs 44 D4
North Kelsey Lincs 90 D4
North Kelsey Moor Lincs 90 D4
North Kessock Highld 151 G9
North Killingholme N Lincs 90 C5
North Kilvington N Yorks 102 F2
North Kilworth Leics 64 F3
North Kirkton Aberds 153 C11
North Kiscadale N Ayrs 143 F11
North Kyme Lincs 78 D4
North Lancing W Sus 17 D5
North Lee Bucks 39 D8
North Leigh Oxon 38 C3
North Leverton with Habblesthorpe Notts 89 F8
North Littleton Worcs 51 E5
North Lopham Norf 68 F3
North Luffenham Rutland 65 D6
North Marden W Sus 16 C2
North Marston Bucks 39 B7
North Middleton Midloth 121 D6
North Middleton Northumb 117 B6
North Molton Devon 10 B2
North Moreton Oxon 39 F5
North Mundham W Sus 16 D2
North Muskham Notts 77 D7
North Newbald E Yorks 96 F5
North Newington Oxon 52 F2
North Newnton Wilts 25 D6
North Newton Som 22 F4
North Nibley Glos 36 E4
North Oakley Hants 26 D3
North Ockendon London 42 F1
North Ormesby Mbro 102 B3
North Ormsby Lincs 91 E6
North Otterington N Yorks 102 F1
North Owersby Lincs 90 E4
North Perrott Som 12 D2
North Petherton Som 22 F4
North Petherwin Corn 8 F4
North Pickenham Norf 67 D8
North Piddle Worcs 50 D4
North Poorton Dorset 12 E3
North Port Argyll 125 C6
North Queensferry Fife 128 F3
North Radworthy Devon 21 F6
North Rauceby Lincs 78 E3
North Reston Lincs 91 F7
North Rigton N Yorks 95 E5
North Rode Ches E 75 C5
North Roe Shetland 160 E5
North Runcton Norf 67 C6
North Sandwick Shetland 160 D7
North Scale Cumb 92 C1
North Scarle Lincs 77 C8
North Seaton Northumb 117 F8
North Shian Argyll 130 E3
North Shields T&W 111 C6
North Shoebury Southend 43 F5
North Shore Blackpool 92 F3
North Side Cumb 98 B2
North Side Pboro 66 E2
North Skelton Redcar 102 C4
North Somercotes Lincs 91 E8
North Stainley N Yorks 95 B5
North Stainmore Cumb 100 C3
North Stifford Thurrock 42 F2
North Stoke Bath 24 C2
North Stoke Oxon 39 F6
North Stoke W Sus 16 C4
North Street Hants 26 F4
North Street Kent 30 D4
North Street Medway 30 B2
North Street W Berks 26 B4
North Sunderland Northumb 123 F8
North Tamerton Corn 8 E5
North Tawton Devon 9 D8
North Thoresby Lincs 91 E6
North Tidworth Wilts 25 E7
North Togston Northumb 117 D8
North Tuddenham Norf 68 C3
North Walbottle T&W 110 C4
North Walsham Norf 81 D8
North Waltham Hants 26 E3
North Warnborough Hants 26 D5
North Water Bridge Angus 135 C6
North Watten Highld 158 E4
North Weald Bassett Essex 41 D7
North Wheatley Notts 89 F8
North Whilborough Devon 7 C6
North Wick Bath 23 C7
North Willingham Lincs 91 F5
North Wingfield Derbys 76 C4
North Witham Lincs 65 B6
North Woolwich London 28 B5
North Wootton Dorset 12 C4
North Wootton Norf 67 B6
North Wootton Som 23 E7
North Wraxall Wilts 24 B3
North Wroughton Swindon 38 F1
Northacre Norf 68 E2
Northallerton N Yorks 102 E1
Northam Devon 9 B6
Northam Soton 14 C5
Northampton Northants 53 C5
Northaw Herts 41 D5
Northbeck Lincs 78 E3
Northborough Pboro 65 D8
Northbourne Kent 31 D7
Northbridge Street E Sus 18 C4
Northchapel W Sus 16 B3
Northchurch Herts 40 D2
Northcott Devon 8 E5
Northdown Kent 31 B7
Northdyke Orkney 159 F3
Northend Bath 24 C2
Northend Bucks 39 E7
Northend Warks 51 D8
Northenden Gtr Man 87 E6
Northfield Aberdeen 141 D8
Northfield Borders 122 C5
Northfield E Yorks 90 B4
Northfield W Mid 50 B5
Northfields Lincs 65 D7
Northfleet Kent 29 B7
Northgate Lincs 65 B8
Northhouse Borders 115 D7
Northiam E Sus 18 C5
Northill C Beds 54 E2
Northington Hants 26 F3
Northlands Lincs 79 D6
Northlea Durham 111 D7
Northleach Glos 37 C8
Northleigh Devon 11 E6
Northlew Devon 9 E7
Northmoor Oxon 38 D4
Northmoor Green or Moorland Som 22 F5
Northmuir Angus 134 D3
Northney Hants 15 D8
Northolt London 40 F4
Northop Flint 73 C6
Northop Hall Flint 73 C6
Northorpe Lincs 65 C7
Northorpe Lincs 78 F5
Northorpe Lincs 90 E2
Northover Som 12 B3
Northover Som 23 F6
Northowram W Yorks 88 B2
Northport Dorset 13 F7
Northpunds Shetland 160 L6
Northrepps Norf 81 D8
Northtown Orkney 159 J5
Northway Glos 50 F4
Northwich Ches W 74 B3
Northwick S Glos 36 F2
Northwold Norf 67 E7
Northwood Derbys 76 C2
Northwood IoW 15 E5
Northwood Kent 31 C7
Northwood London 40 E3
Northwood Shrops 73 F8
Northwood Green Glos 36 C4
Norton E Sus 17 D8
Norton Glos 37 B5
Norton Halton 86 F3
Norton Herts 54 F3
Norton IoW 14 F4
Norton Mon 35 C8
Norton Northants 52 C4
Norton Notts 77 B5
Norton Powys 48 C5
Norton S Yorks 89 C6
Norton Shrops 60 F4
Norton Shrops 61 D5
Norton Shrops 61 D7
Norton Stockton 102 B2
Norton Suff 56 C3
Norton W Sus 16 D3
Norton W Sus 16 E2
Norton Wilts 37 F5
Norton Worcs 50 D3
Norton Worcs 50 E5
Norton Bavant Wilts 24 E4
Norton Bridge Staffs 75 F5
Norton Canes Staffs 62 D4
Norton Canon Hereford 49 E5
Norton Corner Norf 81 E6
Norton Disney Lincs 77 D8
Norton East Staffs 62 D4
Norton Ferris Wilts 24 F2
Norton Fitzwarren Som 11 B6
Norton Green IoW 14 F4
Norton Hawkfield Bath 23 C7
Norton Heath Essex 42 D2
Norton in Hales Shrops 74 F4
Norton-in-the-Moors Stoke 75 D5
Norton-Juxta-Twycross Leics 63 D7
Norton-le-Clay N Yorks 95 B7
Norton Lindsey Warks 51 C7
Norton Malreward Bath 23 C8
Norton Mandeville Essex 42 D
Norton-on-Derwent N Yorks 96 B
Norton St Philip Som 24 D
Norton sub Hamdon Som 12 C
Norton Woodseats S Yorks 88 F

Norwell Notts 77 C7
Norwell Woodhouse Notts 77 C7
Norwich Norf 68 D5
Norwick Shetland 160 B8
Norwood Derbys 89 F5
Norwood Hill Sur 28 E3
Norwoodside Cambs 66 E4
Noseley Leics 64 E4
Noss Shetland 160 M5
Noss Mayo Devon 6 E3
Nosterfield N Yorks 101 F7
Nostie Highld 149 F13
Notgrove Glos 37 B8
Nottage Bridgend 21 B7
Nottingham Nottingham 77 F5
Nottington Dorset 12 F4
Notton W Yorks 88 C4
Notton Wilts 24 C4
Nounsley Essex 42 C3
Noutard's Green Worcs 50 C2
Novar House Highld 151 E9
Nox Shrops 60 C4
Nuffield Oxon 39 F6
Nun Hills Lancs 87 B6
Nun Monkton N Yorks 95 D8
Nunburnholme E Yorks 96 E4
Nuncargate Notts 76 D5
Nuneaton Warks 63 E7
Nuneham Courtenay Oxon 39 E5
Nunney Som 24 E2
Nunnington N Yorks 96 B2
Nunnykirk Northumb 117 E6
Nunsthorpe NE Lincs 91 D6
Nunthorpe Mbro 102 C3
Nunthorpe York 96 D2
Nunton Wilts 14 B2
Nunwick N Yorks 95 B6
Nupend Glos 36 D4
Nursling Hants 14 C4
Nursted Hants 15 B8
Nutbourne W Sus 15 D8
Nutbourne W Sus 16 C4
Nutfield Sur 28 D4
Nuthall Notts 76 E5
Nuthampstead Herts 54 F5
Nuthurst W Sus 17 B5
Nutley E Sus 17 B8
Nutley Hants 26 E4
Nutwell S Yorks 89 D7
Nybster Highld 158 D5
Nyetimber W Sus 16 E2
Nyewood W Sus 16 B2
Nymet Rowland Devon 10 D2
Nymet Tracey Devon 10 D2
Nympsfield Glos 37 D5
Nynehead Som 11 B6
Nyton W Sus 16 D3

O

Oad Street Kent 30 C2
Oadby Leics 64 D3
Oak Cross Devon 9 E7
Oakamoor Staffs 75 E7
Oakbank W Loth 120 C3
Oakdale Caerph 35 E5
Oake Som 11 B6
Oaken Staffs 62 D2
Oakenclough Lancs 92 E5
Oakengates Telford 61 C7
Oakenholt Flint 73 B6
Oakenshaw Durham 110 F5
Oakenshaw W Yorks 88 B2
Oakerthorpe Derbys 76 D3
Oakes W Yorks 88 C2
Oakfield Torf 35 E7
Oakford Ceredig 46 D3
Oakford Devon 10 B4
Oakfordbridge Devon 10 B4
Oakgrove Ches E 75 C6
Oakham Rutland 65 D5
Oakhanger Hants 27 F5
Oakhill Som 23 E8
Oakhurst Kent 29 D6
Oakington Cambs 54 C5
Oaklands Herts 41 C5
Oaklands Powys 48 D2
Oakle Street Glos 36 C4
Oakley Bedford 53 D8
Oakley Bucks 39 C6
Oakley Fife 128 F2
Oakley Hants 26 D3
Oakley Oxon 39 D7
Oakley Poole 13 E8
Oakley Suff 57 B5
Oakley Green Windsor 27 B7
Oakley Park Powys 59 F6
Oakmere Ches W 74 C2
Oakridge Glos 37 D6
Oakridge Hants 26 D4
Oaks Shrops 60 D4
Oaks Green Derbys 75 F8
Oaksey Wilts 37 E6
Oakthorpe Leics 63 C7
Oakwoodhill Sur 28 F2
Oakworth W Yorks 94 F3
Oape Highld 156 J7
Oare Kent 30 C4
Oare Som 21 E7
Oare W Berks 26 B3
Oare Wilts 25 C6
Oasby Lincs 78 F3
Oathlaw Angus 134 D4
Oatlands N Yorks 95 D6
Oban Argyll 124 C4
Oban Highld 147 C11
Oborne Dorset 12 C4
Obthorpe Lincs 65 C7
Occlestone Green Ches W 74 C3
Occold Suff 57 B5
Ochiltree E Ayrs 112 B5
Ochtermuthill Perth 127 C7
Ochtertyre Perth 127 B7
Ockbrook Derbys 76 F4
Ockham Sur 27 D8
Ockle Highld 147 D8
Ockley Sur 28 F2
Ocle Pychard Hereford 49 E7
Octon E Yorks 97 C6
Octon Cross Roads E Yorks 97 C6
Odcombe Som 12 C3
Odd Down Bath 24 C2
Oddendale Cumb 99 C7
Odder Lincs 78 B2
Oddingley Worcs 50 D4
Oddington Glos 38 B2
Oddington Oxon 39 C5
Odell Bedford 53 D7
Odie Orkney 159 F7
Odiham Hants 26 D5
Odstock Wilts 14 B2
Odstone Leics 63 D7
Offchurch Warks 51 C8
Offenham Worcs 51 E5
Offham E Sus 17 C7
Offham Kent 29 D7
Offham W Sus 16 D4
Offord Cluny Cambs 54 C3
Offord Darcy Cambs 54 C3
Offton Suff 56 E4
Offwell Devon 11 E6
Ogbourne Maizey Wilts 25 B6
Ogbourne St Andrew Wilts 25 B6
Ogbourne St George Wilts 25 B7
Ogil Angus 134 C4
Ogle Northumb 110 B4
Ogmore V Glam 21 B7
Ogmore-by-Sea V Glam 21 B7
Ogmore Vale Bridgend 34 E3
Okeford Fitzpaine Dorset 13 C6
Okehampton Devon 9 E7
Okehampton Camp Devon 9 E7
Okraquoy Shetland 160 K6
Old Northants 53 B5
Old Aberdeen Aberdeen 141 D8
Old Alresford Hants 26 F3
Old Arley Warks 63 E6
Old Basford Nottingham 76 E5
Old Basing Hants 26 D4
Old Bewick Northumb 117 B6
Old Bolingbroke Lincs 79 C6
Old Bramhope W Yorks 94 E5
Old Brampton Derbys 76 B3
Old Bridge of Tilt Perth 133 C5
Old Bridge of Urr Dumfries 106 C4
Old Buckenham Norf 68 E3
Old Burghclere Hants 26 D2
Old Byland N Yorks 102 F3
Old Cassop Durham 111 F6
Old Castleton Borders 115 E8
Old Catton Norf 68 C5
Old Clee NE Lincs 91 D6
Old Cleeve Som 22 E2
Old Clipstone Notts 77 C6
Old Colwyn Conwy 83 D8
Old Coulsdon London 28 D4
Old Crombie Aberds 152 C5
Old Dailly S Ayrs 112 E2
Old Dalby Leics 64 B3
Old Deer Aberds 153 D9
Old Denaby S Yorks 89 E5
Old Edlington S Yorks 89 E6
Old Eldon Durham 101 B7
Old Ellerby E Yorks 97 F7
Old Felixstowe Suff 57 F7
Old Fletton Pboro 65 E8
Old Glossop Derbys 87 E8
Old Goole E Yorks 89 B8
Old Hall Powys 59 F6
Old Heath Essex 43 B6
Old Heathfield E Sus 18 C2
Old Hill W Mid 62 F3
Old Hunstanton Norf 80 C2
Old Hurst Cambs 54 B3
Old Hutton Cumb 99 F7
Old Kea Corn 3 B7
Old Kilpatrick W Dunb 118 B4
Old Kinnernie Aberds 141 D6
Old Knebworth Herts 41 B5
Old Langho Lancs 93 F7
Old Laxey IoM 84 D4
Old Leake Lincs 79 D7
Old Malton N Yorks 96 B3
Old Micklefield W Yorks 95 F7
Old Milton Hants 14 E3
Old Milverton Warks 51 C7
Old Monkland N Lanark 119 C7
Old Netley Hants 15 D5
Old Philpstoun W Loth 120 B3
Old Quarrington Durham 111 F6
Old Radnor Powys 48 D4
Old Rattray Aberds 153 C10
Old Rayne Aberds 141 B5
Old Romney Kent 19 C7
Old Sodbury S Glos 36 F4
Old Somerby Lincs 78 F2
Old Stratford Northants 53 E5
Old Thirsk N Yorks 102 F2
Old Town Cumb 99 F7
Old Town Cumb 108 E4
Old Town Northumb 116 E4
Old Town Scilly 2 E4
Old Trafford Gtr Man 87 E6
Old Tupton Derbys 76 C3
Old Warden C Beds 54 E2
Old Weston Cambs 53 B8
Old Whittington Derbys 76 B3
Old Wick Highld 158 E5
Old Windsor Windsor 27 B7
Old Wives Lees Kent 30 D4
Old Woking Sur 27 D8
Old Woodhall Lincs 78 C5
Oldany Highld 156 F4
Oldberrow Warks 51 C6
Oldborough Devon 10 D2
Oldbury Shrops 61 E7
Oldbury W Mid 62 F3
Oldbury Warks 63 E7
Oldbury-on-Severn S Glos 36 E3
Oldbury on the Hill Glos 37 F5
Oldcastle Bridgend 21 B8
Oldcastle Mon 35 B7
Oldcotes Notts 89 F6
Oldfallow Staffs 62 C3
Oldfield Worcs 50 C3
Oldford Som 24 D2
Oldham Gtr Man 87 D7
Oldhamstocks E Loth 122 B3
Oldland S Glos 23 B8
Oldmeldrum Aberds 141 B7
Oldshore Beg Highld 156 D4
Oldshoremore Highld 156 D5
Oldstead N Yorks 102 F3
Oldtown Aberds 140 B4
Oldtown of Ord Aberds 152 C6
Oldway Swansea 33 F6
Oldways End Devon 10 B3
Oldwhat Aberds 153 C8
Olgrinmore Highld 158 E2
Oliver's Battery Hants 15 B5
Ollaberry Shetland 160 E5
Ollerton Ches E 74 B4
Ollerton Notts 77 C6
Ollerton Shrops 61 B6
Olmarch Ceredig 46 D5
Olney M Keynes 53 D6
Olrig Ho. Highld 158 D3
Olton W Mid 62 F5
Olveston S Glos 36 F3
Olwen Ceredig 46 E4
Ombersley Worcs 50 C3
Ompton Notts 77 C6
Onchan IoM 84 E3
Onecote Staffs 75 D7
Onen Mon 35 C8
Ongar Hill Norf 67 B5
Ongar Street Hereford 49 C5
Onibury Shrops 49 B6
Onich Highld 130 C4
Onllwyn Neath 34 C2
Onneley Staffs 74 E4
Onslow Village Sur 27 E7
Onthank E Ayrs 118 E4
Openwoodgate Derbys 76 E3
Opinan Highld 149 A12
Opinan Highld 155 H13
Orange Lane Borders 122 E3
Orange Row Norf 66 B5
Orasaigh W Isles 155 F8
Orbliston Moray 152 C3
Orbost Highld 148 D7
Orby Lincs 79 C7
Orchard Hill Devon 9 B6
Orchard Portman Som 11 B7
Orcheston Wilts 25 E5
Orcop Hereford 36 B1
Orcop Hill Hereford 36 B1
Ord Highld 149 G11
Ordhead Aberds 141 C5
Ordie Aberds 140 D3
Ordiequish Moray 152 C3
Ordsall Notts 89 F7
Ore E Sus 18 D5
Oreton Shrops 61 F6
Orford Suff 57 E8
Orford Warr 86 E4
Orgreave Staffs 63 C5
Orlestone Kent 19 B6
Orleton Hereford 49 C6
Orleton Worcs 49 C8
Orlingbury Northants 53 B6
Ormesby Redcar 102 C3
Ormesby St Margaret Norf 69 C7
Ormesby St Michael Norf 69 C7
Ormiclate Castle W Isles 148 E2
Ormiscaig Highld 155 H13
Ormiston E Loth 121 C7
Ormsaigbeg Highld 146 E7
Ormsaigmore Highld 146 E7
Ormsary Argyll 144 F6
Ormsgill Cumb 92 B1
Ormskirk Lancs 86 D2
Orpington London 29 C5
Orrell Gtr Man 86 D3
Orrell Mers 85 E4
Orrisdale IoM 84 C3
Orroland Dumfries 106 E4
Orsett Thurrock 42 F2
Orslow Staffs 62 C2
Orston Notts 77 E7
Orthwaite Cumb 108 F2
Ortner Lancs 92 D5
Orton Cumb 99 D8
Orton Northants 53 B6
Orton Longueville Pboro 65 E8
Orton-on-the-Hill Leics 63 D7
Orton Waterville Pboro 65 E8
Orwell Cambs 54 D4
Osbaldeston Lancs 93 F6
Osbaldwick York 96 D2
Osbaston Shrops 60 B3
Osbournby Lincs 78 F3
Oscroft Ches W 74 C2
Ose Highld 149 D8
Osgathorpe Leics 63 C8
Osgodby Lincs 90 E4
Osgodby N Yorks 96 F2
Osgodby N Yorks 103 F8
Oskaig Highld 149 E10
Oskamull Argyll 146 G7
Osmaston Derby 76 F3
Osmaston Derbys 76 E2
Osmington Dorset 12 F5
Osmington Mills Dorset 12 F5
Osmotherley N Yorks 102 E2
Ospisdale Highld 151 C10
Ospringe Kent 30 C4
Ossett W Yorks 88 B3
Ossington Notts 77 C7
Ostend Essex 43 E5
Oswaldkirk N Yorks 96 B2
Oswaldtwistle Lancs 86 B5
Oswestry Shrops 60 B2
Otford Kent 29 D6
Otham Kent 29 D8
Othery Som 23 F5
Otley Suff 57 D6
Otley W Yorks 94 E5
Otter Ferry Argyll 145 E8
Otterbourne Hants 15 B5
Otterburn N Yorks 93 D8
Otterburn Northumb 116 E4
Otterburn Camp Northumb 116 E4
Otterham Corn 8 E3
Otterhampton Som 22 E4
Ottershaw Sur 27 C8
Otterswick Shetland 160 E7
Otterton Devon 11 F5
Ottery St Mary Devon 11 E6
Ottinge Kent 31 E5
Ottringham E Yorks 91 B6
Oughterby Cumb 108 D2
Oughtershaw N Yorks 100 F3
Oughterside Cumb 107 E8
Oughtibridge S Yorks 88 E4
Oughtrington Warr 86 F4
Oulston N Yorks 95 B8
Oulton Cumb 108 D2
Oulton Norf 81 E7
Oulton Staffs 75 F6
Oulton Suff 69 E8
Oulton W Yorks 88 B4
Oulton Broad Suff 69 E8
Oulton Street Norf 81 E7
Oundle Northants 65 F7
Ousby Cumb 109 F6
Ousdale Highld 158 H2
Ousden Suff 55 D8
Ousefleet E Yorks 90 B2
Ouston Durham 111 D5
Ouston Northumb 110 B3
Out Newton E Yorks 91 B7
Out Rawcliffe Lancs 92 E4
Outertown Orkney 159 G3
Outgate Cumb 99 E5
Outhgill Cumb 100 D2
Outlane W Yorks 87 C8
Outwell Norf 66 D5
Outwick Hants 14 C2
Outwood Sur 28 E4
Outwood W Yorks 88 B4
Outwoods Staffs 61 C7
Ovenden W Yorks 87 B8
Ovenscloss Borders 121 F7
Over Cambs 54 B4
Over Ches W 74 C3
Over S Glos 36 F2
Over Compton Dorset 12 C3
Over Green W Mid 63 E5
Over Haddon Derbys 76 C2
Over Hulton Gtr Man 86 D4
Over Kellet Lancs 92 B5
Over Kiddington Oxon 38 B4
Over Knutsford Ches E 74 B4
Over Monnow Mon 36 C2
Over Norton Oxon 38 B3
Over Peover Ches E 74 B4
Over Silton N Yorks 102 E2
Over Stowey Som 22 F3
Over Stratton Som 12 C2
Over Tabley Ches E 86 F5
Over Wallop Hants 25 F7
Over Whitacre Warks 63 E6
Over Worton Oxon 38 B4
Overbister Orkney 159 D7
Overbury Worcs 50 F4
Overcombe Dorset 12 F4
Overgreen Derbys 76 B3
Overleigh Som 23 F6
Overley Green Warks 51 D5
Overpool Ches W 73 B7
Overscaig Hotel Highld 156 G7
Overseal Derbys 63 C6
Oversland Kent 30 D4
Overstone Northants 53 C6
Overstrand Norf 81 C8
Overthorpe Northants 52 E2
Overton Aberdeen 141 C7
Overton Ches W 74 B2
Overton Dumfries 107 C6
Overton Hants 26 E3
Overton Lancs 92 D4
Overton N Yorks 95 D8
Overton Shrops 49 B7
Overton Swansea 33 F5
Overton W Yorks 88 C3
Overton = Owrtyn Wrex 73 E7
Overton Bridge Wrex 73 E7
Overtown N Lanark 119 D8
Oving Bucks 39 B7
Oving W Sus 16 D3
Ovingdean Brighton 17 D7
Ovingham Northumb 110 C3
Ovington Durham 101 C6
Ovington Essex 55 E8
Ovington Hants 26 F3
Ovington Norf 68 D2
Ovington Northumb 110 C3
Ower Hants 14 C4
Owermoigne Dorset 13 F5
Owlbury Shrops 60 E3
Owler Bar Derbys 76 B2
Owlerton S Yorks 88 F4
Owl's Green Suff 57 C6
Owlswick Bucks 39 D7
Owmby Lincs 90 D4
Owmby-by-Spital Lincs 90 F4
Owrtyn = Overton Wrex 73 E7
Owslebury Hants 15 B6
Owston Leics 64 D4
Owston S Yorks 89 C6
Owston Ferry N Lincs 90 D2
Owstwick E Yorks 97 F8
Owthorne E Yorks 91 B7
Owthorpe Notts 77 F6
Oxborough Norf 67 D7
Oxcombe Lincs 79 B6
Oxen Park Cumb 99 F5
Oxenholme Cumb 99 F7
Oxenhope W Yorks 94 F3
Oxenton Glos 50 F4
Oxenwood Wilts 25 D8
Oxford Oxon 39 D5
Oxhey Herts 40 E4
Oxhill Warks 51 E8
Oxley W Mid 62 D3
Oxley Green Essex 43 C5
Oxley's Green E Sus 18 C3
Oxnam Borders 116 C2
Oxshott Sur 28 C2
Oxspring S Yorks 88 D3
Oxted Sur 28 D4
Oxton Borders 121 D7
Oxton Notts 77 D6
Oxwich Swansea 33 F5
Oxwick Norf 80 E5
Oykel Bridge Highld 156 J6
Oyne Aberds 141 B5

P

Pabail Iarach W Isles 155 D10
Pabail Uarach W Isles 155 D10
Pace Gate N Yorks 94 D4
Packington Leics 63 C7
Padanaram Angus 134 D4
Padbury Bucks 52 F5
Paddington London 41 F5
Paddlesworth Kent 19 B8
Paddock Wood Kent 29 E7
Paddockhaugh Moray 152 C2
Paddockhole Dumfries 115 F5
Padfield Derbys 87 E8
Padiham Lancs 93 F7
Padog Conwy 83 F8
Padside N Yorks 94 D4
Padstow Corn 4 B4
Padworth W Berks 26 C4
Page Bank Durham 110 F5
Pagham W Sus 16 E2
Paglesham Churchend Essex 43 E5
Paglesham Eastend Essex 43 E5
Paibeil W Isles 148 B2
Paible W Isles 154 H5
Paignton Torbay 7 C6
Pailton Warks 63 F8
Painscastle Powys 48 E3
Painshawfield Northumb 110 C3
Painsthorpe E Yorks 96 D4
Painswick Glos 37 D5
Pairc Shiaboist W Isles 154 C7
Paisley Renfs 118 C4
Pakefield Suff 69 E8
Pakenham Suff 56 C3
Pale Gwyn 72 F3
Palestine Hants 25 E7
Paley Street Windsor 27 B6
Palfrey W Mid 62 E4
Palgowan Dumfries 112 F3
Palgrave Suff 56 B5
Pallion T&W 111 D6
Palmarsh Kent 19 B8
Palnackie Dumfries 106 D5
Palnure Dumfries 105 C8
Palterton Derbys 76 C4
Pamber End Hants 26 D4
Pamber Green Hants 26 D4
Pamber Heath Hants 26 C4
Pamphill Dorset 13 D7
Pampisford Cambs 55 E5
Pan Orkney 159 J4
Panbride Angus 135 F5
Pancrasweek Devon 8 D4
Pandy Gwyn 58 D3
Pandy Mon 35 B7
Pandy Powys 59 D6
Pandy Wrex 73 F5
Pandy Tudur Conwy 83 E8
Panfield Essex 42 B3
Pangbourne W Berks 26 B4
Pannal N Yorks 95 D6
Panshanger Herts 41 C5
Pant Shrops 60 B2
Pant-glâs Powys 58 E4
Pant-glas Carms 33 B6
Pant-glas Gwyn 71 C5
Pant-glas Shrops 73 F6
Pant-lasau Swansea 33 E7
Pant Mawr Powys 59 F5
Pant-teg Carms 33 B5
Pant-y-Caws Carms 32 B2
Pant-y-dwr Powys 47 B8
Pant-y-ffridd Powys 59 D8
Pant-y-Wacco Flint 72 B5
Pant-yr-awel Bridgend 34 F3
Pantgwyn Carms 33 B6
Pantgwyn Ceredig 45 E4
Panton Lincs 78 B4
Pantperthog Gwyn 58 D4
Pantyffynnon Carms 33 C7
Pantymwyn Flint 73 C5
Panxworth Norf 69 C6
Papcastle Cumb 107 F8
Papigoe Highld 158 E5
Papil Shetland 160 K5
Papley Orkney 159 J5
Papple E Loth 121 B8
Papplewick Notts 76 D5
Papworth Everard Cambs 54 C3
Papworth St Agnes Cambs 54 C3
Par Corn 5 D5
Parbold Lancs 86 C2
Parbrook Som 23 F7
Parbrook W Sus 16 B4
Parc Gwyn 72 F2
Parc-Seymour Newport 35 E8
Parc-y-rhôs Carms 46 E4
Parcllyn Ceredig 45 D4
Pardshaw Cumb 98 B2
Parham Suff 57 C7
Park Dumfries 114 E2
Park Corner Oxon 39 F6
Park Corner Windsor 40 F1
Park End Mbro 102 C3
Park End Northumb 109 B8
Park Gate Hants 15 D6
Park Hill N Yorks 95 C6
Park Hill Notts 77 D6
Park Street W Sus 28 F2
Parkend Glos 36 D3
Parkeston Essex 57 F6
Parkgate Ches W 73 B6
Parkgate Dumfries 114 F3
Parkgate Kent 19 B5
Parkgate Sur 28 E3
Parkham Devon 9 B5
Parkham Ash Devon 9 B5
Parkhill Ho. Aberds 141 C7
Parkhouse Mon 36 D1
Parkhouse Green Derbys 76 C4
Parkhurst IoW 15 E5
Parkmill Swansea 33 F6
Parkneuk Aberds 135 B7
Parkstone Poole 13 E8
Parley Cross Dorset 13 E8
Parracombe Devon 21 E5
Parrog Pembs 45 F2
Parsley Hay Derbys 75 C8
Parson Cross S Yorks 88 E4
Parson Drove Cambs 66 D3
Parsonage Green Essex 42 D3
Parsonby Cumb 107 F8
Parson's Heath Essex 43 B6
Partick Glasgow 119 C5
Partington Gtr Man 86 E5
Partney Lincs 79 C7
Parton Cumb 98 B1
Parton Dumfries 106 B3
Parton Glos 37 B5
Partridge Green W Sus 17 C5
Parwich Derbys 75 D8
Passenham Northants 53 F5
Paston Norf 81 D9
Patchacott Devon 9 E6
Patcham Brighton 17 D7
Patching W Sus 16 D4
Patchole Devon 20 E5
Pateley Bridge N Yorks 94 C4
Paternoster Heath Essex 43 C5
Path of Condie Perth 128 C2
Pathe Som 23 F5
Pathhead Aberds 135 C7
Pathhead E Ayrs 113 C6
Pathhead Fife 128 E4
Pathhead Midloth 121 C6
Pathstruie Perth 128 C2
Patna E Ayrs 112 C4
Patney Wilts 25 D5
Patrick IoM 84 D2
Patrick Brompton N Yorks 101 E7
Patrington E Yorks 91 B7
Patrixbourne Kent 31 D5
Patterdale Cumb 99 C5
Pattingham Staffs 62 E2
Pattishall Northants 52 D4
Pattiswick Green Essex 42 B4
Patton Bridge Cumb 99 E7
Paul Corn 2 D3
Paulerspury Northants 52 E5
Paull E Yorks 91 B5
Paulton Bath 23 D8
Pavenham Bedford 53 D7
Pawlett Som 22 E5
Pawston Northumb 122 F4
Paxford Glos 51 F6
Paxton Borders 122 D5
Payhembury Devon 11 D5
Paythorne Lancs 93 D8
Peacehaven E Sus 17 D8
Peak Dale Derbys 75 B7
Peak Forest Derbys 75 B8
Peakirk Pboro 65 D8
Pearsie Angus 134 D3
Pease Pottage W Sus 28 F3
Peasedown St John Bath 24 D2
Peasemore W Berks 26 B2
Peasenhall Suff 57 C7
Peaslake Sur 27 E8
Peasley Cross Mers 86 E3
Peasmarsh E Sus 19 C5
Peaston E Loth 121 C7
Peastonbank E Loth 121 C7
Peat Inn Fife 129 D6
Peathill Aberds 153 B9
Peatling Magna Leics 64 E2
Peatling Parva Leics 64 F2
Peaton Shrops 60 F5
Peats Corner Suff 57 C5
Pebmarsh Essex 56 F2
Pebworth Worcs 51 E6
Pecket Well W Yorks 87 B7
Peckforton Ches E 74 D2
Peckham London 28 B4
Peckleton Leics 63 D8
Pedlinge Kent 19 B8
Pedmore W Mid 62 F3
Pedwell Som 23 F6
Peebles Borders 121 E5
Peel IoM 84 D2
Peel Common Hants 15 D6
Peel Park S Lanark 119 D6
Peening Quarter Kent 19 C5
Pegsdon C Beds 54 F2
Pegswood Northumb 117 F8
Pegwell Kent 31 C7
Peinchorran Highld 149 E10
Peinlich Highld 149 C9
Pelaw T&W 111 C5
Pelcomb Bridge Pembs 44 D4
Pelcomb Cross Pembs 44 D4
Peldon Essex 43 C5
Pellon W Yorks 87 B8
Pelsall W Mid 62 D4
Pelton Durham 111 D5
Pelutho Cumb 107 E8
Pelynt Corn 5 D7
Pemberton Gtr Man 86 D3
Pembrey Carms 33 D5
Pembridge Hereford 49 D5
Pembroke = Penfro Pembs 44 E4
Pembroke Dock = Doc Penfro Pembs 44 E4
Pembury Kent 29 E7
Pen-bont Rhydybeddau Ceredig 58 F3
Pen-clawdd Swansea 33 E6
Pen-ffordd Pembs 32 B1
Pen-groes-oped Mon 35 D7
Pen-llyn Anglesey 82 C3
Pen-lon Anglesey 82 E4
Pen-sarn Gwyn 70 C5
Pen-sarn Gwyn 71 E6
Pen-twyn Mon 36 D2
Pen-y-banc Carms 33 B7
Pen-y-bont Carms 32 B4
Pen-y-bont Gwyn 58 D4
Pen-y-bont Gwyn 71 E7
Pen-y-bont Powys 60 B2
Pen-Y-Bont Ar Ogwr = Bridgend Bridgend 21 B8
Pen-y-bryn Gwyn 58 C3
Pen-y-bryn Pembs 45 E3
Pen-y-cae Powys 34 C2
Pen-y-cae-mawr Mon 35 E8
Pen-y-cefn Flint 72 B5
Pen-y-clawdd Mon 36 D1
Pen-y-coedcae Rhondda 34 F4
Pen-y-fai Bridgend 34 F2
Pen-y-garn Carms 46 F4
Pen-y-garn Ceredig 58 F3
Pen-y-garnedd Anglesey 82 D5
Pen-y-gop Conwy 72 E3
Pen-y-graig Gwyn 70 D2
Pen-y-groes Carms 33 C6
Pen-y-groeslon Gwyn 70 D3
Pen-y-Gwryd Hotel Gwyn 83 F6
Pen-y-stryt Denb 73 D5
Pen-yr-heol Mon 35 C8
Pen-yr-Heolgerrig M Tydf 34 D4
Penallt Mon 36 C2
Penally Pembs 32 E2
Penalt Hereford 36 B2
Penare Corn 3 B8
Penarlâg = Hawarden Flint 73 C7
Penarth V Glam 22 B3
Penbryn Ceredig 45 D4
Pencader Carms 46 F3
Pencaenewydd Gwyn 70 C5
Pencaitland E Loth 121 C7
Pencarnisiog Anglesey 82 D3
Pencarreg Carms 46 E4
Pencelli Powys 34 B4
Pencoed Bridgend 34 F3
Pencombe Hereford 49 D7
Pencoyd Hereford 36 B2
Pencraig Hereford 36 B2
Pencraig Powys 59 B7
Pendeen Corn 2 C2
Penderyn Rhondda 34 D3
Pendine Carms 32 D3
Pendlebury Gtr Man 87 D5
Pendleton Lancs 93 F7
Pendock Worcs 50 F2
Pendoggett Corn 4 B5
Pendomer Som 12 C3
Pendoylan V Glam 22 B2
Pendre Bridgend 34 F3
Penegoes Powys 58 D4
Penfro = Pembroke Pembs 44 E4
Pengam Caerph 35 E5
Penge London 28 B4
Pengenffordd Powys 48 F3
Pengorffwysfa Anglesey 82 B4
Pengover Green Corn 5 C7
Penhale Corn 3 E5
Penhale Corn 4 D4
Penhalvaen Corn 3 C6
Penhill Swindon 38 F1
Penhow Newport 35 E8
Penhurst E Sus 18 D3
Peniarth Gwyn 58 D3
Penicuik Midloth 120 C5
Peniel Carms 33 B5
Peniel Denb 72 C4
Penifiler Highld 149 D9
Peninver Argyll 143 F8
Penisarwaun Gwyn 83 E5
Penistone S Yorks 88 D3
Penjerrick Corn 3 C6
Penketh Warr 86 F3
Penkill S Ayrs 112 E2
Penkridge Staffs 62 C3
Penley Wrex 73 F8
Penllergaer Swansea 33 E7
Penllyn V Glam 21 B8
Penmachno Conwy 83 F7
Penmaen Swansea 33 F6
Penmaenan Conwy 83 D7
Penmaenmawr Conwy 83 D7
Penmaenpool Gwyn 58 C3
Penmark V Glam 22 C2
Penmarth Corn 3 C6
Penmon Anglesey 83 C6
Penmore Mill Argyll 146 F7
Penmorfa Ceredig 46 D2
Penmorfa Gwyn 71 C6
Penmynydd Anglesey 82 D5
Penn Bucks 40 E2
Penn W Mid 62 E2
Penn Street Bucks 40 E2
Pennal Gwyn 58 D4
Pennan Aberds 153 B8
Pennant Ceredig 46 C4
Pennant Denb 72 D4
Pennant Denb 72 F4
Pennant Powys 59 E5
Pennant Melangell Powys 59 B7
Pennar Pembs 44 E4
Pennard Swansea 33 F6
Pennerley Shrops 60 E3
Pennington Cumb 92 B2
Pennington Gtr Man 86 E4
Pennington Hants 14 E4
Penny Bridge Cumb 99 F5
Pennycross Argyll 147 J8
Pennygate Norf 69 B6
Pennygown Argyll 147 G8
Pennymoor Devon 10 C3
Pennywell T&W 111 D6
Penparc Ceredig 45 E4
Penparc Pembs 44 B3
Penparcau Ceredig 58 F2
Penperlleni Mon 35 D7
Penpillick Corn 5 D5
Penpol Corn 3 C7
Penpoll Corn 5 D6
Penpont Dumfries 113 E8
Penpont Powys 34 B3
Penrhôs Mon 35 C8
Penrherber Carms 45 F4
Penrhiw goch Carms 33 C6
Penrhiw-llan Ceredig 46 E2
Penrhiw-pâl Ceredig 46 E2
Penrhiwceiber Rhondda 34 E4
Penrhos Gwyn 70 D4
Penrhos Powys 34 C1
Penrhosfeilw Anglesey 82 C2
Penrhyn Bay Conwy 83 C8
Penrhyn-coch Ceredig 58 F3
Penrhyndeudraeth Gwyn 71 D7
Penrhynside Conwy 83 C8
Penrice Swansea 33 F5
Penrith Cumb 108 F5
Penrose Corn 4 B3
Penruddock Cumb 99 B6
Penryn Corn 3 C6
Pensarn Carms 33 C5
Pensarn Conwy 72 B3
Pensax Worcs 50 C2
Pensby Mers 85 F3
Penselwood Som 24 F2
Pensford Bath 23 C8
Penshaw T&W 111 D6
Penshurst Kent 29 E6
Pensilva Corn 5 C7
Penston E Loth 121 B7
Pentewan Corn 3 B9
Pentir Gwyn 83 E5
Pentire Corn 4 C2
Pentlow Essex 56 E2
Pentney Norf 67 C7
Penton Mewsey Hants 25 E8
Pentraeth Anglesey 82 D5
Pentre Carms 33 C6
Pentre Powys 59 F7
Pentre Powys 60 E2
Pentre Rhondda 34 E3
Pentre Shrops 60 C3
Pentre Wrex 72 F5
Pentre Wrex 73 E6
Pentre-bâch Ceredig 46 E4
Pentre-bach Powys 47 F8
Pentre Berw Anglesey 82 D4
Pentre-bont Conwy 83 F7
Pentre-celyn Denb 72 D5
Pentre-Celyn Powys 59 D5
Pentre-chwyth Swansea 33 E7
Pentre-cwrt Carms 46 F2
Pentre Dolau-Honddu Powys 47 E8
Pentre-dwr Swansea 33 E7
Pentre-galar Pembs 45 F3
Pentre-Gwenlais Carms 33 C7
Pentre Gwynfryn Gwyn 71 E6
Pentre Halkyn Flint 73 B6
Pentre-Isaf Conwy 83 E8
Pentre Llanrhaeadr Denb 72 C4
Pentre-llwyn-llŵyd Powys 47 D8
Pentre-llyn Ceredig 46 B5
Pentre-llyn cymmer Conwy 72 D3
Pentre Meyrick V Glam 21 B8
Pentre-poeth Newport 35 F6
Pentre-rhew Ceredig 47 D5
Pentre-tafarn-y-fedw Conwy 83 E8
Pentre-ty-gwyn Carms 47 F7
Pentrebach M Tydf 34 D4
Pentrebach Swansea 33 D7
Pentrebeirdd Powys 59 C8
Pentrecagal Carms 46 E2
Pentredwr Denb 73 E5
Pentrefelin Carms 33 B6
Pentrefelin Ceredig 46 E5
Pentrefelin Conwy 83 D8
Pentrefelin Gwyn 71 D6
Pentrefoelas Conwy 83 F8
Pentregat Ceredig 46 D2
Pentreheyling Shrops 60 E2
Pentre'r Felin Conwy 83 E8
Pentre'r-felin Powys 47 F8
Pentrich Derbys 76 D3
Pentridge Dorset 13 C8
Pentyrch Cardiff 35 F5
Penuchadre V Glam 21 B7
Penuwch Ceredig 46 C4
Penwithick Corn 4 D5
Penwyllt Powys 34 C2
Penybanc Carms 33 C7
Penybont Powys 48 C3
Penybontfawr Powys 59 B7
Penycae Wrex 73 E6
Penycwm Pembs 44 C3
Penyffordd Flint 73 C7
Penyffridd Gwyn 82 F5
Penygarnedd Powys 59 B8
Penygraig Rhondda 34 E3
Penygroes Gwyn 82 F4
Penygroes Pembs 45 F3
Penyrheol Caerph 35 F5
Penysarn Anglesey 82 B4
Penywaun Rhondda 34 D3
Penzance Corn 2 C3
Peopleton Worcs 50 D4
Peover Heath Ches E 74 B4
Peper Harow Sur 27 E7
Perceton N Ayrs 118 E3
Percie Aberds 140 E4
Percyhorner Aberds 153 B9
Periton Som 21 E8
Perivale London 40 F4
Perkinsville Durham 111 D5
Perlethorpe Notts 77 B6
Perranarworthal Corn 3 C6
Perranporth Corn 4 D2
Perranuthnoe Corn 2 D4
Perranzabuloe Corn 4 D2
Perry Barr W Mid 62 E4
Perry Green Herts 41 C7
Perry Green Wilts 37 F6
Perry Street Kent 29 B7
Perryfoot Derbys 88 F2
Pershall Staffs 74 F5
Pershore Worcs 50 E4
Pert Angus 135 C6
Pertenhall Bedford 53 C8
Perth Perth 128 B3
Perthy Shrops 73 F7
Perton Staffs 62 E2
Pertwood Wilts 24 F3
Peter Tavy Devon 6 B3
Peterborough Pboro 65 E8
Peterburn Highld 155 J12
Peterchurch Hereford 48 F5
Peterculter Aberdeen 141 D7
Peterhead Aberds 153 D11
Peterlee Durham 111 E7
Peter's Green Herts 40 C4
Peters Marland Devon 9 C6
Petersfield Hants 15 B8
Peterston super-Ely V Glam 22 B2
Peterstone Wentlooge Newport 35 F6
Peterstow Hereford 36 B2
Petertown Orkney 159 H4
Petham Kent 30 D5
Petrockstow Devon 9 D7
Pett E Sus 19 D5
Pettaugh Suff 57 D5
Petteridge Kent 29 E7
Pettinain S Lanark 120 E2
Pettistree Suff 57 D6
Petton Devon 10 B5
Petton Shrops 60 B4
Petts Wood London 28 C5
Petty Aberds 153 E7
Pettycur Fife 128 F4
Pettymuick Aberds 141 B8
Petworth W Sus 16 B3
Pevensey E Sus 18 E3
Pevensey Bay E Sus 18 E3
Pewsey Wilts 25 C6
Philham Devon 8 B4
Philiphaugh Borders 115 B7
Phillack Corn 2 C4
Philleigh Corn 3 C7
Philpstoun W Loth 120 B3
Phocle Green Hereford 36 B3
Phoenix Green Hants 27 D5
Pica Cumb 98 B2
Piccotts End Herts 40 D3
Pickering N Yorks 103 F5
Picket Piece Hants 25 E8
Picket Post Hants 14 D2
Pickhill N Yorks 101 F8
Picklescott Shrops 60 E4
Pickletillem Fife 129 B6
Pickmere Ches E 74 B3
Pickney Som 11 B6
Pickstock Telford 61 B7
Pickwell Devon 20 E3
Pickwell Leics 64 C4
Pickworth Lincs 78 F3
Pickworth Rutland 65 C6
Picton Ches W 73 B8
Picton Flint 85 F2
Picton N Yorks 102 D2
Piddinghoe E Sus 17 D8
Piddington Northants 53 D6
Piddington Oxon 39 C6
Piddlehinton Dorset 12 E5
Piddletrenthide Dorset 12 E5
Pidley Cambs 54 B4
Piercebridge Darl 101 C7
Pierowall Orkney 159 D5
Pigdon Northumb 117 F7
Pikehall Derbys 75 D8
Pilgrims Hatch Essex 42 E1
Pilham Lincs 90 E2
Pill N Som 23 B7
Pillaton Corn 5 C8
Pillerton Hersey Warks 51 E8
Pillerton Priors Warks 51 E7
Pilleth Powys 48 C4
Pilley Hants 14 E4
Pilley S Yorks 88 D4
Pilling Lancs 92 E4
Pilling Lane Lancs 92 E3
Pillowell Glos 36 D3
Pillwell Dorset 13 C5
Pilning S Glos 36 F2
Pilsbury Derbys 75 C8
Pilsdon Dorset 12 E2
Pilsgate Pboro 65 D7
Pilsley Derbys 76 B2
Pilsley Derbys 76 C4
Pilton Devon 20 F4
Pilton Northants 65 F7
Pilton Rutland 65 D6
Pilton Som 23 E7
Pilton Green Swansea 33 F5
Pimperne Dorset 13 D7
Pin Mill Suff 57 F6
Pinchbeck Lincs 66 B2
Pinchbeck Bars Lincs 65 B8
Pinchbeck West Lincs 66 B2
Pincheon Green S Yorks 89 C7
Pinehurst Swindon 38 F1
Pinfold Lancs 85 C4
Pinged Carms 33 D5
Pinhoe Devon 10 E4
Pinkneys Green Windsor 40 F1
Pinley W Mid 51 B8
Pinminnoch S Ayrs 112 E1
Pinmore S Ayrs 112 E2
Pinmore Mains S Ayrs 112 E2
Pinner London 40 F4
Pinvin Worcs 50 E4
Pinwherry S Ayrs 112 F1
Pinxton Derbys 76 D4
Pipe and Lyde Hereford 49 E7
Pipe Gate Shrops 74 E4
Piperhill Highld 151 F11
Piper's Pool Corn 8 F4
Pipewell Northants 64 F5
Pippacott Devon 20 F4
Pipton Powys 48 F3
Pirbright Sur 27 D7
Pirnmill N Ayrs 143 D9
Pirton Herts 54 F2
Pirton Worcs 50 E3
Pisgah Ceredig 47 B5
Pisgah Stirling 127 D6
Pishill Oxon 39 F7
Pistyll Gwyn 70 C4
Pitagowan Perth 133 C5
Pitblae Aberds 153 B9
Pitcairngreen Perth 128 B2
Pitcalnie Highld 151 D11
Pitcaple Aberds 141 B6
Pitch Green Bucks 39 D7
Pitch Place Sur 27 D7
Pitchcombe Glos 37 D5
Pitchcott Bucks 39 B7
Pitchford Shrops 60 D5
Pitcombe Som 23 F8
Pitcorthie Fife 129 D7
Pitcox E Loth 122 B2
Pitcur Perth 134 F2
Pitfichie Aberds 141 C5
Pitforthie Aberds 135 B8
Pitgrudy Highld 151 B10
Pitkennedy Angus 135 D5
Pitkevy Fife 128 D4
Pitkierie Fife 129 D7
Pitlessie Fife 128 D5
Pitlochry Perth 133 D6
Pitmachie Aberds 141 B5
Pitmain Highld 138 D3
Pitmedden Aberds 141 B7
Pitminster Som 11 C7
Pitmuies Angus 135 E5
Pitmunie Aberds 141 C5
Pitney Som 12 B2
Pitscottie Fife 129 C6
Pitsea Essex 42 F3
Pitsford Northants 53 C5
Pitsmoor S Yorks 88 F4
Pitstone Bucks 40 C2
Pitstone Green Bucks 40 C2
Pittendreich Moray 152 B1
Pittentrail Highld 157 J10
Pittenweem Fife 129 D7
Pittington Durham 111 E6
Pittodrie Aberds 141 B5
Pitton Wilts 25 F7
Pittswood Kent 29 E7
Pittulie Aberds 153 B9
Pity Me Durham 111 E5
Pityme Corn 4 B4
Pityoulish Highld 138 C5
Pixey Green Suff 57 B6
Pixham Sur 28 D2
Pixley Hereford 49 F8
Place Newton N Yorks 96 B4
Plaidy Aberds 153 C7
Plains N Lanark 119 C7
Plaish Shrops 60 E5
Plaistow W Sus 27 F8
Plaitford Wilts 14 C3
Plank Lane Gtr Man 86 E4
Plas-canol Gwyn 58 C2
Plas Gogerddan Ceredig 58 F3
Plas Llwyngwern Powys 58 D4
Plas Nantyr Wrex 73 F5
Plas-yn-Cefn Denb 72 B4
Plastow Green Hants 26 C3
Platt Kent 29 D7
Platt Bridge Gtr Man 86 D4
Platts Common S Yorks 88 D4
Plawsworth Durham 111 E5
Plaxtol Kent 29 D7
Play Hatch Oxon 26 B5
Playden E Sus 19 C6
Playford Suff 57 E6
Playing Place Corn 3 B7
Playley Green Glos 50 F2
Plealey Shrops 60 D4
Plean Stirling 127 F7
Pleasington Blackburn 86 B4
Pleasley Derbys 76 C5
Pleckgate Blackburn 93 F6
Plenmeller Northumb 109 C7
Pleshey Essex 42 C2
Plockton Highld 149 E13
Plocrapol W Isles 154 H6
Ploughfield Hereford 49 E5
Plowden Shrops 60 F3
Ploxgreen Shrops 60 D3
Pluckley Kent 30 E3
Pluckley Thorne Kent 30 E3
Plumbland Cumb 107 F8
Plumley Ches E 74 B4
Plumpton Cumb 108 F4
Plumpton E Sus 17 C7
Plumpton Green E Sus 17 C7
Plumpton Head Cumb 108 F5
Plumstead London 29 B5
Plumstead Norf 81 D7
Plumtree Notts 77 F6
Plungar Leics 77 F7
Plush Dorset 12 D5
Plwmp Ceredig 46 D2
Plymouth Plym 6 D2
Plympton Plym 6 D3

Ros–Shi 199

Rosehall Highld 156 J7
Rosehaugh Mains Highld 151 F9
Rosehearty Aberds 153 B9
Rosehill Shrops 74 F3
Roseisle Moray 152 B1
Roselands E Sus 18 E3
Rosemarket Pembs 44 E4
Rosemarkie Highld 151 F10
Rosemary Lane Devon 11 C6
Rosemount Perth 134 E1
Rosenannon Corn 4 C4
Rosewell Midloth 121 C5
Roseworth Stockton 102 B2
Roseworthy Corn 2 C5
Rosgill Cumb 99 C7
Roshven Highld 147 D10
Roskhill Highld 149 D7
Roskill House Highld 151 F9
Rosley Cumb 108 E3
Roslin Midloth 121 C5
Rosliston Derbys 63 C6
Rosneath Argyll 145 E11
Ross Dumfries 106 E3
Ross Northumb 123 F7
Ross Perth 127 B6
Ross-on-Wye Hereford 36 B3
Rossett Wrex 73 D7
Rossett Green N Yorks 95 D6
Rossie Ochill Perth 128 C2
Rossie Priory Perth 134 F2
Rossington S Yorks 89 E7
Rosskeen Highld 151 E9
Rossland Renfs 118 B4
Roster Highld 158 G4
Rostherne Ches E 86 F5
Rosthwaite Cumb 98 C4
Roston Derbys 75 E8
Rosyth Fife 128 F3
Rothbury Northumb 117 D6
Rotherby Leics 64 C3
Rotherfield E Sus 18 C2
Rotherfield Greys Oxon 39 F7
Rotherfield Peppard Oxon 39 F7
Rotherham S Yorks 88 E5
Rothersthorpe Northants 52 D5
Rotherwick Hants 26 D5
Rothes Moray 152 D2
Rothesay Argyll 145 G9
Rothiebrisbane Aberds 153 E7
Rothienorman Aberds 153 E7
Rothiesholm Orkney 159 F7
Rothley Leics 64 C2
Rothley Northumb 117 F6
Rothley Shield East Northumb 117 E6
Rothmaise Aberds 153 E6
Rothwell Lincs 91 E5
Rothwell Northants 64 F5
Rothwell W Yorks 88 B4
Rothwell Haigh W Yorks 88 B4
Rotsea E Yorks 97 D6
Rottal Angus 134 C3
Rotten End Suff 57 C7
Rottingdean Brighton 17 D7
Rottington Cumb 98 C1
Roud IoW 15 F6
Rough Close Staffs 75 F6
Rough Common Kent 30 D5
Rougham Norf 80 E4
Rougham Suff 56 C3
Rougham Green Suff 56 C3
Roughburn Highld 137 F6
Roughlee Lancs 93 E8
Roughley W Mid 62 E5
Roughsike Cumb 108 B5
Roughton Lincs 78 C5
Roughton Norf 81 D8
Roughton Shrops 61 E7
Roughton Moor Lincs 78 C5
Roundhay W Yorks 95 F6
Roundstonefoot Dumfries 114 D4
Roundstreet Common W Sus 16 B4
Roundway Wilts 24 C5
Rous Lench Worcs 50 D5
Rousdon Devon 11 E7
Routenburn N Ayrs 118 C1
Routh E Yorks 97 E6
Row Corn 5 B5
Row Cumb 99 F6
Row Heath Essex 43 C7
Rowanburn Dumfries 108 B4
Rowardennan Stirling 126 E2
Rowde Wilts 24 C4
Rowen Conwy 83 D7
Rowfoot Northumb 109 C6
Rowhedge Essex 43 B6
Rowhook W Sus 28 F2
Rowington Warks 51 C7
Rowland Derbys 76 B2
Rowlands Castle Hants 15 C8
Rowlands Gill T&W 110 D4
Rowledge Sur 27 E6
Rowlestone Hereford 35 B7
Rowley E Yorks 97 F5
Rowley Shrops 60 D3
Rowley Hill W Yorks 88 C2
Rowley Regis W Mid 62 F3
Rowly Sur 27 E8
Rowney Green Worcs 50 B5
Rownhams Hants 14 C4
Rowrah Cumb 98 C2
Rowsham Bucks 39 C8
Rowsley Derbys 76 C2
Rowstock Oxon 38 F4
Rowston Lincs 78 D3
Rowton Ches W 73 C8
Rowton Shrops 60 C3
Rowton Telford 61 C6
Roxburgh Borders 122 F3
Roxby N Lincs 90 C3
Roxby N Yorks 103 C5
Roxton Bedford 54 D2
Roxwell Essex 42 D2
Royal Leamington Spa Warks 51 C8
Royal Oak Darl 101 B7
Royal Oak Lancs 86 D2
Royal Tunbridge Wells Kent 18 B2
Royal Wootton Bassett Wilts 37 F7
Roybridge Highld 137 F5
Roydhouse W Yorks 88 C3
Roydon Essex 41 D7
Roydon Norf 68 F3
Roydon Norf 80 E3
Roydon Hamlet Essex 41 D7
Royston Herts 54 E4
Royston S Yorks 88 C4
Royton Gtr Man 87 D7
Rozel Jersey 17
Ruabon = Rhiwabon Wrex 73 E7
Ruaig Argyll 146 G3
Ruan Lanihorne Corn 3 B7
Ruan Minor Corn 3 E6
Ruarach Highld 136 B2
Ruardean Glos 36 C3
Ruardean Woodside Glos 36 C3
Rubery Worcs 50 B4
Ruckcroft Cumb 108 E5
Ruckhall Hereford 49 F6
Ruckinge Kent 19 B7
Ruckland Lincs 79 B6
Ruckley Shrops 60 D5
Rudbaxton Pembs 44 C4
Rudby N Yorks 102 D2
Ruddington Notts 77 F5
Rudford Glos 36 B4
Rudge Shrops 62 E2
Rudge Som 24 D3
Rudgeway S Glos 36 F3
Rudgwick W Sus 27 F8
Rudhall Hereford 36 B3
Rudheath Ches W 74 B3
Rudley Green Essex 42 D4
Rudry Caerph 35 F5
Rudston E Yorks 97 C6
Rudyard Staffs 75 D6
Rufford Lancs 86 C2
Rufforth York 95 D8
Rugby Warks 52 B3
Rugeley Staffs 62 C4
Ruglen S Ayrs 112 D2
Ruilick Highld 151 G8
Ruishton Som 11 B7
Ruisigearraidh W Isles 154 J4
Ruislip London 40 F3
Ruislip Common London 40 F3
Rumbling Bridge Perth 128 E2
Rumburgh Suff 69 F6
Rumford Corn 4 B3
Rumney Cardiff 22 B4
Runcorn Halton 86 F3
Runcton W Sus 16 D2
Runcton Holme Norf 67 D6
Rundlestone Devon 6 B3
Runfold Sur 27 E6
Runhall Norf 68 D3
Runham Norf 69 C7
Runham Norf 69 D8
Runnington Som 11 B6
Runsell Green Essex 42 D3
Runswick Bay N Yorks 103 C6
Runwell Essex 42 E3
Ruscombe Wokingham 27 B5
Rush Green London 41 F8
Rush-head Aberds 153 D8
Rushall Hereford 49 F8
Rushall Norf 68 F4
Rushall W Mid 62 D4
Rushall Wilts 25 D6
Rushbrooke Suff 56 C2
Rushbury Shrops 60 E5
Rushden Herts 54 F4
Rushden Northants 53 C7
Rushenden Kent 30 B3
Rushford Norf 68 F2
Rushlake Green E Sus 18 D3
Rushmere Suff 69 F7
Rushmere St Andrew Suff 57 E6
Rushmoor Sur 27 E6
Rushock Worcs 50 B3
Rusholme Gtr Man 87 E6
Rushton Ches W 74 C2
Rushton Northants 64 F5
Rushton Shrops 61 D6
Rushton Spencer Staffs 75 C6
Rushwick Worcs 50 D3
Rushyford Durham 101 B7
Ruskie Stirling 126 D5
Ruskington Lincs 78 D3
Rusland Cumb 99 F5
Rusper W Sus 28 F3
Ruspidge Glos 36 C3
Russell's Water Oxon 39 F7
Russel's Green Suff 57 B6
Rusthall Kent 18 B2
Rustington W Sus 16 D4
Ruston N Yorks 103 F7
Ruston Parva E Yorks 97 C6
Ruswarp N Yorks 103 D6
Rutherford Borders 122 F2
Rutherglen S Lanark 119 C6
Ruthernbridge Corn 4 C5
Ruthin = Rhuthun Denb 72 D5
Ruthrieston Aberdeen 141 D8
Ruthven Aberds 152 D5
Ruthven Angus 134 E2
Ruthven Highld 138 E3
Ruthven Highld 151 H11
Ruthven House Angus 134 E3
Ruthvoes Corn 4 C4
Ruthwell Dumfries 107 C7
Ruyton-XI-Towns Shrops 60 B3
Ryal Northumb 110 B3
Ryal Fold Blackburn 86 B4
Ryall Dorset 12 E2
Ryarsh Kent 29 D7
Rydal Cumb 99 D5
Ryde IoW 15 E6
Rye E Sus 19 C6
Rye Foreign E Sus 19 C5
Rye Harbour E Sus 19 D6
Rye Park Herts 41 C6
Rye Street Worcs 50 F2
Ryecroft Gate Staffs 75 C6
Ryehill E Yorks 91 B6
Ryhall Rutland 65 C7
Ryhill W Yorks 88 C4
Ryhope T&W 111 D7
Rylstone N Yorks 94 D2
Ryme Intrinseca Dorset 12 C3
Ryther N Yorks 95 F8
Ryton Glos 50 F2
Ryton N Yorks 96 B3
Ryton Shrops 61 D7
Ryton T&W 110 C4
Ryton-on-Dunsmore Warks 51 B8

S

Sabden Lancs 93 F7
Sacombe Herts 41 C6
Sacriston Durham 110 E5
Sadberge Darl 101 C8
Saddell Argyll 143 E8
Saddington Leics 64 E3
Saddle Bow Norf 67 C6
Saddlescombe W Sus 17 C6
Sadgill Cumb 99 D6
Saffron Walden Essex 55 F6
Sageston Pembs 32 D1
Saham Hills Norf 68 D2
Saham Toney Norf 68 D2
Saighdinis W Isles 148 B3
Saighton Ches W 73 C8
St Abbs Borders 122 C5
St Abb's Haven Borders 122 C5
St Agnes Corn 4 D2
St Agnes Scilly 2 F3
St Albans Herts 40 D4
St Allen Corn 4 D3
St Andrews Fife 129 C7
St Andrew's Major V Glam 22 B3
St Anne Ald 16
St Annes Lancs 85 B4
St Ann's Dumfries 114 E3
St Ann's Chapel Corn 6 B2
St Ann's Chapel Devon 6 E4
St Anthony-in-Meneage Corn 3 D6
St Anthony's Hill E Sus 18 E3
St Arvans Mon 36 E2
St Asaph = Llanelwy Denb 72 B4
St Athan V Glam 22 C2
St Aubin Jersey 17
St Austell Corn 4 D5
St Bees Cumb 98 C1
St Blazey Corn 5 D5
St Boswells Borders 121 F8
St Brelade Jersey 17
St Breock Corn 4 B4
St Breward Corn 5 B5
St Briavels Glos 36 D2
St Bride's Pembs 44 D3
St Brides Major V Glam 21 B7
St Bride's Netherwent Mon 35 F8
St Brides super Ely V Glam 22 B2
St Brides Wentlooge Newport 35 F6
St Budeaux Plym 6 D2
St Buryan Corn 2 D3
St Catherine Bath 24 B2
St Catherine's Argyll 125 E7
St Clears = Sanclêr Carms 32 C3
St Cleer Corn 5 C7
St Clement Corn 3 B7
St Clements Jersey 17
St Clether Corn 8 F4
St Colmac Argyll 145 G9
St Columb Major Corn 4 C4
St Columb Minor Corn 4 C3
St Columb Road Corn 4 D4
St Combs Aberds 153 B10
St Cross South Elmham Suff 69 F5
St Cyrus Aberds 135 C7
St David's Perth 127 B8
St David's = Tyddewi Pembs 44 C2
St Day Corn 3 B6
St Dennis Corn 4 D4
St Devereux Hereford 49 F6
St Dogmaels Pembs 45 E3
St Dogwells Pembs 44 C4
St Dominick Corn 6 C2
St Donat's V Glam 21 C8
St Edith's Wilts 24 C4
St Endellion Corn 4 B4
St Enoder Corn 4 D3
St Erme Corn 4 D3
St Erney Corn 5 D8
St Erth Corn 2 C4
St Ervan Corn 4 B3
St Eval Corn 4 C3
St Ewe Corn 3 B8
St Fagans Cardiff 22 B3
St Fergus Aberds 153 C10
St Fillans Perth 127 B5
St Florence Pembs 32 D1
St Genny's Corn 8 E3
St George Conwy 72 B3
St George's V Glam 22 B2
St Germans Corn 5 D8
St Giles Lincs 78 B2
St Giles in the Wood Devon 9 C7
St Giles on the Heath Devon 9 E5
St Harmon Powys 47 B8
St Helen Auckland Durham 101 B6
St Helena Warks 63 D6
St Helen's E Sus 18 D5
St Helens IoW 15 F7
St Helens Mers 86 E3
St Helier Jersey 17
St Helier London 28 C3
St Hilary Corn 2 C4
St Hilary V Glam 22 B2
Saint Hill W Sus 28 F4
St Illtyd Bl Gwent 35 D6
St Ippollytts Herts 40 B4
St Ishmael's Pembs 44 E3
St Issey Corn 4 B4
St Ive Corn 5 C8
St Ives Cambs 54 B4
St Ives Corn 2 B4
St Ives Dorset 14 D2
St James South Elmham Suff 69 F6
St Jidgey Corn 4 C4
St John Corn 6 D2
St John's IoM 84 D2
St John's Jersey 17
St John's Sur 27 D7
St John's Worcs 50 D3
St John's Chapel Durham 109 F8
St John's Fen End Norf 66 C5
St John's Highway Norf 66 C5
St John's Town of Dalry Dumfries 113 F6
St Judes IoM 84 C3
St Just Corn 2 C2
St Just in Roseland Corn 3 C7
St Katherine's Aberds 153 E7
St Keverne Corn 3 D6
St Kew Corn 4 B5
St Kew Highway Corn 4 B5
St Keyne Corn 5 C7
St Lawrence Corn 4 C5
St Lawrence Essex 43 D5
St Lawrence IoW 15 G6
St Leonard's Bucks 40 D2
St Leonards Dorset 14 D2
St Leonards E Sus 18 E4
Saint Leonards S Lanark 119 D6
St Levan Corn 2 D2
St Lythans V Glam 22 B3
St Mabyn Corn 4 B5
St Madoes Perth 128 B3
St Margaret's Hereford 49 F5
St Margarets Herts 41 C6
St Margaret's at Cliffe Kent 31 E7
St Margaret's Hope Orkney 159 J5
St Margaret South Elmham Suff 69 F6
St Mark's IoM 84 E2
St Martin Corn 5 D7
St Martins Corn 3 D6
St Martin's Jersey 17
St Martins Perth 134 F1
St Martin's Shrops 73 F7
St Mary Bourne Hants 26 D2
St Mary Church V Glam 22 B2
St Mary Cray London 29 C5
St Mary Hill V Glam 21 B8
St Mary Hoo Medway 30 B2
St Mary in the Marsh Kent 19 C7
St Mary's Jersey 17
St Mary's Orkney 159 H5
St Mary's Bay Kent 19 C7
St Maughans Mon 36 C1
St Mawes Corn 3 C7
St Mawgan Corn 4 C3
St Mellion Corn 5 C8
St Mellons Cardiff 35 F6
St Merryn Corn 4 B3
St Mewan Corn 4 D4
St Michael Caerhays Corn 3 B8
St Michael Penkevil Corn 3 B7
St Michael South Elmham Suff 69 F6
St Michael's Kent 19 B5
St Michaels Worcs 49 C7
St Michael's on Wyre Lancs 92 E4
St Minver Corn 4 B4
St Monans Fife 129 D7
St Neot Corn 5 C6
St Neots Cambs 54 C2
St Newlyn East Corn 4 D3
St Nicholas Pembs 44 B3
St Nicholas V Glam 22 B2
St Nicholas at Wade Kent 31 C6
St Ninians Stirling 127 E6
St Osyth Essex 43 C7
St Osyth Heath Essex 43 C7
St Ouens Jersey 17
St Owens Cross Hereford 36 B2
St Paul's Cray London 29 C5
St Paul's Walden Herts 40 B4
St Peter Port Guern 16
St Peter's Jersey 17
St Peter's Kent 31 C7
St Petrox Pembs 44 F4
St Pinnock Corn 5 C7
St Quivox S Ayrs 112 B3
St Ruan Corn 3 E6
St Sampson Guern 16
St Stephen Corn 4 D4
St Stephen's Corn 8 F5
St Stephens Corn 6 D2
St Stephens Herts 40 D4
St Teath Corn 8 F2
St Thomas Devon 10 E4
St Tudy Corn 5 B5
St Twynnells Pembs 44 F4
St Veep Corn 5 D6
St Vigeans Angus 135 E6
St Wenn Corn 4 C4
St Weonards Hereford 36 B1
Saintbury Glos 51 F6
Salcombe Devon 6 F5
Salcombe Regis Devon 11 F6
Salcott Essex 43 C5
Sale Gtr Man 87 E5
Sale Green Worcs 50 D4
Saleby Lincs 79 B7
Salehurst E Sus 18 C4
Salem Carms 33 B7
Salem Ceredig 58 F3
Salen Argyll 147 G8
Salen Highld 147 E9
Salesbury Lancs 93 F6
Salford C Beds 53 F7
Salford Gtr Man 87 E6
Salford Oxon 38 B2
Salford Priors Warks 51 D5
Salfords Sur 28 E3
Salhouse Norf 69 C6
Saline Fife 128 E2
Salisbury Wilts 14 B2
Sallachan Highld 130 C3
Sallachy Highld 150 H2
Sallachy Highld 157 J8
Salle Norf 81 E7
Salmonby Lincs 79 B6
Salmond's Muir Angus 135 F5
Salperton Glos 37 B7
Salph End Bedford 53 D8
Salsburgh N Lanark 119 C8
Salt Staffs 62 B3
Salt End E Yorks 91 B5
Saltaire W Yorks 94 F4
Saltash Corn 6 D2
Saltburn Highld 151 E10
Saltburn-by-the-Sea Redcar 102 B4
Saltby Leics 65 B5
Saltcoats Cumb 98 E2
Saltcoats N Ayrs 118 E2
Saltdean Brighton 17 D7
Salter Lancs 93 C6
Salterforth Lancs 93 E8
Salterswall Ches W 74 C3
Saltfleet Lincs 91 E8
Saltfleetby All Saints Lincs 91 E8
Saltfleetby St Clements Lincs 91 E8
Saltfleetby St Peter Lincs 91 F8
Saltford Bath 23 C8
Salthouse Norf 81 C6
Saltmarshe E Yorks 89 B8
Saltney Flint 73 C7
Salton N Yorks 96 B3
Saltwick Northumb 110 B4
Saltwood Kent 19 B8
Salum Argyll 146 G3
Salvington W Sus 16 D5
Salwarpe Worcs 50 C3
Salwayash Dorset 12 E2
Sambourne Warks 51 C5
Sambrook Telford 61 B7
Samhla W Isles 148 B2
Samlesbury Lancs 93 F5
Samlesbury Bottoms Lancs 86 B4
Sampford Arundel Som 11 C6
Sampford Brett Som 22 E2
Sampford Courtenay Devon 9 D8
Sampford Peverell Devon 10 C5
Sampford Spiney Devon 6 B3
Sampool Bridge Cumb 99 F6
Samuelston E Loth 121 B7
Sanachan Highld 149 D13
Sanaigmore Argyll 142 A3
Sanclêr = St Clears Carms 32 C3
Sancreed Corn 2 D3
Sancton E Yorks 96 F5
Sand Highld 150 B2
Sand Shetland 160 J5
Sand Hole E Yorks 96 F4
Sand Hutton N Yorks 96 D2
Sandaig Highld 149 H12
Sandal Magna W Yorks 88 C4
Sandale Cumb 108 E2
Sandbach Ches E 74 C4
Sandbank Argyll 145 E10
Sandbanks Poole 13 F8
Sandend Aberds 152 B5
Sanderstead London 28 C4
Sandfields Glos 37 B6
Sandford Cumb 100 C2
Sandford Devon 10 D3
Sandford Dorset 13 F7
Sandford IoW 15 F6
Sandford N Som 23 D6
Sandford S Lanark 119 E7
Sandford Shrops 74 F2
Sandford on Thames Oxon 39 D5
Sandford Orcas Dorset 12 B4
Sandford St Martin Oxon 38 B4
Sandfordhill Aberds 153 D11
Sandgate Kent 19 B8
Sandgreen Dumfries 106 D2
Sandhaven Aberds 153 B9
Sandhead Dumfries 104 E4
Sandhills Sur 27 F7
Sandhoe Northumb 110 C2
Sandholme E Yorks 96 F4
Sandholme Lincs 79 F6
Sandhurst Brack 27 C6
Sandhurst Glos 37 B5
Sandhurst Kent 18 C4
Sandhurst Cross Kent 18 C4
Sandhutton N Yorks 102 F1
Sandiacre Derbys 76 F4
Sandilands Lincs 91 F9
Sandilands S Lanark 119 F8
Sandiway Ches W 74 B3
Sandleheath Hants 14 C2
Sandling Kent 29 D8
Sandlow Green Ches E 74 C4
Sandness Shetland 160 H3
Sandon Essex 42 D3
Sandon Herts 54 F4
Sandon Staffs 75 F6
Sandown IoW 15 F6
Sandplace Corn 5 D7
Sandridge Herts 40 C4
Sandridge Wilts 24 C4
Sandringham Norf 67 B6
Sandsend N Yorks 103 C6
Sandside Ho. Highld 157 C12
Sandsound Shetland 160 J5
Sandtoft N Lincs 89 D8
Sandway Kent 30 D2
Sandwell W Mid 62 F4
Sandwich Kent 31 D7
Sandwick Cumb 99 C6
Sandwick Orkney 159 K5
Sandwick Shetland 160 L6
Sandwith Cumb 98 C1
Sandy C Beds 54 E2
Sandy Carms 33 D5
Sandy Bank Lincs 79 D5
Sandy Haven Pembs 44 E3
Sandy Lane Wilts 24 C4
Sandy Lane Wrex 73 E7
Sandycroft Flint 73 C7
Sandyford Dumfries 114 E5
Sandyford Stoke 75 D5
Sandygate IoM 84 C3
Sandyhills Dumfries 107 D5
Sandylands Lancs 92 C4
Sandypark Devon 10 F2
Sandysike Cumb 108 C3
Sangobeg Highld 156 C7
Sangomore Highld 156 C7
Sanna Highld 146 E7
Sanndabhaig W Isles 148 D3
Sanndabhaig W Isles 155 D9
Sannox N Ayrs 143 D11
Sanquhar Dumfries 113 D7
Santon N Lincs 90 C3
Santon Bridge Cumb 98 D3
Santon Downham Suff 67 F8
Sapcote Leics 63 E8
Sapey Common Hereford 50 C2
Sapiston Suff 56 B3
Sapley Cambs 54 B3
Sapperton Glos 37 D6
Sapperton Lincs 78 F3
Saracen's Head Lincs 66 B3
Sarclet Highld 158 F5
Sardis Carms 33 D6
Sarn Bridgend 34 F3
Sarn Powys 60 E2
Sarn Bach Gwyn 70 E4
Sarn Meyllteyrn Gwyn 70 D3
Sarnau Carms 32 C4
Sarnau Ceredig 46 D2
Sarnau Gwyn 72 F3
Sarnau Powys 48 F2
Sarnau Powys 60 C2
Sarnesfield Hereford 49 D5
Saron Carms 33 C7
Saron Carms 46 F2
Saron Denb 72 C4
Saron Gwyn 82 E5
Saron Gwyn 82 F4
Sarratt Herts 40 E3
Sarre Kent 31 C6
Sarsden Oxon 38 B2
Sarsgrum Highld 156 C6
Satley Durham 110 E4
Satron N Yorks 100 E4
Satterleigh Devon 9 B8
Satterthwaite Cumb 99 E5
Satwell Oxon 39 F7
Sauchen Aberds 141 C5
Saucher Perth 134 F1
Sauchie Clack 127 E7
Sauchieburn Aberds 135 C6
Saughall Ches W 73 B7
Saughtree Borders 115 E8
Saul Glos 36 D4
Saundby Notts 89 F8
Saundersfoot Pembs 32 D2
Saunderton Bucks 39 D7
Saunton Devon 20 F3
Sausthorpe Lincs 79 C6
Saval Highld 157 J8
Savary Highld 147 G9
Savile Park W Yorks 87 B8
Sawbridge Warks 52 C3
Sawbridgeworth Herts 41 C7
Sawdon N Yorks 103 F7
Sawley Derbys 76 F4
Sawley Lancs 93 E7
Sawley N Yorks 94 C5
Sawston Cambs 55 E5
Sawtry Cambs 65 F8
Saxby Leics 64 C5
Saxby Lincs 90 F4
Saxby All Saints N Lincs 90 C3
Saxelbye Leics 64 B4
Saxham Street Suff 56 C4
Saxilby Lincs 77 B8
Saxlingham Norf 81 D6
Saxlingham Green Norf 68 E5
Saxlingham Nethergate Norf 68 E5
Saxlingham Thorpe Norf 68 E5
Saxmundham Suff 57 C7
Saxon Street Cambs 55 D7
Saxondale Notts 77 F6
Saxtead Suff 57 C6
Saxtead Green Suff 57 C6
Saxthorpe Norf 81 D7
Saxton N Yorks 95 F7
Sayers Common W Sus 17 C6
Scackleton N Yorks 96 B2
Scadabhagh W Isles 154 H6
Scaftworth Notts 89 E7
Scagglethorpe N Yorks 96 B4
Scaitcliffe Lancs 87 B5
Scalasaig Argyll 144 D2
Scalby E Yorks 90 B2
Scalby N Yorks 103 E8
Scaldwell Northants 53 B5
Scale Houses Cumb 109 E5
Scaleby Cumb 108 C4
Scaleby Hill Cumb 108 C4
Scales Cumb 92 B2
Scales Cumb 99 B5
Scales Lancs 92 F4
Scalford Leics 64 B4
Scaling Redcar 103 C5
Scallastle Argyll 124 B2
Scalloway Shetland 160 K6
Scalpay W Isles 154 H7
Scalpay Ho. Highld 149 F11
Scalpsie Argyll 145 H9
Scamadale Highld 147 B10
Scamblesby Lincs 79 B5
Scamodale Highld 130 B2
Scampston N Yorks 96 B4
Scampton Lincs 78 B2
Scapa Orkney 159 H5
Scapegoat Hill W Yorks 87 C8
Scar Orkney 159 D7
Scarborough N Yorks 103 F8
Scarcliffe Derbys 76 C4
Scarcroft W Yorks 95 E6
Scarcroft Hill W Yorks 95 E6
Scardroy Highld 150 F5
Scarff Shetland 160 E4
Scarfskerry Highld 158 C4
Scargill Durham 101 C5
Scarinish Argyll 146 G3
Scarisbrick Lancs 85 C4
Scarning Norf 68 C2
Scarrington Notts 77 E7
Scartho NE Lincs 91 D6
Scarwell Orkney 159 F3
Scatness Shetland 160 M5
Scatraig Highld 151 H10
Scawby N Lincs 90 D3
Scawsby S Yorks 89 D6
Scawton N Yorks 102 F3
Scayne's Hill W Sus 17 B7
Scethrog Powys 35 B5
Scholar Green Ches E 74 D5
Scholes W Yorks 88 B2
Scholes W Yorks 88 D2
Scholes W Yorks 95 F6
School Green Ches W 74 C3
Scleddau Pembs 44 B4
Sco Ruston Norf 81 E8
Scofton Notts 89 F7
Scole Norf 56 B5
Scolpaig W Isles 148 A2
Scone Perth 128 B3
Sconser Highld 149 E10
Scoonie Fife 129 D5
Scoor Argyll 146 K7
Scopwick Lincs 78 D3
Scoraig Highld 150 B3
Scorborough E Yorks 97 E6
Scorrier Corn 3 B6
Scorton Lancs 92 E5
Scorton N Yorks 101 D7
Scotbheinn W Isles 148 C3
Scotby Cumb 108 D4
Scotch Corner N Yorks 101 D7
Scotforth Lancs 92 D4
Scothern Lincs 78 B3
Scotland Gate Northumb 117 F8
Scotlandwell Perth 128 D3
Scotsburn Highld 151 D10
Scotscalder Station Highld 158 E2
Scotscraig Fife 129 B6
Scots' Gap Northumb 117 F6
Scotston Aberds 135 B7
Scotston Perth 133 E6
Scotstoun Glasgow 118 C5
Scotstown Highld 130 C2
Scotswood T&W 110 C4
Scottas Highld 149 H12
Scotter Lincs 90 D2
Scotterthorpe Lincs 90 D2
Scottlethorpe Lincs 65 B7
Scotton Lincs 90 E2
Scotton N Yorks 95 D6
Scotton N Yorks 101 E6
Scottow Norf 81 E8
Scoughall E Loth 129 F8
Scoulag Argyll 145 H10
Scoulton Norf 68 D2
Scourie Highld 156 E4
Scourie More Highld 156 E4
Scousburgh Shetland 160 M5
Scrabster Highld 158 C2
Scrafield Lincs 79 C6
Scrainwood Northumb 117 D5
Scrane End Lincs 79 E6
Scraptoft Leics 64 D3
Scratby Norf 69 C8
Scrayingham N Yorks 96 C3
Scredington Lincs 78 E3
Scremby Lincs 79 C7
Scremerston Northumb 123 E6
Screveton Notts 77 E7
Scrivelsby Lincs 79 C5
Scriven N Yorks 95 D6
Scrooby Notts 89 E7
Scropton Derbys 75 F8
Scrub Hill Lincs 78 D5
Scruton N Yorks 101 E7
Sculcoates Hull 97 F6
Sculthorpe Norf 80 D4
Scunthorpe N Lincs 90 C2
Scurlage Swansea 33 F5
Sea Palling Norf 69 B7
Seaborough Dorset 12 D2
Seacombe Mers 85 E4
Seacroft Lincs 79 C8
Seacroft W Yorks 95 F6
Seadyke Lincs 79 F6
Seafield S Ayrs 112 B3
Seafield W Loth 120 C3
Seaford E Sus 17 E8
Seaforth Mers 85 E4
Seagrave Leics 64 C3
Seaham Durham 111 E7
Seahouses Northumb 123 F8
Seal Kent 29 D6
Sealand Flint 73 C7
Seale Sur 27 E6
Seamer N Yorks 102 C2
Seamer N Yorks 103 F8
Seamill N Ayrs 118 E2
Searby Lincs 90 D4
Seasalter Kent 30 C4
Seascale Cumb 98 D2
Seathorne Lincs 79 C8
Seathwaite Cumb 98 C4
Seathwaite Cumb 98 E4
Seatoller Cumb 98 C4
Seaton Corn 5 D8
Seaton Cumb 107 F7
Seaton Devon 11 F7
Seaton Durham 111 D6
Seaton E Yorks 97 E7
Seaton Northumb 111 B6
Seaton Rutland 65 E6
Seaton Burn T&W 110 B5
Seaton Carew Hrtlpl 102 B3
Seaton Delaval Northumb 111 B6
Seaton Ross E Yorks 96 E3
Seaton Sluice Northumb 111 B6
Seatown Aberds 152 B5
Seatown Dorset 12 E2
Seave Green N Yorks 102 D3
Seaview IoW 15 E7
Seaville Cumb 107 D8
Seavington St Mary Som 12 C2
Seavington St Michael Som 12 C2
Sebergham Cumb 108 E3
Seckington Warks 63 D6
Second Coast Highld 150 B2
Sedbergh Cumb 100 E1
Sedbury Glos 36 E2
Sedbusk N Yorks 100 E3
Sedgeberrow Worcs 50 F5
Sedgebrook Lincs 77 F8
Sedgefield Durham 102 B1
Sedgeford Norf 80 D3
Sedgehill Wilts 13 B6
Sedgley W Mid 62 E3
Sedgwick Cumb 99 F7
Sedlescombe E Sus 18 D4
Sedlescombe Street E Sus 18 D4
Seend Wilts 24 C4
Seend Cleeve Wilts 24 C4
Seer Green Bucks 40 E2
Seething Norf 69 E6
Sefton Mers 85 D4
Seghill Northumb 111 B5
Seifton Shrops 60 F4
Seighford Staffs 62 B2
Seilebost W Isles 154 H5
Seion Gwyn 82 E5
Seisdon Staffs 62 E2
Seisiadar W Isles 155 D10
Selattyn Shrops 73 F6
Selborne Hants 26 F5
Selby N Yorks 96 F2
Selham W Sus 16 B3
Selhurst London 28 C4
Selkirk Borders 115 B7
Sellack Hereford 36 B2
Sellafirth Shetland 160 D7
Sellibister Orkney 159 D8
Sellindge Kent 19 B7
Sellindge Lees Kent 19 B8
Selling Kent 30 D4
Sells Green Wilts 24 C4
Selly Oak W Mid 62 F4
Selmeston E Sus 18 E2
Selsdon London 28 C4
Selsey W Sus 16 E2
Selsfield Common W Sus 28 F4
Selsted Kent 31 E6
Selston Notts 76 D4
Selworthy Som 21 E8
Semblister Shetland 160 H5
Semer Suff 56 E3
Semington Wilts 24 C3
Semley Wilts 13 B6
Send Sur 27 D8
Send Marsh Sur 27 D8
Senghenydd Caerph 35 E5
Sennen Corn 2 D2
Sennen Cove Corn 2 D2
Sennybridge = Pont Senni Powys 34 B3
Serlby Notts 89 F7
Sessay N Yorks 95 B7
Setchey Norf 67 C6
Setley Hants 14 D4
Setter Shetland 160 E6
Setter Shetland 160 H5
Setter Shetland 160 J7
Settiscarth Orkney 159 G4
Settle N Yorks 93 C8
Settrington N Yorks 96 B4
Seven Kings London 41 F7
Seven Sisters Neath 34 D2
Sevenhampton Glos 37 B7
Sevenoaks Kent 29 D6
Sevenoaks Weald Kent 29 D6
Severn Beach S Glos 36 F2
Severn Stoke Worcs 50 E3
Severnhampton Swindon 38 E2
Sevington Kent 30 E4
Sewards End Essex 55 F6
Sewardstone Essex 41 E6
Sewardstonebury Essex 41 E6
Sewerby E Yorks 97 C7
Seworgan Corn 3 C6
Sewstern Leics 65 B5
Sezincote Glos 51 F6
Sgarasta Mhor W Isles 154 H5
Sgiogarstaigh W Isles 155 A10
Shabbington Bucks 39 D6
Shackerstone Leics 63 D7
Shackleford Sur 27 E7
Shade W Yorks 87 B7
Shadforth Durham 111 E6
Shadingfield Suff 69 F7
Shadoxhurst Kent 19 B6
Shadsworth Blackburn 86 B5
Shadwell Norf 68 F2
Shadwell W Yorks 95 F6
Shaftesbury Dorset 13 B6
Shafton S Yorks 88 C4
Shalbourne Wilts 25 C8
Shalcombe IoW 14 F4
Shalden Hants 26 E4
Shaldon Devon 7 B7
Shalfleet IoW 14 F5
Shalford Essex 42 B3
Shalford Sur 27 E8
Shalford Green Essex 42 B3
Shallowford Devon 21 E6
Shalmsford Street Kent 30 D4
Shalstone Bucks 52 F4
Shamley Green Sur 27 E8
Shandon Argyll 145 E11
Shandwick Highld 151 D11
Shangton Leics 64 E4
Shankhouse Northumb 111 B5
Shanklin IoW 15 F6
Shanquhar Aberds 152 E5
Shanzie Perth 134 D2
Shap Cumb 99 C7
Shapwick Dorset 13 D7
Shapwick Som 23 F6
Shardlow Derbys 76 F4
Shareshill Staffs 62 D3
Sharlston W Yorks 88 C4
Sharlston Common W Yorks 88 C4
Sharnbrook Bedford 53 D7
Sharnford Leics 63 E8
Sharoe Green Lancs 92 F5
Sharow N Yorks 95 B6
Sharp Street Norf 69 B6
Sharpenhoe C Beds 53 F8
Sharperton Northumb 117 D5
Sharpness Glos 36 D3
Sharpthorne W Sus 28 F4
Sharrington Norf 81 D6
Shatterford Worcs 61 F7
Shaugh Prior Devon 6 C3
Shavington Ches E 74 D4
Shaw Gtr Man 87 D7
Shaw W Berks 26 C2
Shaw Wilts 24 C3
Shaw Green Lancs 86 C3
Shaw Mills N Yorks 95 C5
Shawbury Shrops 61 B5
Shawdon Hall Northumb 117 C6
Shawell Leics 64 F2
Shawford Hants 15 B5
Shawforth Lancs 87 B6
Shawhead Dumfries 107 B5
Shawhill Dumfries 108 C2
Shawton S Lanark 119 E6
Shawtonhill S Lanark 119 E6
Shear Cross Wilts 24 E3
Shearington Dumfries 107 C7
Shearsby Leics 64 E3
Shebbear Devon 9 D6
Shebdon Staffs 61 B7
Shebster Highld 157 C13
Sheddens E Renf 119 D5
Shedfield Hants 15 C6
Sheen Staffs 75 C8
Sheepscar W Yorks 95 F6
Sheepscombe Glos 37 C5
Sheepstor Devon 6 C3
Sheepwash Devon 9 D6
Sheepway N Som 23 B6
Sheepy Magna Leics 63 D7
Sheepy Parva Leics 63 D7
Sheering Essex 41 C8
Sheerness Kent 30 B3
Sheet Hants 15 B8
Sheffield S Yorks 88 F4
Sheffield Bottom W Berks 26 C4
Sheffield Green E Sus 17 B8
Shefford C Beds 54 F2
Shefford Woodlands W Berks 25 B8
Sheigra Highld 156 C4
Sheinton Shrops 61 D6
Shelderton Shrops 49 B6
Sheldon Derbys 75 C8
Sheldon Devon 11 D6
Sheldon W Mid 63 F5
Sheldwich Kent 30 D4
Shelf W Yorks 88 B2
Shelfanger Norf 68 F4
Shelfield W Mid 62 D4
Shelfield Warks 51 C6
Shelford Notts 77 E6
Shellacres Northumb 122 E4
Shelley Essex 42 D1
Shelley Suff 56 F4
Shelley W Yorks 88 C3
Shellingford Oxon 38 E3
Shellow Bowells Essex 42 D2
Shelsley Beauchamp Worcs 50 C2
Shelsley Walsh Worcs 50 C2
Shelthorpe Leics 64 C2
Shelton Bedford 53 C8
Shelton Norf 68 E5
Shelton Notts 77 E7
Shelton Shrops 60 C4
Shelton Green Norf 68 E5
Shelve Shrops 60 E3
Shelwick Hereford 49 E7
Shenfield Essex 42 E2
Shenington Oxon 51 E8
Shenley Herts 40 D4
Shenley Brook End M Keynes 53 F6
Shenley Church End M Keynes 53 F6
Shenleybury Herts 40 D4
Shenmore Hereford 49 F5
Shennanton Dumfries 105 C7
Shenstone Staffs 62 D5
Shenstone Worcs 50 B3
Shenton Leics 63 D7
Shenval Highld 137 B7
Shenval Moray 139 B8
Shepeau Stow Lincs 66 C3
Shephall Herts 41 B5
Shepherd's Green Oxon 39 F7
Shepherd's Port Norf 80 D2
Shepherdswell Kent 31 E6
Shepley W Yorks 88 D2
Shepperdine S Glos 36 E3
Shepperton Sur 27 C8
Shepreth Cambs 54 E4
Shepshed Leics 63 C8
Shepton Beauchamp Som 12 C2
Shepton Mallet Som 23 E8
Shepton Montague Som 23 F8
Shepway Kent 29 D8
Sheraton Durham 111 F7
Sherborne Dorset 12 C4
Sherborne Glos 38 C1
Sherborne St John Hants 26 D4
Sherbourne Warks 51 C7
Sherburn Durham 111 E6
Sherburn N Yorks 97 B5
Sherburn Hill Durham 111 E6
Sherburn in Elmet N Yorks 95 F7
Shere Sur 27 E8
Shereford Norf 80 E4
Sherfield English Hants 14 B3
Sherfield on Loddon Hants 26 D4
Sherford Devon 7 E5
Sheriff Hutton N Yorks 96 C2
Sheriffhales Shrops 61 C7
Sheringham Norf 81 C7
Sherington M Keynes 53 E6
Shernal Green Worcs 50 C4
Shernborne Norf 80 D3
Sherrington Wilts 24 F4
Sherston Wilts 37 F5
Sherwood Green Devon 9 B7
Shettleston Glasgow 119 C6
Shevington Gtr Man 86 D3
Shevington Moor Gtr Man 86 C3
Shevington Vale Gtr Man 86 D3
Sheviock Corn 5 D8
Shide IoW 15 F5
Shiel Bridge Highld 136 C2
Shieldaig Highld 149 A13
Shieldaig Highld 149 C13
Shieldhill Dumfries 114 F3
Shieldhill Falk 119 B8
Shieldhill S Lanark 120 E3
Shielfoot Highld 147 E9
Shielhill Angus 134 D4
Shielhill Invclyd 118 B2
Shifford Oxon 38 D3
Shifnal Shrops 61 D7
Shilbottle Northumb 117 D7
Shildon Durham 101 B7
Shillingford Devon 10 B4
Shillingford Oxon 39 E5
Shillingford St George Devon 10 F4
Shillingstone Dorset 13 C6
Shillington C Beds 54 F2
Shillmoor Northumb 116 D4
Shilton Oxon 38 D2
Shilton Warks 63 F8
Shilvington Northumb 117 F7
Shimpling Norf 68 F4
Shimpling Suff 56 D2
Shimpling Street Suff 56 D2
Shincliffe Durham 111 E5
Shiney Row T&W 111 D6
Shinfield Wokingham 26 C5
Shingham Norf 67 D7
Shingle Street Suff 57 E7
Shinner's Bridge Devon 7 C5
Shinness Highld 157 H8
Shipbourne Kent 29 D6
Shipdham Norf 68 D2
Shipham Som 23 D6
Shiphay Torbay 7 C6
Shiplake Oxon 27 B5
Shipley Derbys 76 E4
Shipley Northumb 117 C7
Shipley Shrops 62 E2
Shipley W Sus 16 B5
Shipley W Yorks 94 F4
Shipley Shiels Northumb 116 E3
Shipmeadow Suff 69 F6
Shippea Hill Station Cambs 67 F6
Shippon Oxon 38 E4
Shipston-on-Stour Warks 51 E7
Shipton Glos 37 C7
Shipton N Yorks 95 D8
Shipton Shrops 61 E5
Shipton Bellinger Hants 25 E7
Shipton Gorge Dorset 12 E2
Shipton Green W Sus 16 D2
Shipton Moyne Glos 37 F5
Shipton on Cherwell Oxon 38 C4
Shipton Solers Glos 37 C7
Shipton-under-Wychwood Oxon 38 C2
Shiptonthorpe E Yorks 96 E4
Shirburn Oxon 39 E6
Shirdley Hill Lancs 85 C4
Shirebrook Derbys 76 C5

Shiregreen S Yorks 88 E4
Shirehampton Bristol 23 B7
Shiremoor T&W 111 B6
Shirenewton Mon 36 E1
Shireoaks Notts 89 F6
Shirkoak Kent 19 B6
Shirl Heath Hereford 49 D6
Shirland Derbys 76 D3
Shirley Derbys 76 E2
Shirley London 28 C4
Shirley Soton 14 C5
Shirley W Mid 51 B6
Shirrell Heath Hants 15 C6
Shirwell Devon 20 F4
Shirwell Cross Devon 20 F4
Shiskine N Ayrs 143 F10
Shobdon Hereford 49 C6
Shobnall Staffs 63 B6
Shobrooke Devon 10 D3
Shoby Leics 64 C3
Shocklach Ches W 73 E8
Shoeburyness Southend 43 F5
Sholden Kent 31 D7
Sholing Soton 14 C5
Shoot Hill Shrops 60 C4
Shop Corn 4 B3
Shop Corn 8 C4
Shop Corner Suff 57 F6
Shore Mill Highld 151 E10
Shoreditch London 41 F6
Shoreham Kent 29 C6
Shoreham-By-Sea W Sus 17 D6
Shoresdean Northumb 123 E5
Shoreswood Northumb 122 E5
Shoreton Highld 151 E9
Shorncote Glos 37 E7
Shorne Kent 29 B7
Short Heath W Mid 62 D3
Shortacombe Devon 9 F7
Shortgate E Sus 17 C8
Shortlanesend Corn 3 B7
Shortlees E Ayrs 118 F4
Shortstown Bedford 53 E8
Shorwell IoW 15 F5
Shoscombe Bath 24 D2
Shotatton Shrops 60 B3
Shotesham Norf 69 E5
Shotgate Essex 42 E3
Shotley Suff 57 F6
Shotley Bridge Durham 110 D3
Shotley Gate Suff 57 F6
Shotleyfield Northumb 110 D3
Shottenden Kent 30 D4
Shottermill Sur 27 F6
Shottery Warks 51 D6
Shotteswell Warks 52 E2
Shottisham Suff 57 E7
Shottle Derbys 76 E3
Shottlegate Derbys 76 E3
Shotton Durham 111 F7
Shotton Flint 73 C7
Shotton Northumb 122 F4
Shotton Colliery Durham 111 E6
Shotts N Lanark 119 C8
Shotwick Ches W 73 B7
Shouldham Norf 67 D6
Shouldham Thorpe Norf 67 D6
Shoulton Worcs 50 D3
Shover's Green E Sus 18 B3
Shrawardine Shrops 60 C4
Shrawley Worcs 50 C3
Shrewley Common Warks 51 C7
Shrewsbury Shrops 60 C4
Shrewton Wilts 25 E5
Shripney W Sus 16 D3
Shrivenham Oxon 38 F2
Shropham Norf 68 E2
Shrub End Essex 43 B5
Shucknall Hereford 49 E7
Shudy Camps Cambs 55 E7
Shulishadermor Highld 149 D9
Shurdington Glos 37 C6
Shurlock Row Windsor 27 B6
Shurrery Highld 157 D13
Shurrery Lodge Highld 157 D13
Shurton Som 22 E4
Shustoke Warks 63 E6
Shute Devon 10 D3
Shute Devon 11 E7
Shutford Oxon 51 E8
Shuthonger Glos 50 F3
Shutlanger Northants 52 D5
Shuttington Warks 63 D6
Shuttlewood Derbys 76 B4
Siabost bho Dheas W Isles 154 C7
Siabost bho Thuath W Isles 154 C7
Siadar W Isles 155 B8
Siadar Iarach W Isles 155 B8
Siadar Uarach W Isles 155 B8
Sibbaldbie Dumfries 114 F4
Sibbertoft Northants 64 F3
Sibdon Carwood Shrops 60 F4
Sibford Ferris Oxon 51 F8
Sibford Gower Oxon 51 F8
Sible Hedingham Essex 55 F8
Sibsey Lincs 79 D6
Sibson Cambs 65 E7
Sibson Leics 63 D7
Sibthorpe Notts 77 E7
Sibton Suff 57 C7
Sibton Green Suff 57 B7
Sicklesmere Suff 56 C2
Sicklinghall N Yorks 95 E6
Sid Devon 11 F6
Sidbury Devon 11 E6
Sidbury Shrops 61 F6
Sidcot N Som 23 D6
Sidcup London 29 B5
Siddick Cumb 107 F7
Siddington Ches E 74 B5
Siddington Glos 37 E7
Sidemoor Worcs 50 B4
Sidestrand Norf 81 D8
Sidford Devon 11 E6
Sidlesham W Sus 16 E2
Sidley E Sus 18 E4
Sidlow Sur 28 E3
Sidmouth Devon 11 F6
Sigford Devon 7 B5
Sigglesthorne E Yorks 97 E7
Sighthill Edin 120 B4
Sigingstone V Glam 21 B8
Signet Oxon 38 C2
Silchester Hants 26 C4
Sildinis W Isles 155 F7
Sileby Leics 64 C2
Silecroft Cumb 98 F3
Silfield Norf 68 E4
Silian Ceredig 46 D4
Silk Willoughby Lincs 78 E3
Silkstone S Yorks 88 D3
Silkstone Common S Yorks 88 D3
Silloth Cumb 107 D8
Sills Northumb 116 D4
Sillyearn Moray 152 C5
Siloh Carms 47 F6
Silpho N Yorks 103 E7
Silsden W Yorks 94 E3
Silsoe C Beds 53 F8
Silver End Essex 42 C4
Silverburn Midloth 120 C5
Silverdale Lancs 92 B4
Silverdale Staffs 74 E5
Silvergate Norf 81 E7
Silverhill E Sus 18 D4
Silverley's Green Suff 57 B6
Silverstone Northants 52 E4
Silverton Devon 10 D4
Silvington Shrops 49 B8
Silwick Shetland 160 J4
Simmondley Derbys 87 E8
Simonburn Northumb 109 B8
Simonsbath Som 21 F6
Simonstone Lancs 93 F7
Simprim Borders 122 E4
Simpson M Keynes 53 F6
Simpson Cross Pembs 44 D3
Sinclair's Hill Borders 122 D4
Sinclairston E Ayrs 112 C4
Sinderby N Yorks 101 F8
Sinderhope Northumb 109 D8
Sindlesham Wokingham 27 C5
Singdean Borders 115 D8
Singleborough Bucks 53 F5
Singleton Lancs 92 F3
Singleton W Sus 16 C2
Singlewell Kent 29 B7
Sinkhurst Green Kent 30 E2
Sinnahard Aberds 140 C3
Sinnington N Yorks 103 F5
Sinton Green Worcs 50 C3
Sipson London 27 B8
Sirhowy Bl Gwent 35 C5
Sisland Norf 69 E6
Sissinghurst Kent 18 B4
Sisterpath Borders 122 E3
Siston S Glos 23 B8
Sithney Corn 2 D5
Sittingbourne Kent 30 C2
Six Ashes Staffs 61 F7
Six Hills Leics 64 B3
Six Mile Bottom Cambs 55 D6
Sixhills Lincs 91 F5
Sixpenny Handley Dorset 13 C7
Sizewell Suff 57 C8
Skail Highld 157 E10
Skaill Orkney 159 E5
Skaill Orkney 159 G3
Skaill Orkney 159 H6
Skares E Ayrs 113 C5
Skateraw E Loth 122 B3
Skaw Shetland 160 G7
Skeabost Highld 149 D9
Skeabrae Orkney 159 F3
Skeeby N Yorks 101 D7
Skeffington Leics 64 D4
Skeffling E Yorks 91 C7
Skegby Notts 76 C4
Skegness Lincs 79 C8
Skelberry Shetland 160 M5
Skelbo Highld 151 B10
Skelbrooke S Yorks 89 C6
Skeldyke Lincs 79 F6
Skellingthorpe Lincs 78 B2
Skellister Shetland 160 H6
Skellow S Yorks 89 C6
Skelmanthorpe W Yorks 88 C3
Skelmersdale Lancs 86 D2
Skelmonae Aberds 153 E8
Skelmorlie N Ayrs 118 C1
Skelmuir Aberds 153 D9
Skelpick Highld 157 D10
Skelton Cumb 108 F4
Skelton E Yorks 89 B8
Skelton N Yorks 101 D5
Skelton Redcar 102 C4
Skelton York 95 D8
Skelton-on-Ure N Yorks 95 C6
Skelwick Orkney 159 D5
Skelwith Bridge Cumb 99 D5
Skendleby Lincs 79 C7
Skene Ho. Aberds 141 D6
Skenfrith Mon 36 B1
Skerne E Yorks 97 D6
Skeroblingarry Argyll 143 F8
Skerray Highld 157 C9
Skerton Lancs 92 C4
Sketchley Leics 63 E8
Sketty Swansea 33 E7
Skewen Neath 33 E8
Skewsby N Yorks 96 B2
Skeyton Norf 81 E8
Skiag Bridge Highld 156 G5
Skibo Castle Highld 151 C10
Skidbrooke Lincs 91 E8
Skidbrooke North End Lincs 91 E8
Skidby E Yorks 97 F6
Skilgate Som 10 B4
Skillington Lincs 65 B5
Skinburness Cumb 107 D8
Skinflats Falk 127 F8
Skinidin Highld 148 D7
Skinnet Highld 157 C8
Skinningrove Redcar 103 B5
Skipness Argyll 145 H7
Skippool Lancs 92 E3
Skipsea E Yorks 97 D7
Skipsea Brough E Yorks 97 D7
Skipton N Yorks 94 D2
Skipton-on-Swale N Yorks 95 B6
Skipwith N Yorks 96 F2
Skirbeck Lincs 79 E6
Skirbeck Quarter Lincs 79 E6
Skirlaugh E Yorks 97 F7
Skirling Borders 120 F3
Skirmett Bucks 39 F7
Skirpenbeck E Yorks 96 D3
Skirwith Cumb 109 F6
Skirza Highld 158 D5
Skulamus Highld 149 F11
Skullomie Highld 157 C9
Skyborry Green Shrops 48 B4
Skye of Curr Highld 139 B5
Skyreholme N Yorks 94 C3
Slackhall Derbys 87 F8
Slackhead Moray 152 B4
Slad Glos 37 D5
Slade Devon 20 E4
Slade Pembs 44 D4
Slade Green London 29 B6
Slaggyford Northumb 109 D6
Slaidburn Lancs 93 D7
Slaithwaite W Yorks 87 C8
Slaley Northumb 110 D2
Slamannan Falk 119 B8
Slapton Bucks 40 B2
Slapton Devon 7 E6
Slapton Northants 52 E4
Slatepit Dale Derbys 76 C3
Slattocks Gtr Man 87 D6
Slaugham W Sus 17 B6
Slaughterford Wilts 24 B3
Slawston Leics 64 E4
Sleaford Hants 27 F6
Sleaford Lincs 78 E3
Sleagill Cumb 99 C7
Sleapford Telford 61 C6
Sledge Green Worcs 50 F3
Sledmere E Yorks 96 C5
Sleightholme Durham 100 C4
Sleights N Yorks 103 D6
Slepe Dorset 13 E7
Slickly Highld 158 D4
Sliddery N Ayrs 143 F10
Sligachan Hotel Highld 149 F9
Slimbridge Glos 36 D4
Slindon Staffs 74 F5
Slindon W Sus 16 D3
Slinfold W Sus 28 F2
Sling Gwyn 83 E6
Slingsby N Yorks 96 B2
Slioch Aberds 152 E5
Slip End C Beds 40 C3
Slip End Herts 54 F3
Slipton Northants 53 B7
Slitting Mill Staffs 62 C4
Slochd Highld 138 B4
Slockavullin Argyll 124 F4
Sloley Norf 81 E8
Sloothby Lincs 79 B7
Slough Slough 27 B7
Slough Green W Sus 17 B6
Sluggan Highld 138 B4
Slumbay Highld 149 E13
Slyfield Sur 27 D7
Slyne Lancs 92 C4
Smailholm Borders 122 F2
Small Dole W Sus 17 C6
Small Hythe Kent 19 B5
Smallbridge Gtr Man 87 C7
Smallburgh Norf 69 B6
Smallburn Aberds 153 D10
Smallburn E Ayrs 113 B6
Smalley Derbys 76 E4
Smallfield Sur 28 E4
Smallridge Devon 11 D8
Smannell Hants 25 E8
Smardale Cumb 100 D2
Smarden Kent 30 E2
Smarden Bell Kent 30 E2
Smeatharpe Devon 11 C6
Smeeth Kent 19 B7
Smeeton Westerby Leics 64 E3
Smercleit W Isles 148 G2
Smerral Highld 158 G3
Smethwick W Mid 62 F4
Smirisary Highld 147 D9
Smisby Derbys 63 C7
Smith Green Lancs 92 D4
Smithfield Cumb 108 C4
Smithincott Devon 11 C5
Smith's Green Essex 42 B1
Smithstown Highld 149 A12
Smithton Highld 151 G10
Smithy Green Ches E 74 B4
Smockington Leics 63 F8
Smoogro Orkney 159 H4
Smythe's Green Essex 43 C5
Snaigow House Perth 133 E7
Snailbeach Shrops 60 D3
Snailwell Cambs 55 C7
Snainton N Yorks 103 F7
Snaith E Yorks 89 B7
Snape N Yorks 101 F7
Snape Suff 57 D7
Snape Green Lancs 85 C4
Snarestone Leics 63 D7
Snarford Lincs 90 F4
Snargate Kent 19 C6
Snave Kent 19 C7
Snead Powys 60 E3
Sneath Common Norf 68 F4
Sneaton N Yorks 103 D6
Sneatonthorpe N Yorks 103 D7
Snelland Lincs 90 F4
Snelston Derbys 75 E8
Snettisham Norf 80 D2
Sniseabhal W Isles 148 E2
Snitter Northumb 117 D6
Snitterby Lincs 90 E3
Snitterfield Warks 51 D7
Snitton Shrops 49 B7
Snodhill Hereford 48 E5
Snodland Kent 29 C7
Snowden Hill S Yorks 88 D3
Snowdown Kent 31 D6
Snowshill Glos 51 F5
Snydale W Yorks 88 C5
Soar Anglesey 82 D3
Soar Carms 33 B7
Soar Devon 6 F5
Soar-y-Mynydd Ceredig 47 D6
Soberton Hants 15 C7
Soberton Heath Hants 15 C7
Sockbridge Cumb 99 B7
Sockburn Darl 101 D8
Soham Cambs 55 B6
Soham Cotes Cambs 55 B6
Solas W Isles 148 A3
Soldon Cross Devon 8 C5
Soldridge Hants 26 F4
Sole Street Kent 29 C7
Sole Street Kent 30 E4
Solihull W Mid 51 B6
Sollers Dilwyn Hereford 49 D6
Sollers Hope Hereford 49 F8
Sollom Lancs 86 C2
Solva Pembs 44 C2
Somerby Leics 64 C4
Somerby Lincs 90 D4
Somercotes Derbys 76 D4
Somerford Dorset 14 E2
Somerford Keynes Glos 37 E7
Somerley W Sus 16 E2
Somerleyton Suff 69 E7
Somersal Herbert Derbys 75 F8
Somersby Lincs 79 B6
Somersham Cambs 54 B4
Somersham Suff 56 E4
Somerton Oxon 38 B4
Somerton Som 12 B2
Sompting W Sus 17 D5
Sonning Wokingham 27 B5
Sonning Common Oxon 39 F7
Sonning Eye Oxon 27 B5
Sontley Wrex 73 E7
Sopley Hants 14 E2
Sopwell Herts 40 D4
Sopworth Wilts 37 F5
Sorbie Dumfries 105 E8
Sordale Highld 158 D3
Sorisdale Argyll 146 E5
Sorn E Ayrs 113 B5
Sornhill E Ayrs 118 F5
Sortat Highld 158 D4
Sotby Lincs 78 B5
Sots Hole Lincs 78 C4
Sotterley Suff 69 F7
Soudley Shrops 61 B7
Soughton Flint 73 C6
Soulbury Bucks 40 B1
Soulby Cumb 100 C2
Souldern Oxon 52 F3
Souldrop Bedford 53 C7
Sound Ches E 74 E3
Sound Shetland 160 H5
Sound Shetland 160 J6
Sound Heath Ches E 74 E3
Soundwell S Glos 23 B8
Sourhope Borders 116 B4
Sourin Orkney 159 E5
Sourton Devon 9 E7
Soutergate Cumb 98 F4
South Acre Norf 67 C8
South Allington Devon 7 F5
South Alloa Falk 127 E7
South Ambersham W Sus 16 B3
South Anston S Yorks 89 F6
South Ascot Windsor 27 C7
South Ballachulish Highld 130 D4
South Balloch S Ayrs 112 E3
South Bank Redcar 102 B3
South Barrow Som 12 B4
South Beach Gwyn 70 D4
South Benfleet Essex 42 F3
South Bersted W Sus 16 D3
South Brent Devon 6 C4
South Brewham Som 24 F2
South Broomhill Northumb 117 E8
South Burlingham Norf 69 D6
South Cadbury Som 12 B4
South Cairn Dumfries 104 C3
South Carlton Lincs 78 B2
South Cave E Yorks 96 F5
South Cerney Glos 37 E7
South Chard Som 11 D8
South Charlton Northumb 117 B7
South Cheriton Som 12 B4
South Cliffe E Yorks 96 F4
South Clifton Notts 77 B8
South Cockerington Lincs 91 F7
South Cornelly Bridgend 34 F2
South Cove Suff 69 F7
South Creagan Argyll 130 E3
South Creake Norf 80 D4
South Croxton Leics 64 C3
South Croydon London 28 C4
South Dalton E Yorks 97 E5
South Darenth Kent 29 C6
South Duffield N Yorks 96 F2
South Elkington Lincs 91 F6
South Elmsall W Yorks 89 C5
South End Bucks 40 B1
South End Cumb 92 C2
South End N Lincs 90 B5
South Erradale Highld 149 A12
South Fambridge Essex 42 E4
South Fawley W Berks 38 F3
South Ferriby N Lincs 90 B3
South Garth Shetland 160 D7
South Garvan Highld 130 B3
South Glendale W Isles 148 G2
South Godstone Sur 28 E4
South Gorley Hants 14 C2
South Green Essex 42 E2
South Green Kent 30 C2
South-haa Shetland 160 E5
South Ham Hants 26 D4
South Hanningfield Essex 42 E3
South Harting W Sus 15 C8
South Hatfield Herts 41 D5
South Hayling Hants 15 E8
South Hazelrigg Northumb 123 F6
South Heath Bucks 40 D2
South Heighton E Sus 17 D8
South Hetton Durham 111 E6
South Hiendley W Yorks 88 C4
South Hill Corn 5 B8
South Hinksey Oxon 39 D5
South Hole Devon 8 B4
South Holme N Yorks 96 B2
South Holmwood Sur 28 E2
South Hornchurch London 41 F8
South Hykeham Lincs 78 C2
South Hylton T&W 111 D6
South Kelsey Lincs 90 E4
South Kessock Highld 151 G9
South Killingholme N Lincs 91 C5
South Kilvington N Yorks 102 F2
South Kilworth Leics 64 F3
South Kirkby W Yorks 88 C5
South Kirkton Aberds 141 D6
South Kiscadale N Ayrs 143 F11
South Kyme Lincs 78 E4
South Lancing W Sus 17 D5
South Leigh Oxon 38 D3
South Leverton Notts 89 F8
South Littleton Worcs 51 E5
South Lopham Norf 68 F3
South Luffenham Rutland 65 D6
South Malling E Sus 17 C8
South Marston Swindon 38 F1
South Middleton Northumb 117 B5
South Milford N Yorks 95 F7
South Millbrex Aberds 153 D8
South Milton Devon 6 E5
South Mimms Herts 41 D5
South Molton Devon 10 B2
South Moreton Oxon 39 F5
South Mundham W Sus 16 D2
South Muskham Notts 77 D7
South Newbald E Yorks 96 F5
South Newington Oxon 52 F2
South Newton Wilts 25 F5
South Normanton Derbys 76 D4
South Norwood London 28 C4
South Nutfield Sur 28 E4
South Ockendon Thurrock 42 F1
South Ormsby Lincs 79 B6
South Otterington N Yorks 102 F1
South Owersby Lincs 90 E4
South Oxhey Herts 40 E4
South Perrott Dorset 12 D2
South Petherton Som 12 C2
South Petherwin Corn 8 F5
South Pickenham Norf 67 D8
South Pool Devon 7 E5
South Port Argyll 125 C6
South Radworthy Devon 21 F6
South Rauceby Lincs 78 E3
South Raynham Norf 80 E4
South Reston Lincs 91 F8
South Runcton Norf 67 D6
South Scarle Notts 77 C8
South Shian Argyll 130 E3
South Shields T&W 111 C6
South Shore Blackpool 92 F3
South Somercotes Lincs 91 E8
South Stainley N Yorks 95 C6
South Stainmore Cumb 100 C3
South Stifford Thurrock 29 B7
South Stoke Oxon 39 F5
South Stoke W Sus 16 D4
South Street E Sus 17 C7
South Street Kent 30 C5
South Street Kent 30 D4
South Street London 28 D5
South Tawton Devon 9 E8
South Thoresby Lincs 79 B7
South Tidworth Wilts 25 E7
South Town Hants 26 F4
South View Hants 26 D4
South Walsham Norf 69 C6
South Warnborough Hants 26 E5
South Weald Essex 42 E1
South Weston Oxon 39 E7
South Wheatley Corn 8 E4
South Wheatley Notts 89 F8
South Whiteness Shetland 160 J5
South Widcombe Bath 23 D7
South Wigston Leics 64 E2
South Willingham Lincs 91 F5
South Wingfield Derbys 76 D3
South Witham Lincs 65 C6
South Wonston Hants 26 F2
South Woodham Ferrers Essex 42 E4
South Wootton Norf 67 B6
South Wraxall Wilts 24 C3
South Zeal Devon 9 E8
Southall London 40 F4
Southam Glos 37 B6
Southam Warks 52 C2
Southampton Soton 14 C5
Southborough Kent 29 E6
Southbourne Bmouth 14 E2
Southbourne W Sus 15 D8
Southburgh Norf 68 D2
Southburn E Yorks 97 D5
Southchurch Southend 43 F5
Southcott Wilts 25 D6
Southcourt Bucks 39 C8
Southdean Borders 116 D2
Southdene Mers 86 E2
Southease E Sus 17 D8
Southend Argyll 143 H7
Southend W Berks 26 B3
Southend Wilts 25 B6
Southend-on-Sea Southend 42 F4
Southernden Kent 30 E2
Southerndown V Glam 21 B7
Southerness Dumfries 107 D6
Southery Norf 67 E6
Southfield Northumb 111 B5
Southfleet Kent 29 B7
Southgate Ceredig 46 B4
Southgate London 41 E5
Southgate Norf 81 E7
Southgate Swansea 33 F6
Southill C Beds 54 E2
Southleigh Devon 11 E7
Southminster Essex 43 E5
Southmoor Oxon 38 E3
Southoe Cambs 54 C2
Southolt Suff 57 C5
Southorpe Phoro 65 D7
Southowram W Yorks 88 B2
Southport Mers 85 C4
Southpunds Shetland 160 L6
Southrepps Norf 81 D8
Southrey Lincs 78 C4
Southrop Glos 38 D1
Southrope Hants 26 E4
Southsea Ptsmth 15 E7
Southstoke Bath 24 C2
Southtown Norf 69 D8
Southtown Orkney 159 J5
Southwaite Cumb 108 E4
Southwark London 28 B4
Southwater W Sus 17 B5
Southwater Street W Sus 17 B5
Southway Som 23 E7
Southwell Dorset 12 G4
Southwell Notts 77 D6
Southwick Hants 15 D7
Southwick Northants 65 E7
Southwick T&W 111 D6
Southwick W Sus 17 D6
Southwick Wilts 24 D3
Southwold Suff 57 B9
Southwood Norf 69 D6
Southwood Som 23 F7
Soval Lodge W Isles 155 E8
Sowber Gate N Yorks 102 F1
Sowerby N Yorks 102 F2
Sowerby W Yorks 87 B8
Sowerby Bridge W Yorks 87 B8
Sowerby Row Cumb 108 F3
Sowood W Yorks 87 C8
Sowton Devon 10 E4
Soyal Highld 151 B8
Spa Common Norf 81 D8
Spacey Houses N Yorks 95 D6
Spadeadam Farm Cumb 109 B5
Spalding Lincs 66 B2
Spaldington E Yorks 96 F3
Spaldwick Cambs 54 B2
Spalford Notts 77 C8
Spanby Lincs 78 F3
Sparham Norf 68 C3
Spark Bridge Cumb 99 F5
Sparkford Som 12 B4
Sparkhill W Mid 62 F4
Sparkwell Devon 6 D3
Sparrow Green Norf 68 C2
Sparrowpit Derbys 87 F8
Sparsholt Hants 26 F2
Sparsholt Oxon 38 F3
Spartylea Northumb 109 E8
Spaunton N Yorks 103 F5
Spaxton Som 22 F4
Spean Bridge Highld 136 F5
Spear Hill W Sus 16 C5
Speen Bucks 39 E8
Speen W Berks 26 C2
Speeton N Yorks 97 B7
Speke Mers 86 F2
Speldhurst Kent 29 E6
Spellbrook Herts 41 C7
Spelsbury Oxon 38 B3
Spelter Bridgend 34 E2
Spencers Wood Wokingham 26 C5
Spennithorne N Yorks 101 F6
Spennymoor Durham 111 F5
Spetchley Worcs 50 D3
Spetisbury Dorset 13 D7
Spexhall Suff 69 F6
Spey Bay Moray 152 B3
Speybridge Highld 139 B6
Speyview Moray 152 D2
Spilsby Lincs 79 C7
Spindlestone Northumb 123 F7
Spinkhill Derbys 76 B4
Spinningdale Highld 151 C9
Spirthill Wilts 24 B4
Spital Hill S Yorks 89 E7
Spital in the Street Lincs 90 F3
Spithurst E Sus 17 C8
Spittal Dumfries 105 D7
Spittal E Loth 121 B7
Spittal Highld 158 E3
Spittal Northumb 123 D6
Spittal Pembs 44 C4
Spittal Stirling 126 F4
Spittal of Glenmuick Aberds 140 F2
Spittal of Glenshee Perth 133 B8
Spittalfield Perth 133 E8
Spixworth Norf 68 C5
Splayne's Green E Sus 17 B8
Spofforth N Yorks 95 D6
Spon End W Mid 51 B8
Spon Green Flint 73 C6
Spondon Derby 76 F4
Spooner Row Norf 68 E3
Sporle Norf 67 C8
Spott E Loth 122 B2
Spratton Northants 52 B5
Spreakley Sur 27 E6
Spreyton Devon 9 E8
Spridlington Lincs 90 F4
Spring Vale S Yorks 88 D3
Spring Valley IoM 84 E3
Springburn Glasgow 119 C6
Springfield Dumfries 108 C3
Springfield Essex 42 D3
Springfield Fife 128 C5
Springfield Moray 151 F13
Springfield W Mid 62 F4
Springhill Staffs 62 D3
Springholm Dumfries 106 C5
Springkell Dumfries 108 B2
Springside N Ayrs 118 F3
Springthorpe Lincs 90 F2
Springwell T&W 111 D5
Sproatley E Yorks 97 F7
Sproston Green Ches W 74 C4
Sprotbrough S Yorks 89 D6
Sproughton Suff 56 E5
Sprouston Borders 122 F3
Sprowston Norf 68 C5
Sproxton Leics 65 B5
Sproxton N Yorks 102 F4
Spurstow Ches E 74 D2
Spynie Moray 152 B2
Squires Gate Blackpool 92 F3
Srannda W Isles 154 J5
Sronphadruig Lodge Perth 132 B4
Stableford Shrops 61 E7
Stableford Staffs 74 F5
Stacey Bank S Yorks 88 E3
Stackhouse N Yorks 93 C8
Stackpole Pembs 44 F4
Staddiscombe Plym 6 D3
Staddlethorpe E Yorks 90 B2
Stadhampton Oxon 39 E6
Stadhlaigearraidh W Isles 148 E2
Staffield Cumb 108 E5
Staffin Highld 149 B9
Stafford Staffs 62 B3
Stagsden Bedford 53 E7
Stainburn Cumb 98 B2
Stainburn N Yorks 94 E5
Stainby Lincs 65 B6
Staincross S Yorks 88 C4
Staindrop Durham 101 B6
Staines-upon-Thames Sur 27 B8
Stainfield Lincs 65 B7
Stainfield Lincs 78 B4
Stainforth N Yorks 93 C8
Stainforth S Yorks 89 C7
Staining Lancs 92 F3
Stainland W Yorks 87 C8
Stainsacre N Yorks 103 D7
Stainsby Derbys 76 C4
Stainton Cumb 99 B6
Stainton Cumb 99 F7
Stainton Durham 101 C5
Stainton Mbro 102 C2
Stainton N Yorks 101 E6
Stainton S Yorks 89 E6
Stainton by Langworth Lincs 78 B3
Stainton le Vale Lincs 91 E5
Stainton with Adgarley Cumb 92 B2
Staintondale N Yorks 103 E7
Stair Cumb 98 B4
Stair E Ayrs 112 B4
Stairhaven Dumfries 105 D6
Staithes N Yorks 103 C5
Stake Pool Lancs 92 E4
Stakeford Northumb 117 F8
Stalbridge Dorset 12 C5
Stalbridge Weston Dorset 12 C5
Stalham Norf 69 B6
Stalham Green Norf 69 B6
Stalisfield Green Kent 30 D3
Stalling Busk N Yorks 100 F4
Stallingborough NE Lincs 91 C5
Stalmine Lancs 92 E3
Stalybridge Gtr Man 87 E7
Stambourne Essex 55 F8
Stambourne Green Essex 55 E8
Stamford Lincs 65 D7
Stamford Bridge Ches W 73 C8
Stamford Bridge E Yorks 96 D3
Stamfordham Northumb 110 B3
Stanah Cumb 99 C5
Stanborough Herts 41 C5
Stanbridge C Beds 40 B2
Stanbridge Dorset 13 D8
Stanbrook Worcs 50 E3
Stanbury W Yorks 94 F3
Stand Gtr Man 87 D5
Stand N Lanark 119 C7
Standburn Falk 120 B2
Standeford Staffs 62 D3
Standen Kent 30 E2
Standford Hants 27 F6
Standingstone Cumb 107 F7
Standish Gtr Man 86 C3
Standlake Oxon 38 D3
Standon Hants 14 B5
Standon Herts 41 B6
Standon Staffs 74 F5
Stane N Lanark 119 D8
Stanfield Norf 80 E5
Stanford C Beds 54 E2
Stanford Kent 19 B8
Stanford Bishop Hereford 49 D8
Stanford Bridge Worcs 50 C2
Stanford Dingley W Berks 26 B3
Stanford in the Vale Oxon 38 E3
Stanford-le-Hope Thurrock 42 F2
Stanford on Avon Northants 52 B3
Stanford on Soar Notts 64 B2
Stanford on Teme Worcs 50 C2
Stanford Rivers Essex 41 D8
Stanfree Derbys 76 B4
Stanghow Redcar 102 C4
Stanground Phoro 66 E2
Stanhoe Norf 80 D4
Stanhope Borders 114 B4
Stanhope Durham 110 F2
Stanion Northants 65 F6
Stanley Derbys 76 E4
Stanley Durham 110 D4
Stanley Lancs 86 D2
Stanley Perth 133 F8
Stanley Staffs 75 D6
Stanley W Yorks 88 B4
Stanley Common Derbys 76 E4
Stanley Gate Lancs 86 D2
Stanley Hill Hereford 49 E8
Stanlow Ches W 73 B8
Stanmer Brighton 17 D7
Stanmore Hants 15 B5
Stanmore London 40 E4
Stanmore W Berks 26 B2
Stannergate Dundee 134 F4
Stanningley W Yorks 94 F5
Stannington Northumb 110 B5
Stannington S Yorks 88 F4
Stansbatch Hereford 48 C5
Stansfield Suff 55 D8
Stanstead Suff 56 E2
Stanstead Abbotts Herts 41 C6
Stansted Kent 29 C7
Stansted Airport Essex 42 B1
Stansted Mountfitchet Essex 41 B8
Stanton Glos 51 F5
Stanton Mon 35 B7
Stanton Northumb 117 F7
Stanton Staffs 75 E8
Stanton Suff 56 B3
Stanton by Bridge Derbys 63 B7
Stanton-by-Dale Derbys 76 F4
Stanton Drew Bath 23 C7
Stanton Fitzwarren Swindon 38 E1
Stanton Harcourt Oxon 38 D4
Stanton Hill Notts 76 C4
Stanton in Peak Derbys 76 C2
Stanton Lacy Shrops 49 B6
Stanton Long Shrops 61 E5
Stanton-on-the-Wolds Notts 77 F6
Stanton Prior Bath 23 C8
Stanton St Bernard Wilts 25 C5
Stanton St John Oxon 39 D5
Stanton St Quintin Wilts 24 B4
Stanton Street Suff 56 C3
Stanton under Bardon Leics 63 C8
Stanton upon Hine Heath Shrops 61 B5
Stanton Wick Bath 23 C8
Stanwardine in the Fields Shrops 60 B4
Stanwardine in the Wood Shrops 60 B4
Stanway Essex 43 B5
Stanway Glos 51 F5
Stanway Green Suff 57 B6
Stanwell Sur 27 B8
Stanwell Moor Sur 27 B8
Stanwick Northants 53 B7
Stanwick-St-John N Yorks 101 C6
Stanwix Cumb 108 D4
Stanydale Shetland 160 H4
Staoinebrig W Isles 148 E2
Stape N Yorks 103 E5
Stapehill Dorset 13 D8
Stapeley Ches E 74 E3
Stapenhill Staffs 63 B6
Staple Kent 31 D6
Staple Som 22 E3
Staple Cross E Sus 18 C4
Staple Fitzpaine Som 11 C7
Staplefield W Sus 17 B6
Stapleford Cambs 55 D5
Stapleford Herts 41 C6
Stapleford Leics 64 C5
Stapleford Lincs 77 D8
Stapleford Notts 76 F4
Stapleford Wilts 25 F5
Stapleford Abbotts Essex 41 E8
Stapleford Tawney Essex 41 E8
Staplegrove Som 11 B7
Staplehay Som 11 B7
Staplehurst Kent 29 E8
Staplers IoW 15 F6
Stapleton Bristol 23 B8
Stapleton Cumb 108 B5
Stapleton Hereford 48 C5
Stapleton Leics 63 E8
Stapleton N Yorks 101 C7
Stapleton Shrops 60 D4
Stapleton Som 12 B2
Stapley Som 11 C6
Staploe Bedford 54 C2
Staplow Hereford 49 E8
Star Fife 128 D5
Star Pembs 45 F4
Star Som 23 D6
Stara Orkney 159 F3
Starbeck N Yorks 95 D6
Starbotton N Yorks 94 B2
Starcross Devon 10 F4
Stareton Warks 51 B8
Starkholmes Derbys 76 D3
Starlings Green Essex 55 F5
Starston Norf 68 F5
Startforth Durham 101 C5
Startley Wilts 37 F6
Stathe Som 11 B8
Stathern Leics 77 F7
Station Town Durham 111 F7
Staughton Green Cambs 54 C2
Staughton Highway Cambs 54 C2
Staunton Glos 36 B4
Staunton Glos 36 C2
Staunton in the Vale Notts 77 E8
Staunton on Arrow Hereford 49 C5
Staunton on Wye Hereford 49 E5
Staveley Cumb 99 E6
Staveley Cumb 99 F5
Staveley Derbys 76 B4
Staveley N Yorks 95 C6
Staverton Devon 7 C5
Staverton Glos 37 B5
Staverton Northants 52 C3
Staverton Wilts 24 C3
Staverton Bridge Glos 37 B5
Stawell Som 23 F5
Staxigoe Highld 158 E5
Staxton N Yorks 97 B6
Staylittle Powys 59 E5
Staynall Lancs 92 E3
Staythorpe Notts 77 D7
Stean N Yorks 94 B3
Stearsby N Yorks 96 B2
Steart Som 22 E4
Stebbing Essex 42 B2
Stebbing Green Essex 42 B2
Stedham W Sus 16 B2
Steele Road Borders 115 E8
Steen's Bridge Hereford 49 D7
Steep Hants 15 B8
Steep Marsh Hants 15 B8
Steeple Dorset 13 F7
Steeple Essex 43 D5
Steeple Ashton Wilts 24 D4
Steeple Aston Oxon 38 B4
Steeple Barton Oxon 38 B4
Steeple Bumpstead Essex 55 E7
Steeple Claydon Bucks 39 B6
Steeple Gidding Cambs 65 F8
Steeple Langford Wilts 24 F5
Steeple Morden Cambs 54 E3
Steeton W Yorks 94 E3
Stein Highld 148 C7
Steinmanhill Aberds 153 D7
Stelling Minnis Kent 30 E5
Stemster Highld 158 D3
Stemster Ho. Highld 158 D3
Stenalees Corn 4 D5
Stenhousemuir Falk 127 F7
Stenigot Lincs 91 F6
Stenness Shetland 160 F4
Stenscholl Highld 149 B9
Stenso Orkney 159 F4
Stenson Derbys 63 B7
Stenton E Loth 122 B2
Stenton Fife 128 E4
Stenwith Lincs 77 F8
Stepaside Pembs 32 D2
Stepping Hill Gtr Man 87 F7
Steppingley C Beds 53 F8
Stepps N Lanark 119 C6
Sterndale Moor Derbys 75 C8
Sternfield Suff 57 C7
Sterridge Devon 20 E4
Stert Wilts 24 D5
Stetchworth Cambs 55 D7
Stevenage Herts 41 B5
Stevenston N Ayrs 118 E2
Steventon Hants 26 E3
Steventon Oxon 38 E4
Stevington Bedford 53 D7
Stewartby Bedford 53 E8
Stewarton Argyll 143 G7
Stewarton E Ayrs 118 E4
Stewkley Bucks 40 B1
Stewton Lincs 91 F7
Steyne Cross IoW 15 F7
Steyning W Sus 17 C5
Steynton Pembs 44 E4
Stibb Corn 8 C4
Stibb Cross Devon 9 C6
Stibb Green Wilts 25 C7
Stibbard Norf 81 E5
Stibbington Cambs 65 E7
Stichill Borders 122 F3
Sticker Corn 4 D4
Stickford Lincs 79 D6
Sticklepath Devon 9 E8
Stickney Lincs 79 D6
Stiffkey Norf 81 C5
Stifford's Bridge Hereford 50 E2
Stillingfleet N Yorks 95 E8
Stillington N Yorks 95 C8
Stillington Stockton 102 B1
Stilton Cambs 65 F8
Stinchcombe Glos 36 E4
Stinsford Dorset 12 E5
Stirchley Telford 61 D7
Stirkoke Ho. Highld 158 E5
Stirling Aberds 153 D11
Stirling Stirling 127 E6
Stisted Essex 42 B3
Stithians Corn 3 C6
Stittenham Highld 151 D9
Stivichall W Mid 51 B8
Stixwould Lincs 78 C4
Stoak Ches W 73 B8
Stobieside S Lanark 119 F6
Stobo Borders 120 F4
Stoborough Dorset 13 F7
Stoborough Green Dorset 13 F7
Stobshiel E Loth 121 C7
Stobswood Northumb 117 E8
Stock Essex 42 E2
Stock Green Worcs 50 D4
Stock Wood Worcs 50 D5
Stockbridge Hants 25 F8
Stockbury Kent 30 C2
Stockcross W Berks 26 C2
Stockdalewath Cumb 108 E3
Stockerston Leics 64 E5
Stockheath Hants 15 D8
Stockiemuir Stirling 126 F4
Stocking Pelham Herts 41 B7
Stockingford Warks 63 E7
Stockland Devon 11 D7
Stockland Bristol Som 22 E4
Stockleigh English Devon 10 D3
Stockleigh Pomeroy Devon 10 D3
Stockley Wilts 24 C5
Stocklinch Som 11 C8
Stockport Gtr Man 87 E6
Stocksbridge S Yorks 88 E3
Stocksfield Northumb 110 C3
Stockton Hereford 49 C7
Stockton Norf 69 E6
Stockton Shrops 60 D2
Stockton Shrops 61 E7
Stockton Warks 52 C2
Stockton Wilts 24 F4
Stockton Heath Warr 86 F4
Stockton-on-Tees Stockton 102 C2
Stockton on Teme Worcs 50 C2
Stockton on the Forest York 96 D2
Stodmarsh Kent 31 C6
Stody Norf 81 D6
Stoer Highld 156 G3
Stoford Som 12 C3
Stoford Wilts 25 F5
Stogumber Som 22 F2
Stogursey Som 22 E4
Stoke Devon 8 B4
Stoke Hants 15 D8
Stoke Hants 26 D2
Stoke Medway 30 B2
Stoke Suff 57 E5
Stoke Abbott Dorset 12 D2
Stoke Albany Northants 64 F5
Stoke Ash Suff 56 B5
Stoke Bardolph Notts 77 E6
Stoke Bliss Worcs 49 C8
Stoke Bruerne Northants 52 E5
Stoke by Clare Suff 55 E8
Stoke-by-Nayland Suff 56 F3
Stoke Canon Devon 10 E4
Stoke Charity Hants 26 F2
Stoke Climsland Corn 5 B8
Stoke D'Abernon Sur 28 D2
Stoke Doyle Northants 65 F7
Stoke Dry Rutland 65 E5
Stoke Farthing Wilts 13 B8
Stoke Ferry Norf 67 E7
Stoke Fleming Devon 7 E6
Stoke Gabriel Devon 7 D6
Stoke Gifford S Glos 23 B8
Stoke Golding Leics 63 E7
Stoke Goldington M Keynes 53 E6
Stoke Green Bucks 40 F2
Stoke Hammond Bucks 40 B1
Stoke Heath Shrops 61 B6
Stoke Holy Cross Norf 68 D5
Stoke Lacy Hereford 49 E8
Stoke Lyne Oxon 39 B5
Stoke Mandeville Bucks 39 C8
Stoke Newington London 41 F6
Stoke on Tern Shrops 61 B6
Stoke-on-Trent Stoke 75 E5
Stoke Orchard Glos 37 B6
Stoke Poges Bucks 40 F2
Stoke Prior Hereford 49 D7
Stoke Prior Worcs 50 C4
Stoke Rivers Devon 20 F5
Stoke Rochford Lincs 65 B6
Stoke Row Oxon 39 F6
Stoke St Gregory Som 11 B8
Stoke St Mary Som 11 B7
Stoke St Michael Som 23 E8
Stoke St Milborough Shrops 61 F5

Stoke sub Hamdon Som 12 C2
Stoke Talmage Oxon 39 E6
Stoke Trister Som 12 B5
Stoke Wake Dorset 13 D5
Stokeford Dorset 13 F6
Stokeham Notts 77 B7
Stokeinteignhead Devon 7 B7
Stokenchurch Bucks 39 E7
Stokenham Devon 7 E6
Stokesay Shrops 60 F4
Stokesby Norf 69 C7
Stokesley N Yorks 102 D3
Stolford Som 22 E4
Ston Easton Som 23 D8
Stondon Massey Essex 42 D1
Stone Bucks 39 C7
Stone Glos 36 E3
Stone Kent 19 C6
Stone Kent 29 B6
Stone S Yorks 89 F6
Stone Staffs 75 F6
Stone Worcs 50 B3
Stone Allerton Som 23 D6
Stone Bridge Corner Pboro 66 D2
Stone Chair W Yorks 88 B2
Stone Cross E Sus 18 E3
Stone Cross Kent 31 D7
Stone-edge Batch N Som 23 B6
Stone House Cumb 100 F2
Stone Street Kent 29 D6
Stone Street Suff 56 F3
Stone Street Suff 69 F6
Stonebroom Derbys 76 D4
Stoneferry Hull 97 F7
Stonefield S Lanark 119 D6
Stonegate E Sus 18 C3
Stonegate N Yorks 103 D5
Stonegrave N Yorks 96 B2
Stonehaugh Northumb 109 B7
Stonehaven Aberds 141 F7
Stonehouse Glos 37 D5
Stonehouse Northumb 109 D6
Stonehouse S Lanark 119 E7
Stoneleigh Warks 51 B8
Stonely Cambs 54 C2
Stoner Hill Hants 15 B8
Stone's Green Essex 43 B7
Stonesby Leics 64 B5
Stonesfield Oxon 38 C3
Stonethwaite Cumb 98 C4
Stoney Cross Hants 14 C3
Stoney Middleton Derbys 76 B2
Stoney Stanton Leics 63 E8
Stoney Stoke Som 24 F2
Stoney Stratton Som 23 F8
Stoney Stretton Shrops 60 D3
Stoneybreck Shetland 160 N8
Stoneyburn W Loth 120 C2
Stoneygate Aberds 153 E10
Stoneygate Leicester 64 D3
Stoneyhills Essex 43 E5
Stoneykirk Dumfries 104 D4
Stoneywood Aberdeen 141 C7
Stoneywood Falk 127 F6
Stonganess Shetland 160 C7
Stonham Aspal Suff 56 D5
Stonnall Staffs 62 D4
Stonor Oxon 39 F7
Stonton Wyville Leics 64 E4
Stony Cross Hereford 50 E2
Stony Stratford M Keynes 53 E5
Stonyfield Highld 151 D9
Stoodleigh Devon 10 C4
Stopes S Yorks 88 F3
Stopham W Sus 16 C4
Stopsley Luton 40 B4
Stores Corner Suff 57 E7
Storeton Mers 85 F4
Stornoway W Isles 155 D9
Storridge Hereford 50 E2
Storrington W Sus 16 C4
Storrs Cumb 99 E5
Storth Cumb 99 F6
Storwood E Yorks 96 E3
Stotfield Moray 152 A2
Stotfold C Beds 54 F3
Stottesdon Shrops 61 F6
Stoughton Leics 64 D3
Stoughton Sur 27 D7
Stoughton W Sus 16 C2
Stoul Highld 147 B10
Stoulton Worcs 50 E4
Stour Provost Dorset 13 B5
Stour Row Dorset 13 B6
Stourbridge W Mid 62 F3
Stourpaine Dorset 13 D6
Stourport on Severn Worcs 50 B3
Stourton Staffs 62 F2
Stourton Warks 51 F7
Stourton Wilts 24 F2
Stourton Caundle Dorset 12 C5
Stove Orkney 159 E7
Stove Shetland 160 L6
Stoven Suff 69 F7
Stow Borders 121 E7
Stow Lincs 78 F3
Stow Lincs 90 F2
Stow Bardolph Norf 67 D6
Stow Bedon Norf 68 E2
Stow cum Quy Cambs 55 C6
Stow Longa Cambs 54 B2
Stow Maries Essex 42 E4
Stow-on-the-Wold Glos 38 B1
Stowbridge Norf 67 D6
Stowe Shrops 48 B5
Stowe-by-Chartley Staffs 62 B4
Stowe Green Glos 36 D2
Stowell Som 12 B4
Stowford Devon 9 F6
Stowlangtoft Suff 56 C3
Stowmarket Suff 56 D4
Stowting Kent 30 E5
Stowupland Suff 56 D4
Straad Argyll 145 G9
Strachan Aberds 141 E5
Stradbroke Suff 57 B6
Stradishall Suff 55 D8
Stradsett Norf 67 D6
Stragglethorpe Lincs 78 D2
Straid S Ayrs 112 E1
Straith Dumfries 113 F8
Straiton Edin 121 C5
Straiton S Ayrs 112 D3
Straloch Aberds 141 B7
Straloch Perth 133 C7
Stramshall Staffs 75 F7
Strang IoM 84 E3
Stranraer Dumfries 104 C4
Stratfield Mortimer W Berks 26 C4
Stratfield Saye Hants 26 C4
Stratfield Turgis Hants 26 D4
Stratford London 41 F6
Stratford St Andrew Suff 57 C7
Stratford St Mary Suff 56 F4
Stratford Sub Castle Wilts 25 F6
Stratford Tony Wilts 13 B8
Stratford-upon-Avon Warks 51 D6
Strath Highld 149 A12
Strath Highld 158 E4
Strathan Highld 136 E2
Strathan Highld 156 G3
Strathan Highld 157 C8
Strathaven S Lanark 119 E7
Strathblane Stirling 119 B5
Strathcanaird Highld 156 J4
Strathcarron Highld 150 G2
Strathcoil Argyll 124 B2
Strathdon Aberds 140 C2
Strathellie Aberds 153 B10
Strathkinness Fife 129 C6
Strathmashie House Highld 137 E8
Strathmiglo Fife 128 C4
Strathmore Lodge Highld 158 F3
Strathpeffer Highld 150 F7
Strathrannoch Highld 150 D6
Strathtay Perth 133 D6
Strathvaich Lodge Highld 150 D6
Strathwhillan N Ayrs 143 E11
Strathy Highld 157 C11
Strathyre Stirling 126 C4
Stratton Corn 8 D4
Stratton Dorset 12 E4
Stratton Glos 37 D7
Stratton Audley Oxon 39 B6
Stratton on the Fosse Som 23 D8
Stratton St Margaret Swindon 38 F1
Stratton St Michael Norf 68 E5
Stratton Strawless Norf 81 E8
Stravithie Fife 129 C7
Streat E Sus 17 C7
Streatham London 28 B4
Streatley C Beds 40 B3
Streatley W Berks 39 F5
Street Lancs 92 D5
Street N Yorks 103 D5
Street Som 23 F6
Street Dinas Shrops 73 F7
Street End Kent 30 D5
Street End W Sus 16 E2
Street Gate T&W 110 D5
Street Lydan Wrex 73 F8
Streethay Staffs 62 C5
Streetlam N Yorks 101 E8
Streetly W Mid 62 E4
Streetly End Cambs 55 E7
Strefford Shrops 60 F4
Strelley Notts 76 E5
Strensall York 96 C2
Stretcholt Som 22 E4
Strete Devon 7 E6
Stretford Gtr Man 87 E6
Strethall Essex 55 F5
Stretham Cambs 55 B6
Strettington W Sus 16 D2
Stretton Ches W 73 D8
Stretton Derbys 76 C3
Stretton Rutland 65 C6
Stretton Staffs 62 C2
Stretton Staffs 63 B6
Stretton Warr 86 F4
Stretton Grandison Hereford 49 E8
Stretton-on-Dunsmore Warks 52 B2
Stretton-on-Fosse Warks 51 F7
Stretton Sugwas Hereford 49 E6
Stretton under Fosse Warks 63 F8
Stretton Westwood Shrops 61 E5
Strichen Aberds 153 C9
Strines Gtr Man 87 F7
Stringston Som 22 E3
Strixton Northants 53 C7
Stroat Glos 36 E2
Stromeferry Highld 149 E13
Stromemore Highld 149 E13
Stromness Orkney 159 H3
Stronaba Highld 136 F5
Stronachlachar Stirling 126 C3
Stronchreggan Highld 130 B4
Stronchrubie Highld 156 H5
Strone Argyll 145 E10
Strone Highld 136 F4
Strone Highld 137 B8
Strone Involyd 118 B2
Stronmilchan Argyll 125 C7
Strontian Highld 130 C2
Strood Medway 29 C8
Strood Green Sur 28 E3
Strood Green W Sus 16 B4
Strood Green W Sus 28 F2
Stroud Glos 37 D5
Stroud Hants 15 B8
Stroud Green Essex 42 E4
Stroxton Lincs 78 F2
Struan Highld 149 E8
Struan Perth 133 C5
Strubby Lincs 91 F8
Strumpshaw Norf 69 D6
Strutherhill S Lanark 119 E7
Struy Highld 150 H6
Stryt-issa Wrex 73 E6
Stuartfield Aberds 153 D9
Stub Place Cumb 98 E2
Stubbington Hants 15 D6
Stubbins Lancs 87 C5
Stubbs Cross Kent 19 B6
Stubb's Green Norf 69 E5
Stubbs Green Norf 69 E6
Stubhampton Dorset 13 C7
Stubton Lincs 77 E8
Stuckgowan Argyll 126 D2
Stuckton Hants 14 C2
Stud Green Windsor 27 B6
Studham C Beds 40 C3
Studland Dorset 13 F8
Studley Warks 51 C5
Studley Wilts 24 B4
Studley Roger N Yorks 95 B5
Stump Cross Essex 55 E6
Stuntney Cambs 55 B6
Sturbridge Staffs 74 F5
Sturmer Essex 55 E7
Sturminster Marshall Dorset 13 D7
Sturminster Newton Dorset 13 C5
Sturry Kent 31 C5
Sturton N Lincs 90 D3
Sturton by Stow Lincs 90 F2
Sturton le Steeple Notts 89 F8
Stuston Suff 56 B5
Stutton N Yorks 95 E7
Stutton Suff 57 F5
Styal Ches E 87 F6
Styrrup Notts 89 E7
Suainebost W Isles 155 A10
Suardail W Isles 155 D9
Succoth Aberds 152 E4
Succoth Argyll 125 E8
Suckley Worcs 50 D2
Suckquoy Orkney 159 K5
Sudborough Northants 65 F6
Sudbourne Suff 57 D8
Sudbrook Lincs 78 E2
Sudbrook Mon 36 F2
Sudbrooke Lincs 78 B3
Sudbury Derbys 75 F8
Sudbury London 40 F4
Sudbury Suff 56 E2
Suddie Highld 151 F9
Sudgrove Glos 37 D6
Suffield N Yorks 103 E7
Suffield Norf 81 D8
Sugnall Staffs 74 F4
Suladale Highld 149 C8
Sulaisiadar W Isles 155 D10
Sulby IoM 84 C3
Sulgrave Northants 52 E3
Sulham W Berks 26 B4
Sulhamstead W Berks 26 C4
Sulland Orkney 159 D6
Sullington W Sus 16 C4
Sullom Shetland 160 F5
Sullom Voe Oil Terminal Shetland 160 F5
Sully V Glam 22 C3
Sumburgh Shetland 160 N6
Summer Bridge N Yorks 94 C5
Summer-house Darl 101 C7
Summercourt Corn 4 D3
Summerfield Norf 80 D3
Summergangs Hull 97 F7
Summerleaze Mon 35 F8
Summersdale W Sus 16 D2
Summerseat Gtr Man 87 C5
Summertown Oxon 39 D5
Summit Gtr Man 87 D7
Sunbury-on-Thames Sur 28 C2
Sundaywell Dumfries 113 F8
Sunderland Argyll 142 B3
Sunderland Cumb 107 F8
Sunderland T&W 111 D6
Sunderland Bridge Durham 111 F5
Sundhope Borders 115 B6
Sundon Park Luton 40 B3
Sundridge Kent 29 D5
Sunipol Argyll 146 F6
Sunk Island E Yorks 91 C6
Sunningdale Windsor 27 C7
Sunninghill Windsor 27 C7
Sunningwell Oxon 38 D4
Sunniside Durham 110 F4
Sunniside T&W 110 D5
Sunnyhurst Blackburn 86 B4
Sunnylaw Stirling 127 E6
Sunnyside W Sus 28 F4
Sunton Wilts 25 D7
Surbiton London 28 C2
Surby IoM 84 E2
Surfleet Lincs 66 B2
Surfleet Seas End Lincs 66 B2
Surlingham Norf 69 D6
Sustead Norf 81 D7
Susworth Lincs 90 D2
Sutcombe Devon 8 C5
Suton Norf 68 E3
Sutors of Cromarty Highld 151 E11
Sutterby Lincs 79 B6
Sutterton Lincs 79 F5
Sutton C Beds 54 E3
Sutton Cambs 54 B5
Sutton Kent 31 E7
Sutton London 28 C3
Sutton Mers 86 E3
Sutton N Yorks 89 B5
Sutton Norf 69 B6
Sutton Notts 77 F7
Sutton Notts 89 F7
Sutton Oxon 38 D4
Sutton Pboro 65 E7
Sutton S Yorks 89 C6
Sutton Shrops 61 F7
Sutton Shrops 74 F3
Sutton Som 23 F8
Sutton Staffs 61 B7
Sutton Suff 57 E7
Sutton Sur 27 E8
Sutton W Sus 16 C3
Sutton at Hone Kent 29 B6
Sutton Bassett Northants 64 E4
Sutton Benger Wilts 24 B4
Sutton Bonington Notts 64 B2
Sutton Bridge Lincs 66 B4
Sutton Cheney Leics 63 D8
Sutton Coldfield W Mid 62 E5
Sutton Courtenay Oxon 39 E5
Sutton Crosses Lincs 66 B4
Sutton Grange N Yorks 95 B5
Sutton Green Sur 27 D8
Sutton Howgrave N Yorks 95 B6
Sutton In Ashfield Notts 76 D4
Sutton-in-Craven N Yorks 94 E3
Sutton in the Elms Leics 64 E2
Sutton Ings Hull 97 F7
Sutton Lane Ends Ches E 75 B6
Sutton Leach Mers 86 E3
Sutton Maddock Shrops 61 D7
Sutton Mallet Som 23 F5
Sutton Mandeville Wilts 13 B7
Sutton Manor Mers 86 E3
Sutton Montis Som 12 B4
Sutton on Hull Hull 97 F7
Sutton on Sea Lincs 91 F9
Sutton-on-the-Forest N Yorks 95 C8
Sutton on the Hill Derbys 76 F2
Sutton on Trent Notts 77 C7
Sutton Scarsdale Derbys 76 C4
Sutton Scotney Hants 26 F2
Sutton St Edmund Lincs 66 C3
Sutton St James Lincs 66 C3
Sutton St Nicholas Hereford 49 E7
Sutton under Brailes Warks 51 F8
Sutton-under-Whitestonecliffe N Yorks 102 F2
Sutton upon Derwent E Yorks 96 E3
Sutton Valence Kent 30 E2
Sutton Veny Wilts 24 E3
Sutton Waldron Dorset 13 C6
Sutton Weaver Ches W 74 B2
Sutton Wick Bath 23 D7
Swaby Lincs 79 B6
Swadlincote Derbys 63 C7
Swaffham Norf 67 D8
Swaffham Bulbeck Cambs 55 C6
Swaffham Prior Cambs 55 C6
Swafield Norf 81 D8
Swainby N Yorks 102 D2
Swainshill Hereford 49 E6
Swainsthorpe Norf 68 D5
Swainswick Bath 24 C2
Swalcliffe Oxon 51 F8
Swalecliffe Kent 30 C5
Swallow Lincs 91 D5
Swallowcliffe Wilts 13 B7
Swallowfield Wokingham 26 C5
Swallownest S Yorks 89 F5
Swallows Cross Essex 42 E2
Swan Green Ches W 74 B4
Swan Green Suff 57 B6
Swanage Dorset 13 G8
Swanbister Orkney 159 H4
Swanbourne Bucks 39 B8
Swanland E Yorks 90 B3
Swanley Kent 29 C6
Swanley Village Kent 29 C6
Swanmore Hants 15 C6
Swannington Leics 63 C8
Swannington Norf 68 C4
Swanscombe Kent 29 B7
Swansea = Abertawe Swansea 33 E7
Swanton Abbott Norf 81 E8
Swanton Morley Norf 68 C3
Swanton Novers Norf 81 D6
Swanton Street Kent 30 D2
Swanwick Derbys 76 D4
Swanwick Hants 15 D6
Swarby Lincs 78 E3
Swardeston Norf 68 D5
Swarister Shetland 160 E7
Swarkestone Derbys 63 B7
Swarland Northumb 117 D7
Swarland Estate Northumb 117 D7
Swarthmoor Cumb 92 B2
Swathwick Derbys 76 C3
Swaton Lincs 78 F4
Swavesey Cambs 54 C4
Sway Hants 14 E3
Swayfield Lincs 65 B6
Swaythling Soton 14 C5
Sweet Green Worcs 49 C8
Sweetham Devon 10 E3
Sweethouse Corn 5 C5
Sweffling Suff 57 C7
Swepstone Leics 63 C7
Swerford Oxon 51 F8
Swettenham Ches E 74 C5
Swetton N Yorks 94 B4
Swffryd Caerph 35 E6
Swiftsden E Sus 18 C4
Swilland Suff 57 D5
Swillington W Yorks 95 F6
Swimbridge Devon 9 B8
Swimbridge Newland Devon 20 F5
Swinbrook Oxon 38 C2
Swinderby Lincs 77 C8
Swindon Glos 37 B6
Swindon Staffs 62 E2
Swindon Swindon 38 F1
Swine E Yorks 97 F7
Swinefleet E Yorks 89 B8
Swineshead Bedford 53 C8
Swineshead Lincs 78 E5
Swineshead Bridge Lincs 78 E5
Swiney Highld 158 G4
Swinford Leics 52 B3
Swinford Oxon 38 D4
Swingate Notts 76 E5
Swingfield Minnis Kent 31 E6
Swingfield Street Kent 31 E6
Swinhoe Northumb 117 B8
Swinhope Lincs 91 E6
Swining Shetland 160 G6
Swinithwaite N Yorks 101 F5
Swinnow Moor W Yorks 94 F5
Swinscoe Staffs 75 E8
Swinside Hall Borders 116 C3
Swinstead Lincs 65 B7
Swinton Borders 122 E4
Swinton Gtr Man 87 D5
Swinton N Yorks 94 B5
Swinton N Yorks 96 B3
Swinton S Yorks 88 E5
Swintonmill Borders 122 E4
Swithland Leics 64 C2
Swordale Highld 151 E8
Swordland Highld 147 B10
Swordly Highld 157 C10
Sworton Heath Ches E 86 F4
Swydd-ffynnon Ceredig 47 C5
Swynnerton Staffs 75 F5
Swyre Dorset 12 F3
Sychtyn Powys 59 D6
Syde Glos 37 C6
Sydenham London 28 B4
Sydenham Oxon 39 D7
Sydenham Damerel Devon 6 B2
Syderstone Norf 80 D4
Sydling St Nicholas Dorset 12 E4
Sydmonton Hants 26 D2
Syerston Notts 77 E7
Syke Gtr Man 87 C6
Sykehouse S Yorks 89 C7
Sykes Lancs 93 D6
Syleham Suff 57 B6
Sylen Carms 33 D6
Symbister Shetland 160 G7
Symington S Ayrs 118 F3
Symington S Lanark 120 F2
Symonds Yat Hereford 36 C2
Symondsbury Dorset 12 E2
Synod Inn Ceredig 46 D3
Syre Highld 157 E9
Syreford Glos 37 B7
Syresham Northants 52 E4
Syston Leics 64 C3
Syston Lincs 78 E2
Sytchampton Worcs 50 C3
Sywell Northants 53 C6

T

Taagan Highld 150 E3
Tàbost W Isles 155 A10
Tabost W Isles 155 F8
Tackley Oxon 38 B4
Tacleit W Isles 154 D6
Tacolneston Norf 68 E4
Tadcaster N Yorks 95 E7
Taddington Derbys 75 B8
Taddiport Devon 9 C6
Tadley Hants 26 C4
Tadlow C Beds 54 E3
Tadmarton Oxon 51 F8
Tadworth Sur 28 D3
Tafarn-y-gelyn Denb 73 C5
Tafarnau-bach Bl Gwent 35 C5
Taff's Well Rhondda 35 F5
Tafolwern Powys 59 D5
Tai Conwy 83 E7
Tai-bach Powys 59 B8
Tai-mawr Conwy 72 E3
Tai-Ucha Denb 72 D4
Taibach Neath 34 F1
Taigh a Ghearraidh W Isles 148 A2
Tain Highld 151 C10
Tain Highld 158 D4
Tainant Wrex 73 E6
Tainlon Gwyn 82 F4
Tairbeart = Tarbert W Isles 154 G6
Tai'r-Bull Powys 34 B3
Tairgwaith Neath 33 C8
Takeley Essex 42 B1
Takeley Street Essex 41 B8
Tal-sarn Ceredig 46 D4
Tal-y-bont Ceredig 58 F3
Tal-y-Bont Conwy 83 E7
Tal-y-bont Gwyn 71 E6
Tal-y-bont Gwyn 83 D6
Tal-y-cafn Conwy 83 D7
Tal-y-llyn Gwyn 58 D4
Tal-y-wern Powys 58 D5
Talachddu Powys 48 F2
Talacre Flint 85 F2
Talardd Gwyn 59 B5
Talaton Devon 11 E5
Talbenny Pembs 44 D3
Talbot Green Rhondda 34 F4
Talbot Village Poole 13 E8
Tale Devon 11 D5
Talerddig Powys 59 D6
Talgarreg Ceredig 46 D3
Talgarth Powys 48 F3
Talisker Highld 149 E8
Talke Staffs 74 D5
Talkin Cumb 109 D5
Talla Linnfoots Borders 114 B4
Talladale Highld 150 D2
Tallarn Green Wrex 73 E8
Tallentire Cumb 107 F8
Talley Carms 46 F5
Tallington Lincs 65 D7
Talmine Highld 157 C8
Talog Carms 32 B4
Talsarn Carms 34 B1
Talsarnau Gwyn 71 D7
Talskiddy Corn 4 C4
Talwrn Anglesey 82 D4
Talwrn Wrex 73 E6
Talybont-on-Usk Powys 35 B5
Talygarn Rhondda 34 F4
Talyllyn Powys 35 B5
Talysarn Gwyn 82 F4
Talywain Torf 35 D6
Tame Bridge N Yorks 102 D3
Tamerton Foliot Plym 6 C2
Tamworth Staffs 63 D6
Tan Hinon Powys 59 F5
Tan-lan Conwy 83 E7
Tan-lan Gwyn 71 C7
Tan-y-bwlch Gwyn 71 C7
Tan-y-fron Conwy 72 C3
Tan-y-graig Anglesey 82 D5
Tan-y-graig Gwyn 70 D4
Tan-y-groes Ceredig 45 E4
Tan-y-pistyll Powys 59 B7
Tan-yr-allt Gwyn 82 F4
Tandem W Yorks 88 C2
Tanden Kent 19 B6
Tandridge Sur 28 D4
Tanerdy Carms 33 B5
Tanfield Durham 110 D4
Tanfield Lea Durham 110 D4
Tangasdal W Isles 148 J1
Tangiers Pembs 44 D4
Tangley Hants 25 D8
Tanglwst Carms 46 F2
Tangmere W Sus 16 D3
Tangwick Shetland 160 F4
Tankersley S Yorks 88 D4
Tankerton Kent 30 C5
Tannach Highld 158 F5
Tannachie Aberds 141 F6
Tannadice Angus 134 D4
Tannington Suff 57 C6
Tansley Derbys 76 D3
Tansley Knoll Derbys 76 C3
Tansor Northants 65 E7
Tantobie Durham 110 D4
Tanton N Yorks 102 C3
Tanworth-in-Arden Warks 51 B6
Tanygrisiau Gwyn 71 C7
Tanyrhydiau Ceredig 47 C6
Taobh a Chaolais W Isles 148 G2
Taobh a Thuath Loch Aineort W Isles 148 F2
Taobh a Tuath Loch Baghasdail W Isles 148 F2
Taobh a'Ghlinne W Isles 155 F8
Taobh Tuath W Isles 154 J4
Taplow Bucks 40 F2
Tapton Derbys 76 B3
Tarbat Ho. Highld 151 D10
Tarbert Argyll 143 C7
Tarbert Argyll 144 E5
Tarbert Argyll 145 G7
Tarbert = Tairbeart W Isles 154 G6
Tarbet Argyll 126 D2
Tarbet Highld 147 B10
Tarbet Highld 156 E4
Tarbock Green Mers 86 F2
Tarbolton S Ayrs 112 B4
Tarbrax S Lanark 120 D3
Tardebigge Worcs 50 C5
Tarfside Angus 134 B4
Tarland Aberds 140 D3
Tarleton Lancs 86 B2
Tarlogie Highld 151 C10
Tarlscough Lancs 86 C2
Tarlton Glos 37 E6
Tarnbrook Lancs 93 D5
Tarporley Ches W 74 C2
Tarr Som 22 F3
Tarrant Crawford Dorset 13 D7
Tarrant Gunville Dorset 13 C7
Tarrant Hinton Dorset 13 C7
Tarrant Keyneston Dorset 13 D7
Tarrant Launceston Dorset 13 D7
Tarrant Monkton Dorset 13 D7
Tarrant Rawston Dorset 13 D7
Tarrant Rushton Dorset 13 D7
Tarrel Highld 151 C11
Tarring Neville E Sus 17 D8
Tarrington Hereford 49 E8
Tarsappie Perth 128 B3
Tarskavaig Highld 149 H10
Tarves Aberds 153 E8
Tarvie Highld 150 F7
Tarvie Perth 133 C7
Tarvin Ches W 73 C8
Tasburgh Norf 68 E5
Tasley Shrops 61 E6
Taston Oxon 38 B3
Tatenhill Staffs 63 B6
Tathall End M Keynes 53 E6
Tatham Lancs 93 C6
Tathwell Lincs 91 F7
Tatling End Bucks 40 F3
Tatsfield Sur 28 D5
Tattenhall Ches W 73 D8
Tattenhoe M Keynes 53 F6
Tatterford Norf 80 E4
Tattersett Norf 80 D4
Tattershall Lincs 78 D5
Tattershall Bridge Lincs 78 D4
Tattershall Thorpe Lincs 78 D5
Tattingstone Suff 56 F5
Tatworth Som 11 D8
Taunton Som 11 B7
Taverham Norf 68 C4
Tavernspite Pembs 32 C2
Tavistock Devon 6 B2
Taw Green Devon 9 E8
Tawstock Devon 9 B7
Taxal Derbys 75 B7
Tay Bridge Dundee 129 B6
Tayinloan Argyll 143 D7
Taymouth Castle Perth 132 E4
Taynish Argyll 144 E6
Taynton Glos 36 B4
Taynton Oxon 38 C2
Taynuilt Argyll 125 B6
Tayport Fife 129 B6
Tayvallich Argyll 144 E6
Tealby Lincs 91 E5
Tealing Angus 134 F4
Teangue Highld 149 H11
Teanna Mhachair W Isles 148 B2
Tebay Cumb 99 D8
Tebworth C Beds 40 B2
Tedburn St Mary Devon 10 E3
Teddington Glos 50 F4
Teddington London 28 B2
Tedstone Delamere Hereford 49 D8
Tedstone Wafre Hereford 49 D8
Teeton Northants 52 B4
Teffont Evias Wilts 24 F4
Teffont Magna Wilts 24 F4
Tegryn Pembs 45 F4
Teigh Rutland 65 C5
Teigncombe Devon 9 F8
Teigngrace Devon 7 B6
Teignmouth Devon 7 B7
Telford Telford 61 D6
Telham E Sus 18 D4
Tellisford Som 24 D3
Telscombe E Sus 17 D8
Telscombe Cliffs E Sus 17 D7
Templand Dumfries 114 F3
Temple Corn 5 B6
Temple Glasgow 118 C5
Temple Midloth 121 D6
Temple Balsall W Mid 51 B7
Temple Bar Carms 33 C6
Temple Bar Ceredig 46 D4
Temple Cloud Bath 23 D8
Temple Combe Som 12 B5
Temple Ewell Kent 31 E6
Temple Grafton Warks 51 D6
Temple Guiting Glos 37 B7
Temple Herdewyke Warks 51 D8
Temple Hirst N Yorks 89 B7
Temple Normanton Derbys 76 C4
Temple Sowerby Cumb 99 B8
Templehall Fife 128 E4
Templeton Devon 10 C3
Templeton Pembs 32 C2
Templeton Bridge Devon 10 C3
Templetown Durham 110 D4
Tempsford C Beds 54 D2
Ten Mile Bank Norf 67 E6
Tenbury Wells Worcs 49 C7
Tenby = Dinbych-Y-Pysgod Pembs 32 D2
Tendring Essex 43 B7
Tendring Green Essex 43 B7
Tenston Orkney 159 G3
Tenterden Kent 19 B5
Terling Essex 42 C3
Ternhill Shrops 74 F3
Terregles Banks Dumfries 107 B6
Terrick Bucks 39 D8
Terrington N Yorks 96 B2
Terrington St Clement Norf 66 C5
Terrington St John Norf 66 C5
Teston Kent 29 D8
Testwood Hants 14 C4
Tetbury Glos 37 E5
Tetbury Upton Glos 37 E5
Tetchill Shrops 73 F7
Tetcott Devon 8 E5
Tetford Lincs 79 B6
Tetney Lincs 91 D7
Tetney Lock Lincs 91 D7
Tetsworth Oxon 39 D6
Tettenhall W Mid 62 E2
Teuchan Aberds 153 E10
Teversal Notts 76 C4
Teversham Cambs 55 D5
Teviothead Borders 115 D7
Tewel Aberds 141 F7
Tewin Herts 41 C5
Tewkesbury Glos 50 F3
Teynham Kent 30 C3
Thackthwaite Cumb 98 B3
Thainston Aberds 135 B6
Thakeham W Sus 16 C5
Thame Oxon 39 D7
Thames Ditton Sur 28 C2
Thames Haven Thurrock 42 F3
Thamesmead London 41 F7
Thanington Kent 30 D5
Thankerton S Lanark 120 F2
Tharston Norf 68 E4
Thatcham W Berks 26 C3
Thatto Heath Mers 86 E3
Thaxted Essex 55 F7
The Aird Highld 149 C9
The Arms Norf 67 E8
The Bage Hereford 48 E4
The Balloch Perth 127 C7
The Barony Orkney 159 F3
The Bog Shrops 60 E3
The Bourne Sur 27 E6
The Braes Highld 149 E10
The Broad Hereford 49 C6
The Butts Som 24 E2
The Camp Glos 37 D6
The Camp Herts 40 D4
The Chequer Wrex 73 E8
The City Bucks 39 E7
The Common Wilts 25 F7
The Craigs Highld 150 B7
The Cronk IoM 84 C3
The Dell Suff 69 E7
The Den N Ayrs 118 D3
The Eals Northumb 116 F3
The Eaves Glos 36 D3
The Flatt Cumb 109 B5
The Four Alls Shrops 74 F3
The Garths Shetland 160 B8
The Green Cumb 98 F3
The Green Wilts 24 F3
The Grove Dumfries 107 B6
The Hall Shetland 160 D8
The Haven W Sus 27 F8
The Heath Norf 81 E7
The Heath Suff 56 F5
The Hill Cumb 98 F3
The Howe Cumb 99 F6
The Howe IoM 84 F1
The Hundred Hereford 49 C7
The Lee Bucks 40 D2
The Lhen IoM 84 B3
The Marsh Powys 60 E3
The Marsh Wilts 37 F7
The Middles Durham 110 D5
The Moor Kent 18 C4
The Mumbles = Y Mwmbwls Swansea 33 F7
The Murray S Lanark 119 D6
The Neuk Aberds 141 E6
The Oval Bath 24 C2
The Pole of Itlaw Aberds 153 C6
The Quarry Glos 36 E4
The Rhos Pembs 32 C1
The Rock Telford 61 D6
The Ryde Herts 41 D5
The Sands Sur 27 E6
The Stocks Kent 19 C6
The Throat Wokingham 27 C6
The Vauld Hereford 49 E7
The Wyke Shrops 61 D7
Theakston N Yorks 101 F8
Thealby N Lincs 90 C2
Theale Som 23 E6
Theale W Berks 26 B4
Thearne E Yorks 97 F6
Theberton Suff 57 C8
Theddingworth Leics 64 F3
Theddlethorpe All Saints Lincs 91 F8
Theddlethorpe St Helen Lincs 91 F8
Thelbridge Barton Devon 10 C2
Thelnetham Suff 56 B4
Thelveton Norf 68 F4
Thelwall Warr 86 F4
Themelthorpe Norf 81 E6
Thenford Northants 52 E3
Therfield Herts 54 F4
Thetford Lincs 65 C8
Thetford Norf 67 F8
Theydon Bois Essex 41 E7
Thickwood Wilts 24 B3
Thimbleby Lincs 78 C5
Thimbleby N Yorks 102 E2
Thingwall Mers 85 F3
Thirdpart N Ayrs 118 E1
Thirlby N Yorks 102 F2
Thirlestane Borders 121 E8
Thirn N Yorks 101 F7
Thirsk N Yorks 102 F2
Thirtleby E Yorks 97 F7
Thistleton Lancs 92 F4
Thistleton Rutland 65 C6
Thistley Green Suff 55 B7
Thixendale N Yorks 96 C4
Thockrington Northumb 110 B2
Tholomas Drove Cambs 66 D3
Tholthorpe N Yorks 95 C7
Thomas Chapel Pembs 32 D2
Thomas Close Cumb 108 E4
Thomastown Aberds 152 E5
Thompson Norf 68 E2
Thomshill Moray 152 C2
Thong Kent 29 B7
Thongsbridge W Yorks 88 D2
Thoralby N Yorks 101 F5
Thoresway Lincs 91 E5
Thorganby Lincs 91 E6
Thorganby N Yorks 96 E2
Thorgill N Yorks 103 E5
Thorington Suff 57 B8
Thorington Street Suff 56 F4
Thorlby N Yorks 94 D2
Thorley Herts 41 C7
Thorley Street Herts 41 C7
Thorley Street IoW 14 F4
Thormanby N Yorks 95 B7
Thornaby-on-Tees Stockton 102 C2
Thornage Norf 81 D6
Thornborough Bucks 52 F5
Thornborough N Yorks 95 B5
Thornbury Devon 9 D6
Thornbury Hereford 49 D8
Thornbury S Glos 36 E3
Thornbury W Yorks 94 F4
Thornby Northants 52 B4
Thorncliffe Staffs 75 D7
Thorncombe Dorset 11 D8
Thorncombe Dorset 13 D6
Thorncombe Street Sur 27 E8
Thorncote Green C Beds 54 E2
Thorncross IoW 14 F5
Thorndon Suff 56 C5
Thorndon Cross Devon 9 E7
Thorne S Yorks 89 C7
Thorne St Margaret Som 11 B5
Thorner W Yorks 95 E6
Thorney Notts 77 B8
Thorney Pboro 66 D2
Thorney Crofts E Yorks 91 B6
Thorney Green Suff 56 C4
Thorney Hill Hants 14 E2
Thorney Toll Pboro 66 D3
Thornfalcon Som 11 B7
Thornford Dorset 12 C4
Thorngumbald E Yorks 91 B6
Thornham Norf 80 C3
Thornham Magna Suff 56 B5
Thornham Parva Suff 56 B5
Thornhaugh Pboro 65 D7
Thornhill Cardiff 35 F5
Thornhill Cumb 98 D2
Thornhill Derbys 88 F2
Thornhill Dumfries 113 E8
Thornhill Soton 15 C5
Thornhill Stirling 127 E5
Thornhill W Yorks 88 C3
Thornhill Edge W Yorks 88 C3
Thornhill Lees W Yorks 88 C3
Thornholme E Yorks 97 C7
Thornley Durham 110 F4
Thornley Durham 111 F6
Thornliebank E Renf 118 D5
Thorns Suff 55 D8
Thorns Green Ches E 87 F5
Thornsett Derbys 87 F8
Thornthwaite Cumb 98 B4
Thornthwaite N Yorks 94 D4
Thornton Angus 134 E3
Thornton Bucks 53 F5
Thornton E Yorks 96 E3
Thornton Fife 128 E4
Thornton Lancs 92 E3
Thornton Leics 63 D8
Thornton Lincs 78 C5
Thornton Mbro 102 C2
Thornton Mers 85 D4
Thornton Northumb 123 E5
Thornton Pembs 44 E4
Thornton W Yorks 94 F4
Thornton Curtis N Lincs 90 C4
Thornton Heath London 28 C4
Thornton Hough Mers 85 F4
Thornton in Craven N Yorks 94 E2
Thornton-le-Beans N Yorks 102 E1
Thornton-le-Clay N Yorks 96 C2
Thornton-le-Dale N Yorks 103 F6
Thornton le Moor Lincs 90 E4
Thornton-le-Moor N Yorks 102 F1
Thornton-le-Moors Ches W 73 B8
Thornton-le-Street N Yorks 102 F2
Thornton Rust N Yorks 100 F4
Thornton Steward N Yorks 101 F6
Thornton Watlass N Yorks 101 F7
Thorntonhall S Lanark 119 D5
Thorntonloch E Loth 122 B3
Thorntonpark Northumb 122 E5
Thornwood Common Essex 41 D7
Thornydykes Borders 122 E2
Thoroton Notts 77 E7
Thorp Arch W Yorks 95 E7
Thorpe Derbys 75 D8
Thorpe E Yorks 97 E5
Thorpe Lincs 91 F8
Thorpe N Yorks 94 C3
Thorpe Norf 69 E7
Thorpe Notts 77 E7
Thorpe Sur 27 C8
Thorpe Abbotts Norf 57 B5
Thorpe Acre Leics 64 B2
Thorpe Arnold Leics 64 B4
Thorpe Audlin W Yorks 89 C5
Thorpe Bassett N Yorks 96 B4
Thorpe Bay Southend 43 F5
Thorpe by Water Rutland 65 E5
Thorpe Common Suff 57 F6
Thorpe Constantine Staffs 63 D6
Thorpe Culvert Lincs 79 C7
Thorpe End Norf 69 C5
Thorpe Fendykes Lincs 79 C7
Thorpe Green Essex 43 B7
Thorpe Green Suff 56 D3
Thorpe Hesley S Yorks 88 E4
Thorpe in Balne S Yorks 89 C6
Thorpe in the Fallows Lincs 90 F3
Thorpe Langton Leics 64 E4
Thorpe Larches Durham 102 B1
Thorpe-le-Soken Essex 43 B7
Thorpe le Street E Yorks 96 E4
Thorpe Malsor Northants 53 B6
Thorpe Mandeville Northants 52 E3
Thorpe Market Norf 81 D8
Thorpe Marriot Norf 68 C4
Thorpe Morieux Suff 56 D3
Thorpe on the Hill Lincs 78 C2
Thorpe Salvin S Yorks 89 F6
Thorpe Satchville Leics 64 C4
Thorpe St Andrew Norf 69 D5
Thorpe St Peter Lincs 79 C7
Thorpe Thewles Stockton 102 B2
Thorpe Tilney Lincs 78 D4
Thorpe Underwood N Yorks 95 D7
Thorpe Waterville Northants 65 F7
Thorpe Willoughby N Yorks 95 F8
Thorpeness Suff 57 D8
Thorrington Essex 43 C6
Thorverton Devon 10 D4
Thrandeston Suff 56 B5
Thrapston Northants 53 B7
Thrashbush N Lanark 119 C7
Threapland Cumb 107 F8
Threapland N Yorks 94 C2
Threapwood Ches W 73 E8
Threapwood Staffs 75 E7
Three Ashes Hereford 36 B2
Three Bridges W Sus 28 F3
Three Burrows Corn 3 B6
Three Chimneys Kent 18 B5
Three Cocks Powys 48 F3
Three Crosses Swansea 33 E6
Three Cups Corner E Sus 18 C3
Three Holes Norf 66 D5
Three Leg Cross E Sus 18 B3
Three Legged Cross Dorset 13 D8
Three Oaks E Sus 18 D5
Threehammer Common Norf 69 C6
Threekingham Lincs 78 F3
Threemile Cross Wokingham 26 C5
Threemilestone Corn 3 B6
Threemiletown W Loth 120 B3
Threlkeld Cumb 99 B5
Threshfield N Yorks 94 C2
Thrigby Norf 69 C7
Thringarth Durham 100 B4
Thringstone Leics 63 C8
Thrintoft N Yorks 101 E8
Thriplow Cambs 54 E5
Throckenholt Lincs 66 D3
Throcking Herts 54 F4
Throckley T&W 110 C4
Throckmorton Worcs 50 E4
Throphill Northumb 117 F7
Thropton Northumb 117 D6
Throsk Stirling 127 E7
Throwleigh Devon 9 E8
Throwley Kent 30 D3
Thrumpton Notts 76 F5
Thrumster Highld 158 F5
Thrunton Northumb 117 C6
Thrupp Glos 37 D5
Thrupp Oxon 38 C4
Thrushelton Devon 9 F6
Thrussington Leics 64 C3
Thruxton Hants 25 E7
Thruxton Hereford 49 F6
Thrybergh S Yorks 89 E5
Thulston Derbys 76 F4
Thundergay N Ayrs 143 D9
Thundersley Essex 42 F3
Thundridge Herts 41 C6
Thurcaston Leics 64 C2
Thurcroft S Yorks 89 F5
Thurgarton Norf 81 D7
Thurgarton Notts 77 E6
Thurgoland S Yorks 88 D3
Thurlaston Leics 64 E2
Thurlaston Warks 52 B2
Thurlbear Som 11 B7
Thurlby Lincs 65 C8
Thurlby Lincs 78 C2
Thurleigh Bedford 53 D8
Thurlestone Devon 6 E4
Thurloxton Som 22 F4
Thurlstone S Yorks 88 D3
Thurlton Norf 69 E7
Thurlwood Ches E 74 D5
Thurmaston Leics 64 D3
Thurnby Leics 64 D3
Thurne Norf 69 C7
Thurnham Kent 30 D2
Thurnham Lancs 92 D4
Thurning Norf 81 E6
Thurning Northants 65 F7
Thurnscoe S Yorks 89 D5
Thurnscoe East S Yorks 89 D5
Thursby Cumb 108 D3
Thursford Norf 81 D5
Thursley Sur 27 F7
Thurso Highld 158 D3
Thurso East Highld 158 D3
Thurstaston Mers 85 F3
Thurston Suff 56 C3
Thurstonfield Cumb 108 D3
Thurstonland W Yorks 88 C2
Thurton Norf 69 D6
Thurvaston Derbys 76 F2
Thuxton Norf 68 D3
Thwaite N Yorks 100 E3

Walford Heath Shrops 60 C4
Walgherton Ches E 74 E3
Walgrave Northants 53 B6
Walhampton Hants 14 E4
Walk Mill Lancs 93 F8
Walkden Gtr Man 86 D5
Walker T&W 111 C5
Walker Barn Ches E 75 B6
Walker Fold Lancs 93 E6
Walkerburn Borders 121 F6
Walkeringham Notts 89 E8
Walkerith Lincs 89 E8
Walkern Herts 41 B5
Walker's Green Hereford 49 E7
Walkerville N Yorks 101 E7
Walkford Dorset 14 E3
Walkhampton Devon 6 C3
Walkington E Yorks 97 F5
Walkley S Yorks 88 F4
Wall Northumb 110 C2
Wall Staffs 62 D5
Wall Bank Shrops 60 E5
Wall Heath W Mid 62 F2
Wall under Heywood Shrops 60 E5
Wallaceton Dumfries 113 F8
Wallacetown S Ayrs 112 B3
Wallacetown S Ayrs 112 D2
Wallands Park E Sus 17 C8
Wallasey Mers 85 E4
Wallcrouch E Sus 18 B3
Wallingford Oxon 39 F6
Wallington Hants 15 D6
Wallington Herts 54 F3
Wallington London 28 C3
Wallis Pembs 32 B1
Walliswood Sur 28 F2
Walls Shetland 160 J4
Wallsend T&W 111 C5
Wallston V Glam 22 B3
Wallyford E Loth 121 B6
Walmer Kent 31 D7
Walmer Bridge Lancs 86 B2
Walmersley Gtr Man 87 C6
Walmley W Mid 62 E5
Walpole Suff 57 B7
Walpole Cross Keys Norf 66 C5
Walpole Highway Norf 66 C5
Walpole Marsh Norf 66 C4
Walpole St Andrew Norf 66 C5
Walpole St Peter Norf 66 C5
Walsall W Mid 62 E4
Walsall Wood W Mid 62 D4
Walsden W Yorks 87 B7
Walsgrave on Sowe W Mid 63 F7
Walsham le Willows Suff 56 B3
Walshaw Gtr Man 87 C5
Walshford N Yorks 95 D7
Walsoken Cambs 66 C4
Walston S Lanark 120 E3
Walsworth Herts 54 F3
Walters Ash Bucks 39 E8
Walterston V Glam 22 B2
Walterstone Hereford 35 B7
Waltham Kent 30 E5
Waltham NE Lincs 91 D6
Waltham Abbey Essex 41 D6
Waltham Chase Hants 15 C6
Waltham Cross Herts 41 D6
Waltham on the Wolds Leics 64 B5
Waltham St Lawrence Windsor 27 B6
Walthamstow London 41 F6
Walton Cumb 108 C5
Walton Derbys 76 C3
Walton Leics 64 F2
Walton M Keynes 53 F6
Walton Mers 85 E4
Walton Pboro 65 D8
Walton Powys 48 D4
Walton Som 23 F6
Walton Staffs 75 F5
Walton Suff 57 F6
Walton Telford 61 C5
Walton W Yorks 88 C4
Walton W Yorks 95 E7
Walton Warks 51 D7
Walton Cardiff Glos 50 F4
Walton East Pembs 32 B1
Walton-in-Gordano N Som 23 B6
Walton-le-Dale Lancs 86 B3
Walton-on-Thames Sur 28 C2
Walton on the Hill Staffs 62 B3
Walton on the Hill Sur 28 D3
Walton-on-the-Naze Essex 43 B8
Walton on the Wolds Leics 64 C2
Walton-on-Trent Derbys 63 C6
Walton West Pembs 44 D3
Walwen Flint 73 B6
Walwick Northumb 110 B2
Walworth Darl 101 C7
Walworth Gate Darl 101 B7
Walwyn's Castle Pembs 44 D3
Wambrook Som 11 D7
Wanborough Sur 27 E7
Wanborough Swindon 38 F2
Wandsworth London 28 B3
Wangford Suff 57 B8
Wanlockhead Dumfries 113 C8
Wansford E Yorks 97 D6
Wansford Pboro 65 E7
Wanstead London 41 F7
Wanstrow Som 24 E2
Wanswell Glos 36 D3
Wantage Oxon 38 F3
Wapley S Glos 24 B2
Wappenbury Warks 51 C8
Wappenham Northants 52 E4
Warbleton E Sus 18 D3
Warblington Hants 15 D8
Warborough Oxon 39 E5
Warboys Cambs 66 F3
Warbreck Blackpool 92 F3
Warbstow Corn 8 E4
Warburton Gtr Man 86 F5
Warcop Cumb 100 C2
Ward End W Mid 62 F5
Ward Green Suff 56 C4
Warden Kent 30 B4
Warden Northumb 110 C2
Wardhill Orkney 159 F7
Wardington Oxon 52 E2
Wardlaw Borders 115 C5
Wardle Ches E 74 D3
Wardle Gtr Man 87 C7
Wardley Rutland 64 D5
Wardlow Derbys 75 B8
Wardy Hill Cambs 66 F4
Ware Herts 41 C6
Ware Kent 31 C6
Wareham Dorset 13 F7
Warehorne Kent 19 B6
Waren Mill Northumb 123 F7
Warenford Northumb 117 B7
Warenton Northumb 123 F7
Wareside Herts 41 C6
Waresley Cambs 54 D3
Waresley Worcs 50 B3
Warfield Brack 27 B6
Warfleet Devon 7 D6
Wargrave Wokingham 27 B5
Warham Norf 80 C5
Warhill Gtr Man 87 E7
Wark Northumb 109 B8
Wark Northumb 122 F4
Warkleigh Devon 9 B8
Warkton Northants 53 B6
Warkworth Northants 52 E2
Warkworth Northumb 117 D8
Warlaby N Yorks 101 E8
Warland W Yorks 87 B7
Warleggan Corn 5 C6
Warlingham Sur 28 D4
Warmfield W Yorks 88 B4
Warmingham Ches E 74 C4
Warmington Northants 65 E7
Warmington Warks 52 E2
Warminster Wilts 24 E3
Warmlake Kent 30 D2
Warmley S Glos 23 B8
Warmley Tower S Glos 23 B8
Warmonds Hill Northants 53 C7
Warmsworth S Yorks 89 D6
Warmwell Dorset 13 F5
Warndon Worcs 50 D3
Warnford Hants 15 B7
Warnham W Sus 28 F2
Warninglid W Sus 17 B6
Warren Ches E 75 B5
Warren Pembs 44 F4
Warren Heath Suff 57 E6
Warren Row Windsor 39 F8
Warren Street Kent 30 D3
Warrington M Keynes 53 D6
Warrington Warr 86 F4
Warsash Hants 15 D5
Warslow Staffs 75 D7
Warter E Yorks 96 D4
Warthermarske N Yorks 94 B5
Warthill N Yorks 96 D2
Wartling E Sus 18 E3
Wartnaby Leics 64 B4
Warton Lancs 86 B2
Warton Lancs 92 B4
Warton Northumb 117 D6
Warton Warks 63 D6
Warwick Warks 51 C7
Warwick Bridge Cumb 108 D4
Warwick on Eden Cumb 108 D4
Wasbister Orkney 159 E4
Wasdale Head Cumb 98 D3
Wash Common W Berks 26 C2
Washaway Corn 4 C5
Washbourne Devon 7 D5
Washfield Devon 10 C4
Washfold N Yorks 101 D5
Washford Som 22 E2
Washford Pyne Devon 10 C3
Washingborough Lincs 78 B3
Washington T&W 111 D6
Washington W Sus 16 C5
Wasing W Berks 26 C3
Waskerley Durham 110 E3
Wasperton Warks 51 D7
Wasps Nest Lincs 78 C3
Wass N Yorks 95 B8
Watchet Som 22 E2
Watchfield Oxon 38 E2
Watchfield Som 22 E5
Watchgate Cumb 99 E7
Watchhill Cumb 107 E8
Watcombe Torbay 7 C7
Watendlath Cumb 98 C4
Water Devon 10 F2
Water Lancs 87 B6
Water End E Yorks 96 F3
Water End Herts 40 C3
Water End Herts 41 D5
Water Newton Cambs 65 E8
Water Orton Warks 63 E5
Water Stratford Bucks 52 F4
Water Yeat Cumb 98 F4
Waterbeach Cambs 55 C5
Waterbeck Dumfries 108 B2
Waterden Norf 80 D4
Waterfall Staffs 75 D7
Waterfoot E Renf 119 D5
Waterfoot Lancs 87 B6
Waterford Hants 14 E4
Waterford Herts 41 C6
Waterhead Cumb 99 D5
Waterhead Dumfries 114 E4
Waterheads Borders 120 D5
Waterhouses Durham 110 E4
Waterhouses Staffs 75 D7
Wateringbury Kent 29 D7
Waterloo Gtr Man 87 D7
Waterloo Highld 149 F11
Waterloo Mers 85 E4
Waterloo N Lanark 119 D8
Waterloo Norf 68 C5
Waterloo Perth 133 F7
Waterloo Poole 13 E8
Waterloo Shrops 74 F2
Waterloo Port Gwyn 82 E4
Waterlooville Hants 15 D7
Watermeetings S Lanark 114 C2
Watermillock Cumb 99 B6
Waterperry Oxon 39 D6
Waterrow Som 11 B5
Water's Nook Gtr Man 86 D4
Waters Upton Telford 61 C6
Watersfield W Sus 16 C4
Waterside Aberds 141 B9
Waterside Blackburn 86 B5
Waterside Cumb 108 E2
Waterside E Ayrs 112 D4
Waterside E Ayrs 118 E4
Waterside E Dunb 119 B6
Waterside E Renf 118 D5
Waterstock Oxon 39 D6
Waterston Pembs 44 E4
Watford Herts 40 E4
Watford Northants 52 C4
Watford Gap Staffs 62 D5
Wath N Yorks 94 C4
Wath N Yorks 95 B6
Wath N Yorks 96 B2
Wath Brow Cumb 98 C2
Wath upon Dearne S Yorks 88 D5
Watlington Norf 67 C6
Watlington Oxon 39 E6
Watnall Notts 76 E5
Watten Highld 158 E4
Wattisfield Suff 56 B4
Wattisham Suff 56 D4
Wattlesborough Heath Shrops 60 C3
Watton E Yorks 97 D6
Watton Norf 68 D2
Watton at Stone Herts 41 C6
Wattston N Lanark 119 B7
Wattstown Rhondda 34 E4
Wauchan Highld 136 F2
Waulkmill Lodge Orkney 159 H4
Waun Powys 59 D5
Waun-y-clyn Carms 33 D5
Waunarlwydd Swansea 33 E7
Waunclunda Carms 47 F5
Waunfawr Gwyn 82 F5
Waungron Swansea 33 D6
Waunlwyd Bl Gwent 35 D5
Wavendon M Keynes 53 F7
Waverbridge Cumb 108 E2
Waverton Ches W 73 C8
Waverton Cumb 108 E2
Wavertree Mers 85 F4
Wawne E Yorks 97 F6
Waxham Norf 69 B7
Waxholme E Yorks 91 B7
Way Kent 31 C7
Way Village Devon 10 C3
Wayfield Medway 29 C8
Wayford Som 12 D2
Waymills Shrops 74 E2
Wayne Green Mon 35 C8
Wdig = Goodwick Pembs 44 B4
Weachyburn Aberds 153 C6
Weald Oxon 38 D3
Wealdstone London 40 F4
Weardley W Yorks 95 E5
Weare Som 23 D6
Weare Giffard Devon 9 B6
Wearhead Durham 109 F8
Weasdale Cumb 100 D1
Weasenham All Saints Norf 80 E4
Weasenham St Peter Norf 80 E4
Weatherhill Sur 28 E4
Weaverham Ches W 74 B3
Weaverthorpe N Yorks 97 B5
Webheath Worcs 50 C5
Wedderlairs Aberds 153 E8
Wedderlie Borders 122 D2
Weddington Warks 63 E7
Wedhampton Wilts 25 D5
Wedmore Som 23 E6
Wednesbury W Mid 62 E3
Wednesfield W Mid 62 D3
Weedon Bucks 39 C8
Weedon Bec Northants 52 D4
Weedon Lois Northants 52 E4
Weeford Staffs 62 D5
Week Devon 10 C2
Week St Mary Corn 8 E4
Weeke Hants 26 F2
Weekley Northants 65 F5
Weel E Yorks 97 F6
Weeley Essex 43 B7
Weeley Heath Essex 43 B7
Weem Perth 133 E5
Weeping Cross Staffs 62 B3
Weethley Gate Warks 51 D5
Weeting Norf 67 F7
Weeton E Yorks 91 B7
Weeton Lancs 92 F3
Weeton N Yorks 95 E5
Weetwood Hall Northumb 117 B6
Weir Lancs 87 B6
Weir Quay Devon 6 C2
Welborne Norf 68 D3
Welbourn Lincs 78 D2
Welburn N Yorks 96 C3
Welburn N Yorks 102 F4
Welbury N Yorks 102 D1
Welby Lincs 78 F2
Welches Dam Cambs 66 F4
Welcombe Devon 8 C4
Weld Bank Lancs 86 C3
Weldon Northumb 117 E7
Welford Northants 64 F3
Welford W Berks 26 B2
Welford-on-Avon Warks 51 D6
Welham Leics 64 E4
Welham Notts 89 F8
Welham Green Herts 41 D5
Well Hants 27 E5
Well Lincs 79 B7
Well N Yorks 101 F7
Well End Bucks 40 F1
Well Heads W Yorks 94 F3
Well Hill Kent 29 C5
Well Town Devon 10 D4
Welland Worcs 50 E2
Wellbank Angus 134 F4
Welldale Dumfries 107 C8
Wellesbourne Warks 51 D7
Welling London 29 B5
Wellingborough Northants 53 C6
Wellingham Norf 80 E4
Wellingore Lincs 78 D2
Wellington Cumb 98 D2
Wellington Hereford 49 E6
Wellington Som 11 B6
Wellington Telford 61 C6
Wellington Heath Hereford 50 E2
Wellington Hill W Yorks 95 F6
Wellow Bath 24 D2
Wellow IoW 14 F4
Wellow Notts 77 C6
Wellpond Green Herts 41 B7
Wells Som 23 E7
Wells Green Ches E 74 D3
Wells-Next-The-Sea Norf 80 C5
Wellsborough Leics 63 D7
Wellswood Torbay 7 C7
Wellwood Fife 128 F2
Welney Norf 66 E5
Welsh Bicknor Hereford 36 C2
Welsh End Shrops 74 F2
Welsh Frankton Shrops 73 F7
Welsh Hook Pembs 44 C4
Welsh Newton Hereford 36 C1
Welsh St Donats V Glam 22 B2
Welshampton Shrops 73 F8
Welshpool = Y Trallwng Powys 60 D2
Welton Cumb 108 E3
Welton E Yorks 90 B3
Welton Lincs 78 B3
Welton Northants 52 C3
Welton Hill Lincs 90 F4
Welton le Marsh Lincs 79 C7
Welton le Wold Lincs 91 F6
Welwick E Yorks 91 B7
Welwyn Herts 41 C5
Welwyn Garden City Herts 41 C5
Wem Shrops 60 B5
Wembdon Som 22 F4
Wembley London 40 F4
Wembury Devon 6 E3
Wembworthy Devon 9 D8
Wemyss Bay Invclyd 118 C1
Wenallt Ceredig 47 B5
Wenallt Gwyn 72 E3
Wendens Ambo Essex 55 F6
Wendlebury Oxon 39 C5
Wendling Norf 68 C2
Wendover Bucks 40 D1
Wendron Corn 3 C5
Wendy Cambs 54 E4
Wenfordbridge Corn 5 B5
Wenhaston Suff 57 B8
Wennington Cambs 54 B3
Wennington Lancs 93 B6
Wennington London 41 F8
Wensley Derbys 76 C2
Wensley N Yorks 101 F5
Wentbridge W Yorks 89 C5
Wentnor Shrops 60 E3
Wentworth Cambs 55 B5
Wentworth S Yorks 88 E4
Wenvoe V Glam 22 B3
Weobley Hereford 49 D6
Weobley Marsh Hereford 49 D6
Wereham Norf 67 D6
Wergs W Mid 62 D2
Wern Powys 59 C6
Wern Powys 60 C2
Wernffrwd Swansea 33 E6
Wernyrheolydd Mon 35 C7
Werrington Corn 8 F5
Werrington Pboro 65 D8
Werrington Staffs 75 E6
Wervin Ches W 73 B8
Wesham Lancs 92 F4
Wessington Derbys 76 D3
West Acre Norf 67 C7
West Adderbury Oxon 52 F2
West Allerdean Northumb 123 E5
West Alvington Devon 6 E5
West Amesbury Wilts 25 E6
West Anstey Devon 10 B3
West Ashby Lincs 79 B5
West Ashling W Sus 16 D2
West Ashton Wilts 24 D3
West Auckland Durham 101 B6
West Ayton N Yorks 103 F7
West Bagborough Som 22 F3
West Barkwith Lincs 91 F5
West Barnby N Yorks 103 C6
West Barns E Loth 122 B2
West Barsham Norf 80 D5
West Bay Dorset 12 E2
West Beckham Norf 81 D7
West Bedfont Sur 27 B8
West Benhar N Lanark 119 C8
West Bergholt Essex 43 B5
West Bexington Dorset 12 F3
West Bilney Norf 67 C7
West Blatchington Brighton 17 D6
West Bowling W Yorks 94 F4
West Bradford Lancs 93 E7
West Bradley Som 23 F7
West Bretton W Yorks 88 C3
West Bridgford Notts 77 F5
West Bromwich W Mid 62 E4
West Buckland Devon 21 F5
West Buckland Som 11 B6
West Burrafirth Shetland 160 H4
West Burton N Yorks 101 F5
West Burton W Sus 16 C3
West Butterwick N Lincs 90 D2
West Byfleet Sur 27 C8
West Caister Norf 69 C8
West Calder W Loth 120 C3
West Camel Som 12 B3
West Challow Oxon 38 F3
West Chelborough Dorset 12 D3
West Chevington Northumb 117 E8
West Chiltington W Sus 16 C4
West Chiltington Common W Sus 16 C4
West Chinnock Som 12 C2
West Chisenbury Wilts 25 D6
West Clandon Sur 27 D8
West Cliffe Kent 31 E7
West Clyne Highld 157 J11
West Clyth Highld 158 G4
West Coker Som 12 C3
West Compton Dorset 12 E3
West Compton Som 23 E7
West Cowick E Yorks 89 B7
West Cranmore Som 23 E8
West Cross Swansea 33 F7
West Cullery Aberds 141 D6
West Curry Corn 8 E4
West Curthwaite Cumb 108 E3
West Darlochan Argyll 143 F7
West Dean W Sus 16 C2
West Dean Wilts 14 B3
West Deeping Lincs 65 D8
West Derby Mers 85 E4
West Dereham Norf 67 D6
West Didsbury Gtr Man 87 E6
West Ditchburn Northumb 117 B7
West Down Devon 20 E4
West Drayton London 27 B8
West Drayton Notts 77 B7
West Ella E Yorks 90 B4
West End Bedford 53 D7
West End E Yorks 96 F5
West End E Yorks 97 F7
West End Hants 15 C5
West End Lancs 86 B5
West End N Som 23 C6
West End N Yorks 94 D4
West End Norf 68 D2
West End Norf 69 C8
West End Oxon 38 D4
West End S Lanark 120 E2
West End S Yorks 89 D7
West End Suff 69 F7
West End Sur 27 C7
West End W Sus 17 C6
West End Wilts 13 B7
West End Wilts 24 B4
West End Green Hants 26 C4
West Farleigh Kent 29 D8
West Felton Shrops 60 B3
West Fenton E Loth 129 F6
West Ferry Dundee 134 F4
West Firle E Sus 17 D8
West Ginge Oxon 38 F4
West Grafton Wilts 25 C7
West Green Hants 26 D5
West Greenskares Aberds 153 B7
West Grimstead Wilts 14 B3
West Grinstead W Sus 17 B5
West Haddlesey N Yorks 89 B6
West Haddon Northants 52 B4
West Hagbourne Oxon 39 F5
West Hagley Worcs 62 F3
West Hall Cumb 109 C5
West Hallam Derbys 76 E4
West Halton N Lincs 90 B3
West Ham London 41 F7
West Handley Derbys 76 B3
West Hanney Oxon 38 E4
West Hanningfield Essex 42 E3
West Hardwick W Yorks 88 C5
West Harnham Wilts 14 B2
West Harptree Bath 23 D7
West Hatch Som 11 B7
West Head Norf 67 D5
West Heath Ches E 74 C5
West Heath Hants 26 D3
West Heath Hants 27 D6
West Helmsdale Highld 157 H13
West Hendred Oxon 38 F4
West Heslerton N Yorks 96 B5
West Hill Devon 11 E5
West Hill E Yorks 97 C7
West Hill N Som 23 B6
West Hoathly W Sus 28 F4
West Holme Dorset 13 F6
West Horndon Essex 42 F2
West Horrington Som 23 E7
West Horsley Sur 27 D8
West Horton Northumb 123 F6
West Hougham Kent 31 E6
West Houlland Shetland 160 H4
West-houses Derbys 76 D4
West Huntington York 96 D2
West Hythe Kent 19 B8
West Ilsley W Berks 38 F4
West Itchenor W Sus 15 D8
West Keal Lincs 79 C6
West Kennett Wilts 25 C6
West Kilbride N Ayrs 118 E2
West Kingsdown Kent 29 C6
West Kington Wilts 24 B3
West Kinharrachie Aberds 153 E9
West Kirby Mers 85 F3
West Knapton N Yorks 96 B4
West Knighton Dorset 12 F5
West Knoyle Wilts 24 F3
West Kyloe Northumb 123 E6
West Lambrook Som 12 C2
West Langdon Kent 31 E7
West Langwell Highld 157 J9
West Lavington W Sus 16 B2
West Lavington Wilts 24 D5
West Layton N Yorks 101 D6
West Lea Durham 111 E7
West Leake Notts 64 B2
West Learmouth Northumb 122 F4
West Leigh Devon 9 D8
West Lexham Norf 67 C8
West Lilling N Yorks 96 C2
West Linton Borders 120 D4
West Liss Hants 15 B8
West Littleton S Glos 24 B2
West Looe Corn 5 D7
West Luccombe Som 21 E7
West Lulworth Dorset 13 F6
West Lutton N Yorks 96 C5
West Lydford Som 23 F7
West Lyng Som 11 B8
West Lynn Norf 67 B6
West Malling Kent 29 D7
West Malvern Worcs 50 E2
West Marden W Sus 15 C8
West Marina E Sus 18 E4
West Markham Notts 77 B7
West Marsh NE Lincs 91 C6
West Marton N Yorks 93 D8
West Meon Hants 15 B7
West Mersea Essex 43 C6
West Milton Dorset 12 E3
West Minster Kent 30 B3
West Molesey Sur 28 C2
West Monkton Som 11 B7
West Moors Dorset 13 D8
West Morriston Borders 122 E2
West Muir Angus 135 C5
West Ness N Yorks 96 B2
West Newham Northumb 110 B3
West Newton E Yorks 97 F7
West Newton Norf 67 B6
West Norwood London 28 B4
West Ogwell Devon 7 B6
West Orchard Dorset 13 C6
West Overton Wilts 25 C6
West Park Hrtlpl 111 F7
West Parley Dorset 13 E8
West Peckham Kent 29 D7
West Pelton Durham 110 D5
West Pennard Som 23 F7
West Pentire Corn 4 C2
West Perry Cambs 54 C2
West Putford Devon 9 C5
West Quantoxhead Som 22 E3
West Rainton Durham 111 E6
West Rasen Lincs 90 F4
West Raynham Norf 80 E4
West Retford Notts 89 F7
West Rounton N Yorks 102 D2
West Row Suff 55 B7
West Rudham Norf 80 E4
West Runton Norf 81 C7
West Saltoun E Loth 121 C7
West Sandwick Shetland 160 E6
West Scrafton N Yorks 101 F5
West Sleekburn Northumb 117 F8
West Somerton Norf 69 C7
West Stafford Dorset 12 F5
West Stockwith Notts 89 E8
West Stoke W Sus 16 D2
West Stonesdale N Yorks 100 D3
West Stoughton Som 23 E6
West Stour Dorset 13 B5
West Stourmouth Kent 31 C6
West Stow Suff 56 B2
West Stowell Wilts 25 C6
West Strathan Highld 157 C8
West Stratton Hants 26 E3
West Street Kent 30 D3
West Tanfield N Yorks 95 B5
West Taphouse Corn 5 C6
West Tarbert Argyll 145 G7
West Thirston Northumb 117 E7
West Thorney W Sus 15 D8
West Thurrock Thurrock 29 B6
West Tilbury Thurrock 29 B7
West Tisted Hants 15 B7
West Tofts Norf 67 E8
West Tofts Perth 133 F8
West Torrington Lincs 90 F5
West Town Hants 15 E8
West Town N Som 23 C6
West Tytherley Hants 14 B3
West Tytherton Wilts 24 B4
West Walton Norf 66 C4
West Walton Highway Norf 66 C4
West Wellow Hants 14 C3
West Wemyss Fife 128 E5
West Wick N Som 23 C5
West Wickham Cambs 55 E7
West Wickham London 28 C4
West Williamston Pembs 32 D1
West Willoughby Lincs 78 E2
West Winch Norf 67 C6
West Winterslow Wilts 25 F7
West Wittering W Sus 15 E8
West Witton N Yorks 101 F5
West Woodburn Northumb 116 F4
West Woodhay W Berks 25 C8
West Woodlands Som 24 E2
West Worldham Hants 26 F5
West Worlington Devon 10 C2
West Worthing W Sus 16 D5
West Wratting Cambs 55 D7
West Wycombe Bucks 39 E8
West Wylam Northumb 110 C4
West Yell Shetland 160 E6
Westacott Devon 20 F4
Westbere Kent 31 C5
Westborough Lincs 77 E8
Westbourne Bmouth 13 E8
Westbourne Suff 56 E5
Westbourne W Sus 15 D8
Westbrook W Berks 26 B2
Westbury Bucks 52 F4
Westbury Shrops 60 D3
Westbury Wilts 24 D3
Westbury Leigh Wilts 24 D3
Westbury-on-Severn Glos 36 C4
Westbury on Trym Bristol 23 B7
Westbury-sub-Mendip Som 23 E7
Westby Lancs 92 F3
Westcliff-on-Sea Southend 42 F4
Westcombe Som 23 F8
Westcote Glos 38 B2
Westcott Bucks 39 C7
Westcott Devon 10 D5
Westcott Sur 28 E2
Westcott Barton Oxon 38 B4
Westdean E Sus 18 F2
Westdene Brighton 17 D6
Wester Aberchalder Highld 137 B8
Wester Balgedie Perth 128 D3
Wester Culbeuchly Aberds 153 B6
Wester Dechmont W Loth 120 C3
Wester Denoon Angus 134 E3
Wester Fintray Aberds 141 C7
Wester Gruinards Highld 151 B8
Wester Lealty Highld 151 D9
Wester Milton Highld 151 F12
Wester Newburn Fife 129 D6
Wester Quarff Shetland 160 K6
Wester Skeld Shetland 160 J4
Westerdale Highld 158 E3
Westerdale N Yorks 102 D4
Westerfield Shetland 160 H5
Westerfield Suff 57 E5
Westergate W Sus 16 D3
Westerham Kent 28 D5
Westerhope T&W 110 C4
Westerleigh S Glos 23 B9
Westerton Angus 135 D6
Westerton Durham 110 F5
Westerton W Sus 16 D2
Westerwick Shetland 160 J4
Westfield Cumb 98 B1
Westfield E Sus 18 D5
Westfield Hereford 50 E2
Westfield Highld 158 D2
Westfield N Lanark 119 B7
Westfield Norf 68 D2
Westfield W Loth 120 B2
Westfields Dorset 12 D5
Westfields of Rattray Perth 134 E1
Westgate Durham 110 F2
Westgate N Lincs 89 D8
Westgate Norf 80 C4
Westgate Norf 81 C5
Westgate on Sea Kent 31 B7
Westhall Aberds 141 B5
Westhall Suff 69 F7
Westham Dorset 12 G4
Westham E Sus 18 E3
Westham Som 23 E6
Westhampnett W Sus 16 D2
Westhay Som 23 E6
Westhead Lancs 86 D2
Westhide Hereford 49 E7
Westhill Aberds 141 D7
Westhill Highld 151 G10
Westhope Hereford 49 D6
Westhope Shrops 60 F4
Westhorpe Lincs 78 F5
Westhorpe Suff 56 C4
Westhoughton Gtr Man 86 D4
Westhouse N Yorks 93 B6
Westhumble Sur 28 D2
Westing Shetland 160 C7
Westlake Devon 6 D4
Westleigh Devon 9 B6
Westleigh Devon 11 C5
Westleigh Gtr Man 86 D4
Westleton Suff 57 C8
Westley Shrops 60 D3
Westley Suff 56 C2
Westley Waterless Cambs 55 D7
Westlington Bucks 39 C7
Westlinton Cumb 108 C3
Westmarsh Kent 31 C6
Westmeston E Sus 17 C7
Westmill Herts 41 B6
Westminster London 28 B4
Westmuir Angus 134 D3
Westness Orkney 159 F4
Westnewton Cumb 107 E8
Westnewton Northumb 122 F5
Westoe T&W 111 C6
Weston Bath 24 C2
Weston Ches E 74 D4
Weston Devon 11 F6
Weston Dorset 12 G4
Weston Halton 86 F3
Weston Hants 15 B8
Weston Herts 54 F3
Weston Lincs 66 B2
Weston N Yorks 94 E4
Weston Northants 52 E3
Weston Notts 77 C7
Weston Shrops 61 B5
Weston Shrops 61 E5
Weston Staffs 62 B3
Weston W Berks 25 B8
Weston Beggard Hereford 49 E7
Weston by Welland Northants 64 E4
Weston Colville Cambs 55 D7
Weston Coyney Stoke 75 E6
Weston Favell Northants 53 C5
Weston Green Cambs 55 D7
Weston Green Norf 68 C4
Weston Heath Shrops 61 C7
Weston Hills Lincs 66 B2
Weston-in-Gordano N Som 23 B6
Weston Jones Staffs 61 B7
Weston Longville Norf 68 C4
Weston Lullingfields Shrops 60 B4
Weston-on-the-Green Oxon 39 C5
Weston-on-Trent Derbys 63 B8
Weston Patrick Hants 26 E4
Weston Rhyn Shrops 73 F6
Weston-Sub-Edge Glos 51 E6
Weston-super-Mare N Som 22 C5
Weston Turville Bucks 40 C1
Weston under Lizard Staffs 62 C2
Weston under Penyard Hereford 36 B3
Weston under Wetherley Warks 51 C8
Weston Underwood Derbys 76 E2
Weston Underwood M Keynes 53 D6
Westonbirt Glos 37 F5
Westoncommon Shrops 60 B4
Westoning C Beds 53 F8
Westonzoyland Som 23 F5
Westow N Yorks 96 C3
Westport Argyll 143 F7
Westport Som 11 C8
Westrigg W Loth 120 C2
Westruther Borders 122 E2
Westry Cambs 66 E3
Westville Notts 76 E5
Westward Cumb 108 E2
Westward Ho! Devon 9 B6
Westwell Kent 30 E3
Westwell Oxon 38 D2
Westwell Leacon Kent 30 E3
Westwick Cambs 54 C5
Westwick Durham 101 C5
Westwick Norf 81 E8
Westwood Devon 10 E5
Westwood Wilts 24 D3
Westwoodside N Lincs 89 E8
Wetheral Cumb 108 D4
Wetherby W Yorks 95 E7
Wetherden Suff 56 C4
Wetheringsett Suff 56 C5
Wethersfield Essex 55 F8
Wethersta Shetland 160 G5
Wetherup Street Suff 56 C5
Wetley Rocks Staffs 75 E6
Wettenhall Ches E 74 C3
Wetton Staffs 75 D8
Wetwang E Yorks 96 D5
Wetwood Staffs 74 F4
Wexcombe Wilts 25 D7
Wexham Street Bucks 40 F2
Weybourne Norf 81 C7
Weybread Suff 68 F5
Weybridge Sur 27 C8
Weycroft Devon 11 E8
Weydale Highld 158 D3
Weyhill Hants 25 E8
Weymouth Dorset 12 G4
Whaddon Bucks 53 F6
Whaddon Cambs 54 E4
Whaddon Glos 37 C5
Whaddon Wilts 14 B2
Whale Cumb 99 B7
Whaley Derbys 76 B5
Whaley Bridge Derbys 87 F8
Whaley Thorns Derbys 76 B5
Whaligoe Highld 158 F5
Whalley Lancs 93 F7
Whalton Northumb 117 F7
Wham N Yorks 93 C7
Whaplode Lincs 66 B3
Whaplode Drove Lincs 66 C3
Whaplode St Catherine Lincs 66 B3
Wharfe N Yorks 93 C7
Wharles Lancs 92 F4
Wharncliffe Side S Yorks 88 E3
Wharram le Street N Yorks 96 C4
Wharton Ches W 74 C3
Wharton Green Ches W 74 C3
Whashton N Yorks 101 D6
Whatcombe Dorset 13 D6
Whatcote Warks 51 E8
Whatfield Suff 56 E4
Whatley Som 11 D8
Whatley Som 24 E2
Whatlington E Sus 18 D4
Whatstandwell Derbys 76 D3
Whatton Notts 77 F7
Whauphill Dumfries 105 E8
Whaw N Yorks 100 D4
Wheatacre Norf 69 E7
Wheatcroft Derbys 76 D3
Wheathampstead Herts 40 C4
Wheathill Shrops 61 F6
Wheatley Devon 10 E4
Wheatley Hants 27 E5
Wheatley Oxon 39 D5
Wheatley S Yorks 89 D6
Wheatley W Yorks 87 B8
Wheatley Hill Durham 111 F6
Wheaton Aston Staffs 62 C2
Wheddon Cross Som 21 F8
Wheedlemont Aberds 140 B3
Wheelerstreet Sur 27 E7
Wheelock Ches E 74 D4
Wheelock Heath Ches E 74 D4
Wheelton Lancs 86 B4
Wheen Angus 134 B3
Wheldrake York 96 E2
Whelford Glos 38 E1
Whelpley Hill Herts 40 D2
Whempstead Herts 41 B6
Whenby N Yorks 96 C2
Whepstead Suff 56 D2
Wherstead Suff 57 E5
Wherwell Hants 25 E8
Wheston Derbys 75 B8
Whetsted Kent 29 E7
Whetstone Leics 64 E2
Whicham Cumb 98 F3
Whichford Warks 51 F8
Whickham T&W 110 C5
Whiddon Down Devon 9 E8
Whigstreet Angus 134 E4
Whilton Northants 52 C4
Whim Farm Borders 120 D5
Whimble Devon 9 D5
Whimple Devon 10 E5
Whimpwell Green Norf 69 B6
Whinburgh Norf 68 D3
Whinnieliggate Dumfries 106 D4
Whinnyfold Aberds 153 E10
Whippingham IoW 15 E6
Whipsnade C Beds 40 C3
Whipton Devon 10 E4
Whirlow S Yorks 88 F4
Whisby Lincs 78 C2
Whissendine Rutland 64 C5
Whissonsett Norf 80 E5
Whistlefield Argyll 145 D10
Whistlefield Argyll 145 D11
Whistley Green Wokingham 27 B5
Whiston Mers 86 E2
Whiston Northants 53 C6
Whiston S Yorks 88 F5
Whiston Staffs 62 C2
Whiston Staffs 75 E7
Whitbeck Cumb 98 F3
Whitbourne Hereford 50 D2
Whitburn T&W 111 C7
Whitburn W Loth 120 C2
Whitburn Colliery T&W 111 C7
Whitby Ches W 73 B7
Whitby N Yorks 103 C6
Whitbyheath Ches W 73 B7
Whitchurch Bath 23 C8
Whitchurch Bucks 39 B7
Whitchurch Cardiff 35 F5
Whitchurch Devon 6 B2
Whitchurch Hants 26 E2
Whitchurch Hereford 36 C2
Whitchurch Oxon 26 B4
Whitchurch Pembs 44 C2
Whitchurch Shrops 74 E2
Whitchurch Canonicorum Dorset 11 E8
Whitchurch Hill Oxon 26 B4
Whitcombe Dorset 12 F5
Whitcott Keysett Shrops 60 F2
White Coppice Lancs 86 C4
White Lackington Dorset 12 E5
White Ladies Aston Worcs 50 D4
White Lund Lancs 92 C4
White Mill Carms 33 B5
White Ness Shetland 160 J5
White Notley Essex 42 C3
White Pit Lincs 79 B6
White Post Notts 77 D6
White Rocks Hereford 35 B8
White Roding Essex 42 C1
White Waltham Windsor 27 B6
Whiteacen Moray 152 D2
Whiteacre Heath Warks 63 E6
Whitebridge Highld 137 C7
Whitebrook Mon 36 D2
Whiteburn Borders 121 E8
Whitecairn Dumfries 105 D6
Whitecairns Aberds 141 C8
Whitecastle S Lanark 120 E3
Whitechapel Lancs 93 E5
Whitecleat Orkney 159 H6
Whitecraig E Loth 121 B6
Whitecroft Glos 36 D3
Whitecross Corn 4 B4
Whitecross Falk 120 B2
Whitecross Staffs 62 B2
Whiteface Highld 151 C10
Whitefarland N Ayrs 143 D9
Whitefaulds S Ayrs 112 D2
Whitefield Gtr Man 87 D6
Whitefield Perth 134 F1
Whiteford Aberds 141 B6
Whitegate Ches W 74 C3
Whitehall Blackburn 86 B4
Whitehall W Sus 16 B5
Whitehall Village Orkney 159 F7
Whitehaven Cumb 98 C1
Whitehill Hants 27 F5
Whitehills Aberds 153 B6
Whitehills S Lanark 119 D6
Whitehough Derbys 87 F8
Whitehouse Aberds 140 C5
Whitehouse Argyll 145 G7
Whiteinch Glasgow 118 C5
Whitekirk E Loth 129 F7
Whitelaw S Lanark 119 E6
Whiteleas T&W 111 C6
Whiteley Bank IoW 15 F6
Whiteley Green Ches E 75 B6
Whiteley Village Sur 27 C8
Whitemans Green W Sus 17 B7
Whitemire Moray 151 F12
Whitemoor Corn 4 D4
Whitemore Staffs 75 C5
Whitenap Hants 14 B4
Whiteoak Green Oxon 38 C3
Whiteparish Wilts 14 B3
Whiterashes Aberds 141 B7
Whiterow Highld 158 F5
Whiteshill Glos 37 D5
Whiteside Northumb 109 C7
Whiteside W Loth 120 C2
Whitesmith E Sus 18 D2
Whitestaunton Som 11 C7
Whitestone Devon 10 E3
Whitestone Devon 20 E3
Whitestone Warks 63 F7
Whitestones Aberds 153 C8
Whitestreet Green Suff 56 F3
Whitewall Corner N Yorks 96 B3
Whiteway Glos 37 C6
Whiteway Glos 37 E5
Whitewell Aberds 153 B9
Whitewell Lancs 93 E6
Whitewell Bottom Lancs 87 B6
Whiteworks Devon 6 B4
Whitfield Kent 31 E7
Whitfield Northants 52 F4
Whitfield Northumb 109 D7
Whitfield S Glos 36 E3
Whitford Devon 11 E7
Whitford Flint 72 B5
Whitgift E Yorks 90 B2
Whitgreave Staffs 62 B2
Whithorn Dumfries 105 E8
Whiting Bay N Ayrs 143 F11
Whitkirk W Yorks 95 F6
Whitland Carms 32 C2
Whitletts S Ayrs 112 B3
Whitley N Yorks 89 B6
Whitley Reading 26 B5
Whitley Wilts 24 C3
Whitley Bay T&W 111 B6
Whitley Chapel Northumb 110 D2
Whitley Lower W Yorks 88 C3
Whitley Row Kent 29 D5
Whitlock's End W Mid 51 B6
Whitminster Glos 36 D4
Whitmore Staffs 74 E5
Whitnage Devon 10 C5
Whitnash Warks 51 C8
Whitney-on-Wye Hereford 48 E4
Whitrigg Cumb 108 D2
Whitrigg Cumb 108 F2
Whitsbury Hants 14 C2
Whitsome Borders 122 D4
Whitson Newport 35 F7
Whitstable Kent 30 C5
Whitstone Corn 8 E4
Whittingham Northumb 117 C6
Whittingslow Shrops 60 F4
Whittington Glos 37 B7
Whittington Lancs 93 B6
Whittington Norf 67 E7
Whittington Shrops 73 F7
Whittington Staffs 62 F2
Whittington Staffs 63 D5
Whittington Worcs 50 D3
Whittle-le-Woods Lancs 86 B3
Whittlebury Northants 52 E4
Whittlesey Cambs 66 E2
Whittlesford Cambs 55 E5
Whittlestone Head Blackburn 86 C5
Whitton Borders 116 B3
Whitton N Lincs 90 B3
Whitton Northumb 117 D6
Whitton Powys 48 C4
Whitton Shrops 49 B7
Whitton Stockton 102 B1
Whitton Suff 56 E5
Whittonditch Wilts 25 B7
Whittonstall Northumb 110 D3
Whitway Hants 26 D2
Whitwell Derbys 76 B5
Whitwell Herts 40 B4
Whitwell IoW 15 G6
Whitwell N Yorks 101 E7

Whitwell Rutland 65 D6
Whitwell-on-the-Hill N Yorks 96 C3
Whitwell Street Norf 81 E7
Whitwick Leics 63 C8
Whitwood W Yorks 88 B5
Whitworth Lancs 87 C6
Whixall Shrops 74 F2
Whixley N Yorks 95 D7
Whoberley W Mid 51 B8
Whorlton Durham 101 C6
Whorlton N Yorks 102 D2
Whygate Northumb 109 B7
Whyle Hereford 49 C7
Whyteleafe Sur 28 D4
Wibdon Glos 36 E2
Wibsey W Yorks 88 A2
Wibtoft Leics 63 F8
Wichenford Worcs 50 C2
Wichling Kent 30 D3
Wick Bmouth 14 E2
Wick Devon 11 D6
Wick Highld 158 E5
Wick S Glos 24 B2
Wick Shetland 160 K6
Wick V Glam 21 B8
Wick W Sus 16 D4
Wick Wilts 14 B2
Wick Worcs 50 E4
Wick Hill Wokingham 27 C5
Wick St Lawrence N Som 23 C5
Wicken Cambs 55 B6
Wicken Northants 52 F5
Wicken Bonhunt Essex 55 F5
Wicken Green Village Norf 80 D4
Wickenby Lincs 90 F4
Wickersley S Yorks 89 E5
Wickford Essex 42 E3
Wickham Hants 15 C6
Wickham W Berks 25 B8
Wickham Bishops Essex 42 C4
Wickham Market Suff 57 D7
Wickham Skeith Suff 56 C4
Wickham St Paul Essex 56 F2
Wickham Street Suff 55 D8
Wickham Street Suff 56 C4
Wickhambreux Kent 31 D6
Wickhambrook Suff 55 D8
Wickhamford Worcs 51 E5
Wickhampton Norf 69 D7
Wicklewood Norf 68 D3
Wickmere Norf 81 D7
Wickwar S Glos 36 F4
Widdington Essex 55 F6
Widdrington Northumb 117 E8
Widdrington Station Northumb 117 E8
Wide Open T&W 110 B5
Widecombe in the Moor Devon 6 B5
Widegates Corn 5 D7
Widemouth Bay Corn 8 D4
Widewall Orkney 159 J5
Widford Essex 42 D2
Widford Herts 41 C7
Widham Wilts 37 F7
Widmer End Bucks 40 E1
Widmerpool Notts 64 B3
Widnes Halton 86 F3
Wigan Gtr Man 86 D3
Wiggaton Devon 11 E6
Wiggenhall St Germans Norf 67 C5
Wiggenhall St Mary Magdalen Norf 67 C5
Wiggenhall St Mary the Virgin Norf 67 C5
Wigginton Herts 40 C2
Wigginton Oxon 51 F8
Wigginton Staffs 63 D6
Wigginton York 95 D8
Wigglesworth N Yorks 93 D8
Wiggonby Cumb 108 D2
Wiggonholt W Sus 16 C4
Wighill N Yorks 95 E7
Wighton Norf 80 D5
Wigley Hants 14 C4
Wigmore Hereford 49 C6
Wigmore Medway 30 C2
Wigsley Notts 77 B8
Wigsthorpe Northants 65 F7
Wigston Leics 64 E3
Wigthorpe Notts 89 F6
Wigtoft Lincs 79 F5
Wigton Cumb 108 E2
Wigtown Dumfries 105 D8
Wigtwizzle S Yorks 88 E3
Wike W Yorks 95 E6
Wike Well End S Yorks 89 C7
Wilbarston Northants 64 F5
Wilberfoss E Yorks 96 D3
Wilberlee W Yorks 87 C8
Wilburton Cambs 55 B5
Wilby Norf 68 F3
Wilby Northants 53 C6
Wilby Suff 57 B6
Wilcot Wilts 25 C6
Wilcott Shrops 60 C3
Wilcrick Newport 35 F8
Wilday Green Derbys 76 B3
Wildboarclough Ches E 75 C6
Wilden Bedford 53 D8
Wilden Worcs 50 B3
Wildhern Hants 25 D8
Wildhill Herts 41 D5
Wildmoor Worcs 50 B4
Wildsworth Lincs 90 E2
Wilford Nottingham 77 F5
Wilkesley Ches E 74 E3
Wilkhaven Highld 151 C12
Wilkieston W Loth 120 C4
Willand Devon 10 C5
Willaston Ches E 74 D3
Willaston Ches W 73 B7
Willen M Keynes 53 E6
Willenhall W Mid 51 B8
Willenhall W Mid 62 E3
Willerby E Yorks 97 F6
Willerby N Yorks 97 B6
Willersey Glos 51 F6
Willersley Hereford 48 E5
Willesborough Kent 30 E4
Willesborough Lees Kent 30 E4
Willesden London 41 F5
Willett Som 22 F3
Willey Shrops 61 E6
Willey Warks 63 F8
Willey Green Sur 27 D7
Williamscott Oxon 52 E2
Willian Herts 54 F3
Willingale Essex 42 D1
Willingdon E Sus 18 E2
Willingham Cambs 54 B5
Willingham by Stow Lincs 90 F2
Willington Bedford 54 E2
Willington Derbys 63 B6
Willington Durham 110 F4
Willington T&W 111 C6
Willington Warks 51 F7
Willington Corner Ches W 74 C2
Willisham Tye Suff 56 D4
Willitoft E Yorks 96 F3
Williton Som 22 E2
Willoughbridge Staffs 74 E4
Willoughby Lincs 79 B7
Willoughby Warks 52 C3
Willoughby-on-the-Wolds Notts 64 B3
Willoughby Waterleys Leics 64 E2
Willoughton Lincs 90 E3
Willows Green Essex 42 C3
Willsbridge S Glos 23 B8
Willsworthy Devon 9 F7
Wilmcote Warks 51 D6
Wilmington Devon 11 E7
Wilmington E Sus 18 E2
Wilmington Kent 29 B6
Wilminstone Devon 6 B2
Wilmslow Ches E 87 F6
Wilnecote Staffs 63 D6
Wilpshire Lancs 93 F6
Wilsden W Yorks 94 F3
Wilsford Lincs 78 E3
Wilsford Wilts 25 D6
Wilsford Wilts 25 F6
Wilsill N Yorks 94 C4
Wilsley Pound Kent 18 B4
Wilsom Hants 26 F5
Wilson Leics 63 B8
Wilsontown S Lanark 120 D2
Wilstead Bedford 53 E8
Wilsthorpe Lincs 65 C7
Wilstone Herts 40 C2
Wilton Borders 115 C7
Wilton Cumb 98 C2
Wilton N Yorks 103 F6
Wilton Redcar 102 C3
Wilton Wilts 25 C7
Wilton Wilts 25 F5
Wimbish Essex 55 F6
Wimbish Green Essex 55 F7
Wimblebury Staffs 62 C4
Wimbledon London 28 B3
Wimblington Cambs 66 E4
Wimborne Minster Dorset 13 E8
Wimborne St Giles Dorset 13 C8
Wimbotsham Norf 67 D6
Wimpson Soton 14 C4
Wimpstone Warks 51 E7
Wincanton Som 12 B5
Wincham Ches W 74 B3
Winchburgh W Loth 120 B3
Winchcombe Glos 37 B7
Winchelsea E Sus 19 D6
Winchelsea Beach E Sus 19 D6
Winchester Hants 15 B5
Winchet Hill Kent 29 E8
Winchfield Hants 27 D5
Winchmore Hill Bucks 40 E2
Winchmore Hill London 41 E6
Wincle Ches E 75 C6
Wincobank S Yorks 88 E4
Windermere Cumb 99 E6
Winderton Warks 51 E8
Windhill Highld 151 G8
Windhouse Shetland 160 D6
Windlehurst Gtr Man 87 F7
Windlesham Sur 27 C7
Windley Derbys 76 E3
Windmill Hill E Sus 18 D3
Windmill Hill Som 11 C8
Windrush Glos 38 C1
Windsor N Lincs 89 C8
Windsor Windsor 27 B7
Windsoredge Glos 37 D5
Windygates Fife 128 D5
Windyknowe W Loth 120 C2
Windywalls Borders 122 F3
Wineham W Sus 17 B6
Winestead E Yorks 91 B6
Winewall Lancs 94 E2
Winfarthing Norf 68 F4
Winford IoW 15 F6
Winford N Som 23 C7
Winforton Hereford 48 E4
Winfrith Newburgh Dorset 13 F6
Wing Bucks 40 B1
Wing Rutland 65 D5
Wingate Durham 111 F7
Wingates Gtr Man 86 D4
Wingates Northumb 117 E7
Wingerworth Derbys 76 C3
Wingfield C Beds 40 B2
Wingfield Suff 57 B6
Wingfield Wilts 24 D3
Wingham Kent 31 D6
Wingmore Kent 31 E5
Wingrave Bucks 40 C1
Winkburn Notts 77 D7
Winkfield Brack 27 B7
Winkfield Row Brack 27 B6
Winkhill Staffs 75 D7
Winklebury Hants 26 D4
Winkleigh Devon 9 D8
Winksley N Yorks 95 B5
Winkton Dorset 14 E2
Winlaton T&W 110 C4
Winless Highld 158 E5
Winmarleigh Lancs 92 E4
Winnal Hereford 49 F6
Winnall Hants 15 B5
Winnersh Wokingham 27 B5
Winscales Cumb 98 B2
Winscombe N Som 23 D6
Winsford Ches W 74 C3
Winsford Som 21 F8
Winsham Som 11 D8
Winshill Staffs 63 B6
Winskill Cumb 109 F5
Winslade Hants 26 E4
Winsley Wilts 24 C3
Winslow Bucks 39 B7
Winson Glos 37 D7
Winson Green W Mid 62 F4
Winsor Hants 14 C4
Winster Cumb 99 E6
Winster Derbys 76 C2
Winston Durham 101 C6
Winston Suff 57 C5
Winston Green Suff 57 C5
Winstone Glos 37 D6
Winswell Devon 9 C6
Winter Gardens Essex 42 F3
Winterborne Clenston Dorset 13 D6
Winterborne Herringston Dorset 12 F4
Winterborne Houghton Dorset 13 D6
Winterborne Kingston Dorset 13 E6
Winterborne Monkton Dorset 12 F4
Winterborne Stickland Dorset 13 D6
Winterborne Whitechurch Dorset 13 D6
Winterborne Zelston Dorset 13 E6
Winterbourne S Glos 36 F3
Winterbourne W Berks 26 B2
Winterbourne Abbas Dorset 12 E4
Winterbourne Bassett Wilts 25 B6
Winterbourne Dauntsey Wilts 25 F6
Winterbourne Down S Glos 23 B8
Winterbourne Earls Wilts 25 F6
Winterbourne Gunner Wilts 25 F6
Winterbourne Monkton Wilts 25 B6
Winterbourne Steepleton Dorset 12 F4
Winterbourne Stoke Wilts 25 E5
Winterburn N Yorks 94 D2
Winteringham N Lincs 90 B3
Winterley Ches E 74 D4
Wintersett W Yorks 88 C4
Wintershill Hants 15 C6
Winterton N Lincs 90 C3
Winterton-on-Sea Norf 69 C7
Winthorpe Lincs 79 C8
Winthorpe Notts 77 D8
Winton Bmouth 13 E8
Winton Cumb 100 C2
Winton N Yorks 102 E2
Wintringham N Yorks 96 B4
Winwick Cambs 65 F8
Winwick Northants 52 B4
Winwick Warr 86 E4
Wirksworth Derbys 76 D2
Wirksworth Moor Derbys 76 D3
Wirswall Ches E 74 E2
Wisbech Cambs 66 D4
Wisbech St Mary Cambs 66 D4
Wisborough Green W Sus 16 B4
Wiseton Notts 89 F8
Wishaw N Lanark 119 D7
Wishaw Warks 63 E5
Wisley Sur 27 D8
Wispington Lincs 78 B5
Wissenden Kent 30 E3
Wissett Suff 57 B7
Wistanstow Shrops 60 F4
Wistanswick Shrops 61 B6
Wistaston Ches E 74 D3
Wistaston Green Ches E 74 D3
Wiston Pembs 32 C1
Wiston S Lanark 120 F2
Wiston W Sus 16 C5
Wistow Cambs 66 F2
Wistow N Yorks 95 F8
Wiswell Lancs 93 F7
Witcham Cambs 66 F4
Witchampton Dorset 13 D7
Witchford Cambs 55 B6
Witham Essex 42 C4
Witham Friary Som 24 E2
Witham on the Hill Lincs 65 C7
Withcall Lincs 91 F6
Withdean Brighton 17 D7
Witherenden Hill E Sus 18 C3
Witheridge Devon 10 C3
Witherley Leics 63 E7
Withern Lincs 91 F8
Withernsea E Yorks 91 B7
Withernwick E Yorks 97 E7
Withersdale Street Suff 69 F5
Withersfield Suff 55 E7
Witherslack Cumb 99 F6
Withiel Corn 4 C4
Withiel Florey Som 21 F8
Withington Glos 37 C7
Withington Gtr Man 87 E6
Withington Hereford 49 E7
Withington Shrops 61 C5
Withington Staffs 75 F7
Withington Green Ches E 74 B5
Withleigh Devon 10 C4
Withnell Lancs 86 B4
Withybrook Warks 63 F8
Withycombe Som 22 E2
Withycombe Raleigh Devon 10 F5
Withyham E Sus 29 F5
Withypool Som 21 F7
Witley Sur 27 F7
Witnesham Suff 57 D5
Witney Oxon 38 C3
Wittering Pboro 65 D7
Wittersham Kent 19 C5
Witton Angus 135 B5
Witton Worcs 50 C3
Witton Bridge Norf 69 A6
Witton Gilbert Durham 110 E5
Witton-le-Wear Durham 110 F4
Witton Park Durham 110 F4
Wiveliscombe Som 11 B5
Wivelrod Hants 26 F4
Wivelsfield E Sus 17 B7
Wivelsfield Green E Sus 17 B7
Wivenhoe Essex 43 B6
Wivenhoe Cross Essex 43 B6
Wiveton Norf 81 C6
Wix Essex 43 B7
Wixford Warks 51 D5
Wixhill Shrops 61 B5
Wixoe Suff 55 E8
Woburn C Beds 53 F7
Woburn Sands M Keynes 53 F7
Wokefield Park W Berks 26 C4
Woking Sur 27 D8
Wokingham Wokingham 27 C6
Wolborough Devon 7 B6
Wold Newton E Yorks 97 B6
Wold Newton NE Lincs 91 E6
Woldingham Sur 28 D4
Wolfclyde S Lanark 120 F3
Wolferton Norf 67 B6
Wolfhill Perth 134 F1
Wolf's Castle Pembs 44 C4
Wolfsdale Pembs 44 C4
Woll Borders 115 B7
Wollaston Northants 53 C7
Wollaston Shrops 60 C3
Wollaton Nottingham 76 F5
Wollerton Shrops 74 F3
Wollescote W Mid 62 F3
Wolsingham Durham 110 F3
Wolstanton Staffs 75 E5
Wolston Warks 52 B2
Wolvercote Oxon 38 D4
Wolverhampton W Mid 62 E3
Wolverley Shrops 73 F8
Wolverley Worcs 50 B3
Wolverton Hants 26 D3
Wolverton M Keynes 53 E6
Wolverton Warks 51 C7
Wolverton Common Hants 26 D3
Wolvesnewton Mon 36 E1
Wolvey Warks 63 F8
Wolviston Stockton 102 B2
Wombleton N Yorks 102 F4
Wombourne Staffs 62 E2
Wombwell S Yorks 88 D4
Womenswold Kent 31 D6
Womersley N Yorks 89 C6
Wonastow Mon 36 C1
Wonersh Sur 27 E8
Wonson Devon 9 F8
Wonston Hants 26 F2
Wooburn Bucks 40 F2
Wooburn Green Bucks 40 F2
Wood Dalling Norf 81 E6
Wood End Herts 41 B6
Wood End Warks 51 B6
Wood End Warks 63 E6
Wood Enderby Lincs 79 C5
Wood Field Sur 28 D2
Wood Green London 41 E6
Wood Hayes W Mid 62 D3
Wood Lanes Ches E 87 F7
Wood Norton Norf 81 E6
Wood Street Norf 69 B6
Wood Street Sur 27 D7
Wood Walton Cambs 66 F2
Woodacott Devon 9 D5
Woodale N Yorks 94 B3
Woodbank Argyll 143 G7
Woodbastwick Norf 69 C6
Woodbeck Notts 77 B7
Woodborough Notts 77 E6
Woodborough Wilts 25 D6
Woodbridge Dorset 12 C5
Woodbridge Suff 57 E6
Woodbury Devon 10 F5
Woodbury Salterton Devon 10 F5
Woodchester Glos 37 D5
Woodchurch Kent 19 B6
Woodchurch Mers 85 F3
Woodcombe Som 21 E8
Woodcote Oxon 39 F6
Woodcott Hants 26 D2
Woodcroft Glos 36 E2
Woodcutts Dorset 13 C7
Woodditton Cambs 55 D7
Woodeaton Oxon 39 C5
Woodend Cumb 98 E3
Woodend Northants 52 E4
Woodend W Sus 16 D2
Woodend Green Northants 52 E4
Woodfalls Wilts 14 B2
Woodfield Oxon 39 B5
Woodfield S Ayrs 112 B3
Woodford Corn 8 C4
Woodford Devon 7 D5
Woodford Glos 36 E3
Woodford Gtr Man 87 F6
Woodford London 41 E7
Woodford Northants 53 B7
Woodford Bridge London 41 E7
Woodford Halse Northants 52 D3
Woodgate Norf 68 C3
Woodgate W Mid 62 F3
Woodgate W Sus 16 D3
Woodgate Worcs 50 C4
Woodgreen Hants 14 C2
Woodhall Herts 41 C5
Woodhall Invclyd 118 B3
Woodhall N Yorks 100 E4
Woodhall Spa Lincs 78 C4
Woodham Sur 27 C8
Woodham Ferrers Essex 42 E3
Woodham Mortimer Essex 42 D4
Woodham Walter Essex 42 D4
Woodhaven Fife 129 B6
Woodhead Aberds 153 E7
Woodhey Gtr Man 87 C5
Woodhill Shrops 61 F7
Woodhorn Northumb 117 F8
Woodhouse Leics 64 C2
Woodhouse N Lincs 89 D8
Woodhouse S Yorks 88 F5
Woodhouse W Yorks 88 B4
Woodhouse W Yorks 95 F5
Woodhouse Eaves Leics 64 C2
Woodhouse Park Gtr Man 87 F6
Woodhouselee Midloth 120 C5
Woodhouselees Dumfries 108 B3
Woodhouses Staffs 63 C5
Woodhurst Cambs 54 B4
Woodingdean Brighton 17 D7
Woodkirk W Yorks 88 B3
Woodland Devon 7 C5
Woodland Durham 101 B5
Woodlands Aberds 141 E6
Woodlands Dorset 13 D8
Woodlands Hants 14 C4
Woodlands Highld 151 E8
Woodlands N Yorks 95 D6
Woodlands S Yorks 89 D6
Woodlands Park Windsor 27 B6
Woodlands St Mary W Berks 25 B8
Woodlane Staffs 62 B5
Woodleigh Devon 6 E5
Woodlesford W Yorks 88 B4
Woodley Gtr Man 87 E7
Woodley Wokingham 27 B5
Woodmancote Glos 36 E4
Woodmancote Glos 37 B6
Woodmancote Glos 37 D7
Woodmancote W Sus 15 D8
Woodmancote W Sus 17 C6
Woodmancott Hants 26 E3
Woodmansey E Yorks 97 F6
Woodmansterne Sur 28 D3
Woodminton Wilts 13 B8
Woodnesborough Kent 31 D7
Woodnewton Northants 65 E7
Woodplumpton Lancs 92 F5
Woodrising Norf 68 D2
Wood's Green E Sus 18 B3
Woodseaves Shrops 74 F3
Woodseaves Staffs 61 B7
Woodsend Wilts 25 B7
Woodsetts S Yorks 89 F6
Woodsford Dorset 13 E5
Woodside Aberdeen 141 D8
Woodside Aberds 153 D10
Woodside Brack 27 B7
Woodside Fife 129 D6
Woodside Hants 14 E4
Woodside Herts 41 D5
Woodside Perth 134 F2
Woodside of Arbeadie Aberds 141 E6
Woodstock Oxon 38 C4
Woodstock Pembs 32 B1
Woodthorpe Derbys 76 B4
Woodthorpe Leics 64 C2
Woodthorpe Lincs 91 F8
Woodthorpe York 95 E8
Woodton Norf 69 E5
Woodtown Devon 9 B6
Woodtown Devon 9 B6
Woodvale Mers 85 C4
Woodville Derbys 63 C7
Woodyates Dorset 13 C8
Woofferton Shrops 49 C7
Wookey Som 23 E7
Wookey Hole Som 23 E7
Wool Dorset 13 F6
Woolacombe Devon 20 E3
Woolage Green Kent 31 E6
Woolaston Glos 36 E2
Woolavington Som 22 E5
Woolbeding W Sus 16 B2
Wooldale W Yorks 88 D2
Wooler Northumb 117 B5
Woolfardisworthy Devon 8 B5
Woolfardisworthy Devon 10 D3
Woolfords Cottages S Lanark 120 D3
Woolhampton W Berks 26 C3
Woolhope Hereford 49 F8
Woolhope Cockshoot Hereford 49 F8
Woolland Dorset 13 D5
Woollaton Devon 9 C6
Woolley Bath 24 C2
Woolley Cambs 54 B2
Woolley Corn 8 C4
Woolley Derbys 76 C3
Woolley W Yorks 88 C4
Woolmer Green Herts 41 C5
Woolmere Green Worcs 50 C4
Woolpit Suff 56 C3
Woolscott Warks 52 C2
Woolsington T&W 110 C4
Woolstanwood Ches E 74 D3
Woolstaston Shrops 60 E4
Woolsthorpe Lincs 65 B6
Woolsthorpe Lincs 77 F8
Woolston Devon 6 E5
Woolston Shrops 60 B3
Woolston Shrops 60 F4
Woolston Soton 14 C5
Woolston Warr 86 F4
Woolstone M Keynes 53 F6
Woolstone Oxon 38 F2
Woolton Mers 86 F2
Woolton Hill Hants 26 C2
Woolverstone Suff 57 F5
Woolverton Som 24 D2
Woolwich London 28 B5
Woolwich Ferry London 28 B5
Woonton Hereford 49 D5
Wooperton Northumb 117 B6
Woore Shrops 74 E4
Wootten Green Suff 57 B6
Wootton Bedford 53 E8
Wootton Hants 14 E3
Wootton Hereford 48 D5
Wootton Kent 31 E6
Wootton N Lincs 90 C4
Wootton Northants 53 D5
Wootton Oxon 38 C4
Wootton Oxon 38 D4
Wootton Shrops 49 B6
Wootton Shrops 60 B3
Wootton Staffs 62 B2
Wootton Staffs 75 E8
Wootton Bridge IoW 15 E6
Wootton Common IoW 15 E6
Wootton Courtenay Som 21 E8
Wootton Fitzpaine Dorset 11 E8
Wootton Rivers Wilts 25 C6
Wootton St Lawrence Hants 26 D3
Wootton Wawen Warks 51 C6
Worcester Worcs 50 D3
Worcester Park London 28 C3
Wordsley W Mid 62 F2
Worfield Shrops 61 E7
Work Orkney 159 G5
Workington Cumb 98 B1
Worksop Notts 77 B5
Worlaby N Lincs 90 C4
World's End W Berks 26 B2
Worle N Som 23 C5
Worleston Ches E 74 D3
Worlingham Suff 69 F7
Worlington Suff 55 B7
Worlingworth Suff 57 C6
Wormald Green N Yorks 95 C6
Wormbridge Hereford 49 F6
Wormegay Norf 67 C6
Wormelow Tump Hereford 49 F6
Wormhill Derbys 75 B8
Wormingford Essex 56 F3
Worminghall Bucks 39 D6
Wormington Glos 50 F5
Worminster Som 23 E7
Wormit Fife 129 B5
Wormleighton Warks 52 D2
Wormley Herts 41 D6
Wormley Sur 27 F7
Wormley West End Herts 41 D6
Wormshill Kent 30 D2
Wormsley Hereford 49 E6
Worplesdon Sur 27 D7
Worrall S Yorks 88 E4
Worsbrough S Yorks 88 D4
Worsbrough Common S Yorks 88 D4
Worsley Gtr Man 86 D5
Worstead Norf 69 B6
Worsthorne Lancs 93 F8
Worston Lancs 93 E7
Worswell Devon 6 E3
Worth Kent 31 D7
Worth W Sus 28 F4
Worth Matravers Dorset 13 G7
Wortham Suff 56 B4
Worthen Shrops 60 D3
Worthenbury Wrex 73 E8
Worthing Norf 68 C2
Worthing W Sus 16 D5
Worthington Leics 63 B8
Worting Hants 26 D4
Wortley S Yorks 88 E4
Wortley W Yorks 95 F5
Worton N Yorks 100 E4
Worton Wilts 24 D4
Wortwell Norf 69 F5
Wotherton Shrops 60 D2
Wotter Devon 6 C3
Wotton Sur 28 E2
Wotton-under-Edge Glos 36 E4
Wotton Underwood Bucks 39 C6
Woughton on the Green M Keynes 53 F6
Wouldham Kent 29 C8
Wrabness Essex 57 F5
Wrafton Devon 20 F3
Wragby Lincs 78 B4
Wragby W Yorks 88 C5
Wragholme Lincs 91 E7
Wramplingham Norf 68 D4
Wrangbrook W Yorks 89 C5
Wrangham Aberds 153 E6
Wrangle Lincs 79 D7
Wrangle Bank Lincs 79 D7
Wrangle Lowgate Lincs 79 D7
Wrangway Som 11 C6
Wrantage Som 11 B8
Wrawby N Lincs 90 D4
Wraxall Dorset 12 D3
Wraxall N Som 23 B6
Wraxall Som 23 F8
Wray Lancs 93 C6
Wraysbury Windsor 27 B8
Wrayton Lancs 93 B6
Wrea Green Lancs 92 F3
Wreay Cumb 99 B6
Wreay Cumb 108 E4
Wrecclesham Sur 27 E6
Wrecsam = Wrexham Wrex 73 D7
Wrekenton T&W 111 D5
Wrelton N Yorks 103 F5
Wrenbury Ches E 74 E2
Wrench Green N Yorks 103 F7
Wreningham Norf 68 E4
Wrentham Suff 69 F7
Wrenthorpe W Yorks 88 B4
Wrentnall Shrops 60 D4
Wressle E Yorks 96 F3
Wressle N Lincs 90 D3
Wrestlingworth C Beds 54 E3
Wretham Norf 68 F2
Wretton Norf 67 E6
Wrexham = Wrecsam Wrex 73 D7
Wrexham Industrial Estate Wrex 73 E7
Wribbenhall Worcs 50 B2
Wrightington Bar Lancs 86 C3
Wrinehill Staffs 74 E4
Wrington N Som 23 C6
Writhlington Bath 24 D2
Writtle Essex 42 D2
Wrockwardine Telford 61 C6
Wroot N Lincs 89 D8
Wrotham Kent 29 D7
Wrotham Heath Kent 29 D7
Wroughton Swindon 37 F8
Wroxall IoW 15 G6
Wroxall Warks 51 B7
Wroxeter Shrops 61 D5
Wroxham Norf 69 C6
Wroxton Oxon 52 E2
Wyaston Derbys 75 E8
Wyberton Lincs 79 E6
Wyboston Bedford 54 D2
Wybunbury Ches E 74 E4
Wych Cross E Sus 28 F5
Wychbold Worcs 50 C4
Wyck Hants 27 F5
Wyck Rissington Glos 38 B1
Wycoller Lancs 94 F2
Wycomb Leics 64 B4
Wycombe Marsh Bucks 40 E1
Wyddial Herts 54 F4
Wye Kent 30 E4
Wyesham Mon 36 C2
Wyfordby Leics 64 C4
Wyke Dorset 13 B5
Wyke Shrops 61 D6
Wyke Sur 27 D7
Wyke W Yorks 88 B2
Wyke Regis Dorset 12 G4
Wykeham N Yorks 96 B4
Wykeham N Yorks 103 F7
Wyken W Mid 63 F7
Wykey Shrops 60 B3
Wylam Northumb 110 C4
Wylde Green W Mid 62 E5
Wyllie Caerph 35 E5
Wylye Wilts 24 F5
Wymering Ptsmth 15 D7
Wymeswold Leics 64 B3
Wymington Bedford 53 C7
Wymondham Leics 65 C5
Wymondham Norf 68 D4
Wyndham Bridgend 34 E3
Wynford Eagle Dorset 12 E3
Wyng Orkney 159 J4
Wynyard Village Stockton 102 B2
Wyre Piddle Worcs 50 E4
Wysall Notts 64 B3
Wythall Worcs 51 B5
Wytham Oxon 38 D4
Wythburn Cumb 99 C5
Wythenshawe Gtr Man 87 F6
Wythop Mill Cumb 98 B3
Wyton Cambs 54 B3
Wyverstone Suff 56 C4
Wyverstone Street Suff 56 C4
Wyville Lincs 65 B5
Wyvis Lodge Highld 150 D7

Y

Y Bala = Bala Gwyn 72 F3
Y Barri = Barry V Glam 22 C3
Y Bont-Faen = Cowbridge V Glam 21 B8
Y Drenewydd = Newtown Powys 59 E8
Y Felinheli Gwyn 82 E5
Y Fenni = Abergavenny Mon 35 C6
Y Fflôr Gwyn 70 D4
Y Fflint = Flint Flint 73 B6
Y-Ffrith Denb 72 A4
Y Gelli Gandryll = Hay-on-Wye Powys 48 E4
Y Mwmbwls = The Mumbles Swansea 33 F7
Y Pîl = Pyle Bridgend 34 F2
Y Rhws = Rhoose V Glam 22 C2
Y Rhyl = Rhyl Denb 72 A4
Y Trallwng = Welshpool Powys 60 D2
Y Waun = Chirk Wrex 73 F6
Yaddlethorpe N Lincs 90 D2
Yafford IoW 14 F5
Yafforth N Yorks 101 E8
Yalding Kent 29 D7
Yanworth Glos 37 C7
Yapham E Yorks 96 D3
Yapton W Sus 16 D3
Yarburgh Lincs 91 E7
Yarcombe Devon 11 D7
Yard Som 22 F2
Yardley W Mid 62 F5
Yardley Gobion Northants 53 E5
Yardley Hastings Northants 53 D6
Yardro Powys 48 D4
Yarkhill Hereford 49 E8
Yarlet Staffs 62 B3
Yarlington Som 12 B4
Yarlside Cumb 92 C2
Yarm Stockton 102 C2
Yarmouth IoW 14 F4
Yarnbrook Wilts 24 D3
Yarnfield Staffs 75 F5
Yarnscombe Devon 9 B7
Yarnton Oxon 38 C4
Yarpole Hereford 49 C6
Yarrow Borders 115 B6
Yarrow Feus Borders 115 B6
Yarsop Hereford 49 E6
Yarwell Northants 65 E7
Yate S Glos 36 F4
Yateley Hants 27 C6
Yatesbury Wilts 25 B5
Yattendon W Berks 26 B3
Yatton Hereford 49 C6
Yatton N Som 23 C6
Yatton Keynell Wilts 24 B3
Yaverland IoW 15 F7
Yaxham Norf 68 C3
Yaxley Cambs 65 E8
Yaxley Suff 56 B5
Yazor Hereford 49 E6
Yeading London 40 F4
Yeadon W Yorks 94 E5
Yealand Conyers Lancs 92 B5
Yealand Redmayne Lancs 92 B5
Yealmpton Devon 6 D3
Yearby Redcar 102 B4
Yearsley N Yorks 95 B8
Yeaton Shrops 60 C4
Yeaveley Derbys 75 E8
Yedingham N Yorks 96 B4
Yeldon Bedford 53 C8
Yelford Oxon 38 D3
Yelland Devon 20 F3
Yelling Cambs 54 C3
Yelvertoft Northants 52 B3
Yelverton Devon 6 C3
Yelverton Norf 69 D5
Yenston Som 12 B5
Yeo Mill Devon 10 B3
Yeoford Devon 10 E2
Yeolmbridge Corn 8 F5
Yeovil Som 12 C3
Yeovil Marsh Som 12 C3
Yeovilton Som 12 B3
Yerbeston Pembs 32 D1
Yesnaby Orkney 159 G3
Yetlington Northumb 117 D6
Yetminster Dorset 12 C3
Yettington Devon 11 F5
Yetts o'Muckhart Clack 128 D2
Yieldshields S Lanark 119 D8
Yiewsley London 40 F3
Ynys-meudwy Neath 33 D8
Ynysboeth Rhondda 34 E4
Ynysddu Caerph 35 E5
Ynysgyfflog Gwyn 58 C3
Ynyshir Rhondda 34 E4
Ynyslas Ceredig 58 E3
Ynystawe Swansea 33 D7
Ynysybwl Rhondda 34 E4
Yockenthwaite N Yorks 94 B2
Yockleton Shrops 60 C3
Yokefleet E Yorks 90 B2
Yoker W Dunb 118 C5
Yonder Bognie Aberds 152 D5
York York 95 D8
York Town Sur 27 C6
Yorkletts Kent 30 C4
Yorkley Glos 36 D3
Yorton Shrops 60 B5
Youlgreave Derbys 76 C2
Youlstone Devon 8 C4
Youlthorpe E Yorks 96 D3
Youlton N Yorks 95 C7
Young Wood Lincs 78 B4
Young's End Essex 42 C3
Yoxall Staffs 62 C5
Yoxford Suff 57 C7
Yr Hôb = Hope Flint 73 D7
Yr Wyddgrug = Mold Flint 73 C6
Ysbyty-Cynfyn Ceredig 47 B6
Ysbyty Ifan Conwy 72 E2
Ysbyty Ystwyth Ceredig 47 B6
Ysceifiog Flint 73 B5
Yspitty Carms 33 E6
Ystalyfera Neath 34 D1
Ystrad Rhondda 34 E3
Ystrad Aeron Ceredig 46 D4
Ystrad-mynach Caerph 35 E5
Ystradfellte Powys 34 C3
Ystradffin Carms 47 E6
Ystradgynlais Powys 34 C1
Ystradmeurig Ceredig 47 C6
Ystradowen Carms 33 C8
Ystradowen V Glam 22 B2
Ystumtuen Ceredig 47 B6
Ythanbank Aberds 153 E9
Ythanwells Aberds 153 E6
Ythsie Aberds 153 E8

Z

Zeal Monachorum Devon 10 D2
Zeals Wilts 24 F2
Zelah Corn 4 D3
Zennor Corn 2 C3